*Baptist Theology
A Four-Century Study*

Endowed by
TOM WATSON BROWN
and
THE WATSON-BROWN FOUNDATION, INC.

Baptist Theology
A Four-Century Study

by
James Leo Garrett, Jr.

MERCER UNIVERSITY PRESS
Macon, Georgia

MUP/P584

Baptist Theology: A Four-Century Study.
Copyright ©2009
Mercer University Press, Macon GA USA
All rights reserved
Printed in the United States of America
First edition : January 2009
First paperback edition : 2019

The paper used in this publication meets the minimum requirements
of American National Standard for Information Sciences—
Permanence of Paper for Printed Library Materials, ANSI Z39.48–1984.

Library of Congress Cataloging-in-Publication Data

Garrett, James Leo, Jr.
Baptist theology : a four-century study / by James Leo Garrett, Jr.
-- 1st ed.
    p.   cm.
Includes bibliographical references and index.
ISBN-13: 978-0-88146-707-9 (paperback : alk. paper)

 1. Baptists--Doctrines. 2. Baptists--History. I. Title.
BX6331.3.G37 2009
230'.6--dc22
2008031645

Contents

Abbreviations xi
Glossary, by Dongsun Cho xiii
Preface xxv
Dedication xxviii

Chapter 1
The Roots of Baptist Beliefs 1
    The Councils, the Creeds, and the Fathers, 1
    Pre-Reformation Sectarian and Reforming Movements, 5
    The Magisterial Protestant Reformation, 6
    Continental Anabaptism, 8
    English Separatist Puritans and Independents, 16

Chapter 2
English General Baptists 23
    John Smyth (ca. 1570–1612), 23
    Thomas Helwys (1570-ca. 1616), 31
    Other Confessions of Faith, 35
    Thomas Grantham (1634–1692), 42
    Matthew Caffyn (1628–1715), Celestial Flesh, and Socinianism, 44
    Dan Taylor (1738–1816) and the New Connection (1770), 46

Chapter 3
English Particular Baptists 51
    First London Confession (1644, 1646), 53
    Midland (1655) and Somerset (1656) Confessions, 59
    Hanserd Knollys (1609–1691), 62
    William Kiffin (1616–1701), 65
    John Bunyan (1628–1688), 67
    Second London or Assembly Confession (1677, 1689), 71
    Thomas Collier and Arminianized Western Particular Baptists, 80
    Benjamin Keach (1640–1704), 83
    Baptist Hyper-Calvinism (John Skepp, ?–1721,
        John Brine, 1703–1765, and John Gill, 1697–1771), 89

Chapter 4
Early American Baptists 109
    Roger Williams (1603?–1683), 109
    Confessions of Faith and Church Disciplines, 114
    Six Principle, Free Will (or Freewill), and General Baptists, 118
    Elhanan Winchester (1751–1797) and Universalism, 124
    Kehukee and New Hampshire Confessions of Faith, 126
    Francis Wayland (1796–1865), 132
    Southern Calvinist Theologians: Patrick Hues Mell (1814–1888)
        and John Leadley Dagg (1796–1884), 134
    Southern Calvinist Theology: The "Abstract of Principles"
        of the Southern Baptist Theological Seminary (1858)
        and James Petigru Boyce (1827–1888), 145

Chapter 5
Awakening and Missionary Baptists 153
    Isaac Backus (1724–1806) and John Leland (1754–1841), 154
    The Separate Baptists, 163
    English Particular Baptists from Revival to Missions:
        Robert Hall, Sr. (1728–1791), John Collett Ryland (1723–1792),
        John Ryland (1753–1825), and John Sutcliff (1752–1814), 166
    English Particular Baptists from Revival to Missions:
        William Carey (1761–1834), Andrew Fuller (1754–1815),
        Abraham Booth (1734–1806), Robert Hall, Jr. (1764–1831),
        Joseph Kinghorn (1766–1832), Joseph Ivimey (1773–1834),
        and John Rippon (1750–1838), 173
    Strict and Particular Baptists, 198
    Alexander Carson (1776–1844), 200
    Antimissionary Controversy; Primitive Baptists;
        Daniel Parker (1781–1844), 204

Chapter 6
Baptist Landmarkism 213
    Early Landmark History, 213
    The Landmark "Triumvirate": James Robinson Graves (1820–1893),
        James Madison Pendleton (1811–1891),
        and Amos Cooper Dayton (1813–1865), 217
    Later Landmark Controversies, 230
    Non-Landmark Ecclesiology, 242
    Landmark Effects on Twentieth-Century Southern Baptists, 246

Chapter 7
Baptists in Controversy 249
    The Campbells and the Baptists, 249
    Controversies over the Bible: Bible Translation;
        Crawford Howell Toy (1836–1919)
        and Basil Manly, Jr. (1825–1892), 258
    Down Grade Controversy: Charles Haddon Spurgeon (1834–1892)
        and John Clifford (1836–1923), 264
    The Changing Theological Scene, 278
    Northern and Canadian Baptist Conservative Theologians:
        Alvah Hovey (1820–1903), George Dana Boardman Pepper
        (1833–1913), Calvin Goodspeed (1842–1912),
        and Adoniram Judson Gordon (1836–1895), 279
    Northern Baptist Mediating Theologians: Ezekiel Gilman Robinson
        (1815–1894), George Washington Northrup (1826–1900),
        Elias Henry Johnson (1841–1906), Nathan Eusebius Wood
        (1849–1937), Augustus Hopkins Strong (1836–1921),
        and Ebenezer Dodge (1819–1890), 288
    Northern Baptist Liberal Theologians: William Newton Clarke
        (1841–1912), Harry Emerson Fosdick (1878–1969), George Cross
        (1862–1929), and Henry Clay Vedder (1853–1935), 304
    Social Gospel: Walter Rauschenbusch (1861–1918), 314
    Northern and Canadian Baptist Fundamentalist Theologians:
        William Bell Riley (1861–1947), John Roach Straton
        (1875–1929), Thomas Todhunter Shields (1873–1955),
        and Jasper Cortenus Massee (1871–1965), 318
    Baptist Congress, 327
    Northern Baptist Convention Controversy, 1920–1950, 330

Chapter 8
Biblical Theologians 343
    Ezra Palmer Gould (1841–1900), 343
    Archibald Thomas Robertson (1863–1934), 347
    Henry Wheeler Robinson (1872–1945), 350
    Harold Henry Rowley (1890–1969), 355
    Eric Charles Rust (1910–1991), 360
    Ralph Edward Knudson (1897–1987), 363
    Ray Summers (1910–1992);
        Edward Allison McDowell (1898–1975), 364
    Frank Stagg (1911–2001), 369

George Eldon Ladd (1911–1982), 374
Dale Moody (1915–1992); Wayne Eugene Ward (1921–), 377
George Raymond Beasley-Murray (1916–2000), 388
Donald Guthrie (1916–1992), 395
Ralph Lee Smith (1918–1999), 397
Ralph Philip Martin (1925–), 399
Edward Earle Ellis (1926–), 403
Ronald Ernest Clements (1929–), 407
Richard Norman Longenecker (1930–), 410

Chapter 9
Twentieth-Century Southern Baptists 415
Edgar Young Mullins (1860–1928), 415
Doctrinal Statements prior to 1925, 434
The 1925 Baptist Faith and Message Statement, 442
Walter Thomas Conner (1877–1952), 449
Doctrinal Summaries for the Laity and the Convention, 455
The Elliott Controversy, 457
The 1963 Baptist Faith and Message Statement, 462
Herschel Harold Hobbs (1907–1995), 468
Baptist Ideals, 474
Doctrinal Texts for Students and Dismissals of Professors, 475
Wallie Amos Criswell (1909–2002), 481
The *Broadman Bible Commentary* Controversy, 486
Charismaticism, 489
The Inerrancy Controversy, 491
The 2000 Baptist Faith and Message Statement, 506

Chapter 10
*Recovering Evangelicalism
and Reassessing the Baptist Heritage* 515
Carl Ferdinand Howard Henry (1913–2003), 515
Bernard Lawrence Ramm (1916–1992), 520
Millard John Erickson (1932–), 525
Baptist Distinctives, 531
Baptists, Free Churches, and Believers' Churches, 532
Southern Baptists and American Evangelicals, 535
James William McClendon, Jr. (1924–2000), 537
British Baptismal Sacramentalism, 540

Chapter 11
Incursions into Baptist Theology 549
  Modernism, 549
  Dispensationalism, 560
  The English Christological Controversy, 570
  Open Theism, 574

Chapter 12
Missions, Ecumenism, and Globalization 581
  Missiology of William Owen Carver (1868–1954), 581
  European Confessions of Faith, 585
  Baptists and Ecumenism, 591
  The Evangelistic Theology
    of William Franklin (Billy) Graham, Jr. (1918–), 602
  Harvey Gallagher Cox (1929–):
    From the Secular City to Openness to Pentecostalism, 609
  James Deotis Roberts (1927–):
    Afro-American Theology of Liberation/Reconciliation, 613
  Osadolor Imasogie (1928–):
    Contextualized African Theology, 616
  South African Theologians and Doctrinal Statements, 621
  Latin American Confessions and Controversies, 624
    Brazil, 624
    Mexico, 626
    Argentina, 628
  Latin American Theologians:
    Orlando Enrique Costas (1942–1987),
    C. René Padilla (1932–),
    and Samuel Escobar (1934–), 633
  Australia, 644
  Asian Confessions and Monographs, 647
    Korea, 647
    India, 648
    Philippines, 649
    Malaysia and Singapore, 649
  Salvation of the Unevangelized, 651
  Textbook on Missiology, 656

Chapter 13
New Voices in Baptist Theology 661
    John Stephen Piper (1946–):
        Edwardsean Theology of Christian Hedonism, 661
    Thomas Julian Nettles (1946–):
        Repristination of Biblical Inerrancy and Dortian Calvinism, 666
    Donald Arthur Carson (1946–):
        Exemplar of Intelligent and Polemical Evangelicalism, 669
    Paul Stuart Fiddes (1947–):
        The Suffering and Trinitarian God and Ecumenical Theology, 676
    Wayne Arden Grudem (1948–):
        Reformed Theology with Vineyard Refinements, 684
    Nigel Goring Wright (1949–):
        Reinterpreted Baptist Convictions for Post-Christendom, 686
    Stanley James Grenz (1950–2005):
        Reenvisioner of Evangelical Theology for a Postmodern Age, 690
    Timothy Francis George (1950–):
        Evangelical/Calvinist and Baptist Historical Theologian, 696
    Roger Eugene Olson (1952–): Evangelical Arminianism
        and the History of Christian Doctrine, 701
    David Samuel Dockery (1952–):
        Evangelical-Calminian Baptist and the Doctrine of the Bible, 704

Conclusion 713

Index of Persons 727

Abbreviations

ABA	American Baptist Association (USA)
ABFMS	American Baptist Foreign Mission Society (USA)
ABSC	Arkansas Baptist State Convention (USA)
ATR	African Traditional Religion
BBC	Brazilian Baptist Convention
BBHRM/M, RP	British Baptist Historical Resource Materials from Manchester and Regent's Park Colleges
BBM/Angus	British Baptist Materials from the Angus Library of Regent's Park College, Oxford England
BBM/Bodleian	British Baptist Materials from the Bodleian Library of the University of Oxford
BBUNA	Baptist Bible Union of North America
BGC	Baptist General Conference (USA)
BGCT	Baptist General Convention of Texas (USA)
BMAA	Baptist Missionary Association of America (USA)
BUSA	Baptist Union of South Africa
BWA	Baptist World Alliance
C	Nicaeno-Constantinopolitan Creed
CBAA	Conservative Baptist Association of America (USA)
CBF	Cooperative Baptist Fellowship (USA)
CBFMS	Conservative Baptist Foreign Mission Society (USA)
CIA	Central Intelligence Agency (USA)
EBCA	Evangelical Baptist Convention of Argentina
EBP	Early Baptist Publications, University Microfilms (1951)
FMB-SBC	Foreign Mission Board of the SBC
FTL	Fraternidad Teológica Latinoamericana
GARBC	General Association of Regular Baptist Churches (USA)
IBTS	International Baptist Theological Seminary, Buenos Aires
IFES	International Fellowship of Evangelical Students

KJV	King James Version
LC 1644	First London Confession of Particular Baptists
MWJB	*The Miscellaneous Works of John Bunyan*
N	Nicene Creed
NABA	North American Baptist Association (USA)
NABPR	National Association of Baptist Professors of Religion
NBC	National Baptist Convention (Brazil)
NBC	Northern Baptist Convention (USA)
NIV	New International Version
NPNF	*Nicene and Post-Nicene Fathers*, series 1 and 2
SBC	Southern Baptist Convention (USA)
WCC	World Council of Churches

Glossary
by Dongsun Cho

adoption. The divine reception of repentant sinners as sons of God.

adoptionism. The heretical Christology that Jesus was not the incarnated Son of God but was adopted as Christ at his baptism.

amillennialism. The eschatological view that, denying any literal 1,000-year reign of Christ on earth, holds either that the millennial reign is occurring between the two advents of Christ or is a heavenly reign.

Amyraldianism. The peculiar teachings of the French Reformed theologian Moise Amyraut (1596–1664), especially his acceptance of general atonement and his rejection of reprobation, or double predestination, together with his acceptance of the other Synod of Dort teachings.

analogy of faith. The hermeneutical principle presented by the Reformers that argues for "Scripture interprets Scripture," denying the Roman Catholic appeal to the necessity of an authoritative judge—such as the church or the pope—of the interpretation of the Bible.

annihilationism. The belief that since immortality belongs only to God, the existence of the unsaved will be terminated, or totally destroyed, after the final judgment.

antipedobaptist. A person who rejects the baptism of infants or of little children who are unable to confess their faith.

anthropology (as a theological term). The doctrine of man. Its major topics are the image of God, the constituents of the human, and sin.

antinomianism. The disputed view that since Christians are saved by God's grace they are no longer under the obligation of the moral law of God.

Arianism. Taught by Arius in the fourth century, this heretical Christology denied the full divinity of Jesus Christ as equal to that of God the Father and reckoned Jesus to have been a creature of God.

Arminianism. The theological system initiated by James Arminius (1560–1609) that emphasized the role of human free will with regard to salvation so that repentance and faith are human duties and foreseen by God, Christ's death was intended for all humanity, and God's grace can be resisted and possibly abandoned. Later forms of Arminianism did not maintain Arminius's stress on total human depravity and the initiating ministry of the Holy Spirit for regeneration.

apostasy. The deliberate abandonment of the Christian faith which has once been held.

Augustinian or natural headship theory of original sin. Any theory that the sin and guilt of Adam have been imputed to all his descendants, except

Jesus, because all humans sinned in Adam, the seminal head of all human beings.

autographs of the Bible. A term for the *original* manuscripts of the Bible.

baptizand. A person to be baptized.

baptismal regeneration. The view that baptism really effects the forgiveness of sins. The Roman Catholic Church, Lutheran Churches, and Churches of Christ hold to this view.

Bezan Calvinism. Calvinism characterized by Theodore Beza's (1519–1605) supralapsarian context for predestination, which is placed under the doctrine of God rather than under the doctrine of salvation, and by Beza's doctrine of limited atonement.
(See *supralapsarianism.*)

biblical hermeneutics. The science of studying methodologies for interpreting the Bible.

Calminianism. Any set of doctrines that involves a mixing of the teachings of the Synod of Dort and the teachings of the Arminians, or Remonstrants.

Calvinism. (1) The doctrinal teachings of John Calvin (1509–1564). (2) The affirmations of the Synod of Dort (1618–1619), which have been popularly, if not precisely, summarized under the acronym TULIP: total depravity, unconditional election, limited atonement, irresistible grace, and perseverance of all saints. The second definition is applicable in this book.

canonical criticism. The critical methodology in biblical scholarship that focuses on the development of the text in its final form as the canonical Scriptures (including both O.T. and N.T.).

canonicity. The specific identity and the number of those books that constitute the canon of the O.T. and the N.T.; also the attributes of those books that seemingly warranted such inclusion.

Chalcedonian Christology. The doctrine, first formulated by the Council of Chalcedon (451), that Christ's full humanity and full divinity are united in one person without any confusion, change, division, or separation of the natures.

charismaticism. The movement that seeks every gift of the Holy Spirit in the N.T. for today. Unlike Pentecostalism, however, charismaticism does not argue for the necessary identification of speaking in tongues with the baptism of the Holy Spirit.

chiliasm. Another term for millennialism, the eschatological view that the returning Christ will reign with his saints on earth for a thousand years before the final judgment.

Christian apologetics. The effort to present rational explanations of Christian faith in a systematic way.

Christian ethics. The theological discipline that studies right and wrong in human behavior from the Christian perspective.

Christology. The doctrine about Christ. Its major topics are the person and the work of Christ; it may also include the titles ascribed to him and his 'holy history.'

church covenant. The voluntary and official vows of church members to observe the discipline and government of their particular congregation.

close or strict communion. The view that the legitimate recipients of the Lord's Supper must be limited to (a) those baptized upon profession of faith by immersion; (b) the members of churches of the Baptist denomination; or (c) the members of the Baptist congregation observing the Supper.

complementarianism (re male-female issues). The view that men and women are equal in their ontological value before God but have different roles and functions in marriage and in the church.

conditional election. The doctrine that God's election is based on his foreknowledge of a person's faith in or rejection of Jesus Christ.

conditional immortality. The view that only Christians will receive immortal life as a gift of God, who alone is immortal by nature, and non-Christians, therefore, will be annihilated without being raised from the dead. (See *annihilationism.*)

congregational polity. The view of church government according to which the whole congregation has the final authority in decision making, such as concerning doctrine, discipline, ministerial leadership, missions, and property.

contextualization. The contemporization of the gospel for a present-day audience, especially in non-Western cultures.

covenant of Eden (R. C. B. Howell, *The Covenants* [1855]). The view that God's announcement of the seed of Eve and the seed of the serpent (Gen. 3:15) was the divine covenant, in a proper sense, to save men through the Messiah.

covenant of grace (with all penitent believers). The Reformed doctrine that God made a covenant with human beings in which God would save all penitent believers by his grace.

covenant of redemption (within the Trinity). The doctrine that God the Father, God the Son, and God the Holy Spirit made a covenant in eternity for human redemption on the basis of Christ's incarnation and death on the cross.

covenant of works (with Adam and his posterity). The Reformed doctrine that God made a covenant of works with Adam before his fall, providing that on condition of his obedience he and his posterity would attain eternal life and on condition of his disobedience he and his posterity would attain eternal death.

creedalism. The theological commitment to a creed as the nonnegotiable standard of professed faith, usually with some effort at enforcement.

declarative justification. God's act of declaring a sinner as "righteous" not because of his worthiness of divine forgiveness but because of the righteousness of Christ that is imputed to the sinner by faith.

Deism. The view that God created the universe but has not been involved with it after finishing creation.

demythologization. A hermeneutical principle taught by Rudolf Bultmann (1884–1976) that the N.T. contains "myths," and that, therefore, one has to reinterpret the narratives of the N.T. existentially.

dichotomy. The view that humanity consists of two parts: body and "soul." "Spirit" is considered as the synonym of soul.

dispensationalism. The theological movement initiated by John Nelson Darby (1800–1882) that presents several (usually seven) different dispensations in God's dealing with humankind and emphasizes the literal future fulfillment of the O.T. prophecies about Israel, the distinction between Israel and the church, the "rapture" of the church before the great tribulation, and the Jewish nature of the millennial kingdom.

Dissenters. Those who defied the Act of Uniformity (1662) in England because it required ministers to use the revised Prayer Book alone in worship services and to take an oath of ordination administered only by the bishops of the Church of England.

ditheism. A belief that there are two equal deities, one representing good and the other evil.

docetism. The heretical Christology that Jesus did not exist as a real man but just appeared to be so.

dominical (adjective re Christ). Of or belonging to Jesus Christ as Lord.

Dortian Calvinism. Calvinism as it was formulated by the Synod of Dort, which presumably articulated five points: total depravity, unconditional election, limited atonement, irresistible grace, and the perseverance of saints.

double predestination. God preordained not only some to salvation but also others to eternal damnation.

dualism. The view that God (or Spirit) as the force of good and matter as the force of evil eternally exist in conflict.

ecclesiology. The doctrine of the church. Its major topics are the nature, membership, polity, ordinances (baptism, Lord's Supper), worship, mission, and ministry of the church.

ecumenical (patristic era). Of or pertaining to the entire Christian community; as in ecumenical creeds or ecumenical councils.

ecumenical (20th and 21st centuries). Of or pertaining to ecclesiastical efforts to establish the unity of the whole church through authoritative and universally valid doctrinal and practical agreements among the various Christian denominations.

effectual calling. The powerful act of God that does not fail to bring about the repentance of the sinners whom he has elected and their acceptance of the gospel.

egalitarianism (re male-female issues). The view that men and women are equal not only in their ontological value but also in their leadership in marriage and the church.

emanationism. The view that all things of the universe overflow from God and are divine.

epistemology. The study of knowledge. It deals with the sources, forms, and limits of knowledge.

eschatological universalism. The view that all human beings, regardless of their present responses to the gospel, will ultimately be saved by the grace of God.

eschatology. The doctrine of the last things. Its major topics are death, intermediate state, the resurrection, the kingdom of God, Christ's second coming, the final judgment, hell, and heaven.

eternal creation. The view that God created the universe in eternity past out of eternally preexistent matter.

eternal death. The term referring to the eternal punishment of hell.

eternal generation of the Son of God. The doctrine that expresses the distinction and equality between the Father and the Son in eternity by arguing that the Son was generated by and from the Father so that there was no time when the Father existed without the Son.

excommunication. The means of church discipline by which unrepentant members who have embraced doctrinal heresy, committed serious moral infractions, or broken the unity of the church are removed from membership and from participation in the Lord's Supper.

existential fall. The view that regards the fall of Adam in Eden as a symbol of every human's present experience of his or her alienation from God.

fatalism. The view that everything in the universe happens only according to the determination of a powerful and impersonal fate unalterable by human will and actions.

federal theory of original sin. The view, especially as promulgated by Johannes Cocceius (1603–1669), that since Adam, the federal head of all human beings, broke the divine covenant of works, God has imputed the guilt of Adam to his posterity. (Also called the Convenant Theory.)

Fifth Monarchy. The messianic kingdom as it was anticipated by a number of nonconformist or dissenting groups when England was in political and social turmoil from 1649 to 1661. They believed that the messianic kingdom, the fifth monarchy prophesied by Daniel, would be realized by the return of Christ following the English civil wars.

foreordination. God's predestination of everything that will happen in history, including the salvation of human beings.

foundationalism (as used in apologetics). An epistemological view that there are some beliefs, not requiring justification by any external evidence, that are bases for the justification of other beliefs.

general atonement. The doctrine that the death of Jesus Christ was intended to be sufficient for the remission of the sins of all humanity, whether or not persons repent and believe.

Geschichte. The German term referring to the existential meaning of history.

governmental theory of the atonement. The theory of the atonement first promulgated by Hugo Grotius (1583–1645) that God, as a moral governor rather than the party offended by man's sin, exhibits in Christ's sufferings and death the extent of his displeasure toward sin and his determination to punish impenitent sinners.

Half-Way Covenant. (See Edwin Gaustad's *The Great Awakening in New England* [1957].) A form of church membership in seventeenth-century New England Congregationalism in which baptized adults who could not testify to conversion were regarded as "halfway" members, who could bring their children for baptism but neither parents nor children could participate in the Lord's Supper.

hedonism. The view that pleasure or happiness is the ultimate goal of human activities.

heresy. A view or doctrinal position that is opposed or contrary to the orthodox teachings of the church.

historical fall. The view that regards the fall of Adam in Eden as a real event in primeval history.

historicism. The view that anything in history can be explained exclusively by means of its origins, that is, not by divine causation.
Historie. The German term referring to the factuality of history in time and space.
humanism. The view that humanity must be valued as most important and that human reason alone—without God—is able to judge good and evil.
illumination. The ministry of the Holy Spirit to help one to understand the true meaning of the Bible.
(philosophical) idealism. The view that the ideas of the human self constitute absolute reality and are identifiable with the divine self.
immersion. The mode of baptism practiced in the N.T. in which the whole body is put under the water and brought back up again.
imputation of Adam's sin. Any theory that the sin and guilt of Adam have been imputed to all his descendants, except Jesus, either because all humans sinned in Adam himself (Augustinian view) or because the covenant of works was broken and the effects implemented (federal view).
imputation of Christ's righteousness to believers. The doctrine that God imputes Christ's righteousness to sinners who believe in Christ. Since the righteousness of the Christian in justification is not his own but Christ's, it is also called *alien righteousness*.
imputed righteousness. The doctrine referring to the righteousness of Christ, alien to and outside sinners, which God imputes to believers on the basis of their faith, not of their works.
incarnation. The doctrine that God the Son, the second person of the Trinity, became a man by assuming full humanity in Jesus of Nazareth.
inerrancy of the Bible. The view that the Bible is without any error, not only in its salvific data but also in its nonsalvific (historical and scientific) data.
inherent righteousness. The view that the righteousness of the Christian, which is earned by good works and residing within the Christian, makes him really just. God declares him righteous on the basis of his internal righteousness.
infralapsarianism. A view presenting God's decrees in the following logical sequence: Creation → the Divine Permission of the Fall of Human Beings → Election → Redemption.
inspiration (of the Bible). The divine influence over the writers and the writings of the Bible.
intercession of Jesus Christ. The priestly ministry of the ascended Jesus who makes intercession before God on behalf of Christians.

itinerancy. The practice of traveling from place to place to preach that characterized many ministers of the American frontier era. Itinerancy also refers to a Methodist rotation system of itinerating ministers as directed by the bishops.

kenotic, kenoticism. The view that Christ became a true man by emptying (based on Greek *kenosis* in Phil. 2:7) or surrendering some of his divine (esp. omni-) attributes or the independent exercise of such attributes.

limited providence. The view that God cooperates with humans for the things that happen in the world and that the future is open, not closed, because God's sovereign work changes according to the contingencies of his creation.

logical empiricism. The philosophy that bases true knowledge on logical statements, which can be verified through the senses, while denying the veracity of metaphysical truths.

Macedonianism: The heretical movement developed by Macedonius (d. 362), an Arian bishop of Constantinople, that denied the full deity of the Holy Spirit. Members of this sect were called Pneumatomachians, meaning "those who are against the Holy Spirit."

macroevolution. The view that allows not only evolution *within* the same kind but also evolution *among* different kinds.

materialism. The view that the only true reality is matter.

mechanical dictation theory of biblical inspiration. The view that God literally dictated every word of the Bible in its present form to biblical writers, whose function was like that of a pen.

meticulous providence (as used by Roger E. Olson, *The Mosaic of Christian Belief* [2002]). The view that God is in charge of every single detail that happens in the world.

microevolution. The view that allows evolutionary development of species within one kind. It does not result in a product of another kind.

modalism. The heretical view that there is only one person in the Trinity. Father, Son, and the Spirit are not three persons but three different modes of appearance or functions. (See *Sabellianism.*)

monad. A term referring to the one ultimate or indivisible reality of universe. In the philosophy of Spinoza or Leibniz, God is described as the monad of all existing beings.

monogamous marriage. Marriage with only one other person at a time.

monotheism. The belief that there is only one true deity.

Nonconformist(s). A synonym for Dissenter(s).

open communion. The view that the legitimate recipients in the Lord's Supper can be all baptized Christians, whether baptized in infancy or in believer's baptism and whether by sprinkling or immersion.

original sin. The doctrine pertaining to the sinful nature and legal guilt inherited by all human beings from Adam as his descendants.

panentheism. The view that the universe is part of God and, therefore, divine, but God is not restricted to it.

pantheism. The idea that the universe is ontologically identical with God or contains part of his divine nature.

parousia. The term referring to the future second coming of Christ.

particular atonement. The doctrine that the death of Jesus Christ was intended to be sufficient for the remission of the sins of elect humans only, so that the intention and the efficacy of his atonement apply to the same persons.

particular election. The view that God's election means his choice of particular individual persons to salvation, not his making a principle of salvation through prescience.

pedobaptism. The baptism of infants or very young children without their having confessed their own faith in Jesus Christ.

perfectionism. The view that a Christian can attain a sinless life before death.

perseverance. The doctrine that the salvation of all true believers will be preserved by the power of God through faith until the last moment of their lives and into eternity.

personalism. The philosophical view that a person is the ultimate reality and that God and human beings are ontologically similar by virtue of their personhood.

perspicuity of the Bible. The belief that the central message of the Scriptures is clear; also called *claritas Scripturae* ("clarity of Scripture").

plenary-verbal theory of biblical inspiration. The view that all the words of the Bible are fully inspired by God.

pluralism (defined soteriologically, not in reference to the great diversity of religions). The view that all religions can be effective ways leading to salvation and God.

pneumatology. The doctrine of the person and work of the Holy Spirit.

polygenism or *polygeneticism.* The belief that human beings came not from a single source (God as Creator) but from multiple sources (via evolution).

postmillennialism. The eschatological view that the progress of the gospel will Christianize the world and usher in an era of justice and peace before the second coming of Christ.

postmortal evangelism. The view that those who never hear the gospel or who have rejected the gospel will have a second chance to respond to the gospel after death.

posttribulationism. The belief that the church will endure the great tribulation before the second coming of Christ and the millennial kingdom on earth.

pragmatism. A philosophical view that argues for knowledge from experience and regards the utility of knowledge as the ultimate criterion of its truthfulness.

pre-Adamite theory. The hypothesis that there might have been another kind of human beings before the creation of Adam.

predamnation. The opposite of election, it is the doctrine that those who were not elected by God in eternity were already damned before their actual fall.

predestination. The view that salvation depends upon God's decision, prior to creation, to save some to eternal life.

prelapsarian (adjective). Relating to the period before the fall of Adam and Eve.

(historic) premillennialism. The eschatological doctrine that the second coming of Christ will precede the millennium and thus Christ with his saints will reign on the earth during the millennium.

prevenient grace. The grace that God grants to the sinner in the process of justification, prior to any human response to God's calling.

preterition. The Reformed doctrine that some human beings will be eternally damned because the electing God chose to pass over them, thus leaving them in their sins subject to punishment.

pretribulationism. The belief that the rapture of the church will precede a seven-year great tribulation; the church will meet Christ in the air when he secretly returns.

primitivism. Any movement seeking to restore the apostolic church of the N.T. era (AD 30–100).

process philosophy/theology. The view that all realities, including God, are in process of change, and God is becoming in process and does not know the absolute knowledge of the future.

progressive creation. The view that God created the world not in six days but in millions or billions of years. God is the direct creator of the head of each kind, and each individual species has evolved from that head.

propitiation. The term expressing the divine work of the atonement as a sacrifice that is able to turn away the wrath of God.

propositional revelation. The view that the revelation of God can be truly expressed through cognitive and conceptual statements and that the Bible can be a true revelation of God.

providence. The doctrine that God is continually involved with his creation by taking care of and directing it in a way that accomplishes his will.

redaction criticism. The critical methodology in biblical scholarship that views the present form of the biblical text as edited by the writer(s) of that text for, in some instances, presenting the editors' theological agenda(s).

reprobation. The Reformed doctrine that some go to hell because the sovereign God actively assigned them to damnation from eternity.

Sabellianism. The heretical view, held by Sabellius (3rd century), that the Father, the Son, and the Holy Spirit are merely three different historical modes or appearances of the one God and that they are not personally distinct; also called *modalistic monarchianism.*

sacramentalism. The view that the sacraments of the church convey the reality of what they signify and are the actual means of the grace of God.

sanctification. The ongoing work of the Holy Spirit in the lives of Christians to make them holy through faith and obedience.

se-baptism. The doctrine or practice of baptizing oneself.

Socinianism. The view of Faustus Socinus (1539–1604) that denied the divinity of Christ and the penal-substitution view of the atonement. (In America it has been absorbed in Unitarianism.)

soteriology. The doctrine of salvation and the Christian life. Its major topics are regeneration, justification, adoption, union with Christ, sanctification, election, discipleship, and stewardship.

special revelation. God's direct revelation to his chosen people (Israel and the church) through special means (divine oracles, the incarnation, and the Bible) for accomplishing the covenantal relationship between himself and his chosen people.

Stoddardeanism (see Gaustad's *The Great Awakening in New England*): The Congregational view taught by Solomon Stoddard (1643–1728 or 1729), but rejected by his grandson, Jonathan Edwards, Sr. (1703–1758), that those who had not confessed their faith but lived pious lives could be encouraged to partake of the Lord's Supper as an incentive to conversion.

sublapsarianism. A view presenting God's decrees in the following logical sequence: Creation → Divine Permission of the Fall of Human Beings → Redemption → Election.

supralapsarianism. A view presenting God's decrees in the following logical sequence: Election → Creation → Divine Permission of the Fall of Human Beings → Redemption.

syncretism. The ideological process that integrates different or even contradictory ideas into a new one. In this process some essential aspects of the previously unmerged ideas experience significant modification.

Textus Receptus (Latin, "Received Text"). The term referring to the edition of the Greek N.T. text, based on the Byzantine manuscripts, which Luther, Tyndale, and the King James Version utilized for their vernacular translations of the Greek N.T.

theistic evolution. The view that God is the initiating cause of the beginning of life but that nature developed all living species by its own evolutionary process.

theistic existentialism. The philosophy that God created human beings but does not actively direct their lives and that they, as responsible agents, have to find the meaning of their lives.

traducianism. The view that a person's soul is transmitted along with the body from his or her parents at the moment of conception.

trichotomy. The anthropological view that man consists of three parts—body, soul, and spirit.

tritheism. The heretical view that three individual and separate gods make up the Godhead.

typology. The hermeneutical method by which a certain person or event in the O.T. is seen as the prefiguration of a person or event in the N.T.

unconditional election. The doctrine that God's election is based solely on his sovereign will and freedom to choose some for salvation.

Unitarianism. The heretical view that God is only one person, not three persons, on the basis that Jesus is not divine.

universal church. The term referring to all Christians in all ages, whether on earth or in heaven. It can also be used to refer to all present-day professing Christians throughout the world.

warrant (18th-century technical term among Hyper-Calvinists). A necessary preliminary internal and personally validated evidence of being among God's elect rather than a personal response to the objective, biblically based invitation to Christ and the gospel.

Preface

This book is a study of the doctrinal beliefs of the people called Baptists. It is a coordinated consideration of the major sources for such a study, namely, their confessions of faith, the teachings of their major theologians, and their principal theological movements and controversies. It is not a study of Baptist ethics, spirituality, apologetics, or hymnology or a narrative history of the Baptist denomination or of Baptist missionary expansion. It reckons the formation of the earliest identifiable Baptist congregation as having occurred in 1609, and hence it is a four-century study that attempts to treat responsibly each of the four centuries and the Baptists of the world. It has utilized both the primary sources and the secondary literature. I have sought to allow Baptist authors to speak authentically for themselves before assessment or evaluation is undertaken.

During the fall semester of 1950, as a young instructor, I offered a modest two-semester-hour elective course at Southwestern Baptist Theological Seminary on the history of Baptist theology. Although Baptist history and Baptist missions had been in the curricula of the (then only) three Southern Baptist Convention seminaries, apparently this was the first course in Baptist "historical theology." I offered this course, as expanded and developed, at Southwestern during the 1950s and the 1980s and 1990s and at Southern Baptist Theological Seminary during the 1960s and the early 1970s. This book is the sequel to those instructional undertakings, but more specifically it is the product of four years of postretirement research and writing.

I have built upon the foundations laid by my predecessors. For half a century William L. Lumpkin's *Baptist Confessions of Faith* (1959, 1969) has served as the standard collection and treatment of Anglo-American Baptist confessions of faith. A similar service for Continental Europe was rendered by G. Keith Parker in his *Baptists in Europe: History and Confessions of Faith* (1982). James E. Tull examined the thought of nine Baptist thinkers from John Smyth to Martin Luther King, Jr., in his *Shapers of Baptist Thought* (1972). Timothy George and David S. Dockery coedited *Baptist Theologians* (1990), which interpreted thirty-three Baptist theologians from John Bunyan to Clark H. Pinnock, and the same coeditors produced a more concise *Theologians of the Baptist Tradition* (2001), which treated seventeen theologians from John Gill to Millard J. Erickson. Various authors have produced monographs on Baptist Calvinism, Missions and

Antimissions, Landmarkism, Liberalism, Modernism, Fundamentalism, and Ecumenism. William H. Brackney's monumental *A Genetic History of Baptist Thought* (2004), a study limited to Great Britain and North America, was the first comprehensive study of the history of Baptist theology.

Inasmuch as this book is being issued in 2009, it is anticipated that it may be useful in the observance of the Baptist quadricentennial, which hopefully will be both commemorative and forward-looking.

I am deeply indebted to David S. Dockery for reading the entire typescript and offering advice and encouragement; to Dongsun Cho for his painstaking work on the glossary; to Robert G. Collmer for reading the section on Bunyan; to Paul L. Gritz for reading and offering valuable suggestions especially about chapter 9; to Denton Lotz for encouragement and counsel; to Bill W. Lee for loan of materials and recurring counsel; to Justice C. Anderson, Dinorah Mendez, and Terry F. Coy for assistance relative to Latin America; to Craig A. Blaising for providing a postretirement office with computer; to David Allen, Jane Fiscus, and Joan Conley for support; to Cathy Drewry for assistance with the index of persons; and to Marc A. Jolley and Edmon L. Rowell, Jr. of Mercer University Press for their editorial skills and good judgment.

I am pleased to acknowledge with gratitude that the section on Brazil has been written by Jerry S. Key, longtime missionary professor in the Baptist Theological Seminary of South Brazil; that most of the section on South Korea has been cooperatively written by the authors of the respective monographs and gathered and translated by Samuel Byungdoo Nam, all of the Korean Baptist Theological Seminary; and that the section on Walter B. Shurden has been written by John E. Forsythe, a gifted M.Div. student in Southwestern Baptist Theological Seminary.

Particular thanks are due the staff of A. Webb Roberts Library of Southwestern Baptist Theological Seminary, especially to C. Berry Driver, Robert L. Phillips, Joseph Cathey, Helen Bernard, Glenn Wittig, William C. Taylor, Rachael Spriggs, Jeanne Kennedy, Ken Steffen, and Russell Watkins. Indispensable to this project were the scores of books and articles borrowed from or photocopied by the libraries of theological seminaries, universities, and colleges and by other libraries.

I am indebted to those who have assisted me in gathering materials relative to Baptist theology from various parts of the Baptist world:

Africa—John N. Jonsson, Paul H. Miller, Charles W. Parnell, Karen Viljoen

Asia—Ildefonso Alfafara, Brad Beaman, Precy Carorongan, Frederick S. Downs, Russell A. Morris, Samuel Byungdoo Nam, Lydia Penacerrada, Alfredo Saure

Australia—Thorwald Lorenzen, Ken R. Manley

Europe—Geoffrey R. Breed, Paul S. Fiddes, John-Paul Lotz, Susan J. Mills, Malcolm B. Yarnell III

Latin America—Justice C. Anderson, Stanley D. Clark, Terrell F. Coy, Jerry S. Key, Dinorah Mendez

North America—Sean A. Adams, B. S. Coyne, Matthew A. Finn, Curtis W. Freeman, David E. Garland, Joel C. Gregory, Lloyd Harsch, Daniel Holcomb, Betty Layton, Bill W. Lee, Bill J. Leonard, Cindy Meredith, R. Albert Mohler, Jr., Andrew Rawls, Kristi Robinson, Bill Sumners, Wayne E. Ward, Gregory A. Wills

Amy K. Downey has accomplished a magnificent task in turning my intricate manuscript with numerous subsequent changes and additions into a final and corrected typescript. For her loyalty and diligence I am indeed thankful.

My dear wife, Myrta Ann, has been a partner and participant in everything I have undertaken for three score years and has carried a heavy load of family responsibility. This book is no exception. To her I am abidingly grateful.

August 2008   *James Leo Garrett, Jr.*

Dedicated to
and with blessing for

our sons,

James Leo Garrett III
Robert Thomas Garrett
Paul Latimer Garrett

and our grandsons,

James Mark Garrett
William Latimer Garrett
Michael Thomas Garrett
Wyatt David Garrett

Chapter 1

The Roots of Baptist Beliefs

The people called Baptists have often identified their churches as "New Testament churches" and have frequently insisted that they are not a creedal people. Some Baptists have "leapfrogged" over the Christian centuries, while others have posited a "trail of blood" church succession. Consequently one may be prone to assume that they owe nothing to the creeds, the church councils, or the theologians of the sixteen centuries prior to the advent of the Baptist movement. But that assumption needs to be challenged and tested.

The Councils, the Creeds, and the Fathers

The four earliest ecumenical councils constituted efforts to resolve theological controversies after the subsidence of the major persecutions and the advent of favorable treatment of Christians in the Roman Empire. The Council of Nicaea (325) rejected the teachings of Arius (ca. 250–ca. 336), notably that God is an unoriginate and noncommunicable monad and that Jesus was a creature having a beginning and being subject to change and sin, "less than God and more than man."[1] Nicaea responded by affirming that Jesus as "the Son of God" was "of the substance of the Father," "begotten, not made," and "of one substance with the Father."[2] Baptists have repeatedly affirmed the deity and eternality of Jesus as God's Son and his incarnation, thus manifesting only on rare occasions any tendency to resurrect Arianism.[3]

Apollinarius of Laodicea (ca. 310–ca. 390) refused to allow for a human mind in Jesus by holding that the Godhead and Jesus' body were fused into a single reality.[4] The Pneumatomachians, or Macedonians, opposed the full deity of the Holy Spirit, asserting rather that the Spirit was

---

[1] J. N. D. Kelly, *Early Christian Doctrines* (New York: Harper & Brothers, 1958), 226-31; Jaroslav Pelikan, *The Emergence of the Catholic Tradition (100–600)*, vol. 1, *The Christian Tradition: A History of the Development of Doctrine* (Chicago: University of Chicago Press, 1971) 193-200.

[2] "The Nicene Creed," *NPNF*, 2nd ser., 14:3.

[3] Deviations, as in the case of the early eighteenth-century General Baptists, were recognized as heresy by other Baptists.

[4] Kelly, *Early Christian Doctrines*, 289-95.

a creature or a being between God and creatures.⁵ The Council of Constantinople I (381), building on the objections by Gregory of Nyssa and Gregory of Nazianzus,⁶ rejected Apollinarianism and likewise, together with other heresies, condemned the teaching of the Pneumatomachians.⁷ Baptists, as may be seen in their confessions of faith, have affirmed the full or complete humanity of Jesus⁸ and the deity of the Holy Spirit.⁹

Nestorius (ca.381–ca.451) was credited with advancing the view—whether he actually did continues to be debated by today's scholars—that the two natures of Jesus Christ, the divine and human, were veritably two persons and that these two persons, being unaltered, were only "conjoined" or loosely connected. Nestorius rejected the prevailing use of the term *theotokos* (God-bearing) for Mary the virgin, arguing that "God cannot have a mother" and "Mary bore a man, the vehicle of divinity but not God."[10] The Council of Ephesus (431) after no little intrigue rejected Nestorianism

---

⁵Ibid., 259-60.

⁶Ibid., 295-300.

⁷Canons of Constantinople I, 1, 7, *NPNF*, 2nd ser., 14:172, 185.

⁸"Short Confession of Faith in XX Articles by John Smyth," art. 6; "A Declaration of Faith of English People Remaining at Amsterdam in Holland," art. 8; Somerset Confession, art. 13; Second London Confession of Particular Baptists, art. 8, sect. 2; Orthodox Creed of General Baptists, arts. 6, 7; "Treatise and the Faith and Practices of the Free Will Baptists," art. 5, sect. 2, in William L. Lumpkin, *Baptist Confessions of Faith* (Philadelphia: Judson, 1959) 100, 119, 206, 260-61, 300-301, 371; SBC Statement of Baptist Faith and Message (1963)," art. 2, sect. 2, in Lumpkin, *Baptist Confessions of Faith*, rev. ed. (Valley Forge PA: Judson, 1969) 394.

⁹"A Short Confession of Faith" (1610), arts. 2-3; First London Confession of Particular Baptists, art. 2; Orthodox Creed of General Baptists, art. 8; "Principles of Faith of the Sandy Creek Association," art. 1; "Treatise and the Faith and Practices of the Free Will Baptists," art. 7; "Articles of Faith Put Forth by the Baptist Bible Union of America," art. 3, in ibid., 103, 156-57, 301, 358, 372-73, 385; SBC Statement of Baptist Faith and Message (1963), art. 2, sect. 3, in ibid., rev. ed., 394.

¹⁰Kelly, *Early Christian Doctrines*, 310-17. See also J. F. Bethune-Baker, *Nestorius and His Teaching: A Fresh Examination of the Evidence* (Cambridge UK: Cambridge University Press, 1908; repr.: New York: Kraus, 1969); Friedrich Loofs, *Nestorius and His Place in the History of Christian Doctrine* (Cambridge UK: Cambridge University Press, 1914; repr.: New York: Burt Franklin, 1975).

and its followers and deposed and excommunicated Nestorius.[11] Although modern Baptist confessions of faith have tended not to address this issue specifically,[12] there is no evidence of any Baptist effort to disavow the union of the two natures in the one person of Jesus Christ.

Eutyches (ca.378–454), taking the word "nature" to signify "a concrete existence" and denying that Christ's manhood was of the same substance as our manhood, taught the confusion of his natures so as to imply one nature. Under interrogation, Eutyches acknowledged that Christ was "of two natures" but insisted that this was before the union of the natures and that after the union there was only one nature.[13] After being vindicated at the so-called "Robber Synod" of 448, he was deposed and exiled by the Council of Chalcedon (451). The confessional statement adopted by Chalcedon not only rejected Eutychianism but also Arianism, Apollinarianism, and Nestorianism and explicated the doctrine of two natures in the one person.[14] It would prove in later centuries to be common ground for Roman Catholics, Eastern Orthodox, and Protestants.[15] As was noted in respect to Apollinarianism, Baptists have consistently affirmed the genuine and complete humanity of Jesus and have in reality concurred in Chalcedon's definition even when not explicitly stating such.

Hence for Baptists the affirmations of the deity of Christ, the complete humanity of Christ, the one person of Christ, and the two natures of Christ imply some indebtedness to these early councils, whether or not that indebtedness is formally acknowledged. Moreover, concurrent with these councils—Nicaea I through Chalcedon—was the framing of certain widely used Christian creeds.

---

[11]"The Twelve Anathematisms of St. Cyril against Nestorius," and "Decree of the Council against Nestorius" in *NPNF*, 2nd ser., 14:206-19.

[12]"A Short Confession of Faith" (1610); art. 8; "A Declaration of Faith of English People Remaining at Amsterdam in Holland," art. 8; Second London Confession, art. 8, sect. 2; Orthodox Creed of General Baptists, arts. 6, 7, in Lumpkin, *Baptist Confessions of Faith*, 104-105, 119, 260-61, 300-301.

[13]Kelly, *Early Christian Doctrines*, 330-34.

[14]"The Definition of Faith of the Council of Chalcedon," in *NPNF*, 2nd ser., 14:262-65. See also R. V. Sellers, *The Council of Chalcedon: A Historical and Doctrinal Survey* (London: S.P.C.K., 1953).

[15]See James Leo Garrett, "A Reappraisal of Chalcedon," *Review and Expositor* 71 (Winter 1974): 31-42, esp. 42.

That which we call the Apostles' Creed, sometimes called "R" for Old Roman Symbol, developed during the second and third centuries, being expressed in various similar but not identical texts until finally there came to be a single common text. Framed in order to give instruction at baptism or to refute heresies or possibly for both reasons, R had a Trinitarian structure and an extended section on the Son of God.[16] The Nicene Creed (N), the product of the council in 325, was specifically anti-Arian.[17] That which is called the Niceno-Constantinopolitan Creed (C) has a more extended section on the Holy Spirit. It has traditionally been taken to be the product of the Council of Constantinople I, but it did not appear in official conciliar records until the Council of Chalcedon.[18] The "Athanasian" Creed, actually a formulation based on the Trinitarian theology of Augustine of Hippo, probably originated in southern Gaul in the fifth or sixth century.[19]

Baptists in their congregational worship have not normally included the recitation of any creedal or confessional statement. It is, however, worthy of note that the Orthodox Creed of General Baptists (1678) included the texts of the Apostles' Creed, the Nicene Creed, and the Athanasian Creed and declared that these "ought throughly [sic] to be received, and believed," may be proved from the Scriptures, ought to be understood by all Christians, and should be taught by ministers and "in all christian [sic] families."[20] Also at the first world congress of the Baptist World Alliance in 1905, its president, Alexander Maclaren, in the midst of his presidential address asked all those assembled to rise and to repeat the Apostles' Creed.[21]

---

[16]J. N. D. Kelly, *Early Christian Creeds*, 2nd ed. (New York: David McKay, 1960) 100-66.

[17]Ibid., 211-62.

[18]Ibid., 296-357.

[19]J. N. D. Kelly, *The Athanasian Creed* (New York: Harper & Row, 1964).

[20]Art. 38, in Lumpkin, *Baptist Confessions of Faith*, 326-27.

[21]*The Baptist World Congress, London, July 11-19, 1905: Authorised Record of Proceedings* (London: Baptist Union Publication Department, 1905) 20. For a probing treatment of the dependence of Baptist confessions of faith upon patristic theology and possibly more future "interaction" with the patristic tradition, see Steven R. Harmon, "Baptist Confessions of Faith and the Patristic Tradition," *Perspectives in Religious Studies* 29 (Winter 2002): 349-58; and idem, *Towards Baptist Catholicity: Essays on Tradition and the Baptist Vision*, Studies in Baptist History and Thought 27 (Milton Keynes, UK; Waynesboro GA: Paternoster, 2006).

Baptists have consistently affirmed that the canonical Scriptures are always superior to and more authoritative than any or all postbiblical tradition. Such a fact does not prevent or preclude evidence that certain of the church fathers, especially the Latin fathers, seem to have influenced positively the beliefs of the later Baptists. Two examples may be noted. Tertullian, who was the first Latin Christian writer to use the term *trinitas*, pioneered in the use of what became technical terms for the Trinity (one in substance and three persons)[22] and for the person of Christ (two natures, which he preferred to speak of as "two substances,"[23] in one person).[24] Augustine of Hippo, especially in his controversial writings against the Pelagians, set forth the doctrines of the universality of sin and the necessity of divine grace as pardon and power that would so greatly influence all Western Christians that espousal of strictly Pelagian views would be far less likely,[25] and this was true of most Baptists.

Pre-Reformation Sectarian and Reforming Movements

The modern advocates of Baptist church succession,[26] notably the Landmark Baptists, have posited and sought to identify a chain of pre-Reforma-

---

[22]*Unius substantiae; tres dirigens* (*Against Praxeas*, 2:4).

[23]*Utramque substantiam* (*On the Flesh of Christ*, 18:6).

[24]*In uno plane* (*Against Praxeas*, 27:14).

[25]Here we do not consider either Semipelagianism or those aspects of Augustine's theology that pertain to predestination and irresistible grace.

[26]This is the theory that there existed from the apostolic era to the seventeenth century in unbroken fashion churches which in teaching and practice, although not in name, were conformable to Baptists. See, e.g., George Herbert Orchard, *A Concise History of Baptists from the Time of Christ Their Founder to the 18th Century* (repr. with intro. by J. R. Graves: Lexington KY: Ashland Avenue Baptist Church, 1956; first publ. in London in 1838 under title *A Concise History of Foreign Baptists*; also Nashville: Graves and Marks, 1855; under title *A History of the Baptists in England*, Nashville: Southwestern Publishing, 1859); David Burcham Ray, *Baptist Succession: A Handbook of Baptist History* (Cincinnati: G. E. Stevens, 1870; St. Louis: St. Louis Baptist Publishing, 1880; rev. ed.: Parsons KS: Foley, 1912; Rosemead CA: King's, 1949); Willis Anselm Jarrel, *Baptist Church Perpetuity*, or, *The Continuous Existence of Baptist Churches from the Apostolic to the Present Day Demonstrated by the Bible and by History* (Dallas: by the author, 1894; 3rd ed.: Fulton KY: Baptist Gleaner, 1900); James Milton Carroll, *The Trail of Blood* (Lexington KY: American Baptist Publishing Co., 1931; Lexington KY: Ashland Avenue Baptist Church, 1931, 1979).

tion reforming and sectarian movements. Often the claims of identity between such groups and Baptists of the last four centuries have not matched the historical evidence. But the lack of total identity does not preclude a kinship in respect to particular teachings or a common rejection of teachings and practices prevailing in the dominant ecclesiastical system. Albert Henry Newman, a Baptist historian writing more than a century ago, could find no common ground between modern Baptists and such early movements as Montanism, Novatianism, and Donatism or such later movements as the Paulicians and the Cathari. But Newman saw in early reformers such as Aërius, Jovinian, and Vigilantius and in the ancient British church a nascent antiascetic evangelicalism which did not challenge infant baptism, and he found in the followers of Peter de Bruys and Henry of Lausanne, the Waldenses, the Taborites, Peter Chelčický and the Bohemian Brethren, and the Lollards advocates of antisacramentalism, biblical authority, and primitivism, who stopped short of the full recovery of believer's baptism.[27] Baptists have had no interest in kinship with the mystical heresy of the Free Spirit,[28] or with later mystics such as John Tauler, Henry Suso, and John Ruysbroeck,[29] but possibly with late quasi-Evangelicals such as John of Wesel, Wessel Gansfort, and Cornelius Hoen.[30]

The Magisterial Protestant Reformation

Despite modern denials by certain Baptists that Baptists are Protestants,[31] the matrix of the Baptist movement had been powerfully shaped by the

---

[27]Newman, *A History of Anti-Pedobaptism from the Rise of Pedobaptism to A.D. 1609* (Philadelphia: American Baptist Publication Society, 1897) 15-61.

[28]Gordon Leff, *Heresy in the Later Middle Ages: The Relation of Heterodoxy to Dissent, ca.1250–ca.1450*, 2 vols. (Manchester UK: Manchester University Press; New York: Barnes and Noble, 1967) 1:308-407.

[29]*Late Medieval Mysticism*, ed. Ray C. Petry, Library of Christian Classics 13 (Philadelphia: Westminster, 1957) 245-62, 285-320.

[30]A. H. Newman, *A Manual of Church History*, 2 vols., rev. ed. (Philadelphia: American Baptist Publication Society, 1933) 1:620-21; Heiko Augustinus Oberman, ed., *Forerunners of the Reformation: The Shape of Late Medieval Thought* (New York: Holt, Rinehart & Winston, 1966) 63-65, 252-53.

[31]William Owen Carver, "Are Baptists Protestants?" *The Chronicle* 14 (July 1951): 116-20. Carver was refuting those who had given a negative answer largely on the basis of Baptist church successionism. According to Carver, "Anabaptists and Baptists have not improperly been described as 'Protestants of the Protestants'" (117).

Protestant Reformation, and some have even claimed that the Baptists are the truly thoroughgoing Reformers.[32]

Martin Luther's doctrines of the supremacy of the Scriptures over all, especially late, church tradition and of Christ as the center of the Scriptures, of declarative justification by God's grace through faith alone, and of the priesthood of all believers[33] were all affirmed by Baptists, even when no specific acknowledgment was made to Luther. Likewise, Ulrich Zwingli's doctrine of the Lord's Supper as a memorial or symbolic observance[34] proved to be the dominant, though not the sole, theme in the Baptist teaching about the Supper. Moreover, John Calvin's doctrine of predestination,[35] whatever its debt to Augustine of Hippo, Thomas Bradwardine, John Wycliffe, and John Huss, had an impact on the theology of many Anglo-American Baptists. Martin Bucer's teaching that discipline is a mark of the true church,[36] though perhaps routed through Calvin or through the Anabaptists, found acceptance among early Baptists. Among the confessions of faith produced by the magisterial wing of the Reformation the mid-seventeenth century Westminster Confession of Faith (1647)[37] was by far the most influential on early Baptist confessions of faith.[38]

---

[32]John Quincy Adams, *Baptists the Only Thorough Religious Reformers*, rev. ed. (New York: Sheldon, 1876).

[33]Paul Althaus, *The Theology of Martin Luther*, trans. Robert C. Schultz (Philadelphia: Fortress, 1966) 72-102, 224-50, 313-18; A. Skevington Wood, *Captive to the Word: Martin Luther: Doctor of Sacred Scripture* (Exeter UK: Paternoster, 1969) 119-28; E. F. Klug, *From Luther to Chemnitz: On Scripture and the Word* (Grand Rapids MI: Eerdmans, 1971) 51-75.

[34]W. Peter Stevens, *Zwingli: An Introduction to His Thought* (Oxford UK: Oxford University Press, 1992) 94-110, esp. 98-99.

[35]François Wendel, *Calvin: The Origins and Development of His Religious Thought*, trans. Philip Mairet (New York: Harper & Row, 1963) 263-84.

[36]Martin Bucer, *Common Places*, trans. and ed. D. F. Wright, The Courtenay Library of Reformation Classics 4 (Appleford, Berkshire UK: Sutton Courtenay, 1972) intro. by Wright, 31.

[37]For the text, see Philip Schaff, *The Creeds of Christendom*, 3 vols. (New York: Harper & Brothers, 1877) 3:598-704.

[38]Especially the Second London Confession of Particular Baptists and the Orthodox Creed of General Baptists, in Lumpkin, *Baptist Confessions of Faith*, 241-95, 297-334.

Continental Anabaptism

The sixteenth-century Anabaptists on the continent of Europe have played a singular role in the interpretation of Baptist origins. Those advocating different views of origins[39] have treated the Anabaptists differently. Those who have sought to trace Baptists in succession to John the Baptist and the Jerusalem church have regarded the Anabaptists as an essential link in the chain of succession but have usually done little research or exhibited no scholarly acumen in dealing with the Anabaptists. Those who have adhered to the "Anabaptist spiritual kinship" theory have posited on the basis of careful studies not only of sixteenth-century Anabaptists but also various

---

[39]Here we follow the threefold classification of Robert G. Torbet, *A History of the Baptists* (Philadelphia: Judson, 1950) 59-62. In mid-twentieth century and following, the issue of Baptist origins was intensely debated by Baptist scholars. Those advocating Anabaptist influence on English Baptists in terms of teachings, if not an organizational nexus, included Ernest Alexander Payne, *The Free Church Tradition in the Life of England* (London: SCM, 1944) 25, 27-28; idem, *The Baptist Movement in the Reformation and Onwards* (London: Kingsgate, 1947) 20; idem, *The Anabaptists of the 16th Century and Their Influence in the Modern World* (London: Carey Kingsgate, 1949); idem, "Who Were the Baptists?," *Baptist Quarterly* 16 (October 1956): 339-42; Alfred Clair Underwood, *A History of the English Baptists* (London: Carey Kingsgate, 1947) 21-27, 35-55; James D. Mosteller, "Baptists and Anabaptists," *The Chronicle* 20 (January 1957): 3-27; ibid. (July 1957): 100-14; William R. Estep, Jr., "A Baptist Reappraisal of Sixteenth Century Anabaptists," *Review and Expositor* 55 (January 1958): 55-58; idem, *The Anabaptist Story* (Nashville: Broadman, 1963) 200-22; and Glen H. Stassen, "Anabaptist Influence in the Origin of the Particular Baptists," *Mennonite Quarterly Review* 36 (October 1962): 322-48. Those advocating the English Separatist origin of English Baptists with little or no influence from continental Anabaptism included Winthrop Still Hudson, "Baptists Were Not Anabaptists," *The Chronicle* 16 (October 1953): 171-79; idem, "Who Were the Baptists?," *Baptist Quarterly* 16 (July 1956): 303-12; ibid., 17 (April 1957): 53-55; Norman H. Maring, "Notes from Religious Journals," *Foundations* 1 (July 1958): 91-95; Lonnie D. Kliever, "General Baptist Origins: The Question of Anabaptist Influence," *Mennonite Quarterly Review* 36 (October 1962): 291-321; Barrington R. White, *The English Separatist Tradition: From the Marian Martyrs to the Pilgrim Fathers* (London: Oxford University Press, 1971) 161-64; idem, *The English Baptists of the Seventeenth Century*, vol. 1 of *A History of the English Baptists* (London: Baptist Historical Society, 1983) 21-23; and H. Leon McBeth, *The Baptist Heritage* (Nashville: Broadman, 1987) 49-63.

pre-Reformation rebaptizing sects that these were kinspeople to the later Baptists. Those who hold on the basis of research that Baptists derived from English Separatist Puritanism usually have viewed Anabaptists as outside the story of Baptist origins and as not contributing significantly to Baptist theology.[40]

The classification of various types of sixteenth-century Anabaptists has been attempted by modern church historians who have specialized in this field. Their work is important in determining whether and which Anabaptists may have influenced Baptists. A. H. Newman posited a fivefold classification of Anabaptists: "the chiliastic" or millennial, "the soundly biblical," "the mystical," "the pantheistic," and "the anti-trinitarian."[41] George Huntston Williams within the larger framework of a threefold classification of "the Radical Reformation" (Anabaptists, Spiritualists, and Evangelical Rationalists) identified three types of Anabaptists: "revolutionary," "contemplative," " and "evangelical."[42] Newman's "chiliastic" Anabaptists and Williams's "revolutionary" Anabaptists, which included Melchior Hofmann and the Münster kingdom, were virtually identical but did not seemingly shape in a positive way the later Baptists, except at the point of Hofmann's Christology.[43] Williams's "contemplative" Anabaptists included Hans Denck and Ludwig Hetzer, as did Newman's "mystical" Anabaptists, but Williams did not include Newman's "pantheistic" Anabaptists such as David Joris, and Williams considered Caspar Schwenckfeld to have been an "evangelical Spiritualist." None of these can be seen as having significant influence upon the later Baptists. The same may be said of Newman's "antitrinitarian Anabaptists," who may be equated with Williams's "Evangelical Rationalists," whose only traceable influence may have been

---

[40]For a detailed account of the historiography of Anabaptist-Baptist relations, see Goki Saito, "An Investigation into the Relationships between the Early English Baptists and the Dutch Anabaptists" (Th.D. diss., Southern Baptist Theological Seminary, 1974) 11-58.

[41]*A Manual of Church History*, 2:156-200.

[42]Intro. to "Part One," in *Spiritual and Anabaptist Writers*, ed. George Huntston Williams and Angel M. Mergal, The Library of Christian Classics 25 (Philadelphia: Westminster, 1957) 28-31. Williams also set forth a threefold classification of Spiritualists: "revolutionary," "rational," and "evangelical" (ibid., 32-35).

[43]Williams, *The Radical Reformation* (Philadelphia: Westminster, 1962), 328-32; William R. Estep, *The Anabaptist Story: An Introduction to Sixteenth-Century Anabaptism*, 3rd ed. (Grand Rapids MI: Eerdmans, 1996) 290-91.

that of Socinianism on the Mennonite-oriented Rhynsburger community,[44] from which Particular Baptists seemingly derived the practice of baptism by immersion. Hence the focus must clearly rest upon those whom Newman denominated "soundly biblical" Anabaptists, namely, the Swiss Brethren, the Hutterites, the South Germans, and the Mennonites.

Who, then, were the theological writers among these evangelical Anabaptists who may possibly have influenced even indirectly the Baptists? An excellent foretaste of Anabaptist teachings may be seen in George Blaurock's account of his meeting with two Swiss, Conrad Grebel and Felix Manz:

> They came to one mind in these things, and in the pure fear of God they recognized that a person must learn from the divine Word and preaching a true faith which manifests itself in love, and receive the true Christian baptism on the basis of the recognized and confessed faith, in the union with God of a good conscience, prepared) henceforth to serve God in a holy Christian life with all godliness, also to be steadfast to the end in tribulation.[45]

Moreover, when Grebel and his associates wrote to Thomas Müntzer, a revolutionary Spiritualist and antipedobaptist, they urged him: "Go forward with the Word and establish a Christian church with the help of Christ and his rule, as we find it instituted in Matt. 18:15-18 and applied in the Epistles."[46] Reflective of the ecclesiological concerns of the early Swiss Anabaptists were the Schleitheim Articles (1527), probably the work of Michael Sattler, with their sevenfold emphasis: believer's baptism, excommunication, the Lord's Supper, separation from the world, the office of pastor, nonuse of the sword, and nontaking of oaths.[47]

Balthasar Hubmaier wrote his 36-article "On Heretics and Those Who Burn Them," "the first text of the Reformation directed specifically to the

---

[44]On the Rhynsburgers, see Newman, *A History of Anti-Pedobaptism*, 321-22, 387.

[45]Excerpted from the Hutterite *Chronicle*, in *Spiritual and Anabaptist Writers*, 43.

[46]Grebel et al., "Letters to Thomas Müntzer," in *Spiritual and Anabaptist Writers*, 79.

[47]For the text, see Lumpkin, *Baptist Confessions of Faith*, 23-31, and *The Legacy of Michael Sattler*, trans. and ed. John Howard Yoder, Classics of the Radical Reformation 1 (Scottdale PA: Herald, 1973) 34-43.

topic of the liberty of dissent,"[48] four major treatises on baptism,[49] a treatise on excommunication,[50] and "On the Sword,"[51] which was directed against his more pacifist fellow Anabaptists. It is not a question as to whether early English Baptists read the German-language writings by Hubmaier; rather it is whether his concepts of religious freedom, baptism, church discipline, and the rightful use of the sword[52] may have so crossed the English Channel as to make their advocacy by English Baptists something less than an innovation.

Pilgram Marpeck's two major writings contain a recurrent emphasis on the differences between the Old Testament and the New Testament and a rather complete treatment of baptism as "witness" (*Zeugnis*) rather than as "symbol" (*Zeichen*).[53]

---

[48]H. Wayne Pipkin and John Howard Yoder, intro. to "On Heretics and Those Who Burn Them," in *Balthasar Hubmaier: Theologian of Anabaptism*, trans. and ed. Pipkin and Yoder, Classics of the Radical Reformation 5 (Scottdale PA and Kitchener ON: Herald, 1989) 58. H. C. Vedder, *Balthasar Hubmaier: The Leader of the Anabaptists* (New York: G. P. Putnam's Sons, 1905) 84, and William R. Estep, *Revolution within the Revolution: The First Amendment in Historical Context, 1612–1789* (Grand Rapids MI: Eerdmans, 1990) 30, esp. n. 11, have held that Hubmaier was espousing full religious freedom for all humankind, whereas Torsten Bergsten, *Balthasar Hubmaier: Anabaptist Theologian*, trans. Irwin J. Barnes and William R. Estep and ed. William R. Estep (Valley Forge PA: Judson, 1978) 131-32, held that Hubmaier was calling only for religious freedom for the Anabaptists in Waldshut.

[49]"On the Christian Baptism of Believers," "Dialogue with Zwingli's Baptism Book," "Old and New Teachers on Believer's Baptism," and "On Infant Baptism against Oecolampad," in *Balthasar Hubmaier: Theologian of Anabaptism*, 95-149, 170-233, 246-74, 276-95.

[50]"On the Christian Ban," in ibid., 410-25.

[51]In ibid., 494-523. This treatise helps to explain why for modern Mennonites Hubmaier is not such a hero, whereas for Baptists he is. Baptists have followed Hubmaier in holding that a Christian can be a civil magistrate and therein make proper use of the sword.

[52]See Bergsten, *Balthasar Hubmaier: Anabaptist Theologian and Martyr*, 382-98, esp. 385, 387, 397-98.

[53]"Confession of 1532" and "The Admonition of 1542," in *The Writings of Pilgram Marpeck*, trans. and ed. William Klassen and Walter Klaassen, Classics of the Radical Reformation 2 (Scottdale PA, and Kitchener ON: Herald, 1978) 108-57, 160-302; Klassen and Klaassen, intro. to "Confession of 1532," 107. See also David C. Steinmetz, *Reformers in the Wings* (Philadelphia: Fortress, 1971) 219-30.

Among the numerous writings by Menno Simons were his *Foundation of Christian Doctrine*,[54] with its threefold "call to discipleship," refutation of Roman Catholicism," and "appeals for toleration," his *Christian Baptism*,[55] three treatises on church discipline,[56] and three writings expressive of his peculiar view of the incarnation.[57] The argument has been made by Glen Stassen that the First London Confession of Particular Baptists (1644) was indebted to Menno's *Foundation of Christian Doctrine*.[58] Whatever influence his writings on church discipline may have had on early English Baptists such as John Smyth, any such influence stopped short of Baptist acceptance of "shunning," or the social ostracism of those excommunicated, including that of husband and wife.[59] Furthermore, Menno's views of the incarnation, namely, that, since women supposedly produce no seed, the Word became a human being in Mary, but not of or from Mary,[60] being akin to the teaching of Melchior Hofmann[61] as to the celestial flesh of Jesus, posed a problem for the early English General Baptists but did not gain acceptance by them.[62] Dietrich (or Dirk) Philips in his *Enchiridion*

---

[54]In *The Complete Writings of Menno Simons, c.1496–1561*, trans. Leonard Verduin, ed. John Christian Wenger (Scottdale PA: Herald, 1956) 103-226.

[55]In ibid., 227-87.

[56]"A Kind Admonition on Church Discipline," "A Clear Account of Excommunication," and "Instruction on Excommunication," in ibid., 407-18, 455-85, 959-98.

[57]"Brief and Clear Confession," "The Incarnation of Our Lord," and "Reply to Martin Micron," in ibid., 419-54, 783-834, 835-913.

[58]Stassen, "Anabaptist Influence in the Origin of the Particular Baptists," 322-48, esp. 347.

[59]"Short Confession of Faith in XX Articles by John Smyth" (1609), art. 18; "A Short Confession of Faith" (1610), art. 34; "A Declaration of Faith of English People Remaining at Amsterdame in Holland" (1611), art. 18, in Lumpkin, *Baptist Confessions of Faith*, 101, 111, 121. The only confession favorable to shunning seems to have been "Propositions and Conclusions concerning True Christian Religion" (1612–1614), art. 80, in Lumpkin, *Baptist Confessions of Faith*, 139.

[60]J. C. Wenger, intro. to "Brief and Clear Confession," in *The Complete Writings of Menno Simons*, 420. See also Timothy George, *Theology of the Reformers* (Nashville: Broadman, 1988) 281-85.

[61]See Williams, *The Radical Reformation*, 325-32. As to Menno's slight alteration of Hofmann's doctrine, see ibid., 395-96, 503.

[62]Thomas Helwys opposed all forms of denial that Jesus took his human body from Mary in his *An Advertisement or Admonition unto the Congregations, which Men Call the New Fryelers* and "accused John Smyth of accepting the Christology

identified seven "ordinances" of the true church[63] and its twelve "notes,"[64] the latter drawn from the New Testament Apocalypse. The early English Baptists would also identify and characterize the church as distinct from the eschatological kingdom of God. Baptists have not accepted the teaching about the community of goods set forth by the Hutterite theologian, Peter Rideman,[65] but some of his ecclesiological images[66] were employed by later Baptists.

What specific Anabaptist teachings, therefore, can be identified as possibly influencing, even indirectly, the English Baptists? In answering this question, we will utilize two Mennonite confessions of faith, the Waterland Confession (1580) and the Dordrecht Confession (1632).[67] First, there is believer's baptism as constitutive of a gathered or truly ordered church. The Schleitheim Articles[68] and the Waterland Confession[69] specified believer's baptism, and the Dordrecht Confession[70] related it to incorporation into the church. An early Helwys confession[71] was explicit both about

---

of the Mennonites." James Robert Coggins, *John Smyth's Congregation: English Separatism, Mennonite Influence, and the Elect Nation*, Studies in Anabaptist and Mennonite History 32 (Scottdale PA, Waterloo ON: Herald, 1991) 123-26. "A Declaration of Faith of English People Remaining at Amsterdam in Holland," art. 8, in Lumpkin, *Baptist Confessions of Faith*, 119.

[63]Pure doctrine, two sacraments, footwashing, evangelical separation, command of disciples to love one another, keeping of Christ's commandments, and endurance of persecution: "The Church of God," in *Spiritual and Anabaptist Writers*, 240-55.

[64]The Holy City, the New Jerusalem, its having come down from heaven, a bride, the glory of God, high walls, twelve gates, without temple yet purified by tribulation, the gates being open, stream of living water and trees of life, inclusion of Gentiles and exclusion of the wicked, and servants seeing, serving, and reigning with the Lord, in ibid., 255-60.

[65]*Account of Our Religion, Doctrine, and Faith*, trans. Kathleen E. Hasenberg (London: Hodder & Stoughton, 1950) 88-91.

[66]Especially holy people, bride, body, assembly of the true children of God, gathering by the Holy Spirit, light of the world, and community of saints. Ibid., 38-44, 114.

[67]For the texts, see Lumpkin, *Baptist Confessions of Faith*, 44-66, 67-78.

[68]Art. 1, in ibid., 25.

[69]Art. 31, in ibid., 60.

[70]Art. 7, in ibid., 71.

[71]"A Declaration of Faith of English People Remaining at Amsterdam in Holland," arts. 13, 14, in ibid., 120.

believer's baptism and the constituting of churches, whereas other General and Particular Baptist confessions[72] only affirmed believer's baptism. A possible negation of such Mennonite influence comes from Irwin B. Horst's argument that so-called Anabaptists in pre-Elizabethan England did not practice believer's baptism.[73] But the Separatists retained pedobaptism, and John Smyth's congregation was in Amsterdam. For William R. Estep, Jr., there was "little doubt that Mennonite influence played a role in Smyth's rethinking of the biblical teachings on baptism and the church."[74]

Second, there is church discipline as necessary to the life of the true church, especially on the basis of Matt. 18:15-17. Anabaptist confessions[75] clearly specified admonition and excommunication, or the ban, and the same was true of early English General and Particular Baptist confessions.[76]

Third, there is the elevation of the New Testament in authority over the Old Testament, especially in matters of ecclesiology. Marpeck had elevated the New Testament while retaining the canonicity and inspiration of the Old Testament.[77] Although this elevation of the New Testament is not specifically stated in the earliest Baptist confessions of faith, John Smyth's

---

[72]"Propositions and Conclusions concerning True Christian Religion," art. 70; First London Confession of Particular Baptists, art. 39; Second London Confession of Particular Baptists, art. 29, sect. 2, in Lumpkin, *Baptist Confessions of Faith*, 137, 167, 291.

[73]*The Radical Brethren: Anabaptism and the English Reformation to 1558*, Bibliotheca Humanistica et Reformatorica 2 (Nieuwkoop: B. de Graaf, 1972) 178.

[74]*Revolution within the Revolution*, 45. See also Estep, "On the Origins of English Baptists," *Baptist History and Heritage* 22 (April 1987): 19-26.

[75]Schleitheim Articles, art. 2; Waterland Confession, art. 35, in Lumpkin, *Baptist Confessions of Faith*, 25, 62.

[76]"Short Confession of Faith in XX Articles by John Smyth," art. 17; "A Short Confession of Faith" (1610), arts. 33, 34; "A Declaration of Faith of English People Remaining at Amsterdam in Holland," art. 17; First London Confession of Particular Baptists, arts. 42, 43, in ibid., 101, 110-11, 121, 168.

[77]William Klassen, *Covenant and Community: The Life, Writings and Hermeneutics of Pilgram Marpeck* (Grand Rapids MI: Eerdmans, 1968) 105, 124-30; Estep, *The Anabaptist Story: An Introduction to Sixteenth-Century Anabaptism*, 3rd ed., 193-95.

Principles and Inferences concerning the Visible Church (1607)[78] exhibits the much greater reliance on the New Testament.[79]

Fourth, there is the advocacy of religious freedom for all human beings and the absence of persecution. Although the claim that Hubmaier advocated such freedom has been challenged,[80] the advocacy by Menno Simons[81] is rather clear. Likewise, Smyth,[82] Helwys,[83] Mark Leonard Busher,[84] and John Murton[85] were advocates.

Finally, the fact needs to be noted that certain Mennonite teachings and practices, identifiably four, were specifically rejected by the early English Baptists. First, Baptists[86] rejected the Anabaptist teaching[87] that Christians ought not to serve as civil magistrates for they must use the sword, although John Smyth was an exception.[88] Second, Baptists[89] rejected the Anabaptist

---

[78]In *The Works of John Smyth, Fellow of Christ's College, 1594-8*, tercentenary ed. for the Baptist Historical Society, ed. William Thomas Whitley, 2 vols. (Cambridge UK: Cambridge University Press, 1915) 1:249-68. Estep, *Revolution within the Revolution*, 41.

[79]For a modern Baptist exposition of the supremacy of the New Testament, see Henry Cook, *What Baptists Stand For* (London: Kingsgate, 1947) 13-24.

[80]See n. 48 above.

[81]"Foundation of Christian Doctrine," part 3; "A Pathetic Supplication to All Magistrates"; "Brief Defense to All Theologians"; "The Cross of the Saints," in *The Complete Writings of Menno Simons*, 190-226, 525-31, 535-40, 581-622.

[82]"Propositions and Conclusions concerning True Christian Religion," art. 84, in Lumpkin, *Baptist Confessions of Faith*, 140.

[83]Helwys, *A Short Declaration of the Mistery [sic] of Iniquity* (1612) (replica ed.: London: Kingsgate, 1935). Also Helwys, *A Short Declaration of the Mystery of Iniquity (1611/1612)*, ed. and intro. by Richard Groves, Classics of Religious Liberty 1 (Macon GA: Mercer University Press, 1998).

[84]*Religion's Peace; or, A Plea for Liberty of Conscience* (1614), in *Tracts on Liberty of Conscience and Persecution, 1614–1661*, ed. Edward Bean Underhill (London: J. Haddon, 1846) 1-81.

[85]*Objections Answered by Way of Dialogue* . . . (1615) and *A Most Humble Supplication of Many of the King's Majesty's Loyal Subjects* . . . (1620), in ibid., 85-231.

[86]"A Declaration of Faith of English People Remaining at Amsterdam in Holland," art. 24, in Lumpkin, *Baptist Confessions of Faith*, 122-23.

[87]Schleitheim Articles, art. 6; Waterland Confession, art. 37, in ibid., 27-28, 63-64.

[88]"A Short Confession of Faith" (1610), art. 35, in ibid., 111-12.

[89]Second London Confession of Particular Baptists, art. 24, sect. 2, in ibid.,

teaching[90] that Christians ought not to be soldiers but rather be nonresistant. Third, Baptists,[91] with the exception of John Smyth,[92] rejected the Anabaptist teaching[93] that Christians ought not to take civil oaths. Fourth, Baptists rejected, as noted previously,[94] the Mennonite practice[95] of shunning those who have been excommunicated.

English Separatist Puritans and Independents

Separatists we understand to have been those English Puritans who, not being willing to continue to await thoroughgoing reforms in the Church of England, separated therefrom by constituting congregations or conventicles on the basis of a church covenant and congregational polity. B. R. White has insisted that their goal was not so much reformation of the existing church as restitution of New Testament Christianity.[96]

Certain precursors to the Separatists have been identified, although the extent to which the Separatists acknowledged them as their forerunners is disputed. Sectarian "Freewillers"[97] in Kent and Essex during the reign of Edward VI (1547–1553) were cited by Champlin Burrage,[98] but White[99] discounted them as forerunners. The Strangers' Church, composed of foreigners, established by John a Lasco, expelled under Mary, and reconsti-

---

284.

[90] Dordrecht Confession, art. 14, in ibid., 75-76.

[91] "A Declaration of Faith of English People Remaining at Amsterdam in Holland," art. 25, in ibid., 123.

[92] "A Short Confession of Faith" (1610), art. 36; Propositions and Conclusions concerning True Christian Religion," art. 86, in ibid., 112, 140.

[93] Schleitheim Articles, art. 7; Waterland Confession, art. 38; Dordrecht Confession, art. 15, in ibid., 29-30, 64, 76.

[94] See n. 59 above.

[95] Waterland Confession, art. 36; and Dordrecht Confession, art. 17, in ibid., 63, 77.

[96] *The English Separatist Tradition: From the Marian Martyrs to the Pilgrim Fathers*, xii, xiii, 2.

[97] O. T. Hargrave, "The Freewillers in the English Reformation," *Church History* 37 (September 1968): 271-80, who identified these as "Arminians *avant la lettre*" (280).

[98] *The Early English Dissenters in the Light of Recent Research, 1550–1641*, 2 vols. (Cambridge UK: Cambridge University, 1912; repr.: New York: Russell and Russell, 1967) 1:50-53; 2:1-6.

[99] *The English Separatist Tradition*, 2-3.

tuted under Elizabeth I, according to Timothy George, "with their own liturgy and discipline, was itself a source of envy on the part of some who found the pace of reformation in the established Church intolerably slow."[100] Secret conventicles, especially one in the London area, during Mary's reign (1553–1558), which seem to have been distinct from the earlier Freewillers,[101] "were sustained by the ministry of itinerant preachers" and practiced excommunication.[102] During the early Elizabethan era there were congregations that were distinct from the Church of England as to worship and met in private homes, but they left no evidence of any teaching or practice of a covenanted or gathered church.[103] From one of these, the Plumbers' Hall Church in London, Puritan rather than Separatist,[104] which claimed a biblical warrant for church reform and practiced church discipline,[105] some members departed and united with the Privy Church.[106] The latter, led by Richard Fitz, was clearly Separatist vis-à-vis the Church of England,[107] indeed "the first-known congregation in England which had a covenant." "To obey this covenant each member separately pledged himself and then took communion as a ratification of his consent."[108]

Major writings by Separatist authors gave expression to Separatist principles.[109] Robert Harrison (?–1585?) in *A Treatise of the Church and the*

---

[100]*John Robinson and the English Separatist Tradition*, NABPR Dissertation Series 1 (Macon GA: Mercer University Press, 1982) 16.

[101]W. M. S. West, "The Anabaptists and the Rise of the Baptist Movement," in *Christian Baptism: A Fresh Attempt to Understand the Rite in Terms of Scripture, History, and Theology*, ed. Alec Gilmore (Philadelphia: Judson, 1959) 255.

[102]George, *John Robinson and the English Separatist Tradition*, 17-23. White, *The English Separatist Tradition*, 6-14, has treated these as precursors to the Separatists.

[103]West, "The Anabaptists and the Rise of the Baptist Movement," 258.

[104]Burrage, *The Early English Dissenters*, 1:79-86.

[105]George, *John Robinson and the English Separatist Tradition*, 27-31.

[106]Estep, *The Anabaptist Story*, 278.

[107]Burrage, *The Early English Dissenters*, 1:86-93; 2:9-18; White, *The English Separatist Tradition*, 29-32; Estep, *The Anabaptist Story*, 179-80.

[108]West, "The Anabaptists and the Rise of the Baptist Movement," 258-59.

[109]McBeth, *The Baptist Heritage*, 27-32, has labeled Robert Browne's congregation "the pioneer church," Francis Johnson's "the ancient church," John Robinson's "the pilgrim church," and Henry Jacob's "the JLJ church" (so identified by the last initials of its first three pastors: Jacob, Lathrop, Jessey).

Kingdome of Christ (ca.1580) equated the church and the kingdom, enjoined the observance of Matt. 18:15-17, and defended a separated and gathered church.[110] Robert Browne's (1550?–1633) *A Treatise of Reformation without Tarying for Anie* (1582) endorsed the civil duties of the magistrates but denied them the power to reform the church, conceived of the risen Christ as ruling covenanted congregations, and called on Puritans not to "tarry" for magisterial reform.[111] Henry Barrow (1550?–1593) in *Four Causes of Separation* (1587) identified the false manner of worshiping the true God, the ungodly members retained in churches, the anti-Christian ministry imposed on the churches, and the anti-Christian polity of churches.[112] Barrow and John Greenwood (?–1593) in *The True Church and the False Church* (1588) extended the list of marks of the false church to eleven,[113] and Barrow in *A True Description out of the Worde of God, of the Visible Church* (1589) prescribed a fivefold ministry (pastor, doctor, elders, deacons, widows).[114] Barrow's anti-Anglican polemic reached its full expression in *A Brief Discoverie of the False Church* (1590).[115] Henry Ainsworth (1571–1622?) answered the Oxford doctors in *An Apologie or Defence of Such True Christians as One Commonly (but Unjustly) Called Brownists* (1604),[116] whereas Francis Johnson (1562–1618) in *Certayne Reasons and Arguments Proving That It Is Not Lawfull to Heare or Have Any Spiritual Communion with the Present Ministerie of the Church of England* (1608)[117] set forth seven reasons.

The Separatist congregation in London of which Francis Johnson was pastor, but which was exiled in Amsterdam without Johnson and which then

---

[110]For the text, see *The Writings of Robert Harrison and Robert Browne*, ed. Albert Peel and Leland H. Carlson, Elizabethan Nonconformist Texts 2 (London: George Allen & Unwin, 1953) 31-69.

[111]For the text, see ibid., 151-70. White, *The English Separatist Tradition*, 58-62.

[112]For the text, see *The Writings of Henry Barrow, 1587–1590*, Elizabethan Nonconformist Texts 3 (London: George Allen & Unwin, 1962) 54-66.

[113]For the text, see *The Writings of John Greenwood, 1587–1590, together with the Joint Writings of Henry Barrow and John Greenwood, 1587–1590*, Elizabethan Nonconformist Texts 4 (London: George Allen & Unwin, 1962) 98-102.

[114]For the text, see *The Writings of Henry Barrow*, 2:4-23.

[115]For the text, see ibid., 263-673.

[116]Photocopy from Cambridge University Library.

[117]Photocopy from Bodleian Library, Oxford.

chose Henry Ainsworth as pastor, framed in 1596 a confession of faith entitled *A True Confession*. It expressed Calvinistic doctrine and congregational polity and would be used "as a model" by Particular Baptist churches in London when they framed their 1644 Confession.[118] Among its major doctrines were divine foreordination to salvation and to condemnation, the fall of Adam and its consequences, Christ's offices as mediator, prophet, priest, and king, the royal priesthood of the people of God, the identification of the church with Christ's spiritual kingdom, the fivefold ministry, congregational polity, and the duty of civil magistrates to suppress false religions and establish the true religion.[119]

What specific Separatist doctrines may have positively influenced the early English Baptists? First, there is humanity's Adamic disability. The First London Confession of Particular Baptists[120] employed language almost identical to that of *A True Confession*,[121] and the Second London Confession,[122] being a revision of the Westminster Confession of Faith, was even more specific as to humanity's being "in" Adam and Eve when they fell. Second, we take note of the Bible as the rule of faith and practice. *A True Confession* described the Bible as "the rule of this knowledge, faith and obedience,"[123] and the Second London Confession, modifying the Westminster's language, declared "The Holy Scripture is the only sufficient, certain, and infallible rule of all saving Knowledge, Faith, and Obedience."[124] Third, the royal priesthood of all Christians seems to have come to the Baptists from Separatism. Whereas both Anabaptist[125] and Separatist[126] documents referred to the offices of Christ as prophet, priest, and king, only *A True*

---

[118]Lumpkin, *Baptist Confessions of Faith*, 79-81.

[119]For the text, see ibid., 82-97.

[120]Art. 5, in ibid., 158.

[121]Art. 5, in ibid., 83.

[122]Second London, art. 6, esp. sects. 2, 3, in ibid., 258-59; Westminster, art. 6, esp. sects. 2, 3, in Philip Schaff, *The Creeds of Christendom*, 3 vols., 4th ed. (New York: Harper & Brothers, 1919) 3:615-16.

[123]Art. 7, in Lumpkin, *Baptist Confessions of Faith*, 84.

[124]Second London, art. 1, sect. 1, in ibid., 248; Westminster, art. 1, in Schaff, *The Creeds of Christendom*, 3:600-606.

[125]Waterland Confession, arts. 11, 12, 14, in Lumpkin, *Baptist Confessions of Faith*, 50-51.

[126]*A True Confession*, arts. 10, 12-18, in ibid., 85-88.

Confession[127] specifically and in detail taught the universal Christian priesthood. Fourth, there is congregational polity, about which the Separatists were very explicit. *A True Confession*[128] explains the congregation's duties respecting its ministers, excommunication and its careful use, and mutual counsel and help among congregations. A Helwys confession taught that no congregation should assert any "prerogative" over another,[129] the First London Confession spelled out the authority of each congregation to choose its officers,[130] and the Second London Confession taught that congregations have authority over their worship and discipline and for choosing and ordaining both bishops or elders and deacons.[131]

But there were some Separatist teachings which were rejected or at least not accepted by early English Baptists. First, there is double predestination, which was clearly taught in *A True Confession*,[132] whereas the First London Confession[133] referred only to election to salvation and vengeance toward, not foreordination of, the nonelect. According to the Second London Confession[134] the nonelect are "left to act in their sin to their just condemnation" in what some call the doctrine of preterition (passing over). Moreover, the Westminster Confession's references to foreordination "to everlasting death" and ordination to wrath were deleted.[135] The Orthodox Creed of General Baptists, building upon the Westminster, relocated and rewrote the doctrine of divine decrees so as to treat them as conditional.[136] Second, the doctrine of double reconciliation was not retained. According to *A True Confession*,[137] not only are elect human beings reconciled to God through the death of Jesus Christ but also God is reconciled to elect humans

---

[127]Ibid., arts. 14, 17, in ibid., 85-86, 87.

[128]Ibid., arts. 22-25, 38, in ibid., 89-90, 94.

[129]"A Declaration of English People Remaining at Amsterdam in Holland," arts. 11-12, in Lumpkin, *Baptist Confessions of Faith*, 120.

[130]Art. 36, in ibid., 166.

[131]Art. 26, sects. 7-9, in ibid., 286-87.

[132]Art. 3, in ibid., 82-83.

[133]Arts. 5-6, in ibid., 158.

[134]Art. 3, sect. 3, in ibid., 254.

[135]Second London, art. 3, sects. 3, 6-7, in ibid., 254-55; Westminster, art. 3, sects. 3, 7, in Schaff, *The Creeds of Christendom*, 3:608-10.

[136]Arts. 9-10, in Lumpkin, *Baptist Confessions of Faith*, 302-304.

[137]Art. 14, in ibid., 85-86.

through the cross. But the First London Confession[138] referred only to Christ's reconciliation of the elect, and the Second London[139] likewise affirmed single reconciliation. Third, some functions of civil magistrates taught by Separatists were rejected by Baptists. As previously noted, according to *A True Confession*[140] magistrates have the power and function of suppressing false religions and establishing the true religion. On the other hand, the First London Confession[141] acknowledged subjection to king and parliament as to civil laws but declared that conscientious objection to some ecclesiastical laws may be necessary. The framers of the Second London Confession[142] deleted the Westminster doctrine of the suppression of false religions and emphasized generally obedience to and prayer for magistrates. Fourth, whereas *A True Confession*[143] never questioned or deviated from pedobaptism, the earliest Baptist confessions of faith[144] clearly taught believer's baptism. Moreover, some Baptists retained the church covenant, but for them believer's baptism would be constitutive of a truly ordered church.

As will subsequently be made clear, English Independency, from which the earliest Particular Baptists were derived, affirmed Dortian Calvinist rather than Arminian theology, had a more irenic and less hostile attitude toward the Church of England than the Separatists but wanted to be out from under episcopal rule, and practiced congregational polity.

In summary, Baptists have adhered to the Trinitarian and Christological doctrines formulated by the first four ecumenical councils and expressed in the earliest Christian creeds. They have shared with medieval sectarian and

---

[138] Art. 17, in ibid., 160-61.
[139] Art. 8, sect. 5, in ibid., 262.
[140] Art. 39, in ibid., 94-95.
[141] Arts. 49, 52, in ibid., 169, 170.
[142] Art. 24, in ibid., 283-84; Westminster, art. 23, in Schaff, *The Creeds of Christendom*, 3:652-55.
[143] Art. 35, in Lumpkin, *Baptist Confessions of Faith*, 93.
[144] "Short Confessions of Faith in XX Articles by John Smyth," art. 14; A Short Confession of Faith (1610), art. 29; "A Declaration of Faith of English People Remaining at Amsterdam in Holland," art. 14; "Propositions and Conclusions concerning True Christian Religion," art. 70; First London Confession, art. 39; Midland Association Confession, art. 13; Standard Confession of General Baptists, art. 11; Second London Confession, art. 29, sect. 2; and Orthodox Creed of General Baptists, art. 28, in ibid., 101, 109-10, 120, 137, 167, 199, 228-29, 291, 317-18.

reforming groups antiascetical, antisacramental, and primitivist intentions. They seem to have been indebted to various magisterial Reformers: Luther for the supremacy of the Scriptures over tradition, for justification by grace through faith, and the priesthood of all Christians; Zwingli for a memorialist understanding of the Lord's Supper; Bucer for church discipline as essential to the true church, and Calvin for predestination as a major doctrine. Continental Anabaptist influence can most clearly be seen in believer's baptism as constitutive of a truly ordered church, church discipline as necessary, the New Testament as superior to the Old Testament, and religious freedom for all humans. English Separatist influence can be most accurately identified in terms of humanity's Adamic disability, the Bible as the rule of faith and practice, the priesthood of all Christians, and congregational polity. Independency left its imprint on the earliest Particular Baptists through its Dortian Calvinism and its congregational polity.

Chapter 2

English General Baptists

By the recognized standards of historiography the earliest group that can properly be given the name "Baptists"[1] was the General Baptists in England. Some few[2] have sought to deny this by considering the Particular Baptists to be the fountain head of the Baptist movement. As indicated in chapter one, the question of possible/probable theological influences from English Separatism and from continental Anabaptism upon the General Baptists has had to be answered. One other possible theological influence, Dutch Arminianism, must be explored in this chapter.

John Smyth (ca. 1570–1612)

Educated at Christ's College, Cambridge, under Puritan influences and having been an appointed lecturer and subsequently an unlicensed preacher, Smyth became a Separatist and the leader of a covenanting Separatist congregation in Gainsborough in Lincolnshire. By 1608 governmental "harassment" caused Smyth's congregation to emigrate to Amsterdam, where the English Separatist congregation led by Francis Johnson had already settled and the one led by John Robinson was soon to arrive. Within a year Smyth on the basis of his se-baptism and the baptism of other members by affusion constituted a Baptist congregation. Soon thereafter Smyth's congregation divided over the issues of Hofmannite Christology and baptismal succession, and Thomas Helwys became the leader of the separating group. Smyth's remaining congregation applied for membership with the Waterlander Mennonites, Smyth died in 1612, and his congregation was received by the Mennonites in 1615.[3]

---

[1] See Robert B. Hannen, "Historical Notes on the Name 'Baptist,'" *Foundations* 8 (January 1965): 62-71.

[2] John Howard Shakespeare, *Baptist and Congregational Pioneers* (London: National Council of Evangelical Free Churches, 1907), although stating that "John Smyth has a rightful claim to be regarded as the founder of the modern Baptist Churches" (p. 125), went on to declare that Independents and Baptists are "two sections" of Congregationalism (p. 172) and to conclude, "The Calvinists are the real forerunners of the modern [Baptist] Denomination" (p. 180).

[3] Coggins, *John Smyth's Congregation*, 32-37, 43-65, 69-84, 97-103; Estep, *The Anabaptist Story*, 286-93; Underwood, *A History of the English Baptists*, 33-46; Walter H. Burgess, *John Smyth, the Se-Baptist, Thomas Helwys, and the First Baptist Church in England* (London: James Clarke, 1911) 27-97, 145-60, 175-99,

Modern scholars[4] have detected, primarily on the basis of his writings, distinct stages or periods in Smyth's ecclesiological identity: Anglican, Puritan, Separatist, Baptist, and would be Mennonite. From Smyth's Anglican period no writings survive, and from his Puritan period came two writings, *The Bright Morning Starre* (1603),[5] consisting of sermons on Psalm 22, and *A Paterne of True Prayer* (1605),[6] a Calvinistic exposition of the Lord's Prayer as the model prayer.

As a Separatist Smyth wrote three ecclesiological treatises. In *Principles and Inferences concerning the Visible Church* (1607) he, differentiating the catholic or invisible church, composed of all the elect, from the covenanting visible church, proceeded to spell out the visible church's members ("saints"), its inward form (the church covenant), its receiving of members and of officers (by election, examination, and ordination), its casting out of members and of officers when necessary, and its two officers (bishops or elders and deacons) without ruling elders.[7] *The Differences of the Churches of the Seperation* [sic] (1608) dealt with issues between Smyth's congregation and Francis Johnson's Ancient Church, especially Smyth's quest for "spiritual worship." Accordingly, the Scriptures were to be read to the church prior to worship and hence not as a part of worship, even as Jesus closed the scroll in the synagogue at Nazareth, and the minister was to make a fresh translation of the text from the original languages.[8]

226-75; Newman, *A History of Anti-Pedobaptism*, 376-91.

[4]Underwood, *A History of the English Baptists*, 33, noted four periods: Anglican, Puritan, Separatist, and Baptist. James E. Tull, *Shapers of Baptist Thought* (Valley Forge PA: Judson, 1972) 15-29, examined three "phases": Puritan, Separatist, and Baptist. Thomas Julian Nettles, "A Comparative Study of the Historical Stimuli Contributing to the Ecclesiological Views of Francis Johnson, John Smyth, and Roger Williams" (Ph.D. diss., Southwestern Baptist Theological Seminary, 1976) 142, specified four phases: Anglican, Puritan, Separatist, and Anabaptist, whereas James R. Coggins, "The Theological Positions of John Smyth," *The Baptist Quarterly* 30 (April 1984): 247, listed a different four: "a Puritan, a Separatist, a Baptist, and an Anabaptist," and Jason K. Lee, *The Theology of John Smyth: Puritan, Separatist, Baptist, Mennonite* (Macon GA: Mercer University Press, 2003) 41-95, concurred.

[5]In *The Works of John Smyth*, 1:1-66.

[6]In ibid., 1:67-247.

[7]In ibid., 1:249-68. See also Tull, *Shapers of Baptist Thought*, 19-21.

[8]Part 1, chs. 3-20, in *The Works of John Smyth*, 1:269-306. See also Tull, *Shapers of Baptist Thought*, 23-24; Coggins, *John Smyth's Congregation*, 49-56,

Smyth also differentiated the "kingdom" of the saints, that is, the governmental function, from the "priesthood" of the saints, that is, the devotional function,[9] rejected ruling elders,[10] and taught that nonmembers should be discouraged from contributing to the church treasury.[11] *Paralleles [sic], Censures, Observations* (1609) consists chiefly of Smyth's part of a debate with Richard Bernard, a Puritan, in which Smyth rejected the "mixed membership" of the godly and the wicked in a visible church, since only genuine saints should be members of such,[12] taught that church discipline belongs to the whole congregation, and insisted that any ministerial succession from Roman and Anglican churches should be rejected.[13]

In his Baptist phase Smyth authored *The Character of the Beast* (1609), in which he, debating a Separatist, Richard Clifton, expanded his polemic to Separatists, who, he alleged, also bear the "mark of the beast" by retaining infant baptism on the basis of analogy to circumcision. Smyth contended that God made two covenants with Abraham, one with Abraham and his "carnal seed," of which circumcision was the seal, and the other with Abraham and his "spiritual seed," of which the promised Holy Spirit is the seal. Hence baptism, to be true, must be upon confession of one's faith.[14] In his "Short Confession of Faith in 20 Articles" Smyth denied that God is responsible for human sin, rejected the concept of original sin, taught that grace is to be offered to all but may be rejected, and rejected the Mennonite practice of shunning.[15]

58-63, 66; Christa Friel, " 'Spirituall' Worship: John Smyth and Thomas Grantham," Historical Theology 7672, Fall 2002, Scripta, Roberts Library, Southwestern Baptist Theological Seminary, esp. 10-25.

[9]"The Differences of the Churches of the Seperation," part 1, chs. 1–2, in *The Works of John Smyth*, 1:274-75.

[10]Ibid., part 2, sect. 1, chs. 1-6, in ibid., 1:307-15.

[11]Ibid., part 2, sect. 2, chs. 1-7, esp. 4, in ibid., 1:316-20.

[12]Sect. 6, in *The Works of John Smyth*, 2:373-93. See also Tull, *Shapers of Baptist Thought*, 21-22.

[13]Sect. 7 in ibid., 2:393-442. See also Tull, *Shapers of Baptist Thought*, 23.

[14]In *The Works of John Smyth*, 2:563-680. See also Tull, *Shapers of Baptist Thought*, 25-26.

[15]Esp. arts. 3, 5, 8, 9, and 18, in *The Works of John Smyth*, 2:682-84 (Latin original); and in Lumpkin, *Baptist Confessions of Faith*, 100-101 (English translation).

In his "would be" Mennonite phase Smyth wrote in Latin both a defense[16] of the confession by Hans de Ries, a Mennonite, and *Argumenta contra baptismum infantum*[17] and in English *The Last Booke of John Smith, Called the Retractation of His Errours, and the Confirmation of the Truth*.[18] In the last he retracted his censorious spirit but not the substance of his teaching, expressed misgivings about his se-baptism but acknowledged only succession "in the truth," and distanced himself from the Mennonite Christology.[19]

Is there a central doctrinal motif basic to John Smyth's theology that prevailed through the several phases of his theological pilgrimage? Two scholars have arrived at very different answers. B. R. White[20] has found the church covenant to be that central motif, whereas Douglas Shantz has identified the central motif as "the resurrected, ruling Christ."[21] One would hardly dispute the claim, however, that ecclesiology was Smyth's most developed doctrine.[22] He rigorously rejected the baptism of infants, asserted that baptism should only be administered to voluntary or professed believers who are regenerate, retained the baptismal mode of aspersion or affusion, and denied that succession in the administration of baptism was necessary.[23] Such baptisms—and presumably only regenerate persons—are,

---

[16]Selected chapters in *The Works of John Smyth*, 2:685-709.
[17]In ibid., 2:710-32.
[18]In ibid., 2:751-60.
[19]Tull, *Shapers of Baptist Thought*, 28-29.
[20]*The English Separatist Tradition*, 125-29. Lee, *The Theology of John Smyth*, 127-65, esp. 164, has found the covenant to be "vital" for Smyth's ecclesiology but not in his Mennonite phase.
[21]"The Place of the Resurrected Christ in the Writings of John Smyth," *The Baptist Quarterly* 30 (January 1984): 202. See also Coggins, "The Theological Positions of John Smyth," 247.
[22]Richard Andrew Rankin, "The Use of Aristotelian Logic and Metaphysical Principles in the Ecclesiology of John Smyth" (Ph.D. diss., Southwestern Baptist Theological Seminary, 1994), has argued that Smyth's various shifts and ultimate ecclesiology were the "result" of his use of Aristotle's logic and metaphysics.
[23]J. Eric Hankins, "Reformed Sacramental Theology as a Key to Understanding John Smyth's Affirmation of Believers' Baptism," Historical Theology 7672, Fall 2002, Scripta, Roberts Library, Southwestern Baptist Theological Seminary, esp. 24, 17, 25, has contended that Smyth was not so much "a unique and brave trailblazer" as "the final link in completing" the Reformation and hence should be reckoned as "the 'last Radical English Separatist.'"

therefore, constitutive of a truly ordered congregation. Hence for subsequent Baptists the church covenant, although commonly retained, would not be constitutive of the church, as among Congregationalists. Moreover, for Smyth church governance should be congregational in that the congregation receives and dismisses members, elects, examines, ordains, and dismisses its officers, and exercises discipline. The two officers are bishops or elders and deacons. Distinct from the church's governance, according to Smyth, is its worship. His insistence that Bible reading be a prelude to but not an integral part of "spiritual worship" and that the minister make and verbalize a fresh translation of the text from the original languages would not subsequently become Baptist practice.

Smyth and his congregation after coming to a Baptist stance obviously shifted from an earlier Calvinism to a later non-Calvinism, or Arminianism.[24] According to Stephen M. Johnson,[25] the shift occurred between the publication of *The Character of the Beast* and the issuance of "A Short Confession in 20 Articles by John Smyth." In the former Smyth held to

---

[24]"Calvinism" here is to be understood as the teachings of the Synod of Dort (1618–1619), and "Arminianism" has reference to the teachings of the followers of James Arminius (1560–1609), also called Remonstrants, as expressed in the Five Arminian Articles (1610). Although the teachings of Dort have been most often understood during the twentieth century under the acronym of the TULIP (total depravity, unconditional election, limited atonement, irresistible grace, perseverance of the saints), the differences between Dort and the Remonstrants can be more accurately summarized as follows:

Dort		**Remonstrants**
Unconditional	←Predestination→	Conditioned on the foreknowledge of true believers
Death of Christ for the elect	←Atonement→	Death of Christ for all humanity
The gift of God	←Faith→	The response of the believer
Irresistible	←Divine Grace→	Resistible
Certain for all the saints	←Continuance in Grace→	Uncertain as to lapses of certain professed believers

For the respective texts, see Schaff, *The Creeds of Christendom*, 3:545-49, 581-97.

[25]"The Soteriology of the English General Baptists to 1630: A Study in Theological Kinship and Dependence" (Ph.D. diss., Westminster Theological Seminary, 1988) 220-27.

unconditional election and to original sin in the sense that "infants are culpable for Adamic sin prior to actual sin." In the latter he

> affirms universal election (Article 2), denies reprobation (Article 2), denies original sin (Article 5), denies limited atonement (Article 8), asserts free choice by virtue of prevenient grace (Article 9), denies effectual calling (Article 9), and affirms justification before God by virtue of both imputed and inherent righteousness.[26]

What caused such a shift by Smyth? There are at least four possible answers: "from his own study of the Bible," "from the teaching of Peter Baro (1534–1599)" in Cambridge, from the Arminians, or from the Mennonites.[27] Michael R. Watts,[28] Timothy George,[29] Johnson,[30] James R. Coggins,[31] Jason K. Lee,[32] and William H. Brackney[33] have clearly opted for the view that the principal source was the Mennonites. In his defense of the theology of Hans de Ries, Smyth gave final expression to his soteriology by teaching that "sin is the cause of damnation," not a divine decree, and "God simply permits, but does not want or cause sin," by interpreting election as being in Christ, by teaching the salvation of dying infants, by holding that free will, broken by the fall, has been restored through prevenient grace, which itself can be resisted, by interpreting justification as only inherent and not imputed, and by retaining the doctrine of perseverance of true believers.[34]

Smyth's alleged embrace of the Mennonite view that Jesus did not derive his basic humanity from Mary[35] came late in his life. In *The Character*

---

[26]Ibid., 226.

[27]Underwood, *A History of English Baptists*, 41n.1.

[28]*The Dissenters: From the Reformation to the French Revolution*, 2 vols. (Oxford: Oxford University Press, 1978) 1:46.

[29]George, *John Robinson and the English Separatist Tradition*, 182n.48.

[30]"The Soteriology of the English General Baptists to 1630," 9, 220-21.

[31]*John Smyth's Congregation*, 133, 140, 141. As to those who have opted for another source, see ibid., 214n.85, and Johnson, "The Soteriology of the English General Baptists to 1630," 7-10.

[32]*The Theology of John Smyth*, 167-208.

[33]*A Genetic History of Baptist Thought: With Special Reference to Baptists in Britain and North America* (Macon GA: Mercer University Press, 2004) 18-19.

[34]Johnson, "The Soteriology of the English General Baptists to 1630," 227-50.

[35]Thomas Helwys, *An Advertisement or Admonition unto the Congregations, Which Men Call the New Fryelers*, differentiated the Hofmannite view that Jesus

of the Beast he still affirmed that Christ is "the Sonne of Mary his Mother, made of her substance, the Holy Ghost overshadowing her," and "is one person in two distinct natures, the Godhead and manhood, and we detest the contrary errors."[36] Smyth's alleged shift on this doctrine evoked a counterview from Thomas Helwys[37] and contributed to the division between them.[38] Finally Smyth asserted that to know Christ's "spiritual flesh" is better than to know his "naturall flesh."[39] According to Lee, it was this Mennonite distinction between Christ's "natural flesh" and "spiritual flesh" that Smyth embraced, not the Hofmannite view of Christ's celestial flesh.[40]

Whether "Propositions and Conclusions concerning True Christian Religion," consisting of 100 articles, was written by Smyth just prior to his death or was framed subsequently by his followers is a matter of dispute.[41] It continued to express the non-Calvinist teachings of Smyth's final years. It denied any divine foreordination of evil, asserted the free will of fallen humanity, held that any passage of original sin from Adam to his descendants was "stopped" by the death of Jesus, affirmed the salvation of dying

---

brought his "flesh" from heaven, the Schwenckfeldian view that God was "turned into flesh," and the view of those who were unsure of the origin of Jesus' "flesh." Coggins, *John Smyth's Congregation*, 123.

[36] Epistle to the reader of *The Works of John Smyth*, 2:572. See also Burgess, *John Smyth, the Se-Baptist, Thomas Helwys, and the First Baptist Church in England*, 178-79.

[37] "A Declaration of Faith of English People Remaining at Amsterdam in Holland," art. 8, in Lumpkin, *Baptist Confessions of Faith*, 119.

[38] Underwood, *A History of the English Baptists*, 39, 43-44.

[39] "The Last Booke of John Smith" in *The Works of John Smyth*, 2:759-60.

[40] *The Theology of John Smyth*, 209-43.

[41] W. T. Whitley as editor of *The Works of John Smyth*, 2:733-50, considered it as one of Smyth's writings; Burgess, *John Smyth, the Se-Baptist, Thomas Helwys, and the First Baptist Church in England*, 236, held that it was written by Smyth during "the last year of his life"; Tull, *Shapers of Baptist Thought*, 26, stated that Smyth wrote it and published it in 1610; Johnson, "The Soteriology of the English General Baptists to 1630," 228, 334, 346, concluded that it was written by Smyth but published posthumously, first as 102 articles and later as 100, and Lee, *The Theology of John Smyth*, 91, assumed Smyth's authorship. But Lumpkin, *Baptist Confessions of Faith*, 123-24, asserted that it was written by "Smyth's followers," although it may have been a modification of a confession in Dutch by Smyth and "was an elaboration of the articles of [Mennonites] John de Ries and Lubbert Gerrits."

infants, taught that election is God's determining the way of salvation in Christ and foreseeing who would believe, rejected reprobation, and taught single reconciliation.[42] On the other hand, repentance and faith are "the conditions to be performed on our behalf" "by the preaching of the word,"[43] and general atonement is inferred but not clearly stated.[44] Being quickened or raised with Christ and being born again are recurring themes.[45] As to ecclesiology the visible church and the invisible church are differentiated,[46] the baptism of John the Baptist is reckoned to be very different from that of Jesus,[47] water baptism is only for penitent believers and a figure of the baptism of the Holy Spirit,[48] excommunication and shunning are enjoined,[49] and there is to be a twofold ministry with both male and female deacons.[50] Christians are supposed to marry Christians and not take their disputes to civil courts.[51] Three eschatological events are emphasized: bodily resurrection, the general and separative judgment, and the second coming of Christ.[52] Christians cannot rightly serve as civil magistrates.[53] The truly unique article is 84:

> That the magistrate is not by virtue of his office to meddle with religion, or matters of conscience, to force or compel men to this or that form of religion, or doctrine: but to leave Christian religion free, to every man's conscience, and to handle only civil transgressions . . . , injuries and wrongs of man against man, in murder, adultery, theft, etc., for Christ only is the king, and lawgiver of the church and conscience. . . .[54]

---

[42] Arts. 10, 14-17, 18-19, 20, 26, 25, 32, in Lumpkin, *Baptist Confessions of Faith*, 125-29.
[43] Arts. 57-58, in ibid., 134-35.
[44] Art. 27, in ibid., 128.
[45] Arts. 41-42, 44-47, in ibid., 131-32.
[46] Arts. 64-65, in ibid., 136.
[47] Arts. 54-56, in ibid., 134.
[48] Arts. 70-71, in ibid., 137.
[49] Arts. 77-80, in ibid., 138-39.
[50] Art. 76, in ibid., 138.
[51] Arts. 87, 86, in ibid., 140.
[52] Arts. 91-100, in ibid., 141-42.
[53] Art. 85, in ibid., 140.
[54] In ibid. See Timothy George, "Between Pacifism and Coercion: The English Baptist Doctrine of Religious Toleration," *Mennonite Quarterly Review* 58 (January 1984): 30-49, who concluded (48): "By maintaining a fundamentally positive view of the state, while at the same time sharply separating the spiritual and temporal

This 100-article confession was probably the first Christian confession of faith to affirm and prescribe religious liberty, or freedom of conscience, vis-á-vis civil government[55] and the first such claim in the English language.[56] Lee has argued for continuity in Smyth's concept of church-state separation but for Mennonite influence on his late view of the magistracy and religious freedom.[57]

A. C. Underwood called John Smyth "the fountain-head of consecutive Baptist history" and "the father and founder of the organized Baptists of England and of the General Baptists in particular."[58] James E. Tull modified that assessment by noting that "the General Baptist communion which Smyth founded was almost extinct by the end of the seventeenth century" and "the Particular Baptists . . . had little connection with Smyth."[59]

Thomas Helwys (1570-ca. 1616)

Helwys, reared in Nottinghamshire and educated at Gray's Inn, London, a college for lawyers, together with his wife Jane became members of the Separatist congregation in Gainsborough led by Smyth, provided funds for that congregation's emigration to Amsterdam, received believer's baptism from Smyth, and belonged to the reconstituted congregation. But, after Smyth opened correspondence with Mennonites, Helwys and about ten others separated from and excommunicated Smyth's congregation and subsequently returned to England.[60] Helwys's theological agreements with and differences from Smyth were expressed in his writings.

In his *Synopsis fidei verae Christianae Ecclesiae Anglicanae* (1610), consisting of nineteen articles, Helwys denied any divine necessity of sinning or any hereditary sin, affirmed that God desires all human beings to be saved, and held that humans can repent, believe, and persevere yet can also resist the Holy Spirit and depart from God. A church is to consist only

---

realms, the Baptists positioned themselves between the radical pacifism of the Anabaptists and the Calvinist tradition of magisterial reformation."

[55]Lumpkin, *Baptist Confessions of Faith*, 124.
[56]Underwood, *A History of the English Baptists*, 42.
[57]*The Theology of John Smyth*, 274-79.
[58]Ibid., 45.
[59]*Shapers of Baptist Thought*, 30.
[60]Underwood, *A History of the English Baptists*, 34-35, 37, 39-40, 46; Ernest A. Payne, *Thomas Helwys and the First Baptist Church in England*, 2nd ed. (London: Baptist Union of Great Britain and Ireland, 1966).

of believers and to be governed congregationally, practicing excommunication but not shunning. Baptism, a sign of the remission of sin, is not to be given to infants, and in the twofold ministry deacons may be "men" or "widows."[61] In *An Advertisement or Admonition unto the Congregations, Which Men Call the New Fryelers*, Helwys identified four errors of the Mennonites: concerning the incarnation and Jesus' human nature, concerning their lax observance of the Sabbath, concerning their insistence on succession in baptism and ordination, and concerning their practice of excluding magistrates from the church.[62]

A Declaration of Faith in English People Remaining at Amsterdam in Holland (1611), consisting of twenty-seven articles, took positions contrary to Mennonite beliefs and positions contrary to Bezan Calvinism. As to the first, it rejected the view that Jesus' body was unlike ours, the practice of shunning, the position that Christians should not serve as civil magistrates, and the avoidance of oaths.[63] As to the second, it seemed to teach a general atonement in that by the "obedience" of Christ all human beings "are made righteous," it reckoned predestination to mean God's ordaining "that all that believe in him shall be saved" and all "that believe not shall be damned" and clearly rejected reprobation, and it affirmed that humans may resist God's grace and true believers may fall from grace.[64] On the contrary, Helwys retained certain aspects of the Augustinian-Calvinist tradition: the sin of Adam was imputed to all human beings and so death came to all, and fallen humans have "all disposition" to evil and "no disposition or will" to any good.[65] Furthermore, believer's baptism is constitutive of the church, the Lord's Day is to be for worship and abstinence from labor, congregations are not to be so large as to prevent knowing and caring for one another, and there may be women as well as men serving as deacons but no

---

[61] Arts 3-5, 8-9, 15-16, 10, 13, in English translation by Saito, "An Investigation into the Relationship between the Early English Baptists and the Dutch Anabaptists," 198-200. Saito, 104, found that Helwys agreed with Smyth's "Short Confession of Faith in XX Articles" as to non-Calvinism, the Trinity, and the *imago Dei* but placed more stress on human sinfulness and less on the human free will.

[62] Coggins, *John Smyth's Congregation*, 97-101.

[63] Arts. 8, 18, 24, and 25, in Lumpkin, *Baptist Confessions of Faith*, 119, 121, 122-23. On the magistracy, Helwys's position was close to that of Hubmaier, as Estep, *The Anabaptist Story*, 295, noted.

[64] Arts. 3, 5, 4, and 7, in Lumpkin, *Baptist Confessions of Faith*, 117-19.

[65] Arts. 2 and 4, in ibid., 117-18.

ruling elders.[66] The Scriptures, being "written for our instruction," testify of Christ and are to be used reverently for they contain the Word of God, which alone is "our direction" in all things.[67]

A brief tract entitled *A Short and Plaine Proof by the Word and Workes of God that Gods Decree is Not the Cause of Anye Mans Sinne or Condemnation* (1611) "argued that no particular persons were elected or reprobated" and that the Calvinist/Puritan doctrine of predestination is "presumptuous," for it makes God the author of sin.[68] Helwys may have alluded in the preface to the teachings of the Remonstrants, or Arminians.[69]

Helwys's final publication, *A Short Declaration of the Mistery of Iniquity* (1612), addressed to King James I of England and of which a copy was delivered to him, was a bold advocacy of religious freedom.

> The king is a mortall man, and not God; therefore hath no power over ye immortall soules of his subjects, to make lawes and ordinances for them, and to set spirituall Lords over them. . . .[70]
>
> . . . for our lord the King is but an earthly King, and he hath no authority as a King but in earthly causes, and if the Kings people be obedient and true subjects, obeying all humane lawes made by the King, our lord the King can require no more: for men's religion to God, is betwixt God and themselves; the King shall not answere for it, neither may the King be jugd betwene God and man. Let them be heretikes, Turcks, Jewes, or whatsoever it apperteynes not to the earthly power to punish them in the least measure.[71]

Like the Separatists, Helwys identified the Roman Catholic Church with the first beast of Revelation 13 and the Church of England with the second beast,[72] but the Puritans and the Separatists were also criticized.[73] This book

---

[66]Arts. 14, 13, 19, 16, 20, and 21, in ibid., 120-22.

[67]Art. 23, in ibid., 122.

[68]Dewey D. Wallace, Jr., *Puritans and Predestination: Grace in English Protestant Theology, 1525–1695* (Chapel Hill: University of North Carolina Press, 1982) 107.

[69]Coggins, *John Smyth's Congregation*, 138-39, 141.

[70]Replica ed. (London: Kingsgate, 1935) unnumbered page.

[71]Ibid., 69.

[72]Ibid., unnumbered page. See Coggins, *John Smyth's Congregation*, 105; Estep, *The Anabaptist Story*, 294.

[73]Coggins, *John Smyth's Congregation*, 105.

constituted "the first demand made in England for universal religious liberty"[74] and was a major milestone in the entire struggle for religious liberty.

In 1615 Helwys's congregation published *Objections: Answered by Way of Dialogue*—whether it was written in prison by Helwys or written by John Murton is not certain—as a reply to various objections by the king's supporters.[75] For example, the royalists were saying that Helwys's people must attend the Anglican worship because it is law, the king is "head over the Church under Christ," and otherwise they must go to prison, that a heathen king cannot compel in matters religious but a Christian king can, that freedom of religion would bring divisions and "sedition" to the state and would endanger the king in respect to treachery or treason, and that the parable of the tares mandates that the good and the bad in the church must be allowed to grow without hindrance.[76] In reply the Helwys group declared, "It is a sure rule in divinitie [sic], that God loves not to plant his church by violence and bloodshed."[77]

Other appeals for universal religious liberty were issued by those who succeeded Helwys, notably Mark Leonard Busher's *Religion's Peace: A Plea for Liberty of Conscience* (1614)[78] and Murton's *A Most Humble Supplication of Many of the King's Majesty's Loyal Subjects* (1620).[79]

---

[74]Underwood, *A History of the English Baptists*, 47.

[75]Coggins, *John Smyth's Congregation*, 106; Burgess, *John Smyth, the Se-Baptist, Thomas Helwys, and the First Baptist Church in England*, 303, and McBeth, *The Baptist Heritage*, 105, have identified Murton as the author.

[76]*Objections: Answered by Way of Dialogue*, facsimile ed. (Amsterdam: Theatrum Orbis Terrarum; New York: Da Capo, 1973) 1, 3, 8, 35, 27, 30-31, 13-14, 18.

[77]Ibid., preface, (v).

[78]In *Tracts on Liberty of Conscience and Persecution, 1614–1661*, ed. Edward Bean Underhill (London: J. Haddon, 1846) 1-81. According to McBeth, *The Baptist Heritage*, 104, "Like Smyth and Helwys, Busher argued for religious liberty on the grounds of Scripture, logic, and history," pressing even more "the civil and national advantages of liberty" and using the analogy of "forced religion" as "spiritual rape."

[79]In *Tracts on Liberty of Conscience and Persecution, 1614–1661*, 183-231. Stephen Wright, *The Early English Baptists, 1603–1649* (Woodridge, Suffolk UK: Boydell and Brewer, 2006) 11-12, 99-102, 142, has recently expressed doubt that there was conscious continuity or any denominational connection among General Baptist churches prior to the 1640s.

Other Confessions of Faith

After the time of Smyth and Helwys the General Baptist churches in England, so-called because of their affirming a general atonement, composed and adopted four noteworthy confessions of faith.

The Faith and Practice of Thirty Congregations, Gathered according to the Primitive Pattern, consisting of 75 articles, was framed and adopted by 30 General Baptist churches in the Midlands at their associational meeting in 1651. According to William L. Lumpkin, its importance rests on the fact that it was "the first General Baptist statement representing the views of more than one church." It also "shows essential agreement with" Helwys's *A Declaration of Faith of English People Remaining at Amsterdam in Holland*.[80] Certain Calvinist teachings were included, notably that all humankind shares Adam's death, which resulted from Adam's sin,[81] and that free will seems to be repudiated.[82] Moreover, there is silence as to apostasy. On the other hand, the confession seems to teach general atonement[83] and to follow John Smyth's concept of "spiritual worship."[84] Lumpkin's statement that articles 4-16 were "a pioneer statement of the Baptist doctrine of soul competency"[85] may be a reading back into this confession of the thought of Edgar Young Mullins[86] at the beginning of the twentieth century. Perhaps human accountability would be a more apt identification of the theme of these articles, wherein God's self-revelation through the created order, the human repudiation of that revelation, and the fall of Adam and its resultant death are taught.[87] Lumpkin[88] has found articles 45-75 to have been "directed" against the Quakers, who were numerous in the Midlands. Article 48[89] seems to prescribe immersion as the form of baptism, thus reflecting the influence of the Particular Baptists, who

---

[80] *Baptist Confessions of Faith*, 173.
[81] Art. 16, in ibid., 178.
[82] Arts. 25, 31, in ibid., 179-80.
[83] Art. 18, in ibid., 178.
[84] Art. 21, in ibid.
[85] *Baptist Confessions of Faith*, 173.
[86] *The Axioms of Religion: A New Interpretation of the Baptist Faith* (Philadelphia: Judson, 1908) 44-69.
[87] Arts. 4-16, in ibid., 176-78. The *imago Dei* is identified as dominion. Art. 11, in ibid., 177.
[88] *Baptist Confessions of Faith*, 173.
[89] In ibid., 182.

had adopted immersion, on the General Baptists. Worship has an ethical purpose,[90] and the Lord's Supper is a "memorial" of Christ's suffering.[91] The poor are to be cared for, especially through male deacons, but the unemployed who are able to work are to be exhorted to work on penalty of excommunication.[92] Both ministerial support by the congregation and ministerial self-support are taught,[93] church judges are to resolve disputes among Christians,[94] and the associational principle is affirmed.[95]

The True-Gospel Faith, consisting of 30 articles, was originally written by Thomas Lover, presumably "an early leader among General Baptists," and may have been either his private confession or one "adopted by one or more churches." Lover had indicated that his purposes were "partly apologetic and partly missionary." This confession was taken over and adopted in 1654 by certain London area General Baptist leaders in order to meet and withstand the "inroads" of the newly founded Quakers in London and elsewhere.[96] One of these leaders, John Griffith (1622?–1700), had authored an attack[97] on the Quakers for rejecting the Lord's Supper, for being proud and boastful, and for rejecting the Scriptures. All humanity is subject to death as the consequence of Adam's sin, and no self-redemption from that death is possible, but Christ's death is "for the sins of all men under the first Covenant," indeed "for every man."[98] Immersion as the mode of baptism is taught, and so is the laying on of hands after baptism.[99] This is "the first Baptist Confession to prescribe the laying on of hands for all baptized believers," but not all General Baptists at this time seem to have adopted the practice.[100] Believer's immersion is constitutive of a truly ordered congregation, every member should "exercise his gift for the benefit of others," hearing non-Baptist teachers should be avoided, and marriage outside the

---

[90] Art. 52, in ibid., 183.
[91] Art. 53, in ibid.
[92] Arts. 57, 64, 68, in ibid., 184, 185, 186.
[93] Arts. 59-61, in ibid., 184-85.
[94] Art. 67, in ibid., 186.
[95] Arts. 70, 72, in ibid., 186, 187.
[96] Lumpkin, *Baptist Confessions of Faith*, 190, 189.
[97] *A Voice from the Word of the Lord to Those Grand Imposters Called Quakers* (London, 1654) BBM/Angus, microform publ. no. 5855, reel 2, item 6.
[98] Arts. 2-4, in Lumpkin, *Baptist Confessions of Faith*, 192-93.
[99] Arts. 11-12, in ibid., 193.
[100] Lumpkin, *Baptist Confessions of Faith*, 191.

English General Baptists

General Baptist fellowship likewise forbidden.[101] In contrast to John Smyth's twofold ministry of pastor and deacons, this confession prescribed three offices: "Messengers, Pastors, and Teachers."[102] Eschatological themes that were affirmed are the second coming of Christ, the general resurrection, the general judgment, hell, and final salvation.[103]

In March 1660 the General Assembly of General Baptists, meeting in London, framed and adopted a 25-article confession in order to answer the criticisms and misunderstandings of the Baptists, often called "Anabaptists," at the end of the Commonwealth and Protectorate and at the time of the restoration of the Stuart monarchy. It was signed by 40 men who were "fairly representative" but not really inclusive of the General Baptists of the time. London was well represented but not the Midlands or Wales. One signatory, William Jeffrey, was a known author, but Thomas Grantham did not sign, and neither did John Griffith and his supporters, the latter probably because the confession did not include the six principles of Heb. 6:1-2.[104] William J. McGlothlin regarded Grantham as the author of this confession,[105] but Lumpkin has rightly corrected such attribution.[106] The confession was presented to King Charles II in July 1660, and at the next meeting of the assembly in 1663 it was "slightly revised and reaffirmed by a larger circle" so that it became known as the Standard Confession of General Baptists. In 1678 Thomas Grantham edited this confession with supplements, and his changes "were approved by the Assembly in 1691." At the assembly's request Thomas Hooke revised it about 1700.[107]

---

[101] Arts. 13, 25, and 26, in ibid., 194-95.

[102] "Messengers" were denominational servants who were general evangelists and church planters. See Underwood, *A History of the English Baptists*, 119-23.

[103] Arts. 27-28, 30, 29, in Lumpkin, *Baptist Confessions of Faith*, 195.

[104] Lumpkin, *Baptist Confessions of Faith*, 220-23. In 1655 Griffith had published *God's Oracle and Christ's Doctrine, or the Six Principles of the Christian Religion*. "Because the Assembly churches would not accept the Six Principles as the authoritative and only official platform, though they agreed to the laying on of hands, the Griffith group withdrew." Lumpkin, *Baptist Confessions of Faith*, 222-23.

[105] *Baptist Confessions of Faith* (Philadelphia: American Baptist Publication Society, 1911) 109. McGlothlin was following Adam Taylor, *The History of the English General Baptists* (London, 1818) 1:366, who stated that Grantham "is supposed to have drawn up this Confession."

[106] *Baptist Confessions of Faith*, 221.

[107] Ibid., 223.

Lumpkin's description of this confession as "mildly Arminian"[108] is confirmed by examination of the text. General atonement is affirmed in a context in which "unbelief" is said to be the sole basis of human condemnation. Election is God's choosing "before the foundation of the world . . . to eternal life, such as believe, and so are in Christ," yet this election does not arise "from foreseen faith" or from works of human righteousness. To believe is to "assent to gospel truth" and to trust "that there is remission of sins, and eternal life to be had in Christ," but nothing is said as to faith's being given by God. Infants dying in infancy shall not suffer in hell for Adam's sin, and falling from grace is taught but assurance is given to those who persevere.[109] Churches are properly gathered by gospel preaching, the baptism of repentant believers, prayer and the laying on of hands for receiving the Holy Spirit, fellowship, and the godly Christian life.[110] "Elders or Pastors" are to be converted persons, chosen, ordained, and financially supported.[111] Civil magistrates are needed but not to be obeyed in religious matters, and liberty of conscience in religious matters is affirmed on the basis of the Golden Rule (Matt. 7:12) and the parable of the wheat and the tares (Matt. 13:29-30, 38-39).[112] The latter is "one of the clearest statements of the seventeenth century in favor of absolute liberty of conscience."[113] In addition to affirmations about the general resurrection, the second coming of Christ, and the general judgment, this confession, although making no reference to Rev. 20:1-7, so refers to Christ's reigning with believers on the earth and over the nations as to be consonant with premillennial teaching.[114] This confession, Lumpkin declared, "proved to be exceedingly important in the life of General Baptists, serving as a basis of union for over forty years, "especially during persecution."[115]

The "common sufferings" of all Nonconformists in England after the Stuart restoration and after the Fifth Monarchy uprising in 1661 led such

---

[108]Ibid., 221.

[109]Arts, 4, 8, 6, 10, 18 in ibid., 225-26, 227, 226-27, 228, 230.

[110]Arts. 11-14, in ibid., 228-29.

[111]Arts, 5, 15, 16, in ibid., 226, 229-30. Here tithes for maintaining "Gospel Ministers" in the sense of the tithe as a tax for the clergy of the established church are rejected.

[112]Arts. 25, 24, in ibid., 233, 232-33.

[113]Ibid., 221.

[114]Arts. 20-22, in ibid., 231-32.

[115]Ibid., 223.

groups to seek "closer relations" with each other and to stress their "points of agreement" more than their "differences." Both the Particular Baptists and the General Baptists sought to show their "large agreement with Presbyterians and Congregationalists" by framing new confessions of faith that were built upon and were slight revisions of the Westminster Confession (1648).[116] In 1678 Thomas Monck[117] seemingly prepared a draft, and it was signed by 54 "more earnestly orthodox" Baptist leaders from the Midlands. Called *An Orthodox Creed*, it professed to "unite and confirm all true Protestants in the fundamental articles of the Christian religion, against the errors and heresies of Rome."[118] It came to as close agreement as possible to "the Calvinistic position" and was "the first attempt at that compromise between the two great systems of theology [Calvinism and Arminianism] which was . . . the work of Andrew Fuller and others in the latter part of the eighteenth century."[119] It also sought to refute the Hofmannite Christology of Matthew Caffyn (1628–1715), a General Baptist messenger. Consisting of 50 articles, it "followed less closely" the Westminster Confession than did the Second London Confession of Particular Baptists (1677) inasmuch as there were changes both in order of articles and in content of articles.[120]

After articles on God's essence and attributes and the Trinity, *An Orthodox Creed* proceeded to identify the Son of God as "very and true God," "not a God by office, but a God by nature, coequal, coessential, and coeternal" with the Father and the Holy Spirit. He "took to himself a true, real, and fleshly body, and reasonable soul . . . and became very and true man like unto us in all things, even in our infirmities, sin only excepted." His divine and human natures were united but not fused.[121] *An Orthodox Creed*

---

[116]McGlothlin, *Baptist Confessions of Faith*, 122-23.

[117]A Buckinghamshire farmer and messenger who had published in 1673 *A Cure for the Cankering Error of the New Eutychians*.

[118]Lumpkin, *Baptist Confessions of Faith*, 295, 297.

[119]McGlothlin, *Baptist Confessions of Faith*, 123.

[120]Lumpkin, *Baptist Confessions of Faith*, 295, 296. For the full original text, including the preface, an advertisement to the reader (including the signatures), and the postscript, which three items were omitted from Thomas Crosby's and subsequent reprintings, see W. Madison Grace II, "Transcriber's Preface to *An Orthodox Creed*: An Unabridged 17th Century General Baptist Confession," *Southwestern Journal of Theology* 48 (Spring 2006): 127-82.

[121]Arts. 1-7, in Lumpkin, *Baptist Confessions of Faith*, 298-301.

"is alone among Baptist confessions in including and setting forth the Apostles', the Nicene, and the Athanasian Creeds."[122] Rejecting any "pretended immediate inspirations" or general revelation through "the works of creation" or "the law written on the heart" as salvific, it affirmed the inspired Scriptures as containing "all things necessary for salvation" and as "the Rule of faith and life." They are to be interpreted not privately but "according to the analogy of faith." The Bible "is the best interpreter of itself, and is sole judge in controversy." The two testaments through types and antitypes are in agreement and "hold forth the self-same gospel."[123]

An Orthodox Creed reflects the magisterial Reformation in its doctrines of repentance, faith, declarative justification through the active and passive obedience of Christ, double reconciliation, adoption, and sanctification[124] and reflects English Puritanism in its doctrines of the Christian sabbath, prayer, and fasting.[125] Concerning the doctrines common to the Augustinian-Calvinist tradition and those on which Synod of Dort Calvinists and the Arminians differed, this confession has a mixture of responses. Predestination "unto life" is God's choice of his elect in Christ, but not on the basis of "foreseen holiness," and the everlasting punishment of the wicked "is of themselves, not the result of a decree." God's covenant of works with "man" was affirmed, God "foresaw" but did not "decree" Adam's fall, and the covenant of grace is the new covenant in Christ. The fall brought physical and spiritual death to Adam and his posterity, and original sin is universal human corruption that came "from Adam by natural generation." Hence fallen humanity has lost the freedom of the will "to any spiritual good" or "eternal salvation," thus being incapable of self-conversion. Christ's death is sufficient "for the sins of the whole world." There are both a general call and an effectual call, and those effectually called "shall certainly persevere unto eternal life."[126]

An Orthodox Creed introduced the doctrine of the universal church, consisting of "the whole number of the elect" past, present, and future, and identified the visible church as "made up of several distinct congregations," the four marks of which are right preaching, true "sacraments," church

---

[122]Ibid., 296; art. 38, in ibid., 326-27. See above, 4.

[123]Arts. 37, 19, in ibid., 324-26, 311-12.

[124]Arts. 22-26, 17, in ibid., 313-17, 310.

[125]Arts. 40-42, in ibid., 327-29.

[126]Arts. 9, 10, 13, 14, 16, 15, 20, 18, 21, and 36, in ibid., 302-4, 305-306, 307-308, 306-307, 312-13, 310-11, 313, 324.

discipline, and congregational polity. Such congregations are "not infallible," but their "errors" are "not fundamental," and no one "ought . . . schismatically to separate" therefrom. Three church offices are prescribed: "Bishops, or Messengers; and Elders, or Pastors; and Deacons, or Overseers of the poor," with financial support of messengers and pastors. The "executive part" of congregational church discipline is committed to the ministers, and to the general assembly is ascribed the right to arbitrate and excommunicate. The two "sacraments" are of perpetual obligation. Baptism by immersion of those professing repentance and faith is "a sign" of "entrance into the covenant of grace and of ingrafting into Christ and his church, of remission of sin, of fellowship with Christ's death and resurrection, and of "rising to newness of life." The Lord's Supper is to show forth Christ's sacrificial death, to confirm believers in the benefits of his death and resurrection, to provide "spiritual nourishment and growth" in Christ, to seal the continuance of believers, to pledge communion with and obedience to Christ, and to pledge "communion and union" with fellow believers.[127] Christians can hold civil office, the taking of oaths before magistrates is allowable, and Christians are to enjoy liberty of conscience under Christ, the "only Lord of Conscience."[128] General Baptist distinctives are reflected in the laying on of hands on the baptized and in marriage within the General Baptist fellowship.[129] One general resurrection and one general judgment are the only eschatological teachings.[130]

The General Baptist confessions of the seventeenth century did exhibit the major emphases of the General Baptist theology: general atonement, together with its related doctrines; liberty of conscience vis-á-vis civil government; and believer's baptism, ultimately by immersion.[131]

---

[127]Arts. 29, 30, 31, 34, 39, 27, 28 and 33, in ibid., 318-20, 322-23, 327, 317-18, 321-22.

[128]Arts. 45, 48, and 46, in ibid., 331, 332-33, 331-32.

[129]Arts. 32 and 47, in ibid., 320-21, 332.

[130]Arts. 49-50, in ibid., 333-34.

[131]Murray M. Tolmie, *The Triumph of the Saints: The Separate Churches of London, 1616–1649* (London: Cambridge University Press, 1977) 72, regarded "the doctrine of general redemption" as the "fundamental tenet" of the early General Baptists because they "reopened negotiations" with the Mennonites "in the 1620s" and "refused to accept the Calvinist Baptists as fellow Christians." Johnson, "The Soteriology of the English General Baptists to 1630," 327, although concurring, stressed the antipedobaptist trajectory that led to believer's baptism. On freedom of conscience, see Underwood, *A History of the English Baptists*, 47-49. Perhaps the

Thomas Grantham (1634–1692)

The leading General Baptist theologian during the last half of the seventeenth century was Thomas Grantham, a Lincolnshire farmer-tailor and pastor who was ordained a messenger in 1666. A frequent debater with those of other religious persuasions and a spokesman in behalf of the persecuted General Baptists to King Charles II, he was a prolific author.[132] His most lengthy production was the 602-page *Christianismus Primitivus. or, The Ancient Christian Religion in Its Nature, Certainty, Excellency, and Beauty. . . .*[133] It seemingly was the first treatise written by a Baptist which can be reckoned as a systematic theology.[134] It consists of four books, the second book having two parts, the contents of which may be identified as follows:

Book I	Book II, 1st part	Book II, 2nd part	Book III	Book IV
Christian Apologetics	Christian Doctrine	Ecclesiology	Christian Ethics	Baptist Polemics

Grantham's apologetic centered in the life, miracles, death, and resurrection of Jesus and in the excellence of Christian worship, forgiveness, marriage, stewardship, and evangelization.[135] Having dealt in his introduction with the divine authority and correct translation of the Old and the New Testaments as the Word of God,[136] he proceeded under doctrine to interpret the doctrines of God, Jesus Christ,[137] sin, the Christian life (including last things), and angels.[138] His lengthy ecclesiological section expounded the gathered church, believer's baptism by immersion, laying of hands on the

---

earliest summary of General Baptist doctrines and polity was that by Taylor, *The History of the English General Baptists*, 1:356-480.

[132]Samuel Edward Hester, "Advancing Christianity to Its Primitive Excellency: The Quest of Thomas Grantham, Early English General Baptist" (Th.D. diss., New Orleans Baptist Theological Seminary, 1972) 8-32.

[133](London, 1678).

[134]See below, ch. 3, fns. 168, 249.

[135]Book 1.

[136]Introduction.

[137]Richard Andrew Rankin, "The Person and Work of the Holy Spirit in Thomas Grantham." Historical Theology, 471-767, Fall 1991, Scripta, Roberts Library, Southwestern Baptist Theological Seminary, found in Grantham's writings a considerable doctrine of the work of the Holy Spirit centered in revelation, salvation, and the church.

[138]*Christianismus Primitivus*, book 2, part 1.

baptized,[139] separation from the world, church fellowship, opposition to fixed or liturgical prayers, the Lord's Supper as commemorative, singing in worship,[140] church officers (messengers, elders, deacons), general assemblies,[141] church discipline, the Lord's Day, the absence of holy places, and the financial support of and brotherly respect for ministers.[142] The ethical teaching by Grantham, which he called "cases of conscience," embraced Baptists' nonseditious obedience to civil government, the duties of civil magistrates as not including the making of "spiritual laws," the validity of oaths for Christians, Christian "moderation" toward Christians of other denominations, marriage and divorce, the role of women in church meetings,[143] civil restrictions on church meetings, the duties of Christians to serve as civil magistrates and as soldiers in just wars, the use by Baptist churches of civil laws concerning the relief of the poor and the burial of the dead, the prohibition of usury, the government of Christian families,[144] and the control of one's tongue.[145] Grantham's Baptist polemical writing was addressed to a Roman Catholic priest, the Quakers, all pedobaptists, Presbyterians, Baptists who do not practice the laying on of hands, and the opponents of separatism, who fail to take seriously the restoration of baptism and the ungodliness and innovations in the established church.[146] Grantham consistently sought biblical support for his theological and ethical teachings. Of great concern to him, as for John Griffith, was the advocacy and practice of the laying of hands on the newly baptized.

---

[139]See also Grantham, *A Sigh for Peace* . . . (1671), BBM/Angus, microform publ. no. 5855.

[140]Grantham favored singing by an individual of paraphrased Davidic Psalms or biblical hymns and disfavored congregational singing (ch. 8).

[141]Grantham ascribed to a general assembly the authority to decide controversies arising in local churches (ch. 10).

[142]Book 2, part 2. Grantham urged ministerial support but denied that tithes are obligatory under the law of God (ch. 15).

[143]Women were forbidden to preach or teach, as the Quakers allowed, and were to be veiled (ch. 7).

[144]The husband was said to be the head and ruler of the family, and the wife to be subject and obedient (ch. 12).

[145]Book 3.

[146]Book 4.

Matthew Caffyn (1628–1715), Celestial Flesh, and Socinianism

Matthew Caffyn, farmer-pastor at Horsham and a General Baptist messenger, evoked doctrinal controversy in the General Assembly of General Baptists by advocating in the churches of Kent and Sussex Christological doctrine which has been identified both with that of the Anabaptist Melchior Hofmann[147] and with that of the Antitrinitarian Faustus Socinus. As already noted,[148] the refutation of Caffyn's Christology was one of the purposes of the Orthodox Creed of 1678. But five years earlier Thomas Monck had published a 219-page tractate entitled *A Cure for the Cankering Error of the New Eutychians*.[149] On the one hand, Monck clearly identified as heretical the teaching that Christ "did not take his flesh of the Virgin Mary, nor of David,"[150] which can be traced to Hofmann's doctrine of celestial flesh and on back to Valentinian Gnosticism,[151] while taking as a label for his opponents Eutyches, for whom Jesus' humanity was absorbed by his deity.[152] On the other hand, Monck also accused Caffyn and his followers of teaching that the divine nature of the eternal Word was turned into flesh so that the Creator became a creature, a position that Monck identified with Arians and Socinians,[153] neither of whom ascribed to Jesus a divine nature. In refuting the doctrine of celestial flesh, Monck specified

---

[147]See above, 9, 12.

[148]See above, 39.

[149](London, 1673), BBM/Bodleian, microform publ. no. 5877, reel 3, item 10.

[150]Ibid., "Author to the Reader," back of A2.

[151]Williams, *The Radical Reformation*, 329.

[152]According to Kelly, *Early Christian Doctrines*, 331, 333, Eutyches "counts as the founder of an extreme and virtually Docetic form of monophysitism [one-nature doctrine], teaching that the Lord's humanity was totally absorbed by His divinity," and yet Eutyches "was no Docetist or Apollinarian."

[153]*A Cure for the Cankering Error of the New Eutychians*, "Author to the Reader," A2, A3. Underwood, *A History of the English Baptists*, 106-107, 127, did not take note of the Socinian aspect of Monck's polemic and alleged that Caffyn shifted from Hofmannism to Socinianism. Arians "acknowledged the preexistence of Christ" and reckoned him as quasi-divine, whereas "the more radical Socinians denied both the divinity and the preexistence of Christ." Arian views were being set forth by such Anglican authors as William Whiston, author of *Primitive Christianity Revived* (1711), and Samuel Clarke, *The Scripture-doctrine of the Trinity* (1712). Watts, *The Dissenters*, 1:371, 373.

both the Valentinian idea that the Word passed through Mary as "through a Conduit" and the docetic idea that Jesus' body was "imaginary," not "real." He also sought to put the Caffynites on the horns of a dilemma: "if Christ be only God, then he could not die . . . ; if only Man, then he cannot raise himself from the dead."[154] Adam Taylor, writing in 1818, thought that Caffyn's difficulties had begun with his effort "to reconcile the assertion, that Christ was free from sin, with the fact of his being conceived of the virgin" and such led to his dislike of the Athanasian Creed.[155] Sin as the starting point for Caffyn differs from George Huntston Williams's verdict that for the sixteenth-century Radical Reformers the doctrine of the celestial flesh of Jesus was "an effort to restate the Christological problem in the language of Eucharistic piety."[156]

Caffyn's views ultimately became a major issue for the General Assembly of General Baptists. Joseph Wright of Maidstone became during the 1680s his accuser before the assembly, charging him with denial of both the deity and the humanity of Christ and calling for his expulsion from the assembly and excommunication by General Baptist churches. Caffyn defended himself by claiming submission to biblical authority and professing to regard Jesus "both as God and man." The assembly acquitted Caffyn and censured Wright "for want of charity." After Caffyn had stated his views more openly, the 1693 assembly again considered the charges against Caffyn, but the majority found him not guilty, while declaring that the views expressed in the charges were indeed heretical. Sixteen members signed a protest. Another trial and acquittal took place in the 1696 assembly, but those in protest seceded and formed the General Association of General Baptists. In 1700 an effort was made to reconcile and reunite the association and the assembly, but it failed, with the association wanting a heresy trial and the assembly wanting to preserve peace. Northamptonshire and Lincolnshire churches then shifted from the assembly to the association. In 1704 a reunification was actually effected on the basis of a document entitled *The Unity of the Churches*, but it lasted only a short time. The association resumed its separate meetings, and an attempt at reconciliation in 1709 was futile. Leaders such as Grantham died, and there came those who became more extreme than Caffyn.[157] The assembly and the association

---

[154] *A Cure for the Cankering Error of the New Eutychians*, 104, 96.
[155] *The History of the English General Baptists*, 1:464-65.
[156] *The Radical Reformation*, 327.
[157] Taylor, *The History of the English General Baptists*, 1:466-80.

continued to hold separate meetings until the reunification of 1731, on the basis of Hebrews 6:1-2,[158] but some General Baptist leaders participated in the Nonconformist ministers' meeting at Salters' Hall, London, in 1719. There by vote of 57 to 53 the majority decided against any "human compositions, or interpretations of the doctrine of the Trinity." The minority subscribed to a Trinitarian declaration. One General Baptist subscribed, and fourteen were nonsubscribers.[159] The General Baptists continued on their debilitating trek toward being a Unitarian denomination.[160]

Dan Taylor (1738–1816) and the New Connection (1770)

But the Arminian type of English Baptists was destined to have a new beginning. A Yorkshire coal miner's son under the impact of the Wesleyan Revival, Dan Taylor broke with John Wesley over disciplinary issues and became pastor of Wesleyan seceders at Wadsworth who came to accept believer's baptism. He himself sought and obtained immersion from a General Baptist pastor in Nottinghamshire and joined the Lincolnshire Association of General Baptists. Having less affinity for the "conservative customs" and "liberal theology" of many General Baptists and more affinity with the "evangelistic fervour" of the so-called Independent churches in Leicestershire which had sprung from the ministry of David Taylor, Dan Taylor in 1770 gathered the pastors of the Independent group and the pastors of more orthodox congregations affiliated with the General Assembly of General Baptists into a new body which would ultimately be called the New Connection of General Baptists.[161] The new body adopted six brief articles of faith dealing with the fall of humanity, "the nature and perpetual obligation of the moral law," the divine and human natures of the one person, Jesus, and his universal atonement, salvation through faith, re-

---

[158]Whitley, *A History of British Baptists*, 174. According to McBeth, *The Baptist Heritage*, 157, "two General Baptist denominations existed, the more orthodox centered in Buckinghamshire and the Midlands, the less orthodox drawing its strength more from Kent, Sussex, Essex, and the West Country."

[159]Watts, *The Dissenters*, 1:374-76; Curtis W. Freeman, "God in Three Persons: Baptist Unitarianism and the Trinity," *Perspectives in Religious Studies* 33 (Fall 2006): 324-30.

[160]Although Arian or Socinian theology is only one of seven causes of the decline of General Baptists identified by Underwood, *A History of the English Baptists*, 126-27, it was surely a major one.

[161]Watts, *The Dissenters*, 1:454-55.

generation unto holiness, and believer's baptism by immersion as prerequisite to church membership.[162] Although Taylor attended and even presided over the General Assembly toward the end of the century, efforts to unite that body and the New Connection did not succeed and ceased in 1802, when William Vidler, a Unitarian and a Universalist, was admitted to the General Assembly.[163]

Taylor's Wesleyan-shaped Arminianism was focused on the general scope of the atonement of Christ, although he did write on related doctrines. For Taylor, the sin of Adam and Eve brought depravity to all humankind, but he espoused no theory of imputed guilt for such sin.[164] Although all human beings have sinned and are spiritually dead, they, according to Taylor, have "moral ability," which he defined not as "a power to keep the law; but a power, by grace, to receive the gospel."[165] Faith is prior to regeneration, and the agency of the Holy Spirit is never insufficient.[166] Agreeing with Andrew Fuller, a Particular Baptist theologian, that faith is not only belief of the truth but also dependence upon Christ,[167] Taylor unsuccessfully nudged Fuller beyond their agreement as to universal invitations to the gospel toward Fuller's acceptance of God's universal love and the general or universal atonement.[168]

Two ecclesiological subjects were argued in detail by Taylor: baptism and singing in worship. Of his three treatises on baptism, the first primarily argued for the mode of immersion and somewhat secondarily defended the baptism of only professed believers. Contending that the Greek verb *baptizein* means "to immerse" and that immersion was the only mode practiced by the apostles, Taylor noted that pouring had not been replaced by sprinkling until the 1640s and that pouring and sprinkling had never been adopted by Eastern Orthodoxy. He answered contentions by pedo-

---

[162]Lumpkin, *Baptist Confessions of Faith*, 342-44.
[163]Watts, *The Dissenters*, 1:455-56.
[164]*Fundamentals of Religion in Faith and Practice* . . . (Leeds, 1775) 52-85.
[165]*Observations on the Rev. Andrew Fuller's "Reply to Anthropos,"* 2nd ed. (London, 1788) BBHRM/M,RP, microfilm publ. no. 946, reel 11, item 14, 59-61.
[166]Ibid., 10-35.
[167]Ibid., 7.
[168]*Observations on the Rev. Andrew Fuller's Late Pamphlet Entitled "The Gospel of Christ Worthy of All Acceptation"* . . . (London, 1785) BBHRM/M,RP, microfilm publ. no. 946, reel 11, item 13. See also *Fundamentals of Religion in Faith and Practice*, 207-14.

baptists concerning circumcision, Jewish proselyte baptism, the bringing of young children to Jesus, and 1 Cor. 7:14.[169] In the second treatise Taylor advocated infant dedication in place of infant baptism, which he declared to be without "divine authority."[170] In his third treatise Taylor began with the question of the proper recipients of baptism, that is, believers only, which practice is a "duty" and not a matter of "indifference," then proceeded to defend immersion and to assert the harmfulness of alternative modes, and finally asserted the needed perpetuity of the practice of baptism throughout "the Christian dispensation."[171]

Taylor authored two treatises on singing in the public worship of God. "Singing of the praises of God" is "plainly and frequently recommended" throughout the Bible and was "not peculiar to the Jewish dispensation." It was an "ancient" or patristic practice, "if not universal," and was restored in the Protestant Reformation. Unlike Grantham, Taylor favored singing by multiple voices, but he set limits. Organs or musical instruments were not to be used, and unconverted persons were not to participate in or direct such singing, but nonmembers should be allowed to join in the singing.[172] He seems to have shifted from an initial refusal to allow anthems and prose compositions[173] to a later acceptance of humanly composed hymns.[174]

Taylor also addressed the doctrines of the Scriptures and of last things. In treating the inspiration of the Bible in the light of 2 Pet. 1:16-21, he dealt not with the mode or manner of inspiration but with the veracity and reliability of the biblical books. He attempted to use the confirmatory value of Jesus' transfiguration but then fell back on the Old Testament prophets as

---

[169]*A Humble Essay on Christian Baptism*, 2nd ed. (London, 1777), BBHRM/M,RP, microfilm publ. no. 946, reel 11, item 16, esp. 10, 19, 28, 31, 32.

[170]*Strictures on the Rev. Stephen Addington's Late Summary of the Christian Minister's Reasons for Baptizing Infants, and for Administering the Ordinances by Sprinkling or Pouring of Water* (London, 1777) BBHRM/M,RP, microfilm publ. no. 946, reel 11, item 17, 18, 26.

[171]*A Compendious View of the Nature and Importance of Christian Baptism . . .* (London, 1789) BBHRM/M,RP, microfilm publ. no. 946, reel 11, item 18, 4-10, 21, 10-15, 17-20, 15-17.

[172]*A Dissertation on Singing in the Worship of God . . .* (London, 1786) BBHRM/M,RP, microfilm publ. no. 946, reel 11, item 20, 8, 21, 14, 26, 50-51, 63, 68, 65.

[173]Ibid., 61.

[174]*A Second Dissertation on Singing in the Worship of God* (London, 1787) EBP, UM 1951, reel 23, item, 30, 71.

more convincing evidence of the truth of Christianity.[175] Taylor explicated four eschatological themes: death, judgment (both particular at death and the last or universal judgment), to which he attached brief references to the second coming of Christ and final resurrection, heaven, and hell.[176] He also wrote in defense of the eternal punishment of the wicked, building his case chiefly on the meaning of "everlasting" in Matt. 25:46 and other texts.[177]

From Smyth through Dan Taylor the English General Baptists were increasingly committed to those doctrines which in the Reformed heritage were being labeled "Arminian." Although Smyth may have been shaped on such doctrines more by contacts with Dutch Mennonites than by any such with Dutch Arminians, his successors were more emphatic about the general or universal provision of Christ's atoning death than about teaching that true believers do fall from grace unto perdition. Some mixing of Calvinist with Arminian teachings can be observed in the unfolding of the General Baptists, especially in respect to the doctrine of sin. Smyth's convictions about worship were not retained by General Baptists, but the issue of singing proved to be controversial. The strong stance of Smyth and Helwys on religious freedom continued to be embraced by General Baptists, who uniquely employed the office of "messengers" and under Griffith and Grantham inclined to insist on the laying of hands on the newly baptized. The Mennonite Christology of the celestial flesh of Jesus as advocated by Caffyn was resisted, but the Socinian denial of the deity of Jesus Christ by Caffyn and his successors provided the slippery slope on which most of the original General Baptists went down into Unitarian oblivion. A new and more orthodox beginning with Wesleyan and revivalist impetus under Dan Taylor reinvigorated and extended the Arminian Baptist heritage.

---

[175]*An Essay on the Truth and Inspiration of the Holy Scriptures: An Antidote against Deism* (London, 1819) BBHRM/M,RP, microfilm publ. no. 946, reel 11, item, 9, esp. sections 3-9, 17.

[176]*Fundamentals of Religion in Faith and Practice*, 312-47.

[177]*The Eternity of Future Punishment* . . . (London, 1789), BBHRM/M,RP, microfilm publ. no. 5855, reel 3, item 5. This 1789 tract was seemingly a refutation of the eschatological universalism of Elhanan Winchester, Baptist pastor in Philadelphia. Adam Taylor, *The History of the English General Baptists*, part 2, 188-91; Joe Render Lovelady, "Dan Taylor: His Life and Relationship to the New Connection of General Baptists" (Th.M. thesis, New Orleans Baptist Theological Seminary, 1961) 31-32, 47. See below, 124-26.

Chapter 3

English Particular Baptists

A second body of Baptists in England evolved from Independency, which affirmed Calvinist rather than Arminian theology and held to a more irenic and less hostile attitude toward the Church of England than Separatism.[1] Independent churches desired to have congregational polity and to be out from under episcopal government while not denying that the Church of England was in some sense a true church.

Noteworthy is the Independent church founded in London in 1616 and known because of its first three pastors as the Jacob-Lathrop-Jessey (J-L-J) Church. Henry Jacob,[2] an Oxford graduate who had been in exile in Holland, emigrated to Virginia about 1622 and died in 1624, whereas John Lathrop and thirty church members departed for New England in 1634.[3] Before Lathrop's departure, in September 1633, seventeen members were dismissed to constitute another church; in the latter, led by Samuel Eaton, some members received a "further baptism." Whether this was a baptism not performed in the Church of England or a baptism on confession of personal faith (to replace pedobaptism) is not clear. In 1638, a year after Henry Jessey became pastor, six members having the same view about baptism as Samuel Eaton were dismissed and joined with John Spilsbury (1593–1668). Whether "Spilsbury had succeeded Eaton as pastor of the 1633 group"[4] or was pastor of another Independent church that had adopted believer's baptism is not clear. "At any rate," Leon McBeth has concluded, "by 1638, and possibly by 1633, there was a Particular Baptist church formed in London."[5]

The name "Particular" was derived from the belief that Christ's death was intended for and is efficacious only among the elect. The adoption of

---

[1]Hugh Wamble, "Inter-Relations of Seventeenth Century English Baptists," *Review and Expositor* 54 (July 1957): 407-25, esp. 408, differentiated the "radical separation" of the General Baptists from the Church of England and non-Separatist Puritanism from the "gradual evolution" of the Particular Baptists.

[2]Slayden A. Yarbrough, "Henry Jacob, a Moderate Separatist, and His Influence on Early English Congregationalism" (Ph.D. diss., Baylor University, 1972) labeled Jacob a "moderate Separatist."

[3]Tolmie, *The Triumph of the Saints*, 7-27.

[4]McBeth, *The Baptist Heritage*, 44.

[5]Ibid.

believer's baptism by one or two Calvinist churches that had arisen out of Independency was soon followed by a second innovation during 1640-41 with respect to Christian baptism, namely, the adoption of immersion as the proper and normative mode of baptism. Richard Blunt, having become convinced that baptism should be by immersion so as to resemble burial and resurrection (Col. 2:12; Rom. 6:4), was sent by the Jessey Church to the Rhynsburgers in the Netherlands with letters of commendation and, after being well received, returned with letters. Whether Blunt was actually immersed by the Rhynsburgers or only received instructions is not certain, but the words "Mr. Blunt being Baptized" in the Kiffin Manuscript[6] can be taken to support his having been immersed in the Netherlands. Blunt, upon return to London, immersed a fellow believer named Blacklock, and the two proceeded to immerse some 53 others.[7]

But Spilsbury had a different view, namely, that in the reintroduction of immersion succession in administration is not essential, or in the words of Thomas Crosby, "after a general corruption of baptism, an unbaptized person might warrantably baptize."[8] Hence Spilsbury proceeded to immerse *de novo* so as to reform the practice of baptism. Spilsbury argued that succession in the administration of baptism would necessitate tracing the succession through the Roman Catholic Church so as "to keep the Pope upon the throne of Christ."[9]

Like other Particular Baptists, Spilsbury taught that Christ died only for the sins of elect human beings. His treatment of this subject consisted of answers to the use of thirty-seven biblical texts by defenders of a general

---

[6] For the text, see Burrage, *The Early English Dissenters in the Light of Recent Research (1550–1651)*, 2:302-305. See also B. R. White, "Who Really Wrote the 'Kiffin Manuscript'?" *Baptist History and Heritage* 1 (October 1966): 3-10, 14; idem, "Baptist Beginnings and the Kiffin Manuscript," ibid. 2 (January 1967): 27-37.

[7] McBeth, *The Baptist Heritage*, 45-46. According to Wright, *The Early English Baptists*, 81, the recovery of immersion by General Baptists occurred about the same time as among Particular Baptists.

[8] *The History of the English Baptists, from the Reformation to the Beginning of the Reign of King George I* (London, 1738) 1:103.

[9] *A Treatise concerning the Lawfull Subject of Baptisme* (London, 1643), EBP (1951), reel 3, item 25, 39. Unlike the later nineteenth-century Landmark Baptists, Spilsbury did not exercise the option of positing a Baptist baptismal succession. See W. Morgan Patterson, *Baptist Successionism: A Critical View* (Valley Forge PA: Judson, 1969) 16-19.

atonement.[10] He also taught that Christ died in his human nature, not in his divine nature, and that "by his divine nature he overcame death."[11]

First London Confession (1644, 1646)

In 1644 seven Particular Baptist churches in London composed and distributed a confession of faith consisting of 53 articles.[12] Its fifteen signatories included such well-known pastors as Spilsbury, William Kiffin, and Samuel Richardson. Although it would serve as a didactic instrument for the members of these struggling young congregations, its chief purpose, as indicated in its preface, was to refute as untrue certain charges that had been made in the English Calvinist context against the Particular Baptists. Jay T. Collier[13] has grouped these charges as follows:

Arminian/Pelagian or General Baptist heresy:
    Doctrine of free will
    Doctrine of falling from grace
    Denial of doctrine of original sin
Anabaptist heresy:[14]
    Rejection of civil magistracy
    Refusal to obey lawful commands of magistrates
Particular Baptist immorality:
    Immodesty in administration of immersion[15]

---

[10] *Gods Ordinance, the Saints Priviledge* . . . (London, 1646), EBP (1951), reel 5, item 7, 39-80.

[11] *To Sions Virgins: or a Short Forme of Catechisme of the Doctrine of Baptisme* . . . ([London], 1644), EBP (1951), reel 28, item 28, 10. Wright, *The Early English Baptists*, 11, has found that Particular Baptists were not a "self-conscious group" before 1644.

[12] For the text, see McGlothlin, *Baptist Confessions of Faith*, 171-89; Lumpkin, *Baptist Confessions of Faith*, 153-71. The text has been rewritten in modern English by Sidney Maurice Houghton: *A Faith to Confess: The Baptist Confession of Faith of 1689* (Haywards Heath, Sussex UK: Carey Publications, 1975).

[13] "The Purpose and Sources behind the First London Confession," Historical Theology 4373, Fall 2000, Scripta, Roberts Library, Southwestern Baptist Theological Seminary, 3-7.

[14] The confession's title was *The Confession of Faith, of Those Churches Which Are Commonly (though Falsly [sic]) Called Anabaptists*. As to the anti-Anabaptist tracts recently published in England, see Lumpkin, *Baptist Confessions of Faith*, 145.

[15] Accusations were made as to dangers to health from immersion in rivers in

The contents of the 1644 confession can best be treated topically. First, there are the doctrines on which Calvinists differed from Arminians. Predestination is defined as the foreordination of "some [particular] men" unto eternal life through the grace of Christ, and the nonelect are said to be left "in their sinne to their just condemnation." The latter teaching is, therefore, that of preterition rather than reprobation. The fall of Adam and Eve is taught with the result "that all since the Fall are conceived in sinne, and brought forth in iniquitie, and so by nature children of wrath, and . . . subjects of death." No specific theory of imputation is defended. Christ died as "an acceptable sacrifice" that he might reconcile only "his elect" and did so reconcile only the elect. Faith is God's gift to the elect, wrought by the Holy Spirit, "whereby they come to see, know, and beleeve the truth of the Scriptures" and are enabled "to cast the weight of their soules upon this truth beleeved." This rather cognitive gift of faith is said to be "ordinarily begot by the preaching of the Gospel" and to be given to unbelievers who are "wholly passive" in its receipt and in their conversion. All believers, aided by Christ, will continue to wage spiritual warfare until the second coming of Christ and will "never finally nor totally fall away," being kept by God's power and having been engraved upon the palms of God's hands (Isa. 49:16).[16]

Second, the Bible is "the Rule of this Knowledge, Faith, and Obedience" for the worship of God and for Christian ethics. Rather than on any human traditions, written or unwritten, Christians are to rely only on "the word of God contained in the Canonicall Scriptures."[17] Therein God has "plainly revealed" all we need to know and believe about "the Nature and Office of Christ."[18]

---

winter and as to immoral activities associated with nude immersions at night. See Henry Martyn Dexter, *The True Story of John Smyth, the Se-Baptist, as Told by Himself and His Contemporaries* . . . (Boston: Lee and Shepard, 1881) 56-61; J. F. McGregor, "The Baptists: Fount of All Heresy," in *Radical Religion in the English Revolution*, ed. McGregor and B. Reay (Oxford: Oxford University Press, 1984) 41-42.

[16]Arts. 3, 4-5, 17, 21-22, 24-25, 31-32, 23, 26.

[17]See Thomas Helwys, *A Declaration of Faith of English People Remaining at Amsterdam in Holland*, art. 23, in McGlothlin, *Baptist Confessions of Faith*, 91, and Lumpkin, *Baptist Confessions of Faith*, 122.

[18]Arts. 7-8.

Third, there is considerable teaching concerning the person and work of Christ. The preexistent Son of God in the fulness of time "was made man of a woman," that is, Mary the virgin, and was "in all things like unto us, sinne only excepted." He was foreordained, called, and anointed to be the Mediator of the new covenant and to exercise three offices (prophet, priest, king) that grew out of human need and are not transferable to others. The prophetic office was revelatory of God's will and necessitated that he be both God and man. The priestly office was exercised both in his once-for-all sacrifice of himself and in his heavenly intercession. Being a Melchizedekan priest, he was simultaneously "Priest, Sacrifice, and Altar" and bestowed on believers the royal priesthood. The kingly office was manifested in his resurrection, ascension, and heavenly session at the Father's right hand, is exercised over both angels and men, both good and evil, and will be perfected at the second coming and reign of Christ.[19]

Fourth, the confession gives expression to a mild form of the *ordo salutis*, or sequencing of God's acts in applying the gospel to believers: salvation, union with Christ and adoption, justification, sanctification, and reconciliation.[20]

Fifth, the confession provides detailed attention to ecclesiological teachings. Commencing with a definition of Christ's present spiritual kingdom, it proceeds to define a "visible" or particular church as "a company of visible Saints, called and separated from the world, by the word and Spirit of God, to the visible profession of the faith of the Gospel, . . . joyned to the Lord, and each other, by mutuall agreement." Receiving Christ's promises and the signs of his covenant, it is a "walled sheepfold, and watered garden" and is the locale for the exercise of spiritual gifts. The confession does not refer to or define the invisible or universal church.[21] Baptism is to be only of professed believers or instructed disciples and by the mode of immersion as administered by "a preaching Disciple" who is not necessarily an officer of a particular congregation. Immersion is said to be a threefold sign: of "the washing the whole soule in the bloud of Christ" (Rev. 1:5; 7:14; Heb. 10:22), of "that interest the Saints have in the death, buriall, and resurrection" of Christ (Rom. 6:3-5), and of "a confirmation of our faith" in our

---

[19] Arts. 9-20.
[20] Arts. 21, 27-30.
[21] Hence Lumpkin, *Baptist Confessions of Faith*, 146, is hardly correct when stating that it "includes the concept of the invisible Church," although it did refer once to Christ's "whole Church" (art. 42).

future bodily resurrection (1 Cor. 15:28-29). There is a strange silence concerning the Lord's Supper.[22] Every congregation has from Christ the "power" to "choose" "Pastors, Teachers, Elders, Deacons" "for the feeding, governing, serving, and building up of his Church." Such ministers are appointed by the congregations, are obliged to exercise their calling, and are to be financially supported by the voluntary gifts of members. All members have the authority and duty "to watch over one another," each member is subject to the "censure and judgement of Christ" through the church, and every congregation, having the "power" of excommunication, "ought with great care and tendernesse, with due advice to proceed against her members." There should be no schismatic separation "for faults and corruptions" until such persons "have in due order sought redresse thereof," and the association of churches for counsel and help is affirmed. The civil magistracy is divinely ordained and to be obeyed. King and parliament ought to be obeyed in all civil laws, but not in ecclesiastical laws. The highest loyalty is to God, and believers ought to have "a cleare conscience void of offense towards God and towards man," rendering to Caesar what is Caesar's and to God what is God's.[23]

The 1644 confession has been described as "moderately Calvinistic."[24] It was "the first Confession of [Christian] history to prescribe a single immersion as the form of baptism"[25] and "the first Baptist Confession to pronounce in favor of immersion as the proper mode of baptism."[26] To it have been attributed both immediate and long-range effects. It "was one of the most effective bits of propaganda both for winning a toleration for Baptists and for winning converts to the Baptist position."[27] It has been called "the

---

[22] Arts. 33-35, 39-41.

[23] Arts. 36, 45, 37-38, 44, 43, 42, 46-47, 48, 52, 49, 41, 53. Articles 1-2 on God and the Trinity and article 6 on heaven and hell are not treated in this summary.

[24] McGlothlin, *Baptist Confessions of Faith*, 169; Lumpkin, *Baptist Confessions of Faith*, 146. This descriptive label was doubtless applied by comparison with the Second London Confession of Particular Baptists (1677, 1689).

[25] McGlothlin, *Baptist Confessions of Faith*, 169. The (Eastern) Orthodox Confession of 1643, art. 102, framed by or under the direction of Peter Mogilas, metropolitan of Kiev, and approved by the Synod of Jassy (1643) and by the Synod of Jerusalem (1672), taught trine immersion. Schaff, *The Creeds of Christendom*, 2:375-76.

[26] Lumpkin, *Baptist Confession of Faith*, 146.

[27] Ibid., 152.

doctrinal standard for the first period of their [Particular Baptist] expansion"[28] and "one of the chief landmarks of Baptist history."[29] "Perhaps no Confession of Faith has had so formative influence on Baptist life as this one."[30] Three centuries later an American Baptist would declare that it "embodies practically every doctrine that present-day Baptists hold dear."[31]

The probable source or sources for the 1644 confession have posed a major question for present-day scholars. Jay T. Collier has wisely differentiated three types of dependence for such confessions: the "theological," the "structural," and the "verbal."[32] As previously noted,[33] the Separatist *A True Confession* (*TC*) (1596) served "as a model"[34] for the 1644 Particular Baptist Confession (*LC*). In the structure of the two confessions and on the threefold office of Christ,[35] one finds theological, literary, and verbal dependences. But there are major differences between the two confessions: the civil government's involvement in church reform (*TC*),[36] the death-burial-resurrection interpretation of baptism (*LC*),[37] reprobation, or double predestination (*TC*),[38] double reconciliation (*TC*),[39] and applied soteriology (*LC*).[40]

What source or sources were likely utilized by the framers of the 1644 Confession for the composition of those articles which were not derived from *A True Confession*? One scholar has claimed some likely structural and verbal indebtedness to the ten articles of faith placed at the end of John

---

[28]B. R. White, "The Doctrine of the Church in the Particular Baptist Confession of 1644," *Journal of Theological Studies* n.s. 19 (October 1968): 570.

[29]Henry C. Vedder, *A Short History of the Baptists* (Philadelphia: American Baptist Publication Society, 1907) 211.

[30]Lumpkin, *Baptist Confessions of Faith*, 152.

[31]Harold Brown, "The History of the Baptists in England to 1644," *The Chronicle* 8 (January 1945): 14.

[32]"The Sources behind the First London Confession," *American Baptist Quarterly* 21 (June 2002): 198.

[33]See above, 18-21.

[34]Lumpkin, *Baptist Confessions of Faith*, 81.

[35]*TC*, arts. 12-17; *LC*, arts. 10-20.

[36]*TC*, arts. 39-41; *LC*, art. 49.

[37]*LC*, art. 40.

[38]*TC*, art. 3; *LC*, art. 3.

[39]*TC*, art. 14; *LC*, art. 17.

[40]*LC*, arts. 21-32.

Spilsbury's treatise relative to baptism.[41] A similarity between William Ames's *The Marrow of Divinity* and the 1644 Confession as to the doctrines of God and soteriology has been noted.[42] Likewise, structural similarities between sections of the 1616 Aberdeen Confession of the Church of Scotland and sections of the 1644 Confession have been identified.[43] Another possible linkage is with Henry Jacob's *Confession and Protestation* (1616).[44]

The two more probable sources for the distinctive material on baptism in the 1644 Confession are Menno Simons's *Foundation—Book* (1539), with which there are theological similarities,[45] and the treatise by the Independent, Praisegod Barebone, entitled *A Discourse Tending to Prove the Baptisme in, or under the Defection of Antichrist to Be the Ordinance of Jesus Christ* (1642), with which there are structural similarities.[46]

The revision of the 1644 Confession which was issued in 1646 in reply to the polemical attack by an Anglican, Daniel Featley,[47] on the 1644 Con-

---

[41] Lumpkin, *Baptist Confessions of Faith*, 145. But see the refutation on the basis of lack of evidence in Collier, "The Sources behind the First London Confession," 209-11.

[42] Glen H. Stassen, "Anabaptist Influence in the Origin of the Particular Baptists," *Mennonite Quarterly Review* 36 (October 1962): 332; Stanley A. Nelson, "Reflecting on Baptist Origins: The London Confession of Faith of 1644," *Baptist History and Heritage* 29 (April 1994): 34-35, 38-43.

[43] Robert B. Hannen, "A Suggested Source of Some Expressions in the Baptist Confession of Faith, London, 1644," *Baptist Quarterly* 12 (April-July 1948): 389-99. Hannen even conjectured that the Scot who brought the Aberdeen Confession to the attention of Particular Baptists in London was Gilbert Gardin of Aberdeenshire, who was accused of "Brownism" in 1643 and later identified as a Baptist.

[44] White, "The Doctrine of the Church in the Particular Baptist Confession of 1644," 575, 586-89.

[45] Stassen, "Anabaptist Influence in the Origin of the Particular Baptists," 341-48; Stassen, "Opening Menno Simons's *Foundation—Book* and Finding the Father of Baptist Origins alongside the Mother—Calvinist Congregationalism," *Baptist History and Heritage* 33 (Spring 1998): 34-44; Stassen, "Revisioning Baptist Identity by Naming Our Origin and Character Rightly," ibid., 45-54.

[46] James M. Renihan, "An Examination of the Possible Influence of Menno Simons's *Foundation Book* upon the Particular Baptist Confession of 1644," *American Baptist Quarterly* 15 (September 1996): 200-204; Collier, "The Sources behind the First London Confession," 207-208.

[47] McGlothlin, *Baptist Confessions of Faith*, 189-90.

fession contained some deletions and additions as well as stylistic refinements. The deletions included Christ's reconciliation of "his elect onely," his heavenly session at the Father's right hand, sanctification as the means whereby the believer is "separated" from all sin and "dead works," the significance of baptism as "the washing the whole soule in the bloud of Christ," the Great Commission, and specific allusion to rendering to Caesar and rendering to God.[48] The additions included a new article on providence, New Testament references supportive of the deity and the humanity of Christ, Christ's heavenly intercession, the "gifts" and "graces" given to believers, proper clothing for the administrator and the recipient of immersion, biblical texts concerning the civil magistracy, the lawfulness of a Christian to serve as civil magistrate and to take oaths, and future resurrection and final judgment.[49] Of note also is the change from "Pastors, Teachers, Elders, Deacons" to "elders and deacons."[50]

Midland (1655) and Somerset (1656) Confessions

Two Particular Baptist confessions were written and adopted during the Commonwealth era, the one briefer and more strictly Calvinistic and the other more lengthy and innovative as to the missionary mandate. In 1655 seven of the fourteen Particular Baptist churches in four Midlands counties formed an association and adopted a relatively brief 16-article confession. Framed by laymen or lay preachers, it avoided technical language and sought to instruct church members rather than to engage in controversy with their opponents. Although it "must have been modeled on the London Confession of 1644, . . . its statements are original."[51] The Scriptures are said "to be the word and revealed mind of God, which are able to make men

---

[48]First London Confession of Particular Baptists, arts. 17, 19, 29, 40, 51, 52, in Lumpkin, *Baptist Confessions of Faith*, 160-61, 161-62, 164, 167, 170; *The First London Confession of Faith, 1646 Edition, with an Appendix by Benjamin Cox, 1646* (Rochester NY: Backus, 1981) arts. 17, 19, 29, 40, 49, 52, on pp. 7, 8, 11, 14-15, 18-19.

[49]First London Confession of Particular Baptists, arts. 16, 19, 23, 40, 49-50, 52b, in Lumpkin, *Baptist Confessions of Faith*, 160, 161-62, 163, 167, 169-70, 170-71; *The First London Confession of Faith, 1646 Edition*, arts. 5, 16, 19, 23, 40, 48, 50, 52, on pp. 2-3, 6-7, 8, 9, 14-15, 17-18, 19.

[50]First London Confession of Particular Baptists, art. 36, in Lumpkin, *Baptist Confessions of Faith*, 166; *The First London Confession of Faith, 1646 Edition*, art. 36 on pp. 13-14.

[51]Lumpkin, *Baptist Confessions of Faith*, 195-98.

wise unto Salvation . . . ; and . . . they are given by inspiration of God . . . ; and by them we are (in the strength of Christ) to try all things whatsoever are brought to us, under the pretence of truth." By Adam's fall not only he "but his posterity" were made "sinners by his disobedience." "God elected and chose . . . some persons to life and salvation," not because of "any forseen [sic] works of faith," and them he does "and will effectually call," but nothing is said about the nonelect. Nor is particular atonement mentioned. Faith "is the free gift of God, and the mighty work of God in the soul" but is not given to all humankind. Human beings are justified by Christ through faith and subsequently to "abound in" good works. Those effectually called God "will certainly keep" to final salvation. Those whose faith has been made evident by "fruits" ought to be baptized by immersion as the representation of Christ's death, burial, and resurrection, and those so baptized should constitute "distinct churches." Christ's second coming, the general resurrection of the "just and unjust," and the final judgment are affirmed.[52]

In 1656 sixteen Particular Baptist churches located in five western counties of England at the seventh meeting of their Western or Somerset Association adopted a 45-article confession which may have been composed as early as 1653. Thomas Collier (?–1691), their "General Superintendent and Messenger," seems to have been the primary author of the confession.[53] In its "Epistle Dedicatory" two reasons were given for the composition of the confession. First, the framers wished to refute "the general charge" that they were Arminian and thus were not in accord with the London Particular Baptist churches and their 1644 Confession. Second, they wanted to testify to the truth in face of the divisiveness of the Quaker movement in the western counties.[54] Although the framers sought "to approximate the theological position" of the 1644 Confession, "there is complete independence of expression, and there are some noteworthy omissions of material of the older document." Lumpkin's assessment that the Calvinism of the Somerset Confession "was not of a rigid type," that it was open to the General Baptist critique of particular atonement, and that it "probably represents an attempt to comprehend all Baptists of the district

---

[52]Midland Association Confession, arts. 3-6, 8, 10, 12, 5, 13-16, in ibid., 198-200.

[53]Ibid., 200-201.

[54]In *Confessions of Faith, and Other Public Documents, Illustrative of the History of the Baptist Churches of England in the 17th Century*, ed. Edward Bean Underhill (London: Haddon Brothers, 1854) 63-64.

irrespective of their Calvinism or Arminianism"⁵⁵ must be balanced by the absence of major Arminian doctrines.

Adam's breaking of the law "brought himself and his posterity under the guilt and judgment denounced." Mosaic law was "not for justification to eternal life . . . , but that all might appear guilty before the Lord by it." There is no possibility of self-salvation. God elected and chose in Christ "some to himself before the foundation of the world," and they "shall never finally fall from him." The Holy Spirit "is administred [*sic*] by or through the word of faith preached" and works in us "faith in Christ," through which we are justified and which produces in us "conformity . . . to the Lord Jesus."⁵⁶

The Somerset Confession delineates the 'holy history' of Jesus Christ: conception and birth, true deity and true humanity, baptism and manifestation as Messiah, passion and death, burial, resurrection, appearances, ascension, heavenly session, and exaltation in his threefold office. Its ecclesiology was even more significant for the future of Baptists. Every repentant, believing person has "the duty" to be immersed "in the name of our Lord Jesus (Acts 8:16), or in the name of the Father, Son, and Holy Spirit (Matt. 28:19)." Every church and every minister have "the duty" in admitting members to "be careful they receive none but such as do make forth evident demonstration of the new birth." The congregation is to choose, "approve and ordain" its ministers, submit to the authority of Christ through them, and financially support them except for self-support "in cases of necessity." The Somerset Confession 136 years before William Carey sailed for India taught that churches have "the duty . . . to send forth such brethren as are fitly gifted and qualified through the Spirit of Christ to preach the gospel to the world." Unique among Baptist confessions of faith is its article enjoining compassion toward, prayer for, and expectation of the conversion of Jews to Christ.⁵⁷

Following teaching on angels and Satan, the Somerset Confession concluded with the last things: the second coming; the resurrection of the saints, their reign with him and judgment of the nations;⁵⁸ the resurrection

---

⁵⁵Lumpkin, *Baptist Confessions of Faith*, 201, 202.

⁵⁶Somerset Confession, arts. 4, 6-7, 9, 19-23, in Lumpkin, *Baptist Confessions of Faith*, 204-205, 208-209.

⁵⁷Ibid., arts. 12-18, 24, 25 (sect. 21), 31, 33, 32, 34-35, in Lumpkin, *Baptist Confessions of Faith*, 206-208, 211, 212-13; also 202.

⁵⁸One of the seventeen biblical texts cited is Rev. 20:6.

of the unrighteous and their judgment; heaven; and hell.[59] Here the temporal differentiation between the resurrection of the redeemed and the resurrection of the wicked entered Baptist confessional history.

Hanserd Knollys (1609–1691)

The son of a Church of England clergyman in Lincolnshire who himself was ordained at the age of thirty both a deacon and a priest on successive days, Knollys, after studying at Cambridge and becoming a Puritan in his initial Anglican charge, had sojourned in New England as a pastor for three years before joining the JLJ Church and then becoming a Baptist about 1644 and assuming a pastorate in London.[60]

Knollys's writings on baptism were more reflective of his new Particular Baptist identity than his writings on church polity. Writing to refute John Saltmarsh, arguing as if a Seeker, who "denied the need for ordinances at all,"[61] Knollys insisted that Matt. 28:19 refers to water baptism, not, as Saltmarsh alleged, to a baptism of spiritual gifts limited to the apostolic era.[62] In response to John Bastwick's defense of Presbyterian polity, wherein he had argued that the several congregations in Jerusalem constituted one Church and had synodical government, Knollys contended for the independence of each congregation. The Great Commission was not given only to apostles and ministers, and ministers alone are not to admit

---

[59]Somerset Confession, arts. 37-42, in McGlothlin, *Baptist Confessions of Faith*, 212-13; Lumpkin, *Baptist Confessions of Faith*, 213-14.

[60]Dennis C. Bustin, *Paradox and Perseverance: Hanserd Knollys, Particular Baptist Pioneer in Seventeenth-Century England*, Studies in Baptist History and Thought 23 (Milton Keynes UK, Waynesboro GA: Paternoster, 2006); Barry H. Howson, *Erroneous and Schismatical Opinions: The Question of Orthodoxy regarding the Theology of Hanserd Knollys (ca.1599–1691)*, Studies in the History of Christian Thought 98 (Leiden: Brill, 2001) 54-64; James Culross, *Hanserd Knollys: "A Minister and Witness of Jesus Christ," 1598–1691*, Baptist Manuals: Historical and Biographical 2 (London: Alexander and Shepheard, 1895) 1-40; Pope A. Duncan, *Hanserd Knollys: Seventeenth-Century Baptist*, Broadman Historical Monographs (Nashville: Broadman, 1965) 8-11; Muriel James, *Religious Liberty on Trial: Hanserd Knollys—Baptist Hero* (Franklin TN: Providence House, 1997). We accept Bustin's argument for 1609 as the year of Knollys's birth rather than the traditional ca. 1599. *Paradox and Perseverance*, 324-28.

[61]Howson, *Erroneous and Schismatical Opinions*, 66.

[62]*The Shining of a Flaming Fire in Zion* (1646), as interp. by Culross, *Hanserd Knollys*, 52-54.

and excommunicate members.⁶³ But on the basis of all of Knollys's writings, Barry Howson has concluded that he "was committed to a Presbyterian style of church government within each church."⁶⁴ In his commentary on the Song of Solomon Knollys employed the medieval method, especially that of Hugh of St. Victor (ca.1096–1141), of the threefold meaning of the text: the literal, Israel and her Messiah as pointing to the church and Christ; the prophetical, the churches from the apostolic era to the seventeenth century; and the spiritual, Christ and the individual soul.⁶⁵

All of Knollys's eschatological teachings were not shared, it would seem, by all other Particular Baptists. He interpreted the parable of the five wise and the five foolish virgins (Matt. 25:1-13) as a call to the restoration of primitive Christianity and "the power of godliness" and so that the bridegroom's coming is his "spiritual, powerful, and glorious coming" with "the living saints," not his later personal and physical coming to earth, the two comings being separated by the Davidic millennial reign. Hence with the incarnation Knollys taught three comings of Christ.⁶⁶ Signs of the end of time, according to Knollys, will be three: the apostasy of professing Christians together with the lukewarmness of both ministers and members, the abundant iniquity of unbelievers, and the great tribulation.⁶⁷ Knollys applied to the New Testament Apocalypse both the continuous-historical and the "symbolic-figurative" methods of interpretation.⁶⁸ The seven seals, seven trumpets, and seven vials, or bowls, represent successive periods of Christian history. The 1,260 days of Rev. 11:3 and 12:6 are taken to symbolize 1,260 literal years. Knollys posited the beginning of papal Rome

---

⁶³*A Moderate Answer unto Dr. Bastwick's Book, Called, Independency Not God's Ordinance* (1645), EBP (1951), reel 2, item 11, esp. 15, 17; Howson, *Erroneous and Schismatical Opinions*, 65, 224n.92, 225.

⁶⁴*Erroneous and Schismatical Opinions*, 224.

⁶⁵Jay T. Collier, "Hanserd Knollys as Interpreter of Scripture: An Examination of His 'An Exposition of the First Chapter of the Song of Solomon' " *Eusebeia* no. 5 (Autumn 2005): 5-32.

⁶⁶*The Parable of the Kingdom of Heaven Expounded, or, An Exposition of the First Thirteen Verses of the Twenty-Fifth Chapter of St. Matthew* (London, 1813) esp. 86-87, 90-93, 98, 107-108; *The World That Now Is, and the World That Is to Come: On the First and Second Coming of Jesus Christ* (London, 1681), BBHRM/M, RP, microform publ. no. 946, reel 45, item 1, part 2, esp. 39-41.

⁶⁷*The World That Now Is, and the World That Is to Come*, part 1, 81-95.

⁶⁸*An Exposition of the Whole Book of Revelation* (London, 1689) preface, as quoted by Howson, *Erroneous and Schismatical Opinions*, 258-59.

during AD 407–428, and thus 1,260 years later would be AD 1667–1688. Unlike other contemporary Protestants, he held that the seventh trumpet had not yet sounded and the vials were not yet poured out. Like other Protestants, he identified the Antichrist, the red dragon (Rev. 12), the two beasts (Rev. 13), Babylon (Rev. 14, 16-18), the false prophet (Rev. 16), and the great prostitute riding the beast (Rev. 17) variously with the Roman Catholic Church.[69] The two witnesses (Rev. 11), representative of the true church, were yet to be martyred and raised. The Battle of Armageddon, at which both the Turks and the Papacy would be defeated, would occur at the outpouring of the sixth vial, along with the conversion of the Jews and their return to Palestine, and at the beginning of the millennial reign of the saints, the "thousand years" of Rev. 20:1-7 being interpreted literally. At the end of the millennium, according to Howson's rendering of Knollys, Christ will come personally and visibly with his resurrected and living saints, the universal judgment will occur, the heavens and the earth will be dissolved, "and the eternal kingdom will begin."[70] On the other hand Bustin has contended that Knollys in his last eschatological treatises, *The World That Now Is and the World That Is to Come* and *An Exposition of the Whole Book of Revelation*, "abandoned" his earlier two-comings view and affirmed only one personal, physical second coming of Christ.[71]

Concerning the charge, made both in the seventeenth century and in the twentieth century, that Knollys was a Fifth Monarchist, or one who advocated human and even violent efforts to establish Christ's millennial rule as the fifth kingdom in succession to Daniel's four kingdoms (Daniel 2), Howson, while acknowledging some commonalities, has concluded that Knollys was not a Fifth Monarchist, despite his incarceration, because he did not advocate the use of force to establish the kingdom and did not major on English political and economic events, people, and institutions.[72]

---

[69]Howson, *Erroneous and Schismatical Opinions*, 248-49, 260-62, 270-72.

[70]Ibid., 260-61, 263, 273-74, 275-76, 277-79.

[71]Neither Howson, *Erroneous and Schismatical Opinions*, 278, nor Bustin, *Paradox and Perseverance*, 223-28, was precisely correct in labeling the earlier view "postmillennial," but Bustin was probably correct in describing the later as "premillennial."

[72]Howson, *Erroneous and Schismatical Opinions*, 284-305. B. R. White, *Hanserd Knollys and Radical Dissent in the 17th Century* (London: Dr. Williams's Trust, 1977) 17, 18, 24, agreed that Knollys "drew back from involvement in revolutionary politics" and was not "anywhere near the heart of the Fifth Monarchy

Similarly Howson has exonerated Knollys of the charge, made both in New England and England, that he was an Antinomian[73] and, agreeing with both Joseph Ivimey[74] and Culross,[75] has exonerated him of the charge that he was "a forerunner of eighteenth-century Hyper-Calvinism," while acknowledging that he was a High Calvinist.[76] Only with respect to the charge that Knollys was an Anabaptist has Howson acknowledged any validity to the various charges. But even here Knollys's agreement with Anabaptists was qualified; that is, not on Arminian-type teachings and not on anti-Trinitarianism, oaths, magistracy, or communion of goods but on believer's baptism, the gathered church, lay preaching, and separation of church and state.[77]

William Kiffin (1616–1701)

A poor boy orphaned at nine who became a wealthy wool merchant and a Nonconformist who endured arrest and imprisonment but became a member of Parliament, alderman of London, and confidant of royalty, William Kiffin served as pastor of the same Baptist church in Devonshire Square, London, for about sixty years and, together with Knollys, gave leadership to Particular Baptists from the inception of the movement to the end of the century. A signatory to both the First London and the Second London confessions, Kiffin embraced the high Calvinism of Particular Baptists, but his writings, less extensive than Knollys's, focused on ecclesiology.[78]

---

movement." Bustin, *Paradox and Perseverance*, 169, called Knollys "a mild Fifth Monarchist sympathiser." Concerning the Fifth Monarchy eschatology, see B. S. Capp, "Extreme Millenarianism," in Peter Toon, ed., *Puritans, the Millennium and the Future of Israel: Puritan Eschatology 1600 to 1660* (Cambridge: James Clarke, 1970) 66-90.

[73]Howson, *Erroneous and Schismatical Opinions*, 79-132, esp. 131-32.

[74]*A History of the English Baptists* 4 vols. (London: various printers, 1811–1830) 3:364-65.

[75]*Hanserd Knollys*, 36-37.

[76]Howson, *Erroneous and Schismatical Opinions*, 133-93, esp. 192-93. The major evidence for the charge was the fact that John Skepp, a Hyper-Calvinist, in his *Divine Energy* (1722) claimed to be building on the foundation laid by Hanserd Knollys (Howson, 133).

[77]Ibid., 194-242, esp. 241-42.

[78]William Orme, *Remarkable Passages in the Life of William Kiffin, Written by Himself, and Edited from the Original Manuscript, with Notes and Additions* (London, 1823); Joseph Ivimey, *The Life of Mr. William Kiffin*... (London, 1833);

Joining with Benjamin Coxe and Knollys, Kiffin contributed to the antipedobaptist argument of a scheduled but never held debate with pedobaptists on "Whether the Infants of believing Parents ought to be baptized." Baptism should be administered solely to believers, and to administer it contrary to the teaching of Jesus and "his Disciples" is unlawful. Only the seed of Abraham, either according to the flesh or through faith, should be baptized, and this excludes the infants of believing Gentiles. Jesus did not command infant baptism, and it is "no part of the revealed counsell of God."[79] In confrontation with Robert Poole he answered Poole's critical queries about why the Particular Baptists had separated from Independency—branded by Poole as "defection from all the Reformed Churches"—and pressed Poole to disconnect circumcision and baptism and to acknowledge that baptism is only for "Persons Discipled or taught" and that ordinances are not means to confer grace but signs to confirm the grace which has been conferred.[80]

Kiffin's longest writing was a book[81] defending close communion in opposition to John Bunyan's advocacy of open communion. His thesis was that "no Unbaptized person may be Regularly admitted to the Lord's Supper" because this was the practice of primitive Christianity and later Christian history and because, since infant baptism is not genuine baptism, those having such are unbaptized. Admitting the unbaptized to the Supper destroys the initiatory nature of baptism, the foundation principle of Heb.

B. A. Ramsbottom, *Stranger than Fiction: The Life of William Kiffin* (Harpenden, Hertfordshire UK: Gospel Standard Trust Publications, 1989); B. R. White, "William Kiffin: Baptist Pioneer and Citizen of London," *Baptist History and Heritage* 2 (July 1967): 91-103, 126; idem, "How Did William Kiffin Join the Baptists?" *Baptist Quarterly* 23 (January 1970): 201-207.

[79]Benjamin Coxe, Hanserd Knollys, William Kiffin, et al., *A Declaration concerning the Publike Dispute Which Should Have Been . . . Concerning Infants-Baptisme . . .* (London, 1645), EBP (1951), reel 3, item 17. Kiffin had already debated Daniel Featley, the author of *The Dippers Dipt, or, the Anabaptists Duck'd and Plunged over Head and Eares*, in 1642. Underwood, *A History of the English Baptists*, 66-67.

[80]*A Briefe Remonstrance of the Reasons and Grounds of Those People Commonly Called Anabaptists, for their Separation, etc., or Certaine Queries concerning Their Faith and Practice Propounded by Mr. Robert Poole, Answered and Resolved* ([London], 1645), EBP (1951), reel 2, item 12, esp. 2-3.

[81]*A Sober Discourse of Right to Church-Communion . . .* (London, 1681), EBP (1951), reel 16, item 13.

6:2, and "the right Gospel Order" (faith, baptism, Lord's Supper). Believer's baptism by immersion was never intended by God to be "a Wall of Division" to exclude "other Christians from our Love, Charity, and Christian-Communion," but only to exclude "from immediate Church-fellowship." Kiffin's use of biblical texts to support his thesis is not impressive, but he cited various church fathers and several non-Baptist authors to confirm that baptism ought to precede the Lord's Supper. He answered eleven objections to his position such as the assumption that what is not forbidden in the Scriptures is permitted, the view that Spirit baptism (1 Cor. 12:13) "is the Inchurching ordinance," the idea that Paul was not interrogated by the Jerusalem church (Acts 9:26) as to his baptism, but only as to discipleship, the concept that union with Christ "gives a Right to all the Ordinances of Christ," and the objection that close communion violates the "one baptism" of Eph. 4:4-6.[82]

John Bunyan (1628–1688)

Whether Bunyan ought to be included in the history of Baptist theology depends upon one's answer to the question, raised in his own time and continued to be pursued until today, as to whether open membership, or the practice of not requiring believer's baptism by immersion of all members of a congregation, does or does not disqualify the congregation to be regarded as Baptist.[83] The son of a poor brazier or tinker and having a limited education, Bunyan underwent religious doubt and despair before his assurance of conversion and joining the Independent congregation in Bedford. He became preacher for that church, despite criticism of his lack of formal training, until his two imprisonments (1660–1672 and 1676) and then in 1672 became its pastor and served there until his death.[84] Of

---

[82]Ibid., title page, 10, 13, 16-17, 18-19, 33-110, 120, 132, 146, 151, 154-55. Among certain modern, especially non-Baptist, authors there has been a scornful disdain for Kiffin's position. A Methodist, Gordon Wakefield, *Bunyan the Christian* (London: HarperCollins Religious, 1992) 70, has compared it with the exclusivism "of ritualistic High Churchmen" and with "those condemned by Jesus Christ who tithe mint and anise and cummin and neglect judgement and the love of God."

[83]The inclusion of Bunyan in this book is, however, not predicated on full acceptance of open membership as qualification for Baptist identity.

[84]Richard L. Greaves, *John Bunyan*, Courtenay Studies in Reformation Theology 2 (Grand Rapids MI: Eerdmans, 1969) 15-23; Michael Mullett, *John Bunyan in Context*, Studies in Protestant Nonconformity (Pittsburgh: Duquesne University

Bunyan's voluminous writings[85] it was *The Pilgrim's Progress* (1678, 1684) that caused him to be well known and widely read.[86] These writings have been classified as either "Experimental, Doctrinal, and Practical" or "Allegorical, Figurative and Symbolical."[87]

Bunyan's earliest writing was in refutation of the Quaker doctrine of the Inner Light and in defense of the human, physical, and historical Jesus, together with his death, burial, resurrection, ascension, and intercession,[88] and some of his last works expounded Christ's role as advocate-intercessor and high priest.[89] Underlying all of his writings was his commitment to the truth, the power, and the relevance of the Bible, whose interpretation, for Bunyan, combined the literal and the typological.[90] He particularly utilized Luke, Acts, and Hebrews, making the Bible "into a story that had foreseen his very retelling of it as an authentic part of the further reformation."[91]

Press, 1997) 9-125.

[85]*The Miscellaneous Works of John Bunyan*, hereafter MWJB, Roger Sharrock, gen. ed (London: Oxford University Press, 1976–1994) consists of thirteen volumes.

[86]Mullett, *John Bunyan in Context*, 191.

[87]This distinction was made by George Offor, the editor of *Works of John Bunyan*, 3 vols. (Glasgow: W. G. Blackie, 1854; repr.: Grand Rapids MI: Baker, 1977; repr.: Edinburgh, Carlisle PA: Banner of Truth Trust, 1991). Mullett, *John Bunyan in Context*, 291.

[88]*Some Gospel-Truths Opened* (1656) and *A Vindication of Some Gospel-Truths Opened* (1657), in MWJB vol. 1, ed. T. L. Underwood (Oxford: Oxford University Press, 1978) 5-220. Concerning Bunyan's relationships with both Ranters and Quakers, see Christopher Hill, *A Tinker and a Poor Man: John Bunyan and His Church, 1628–1688* (New York: Alfred A. Knopf, 1989) 75-84.

[89]*The Advocateship of Jesus Christ* (1688), in MWJB vol. 11, ed. Richard L. Greaves (Oxford: Oxford University Press, 1985) 99-216; *Christ a Compleat Saviour* (1692), in MWJB vol. 13, ed. W. R. Owens (1994), 257-333; *The Saints Privilege and Profit* (1692), in ibid., 165-252.

[90]John R. Knott, Jr., "'Thou Must Live upon My Word': Bunyan and the Bible," in *John Bunyan, Conventicle and Parnassus: Tercentenary Essays*, ed. N. H. Keeble (Oxford: Oxford University Press, 1988) 156-64. Also see Richard L. Greaves, intro. to vol. 8 of MWJB (Oxford: Oxford University Press, 1979) xliii-l.

[91]Dayton Haskin, "Bunyan's Scriptural Acts," in *Bunyan in Our Time*, ed. Robert G. Collmer (Kent OH and London: Kent State University Press, 1989) 61-92, esp. 63.

Bunyan has been said to belong to the "strict Calvinist" and "Antinomian" wing rather than to the "moderate Calvinist" and "Arminian" wing of English Calvinism.[92] His doctrine of election, namely, that God decreed "to grant to certain men eternal life" was set in an infralapsarian context inasmuch as election in the scheme of divine decrees "was subsequent to God's foreknowledge of the fall, but prior to the fall itself," but his doctrine pertaining to the nonelect was preterition, or God's leaving sinners in their sins so that they would perish under divine judgment, though this was modified by God's hardening of the hearts of the nonelect.[93] Bunyan's doctrine of two covenants, that of works and that of grace, had two important features. First, the covenant of grace actually preceded the covenant of works because it was "first formed [in eternity] between the Father and the Son." Second, Bunyan's covenantal doctrine belonged to the "promissory" or "unilateral" view of the covenant of grace set forth by John Calvin rather than to the "contractual" or "reciprocal" view traceable to Ulrich Zwingli, Henry Bullinger, and William Tyndale. Thus the covenant of grace gave basis to assurance for the elect.[94] Moreover, Bunyan could deny holding to human free will vis-à-vis salvation, while calling his readers to repentance.[95]

In rebuttal of *The Design of Christianity*, written by Edward Fowler, a Presbyterian turned Anglican who gave support to Latitudinarianism, Bunyan defended the imputation of Christ's righteousness "to the ungodly while they are still ungodly" and "true Gospel righteousness" against Fowler's "natural human righteousness."[96] Bunyan, who had earlier taught that faith as God's gift precedes in time one's justification,[97] by 1685 shifted to the more antinomian position that justification precedes faith so that the justified, being still "ungodly," knows nothing about his justification.[98]

---

[92]Greaves, *John Bunyan*, 24-25.

[93]Ibid., 49-67, esp. 52, 57.

[94]Richard L. Greaves, intro. to vol. 2 of MWJB (Oxford: Oxford University Press, 1976) xxi-xxviii.

[95]Greaves, *John Bunyan*, 58-61.

[96]T. L. Underwood, intro. to vol. 4 of MWJB (Oxford: Oxford University Press, 1989) xx-xxv. See also Isabel Rivers, "Grace, Holiness, and the Pursuit of Happiness: Bunyan and Restoration Latitudinarianism," in Keeble, ed., *John Bunyan, Conventicle and Parnassus*, 45-69. On the imputed righteousness of Christ, see also Bunyan's *Of Justification by an Imputed Righteousness* (1692), in MWJB vol. 12, ed. W. R. Owens (Oxford: Oxford University Press, 1994) 283-352.

[97]*Instruction for the Ignorant* (1675), in MWJB vol. 8, ed. Greaves, 30, 33.

[98]*A Discourse upon the Pharisee and the Publican*, in MWJB vol. 10, ed. Owen

Despite the fact that other seventeenth-century authors had made the "salvific journey" to be "a commonplace,"⁹⁹ Bunyan placed later Christians in his debt by his predominating theme of the Christian life as pilgrimage—a venture with vicissitudes¹⁰⁰—in *The Pilgrim's Progress*.

Probably Bunyan's most significant contribution to Baptist theology was his case for open communion and open membership, which he made as a quasi-Baptist or Congregationalist. Defining communion as "fellowship *in the things of the Kingdom of Christ*," Bunyan made only sainthood, or holiness, not water-baptism, essential to church membership and, magnifying Spirit-baptism, denied that water baptism is "the initiating or entering ordinance." Rather it confirms the believer's faith as a sign of his death, burial, and resurrection with Christ. Consequently saints not immersed as believers should not be barred from receiving the Lord's Supper.¹⁰¹ Bunyan, replying to his author-critics,¹⁰² who utilized the Great Commission and New Testament church practice, argued that churches are not forbidden to, but rather required to, accept pedobaptist saints at the Lord's Supper and not make "a Wall of Division."¹⁰³ He decried such "Factious Titles" as "*Anabaptists, Independents,* [and] *Presbyterians*," preferring only "*to be called a Christian.*"¹⁰⁴ Even so, after 1672 Bunyan clearly defended Independency's separation from the Church of England.¹⁰⁵ He also wrote against the observance of a seventh-day Sabbath.¹⁰⁶

C. Watkins (Oxford: Oxford University Press, 1988) 194-95. Brackney, *A Genetic History of Baptist Thought*, 109, has found Bunyan dependent on Luther, especially as to wrath and grace and law and grace.

⁹⁹Monica Furlong, *Puritan's Progress: A Study of John Bunyan* (London: Hodder & Stoughton, 1975) 94.

¹⁰⁰Gordon S. Wakefield, " 'To Be a Pilgrim': Bunyan and the Christian Life," in *John Bunyan, Conventicles and Parnassus*, ed. Keeble, 115-20.

¹⁰¹*A Confession of My Faith, and a Reason of My Practice* (1672) in MWJB, 4:154, 162, 171-72, 183.

¹⁰²Thomas Paul and William Kiffin.

¹⁰³*Differences in Judgment about Water-Baptism, No Bar to Communion* (1673) in MWJB, 4:235-36, 238, 233, 243.

¹⁰⁴*Peaceable Principles and True* (1674), in MWJB, 4:270.

¹⁰⁵Greaves, *John Bunyan*, 125-27.

¹⁰⁶*Questions about the Nature and Perpetuity of the Seventh-Day Sabbath* (1685), in MWJB, 4:331-89. Authors defending the views of Seventh Day Baptists included Thomas Tillam, Francis Bampfield, Edward Stennett, and Peter Chamberlen. T. L. Underwood, intro. to vol. 4 of MWJB, xlvii-l.

Bunyan early set forth in poetry his four eschatological essentials: death, judgment, heaven, and hell,[107] and concurrently he expounded the New Jerusalem in an anti-Catholic, postmillennial framework, devoid of Fifth Monarchism, as "the gathered Church fortified against persecution" with "its doctrinal and liturgical perfection."[108] Peculiar to Bunyan was his periodization of church history as predicted in the book of Revelation: "Altar-work" for the reformation undertaken from Wycliffe through the Marian martyrs; "Temple-work" for the separatist movements, and "City-work" for the yet-to be finished work of making safe the gathered church.[109] Likewise, refuting the Ranters, who denied a future bodily resurrection, Bunyan set forth resurrection in "this Body and not another," gloriously transformed and devoid of deformities, and final judgment as the opening of four books.[110] Posthumously published was his treatise on the imminent destruction of the Antichrist.[111]

Second London or Assembly Confession (1677, 1689)

The restoration of the Stuart monarchy with the return (1660) of Charles II as king was followed by Venner's Fifth Monarchy rebellion in January 1661 and a series of parliamentary acts designed to suppress Nonconformists or Dissenters and to bolster the Church of England: the Corporation Act (1661), the Act of Uniformity (1662), the Conventicle Act (1664), the Five-Mile Act (1665), and the Test Act (1673). Even the king's 1672 Declaration of Indulgence did little to alter the circumstances faced by Dissenters.[112]

The common experience of persecution brought Dissenters closer to one another than previously and made desirable expressions of unity, especially among Presbyterians, Congregationalists, Particular Baptists, and General Baptists. The Congregationalists as early as 1658 had adopted at Savoy the

---

[107]*One Thing Is Needful: or, Serious Meditations upon the Four Last Things, Death, Judgment, and Heaven, Hell* (1665), in MWJB vol. 6, ed. Graham Midgley (Oxford: Oxford University Press, 1980) 63-102.

[108]J. Sears McGee, intro. to MWJB vol. 3, ed. McGee (Oxford: Oxford University Press, 1987) xxxvi-xli.

[109]*The Holy City: or, The New Jerusalem* (1665) in MWJB, 3:134-36.

[110]*The Resurrection of the Dead, and Eternall Judgement* (1665), in MWJB, 3:221-24, esp. 223; 252-92; i.e., "the Book of the *Creatures*," "the Book of *Gods Remembrance*," "the Book of the Law," and the "Book of Life."

[111]*Of Antichrist, and His Ruine* (1692) in MWJB 13:421-504.

[112]McBeth, *The Baptist Heritage*, 113-20.

Presbyterian-shaped Westminster Confession (1647) with some alterations. It was not, therefore, altogether surprising that a group of assembled Particular Baptists should overhaul the Westminster Confession, especially by inserting distinctive Baptist doctrines, and thereby demonstrate the basic Christian orthodoxy and kinship to other Dissenters of the Particular Baptists. This was accomplished in 1677 with William Collins as the principal drafter, and the product was published "by the Elders and Brethren of many Congregations of Christians (baptized upon Profession of their Faith) in London and the Country."[113]

The Particular Baptist representatives, having noted that the 1644 confession was not now readily available, insisted that their new confession agreed in substance but differed in manner of expression from that of 1644 and defended their following the order of topics and much of the language of the Westminster and Savoy confessions, although with Baptist-oriented changes.[114] A second edition was published in 1688, and in September 1689, soon after parliamentary enactment of the Act of Toleration, the first assembly of English Particular Baptists adopted this confession and published it without its appendix and with a new preface.[115]

In actuality, there were, as Lumpkin has noted, "numerous and marked differences" between the 1644 and 1677 confessions. First, new topics were included in the 1677 confession, namely, the Scriptures, the Sabbath, and marriage. Second, the treatment of the doctrine of the church was more extensive in the 1677. Third, the Calvinism in the 1677 was "more pronounced." Fourth, the 1677 confession followed the sequence of topics of the Westminster Confession. Fifth, the 1677 was more complete in its treatment of some other topics, notably the Lord's Supper.[116]

---

[113]Lumpkin, *Baptist Confessions of Faith*, 235-36. For the text of the Second London Confession, see ibid., 241-95, and McGlothlin, *Baptist Confessions of Faith*, 220-89.

[114]"To the Judicious and Impartial Reader" (preface to the Second London Confession), in McGlothlin, *Baptist Confessions of Faith*, 223-25; Lumpkin, *Baptist Confessions of Faith*, 244-46.

[115]Ibid., 238-39.

[116]Ibid., 237. The 1644 Confession was marked by its silence about the Lord's Supper and its lack of endorsement of William Kiffin's later-to-be expressed (1681) teaching of close communion. The 1646 revision did add to the article (39) on baptism the words "and after to partake of the Lord's Supper."

There were also marked differences between the 1677 and the Westminster confessions. First, there were some exceptions to the Westminster's order of topics.[117] Second, the 1677 confession deleted certain sections within the chapters of the Westminster, notably on reprobation, the covenant of works, "the duties of the civil magistrate to preserve peace in the Church, to suppress heresies and corruptions, and to call and order synods,"[118] and the forbidding of revolt against civil or ecclesiastical authorities.[119] Third, the 1677 confession greatly expanded the Westminster's chapters on the church from six to fifteen sections, thus incorporating Baptist teachings on membership, polity, elders and deacons, and discipline, and made significant additions relative to perseverance of the saints.[120] Fourth, some articles, notably those on repentance and on baptism and the Lord's Supper—devoid of sacramental language, were completely rewritten for the 1677 confession.[121] Fifth, the 1677 confession introduced certain Baptist themes: the singing of hymns and spiritual songs as well as psalms and lay preaching.[122]

The 1677 confession's new article on the gospel was taken verbatim from the Savoy Declaration,[123] and its statement on kingdom continuity rather than church continuity through history followed the Savoy rather than the Westminster.[124]

---

[117]The 1677 Confession added a chapter on "Of the Gospel, and of the extent of the Grace Thereof" (ch. 20) and deleted Westminster's chapters "Of Church Censures" (ch. 30) and "Of Synods and Councils" (ch. 31). Ibid. See Schaff, *The Creeds of Christendom*, 3:600-673, for the text of the Westminster Confession.

[118]Lumpkin, *Baptist Confessions of Faith*, 237.

[119]Westminster Confession, ch. 3, sect. 7, which was subsumed under 1677, ch. 3, sect. 3; ch. 7, sect. 2; ch. 23, sect. 3, which was deleted and into which a newly composed text was inserted; and ch. 20, sect. 4.

[120]Ibid., chs. 25, 17; Second London Confession, chs. 26, 17.

[121]Westminster Confession, chs. 15, 27; Second London Confession, chs. 15, 28.

[122]Second London Confession, ch. 22, sect. 5; ch. 26, sect. 11. Lumpkin, *Baptist Confessions of Faith*, 237-38, 281, 288; McGlothlin, *Baptist Confessions of Faith*, 260, 267.

[123]Savoy Declaration, art. 20, in Schaff, *The Creeds of Christendom*, 3:718-19; Second London Confession, ch. 20. Only the work of the Holy Spirit as "irresistible" was changed to "insuperable."

[124]Westminster Confession, ch. 25, sect. 5; Savoy Declaration, ch. 26, sect. 3, in Schaff, *The Creeds of Christendom*, 3:722; Second London Confession, ch. 26,

The teachings of the Second London Confession can best be expressed under an eightfold topical arrangement. First, the confession began with a tenfold treatment of "the Holy Scriptures,"[125] taken almost verbatim from the Westminster Confession. The major differences are in subsection one, where the 1677 inserted the statement, "The Holy Scripture is the only sufficient, certain, and infallible rule of all saving Knowledge, Faith, and Obedience,"[126] and in subsection ten, where the Westminster's assertion that the supreme judge of all controversies is "the Holy Spirit speaking in the Scriptures" was changed to "the Holy Scripture delivered by the Spirit, into which Scripture so delivered, our faith is finally resolved."[127] The former affirmed the Bible's role as the "infallible rule" of faith, whereas the latter made the Spirit-inspired Scripture rather than the Scripture-employing Spirit to be the final arbiter. The content drawn from the Westminster Confession included the insufficiency of general revelation and hence the need for special revelation, the list of the canonical books, the nature and role of the Old Testament Apocrypha, the Bible as the Word of God because God is its Author, the internal testimony of the Holy Spirit to the Scriptures as the Word of God, the necessary illumination of the Spirit for scriptural understanding, the perspicuity of the Scriptures, the necessity of translation of the Bible into the common language "of every nation," and the infallible hermeneutical method of interpreting a biblical text in the light of other pertinent biblical texts.[128] The Second London Confession was the first Baptist confession to apply the word "infallible" to the Bible. Whereas the Westminster Confession used it twice in its lengthy article on the Scripture, the 1677 used it three times:[129] to qualify the Bible as the rule of faith, to characterize the truth as witnessed to by the Holy Spirit, and to describe the hermeneutical principle of interpreting Scripture in the light of other scriptural texts.[130]

---

sect. 3.

[125]Second London Confession, ch. 1; Westminster Confession, ch. 1.

[126]Second London Confession, ch. 1, sect. 1.

[127]Ibid., ch. 1, sect. 10; Westminster Confession, ch. 1, sect. 10.

[128]Second London Confession, ch. 1, sects. 1-9.

[129]Westminster Confession, ch. 1, sects. 5, 9; Second London Confession, ch. 1, sects. 1, 5, 9.

[130]See James Leo Garrett, "Biblical Authority according to Baptist Confessions of Faith," *Review and Expositor* 76 (Winter 1979): 43-54, esp. 45-48, wherein the "*functional* infallibility" of the 1677 confession is contrasted with the "*modal*

Second, the Second London Confession expounded in detail the High Calvinism which Particular Baptists shared with English Presbyterians. It affirmed God's decree of predestination of "some men and Angels . . . to Eternal Life, through Jesus Christ" and God's decreeing to leave others "to act in their sin to their just condemnation." The number of those so predestinated was said to be "certain" and "definite," and the "means" of election also to be "foreordained," but the Westminster statement on foreordination to "everlasting death" was rewritten in favor of preterition.[131] The fall of the first humans and all the sins of human beings and angels are encompassed in God's providence, but God is not "the author or approver of sins." By sinning Adam and Eve "fell from their original righteousness and communion with God, and we in them, whereby death came upon all," so that all became totally defiled. The "guilt" of the first sin "was imputed, and corrupted nature conveyed, to all . . . posterity." From that "original corruption" "proceed all actual transgressions."

The Westminster's teaching about a covenant of works was omitted,[132] but the covenant of grace was still founded on the eternal covenant between the Father and the Son and still traced to the promise of salvation to Adam through the seed of Eve. None has ever been saved apart from this covenant.[133] God has bestowed on human wills "that natural liberty, that is neither forced nor by any absolute necessity of nature determined to good or evil." Following the Westminster, the 1677 confession demarcated four stages respecting sin: innocence, sin, grace, and glory.[134]

God's elect humans, unlike the nonelect, are effectually called by the word and the Spirit of God, not on the basis of any foreseen merit or human agency, "to grace and salvation" through Christ, and so are "elect infants,

---

infallibility" of twentieth-century Landmark and Fundamentalist confessions. L. Russ Bush and Tom J. Nettles, *Baptists and the Bible: The Baptist Doctrines of Biblical Inspiration and Religious Authority in Historical Perspective* (Chicago: Moody, 1980) 392-94, were inclined to reject such a distinction as apt for Baptist confessions.

[131] Second London Confession, ch. 3; Westminster Confession, ch. 3.

[132] Second London Confession, ch. 5, sect. 4; ch. 6, sects. 2-4; it did omit the Westminister's first section on guilt (ch. 6, sect. 6).

[133] Westminister Confession, ch. 7, sect. 2; Second London Confession, ch. 7, sect. 3.

[134] Westminister Confession, ch. 9; Second London Confession, ch. 9.

dying in infancy."[135] Saving faith is the work of the Holy Spirit, "ordinarily wrought by the Ministry of the Word," it being both the acceptance of the truth of God's Word, the embrace of God's promises, and "receiving and resting upon" Christ "alone."[136] The other "evangelical Grace," repentance, is given to the elect who are being effectually called "in riper years." It means being made "sensible of" and sorrowful for one's sins, praying for pardon, and endeavoring to walk by the Spirit before God.[137] Likewise the elect and effectually called "can," despite temptations and backslidings, "neither totally nor finally fall from the state of grace" but "shall certainly persevere . . . and be eternally saved." This is because of "the immutability of the decrees of Election," the "efficacy" of the work of Christ, and "the nature of the Covenant of Grace."[138] True believers "may in this life be certainly assured that they are in the state of Grace" on the basis of the saving work of Christ, the possession of spiritual graces, and the Spirit's testimony as to adoption. Such assurance, not being of "the essence of faith," is to be sought and may be obtained after conversion, and, being "shaken" or "diminished," "may in due time be revived."[139]

The Second London Confession, thirdly, affirmed various Christian doctrines of a classic nature common to various confessions or denominations. Various attributes are ascribed to the one true God, and he is said to exercise dominion over all creatures and to be worthy of the worship and service of angels and human beings. He is the triune God "of one substance" but having "three subsistences," with the Son being "Eternally begotten of the Father" and the Spirit "proceeding from the Father and the Son."[140] All things were created by the triune God in six days. Human beings were created male and female with immortal souls "after the image of God" and with dominion over other creatures, having God's law written on their hearts and yet the possibility of voluntary transgression.[141] As the eternal Son of God Jesus Christ in his incarnation through virginal conception became fully man, except for sin, and thus had two distinct natures, divine and human, united in one person. He was "the only Mediator

---

[135] Second London Confession, ch. 10.
[136] Ibid., ch. 14.
[137] Ibid., ch. 15.
[138] Ibid., ch. 17.
[139] Ibid., ch. 18.
[140] Ibid., ch. 2.
[141] Ibid., ch. 4.

between God and Man," having the offices of prophet, priest, and king. His mediatorship was to be exercised by his substitutionary death, resurrection, ascension, heavenly intercession, and second coming, and its benefits made applicable to God's elect.[142] Marriage, which is to be monogamous, has three purposes: "the mutual help of Husband and Wife," the bearing and rearing of children, and the "preventing of uncleanness." A Christian should marry a Christian, not a Roman Catholic, a wicked person, or a heretic, and marriage is forbidden within the "degrees" of consanguinity or affinity or for incest.[143]

Fourth, certain Protestant doctrines were expounded in some detail. Those effectually called are justified, not by the infusion of righteousness into them, but by the declaration of their righteousness on the basis of the imputation of Christ's active and passive righteousness, and this through their faith, which works through love. Christ in his death made "full satisfaction to God's justice" and expressed the "rich Grace of God." This justification, although decreed from eternity for the elect, does not occur until the Holy Spirit "doth in due time actually apply Christ unto them."[144] Those justified by adoption become the children of God with access in prayer to Abba and being sealed unto final redemption.[145] They are sanctified by the word and the Spirit of God so that the "dominion" of sin is "destroyed," lusts are weakened and put to death, and the saints are strengthened for the practice of holiness. Yet they are imperfect with "remnants of corruption," out of which comes a struggle between flesh and the Spirit, and must press on toward heaven.[146] Good works performed by believers under the influence of the Holy Spirit are "fruits" and "evidences" of genuine faith. They cannot be "more than God requires" and cannot "merit" forgiveness of sin or eternal life but are acceptable to God, who "looks upon" such works "in his Son," whereas works by the unregenerate are "sinful and cannot please God."[147] The law of God, first written on the heart of Adam and later delivered through Moses at Mount Sinai, with respect to moral law, though not in regard to ceremonial laws or judicial laws, is still obligatory for Christians as well as non-Christians, for it serves

---

[142]Ibid., ch. 8.
[143]Ibid., ch. 25.
[144]Ibid., ch. 11.
[145]Ibid., ch. 12. The confession contains no chapter on regeneration.
[146]Ibid., ch. 13.
[147]Ibid., ch. 16.

instructional, convictive, and restraining purposes.[148] The gospel, which began with the promise relative to the seed of woman (Gen. 3:15) and derives not from general revelation, is made known both by the outward preaching of it and by the inward rebirth by the Spirit.[149] Christian liberty was defined as freedom from guilt, divine wrath, "bondage to Satan," the fear of death, hell, and the like, plus deliverance from ceremonial laws and from human "Doctrines and Commandments" "contrary to" or "not contained in" the Word of God. The purpose of such liberty is destroyed by those who under its pretense practice sin or cherish lust.[150]

Fifth, one specifically Puritan doctrine was set forth in the 1677 confession. The "acceptable way of worshipping the true God" is prescribed in the Bible and involves worship of the triune God, not of angels, saints, or other human beings. It should include prayer, but not for the deceased or those who have "sinned the sin unto death," the "reading, preaching, and hearing" of the Scriptures, the singing of psalms, hymns, and spiritual songs, baptism, and the Lord's Supper. From creation to the resurrection of Jesus the day of worship was "the last day of the week," but from Jesus' resurrection to now and to the end of the world it has been and shall be "the first day of the week." The Sabbath should be observed by resting from work and "recreations," engaging in public and private worship, and performing "the duties of necessity and mercy."[151]

Sixth, two doctrines were anti-Anabaptist in nature. Lawful oaths "for confirmation of truth" are warranted by Scripture and should be taken "without equivocation, or mental reservation." Likewise, religious vows made "to God alone" are valid, but monastic vows of perpetual nature are "sinful snares."[152] The civil magistracy, being ordained by God, may be undertaken by Christians, Christians may also engage in military service in "just and necessary" wars, and they ought not only to obey the civil magistrates but also to pray for them.[153]

---

[148]Ibid., ch. 19. The confession contains a residue of teaching about a covenant of works in chs. 19 and 20.

[149]Ibid., ch. 20.

[150]Ibid., ch. 21. By contrast art. 46, "Of Liberty of Conscience," in the Orthodox Creed of General Baptists deals with liberty of conscience via-à-vis civil government.

[151]Second London Confession, ch. 22.

[152]Ibid., ch. 23.

[153]Ibid., ch. 24.

Seventh, the ecclesiological teachings of the 1677 confession exhibited the Baptist distinctives. The universal or invisible church "consists of the whole number of the Elect, that have been, are, or shall be gathered into one, under Christ the head thereof." "Visible saints" are those "throughout the world" who profess "the faith of the Gospel" and have not destroyed that profession by any doctrinal errors or unholy living; "of such ought all particular Congregations to be constituted." "The purest Churches under heaven," however, "are subject to mixture, and error." Some have even "degenerated" into "Synagogues of Satan," but Christ's kingdom will continue. Christ is "the Head of the Church," and the pope of Rome is not only not its head but is the Antichrist. The elect are called out of the world "to walk together in particular societies, or Churches" for "mutual edification" and public worship.[154] The communion of saints was affirmed in terms of fellowship, the mutual exercise of "gifts" and "graces," and sharing with the needy but not in terms of community property.[155] The officers of a "particular Church," congregationally governed, should be bishops or elders and deacons, who are to be "chosen . . . by the common suffrage of the Church" and "set apart" by "Prayer, with imposition of hands of the Eldership." Pastors are to be financially supported by the congregation, and lay preaching is encouraged. All church members are subject to church discipline and are expected to attend church meetings. Associations of churches have an advisory role in resolving conflicts but no "Church-power" or "jurisdiction over the Churches themselves."[156]

Baptism and the Lord's Supper are "ordinances" "appointed" by the Lord Jesus and are to be practiced "to the end of the world" and administered only to those qualified. Baptism, which is to be by immersion in the name of the triune God, is to be administered only to those who "profess repentance towards God, faith in, and obedience, to our Lord Jesus." It is a sign of the baptizand's "fellowship" with Christ in his death and resurrection, of his being "engrafted" into Christ, of the "remission of sins," and of his surrender "to live and walk in newness of Life." The Lord's Supper was interpreted in Calvinistic as well as Zwinglian terms inasmuch as the Supper is not only a memorial of the death of Christ but also the locale of his spiritual presence and the occasion of spiritual nourishment. "Worthy receivers, outwardly partaking of the visible Elements . . . , do

---

[154]Ibid., ch. 26, sects. 1-5.
[155]Ibid., ch. 27.
[156]Ibid., art. 26, sects. 7-15.

then also inwardly by faith, really and indeed, yet not carnally, and corporally, but spiritually receive, and feed upon Christ crucified and all the benefits of his death." The Supper as a propitiatory sacrifice and transubstantiation were specifically rejected. The issue as to whether the reception of the elements should be limited to those baptized by immersion on profession of faith was not addressed.[157]

Finally, the 1677 confession exposited briefly certain central eschatological teachings. At death the immortal souls of the righteous are received into paradise, where they "are with Christ," "behold the face of God," and await their resurrection. At death the souls of the wicked "are cast into hell," where they are "in torment" and await the last judgment. Resurrection of the righteous and of the wicked will occur at "the last day," and Christ will judge all human beings and the evil angels at the last judgment, after which those judged will go to their separate destinies, either "Eternal Salvation" and "Eternal Life" or "Eternal torments."[158]

Later editions of the 1677/1689 confession were issued in 1693, 1699, 1719, 1720, 1791, and 1809,[159] and a revision by Benjamin Keach would eventuate in the Philadelphia Confession in the American colonies.

Thomas Collier and Arminianized Western Particular Baptists

In the western counties of England toward the end of the seventeenth century there came to be an Arminianizing movement among the Particular Baptists, especially because of the leadership of Thomas Collier, sometimes called "the Baptist 'Apostle to the West,'"[160] for he superintended the Western Association.[161] Ordained in 1654 after already having served as an evan-

---

[157]Ibid., chs. 28-30.

[158]Ibid., chs. 31-32. Only a brief allusion is made to the second coming, and nothing is said as to a millennium.

[159]Lumpkin, *Baptist Confessions of Faith*, 239, 348-49.

[160]McBeth, *The Baptist Heritage*, 67. The most complete study of Collier is Richard Dale Land, "Doctrinal Controversies of English Particular Baptists (1644–1691) as Illustrated by the Career and Writings of Thomas Collier" (D.Phil. diss., University of Oxford, 1979).

[161]Ronald W. Thomson, *Heroes of the Baptist Church* (London: Carey Kingsgate, 1937) 41.

gelist or church planter,[162] he early wrote on the doctrine of the Scriptures[163] and on Baptist church order[164] and resisted the Fifth Monarchy movement.[165]

But Collier's principal significance for Baptist theology rests on those doctrinal issues which differentiated the Synod of Dort Calvinists from James Arminius. In his own confession of faith, published in 1678, Collier set forth three unitary foundations of gospel preaching,[166] criticized the doctrine of reprobation as providing for the salvation of the few, formulated a doctrine of free will, and was open to the apostasy of true believers.[167] Collier's *The Marrow of Divinity*[168] expounded man's fall and consequent misery, Christ's purchase of his Church, the gift of faith, union with Christ, and the latter-day glory of "the Spiritual kingdom of Christ," which is his Church. In a postscript to his confession he refuted seven teachings which he found in the Second London Confession: eternal reprobation of the nonelect, limited atonement, the necessity of miraculous power for true

---

[162]B. R. White, *The English Baptists of the 17th Century*, vol. 1 of *A History of the English Baptists* (London: Baptist Historical Society, 1983) 74.

[163]McBeth, *The Baptist Heritage*, 72-73, based on Collier's *A Generall Epistle to the Universall Church of the First Born* (1648).

[164]*The Right Constitution and True Subjects of the Visible Church of Christ* . . . (London, 1654), EBP (1951), reel 7, item 12. Collier identified ten ordinances (baptism, prayer, singing of praise, preaching, the Lord's Supper, assembling together, restoration of fallen members, excommunication, distribution to the needy, good works), held to the additional "ordinance" of contemporary prophecy, and rejected the laying of hands on all baptized believers (chs. 3, 5, 8).

[165]McBeth, *The Baptist Heritage*, 89, 91.

[166]*A Confession of Faith, Published on Special Occasion* (London, 1678), EBP (1951), reel 8, item 14, 6-7: "the general love of God to the World in the gift of his Son," "Christ giving himself a Sacrifice for the sins of the world," and "the general Commission for publishing" the gospel "to the World."

[167]Ibid., 10-11, 17-18, 20-21.

[168]Subtitle: *or, A Spiritual Discovery of Some Principles of Truth, Meet to Be Known of All the Saints* (London: Giles Calvert, 1651; first publ. 1647; Early English Books, 1641–1700, reel 1420, items 5267A, 5292, University Microfilms International, 1983). Collier wrote nothing of the doctrines of God, the Trinity, the person of Christ, the person of the Holy Spirit, or the Bible. Although this treatise may point toward systematic theology, it is best to reckon Thomas Grantham's *Christianismus Primitivus* (1678) as the first Baptist systematic theology. See above, 42, and below, 94, n. 249.

faith, justification by faith without respect to works, the impossibility of apostasy, God's eternal, unchangeable decreeing of all things that happen, and the inclusion of sin in the latter.[169]

Under Collier's leadership Particular Baptist churches in the western counties adopted in 1691 *A Short Confession or a Brief Narrative of Faith*,[170] sometimes called the "Somerset Confession" but not to be confused with the 1656 Somerset Confession.[171] It was designed to give answer to the Assembly's approval in London in 1689 of the 1677 confession.[172] It specifically espoused Arminian positions and can hardly be said to "speak for both Particular and General Baptists"[173] or "to accommodate both types of Baptists."[174] It declared the love of God to be "the foundation of all gospel grace," taught general atonement and asserted that the human will, though "greatly debilitated" by the fall, had not been "wholly lost" so that man can "bring his will" to "seeking after his eternal well-being." It defined faith in cognitive terms and called repentance a "great duty," affirmed the possibility of the apostasy of "true believers," and, denying that there is a "secret will" in God contrary to his "revealed will," taught that not all things that happen have been decreed by God. Moreover, the number of the elect is not fixed, and God has elected from eternity "those that in time do believe," "obey, and continue to the end."[175] In addition to these Arminian positions the 1691 confession rejected infant damnation for original sin, insisted that justification through faith must issue in good works, and denied that the eschatological kingdom is to be established by the sword.[176] Collier

---

[169]Ibid., 42-64.

[170]For the complete text, see Crosby, *The History of the English Baptists*, vol. 3, appendix no. 1, 1-42.

[171]Lumpkin, *Baptist Confessions of Faith*, 334-35. Here we reject the view of McGlothlin, *Baptist Confessions of Faith*, 161, who attributed this confession to the General Baptists, and agree with Lumpkin that it derived from Particular Baptists.

[172]Lumpkin, *Baptist Confessions of Faith*, 335. See Crosby, *The History of the English Baptists*, 3:259-61.

[173]Lumpkin, *Baptist Confessions of Faith*, 335.

[174]McBeth, *The Baptist Heritage*, 67.

[175]*A Short Confession or a Brief Narrative of Faith*, chs. 5, 6, 8, 10, 11, 17, 18, 19, 20, and 21.

[176]Ibid., chs, 4, 21, 15, 27. According to Land, "Doctrinal Controversies of English Particular Baptists," 328, 330, Collier in the last phase of his teaching taught that the fifth kingdom had already begun and "would be perfected at the Lord's coming" and that in the world to come there would be three destinies: that

may have been the first Baptist author to declare that Baptist deacons are to serve three tables: the Lord's Table (that is, the Lord's Supper), the table of the minister, and the table of the poor.[177]

Benjamin Keach (1640–1704)

One of the leading Particular Baptist pastor-theologians, Benjamin Keach, came from a General Baptist background in Buckinghamshire and led in greater London a General Baptist congregation to become Particular Baptist at Horsleydown in Southwark[178] that in later centuries would be led by John Gill and Charles Haddon Spurgeon. While still a General Baptist, he was jailed, fined, and put in the pillory for his children's primer, with its Baptist view of baptism.[179] Like and even prior to Bunyan, he employed allegory and his imagination in the writing of books on the Christian life.[180] Keach produced a detailed study of Jesus' parables,[181] coauthored a study of bibli-

---

of believers, that of those eternally punished, and that of those temporarily punished but afterward blessed.

[177] *The Right Constitution and True Subjects of the Visible Church of Christ*, 30-31.

[178] According to J. Barry Vaughn, "Benjamin Keach," in *Baptist Theologians*, ed. Timothy George and David S. Dockery (Nashville: Broadman, 1990) 52, "The date and circumstance of Benjamin Keach's acceptance of Calvinism is the greatest puzzle of his life." Yet Underwood, *A History of the English Baptists*, 112, noted "contacts with Kiffin and Knollys and the influence of his Calvinistic second wife." After three centuries there is now a full-length biography of Keach: Austin Walker, *The Excellent Benjamin Keach* (Dundas ON: Joshua, 2004). Walker does not resolve this question (101-104), but he asserts that the eternal covenant of grace between the Father and the Son and with the aid of the Holy Spirit "became the cornerstone" of Keach's theology (103, 107-15, 251-55).

[179] Vaughn, "Benjamin Keach," 50, 52; Michael A. G. Haykin, *Kiffin, Knollys and Keach: Rediscovering Our English Baptist Heritage* (Leeds UK: Reformation Today Trust, 1996) 84-85.

[180] Vaughn, "Benjamin Keach," 67; Haykin, *Kiffin, Knollys and Keach*, 83. Included were Keach's *War with the Devil* (1674), *The Glorious Lover* (1679), *The Travels of True Godliness* (1683), and *The Progress of Sin* (1684).

[181] *Gospel Mysteries Unveil'd; or an Exposition of All the Parables and Many Express Similitudes Contained in the Four Evangelists Spoken by Our Lord and Saviour Jesus Christ* (1701); published under the title, *Exposition of the Parables in the Bible* (Grand Rapids MI: Kregel, 1974).

cal metaphors,[182] and refuted Quakers,[183] the Roman Catholic Church,[184] and the sabbatarian teaching of Seventh-Day Baptists.[185]

The theological significance, however, of Keach's work is to be found chiefly in three areas: Baptist ecclesiology, Calvinist soteriology, and congregational hymn singing. His brief booklet on the constituting, the officers, and the discipline of "a true church"[186] has been called "the first Calvinistic Baptist treatise specifically devoted to ecclesiastical polity."[187] He as a Particular Baptist defended as a church ordinance the laying on of hands upon newly baptized believers[188] and a congregation's financial support of its minister(s).[189] Keach's most extensive ecclesiological work pertained to Christian baptism, concerning which he authored eight treatises. Replying

---

[182] With Thomas Delaune, *Tropologia, or a Key to Open Scripture Metaphors* (1681; London: William Hill Collingridge, 1856). Vaughn, "Benjamin Keach," 69.

[183] *The Grand Impostor Discovered, or the Quakers Doctrine Weighed in the Ballance, and Found Wanting* (1675), BBM/Bodleian, microform publ. no. 5877, reel 3, item 3.

[184] *Antichrist Stormed, or Mystery Babylon, the Great Whore, and Great City, Proved to Be the Present Church of Rome* (London, 1689). Like other seventeenth-century English Protestant authors, Keach followed postmillennialism and a continuous-historical interpretation of the Book of Revelation, in which he identified the Antichrist and the harlot of Revelation 17 as the Roman Catholic Church. What was different about Keach was that he interpreted the ascension of William of Orange to the English throne in 1688 as the sounding of the seventh trumpet and the forthcoming year 1697 as the time of the fall of the Antichrist and the beginning of the millennium. Kenneth G. C. Newport, "Benjamin Keach, William of Orange, and the Book of Revelation: A Study in English Prophetical Exegesis," *Baptist Quarterly* 36 (1995–1996): 43-51.

[185] *The Jewish Sabbath Abrogated, or the Saturday Sabbatarians Confuted* (London, 1700).

[186] *The Glory of a True Church and Its Discipline Display'd* (1668), BBM/Angus, microfilm pub. no. 5855, reel 1, item 16.

[187] Haykin, *Kiffin, Knollys and Keach*, 83.

[188] *Darkness Vanquished: or, Truth in It's Primitive Purity*... (1675), EBBM, reel 26, item 34; republished under the title, *Laying on of Hands upon Baptized Believers, as Such, Proved an Ordinance of Christ*... (1698), EBBM, reel 17, item 13. Keach appealed to Acts 8:16-17 and 19:6.

[189] *The Gospel Minister's Maintenance Vindicated*... (1689), BBM/Angus, microfilm pub. no. 4265, reel 5, item 69. This book was endorsed by the General Assembly of Particular Baptists in 1689. Hugh Martin, *Benjamin Keach (1640–1704): Pioneer of Congregational Hymn Singing* (London: Independent, 1961) 7.

to pedobaptist authors, he set forth views common to his fellow Baptists. Baptism is to be observed until the end of the world.[190] Immersion as its proper mode is defended from the Greek word *baptizein*, from primitive church practice, and from metaphorical uses of baptism in the New Testament (for example, as suffering and by the Holy Spirit and fire).[191] That only believers are proper "subjects" of baptism is defended from the Great Commission, apostolic teaching and practice, and the "special ends" of baptism. Infant baptism is said to have no word of institution and no biblical precedent. There are no commands and promises for its practice and no rebukes or threats for its neglect. Only believers can repent and believe.[192] The pedobaptist argument from the covenant with Abraham suffers from its failure to identify two covenants with Abraham, one with his natural seed and the other with his spiritual seed. But the infants of Gentile believers belong under neither covenant.[193] Infant baptism, which was not practiced in the first two centuries of the Christian era, not only is not useful but also brings evil consequences.[194] In respect to close communion Keach agreed with but went beyond Kiffin by insisting that not only believer's immersion but also laying on of hands be prerequisite to receiving the Lord's Supper.[195]

---

[190]*Gold Refin'd; or Baptism in Its Primitive Purity* . . . (1689), Selected Works of Benjamin Keach and Other Authors (microfilm), Roberts Library, Southwestern Baptist Theological Seminary, ch. 1; *Light Broke Forth in Wales, Expelling Darkness* . . . (London, 1696) ch. 2.

[191]*Gold Refin'd*, chs. 2-5; *The Rector Rectified and Corrected; or Infant-Baptism Unlawful* . . . (1692), BBM/Bodleian, microform publ. no. 5877, reel 3, item 4, chs. 7-9; *Light Broke Forth in Wales*, chs. 3-5.

[192]*Gold Refin'd*, chs. 6-9.

[193]Ibid., ch. 10; *The Rector Rectified and Corrected*, ch. 2; *The Ax Laid to the Root: or, One Blow More at the Foundation of Infant Baptism, and Church-Membership* (1693), BBM/Bodleian, microform publ. no. 5877, reel 3, item 1, consisting of two sermons on Matt. 3:10, passim; *A Counter-Antidote, to Purge out the Malignant Effects of a Late Counterfeit Prepared by Mr. Gyles Shute* . . . (1694), BBM/Bodleian, microform publ. no. 5877, reel 3, item 1, ch. 3; *Light Broke Forth in Wales*, chs. 6-7.

[194]*Gold Refin'd*, ch. 13; *The Rector Rectified and Corrected*, ch. 6; *Light Broke Forth in Wales*, ch. 17.

[195]David A. Copeland, *Benjamin Keach and the Development of Baptist Traditions in Seventeenth-Century England*, Studies in Religion and Society 48 (Lewiston NY: Edwin Mellen, 2001) 56-60.

Keach authored five books[196] in which he defended the high Calvinist doctrines, especially unconditional justification, against the "middle way" of Richard Baxter. For Keach, justification is by the imputation of Christ's righteousness—both his active obedience (fulfillment of the law) and his passive obedience (death as penal substitution)—and is wrought through Christ's priestly office. Faith, the primary means of justification, is only an "instrumental" cause, not a "material" cause of justification.[197] Similarly, regeneration is totally the work of God with the recipient being entirely passive, but conversion has two aspects, the passive and the active.[198] Assurance, for Keach, is based not only on sanctification but also on the joint testimony of the Holy Spirit.[199] According to J. Barry Vaughn, the "danger of Keach's high Calvinism was that it could slip over into hyper-Calvinism," for the "distance between the doctrine of *unconditional* justification (which Keach held) and the doctrine of *eternal* justification (which Keach rejected) is not great."[200]

"Keach's present-day fame, however, rests upon his place, real and alleged, in the history of English hymnody." Although other claims have been made for him, it is best to conclude "that he was the first to introduce the regular singing of hymns into the normal worship of an English congregation," and this applied to other denominations as well as to Baptists. "In 1673 he introduced [in his Horselydown congregation] the singing of a hymn at the conclusion of the Lord's Supper," citing Matt. 26:30.[201] After

---

[196] *The Marrow of True Justification* (1692), in which he defended particular atonement; *The Everlasting Covenant* (1693), which marked Keach's shift from three covenants (covenant of works with Adam, covenant of redemption among the Father, the Son, and the Holy Spirit, and covenant of grace) to two covenants (covenant of works, covenant of grace); *Christ Alone the Way to Heaven* (1698), in which he supported perseverance; *The Display of Glorious Grace* (1698), in which he refuted universal salvation; and *A Medium betwixt Two Extremes* (1698), in which Keach attacked Arminianism. Vaughn, "Benjamin Keach," 57; Copeland, *Benjamin Keach and the Development of Baptist Traditions*, 30-43.

[197] Vaughn, "Benjamin Keach," 56-59.

[198] Haykin, *Kiffin, Knollys and Keach*, 87-90, based on Keach, *Gospel Mysteries Unveil'd* (1815 ed.) 2:392-412.

[199] Vaughn, "Benjamin Keach," 59-60.

[200] Ibid., 60.

[201] Martin, *Benjamin Keach (1640–1704)*, 9-10. Regular every-Sunday singing of hymns by Keach's congregation did not commence for nearly twenty years. Twenty-two members did withdraw in 1691 in opposition to the practice and joined

hymn singing became officially an every-Sunday practice in 1691 in Keach's congregation, controversy erupted among Particular Baptists. The most prolific author opposing the practice was a wealthy jeweler, Isaac Marlow (1649–1719), who wrote eleven books on this matter. The controversy divided Particular Baptists for about a decade.[202]

The arguments set forth by Marlow and his supporters have been summarized by Murdina D. MacDonald. First, using "a precomposed hymn produces the same effect as the reading of a written prayer," that is, "formalism." Second, "examples of singing in the New Testament era" occurred as "the exercise of an 'extraordinary' spiritual gift," and since such extraordinary gifts are no longer being given, such examples are not proper precedents for Marlow's day. Third, since congregational hymn singing may involve participation by unbelievers, it stains the purity of the church. Fourth, the early church had singing only "by a single voice." Fifth, when women engage in congregational hymn singing, it violates the Pauline admonitions for women to keep silent in the churches and not to teach or have authority over men (1 Cor. 14:34 and 1 Tim. 2:11-12).[203]

---

another congregation whose pastor, Robert Speed, had written against hymn singing. See Crosby, *The History of the English Baptists*, 4:298-301; Horton Davies, *Worship and Theology in England*, vol. 2, *From Andrewes to Baxter to Fox, 1603–1690* (Princeton NJ: Princeton University Press, 1975) 499. See also David W. Music and Paul A. Richardson, "Benjamin Keach" in *"I Will Sing the Wondrous Story": A History of Baptist Hymnody in North America*, 12-17 et passim (Macon GA: Mercer University Press, 2008).

[202]Haykin, *Kiffin, Knollys and Keach*, 92-93. Marlow's first book was *A Brief Discourse concerning Singing in the Public Worship of God in the Gospel Church* (London, 1690). The General Assembly of Particular Baptists in 1692 censured both parties to this controversy. Robert H. Young, "History of Baptist Hymnody in England from 1612 to 1800" (Ph.D. diss., University of Southern California, 1959) 43-44, as quoted by James Patrick Carnes, "The Famous Mr. Keach: Benjamin Keach and His Influence on Congregational Singing in Seventeenth Century England" (M.A. thesis, North Texas State University, 1984) 61. For detailed analyses of all these controversial writings during the 1690s, see Carry Edward Spann, "The Seventeenth Century English Baptist Controversy concerning Singing" (M.C.M. thesis, Southwestern Baptist Theological Seminary, 1965) chs. 4-6.

[203]Haykin, *Kiffin, Knollys and Keach*, 93, summarizing MacDonald, "London Calvinistic Baptists, 1689–1727: Tensions within a Dissenting Community under Toleration" (D.Phil. diss., University of Oxford, 1982) 53-54.

Keach's case for congregational hymn singing was extensively made in *The Breach Repaired in God's Worship: or, Singing of Psalms, Hymns, and Spiritual Songs, Proved to Be an Ordinance of Jesus Christ.*[204] Keach and Marlow differed as to the nature of spiritual worship.[205] For Marlow, singing is only "an inward spiritual Exercise of the Soul or Mind of Man" which need not be vocalized, whereas for Keach the tongue and the voice were essential.[206] Marlow was close to the Quaker dichotomy of nature and Spirit. Keach contended that singing was both a moral duty, derived from natural law, and an ordinance specifically commanded by God.[207] Keach traced singing to the angels and to Moses, Deborah, and Barak as well as to the psalms of David.[208] From the New Testament Keach majored on the singing at the Last Supper (Matt. 26:30) and on three admonitions (Eph. 5:19; Col. 3:6; and James 5:13), which he interpreted as enjoining the collective singing of "psalms, hymns, and spiritual songs."[209] To Marlow's objection based on singing in the New Testament as by an "extraordinary" gift of the Spirit, Keach found that preaching, praying, prophesying, and interpreting Scripture in the New Testament era were similarly given and yet such practices continue to Keach's times.[210] To the objectors who decried humanly composed hymns Keach noted that preaching has the element of human composition and insisted that hymns, like sermons, when taken from the Scriptures, "may as truly be called the Word of Christ."[211] For an unbeliever to sing during congregational worship is no more of a problem than for him to join in prayer or hear the preaching,[212] and for women to sing is no more of a problem than their testifying to their conversion when applying for church membership.[213]

---

[204](London, 1691), British Museum photocopy, no. 1018, g21.

[205]John Smyth had dealt extensively with this subject. See above, 24, 27.

[206]*The Breach Repaired in God's Worship*, 7-12, 121-27; Vaughn, "Benjamin Keach," 65.

[207]*The Breach Repaired in God's Worship*, 28-41, 163; Vaughn, "Benjamin Keach," 64.

[208]*The Breach Repaired in God's Worship*, 22-27, 42-44, 74, 146, 45-54.

[209]Ibid., 44, 150-51, 49, 54-59, 91, 114, 133, 172-73; Haykin, *Kiffin, Knollys and Keach*, 94, 95.

[210]*The Breach Repaired in God's Worship*, 62-64, 115; Haykin, *Kiffin, Knollys and Keach*, 94.

[211]*The Breach Repaired in God's Worship*, 134-39, 94.

[212]Ibid., 105-10; Haykin, *Kiffin, Knollys and Keach*, 94-95.

[213]*The Breach Repaired in God's Worship*, 139-42; Haykin, *Kiffin, Knollys and*

Thomas Grantham as a General Baptist was allowing singing by one vocalist of paraphrased biblical psalms or hymns.[214] Congregationalists and Presbyterians were permitting the congregational singing of Old Testament Psalms, and Knollys had allowed for solo singing if the song had been dictated by the Holy Spirit.[215] But it was Keach, Baptist and Calvinist, who opened the door for that congregational hymn singing to which Isaac Watts and Charles Wesley would so significantly contribute and which would become normative for later Baptist worship.

Baptist Hyper-Calvinism (John Skepp, ?–1721; John Brine, 1703–1765; and John Gill, 1697–1771)

Modern scholars have increasingly agreed that the High Calvinism found among the English Particular Baptists, Congregationalists, and Presbyterians of the seventeenth century—a Calvinism not significantly different from the canons of the Synod of Dort (1618–1619) in the Netherlands—was early in the eighteenth century transformed into something that can more precisely be called Hyper-Calvinism, which can accurately be identified by five teachings: the prioritizing of the eternal divine decree to elect some human beings and to reprobate others (supralapsarianism), an eternal covenant among the Father, the Son, and the Holy Spirit for the redemption of the elect through the Son (covenant of redemption), the justification of the elect occurring in eternity past and being only manifested in time (eternal justification), since grace is irresistible, grace is not to be offered to any but the elect (no general offers of grace), and playing down any role of the law in guiding the Christian's life (antinomianism). These five doctrines may be utilized as indicators of Hyper-Calvinism.

Although the fact that certain Particular Baptist pastors became Hyper-Calvinists is rather well established, the nature and extent of the influence of certain non-Baptist authors upon them is not so clear. Tobias Crisp (1600–1644), an Anglican, and Joseph Hussey (1660–1726), a Presbyterian turned Congregationalist, have been identified by Peter Toon as major contributors to the shift from High Calvinism to Hyper-Calvinism.[216]

Keach, 95.

[214]See above, ch. 2, n. 140. See also Bustin, *Paradox and Perseverance*, 293-300.

[215]Haykin, *Kiffin, Knollys and Keach*, 91-92.

[216]*The Emergence of Hyper-Calvinism in English Nonconformity, 1689–1765* (London: Oliver Tree, 1967) 28, 43, 49-50, 54-66, 70-85, 99, 145-46.

Similarly, Leon McBeth has concluded that the Hyper-Calvinism of Particular Baptists "came primarily from non-Baptist sources," particularly, Crisp and Hussey.[217]

A careful examination of Crisp's 52 extant sermons,[218] published a half century after his death by his son and later by John Gill, yields no espousal of the differentiating tenets of Hyper-Calvinism. There is no discussion of the order of divine decrees, of eternal justification,[219] or of a Trinitarian covenant. Crisp differentiated the covenant of works and two different covenants of grace, that of the Jews and that of Christ.[220] In respect to the use of the law Crisp called it "a handmaid" to the gospel so as to convict and guide Christians.[221] His reference to Christ's "advocateship" for the elect only[222] was in line with Dortian Calvinism, and his doctrine of assurance that combined "the voice of the Spirit of God to a man's own spirit" and "the faith of a believer," supplemented by sanctification,[223] was not unlike William Perkins's (1558–1602) twofold assurance through the "witness of the Spirit" and "the effects of sanctification."[224] Crisp was

---

[217] *The Baptist Heritage*, 173-74. Crisp, he stated, "became the fountain of much of the hyper-Calvinism that marked Baptists later."

[218] *Christ Alone Exalted, in the Perfection and Encouragement of the Saints, Notwithstanding Sins and Trials; Being the Complete Works of Tobias Crisp, D.D.*, 2 vols., 7th ed. (London: John Bennett, 1832).

[219] Raymond Brown, *The English Baptists of the Eighteenth Century*, vol. 2 of *A History of the English Baptists* (London: Baptist Historical Society, 1986) 73, has suggested that Crisp taught eternal justification but did not cite Crisp's sermons.

[220] *Christ Alone Exalted*, sermon 16, 1:245-62.

[221] Ibid., sermon 51, 2:396-403, esp. 398. Alan P. F. Sell, *The Great Debate: Calvinism, Arminianism, and Salvation* (Grand Rapids MI: Baker, 1983) 47, has found Crisp to have been "ambiguous" on the antinomian issue, "genuinely" intending "to ascribe salvation solely to God's grace" but "resisting the believer's desire to verify his assurance from those spiritual graces which the Spirit imparted to him." But John Gill strongly defended Crisp against the charge of being antinomian. See John Rippon, *A Brief Memoir of the Life and Writings of the Late Rev. John Gill, D.D.* (London: John Bennett, 1838) 66-71.

[222] *Christ Alone Exalted*, sermon 36, 2:191-203. Seven of his sermons (34-40) had as their text 1 John 2:1-2a, but Crisp never quoted 2b.

[223] Ibid., sermons 30, 31, 2:79-110, esp. 82-83, 97-99, 100.

[224] R. T. Kendall, *Calvin and English Calvinism to 1649* (Oxford: Oxford University Press, 1979) 69-75.

explicit that grace is free and unconditional[225] and that election provides great security. Indeed there "is no danger of miscarriage in Christ,"[226] for "the state of the unconverted elect person, is as sure from danger of final miscarriage, as the estate of a saint in glory."[227] Interpreting Isa. 53:6b, Crisp took the Lord's laying on the Servant "the iniquity of us all" to mean the laying of the sins of the elect upon Christ, who bears them, but Crisp stopped short of saying that these sins were "imputed" to Christ or that Christ became a sinner, except in the sense of "God's determining and judging Christ to bear sin."[228] This is an expression of penal substitution in the work of Christ, but it is not Hyper-Calvinism.

Joseph Hussey exhibited more of the defining teachings of Hyper-Calvinism[229] after undergoing a theological shift. In 1693 in *The Gospel Feast Opened* he likened the gospel to a gigantic feast with "all kinds of spiritual provision," now available and to which sinners are invited.[230] By 1706 in *The Glory of Christ Unveil'd, or The Excellency of Christ Vindicated*, Hussey had adopted supralapsarianism,[231] and in the next year in *God's Operations of Grace but No Offers of Grace*[232] he had rejected "offers of grace" as "antievangelical." Sharply differentiating offering the gospel or salvation from preaching the gospel or preaching Christ and distinguishing external offers from the Spirit's enabling sinners "to close savingly with the offer," Hussey contended that "an offer of grace is no gift of grace" and sought to explain how to preach the gospel without offering grace. Only God's operations through the preaching of the gospel can bring the conversion of the elect.[233]

The earliest Baptist Hyper-Calvinist was seemingly John Skepp, the pastor of the Particular Baptist church in Cripplegate, London,[234] whose only publication, *Divine Energy*,[235] appeared posthumously in 1722. Taking

---

[225]*Christ Alone Exalted*, sermons 3, 12, 1:29-45, 184-97, esp. 36, 196.
[226]Ibid., sermon 3, 1:41.
[227]Ibid., sermon 36, 2:198.
[228]Ibid., sermon 17, 1:267; sermon 19, 1:291-92.
[229]Toon, *The Emergence of Hyper-Calvinism*, 83.
[230]Ibid., 73.
[231]Ibid., 75-76.
[232]Abr. ed. (Elon, NC: Primitive Publications, 1973).
[233]Ibid., chs. 2-6, esp. pp. 24, 41, 61, 81, 124.
[234]Toon, *The Emergence of Hyper-Calvinism*, 85.
[235]*Divine Energy: or the Efficacious Operations of the Spirit of God upon the*

as his text Eph. 1:19, Skepp sought to correct the concept that true conversion can occur by "moral suasion" and to prove that it occurs only by the internal operation of God's power on the heart and soul of the sinner. Conversion is not to be equated with the use of general revelation, a "sober religious . . . life," mere doctrinal conversion, mere moral reformation, baptism and nurture alone, or mere confession of Jesus as Messiah.[236] Skepp's "moral suasion," which he defined as self-conversion,[237] has been translated by McBeth[238] into the twentieth-century vocabulary of "gospel invitations." Such "moral suasion," according to Skepp, is "not only deficient but culpable" and "no more than a dead and helpless exhortation."[239] Skepp proceeded to teach that in true conversion the human will "is not forced" and its "natural liberty" not "in the least infringed but by grace" "made truly and spiritually free." But the sinner is utterly passive in receiving the Holy Spirit, in "receiving vital union with Christ, in regeneration, and in subsequent workings of grace, whereas God's power and efficacious grace are absolutely necessary. The Holy Spirit works from regeneration through sanctification and the giving of spiritual gifts to glorification.[240] Skepp did not probe the order of eternal divine decrees or a Trinitarian covenant of redemption, but his teaching about passivity, unaccompanied by any recognition of the obligation to repent and believe and coupled with Hussey's "no offers of grace," seemingly led to the wider embrace of Hyper-Calvinism.

John Brine (1703–1765), who had been nurtured under the ministry of John Gill in Kettering and succeeded Skepp as the pastor at Cripplegate, expressed Hyper-Calvinism in several booklets. Faith, he contended, is not "the impulsive or moving cause," "the matter," or "the instrumental cause of justification," for "Christ's righteousness alone is the matter and cause"; rather faith is "the eye of our souls, by which we . . . discern the justifying [and imputed] righteousness of Christ." Moreover, justification, being an

---

Soul of Man in His Effectual Calling and Conversion, Stated, Proved, and Vindicated . . . Being an Antidote against the Pelagian Error, 3rd. ed. rev. by James Upton (London, 1815). John Gill wrote a "recommendatory preface" for the 1751 edition.

[236] Ibid., 12, 14-31.
[237] Ibid., 58.
[238] *The Baptist Heritage*, 175.
[239] Skepp, *Divine Energy*, 59, 81.
[240] Ibid., 12-14, 158-206, 206-56, 256-78, 278-301.

"immanent," not a "transient" act of God, occurred from eternity since God's choice of the elect and his decree "not to punish sin in His people, but in His Son" were "in the eye of God from eternity."[241] Brine affirmed a "covenant of Grace" made in eternity between God and Christ and with the elect, to which personal consent was not necessary, and contended that there is no difference between "the Covenant of Redemption" and "the Covenant of Grace." Hence there have been only two covenants, those of Works and Grace, not three.[242] Brine defended supralapsarianism against an anonymous polemicist and proceeded also to defend eternal reconciliation and eternal adoption prior to faith.[243] He responded to the "modern question," that is, whether "evangelical Repentance" and "Special Faith" are indeed the "Duties of all who hear the Gospel," with a resounding "No." Labeling such as Arminianism, Brine insisted that the unconverted must have a "Warrant," that there is no preparatory work of the Holy Spirit, that there are to be no "Offers and Tenders of Mercy and Salvation to Sinners," and that if repentance and faith are to be taken as "Conditions of Life," one would have salvation or justification by works.[244]

John Gill's birth in Kettering in 1697 was contemporaneous with the publication of *Christianity Not Mysterious* (1696) by the English Deist John Toland.[245] The son of a Baptist deacon in the Particular Baptist congregation in Kettering, John was a precocious lad who mastered "the rudiments of Latin and Greek" and "read through the entire Greek New Testament" before he was eleven. Quickened by a sermon when he was about twelve, he was not immersed until almost nineteen. After serving as assistant pastor

---

[241]*A Defence of the Doctrine of Eternal Justification* . . . (London, 1732) 1-17; ibid., Baptist Tract Series, no. 4 (Paris AR: Baptist Standard Bearer, 1987) 1-13.

[242]*The Covenant of Grace Open'd: in a Sermon Occasioned by the Death of Mrs. Margaret Busfield, Who Departed This Life, May 13th, 1734* (London, 1734?) 7-10, 17-18.

[243]*Remarks upon a Pamphlet, Intitled, Some Doctrines in the Superlapsarian [sic] Scheme Impartially Examin'd by the Word of God* (London, 1736).

[244]*A Refutation of Arminian Principles, Delivered in a Pamphlet, Intitled, the Modern Question concerning Repentance and Faith, Examined with Candour* (London, 1743). Brine differentiated "natural Repentance" from "evangelical Repentance" and "historical Faith" from "special Faith." Brine was responding to Abraham Taylor's *The Modern Question concerning Repentance and Faith Examined* (1735).

[245]Timothy George, "John Gill," in *Baptist Theologians*, ed. George and Dockery, 85.

in two churches in the Kettering area, Gill was called in 1719 to the Particular Baptist church at Horsleydown, Southwark, London, which Keach and his son-in-law Benjamin Stinton had served. The call, however, was a divided vote, and a church split resulted. For about 52 years Gill served as pastor of that one congregation. He influenced non-Baptists in the London area by his weekly Wednesday evening lectures for about 27 years at Great Eastcheap, and his mastery of Hebrew and his use of the Mishnah and the Talmud in his biblical studies led to his being awarded the honorary degree of Doctor of Divinity by Marischal College of the University of Aberdeen.[246]

Gill, a prolific author, is said to have had "more than ten thousand pages" of his writings published "during his lifetime."[247] Early he produced *The Prophecies of the Old Testament respecting the Messiah* (1728), *An Exposition of the Book of Solomon's Song Commonly Called Canticles* (1728), and *The Doctrine of the Trinity Stated and Vindicated* (1731). *The Cause of God and Truth* (1735–1738), written to refute Daniel Whitby's *Discourse on the Five Points* (1733 or 1734?), was a "classic defense of Calvinist soteriology."[248] His three-volume *Exposition of the New Testament* appeared during 1746-48, his two-volume *An Exposition of the Books of the Prophets of the Old Testament* was printed during 1757-58, and his four-volume *Exposition of the Old Testament* was issued during 1763-66. Gill completed *A Body of Doctrinal Divinity* in two volumes in 1769, and *A Body of Practical Divinity* in 1770. He was, as Timothy George has noted, "the first Baptist to write a verse-by-verse commentary on the entire Bible."[249] Gill in 1729 led his congregation to adopt a twelve-article "declaration of faith and practice," which serves as a summary of Gill's own theology.[250]

---

[246]Ibid., 78, 80-82.

[247]Ibid., 77, based on Rippon, *A Brief Memoir*, 111.

[248]Ibid., 82.

[249]Ibid., 77. We differ with George's assertion that Gill was "the first Baptist to develop a complete systematic theology" by ascribing such to Thomas Grantham. See above, 42. Rippon, *A Brief Memoir*, 76, claimed that Gill was the first to complete a verse-by-verse commentary "in the English language."

[250]The text is included in Rippon, *A Brief Memoir*, 14-18. The confession taught God's election "before the world began" of "a certain number of men," affirmed "corporeal death," "spiritual" death, and "eternal death," denied any preincarnate humanity of Jesus, taught limited atonement, reckoned "regeneration,

The doctrine of the Scriptures, for Gill, included a statement about the canon and the inspiration of the Bible in its "original languages," though without commitment to any theory of its mode, the delineation of various proofs for the authority of the Bible, and the affirmation of the "*perspicuity*" and the revelatory necessity of the Bible vis-à-vis "the light of nature."[251]

Gill began his *A Body of Doctrinal Divinity* with a detailed exposition of twenty-seven attributes of God.[252] He began his exposition of the Trinity by affirming the unity of God, which Christianity shares with Judaism and which is to be differentiated from Arian,[253] Sabellian, and tritheistic alternatives.[254] God's plurality he sought to establish from the plural names of God in the Old Testament, the "us" and "our" language, and the Angel of Jehovah texts. God's threefoldness has been manifested in the works of creation, of providence, of grace, of Christ as Redeemer, of justification, regeneration, and adoption, and of worship and is an eternal distinction.[255] Gill elaborated on the eternal generation of the Son and explicated the "distinct personality" and the deity of each: Father, Son or Word (contrary to the Socinians), and Holy Spirit (contrary to the Macedonians).[256] Gill demonstrated "remarkable respect for the doctrinal consensus of the early

---

conversion, sanctification, and faith" as the work of the "irresistible grace of God," prescribed close communion, and allowed for the vocal "singing of psalms, hymns, and spiritual songs" (arts. 3-6, 8, 11-12).

[251]*A Complete Body of Doctrinal and Practical Divinity* (Paris AR: Baptist Standard Bearer, 1989) doct. div., book 1, ch. 2.

[252]Book 1, chs. 1, 4-25. These are: being, spirituality, simplicity, immutability, omnipresence, eternity, life, omnipotence, omniscience, wisdom, will, love, grace, mercy, longsuffering, goodness, anger, wrath, hatred, joy, holiness, justice or righteousness, veracity, faithfulness, sufficiency, perfection, and blessedness.

[253]Gill somewhat mistakenly identified the Arian view as that of "one supreme God" and "two subordinate or inferior ones." Ibid., book 1, ch. 26. For Arius both Jesus and the Spirit were outside the realm of deity. See Kelly, *Early Christian Doctrines*, 226-31.

[254]*A Body of Doctrinal Divinity*, book 1, ch. 26; *The Doctrine of the Trinity Stated and Vindicated* . . . , 2nd ed. (1752) ch. 1.

[255]*A Body of Doctrinal Divinity*, book 1, ch. 27; *The Doctrine of the Trinity Stated and Vindicated*, chs. 2–3.

[256]*A Body of Doctrinal Divinity*, book 1, chs. 28-31; *The Doctrine of the Trinity Stated and Vindicated*, chs. 4-9.

Fathers"[257] by referring to the Father's "begetting," the Son's being "begotten," and the Spirit's breathing.[258]

In his pre-Darwinian setting Gill interpreted the work of each day of creation as momentary, the first day being creation out of nothing and the other five days being "mediate" creation. Creation's end is the glory of God. Human beings were created with body and soul, the soul having been directly created by God, and as male and female. The image of God, located "in the whole man," consists of certain qualities together with immortality and dominion. In his prelapsarian happiness Adam as federal head received from God the law in the form of a covenant of "friendship" or "innocence." First Adam, then Eve ate the forbidden fruit, being tempted by Satan, and then both came under the curse of death and were ejected from paradise. Their sin was imputed to their posterity as well as to themselves, and all humankind became depraved, out of which condition actual sins are committed—against God, against other humans, and against oneself. Punishments for sin are both temporal and eternal; the temporal are either internal (loss of the image, of freedom of will, of knowledge of divine things, and of communion with God) or external (loss of immortality, toil and fatigue, loss of dominion, personal distresses, public calamities).[259]

Like Augustine of Hippo, Gill made the title and role of Mediator to be central to his Christology. Fitted for mediatorship by being both the Son of God and the son of man, Christ as the "one and only" and "everlasting" Mediator effected reconciliation, satisfaction, and intercession, being both the "Surety" and "Testator" of the covenant of grace.[260] Gill quoted extensively from the Church Fathers in making his case for the eternal generation of the Son of God[261] and yet reckoned the "fulness" in Col. 1:19 to be "a dispensatory, communicative fulness . . . put into the hands of Christ, to be distributed to others."[262] The eternal Son or Word "became flesh" by assuming "a whole individual of human nature, consisting of [a reasonable] soul and [a true] body," being conceived by Mary the virgin

---

[257]George, "John Gill," 89.
[258]*A Body of Doctrinal Divinity*, book 1, ch. 28.
[259]Ibid., book 3, chs. 1, 3, 6-13.
[260]Ibid., book 2, chs. 11-13.
[261]*A Dissertation concerning the Eternal Sonship of Christ* (London, 1768).
[262]*The Fulness of the Mediator: A Sermon Preach'd June 15, 1736, to the Society That Supports the Lord's-Day Evening Lecture, near Devonshire-Square* (London: Aaron Ward, 1736) esp. 11.

with the overshadowing of the Holy Spirit and born "after the manner of other men." The result was a union of the two natures, divine and human, in one person but with an exchange of the properties of the two natures. In his state of humiliation, which extended from his conception to his burial,[263] Jesus actively obeyed the Father by perfectly fulfilling the law—civil, ceremonial, and moral—and passively obeyed by his death. His state of exaltation began with his resurrection and included his ascension and heavenly intercession. Concurrently he exercised his three offices: prophetic, priestly, and kingly.[264] Although "redemption" was Gill's most frequently used term in reference to the death of Jesus, his interpretation centered in Jesus's satisfaction—not, as with Anselm of Canterbury, the satisfaction of God's offended honor but, more like John Calvin, the substitutionary and propitiatory satisfaction of God's justice in punishment for sin, a position denied by the Socinians.[265]

How specifically did Gill embrace or embody the soteriological heritage of Calvinism as delivered through English Puritanism and Particular Baptists? First, he set forth an *ordo salutis*: forgiveness, justification, adoption, regeneration, effectual calling, conversion, sanctification, and perseverance.[266] Second, Gill embraced the particular tenets of the Synod of Dort.[267] Election, being one of the eternal decrees of God, is "the choice of certain persons by God, from all eternity, to grace and glory," not because they would be "called" and "converted" but "of God's good will and pleasure."[268] Gill set forth a detailed refutation of general atonement, which he described as "universal redemption," by alleging that it adversely

---

[263] Gill interpreted the "descent into hell" (1 Pet. 3:19-20) as "his preaching by his Spirit, to the disobedient ones, who lived in the times of Noah: whose spirits, for their disobedience . . . were, in the apostle's time, in the prison of hell." *A Body of Doctrinal Divinity*, book 5, ch. 5, p. 406. See Richard A. Muller, "John Gill and the Reformed Tradition," in *The Life and Thought of John Gill (1697–1771): A Tercentennial Appreciation*, ed. Michael A. G. Haykin, Studies in the History of Christian Thought 77 (Leiden: Brill, 1997) 65-66.

[264] *A Body of Doctrinal Divinity*, book 5, chs. 1-13.

[265] Ibid., book 6, chs. 1-3, 5-6; *The Necessity of Christ's Making Satisfaction for Sin, Proved and Confirmed* (London: George Keith, 1766).

[266] *A Body of Doctrinal Divinity*, book 6, chs. 7-15.

[267] See above, ch. 2, n. 24.

[268] *A Body of Doctrinal Divinity*, book 2, chs. 1–2, esp. pp. 180, 182; also *The Cause of God and Truth* (London: W. H. Collingridge, 1855; repr.: Streamwood IL: Primitive Baptist Library, 1978) part 2, ch. 2; part 3, ch. 2.

reflects on the attributes of God and on the work of Christ and by answering the use of the "all men" and "world" passages in the New Testament and asserted that "the objects of election and redemption are the same."[269] Gill's detailed exposition of justification has little to say about faith, but in treating conversion he did allow that it consists of God's act upon men, in turning them, and of acts done by men under the influence of converting grace."[270] Furthermore, effectual calling is an "internal call" and "an act of efficacious and irresistable [sic] grace."[271] Finally, Gill taught the final perseverance of all "who are truly regenerated, effectually called, . . . really converted, and internally sanctified."[272]

Somewhat controversial is the third question, namely, whether Gill embraced all the positions characteristic of Hyper-Calvinism. Did Gill advocate the supralapsarian ordering of divine decrees? He discussed both supralapsarian and sublapsarian positions, noting the great extent of their agreements and how the one focuses on "the decree of the end" and the other on "the decree of the means." He concluded: "for my own part, I think both may be taken in."[273] Yet Gill's doctrine of reprobation or "rejection" is more difficult to harmonize with sublapsarianism, for he included in reprobation not only God's preterition, or passing over of the nonelect, but also

---

[269] *A Body of Doctrinal Divinity*, book 6, chs. 3-4; also *The Cause of God and Truth*, part 2, ch. 3, where (p. 98) Gill agreed with Daniel Whitby in rejecting the distinction that Christ died "*sufficiently* for all but *intentionally* only for the elect;" part 3, ch. 3.

[270] *A Body of Doctrinal Divinity*, book 6, chs. 8, 13, esp. p. 545. Watts, *The Dissenters*, 1:458, ascribes to Gill the view that faith is "a gift bestowed only on the elect."

[271] *A Body of Doctrinal Divinity*, book 6, ch. 12, esp. pp. 541-42, 544; also *The Cause of God and Truth*, part 2, ch. 4; part 3, ch. 4.

[272] *A Body of Doctrinal Divinity*, book 6, ch. 15, esp. p. 559; also *The Cause of God and Truth*, part 2, ch. 6; part 3, ch. 6, and *The Doctrine of the Saints Final Perseverance, Asserted and Vindicated* (London: George Keith, 1752), written in response to John Wesley.

[273] *A Body of Doctrinal Divinity*, book 2, ch. 2, pp. 183-85. Thomas J. Nettles, *By His Grace and for His Glory: A Historical, Theological, and Practical Study of the Doctrine of Grace in Baptist Life* (Grand Rapids MI: Baker Book House, 1986) 89-91, has held that Gill cannot be categorized as "rigidly supralapsarian" but "evidently preferred that view."

predamnation, or God's preordaining of the nonelect to condemnation for sin by the "moving cause" of "the good pleasure of his will."[274]

Gill clearly taught an eternal covenant of redemption or grace, growing out of the council involving the Father, the Son, and the Holy Spirit.[275] He also interpreted justification, adoption, and union with Christ as eternal acts immanently executed by God.[276]

What was Gill's attitude toward general "offers of grace" or "tenders of the gospel"? In treating reprobation he declared that the "gospel is not tendered to the elect" but rather God's grace "is bestowed upon them, applied to them and wrought in them, but not offered."[277] He also denied that preachers should exhort to repentance, whether "evangelical" or "legal," as being "within . . . the power of man's will, . . . a term of acceptance with God, and in order to make peace with God."[278] Thomas J. Nettles has made an elaborate defense of Gill, arguing that "offers of grace" were different from preaching the gospel, that Gill commended Christian zeal, and that Gill held that "rejecting the gospel aggravated the guilt of man."[279] But Gill's rejection of "offers" and "tenders" with its implications for preaching means that he can hardly be removed from the ranks of the Hyper-Calvinists.[280]

Was Gill an antinomian? Alan P. F. Sell has declared:

> Like many High Calvinists before them Gill and Brine were accused of antinomianism; and like most High Calvinists they were blameless as far as practical antinomianism was concerned. . . . Although Gill might be thought to have added fuel to the fire by republishing Crisp's *Works* in

---

[274]*A Body of Doctrinal Divinity*, book 2, ch. 3, esp. pp. 194, 197; also *The Cause of God and Truth*, part 3, ch. 1, and *The Doctrine of Predestination Stated, and Set in the Scripture-Light; in Opposition to Mr. Wesley's Predestination Calmly Considered* (London, 1752) 6-14.

[275]*A Body of Doctrinal Divinity*, book 2, chs. 6-15.

[276]Ibid., book 2, chs. 4-5.

[277]*The Cause of God and Truth*, part. 3, ch. 1, p. 156.

[278]*The Doctrines of God's Everlasting Love to His Elect, and Their Eternal Union with Christ . . . in a Letter to Dr. Abraham Taylor* (London: George Keith, 1732; repr.: Paris AR: Baptist Standard Bearer, 1987) 59-60.

[279]*By His Grace and for His Glory*, 99-106.

[280]See George, "John Gill," 92-93.

1755, . . . his avowed intention was to *clear* Crisp of the charge of antinomianism by annotating the works.[281]

Rippon quoted Gill as having written: "I *abhor* the thoughts of setting the law of God aside as the rule of walk and conversation; and constantly affirm that all who believe in Christ for righteousness should be careful to maintain good works, for necessary uses."[282] Peter Toon[283] has retained the charge that Gill was antinomian by citing his *The Doctrines of God's Everlasting Love to His Elect and Their Eternal Union with Christ*,[284] but in that treatise Gill supported eternal union and limited the idea that "sin could do a believer no harm" to "the hurt of punishment," lamenting that opponents had ever associated the two concepts.[285] George,[286] Nettles,[287] and Curt Daniel[288] have carefully concluded that Gill was not antinomian, and Gill's sermons on Rom. 3:31[289] and Deut. 20:5[290] strongly support that conclusion.

Hence Gill can be reasonably described either as three-fifths or as four-fifths a Hyper-Calvinist, he not being an antinomian and being ambiguous on supralapsarianism.[291]

---

[281] *The Great Debate: Calvinism, Arminianism and Salvation*, 79.

[282] *A Brief Memoir*, 56.

[283] *The Emergence of Hyper-Calvinism in English Nonconformity*, 145-46.

[284] (London, 1733; repr.: Paris AR: Baptist Standard Bearer, 1987).

[285] Ibid., esp. 2-3, 8, 11.

[286] "John Gill," 92.

[287] *By His Grace and for His Glory*, 91-94.

[288] "John Gill and Calvinistic Antinomianism," in Haykin, ed., *The Life and Thought of John Gill*, 171-90, esp. 187, 190. Daniel places Gill in the larger context of antinomian controversies from Luther to Gill.

[289] *The Law Established by the Gospel: A Sermon Preached March the 22nd, 1738-9, at a Monthly Exercise of Prayer, at the Rev. Mr. Wilson's Meetinghouse in Goodman's Fields*, 2nd ed. (London: George Keith, 1756; first publ. 1739). Gill held that the covenant of works and the Mosaic administration of law were abolished and the ceremonial law was voided by being fulfilled in Christ but that the moral law is "not made null and void" but is "established" by the gospel, its "*perpetuity*" being maintained and its "*spirituality*" being secured "in the hands of Christ" (esp. 26-28, 13-14, 32-34, 35).

[290] *The Law in the Hand of Christ; A Sermon, Preached May 24, 1761, at Broad-mead, in Bristol* (London: George Keith, 1761).

[291] George M. Ella, "John Gill and the Charge of Hyper-Calvinism," *Baptist Quarterly* 36 (October 1995): 160-77, has tried to establish that Gill was in no sense a Hyper-Calvinist.

Gill differentiated the "general" from the "particular" usage of the term "church" and held that a particular church should be composed of "regenerate persons," "called ones," real saints, believers in Christ, those saved, and those knowledgeable of divine things who have been baptized by immersion upon a profession of faith. Members are to love, be unified with, sympathize with, share materially and spiritually with, watch over, bear with, pray for, assemble with, have no respect of persons among, strive for the gospel with, and be an example for one another. Pastors and deacons[292] are the "ordinary officers" of a particular church; pastors must have both an internal call through the recognition of gifts and the external call from the church, and their task is to "feed the church of God," or "their respective flocks." Members are to know, esteem, remember, obey, and pray for their pastor. Gill denied that Matt. 18:17, 1 Cor. 5:3, 5, and Tit. 3:10 apply to excommunication.[293] Gill's arguments in defense of separation from the Church of England were as elaborate as those by seventeenth-century Separatists and General Baptists.[294]

Gill's earliest treatises on baptism were defenses of the mode of immersion in which he focused on the New Testament practice of baptism, baptism's end vis-à-vis Jesus's death and burial, and the meaning of the word *baptizein*.[295] Subsequently he sought to invalidate infant baptism either by

---

[292]Gill, without citing Collier, repeated his threefold identification of the work of deacons: "the Lord's table," "the minister's table," and "the poor's table." *A Body of Practical Divinity*, book 2, ch. 5, p. 883. See above, 82-83.

[293]Ibid., book 2, chs. 1-6.

[294]*The Dissenters Reasons for Separation from the Church of England, Occasioned by a Letter Wrote by a Welch Clergyman on the Duty of Catechising Children* (1751), in BBHRM/M,RP, reel 4, item 1; also summarized by George M. Ella, *John Gill and the Cause of God and Truth* (Eggleston UK: Go Publications, 1995) 117-28. The Church of England (1) has a human constitution based on "the law of man"; (2) is a "national" church, not a "congregational" church; (3) has "the whole nation" as its members rather than believers only; (4) has corrupt and incomplete doctrine; (5) does not rightly administer baptism and the Lord's Supper; (6) has offices not mentioned in the Scriptures; (7) has a temporal head (king or queen) rather than Christ as head; (8) lacks proper church discipline; (9) has rites and ceremonies that are pagan, Jewish, or papal; (10) uses the *Book of Common Prayer*, to which numerous objections are raised; and (11) has been a persecuting church.

[295]*The Ancient Mode of Baptizing by Immersion, Plunging, or Dipping into Water, Maintained and Vindicated* (London, 1726), in BBHRM/M, RP, reel 4, item 1; *A Defence of a Book, Intitled, The Ancient Mode of Baptizing by Immersion,*

the dubious effort to show that the early Waldenses practiced believer's baptism or by the more fruitful efforts to reinterpret the Abrahamic covenant,[296] to answer pedobaptist arguments in detail,[297] to press for any evidence that infant baptism was practiced prior to Tertullian,[298] and to enjoin believer's baptism on the basis of loving obedience to the divine command.[299] Finally Gill argued that infant baptism was "part and pillar" of the Roman Catholic system and that by retaining it Protestantism "keeps in her very citadel the chief supporter and prime minister of the foe."[300] Moreover, the baptism of Gentile proselytes into Judaism cannot be found in the Old Testament, the Old Testament Apocrypha, the New Testament, Philo, Josephus, the Targums, the Mishnah, or the early Church Fathers, but only in the Talmuds, and hence it cannot have been the basis for Christian baptism.[301] Gill's position that baptism is "not a church-ordinance," although "an ordinance of God," and not to be "administered in the church, but out of it, and in order to admission into it" would not be accepted by the great majority of later Baptists.[302]

Plunging, or Dipping in Water, etc., against Mr. Matthias Maurice's Reply, Called, Plunging into Water No Scriptural Mode of Baptizing (London, 1727), in ibid., reel 4, item 1.

[296] *The Divine Right of Infant-Baptism, Examined and Disproved: Being an Answer to a Pamphlet, Intitled, A Brief Illustration and Confirmation of the Divine Right of Infant-Baptism* (London, 1749), in BBHRM/M, RP, reel 4, item 1.

[297] *An Answer to a Welch Clergyman's Twenty Arguments in Favour of Infant-Baptism* (London, 1751), in BBHRM/M, RP, reel 4, item 1; also reel 4, item 3.

[298] *Antipaedobaptism; or Infant-Baptism an Innovation: Being a Reply to a Late Pamphlet, Intitled, Paedobaptism; or, a Defence of Infant-Baptism, in Point of Antiquity, etc.* (London, 1753), in BBHRM/M, RP, reel 4, item 1; also reel 4, item 4.

[299] *Baptism a Divine Command to Be Observed: Being a Sermon Preached at Barbican, October 9, 1765, at the Baptism of the Reverend Mr. Robert Carmichael, Minister of the Gospel in Edinburgh* (1765), in BBHRM/M, RP, reel 4, item 1.

[300] *Infant Baptism a Part and Pillar of Popery*, rev. and ed. George B. Ide (Philadelphia: American Baptist Publication Society, 1851; orig., London, 1766) esp. 124.

[301] *A Dissertation concerning the Baptism of Jewish Proselytes* (London, 1771), in BBHRM/M, RP, reel 4, item 12; also bound with *A Body of Doctrinal and Practical Divinity* (1989 ed.) 995-1023.

[302] *A Body of Practical Divinity*, book 3, ch. 1, p. 896. Ella, *John Gill and the Cause of God and Truth*, 121-22; Stanley K. Fowler, "John Gill's Doctrine of Believer Baptism," in Haykin, ed., *The Life and Thought of John Gill*, 88-90.

Gill expressed a symbolic view of the Lord's Supper and regarded the public ministry of the word (preaching) and the public hearing of the word as also being ordinances "under the gospel-dispensation." Although allowing for postbiblical hymns in public worship, Gill favored the singing of Old Testament Psalms.[303]

Gill's doctrine of last things is classic Protestant eschatology except that, as to the millennial reign, there are within a premillennial structure postmillennial features. Interpreting the seven letters in Revelation 2–3 as indicative of seven successive epochs of church history, he taught that he was living in the age of Sardis, which had begun with the Protestant Reformation, that the age of Philadelphia would bring the "latter glory" of the church, and that the age of Laodicea would precede the second advent of Christ.[304] The age of Philadelphia, which is to be that of the "spiritual reign" of Christ, will be marked by the destruction of the two Antichrists, the pope and the Turk, with the pouring out of the seven vials (bowls) (Revelation 16), by "a general spread of the gospel . . . into the several nations of the world," by numerous conversions throughout the world, and by the full effusion of God's Spirit (Joel 3:1-5; Acts 2:16-21).[305]

According to Gill, between death and resurrection there will be a disembodied state for immortal human souls, either of "happiness" or of

---

[303] *A Body of Practical Divinity*, book 3, chs. 2–4, 7.

[304] *The Glory of the Church in the Latter Day: A Sermon Preached to the Society Which Supported the Wednesday's Evening Lecture in Great Eastcheap, Dec. 27th, 1752*, 6th ed. (London, 1812; first publ. 1753) 10, 19, 25-27; *The Watchman's Answer to the Question, What of the Night? A Sermon Preached to the Society Which Supported the Wednesday's Evening Lecture in Great Eastcheap, Dec. 27th 1750*, 6th ed. (London, 1812; first publ. 1751) 24-26, 32, 34; *The Practical Improvement of the Watchman's Answer to the Question, What of the Night? A Sermon Preached to the Society Which Support the Wednesday's Evening Lecture in Great Eastcheap, January 1, 1752* (London: George Keith et al., 1752) 11-12. Barry H. Howson, "The Eschatology of the Calvinistic Baptist John Gill (1697–1771) Examined and Compared," *Eusebeia* no. 5 (Autumn 2005): 33-66, agreeing that in Gill there was a "conflation of postmillennialism with premillennialism," also concluded that Gill's date setting, especially 1866, had a stifling effect on any missionary endeavor and helps to explain later Gillite opposition to William Carey's mission.

[305] *The Glory of the Church in the Latter Day*, 7-27. Gill calculated that the destruction of the Antichrists would occur in the year 1866. *A Body of Practical Divinity*, book 7, ch. 6, sect. 5.

"woe."[306] The certain, personal, and visible second coming of Christ in glory is to be followed by the "universal conflagration" (2 Pet. 3:10, 12), by the resurrection of believers in the same but transformed body, and by the creation of the "new heavens and a new earth" (Isa. 65:17; Rev. 21:1).[307] Then will follow the "personal reign" of Christ, or the millennium (Rev. 20:2-7) on the new earth, during which Satan is bound, to be terminated by the Satanic rebellion and followed by the resurrection of all the wicked, the last judgment, and the final states of hell and heaven.[308]

Gill's teachings and ministry have evoked diverse and contradictory evaluations for two centuries. The more negative assessments have come chiefly from historians of the Baptists who have related Gill to the spiritual decline of the Particular Baptists of his day, whereas the more positive assessments have been given by theologians who have majored on extensive reading of Gill's writings. The negative evaluations began with Robert Hall's often-quoted reference to *A Body of Doctrinal and Practical Divinity* as "a continent of mud."[309] Joseph Ivimey acknowledged that Gill recognized antinomianism as a "very dangerous error" but noted his zeal for eternal justification and strongly asserted that Gill "adopted the noninvitation scheme" with its lack of call to repentance.[310] According to Thomas Armitage, Gill was a supralapsarian, was "hard to distinguish from an Antinomian," particularly because of his publication of Crisp's sermons, and left a diminished congregation.[311] For Henry C. Vedder, Gill was "a great scholar" and "an industrious writer of books" but he set forth a "supralapsarian" "Hyper-Calvinism," which for Vedder was "blighting" and "false" doctrine and which could hardly "be distinguished from fatalism and

---

[306]*A Body of Doctrinal Divinity*, book 7, chs. 1-4.

[307]Ibid., chs. 5-7.

[308]Ibid., chs. 8-11. See also Gill's *The Doctrine of the Resurrection, Stated and Defended; in Two Sermons, Preached at a Lecture in Lime-Street*, 2nd ed. (London: G. Keith and J. Robinson, 1750; first publ. 1731?), photocopy suppl. by Brown University Library, for his assertion of the "credibility" and "certainty" of eschatological resurrection (11-30), his defense of two distinct times of resurrection, for the righteous and for the wicked (31-43), and his rejection of the death of the soul, the sleep of the soul, and annihilation (43-67).

[309]*The Works of Robert Hall, A.M.*, 6 vols., ed. Olinthus Gregory (London: Samuel Holdsworth, 1839) 1:175. See below, 193.

[310]*A History of the English Baptists*, 3:440, 448-50, 272, 273, 275.

[311]*A History of the Baptists* (New York: Bryan, Taylor, and Co., 1887), 561.

antinomianism," and his noninvitation to sinners was "practically to nullify the Great Commission."³¹² Robert Edward Seymour thought that Gill "leaned over backwards in an impossible attempt to exonerate" Crisp of antinomianism and was not clear concerning and advocated both supralapsarianism and sublapsarianism. Furthermore Gill's theology, which Seymour labeled "cold and abstract," "had a withering effect upon the Particular Baptists of England" and "contributed nothing toward overcoming the religious apathy of the age."³¹³ According to Alan Sell, "No matter how much we may respect Gill for his prodigious labours, . . . the fact remains that for all his assertion of the need to *declare* the gospel, he does seem to have underemphasized the gospel *call*." Such neglect "led . . . to undue introspection at the expense of Christ-centeredness."³¹⁴ Leon McBeth concluded that "Gill . . . perhaps did more than . . . [Skepp and Brine] to spread hyper-Calvinism among the Particular Baptists" and Gill's Hyper-Calvinism was a considerable departure from the Calvinism of Knollys.³¹⁵

The positive evaluations of Gill began with his Anglican friend, Augustus M. Toplady, who wrote in 1772:

> His Doctrinal and Practical Writings will live, and be admired, and be a standing blessing to posterity. . . . While true Religion, and sound Learning have a single friend remaining in the British Empire, the works and name of *Gill* will be precious and revered.³¹⁶

William Cathcart declared of Gill in 1883: "His 'Body of Divinity' . . . is a work without which no theological library is complete. His grand old doctrines of grace . . . sweep all opposition before them," especially Arminianism. His commentary "is the most valuable exposition of the Old and New Testaments ever published."³¹⁷ Recent authors have mostly assumed the roles of reassessor and defender of Gill. Timothy George successfully refuted the charge that Gill was an antinomian but acknowledged that Gill's doctrine of eternal justification "was a perilous teaching,

---

³¹²*A Short History of the Baptists*, 239-41.
³¹³"John Gill: Baptist Theologian, 1697–1771" (Ph.D. diss., University of Edinburgh, 1954) 82, 91-94, 311, 310, 311.
³¹⁴*The Great Debate: Calvinism, Arminianism, and Salvation*, 82.
³¹⁵*The Baptist Heritage*, 176-77, 178.
³¹⁶Quoted in Rippon, *A Brief Memoir*, 140.
³¹⁷Cathcart, ed., *The Baptist Encyclopedia*, rev. ed. (Philadelphia: Louis H. Everts, 1883) 453, 454.

insofar as it encouraged sinners to think of themselves as actually justified regardless of their personal response to Christ and the gospel." George found some distance between Gill and Hussey on coming to Christ but stated that Gill could not be exonerated for helping to foster a climate in which preaching "the missionary mandate of the church" could be seen as "a threat to . . . the gospel of grace." Moreover, Gill's followers carried certain of Gill's teachings "to extremes he would not, or at least did not, himself embrace."[318] Thomas J. Nettles, finding Gill to be indecisive about but preferring supralapsarianism and to have been no antinomian, went on to insist that Gill did not reject "duty-faith" and "duty-repentance" and that Gill believed in preaching the gospel but not in "offers of grace."[319] Peter Naylor, equating "high Calvinism" with Hyper-Calvinism, regarded Gill as having been "confused" by teaching "that before conversion elect believers were simultaneously in both a state of condemnation and a state of justification," as having been insensitive to biblical teaching as to "the point in time when God justifies the elect sinner," and as having been "perhaps, somewhat misleading when he taught that salvation (as distinct from 'grace') should never be offered."[320] George M. Ella in an extensive recent study of Gill has sought to disprove the classification of Gill as a "Hyper-Calvinist" by denying that Gill was a supralapsarian and insisting that supralapsarianism is not synonymous with Hyper-Calvinism, by defending Gill's doctrine of eternal justification but noting that Gill connected it with faith in time, and by stressing that Gill issued the gospel call without being a participant in the debate about duty-faith. Ella's study is predicated on demonstrating the truth of Gill's theology and denigrating that of Andrew Fuller. Thus he has concluded that Gill "served the Baptist cause in an unparalleled way" and "provided all evangelicals with a body of divinity second to none."[321]

---

[318]"John Gill," 92, 93-94, 78.

[319]*By His Grace and for His Glory*, 89-106. See also Nettles's more recent "John Gill and the Evangelical Awakening," in Haykin, ed., *The Life and Thought of John Gill*, 131-70.

[320]*Picking Up a Pin for the Lord: English Particular Baptists from 1688 to the Early Nineteenth Century* (Darlington UK: Grace Publications, 1992) 145, 179, 184, 162.

[321]*John Gill and the Cause of God and Truth*, 159-74, 178-83, 264, 254-57, 269.

Particular Baptists emerged from the less polemical Independents during the 1630s, retaining a theology mostly consonant with the Synod of Dort, especially as to limited atonement, but insisted on believer's baptism by the mode of total immersion, likely derived from the Dutch Rhynsburgers. Some also insisted upon believer's immersion as prerequisite to receiving the Lord's Supper. Their 1644 confession, framed for defensive and didactic purposes and somewhat dependent on Separatism's *A True Confession* and other sources, was "moderately Calvinistic" and expressed Baptist ecclesiology, being the first Christian confession to prescribe single immersion for baptism. The Midland Confession was a brief document in lay language, whereas the Somerset Confession resisted the Quakers, dispelled charges of Arminian tendencies, and affirmed the mandate of missions. Hanserd Knollys as to Christ's second coming differentiated his "spiritual coming" from his personal, physical coming, they being separated by the millennial reign, and calculated that the former would occur between AD 1667 and 1688. Knollys had affinities for Fifth Monarchy leaders but did not espouse violence. William Kiffin refuted pedobaptism and strongly defended in opposition to John Bunyan close communion. Bunyan, prolific author and allegorist, answered the Quaker claims for the Inner Light, was infralapsarian with stress on an eternal covenant between the Father and the Son, defended the imputation of Christ's righteousness, shifted to the position that justification precedes faith, magnified the Christian life as pilgrimage, and strongly espoused open communion and open membership while decrying sectarian labels.

The 1677 confession was a modification of the Westminster Confession to show Particular Baptist solidarity with other Dissenters. Opening with a detailed article on the Scriptures, it mostly affirmed the doctrines of high Calvinism, classic orthodoxy, Protestantism, Puritanism, and anti-Anabaptism. It exhibited a distinctive Baptist ecclesiology but was more Calvinist than Zwinglian on the Lord's Supper. Thomas Collier and Western Baptists embraced an Arminianized theology as Particular Baptists. Benjamin Keach defended the laying on of hands on the newly baptized, Baptist views on baptism, and the doctrines of high Calvinism, but his most distinctive contribution was in defending and instituting congregational hymn singing during congregational worship. The Hyper-Calvinists among Particular Baptists (John Skepp, John Brine, John Gill) were reportedly greatly influenced by an Anglican, Tobias Crisp, and a Congregationalist, Joseph Hussey. Hyper-Calvinist distinctives are difficult to find in Crisp's writings, but Hussey was more clearly Hyper-Calvinist, especially as to "offers of grace." Skepp insisted that conversion does not come by "moral suasion," for the sinner must be utterly passive. Brine taught eternal justification and an eternal Trinitarian covenant, which he equated with the covenant of grace in time, in a supralapsarian framework and answered the "modern question" by insisting on a "warrant" and rejecting the dutiful nature of repentance and faith. Gill, a prolific author who wrote both a commentary on the entire Bible and a systematic theology, defended the Trinity, the eternal sonship of Christ, the covenant of "innocence" (works), Chalcedonian Christology, and substitutionary satisfaction as the atonement. Gill squared with the *ordo salutis* of Calvinism and the five tenets of Dort and seemingly embraced either three or four of the five distinctives of Hyper-Calvinism. He also defended believer's immersion and criticized pedobaptism. Gill has continued to have his critics, who have majored on his impact on Particular Baptists in an era of decline, and his defenders, who have reexamined his writings so as to foster his rehabilitation. Thus the review of Particular Baptist theology ends on the eve of the Evangelical Revival.

Chapter 4

Early American Baptists

Baptists in constituting churches in the American colonies brought with them from England those theological differences that had distinguished the General and Particular Baptists, issues of Arminianism and Calvinism, and these, together with the ecclesiological distinctives of the Baptists, also derived from England, and the new American concerns for freedom, church, and government would constitute the principal subject matter of Baptist theology during the colonial and early national periods. Baptist theology in the colonies had its beginning in New England in the life and writings of Roger Williams.

Roger Williams (1603?–1683)

Reared in London, educated at Cambridge, and ordained as an Anglican, Williams had become a Puritan and a Separatist before sailing to Boston in 1630–1631. His successive ministries at Salem in Massachusetts Bay Colony, in Plymouth in Plymouth Colony, and again in Salem were marked by increasing tension with the Massachusetts Bay authorities over his thoroughly separatist views.[1] Hence, lest he be sent back to England, Williams fled from Salem in the winter of 1636 into "the howling wilderness" and settled in Providence in what would become the Rhode Island Colony. He made two trips to England (1643–1644; 1651–1654), the first to obtain a parliamentary charter for the new colony and the second to save that charter. During these sojourns in England he published most of his books.[2] He served three years as "president" of the colony, continued to be

---

[1]Hugh Spurgin, *Roger Williams and Puritan Radicalism in the English Separatist Tradition*, Studies in American Religion 34 (Lewiston NY: Edwin Mellen, 1989) 21-28.

[2]*A Key into the Language of America* (London, 1643); *Mr. Cottons Letter Lately Printed, Examined, and Answered* (London, 1644); *Queries of Highest Consideration* (London, 1644); *The Bloudy Tenent, of Persecution, for Cause of Conscience, Discussed, in a Conference betweene Truth and Peace* (London?, 1644); *Christenings Make Not Christians, or a Brief Discourse concerning That Name Heathen, Commonly Given to the Indians* (London, 1645); *A Letter of R. Williams of Providence in New England, to Major Endicot, Governour of Massachusets, upon Occasion of the Late Persecution against Mr. Clarke and Obadiah Holmes, and Others at Boston . . .* (1651?); *The Bloody Tenent Yet More Bloody* (London, 1652); *Experiments of Spiritual Life and Health and Their*

a mediator between the colonists and the Indians, and later publicly debated Quakers.[3] Perry Miller[4] applied the term "prophet" to Williams, whereas Edwin S. Gaustad[5] has used the term "exile."

By 1639 Williams led in the formation of a Baptist church in Providence—the first in the American colonies, but he remained a Baptist and member of that congregation "for only a few months," the alleged reason being the lack of authority via succession from the apostles for its baptisms and the absence of any new apostle to restore baptism. Williams "retained many Baptist convictions to the day of his death."[6] Whether Williams later joined the English sect known as Seekers is uncertain, and it seems best to assume that he never joined any other church.[7]

In interpreting the thought of Williams, one needs to ask two preliminary questions. What was his biblical interpretation, and what was his basic theological orientation? First, Perry Miller[8] asserted that Williams followed the typological method of biblical interpretation—not so much as the means of understanding specific texts as the means of relating the two testaments,

---

Preservatives... (London, 1652); *The Fourth Paper, Present by Maior Butler to the Honourable Committee of Parliament, for the Propagating the Gospel of Christ Jesus* (London, 1652); *The Hireling Ministry None of Christs, or a Discourse Touching the Propagating the Gospel of Christ Jesus* (London, 1652); *The Examiner Defended, in a Fair and Sober Answer to the Two and Twenty Questions Which Lately Examined the Author of 'Zeal Examined'* (London, 1652).

[3]Tull, *Shapers of Baptist Thought*, 31-34; McBeth, *The Baptist Heritage*, 124-30. See also Thomas S. Kidd, " 'Is It Worse to Follow Mahomet than the Devil?' Early American Uses of Islam," *Church History* 72 (December 2003): 777-78. "Williams contrasted the Roman church, Islam, and Quakerism, all deceitful human systems, with the true religion of Christ."

[4]*Roger Williams: His Contribution to the American Tradition* (Indianapolis: Bobbs-Merrill, 1953). Note the titles to chs. 2, 3, and 4.

[5]*Liberty of Conscience: Roger Williams in America* (Grand Rapids MI: Eerdmans, 1991). Note the titles to chs. 1-5, 7.

[6]McBeth, *The Baptist Heritage*, 130-32; Gaustad, *Liberty of Conscience*, 90-91.

[7]Spurgin, *Roger Williams and Puritan Radicalism in the English Separatist Tradition*, 29-30; Gaustad, *Liberty of Conscience*, 98. But John Garrett, *Roger Williams: Witness beyond Christendom, 1603–1683* (New York: Macmillan, 1970) 48, quoting Cotton Mather and Richard Baxter, has inclined to a connection with the English Seekers.

[8]*Roger Williams: His Contribution to the American Tradition*, 32-38, 89.

and James Tull agreed.⁹ Whereas most typologists, including those in New England, posited both a continuity of the covenant of grace and a continuity between the two testaments, Williams held to a discontinuity between the Abrahamic covenant and the new covenant in Christ and between the testaments. Hence the kings of Israel and Judah are not to be taken as examples for magistrates in the seventeenth century or as the basis for religious persecution, and Old Testament types are to be interpreted figuratively. The Epistle to the Hebrews, "used repeatedly" by Williams, was the "main charter" for Williams's typological interpretation.¹⁰ Second, Williams's basic theological orientation was Calvinist or Dortian Calvinist,¹¹ as his views of anthropology, predestination, providence, and perseverance indicate. His contribution to Baptist theology, however, does not rest in the preservation of these beliefs.

Williams was more able to delineate the marks of that which he denominated as false churches and false ministries than to demarcate the truly gathered church and its ministry.¹² In *Queries of Highest Consideration* (1644) he identified synods, assemblies, national churches, suppression of "heresy," and two kinds of baptism as not to be found in the teaching of Jesus.¹³ In *The Hireling Ministry None of Christs* (1652) he specified four defects in contemporary ministries: no "gifts" (no apostolic succession), no "calling" (prior to gathering of churches), no work (Great Commission) and no "wages" (tithes collected by civil governments).¹⁴

Building, although perhaps unknowingly, on Bathasar Hubmaier and citing John Murton,¹⁵ Williams laid out a detailed case against persecution

---

⁹*Shapers of Baptist Thought*, 45-47.

¹⁰Garrett, *Roger Williams: Witness beyond Christendom*, 43, 44.

¹¹Ibid., 20, 30, 162, 181, 213, 236; Tull, *Shapers of Baptist Thought*, 35.

¹²Williams did offer a definition of the true church: "The Church of Christ is a congregation of Saints, a flock of sheep, humble, meek, patient, contented, with whom it is monstrous and impossible, to couple cruel and persecuting lyons, subtle and hypocritical Foxes, contentious biting dogs or greedy and rooting swine, so visibly declared and apparant." *The Bloody Tenent Yet More Bloody* (1652), in *The Complete Works of Roger Williams*, 4:143.

¹³In *The Complete Writings of Roger Williams* 2:257-60, 264-66, 270-73.

¹⁴In ibid., 7:162-63; Gaustad, *Liberty of Conscience*, 90-96.

¹⁵Williams referred to Murton as the "close prisoner of Newgate." *The Blovdy Tenent, of Persecution, for Cause of Conscience, Discussed, in a Conference betweene Truth and Peace,* in *The Complete Writings of Roger Williams*, 3:61.

in *The Bloudy Tenent, of Persecution, for Cause of Conscience* (1644). It is contrary to certain New Testament texts; the blood of many martyrs has been shed; civil magistrates ought not to govern Christian faith and worship; there is a marked difference between a literal sword and the sword of the Spirit (the Word of God); and religious uniformity is provocative of civil wars, discourages the conversion of Jews to Christ, and confuses the civil and the religious.[16]

In addition to answering John Cotton's argument, Williams gave attention to particular New Testament passages,[17] two of which were treated in detail: the parable of the tares and Romans 13:1-7. Although Williams did not fully explain the interpretation of his predecessors, except for Cotton, he did, as James P. Byrd, Jr.,[18] has recently demonstrated, set out a carefully nuanced interpretation of the parable of the tares (weeds). Contrary to John Calvin and John Cotton, who insisted that "the field" is the church, Williams, like Menno Simons and Henry Barrow, held that "the field" is the world. Unlike Calvin, who interpreted the tares as immoral but not heretical persons, and unlike John Cotton, who found the tares to be hypocrites in the church, Williams, like Menno, who understood the tares as those accused of heresy, identified them as "Idolaters, False-worshippers, [and] Antichristians." For Calvin, the parable was intended to help weak Christians to cope with the tares. For Barrow, the parable, being "a command to endure sin in the civil sphere," did not inhibit the full exercise of church discipline, whereas for Cotton the parable was designed to correct "overly harsh" church discipline. Williams, on the other hand, deplored the past misuse of the parable to justify persecution and, taking the servants to be Christian ministers, saw the parable as admonishing them not to incite magistrates to persecution and to pray for the future salvation, not the present destruction, of the tares.

Rom. 13:1-7, according to Williams, a "fort" amid controversies, pertains not at all to the first table of the Ten Commandments but only to the second, commands obedience to emperors and magistrates who are non-

---

[16]Taken from the introductory twelve-point summary. Ibid., 3:3-4.

[17]Ibid., 3:97-164.

[18]*The Challenges of Roger Williams: Religious Liberty, Violent Persecution, and the Bible* (Macon GA: Mercer University Press, 2002) 87-127; Williams, *The Bloudy Tenent, of Persecution* in *The Complete Writings of Roger Williams*, 3:97-119, esp. 109, 107, 115-16. See also Williams, *The Bloody Tenent Yet More Bloody*, in *The Complete Writings of Roger Williams*, 4:114-55.

Christians and persecute Christians, refers (v. 4) to "the Sword of Civill justice," implies that only civil work should be done by those who receive such civil wages as "tribute" and "customs" (v. 6), and recognizes magistrates as civil ministers of God distinct from spiritual ministers in churches.[19]

Although Williams quoted from the New Testament Apocalypse "much more often than from any other biblical book," citing chapters 2–3 and 17 most often, and gave to it a continuous-historical interpretation,[20] he seems not to have set forth any coherent or comprehensive eschatology. Like Puritans, he identified the "great whore" of Babylon with the Roman Catholic Church, and to the dismay of Massachusetts Bay authorities he specified one of the ten horns of the beast as the kingdom of King Charles I.[21] W. Clark Gilpin has contended that Williams's millennialism differed from the prevailing Puritan view in that the millennium is to bring a restored apostolic Christianity with outward ordinances, not a reign "over both state and church."[22]

The influence of Roger Williams has been assessed both with respect to the American nation and to the Baptist denomination. The history of the former assessment, traced by Edwin S. Gaustad,[23] extends from George Bancroft's acclaim of Williams as "the first person in modern Christendom to assert in its plenitude the doctrine of the liberty of conscience, the equality of opinions before the law,"[24] through the late nineteenth- and early twentieth-century identification of Williams with "democratic reform and social progress" to the mid-twentieth century recovery of Williams as theologian led by Perry Miller. According to Edmund S. Morgan, Williams's concept of conscience was thoroughly Puritan, including the ideas that conscience can err and violators of the moral code of the second table can be punished, but he differed in that only *"religious* conscience" cannot be violated by government and is correctable only by persuasion. His

---

[19]*The Bloudy Tenent, of Persecution,* in *The Complete Writings of Roger Williams,* 3:150-64. See also Williams, *The Bloody Tenent Yet More Bloody,* in *The Complete Writings of Roger Williams,* 4:262-83.

[20]Byrd, *The Challenges of Roger Williams,* 156.

[21]Ibid., 173-75.

[22]*The Millenarian Piety of Roger Williams* (Chicago: University of Chicago Press, 1979) 56-62, esp. 61.

[23]*Liberty of Conscience,* 199-219, esp. 212, 215, 217.

[24]*History of the United States, from the Discovery of the American Continent,* 10 vols., 10th ed. (Boston: Charles C. Little and James Brown, 1842) 1:375-76.

defense of liberty of conscience was seemingly "more limited" than that later offered by Thomas Jefferson and James Madison.[25] James E. Ernst stated: "In the constitution [Rhode Island] adopted we have prefigured the constitutions of the United States and the several states."[26] For John Garrett, "Williams's originality lay in his explicit use of the word 'Christendom' and the idea of 'christening' as targets for attack,"[27] whereas Hugh Spurgin has concluded that Williams as a Separatist created and espoused "a more extreme, more pervasive, and eventually more tolerant understanding of separateness."[28] The major influence of Williams upon Baptists, especially in the American colonies and in the United States, has been identified by James E. Tull as his being "a foremost representative of one of the Baptists' most cherished convictions," that is, religious liberty.[29]

Confessions of Faith and Church Disciplines

Although only the confession adopted by the Philadelphia Baptist Association in 1742 was widely circulated and adopted by various Baptist associations and churches,[30] the confession framed and adopted by the First Baptist Church of Boston, Massachusetts, in 1665 is worthy of note. Consisting of eight articles, with biblical references attached to each, it affirmed the triune God as knowable only through Jesus Christ, the rule of the Bible as "the written Word of God," Christ as "that great Prophet" who is to be heard and obeyed, the Great Commission and the gathering of visible churches, the congregational selection and ordination of church officers, the reception and dismissal of members and corporate worship, the civil magistracy as a God-given ordinance, and a clear conscience and the final resurrection of both just and unjust.[31] This confession, which was presented by the church to the

---

[25]*Roger Williams: The Church and the State* (New York: Harcourt, Brace and World, 1967) 130-42, esp. 133, 134, 135, 136, 139, 141.

[26]*Roger Williams: New England Firebrand* (New York: Macmillan, 1932) 274.

[27]*Roger Williams: Witness beyond Christendom*, 241.

[28]*Roger Williams and Puritan Radicalism*, 145-46.

[29]*Shapers of Baptist Thought*, 52-53.

[30]James L. Clark, *"To Set Them in Order": Some Influences of the Philadelphia Baptist Association upon Baptists of America to 1814*, suppl. and ed. Terry L. Wolever (Springfield MO: Particular Baptist, 2001) 132-37.

[31]For the text, see *Manual, with Historical Sketch, of the First Baptist Church, Boston* (Boston: Rand, Avery, and Co., 1880) 9-11, and Nathan E. Wood, *The History of the First Baptist Church of Boston (1665–1899)* (Philadelphia: American Baptist Publication Society, 1899) 65-66. The church also adopted in 1665 a church

Massachusetts Bay Court so as "to let the world know" that its "faith & order" can be "proved from the word of God,"[32] avoided any reference to Calvinist-Arminian issues. Also the two earliest pastors of the First Baptist Church in Newport, Rhode Island—John Clarke and Obadiah Holmes—composed their own confessions of faith.[33]

That which became known as the Philadelphia Confession of Faith had its origin in England. Benjamin Keach condensed the Second London Confession and added two articles, one on the singing of "psalms, hymns, and spiritual songs" in congregational worship, and the other on the laying on of hands on the newly baptized. His congregation and the one served by his son Elias, both in London, adopted this confession, and it was published in London in 1697.[34] To this confession, as published, was attached Benjamin Keach's *The Glory and Ornament of a True Gospel-constituted Church*, which was "a vigorous attack on infant baptism."[35] This confession was most likely brought to the Philadelphia area by or under the influence of Elias Keach, who was pastor of churches in the Philadelphia area from 1687 to 1692.[36] When the church in Middletown, New Jersey, had doctrinal difficulty, the council assisting the church advised its members to "'subscribe to Elias Keach's Confession of Faith, at the least the covenant annexed to it,'" and those who subscribed were reckoned "as the Baptist church."[37] Abel Morgan translated the Keach Confession into Welsh, it was

---

covenant, then reaffirmed its confession in 1878, and added in 1880 an "Explanatory Note" which specified believer's baptism by immersion and close communion (*Manual*, 12-15, 9, 11). In the interim the church yielded neither to Universalism nor to Unitarianism. Wood, *History*, 348.

[32]Wood, *History*, 65.

[33]Isaac Backus, *A History of New England, with Particular Reference to the Denomination of Christians Called Baptists* (Boston: Edward Draper, 1777) 1:222-24, 256-60; 2nd ed. (Newton MA: Backus Historical Society, 1871) 1:182-84, 206-209.

[34]McGlothlin, *Baptist Confessions of Faith*, 293-94; Lumpkin, *Baptist Confessions of Faith*, 239-40. The text of the two articles added by Keach and by the Philadelphia Confession of Faith has been published in McGlothlin, *Baptist Confessions of Faith*, 297-98, and in Lumpkin, *Baptist Confessions of Faith*, 351. The full text of the Philadelphia Confession has been published in facsimile in Clark, *"To Set Them in Order,"* 149-262.

[35]Lumpkin, *Baptist Confessions of Faith*, 240.

[36]Clark, *"To Set Them in Order,"* 7, 10-11.

[37]McGlothlin, *Baptist Confessions of Faith*, 294.

adopted by the Welsh Tract Church in Delaware in 1716,[38] and that church helped to spread the somewhat limited observance of congregational singing and laying on of hands.[39] Although there are references to a confession "owned by us" in the Philadelphia Association records of 1724, it was not until 1742 that the Philadelphia Association, which had been organized in 1707, formally adopted the Keach Confession and ordered its printing.[40] The article on congregational singing would in the future have a much wider acceptance among Baptists in North America than the article on laying on of hands. Baptist associations began to adopt the Philadelphia Confession, notably the Ketockton (Virginia), the Warren (Rhode Island), the Charleston (South Carolina), the Elkhorn (Kentucky), and the Holston (Tennessee). But Charleston omitted the article on laying on of hands, and the considerable revision published by the Ketockton and Culpepper (Virginia) associations in 1806 did likewise.[41]

In 1742 the Philadelphia Association authorized Jenkin Jones and Benjamin Griffith to prepare a treatise concerning church discipline so that it could be adopted and attached to the Philadelphia Confession of Faith. Griffin actually composed the treatise, *A Short Treatise of Church-Discipline*,[42] and it was approved in 1743 and added to the confession of faith. This document first describes the constituting of a truly ordered "visible Gospel Church" after fasting and prayer and then treats the trying, choice, and ordination of ministers and their duties—preaching, overseeing, visitation, administration of two ordinances, prayer, and example of life. The duties of ruling elders (assistance to the pastor in governance) and of deacons (the three tables) are described. There follows a detailed account of the proper examination of prospective members as to their repentance and faith, doctrinal knowledge, and life-style and their admission by the congregation, together with details as to letters of transfer from sister

---

[38]Ibid.

[39]Clark, *"To Set Them in Order,"* 11; McGlothlin, *Baptist Confessions of Faith*, 295.

[40]McGlothlin, *Baptist Confessions of Faith*, 295; Lumpkin, *Baptist Confessions of Faith*, 349.

[41]Lumpkin, *Baptist Confessions of Faith*, 352-53.

[42](Philadelphia: Benjamin Franklin, 1743) iv. Griffith utilized the writings of Elias Keach and Abel Morgan and of two non-Baptists, John Owen and Thomas Goodwin (ibid., v). Also republished in facsimile in Clark, *"To Set Them in Order,"* 263-324.

churches and pertaining to the obligation to unite with the "orderly" church that meets nearest one's place of residence. Then the duties of members toward "Elders, Teachers, Ministers and Pastors" (prayer, obedience, following of example, support during difficulties, noncriticism for weaknesses, and contributions toward maintenance) are delineated, and their duties to fellow members (love, unity, edification, oversight, prayer, attendance of worship, clean living, and advocacy of the truth) defined. Church censures are carefully to be observed, when necessary, on three levels: admonition, suspension, and excommunication, and various disorders in the church, including Arminian and Socinian errors, are identified. Finally, each congregation has authority to choose its leaders and to apply censures, yet such congregations, being "equal in Power and Dignity," "ought to maintain Communion together" in ways mutually helpful but without their "Messengers and Delegates" having "coercive Power, or any superior Jurisdiction."[43] Thus Baptist associations were both affirmed and delimited in authority.

In 1795 the Philadelphia Association authorized Samuel Jones to undertake a revision of its 1743 *Short Treatise*; such was approved in 1797[44] and published in 1798.[45] The revision differed from the original in five ways. Churches are said to have Christ's executive power but not his legislative power. Ministerial maintenance by the congregation is the ideal, but, when necessary, ministers may take secular employment to supplement their income. The office of ruling elder is to be found in some but not all churches. Deacons are to be ordained. A distinction is made between admonition and rebuke, and excommunication is to be used less frequently.[46]

The Charleston Association in 1767, having adopted the Philadelphia Confession with the omission of its article on the laying on of hands, appointed Oliver Hart and Francis Pelot to compose a treatise on church

---

[43]Ibid.

[44]James Leo Garrett, Jr., ed., *Baptist Church Discipline*, Broadman Historical Monographs (Nashville: Broadman, 1962) 16; rev. ed. (Paris AR: Baptist Standard Bearer, 2004) 17.

[45]Published within *A Confession of Faith, Put Forth by the Elders and Brethren of Many Congregations of Christians (Baptized upon Profession of Their Faith) in London and the Country. Adopted by the Baptist Association Met at Philadelphia, September 25, 1742)*, 9th ed. (Philadelphia: Stephen C. Ustick, 1798) 28 pp.

[46]Robert T. Handy, "The Philadelphia Tradition," in *Baptist Concepts of the Church*, ed. Winthrop Still Hudson (Philadelphia: Judson, 1959) 37, 39, 40, 44.

discipline. Their draft, presented in 1772, was revised with the help of Morgan Edwards and David Williams, adopted in 1773, and published in 1774.[47] How did the Charleston *Summary* differ from the 1743 Philadelphia *Treatise*?[48] First, "The *Summary* contains a more systematically thought out and applied theology than does the *Treatise*," including some dependence on John Gill and the differentiation of particular churches and the universal church. Second, "in constituting a church the *Treatise* emphasizes that candidates" for membership "are 'first orderly baptized,' while the *Summary* calls for subscription to a written covenant" and participation in the Lord's Supper. Third, "the *Summary* alone specifically declares that women are not to share in the government of the congregation." Fourth, "the *Treatise* contains an article on ruling elders, while the *Summary* makes no mention of such." Fifth, the *Treatise* enjoins the laying on of hands "on candidates after the act of baptism, but on this the *Summary* does not speak." Sixth, the *Treatise* alone allows for ministers to take up supplementary secular employment. Seventh, the *Treatise* alone provides that when a member is being investigated for an offense, that member "should be immediately suspended" from the Lord's Supper. Eighth, whereas the *Treatise* takes 1 Cor. 5:5 as applicable to modern excommunication, the *Summary* does not.[49] Both Philadelphia and Charleston Baptists were quite intentional concerning church discipline.

Six Principle, Free Will (or Freewill), and General Baptists

Divisions within the Baptist churches in Providence and in Newport, Rhode Island, the one in the 1650s and the other ca.1665, led to the formation of a small group of General Six Principle Baptist churches, first in New England and later in the middle colonies. These churches were mostly Arminian in theology and gave high priority to Heb. 6:1-2.[50] Six Principle

---

[47]Garrett, ed., *Baptist Church Discipline*, 16-17; rev. ed., 17-18; *A Confession of Faith . . . [and] A Summary of Church Dicipline [sic] Shewing the Qualifications and Duties of the Officers and Members of a Gospel-Church by the Baptist-Association in Charleston, SC* (Charleston: David Bruce, 1774). The text has been republished in Garrett, ed., *Baptist Church Discipline*, 27-52; rev. ed., 29-60.

[48]William David May, "The Philadelphia and Charleston Baptist Church Disciplines: A Theological Analysis" (Th.M. thesis, Southern Baptist Theological Seminary, 1961). May's nine differences are here reduced to eight.

[49]Garrett, ed., *Baptist Church Discipline*, 18-19; rev. ed., 20-21.

[50]McBeth, *The Baptist Heritage*, 136, 139, 703; Vedder, *A Short History of the Baptists*, 293, 295, 302; William H. Brackney, ed., *Baptist Life and Thought, 1600–*

churches did not produce a systematic theologian, but they were differentiated by their insistence upon laying on of hands as the second of three ordinances and as a prerequisite to partaking of the Lord's Supper.[51] A separation from the Newport Six Principle church in 1671 led by Stephen Mumford (1639–1707) resulted in Seventh Day Baptist churches in the colonies.[52]

General or Free Will Baptist churches in the American colonies trace their origins to Burley in Isle of Wight County in Virginia ca.1714 and to Chowan County in North Carolina in 1727, the latter church being founded by Paul Palmer, a church planter who "considered willingness to be baptized a sufficient evidence of conversion."[53] Beginning in 1755, under the influence of missionaries from the Philadelphia Association such as John Gano, numerous General Baptist churches in North Carolina were, often after division, reconstituted as Regular or Calvinistic Baptist churches. The remnant of General Baptist leaders pioneered in the recovery which became the surviving Free Will Baptists.[54]

1980: A Source Book (Valley Forge PA: Judson, 1983) 98.

[51]Nelson Robert Elliott, "A History of the General Six Principle Baptists in America" (Th.D. diss., Southwestern Baptist Theological Seminary, 1958) 150, 153-155, 161. During the 1850s they had a temporary schism over open communion (134-39).

[52]McBeth, *The Baptist Heritage*, 139, 706-11. Mumford had come from London, where the first Seventh-Day Baptist congregation had been constituted in 1653. Albert N. Rogers, Evalois St. John, and Rex Zwiebel, "Seventh Day Baptist General Conference," in *Baptist Advance: The Achievements of the Baptists of North America for a Century and a Half* (Nashville: Broadman, 1964) 251. Seventh Day Baptists have continued to the twenty-first century as a tiny minority movement, differing from other Baptists on the major issue of the Saturday Sabbath. In the nineteenth century they influenced the adoption of the seventh day Sabbath by Seventh-Day Adventists, and in the twentieth century they participated in the Ecumenical Movement.

[53]Damon C. Dodd, *The Free Will Baptist Story* (Nashville: Executive Department of the National Association of Free Will Baptists, 1956) 32-41, esp. 39; William Franklin Davidson, *An Early History of Free Will Baptists: The Original Free Will Baptists in America a Continuing Witness from Infancy to Identity (1727–1830)* (Nashville: Randall House, 1974) 8-17, 39-56. Davidson, 94-96, 182-85, has argued for the continuity of Southern Free Will Baptists out of the initial General Baptist movement.

[54]Davidson, *An Early History of Free Will Baptists*, 97-130; Dodd, *The Free*

The Bethel Conference of Free Will Baptists in North Carolina adopted in 1812 on the basis of the authorized work of Jesse Heath and James Roach a thirteen-article confession of faith which was a revision of the Standard Confession (1660) of General Baptists in England. The articles on God the Father (1), the original state of human beings (4), God's desire for all humans to be saved (5), general atonement and the universal capacity for salvation (6), election on the basis of God's mercy rather than on foreseen faith of the elect (11), and apostasy (12) were virtually identical with those in the 1660 confession. To the article on Christology (2) were added references to Christ's second coming and final judgment. Whereas in 1660 the Holy Spirit was said to be the agent of sanctification and perseverance who honors the Father and the Son, now (3) the Spirit is said to quicken and draw sinners to God. The article on the Scriptures (7) was considerably shorter, but it added that they "are infallibly true," and the article on perseverance (10) was greatly abbreviated. The lengthy 1660 article on justification (8) was replaced by a brief affirmation of God's "general Provision" for all who repent and believe, and the article (13) on unbaptized infants who die during infancy not suffering in hell omitted the earlier rebuke of pedobaptists who hold to limited atonement.[55]

Another Freewill Baptist movement arose in New England. Benjamin Randall (1749–1808), who, having been converted by the news of the death of the Calvinist evangelist, George Whitefield, whose preaching he had just heard, and having left Congregationalism, sought believer's immersion, heeded a call to preach, and constituted in New Durham, New Hampshire, in 1780 the first Freewill Baptist congregation in New England.[56] Although Randall's separation from Calvinist Baptists was due to his rejection of

---

Will Baptist Story, 48-54; Michael R. Pelt, *A History of Original Free Will Baptists* (Mount Olive NC: Mount Olive College Press, 1996) 56-71, 102-107.

[55]Davidson, *An Early History of Free Will Baptists*, 172-81, based on *An Abstract of the Former Articles of Faith Confessed by the Original Baptist Church Holding the Doctrine of General Provision with a Proper Code of Discipline*, 2nd ed. (Newbern NC: Salmon Hall, 1814).

[56]Norman Allen Baxter, *History of the Freewill Baptists: A Study in New England Separatism* (Rochester NY: American Baptist Historical Society, 1957) 1-24; I. D. Stewart, *The History of the Freewill Baptists, for Half a Century*, vol. 1 (Dover NH: Freewill Baptist Printing, 1862) 32-73.

Calvinist doctrine, the movement which he founded did not produce theological writings until after his death.[57]

Samuel Shepard (1739–1815), the Calvinist pastor-physician who baptized Randall and joined with him in revival preaching, rejected the claims of Universalists that the nations of Matt. 25:32 are human lusts and sins, not persons, and that "eternal" (αἰώνιος) in the New Testament can refer to a limited duration of punishment.[58] Shepard, teaching a general atonement, went on to differentiate the "decreeative" will of God, which is "intentional, eternal, unalterable, but beyond our knowledge," from his "perceptive" will, which can be discerned through "proclamations, commands, precepts, and promises." The perceptive will provides all that one needs to accept or reject the gospel and "exhorts all men to repent."[59] Hosea Quinby (1804–1878) articulated against Calvinists certain basic distinctives of Freewill Baptists: (1) humans are depraved but not guilty of Adam's sin, and hence guilt is not imputed until one voluntarily rejects the gospel; (2) repentance precedes regeneration, and thus sinners are obliged to seek the Lord and pray to him; (3) God's predetermination of the damnation of the nonelect is to be rejected in favor of a conditional election; and (4) some true believers do commit a final apostasy.[60]

In 1832 the General Conference of Freewill Baptists authorized the preparation of a statement on doctrine and practice, and two years later it adopted and published the sixteen-article Treatise on the Faith of the Freewill Baptists. It included general Christian teachings (the attributes of God; creation; the primitive state, fall, and depravity; Christology; the Holy Spirit and the Trinity; and death, resurrection, and general judgment). Protestant doctrines (regeneration; justification; sanctification), and one Puritan doctrine (the Sabbath). It expressed specifically Arminian doctrines

---

[57]Baxter, *History of the Freewill Baptists*, 55-59.

[58]*The Principle of Universal Salvation Examined and Tried by the Law and Testimony, and Found to Be a Direct Contradiction to the Doctrine of Christ and His Inspired Witnesses* (Exeter NH: Henry Ranlet, 1798) esp. 4, 6-8, 10, 14-15, 17-18, 27.

[59]Baxter, *History of the Freewill Baptists*, 119-20, based on Shepard, *The Principle of Universal Salvation*, 27-36.

[60]*A Letter to the Rev. J. Butler, Containing a Review of His "Friendly Letters to a Lady," together with a General Outline of the Doctrine of the Freewill Baptists* (Limerick ME: Silas Curtis, 1832) Historical Commission of the SBC, microform publ. no. 4105 (1974), 24-38, 43-64, 88-140, 156-60.

(general atonement; general gospel call; repentance and faith as human responses as well as divine gifts; and uncertain perseverance). It articulated the Freewill Baptist ecclesiology (general church and particular churches; bishops or elders and deacons as officers; four ordinances: believer's immersion, commemorative Lord's Supper open to all believers, washing of feet of believers, and public worship).[61] The Treatise was revised by the General Conference in 1848, 1865, 1868, and 1889.[62] The 1889 revision added three new articles (the Holy Scriptures, divine government and providence,[63] and the second coming of Christ), rewrote articles or sections (sanctification, perseverance, Sabbath,[64] Lord's Supper, death,[65] and resurrection[66]) and condensed certain articles (gospel call, church offices).[67] In 1948 the National Association of Free Will Baptists, a Southern and Western body, adopted a slight revision of the 1889 revision.[68] It contained new articles on tithing and about infants dying in infancy not suffering in hell for the guilt of Adam's sin, and it reinserted a section on footwashing that was more complete than that of 1834. The articles on sanctification and on the church were rewritten,[69] and the articles on the Scriptures,[70] the Holy Spirit, and resurrection[71] slightly altered.[72]

The leading systematic theologian of the Freewill Baptists, John Jay Butler (1814–1891), in his *Natural and Revealed Theology*[73] explicated those doctrines which had been affirmed in the 1834 Treatise—those

---

[61]The text of the 1834 Treatise is given by McGlothlin, *Baptist Confessions of Faith*, 310-29. Each of the articles has its list of related biblical passages.

[62]*A Treatise on the Faith and Practice of the Free Baptists, . . . together with Usages of the Free Baptist Connection* (Boston: Morning Star, ca. 1889) 7-37.

[63]So as to specify God's foreknowledge but not his foreordination of all things.

[64]So as to specify first-day observance.

[65]So as to make the intermediate state more explicit.

[66]So as to make one general resurrection more explicit.

[67]*A Treatise on the Faith and Practice of the Free Baptists*, 7, 10-11, 35, 27-30, 33-35, 36, 23, 31-32.

[68]Lumpkin, *Baptist Confessions of Faith*, 369. Lumpkin, 369-76, included the 1948 text.

[69]Ibid., 375, 372, 376, 374, 375.

[70]So as to change "contain God's revealed will to man" to "are God's revealed word to man."

[71]So as to be less specific as to one general resurrection.

[72]Lumpkin, *Baptist Confessions of Faith*, 369, 372-73, 376.

[73](Dover NH: Freewill Baptist Printing, 1861).

affirmed generally by all Christians, those of a Protestant character, those essentially Arminian,[74] and those peculiarly Baptist. In distinction from the Treatise, Butler set forth an elaborate doctrine of revelation and the Scriptures[75] and added a chapter on the millennium that espoused postmillennialism.[76] Butler's treatment of baptism[77] and Quinby's booklet on baptism[78] were similar in content to English Particular Baptist treatments of an earlier time.

At a time when few General Baptist churches had survived in the United States, a new thrust of General Baptist churches, destined to spread in the Midwestern states, began with the ministry of Kentucky-born Benoni Stinson (1798–1869), who by 1823 had constituted Liberty Church in southern Indiana and the next year a Liberty Association.[79] The articles of faith of that church and association affirmed general atonement but retained the doctrine of perseverance of all saints. The church's articles also retained close communion.[80] In some other General Baptist associations the washing of disciples' feet was considered to be a third ordinance.[81] When the General Association of General Baptists was organized in 1870, its articles affirmed "that he that shall endure to the end, the same shall be saved."[82]

---

[74]In particular unconditional and conditional decrees and hence conditional election, free will as the "power of contrary choice" or "self-determination," nonimputational depravity, general atonement, and apostasy. Ibid., 152-53, 300, 166, 206-7, 225-29, 309-14.

[75]In particular authenticity, miracles, prophecy, difficulties, and inspiration. Ibid., 63-109.

[76]Ibid., 430-38.

[77]Ibid., 403-19.

[78]*A Short Examination of the Scriptural Subjects, Act, and Design of Christian Baptism* . . . (Dover NH: Trustees of the Freewill Baptist Connection, 1839).

[79]McBeth, *The Baptist Heritage*, 705; Theophilus Alexander Hall Laslie, *History of the General Baptists*, rev. by L. O. Roberts and E. Y. Laslie (Poplar Bluff MO: General Baptist Publishing House, 1938) 203-17.

[80]Laslie, *History of the General Baptists*, 206-207, 214; Ollie Latch, *History of the General Baptists* (Poplar Bluff MO: General Baptist, 1954) 123-24, 129-30. Articles 5, 6, and 9 in the church's articles; articles 5 and 11 in the association's articles.

[81]Laslie, *History of the General Baptists*, 216-17, 231-32, 267, 335, 355, 358; Latch, *History of the General Baptists*, 7.

[82]Latch, *History of the General Baptists*, 200. Art. 5.

Such a doctrine of apostasy was grounded on a concept of free will.[83] By 1954, if not earlier, an article espousing open communion had been added.[84] The General Baptists inclined toward a pre-Reformation "succession of truth" regarding antipedobaptism.[85]

Elhanan Winchester (1751–1797) and Universalism

Although the atonement teaching of General Baptists would seem logically to afford a more likely matrix for any Baptist to embrace the eschatological salvation of all human beings, it was a General Baptist who had embraced Calvinism, Elhanan Winchester, who became the first Baptist leader to espouse such universalism.[86] Winchester, a native of Massachusetts, after a pastorate and revival preaching in that state and a pastorate in South Carolina, accepted the pastorate of the First Church of Philadelphia in the autumn of 1780.[87] Winchester's gradual abandonment of Calvinism grew out of his evangelistic preaching, and his interest in universalism was fostered by reading while still in South Carolina Paul Siegvolck's[88] *The Everlasting Gospel . . .*[89] and by reading James Stonehouse's *Universal Restitution Vindicated against the Calvinists*[90] just after assuming the Philadelphia pastorate.[91] Winchester's espousal of universalism led to a division in the Philadelphia church with the result that in 1781 the opposition (minority) separated from Winchester and his supporters (majority),

---

[83]Robert F. Head, *Theology of General Baptists* (Poplar Bluff MO: General Baptist, 1963) 82-84.

[84]Latch, *History of the General Baptists*, 201-205. Art. 13. See also Head, *Theology of General Baptists*, 114-15.

[85]Laslie, *History of the General Baptists*, 136-38; Latch, *History of the General Baptists*, 74-75.

[86]Edwin Martin Stone, *Biography of Rev. Elhanan Winchester* (Boston: H. B. Brewster, 1836) 23; Joseph R. Sweeny, "Elhanan Winchester and the Universal Baptists" (Ph.D. diss., University of Pennsylvania, 1969) 23-24.

[87]Stone, *Biography*, 13, 23-29, 40-41, 53; Sweeny, "Elhanan Winchester and the Universal Baptists," 22-23, 25-27, 29, 35-36.

[88]Pseudonym for Georg Klein-Nicolai. Sweeny, "Elhanan Winchester and the Universal Baptists," 37n.45.

[89]Trans. from German by John Sechla (Germantown PA: Christopher Sower, 1753; also London, 1792).

[90](Bristol, London, 1773).

[91]Stone, *Biography*, 34, 41-42; Sweeny, "Elhanan Winchester and the Universal Baptists," 36.

declared the pulpit vacant, and retained the meeting house. Both the Philadelphia and the Warren associations refuted universalism as erroneous and sustained the church. Winchester, continuing to lead his Society of Universal Baptists in Philadelphia, allied himself with such Universalist leaders as John Murray in America and William Vidler in England.[92]

Winchester asserted from the protevangelium (Gen. 3:15) that the promise that the seed of the woman would bruise the serpent's head was made on the supposition of "universal Restoration" and cannot be fulfilled without such.[93] His collection of biblical texts alleged to support universalism was drawn more from the Old Testament prophets (Hosea, Isaiah, Jeremiah, Ezekiel, and Zechariah) and included passages affirming the restoration of Israel or Judah.[94] Winchester's case was built on the love of God as central attribute, general atonement, and inclusive salvation.[95] He insisted that the New Testament, especially Paul,[96] teaches both "*particular* redemption" and "*general* redemption," and hence these are not alternatives. Refusing to take either the label "Calvinist" or "Arminian" and holding that both camps are right on some matters and likely wrong on others, Winchester declared that he wanted "to be called a Christian."[97] The "all men" texts in the New Testament are never used "in a limited sense,"[98] but the word "everlasting" in both testaments, he argued, is sometimes used "in a limited sense."[99] The punishment of unquenchable fire will cease when Christ shall deliver the kingdom to the Father, and the great gulf that is impassable shall have been passed by Christ when he has preached to the

---

[92]Stone, *Biography*, 53-57, 76-94, 209-12; Sweeny, "Elhanan Winchester and the Universal Baptists," 41-49.

[93]*The Seed of the Woman Bruising the Serpent's Head*... (Philadelphia, 1783), BBM/BM, microform no. 4264, reel 5, item 42, p. 7.

[94]*An Attempt to Collect the Scripture Passages in Favour of the Universal Restoration, as Connected with the Doctrine of Rewards and Punishments* . . . (Providence, 1786) BBM/BM, microform no 4264, reel 5, item 40, passim.

[95]Ibid., 5-23.

[96]He declared that both are also taught in 1 John 2:1-2, 1 Pet. 2:9, and James 1:18. *The Gospel Preached by the Apostles, and Especially St. Paul . . . Proving that This Great Apostle Held, and Taught, Both Particular and General Redemption and Salvation* 2nd ed. (London, 1788) 17-21.

[97]Ibid., 11.

[98]Ibid., 13-17; *The Universal Restoration, Exhibited in Four Dialogues between a Minister and His Friend*... (Philadelphia: T. Dobson, 1792) 38-40.

[99]*The Universal Restoration*, 2-31.

spirits in prison. Belief in universal restoration does not, as charged, encourage wicked living but fosters godliness. Limited punishment is more restraining than endless punishment, and the doctrine of hell is the major cause of disagreement among Christians. Winchester declared that annihilationism is unbiblical and answered the argument that sin as infinite deserves infinite punishment by saying that it destroys the degrees of sin.[100] In his reply to Dan Taylor, the English General Baptist, Winchester, after examining in detail the uses of αἰών and αἰώνιος in the New Testament, concluded that "age" and "age-lasting" are the basic meanings, so as to eliminate any concept of "endless damnation."[101]

Of lesser significance for the later course of Baptist theology were Winchester's defense of the deity of Christ[102] and his premillennialism with its expectation of the Turks' capture of Jerusalem and their subsequent defeat.[103]

Kehukee and New Hampshire Confessions of Faith

American Calvinistic Baptists, both North and South, toward the latter half of the eighteenth century and the first half of the nineteenth at times found it needful and expedient to compose new confessions of faith, especially in order to restate in new settings their beliefs on Calvinist-Arminian issues. Two examples in particular are noteworthy. One of these confessions was framed and adopted by a single association—probably the first such in America,[104] and its influence was largely limited to the Carolinas and Virginia. The other was framed and adopted by a state convention, a new nineteenth-century Baptist phenomenon, New Hampshire, and its influence was to be felt in states far removed from New England.

The Kehukee Association in North Carolina and Virginia "was formed in 1769 of churches which missionaries of the Philadelphia and Charleston Associations had helped build." These were Regular, or Calvinist, churches,

---

[100]Ibid., 57-58, 69-70, 93-98, 128-33, 143, 199-203.

[101]*The Restitution of All Things . . . Defended: Being an Attempt to Answer the Reverend Dan Taylor's Assertions and Re-Assertions in Favour of Endless Misery* (London, 1790) letter 1, esp. pp. 1, 5-6, 12, 18.

[102]*The Divinity of Christ, Proved from the Scriptures of the Old and New Testament* (Philadelphia, 1784), BBM/BM, microform no. 4264, reel 5, item 31.

[103]*A Course of Lectures on the Prophecies that Remain to Be Fulfilled . . .* (Norwich UK: John Trumbull and John Sterry, 1794), esp. 139-61.

[104]Lumpkin, *Baptist Confessions of Faith*, 354.

some of which had formerly been General Baptist churches. In the latter churches reception into membership of persons who had not clearly professed "conversion prior to baptism" had left a residual problem about the claim to a regenerate church membership. Concurrently the Separate Baptist churches of the area, being the product of the Great Awakening in New England, were reluctant to identify with the Regular Baptists because of the aforementioned issue of members "baptized in a state of unbelief" and other issues. In 1774 a majority of the Kehukee Association sought to institute a reform as to believer's baptism and church membership, but a minority objected and separated. On the other hand, several Separate churches united with the reforming Kehukee Association. In order to win back the dissident churches and to encourage Separate churches to affiliate, the association in 1777 adopted a newly composed, relatively brief seventeen-article confession of faith. It, according to Lumpkin, "was designed to meet the objections of the Separates to the Philadelphia Confession and, at the same time, to declare against Arminianism and lax disciplining standards" and hence "served as the principal instrument for restoring harmony to the" Kehukee churches.[105]

The new confession affirmed "particular" and "unconditional" election (art. 3), the guilt of all "the natural offspring" of Adam, who was "the federal head, or representative" of humanity, for Adam's sin and the resultant spiritual death (arts. 4-5), and the impotence of fallen human beings to keep God's law perfectly and to repent and believe without being drawn by the Holy Spirit (art. 6). Moreover, the elect in "God's appointed time" and through his means will be effectually called, justified by "the imputed righteousness of Jesus Christ," converted, sanctified, and kept unto final salvation (arts. 7-11). Believer's baptism was affirmed in contrast to being "sprinkled or dipped while in unbelief" (art. 12), and the two ordinances are to be administered by ordained ministers (art. 16). "Every church is independent in matters of discipline," and associations are to be advisory, not coercive (arts. 13, 17). One general resurrection, one general judgment, and eternal hell and heaven were affirmed (arts. 14-15).[106] During the Missionary-Antimissionary controversy of the 1820s, the majority of churches in the Kehukee Association, being missionary, seceded so that the

---

[105]Ibid., 353-54.
[106]Ibid., 355-57.

residual minority became the Kehukee Primitive Baptist Association. But the 1777 confession was never altered or revoked.[107]

The New Hampshire Baptist Convention, which had been organized in 1825,[108] in 1830 appointed a committee of three to prepare "a Declaration of Faith and Practice, together with a Covenant, as may be thought agreeable and consistent with the views of all churches in this state."[109] Certain twentieth-century scholars were convinced that the Arminianism of Freewill Baptists had caused the Calvinistic Baptists to "react to" the Freewill position[110] and to "revolt against" strict Calvinism so as to espouse a "modified"[111] Calvinism which needed to be expressed in a new confession. When the committee was unable to complete its work, the convention appointed I. Person to finish the task and report to the board of the convention. Person's draft was presented to the board in 1832 and referred to a committee consisting of Baron Stow, John Newton Brown (1803–1868),[112] Jonathan Going, and Person. That committee reported that the articles with "slight alterations" should be adopted by the board. The board, after authorizing Stow and Brown to undertake "further revision" and after more alterations, requested that Brown prepare a final copy. Such was presented to the board, approved, and "recommended to the churches for adoption" in 1833, the convention taking no further action.[113] The confes-

---

[107]Ibid., 354-55.

[108]William Hurlin, "The State Convention," in Hurlin, O. C. Sargent, and W. W. Wakeman, *The Baptists of New Hampshire* (Manchester NH: New Hampshire Baptist Convention, 1902) 19-23. At least two Calvinistic Baptist congregations in the state had previously composed and adopted confessions of faith: the church at Exeter in 1800 and the church at Sutton about 1822. *An Anthology of Early Baptists in New Hampshire*, ed. Terry L. Wolever (Springfield MO: Particular Baptist, 2001) 543-54, 517-23.

[109]New Hampshire Baptist Convention, *Minutes*, 1830, as quoted by Hurlin, "The New Hampshire Declaration of Faith," in *The Baptists of New Hampshire*, 51.

[110]Gilbert Rimel Englreth, "American Baptists and Their Confessions of Faith" (Ph.D. diss., Temple University, 1969) 282.

[111]Lumpkin, *Baptist Confessions of Faith*, 360.

[112]William Henry Brackney, *The Baptists*, Denominations in America 2 (Westport CT: Greenwood, 1988) 135.

[113]Hurlin, "The New Hampshire Confession of Faith," 51-57; Lumpkin, *Baptist Confessions of Faith*, 360; Englerth, "American Baptists and Their Confessions of Faith," 282-83, 284-85. No copies of the original printing of the confession seem to be extant.

sion originally consisted of sixteen articles. In 1853, while serving as editorial secretary of the American Baptist Publication Society, Brown "on his own authority" emended the confession and added two new articles, one on "Repentance and Faith" and the other on "Sanctification," so as to make a total of eighteen articles.[114] He published the revised confession in his *The Baptist Church Manual*,[115] and subsequently it was included in other Baptist church manuals, notably those by James Madison Pendleton (1811–1891)[116] and by Edward Thurston Hiscox (1814–1901).[117] This confession, apart from Brown's work, "might never have been known outside of New Hampshire,"[118] but it became "perhaps the most widely used and influential statement of doctrine among American Baptists" at the beginning of the twentieth century.[119]

The New Hampshire Confession began with an article on "the Scriptures," not with an article on God.[120] It was destined to be utilized, analyzed, and discussed until the advent of the twenty-first century.

> We believe the Bible was written by men divinely inspired, and is a perfect treasure of heavenly instruction; that it has God for its author, salvation for its end, and truth, without any mixture of error, for its matter; that it reveals the principles by which God will judge us; and therefore is, and shall remain to the end of the world, the true centre of Christian union, and the supreme standard by which all human conduct, creeds, and opinions, should be tried.[121]

---

[114]Hurlin, "The New Hampshire Confession of Faith," 57; Lumpkin, *Baptist Confessions of Faith*, 360-61; Englerth, "American Baptists and Their Confessions of Faith," 285.

[115](Philadelphia: American Baptist Publication Society, 1853) 5-22.

[116]*Church Manual: Designed for the Use of Baptist Churches* (Philadelphia: American Baptist Publication Society, 1867) 44-61.

[117]*The Baptist Church Directory: A Guide to the Doctrines and Discipline, Officers and Ordinances, Principles and Practices, of Baptist Churches* (New York: Sheldon and Co., 1860) 154-75.

[118]Lumpkin, *Baptist Confessions of Faith*, 360.

[119]McGlothlin, *Baptist Confessions of Faith*, 299.

[120]Torbet, *A History of the Baptists*, 475-76.

[121]McGlothlin, *Baptist Confessions of Faith*, 301-302; Lumpkin, *Baptist Confessions of Faith*, 361-62. G. Hugh Wamble, Letter to Editor, *Baptist Standard*, 17 September 1986, 2, traced the words "it has God for its author . . . for its matter" to a letter written in 1703 by John Locke (1632–1704). *The Works of John Locke*, 10 vols., 11th ed. (London: W. Otridge and Sons, 1812) 10:306. Per Paul L. Gritz.

The doctrine of God (art. 2)[122] is Trinitarian,[123] but there is no accompanying article on the person of Christ or on the person and work of the Holy Spirit. The article on the church (art. 13) mentions only a "visible" or particular church and is silent as to the universal church—a fact that made the New Hampshire Confession quite acceptable to Landmark Baptists.[124] A church's "proper officers" are "Bishops or Pastors, and Deacons." Baptism (art. 14) is "the immersion of a believer in water" according to the Trinitarian formula, is the "emblem" of "our faith in a crucified, buried, and risen Saviour," and is prerequisite to church membership and to participation in the Lord's Supper, which is a commemoration by church members of "the dying love of Christ," "preceded always by solemn self-examination." The Lord's Day (art. 15) "is to be kept . . . by abstaining from secular labor and [secular] recreations; by the devout observance of all the means of grace," and by "preparation" for eternal rest. Civil government (art. 16) "is of divine appointment" and for the "good order of human society," and "magistrates are to be prayed for, conscientiously honored, and obeyed, except [only] in things opposed to the will of" Christ. The righteous and the wicked are to be distinguished "both in and after death" (art. 17), and Christ's second coming, one general resurrection, one general judgment, and endless separation in hell and in heaven were affirmed (art. 18).[125]

How does the New Hampshire Confession treat the Calvinist-Arminian issues and related matters? There are no articles on divine decrees or on providence, as in the Philadelphia Confession (art. 3).[126] Whereas the Philadelphia Confession (art. 6) taught that to all humankind was imputed not only depravity but also the guilt of the sin of Adam and Eve,[127] the New Hampshire Confession teaches (art. 3) that in "consequence" of the sin of

---

[122]Article numbers will be those of the 1853 edition; bracketed words have been added in the 1853 edition.

[123]McGlothlin, *Baptist Confessions of Faith*, 302; Lumpkin, *Baptist Confessions of Faith*, 362.

[124]Lumpkin, *Baptist Confessions of Faith*, 361; Englerth, "American Baptists and Their Confessions of Faith," 293-95.

[125]McGlothlin, *Baptist Confessions of Faith*, 302, 305-307; Lumpkin, *Baptist Confessions of Faith*, 362, 365-67.

[126]McGlothlin, *Baptist Confessions of Faith*, 233-34, 235-37; Lumpkin, *Baptist Confessions of Faith*, 254-55, 256-58.

[127]McGlothlin, *Baptist Confessions of Faith*, 237-38; Lumpkin, *Baptist Confessions of Faith*, 258-59.

Adam and Eve "all mankind are now sinners, not by constraint but choice" as depraved persons "under just condemnation to eternal ruin."[128] In treating the atoning work (art. 4) of Christ the New Hampshire Confession avoids any statement as to particular or universal atonement by referring to "atonement for our sins by his death."[129] Justification (art. 5) is essentially divine pardon "solely through" Christ's "redemption and righteousness," and regeneration (art. 7) is the incomprehensible gift of "a holy disposition to the mind" "by the power of the Holy Spirit."[130] Since "the blessings of salvation are made free to all by the Gospel, . . . it is the immediate duty of all to accept them by . . . faith." Hence "nothing prevents," including a decree of reprobation, "the salvation of the greatest sinner on earth except his own [inherent depravity and] voluntary refusal to submit to" Christ (art. 6).[131] Repentance and faith (art. 8) are given a both/and definition in that they "are sacred duties, and also inseparable graces, wrought in our souls by the regeneratng Spirit of God."[132] Election, treated late in the confession (art. 9), is "the gracious purpose of God, according to which he . . . regenerates, sanctifies, and saves sinners," this "being perfectly consistent with the free agency of man," encompassing the God-appointed "means," and providing "the foundation of Christian assurance."[133] Sanctification (art. 10) is "the process" or "progressive work" "by which . . . we are made partakers of" God's "holiness" through the agency of the Holy Spirit and the "use of the appointed means," and the inability of "fallen men" to fulfill the law of God is remedied through the mediatorship of Christ as "the one great end of the Gospel" (art. 12).[134] In contrast to the Philadelphia

---

[128]McGlothlin, *Baptist Confessions of Faith*, 302; Lumpkin, *Baptist Confessions of Faith*, 362.

[129]McGlothlin, *Baptist Confessions of Faith*, 302-303; Lumpkin, *Baptist Confessions of Faith*, 362-63.

[130]McGlothlin, *Baptist Confessions of Faith*, 303-304; Lumpkin, *Baptist Confessions of Faith*, 363-64.

[131]McGlothlin, *Baptist Confessions of Faith*, 303; Lumpkin, *Baptist Confessions of Faith*, 363.

[132]McGlothlin, *Baptist Confessions of Faith*, 304; Lumpkin, *Baptist Confessions of Faith*, 364.

[133]McGlothlin, *Baptist Confessions of Faith*, 304; Lumpkin, *Baptist Confessions of Faith*, 364.

[134]McGlothlin, *Baptist Confessions of Faith*, 305; Lumpkin, *Baptist Confessions of Faith*, 365.

Confession's basing perseverance of the saints (art. 17) on "the immutability of the decree of Election" and "the efficacy of the merit and intercession of Jesus Christ and Union with him,"[135] the New Hampshire Confession affirms that "such only are real believers as endure to the end; that their persevering attachment to Christ is the grand mark which distinguishes them from mere professors" of faith; and "[that] they are kept by the power of God through faith unto salvation" (art. 11).[136]

Lumpkin identified the theology of the New Hampshire Confession as that of a "very moderate" Calvinism,[137] and McGlothlin had used the same words "very moderately Calvinistic," while expressing doubt as to whether the confession "ought to be called Calvinistic."[138] Since the confession is silent as to the extent of the atonement, interprets repentance and faith as both human duties and divine graces, gives no indication of teaching irresistible grace, does not interpret election as God's choice from eternity of particular human beings for salvation, and interprets perseverance both in terms of endurance to the end and being kept by the power of God, one can conclude that the label "moderately Arminian" would be as accurate as the term "moderately Calvinistic."

Francis Wayland (1796–1865)

The emphasis of the New Hampshire Confession on the local or particular church with its silence as to the universal church found advocacy by another New England Baptist, Francis Wayland. The son of a business man turned Baptist pastor and a graduate of Union College who had one year of study at Andover (Congregational) Theological Seminary under its biblical scholar, Moses Stuart, Wayland served as pastor of First Baptist Church, Boston (1821–1826) before assuming the presidency of Brown University (1827–1855).[139]

---

[135]McGlothlin, *Baptist Confessions of Faith*, 251-53; Lumpkin, *Baptist Confessions of Faith*, 272-74.

[136]McGlothlin, *Baptist Confessions of Faith*, 305; Lumpkin, *Baptist Confessions of Faith*, 365. Oates Charles Symonds Wallace (1856–1947) produced an interpretative commentary on the New Hampshire Confession: *What Baptists Believe: The New Hampshire Confession: An Exposition* (Nashville: Sunday School Board of the SBC, 1913; abridged and rev. ed., 1934).

[137]*Baptist Confessions of Faith*, 360.

[138]*Baptist Confessions of Faith*, 299.

[139]Francis Wayland [Jr.] and H. L. Wayland, *A Memoir of the Life and Labors of Francis Wayland, D.D., LL.D.*, vol. 1 (New York: Sheldon and Co., 1867) 11-

Wayland in his *Notes on the Principles and Practices of Baptist Churches*[140] advocated the "independence" of the churches as a basic Baptist tenet.

> By this, we mean that every church of Christ, that is, every company of believers united together according to the laws of Christ, is wholly independent of every other; that every church is perfectly capable of self-government; and that, therefore, no one acknowledges any higher authority, under Christ, than itself; that with the church all ecclesiastical action commences, and with it it terminates, and hence, that the ecclesiastical relations proper, of every member, are limited to the church to which he belongs.[141]

Wayland defended church independence on several grounds: (1) that religion "concerns exclusively the relations between an individual and his Maker"; (2) how God desires human beings to serve him "must be made known to us by God himself"; (3) in the New Testament we have God's "perfect rule of duty"; (4) "every individual is under obligation to understand" God's revelation "for himself" and "govern his conduct" accordingly; and (5) church members are obligated to the laws of Christ, but they have no "power of original legislation over each other."[142] Hence, for Wayland, the only bond that unites Baptists in various congregations is their love for Christ,[143] there being no ecclesiological bond. Baptist associations, state conventions, and/or societies, therefore, are not to be composed of "representatives" from Baptist churches but of financial contributors.[144] Wayland rejected the distinction and sometimes conflict in his day between

---

219; James Ormsbee Murray, *Francis Wayland* (Boston: Houghton, Mifflin, and Co., 1891) 1-114; Brackney, *The Baptists*, 278-79.

[140](New York: Sheldon, Blakeman, and Co., 1857).

[141]Ibid., 177-78.

[142]Ibid., 178-80.

[143]Ibid., 190-91.

[144]Ibid., 180-90. Winthrop S. Hudson, "Stumbling into Disorder," *Foundations* 1 (April 1958): 45-71, esp. 69-71, offered a strong critique of Wayland's role in the transformation of the "Triennial" Convention's representation basis of membership into the American Baptist Foreign Mission's Society lifetime individual membership by contribution, charging that Wayland misrepresented his own views as having been commonly held by previous Baptists.

the "church" as the body of regenerate members and the society of pewholders, a practice that made possible larger meeting houses.[145]

Wayland's individualism and congregationalism were also made evident in his delineation of the Baptist distinctives: the "spirituality of the church" (that is, a regenerate membership); the priesthood of all believers as access to God without human mediators; "the absolute right of private judgment in all matters of religion"; "the perfect sufficiency of the Scriptures," especially the New Testament; the church as "wholly and absolutely independent of the civil power"; believer's baptism and the rejection of hereditary church membership; baptism by immersion; ministers as necessarily called by God and by a church; and the impossibility of a denomination-wide Baptist confession of faith in deference to adherence to "the *New Testament,* the *whole* New Testament, and *nothing but the* New Testament."[146]

Southern Calvinist Theologians: Patrick Hues Mell (1814–1888) and John Leadley Dagg (1796–1884)

The influence of Calvinism upon Baptist theology was extended through the nineteenth century, especially in the South, as can be seen from the writings of three Southern theologians: Patrick Hues Mell, John Leadley Dagg, and James Petigru Boyce, and their associates.

Mell, orphaned as a teenager and baptized at eighteen, studied for two years in Amherst College in Massachusetts with the support of a rich benefactor. Returning to Georgia and reaffirming his Christian faith after a period of doubt, he held the professorship of ancient languages at Mercer University, then located at Penfield, from 1841 to 1855, while concurrently serving as pastor of rural Baptist churches, but in 1855 he resigned from Mercer after conflict with the newly elected president. In 1857 Mell became professor of ancient languages at the University of Georgia at Athens; subsequently he was professor of ethics and metaphysics, vice chancellor (1860–1872) and chancellor (1878–1887). He served as moderator of the Georgia Baptist Association for 28 years, as president of the Georgia Baptist Convention for 24 years, and as president of the Southern Baptist Convention for 14 years, while becoming increasingly recognized as a

---

[145]*Notes on the Principles and Practices of Baptist Churches*, 165-71. Pewholders paid for the use of their pews but were not necessarily church members.

[146]Ibid., 130-31, 140-41, 131-38, 93-99, 87-92, 106-13, 13-16, 85-86.

skilled parliamentarian. He was the author of "popular tracts and essays" on Calvinistic doctrine, baptism, and church discipline.[147]

Mell wrote in response to the anti-Calvinist sermons in Georgia by Russell Reneau, which focused on predestination and perseverance, and because he deplored the public neglect by pastors of "the doctrines of Grace," which neglect he traced to their false conclusion that "the doctrines of Grace are synonymous with Antinomianism."[148] Mell adopted the definition of "predestination" which had been framed by the Italian-born Reformed theologian Jerome Zanchi (1516–1590), which definition applies to what other theologians have called "foreordination":

> Predestination is that eternal, most wise, and immutable decree of God, whereby he did, form before all time, determine and ordain to create, dispose of, and direct to some particular end, every person and thing to which he has given, or is yet to give, being; and to make the whole creation subservient to, and declarative of, his own glory.[149]

Mell's doctrine was based on God's knowledge of "not only all things that have existed" but also of "all things possible," and hence God ordained this kind of world. Mell declared that moral evil came into the world as designed by God and yet denied that God is "the author of sin." Such moral evil was foreseen and permitted by God. Predestination, moreover, applies both to the election and the nonelection of human beings to salvation. Election was not based on God's foreseeing of the faith of the elect but was "an immutable decree" and yet did envision the means of its implementation. Nonelection, according to Mell, consists of God's passing over such as are nonelect (preterition) and God's condemnation and punishment of the nonelect. Predestination does not destroy human free agency but rather establishes free agency, Mell argued, citing biblical examples.[150] Later Mell

---

[147]P. H. Mell, Jr., *Life of Patrick Hues Mell* (Louisville: Baptist Book Concern, 1895); Paul A. Basden, "Patrick Hues Mell," in *Baptist Theologians*, ed. George and Dockery, 205-206; P. H. Mell, *Predestination and the Saints' Perseverance, Stated and Defended* . . . (repr.: [Fort Worth TX]: Wicket Gate, 1983?) 3-4.

[148]*Predestination and the Saints' Perseverance, Stated and Defended* . . . (Charleston SC: Southern Baptist Publication Society, 1851) iii-iv.

[149]Ibid., 22-23; Jerome Zanchius, *The Doctrine of Absolute Predestination Stated and Asserted*, trans. Augustus Montague Toplady (London: Sovereign Grace Union, 1930; repr.: Grand Rapids MI: Baker Book House, 1977) 83. Mell's word "form" (line 2) is "from" in the translation of Zanchius (p. 83).

[150]*Predestination and the Saints' Perseverance* (1851), 23, 24, 37-38, 26-27,

more explicitly defined the differentiating characteristic of Calvinism as "God's sovereignty over all things, sin not excepted," in that his will "is shown either efficiently or permissively in all existences and all events on earth." Calvinism, Mell asserted, is "a sovereign remedy" for "two great heresies," namely "ritualism" and "rationalism."[151]

Mell's treatment of perseverance was brief, perhaps because for him it was a derivative divine decree. He taught that Christians do not "totally fall" from grace, he sought to show that King David did not totally fall, he taught that Christians do not "finally fall," and he asserted that Judas Iscariot, Hymenaeus, and Alexander were never Christians.[152]

The Georgia theologian's exposition of Christian baptism[153] was not unlike that of his Baptist predecessors who had written about baptism. But he did employ his lexical skill on the usages of *baptizein*, equate the baptism of John the Baptist with Christian baptism, argue principally from the Scriptures, and answer various objections to believer's baptism by immersion such as the "abhorrence of the bigotry and exclusiveness" of the Baptists and "The Baptists make immersion a saving ordinance."[154]

Majoring on the corrective aspects of church discipline, Mell sharply differentiated "private offences" from "public offenses" and the "universal" church as unorganized from the "local" church and counseled pastors how to conduct themselves with respect to corrective discipline. He held to unanimity as the ideal, to the prevailing of the majority when divided, and to the right of the minority to declare that the majority is no longer "a Baptist church." Excommunicated members should not seek or obtain

---

24, 53, 49-50, 47-49.

[151]*Calvinism: An Essay Read before the Georgia Baptist Ministers' Institute, at Marietta, GA, August 13, 1868* (Atlanta: George C. Connor, 1868; Savannah GA: J. H. Estill, 1875) 3, 12.

[152]*Predestination and the Saints' Perseverance* (1851) 72-92. Mell argued against final apostasy from "the perfections of God," "the immutability of His decrees," "the covenant of redemption" (Father, Son, Spirit), "the covenant of grace," the full payment of Christ's atonement, the intercession by Christ, and "the distinct and explicit declarations" of the Bible (67). Nettles, *By His Grace and for His Glory*, 184, has interpreted Mell as having taught that the atonement was limited as to its intention (efficient) but infinite as to its merit (sufficient).

[153]*Baptism in Its Mode and Subjects* (Charleston SC: Southern Baptist Publication Society, 1853).

[154]Ibid., 7-18, 61-80, 299, 172-89, 195-97.

redress from an association, and ordained ministers, when accused, can be tried by the congregation without assistance of a presbytery.[155]

A more complete body of theological writings expressive of Baptist Calvinism came from the pen of John Leadley Dagg. Born in Middleburg, Virginia, Dagg was converted at fifteen and after coming to Baptist convictions was baptized at eighteen. Soon orphaned, he was ordained to the pastoral ministry at 23, and despite limited formal education persisted to learn Greek, Hebrew, and Latin. After pastorates in Virginia he served the Fifth Baptist Church in Philadelphia (1825–1834), and subsequently he was president of Haddington Institute in Philadelphia (1834–1836) and of Alabama Female Athenaeum (1836–1844) at Tuscaloosa. In 1844 Dagg became professor of theology in and president of Mercer University in Penfield, Georgia. During his tenure Mercer began to offer theological degrees. In 1854 Dagg resigned[156] his presidency and two years later retired as professor.[157] Despite multiple physical infirmities during the next thirteen years Dagg wrote four major volumes that represented the systematic theological curriculum of his time: doctrine, *A Manual of Theology*;[158] ecclesiology, *A Treatise on Church Order*;[159] ethics, *The Elements of Moral*

---

[155]*Corrective Church Discipline: With a Development of the Scriptural Principles upon Which It Is Based* (Charleston SC: Southern Baptist Publication Society, 1860) 8-15, 48-61, 76-83, 118-22, 84-98.

[156]Robert G. Gardner, "John Leadley Dagg: Pioneer American Baptist Theologian" (Ph.D. diss., Duke University, 1957) 23n.44, has concluded that the trustees asked for Dagg's resignation.

[157][John L. Dagg], *Autobiography of Rev. John L. Dagg, D.D.* (Rome GA: J. F. Shanklin, 1886); Gardner, "John Leadley Dagg: Pioneer," 2-49; Mark E. Dever, "John L. Dagg," in *Baptist Theologians*, ed. George and Dockery, 165-66; Nettles, *By His Grace and for His Glory*, 168.

[158](Charleston SC: Southern Baptist Publication Society, 1857; Philadelphia: American Baptist Publication Society, 1871; Harrisonburg VA: Gano Books, 1982). This volume was used as a text by James P. Boyce during the earliest years (1859–1861 or up to 1869) of the Southern Baptist Theological Seminary in Greenville SC. Dever, "John L. Dagg," 185n.9; Gardner, "John Leadley Dagg," *Review and Expositor* 54 (April 1957): 262.

[159](Charleston SC: Southern Baptist Publication Society, 1858; Philadelphia: American Baptist Publication Society, 1871; Harrisonburg VA: Gano Books, 1982).

Science;[160] and apologetics, *The Evidences of Christianity*.[161] Dagg helped to establish and/or strongly supported various Baptist denominational entities.[162]

Dagg began *A Manual of Theology* by affirming the obligation to approach religious truth not with curiosity or for speculation but in the awareness of human immortality and moral government. The sources of religious knowledge are twofold: "Natural Religion," consisting of "our moral and religious feelings" (conscience), those "feelings of our fellow-man," and "the course of Nature" "(the predictable results of certain behavior), and "Divine Revelation," consisting of the Old and the New Testaments.[163] Natural religion teaches God's existence,[164] a "code of ethics,"[165] and final judgment and immortality.[166] But natural religion, as Robert Gardner noted, has for Dagg "four major defects": "it is insufficient to restore man to perfect virtue";[167] it "is defective in its mode of teaching";[168] it "is inadequate in the content of its teaching";[169] and its "insufficiency" is proved by the granting of divine revelation.[170] E. Brooks

---

[160](New York: Sheldon and Co., 1859; Macon GA: J. W. Burke and Co., 1883; rev. ed., 1888).

[161](Macon GA: J. W. Burke and Co.; Philadelphia: Claxton, Remsen, and Haftelfinger, 1869). See also Thomas E. Cuttino, "A Study of the Theological Works of John Leadly [*sic*] Dagg" (Th.M. thesis, Southern Baptist Theological Seminary, 1954).

[162]Notably the General Association of Baptists in Virginia, the "Triennial" Convention, the Philadelphia Baptist Missionary Society, the Baptist General Tract Society, the American Baptist Home Mission Society, the Alabama Baptist State Convention, the Georgia Baptist Convention, and the Southern Baptist Convention. Gardner, "John Leadley Dagg," 265-38.

[163]*A Manual of Theology*, 13-23.

[164]Ibid., 50-53.

[165]*The Elements of Moral Science*, 101-109.

[166]*The Elements of Moral Science*, 108, 112; *A Manual of Theology*, 341, 364-65; Robert G. Gardner, " 'The Bible . . . A Revelation from God, Supplying the Defects of Natural Religion,' " *Foundations* 4 (July 1961): 243-45.

[167]*A Treatise on Church Order*, 160-61; *The Elements of Moral Science*, 113; *The Evidences of Christianity*, 68-69.

[168]*The Elements of Moral Science*, 114-15.

[169]Ibid., 117-18; *The Evidences of Christianity*, 68-71.

[170]*The Elements of Moral Science*, 115-16; Gardner, " 'The Bible . . . a Revelation from God,' " 245-46.

Holifield, despite Dagg's tendency to theologize solely from biblical texts and to "restrain . . . philosophy within due bounds,"[171] has concluded that Dagg was influenced by the Scottish Common Sense Realism of Thomas Reid (1710–1796) and John Witherspoon (1723–1794) not only in respect to piety and the duties corresponding to each Christian doctrine but also in defense of the bondage of the will and the need for repentance.[172] Similarly, Mark E. Matheson has argued that Dagg had an epistemological debt to Scottish Realism in four aspects: his "methodological" emphasis on empiricism and the usefulness of the sciences; his "empirical-psychological emphasis" with "self-evident principles"; his "commonsensical-rationalistic emphasis" that veered toward individualism and anthropocentrism; and his "moralistic emphasis" relative to conscience and a moral order.[173]

Dagg's doctrine of the Bible, as first expressed in a pamphlet in 1853, focused on the divine "origin" and essential "authority" of the Scriptures. The divine origin was, for Dagg, proved by the character of its revelation of God, by the "blessings" which the Bible has conferred on humanity, by the attestation of its miracles, and by the fulfilment of its prophecies.[174] As to its authority,

> The Bible contains the *testimony* of God, and is therefore a Rule of *Faith.* . . . The Bible contains the *precepts* of God, and is therefore a Rule of *Duty.* . . . The Bible contains the *promises* of God, and is therefore a Rule of *Hope.*[175]

Its authority is *"supreme," "independent,"* and *"immediate."* Dagg espoused the "plenary" view of biblical inspiration, according to which the human authors were conscious and employed their memories and "mental powers," but the transcription, preservation, and translation of the Bible have been providential but not miraculous.[176] Dagg's *The Evidences of Christianity*

---

[171]*A Manual of Theology*, 133.

[172]Holifield, *The Gentlemen Theologians: American Theology in Southern Culture, 1795–1860* (Durham NC: Duke University Press, 1978) 120, 122-25.

[173]"Religious Knowledge in the Theologies of John Leadley Dagg and James Petigru Boyce: With Special Reference to the Influence of Common Sense Realism" (Ph.D. diss., Southwestern Baptist Theological Seminary, 1984) 135-39.

[174]*Origin and Authority of the Bible* (Charleston SC: Southern Baptist Publication Society; Richmond VA: Virginia Baptist Sunday School and Publication Society, 1853) 3-27; incorporated into *A Manual of Theology*, 26-39.

[175]Ibid., 28-29; ibid., 40.

[176]Ibid., 29-32; ibid., 40-42.

was essentially the use of the Bible as the central Christian apologetic. He set forth its "prominent singularities," its "beneficial effects," its "perfect morality," and its "superhuman doctrine"[177] before defending the historical credibility of the four Gospels and Acts and elaborating on prophecy,[178] miracles, authenticity, and inspiration.[179] Finally Dagg sought to show how the Bible is in harmony with geography, natural history, astronomy, geology,[180] and anthropology.[181] Dwight A. Moody has concluded that Dagg provided no "discussion of the nature of revelation" but assumed that "revelation" is "a body of religious information communicated from God to humankind," that Dagg held that divine revelation "can be rationally and logically demonstrated," that Dagg was ambigious as to any "distinction between revelation and inspiration," that Dagg took "plenary inspiration" to mean verbal inspiration wherein the human author is deemphasized and God elevated, and that Dagg used "infallibility" to mean inerrancy.[182]

Dagg's doctrine of God as Father, Son, and Holy Spirit presents little that is distinctive to Dagg. God's existence is affirmed on the basis of natural religion as well as the Scriptures, and the attributes of God treated by Dagg are predominantly what E. Y. Mullins[183] would call "natural" rather than "moral" attributes. God's "will of purpose," which refers to God's own actions and "always takes effect," is differentiated from the "will of command," which "refers to the actions of his creatures" and may fail "to take effect." Providence includes God's preservation of that which has been created and sovereign rule over nature and creatures, including sin, and "moral necessity" is favored instead of "absolute contingency."[184]

Dagg's treatment of the person of Christ is classical with much more attention being given to the "divinity" than to the humanity or the union of

---

[177] *The Evidences of Christianity*, 13-83.

[178] Especially the prophecies in the New Testament book of Revelation.

[179] *The Evidences of Christianity*, 84-230.

[180] Dagg posited pre-Adamite beings and interpreted the "days" of Genesis 1 to refer to "a long geological period." Ibid., 242-48, 250-51.

[181] Ibid., 231-70.

[182] "Doctrines of Inspiration in the Southern Baptist Theological Tradition" (Ph.D. diss., Southern Baptist Theological Seminary, 1982) 36, 39, 38, 42, 44-45, 46-47.

[183] *The Christian Religion in Its Doctrinal Expression* (Philadelphia: Roger Williams, 1917) 223-43.

[184] *A Manual of Theology*, 50-94, 99-137.

natures. The states of Christ are three (original glory, humiliation, and exaltation), and the offices of the Mediator likewise three (prophet, priest, king).[185] The exposition of the Holy Spirit is limited to the Spirit's "personality" and "divinity" and to the singular "office of the Spirit" as "the Sanctifier and Comforter of God's people."[186] Dagg's brief discussion of the Trinity does include refutation of modalism and tritheism, but not of unitarianism, and acceptance of nonbiblical terms such as "Trinity" and "person," but, following Dagg's aversion to the history of Christian doctrine, his exposition in lacking is depth and clarity.[187]

Dagg's doctrines of man and sin were indebted to the Augustinian-Calvinist lineage and to the Continental Reformed and English Puritan theologians. His understanding of the *imago Dei* was pluriform; it included "mental endowments," "dominion . . . over all inferior creatures," "spirituality," and "immortality."[188] God made a "covenant of *works*"[189] with Adam, Dagg asserted, citing Hos. 6:7. The fall was historical, not "mythical." Dagg was certain that the fall brought spiritual death but not so certain that it brought physical death.[190] All humans have sinned, and human depravity is total, universal, and "natural" (that is, unacquired) and passes from parent to child.[191] Adam was the federal head of the human race, and all humans are bound to him by a moral union and a natural union as well as a federal

---

[185]Ibid., 179-229. See also Gardner, "John Leadley Dagg: Pioneer," 151-59, 164-76.

[186]*A Manual of Theology*, 236-43. See also Dever, "John L. Dagg," 171.

[187]*A Manual of Theology*, 246-53.

[188]Ibid., 141-44. Leighton Paige Patterson, "An Evaluation of the Soteriological Thought of John Leadley Dagg, Baptist Theologian of Nineteenth-Century America" (Th.D. diss., New Orleans Baptist Theological Seminary, 1973) 57, on the basis of all of Dagg's writings has concluded that he was seemingly a dichotomist.

[189]The concept of the covenant of works can be traced to the Reformed theologian and federalist, Johannes Cocceius (1603–1669). See Willem J. van Asselt, "Cocceius, Johannes (1603–1669)," in *The Dictionary of Historical Theology*, ed. Trevor A. Hart (Carlisle UK: Paternoster Press; Grand Rapids MI: Eerdmans, 2000) 131-33.

[190]*A Manual of Theology*, 144-50.

[191]Dagg also accepted the traducian view of the origin of human souls. Ibid., 155-56.

union. Adam's sin was imputed to all his descendants, and thus they cannot "free themselves" from "condemnation" or "depravity."[192]

How closely did Dagg adhere to the Calvinist tenets defended by the Synod of Dort? First, for Dagg, election is God's eternal choice by grace of "those only who will finally be saved" and that according to his foreknowledge and not on the basis of "foreseen faith and obedience."[193] Second, redemption "cannot have been universal in its purpose" because it "will not be universal in its consummation." Hence Christ's atonement is "particular," or limited to the elect.[194] Third, sovereignly "the Holy Spirit effectually calls all the elect to repent and believe," and thus God's grace is "efficacious" and not resistible by the elect.[195] Fourth, all those who have been regenerated will continue in sanctification until death, God's warnings to his people being a "part of the means" of the perseverance, and any "final apostasy" means "an absence of true religion."[196] Fifth, only with respect to repentance and faith did Dagg deviate from Dortian Calvinism by his identifying these more as human duties than as divine graces.[197] Only by his teaching an eternal "covenant of grace" made by the Father, the Son, and the Spirit did Dagg embrace one of the tenets of Hyper-Calvinism.[198]

For Dagg, the sacrificial death of Jesus was atoning, propitiatory, and substitutionary; indeed this doctrine "is the grand peculiarity of the Christian scheme."[199] The benefits of this great sacrifice are made available to the elect under Dagg's *ordo salutis*—from pardon and justification through adoption and regeneration to sanctification, final perseverance, and perfection.[200]

---

[192]Ibid., 150-71. See also Gardner, "John Leadley Dagg: Pioneer," 107-28, and Mark E. Dever, "Representative Aspects of the Theologies of John L. Dagg and James P. Boyce: Reformed Theology and Southern Baptists" (Th.M. thesis, Southern Baptist Theological Seminary, 1987) 39-53, 68-72.

[193]*Manual of Theology*, 309-23, esp. 309, 310, 312. Dagg discussed election not under the doctrine of God, but under soteriology and prior to eschatology.

[194]Ibid., 324-31, esp. 324.

[195]Ibid., 331-35.

[196]Ibid., 287-300, esp. 287, 296, 289.

[197]Ibid., 138-41, 175-78, 263.

[198]Ibid., 253-57. Dagg specifically rejected "justification in eternity past." Ibid., 274.

[199]Ibid., 210-19, esp. 211, 213.

[200]Ibid., 262-304. Dagg, using New Testament texts, the earliest church fathers, and John Calvin, had contended for a metaphorical, nonbaptismal, regenerational

Ecclesiology, according to Dagg, was a subject outside of but parallel to the scope of doctrinal theology. He clearly differentiated "local churches" from "the church universal." The Greek noun *ekklēsia* was used in the New Testament to refer to particular or local churches, not to a territorial or denominational body. Such local churches, composed solely of those who had repented, had believed in Christ, and had been baptized, were organized bodies, but each "was independent of every other church," and all were under the rule of Christ.[201] On the other hand, "the church universal is the whole company of those who are saved by Christ." It is "visible" because its members "are known by their profession of Christ and their obedience to his commands"; its unity is spiritual, and it "has no external organization"; and it is now under construction, "will be completed at the end of the world," and then, like the kingdom of God, "will endure forever."[202] Dagg's doctrine of the church universal was contrary to the denial of any such by the Landmark Baptists.[203] "Almost all" contemporary Baptists "except the Landmarkers" adopted "some form of this doctrine," Gardner, has contended, "but Dagg alone made extensive use of it."[204]

"Water baptism," Dagg held, "is a Christian ordinance of perpetual obligation" and not to be displaced by Spirit baptism. At great length[205] Dagg expounded, especially by word studies, that baptism is necessarily immersion. Baptism's only "proper subjects" are those "who repent of sin and believe in Christ," and it "was designed to be the ceremony of Christian

---

interpretation of John 3:5. *An Interpretation of John III:5* (Philadelphia: author, 1839) BBHRM/M, RP, microfilm publ. no. 946, reel 3, item 25.

[201] *A Treatise on Church Order*, 74-99.

[202] Ibid., 100-43, esp. 100, 121, 125, 128, 141-42, 137. Dagg specifically rejected "the distinction between the church visible and the church invisible" and any use of the term "the Visible Church Catholic." Ibid., 121, 130, 132.

[203] Especially Amos Cooper Dayton in his novel, *Theodosia Ernest: or, The Heroine of Faith* (Nashville: Graves, Marks, and Rutland; New York: Sheldon, Blakeman and Co., 1856). See below, 216n.16. See Gardner, "John Leadley Dagg: Pioneer," 306-16.

[204] "John Leadley Dagg," 246.

[205] Charles D. Phillips, "The Southern Baptist View of the Church: As Reflected in the Thought of J. L. Dagg, E. C. Dargan, and H. E. Dana" (Th.M. thesis, Southern Baptist Theological Seminary, 1957) 62-63, stated but did not demonstrate that Dagg's lengthy treatment of baptism was due to the impact of Campbellism and Landmarkism rather than to the various pedobaptist denominations.

profession."[206] Hence no infant baptism and no infant church membership are allowable.[207] Moreover, "the authority to administer baptism is conferred in the ordinary course of the ministerial succession," that is, by the call and by ordination, but not through what has been called "apostolic succession."[208] Bishops or pastors are "to teach and rule" the members of the congregation, and deacons are "to minister in secular affairs."[209] The Lord's Supper is to be observed publicly in Christ's churches and, contrary to Quakers, "till the end of the world." It was "designed to be a memorial" of Christ's death, "a representation that the communicant receives spiritual nourishment from" Christ, and "a token of fellowship among the communicants." Dagg defended strict, or close, communion, or the requirement that believer's baptism by immersion be required of all communicants.[210] The washing of disciples' feet was not "designed" as "a religious ceremony, but to enforce a whole class of moral duties."[211] The first day of the week, being "the Christian sabbath," "is specially appropriate for the public worship of God," and "public worship should include prayers, songs of praise, and the reading and expounding of God's word."[212]

Dagg's treatment of the last things includes the existence of immortal human souls after death either in paradise or with Satan and his servants, the resurrection of the changed bodies of all human beings,[213] the final judgment preceded by Christ's second coming, heaven, and hell, whose punitive suffering will be "eternal," nonpurifying, and nonannihilating.[214]

---

[206] *A Treatise on Church Order*, 13-73, esp. 13, 15-16, 21, 68, 70.

[207] Ibid., 144-202. Dagg turned a pedobaptist proof text, 1 Cor. 7:14, against pedobaptism by interpreting the children as children of the whole Corinthian congregation and the sanctification of the unbelieving spouse as the legitimacy of marital intercourse and by denying that the holiness of the children is an "effect" of the sanctification of the unbelieving parent. *A Decisive Argument against Infant Baptism, Furnished by One of Its Own Proof-Texts* (Charleston SC: Southern Baptist Publication Society, 1850) esp. 13, 15, 23, 49.

[208] Ibid., 254-62.

[209] Ibid., 263-67.

[210] Ibid., 203-25, esp. 203, 212, 205, 209, 214. Dagg had previously written *An Essay in Defence of Strict Communion* (Penfield GA: Benjamin Brantly, 1845).

[211] *A Treatise on Church Order*, 226-31, esp. 226.

[212] Ibid., 232-40, esp. 232, 238.

[213] Dagg inclined to but was not certain of the doctrine of one general resurrection of righteous and wicked at the same time. *A Manual of Theology*, 355.

[214] Ibid., 341-75.

Dagg's theology has been labelled by Thomas J. Nettles "moderate Calvinistic Augustinianism."[215] Dagg, according to Mark E. Dever, is "almost unsurpassed among Baptists as a doctor in the purpose of theology," if not in its content.[216] Robert G. Gardner found Dagg to have been "closer to Gill than to [Andrew] Fuller" and typical of Baptists in the pre-Civil War South at all major points with the single exception of his emphasis on the church universal.[217] Hence by his clear "maintenance" of Calvinism and his "rebuttal" of Landmarkism he was, according to Dever, defending "an earlier version of baptistic Christianity."[218]

Southern Calvinist Theology: The "Abstract of Principles" of the Southern Baptist Theological Seminary (1858) and James Petigru Boyce (1827–1888)

"The oldest effort within the Southern Baptist Convention to formulate what Baptists believe and teach is to be found in the Abstract of Principles of the Southern Baptist Theological Seminary," which was included in the institution's charter.[219] The seed for the Abstract of Principles for a "central theological school" for Southern Baptists[220] was James Petigru Boyce's 1856 inaugural address at Furman University in Greenville, South Carolina, entitled *Three Changes in Theological Institutions*.[221] The third of these changes was that there be "an Abstract of Principles, . . . which every professor . . . must sign when inaugurated, so as to guard against the rise of erroneous and injurious instruction. . . ."[222] Boyce argued that even as every congregation should have its "statement of doctrine" and every man to be

---

[215]"Preface" to Dagg, *A Manual of Theology* (1982) ii.

[216]"John L. Dagg," 182.

[217]"John Leadley Dagg: Pioneer," iv-v.

[218]"John L. Dagg," 181.

[219]Duke K. McCall, "What Southern Baptists Believe and Teach," *Sunday School Builder* 33 (December 1952): 4. This was true because the Southern Baptist Convention in its origin in 1845 had adopted no confessional statement.

[220]John A. Broadus, *Memoir of James Petigru Boyce, D.D., LL.D.* (New York: A. C. Armstrong and Son, 1893) 115.

[221]Subtitle: *An Inaugural Address Delivered before the Board of Trustees of the Furman University, the Night before the Annual Commencement, July 31, 1856* (Greenville SC: C. J. Elford, 1856). Reprinted in *James Petigru Boyce: Selected Writings*, ed. Timothy George (Nashville: Broadman, 1989) 29-59. Subsequent references are to this 1989 edition.

[222]Broadus, *Memoir of James Petigru Boyce*, 121.

ordained as a minister should be carefully examined, even more "we ought to ascertain and guard the doctrinal soundness of a theological instructor."[223] Moreover, according to Boyce, church history is replete with instances of error commencing with individual human beings having "power and ability."[224] Finally, the Abstract's adoption is "in perfect consistency with the position of Baptists, as well as of Bible Christians."[225] But such a subscribed confessional document was not the normal usage among Baptist institutions in the 1850s. Neither Newton Theological Institution nor Brown University nor Furman University employed such a document,[226] but Princeton Theological Seminary, in which both Boyce and Basil Manly, Jr. (1825–1892) had studied,[227] did employ such.[228]

In 1858 Boyce "assigned [to Manly] the task of drafting the confession," and after completing the draft Manly submitted it for considerable revision to a committee of the Southern Baptist Education Convention.[229] Of all the revisions the most thorough was seemingly in the article on "The Fall of Man," the content of which became less Augustinian and Calvinist.[230] It is worthy of note that the committee changed "infallible" to "authoritative" in respect to the Bible's being the "rule of all saving knowledge, faith and obedience" and changed under providence "God . . . willed all things that come to pass" to "God . . . decrees or permits all things that come to pass."[231] Manly had operated under three guidelines: (1) to set forth "the fundamental doctrines of grace"; (2) to explicate "the practices universally prevalent among us"; and (3) to take no position on any issue "upon which the denomination is divided."[232] Under the third guideline

---

[223] Ibid., 139.

[224] *Three Changes in Theological Institutions*, 51.

[225] Ibid., 56.

[226] Danny Martin West, "The Origin and Function of the Southern Baptist Theological Seminary's 'Abstract of Principles,' 1858–1859" (Th.M. thesis, Southern Baptist Theological Seminary, 1983) 40-42.

[227] William A. Mueller, *A History of Southern Baptist Theological Seminary* (Nashville: Broadman, 1959) 20, 88-89.

[228] West, "The Origin and Function," 16-18.

[229] See William Wright Barnes, *The Southern Baptist Convention, 1845–1953* (Nashville: Broadman, 1954) 129-33; Robert Andrew Baker, *The Southern Baptist Convention and Its People, 1607–1972* (Nashville: Broadman, 1974) 200-201.

[230] West, "The Origin and Function," 1, 22-35.

[231] Ibid., 26, 27.

[232] James P. Boyce, "Two Objections to the Seminary," *Western Recorder*, 20

Manly avoided either pro-Landmark or anti-Landmark[233] statements by defining "the Church" as "composed of all his [Christ's] true disciples" but not calling it "universal" or "invisible," by referring to "particular societies or churches," by affirming believer's baptism by immersion but not treating the question of "alien" or non-Baptist immersions, by prescribing close communion among the properly baptized but interpreting the Lord's Supper in terms of "communion" with Christ and "church fellowship."[234] But the third guideline did not permit any clear espousal of Arminian tenets. The Abstract contains a strong article on perseverance of the saints, a doctrine of eternal election of "some persons unto everlasting life," and reference to repentance as "an evangelical grace" and to "faith" as "wrought . . . by the Holy Spirit" and "accompanied by all other saving graces." Christ, however, died "for the salvation of sinners," but not specifically for the elect, and there is no allusion to irresistible grace.[235] Hence the label "moderately Calvinistic"[236] is appropriate for the Abstract.

Even so, the influence of the Second London Confession upon the Abstract was greater than that of the Westminster or the New Hampshire confessions.[237] The Abstract, in conclusion, was able to accomplish initially three purposes: to prevent heresy in the new seminary's faculty, for Boyce had even warned of heresy on the basis of Alexander Campbell's having "threatened at one time the total destruction of our [Baptist] faith,"[238] to

---

June 1874, 2, as incl. in *A Baptist Source Book: With Particular Reference to Southern Baptists*, ed. Robert A. Baker (Nashville: Broadman, 1966) 139-41.

[233]See above, 143, and below, 226, 235, 245.

[234]"Abstract of Principles," arts. 14-16.

[235]Ibid., arts. 13, 5, 9, 10, 7.

[236]David S. Dockery, "The Broadus-Robertson Tradition," in *Theologians of the Baptist Tradition*, ed. Timothy George and David S. Dockery (Nashville: Broadman & Holman, 2001) 103.

[237]Hence we differ from West, "The Origin and Function," 8, who stated that "both structurally and theologically, the Westminster Confession is the most important single document that influenced the 'Abstract of Principles.' " West's point as to structure may be valid, but the moderate Calvinism and the ecclesiological teachings of the Abstract do not support his conclusion.

[238]*Three Changes in Theological Institutions*, 51. But West, "The Origin and Function," 47-54, may have overplayed the idea that Manly and the committee deliberately sought to controvert Campbellite teaching because of the paucity of evidence in the text of the Abstract.

148 Baptist Theology

contribute to denominational unity, and to guarantee to its monetary contributors sound doctrinal instruction.[239]

But the seminary's chairman of faculty, Boyce, in his systematic theology exhibited even stauncher adherence to Dortian Calvinism than the Abstract of Principles.[240] Born in Charleston, South Carolina, the son of a wealthy business man and a Baptist mother, he had been under the pastoral influence of Basil Manly, Sr., and William Theophilus Brantly, Sr. Privileged as to formal education, Boyce studied at Charleston College, Brown University, during which time he was converted to Christ, and Princeton Theological Seminary, where his teachers included Charles Hodge. After a four-year pastorate in Columbia, South Carolina, and two years as professor of theology in Furman University, Boyce began in 1857 to engender support for and prepare for the opening of the Southern Baptist Theological Seminary in 1859. Administrative duties, especially the reopening after the Civil War and the removal from Greenville, South Carolina, to Louisville, Kentucky, in 1877, claimed much of Boyce's energies,[241] but his theological thought was ultimately incorporated in his textbook, *Abstract of Systematic Theology* (1882).[242]

Both Boyce[243] and the seminary's Abstract of Principles[244] strongly affirmed the perseverance of the saints and avoided the issue of irresistible grace. But Boyce set forth an explicit doctrine of reprobation, or double

---

[239]West, "The Origin and Function," 40-47.

[240]Z. T. Cody, "James Petigru Boyce," *Review and Expositor* 24 (April 1927): 160, called Boyce "a wholehearted Calvinist," and Timothy George, "James Petigru Boyce," in *Baptist Theologians*, ed. George and Dockery, 260, has identified him as "a strict (though no hyper-) Calvinist," but David M. Ramsey, *James Petigru Boyce: God's Gentleman* (Nashville: Sunday School Board of the SBC, 1924) 15, without supporting evidence declared that "Boyce accepted a somewhat modified form" of Calvinism.

[241]Broadus, *Memoir of James Petigru Boyce*, 1-303; Cody, "James Petigru Boyce," 145-66; George, "James Petigru Boyce," 249-55; George, "Soli Deo Gloria! The Life and Legacy of James Petigru Boyce," in George, ed., *James Petigru Boyce: Selected Writings*, 14-22.

[242]Two vols. (Louisville: C. T. Dearing, 1882); 1 vol. (Philadelphia: American Baptist Publication Society, 1887). Subsequent pagination is that of the 1887 edition.

[243]Ibid., 425-36 and passim. Although Boyce did not teach irresistible grace, he did expound effectual calling. Ibid., 371-73.

[244]Arts. 13, 8-11.

predestination,[245] whereas the Abstract alluded only to election "unto everlasting life,"[246] and Boyce expounded limited atonement, using the "sufficient"/"efficient" language,[247] whereas the Abstract was not specific as to limited atonement.[248] Only in respect to repentance and faith was the Abstract[249] more in line with the canons of Dort in that it denominated them "graces" while Boyce[250] called repentance a "duty" and stressed the triune God as the "object" of faith with no uses of "graces."

That Boyce was deeply indebted to Charles Hodge for his Dortian Calvinism has been established by Walter Wiley Richards.[251] Boyce specifically followed Hodge by utilizing the distinction between the "secretive" will of God, which is absolute and unchangeable, and the "preceptive will of God, which can be thwarted by creatures, by following the infralapsarian order of divine decrees, by teaching the atonement as limited satisfaction for sin that actually secured the salvation of the elect,[252] and by holding that regeneration precedes repentance and faith.[253] Whereas Hodge taught three covenants (of works, of [eternal] redemption, and of grace [in Christ]), Boyce taught two covenants (of works, of grace).[254] Boyce's debt to Hodge extended beyond the tenets of Dort so as to include the creationist view of the origin of human souls, the dichotomous view of human personhood, and the federal headship of Adam.[255] Richards extended

---

[245]*Abstract of Systematic Theology*, 341-67.
[246]Art. 5.
[247]*Abstract of Systematic Theology*, 337-40.
[248]Art. 7.
[249]Arts. 9, 10.
[250]*Abstract of Systematic Theology*, 384, 387-88.
[251]"A Study of the Influence of Princeton Theology upon the Theology of James Petigru Boyce and His Followers with Special Reference to the Work of Charles Hodge" (Th.D. diss., New Orleans Baptist Theological Seminary, 1964).
[252]That Boyce taught that the death of Christ "effected actual reconciliation" of the elect has been emphasized by Walter D. Draughon III, "A Critical Evaluation of the Diminishing Influence of Calvinism on the Doctrine of Atonement in Representative Southern Baptist Theologians: James Petigru Boyce, Edgar Young Mullins, Walter Thomas Conner, and Dale Moody" (Ph.D. diss., Southwestern Baptist Theological Seminary, 1987) esp. 33.
[253]Richards, "A Study of the Influence of Princeton Theology," 36, 47-48, 54-55, 58, 64, 71, 72, 73-74, 76-77.
[254]Ibid., 49, 57, 77.
[255]Ibid., 61, 69-70, 76, 51, 57, 75-76.

his argument for Hodge's weighty influence by evidence that the Baptist pastors[256] who influenced the young Boyce were not strong Calvinists and by evidence that most of Boyce's immediate successors on the faculty of Southern Baptist Theological Seminary[257] did not fully retain his Dortian Calvinism.

Boyce's apparent embrace of Thomas Reid's Common Sense Realism, whether mediated through Francis Wayland or Charles Hodge or both, seemingly influenced his epistemology and his theological method.[258]

The theology of American Baptists reflected the differences between the Calvinism of English Particular Baptists and the Arminianism of English General Baptists together with the English-derived ecclesiological distinctives of Baptists and the new American concern for freedom, church, and government. Roger Williams, only briefly a Baptist, utilizing a typological hermeneutic, posited a discontinuity between the Abrahamic covenant and the new covenant in Christ and between the two testaments so that persecution could not be supported from the Old Testament and false churches could be identified. His major contribution was his detailed case against religious persecution and for religious liberty. In the parable of the tares "the field" is the world and the tares represent those accused of heresy but not subject to civil authorities, and Williams found Rom. 13:1-7 to be applicable only to the second table of the Decalogue.

The Philadelphia Confession (1742) was Benjamin Keach's condensation of the Second London Confession with the addition of articles on hymn singing and laying on of hands on the newly baptized. The Philadelphia Association likewise drafted and adopted (1743) a document on church discipline, and the Charleston (SC) Association produced another such document, similar but different, in 1774.

The Six-Principle Baptists and the earliest General Baptists in the South produced some confessions of faith but little theological writing, but northern Freewill Baptists produced a major systematic theologian, John

---

[256]Ibid., 105-31. Namely, W. T. Brantly, Richard Fuller, and Francis Wayland. Nathaniel Macon Crawford, a Synod of Dort Calvinist, was pastor in Charleston during the two years of Boyce's study at Brown University.

[257]Ibid., 132-65. Namely, Edwin Charles Dargan, Edgar Young Mullins, Archibald Thomas Robertson, and Franklin Howard Kerfoot. One need not accept Richards's view (xiv-xv) that Calvinism peaked among Baptists in the South ca. 1800 to accept his conclusions about Boyce's professorial successors ca. 1900.

[258]Matheson, "Religious Knowledge," 140-97.

Jay Butler, who expounded a detailed treatment of revelation and the Bible, Arminian theology, Baptist ecclesiology, and postmillennialism.

In Philadelphia Elhanan Winchester embraced and defended eschatological universalism, thus dividing (1781) his Baptist congregation, leading his followers to become Universalists, and conducting a debate with Dan Taylor of England.

The Kehukee (NC and VA) Confession (1777) grew out of efforts to lead General Baptist churches to Calvinism and a regenerate church membership and to attract Separate Baptist churches. The New Hampshire Confession (1833), which would later be widely adopted in the states of the Mid-South and Southwest, was the product of a state convention and was possibly framed in response to the Arminianism of the Freewill Baptists. To it John Newton Brown added in 1853 two articles. Its article on the Bible would be adopted by later Baptist confessions, and its definition of the church as purely local or particular would make it acceptable to Baptist Landmarkers. Although called "moderately Calvinistic," it could as well be denominated "moderately Arminian."

Francis Wayland strongly advocated the thoroughgoing independence of Baptist churches with a rationale expressive of individualism and held that Baptist associations and conventions are to be composed of financial contributors, not of representatives of churches.

Nineteenth-century Baptist Calvinism in the South had its representatives: Patrick Hues Mell, who defended predestination and perseverance, believer's immersion, and corrective church discipline; John Leadley Dagg, who was the first Baptist to publish works reflective of the entire systematic curriculum of his day (doctrine, ecclesiology, ethics, apologetics), who only slightly deviated from Dortian Calvinism, and who embraced the doctrine of the universal church; the Abstract of Principles of Southern Baptist Theological Seminary (1858), framed largely by Basil Manly, Jr., with its moderate Calvinism and avoidance of Landmark Baptist issues; and James Petigru Boyce, whose Calvinism was deeply indebted to his Princeton teacher, Charles Hodge.

Chapter 5

Awakening and Missionary Baptists

The British happening known as the Evangelical Revival and its American counterpart, usually called the (first) Great Awakening, had varied impact on the Baptists in England and the American colonies. The former movement was to a considerable extent identified with the ministries of two Anglicans, George Whitefield (1714–1770), a Calvinist, and John Wesley (1703–1791), an Arminian,[1] and the latter movement was led by such Americans as Theodore Frelinghuysen (1691–1747), Dutch Reformed, Gilbert Tennent (1703–1764), Presbyterian, and Jonathan Edwards, Sr. (1703–1758), Congregationalist, and by the itinerating Whitefield.[2] As already noted, the General Assembly of General Baptists had so embraced Unitarianism that it was not positively influenced by the Evangelical Revival, but Wesley's ministry did influence David Taylor and Dan Taylor, the organizer of the New Connection of General Baptists.[3] For Particular Baptists not only the baptismal issue but also the Arminian theology stood in the way of an immediate and sympathetic response to the Wesleys, although the latter issue was not a barrier to Whitefield.[4] Indeed John Gill defended final perseverance[5] and particular election[6] against John Wesley.

---

[1] A. Skevington Wood, *The Inextinguishable Blaze: Spiritual Renewal and Advance in the Eighteenth Century* (London: Paternoster Press; Grand Rapids MI: Eerdmans, 1960) 78-113, 162-88.
[2] Ibid., 53-66; McBeth, *The Baptist Heritage*, 202-203.
[3] See above, 46. But Gilbert Boyce, a General Baptist messenger, did refute Wesley's stance on infant baptism in Boyce, *A Serious Reply to the Rev. Mr. John Wesley in Particular, and to the People Called Methodists in General* (Boston UK: C. Preston, 1770). Underwood, *A History of the English Baptists*, 149, 153.
[4] Underwood, *A History of the English Baptists*, 159-60.
[5] Gill, *The Doctrine of the Saints Final Perseverance, Asserted and Vindicated: In Answer to a Late Pamphlet, Called Serious Thoughts, on That Subject*, 3rd ed. (London, 1754; orig., 1752) 3-25, refuted Wesley's use of eight biblical texts against perseverance (Ezek. 18:24; 1 Tim. 1:19-20; Rom. 11:17-24; John 15:1-5; 2 Pet. 2:20-21; Heb. 6:4-6; 10:38, 29), in Wesley, "Serious Thoughts upon the Perseverance of the Saints," in *The Works of John Wesley*, 14 vols. (Grand Rapids MI: Zondervan, 1958) 10:284-98, and then defended perseverance from the perfections, or attributes, of God, God's everlasting love of his people, the decrees of God (esp. election), the eternal, unconditional covenant of grace, the biblical promises of perseverance, God's acts of grace toward his people, Christ's loving

Nevertheless, as shall become evident, Particular Baptists would become susceptible to revival influences, as new life began to emerge after "the winter of hyper-Calvinism."[7] In New England, as already described, the news of Whitefield's death would be the occasion of the conversion of Benjamin Randall, the founder of the Freewill Baptist movement in the Northern states.[8] But the Calvinistic Baptists in the American colonies experienced great numerical growth following the Great Awakening, even by Calvinizing General Baptist congregations,[9] and a new Baptist movement, the Separate Baptists, emerged from the Separate Congregational churches of New England, the product of the Great Awakening, and would find their center of gravity in the South.[10]

Isaac Backus (1724–1806) and John Leland (1754–1841)

"Born into the ruling elite of [Norwich,] Connecticut," Backus was baptized as an infant in the local Congregational church "of the Standing Order," having farming parents who had experienced conversion, and was educated in the local school. At seventeen, following Whitefield's first tour of New

---

care of the saints, the work of the Holy Spirit in the saints, the glory of the triune God, and the distress of dreading apostasy (25-26).

[6]Gill, *The Doctrine of Predestination Stated, and Set in the Scripture-Light; In Opposition to Mr. Wesley's Predestination Calmly Considered* . . ., 4th ed. (London, 1770; orig., 1752) 3-33, defined God's predetermination of all things, his predestination of Jesus Christ, of good angels, and of human beings, either by election of some by grace and not because of faith with the means and the end secure or by reprobation of others, both in the sense of preterition (or passing by the nonelect) and predamnation (God's decree to condemn and punish them for their sin). Then he treated various biblical texts which Wesley had alleged to be contrary to reprobation. See Wesley, "Predestination Calmly Considered," in *John Wesley*, ed. Albert C. Outler, A Library of Protestant Thought (New York: Oxford University Press, 1964) 427-72.

[7]Underwood, *A History of the English Baptists,* 160. According to Peter J. Morden, *Offering Christ to the World: Andrew Fuller (1754–1815) and the Revival of Eighteenth-Century Particular Baptist Life*, Studies in Baptist History and Thought 9 (Carlisle UK, Waynesboro GA: Paternoster, 2003) 5, "the revitalization of Particular Baptist life was both fed by the Evangelical Revival and was itself part of the wider Evangelical Revival."

[8]See above, 120.

[9]See above, 119-20.

[10]Baker, *The Southern Baptist Convention and Its People, 1607–1972*, 41-58.

England, he experienced conversion. Then, after itinerating, untrained revivalists had stirred the people's emotions and the newly converted had become aware how many unconverted persons held church membership—the effect of the Half-Way Covenant, he ten months later reluctantly joined Norwich's Congregational Church. After an unsuccessful effort to limit admission to membership to the professedly converted, Backus and others left this parish church in 1745 to hold separate worship and next year constituted a New Light congregation. Being called to preach, Backus did itinerant preaching before being called and ordained, without a college education, as pastor of a newly constituted New Light or Separate church at Titicut, Massachusetts, in 1748. Beset with the demand of being taxed to build an edifice for the parish church, the Separates asked Backus to write the first of his numerous petitions to governmental authorities. When two of his church members began to set forth antipedobaptist views, Backus initially resisted and only slowly became convinced of their validity. After struggle by 1751 he came to reject infant baptism and subjected himself to believer's immersion. Councils of the Separates voted that they could not observe the Lord's Supper with any who rejected infant baptism.

Finally in 1756 Backus led in the formation of the First Baptist Church of Middleborough, Massachusetts, a Separate Baptist congregation. He cultivated relations with the few older, pre-Awakening Baptist churches in New England, encouraging them to be more Calvinist, and with the newer Separate Baptist churches, encouraging them to shift from open communion to close communion. Backus served on the board of Rhode Island College (later Brown University) and after initial fear of its becoming a "presbytery" led the Middleborough church to join the Warren Baptist Association. In addition to his fifty-year pastorate and his extensive travels by horseback, estimated at 67,600 miles, to assist churches in baptisms, ordinations, revivals, constituting new churches, and settling disputes, Backus was a persistent and prolific advocate of church tax exemptions for Separate Baptists, of liberty of conscience as a universal right, and of the ultimate disestablishment (1818, 1833) of the Congregational churches in Connecticut and Massachusetts. At the same time he maintained a Calvinist theology, authored a notable history of New England Baptists[11] and

---

[11] *A History of New England, with Particular Reference to the Denomination of Christians Called Baptists*, 2 vols., 2nd ed., with notes by David Weston (Newton MA: Backus Historical Society, 1871).

numerous tracts,[12] and coupled with his disestablishment viewpoint the concept of America as a Christian nation.[13]

As he was emerging first as a Separate or New Light Congregationalist and then as a Separate Baptist, Backus began to write on themes germane to those movements. In 1754 as a Separate Backus affirmed the internal God-derived call of the minister in addition to the outward or ecclesiastical call as being thoroughly biblical and as given as well in the day of Backus. This call is given to true saints, who are quite aware of the true state of God's people, have received the treasure of the gospel, and have been given a divine command. The truly called preach "the whole counsel of God," practice what they preach, and have the accompanying presence of Christ. They are not inspired writers of the Scriptures or miracle workers, they do need qualifications, and their ministries do not rest on so-called apostolic succession. The examination of ministers is not dispensed with, and college education is not a substitute for conversion.[14] Later Backus advocated the voluntary support of ministers apart from any taxation[15] and the ordination of a minister solely by a congregation.[16]

Then in 1756 as a Separate Baptist Backus rejected infant baptism and made a corresponding reinterpretation of biblical covenants. Taking as his text Gal. 4:31, he differentiated the "bondwoman," or the covenant of works together with the moral law, the ceremonial law, and "the *Jewish* church in her legal standing," from the "freewoman," or the eternal covenant between the Father and the Son and "the Gospel-church in her pure standing."

---

[12]Thirty-five are listed by Stanley J. Grenz, *Isaac Backus—Puritan and Baptist: His Place in History, His Thought, and Their Implications for Modern Baptist Theology*, NABPR Dissertation Series 4 (Macon GA: Mercer University Press, 1983) 331-34.

[13]William Gerald McLoughlin, *Isaac Backus and the American Pietistic Tradition*, Library of American Biography (Boston: Little, Brown and Co., 1967). See also Alvah Hovey, *A Memoir of the Life and Times of the Rev. Isaac Backus, A.M.* (Boston: Gould and Lincoln, 1858).

[14]*A Discourse Showing the Nature and Necessity of an Internal Call to Preach the Everlasting Gospel* (Boston), in *Isaac Backus on Church, State, and Calvinism: Pamphlets, 1754–1789*, ed. William G. McLoughlin, The John Harvard Library (Cambridge MA: Belknap Press of Harvard University Press, 1968) 69-113.

[15]Grenz, *Isaac Backus*, 90, based on Backus, *The Liberal Support of Gospel Ministers Opened and Inculcated* (Boston, 1790). See also Backus, *A Fish Caught in His Own Net* (Boston, 1768), in *Pamphlets*, ed. McLoughlin, 237-43.

[16]Grenz, *Isaac Backus*, 137.

Likewise the children of the bondwoman, "born after the flesh," are to be distinguished from the children of the freewoman, who are free from guilt, Satan, and "the dominion of sin" with *"open access to God"* and walking in God's ways under the "law of liberty." Typologically, the Jewish church is demarcated from "the Gospel-Church" even as the old covenant is from the new. Neither baptism nor the Lord's Supper, contra Stoddardeanism, is a converting ordinance, for they require "spiritual cleanness." Infants did not go into Noah's ark, and all Christians are Abraham's spiritual seed. Children of believers have the advantages of godly examples and instruction. Backus, taking note of the writing of the Congregationalist Peter Clark (1694–1768),[17] who wrote to answer John Gill on pedobaptism, agreed that there is no evidence of the practice of infant baptism during the first two centuries of the Christian era. Circumcision and baptism differ as to recipients (male only vs. male and female), as to administrators, and as to time of administration; circumcision is "a type of what should come," whereas baptism is "an outward sign . . . of what is inwardly wrought." The Half-Way Covenant brought "a sort of *Purgatory* or half way between the Church and the world." Yet Backus wrote more irenically than polemically even as he rejected the Puritan doctrine that the covenant of grace was virtually the same in both testaments.[18]

Other ecclesiological themes were treated by Backus. The membership of visible churches should be restricted to "regenerate souls."[19] Following John Locke,[20] he reckoned a church to be a "voluntary society"[21] which could also be understood as "a corporation," like a city, "with the power to discipline its own members."[22] Contending that "only the true church endeavors to keep to the divine pattern"[23] and that "Christ is the only

---

[17] *A Defense of the Divine Right of Infant Baptism* (Boston, 1752).

[18] *A Short Description of the Difference between the Bondwoman and the Free* (Boston) in *Pamphlets*, ed. McLoughlin, 134-65; "Editor's Introduction," in ibid., 130.

[19] *A Fish Caught in His Own Net*, in *Pamphlets*, ed. McLoughlin, 255.

[20] *A Letter concerning Toleration* in *The Works of John Locke*, 10 vols., 11th ed. (London: W. Otridge and Son et al., 1812) 6:13.

[21] *Policy, as well as Honesty, Forbids the Use of Force in Religious Affairs* (Boston, 1779), in *Pamphlets*, ed. McLoughlin, 376-77.

[22] *The Nature and Necessity of an Internal Call to Preach the Everlasting Gospel*, 2nd ed. (Boston, 1792), 41, as paraphrased by Grenz, *Isaac Backus*, 129.

[23] *A Fish Caught in His Own Net*, in *Pamphlets*, ed. McLoughlin, 182.

lawgiver to his Church,"[24] Backus espoused what Stanley Grenz has called "a radical Congregationalism in which each particular church is self-governing and the governmental power in each rests in the people themselves." Ministers are to be subject to congregational discipline.[25]

> Ministers should be burning and shining lights, and rule the church as the sun rules the day, by holding forth light and heat, to direct and quicken men in their walk and work. This is to be done by word and example, Matt. 5:14–16; Heb. 13:7-8, 17.[26]

When Backus formed a Baptist church in Middleborough, he embraced close communion on the basis that baptism must precede participation in the Lord's Supper and infant baptism is not true baptism.[27]

As already noted, Backus's rejection of infant baptism led him to revise the Puritan doctrine of covenants and embrace to a degree a typological interpretation of the Bible. What else needs to be said of his hermeneutic? According to Grenz, for Backus the Holy Spirit is essential to biblical interpretation by his work of illumination and guidance, which is provided to all believers, "not merely those with knowledge of the ancient languages." But this does not mean "that every Bible interpretation which the Christian may hold is actually the correct one."[28] Backus avoided subjectivism by rejecting the "'voice within'" when set above the Scriptures.[29]

That Backus was a Calvinist is widely accepted, but what kind of Calvinist he was must be determined. He did not expound the five leading tenets of Dortian Calvinism in any specific, holistic exposition. As to particular election, he denied that the doctrine of immutable decrees makes God the author of sin, for "sin is a defect and God is the author of all

---

[24]*The Doctrine of Particular Election and Final Perseverance* (Boston, 1789) in *Pamphlets*, ed. McLoughlin, 457.

[25]*Isaac Backus*, 133, 138. It was "radical" in comparison with the modified congregational polity of the Standing Order with its synods and consociations.

[26]*A Discourse, concerning the Materials, the Manner of Building, and Power of Organizing of the Church of Christ* . . . (Boston, 1773) as quoted by Grenz, *Isaac Backus*, 138.

[27]Grenz, *Isaac Backus*, 71, 144; McLoughlin, *Isaac Backus and the American Pietistic Tradition*, 87-88. Backus also refuted Stoddardeanism. *True Faith Will Produce Good Works* . . . (Boston: D. Kneeland, 1767) 67-68.

[28]*Isaac Backus*, 120-21.

[29]*The Sovereign Decrees of God, Set in a Scriptural Light* . . . (Boston, 1773) in *Pamphlets*, ed. McLoughlin, 294-95.

efficiency but not of any defect at all."[30] He likewise refuted John Wesley's doctrine that election is a conditional decree and does not precede the believer's exercise of faith.[31] Backus was insistent that faith is the work of God, even as the will of the unrepentant and unbelieving is bound rather than free.[32] True faith, he contended, is receiving divine "witness and testimony,"[33] and, like John Calvin,[34] he insisted that faith precedes repentance.[35] Backus deplored as wrong any attempts "to represent irresistible grace to be inconsistent with the soul's liberty of choice," for there is no violence against a man's will, for he "is slain and made alive by the power of truth," and a rational man "is always governed" in his choice by "the present ideas . . . of what is best."[36] The Middleborough pastor refuted Wesley's doctrine of universal atonement[37] and the doctrine of eschatological universalism as set forth by James Relly (1722?–1778)[38] and Elhanan Winchester,[39] thereby indicating his espousal of limited atonement.[40] Backus rejected Wesley's doctrine of possible apostasy and

---

[30]Ibid., 299.

[31]*The Doctrine of Particular Election and Final Perseverance*, in *Pamphlets*, ed. McLoughlin, 456-57.

[32]*The Doctrine of Sovereign Grace Opened and Vindicated...* (Providence RI: John Carter, 1771) 8-21. Backus asserted that the advocates of free will are really Deists (15).

[33]Ibid., 25.

[34]*Institutes of the Christian Religion* (1559 ed.) bk. 3, chs. 2–3.

[35]*The Doctrine of Sovereign Grace*, 55-56.

[36]Ibid., 56, 59.

[37]*The Doctrine of Particular Election and Final Perseverance*, in *Pamphlets*, ed. McLoughlin, 453-55.

[38]*Union: or, A Treatise of the Consanguinity and Affinity between Christ and His Church* (Providence RI: John Carter, 1782; orig., 1759).

[39]Backus, *The Doctrine of Universal Salvation Examined and Refuted, Containing a Concise and Distinct Answer to the Writings of Mr. Relly, and Mr. Winchester, upon That Subject* (Providence RI: John Carter, 1782). Backus also pointed out six theological differences between Relly and Winchester (20-21).

[40]Backus used the language of substitution, *The Doctrine of Sovereign Grace*, 52, and refuted the concept of John Remmele that "atonement consisted wholly in the excellency of Christ's teaching and example, in his life and death, and not at all in his suffering the penalty of the law for sinners," *The Atonement of Christ, Explained and Vindicated, against Late Attempts to Exclude It out of the World* (Boston: Samuel Hall, 1787) esp. 5.

stated his own embrace of perseverance.[41] Therefore, we can conclude that Backus was a Dortian Calvinist.

Backus repeatedly hammered out his concept of liberty of conscience vis-à-vis civil government. As early as 1770 he "cited Paul to show that forcing one to act against conscience is to cause him to sin."[42] In 1773 he espoused civil disobedience when the state interferes with the role of the church.[43] Indeed "the conscience must be left free" because "'true religion is a voluntary obedience unto God.'"[44] While calling for disestablishment of the Standing Order, Backus agreed with his adversaries that "religion is . . . necessary for the well-being of human society"[45] and advocated a "sweet harmony" between church and state.[46]

In a postmillennial framework Backus anticipated after the gradual overcoming of Antichrist[47] a golden age in which the sword would be laid aside[48] and wars would cease.[49] He found multiple meanings for the kingdom of God, one of which will be eschatological.[50] Prior to the expected millennial age, Backus looked to an advance of Baptist principles

---

[41]*The Doctrine of Particular Election and Final Perseverance*, in *Pamphlets*, ed. McLoughlin, 458-61.

[42]Grenz, *Isaac Backus*, 86, based on Backus, *A Seasonable Plea for Liberty and Conscience* (Boston).

[43]*An Appeal to the Public for Religious Liberty*, in *Pamphlets*, ed. McLoughlin, 332-35.

[44]Grenz, *Isaac Backus*, 87, quoting Backus, *Government and Liberty Described . . .* (Boston, 1778) in *Pamphlets*, ed. McLoughlin, 351.

[45]*Policy, as well as Honesty*, in *Pamphlets*, ed. McLoughlin, 371.

[46]McLoughlin, intro. to *Pamphlets*, ed. McLoughlin, 61.

[47]*A Discourse Showing the Nature and Necessity of an Internal Call*, in *Pamphlets*, ed. McLoughlin, 107. The Antichrist, for Backus, was not the pope but "the mingling of church and state," and, while the first beast of Revelation 13 was the pope, the second beast was the Protestant "mingling [of] church and state." Grenz, *Isaac Backus*, 231-32.

[48]*Policy, as well as Honesty*, in *Pamphlets*, ed. McLoughlin, 382; *Truth Is Great, and Will Prevail* (Boston, 1781) in ibid., 425; *A Door Opened for Christian Liberty* (Boston, 1783) in ibid., 438.

[49]*The Doctrine of Particular Election and Final Perseverance*, in *Pamphlets*, ed. McLoughlin, 468.

[50]*The Kingdom of God, Described by His Word, with Its Infinite Benefits to Human Society* (Boston, 1792) 8-14, Evans, Early American Imprints, 1639–1800, no. 24061.

in America both by Baptists' leading the recovery of New Testament Christianity and by the completion of the Protestant Reformation.[51]

Thomas B. Maston, who was primarily interested in Backus's views on liberty of conscience and church and state, concluded:

> Backus brought together the theological and ethical theories of the 'New Divinity' [Edwards et al.], the congregational ecclesiastical polity of the Baptists, and the political philosophy of John Locke, and welded them into a more or less consistent system. . . .[52]

According to Stanley Grenz, Backus stood in the Puritan heritage. He even "brought" the Separate Baptists "into the Puritan myth of the day." Backus, he insisted, made three major contributions: "his [Calvinist] theology, church-state theory, and understanding of the role of the Baptist movement in the on-going reformation." But Arminianism would become very influential in America before Backus's death, and his own stress on individual reason paved the way for revivalism. Backus was much more successful in getting his church-state views adopted. On the contrary, believer's baptism would not be universally accepted, "the reformation of the one church which he envisioned never came about and the Millennium never arrived."[53] W. G. McLoughlin has seen Backus as "an exponent of American evangelical pietism" rather than as a Puritan. He "provided a more viable alternative to deism than the Puritanism of Cotton Mather or than the new 'liberal Christianity' of Unitarianism."[54] Backus's

> career demonstrates that fundamental polarity in American pietism between the Antinomian or anarchistic pietist who seeks complete moral and spiritual freedom for the individual and the theocratic or authoritarian pietist who seeks a perfect moral order for the state. . . . He . . . worked to exalt the religious liberty of the individual above the church and the state, yet he always asserted the necessity for a Christian state subservient to the ultimate moral authority of God's law. He sought a 'sweet harmony' for the new American republic . . . , but he helped to produce the cacophony of sectarianism and pluralism.[55]

---

[51]Grenz, *Isaac Backus*, 168-69, 232.

[52]*Isaac Backus: Pioneer of Religious Liberty* (London: James Clarke, Rochester NY: American Baptist Historical Society, 1962) 106.

[53]*Isaac Backus*, 168-69, 326, 329; Grenz, "Isaac Backus," in *Baptist Theologians*, ed. George and Dockery, 115-17.

[54]*Isaac Backus and the American Pietistic Tradition*, 233, 232.

[55]McLoughlin, intro. to *Pamphlets*, ed. McLoughlin, 61.

James T. Draper, Jr. and Forrest E. Watson have concluded:

> Backus did not understand separation of Church and State to mean that the State should not uphold the Christian religion in general. He was a supporter of laws against blasphemy, profanity, gambling, card-playing, and theatergoing.... The Baptist position [for Backus] was separation of *Church* and *State*, not separation of *Christianity or the Bible* and the State.[56]

Another major Baptist advocate of religious liberty in early America was John Leland. Born in Massachusetts and converted at eighteen under the preaching of Elhanan Winchester, he soon began to preach and served as pastor and itinerant evangelist, first in Virginia and later in Massachusetts. He became involved in the Virginia struggle for disestablishment and religious freedom, being influenced by Thomas Jefferson and associated with James Madison, and was credited with helping to secure Virginia's ratification of the U.S. Constitution on Madison's promise to secure a bill of rights.[57]

Leland defined "conscience" as "*common science*; a court of judicature, erected by God in every human breast," which "can give wrong judgment" but "should be free from human control" and "in strict subordination to the law of God."[58] Constantine's "error" had been his putting "the same fatal dagger" used to put to death Christians into the hands of Christians; hence "the shocking monster of *Christian nation*."[59] Human beings ought not to surrender conscience to government because everyone "must give an account of himself to God," conscience is "to be kept sacred by God," it would be "very iniquitous to bind the conscience of" one's "children," and "religion is a matter between God and individuals."[60] Leland, being more

---

[56]*If the Foundations Be Destroyed* (Nashville: Thomas Nelson, 1984) 99.

[57]John Leland, "Events in the Life of John Leland Written by Himself," in *The Writings of the Late Elder John Leland*, ed. L. F. Greene (New York: G. W. Wood, 1845; repr.: New York: Arno, 1980) 9-40; Lyman H. Butterfield, "Elder John Leland, Jeffersonian Itinerant," *Proceedings of the American Antiquarian Society* 62 (Worcester MA, 1952); repr. in *Colonial Baptists and Southern Revivals* (New York: Arno, 1980) 160-242.

[58]"The Virginia Chronicle," in *Writings*, 123.

[59]"Short Essays on Government...," in ibid., 476. Leland was not precise in differentiating the roles of Constantine and Theodosius I.

[60]"The Rights of Conscience Inalienable, and, Therefore, Religious Opinions Not Cognizable by Law...," in ibid., 181.

Jeffersonian than Backus, opposed legislative and military chaplains paid by the government[61] and legislation as to Sabbath observance.[62] Edwin S. Gaustad has utilized the term "the Backus-Leland tradition,"[63] but Barry Hankins has more recently challenged the usage on the basis that Backus accepted and Leland rejected the concept of "Christian nation."[64]

Christ's rule over the church, Leland taught, is like both a monarchy and a democracy. It is "a divine Christocracy," and it is through congregational governance. Hence "all state establishments of Christianity . . . are . . . Anti-Christocracies."[65] Leland's congregationalism led him to be hesitant about national Baptist societies lest they exercise control over congregations.[66]

The Separate Baptists

The Separate Baptist movement, derived from the New Light or Separate Congregationalists of New England, was destined to have an even greater impact on the South than on New England. Particularly was this so because of the migration of Shubael Stearns (1706–1771) and his brother-in-law Daniel Marshall (1706–1784) from Connecticut to northern Virginia and then to Sandy Creek in central North Carolina. The Sandy Creek Church (1755) and the Sandy Creek Association (1758) were the nerve center of the expanding church-planting Separate Baptists, who were to be found also in Virginia, South Carolina, and Georgia and later in Tennessee and Kentucky.[67]

---

[61]Edwin Scott Gaustad, "The Backus-Leland Tradition," *Foundations* 2 (April 1959): 148.

[62]"On Sabbatical Laws," in *Writings*, 440-46.

[63]Gaustad, "The Backus-Leland Tradition," 131-52.

[64]*Uneasy in Babylon: Southern Baptist Conservatives and American Culture* (Tuscaloosa: University of Alabama Press, 2002) 127-32. Hankins rightly notes that today the term "Christian nation" must be precisely defined either "demographically" or "legally" or soteriologically (p. 128). See also Gaustad, "Religious Liberty: Baptists and Some Fine Distinctions," *American Baptist Quarterly* 6 (December 1987): 215-25.

[65]"The Government of Christ a Christocracy," in *Writings*, 275, 277, 281.

[66]Gaustad, "The Backus-Leland Tradition," 144.

[67]William L. Lumpkin, *Baptist Foundations in the South: Tracing through the Separates the Influence of the Great Awakening, 1754–1787* (Nashville: Broadman, 1961) 1-59, 87-132; Lumpkin, "Separate Baptists," in *Encyclopedia of Southern Baptists* (Nashville: Broadman, 1958) 2:1190-91; J. Allen Easley, "Stearns,

"Separate Baptists," according to William L. Lumpkin, "emphasized the necessity of the new birth, the authority of the Scriptures, and the leadership of the Holy Spirit in the lives of God's people."[68] Other emphases included human depravity, Christ's atonement, and baptism as the outward sign of an inward change.[69] Stearns and Marshall having been influenced by George Whitefield, the Separate Baptists were "modified Calvinists"[70] in the sense that they preached salvation by grace alone[71] and the perseverance of all true believers but "either rejected or had little to say about" such doctrines as "predestination" and "limited atonement."[72] They tended to be anti-creedal and formed no complete system of theology.[73] John Sparks has noted that the preamble to an early church covenant which Stearns seemingly wrote was a statement of the six principles of Heb. 6:1-2.[74]

The Sandy Creek Church observed as many as nine ordinances: "baptism, the Lord's Supper, the love feast, laying on of hands, the washing of feet, anointing of the sick, the right hand of fellowship, the kiss of charity, and devoting children."[75] Those professing faith were examined carefully before admission to church membership, and the association, at least initially, exercised authority in respect to ordination of ministers and the manner of constituting new churches.[76]

The Sandy Creek Association, however, did in 1816, probably under the influence of Luther Rice (1783–1836), adopt ten brief articles of faith.[77] After affirming the Trinity (art. 1) and the Scriptures as "the word of God" and the "only rule of faith and practice" (art. 2), the confession taught

---

Shubal," in ibid., 2:1298; Malcolm Lester, "Marshall, Daniel," in ibid., 2:824.

[68]Lumpkin, *Baptist Foundations in the South*, 63.

[69]Lumpkin, "Separate Baptists," 2:1191.

[70]Lumpkin, *Baptists Foundations in the South*, 62.

[71]Albert Henry Newman, *A History of the Baptist Churches in the United States*, American Church History Series 2 (New York: Christian Literature Co., 1894) 302.

[72]Lumpkin, *Baptist Foundations in the South*, 62.

[73]Ibid., 63, 62, 153.

[74]*The Roots of Appalachian Christianity: The Life and Legacy of Elder Shubal Stearns* (Lexington: University Press of Kentucky, 2001) 45-46. Per Paul L. Gritz.

[75]Ibid., 38-39. The same nine were affirmed by Morgan Edwards (1722–1795) of Philadelphia. Thomas R. McKibbens and Kenneth L. Smith, *The Life and Works of Morgan Edwards* (New York: Arno, 1980) 129-30.

[76]Sparks, *The Roots of Appalachian Christianity*, 40, 57-59, 159-60.

[77]Lumpkin, *Baptist Confessions of Faith*, 357.

Adamic guilt and the lack of human free will vis-à-vis salvation (art. 3), particular election from eternity, effectual calling, justification through "the imputation of Christ's righteousness," and final perseverance (art. 4), and resurrection, the general judgment, heaven, and hell (art. 5). The visible church is "a congregation of faithful persons, who have . . . given themselves up to the Lord and one another" and "agreed to keep up a godly discipline" (art. 6). Christ is "the great head of the church," and church polity is congregational (art. 7). Baptism and the Lord's Supper are to be perpetually observed until Christ's second coming (art. 8). Baptism is only for "true believers" and by the mode of immersion (art. 9), and participants in the Supper are only to be "regular baptized church members" (art. 10).[78]

The Separate Baptist General Association of Virginia did in 1783 "adopt the Philadelphia Confession, with the proviso that the acceptance did"[79]

> not mean that every person is to be bound to the strict observance of everything therein contained, nor do we mean to make it in any respect superior or equal to the Scriptures in matters of faith and practice. . . .[80]

When the Elkhorn (Regular) Association and the South Kentucky (Separate) Association sought a theological basis for their union, it was decided that new articles were needed inasmuch as the Separate Baptists were "unwilling to accept the Philadelphia Confession." Hence in 1801 eleven articles were framed and adopted.[81] Quite similar to the later Sandy Creek articles, they did identify the Scriptures as "the infallible word of God" (art. 1), omit any reference to Adamic guilt or lack of free will while affirming depravity (art. 3), state that preaching that "Christ tasted death for every man, shall be no bar to communion" (art. 9), and declare that each association may retain its own form of church and associational polity (art. 10).[82] It is commonly accepted that Stearns fathered the Separate Baptist

---

[78]"Principles of Faith of the Sandy Creek Association," in ibid., 358, copied from George W. Purefoy, *A History of the Sandy Creek Baptist Association, from Its Organization in A.D. 1758, to A.D. 1858* (New York: Sheldon and Co., 1859) 104-105.

[79]Lumpkin, *Baptist Confessions of Faith*, 353.

[80]Robert Naylor Semple, *A History of the Rise and Progress of the Baptists in Virginia*, rev. G. W. Beale (Richmond: Pitt and Dickinson, 1894) 93.

[81]Lumpkin, *Baptist Confessions of Faith*, 358-59.

[82]"Terms of Union between the Elkhorn and South Kentucky, or Separate, Associations," in ibid., 359, copied from John H. Spencer, *A History of Kentucky*

movement in the South; Sparks would have us acclaim him as "the father of Appalachian religion."[83]

English Particular Baptists from Revival to Missions: Robert Hall, Sr. (1728–1791), John Collett Ryland (1723–1792), John Ryland (1753–1825), and John Sutcliff (1752–1814)

Attention has already been given[84] to the impact of the Evangelical Revival upon the General Baptists leading to the formation of the New Connection of General Baptists. But other Dissenting or Nonconformist bodies, including Particular Baptists, more slowly responded to the "stirrings of new life."[85] As David Bebbington has recently noted, "The impact of Evangelicalism on orthodox Dissent in England and Wales did not become general until the last years of the eighteenth century."[86]

An early indication of the theological revision influenced by the Evangelical Revival was the sermon preached by Robert Hall, Sr., Particular Baptist pastor in the village of Arnesby near Leicester,[87] at the meeting of the Northamptonshire Baptist Association in 1779 and then expanded and published as *Help to Zion's Travellers* (1781).[88] Taking as his text Isa. 57:14, Hall sought to remove the "stumbling blocks" impeding his fellow Dissenters of the Hyper-Calvinist type, and these were "doctrinal," "experimental," and "practical." He identified six doctrinal stumbling blocks. The first was Socinian denial of the deity of Jesus Christ, either by positing that "inferiority of office" means "inferiority of nature," by perverting the language of "one essence" and "three persons," by presupposing that the preexistent Logos had a human soul, or by depreciating the

---

Baptists from 1769 to 1885, 2 vols, rev. by Burrilla B. Spencer (Cincinnati: pvt. prtg., 1886) 1:546.

[83]Loyal Jones, foreword to *The Roots of Appalachian Christianity*, xii.
[84]See above, 46, 153.
[85]Underwood, *A History of the English Baptists*, 160.
[86]*Evangelicalism in Modern Britain: A History from the 1730s to the 1980s* (London: Unwin Hyman/Routledge, 1989; Grand Rapids MI: Baker, 1992) 32.
[87]Michael A. G. Haykin, "Robert Hall, Sr. (1728–1791)," in Haykin, ed., *The British Particular Baptists 1638–1910*, 3 vols. (Springfield MO: Particular Baptist, 1998) 1:202-10.
[88]Underwood, *A History of the English Baptists*, 160-61.

bodily nature of Jesus. Second, some objected to the unchangeable character of God's love by reckoning such love as antithetical to and not confluent with God's hatred of sin. Third, the doctrine of election was being misinterpreted by failure to recognize the freedom of the One who elects and the passive role of the elected, by failing to discern the difference between election to "privileges" and to "office" and election to salvation, and by various distorted understandings of reprobation. Fourth, disputes over union with Christ, especially as to whether it is eternal or comes only at or after believing have beclouded the "visible," "vital" and "virtual" (or final) nature of such union. Likewise, some have failed properly to differentiate adoption and regeneration. Finally, the penal, meritorious, and substitutionary nature of Christ's atonement, vindicative of God's righteousness, was being threatened by those who see the atonement as only an act of God's clemency or an act of his will or who contend against atonement on the basis that "Deity could not die."[89]

Christian experience in his day posed stumbling blocks which Hall sought to remove. The "warrants" said to be necessary for "a sinner to apply to Jesus as Savior" took several forms. Some were saying that unconverted persons ought not to pray, but this, for Hall, could lead to "pharisaism" and "fatal security." Others were claiming that one cannot genuinely repent until he believes in Christ and has hope of forgiveness of sin, whereas Hall found repentance and faith to be connected and to accompany each other. Still others were declaring that one cannot have "a true faith in Christ" without knowing of an "interest" in Christ or considering Christ "as a person's own," while Hall affirmed that the way for sinners to Jesus is open "for *whosoever will*." For some Christians not to know the exact time of their being born again was a problem, for others the difficulty was the lack of "strong consolation" and the brevity of their joy, and for yet others the issue was a deep sense of personal sinfulness. Hall especially sought to remove the stumbling block that the doctrines of grace are "inimical to experimental religion" so "as to supersede personal holiness, and render internal conformity to God unnecessary." Hall dealt with "*imputed*" righteousness and "*imparted* righteousness, showed that God's efficacious grace in conversion is "consistent with the natural freedom of the human will," recast election from being a discouraging to an encouraging doctrine, and

---

[89]*Help to Zion's Travellers: Being an Attempt to Remove Various Stumbling Blocks out of the Way relating to Doctrinal, Experimental, and Practical Religion*, 5th ed. (London: Hamilton, Adams, and Co., 1825) 1-94.

was certain that a recast doctrine of election would not undermine redemption through Christ's death. Moreover, when God's particular providences seem to be contrary to his promises, believers need to be patient, slow to pass judgment, willing to correct their views of God's promises, and aware that God tests believers "by a suspension of promised mercies."[90]

Practically speaking, some professing Christians, either by denigrating weaker Christians or by their "loose" living, constitute stones of stumbling. Suffering "reproach and persecution" for Christ and the cross is hard for some. Others are misled by antinomianism or are disobedient concerning baptism and the Lord's Supper. But Hall's climactic word was his distinguishing, as had Jonathan Edwards, Sr., between natural and moral inability and ability. For him the distinction makes sovereign grace "not only defensible" but also "infinitely great" and the source of much encouragement and comfort.[91]

The author's son, Robert Hall, Jr. (1764–1831), wrote in 1824 that his father, whose "sentiments . . . were decidedly Calvinistic," had not written "so much to recommend that system in general, as to disengage it from certain excrescences."[92] *Help to Zion's Travellers* not only greatly impacted William Carey.[93] It was veritably an early great trumpet sound for the theological renovation out of which came the impetus for the worldwide Protestant missionary movement.

An important participant in the emerging Particular Baptist missionary movement was John Ryland, the son of John Collett Ryland. The elder Ryland, trained at the Bristol Baptist Academy and pastor briefly at Warwick and for twenty-six years in Northampton,[94] represented the older Calvinism[95] out of which the missionary impulse came. It was he who said

---

[90]Ibid., 94-155.

[91]Ibid., 155-222.

[92]Preface to the 3rd ed. of *Help to Zion's Travellers*, as publ. in the 5th ed., xviii.

[93]Underwood, *A History of the English Baptists*, 161.

[94]James Culross, *The Three Rylands: A Hundred Years of Various Christian Service* (London: Elliot Stock, 1897) 15-37; Peter Naylor, "John Collett Ryland (1723–1792)," in *The British Particular Baptists*, ed. Haykin, 1:184-201.

[95]Ryland has been described as one who agreed with Joseph Hussey about "offers of grace" and "definitely favoured the High Calvinism of Brine and Gill." Michael A. G. Haykin, *One Heart and One Soul: John Sutcliff of Olney, His Friends and His Times* (Darlington UK: Evangelical, 1994) 81, 71, 73.

to William Carey at a meeting of ministers, "'Young man, sit down, sit down. You're an enthusiast.'"[96] The elder Ryland spelled out the insufficiencies of reason in that it cannot provide the love and true worship of God, the happiness of human beings, a complete morality, powerful motives to virtue, assistance toward obedience, pardon of sin, transformation of the heart, support amid troubles or at death, or clarity as to future rewards and punishments.[97] He sought to demonstrate the existence of God by drawing from every aspect of the created order and employing the teleological argument.[98] Ryland treated extensively the doctrine of the Bible, whose authority, he stated, derives from its right and power to be "regarded by man as true and . . . divine" and "to demand obedience" in God's name. Defining inspiration as "the infusion" of biblical "thoughts and words" "into the minds of the prophets and apostles, by the Spirit of God," he did not espouse a particular theory as to its mode but allowed for differing degrees of inspiration and denied that the Holy Spirit destroyed the writers' differing "natural faculties and abilities," while affirming the inerrancy of the Bible.[99] Ryland laid out four major demonstrable evidences for inspiration: the salvific effectiveness of the biblical message, the occurrence of biblical miracles, the fulfillment of prophetic predictions, and the clear differentiation of the character of good and evil human beings and delineation of the "divine and moral character" of Jesus Christ.[100] Claims of contemporary inspiration were, for Ryland, "wild enthusiasm," but the Scriptures "enforce" and "enlarge the *law of nature*" and furnish a complete "system of *natural religion* and *moral philosophy*."[101]

---

[96]Quoted by Underwood, *A History of the English Baptists*, 142.

[97]*Contemplation on the Insufficiency of Reason, and the Necessity of Divine Revelation to Enable Us to Attain Eternal Happiness* (London: Vallance and Simmons, 1775) BBM:Angus, microform publ. 5855, reel 3, item 3.

[98]*A Contemplation on the Existence and Perfections of God, Drawn from the Several Parts of the Visible World, the Structure of the Human Body, and the Wonderful Powers of the Soul . . .* (London: Vallance and Simmons, 1774) BBM:Angus, microform publ. 5855, reel 2, item 31, esp. 1-18.

[99]*Contemplations on the Beauties of Creation, and on All the Principal Truths and Blessings of the Glorious Gospel: with the Sins and Graces of Professing Christians*, vol. 1 of 3, 3rd ed. (London: Edward and Charles Dilly, 1777) 140, 139, 189, 192, 201-202, 203.

[100]Ibid., 227-74; vol. 2 (Northampton: Thomas Dicey, 1779) 5-218.

[101]Ibid., 1:220, 285.

The elder Ryland dwelt upon the awesome nature of sin,[102] and, borrowing from John Owen (1616–1683), laid out an extensive critique of the Socinianism of some of his English contemporaries. It subverts biblical authority, denies the Trinity, holds that God has no genuine knowledge of further events, denies human depravity, makes Christ to be mere man, not pre-existent and not virginally conceived, and anticipates annihilationism. But his central argument against Socinians was their denial of the "necessity, reality, and perfection of the satisfaction of Christ" by his death and hence of the punitive justice of God.[103] For the elder Ryland baptism is "a solemn act of worship," a "lively representation" of Christ's passion, death, and resurrection, "the answer . . . of a good conscience towards God," "an emblem of regeneration and sanctification," "a powerful obligation" to that "evangelical disobedience" that differentiates the church from the world, and "a lively resemblance" to the believer's physical death and "emblem" of his future resurrection.[104] Ryland embraced open communion, probably before leaving Warwick, and he and Daniel Turner (1710–1798) published concurrently almost identical pseudonymous tracts[105] defending it.[106]

---

[102]*A Demonstration of the Horrid Nature of Sin* (London: John Robinson et al., 1755) BPB/Angus, reel 1, item 22; *Threatenings of Divine Justice, against Particular Sins* (London: W. Justins, 1787) BBM:Angus/Whitley, microform publ. 1975, reel 1, item 25.

[103]*Contemplations on the Eternal and Immutable Justice of God; from the Latin Dissertations of Dr. John Owen . . . , Designed as a Full Answer to the Essential Parts of Socinianism . . .* (London: W. Justins, 1787) x, xi, and *A View of the Corrupt Principles of Socinianism, Designed as an Introduction to Dr. John Owen, On Divine Justice, and His Answer to Biddle . . .* (London: W. Justins, 1787?) 1-4, 16-17, both in BBM:Angus/Whitley, microform no. 1975, reel 1, items 24, 25.

[104]*Six Views of Believer's Baptism*, with additions by Dr. Ryland (London: Baptist Tract Society, 1841; orig., 1774) BBHRM:M/RP, microform publ. 946, reel 16, item 41.

[105](Ryland) *A Modest Plea for Free Communion at the Lord's Table; Between True Believers of All Denominations* by Pacificus (1772), and (Turner), *A Modest Plea for Free Communion at the Lord's Table, Particularly between the Baptists and Paedobaptists*, by Candidus (1772).

[106]Haykin, *One Heart and One Soul*, 71-72, 293-94; Brown, *The English Baptists of the Eighteenth Century*, 130; Robert W. Oliver, "John Collett Ryland, Daniel Turner and Robert Robinson and the Communion Controversy, 1772-1781," *Baptist Quarterly* 29 (April 1981): 77-79; Geoffrey Ralph Breed, *Particular Baptists in Victorian England and Their Strict Communion Organizations* (Didcot

The younger Ryland, who served first as his father's assistant, was then pastor in Northampton and helped to found the Baptist Missionary Society before moving to the pastorate of Broadmead Church, Bristol, where he also served as president of Bristol Baptist Academy.[107] He continued within the Calvinistic heritage in that he held to the covenant of redemption (within the Trinity), the covenant of works (with Adam and his posterity), and the covenant of grace (with all penitent believers)[108] and by affirming that "sovereign Grace" is "the impulsive Cause" of salvation, the "Blood of Christ" is "the meritorious Cause," and the Holy Spirit is "the only efficient Cause."[109] Yet the Scriptures need to be confirmed not only by external evidence but also by Christian experience,[110] and Ryland countered antinomianism by insisting that there is no "contradiction" between the moral law and the gospel, for the gospel only opposes justification by works of the law, and the gospel provides "not only . . . a Saviour" but also "a Sanctifier."[111] Redemption from the curse of the law does not mean that "*Christ has cancelled or lessened*" the "obligations to obedience."[112] Divine decrees do not exclude "the use of means" or "the propriety of warning, invitation, expostulation, and reproof."[113] Like his father, the younger

---

UK: Baptist Historical Society, 2003) 14-15.

[107]Culross, *The Three Rylands*, 73-81; Grant Gordon, "John Ryland, Jr. (1753–1825)," in *The British Particular Baptists*, ed. Haykin, 2:76-95.

[108]*The Law Not against the Promises of God: A Sermon Delivered at . . . Leicester, May 30, 1787* (London: J. Buckland, 1787?) BM:Angus, microform publ. no. 5855, reel 2, item 13, 9-10; *A Candid Statement of the Reasons Which Induce the Baptists to Differ in Opinion and Practice from So Many of Their Christian Brethren* (London: W. Button, 1814) BBM:Angus, microform publ. no. 5855, reel 3, item 7, 30-33.

[109]*The Necessity of the Trumpet's Giving a Certain Sound: A Sermon Preached . . . at Lyme on Thursday, June 10th, 1813* (Bristol; E. Bryan, 1813?) BBHRM:M/-RP, microform publ. no. 946, reel 16, item 6, 20.

[110]*The Faithfulness of God in His Word Evinced: or, the Fulfilling of the Scriptures in the Believer's Own Experience* . . . (London: J. Pasham, 1773) BBM:Angus, microform publ. no. 5855, reel 2, item 1, lines 22-42, 480-500.

[111]*The Law Not against the Promises of God*, 32-33, 35.

[112]*Redemption from the Curse of the Law: A Sermon Preached at Cheltenham, Sept. 18th 1820* . . . (London: B. J. Holdsworth, 1820) BBM:Angus, microform publ. no. 5855, reel 3, item 29, 35.

[113]*Serious Remarks on the Different Representations of Evangelical Doctrine by the Professed Friends of the Gospel* (Bristol: J. G. Fuller, 1817) BBM:Angus,

Ryland engaged in polemic against the Socinians. Why, he asked, is their zeal "against making too much of Christ" not "fully matched" by their zeal against the great moral evils of the day? If "the Socinians are right in their ideas of" Christ's "person, Christ has been *idolized* for at least *sixteen hundred* years."[114] He called upon pastors to be "nursing fathers" (Num. 11:12) to their congregations,[115] defended immersion as the true mode of baptism and practiced open communion,[116] and anticipated a great "increase of the Messiah's kingdom" before "the end of time" without specific reference to a thousand-year reign.[117]

Another participant in the circle of Particular Baptist pastors awakened to evangelical zeal and missionary activity was John Sutcliff. A native of Yorkshire and converted at fifteen or sixteen, he studied at Bristol Baptist Academy. After pastorates at Shrewsbury and Birmingham, he began in 1775 a ministry in Olney which would continue until his death. In intimate friendship with John Ryland, Andrew Fuller, and William Carey, and under the influence of the writings of Jonathan Edwards, Sr., he joined with these friends in issuing the Prayer Call of 1784 and was one of the founders of the Baptist Missionary Society.[118]

Sutcliff replied to Thomas Paine's Deism by appealing to biblical miracles and fulfilled predictive prophecies to validate the revelatory nature of the Scriptures,[119] demonstrated, as did Fuller, a willingness to embrace the governmental theory of the atonement,[120] and expounded "jealousy for

---

microform publ. no. 5855, reel 3, item 26, 30.

[114]*The Partiality and Unscriptural Direction of Socinian Zeal: Being a Reply to the Rev. Mr. Rowe's Letter* . . . (Bristol: Biggs and Cottle, 1801) BBM:Angus, microform publ. no. 5855, reel 3, item 28, esp. 43, 47.

[115]*The Duty of Ministers to Be Nursing Fathers to the Church; and the Duty of Churches to Regard Ministers as the Gift of Christ* . . . (London: Button, 1796) BBM:Angus, microform publ. no. 5855, reel 4, item 4, esp. 16.

[116]*A Candid Statement of the Reasons*, 7-16, xi.

[117]*The Certain Increase of the Glory and Kingdom of Jesus: A Sermon, Preached at Chard, . . . July 11th 1794* . . . (Bristol: John Rose, 1794) esp. 15, 22.

[118]Haykin, *One Heart and One Soul*, 36-67, 85-98, 115-20, 334-39, 82-84, 139-42, 153-71, 176-78, 182-89, 212-23; also idem, "John Sutcliff (1752–1814)," in Haykin, ed., *The British Particular Baptists*, 3:20-41.

[119]*The Divinity of the Christian Religion Considered and Proved in a Letter from the Baptist Association of Leicester, 1797* (Nottingham: T. Dicey and Co., 1797); also Haykin, *One Heart and One Soul*, 286-89.

[120]*The Ordinance of the Lord's Supper Considered* (Dunstable UK: J. W.

God" as a leading motif of the Christian life.[121] He held that only "visible," "sincere," and "spiritual" Christians who make a credible personal profession of genuine repentance and faith should be admitted to church membership[122] and emphasized that baptism and the Lord's Supper "are memorials of the absent Saviour" to be observed "to the close of time" "in their primitive purity and uncorrupted simplicity."[123] Unlike earlier Baptists, Sutcliff had fellowship with individual Anglican and Nonconformist Evangelicals in a context of "evangelical catholicity."[124]

English Particular Baptists from Revival to Missions: William Carey (1761–1834), Andrew Fuller (1754–1815), Abraham Booth (1734–1806), Robert Hall, Jr. (1764–1831), Joseph Kinghorn (1766–1832), Joseph Ivimey (1773–1834), and John Rippon (1750–1836)

Central to the great transition from Hyper-Calvinism to evangelical and missionary Calvinism was William Carey. Born in the Northamptonshire village of Paulerspury and the son of a weaver who had become master of a charity school, Carey was baptized as an infant and reared in the Church of England with a disdain for Dissenters, was, after Christian conversion in 1779, then immersed in 1783 by John Ryland, Jr., worked as a shoemaker,

---

Morris, 1803), as interp. by Haykin, *One Heart and One Soul*, 300-302. See below, 180.

[121]*Jealousy for the Lord of Hosts Illustrated* (London: W. Button, 1791) as reprinted by Haykin, *One Heart and One Soul*, 355-65.

[122]*Qualifications for Church Fellowship: The Circular Letter from . . . the Northamptonshire Association, Assembled at Nottingham, June 3, 4, 5, 1800*, EBP (1951) reel 13, item 19, 4, 6, 7.

[123]*On Obedience to Positive Institutions: The Circular Letter from . . . the Northamptonshire Association, Assembled at Olney, June 7, 8, 9, 1808*, in EBP (1951) reel 13, item 22, 6, 8; *The Ordinance of the Lord's Supper Considered*, 7, 9, 2, as interp. by Haykin, *One Heart and One Soul*, 298. Haykin, "'His Soul-Refreshing Presence': The Lord's Supper in Calvinistic Baptist Thought and Experience in the 'Long' Eighteenth Century," in *Baptist Sacramentalism*, ed. Anthony R. Cross and Philip E. Thompson, Studies in Baptist History and Thought 5 (Carlisle UK; Waynesboro GA: Paternoster, 2003) 188-93, extended his lament that Sutcliff had constricted the Lord's Supper by his almost completely Zwinglian or memorialist view with its absent Christ at a time when evangelization was becoming paramount for Particular Baptists.

[124]Haykin, *One Heart and One Soul*, 292-93, 165.

and served successively as pastor of three Particular Baptist churches. In May 1792 he preached to the Northamptonshire Association his sermon from Isa. 54:2-3 with its climactic "Expect great things. Attempt great things," and the association at Carey's urging registered its intention to form a Baptist missionary society. Inspired by the missionary examples of John Eliot (1604–1690) and David Brainerd (1718–1747) and assisted by Hall's *Help to Zion's Travellers* and the developing theology of Andrew Fuller,[125] Carey published in 1792 *An Enquiry into the Obligations of Christians, to Use Means for the Conversion of the Heathens.*[126] On 2 October he and others formed the Particular Baptist Society for the Propagation of the Gospel amongst the Heathen. In June 1793 Carey and his family and John Thomas, a physician, sailed for India, where Carey would labor for the rest of his life as preacher, church planter, Bible translator, publisher, teacher, and school founder. Carey and his colleagues "translated the Bible into some 40 languages and dialects," and he, who had had no collegiate education, became professor in Fort William College, Calcutta, and founded Serampore College.[127]

Carey's eighty-seven-page *Enquiry* was not essentially a doctrinal treatise, but it would help to turn missiology into a theological discipline. First, inasmuch as most heirs of the Protestant Reformation had assumed that the Great Commission had been fulfilled in the age of the apostles, Carey was compelled to contend that it rather was still binding on Christians of his day. If, he argued, the Great Commission were in fact limited in application to the apostolic era, then all baptisms in Carey's day would be wrongly administered, all postapostolic missionaries would "have acted without a warrant," and the promised presence of the risen, ascended Christ would also have been so limited. The commission has not been "repealed," Rev. 11:1-10 is not a hindrance to modern missions, and missionary work

---

[125]Timothy George, *Faithful Witness: The Life and Mission of William Carey* (Birmingham AL: New Hope, 1991) 2-12, 15-33, 42-45, 55-57; S. Pearce Carey, *William Carey, D.D., Fellow of Linnean Society* (London: Hodder & Stoughton, 1923) passim; Brown, *The English Baptists of the Eighteenth Century*, 90, 115-17, 119-20.

[126](Leicester UK: Ann Ireland, 1792; repr., 1818; facsimile eds. by Baptist Missionary Society, London, 1892, 1934, 1942; repr. as appendix to George, *Faithful Witness*).

[127]George, *Faithful Witness*, 67-69, 81-93, 137-48.

cannot be deferred to a latter-day age of the Spirit.[128] Second, Carey reviewed the history of Christian missions from the New Testament era until the end of the eighteenth century.[129] Third, he provided statistical estimates on world population by nations and colonies and on religious affiliations.[130] Fourth, Carey answered the major objections to a contemporary renewal of missionary activity: the distance of pagan lands from Europe, the "uncivilized" and "barbarous" lifestyle in pagan lands, the danger that missionaries will be killed, the difficulty of obtaining life's necessities, especially European cuisine, and the difficulty of learning other languages.[131] Finally, the cobbler-pastor addressed the question of "means" of implementation: "fervent and united prayer," in which all Christians can be engaged; the formation of a society for the employment and support of foreign missionaries; and regular monetary contributions. While desiring that all Christians should be involved in such missionary support, Carey, recognizing "the present divided state of Christendom," proposed that the society "be formed amongst the *particular baptist denomination*."[132]

In the person and writings of Andrew Fuller the influence of the Evangelical Revival upon Particular Baptists and their sympathy toward such revival would be significantly increased. Born the son of farming parents who were of Calvinist Baptist persuasion in the Cambridgeshire village of Wicken, Fuller, growing up in the village of Soham, was delayed in his Christian conversion by protracted anguish over his lack of a "warrant," or an inward persuasion of divine election. Baptized at sixteen and ordained at 21, he served as pastor of the Baptist church in Soham from 1775 to 1782 and then at Kettering from 1782 to his death. Whether the ecclesial setting of Fuller's youth should be described as High Calvinist or Hyper-Calvinist can be debated, but clearly calling upon unbelievers to repent and to believe was disfavored. Yet slowly but certainly Fuller shifted toward a theologically based advocacy of "indiscriminate gospel preaching."[133] His grandson[134] cited four factors contributing to this change:

---

[128]*An Enquiry into the Obligations of Christians*, 7-13.
[129]Ibid., 14-37.
[130]Ibid., 38-66.
[131]Ibid., 67-76.
[132]Ibid., 77-87, esp. 84.
[133]Andrew Gunton Fuller, "A New Memoir of His Life," in *The Complete Works of the Rev. Andrew Fuller*, rev. by Joseph Belcher (Philadelphia: American Baptist Publication Society, 1845?; repr.: Harrisonburg VA: Sprinkle Publications,

Fuller's reading books that argued for the new position from the Scriptures,[135] his examining carefully the pertinent biblical texts, the success of the preaching of missionaries such as John Eliot and David Brainerd, and the companionship of men such as John Sutcliff and Robert Hall, Jr. Also important was Fuller's reading of writings by John Bunyan and by Jonathan Edwards, Sr.[136] In the Northamptonshire Baptist Association Fuller came to be associated with Carey, Sutcliff, Hall, and John Ryland, Jr., and participated in the formation of the Particular Baptist Society for the Propagation of the Gospel amongst the Heathen (1792), which he then faithfully and sacrificially served as "secretary" and fund-raiser for the rest of his life.[137]

Fuller's writings, which extend to 2,419 pages,[138] consist of seven major theological discourses,[139] two biblical commentaries,[140] nine circular letters of Northamptonshire Association, more than ninety sermons, half a dozen briefer theological writings in the form of letters, an apology for Indian

---

1988) 1:1-44; Thomas Elkins Fuller, *A Memoir of the Life and Writings of Andrew Fuller* (London: J. Heaton and Son, 1863) 1-48; R. Philip Roberts, "Andrew Fuller," in *Baptist Theologians*, ed. George and Dockery, 121-24; Gilbert Laws, *Andrew Fuller: Pastor, Theologian, Ropeholder* (London: Carey, 1942).

[134]T. E. Fuller, *A Memoir*, 27-29.

[135]Such as Abraham Taylor, *The Modern Question concerning Repentance and Faith, Examined with Candour in Four Dialogues* (London, 1742).

[136]A. G. Fuller, "A New Memoir of His Life," 3, 14-15.

[137]John Ryland, *The Work of Faith, the Labour of Love, and the Patience of Hope, Illustrated in the Life and Death of the Rev. Andrew Fuller . . .* (Charlestown MA: Samuel Etheridge, 1818) 136-200; Underwood, *A History of the English Baptists*, 164-65; F. Townley Lord, *Achievement: A Short History of the Baptist Missionary Society, 1792–1942* (London: Carey, 1942) 7-17, 19, 22-23, 100; Brian Stanley, *The History of the Baptist Missionary Society, 1792–1992* (Edinburgh: T.&T. Clark, 1992) 9-12, 15-35.

[138]Roberts, "Andrew Fuller," 122. See *The Complete Works*, 3 vols.

[139]*The Gospel Worthy of All Acceptation . . .* (1785); *A Defence of a Treatise Entitled 'The Gospel Worthy of All Acceptation' . . .* (1787); *The Calvinistic and Socinian Systems Examined and Compared as to Their Moral Tendency* (1792); *Socinianism Indefensible . . .* (1797); *The Gospel Its Own Witness* (1800); *Letters to Mr. Vidler on Universal Salvation* (1802); *Strictures on Sandemanianism . . .* (1810).

[140]*Expository Discourses on the Book of Genesis* (1806); *Expository Discourses on the Apocalypse* (1815).

missions, the memoirs of Samuel Pearce, and a multitude of essays, tracts, and biblical textual pieces.

Fuller's twenty-article personal confession of faith, which he set forth at his induction to his pastorate at Kettering, was weighted toward soteriology inasmuch as six of the twenty articles pertain to salvation, when that subject is differentiated from the doctrines of man and sin and from God's eternal plan.[141]

The Kettering pastor assumed the role of a Christian apologist vis-à-vis Deism.[142] His anti-Deistical argument was twofold: Christianity is marked by holiness, but Deism is characterized by immorality; and the harmony and rationality of biblical history and teaching give evidence favorable to the claims of Christianity. As to the first argument, Fuller contended that whereas Christianity reveals a God of *"moral* perfections," Deism is deficient as to such; that whereas Christians seek to worship and serve the God whom they profess, Deists refuse to worship the deity of whom they speak; that Christian morality is rooted in the commands to love God and neighbor, whereas Deism's morality does not rise above civil laws, human feelings, or *"the law and light of nature"*; and that Christianity offers numerous admonitions and motivations to morality which Deism, despite its appeal to postmortal rewards and punishments, does not. Moreover, the lives of Deism's leaders pale before the higher morality of numerous Christians, Christianity has elevated morality of societies above the practices of ancient Greece and Rome and without comparable results from Deism, and the Christian gospel brings happiness with its peace of mind, perpetuity, meeting of needs, and relief of miseries, and Deism does not.[143] Fuller's second argument majored on fulfilled biblical prophecies, on Christianity's credible and realistic assessment of societal ills as rooted in human depravity and idolatry, on the rational necessity of the Christian doctrine of atonement/propitiation/satisfaction/redemption in contrast to the inadequacy of efforts "to bestow pardon without a mediator." Indeed the

---

[141] This confession may be found in Ryland, *The Work of Faith*, 54-59.

[142] *The Gospel Its Own Witness; or, the Holy Nature and Divine Harmony of the Christian Religion Contrasted with the Immorality and Absurdity of Deism*, in *Complete Works*, 2:1-107, was directed particularly to Tom Paine's *The Age of Reason* but also constituted an answer to "Shaftesbury, Tindal, Morgan, Bolingbroke, Voltaire, Hume and Gibbon" (introduction).

[143] Ibid., part 1.

Christian doctrine of redemption is not inconsistent with the modern view of an enlarged universe but is even strengthened by such a modern view.[144]

Fuller differentiated and affirmed what twentieth-century theologians would call "general revelation" and "special revelation," the human corruption of the former making necessary the latter.[145] In refuting the Socinian Joseph Priestley, Fuller declared: "As the sacred writers considered themselves as Divinely inspired, so they represented their writings as the infallible test of Divine truth, to which all appeals were to be made, and by which every controversy in religious matters was to be decided." To venerate the Bible's authority, one must "receive it as *being what it professes to be, and for all the purposes for which it professes to be written.*"[146] In a sermon he insisted that "*all Divine knowledge is to be derived from the oracles of God,*" that is, the Scriptures. To neglect them is "*a heinous sin,*" for they are "*a means of sanctification*" and "*the great source of Christian enjoyment.*"[147] Norman Hill Maring has noted that Fuller "pointed out that although the Bible contains a system of revealed truth, yet it is not presented in systematic form."[148] According to R. Philip Roberts, Fuller's theological work "was primarily polemical," for he "was not a systematizer like John Gill."[149] In the confluence of these two assessments, we seek now to interpret Fuller in a systematic framework.

The attributes of God and the doctrine of the Trinity were more assumed by Fuller than explicated by him.[150] Nor did Fuller treat in detail those Christological concerns that occupied center stage in the patristic era. His refutation of Socinianism was much more focused on its fruits than on its roots. It does not adequately lead to repentance toward God and faith toward the Lord Jesus Christ. It is not essentially missionary, and any argument from the number and nature of its converts is dubious. It is inferior in

---

[144]Ibid., part 2; Bush and Nettles, *Baptists and the Bible*, 113-16.

[145]Personal confession of faith, arts. 1-2, in Ryland, *The Work of Faith*, 54; Tull, *Shapers of Baptist Thought*, 93.

[146]*The Calvinistic and Socinian Systems Examined and Compared, as to Their Moral Tendency*, letter 12, in *Complete Works*, 2:196.

[147]*The Nature and Importance of an Intimate Knowledge of Divine Truth*, in *Complete Works*, 1:160, 168, 169, 170.

[148]"Andrew Fuller's Doctrine of the Church," in *Baptist Concepts of the Church*, ed. Winthrop Still Hudson (Philadelphia: Judson, 1959) 75.

[149]"Andrew Fuller," 125.

[150]Personal confession of faith, art. 3, in Ryland, *The Work of Faith*, 54.

promoting morality, evoking love to God, engendering love toward Christ, producing humility, bringing happiness, or motivating human beings. It rejects Christ as "the *rule* of faith, the *ground* of hope, and the *object* of worship." It even closely resembles Deism.[151] Fuller did insist that the doctrine of the atonement is "necessarily connected with the Divinity of Christ," refuting the argument that only the human, which only is capable of suffering, is needed to make atonement, and that atonement is "essential to our calling on his name and trusting in him for salvation."[152]

Fuller seemingly derived from his Particular Baptist roots some adherence to penal substitution as the central meaning of Christ's atonement, although he avoided the subject in his personal confession of faith.[153] In refuting Socinianism he insisted that the love of God is the "cause" of the atonement and not that the death of Christ obtained the love of God.[154] In writing to John Ryland, he denied "that God for one moment was angry or displeased with" Jesus. Since "*imputation* ought not to be confounded with *transfer*," then "all that is transferred in the imputation of sin is its penal effects," and thus Jesus himself was not guilty of the sins of the elect—a view that Fuller attributed to Tobias Crisp.[155] In answering the Deists, Fuller asserted that "debt" and "ransom" are terms "borrowed from pecuniary transactions" and used "metaphorically." "As sin is not a pecuniary, but a moral debt, so the atonement for it is not a pecuniary, but a moral ransom."[156] Along with this honed penal substitutionary view Fuller came to embrace aspects of the governmental or penal example theory, first set forth by the Dutch jurist Hugo Grotius (1583–1645), according to which the necessity for the death of Jesus lay in the rectoral duties of the benevolent God and his intention to discourage human sin by the public exhibition of his subjection of his Son to cruel death.[157] The governmental theory was

---

[151]*The Calvinistic and Socinian Systems Examined and Compared*, letters 2-4, 6-7, 11, 9, 13-14, 10, 15, in *Complete Works*, 2:115-36, 141-61, 188-95, 170-74, 206-20, 180, 220-33.

[152]*The Deity of Christ*, in *Complete Works*, 3:693-97.

[153]In Ryland, *The Work of Faith*, 54-59.

[154]*The Calvinistic and Socinian Systems Examined and Compared*, letter 7, in *Complete Works*, 2:154.

[155]*Six Letters to Dr. Ryland respecting the Controversy with the Rev. A. Booth*, letter 2 (8 January 1803) in *Complete Works*, 2:705.

[156]*The Gospel Its Own Witness*, part 2, ch. 4, in *Complete Works*, 2:80-81.

[157]See Sydney Cave, *The Doctrine of the Work of Christ* (London: University

most likely mediated to Fuller through certain New England theologians who had embraced it: Joseph Bellamy (1719–1790), Samuel Hopkins (1721–1803), Stephen West (1735–1819), and Jonathan Edwards, Jr. (1745–1801).[158] Hence Fuller wrote:

> The incapacity of God to show mercy without an atonement, is no other than that of a righteous governor, who, whatever good-will he may bear to an offender, cannot admit the thought of passing by the offense, without some public expression of his displeasure against it; that, while mercy triumphs, it may not be at the expense of law and equity, and of the general good.[159]

But Fuller's commitment to Dortian Calvinism was retained at the point of his holding to a limited atonement. Dan Taylor's refutation[160] of Fuller's

---

of London Press, 1937) 176-82; Robert H. Culpepper, *Interpreting the Atonement* (Grand Rapids MI: Eerdmans, 1966) 105-108; James Leo Garrett, Jr., *Systematic Theology: Biblical, Historical, and Evangelical*, 2nd ed. (North Richland Hills TX: BIBAL, 2001) 2:26-28. Edwin Allen Reed, "A Historical Study of Three Baptist Doctrines of Atonement as Seen in the Writings of John Smyth and Thomas Helwys, John Gill, and Andrew Fuller" (Th.M. thesis, Golden Gate Baptist Theological Seminary, 1965) 110, 126, 131, concluded that Fuller strained "the limits of his Anselmic-Calvinistic heritage" and "was influenced by the governmental theory of Grotius."

[158]See Frank Hugh Foster, *A Genetic History of the New England Theology* (Chicago: University of Chicago Press, 1907; repr.: New York: Garland Publishing, 1987) 113-17, 177-82; Joseph A. Conforti, *Samuel Hopkins and the New Divinity Movement: Calvinism, the Congregational Ministry, and Reform in New England between the Great Awakenings* (Washington DC: Christian College Consortium, 1981) 163-64; Dorus Paul Rudisill, *The Doctrine of the Atonement in Jonathan Edwards and His Successors* (New York: Poseidon Books, 1971) esp. 36-37, 51, 63-64, 77-78, 85-86, 92-109; Morden, *Offering Christ to the World*, 89-92.

[159]*The Calvinist and Socinian Systems Examined and Compared*, letter 7, in *Complete Works*, 2:154-55. R. Philip Roberts, *Continuity and Change: London Calvinistic Baptists and the Evangelical Revival, 1760–1820* (Wheaton IL: Richard Owen Roberts, 1989) 168-69, has implied that the second revised edition (1801) of *The Gospel Worthy of All Acceptation* marked the clear advent of Fuller's espousal of the governmental theory, but our quotation from Fuller, dated 1792, is evidence of earlier commitment to the theory.

[160]*Observations on the Rev. Andrew Fuller's Late Pamphlet Entitled the Gospel Worthy of All Acceptation* (London, 1786) in BBHRM:M/RP, microform publ. no. 946, reel 11, item 13.

Calvinism as expressed in *The Gospel Worthy of All Acceptation* included a critical wooing of him from limited atonement. Fuller's reply contained a sevenfold defense of Christ's death for the elect.[161] Indeed, "Christ, in his death, absolutely designed the salvation of all those who are finally saved."[162] Thomas J. Nettles has affirmed that Fuller's doctrine was fully "consistent" with the historical formula, traceable at least to Peter Lombard (ca.1100–1160), "sufficient for all but efficient only for the elect."[163]

Fuller's protracted and agonizing conversion in which he found gracious acceptance by Christ without a "warrant" was for some time in conflict with the practices of the High or Hyper-Calvinism in which he had been nurtured. He continued to refrain from inviting the unconverted to come to Jesus. But through biblical study and theological reflection he began to compose a soteriological revision, and after about five years this was published as *The Gospel Worthy of All Acceptation, or the Duty of Sinners to Believe in Jesus Christ* (1785).[164] After explaining his subject and defining the pertinent terms, Fuller proceeded to the heart of this treatise: six "arguments to prove that faith in Christ is the duty of all men who hear, or have opportunity to hear, the gospel":

1. "Unconverted sinners are commanded, exhorted, and invited to believe in Christ for salvation."[165]
2. "Every man is bound cordially to receive and approve whatever God reveals."

---

[161] *A Defence of a Treatise Entitled the Gospel Worthy of All Acceptation: Containing a Reply to Mr. Button's Remarks and the Observations of Philanthropos*, reply to Philanthropos, sect. 4, in *Complete Works*, 2:490-94. For a summary of these arguments, see Nettles, *By His Grace and for His Glory*, 123-26, and Morden, *Offering Christ to the World*, 68-72, although Morden mistakenly concludes (70, 76) that Fuller fully embraced general atonement.

[162] *The Reality and Efficacy of Divine Grace, with the Certain Success of Christ's Kingdom . . .* , letter 12, in *Complete Works*, 2:551.

[163] Nettles, *By His Grace and for His Glory*, 123.

[164] John W. Eddins, Jr., "Andrew Fuller's Theology of Grace" (Th.D. diss., Southern Baptist Theological Seminary, 1957) 39, 41. The text of the original edition was included in *The Baptist Library: A Republication of Standard Baptist Works*, ed. Charles G. Sommers, William R. Williams, and Levi L. Hill (Prattsville NY: Robert H. Hill, 1843) 2:375-411. The text of the second or revised edition of 1801 appears in *Complete Works*, 2:328-416. Concerning the changes in the second edition, see Morden, *Offering Christ to the World*, 73-75.

[165] See Psa. 2:11-12; Isa. 45:1-7; Jer. 6:16; John 12:3b; 6:29; 5:23.

3. "Though the gospel, strictly speaking, is not a law, but a message of pure grace; yet it virtually requires obedience, and such an obedience as includes saving faith."
4. "The want of faith in Christ is ascribed in the Scriptures to men's depravity, and is itself represented as a heinous sin."[166]
5. "God has threatened and inflicted the most awful punishments on sinners for their not believing on the Lord Jesus Christ."[167]
6. "Other spiritual exercises, which sustain an inseparable connexion with faith in Christ, are represented as the duty of men in general."[168]

Then Fuller posed and answered objections to duty-faith: the holiness possessed by prelapsarian Adam was not conducive to living "through a mediator," and his posterity are not commanded so to live; a general invitation to sinners is "inconsistent" with the divine decrees, with particular atonement, and with living under the covenant of works. Sinners lack the ability to believe in Christ and hence are not obligated to believe. Repentance and faith are the work of the Holy Spirit, not "*duties* required of sinners," for indeed a "divine principle" or "influence" is necessary for believing.[169]

Objections to Fuller's treatise soon followed. William Button, a London pastor, differentiated supernatural "saving faith," possible only for the elect, from "general faith in God," objected to Fuller's use of Jonathan Edwards's distinction between natural and moral inability, and asserted that "God never requires what man cannot do in and of himself."[170] Fuller, in amicably

---

[166] In addition to depravity: "*voluntary ignorance,*" "*pride,*" "*dishonesty* of heart," "*aversion of heart,*" "*a voluntary and judicial blindness, obstinacy, and hardness of heart,*" and "unbelief."

[167] See Mark 16:15-16; Psa. 37:18, 20; 147:6; 145:20; John 3:18; Luke 19:27; 2 Thess. 2:10-12.

[168] That is, "*the love of God,*" "*love to Christ,*" "*the fear of God,*" repentance, and humility. *The Gospel Worthy of All Acceptation*, part 2, in *Complete Works*, 2:343-66.

[169] Ibid., part 3, in *Complete Works*, 2:366-82. Thomas Kennedy Ascol, "The Doctrine of Grace: A Critical Analysis of Federalism in the Theologies of John Gill and Andrew Fuller" (Ph.D. diss., Southwestern Baptist Theological Seminary, 1989) has contended that Fuller adhered to covenantal theology more than Gill by his balancing divine sovereignty and human responsibility.

[170] Button, *Remarks on a Treatise Entitled the Gospel Worthy of All Acceptation* . . . (London, 1785) as interpreted by Roberts, *Continuity and Change*, 163-64. See also Morden, *Offering Christ to the World*, 55-61.

Awakening and Missionary Baptists   183

replying to Button,[171] answered point-by-point, making the biblical basis for his own views more emphatic than the rational.[172] Another London pastor, John Martin (1741–1820), criticized Fuller's position by objecting that faith is not biblically commanded of unbelievers and by denying that all humans are "bound" "to receive and approve whatever God reveals."[173] Fuller's terse reply, accusing Martin of misrepresentations and similar to his reply to Button, saw him claim the support of certain Particular Baptist leaders and defend his reading and use of writings by Americans, Jonathan Edwards, Sr., and Joseph Bellamy.[174] Dan Taylor's critique, already mentioned,[175] agreed on duty-faith but declared that the universal offer of salvation by removing ignorance removed the inability to believe.[176] Fuller, in replying to "Philanthropos" (or Taylor), insisted that the Holy Spirit is the "efficient cause of a sinner's believing in Jesus Christ," not merely the dispenser of a "holy influence," and hence regeneration precedes repentance and faith; that depravity bears guilt; that faith in Christ is "a requirement of the moral law," and unbelief is "a breach of the law of Moses;" that Christ was absolutely determined by his death to save the elect;[177] and that the effectual operations of the Holy Spirit are irresistible.[178]

---

[171]*A Defence of a Treatise Entitled the Gospel Worthy of All Acceptation, Containing a Reply to Mr. Button's Remarks and the Observations of Philanthropos* in *Complete Works*, 2:417-59.

[172]Roberts, *Continuity and Change*, 164.

[173]Martin, *Thoughts on the Duty of Man relative to Faith in Jesus Christ; in which Mr. Fuller's Leading Propositions on That Subject Are Considered* . . . (1788–1791), as interpreted by Roberts, *Continuity and Change*, 165.

[174]*Remarks on Mr. Martin's Publication, Entitled, "Thoughts on the Duty of Man relative to Faith in Jesus Christ"* . . . in *Complete Works*, 2:716-36, esp. 717, 718. Martin wrote two other treatises against Fuller, but Fuller responded to neither. Roberts, *Continuity and Change*, 165-66. On Button and Martin see Robert W. Oliver, *History of the English Calvinistic Baptists, 1771–1892: From John Gill to C. H. Spurgeon* (Edinburgh; Carlisle PA: Banner of Truth Trust, 2006) 99-107.

[175]See above, 181n.160.

[176]*Observations on the Rev. Andrew Fuller's Late Pamphlet Entitled The Gospel Worthy of All Acceptation*, in BBHRM:M/RP, microfilm publ. no. 946, reel 11, item 13, as interpreted by Roberts, "Andrew Fuller," 127.

[177]*A Defence of a Treatise Entitled*, in *Complete Works*, 2:459-511.

[178]*The Reality and Efficacy of Divine Grace*, letter 2, in *Complete Works*, 2:518-19. See also Morden, *Offering Christ to the World*, 63-68.

Fuller also received criticism from outside Baptist ranks, that is, from the form of Scottish Independency which began with the ministries of John Glas (1695–1773) and his son-in-law Robert Sandeman (1718–1771)[179] and impacted Fuller through the writing[180] of Archibald McLean (1733–1812). As a Calvinist, McLean agreed with Fuller that regeneration precedes repentance and faith, but as a Sandemanian he held tenaciously that faith is nothing more than the intellectual acceptance of the gospel revelation.[181] Hence "saving faith is simply an act of man's mind by which he believes the testimony of Jesus Christ, and . . . it differs from any ordinary act of belief only in being belief of the evidence about a saving fact."[182] Fuller's first reply[183] to McLean argued that "a holy disposition of heart" is necessary to genuine faith. Nearly a decade later Fuller wrote *Strictures on Sandemanianism*, in which he elaborated the differing views on faith, charged McLean with inverting the New Testament sequence of repentance and faith, taught that "spiritual understanding" differs from "*notional understanding*" and justifying faith involves "the *holy exercises* of the will and affections," and found the Sandemanians to be too "punctilious" about family prayer, the Lord's Day, washing of disciples' feet, and the holy kiss,

---

[179]See Winfred Ernest Garrison and Alfred T. DeGroot, *The Disciples of Christ: A History*, rev. ed. (St. Louis: Bethany, 1958) 46-50; William Heth Whitsitt, *Origin of the Disciples of Christ (Campbellites): A Contribution to the Centennial Anniversary of the Birth of Alexander Campbell* (New York: A. C. Armstrong and Son, 1888) 1-22.

[180]*The Commission Given by Jesus Christ to His Apostles Illustrated*, 4th ed. (London, 1819; orig., 1786) 71-83. "Every body knows that faith or belief, in the ordinary sense of the word, is that *credit* which we give to the truth of any thing which is made known to us by report or testimony, and is grounded either on the veracity of the speaker, or on the evidence by which his words are confirmed. But many are of opinion, that justifying faith must be something more than this. . . . The word *pistis faith* or *belief*, is evidently used by the inspired writers in the same sense in which it is commonly used and understood among men in ordinary cases" (74, 77). See below, 249-51.

[181]Roberts, "Andrew Fuller," 127-28.

[182]Garrison and DeGroot, *The Disciples of Christ*, 48.

[183]"Appendix: On the Question whether the Existence of a Holy Disposition of Heart Be Necessary to Believing" to the second (1801) edition of *The Gospel Worthy of All Acceptation*, in *Complete Works*, 2:393-416.

too lax in following New Testament church polity, and more given to proselytism than to evangelism.[184]

Fuller's teaching that regeneration precedes repentance and faith also somewhat surprisingly evoked criticism from another London Particular Baptist pastor, Abraham Booth, formerly a General Baptist. In his *Glad Tidings to Perishing Sinners* (1796)[185] Booth accused Fuller of making regeneration a barrier to the free invitation of the gospel. "The genuine gospel," he asserted, is "a complete warrant for the most ungodly person to believe in Jesus," and "no degree of holiness" [that is, regeneration] is "previously necessary" for such believing.[186] Fuller, whose youthful conversion had meant acceptance of Christ without a "warrant," was now being accused of making regeneration a "warrant."[187] These controversies with Taylor, McLean, and Booth, according to Philip Roberts, "demonstrated the triumph of evangelical Calvinism because the issue was no longer . . . whether or not to offer the gospel but was an attempt to remove all hindrances to such ministry."[188]

Ecclesiology was a subject treated by Fuller, but not a major focus of his writings. He did not find it necessary to make a detailed defense of believer's baptism or baptism by immersion but instead dealt with the "*influence*" and "effects" of baptism. It is a "*solemn and practical profession of the Christian religion*," a motivation for holy living and "*separation from the world*," and a line of demarcation "between *the kingdom of Christ and the kingdom of Satan*."[189] Infant communion is no more defensible than infant baptism.[190] Fuller defended "strict" communion and opposed "open" communion on the grounds that true baptism is prerequisite to participation in the Lord's Supper, that immersion is necessary to true baptism, and that

---

[184]*Strictures on Sandemanianism*, esp. letters 2, 3, 5, 6, 8, 9, 10, and 11, in *Complete Works*, 2:561-646. See below, 250-51.

[185]Subtitle: *or, The Genuine Gospel a Complete Warrant for the Ungodly to Believe in Jesus* (Philadelphia: Shadrach Taylor, 1833; orig., 1796).

[186]Ibid., 18, 55.

[187]Fuller's reply to Booth was briefly incorporated in his reply to McLean, i.e., the 1801 appendix (*Complete Works*, 2:397, 413-14) and more fully expressed in *Six Letters to Dr. Ryland respecting the Controversy with the Rev. A. Booth*, letters 1-5 (*Complete Works*, 2:699-714).

[188]"Andrew Fuller," 129.

[189]*The Practical Uses of Christian Baptism* (1802), *Complete Works*, 3:339-45.

[190]*Terms of Communion* in *Complete Works*, 3:499-501.

a Baptist church and not solely a paedobaptist Christian should settle this issue.[191] There is seemingly no evidence that Fuller did not adhere to congregational polity, although he wrote little about it, for he did call for a return to the discipline of the primitive churches.[192] Rather he frequently preached about the pastoral ministry.[193] Fuller preferred the singing of biblical texts but allowed for hymns if properly matched with appropriate tunes. Instrumental music in public worship he strongly rejected as "utterly unsuited to the genius of the gospel dispensation."[194]

Fuller's eschatological thought centered on the espousal of postmillennialism and the refutation of eschatological universalism. Adhering to the continuous-historical method of interpreting the New Testament book of Revelation, which he reckoned to be a book of "prophecy," he, contra Gill, rejected that interpretation of the letters to the seven churches as predictive of seven ages in the later history of Christianity. Fuller regarded "the book of *seven seals*" as containing "the whole of the prophecy" and identified his own lifetime with the period of the sixth vial (Rev. 16:12-16), including "the overthrow of the temporal power of Antichrist." Furthermore, the "thousand years" of Rev. 20:1-7, taken literally and being identical with the marriage supper of the Lamb and the "first resurrection," will follow the latter-day "prosperity" of the church and worldwide spread of the gospel and

---

[191]*Strictures on the Rev. John Carter's "Thoughts on Baptism and Mixed Communion...," Thoughts on Open Communion* (1800), *Strict Communion in the Mission Church at Serampore* (1814), and *The Admission of Unbaptized Persons to the Lord's Supper Inconsistent with the New Testament* (1814), in *Complete Works*, 3:501-15.

[192]*The Discipline of the Primitive Churches Illustrated and Enforced* (1799) in *Complete Works*, 3:331-38.

[193]For example, *Pastors Required to Feed the Flock of Christ, Spiritual Knowledge and Love Necessary for the Ministry, Ministers Appointed to Root out Evil and to Cultivate Good, Ministers Fellow Labourers with God, The Work and Encouragements of the Christian Minister, Habitual Devotedness to the Ministry, Affectionate Concern of a Minister for the Salvation of His Hearers, The Christian Ministry a Great Work, Christian Churches Fellow Helpers with Their Pastors to the Truth, The Reward of a Faithful Minister,* and *The Obedience of Churches to Their Pastors Explained and Enforced* in *Complete Works*, 1:477-82, 486-89, 491-94, 496-501, 506-10, 513-15, 524-26, 542-43, 196-202.

[194]*Instrumental Music in Christian Worship* and *Thoughts on Singing* in *Complete Works*, 3:515-23.

will be succeeded by the general resurrection and general judgment. For Fuller, then, Christ's millennial reign will be "spiritual," not "personal."[195]

In a more polemical vein Fuller refuted the eschatological universalism of William Vidler.[196] According to Fuller, Vidler's teaching was contrary to that of the Scriptures: some passages "describe the future state of men in [marked] contrast"; other passages, using "everlasting," "forever," and similar terms, teach "the duration of future punishment"; still others imply "the duration of eternal punishment"; yet others indicate that a "change of heart" and of destiny can occur only in the present life. Fuller even suggested that Vidler was opting for annihilationism as well as for universalism.[197] Fuller also set forth a doctrine of heavenly rewards and different degrees of heavenly glory.[198]

How does one categorize and evaluate the theological work of Fuller? One can begin with Fuller's threefold classification of Calvinists in his day: "high" Calvinists, who were "more Calvinistic than Calvin himself"; "moderate" Calvinists, who were "half-Arminian[s]"; and "strict" Calvinists, who held to "the system of Calvin." Fuller identified himself with the third group.[199] Certain studies have sought to demonstrate Fuller's reading of and debt to Calvin.[200] Baptist historians in the United States[201] have tended to label Fuller a "moderate" or "modified" Calvinist, whereas British Baptist authors[202] have preferred to call him an "evangelical Calvinist."

---

[195]*Expository Discourses on the Apocalypse*, scheme of the prophecy and discourses, 2, 24, 25, 26, 28, 29, in *Complete Works* 3:202-207, 210, 276-87, 291-97.

[196]Vidler, *God's Love to His Creatures Asserted and Vindicated* (London, 1799).

[197]*Letters to Mr. Vidler, on the Doctrine of Universal Salvation*, esp. letters 5, 3, in *Complete Works*, 2:306-12, 300-302.

[198]*The Heavenly Glory* in *Complete Works*, 3:725-44; esp. 732, 741-43.

[199]Ryland, *The Work of Faith*, 346. See also Arthur H. Kirkby, "Andrew Fuller—Evangelical Calvinist," *Baptist Quarterly* 15 (January 1954): 195.

[200]Kirkby, "Andrew Fuller—Evangelical Calvinist," 198; Ernest F. Clipsham, "Andrew Fuller and Fullerism: a Study in Evangelical Calvinism" (II), *Baptist Quarterly* 20 (October 1963): 146-54. But Morden, *Offering Christ to the World*, 33-35, 87-89, played down any originating influence of Calvin.

[201]Vedder, *A Short History of the Baptists*, 249; Torbet, *A History of the Baptists*, 103; McBeth, *The Baptist Heritage*, 182, 774.

[202]Kirkby, "Andrew Fuller—Evangelical Calvinist," 202; Clipsham, "Andrew Fuller and Fullerism," 146; Morden, *Offering Christ to the World*, 51, 92-93, 102,

Fuller's "main work and contribution" have been said to be "soteriological."[203] With respect to Particular Baptists his contribution has been described as helping to "stave off the paralysis of hyper-Calvinism,"[204] as "freeing the denomination from the imprisonment of hyper-Calvinism" and "launching . . . a new era of evangelism and missions,"[205] as uniting "doctrinal strength" and "evangelistic fervour,"[206] as restoring "moral obligation and human responsibility to the very centre of their theology of salvation,"[207] as properly "determining . . . the relation between the grace of God and the responsibility of man in the salvation of the race,"[208] as bringing "to an end the reign of hyper-Calvinism among the great majority of Particular Baptist ministers and churches,"[209] and as their "premier theologian" and a true Evangelical.[210] But one identification of Fuller as "the chief cause for the awakening of . . . [the] missionary impulse among Particular Baptists"[211] must be balanced by the judgment of another that Robert Hall, Sr., and Fuller were "more symptomatic than causative" of the new evangelism.[212] Fuller has been called "one of the most widely read and influential theological writers of England and America,"[213] "the soundest and most creatively useful the Particular Baptists . . . ever had,"[214] and "perhaps the greatest theologian English Baptists ever produced."[215]

But Fuller has not been without his critics, especially as "Gillites" began to controvert "Fullerites" and as later Strict and Particular Baptists in England took an anti-Fuller stance.[216] The zenith of criticism of Fuller's

---

180-84.

[203]Roberts, "Andrew Fuller," 132.
[204]McBeth, *The Baptist Heritage*, 182.
[205]Tull, *Shapers of Baptist Thought*, 98.
[206]Whitley, *A History of British Baptists*, 232.
[207]Stanley, *The History of the Baptist Missionary Society*, 5-6.
[208]Kirkby, "Andrew Fuller—Evangelical Calvinist," 197.
[209]Underwood, *A History of the English Baptists*, 164.
[210]Morden, *Offering Christ to the World*, 100, 181-84.
[211]Torbet, *A History of the Baptists*, 103.
[212]Olin C. Robison, "The Particular Baptists in England, 1760–1820" (D.Phil. diss., University of Oxford, 1963) 38, as quoted by Roberts, *Continuity and Change*, 176.
[213]Vedder, *A Short History of the Baptists*, 249.
[214]Underwood, *A History of the English Baptists*, 166.
[215]McBeth, *The Baptist Heritage*, 182.
[216]Tull, *Shapers of Baptist Thought*, 99; see below, 198, 199.

theology is undoubtedly the recent monograph by George M. Ella.[217] He has severely indicted Fuller for his false views of Adamic guilt, the punishment of sin, the separation of the justice and the righteousness of God, the effects of the fall of humankind (with the consequent exaltation of reason and natural theology), reconciliation, justification, and sanctification and has identified the central defect as Fuller's critique of the "commercial" view and his embrace of Grotius's view of the atonement by means of his effort to "demetaphorise" the New Testament. Exalting Gill while denigrating Fuller, Ella has labeled Fuller "Antinomian," Baxterian, and "Calminian," tending toward Socinianism, while charging his modern followers with trying to combine "the doctrines of grace *and* the doctrines of works-righteousness." Ella has concluded that "Fullerism" is "a humanistic message which is . . . of no saving value" and is "completely different" from the gospel commanded by Jesus in his Great Commission.

To the company of evangelical Particular Baptist pastor-theologians was added one whose roots were in the soil of the General Baptists, Abraham Booth. Born in Derbyshire but reared in Nottinghamshire by farming Anglican parents, he was converted at twelve, wrote a poem against predestination at 20, was baptized by a General Baptist at 21, and became a preacher to two General Baptist congregations before a shift to deep Calvinist convictions compelled him to resign. He then gathered a Particular Baptist congregation at Sutton Ashfield and published *The Reign of Grace from Its Rise to Its Consummation* (1768) after being befriended by Henry Venn, an Evangelical Anglican. Called to and ordained for the pastorate of Little Prescot-Street Baptist Church in London, he continued in that ministry for 37 years until his death. He secured a tutor to help him to learn Latin, and he acquired some knowledge of Greek and Hebrew. Unlike numerous other London pastors, Booth supported from the beginning the society that sent out Thomas and Carey, and he was instrumental in initiating the itinerant preaching that became the Baptist Home Mission Society and the educational efforts that ultimately became Regent's Park College.[218]

---

[217]*Law and Gospel in the Theology of Andrew Fuller* (Eggleston UK: Go Publications, 1996) esp. 154-55, 29-37, 60-67, 69-71, 77-78, 109-45, 21, 67-69, 74-75, 92-97, 30, 185-99, 56-57, 146-50, 151, 200, 204.

[218]William Jones, *An Essay on the Life and Writings of Mr. Abraham Booth, Late Pastor of the Baptist Church in Little Prescot-Street, Goodman's Fields, London* (Liverpool: James Smith, 1808) 3-25; K. F. T. Matrunola, *A Brief Account of the Life and Labours of Abraham Booth, 1734–1806* (Rushden UK: Fauconberg

In *The Reign of Grace* Booth defined grace as "the eternal and absolutely free favour of God, manifested in the vouchsafement of spiritual and eternal blessings to the guilty and the unworthy" and noted that the "gospel of Reigning Grace ... has ever been the object of the world's contempt."[219] He then proceeded to explicate grace in respect to each of the categories of his *ordo salutis*: election, effectual calling, pardon, justification, adoption, sanctification, perseverance, and consummation. All of this was through the person and work of the non-Socinian and righteous Jesus Christ.[220] Booth's confession of faith presented at his ordination treated in detail the revelatory nature of biblical teachings and affirmed the federal imputation of Adam's sin and particular election but was silent as to limited atonement and did not address the issue of strict or open communion.[221] Seeking to avoid the "fatal extremes" of "Arminian legality" and "Antinomian licentiousness," Booth in *The Death of Legal Hope* asserted that unregenerate sinners are alive to the moral law in that they seek to be justified by it, they become dead to that moral law when they are born again and that law is dead to them so that they may live to God in "holy" "obedience," and yet all believers are commanded to heed the moral law as "a rule of conduct."[222] In *Glad Tidings to Perishing Sinners* he strongly contended that "the genuine gospel" is "a complete warrant for the most ungodly person to believe in Jesus" and that no antecedent "holy disposition" or "degree of holiness" is necessary as a warrant.[223] In addition to such refutation of the earlier Hyper-Calvinism and of Fuller, Booth supplied a detailed critique of certain teachings of Samuel Hopkins, namely, that regeneration is by the Holy Spirit and not through the

---

Press for the Strict Baptist Historical Society, 1981); Underwood, *A History of the English Baptists*, 179-80, 198-99; Robert W. Oliver, "Abraham Booth (1734–1806)," in *The British Particular Baptists*, ed. Haykin, 2:30-40.

[219](Leeds: E. and C. Dilley, 1768); (repr.: Paris AR: Baptist Standard Bearer, 1995) 47, 39.

[220]Ibid., 53-291.

[221]*A Charge and Sermon together with an Introductory Discourse and Confession of Faith Delivered at the Ordination of the Rev. Mr. Abraham Booth, Feb. 16, 1769*... (London: G. Keith et al., 1769) BBM:Bodleian, microform publ. no. 5877, reel 5, item 2, 11-26.

[222]*The Death of Legal Hope, the Life of Evangelical Obedience: An Essay on Galatians 2:19*... (London: E. and C. Dilly et al., 1770) esp. iv, 15, 28-30, 66-67, 77-78, 94, 105.

[223]*Glad Tidings to Perishing Sinners*, esp. 18, 11, 55. See above, 185.

word of God, that regeneration is "a change of the *will* or *heart*" but not of the intellect or mind, that prior to faith "'there must be knowledge . . . of the divine character and law,'" and that prior to justification the sinner must exercise "'virtue,'" so that he may be "united to the Mediator."²²⁴ In a late sermon the London pastor asserted that "justice is essential" to the character of God and "must be displayed in the punishment of sin," that justice "pleads the necessity" of a vicarious, substitutionary atonement, and that it infers a particular or limited atonement.²²⁵

Booth also was prolific in defense of the Baptist distinctives. *An Apology for the Baptists* (1778) was not directed, as a modern reader might surmise, against Paedobaptists but rather against those contemporary Baptists who were practicing "free" or open communion. Controverting John Bunyan and John Collett Ryland, he argued that open communion Baptists inconsistently say that infant baptism is not true baptism and yet welcome to the Lord's Supper those baptized as infants and even those with no baptism. The historic Christian position, he affirmed, has been that baptism must always precede participation in the Supper. For Baptists, only the immersion of a professing believer is Christian baptism. Hence strict communion Baptists maintain the high significance of baptism, whereas open communion Baptists are "latitudinarian."²²⁶

Having gathered an extensive collection of statements concerning Christian baptism by Paedobaptist authors, chiefly Protestant but occasionally Roman Catholic, Booth arranged these under the various facets of the doctrine of baptism so as to exhibit some support for the Baptist position and offered his own reflections.²²⁷ Yet he contended "that there is a

---

²²⁴Ibid., 107, 108, 112, 119.

²²⁵*Divine Justice Essential to the Divine Character: A Sermon Preached in Mr. Timothy Thomas's Meeting-House, near Devonshire-Square, at the Baptist Monthly Meeting, Sept. 22, 1803* (London: C. Whittingham, 1804) BBM:Bodleian, microform publ. no. 5877, reel 1, item 11, esp. 5, 46-47, 64, 86, 102.

²²⁶Subtitle: *In Which They Are Vindicated from the Imputation of Laying an Unwarrantable Stress on the Ordinance of Baptism; and against the Charge of Bigotry in Refusing Communion at the Lord's Table to Paedobaptists* (London: E. and C. Dilly et al.); repr.: under title, *A Defense for the Baptists* (Paris AR: Baptist Standard Bearer, 1995). Booth claimed that the open communion objection that strict communionists invite Paedobaptist ministers to their pulpits did not pose a parallel issue (103-107).

²²⁷*Paedobaptism Examined on the Principles, Concessions, and Reasonings of the Most Learned Paedobaptists* (London: author, 1784; 2nd ed., 1787). The edition

remarkable similarity between the arguments used by Roman Catholics in defence of Popery; by our Conformists, in support of their Establishment; and by Paedobaptists in general, in favour of infant sprinkling."[228] Booth first defended the mode of immersion by treating the Greek words for "baptism" and "baptize," by explicating baptism as the representation of Christ's death, burial, and resurrection, by examining the practice according to the New Testament and in the later Greek and Oriental churches, by asserting that the design of baptism is "more fully expressed by immersion," and by tracing the rise and practice of pouring or sprinkling back to Novatian.[229] Then he defended believer's baptism chiefly by a critique of infant baptism. There is no "express precept" for nor "plain example" of infant baptism in the New Testament and no evidence of its practice prior to the end of the second or beginning of the third centuries. Jewish proselyte baptism was a "civil" rather than a "religious rite"; there is no evidence of its practice in the time of Jesus, for the earliest accounts are in the Talmuds. Circumcision was "a mark of national distinction," whereas baptism is "purely religious." Booth examined nine biblical passages allegedly supportive of infant baptism, questioned paedobaptist usage of "apostolic tradition," and found that infant communion was introduced about the same time as and supported by the same arguments as infant baptism.[230]

Because Booth's book was answered by Edward Williams (1750–1813) and by Peter Edwards, Booth was compelled to write replies to each. In reply to Williams,[231] he offered certain new arguments; for example, Paedobaptists wrongly emphasize the discretionary power of the administrator of baptism; neither the baptism by John the Baptist nor Christian baptism ought to be described as a "purification"; and infants have no "legal title" to participate in the Lord's Supper, which Williams denied to them on the ground of expediency. Booth answered[232] Edwards's argument that the

---

used here was included in Booth, *Paedobaptism Examined; with Replies to the Arguments and Objections of Dr. Williams and Mr. Peter Edwards*, 3 vols. (London: Ebenezer Palmer, 1829) 1:1-443; 2:1-343.

[228]Ibid., 1:xiii.
[229]Ibid., 1:1-300.
[230]Ibid., 1:303-411; 2:1-33 (esp. 15), 68-97 (esp. 80-85), 97-279.
[231]*A Defence of Paedobaptism Examined: or, Animadversions on Dr. Edward Williams's Antipaedobaptism Examined* (London: author, 1792) esp. 141, 371, 302, 314, 337, 475.
[232]*The Principles of Antipaedobaptism, and the Practice of Female Commu-*

Baptist practice of admitting females to the Lord's Supper was contradictory to Baptist insistence on an "explicit divine precept" in the New Testament or "a plain apostolic example" by his reckoning sexual difference at the Lord's Supper as "a *mere circumstance*," by interpreting "disciples" as inclusive of women, and by connecting 1 Cor. 11:33-34 with 1 Cor. 14:33b-35.

The kingdom of Christ is essentially "not of this world" (John 18:36) and "is none other than the gospel Church."[233] Booth's exposition delineated contrasts between Christ's kingdom and political or secular kingdoms, including "the ancient Israelitish theocracy" and established churches. They differ as to origin, as to subjects or members, as to means of establishment and enlargement, as to their laws, as to splendor or simplicity, as to the nature of their riches and honors, and as to their duration.[234]

Also to be noted among the Particular Baptist pastor-theologians was Robert Hall, Jr. Educated at Bristol Academy and King's College, Aberdeen, he served as pastor in Cambridge, Leicester, and Bristol. It was he who once called John Gill's writings "a continent of mud."[235] In his *On Terms of Communion* (1815)[236] he both refuted in detail Booth's arguments for strict communion and set forth his own case for open communion. Hall summarized his book in these words:

---

nion, *Completely Consistent: In Answer to the Arguments and Objections of Mr. Peter Edwards in His Candid Reasons* . . . (London, 1795); in *Paedobaptism Examined; With Replies to the Arguments and Objections of Dr. Williams and Mr. Peter Edwards*, 3:389-460, esp. 391-92, 396, 400-411.

[233] *An Essay on the Kingdom of Christ* (London: Houlston and Stoneman, 1788); repr.: in Booth, *A Defense for the Baptists* (1985), 3, 4. Although Booth interpreted heaven as the goal of Christ's kingdom, his was essentially a noneschatological view of the kingdom itself.

[234] Ibid., 5-76.

[235] Olinthus Gregory, "A Brief Memoir of the Rev. Robert Hall, A.M.," in *The Works of the Rev. Robert Hall, A.M.*, 3 vols., ed. Olinthus Gregory (New York: Harper & Brothers, 1835) 3:1-75; Underwood, *A History of the English Baptists*, 169-70; Whitley, *A History of British Baptists*, 245-46, 306-307. See above, 104.

[236] Subtitle: *With a Particular View to the Case of the Baptists and Pedobaptists*, in *Works*, 1:283-362. Breed, *Particular Baptists in Victorian England and Their Strict Communion Organizations*, has called the book "a masterly justification of open communion."

We have endeavoured to show that the practice of strict communion derives no support from the supposed priority of baptism to the Lord's Supper in the order of institution, which order is exactly the reverse;[237] that it is not countenanced by the tenor of the apostles' commission [= Great Commission], nor by apostolic precedent, the spirit of which is in our favour . . . ; that the opposite practice is enforced by the obligations of Christian charity [= love]; that it is indubitably comprehended within the canon which enjoins forbearance towards mistaken brethren; that the system of our opponents *unchurches* every Pedobaptist community; that it rests on no general principle; . . . that it inflicts a punishment [on Pedobaptists] which is capricious and unjust; and finally, that by fomenting prejudice and precluding the most effectual means of conviction, it defeats its own purpose [of leading Pedobaptists to believer's immersion].[238]

Rebuttal to Hall's open communion came from Joseph Kinghorn, who, after studying at Bristol Academy, served as pastor of St. Mary's Church in Norwich for the remainder of his life, that is, 42 years,[239] and wrote three substantive books defending strict communion. His *Baptism a Term of Communion at the Lord's Table* (1816)[240] was a reply to Hall's *On Terms of Communion*. The issue was: "whether persons who are acknowledged to be unbaptized ought to come to the Lord's table." Strict communion builds on New Testament precedents, and open communion may cause Paedobaptists to have to answer whether infant baptism has any use. Hall's argument from brotherly love should not overrule obedience to the will of Christ. Hall was wrong to argue that strict communion Baptists attack the liberty of others when they are preserving their own. Open or "mixed" communion

---

[237]Hall extended this argument that John's baptism was quite distinct from Christian baptism and that the latter was not initiated until after Jesus' postresurrection Great Commission in his *The Essential Difference between Christian Baptism and the Baptism of John, More Fully Stated and Confirmed; in Reply to a Pamphlet, Entitled 'A Plea for Primitive Communion'*, in *Works*, 1:363-90.

[238]*On Terms of Communion*, 1:359.

[239]Underwood, *A History of the English Baptists*, 170-72, 206; Brown, *The English Baptists of the Eighteenth Century*, 130; Breed, *Particular Baptists in Victorian England and Their Strict Communion Organizations*, 19; Dean Olive, "Joseph Kinghorn (1766–1832)," in *The British Particular Baptists*, ed. Haykin, 3:84-11.

[240](Norwich: Bacon, Kinnebrook, and Co., 1816) BBHRM:M/RP, microform publ. no. 946, reel 6, item 6.

was unknown in the apostolic or patristic ages, undermines the case of paedobaptist Nonconformists for their separation from the Church of England, and surrenders the chief Baptist denominational distinctive. It is doubtful that open membership will increase the membership of Baptist churches.[241] Kinghorn's *A Defence of "Baptism a Term of Communion": In Answer to the Rev. Robert Hall's Reply* (1820)[242] was a rejoinder to Hall's *A Reply to the Rev. Joseph Kinghorn: Being a Further Vindication of the Practice of Free Communion* (1817).[243] Here Kinghorn pressed the idea that New Testament precedents relative to baptism and the Lord's Supper are "interpretations of the will of Christ." He charged Hall with misinterpreting the statement "that Baptism is a term of christian profession" and insisted, contra Hall, that the New Testament does not state that baptism is "an evidence of faith" but serves only "to evince the possession of christian sincerity." Rom. 14:7 applies to the weak in faith, not to the unbaptized. The objection to communion with Paedobaptists does not rest on "'suspicions attaching to their *christian character*'" but on "'deviation from . . . the *original constitution of the church.*'"[244] In *Arguments against the Practice of Mixed Communion and in Support of Communion on the Plan of the Apostolic Church*,[245] Kinghorn answered Hall's charge that strict communion was "party" communion by affirming that such "party" communion was actually the "primitive" communion. To the charge that strict communion will produce "disunion" between Baptists and Paedobaptists, he replied by declaring that open or "mixed" communion will tend to produce dissension among Baptists and likely result in the loss of the name "Baptist."[246]

Kinghorn also wrote to answer the Paedobaptist argument from circumcision.

---

[241]Ibid., 10, 24, 22, 39, 56-57, 92, 143ff., 119-31, 95, 106-109.

[242](Norwich: Wilkin and Youngman) BBHRM:M/RP, microform publ. no. 946, reel 6, item 5.

[243](Leicester: Thomas Combe, 1818). See also *The Works of the Rev. Robert Hall*, 1:391-504.

[244]*A Defence of "Baptism a Term of Communion,"* 47, 59, 84, 87, 164-65, 185.

[245]Subtitle: *With Preliminary Observations on Rev. R. Hall's Reason for Christian, in Opposition to Party Communion* (London: Wightman and Cramp, 1827) BBM:Angus, microform publ. no. 5855, reel 1, item 18.

[246]Ibid., 12, 5, 51-60, 19.

Circumcision was a *sign* of the covenant which God made with Abraham, and a *seal* of the righteousness of that faith which *he* had *before* he was circumcised.... But it could not be a *seal* of the righteousness of the faith of his infant posterity, nor of [the children of his slaves]....[247]

Indeed the covenant associated with circumcision was a "national" covenant, with which "*compulsion*" or "*force*" was employed, and "there was no injunction to attempt to gain proselytes from the surrounding nations by circumcision."[248]

Further defense of strict communion was made by Joseph Ivimey, a former tailor who served as pastor of Eagle Street Church, London, for thirty years, wrote a four-volume *A History of the English Baptists*[249] and biographies of Kiffin,[250] Bunyan,[251] and John Milton,[252] and helped to organize in 1813 and gave leadership to the General Union[253] of [Particular] Baptist Ministers and Churches.[254] Writing in answer to Robert Hall, Jr., Ivimey added to Kinghorn's case for strict communion by supplying three arguments. First, strict communion rests both on the exercise of conscience and "right of private judgment" and on the sufficiency of the Scriptures alone as "the rule of faith and practice."[255] Second, open communion

---

[247] *The Argument in Support of Infant Baptism, from the Covenant of Circumcision, Examined and Shewn to Be Invalid* (London: John Offer, n.d.) BBHRM:M/RP, microform publ. no. 946, reel 42, item 26, 5-6.

[248] Ibid., 11, 14, 8.

[249] See above, ch. 3, n. 74.

[250] *The Life of Mr. William Kiffin; Upwards of Sixty Years Pastor of the Baptist Church, Devonshire Square, London, from 1639 to 1701* (London: author, 1833).

[251] *The Life of Mr. John Bunyan, Minister of the Gospel at Bedford...* (London: R. Edwards for Button and Burditt, 1809).

[252] *John Milton: His Life and Times, Religious and Political Opinions...* (London: Effingham Wilson, 1833).

[253] Later to be called the Baptist Union of Great Britain and Ireland.

[254] Underwood, *A History of the English Baptists*, 182-84; J. C. Doggett, "Joseph Ivimey (1773–1834)," in *The British Particular Baptists*, ed. Haykin, 3:112-31.

[255] *Baptism the Scriptural and Indispensable Qualification for Communion at the Lord's Table...; Including Animadversions on the "Preface, etc." of the Rev. Robert Hall's "Reply" to the Rev. Joseph Kinghorn's Work on "Baptism a Term of Communion"* (London: John Offor, 1824) BBHRM:M/RP, microform publ. no. 946, reel 16, item 58, iv-v, 1-5, 50.

Baptists cannot justify planting new congregations in neighborhoods having evangelical Independent or Congregational churches unless on the basis of population growth or major doctrinal deviancy.[256] Third, Hall's criticism of Particular Baptist strict communion as "party communion" rather than "Christian communion" runs afoul of the fact that most all Christians of whatever denomination have never experienced anything but a form of "party communion."[257]

Atypical of Baptist writings was Ivimey's treatise in defense of the Protestant canon of the Old Testament. Its occasion was the decision of the British and Foreign Bible Society to distribute to Roman Catholics on the European continent German Bibles containing the books of the Old Testament Apocrypha intermixed, "interspersed," or "intermingled" with other Old Testament books and not placed in a separated section. Ivimey strongly opposed this action as contrary to the society's founding documents, as espousing a *"false canon of Scripture,* and as assisting in the circulation of *"human and erroneous writings as inspired truth."*[258]

Another London pastor for 63 years, the successor of John Gill, John Rippon, planted the seed for a worldwide Baptist body such as the Baptist World Alliance would become in 1905. Writing as editor in the initial issue of *The Baptist Annual Register* in 1790, he dedicated the magazine

> to all the baptized ministers and people in America, England, Ireland, Scotland, Wales, the United Netherlands, France, Switzerland, Poland, Russia, Prussia, and elsewhere . . . with a desire of promoting an universal interchange of kind offices among them and in serious expectation that before many years elapse . . . a deputation from all these climes will meet probably in London to consult the ecclesiastical good of the whole.[259]

---

[256]Ibid., iii, 5-11.

[257]*Communion at the Lord's Table, Regulated by the Revealed Will of Christ, Not Party, but Christian Communion: A Reply to the Rev. Robert Hall's Pamphlet, Entitled "Reasons for Christian in Opposition to Party Communion"* (London: Wightman and Cramp, 1826) BBM:Angus, microform publ. no. 5855, reel 5, item 3, 11, 15.

[258]*A Plea for the Protestant Canon of Scripture, in Opposition to the Popish Canon, of Which the Apocrypha Makes an Integral Part, or, A Succinct Account of the Bible Society Controversy* . . . (London: Wightman and Cramp, 1825) esp. i-iii, 1-11, 12, 23, 34, 35, 94.

[259]Quoted by Underwood, *A History of the English Baptists*, 178-79; see also 250-51; F. Townley Lord, *Baptist World Fellowship: A Short History of the Baptist World Alliance* (Nashville: Broadman, 1955) 1-2; Kenneth R. Manley, "John

Strict and Particular Baptists

The rejection of the theology of Andrew Fuller and of the work of the Baptist Missionary Society crystallized in a body of churches known as Strict and Particular Baptists or Gospel Standard churches. The pioneer of this movement was a Warwickshire native, William Gadsby (1773–1844), who, having been an apprentice to a ribbon weaver and baptized at twenty, served as pastor of a Particular Baptist church, Back Lane Chapel, in Manchester from 1805 to his death.[260] Gadsby seemingly had been influenced by the theology of William Huntington (1745–1813), an Independent pastor in London who blended an antinomian high Calvinism with an extreme subjectivism with its claims of remarkable "providences" but who had little interest in baptism.[261] "Gadsby was not an organizer" and neither joined nor formed any association of churches; but he was a planter of churches and supported Sunday Schools but opposed missionary societies and theological education. A magazine, *The Gospel Standard*, founded by Gadsby's son John in 1835, helped to give cohesion to the movement.[262]

Gadsby's Hyper-Calvinism included a deep conviction of sin, man's total inability, a stereotypical experience of conversion, and a form of antinomianism. According to Kenneth Dix, Gadsby, whose preaching drew large audiences, taught that invitations were to be given only to "'sensible sinners,'" or "those who felt they were lost and hopeless," and, for Gadsby, the "biblical call to faith was largely displaced by introspection."[263] Gadsby published extensively in defense of those falsely accused of preaching "*foul*

Rippon and American Baptists," *The Quarterly Review* 41 (October-November-December 1980): 61; idem, "John Rippon and Baptist Historiography," *Baptist Quarterly* 28 (July 1979): 109, 122; Sharon James, "John Rippon (1751–1836)," in *The British Particular Baptists*, ed. Haykin, 2:56-75.

[260] Kenneth Dix, *Strict and Particular: English Strict and Particular Baptists in the Nineteenth Century* (Didcot UK: Baptist Historical Society for the Strict Baptist Historical Society, 2001) 32-36; B. A. Ramsbottom, "William Gadsby (1773–1844)," in *The British Particular Baptists*, ed. Haykin, 3:132-49; William H. Brackney, *Historical Dictionary of the Baptists*, Historical Dictionaries of Religions, Philosophies, and Movements 25 (Lanham MD: Scarecrow, 1999) 177-78.

[261] Dix, *Strict and Particular*, 13-29; Oliver, *History of the English Calvinistic Baptists*, 119-45.

[262] Dix, *Strict and Particular*, 59-60.

[263] Ibid., 36-41.

dogmas" and being "*pulpit libertines*" and of the position that "the perfect law of liberty" is not "the moral law" but the gospel of Christ. Indeed "the believer is dead to Moses, his first husband, and married to Christ . . . [and] is ruled by the precious laws of Christ, his second Husband."[264] Gadsby refuted the Sandemanian view of faith[265] and strongly defended strict communion.[266] The experiential subjectivism of Gadsby was taken up by a former Anglican, Joseph Charles Philpot (1802–1869), who, unlike the churches of Suffolk and Norfolk,[267] opposed the sending of missionaries and defended the eternal generation of the Son of God.[268] On the other hand, overt evangelistic endeavor was espoused by John Stevens (1776–1847), a London pastor who wrote against Fuller's teaching of duty-faith, against Huntington's antinomianism, and against Edward Irving's (1792–1834) teaching that the Son of God assumed depraved human nature. Stevens advocated the view that "Christ's human soul was formed before the creation of the world" while denying his eternal generation.[269]

The Strict Baptist Aid Society adopted in 1872 a seventeen-article confession of faith which had been drawn up in 1843 by Philpot on the basis of John Gill's confession for his church in London. The teachings affirmed included particular election, a covenant of grace made by the Father, the Son, and the Holy Spirit, the human soul of Jesus as created in the incarnation, particular atonement, regeneration and sanctification as works by God, certain perseverance of the elect, and strict communion. There were specific denials of duty-faith, duty-repentance, divine enlightenment of the nonelect,

---

[264]*The Gospel the Believer's Rule of Conduct, Being a Few Remarks upon a Letter by Gaius; The Present State of Religion, or What Are the People Miscalled Antinomians? . . . ; The Perfect Law of Liberty, or The Glory of God Revealed in the Gospel* in *The Works of the Late William Gadsby, Manchester*, 2 vols. (London: J. Gadsby, 1851) 1:6, 7, 53-54, 101-54.

[265]*What Is Faith? or the Faith of the Sandemanians Found Wanting . . .* in *The Works of the Late William Gadsby*, 1:277-315; Oliver, *History of the English Calvinistic Baptists*, 187-93.

[266]Dix, *Strict and Particular*, 41-43.

[267]Ibid., 146-54.

[268]Ibid., 67, 67-71, 76-78, 80-112. On Philpot see B. A. Ramsbottom, "Joseph Charles Philpot (1802–1869)," in *The British Particular Baptists*, ed. Haykin, 3:196-209, and Oliver, *History of the English Calvinistic Baptists*, 288-311.

[269]Dix, *Strict and Particular*, 173-77, 275. Stevens's denial of eternal generation found support in the magazine *The Earthen Vessel*. Ibid., 94-96, 186-88. See also Oliver, *History of the English Calvinistic Baptists*, 200-27.

and offers of grace.[270] Revisions of these articles in 1866 included the teaching that Jesus' "human nature was not peccable or mortal, but capable of death by a voluntary act," "that faith is the gift of God," and that baptismal regeneration is a "blasphemous" doctrine. The denial of offers of grace was coupled with the statement "the Gospel is to be preached to all the world."[271] Revisions in 1872 denied both "progressive sanctification" and "perfection in the flesh" and affirmed that the elect can backslide and that God does "chastise His people for sin."[272] Revisions in 1878 further defined the limits on a pastor's addressing the unconverted and affirmed that "there are various degrees of faith."[273]

Whereas the Gadsbyite Strict and Particular Baptists, thus described, sought to reactivate the eighteenth-century Hyper-Calvinist posture of Brine and Gill and to continue in the strict communion view of Booth, Kinghorn and Ivimey, there were other Particular Baptist churches in nineteenth-century England which retained strict communion but not Hyper-Calvinism and supported both the Baptist Missionary Society and the Baptist Union of Great Britain and Ireland.[274]

Alexander Carson (1776–1844)

Although Baptist churches had been planted in Scotland by soldiers in Oliver Cromwell's army during the 1650s, such churches soon became extant. The adherents of Archibald McLean, known as "Scotch Baptists," had appeared during the 1760s, but only with the ministry of the Haldane brothers, Robert (1764–1842) and James Alexander (1768–1851), who became Baptists in 1808, did Baptist churches have a continuous history in

---

[270]Ibid., 297-303; articles 3, 5, 6, 8, 9, 14, 15.
[271]Ibid., 303-5; articles 5, 13, 15.
[272]Ibid., 305-9; articles 20, 21, 22.
[273]Ibid., 309-10; articles 32-35.
[274]The latter, which inaugurated the *Primitive Church Magazine* and formed the Baptist Tract Society in 1841 and formed the Strict Baptist Society in 1845, have been the subject of Geoffrey R. Breed's recent study: *Particular Baptists in Victorian England and Their Strict Communion Organizations*.

Scotland.²⁷⁵ Baptists in Ireland also trace their origins to the 1650s, but the early nineteenth century brought renewal to Irish Baptists.²⁷⁶

The most prolific and influential theologian among Scottish and Irish Baptists was Alexander Carson, an Irishman from a Presbyterian family who after university studies in Glasgow and a Presbyterian pastorate had become first a Congregationalist and then a Baptist, serving the Baptist church in Tobermore in northern Ireland until his death.²⁷⁷ His writings were widely circulated in North America as well as in the British Isles.

Anticipating somewhat the controversies of the latter nineteenth century concerning the Bible, Carson wrote in detail about biblical interpretation and biblical hermeneutics. He defended the plenary-verbal view of

---

²⁷⁵George McGuinness, "Robert (1764–1842) and James Haldane (1768–1851)," in *The British Particular Baptists*, ed. Haykin, 2:223-29; D. B. Murray, "The Seventeenth and Eighteenth Centuries," in *The Baptists in Scotland: A History*, ed. David William Bebbington (Glasgow: Baptist Union of Scotland, 1988) 9-25; McBeth, *The Baptist Heritage*, 308-12. The Haldanes not only sponsored practical, church-related theological training in Scotland but also were authors, especially after becoming Baptists. Robert defended the plenary-verbal theory of biblical inspiration and the Protestant canon of the Old Testament (*The Books of the Old and New Testaments Proved to Be Canonical, and Their Verbal Inspiration Maintained*, 3rd ed. [Edinburgh: William Whyte and Co., 1830]; *The Authenticity and Inspiration of the Holy Scriptures* [Edinburgh: William Whyte and Co., 1845]; Minneapolis: Klack and Klack Christian Publishers, 1985]) and wrote a major commentary on the Epistle to the Romans while refuting certain contemporary commentators (*Exposition of the Epistle to the Romans: With Remarks on the Commentaries of Dr. MacKnight, Professor Moses Stuart and Professor Tholuck*, 3 vols., 2nd ed. [London: Hamilton, Adams and Co., 1836–1839]). James Alexander defended the immersion of believers (*Reasons of a Change of Sentiment and Practice on the Subject of Baptism* [Edinburgh: J. Ritchie, 1809]) and wrote on the atonement (*The Doctrine of the Atonement: With Strictures on the Recent Publications of Drs. Wardlaw and Jenkyn*, 2nd ed. [Edinburgh: William Whyte, 1847]) and on the Epistle to the Galatians (*An Exposition of the Epistle to the Galatians, Showing That the Present Divisions among Christians Originate in Blending the Ordinances of the Old and New Covenants* [Edinburgh: William Whyte, 1848; Springfield MO: Particular Baptist, 2002]).

²⁷⁶McBeth, *The Baptist Heritage*, 312-14.

²⁷⁷Robert Briggs, "Alexander Carson (1776–1844)," in *The British Particular Baptists*, ed. Haykin, 3:152-61; George C. Moore, *The Life of Alexander Carson, LL.D.* (New York: Edward H. Fletcher; London: Benjamin L. Green, 1851).

inspiration[278] by a critique of the views held by those "overawed by German neology,"[279] namely, Daniel Wilson (1778–1858),[280] F. D. E. Schleiermacher (1768–1834),[281] John Pye Smith (1774–1851),[282] and John Dick (1764–1833).[283] He refuted as "neological" the hermeneutical principles set forth by Johann August Ernesti (1707–1781), Christoph Friedrich Ammon (1766–1849), and Moses Stuart (1780–1852),[284] although at times agreeing with Ernesti as to the single sense of a biblical text, the use of the grammatical factor, and the avoidance of excessive typology.[285]

Carson expounded ten attributes of God[286] not on the basis of biblical texts but in dialogue with contemporary authors and then, after interpreting the Trinity in respect to plurality of persons, sought to show how God's mercy, justice, wisdom, power, holiness, and sovereignty are manifested in the gospel of Christ. The Father's character has been supremely manifested in his Son. Finally by examining specific biblical texts Carson sought to show the biblical evidence for the gospel's manifesting God's character.[287] In writing on the atonement, the Irish theologian did not defend any motif or theory, although he seemingly accepted penal substitution, but focused

---

[278]*The Inspiration of the Scriptures: A Review of the Theories of the Rev. Daniel Wilson, Rev. Dr. Pye Smith, and the Rev. Dr. Dick, and Other Treatises*, 4th ed. (New York: Edward H. Fletcher, 1857; orig., 1830) 86, 118-20, 150, 152, 201, 234, 243.

[279]Ibid., 6.

[280]Ibid., 5-96, esp. 7. Wilson held that the Bible is "human in manner, divine in matter."

[281]Ibid., 97-115, Schleiermacher reckoned the Gospels to be compilations of fragments of apostolic origin with "*poetic allegories.*"

[282]Ibid., 117-220, esp. 118-23. Smith held that the "thoughts" of the Bible were inspired but not the "words."

[283]Ibid., 221-52, esp. 222-30. Dick held to three "degrees" of inspiration: that known or knowable "by ordinary means," that knowable by supernatural endowment, and that "directly revealed" to the writers.

[284]*Examination of the Principles of Biblical Interpretation of Ernesti, Ammon, Stuart, and Other Philogists* . . . (New York: Edward H. Fletcher, 1857; orig., 1836).

[285]Ibid., 43, 85-87, 89.

[286]Unity, spirituality, omniscience, omnipotence, eternity, goodness, justice, omnipresence, sovereignty, and life.

[287]*The Knowledge of Jesus the Most Excellent of the Sciences* (New York: Edward H. Fletcher, 1853?).

on universal human guilt, the exclusivity of the death of Christ for atonement, faith as the necessary and transformative means of appropriating its effects, and the eternal destiny-determining results of one's response to the atonement-centered gospel.[288] Twice Carson wrote on the providence of God as the divine government expressed as God's overruling and directing all things: first by examining 139 biblical passages treated in their canonical order[289] and then through a study of the book of Esther.[290]

Twice Carson addressed Christian baptism. In what may have been his most influential book he probed the mode of baptism, examining the uses of the Greek verbs *baptō* and *baptizō* and refuting the writings of Ralph Wardlaw (1779–1853), Scottish Congregationalist, and Greville Ewing (1767–1841), a Haldanian Sandemanian, and defended believers only as the proper "subjects" of baptism, continuing to answer Wardlaw and Ewing.[291] Carson also wrote a rebuttal[292] to Edward Beecher (1803–1895), American Congregationalist who had sought[293] "to prove" that *Baptismos* "refers not to mode at all, but signifies purification in general."[294]

In his polemic against the Roman Catholic Church the Irish pastor majored on transubstantiation, the right and duty of all human beings to read the Bible, and the irreconcilable nature of salvation by law and salvation by grace.[295]

---

[288]*The Doctrine of the Atonement and Other Treatises*, 3rd ed. (New York: Edward H. Fletcher, 1854).

[289]*History of Providence, as Manifested in Scripture; or Facts from Scripture Illustrative of the Government of God* (New York: Edward H. Fletcher, 1852).

[290]*History of Providence as Unfolded in the Book of Esther*, 5th ed. (New York: Edward H. Fletcher, 1854) repr. under title *Confidence of God in Times of Danger* (Swengel PA: Reiner Publications, 1975).

[291]*Baptism in Its Mode and Subjects Considered, and the Arguments of Mr. Ewing and Dr. Wardlaw Refuted* . . . (New York: C. C. P. Crosby, 1832; Philadelphia: American Baptist Publication Society, 1844; repr. as *Baptism: Its Mode and Its Subjects*: Evansville IN: Sovereign Grace Book Club, 1957).

[292]*Baptism Not Purification, in Reply to President Beecher* (London: Simpkin and Marshall, and G. Wightman, 1841).

[293]*Baptism with Reference to Its Impact and Modes* (New York, London: J. Wiley, 1849).

[294]*Baptism Not Purification*, 3.

[295]*The Romish Controversy: Being a Series of Essays and Letters on Some of the Leading Doctrines of the Church of Rome* . . . (New York: Sheldon, Lamport, and Blakeman, 1854).

Antimissionary Controversy; Primitive Baptists; Daniel Parker (1781–1844)

Baptists in the young American nation, being aroused to the foreign mission imperative, especially by the knowledge of and some monetary support of the Baptist Missionary Society and Carey's work in India, after the formation of some Baptist missionary societies in the Northern states,[296] organized, after the prodding of Luther Rice, in Philadelphia in 1814 the General Missionary Convention of the Baptist Denomination in the United States of America for Foreign Missions—popularly known as the Triennial Convention, but actually a foreign mission society. The Triennial Convention undertook home missions for a brief period until the formation of the American Baptist Home Mission Society in 1832. Concurrently Baptist state conventions were being constituted for missionary and educational purposes, the first being in South Carolina in 1821, and Baptist colleges and seminaries were being established.[297]

But the supporters of the new structures in Baptist life were by no means the majority of Baptists; A. H. Newman labeled the supporters "a small minority of the denomination."[298] "By the 1820s, articulate spokesmen arose to undermine missions; what began as scattered dissent mushroomed into a full-fledged antimission movement."[299] Baptist historians have been quick to point out that the causes of the antimissionary controversy were diverse and not strictly theological or ecclesiological.[300]

---

[296] Albert L. Vail, *The Morning Hour of American Baptist Missions* (Philadelphia: American Baptist Publication Society, 1907) 96-156.

[297] Albert Henry Newman, *A History of the Baptist Churches in the United States*, American Church History Series (New York: Christian Literature Co., 1894) 388-423; Torbet, *A History of the Baptists*, 261-71; Baker, *The Southern Baptist Convention and Its People*, 98, 104-13, 114-17; McBeth, *The Baptist Heritage*, 343-61; Jesse C. Fletcher, *The Southern Baptist Convention: A Sesquicentennial History* (Nashville: Broadman & Holman, 1994) 33-39.

[298] *A History of the Baptist Churches in the United States*, 433.

[299] McBeth, *The Baptist Heritage*, 371. Byron Cecil Lambert, *The Rise of the Anti-Mission Baptists: Sources and Leaders, 1800–1840*, The Baptist Tradition series (New York: Arno, 1980; orig. the author's Ph.D. diss., University of Chicago, 1957) iii-v, 1-234, interpreted Baptist antimissions as a part of the larger Protestant resistance to home mission societies and as having been fostered earlier by John Leland.

[300] Newman, *A History of the Baptist Churches in the United States*, 438-39;

Representative of the nontheological critique was *Thoughts on Missions*[301] by John Taylor (1752–1835),[302] a Virginian-born pastor and farmer in Kentucky, who labeled as "deadly evil" "*Missionary Boards, Conventions, Societies,* and *Theological Schools.*" Taylor focused his attack upon Rice and upon Adoniram Judson (1788–1850), the Triennial Convention's second missionary. He called Rice "a modern Tetzel" and charged that Judson "had the same taste for money that the horse leech has for blood." Seeking money and power, he alleged, the missionaries were seeking "Lordship over God's heritage." Sectional bias was reflected in Taylor's statement: "I did begin strongly to smell the *New England Rat.*" Jesus employed no theological school in sending out the Seventy and did not train the Twelve "in literature." Taylor's aim was "to drive these presumptuous men . . . out of Baptist associations."[303]

Allegedly reflective of a theological basis for antimissions but actually more derivative from Baptist ecclesiology were the thoughts of Daniel Parker, Virginia-born, Georgia-reared frontier Baptist preacher-pastor-author who served in Tennessee, Illinois, and Texas.[304] Baptist historians for more than a century after Parker's lifetime,[305] relying on secondary sources more than on Parker's somewhat scarce writings, almost uniformly connected his doctrine of the two seeds with his anti-Triennial Convention

---

Torbet, *A History of the Baptists*, 285-86; Baker, *The Southern Baptist Convention and Its People*, 150; McBeth, *The Baptist Heritage*, 375-76.

[301](Franklin County KY: author, 1820) University of Chicago microfilm no. G748.

[302]Leo T. Crismon, "Taylor, John," in *Encyclopedia of Southern Baptists* (Nashville: Broadman, 1958) 2:1347-48.

[303]*Thoughts on Missions*, 4, 9, 6, 25, 6, 23, 33. See also B. H. Carroll, Jr., *The Genesis of American Anti-Missionism* (Louisville: Baptist Book Concern, 1902) 87, 97-107.

[304]Guy Small, "The Life of Daniel Parker" (M.A. thesis, East Texas Baptist College, 1954); Lambert, *The Rise of the Anti-Mission Baptists*, 252-88; A. B. Rutledge and W. Fred Kendall, "Parker, Daniel," *Encyclopedia of Southern Baptists*, 2:1071; McBeth, *The Baptist Heritage*, 373-74, 375, 720-21; W. Morgan Patterson, "Parker, Daniel (1781–1844)," *Dictionary of Christianity in America*, ed. Daniel G. Reid (Downers Grove IL: InterVarsity, 1990) 867; Brackney, *The Baptists*, 241-42; Joseph E. Early, Jr., *A Handbook of Texas Baptist Biography* (Williamsburg KY: author, 2004) 180-81.

[305]Probably traceable to the 1837 circular letter of the General Association of Baptists in Kentucky.

stance, some making the former a basis or cause of the latter.[306] Only with the groundbreaking research of O. Max Lee[307] in 1960s, anticipated by the work of B. H. Carroll, Jr.,[308] in 1902, has Parker's theology been more accurately interpreted.[309]

Although he had voiced opposition to Luther Rice as early as 1815,[310] Parker, replying to a Triennial Convention missionary, Isaac McCoy,[311] published in 1820 *A Public Address to the Baptist Society, and Friends of Religion in General on the Principle and Practice of the Baptist Board of Missions for the United States of America*.[312] His was a sevenfold argument: self-defense by differentiating his opposition to "the mission plan" from his support of the missionary objective; critique of recruitment of missionaries from seminaries; "the mission plan" as a denial of congregational polity; neither Abraham nor Jonah was sent by a society or board, while Jesus established no theological school; the Scriptures can be used rationally to convince the "natural man" of error; the Triennial Convention makes membership to depend on money donated and accepts it from slaveholders;

---

[306]William Cathcart, *The Baptist Encyclopedia* . . . (Philadelphia: Louis H. Everts, 1881) 883-84; Newman, *A History of the Baptist Churches in the United States*, 439-40; Vedder, *A Short History of the Baptists*, 389; Torbet, *A History of the Baptists*, 279, 286-87; Barnes, *The Southern Baptist Convention, 1845–1953*, 98; Baker, *The Southern Baptist Convention and Its People*, 150-51, 208; McBeth, *The Baptist Heritage*, 373-74, 375, 720-21; Fletcher, *The Southern Baptist Convention*, 372-73; Albert W. Wardin, ed., *Baptists around the World: A Comprehensive Handbook* (Nashville: Broadman & Holman, 1995) 422.

[307]"Daniel Parker's Doctrine of the Two Seeds" (Th.M. thesis, Southern Baptist Theological Seminary, 1962).

[308]*The Genesis of American Anti-Missionism.*

[309]Dan B. Wimberly, "Daniel Parker: Pioneer Preacher and Political Leader" (Ph.D. diss., Texas Tech University, 1995), who utilized Parker's writings and was aware of Lee's thesis, nevertheless has discounted Lee's conclusions. Wimberly refers to Parker's "self-conceived hyper-Calvinistic dualism" and describes his two-seed doctrine as "a hybrid of dualism and hyper-Calvinism," as "a convoluted attempt to refute Arminian free will," and as having "justified opposition to missionary societies" (2, 19, 169, 170). Wimberly helpfully explores Parker's probable indebtedness to Richard M. Newport for an aspect of his two-seed doctrine (168-69, 294-95).

[310]Lambert, *The Rise of the Anti-Mission Baptists*, 257.

[311]Ibid., 262.

[312](Vincennes IN: Stout and Osborn).

and Baptists have declined by apostasy to the new societies and can only be delivered by persecution.[313] Indeed, for Parker, "all mission activity should center in and be controlled by the Church," not by separated societies. These views were further developed in *Plain Truth* (1823)[314] and *The Author's Defence by Explanations and Matters of Fact* . . . (1824).[315] Not until six years after *A Public Address* did Parker publish his first treatise on the two seeds. In pursuit of his own plan he moved the Pilgrim Regular Predestinarian Baptist Church, constituted in Illinois, to Texas and subsequently planted seven or nine churches in Texas. Moreover, "Parker's antimissionism and his two-seed views . . . were never intentionally related to each other by Parker himself."[316]

Parker, building his doctrine of two seeds on Gen. 3:15 but positing that God and Satan are both eternal and self-existent, taught in three treatises[317] that elect humans derived from God's seed and nonelect humans derived from Satan's seed. Satan could beget but not create. Accordingly, Eve bore both the seed of the elect and the seed of the nonelect. No divine decree prevents the salvation of the nonelect, they are condemned for their sin, and every Christian should witness to nonbelievers. Parker's crucial point was that the Holy Spirit prompts the elect via the preached word but does not prompt the nonelect. Each of the "nonelect will refuse to believe in Jesus Christ."[318] Parker's two-seed teaching has been rightly called "a modification of ancient Manichaeism"[319] but wrongly identified as "hyper-Calvinistic,"[320] for Parker, as Lee has contended, "sought to modify the extremes of hyper-Calvinism."[321]

---

[313] As summarized by Lambert, *The Rise of the Anti-Mission Baptists*, 262-68.

[314] No publication data available. As to the content of this treatise, see Wimberly, "Daniel Parker: Pioneer Preacher and Political Leader," 160-61.

[315] (Vincennes IN: Elihu Stout, 1824).

[316] Lee, "Daniel Parker's Doctrine of the Two Seeds," 22, 34, 24.

[317] *Views on the Two Seeds Taken from Genesis 3rd Chapter, and Part of the 15th Verse*, including "A Supplement or Explanation of My Views on the Two Seeds" (Vandalia IL: Robert Blackwell, 1826); *The Second Dose of Doctrine on the Two Seeds* . . . (Vincennes IN: Elihu Stout, 1826).

[318] Lee, "Daniel Parker's Doctrine of the Two Seeds," 25, 11, 26-30.

[319] Ibid., 11.

[320] William Warren Sweet, *Religion in the Development of American Culture, 1765–1840* (New York: Scribner's, 1952) 274; also Brackney, *A Genetic History of Baptist Thought*, 237.

[321] Lee, "Daniel Parker's Doctrine of the Two Seeds," 30. Lee, 32-33, correctly

The tiny Baptist group, Two-Seed-in-the-Spirit Predestinarian Baptists, seemingly derived its two-seed doctrine from Parker but also held to distinctive doctrines: Jesus in his incarnate state had only a spiritual body, did not die, and was not raised bodily.[322]

Also reflective of the ecclesiological basis for antimissions was the thought of Alexander Campbell (1788–1866), whose basic theology and relationship with the Baptists will be examined subsequently.[323] Peculiar to Campbell among antimission Baptist spokesmen was his insistence in the pages of his publication, *The Christian Baptist*, that Christian unity be a prerequisite to missionary activity, and hence sectarian missionary societies impede that unity, and since the apostolic age only churches have had the missionary mandate.[324] Campbell also employed critiques common to Taylor and Parker: "the missionary schemes" are "Catholic," "Episcopalian," and "Presbyterian" in nature;[325] theological education and home missions are not needed; and to be biblically based, modern missionaries would need to work miracles. Citing the difficulties between the Serampore Mission and the Baptist Missionary Society, Campbell even charged mismanagement of funds. Campbell excelled in the use of ridicule.[326] His own plan was for an entire congregation to resettle in a non-Christian nation and use its example of Christian living as testimony.[327] Later, in 1849, Campbell reversed his thought sufficiently so as to participate in the formation of the American Christian Missionary Society.[328]

Those Baptist churches in the United States which deliberately opposed the Triennial Convention and its related societies, the Baptist state

---

noted that Parker and John Calvin "disagreed sharply" on the reprobation of the nonelect, but Lee, not having access to Kendall, *Calvin and English Calvinism to 1649*, 16-18, did not note the similarity between the ascended Christ's intercession only for the elect (Calvin) and the Holy Spirit's prompting of the elect (Parker).

[322]Wardin, ed., *Baptists around the World*, 422.

[323]See below, 249-57.

[324]Carroll, *The Genesis of American Anti-Missionism*, 148-49; Lambert, *The Rise of the Anti-Mission Baptists*, 289-91.

[325]Carroll, *The Genesis of American Anti-Missionism*, 125, quoted from *The Christian Baptist* 1 (2nd ed.): 208.

[326]Ibid., 131-37, 149-51, 145-48.

[327]Ibid., 152-53, quoted from *The Christian Baptist* 1 (2nd ed.): 41-43; Lambert, *The Rise of the Anti-Mission Baptists*, 297-98.

[328]Lambert, *The Rise of the Anti-Mission Baptists*, 310-11.

conventions, and Baptist colleges and seminaries between 1820 and 1840 came to have a separate existence and chose to be called Primitive Baptists on the assumption that Missionary Baptists were innovators, whereas they represented the original Baptist movement.[329] One recent Primitive Baptist author has found the necessity for Primitive Baptists in the early nineteenth-century acceptance among American Baptists of the "Arminianism" of Carey and Fuller, especially the "teaching that eternal salvation . . . depends to some extent on the will of the person being saved."[330] The Kehukee Primitive Baptist Association in North Carolina[331] in 1827 circulated Joshua Lawrence's (1778–1843) "Declaration of the Reformed Baptist Churches in the State of North Carolina." It anticipated or expressed "virtually all Primitive Baptist arguments against Missionary Baptist practice: lack of a definite biblical mandate, overemphasis on money, overevaluation of secular learning, large and potentially subversive organizations, and friendship with 'the world.' "[332] Yet Primitive Baptists have been reluctant to frame and adopt new confessions of faith. Some have been prone to cite or quote from the Philadelphia Confession,[333] whereas others[334] have reckoned as parallel to and reflective of Primitive Baptist beliefs three confessions: the 1655 Midland Association Confession of England,[335] the 1777 Kehukee Association Confession of Faith,[336] and the Principles of

---

[329]Carroll, *The Genesis of American Anti-Missionism*, 156-219.

[330]E. D. McCutcheon, *What Primitive Baptists Believe and Why They Believe It* (Thaxton MS: Primitive Baptist Church, 1983) 1.

[331]See above, 127-28.

[332]John G. Crowley, *Primitive Baptists of the Wiregrass South: 1815 to the Present* (Gainesville: University Press of Florida, 1998) 59.

[333]McCutcheon, *What Primitive Baptists Believe*, 2, 5, 8.

[334]Michael N. Ivey, *Welsh Succession of Primitive Baptist Faith and Practice* (Fort Worth TX?: author, 1994) 144-82.

[335]See above, 59-60.

[336]This 17-article confession affirmed single, "particular," and "unconditional election" (3), the federal headship of Adam and original sin as guilt (4-5), the inability of humans to repent and believe without the drawing of the Holy Spirit (6), irresistible grace (7), regeneration by the Holy Spirit (9), certain perseverance (10), the necessity of obedience but as "reckoned by grace" (11), conversion as prerequisite to baptism (12), church independence (13), general resurrection and general judgment (14), eternal hell (15), only ordained ministers to administer the ordinances (16), and associations as advisory (17). Ivey, *Welsh Succession of Primitive Baptist Faith and Practice*, 167-77.

Faith of the Sandy Creek Association.[337] Normally Primitive Baptists have held to the existence of a succession of Primitive Baptist churches from the New Testament era, especially through the Waldenses or the Welsh Baptists.[338] Early on Primitive views were expressed through two periodicals, the *Primitive Baptist* in North Carolina and Gilbert Beebe's *Signs of the Times* in New York. After the Civil War Primitive Baptists in Georgia and Florida expelled leaders and churches for espousing general atonement, election as conditioned on foreseen faith, permitting Sunday Schools, receiving Missionary Baptists without reimmersion, and accepting Parker's doctrine of two seeds.[339] Late in the nineteenth century a group of Appalachian Primitive Baptists rejected eternal punishment and espoused eschatological universalism.[340]

Calvinistic Baptists in England were slow to respond positively to the Evangelical Revival or to emerge from "the winter of hyper-Calvinism." In colonial America Calvinistic Baptists experienced numerical growth, and the Separate Baptists metamorphosed from the Great Awakening's New England adherents. Isaac Backus, who was successively "Old Light" Congregationalist, "New Light" Congregationalist, and Separate Baptist, maintained a Dortian Calvinist theology, insisted on a converted and divinely called pastoral ministry, advocated liberty of conscience, sought church tax exemptions for Baptists, supported congregational polity and close communion, and worked for the disestablishment of Congregationalism in Connecticut and Massachusetts, while retaining the concept of a Christian nation. John Leland joined the struggle for liberty of conscience, was leery of the concept of a Christian nation, and was so insistent on congregational polity as to be hesitant about national Baptist societies. Shubael Stearns and Daniel Marshall spread the Separate Baptist cause to and in the South through church planting from the Sandy Creek Church

---

[337] See above, 164-65.

[338] J. D. Holder, *Principles and Practices of the Church* (Elon College NC: Primitive Baptist Publishing House, 1961) 13-30, 33-34, 41, 64-77, 197-201; Ivey, *Welsh Succession of Primitive Baptist Faith and Practice*, 4-6, 3-8, 43-61.

[339] Crowley, *Primitive Baptists of the Wiregrass South*, 75-76, 99-133.

[340] Howard Dorgan, *In the Hands of a Happy God: The "No-Hellers" of Central Appalachia* (Knoxville: University of Tennessee Press, 1997). Per Robert L. Uzzel. For the beliefs of the Primitive Baptist Universalists, see 86-99, and for the early leadership of William Hale (1838–1906) in Washington County, Tennessee, see 117-19.

(NC) and Association. Espousing a "modified" Calvinism and an anti-creedal stance and practicing as many as nine ordinances, the Separate Baptists ultimately adopted brief articles of faith.

An early trumpet sound of Particular Baptist awakening and theological revision came with Robert Hall, Sr., in his *Help to Zion's Travellers*, an effort to remove doctrinal, experiential, and practical "stumbling blocks"—whether Hyper-Calvinist or Socinian. More representative of the older Calvinism was John Collett Ryland, who spelled out the insufficiencies of reason and used the teleological argument for God's existence, elaborated a doctrine of biblical inspiration, critiqued Socinianism, especially on the atonement, and advocated open communion. John Ryland, Jr., maintained his father's Calvinism, though countering antinomianism, his critique of Socinianism, and his open communion, but he was a strong supporter of the emerging missionary movement. Another such missionary advocate, John Sutcliff, replied to Tom Paine's Deism, emphasized a regenerate church membership and the ordinances as "memorials of the absent Saviour," and demonstrated evangelical catholicity. William Carey's *Enquiry* provided a missiological rationale centered in the continuing obligation of the Great Commission for the formation of what was later called the (Particular) Baptist Missionary Society. But it was Andrew Fuller, who had struggled to conversion out of the Hyper-Calvinist insistence on a "warrant," who slowly but certainly shifted to an evangelical Calvinism which undergirded indiscriminate gospel preaching and provided a theological foundation for the new missionary endeavor. A prolific author not so well known for his apology against Deism or his polemic against Socinianism, he was best known for his soteriological *The Gospel Worthy of All Acceptation*, in which he argued for the universal duty to repent and believe the gospel. Under the influence of New England theologians Fuller embraced the governmental view of the atonement. He had his critics—William Button and John Martin from Hyper-Calvinism, Dan Taylor from the General Baptists, Archibald McLean from Sandemanianism, and Abraham Booth for making regeneration to be a warrant. A postmillennialist, Fuller rejected the universalism of William Vidler. Booth, who shifted from General Baptist to Particular Baptist and consistently supported the emerging missionary enterprise, authored *The Reign of Grace* with its *ordo salutis*, controverted Samuel Hopkins on regeneration, and strongly defended close communion and believer's baptism. Countering Booth on close communion was Robert Hall, Jr., who set forth an elaborate defense of open communion. Subsequently Joseph Kinghorn defended close communion as close baptism, and

Joseph Ivimey joined in that cause, while John Rippon was planting the seed for the Baptist World Alliance.

The continuing opponents of "Fullerism" in England under the pioneering leadership of William Gadsby and the influence of a non-Baptist, William Huntington, emerged as the Strict and Particular Baptists or Gospel Standard Baptists. Opposing the offers of the gospel, fostering introspective conversion, inclining to antinomianism, and retaining strict communion, these Gadsbyite churches had no part in the Baptist Union, formed by Particular Baptists in 1812, although some strict communion Particular Baptist churches did affiliate with the Baptist Union. Carson, a former Presbyterian, anticipated later controversy by defending biblical inspiration and addressing hermeneutics, wrote on the atonement and on providence, and defended the Baptist stance on baptism against pedobaptists.

In the United States the opponents of the Triennial Convention and its related societies, the state conventions, and college and seminaries mounted a campaign of resistance. John Taylor offered a stinging not-so-theological but monetary attack. Daniel Parker presented the alternative of church-controlled church planting seemingly without connecting his opposition to "the mission plan" with his doctrine of the two seeds, marked by the Holy Spirit's prompting of the good seed. Alexander Campbell ascribed the missionary mandate only to churches, argued that Christian unity must precede missionary work, and charged mismanagement of mission funds. These opposing churches, taking the name Primitive Baptists, were suspicious of the slightest move toward Arminianism, were anti-Carey, anti-Fuller, and anti-Rice, and were reluctant to frame new confessions of faith but held to a historical succession of Primitive Baptist churches from the New Testament era. But the Primitives were destined to have a diminishing influence on Baptist life as Missionary Baptists became the mainstream.

Chapter 6
Baptist Landmarkism

In the middle of the nineteenth century there arose in the American South an ecclesiological movement among Baptists which William Wright Barnes (1883–1960) and James Estol Tull (1913–1989) much later described as "High Church"[1] and which would profoundly impact for more than a century both Southern Baptists and those Landmark Baptists who at the beginning of the twentieth century separated therefrom. The leaders of this movement, Landmarkism, asserted that it was a repristination or perpetuation of earlier Baptist views—indeed a resetting of the "old landmarks,"[2] whereas Tull, Gaston Hugh Wamble (1923–1991), and others have argued at length that Landmark ecclesiology was a major departure from historic, or earlier, Baptist ecclesiology.[3]

Early Landmark History

Landmarkism seems to have arisen from "a query sent by a church to the annual meeting of the Muscle Shoals Association, Alabama, in 1847" concerning the validity or invalidity of immersions of those who make "'a credible profession of faith in Christ'" by pedobaptist ministers who themselves have not been immersed and the two responses made to such a query. The query being addressed to the *Western Baptist Review* in Louisville, Kentucky, its editor John Lightfoot Waller (1809–1854), responded by tracing historically this question, by asserting that the question should be resolved by the congregation, not by the association, and by suggesting that only those who can trace successionally the validity of their own immer-

---

[1]Barnes, *The Southern Baptist Convention*, 102-107; Tull, "A Study of Southern Baptist Landmarkism in the Light of Historical Baptist Ecclesiology" (Ph.D. diss., Columbia University, 1960) 1976; idem, *High-Church Baptists in the South: The Origin, Nature, and Influence of Landmarkism*, ed. Morris Ashcraft (Macon GA: Mercer University Press, 2000) vii, ix, 59, 61.

[2]James Madison Pendleton, *An Old Landmark Reset*, 2nd ed. (Nashville: SouthWestern Publishing House, 1855; orig., 1854). Landmarkers were prone to cite Prov. 22:28: "Remove not the ancient landmarks, which thy fathers have set," and Job 24:2a, "Some remove the landmarks." Tull, *High-Church Baptists*, 1.

[3]Tull, "A Study of Southern Baptist Landmarkism," esp. 149-50, 257-451; Tull, *High-Church Baptists*, 13, 44-46, 48-52, 66-72, 76-82; Wamble, "Landmarkism: Doctrinaire Ecclesiology among Baptists," *Church History* 33 (December 1964): 429-47.

sions should attempt to disfellowship churches and ministers who recognize pedobaptist immersions.⁴ But one "Fidus," who was James Robinson Graves (1820–1893), writing in the *Tennessee Baptist*, expressed a different view, stating that the "'unbroken practice of the Baptist Church, from deep antiquity till now or within a few years, is higher authority than scores of Reviews.'"⁵

Three years later Graves called a meeting of Baptists in Cotton Grove, Tennessee, and posed to such assembled Baptists the compound question as to whether "those societies, not organized according to the pattern of the Jerusalem church, but possessing . . . different *government*," "*officers*," "*class of memberships*," "*ordinances, doctrines,* and *practices*," should be recognized by Baptists as "Gospel Churches," their ministers be recognized as "gospel ministers" and invited to Baptist pulpits, and their members be addressed "as brethren."⁶ Referred to a rally at the annual meeting of the Big Hatchie Association, assembled in Bolivar, Tennessee, 28 July 1851, these questions with their intended negative answers were unanimously adopted. Barnes called these Cotton Grove questions "the first official pronouncement of Landmarkism."⁷

James Madison Pendleton (1811–1891), pastor in Bowling Green, Kentucky, invited Graves to conduct revival services in his church in February 1852.⁸ In doing so, Graves was able to elicit Pendleton's acceptance of Graves's views as to noninvitation of pedobaptist ministers to Baptist pulpits (antipulpit affiliation) and nonacceptance by Baptist churches of immersions administered by nonimmersed pedobaptists (antialien immersion).⁹ At the request of Graves, Pendleton then wrote a pamphlet which Graves published in 1854 under the title, *An Old Landmark Reset*.¹⁰ The

---

⁴Barnes, *The Southern Baptist Convention*, 102-103, quoting from *Western Baptist Review* 3 (March 1848): 276.

⁵Ibid., quoting from *Tennessee Baptist* 1 (25 May 1848): 2.

⁶Ibid., 103-104.

⁷Ibid., 104. See also W. Morgan Patterson, "Landmarkism," *Encyclopedia of Southern Baptists* 2:757.

⁸Pendleton, *Reminiscences of a Long Life* (Louisville: Baptist Book Concern, 1891) 101-103.

⁹Leo T. Crismon and Harold Stephens, "Pendleton, James Madison," *Encyclopedia of Southern Baptists* 2:1082.

¹⁰(1899 edition; repr.: Walker WV: Truth Publications, n.d.) 11-21. The original title of Pendleton's essay was "Ought Baptists to Recognize Pedobaptist Preachers as Gospel Ministers?" and is now available in *Selected Writings of James*

pamphlet was designed to answer the question, "Ought Baptists to invite pedobaptists to preach in their pulpits?" Taking the premise that "'where there is no baptism there are no visible churches,'"[11] Pendleton noted that pedobaptists practice sprinkling rather than immersion and infant baptism rather than believer's baptism (and thus have infant membership) and then concluded that such "societies" are not "gospel organizations," or true churches. Furthermore, because pedobaptist ministers cannot derive their ministerial authority from true churches, they lack "evangelical authority." Since pedobaptist societies would not ordain and recognize as a minister one who is unbaptized, why should Baptists? Thus pedobaptist ministers should not be invited to preach in Baptist pulpits because they have not "membership in the church of Christ." To do so would be to proclaim the "nonessentiality" of the differences between pedobaptists and Baptists and "obliterate the line of demarcation between truth and error." Pendleton disparaged "Union Meetings" and argued that it was inconsistent to deny to pedobaptists access to the Lord's Supper in Baptist churches while inviting pedobaptist ministers to the same pulpits. Since the official acts of pedobaptist ministers are invalid, the immersions which they have administered are invalid and should cease to be practiced. Pendleton sought to anticipate and answer potential objections to his argument relative to repelling pedobaptists, denying gospel "charity," and upsetting "social ties." He was prepared to extend the ban on pulpit affiliation to the adherents of Alexander Campbell, but for different reasons.[12] Recognition of pedobaptist ministers then became the subject of a day-long debate at the 1855 meeting of the Southern Baptist Convention in Montgomery, Alabama.[13]

Graves's next step took Landmarkism beyond antipulpit affiliation and antialien immersion. He republished in 1855 *A Concise History of Foreign*

Madison Pendleton, 3 vols., comp. and ed. by Thomas White (Paris AR: Baptist Standard Bearer, 2006).

[11]The words of a pedobaptist, President Edward Dorr Griffin of Williams College in Massachusetts.

[12]*An Old Landmark Reset*. See also Tull, "A Study of Southern Baptist Landmarkism," 201-206. According to James E. Hill, Jr., "James Madison Pendleton's Theology of Baptism" (Th.M. thesis, Southern Baptist Theological Seminary, 1958) esp. 49-52, 59-60, Pendleton's doctrine of baptism, i.e., antipedobaptism and immersion, provided the foundation for his pulpit nonaffiliation.

[13]Barnes, *The Southern Baptist Convention*, 106; Tull, "A Study of Southern Baptist Landmarkism," 197-98.

Baptists . . .[14] by George Herbert Orchard (1796–1861), an English Baptist pastor in Bedfordshire, which volume had initially been published in London.[15] Orchard sought to trace Baptist churches from the time of John the Baptist through such groups as the Montanists, Novatianists, Donatists, Paulicians, Patarines, Petrobrusians, Arnoldists, Albigenses, Waldenses, *Unitas Fratrum*, Lollards, and Anabaptists. Thereby Baptist church successionism was added to the body of Landmark beliefs.

The Landmark cause was advanced by Amos Cooper Dayton's (1813–1865) two-volume novel, *Theodosia Ernest*.[16] In volume 1 Theodosia of Presbyterian upbringing is led through ten nights of study to reject pedobaptist teachings about Christian baptism and to be immersed, and in volume two a "converted infidel" is led through ten days of travel to seek and find the true church with its historic succession,[17] that is, the Baptist churches.

Graves's Landmarkism led him to oppose as unbiblical the "board" method of foreign missionary appointment and support being pursued by the Foreign Mission Board of the newly formed Southern Baptist Convention. In this he was influenced by the writing of Francis Wayland[18] and by the agitation of Nathaniel Macon Crawford (1811–1871), the president of Mercer University. Consequently the convention was compelled in 1859, after Graves was unsuccessful in getting the board abolished, to instruct the

---

[14](Nashville: Graves, Marks and Rutland).

[15](George Wightman, 1838). But Orchard's book was not the first espousal of Baptist church succession among English Baptists. See John Spittlehouse and John More, *A Vindication of the Continued Succession of the Primitive Church of Jesus Christ (Now Scandalously Termed Anabaptists) from the Apostles unto This Present Time* (London: Gertrude Dawson, 1652; repr.: Victoria BC: Providence Strict Baptist Assembly, 2001).

[16]Subtitle: *or, The Heroine of Faith* (see above, 143n.203); vol. 2, *or, Ten Days' Travel in Search of the Church* (Nashville: Graves, Marks and Rutland, 1856).

[17]See W. Morgan Patterson, *Baptist Successionism: A Critical View* (Valley Forge PA: Judson, 1969); James Edward McGoldrick, *Baptist Successionism: A Crucial Question in Baptist History*, ATLA Monograph Series 32 (Metuchen NJ and London: Scarecrow, 1994); Fletcher, *The Southern Baptist Convention: A Sequicentennial History*, 27-28.

[18]Especially Wayland's pamphlet, *Thoughts on the Missionary Organizations of the Baptist Denomination* (New York: Sheldon, Blakeman and Co., 1859). See also Adrian Lamkin, Jr., "The Gospel Mission Movement within the Southern Baptist Convention" (Ph.D. diss., Southern Baptist Theological Seminary, 1980) 32-41.

board to establish a secondary or "Landmark plan," according to which "churches and associations would appoint their missionaries and send their funds through the facilities of the Board."[19]

Furthermore, Graves and his followers sought repeatedly to alter the basis of membership in the Southern Baptist Convention. Originally the convention was composed of "individuals sent by [contributory] churches and other contributors to" its "mission work," and thus it was following a societal method. Graves insisted that the convention should consist of churches and thus become more strictly "an ecclesiastical body." Such agitation for change long continued after Graves's death until it became partially successful in 1931, when membership in the convention became "a *designated* church representation," though not a Landmark "*delegated* church representation."[20]

Landmarkers, especially Dayton, came to leadership in the SBC's Bible Board (1851–1863) and in the extra-convention Southern Baptist Sunday School Union (1857–1862?).[21]

The Landmark "Triumvirate":[22]
James Robinson Graves,
James Madison Pendleton,
and Amos Cooper Dayton

The three original leaders of Baptist Landmarkism have been given descriptive identifications: Pendleton as "the prophet," Graves as "the warrior," and Dayton as "the sword-bearer."[23] Because Pendleton on account of his advocacy of the gradual emancipation of slaves, though not the immediate abolition of slavery, and his lack of sympathy for the Confederate States lived in Ohio and Pennsylvania from 1862 to 1883,[24] and because of the

---

[19]Barnes, *The Southern Baptist Convention*, 109-12; Fletcher, *The Southern Baptist Convention*, 65.

[20]Barnes, *The Southern Baptist Convention*, 113; Baker, *The Southern Baptist Convention and Its People*, 405. See below, 246-47.

[21]Barnes, *The Southern Baptist Convention*, 83-86; Baker, *The Southern Baptist Convention and Its People*, 207, 199.

[22]Orren Luico Hailey, *J. R. Graves: Life, Times and Teachings* (Nashville: author, 1929) 72; Barnes, *The Southern Baptist Convention*, 103.

[23]Barnes, *The Southern Baptist Convention*, 103.

[24]Pendleton, *Reminiscences of a Long Life*, 112-14, 118-28, 131, 160, 163. For the details of Pendleton's life, see William C. Huddleston, "James Madison Pendleton: A Critical Biography" (Th.M. thesis, Southern Baptist Theological Seminary,

death of Dayton in 1865, Graves became the singular leader of Landmarkism after the Civil War.

A native of Vermont and of Congregational parentage, his father having died shortly after his birth, Graves united with a Baptist church when fifteen and at nineteen moved with his family to Ohio. Studiously self-educated, he became a school principal first in Ohio and then in Kentucky, where he was licensed and ordained as a Baptist minister. After moving to Nashville, Tennessee, in 1845, he first joined the First Church and then served briefly as pastor of the Second Church. After returning to First Baptist Church and after Robert Boyté Crawford Howell's (1801–1868) commencing of his second pastoral tenure in 1857, Graves entered into personal conflict with Howell. Excommunicated, Graves and his followers formed Spring Street Church, which rather than First Church was recognized by state and associational bodies. Having become in 1848 the editor of *The Baptist*, later *The Tennessee Baptist*, he continued in that role until 1889, and he relocated in Memphis, Tennessee, in 1867. Active in various publication efforts and in considerable demand as a preacher, Graves exerted great influence on the Baptists of the Southwest.[25]

Graves was a prolific polemicist against other Protestant denominations in America. In 1855 he issued *The Great Iron Wheel*[26] against the Methodist Episcopal Church, South. Methodism, he argued, was "not a Church of Christ" because it was "christened" in America and was only 68 years old, had a human founder John Wesley, and came "by accident." It was "not a Christian ... Society" since it does not *"require a profession of religion as a condition of membership,"* and Wesley never claimed to be "originating a Church." Wesley did not interpret as biblical the threefold ministry (bishops, elders, deacons), did not leave such in England, and sent Thomas Coke and Francis Asbury to America as "joint superintendents." The "great iron wheel" is Methodist "itinerancy," and the "great outer wheel" is its

---

1962); and Bob D. Compton, "J. M. Pendleton: A Nineteenth-Century Baptist Statesman (1811–1891)," *Baptist History and Heritage* 10 (January 1975): 28-35.

[25]Harold Stewart Smith, "A Critical Analysis of the Theology of J. R. Graves" (Th.D. diss., Southern Baptist Theological Seminary, 1966) 1-53; Homer L. Grice and R. Paul Caudill, "Graves-Howell Controversy (1857–1862)," *Encyclopedia of Southern Baptists* 1:580-85; idem, "Graves, James Robinson," 576-77.

[26]Subtitle: *or, Republicanism Backwards and Christianity Reversed...* (Nashville: Graves and Marks, 1855). It consisted of forty letters addressed to Joshua Soule (1781–1867), senior bishop of the Methodist Episcopal Church, South.

episcopacy. Indeed it is "a monstrous system of clerical usurpation and despotism," veritably "the Popery of Protestantism." Bishops are elected by the general conference, presiding elders are subbishops," travelling preachers exercise authority over class leaders and stewards, and ministers have the right to admit and exclude members. Wesley opposed the American War of Independence, and Methodism denies freedoms of thought, speech, and press and to its members the election of their preachers. Not essentially "republican," Methodist polity is "the antipode of the American political system." Methodism, like the Church of England, has "'a Calvinistic creed, a popish liturgy, and an Armenian [that is, Arminian] clergy.'" It has two baptisms, infant and adult, is divided as to whether the primitive mode was immersion, and practices close communion while avowing open communion.[27]

The Little Iron Wheel (1856)[28] consisted of a declaration of rights written by a Methodist author, Henry Bidleman Bascom (1796–1850), together with Graves's applications to and illustrations of Methodism's "despotism" and further articles by Bascom and charges and defenses by Graves. Bascom affirmed popular sovereignty in both church and the civil order. Hence "representative government is the only legitimate human rule," and legislation should be by consent of the people. Church members have the right to think and decide on matters of faith and morality, and oppressive church polity is not to be justified by the Bible. Church members should resist ministerial "errors, oppressions, and usurpations," and not to do so contradicts the Protestant principle. Graves, agreeing with and utilizing Bascom, time and again scored Methodism's "despotism" as being contrary

---

[27]Ibid., 22, 41-42, 47, 57, 66, 114, 122, 73-74, 81, 157, 163, 169, 186, 195-98, 218-19, 234-46, 154-56, 288-92, 297-301, 156, 308-26, 319, 329, 415-21, 453-63, 471, 478-79. Smith, "A Critical Analysis of the Theology of J. R. Graves," 106-108, has found Fred A. Rose, a Presbyterian editor, to have been a major source for the content of this book. See also ibid., 137-40.

[28]Subtitle: *A Declaration of Christian Rights, and Articles Showing the Despotism of Episcopal Methodism* [with] *Notes of Application and Illustration by J. R. Graves* (Nashville: South Western Publishing House). Bascom was one of a group of Methodist Episcopal Church ministers who sought reform of polity during 1824–1827. When this effort was not successful, some of these ministers who were adamant were excommunicated and then formed in 1828 the Protestant Methodist Church. Bascom remained in the church and, after further division over slavery, became a bishop in the Methodist Episcopal Church, South. Ibid., iii-v. Graves affirmed his total support of the institution of slavery. Ibid., 8-19.

to that republican government that is essentially American as well as contravening the New Testament.[29]

In Graves's lengthy debate in Carrollton, Missouri, with a Methodist, Jacob Ditzler, the two addressed six propositions. Immersion as the Christ-commanded mode of baptism was argued most extensively, with Graves presenting the most elaborate defense of immersion to be found in his writings. Graves refuted in some detail pedobaptism, defended more succinctly close communion, believer's baptism, and perseverance, and contended that Methodist polity was unbiblical.[30] *The New Great Iron Wheel* (1884)[31] was similar in content to and essentially a reorganization of *The Great Iron Wheel* with more material on the Methodist Episcopal Church, South, and on Arminianism.[32]

Graves's polemic against Presbyterianism was connected with his anti-Roman Catholic polemic in *The Trilemma; or, Death by Three Horns* (1890).[33] He posited that Protestants cannot adequately answer the question as to whether Roman Catholic baptism is valid. Noting the nineteenth-century debates within the general assemblies of both Old School and New School Presbyterianism on this issue and the reaffirmation of negative answers, Graves argued that not only had the baptisms of Luther, Calvin, Zwingli, Beza, and Knox been "papal" baptisms and therefore invalid but also are Presbyterian baptisms in the nineteenth century invalid. Graves's premise was that only a true, visible church of Christ can administer Christian baptism, and thus if a baptism is to be "considered scriptural and valid, the society administering it must be acknowledged and treated as a true church of Christ." But Presbyterians did not regard the Roman Catholic Church as a true church.[34] For them

---

[29]Ibid., esp. 26, 29-30, 46-47, 60, 61-62, 70-71, 77-78. These two anti-Methodist books by Graves were answered in two books by a Methodist, William G. Brownlow. Smith, "A Critical Analysis of the Theology of J. R. Graves," 139-40.

[30]*The Graves-Ditzler*, or, *Great Carrollton Debate . . . between J. R. Graves, LL.D., and Jacob Ditzler, D.D.* (Memphis: Southern Baptist Publication Society, 1876). (The text of the debate runs to 1,175 pages.)

[31]Subtitle: *An Examination of the New M. E. Church South, in a Series of Letters Addressed to Bishop* [H. N.] *McTyeire* (Memphis: Baptist Book House, 1884).

[32]Ibid., esp. 57-102, 111-53, 513-70.

[33](Memphis: J. R. Graves and Son).

[34]Ibid., 15-78, 12-13.

The Tri-lemma is the middle horn: the confession of the General Assembly of its inability to decide whether its own ministers are baptized, or have authority to baptize, and consequently, whether their societies are visible Churches of Christ.[35]

Graves has presupposed Baptist historical succession from the New Testament era with no connection with "the Papal Church." He challenged all Protestants to identify the Church of Rome as "the mother of harlots" (Rev. 17:5), to deny its claim to antiquity, its sacraments, and its priestly ministers and clericalism, and to reject its papal head, its placement of traditions above the Scriptures, its resistance to Bible translation, its unions of church and state, and its opposition to civil and religious liberty and individualism.[36]

In Graves's literary debate with Alexander Campbell, his most repeated polemic was his accusation that Campbell was teaching that the "*actual*," not the "*figurative* or *declarative*," remission of sins comes in immersion. Hence the efficacy of Christ's blood is brought into contact with the conscience of the believer while the believer is buried through immersion, and thus salvation in heaven requires immersion on earth. Graves also criticized Campbell for inconsistently teaching that one must have the aid of the Holy Spirit to remain a Christian but not to become a Christian; even Roman Catholics honor the Holy Spirit in baptism as Campbell does not. Graves faulted Campbell for defective theology as to justification, faith, and repentance. Campbell insisted that by the act of going into water one obtains the remission of sins, that there can be no regeneration or remission prior to immersion, and that he was as orthodox as the Baptist leaders prior to Graves.[37]

Graves had in 1878 an in-depth literary debate with John C. Burruss, editor of *The Universalist Herald* of Notasulga, Alabama, on the proposition, "The Scriptures teach the endless punishment of some portion of the

---

[35]Ibid., 72.

[36]Ibid. 80-118. See Tull, "A Study of Southern Baptist Landmarkism," 237-39. In *The Trilemma*, 187-207, Graves argued that Freewill Baptists, Campbellites, and Anti-Missionary Baptists are not true churches of Christ and cannot administer valid baptisms.

[37]Graves, *Campbell and Campbellism Exposed: A Series of Replies to A. Campbell's Articles in the Millennial Harbinger* (Nashville: Graves and Marks, 1854) esp. 21, 10-11, 22, 46, 88, 148, 47, 80, 170-77, 53, 109, 145, 230-32, 41, 45, 219, 28.

human race." Graves offered a barrage of New Testament quotations, and Burruss insisted that Universalists believe in "just retribution for all sins committed" and in postmortal but not endless punishment. Graves countered that Boston Universalism was denying postmortal punishment. Burruss challenged Graves to produce a single biblical text saying that "sin is infinite" and "deserves infinite punishment." Graves argued that limited punishment violates the law and divine justice and that belief in eternal punishment restrains from sin and protects humankind. Burruss put less emphasis than other Universalists on God's almighty love. Graves was unable to answer Burruss's assertion that various pre-Augustinian church fathers taught universalism, but Graves seems to have had the upper hand in their lengthy exchange as to the usages and meanings of "eternal" or "everlasting" (αἰώνιος).[38]

In the context of expounding his own doctrine of the intermediate state between death and resurrection—which he called "the middle life," Graves refuted the teachings of Spiritism and of Swedenborgianism. Because of the lack of biblical support the teaching of these two systems that "all angels, good and bad, are but the spirits of dead men" is to be rejected. Moreover, it is impossible for either "the spirits of wicked men" or "the spirits of saints" "to communicate with or disturb the living."[39]

Some aspects of Graves's theology had no essential connection with Landmarkism. Graves held to the plenary-verbal theory of biblical inspiration and inclined to literal interpretation "unless a figure occurs in the passage." Although teaching the eternal existence of the Trinity, he insisted that the Father-Son-Holy Spirit relationships "*are not* eternal" and "are relevant to . . . time and history." Rejecting evolution, he taught that "humans were created by an immediate act of God" and "located the origin of evil after the creation of the heavenly hosts and before the creation of man." Adam, but not Eve, was placed under the covenant of works, and, he being the federal head of humankind, his fall "brought depravity and woe to all

---

[38]Graves and Burruss, *A Discussion of the Doctrine of Endless Punishment* (Atlanta: J. O. Perkins and Co., 1880) title page, 11-16, 19-20, 61-62, 24, 79, 28-33, 72, 43-49, 24, 148, 41, 96-97, 62, 56, 57-58, 66-67, 104-19, 120-21, 123-26, 132-47, 149-58.

[39]*The Bible Doctrine of the Middle Life, as Opposed to Swedenborgianism and Spiritism* (Memphis: Southern Baptist Publication Society, 1873) 18, 15, 99-101. Graves, 79-88, esp. 80, utilized the parable of the rich man and Lazarus and, noting that it is a parable, declared: "The Savior never built a parable upon a falsehood."

his descendants." Noah had a white son, a "copper-colored" son, and a "black son." Having entered into the covenant of redemption in eternity, the second person of the Trinity by his incarnation "*became* the Son of the first person." Graves was accused of and had to defend himself against Arian heresy. More accurate would have been the charges of Apollinarianism and/or Nestorianism, for Graves denied that Jesus had a human soul, and the "dichotomy of human and divine" may be seen in Graves's insistence that, without a human soul, Jesus suffered in his divine nature. Using the language of satisfaction first developed by Anselm of Canterbury, Graves set forth what Harold S. Smith has called "a sacrificial-substitutionary-satisfaction theory" of the atonement. The atonement is limited to the elect and was completed in Jesus' resurrection and ascension. Holding to the doctrine of perseverance, Graves preferred to speak of the security of the believer.[40]

In *Old Landmarkism: What Is It?*[41] Graves expounded full-orbed Landmarkism. Jesus "while on earth" set up one kingdom and built one church, and that kingdom was not to consist of antagonistic parts. Graves rejected "church-branch" and "church-army" theories as well as any concept of a universal church. "The apostles built churches by a divine model," and the name "church" should not be given to any organization that is not "conformed to that model." There were, for Graves, seven marks of an apostolically modeled church:

1. "The Church and Kingdom of Christ is a Divine Institution."[42]
2. "It is a Visible Church."[43]
3. "Its Locality is upon this Earth."[44]
4. "It was a Local Organization, a Single Congregation."[45]

---

[40]Harold S. Smith, "J. R. Graves," in *Baptist Theologians*, ed. George and Dockery, 230-38. As to Graves's dispensational premillennialism, see below, 562-63.

[41]2nd ed. (Memphis: Baptist Book House, 1881; orig., 1880).

[42]Graves cited Dan. 2:44-45; Matt. 16:19; and Heb. 3:3-6.

[43]Hence Christ "has no invisible kingdom or church" (ibid., 32).

[44]"Church" and "Kingdom" were "synonymous terms . . . so long as Christ had but *one* organized Church." "The Kingdom embraced the first church, and now it embraces all the churches" (ibid., 33).

[45]Graves refuted "the Catholic or Universal" Theory (Roman Catholic Church) and "the National or Provincial theory" (Church of England, Old School Presbyterians, Methodist Episcopal Church) (ibid., 36-38). This local church alone is "commissioned to preach the Gospel," ordain its officers, "receive, discipline, and

5. "The membership [is] all professedly regenerate in heart before baptized into it."[46]
6. "Its baptism is the profession, on the part of the subject, of the faith of the Gospel by which he is saved."[47]
7. "The Lord's Supper[48] was observed as a local church ordinance, commemorative only of the sacrificial chastisement of Christ for his people, never expressive of personal fellowship, or of courtesy for others, or used as a sacrament."[49]

Graves insisted that Landmarkism was "not the denial of spiritual regeneration" to non-Baptists, was "not the denial of the honesty and conscientiousness of Pedobaptists and Campbellites," was "not a proof" of the "uncharitableness" of Landmarkers, and "not the denial to others" of civil and religious liberties.[50] He referred to Baptists who were not Landmarkers as "our 'liberal' brethren" and as "Affiliationists"[51] and sought evidence that at least some Landmark teachings had been held among New England, Virginia, and Philadelphia Baptists.[52]

In numerous monographs Graves expounded in detail his doctrines of baptism and the Lord's Supper, at times reemploying materials that he had previously published. Baptism is the important act of immersion, the mode constituting and being the "essence" of the ordinance, the act symbolizing death, burial, and resurrection, the observance being obedience to Christ,

---

exclude members," and administer the two ordinances (ibid., 43-52).

[46]Graves opposed the Roman Catholic instrumental view of the church and the sacraments, the Presbyterian view of the church as consisting of "believers and *their* children," and the practice of infant baptism (ibid., 55-63).

[47]Graves rejected Eastern Orthodox and Roman Catholic sacramental theologies of baptism, Campbellite immersion "for the remission of sin" as tantamount to "baptismal regeneration," Methodist Episcopal retention of Anglican adherence to baptismal regeneration and the candidate's necessarily professing to be unregenerate, and Presbyterian interpretation of baptism as *sacrament* and *seal* (ibid., 69-76).

[48]Graves espoused the view that participation in the Lord's Supper should be restricted to the members of the observing local church and wrote extensively of the "objections" to, the "inconsistencies" in, and the "evils" of "intercommunion" (ibid., 83-85, 105-20).

[49]Ibid., 17-130.
[50]Ibid., 131-38.
[51]Ibid., 149, 166, 173, 218, 219, 220, 222, 225.
[52]Ibid., 183-214.

and its administration being limited to Baptist churches.[53] Indeed it is "the profession" on the part of the baptized of "the faith of the gospel."[54] Baptism is not a "means to secure the actual remission" of sins or cleansing from sins, or the means of receiving the promise of the Holy Spirit, the new birth, union with Christ, or the grace of God, or "a seal" of "the Covenant of Grace."[55] Furthermore, the ministry of John the Baptist and hence the baptism administered by him belong not to the Jewish dispensation or some "intermediate" dispensation but rather to the Christian dispensation.[56]

The Lord's Supper, for Graves, should be observed with one unleavened and unbroken, but to be broken, loaf of wheat bread and the one cup of "the fermented juice of the grape." Remembrance is central to the Supper, which is to be partaken worthily.[57] The Supper, Graves asserted, is an ordinance of the local church, and, since only that church can discipline its members, only its members should partake of the Supper.[58] Moreover, "intercommunion" was not practiced by the apostolic churches, and it abrogates congregational independence, subverts congregational discipline, and is divisive among Baptists.[59]

Pendleton during his Bowling Green pastorate authored *Three Reasons, Why I Am a Baptist*.[60] His first reason was believer's baptism and the consequent rejection of pedobaptism. He opposed the baptism of infants because

---

[53] *The Act of Christian Baptism* (Memphis: Baptist Book House, 1881).

[54] *Christian Baptism, the Profession of the Faith of the Gospel* (Memphis: Baptist Book House, 1881).

[55] *The Relation of Baptism to Salvation* (Memphis: Baptist Book House, 1881), 24-41.

[56] *John's Baptism: Was It from Moses or Christ? Jewish or Christian?* (Memphis: J. R. Graves and Son, 1891) 22-83.

[57] *The Symbolism of the Supper: What Is It to Eat and Drink Unworthily?* (Memphis: Baptist Book House, 1881).

[58] *The Lord's Supper a Church Ordinance, and So Observed by the Apostolic Churches* (Memphis: Baptist Book House, 1881). Seemingly Graves did not fully embrace the restriction of partaking to members of the observing church until ca. 1875. See the present author's *Systematic Theology: Biblical, Historical, and Evangelical*, 2nd ed. (North Richland Hills TX: BIBAL, 2001) 2:676n.104.

[59] *Intercommunion Inconsistent, Unscriptural, and Productive of Evil*, 2nd ed. (Memphis: Baptist Book House, 1882; orig., 1881) 286-323.

[60] (Cincinnati: Moore, Anderson and Co., 1853). Republished as *Distinctive Principles of Baptists* (Philadelphia: American Baptist Publication Society, 1882; repr.: Paris AR: Baptist Standard Bearer, 2006).

of the absence of evidence of its practice in the New Testament, the failure of its advocates to agree as to its meaning, its tendency to "unite" the church and the world, its giving to infants a "delusive belief" of having a "more hopeful salvation," and its often supplanting believer's baptism. Indeed the Christian church is not identical with the "Jewish Church," and baptism was not substituted for circumcision.[61] His second reason, immersion as the only mode of baptism, was defended by lexical considerations, the design of baptism (that is, burial and resurrection), the location of baptisms in the New Testament near water, and the thirteen-century history of its practice.[62] Congregational polity was Pendleton's third reason. In contradistinction from episcopal and presbyterian polities, this means that "the governmental power is in the hands of the people," the rule of the majority prevails, and church power "cannot be transferred or alienated "and hence congregational action is final.[63] Pendleton added a fourth reason, namely, the Lord's Supper with participation, contra Graves, extended to fellow Baptists.[64] Jerry Thomas White has agreed with Tull as to three major differences between Pendleton and Graves: Pendelton's retention of the doctrine of the universal church, his refusal "to equate the Kingdom of God with the aggregate of Baptist churches," and his nonespousal of Baptist church succession.[65] In his *Church Manual*[66] Pendleton reiterated his views on the ordinances and on polity and dealt with membership and discipline.

In 1878 Pendleton issued a one-volume systematic theology[67] which was moderately Calvinistic and distinctively Baptist and interacted neither with Darwinian evolution nor biblical criticism. His doctrine of revelation and the Bible addressed why revelation was needed and evidence for the divine origin of the Bible. God's attributes were classified as "natural" and

---

[61]Ibid., 5-29, 74-82, 32-54, 60-62.

[62]Ibid., 82-137.

[63]Ibid., 148-71, esp. 153.

[64]*Three Reasons Why I Am a Baptist, with a Fourth Reason Added on Communion* (St. Louis: National Baptist Publishing House, 1879).

[65]"James Madison Pendleton and His Contributions to Baptist Ecclesiology" (Ph.D. diss., Southeastern Baptist Theological Seminary, 2005; Ann Arbor: University Microfilms International, 2005) 9, citing Tull, *High-Church Baptists*, 44.

[66]Subtitle: *Designed for the Use of Baptist Churches* (Philadelphia: American Baptist Publication Society, 1867) 64-117, 8-21, 118-47.

[67]*Christian Doctrines: A Compendium of Theology* (Philadelphia: American Baptist Publication Society).

"moral," the Trinity was said to be biblically based, the deity of Christ was defended, and his humanity, including a human soul, was expounded, and the doctrine of the Holy Spirit was limited to personality and deity. Pendleton referred to God's "purposes" rather than "decrees," taught particular election not based on the divine foreseeing of faith and good works, understood reprobation as God's execution of punishment for sin, and defined providence as preservation of the created, control of the created, and "the ordering of all events." The image of God is both "rational" and "moral," the latter having been lost by the fall and capable of being restored in Christ. In the exercise of free will, Adam, both the natural and the federal head of humanity, sinned. That sin issued in both physical and spiritual death, and Adam's depraved descendants "endorsed" his sin "as soon as they are able to discern between good and evil." In his "general" office of mediator and his "subordinate" offices of prophet, priest, and king, Christ made the atonement—by expiation, satisfaction, and substitution, a sacrifice "sufficient" for the salvation of humanity, and continues his intercessory work for his elect people. Pendleton's *ordo salutis* was: regeneration ("with its attendants, repentance and faith"), justification, adoption, sanctification, good works, and perseverance. Between death and the general resurrection the conscious souls of believers will be with Christ in heaven—not in Paradise, as Graves held. The second coming of Christ will follow the millennium, and the general judgment will be followed by heaven and hell.[68]

Dayton, a native of New Jersey and formerly a Presbyterian, had become a Baptist in 1852. Following his widely circulating *Theodosia Ernest*,[69] he wrote at the urging of Graves *Pedobaptist and Campbellite Immersions*.[70] He included lengthy quotations from Baptist authors in the South who favored receiving "alien immersions" and then offered refutation of each. In reply to John L. Waller he contended that Pedobaptist and Campbellite churches are not truly constituted churches, insisted that lay-

---

[68]Ibid., 63-90, 198-207, 91-114, 128-37, 157-75, 208-328, 368-410. Pendleton amplified ch. 16 so as to produce his monograph, *The Atonement of Christ* (Philadelphia: American Baptist Publication Society, 1885); James E. Taulman, "The Life and Writings of Amos Cooper Dayton (1813–1865)," *Baptist History and Heritage* 10 (January 1975): 36-43.

[69]J. Clark Hensley and Homer L. Grice, "Dayton, Amos Cooper," *Encyclopedia of Southern Baptists* 1:351-52.

[70](Nashville: South-Western Publishing House, 1858).

administered baptism is not a disputed issue, claimed that in the New Testament baptism was administered by disciples who were baptized members "of Christ's visible church," and argued in the context of Baptist church succession from the apostolic age that baptismal validity depends more upon the proper authority to baptize than upon succession in the administrator's own baptism or ordination.[71] Richard Fuller (1804–1876), pastor of Seventh Church, Baltimore, Maryland, having himself been immersed as a Baptist after having been immersed as a believer in a pedobaptist church, advised a Baptist pastor's wife who had received believer's immersion in a Methodist church that further immersion was not needed if she were personally "satisfied." Dayton countered that baptism is not so much a personal duty as a church ordinance and that the wife should receive Baptist immersion. Baptism as initiation to God's kingdom he likened to the civil oath of allegiance. Fuller had said that the authority to baptize is in the Great Commission; Dayton asserted that the Great Commission was given to the baptized. Dayton also insisted that Fuller must locate or identify any "broken link" in Baptist church succession.[72] William Bullein Johnson (1782–1862), who had had a long pastorate in Edgefield, South Carolina, having noted that John the Baptist, Luther, Knox, Whitefield, and Edwards had not been immersed as believers, had asked whether, if pedobaptist preaching has resulted in the salvation of persons, there should be Baptist resistance to immersions administered by nonimmersed ministers, for conversion is greater than baptism. Dayton responded by claiming that in the New Testament there is no reference to "unbaptized Evangelists" or to their duties or to any command that they baptize believers. John the Baptist he allowed as an exception that "stands alone." Moreover, every one who is authorized to preach or evangelize is not also authorized to baptize.[73] Alvin Peter Williams (1813–1868), Missouri pastor, having acknowledged that Pedobaptist churches are not "Scripturally organized churches" and that immersions administered by pedobaptists are "irregular," had explored the New Testament texts so as to conclude that the baptismal candidate was not responsible "for any *unknown* disqualification in the administrator." Hence Williams favored receiving alien immersions, for a second believer's immersion would be repetitious. Dayton sought to move the debate from the candidate-administrator to church duty. If an administrator lacks church

---

[71]Ibid., 41-64, 117-56, esp. 54-57, 62-63, 127-28.
[72]Ibid., 65-91, esp. 65-69, 83, 74, 77-80, 76, 81, 88-90.
[73]Ibid., 92-116, esp. 93-95, 100-105, 112.

membership and proper ordination, such is not an "unknown disqualification." There are biblical qualifications for administering baptism, and hence administration is not "open to all" but "limited," and unauthorized administrators mean invalid baptism.[74]

Dayton concluded his book by setting forth ten "commonsense" arguments against alien immersions and by treating the biblical texts alleged by his opponents to support their positions and those Dayton advanced as supporting his case. Whoever receives the profession of faith of a penitent believer has authority to baptize, and for Dayton this means a Baptist church. Having differentiated the invisible kingdom of God and the visible, Dayton asserted that one cannot be an officer of the visible kingdom if one is not a member. Administering baptism is an "official act," and true ministers baptize by a church authorization conferred by Christ. Baptist churches reordain pedobaptist ministers who became Baptists and seek to minister. To admit the actions of bishops, synods, or presbyteries in appointing administrators of baptism is to admit their authority. If a pedobaptist minister were in a Baptist church teaching and practicing infant baptism and/or sprinkling, he would be deposed. Strict communion Baptist churches do not commune at the Lord's Supper with pedobaptists and Campbellites because they regard them as not being "Scriptural Churches of Jesus Christ." If such churches receive alien immersions, they should for the sake of consistency practice open communion. Indeed receiving alien immersions has become a divisive issue among Baptist churches.[75]

As to the Scriptures, Dayton first asked as a rhetorical question whether the New Testament contains a single text which authorizes a nonbaptized person to administer Christian baptism.[76] Then he proceeded to answer respecting each text cited by the Baptist authors whom he had quoted at length in favor of receiving alien immersions.[77] For his own case Dayton argued that the Great Commission did not authorize everybody to baptize and then reviewed eleven baptismal texts from the baptizing by John the Baptist to the rebaptisms in Acts 19 so as to conclude that all such baptisms

---

[74] Ibid., 157-81, esp. 158-62, 164, 166-69, 173-74.
[75] Ibid., 184-220.
[76] Ibid., 223-24.
[77] Ibid., 225-39. Wayland re Gal. 5:1; Johnson re 1 Cor. 14; Walker re Great Commission texts; Fuller re 1 Pet. 3:21 and 1 Cor. 10:2; Williams re various texts.

had proper administrators. Finally, he explored eight case studies of immersions, six of which he concluded were invalid.[78]

Later Landmark Controversies

Landmarkism had its lingering effects, both as a major influence upon and as the cause of controversy among Southern Baptists, after the deaths of its triumvirate founders. There were four major Landmark-related controversies.

Gospel Missionism represented a conflation of Landmark ecclesiology with the missionary methodology of John Livingston Nevius (1829–1893),[79] a Presbyterian missionary in China. It was advocated and led by Tarleton Perry Crawford (1821–1902), an FMB-SBC missionary in China for forty-one years. Back in the U.S. in 1859, he had heard J. R. Graves challenge the FMB and its policies at that year's SBC session. Crawford came to the view that churches, not mission boards, should appoint and support foreign missionaries, for boards represent an un-Baptistic centralization that threatened local church autonomy.[80] From Nevius and a book by C. H. Carpenter,[81] Crawford, who had initially observed in China dishonesty among national workers, derived the idea that churches on mission fields should from the beginning be self-supporting and self-governing. Schools should be closed, and the clothing, food, and housing of missionaries should be the same as those of nationals. Crawford's efforts in 1879 and 1886 to get the SBC to adopt his principles failed, and he formed in 1890 with a few missionaries and nationals the Gospel Mission Association in North China, but the latter survived only through the first decade of the twentieth century. Ironically, Crawford's missiology, if not ecclesiology,

---

[78]Ibid., 241-65.

[79]*The Planting and Development of Missionary Churches*, 3rd ed. (New York: Student Volunteer Movement for Foreign Missions, 1899); orig., under the title, *Methods of Mission Work* (Shanghai, 1886).

[80]Crawford, *Churches to the Front!* ([Chefoo?], China: author, 1892); condensed text in Robert A. Baker, ed., *A Baptist Source Book: With Particular Reference to Southern Baptists* (Nashville: Broadman, 1966) 177-80; idem, "Churches and the Commission," in *The Crisis of the Churches: A Collection of Earnest Articles and Extracts from Earnest Men on Matters of Vital Concern to Baptists*, ed. Crawford (Chefoo, China: author, 1894) 52-63.

[81]*Self-Support, Illustrated in the History of the Bassein Karen Mission from 1840 to 1880* (Boston: Rand, Avery, and Co., 1883) 147-51, 161-70, 323-407.

would find acceptance among Southern Baptists toward the end of the twentieth century.[82]

A second controversy impinging Landmarkism marked the intersection of Landmark Baptist church successionism and the new historiography of the Baptists and centered in the life and writings of William Heth Whitsitt (1841–1911). A native of Tennessee, Whitsitt graduated from Union University in Murfreesboro in 1861, served in the Confederate Army, studied at the University of Virginia (1866) and the Southern Baptist Theological Seminary (1866-68), and finally spent two years (1869-71) at the universities of Berlin and Leipzig. He joined the faculty of Southern Baptist Theological Seminary in 1872 as professor of ecclesiastical history but also taught other subjects. He became the seminary's third president in 1895.[83]

Whitsitt's method of studying and teaching church history had seemingly been influenced by his studies in Germany—a method that W. W. Barnes

---

[82]L. S. Foster, *Fifty Years in China: An Eventful Memoir of Tarleton Perry Crawford, D.D.* (Nashville: Bayless-Pullen Co., 1909) 169-71, 177-78, 181, 184-85, 187-91, 203, 209, 213-43, 246, 256, 270; Barnes, *The Southern Baptist Convention*, 113-16; W. B. Glass, "Crawford, Tarleton Perry," *Encyclopedia of Southern Baptists* 1:329; Baker, *The Southern Baptist Convention and Its People*, 247, 278-80; McBeth, *The Baptist Heritage*, 416, 457, 751; Fletcher, *The Southern Baptist Convention*, 101-102; William R. Estep, Jr., *Whole Gospel—Whole World: The Foreign Mission Board of the Southern Baptist Convention, 1845–1995* (Nashville: Broadman & Holman, 1994) 106, 139-44, 382; Tull, *High-Church Baptists*, 136-38. Lamkin, "The Gospel Mission Movement within the Southern Baptist Convention," 208-209, 47, 202, 201, has played down the influence of Graves and Landmarkism upon the formation of Crawford's views while acknowledging that Crawford "was provided with ammunition from the earlier efforts" of Graves and that Landmark Baptists utilized Gospel Missionism "in their effort to control the Southern Baptist Convention or to displace it." Lamkin was surely correct to conclude that Gospel Missionism as expressed by Crawford "challenged the right" to exist of both the Foreign Mission Board and the SBC.

[83]E. B. Pollard, "The Life and Work of William Heth Whitsitt," *Review and Expositor* 9 (April 1912): 159-84; Rufus W. Weaver, "Life and Times of William Heth Whitsitt," *Review and Expositor* 37 (April 1940): 115-20; Gaines S. Dobbins, "Whitsitt, William Heth," *Encyclopedia of Southern Baptists* 2:1496; Tull, "A Study of Southern Baptist Landmarkism," 577-78; Charles Basil Bugg, "The Whitsitt Controversy: A Study in Denominational Conflict" (Th.D. diss., Southern Baptist Theological Seminary, 1972) 111-18; Rosalie Beck, "The Whitsitt Controversy: A Denomination in Crisis" (Ph.D. diss., Baylor University, 1984) 3-12; Fletcher, *The Southern Baptist Convention*, 68-69, 104-105.

identified as "the historical-scientific"—possibly by the model of Philip Schaff.[84] James E. Tull toyed with the idea that Whitsitt could have been the author in 1876 of the pseudonymous "Pike" articles against Landmarkism, which dated the recovery of immersion ca.1640.[85] Whitsitt later acknowledged that he had been the anonymous author of editorials appearing, after his summer of study in the British Museum and the Bodleian Library, in 1880 in *The Independent*, a Congregational periodical published in New York. The editorials stated that certain English Independents reinstated immersion as the form of baptism in 1641 and thus became Baptists in 1641 and that Roger Williams was baptized by aspersion or affusion in 1639.[86] In 1893 Whitsitt published a signed article on Baptists in *Johnson's Universal Encyclopedia*, in which he reiterated his earlier findings as to the recovery of immersion.[87] By early 1896 a flood of criticism of this article erupted, not only from Southern Baptists but also from Henry Melville King (1838–1919),[88] pastor of First Baptist Church, Providence, Rhode Island, and Whitsitt apologized in 1897 to the seminary trustees for the publicational location of his article.[89] After having published two pamphlets about the church ordinances,[90] Whitsitt issued in 1896 *A Question of Baptist*

---

[84]Barnes, *The Southern Baptist Convention*, 136-37; Bugg, "The Whitsitt Controversy," 115-18.

[85]"A Study of Southern Baptist Landmarkism," 580-82, citing *The Religious Herald* (23 March 1876) 1. See Bugg, "The Whitsitt Controversy," 119-23, for a rejection of Tull's hypothesis.

[86]Tull, "A Study of Southern Baptist Landmarkism," 579, 582-83; Bugg, "The Whitsitt Controversy," 70-81. These editorials were reprinted in Jesse Burgess Thomas, *Dr. Whitsitt's "Question"* (Louisville: Baptist Book Concerns, 1897) 75-83, 92-97.

[87]Tull, "A Study of Southern Baptist Landmarkism," 582-83; Bugg, "The Whitsitt Controversy," 81-85, citing Whitsitt, "Baptists," *Johnson's Universal Encyclopedia* 1:489-93.

[88]*The Baptism of Roger Williams: A Review of Rev. Dr. W. H. Whitsitt's Inference* (Providence RI: Preston and Rounds Co., 1897). King defended Williams's baptism by immersion (3-4, 33-34, 50, 59-60, 66, 90-91, 95, 98, 113-14, 116).

[89]Bugg, "The Whitsitt Controversy," 71, 81-85.

[90]*The Origin of Infant Baptism* (Louisville: Caperton and Cates, 1878; Charles T. Dearing, 1897); *The History of Communion among Baptists* (New York: J. K. Lees, 1880). In the latter he strongly defended strict communion and severely critiqued and deplored Bunyan and the open communion tradition.

History,[91] in which he showed that his date of 1641 differed from the 1633 date proposed by Robert Barclay (1833–1876)[92] and agreed with the about 1641 date proposed by Henry Martyn Dexter (1821–1890).[93] He also held that the Church of England had long ago abandoned immersion, that few Continental and none of the English Anabaptists of the sixteenth century had been immersionists, and that John Smyth, Thomas Helwys, and their followers did not practice immersion. Whitsitt built his case for the reintroduction of immersion through Richard Blunt's visit to the Rhynsburgers chiefly on the records of the J-L-J church, the so-called Kiffin Manuscript as preserved in Ivimey's history,[94] the First London Confession (1644), and the writing of a non-Baptist, Praisegod Barebone (1596?–1679) in 1642.[95]

Whitsitt's conclusions about the restitution of immersion were both supported and rejected, his three principal literary respondents being two Southern Baptist pastors and a Northern Baptist professor. George Augustus Lofton (1839–1914) of Nashville supported Whitsitt's case for the reintroduction of immersion in England in 1641 in a context of affirming a "personal and doctrinal," though not an "external," succession through the centuries, but he differed with Whitsitt by being open to Williams's baptism by immersion.[96] He also affirmed the genuineness of the Kiffin Manuscript.[97] On the contrary, John Tyler Christian (1854–1925), pastor of East Church, Louisville, Kentucky, assembling a great body of quotations, asserted that "English Baptists did not all originate with John Smyth," that Leonard Busher was immersed, and that Roger Williams was immersed.[98] He sought

---

[91]Subtitle: *Whether the Anabaptists in England Practiced Immersion before the Year 1641?* (Louisville: C. T. Dearing, 1896).

[92]*The Inner Life of the Religious Societies of the Commonwealth*... (London: Hodder & Stoughton, 1879) 73-75.

[93]*The True Story of John Smyth, the Se-Baptist, as Told by Himself and His Contemporaries*..., 42-53.

[94]*A History of the English Baptists*... 2:298-311.

[95]*A Question in Baptist History*, 9-92, 101-10.

[96]*A Review of the Question* (Nashville: University Press Co., 1897) esp. 113, 210-11. See also Tull, "A Study of Southern Baptist Landmarkism," 596-98.

[97]*English Baptist Reformation (from 1609 to 1641 A.D.)* (Louisville: Charles T. Dearing, 1899) 91-115.

[98]*Did They Dip? or, An Examination into the Act of Baptism as Practiced by the English and American Baptists before the Year 1641* (Louisville: Baptist Book Concern, 1896) esp. 81, 98, 221-31.

to discredit both the records of the J-L-J church and the Kiffin Manuscript,[99] labelling the latter "a fraud and of no value" and "false and unauthoritative."[100] Christian's vindicative position was conformable to Landmark church successionism. Jesse Burgess Thomas (1832–1915) of Newton Theological Seminary, with a similar downplaying of documents used by Whitsitt and finding some evidence of immersion among the continental Anabaptists, concluded that Whitsitt had not succeeded in his "Herculean task" of demonstrating "that there were never any Baptists whatever (that is antipedobaptist immersionists) either in England or Holland before . . . 1641" and reversing "the conclusions of all Baptist historians from Crosby in 1738 to Evans in 1862."[101]

Baptist weekly papers, Baptist state conventions, and Baptist associations became involved in the Whitsitt Controversy, reflecting pro-Whitsitt, anti-Whitsitt, and neutral stances, with the result that a collateral polity issue loomed large, namely, the governance of the Southern Baptist Theological Seminary by only the SBC through its nomination of trustees.[102]

Two Southern Baptist pastors served in activist roles in the Whitsitt Controversy so as to secure the resignation of Whitsitt from his seminary presidency and professorship. Thomas Treadwell Eaton (1845–1907), whose background was somewhat non-Landmark[103] and who was the longtime friend and pastor of Whitsitt,[104] was pastor of Walnut Street Church, Louisville, editor of the Kentucky Baptist paper, the *Western Recorder*, and a seminary trustee.[105] Utilizing the editorial pages of his paper, he criticized Whitsitt's findings and fostered his resignation.[106] A belated collaborator

---

[99]Ibid., 142-58.

[100]*Baptist History Vindicated* (Louisville: Baptist Book Concern, 1899) esp. 14, 146. See also Tull, "A Study of Southern Baptist Landmarkism," 593-96, who noted Christian's claim that prior to 1641 immersion had been the general practice of "Episcopalians, Catholics, Independents or Presbyterians, and of the Baptists themselves" (Christian, 75-76).

[101]*Dr. Whitsitt's "Question,"* esp. 10-12, 15-17, 59-74, 2, 51.

[102]Beck, "The Whitsitt Controversy," 78-213.

[103]Baker, *The Southern Baptist Convention and Its People*, 281.

[104]Bugg, "The Whitsitt Controversy," 94-100.

[105]Leo T. Crismon, "Eaton, Thomas Treadwell," *Encyclopedia of Southern Baptists* 1:385; C. Ferris Jordan, "Thomas Treadwell Eaton: Pastor, Editor, Controversialist, and Denominational Servant" (Th.D. diss., New Orleans Baptist Theological Seminary, 1965) 2-15.

[106]Crismon, "Eaton, Thomas Treadwell," 385; Tull, *High Church Baptists*, 141-

with Eaton in the anti-Whitsitt effort was Franklin Howard Kerfoot (1847–1901), professor of systematic theology at the seminary.[107] Both Eaton and Kerfoot were candidates for the seminary presidency when Whitsitt was elected in 1895, and Kerfoot was a candidate when Whitsitt's successor, Edgar Young Mullins (1860–1928), was elected in 1899.[108] Early in the controversy Benajah Harvey Carroll (1843–1914), longtime pastor of First Church, Waco, Texas, and a seminary trustee, took a "moderate stand," reckoning the issue to be historical and not doctrinal and leaving it with the seminary trustees. After Carroll was unable in 1897 to get the trustees to act decisively, his stance became anti-Whitsitt as he expressed fear of denominational schism. At the 1898 SBC session he announced his intention to introduce in 1899 a motion to sever the ties between the SBC and the seminary. Shortly thereafter Whitsitt tendered his resignation to be effective in 1899.[109] Was Carroll motivated by Landmark beliefs in calling for Whitsitt's termination? A definitive answer is difficult, but it is possible to identify how Carroll was and was not a Landmarker. He agreed with Landmarkism in denying a universal church, in emphasizing the local church, in rejecting "alien" immersions, and in positing a succession of churches "resembling Baptists" from "the apostolic era."[110] He was not a Landmarker in that he did not "equate local churches with the kingdom of God," did foster "associational discipline and cooperation," and "allowed Baptists from

---

42; Jordan, "Thomas Treadwell Eaton," 97-114.

[107]Bugg, "The Whitsitt Controversy," 100-10; Leo T. Crismon, "Kerfoot, Franklin Howard," *Encyclopedia of Southern Baptists* 2:749.

[108]Bugg, "The Whitsitt Controversy," 90, 97-98, 102-103, 107-109; Fletcher, *The Southern Baptist Convention*, 105; William A. Mueller, *A History of Southern Baptist Theological Seminary* (Nashville: Broadman, 1959) 176; Jordan, "Thomas Treadwell Eaton," 126-29.

[109]Alan J. Lefever, *Fighting the Good Fight: The Life and Work of Benajah Harvey Carroll* (Austin TX: Eakin, 1994) 84-94.

[110]B. H. Carroll's brother, James Milton Carroll (1852–1931), was the author of *The Trail of Blood: Following the Christians down through the Centuries . . . or the History of Baptist Churches from the Time of Christ, Their Founder, to the Present Day* (Lexington KY: Ashland Avenue Baptist Church, 1931, 1979).

other churches" to partake of the Lord's Supper.[111] Carroll had a pronounced effect upon the theology of Baptists in Texas and the Southwest.[112]

The results of the Whitsitt Controversy have been assessed somewhat differently. According to Rufus W. Weaver, Southern Baptist Theological Seminary "lost its president, but did not lose its soul."[113] Similarly Barnes declared: "Landmarkism won the battle, but lost the war."[114] Corroborative of this assessment is the fact that Whitsitt's successor as professor of church history, William Joseph McGlothlin (1867–1933), taught the same view of Baptist origins as Whitsitt[115] and in most all Baptist seminaries since 1899 either the English Separatist descent view or the Anabaptist spiritual kinship

---

[111]James T. Spivey, "Benajah Harvey Carroll," in *Baptist Theologians*, ed. George and Dockery, 318-19; idem, "Benajah Harvey Carroll" in *The Legacy of Southwestern: Writings That Shaped a Tradition*, ed. James Leo Garrett, Jr., et al. (North Richland Hills TX: Smithfield, 2002) 8-9. Carroll, *Ecclesia: The Church* (Louisville: Baptist Book Concern, 1903) 6-24, interpreted the New Testament uses of *ekklēsia* which others apply to a present universal church as referring to Christ's "*general assembly* in glory." On Carroll, see also James A. Leddon, Jr., "Texas Baptists and the Whitsitt Controversy" (M.A. thesis, Texas Western College, 1964) 87-115.

[112]Carroll held to the plenary-verbal view of biblical inspiration, the infallibility of the Bible, and the primacy of the New Testament. For him actual sin, not Adamic sin, brings guilt to humanity. Carroll was a "moderate Calvinist," holding to the single predestination of the elect and general atonement. Sanctification is a "lifelong process," and the baptism of the Holy Spirit was for the whole church in the apostolic age. Carroll's postmillennialism was built on the power of the Holy Spirit, the missionary purpose of the church, and "the gradual consummation of the kingdom of God." Spivey, "Benajah Harvey Carroll," 6-9. According to J. B. Gambrell, "President Carroll, Bible in hand, standardized orthodoxy in Texas." "The Home-Going of B. H. Carroll," in *Dr. B. H. Carroll: The Colossus of Baptist History*, ed. J. W. Crowder (Fort Worth TX: pvt. prtg., 1946) 103, as quoted by Spivey, "Benajah Harvey Carroll," 9. George Benjamin Macklin, "Pneumatology: A Unifying Theme of B. H. Carroll's Theology" (Ph.D. diss., Southwestern Baptist Theological Seminary, 2007) has recently contended that the Holy Spirit was the unifying center of Carroll's theology, especially as to soteriology, ecclesiology, and eschatology.

[113]"Life and Times of William Heth Whitsitt," 130.

[114]*The Southern Baptist Convention*, 138.

[115]Ibid.; Lefever, *Fighting the Good Fight*, 93-94; Tull, "A Study of Southern Baptist Landmarkism," 616. In 1897 Albert Henry Newman (1852–1933) of Toronto was issuing his non-Landmark *A History of Anti-Pedobaptism from the Rise of Pedobaptism to A.D. 1609* (Philadelphia: American Baptist Publication Society).

view[116] has been standard teaching. On the contrary, James E. Tull, rejecting Barnes's verdict, concluded that the controversy made the seminary in Louisville "virtually the only citadel left" in the SBC "for the defense of the historic Baptist ecclesiology," gave "the Landmark Southwest" a victory over "the non-Landmark Southeast," and turned Landmarkism from "an alien infection in the Southern Baptist body" to "a chronic infection" in the denominational "blood-stream."[117] Supportive of Tull's verdict is the continuing influence of Landmarkism upon Southern Baptists during most of the twentieth century. William Edward Hull (1930–) in a recent study of Whitsitt found ten lessons to be learned by present-day Baptist "moderates."[118]

A third Landmark-related controversy was confined to Texas and centered in the ministry of Samuel Augustus Hayden (1839–1918). A native of Louisiana and a Civil War veteran, Hayden held two pastorates in Texas before becoming pastor of a Landmark-inclined congregation in Dallas that had resulted from a rupture in First Church, Dallas, a division reflective of two rival state Baptist bodies. After helping the two congregations to reunite, Hayden bought and become editor of the *Texas Baptist* and aided in the unification of several Baptist state bodies in 1886 so as to form the Baptist General Convention of Texas (BGCT). After another Baptist paper, the *Baptist Standard*, came on the scene, he and its editor, James Britton Cranfill (1858–1942), engaged in a newspaper war. Hayden directed vicious attacks against the leaders and policies of the BGCT and was denied a seat in that convention in 1897. Hayden's followers organized in 1900 what was soon to be called the Baptist Missionary Association of Texas.[119]

---

[116] Torbet, *A History of the Baptists*, 60-61.

[117] "A Study of Southern Baptist Landmarkism," 616-17.

[118] "William Heth Whitsitt: Martyrdom of a Moderate," in *Distinctively Baptist: Essays on Baptist History: A Festschrift in Honor of Walter B. Shurden*, ed. Marc A. Jolley with John D. Pierce (Macon GA: Mercer University Press, 2005) 237-78, esp. 277-78. Hull incisively summarized Landmarkism in terms of "successionism," "localism," and "exclusivism," and probed the mind and conscience of Whitsitt but failed to utilize the recent scholarship on Carroll (251, 254-55, 242-50, 272).

[119] Joseph E. Early, Jr., "The Hayden Controversy: A Detailed Examination of the First Major Internal Altercation of the Baptist General Convention of Texas" (Ph.D. diss., Southwestern Baptist Theological Seminary, 2001), rev. as *A Texas Baptist Power Struggle: The Hayden Controversy* (Denton: University of North Texas Press, 2005); idem, *A Handbook of Texas Baptist Biography* (Williamsburg KY: author, 2004) 113-15; Baker, *The Southern Baptist Convention and Its People*,

The Hayden Controversy has been variously assessed. N. D. Timmerman and Alan J. Lefever have regarded the controversy as essentially a newspaper conflict. Focusing on the conflict between Hayden and Cranfill, Timmerman asserted that, after his being unseated, Hayden "resorted to the expediency of shoving the explosive matter of 'church sovereignty' into the Controversy."[120] According to Lefever, "Hayden's real fight . . . was actually a personal vendetta against a group of men who he believed were trying to decrease his influence among Texas Baptists by weakening his newspaper." For B. H. Carroll and others, removing Hayden was the removal of a "cancer" from the denominational body.[121] Robert A. Baker and H. Leon McBeth have understood the controversy as ecclesiological in nature and Landmark-related. For Baker, "Haydenism" "provided the determinative answer to the ecclesiological issue" as to "whether sovereign churches made up the state bodies [Hayden's view], or . . . the Convention was composed of individual messengers who neither brought authority from the churches nor carried authority back from the Convention [Hayden's opponents' view]." Moreover, the controversy "articulated the basic eccesiology that has been held by Texas Baptists since that time."[122] According to McBeth, the Hayden Controversy was an "eruption" or "'outcropping'" of Landmarkism, for Hayden's "proposed reforms" in 1894 "amounted to adoption of Landmark practices by the BGCT."[123]

The most recent and most comprehensive study of this controversy, that by Joseph E. Early, Jr., has embraced the conclusion that it was not so much "an outbreak of radical Landmarkism" as a two-decade-long struggle between Dallas and Waco as the center of Texas Baptist life, correlated with

---

281-82; McBeth, *The Baptist Heritage*, 458, 749-51; idem, *The First Baptist Church of Dallas: Centennial History (1868–1968)* (Grand Rapids MI: Zondervan, 1968) 73-80, 133-35.

[120]Timmerman, "The Hayden-Cranfill Controversy" (Th.D. diss., Southwestern Baptist Theological Seminary, 1936) 5; also see 204-35.

[121]Lefever, *Fighting the Good Fight*, 73.

[122]*The Blossoming Desert: A Concise History of Texas Baptists* (Waco TX: Word, 1970) 157-62, esp. 158, 162; also idem, *The Southern Baptist Convention and Its People*, 281-82. For a Hayden editorial in 1900, see Baker, ed., *A Baptist Source Book*, 186.

[123]*The Baptist Heritage*, 458-59. McBeth has placed somewhat less emphasis on the Landmark dimension in his *Texas Baptists: A Sesquicentennial History* (Dallas: Baptistway, 1998) 119-21.

rivalries between Baptist state bodies, Baptist papers, and Baptist leaders.[124] Whether a consensus as to the nature of the Hayden Controversy can be realized is problematic, but clearly the resultant Baptist Missionary Association of Texas became a Landmark body.

A fourth controversy resulted in a permanent separation from the Southern Baptist Convention. A man with strong Landmark convictions, Kentucky-born Benjamin Marquis Bogard (1868–1951), became pastor in Searcy, Arkansas, in 1899.[125] Although initially supporting the work of the Arkansas Baptist State Convention (ABSC), in 1901 he joined with William Allen Clark, an editor who was leading an agrarian Baptist resistance, in opposition to an Executive Board policy statement that sought to balance local church autonomy and cooperation among the churches. Bogard's followers organized in April 1902 the General Association of Baptist Churches in Arkansas. Efforts at reconciliation were ineffective as the Bogard group insisted that churches only should commission missionaries, that each church should have equal representation in an association or convention, that the office of corresponding secretary be abolished, that churches should be able to instruct their messengers, and that cooperation with the two mission boards of the SBC be terminated.[126] Christopher Bart Barber has recently argued that the Bogard schism was not due to Landmark teachings per se, for both groups were essentially Landmark, but due rather to the "agrarian revolt" led by Clark and Bogard against the "New South" direction of the ABSC.[127]

In March 1905 under Bogard's leadership about 150 messengers from 52 Arkansas churches, meeting in Texarkana, issued a "memorial" to the SBC, asking for its "money and associational basis of representation [to] be eliminated in favor of a church basis" and for the two mission boards of the SBC to be denied authority to appoint and remove missionaries and to avoid any impact of "denominational comity."[128] A committee of the SBC then successfully recommended "courteously but firmly" that the memorial's requests be denied on the basis that the principles undergirding the work of

---

[124]Early, "The Hayden Controversy," 1-2.

[125]Baker, *The Southern Baptist Convention and Its People*, 283.

[126]Edward Glenn Hinson, *A History of Baptists in Arkansas, 1818–1978* (Little Rock: Arkansas State Baptist Convention, 1979) 172-79.

[127]"The Bogard Schism: An Arkansas Baptist Agrarian Revolt" (Ph.D. diss., Southwestern Baptist Theological Seminary, 2006).

[128]Baker, *The Southern Baptist Convention and Its People*, 283.

the SBC were "in accord with the teaching of God's Word, and in harmony with Baptist history, Baptist usage, and Baptist doctrine."[129] In November of the same year messengers "from 107 churches in 12 states and territories"[130] organized in Texarkana a national Landmark body, the Baptist General Association.[131] It adopted a concise twelve-article "doctrinal statement," three articles of which were distinctly Landmark: that since the Great Commission was given only to churches, the church is the "only unit" in "kingdom activities," and thus churches have "equal authority and responsibility" (art. 10); that associations and conventions "should be" "the servants of the churches" (art. 11); and that "there has been a succession of missionary Baptist churches from the days of Christ down to this day" (art. 12).[132] In 1924 with additional Texas churches the Baptist General Association changed its name to the American Baptist Association (ABA).[133]

Bogard, a pamphleteer and debater, was the leading twentieth-century Landmark ideologue.[134] He identified four reasons for being Baptist,[135] opposed interdenominational church union,[136] espoused Baptist church succession,[137] attacked Primitive Baptists as heretical,[138] set forth a detailed

---

[129]McBeth, *The Baptist Heritage*, 752-53, quoting *SBC Annual*, 1905, 42.

[130]Baker, *The Southern Baptist Convention and Its People*, 283.

[131]J. Don Hook, "American Baptist Association," *Encyclopedia of Southern Baptists* 1:36. This action did not mean the dissolution of the Texas body, the Baptist Missionary Association of Texas. C. E. Colton, "Baptist Missionary Association," *Encyclopedia of Southern Baptists* 1:118-19.

[132]Lumpkin, *Baptist Confessions of Faith*, 378-79.

[133]McBeth, *The Baptist Heritage*, 753, 459.

[134]Bogard had studied for one year at Georgetown College and for two years at Bethel College and had been pastor in Fulton, Ky., and Charleston, Mo. Barber, "The Bogard Schism," 126-30.

[135]*Four Reasons Why I Am a Baptist* (Princeton KY: T. E. Richey, 1892). They were *regeneration, baptism by immersion, believer's baptism,* and *close communion*.

[136]*Christian Union; or the Problem Solved* (Louisville KY: Baptist Book Concern, 1899).

[137]*Baptist Churches in All Ages: An Unbroken Chain of Baptist Churches from the Apostolic Age to the Present Time* (Little Rock AR: Ben M. Bogard, 1941; Texarkana AR/TX: Bogard, 1974).

[138]*The Hardshell Heresy* (Texarkana TX/AR: Baptist Sunday School Committee, n.d.).

criticism of Alexander Campbell's teaching,[139] and fought the "conventionism" of Southern Baptists.[140] His most cited writing was likely *The Baptist Way-Book*,[141] and his longest book was a compilation of biographical sketches about and excerpted writings by seventeen nineteenth-century Baptist leaders in the South.[142]

In 1950 828 messengers from 463 ABA churches in 16 states, meeting in Little Rock, formed a separate body, the North American Baptist Association (NABA),[143] allegedly because of a "one-church dictatorship" in the ABA[144] or because of a dispute over requiring "all messengers to be members of the churches which elected them."[145] Its 25-article "doctrinal statement," according to Leon McBeth, "reflects as much modern Fundamentalism as old Landmarkism."[146] Nevertheless the Landmark tenets are evident. In addition to the three Landmark beliefs affirmed by the ABA, this document forbids receiving "alien" or non-Baptist-administered immersions (art. 12), advocates the Lord's Supper being given only to "baptized believers" (art. 13), and rejects "pulpit affiliation" with heretics, "unionism," "modernism," and "modern conventionism" (art. 20).[147] The NABA undertook extensive denominational work and in 1969 changed its name to the Baptist Missionary Association of America (BMAA).[148] In 1988 the

---

[139]*Campbellism Exposed: One Hundred One Reasons for Not Being a Campbellite* (Texarkana TX: Bogard, n.d.).

[140]*The Baptist Way-Book: Designed for Use in Baptist Churches* (Little Rock AR: Baptist Publishing Co., 1908; with subtitle, *A Manual Designed for Use in Baptist Churches* (Texarkana AR/TX: Baptist Sunday School Committee, 1928) 50-51; "The Origin of Conventionism" in Ben M. Bogard, J. A. Smith, M. P. Matheny, and G. S. Anderson, *Conventionism from 4 Angles* (Texarkana AR/TX: Baptist Commoner, n.d.) 2-8.

[141]See n. 140 above.

[142]*Pillars of Orthodoxy, or Defenders of the Faith* (Fulton KY: National Baptist Publishing House, 1901).

[143]Don Hook, "North American Baptist Association," *Encyclopedia of Southern Baptists* 2:984.

[144]Lumpkin, *Baptist Confessions of Faith*, 379.

[145]Hook, "North American Baptist Association," 984.

[146]*The Baptist Heritage*, 754.

[147]Lumpkin, *Baptist Confessions of Faith*, 380-81.

[148]McBeth, *The Baptist Heritage*, 754; Leon Gaylor, "Baptist Missionary Association of America," *Encyclopedia of Southern Baptists* 3:1597-98; Louis F. Asher, "Baptist Missionary Association of America," *Encyclopedia of Southern*

BMAA adopted a detailed, newly written, twelve-article "doctrinal statement," which shows the influence of the New Hampshire Confession. It affirmed the Trinity, biblical inspiration and inerrancy, the image of God as "marred" by the fall but supportive of human "dignity and worth," a personal Satan, general atonement, declarative justification, initial and durative sanctification, perseverance of all the reborn, and the institutional separation of churches and government but with the involvement of Christians in government. Landmark distinctives were somewhat muted: the church is defined only as "a local congregation"; "true churches have continued to the present and will continue until Jesus returns"; and believer's immersion "is prerequisite to church membership and participation in the Lord's Supper." An addendum indicated that "the preponderance of opinion" among BMAA churches was to affirm premillennialism and separate resurrections of the righteous and of the wicked. In 1990–1991 a revision substituted for the original article on "the purpose of salvation" (election) a new article on the "complementary" nature of "divine sovereignty and human freedom."[149]

Non-Landmark Ecclesiology

John L. Dagg, as previously noted,[150] during the rise of Landmarkism had set forth a carefully crafted doctrine of the universal church. During the latter nineteenth century other Baptists in the South adopted and articulated views that denied or at least differed from aspects of Landmarkism and reflected pre-Landmark Baptist ecclesiology.

William Williams (1821–1877), a graduate of the University of Georgia and of Harvard University in law, had succeeded Dagg in 1856 as professor of theology in Mercer University and became in 1859 one of the founding professors of the Southern Baptist Theological Seminary in Greenville, South Carolina, teaching ecclesiastical history, church government, and pastoral duties.[151] His advocacy of the acceptance of non-Baptist or "alien" immersions in Baptist churches evoked in 1872 Landmark criticism and led to his transfer to the chair of theology with the support of James P.

Baptists 4:2105-106.

[149]*Yearbook of the Baptist Missionary Association of America* (1988) 35-41; (1990) 33, 45; (1991) 33, 43. Per Jack Henry Downey and Amy K. Downey.

[150]See above, 143.

[151]Leo T. Crismon, "Williams, William," *Encyclopedia of Southern Baptists* 2:1503.

Boyce.[152] In his brief treatise, *Apostolic Church Polity*, Williams concluded that "in most, if not all the apostolic churches, there was a plurality of elders," but he doubted that the New Testament decisively differentiated preaching elders from ruling elders. Refuting the view of Francis Wayland that the New Testament has no pattern of church polity, he opted for New Testament "principles" without a "system."[153]

R. B. C. Howell, who was twice pastor of First Church, Nashville, Tennessee, and once pastor of Second Church, Richmond, Virginia, and was the antagonist of J. R. Graves,[154] espoused a non-Landmark ecclesiology. In his defense of close communion he followed in the tradition of Kiffin, Booth, and Kinghorn by contending that infant baptism and baptism by sprinkling or pouring are not true Christian baptism and hence their recipients should not be admitted to the Lord's Supper in Baptist churches.[155] Similarly, Howell offered a nineteen-point critique of the "evils" of infant baptism.[156] In interpreting the deaconship he, while denying that deacons are "ruling elders," assigned to them the 'temporal affairs of the church" and called them "a board of officers, or the executive board of the church." He interpreted 1 Tim. 3:11 to refer to deaconesses, not to wives of deacons.[157]

Howell made other theological contributions. In a monograph on biblical covenants he identified the covenant of works (Gen. 2:16-17), the

---

[152]Tull, *High-Church Baptists*, 108; Fletcher, *The Southern Baptist Convention*, 76. Crismon reported a different reason for Williams's transfer, i.e., Boyce's preoccupation with fundraising.

[153](Philadelphia: American Baptist Publication Society, 1874); reprinted in *Polity: Biblical Arguments on How to Conduct Church Life*, ed. Mark Edward Dever (Washington DC: Center for Church Reform, 2001), 531, 533-35, 546.

[154]Homer L. Grice, "Howell, Robert Boyté Crawford," *Encyclopedia of Southern Baptists* 1:656-57; Grice and R. Paul Caudill, "Graves-Howell Controversy (1857-62)," ibid. 1:580-85; Linwood Tyler Horne, "A Study of the Life and Work of R. B. C. Howell" (Th.D. diss., Southern Baptist Theological Seminary, 1958). Howell never employed or mentioned Baptist church succession.

[155]*The Terms of Communion at the Lord's Table* (Philadelphia: American Baptist Publication Society, 1846; repr.: Watertown WI: Baptist Heritage Publications, 1987) 131-79. This title was preceded by *Terms of Sacramental Communion* (Philadelphia: American Baptist Publication Society, 1841).

[156]*The Evils of Infant Baptism* (Charleston SC: Southern Baptist Publication Society, 1854).

[157]*The Deaconship* (Philadelphia: American Baptist Publication Society, 1851) 79, 18, 31, 122-23, 34-38.

covenant of Eden (Gen. 3:8-19), the precreational covenant of redemption among the Father, the Son, and the Holy Spirit, the covenant with Abraham (Gen. 12:1-3) and its repetition and transfer to Isaac (Gen. 26:1-5), Jacob (Gen. 28:3-5), Judah (Gen. 49:10), and David (2 Sam. 23:5), the legal covenants concerning Canaan (Gen. 15:1-18), about circumcision (Gen. 17:4-14), and at Sinai (Exod. 19:5-8), and the new covenant in Christ.[158] He rejected the imputation of the guilt of Adam's sin to the human race; instead we are "personally sinners" under the influence of that depravity which derives from the first humans.[159] For Howell the cross of Christ, being designed through the covenant of redemption, harmonizes God's justice and the salvation of sinners, reveals the infinite love of the Father, the Son, and the Spirit, is the medium for necessary spiritual change and the only power that can move human beings to "holy action," brings to believers "an indelible abhorrence of sin" and "ample instruction for the formation of Christian character," gives character to baptism and the Lord's Supper, and provides access to heaven.[160]

Jeremiah Bell Jeter (1802–1880), the pastor of First Church and Grace Street Church, Richmond, Virginia, and of Second Church, St. Louis, Missouri,[161] and John Lansing Burrows (1814–1893), the pastor of Sansom Street and Broad Street churches, Philadelphia, Pennsylvania, First Church, Richmond, Virginia, Broadway Church, Louisville, Kentucky, and Freemason Street Church, Norfolk, Virginia,[162] contributed volumes of a non-Landmark nature to the developing genre of Baptist writings on the doctrinal distinctives of Baptists.[163] It is noteworthy that the era of the

---

[158] *The Covenants* (Charleston SC: Southern Baptist Publication Society, 1855; repr.: Conrad MT: Triangle, 1991).

[159] *The Way of Salvation* (Charleston SC: Southern Baptist Publication Society, 1849) 18.

[160] *The Cross* (Charleston SC: Southern Baptist Publication Society, 1854).

[161] Jeter, *The Recollections of a Long Life* (Richmond: Religious Herald Co., 1891); William Eldridge Hatcher, *Life of J. B. Jeter, D.D.* (Baltimore: H. M. Wharton, 1887); E. C. Routh, "Jeter, Jeremiah Bell," *Encyclopedia of Southern Baptists* 1:706-707; James Lance Cunningham, "The Contributions of Jeremiah Bell Jeter to Southern Baptists" (Th.D. diss., New Orleans Baptist Theological Seminary, 1987) esp. 107-22, 134-79.

[162] J. L. Rosser, "Burrows, John Lansing," *Encyclopedia of Southern Baptists* 1:210-11.

[163] Jeter, *Baptist Principles Reset: Consisting of a Series of Articles on Distinctive Baptist Principles* (Richmond: Religious Herald, 1901); enl. ed. under title

Baptist Landmarkism   245

flourishing of this genre (ca.1850–ca.1950) for all Baptists[164] coincided with the era of the flourishing of Landmarkism.

The second major monograph on ecclesiology by a Southern Baptist, following Dagg, was by Edwin Charles Dargan (1852–1930), professor of homiletics and ecclesiology at Southern Baptist Theological Seminary. He had formerly served as pastor of First Church, Petersburg, Virginia, and Citadel Square Church, Charleston, South Carolina, and would later be pastor of First Church, Macon, Georgia, and editorial secretary of the SBC's Sunday School Board.[165] Designed for textbook usage, *Ecclesiology: A Study of the Churches*[166] treated the polity, the ordinances, the work, and the worship of Baptist churches. In delineating the local uses of *ekklēsia* in the New Testament, Dargan differentiated "particular' or named churches, singular and plural, from "nonparticular" or unnamed churches, singular and plural, and respecting the "general" uses of *ekklēsia* he distinguished generic,[167] collective,[168] and universal[169] meanings. He acknowledged that there were both "resemblances" and "divergences" when comparing Baptist

---

Baptist Principles Reset (Dallas: Standard Publishing Co., 1902) 9-135. Jeter focused on the ordinances, membership, and religious liberty. But, Jeter, like the later Graves, limited participation in the Supper to members of the observing congregation. Irvin Hugh Acree, "A Critical Examination of the Ecclesiological Thought of Jeremiah Bell Jeter" (Th.M. thesis, Southeastern Baptist Theological Seminary, 1962) 120-23. Burrows, *What Baptists Believe and Other Discourses* (Baltimore: H. M. Wharton and Co., 1887); under title *What Baptists Believe* (Baltimore: R. H. Woodward Co., 1894). Burrows majored on the ordinances, polity, and membership.

[164]Robert Stanton Norman, "A Critical Analysis of the Intentional Efforts of Baptists to Distinguish Themselves Theologically from Other Christian Denominations" (Ph.D. diss., Southwestern Baptist Theological Seminary, 1997). See below, 531-32.

[165]John D. Freeman, "Dargan, Edwin Charles," *Encyclopedia of Southern Baptists* 1:348. Dargan also wrote *A History of Preaching*, 2 vols. (New York: A. C. Armstrong, 1905; London: Hodder & Stoughton; New York: G. H. Doran, 1905, 1912; Grand Rapids MI: Baker, 1954) and *The Doctrines of Our Faith* (Nashville: Sunday School Board of the SBC, 1905; rev. ed., 1920).

[166](Louisville: Charles T. Dearing, 1897) esp. 27-34, 112-16, 204-303, 325-29, 216-17, 366-68, 358-60, 527.

[167]1 Tim. 3:15; Matt. 18:17; 1 Cor. 12:28; James 5:14.

[168]Acts 9:31; Rom. 16:23; 1 Cor. 10:32.

[169]Matt. 16:18; Acts 20:28; Eph. 1:22; 3:10, 21; 5:23-32; Col. 1:18, 24; Heb. 12:23.

polity in the 1890s with the New Testament "model." His thorough treatment of immersion and of believer's baptism followed the pattern of preceding Baptist authors. The "declarative" or "symbolic" view was taken to be normative for Baptists, but Dargan included the arguments for infant baptism. Although he specified that a proper administrator of baptism should be a true Christian who has himself been baptized and has local church authorization to baptize, he avoided taking a position as to the issue of "alien" immersions and urged tolerance on the question. Dargan took the Zwinglian view of the Lord's Supper to be normative for Baptists and favored close communion on the basis of a strict definition of baptism but not confining participation to members of the observing congregation. He insisted on "four great elements" in biblically based Christian worship: "prayer, praise, the reading of Scripture, and teaching or preaching."

Landmark Effects on Twentieth-Century Southern Baptists

The separation led by Bogard did not terminate the influence of Landmarkism upon Southern Baptists. Rather it had a lingering influence through at least two-thirds of the twentieth century. That influence may be seen in four particulars. First, where Landmark influence prevailed, Baptist churches did not receive into membership persons who had been immersed by non-Baptist administrators but insisted that they receive Baptist-administered immersion. This was true even when all other aspects of the previous immersion were deemed to be valid and even though Baptists were inept in providing a rationale for the second immersion.[170]

Second, Landmark influence impacted the changes in the basis for representation in the SBC itself. In its founding in 1845 the SBC had established a financial basis of representation (gifts to missionary causes) which included missionary societies and individuals besides local churches. Efforts by Graves and/or other Landmarkers in 1859, 1869, 1874, and 1905 to reduce or eliminate the financial basis and to substitute a church basis of representation had not been successful. But in 1931, in language forged by Eugene Coke Routh (1874–1966), Oklahoma editor, the SBC changed its basis of representation so as to include as "messengers" only those "who are members of missionary" and "cooperating" Baptist churches with provision for one messenger for each "contributing" church and "one additional mes-

---

[170]W. W. Barnes, "Alien Immersion," *Encyclopedia of Southern Baptists* 1:32; James E. Tull, "Alien Immersion," ibid. 3:1563. Barnes did not reckon the issue to have been especially Landmark-derived.

senger for every $250" contributed during the year up to a maximum of three messengers per church. In 1933 the limit of three was raised to ten. Although these "messengers" were not to be "delegates" of churches in the Landmark sense, these changes moved the SBC from its earlier vestiges of the society method toward a convention of mission-contributing churches.[171]

Third, lingering Landmark influence[172] can be seen in the decisions of the SBC not to join the World Council of Churches (1939–1940, 1948) or the National Council of the Churches of Christ in the U.S.A. (1950–1953) and in the disinterest or distrust of many Southern Baptists in conciliar ecumenism.[173] Fourth, Landmarkism seemingly contributed to the twentieth-century denominational solidarity and loyalty of Southern Baptists. This factor has been called "a sense of unity and corporate consciousness,"[174] the awakening "to a needed self-consciousness,"[175] the shaping of a "self-identity,"[176] and the putting of "iron" in "the Baptist bloodstream."[177]

Landmarkism, which arose and flourished in the American South, was hailed by its leaders as a perpetuation of the "old landmarks" of Baptist ecclesiology but branded by its opponents and later critics as a new high-church ecclesiology unknown to earlier Baptists. Stemming from a query concerning what came to be called "alien immersions," the movement under Graves embraced the idea that non-Baptist churches are not true churches and that their ministers are not true ministers and should not be invited to Baptist pulpits. These views called forth the pen of Pendleton. Graves then espoused Baptist church succession when republishing Orchard's earlier volume. Dayton in his novel *Theodosia Ernest* popularized Landmark beliefs. Graves sought unsuccessfully to get abolished the appointive

---

[171]Barnes, *The Southern Baptist Convention*, 33-34; Baker, *The Southern Baptist Convention and Its People*, 313-16, 404-406; McBeth, *The Baptist Heritage*, 614-16; Fletcher, *The Southern Baptist Convention*, 150-53; G. Hugh Wamble, "History of Messengers to Baptist Denominational Bodies," *Baptist History and Heritage* 22 (April 1987): 10-13; Terry L. Jones, "Routh, Eugene Coke," *Encyclopedia of Southern Baptists* 3:1945-46.

[172]Tull, "A Study of Southern Baptist Landmarkism," 659-64, noted that there were also non-Landmark influences upon these SBC decisions.

[173]See below, 596-97.

[174]Barnes, *The Southern Baptist Convention*, 117.

[175]Smith, "A Critical Analysis of the Theology of J. R. Graves," 330.

[176]McBeth, *The Baptist Heritage*, 447.

[177]Quoted by ibid., 461.

powers of the Foreign Mission Board or the board itself and to change the basis of representation in the SBC.

Graves as author-polemicist engaged in controversies with Methodism, Presbyterianism, Campbellism, Universalism, Spiritism, and Swedenborgianism. Much of Graves's theology had no direct relation to Landmarkism, and on Christology he had to defend himself against charges of heresy. Graves's Landmarkism came to fullest expression in *Old Landmarkism: What Is It?*, in which he defined the kingdom of God as composed of Baptist churches and limited participation in the Lord's Supper to members of the observing congregation. Pendleton wrote a one-volume systematic theology, and Dayton wrote in depth against alien immersions.

Four Southern Baptist controversies at the end of the nineteenth century seemingly had Landmark involvement. Gospel Missionism under T. P. Crawford in North China was a blend of Landmark ecclesiological features and the missiology of Nevius and others. The Whitsitt Controversy centered in the dating of the beginning of the practice of baptism by immersion among English Baptists and its impact on Landmark espousal of Baptist church succession. Whitsitt elicited historical support from Lofton and criticism from Christian and Thomas, and Eaton and Carroll were active in bringing about Whitsitt's resignation. The nature of the Hayden Controversy in Texas, which led to a separation from Texas Baptists and a distinctive Landmark body, is somewhat disputed. Bogard's strong leadership, whether driven by Landmark or agrarian motivation, led to separation first in Arkansas and then from the SBC. This distinctively Landmark national body itself divided in the middle of the twentieth century.

Non-Landmark ecclesiologies included the pro-alien immersion stance of Williams and the writings of Howell, Jeter, and Burrows. But it was Dargan, following Dagg, who provided the major non-Landmark ecclesiological treatise. The lingering influence of Landmarkism upon Southern Baptists during most of the twentieth century can be seen in the commonly but not universally held antialien immersion stance, significant changes in the basis of representation in the SBC, the rejection of conciliar ecumenism, and a strong denominational identity and loyalty.

Chapter 7

Baptists in Controversy

Baptists during the nineteenth and the early twentieth centuries became engaged in various theological controversies, most of which pertained to the Bible or soteriology or Christology rather than to the historic Calvinist-Arminian issues or to the Baptist differences from Paedobaptists. The first of these was played out chiefly in the United States, although it had roots in Scotland and Northern Ireland.

The Campbells and the Baptists

The alliance of Thomas (1763–1854) and Alexander (1788–1866) Campbell, father and son, and the churches derived from their ministries with the Baptists for less than two decades and the tensions marking both that period and the era following their separation from the Baptists constituted one of the major controversies in Baptist history.[1]

John Glas, a minister in the Church of Scotland, had come to the conclusion that the New Testament knew nothing of a state-established church. Being dissatisfied with both the position of the Church of Scotland and that of the Covenanters or Cameronians, he had organized in 1725 a "church within a church" composed of those whom he deemed to be regenerate. Glas was deposed by the Church of Scotland, and other kindred congregations of Independents were formed in Scotland, but these had no connection with Independents or Congregationalists in England.[2]

In his quest to restore the "ancient order of things," Glas found fourteen indicia or marks of the New Testament church and sought to implement these. Two of these were later tried and then abandoned by the Campbells: mutual exhortation in worship (1 Cor. 14:31) and the dislike of the presence of unbelievers in worship services. Five of these were adopted and practiced by the Campbells: the plurality of teaching/preaching elders (after the abolition of ruling elders), the observance of the Lord's Supper every Lord's Day, the self-support of elders by trade or profession, the rejection of all creeds and confessions of faith, and reckoning Sunday as the Lord's

---

[1] Austin Bennett Amonette, "Alexander Campbell among the Baptists: An Examination of the Beginning, Ambiguity, and Deterioration of Their Relationship, 1812–1830" (Ph.D. diss., New Orleans Baptist Theological Seminary, 2002).

[2] Whitsitt, *Origin of the Disciples of Christ (Campbellites): A Contribution to the Centennial Anniversary of the Birth of Alexander Campbell*, 1-5.

Day, not the Sabbath, with obligation for worship but no prohibition of pleasures.³

The son-in-law of Glas, Robert Sandeman, who eventually moved to Connecticut,⁴ having rejected the idea that saving faith necessarily involves an operation of the Holy Spirit and a persuasion that Jesus shed his blood for the believer, came to espouse the view that faith is believing the record of revelation, or taking as credible the testimony of God. As a corollary, the Holy Spirit was said to speak no word to any human being other than that which he spoke in the Scriptures. The Glasite churches took the name Sandemanian,⁵ and the Campbells would embrace the Sandemanian view of faith.⁶ But W. H. Whitsitt's assertion that the Disciples of Christ "are an offshoot of the Sandemanian sect"⁷ was rebutted in 1889 by a Disciples of Christ author, George W. Longan,⁸ who pointed to dissimilarities, especially as to Christian unity.⁹

The Sandemanians were Paedobaptists, but two of their converts, Robert Carmichael (?–1774) and Archibald McLean, soon left the movement and then embraced believer's baptism by immersion and a stricter lifestyle.¹⁰ They became coelders of an Edinburgh church, and "Scotch Baptist" or "Sandemanian Baptist" churches were formed elsewhere in

---

³Ibid., 6-15.

⁴Garrison and DeGroot, *The Disciples of Christ: A History*, 50.

⁵Whitsitt, *Origin of the Disciples of Christ*, 16-21; Robert Sandeman, *Letters on Theron and Aspasio: Addresses to the Author*, 4th ed. (London: T. Vernor and J. Chater, 1768) 2:35-38, 170-71.

⁶Garrison and DeGroot, *The Disciples of Christ*, 49. There was an Independent or Glasite church in Rich-Hill, the community in Northern Ireland in which the Campbells lived prior to emigrating to the United States. Edward Roberts-Thomson, *Baptists and Disciples of Christ* (London: Kingsgate, 1951) 35.

⁷*Origin of the Disciples of Christ*, 1.

⁸*Origin of the Disciples of Christ: A Review of Prof. W. H. Whitsitt's Volume Entitled "Origin of the Disciples of Christ"* (St. Louis: Christian Publishing Co., 1889).

⁹Ibid., 106-18; Garrison and DeGroot, *The Disciples of Christ*, 49-50.

¹⁰Whitsitt, *Origin of the Disciples of Christ*, 23-27; Underwood, *A History of the English Baptists*, 188-90; Roberts-Thomson, *Baptists and Disciples of Christ*, 36-37. Carmichael was immersed by John Gill in London in 1765. McLean and Carmichael objected to the expensive clothing, theater attendance, and love of dancing of the Sandemanians. See above, 184-85, for Andrew Fuller's interchange with McLean.

Scotland. But Carmichael reverted to the Sandemanians, leaving McLean as the sole leader of the movement.[11] McLean introduced some innovations into Sandemanianism that would be embraced by the Campbells. The chief of these was the belief that water baptism is essential to the remission of sins (Acts 2:38). This was not baptismal regeneration but the effecting of "remission of sins after the act of mere belief."[12] McLean wrote in defense of believer's baptism.[13]

After Alexander Campbell, his mother, and six younger siblings en route to the United States to join Thomas Campbell shipwrecked in October 1808 in the Hebrides off the coast of Scotland, the family's delay until next year for passage to America afforded to Alexander a year of study in the University of Glasgow. During this time he came under the influence of Greville Ewing, the pastor of an Independent congregation and associate of the Haldane brothers, Robert and James Alexander, wealthy laymen in the Church of Scotland. The Haldanes had led a reformatory and evangelistic movement that spawned congregations in Scotland and the United States. Through Ewing's influence and that of a Scotch Baptist, Charles Stuart, they had adopted congregational polity and weekly observance of the Lord's Supper, but when the Haldanes adopted believer's immersion, Ewing resisted. The influence of Ewing, whose roots were in Sandemanianism, on the young Campbell reached its climax when he cast his token into the plate, thus declining to receive communion in the Seceder Presbyterian Church, of which his father was a minister.[14]

By the time Alexander Campbell had arrived in 1809 in the United States, his father's ties with the American counterpart to Seceder Presby-

---

[11] Whitsitt, *Origin of the Disciples of Christ*, 27; Roberts-Thomson, *Baptists and Disciples of Christ*, 36-37.

[12] Whitsitt, *Origin of the Disciples of Christ*, 27-32. W. E. Garrison, a Disciples theologian, in his *The Sources of Alexander Campbell's Theology* (St. Louis: Christian Publishing Co., 1900) 245-47, concurred.

[13] *Letters Addressed to John Glas in Answer to His Dissertation on Infant-Baptism* (Glasgow: n.p., 1767); *Nature and Import of Baptism, with Its Indispensible Obligation . . .* (Edinburgh: n.p., 1786); *A Defence of Believer-Baptism in Opposition to Infant Sprinkling . . .* (Edinburgh: n.p., 1777; Liverpool: W. Jones, 1800).

[14] Whitsitt, *Origin of the Disciples of Christ, 33-61*; Garrison and DeGroot, *The Disciples of Christ*, 50-53, 141-44; Leroy Garrett, *The Stone-Campbell Movement: An Anecdotal History of Three Churches* (Joplin MO: College Press Publishing Co., 1981) 53-57, 166-72. See above, 200-201.

terianism had been severed, Thomas had formed the Christian Association of Washington, Pennsylvania, and the father had written his "Declaration and Address," with its "tripod": private interpretation of the Scriptures, Christian unity, and restitution of the New Testament pattern of church order. By 1811 the association had become Brush Run Church.[15] The birth of Alexander Campbell's first child, a daughter, led him—there were members advocating immersion—to reassess infant baptism and to finalize his affirmation of believer's baptism by immersion as the true baptism, not a "rebaptism." Alexander turned to a nearby Baptist minister, Matthias Luce, for the administration of immersion. Although Luce desired to examine Campbell on the basis of the Philadelphia Confession and for him to subscribe thereto, Campbell prevailed in his insistence upon being immersed only on the basis of Peter's Caesarean confession (Matt. 16:16). Hence on 12 June 1812 most all of the members of the Brush Run Church were so immersed.[16]

The Redstone Baptist Association in 1813 received the Brush Run Church into its fellowship without adherence to the Philadelphia Confession, but after a few years it became apparent that, although agreed on the mode of immersion, the Campbells and the Baptists had substantive differences.[17] During 1811–1812 Alexander had embraced the Sandemanian view of faith with its indebtedness to John Locke's epistemology and/or Scottish realism.[18] In his 1816 associational sermon on "The Law and the Gospel," Campbell differentiated three dispensations—patriarchal, Mosaic, and Christian—and rejected the distinctions relative to the Old Testament between the moral law, the ceremonial law, and the civil or judicial law. For Campbell the moral law was much older than Mosaic law and not a part of Mosaic law. Although Alexander agreed with his father's dictum, "Where

---

[15]Garrison and DeGroot, *The Disciples of Christ*, 129-41, 145-46.

[16]Garrison and DeGroot, *The Disciples of Christ*, 158-60; Roberts-Thomson, *Baptists and Disciples of Christ*, 30-32; Jesse R. Kellems, *Alexander Campbell and the Disciples* (New York: Richard R. Smith, Inc., 1930), 248-54; Whitsitt, *Origins of the Disciples of Christ*, 76-81.

[17]Whitsitt, *Origin of the Disciples of Christ*, 88-89; Garrison and DeGroot, *The Disciples of Christ*, 161; Roberts-Thomson, *Baptists and Disciples of Christ*, 32-33; Torbet, *A History of the Baptists*, 288; McBeth, *The Baptist Heritage*, 378; Garrett, *The Stone-Campbell Movement*, 182-83.

[18]Whitsitt, *Origin of the Disciples of Christ*, 87-88; Kellems, *Alexander Campbell and the Disciples*, 201-207; McBeth, *The Baptist Heritage*, 378.

the Scriptures speak, we speak; and where the Scriptures are silent, we are silent," for him "the seat of Christian doctrine" is in the New Testament. Some who heard the sermon thought it was heretical.[19]

Alexander Campbell represented Baptists well in his 1820 debate on baptism with John Walker, a Presbyterian, for he dealt with circumcision, household baptisms, believer's baptism, and immersion.[20] In the same year, however, he received and began to find concurrence with a pamphlet from the Scotch Baptist Church in New York City, which taught that baptism is "for the remission of sins" in the sense that baptism "applies" the promise of remission and "represents its *actual accomplishment* to an individual believer."[21] In debating another Presbyterian, W. L. Macalla, Alexander declared, "The water of baptism . . . *formally* washes away our sins" and the "blood of Christ *really* washes away our sins."[22] By 1823 he had begun to publish *The Christian Baptist*, in which he attacked Baptist associations and missionary societies, Baptist pastors as "hireling priests," and the current use of confessions of faith.[23] In 1825 the Brush Run Church and twelve other related churches, having been excluded from the Redstone Association, joined the Mahoning Baptist Association of Ohio.[24] In 1827 Walter Scott, Campbell's associate who had become evangelist for the Mahoning Association, expressed the restored "Ancient Gospel" in terms of the "five-finger exercise": faith, repentance, baptism, remission of sins, and the gift

---

[19]Roberts-Thomson, *Baptists and Disciples of Christ*, 44-50; Garrett, *The Stone-Campbell Movement*, 182-87; Kellems, *Alexander Campbell and the Disciples*, 133, 149-51, 155-56; D. Ray Lindley, *Apostle of Freedom* (St. Louis: Bethany, 1957), 42; McBeth, *The Baptist Heritage*, 378.

[20]*Debate on Christian Baptism, between Mr. John Walker, a Minister of the Secession, and Alexander Campbell, Held at Mount-Pleasant, on the 19th and 20th June, 1820* . . . , 2nd ed. (Pittsburgh: Eichbaum and Johnston, 1822).

[21]Whitsitt, *Origin of the Disciples of Christ*, 91-94.

[22]*A Debate on Christian Baptism, between the Rev. W. L. Maccalla, a Presbyterian Teacher, and Alexander Campbell, Held at Washington, Ky. Commencing on the 15th and Terminating on the 21st Oct. 1823* . . . (Buffaloe VA: Campbell and Sala, 1824), 135.

[23]Garrison and DeGroot, *The Disciples of Christ*, 175-78.

[24]Ibid., 178.

of the Holy Spirit.[25] Whitsitt called this "the natal day of the modern Disciple movement."[26]

Differences and tensions between the followers of the Campbells and the Baptists increased so as to result in separation, which occurred not at one given moment but over a period of three or four years.[27] As early as 1826, the churches whose messengers were not seated by the Redstone Association for nonaffirmation of the Philadelphia Confession formed the Washington Association.[28] In 1829 the Beaver Association in western Pennsylvania anathematized Campbell and the Mahoning Association by charging them with eight doctrinal errors: no "evidence of interest in Christ" needed except the Bible; no direct activity of the Holy Spirit prior to baptism; baptism to be administered by any baptized person; no examination of a baptismal candidate except his confession of Jesus as "the Son of God"; "no promise of salvation without baptism"; baptism as procuring "'the remission of sins and the gift of the Holy Spirit'"; obedience as activating God's election of human beings to salvation; and creeds/confessions as nonessential.[29] Other Baptist associations in Kentucky and Virginia adopted the Beaver anathemas.[30] In the Tate's Creek Association in Kentucky in 1829 ten churches disfellowshiped sixteen churches that agreed with the Campbells[31] and identified four more errors held by Campbell's followers: "no special call to the [pastoral] ministry," the abolition of the Mosaic law, "experimental religion" reckoned as enthusiasm," and "no mystery" in the Bible.[32] In reaction to these events the Mahoning Association dissolved and became "an Annual Meeting of

---

[25]Walter Scott, *The Gospel Restored* . . . (Cincinnati: O. H. Donogh, 1836), 225-548; Garrett, *The Stone-Campbell Movement*, 205-22, esp. 218; Roberts-Thomson, *Baptists and Disciples of Christ*, 74-75.

[26]*Origin of the Disciples of Christ*, 99.

[27]Roberts-Thomson, *Baptists and Disciples of Christ*, 73, stated that "the separation began in 1828, reached its peak in 1830, and was made final in 1832."

[28]Errett Gates, *The Disciples of Christ* (New York: Baker and Taylor Co., 1905), 160.

[29]Errett Gates, *The Early Relation and Separation of Baptists and Disciples* (Chicago: Christian Century Co., 1904) 92.

[30]Garrett, *The Stone-Campbell Movement*, 226.

[31]Garrison and DeGroot, *The Disciples of Christ*, 193-94.

[32]Gates, *The Disciples of Christ*, 162-63.

Disciples of Christ."[33] Disciples historians have tended to identify the year 1830 as "the beginning of the Disciples of Christ."[34]

The Appomattox Association in Virginia in 1830, in adopting the Beaver anathemas, "added three resolutions: to discountenance the writings of Alexander Campbell; to discourage the use of his new translation" of the New Testament; and "not to invite into its pulpits any minister who holds Campbell's views."[35] Campbell's *Millennial Harbinger* replaced *The Christian Baptist* in 1830.[36] In December 1830 the Dover Association of Virginia, including such Baptist leaders as Robert Baylor Semple (1769–1831) and Andrew Broaddus, Sr. (1770–1848), identified the following four Campbellite errors: "'denial of the influence of the Holy Spirit in the salvation of man'"; "'the substitution of baptism and regeneration'" for conversion; "'the substitution of reformation for conversion and repentance,'" and "'the Pelagian doctrine of the sufficiency of man's natural powers to effect his own salvation.'" It also advised as to how to excommunicate, to deal with the "disorderly" conduct of, and receive members from the Campbellite churches.[37] In 1832 the Dover Association recommended to its churches actual separation. Other Baptist churches and associations were influenced by the Dover actions.[38] The Baptist-Disciple separation was virtually completed when Campbell's followers and those of Barton Warren Stone (1772–1844) united in 1832.[39]

Separation of the churches did not mean the end of Baptist polemical writings against the teachings of Alexander Campbell. Attention has already been given to the polemical writings by J. R. Graves[40] and Benjamin M.

---

[33] Roberts-Thomson, *Baptists and Disciples of Christ*, 78-79.

[34] Gates, *The Early Relation and Separation*, 102; William E. Tucker and Lester G. McAllister, *Journey in Faith: A History of the Christian Church (Disciples of Christ)* (St. Louis: Bethany, 1975) 16; Garrett, *The Stone-Campbell Movement*, 230. But, contra, Garrison and DeGroot, *The Disciples of Christ*, 192.

[35] Garrison and DeGroot, *The Disciples of Christ*, 195-96.

[36] Ibid, 206-207.

[37] Gates, *The Early Relation and Separation*, 94-97; Roberts-Thomson, *Baptists and Disciples of Christ*, 79-81; Garrison and DeGroot, *The Disciples of Christ*, 196.

[38] Roberts-Thomson, *Baptists and Disciples of Christ*, 82. Gates, *The Disciples of Christ*, 169-73, listed from the Disciples perspective three doctrinal and four practical differences leading to the separation.

[39] Gates, *The Disciples of Christ*, 177-211; Garrison and DeGroot, *The Disciples of Christ*, 207-17.

[40] See above, 221.

Bogard[41] as well as to Campbell's own opposition to organized Baptist missionary efforts.[42] At the time of the schism Andrew Broaddus of Virginia labeled Campbell's view as baptismal regeneration, insisted that faith only is the instrument of justification or the remission of sin, critiqued Campbell's doctrine of faith as Sandemanian, and insisted on the necessity of the Holy Spirit's work in regeneration.[43] J. B. Jeter in his multifaceted treatment majored on five doctrinal issues: the work of the Holy Spirit in conversion, prayer as not a duty of the unbaptized, making regeneration and conversion to be identified with baptism, the remission of sins in baptism, and weekly observance of the Lord's Supper.[44] In responding to Campbell's critique of his first book, Jeter tried to find common ground on the work of the Spirit in conversion and introduced Campbell's rejection of progressive sanctification.[45] A. P. Williams wrote in reply to a critical review of Jeter's book by Moses Easterly Lard (1818–1880), a Disciples editor.[46] David Burcham Ray (1830–1922) of Tennessee, while giving major attention to issues related to baptism and to the Holy Spirit,[47] criticized "Campbellites" for teaching that the kingdom of God was established by the apostles on the Day of Pentecost, that Baptists were derived from the Roman Catholic Church, and that salvation is to be found only in "the Campbellite Society."[48] Willis Anselm Jarrel (1849–1927) of Texas, who, together with Ray, wrote from a Landmark perspective, made extreme charges: that Campbell's movement "was developed out of" Stone's movement, that the Campbellites were "never Baptists, but only "apostate Presbyterians," that

---

[41] See above, 240-41.

[42] See above, 208.

[43] *A Reply to Mr. A. Campbell's M. Harbinger, Extra, on the Remission of Sins, etc.* (Richmond: Religious Herald, 1831) esp. 8, 18, 19, 22, 28, 36-37, 43, 50, 55.

[44] *Campbellism Examined* (New York: Sheldon, Lamport, and Blakeman, 1855) esp. 76-291. Jeter, 197, declared that Alexander Campbell had been "unfairly charged with teaching *baptismal regeneration.*"

[45] *Campbellism Reexamined* (New York: Sheldon, Blakeman, and Co., 1856) 37-63, 86-89.

[46] *Campbellism Exposed, in an Examination of Lard's Review of Jeter* (Memphis: Graves and Mahaffy, 1866). On Lard, see Garrett, *The Stone-Campbell Movement,* 465, 468b, and Garrison and DeGroot, *The Disciples of Christ,* 384, who call Lard "superorthodox."

[47] *Text-book on Campbellism* (Memphis: South-Western Publishing Co., 1870) 174-257, 266-303.

[48] Ibid., 44-68, 82-88, 128-39.

the Disciples were eighteen centuries too late to be "regarded as the Church of Christ," that Campbell taught "baptismal regeneration,"[49] that Stone looked upon the eternal Sonship of Christ and the Trinity as speculative, not necessarily biblical, truth, that Campbell reckoned the atonement as not substitutionary, and that Campbellism through Sidney Rigdon helped to spawn Mormonism.[50]

Although separation of the Baptists and the Disciples brought division, especially on the Western frontier, both North and South, the Campbells may have left a greater impact on Southern Baptists than on Northern Baptists.[51] James E. Tull saw positive results from this controversy such as the greater willingness of Baptists to elevate the authority of the New Testament above that of the Old Testament and the abandonment by some Baptists of waiting in "supine helplessness for the moving of the Spirit" in favor of a more active exercise of faith.[52] But more negative effects have also been cited. For Southern Baptists, Tull saw both a lessened interest in Christian unity and a reduction of baptism to a "mere symbol" as likely, though not certain, results of the controversy with the Campbells.[53] Tull,[54] Timothy George,[55] and Jesse Fletcher[56] have concurred in the conclusion that resistance to or indifference toward confessions of faith was a major result for Southern Baptists, but such a conclusion was more valid for the latter nineteenth century than for most of the twentieth.

---

[49]See above, n. 43.

[50]*"The Gospel in Water," or Campbellism: Being an Exposition and Refutation of Campbellism, and an Exposition and a Vindication of the Gospel and the New Testament Church* (St. Louis: National Baptist Publishing Co., 1886) esp. 1, 26, 62-63, 32, 92-96, 274-411, 21-24, 533-36, 582-91.

[51]Torbet, *A History of the Baptists*, 287-93, did not address the question of long-term effects on Northern Baptists.

[52]*Shapers of Baptist Thought*, 126.

[53]Ibid., 126, 127.

[54]Ibid., 126.

[55]"Conflict and Identity in the SBC: The Question for a New Consensus," in *Beyond the Impasse? Scripture, Interpretation, and Theology in Baptist Life*, ed. Robison B. James and David S. Dockery (Nashville: Broadman, 1992) 204.

[56]*The Southern Baptist Convention*, 48, 365.

Controversies over the Bible: Bible Translation; Crawford Howell Toy (1836–1919) and Basil Manly, Jr.

Baptists in both England and the United States became involved during the nineteenth century in controversy over a translation of the Bible into the Bengali language. William Yates, a Baptist missionary in Calcutta, had prepared the translation, in which he translated the Greek *baptizein* by the equivalent of "immerse" rather than transliterate it by the equivalent of "baptize," just as Adoniram Judson had done in his Burmese translation. When Baptists asked the British and Foreign Bible Society to help to pay for and to distribute the Bengali translation, that society declined to do so, appealing to the translation policy of the KJV. Indignant English Baptists then formed the Bible Translation Society as an instrument for distribution of "faithful and thorough translations." Likewise American Baptists in 1835 requested the American Bible Society to appropriate funds to assist in the publication of Yates's Bengali Bible. This society voted to appropriate $5000 to the Triennial Convention on the condition that KJV policy be followed so that all denominations supporting the society would be willing to circulate and use its products. The Triennial Convention declined to accept the offer and sought to increase its funds for the Bengali project. In 1837 representatives of Baptist churches in twenty-three states met in Philadelphia to form their own Baptist society, entitled the American and Foreign Bible Society. When in 1850 that society declined to issue an English translation using the word "immerse," those members who dissented formed the American Bible Union. "Neither society made out well financially," and in 1883 in Saratoga, New York, the decision was made that domestic Bible distribution should be the responsibility of the American Baptist Publication Society and foreign Bible distribution should be the duty of the American Baptist Missionary Union, thus allowing for different policies. The Southern Baptist Convention established its Bible Board in 1851.[57]

The second nineteenth-century controversy with respect to the Bible occurred in the Southern Baptist Convention and centered in the teachings and professorial career of Crawford Howell Toy. A native of Virginia and

---

[57]Whitley, *A History of British Baptists*, 315-16; Torbet, *A History of the Baptists*, 295-96; Winthrop S. Hudson, *American Protestantism*, The Chicago History of American Civilization (Chicago: University of Chicago Press, 1961) 109; Baker, *The Southern Baptist Convention*, 148, 203, 207.

a graduate of the University of Virginia and of the Southern Baptist Theological Seminary at its inception, he had studied, especially ancient languages, for two years at the University of Berlin before joining the faculty of Southern Baptist Theological Seminary in 1869.[58] In his inaugural address, *The Claims of Biblical Interpretation on Baptists*,[59] Toy declared that because they do not rely upon church councils or merely "human authority" and "have always maintained to the full the necessity of Scriptural grounds for all beliefs and practices," Baptists are especially obligated to engage in able interpretation of the Bible, even though in the past they had contributed less to biblical scholarship than to biblical proclamation and application. He affirmed the twofold nature of the Bible: the "external" aspect dealing with facts and words and subject to critical inquiry and the "internal" aspect, or having the Holy Spirit as a guide. These must be united. After reviewing the history of biblical hermeneutics from the early Jewish to the Christian of the nineteenth century, Toy defined biblical inspiration as meaning that "the Bible . . . is in every iota of its substance absolutely and infallibly true" and warned Baptists to avoid two errors: turning "illumination" into "fanaticism" and neglecting serious study of the Bible.[60] The inaugural address, when delivered, received praise rather than criticism.[61] As a seminary professor Toy was known to be a knowledgeable scholar, especially gifted in Semitic languages, an able teacher, and a pious Christian.[62] But before the end of a decade of teaching he embraced and articulated views that were reckoned to be at variance with Baptist views of

---

[58]David Gordon Lyon, "Crawford Howell Toy," *Harvard Theological Review* 13 (January 1920): 1-6; Billy Grey Hurt, "Crawford Howell Toy: Interpreter of the Old Testament (Th.D. diss., Southern Baptist Theological Seminary, 1965) 10-50; Pope A. Duncan, "Crawford Howell Toy: Heresy at Louisville," *American Religious Heretics: Formal and Informal Trials*, ed. George H. Shriver (Nashville: Abingdon, 1966) 56-59. Toy was named for R[obert]. B[oyte]. C[rawford]. Howell, the husband of Toy's aunt. Horne, "A Study of the Life and Work of R. B. C. Howell," 5.

[59]Subtitle: *Being the Inaugural Address of Rev. C. H. Toy, on His Induction into the Professorship of Old Testament Interpretation in the Southern Baptist Theological Seminary, at Greenville, S.C., September 1st, 1869* (New York: Lange and Hillman, 1869).

[60]Ibid., 5-6, 53, 7-11, 52-56, 11-42, 44, 55-56.

[61]Hurt, "Crawford Howell Toy," 122-26.

[62]Lyon, "Crawford Howell Toy," 6-7, 9.

the inspiration of the Scriptures.[63] These included exploring various alternatives to a literal interpretation of the days of Genesis 1, Darwinian evolution, the Graf-Kuenen-Wellhausen documentary hypothesis (J, E, D, P) concerning the Pentateuch, denying that Psalm 16 has reference to Jesus' resurrection, teaching that the Servant in Isa. 42:1-4 and 53:1-2 meant Israel as a people with a later fulfillment in Jesus Christ,[64] "the rationalist reconstruction of the history of Israel," and the later dating of Old Testament books.[65] Toy's views posed a problem not only inherently but also for the seminary, which had in 1877 moved from Greenville, South Carolina, to Louisville, Kentucky, for with ninety students, the largest enrollment of any Baptist seminary in the nation, it had financial needs and was dependent on its supporters.[66] In May 1879 Toy submitted to the seminary's trustees a carefully crafted letter in which he affirmed the article on the Scriptures in the seminary's Abstract of Principles, offered brief exposition of his views, and tendered his resignation.[67] The trustees with two negative votes and without pressing any charges via-à-vis the Abstract of Principles accepted Toy's resignation.[68] John A. Broadus, who had baptized Toy and been his pastor in Charlottesville, Virginia, and his professor in Greenville, was with James P. Boyce to bid farewell to Toy at the railway station in Louisville, when Boyce said, "Oh, Toy, I would freely give . . . [my left] arm to be cut off if you could be where you were five years ago, and stay there."[69] Baptist denominational papers in the South, following Toy's resignation, at first expressed bewilderment and then began to discuss biblical inspiration.[70] In 1880 Toy became Hancock Professor of Hebrew and Other Oriental Languages and Dexter Lecturer on Biblical Literature in the Divinity School of Harvard University and continued until retirement in 1909. The first non-Unitarian professor in the Divinity School, Toy remained a Baptist for eight years and then became a Unitarian.[71] He greatly expanded the curricular

---

[63]Hurt, "Crawford Howell Toy," 145.
[64]Duncan, "Crawford Howell Toy," 62-66.
[65]Barnes, *The Southern Baptist Convention*, 136.
[66]Hurt, "Crawford Howell Toy," 175-82.
[67]The full text is appended to Duncan, "Crawford Howell Toy," 79-84.
[68]Hurt, "Crawford Howell Toy," 140-41, 148.
[69]John A. Broadus, *Memoir of James Petigru Boyce, D.D., LL.D.* (New York: A. C. Armstrong and Son, 1893) 263-64.
[70]Hurt, "Crawford Howell Toy," 142-73.
[71]Mueller, *A History of Southern Baptist Theological Seminary*, 142.

offerings in Semitic languages and published an extensive corpus of books, articles, and reviews.[72]

Basil Manly, Jr., whose role in framing the Abstract of Principles of Southern Baptist Theological Seminary has already been noted,[73] played a strategic role in the seminary's response to the teachings of Toy. The son of an influential Charleston, South Carolina, pastor, the younger Manly, educated in the University of Alabama, Newton Theological Institution, and Princeton Theological Seminary and a pastor, educator, and hymn writer, had been one of the four original faculty members of the seminary, occupying the chair of biblical introduction and Old Testament interpretation. But in 1871 he had left the seminary to become president of Georgetown College in Kentucky.[74] Two days after accepting Toy's resignation in May 1879,[75] the trustees reelected Manly, and he returned to the seminary faculty.[76]

Nine years later Manly published *The Bible Doctrine of Inspiration Explained and Vindicated.*[77] Although for Manly inspiration was not absolutely "essential . . . to the historical credibility of Scripture," an uninspired

---

[72]Lyon, "Crawford Howell Toy," 13, 14, 16, 15, 14-15. His books produced at Harvard were: *History of the Religion of Israel: An Old Testament Primer* (Boston: Unitarian Sunday-School Society, 1882); *Quotations in the New Testament* (New York: Scribner's, 1884); *Judaism and Christianity: A Sketch of the Progress of Thought from Old Testament to New Testament* (Boston: Little, Brown, and Co., 1890); *The Book of the Prophet Ezekiel: Critical Edition of the Hebrew Text, with Notes* (Leipzig: J. C. Hinrichs; Baltimore: Johns Hopkins University Press, 1899); *The Book of the Prophet Ezekiel: A New English Translation, with Explanatory Notes and Pictorial Illustrations* (New York: Dodd, Mead: London: James Clarke, 1899); *A Critical and Exegetical Commentary on the Book of Proverbs*, International Critical Commentary 16 (New York: Scribner's, 1899).

[73]See above, 146-47.

[74]Mueller, *A History of Southern Baptist Theological Seminary*, 2, 52, 84-89; Joseph Powhatan Cox, "A Study of the Life and Work of Basil Manly, Jr." (Th.D. diss., Southern Baptist Theological Seminary, 1954) 1-234; idem, "Manly, Basil, Jr.," *Encyclopedia of Southern Baptists* 2:817-18.

[75]Hurt, "Crawford Howell Toy," 197.

[76]Mueller, *A History of Southern Baptist Theological Seminary*, 96; Cox, "A Study of the Life and Work of Basil Manly, Jr.," 277-84.

[77](New York: A. C. Armstrong, 1888; repr.: Harrisonburg VA: Gano Books, 1985). On the events leading to the writing of this book, see Cox, "A Study of the Life and Work of Basil Manly, Jr.," 318-23.

Bible would "furnish no infallible standard of truth," "present no authoritative rule for obedience," or "offer no suitable means for . . . drawing" the human soul "to its Heavenly Father." Inspiration implies genuine "supernatural interposition," may be regarded as both an "act" and a "result," and "implies" a "double authorship," divine and human. Manly insisted that "revelation," or the "direct divine influence that imparts truth to the mind," must be differentiated from "inspiration," or the "divine influence that secures the accurate transference of truth into human language by a speaker or writer, so as to be communicated to other men." Likewise, inspiration must be distinguished from "illumination," or the "influence of the Holy Spirit under which all the children of God receive, discern, and feed upon the truth communicated to them."[78]

Manly explained six different theories of biblical inspiration and espoused the sixth. The "mechanical" theory posits dictation by the Holy Spirit so as to ignore "any real human authorship whatever." The "partial" theory limits inspiration to "certain parts or sorts of the sacred writings; for example, to doctrinal sections but not to narrative or exhortation, or only to "the things naturally unknown," or to "ideas . . . but not to the language." According to the theory of "different degrees" or levels, portions of the Bible differ as to the extent of God's control of the human authors; for example, "superintendence, elevation, direction, [and] suggestion." The "natural" theory takes biblical inspiration to be no different from that of heroes, poets, or men of genius" or the sacred books of non-Christian religions. According to the "universal Christian" theory, the agency of the Holy Spirit in biblical inspiration is "the same in kind with the ordinary illumination of every Christian." Finally Manly defended the "plenary" theory, though not attaching the word "verbal," and defined it as the view "that the Bible as a whole is the Word of God, so that in every part of Scripture there is both infallible truth and divine authority." Then the Louisville professor sought to identify and alleviate some nine misconceptions of inspiration.[79]

The book's second part is a treatment of "proofs of inspiration." Manly used the "presumptive argument" that a God who revealed himself effectively would surely authenticate its transference to peoples and different ages of human history. But direct proofs must be taken from the Scriptures: "the veracity of the historical record in the Scriptures," the

---

[78]*The Bible Doctrine of Inspiration Explained and Vindicated*, 15-18, 23-43.
[79]Ibid., 44-89.

testimony of the prophet and of God, the testimony of miracles, "manifold allusions and references of one part of Scripture to another," the "*phenomena*" of the Scriptures, and the cumulative effect of such argument for proofs. The "high and peculiar" claims of the Bible as to itself, however, are "usually" "incidental and simple." The manner in which biblical authors quote from other biblical books points to inspiration. The same is true of terms such as "*the Scripture(s)*," "*prophecy*" or "*the prophets*," "*the Word of God*," and "*the oracles of God*." There are texts that affirm the inspiration of "particular" persons or singular texts. Other texts more generally promise divine inspiration. Manly cited fifteen New Testament texts as asserting biblical inspiration.[80]

Consideration of objections to biblical inspiration occupies the final part of Manly's monograph. Some New Testament texts, it is alleged, actually "disclaim inspiration." Alleged "discrepancies" or "mistakes" in the Bible are taken by Manly to be due to misinterpretation of a text itself or of historical facts, to the inability to harmonize, or to failure to recognize different authorial purposes or different "readers or hearers." Moral objections to conduct recorded in the Bible can be categorized variously so as to maintain the "moral grandeur" of biblical ethics. Textual criticism was not posing major problems, and some issues raised by "Higher Criticism" actually applied to the canon or to authorship, not to inspiration, but Manly saw denial of the Mosaic authorship of "the body of the Pentateuch" as a threat to the doctrine of inspiration. Relative to scientific objections he noted that "our interpretations of Scripture may be erroneous" and that scientific "conclusions" have had to be revised or corrected. Moreover, in describing the realm of nature, biblical writers used "the language of appearances," and the agreements between biblical studies and the sciences are notable.[81]

Manly's book on inspiration compensated for the lack of attention to the subject in Boyce's *Abstract of Systematic Theology*[82] and was consonant with the work of the Princeton theologians,[83] but Joseph P. Cox has contended that "it provided a comprehensive, though not exhaustive treatment

---

[80] Ibid., 93-175.
[81] Ibid., 177-250.
[82] George, "James Petigru Boyce," 258.
[83] For example, Archibald Alexander Hodge and Benjamin Breckinridge Warfield, *Inspiration* (Philadelphia: Presbyterian Board of Publication, 1881; repr.: Grand Rapids MI: Baker Book House, 1979).

of the doctrine."[84] At least one contemporary review contended that Manly had not made his case that inspiration requires infallibility.[85]

Down Grade Controversy:
Charles Haddon Spurgeon (1834–1892) and John Clifford (1836–1923)

One of the most significant controversies among Baptists occurred in England during the latter part of the ninth decade of the nineteenth century. The principal participants were Charles Haddon Spurgeon and John Clifford.[86] Their roles in the controversy need to be explained, but the theology of each these is in its own right worthy of exposition.

Spurgeon was born in Kelvedon in Essex to devout parents, his father and his paternal grandfather being Independent (or Congregational) pastors.[87] He was converted to Christ at the age of fifteen on a snowy January Sunday in a Primitive Methodist chapel in Colchester, Essex, with the sermon on Isa. 45:22 being delivered by a lay preacher.[88] Four months later, having become convinced of the obligation of immersion, he was immersed on confession of his faith by a Baptist pastor in the River Lark. In October he joined St. Andrew's Street Baptist Church in Cambridge. A year later he became pastor of a Baptist chapel in the nearby village of Waterbeach.[89] In 1854, while yet nineteen, Spurgeon was called to be pastor of New Park Street Church in London, whose pulpit had been filled by Keach, Gill, and Rippon.[90] There ensued a ministry that brought an expanding congregation to more than five thousand members,[91] the construction of the Metropolitan Tabernacle,[92] the establishment of the

---

[84]Cox, "Manly, Basil, Jr.," 818.

[85]Cox, "A Study of the Life and Work of Basil Manly, Jr.," 327-28.

[86]Participating with Spurgeon, at least to an extent, was Samuel Harris Booth, and participating with Clifford were Alexander Maclaren, Charles Williams, James Culross, and T. Vincent Tymns. Lewis A. Drummond, *Spurgeon: Prince of Preachers* (Grand Rapids MI: Kregel Publications, 1992) 669-73, 685, 697, 714; 691, 695, 698, 701; 701, 704; 696-98; 664.

[87]Ibid., 74-82.
[88]Ibid., 113-31.
[89]Ibid., 136, 142, 153-62.
[90]Ibid., 177-99.
[91]Ibid., 284-87.

[92]Ibid., 335-55; Eric W. Hayden, *A Centennial History of Spurgeon's Tabernacle* (Pasadena TX: Pilgrim Publications, 1971; orig., U.K., 1962).

pastor's college,[93] an orphanage,[94] sermon publication and distribution,[95] and the planting of new Baptist churches in greater London.[96]

At least four major influences on the theology of Spurgeon can be identified. First was the English Bible, coupled with Spurgeon's own penchant for Anglo-Saxon English. Second, was the theology of John Calvin. One of Spurgeon's wife's first gifts to him was a set of the complete works of Calvin. Spurgeon at 24 "preached twice in Calvin's pulpit in Geneva, and even wore Calvin's gown."[97] Spurgeon said of Calvinism that it "is neither more nor less than the good old gospel of the Puritans, the Martyrs, the Apostles, and of our Lord Jesus Christ."[98] He also declared: "I am never ashamed to avow myself a Calvinist, although I claim to be rather a Calvinist according to Calvin, than after the modern debased fashion."[99] Whether Spurgeon was thereby alluding to Arminianism or to Hyper-Calvinism may not be certain, but he did reject both.[100] According to Ernest Bacon, the early Spurgeon had a "stronger and more aggressive" Calvinism and the later Spurgeon a "more moderate" Calvinism.[101] For Lewis A. Drummond the shift was from a stress on Calvinist soteriology to a stress on orthodox Christology.[102] But J. C. Carlile concluded that Spurgeon inter-

---

[93]Drummond, *Spurgeon: Prince of Preachers*, 405-19.

[94]Ibid., 420-30.

[95]Ibid., 215-18, 320-30.

[96]Ibid., 285, 467-68, 499, 713. Michael K. Nicholls, "Charles Haddon Spurgeon, 1834–1892: Church Planter," in *Mission to the World: Essays to Celebrate the 50th Anniversary of the Ordination of George Raymond Beasley-Murray to the Christian Ministry*, ed. Paul Beasley-Murray (Didcot UK: Baptist Historical Society, 1991) 20-29.

[97]Ernest W. Bacon, *Spurgeon: Heir of the Puritans* (London: George Allen & Unwin, 1967) 43, 61; Richard Ellsworth Day, *The Shadow of the Broad Brim: The Life Story of Charles Haddon Spurgeon, Heir of the Puritans* (Philadelphia: Judson, 1934) 142.

[98]Quoted by George John Stevenson, *Sketch of the Life and Ministry of the Rev. C. H. Spurgeon: From Original Documents* (New York: Sheldon, Blakeman and Co., 1858) 103.

[99]Bacon, *Spurgeon: Heir of the Puritans*, 67.

[100]Spurgeon "kept clear of the Hyper-Calvinistic Scylla; and he was equally careful to eschew the Arminian Charybdis." James Douglas, *The Prince of Preachers: A Sketch; a Portraiture; and a Tribute* (London: Morgan and Scott, 1900) 106.

[101]Bacon, *Spurgeon: Heir of the Puritans*, 87.

[102]*Spurgeon: Prince of Preachers*, 660.

preted "the sterner doctrines" of Calvinism "with the tenderness of mysticism."[103] The third influence was Puritanism, which in some sense was an extension of Calvinism. Spurgeon built a massive library of Puritan authors,[104] and his wife read to him from Puritan authors on Saturday evenings.[105] "Few men possessed anything like his acquaintance" with Puritan authors,[106] and at the time of his death it was said that he "knew more about Puritanism than any of the Puritans themselves."[107] Spurgeon has been called "a Puritan of the Puritans,"[108] "the heir of the Puritans,"[109] "the last of the Puritans,"[110] and "the first of a new Puritanism."[111] Fourth, Spurgeon was a Particular Baptist during the time when the differences from General Baptists were still recognized, but he was a Particular Baptist of the open communion type that did not embrace open membership.[112]

What were the doctrines emphasized by Spurgeon, and how does one ascertain such? First, Spurgeon composed and published in 1855 a condensation and revision of the 32-article Second London Confession of Particular Baptists.[113] Second, biographers of Spurgeon have listed and discussed the key doctrines of Spurgeon.[114] Volumes of Spurgeon's sermons

---

[103]*C. H. Spurgeon: An Interpretive Biography* (London: Religious Tract Society and Kingsgate, 1933) 140.

[104]Day, *The Shadow of the Broad Brim*, 122.

[105]Bacon, *Spurgeon: Heir of the Puritans*, 46.

[106]Carlile, *C. H. Spurgeon*, 212.

[107]*Christian Commonwealth*, 4 Feb. 1892, as quoted by W. Y. Fullerton, *C. H. Spurgeon: A Biography* (London: Williams and Norgate, 1920) 195.

[108]Day, *The Shadow of the Broad Brim*, 22.

[109]Ibid., 121.

[110]Carlile, *C. H. Spurgeon*, 292.

[111]Ibid.

[112]Heman Lincoln Wayland, *Charles H. Spurgeon: His Faith and Works* (Philadelphia: American Baptist Publication Society, 1892) 191-95, 216; Fullerton, *C. H. Spurgeon*, 291. For the assertion that the "pietism of the evangelical revivals" affected Victorian England and hence Spurgeon, see Duncan S. Ferguson, "The Bible and Protestant Orthodoxy: The Hermeneutics of Charles Spurgeon," *Journal of the Evangelical Theological Society* 25 (December 1982): 455-66.

[113]Stevenson, *Sketch of the Life and Ministry*, 118-22. Only a few deviations from the Second London can be detected, such as the omission of the bondage of the human will after the fall (art. 9) and the addition that the gospel revelation "is sufficient to the saving of all men" (art. 20).

[114]Bacon, *Spurgeon: Heir of the Puritans*, 110-19, included eleven: "The

organized around a single doctrinal subject have been published. Among such volumes those on the person and work of Christ[115] and on soteriology in the broad sense[116] predominate, while there have been fewer volumes on last things,[117] the ordinances,[118] the Holy Spirit,[119] and Satan.[120]

Divine Inspiration and Authority of Scripture," "The Sovereignty of God," "Predestination and Election," "The Deity of Christ," "The Substitutionary Atonement of Christ," "Justification of Faith only," "The Work of the Holy Spirit," "Holiness," "The Loveliness of Christ," "The Final Perseverance of the Saints," and "The Return of the Lord." Drummond, *Spurgeon: Prince of Preachers*, 570-72, 615-29, 291-94, 629-53, treated the Scriptures, God, the person and work of Christ, the Holy Spirit, covenants, angels-Satan-demons, "doctrines of grace" (five points of the Synod of Dort), the church, and last things.

[115] *12 Christian Sermons* (Grand Rapids MI: Baker, 1994) esp. 79-102; *C. H. Spurgeon's Sermons on Christ's Name and Titles*, ed. Charles T. Cook, Library of Spurgeon's Sermons 16 (Grand Rapids MI: Zondervan, 1961); *C. H. Spurgeon's Sermons on the Miracles*, ed. Charles T. Cook, Library of Spurgeon's Sermons 3 (Grand Rapids MI: Zondervan, 1958); *Sermons on the "Cries from the Cross"* (Grand Rapids MI: Baker, 1994); *12 Sermons on the Passion and Death of Christ* (Grand Rapids MI: Baker, 1994); *C. H. Spurgeon's Sermons on the Blood and Cross of Christ*, ed. Charles T. Cook, Library of Spurgeon's Sermons 12 (Grand Rapids MI: Zondervan, 1961); *Christ's Glorious Achievements* (London: Oliphants, 1954); *12 Sermons on the Resurrection* (Grand Rapids MI: Baker, 1994).

[116] *12 Sermons on Faith* (Grand Rapids MI: Baker, 1975); *Twelve Sermons on Repentance* (#1) (N.p., n.d.); *Twelve Sermons on Repentance* (#2) (Grand Rapids MI: Baker, 1974); *Twelve Sermons on Conversion* (Grand Rapids MI: Baker, 1974); *Twelve Sermons on Decision* (Grand Rapids MI: Baker, 1971); *Twelve Sermons on the Plan of Salvation* (New York: F. H. Revell, 1890?); *All of Grace: An Earnest Word with Those Who Are Seeking Salvation by the Lord Jesus Christ* (New York: F. H. Revell, 188?); *Spurgeon on the Five Points* (MacDill AFB FL: Tyndale Bible Society, n.d.); *12 Sermons on Commitment* (Grand Rapids MI: Baker, 1978); *Twelve Sermons on Holiness* (London: Marshall, Morgan, and Scott, 18__?); *C. H. Spurgeon's Sermons on Sin, Salvation and Service*, ed. Charles T. Cook, Library of Spurgeon's Sermons 15 (Grand Rapids MI: Zondervan, 1961); *Twelve Sermons on Prayer* (London: Marshall, Morgan, and Scott, n.d.); *C. H. Spurgeon's Sermons on Prayer*, ed. Charles T. Cook, Library of Spurgeon's Sermons 7 (Grand Rapids MI: Zondervan, 1959); *Twelve Sermons on Backsliding* (Grand Rapids MI: Baker, 1979); *Able to the Uttermost: Twenty Gospel Sermons* (London: Marshall, Morgan, and Scott, 1920?).

[117] *12 Sermons on Hope* (Grand Rapids MI: Baker, 1979); *C. H. Spurgeon's Sermons on the Book of Revelation*, ed. Charles T. Cook, Library of Spurgeon's

Specific doctrinal positions of Spurgeon have been given identifying labels. His plenary-verbal view of biblical inspiration has been identified with its exposition by Louis Gaussen.[121] His Christology has been said to have been agreeable to the Chalcedonian Symbol.[122] Spurgeon's doctrine of the atonement has been readily identified as that of penal substitution, with its satisfaction of divine justice.[123] But he also preached on Christ's overcoming Satan, the world, principalities and powers, and death.[124] Spurgeon has been identified as holding to the five positions set forth by the Synod of Dort vis-à-vis the Remonstrants.[125] This is defensible, but at the same time Spurgeon in his preaching tended to qualify these positions. He did not embrace reprobation, or double predestination,[126] he did allow for the merits of Christ's sacrificial death to be infinite,[127] and he called faith a

---

Sermons 20 (Grand Rapids MI: Zondervan, 1962); *C. H. Spurgeon's Sermons on the Second Coming and the Last Things*, ed. Charles T. Cook, Library of Spurgeon's Sermons 18 (Grand Rapids MI: Zondervan, 1962); *12 Sermons on the Second Coming of Christ* (Grand Rapids MI: Baker, 1976); *C. H. Spurgeon's Sermons on Heaven and Hell*, ed. Charles T. Cook, Library of Spurgeon's Sermons 17 (Grand Rapids MI: Zondervan, 1962).

[118]*Spurgeon on Baptism* (Worthing UK: Henry E. Walter, 1971?); *"Till He Come": Communion Meditations and Addresses* (London: Passmore and Alabaster, 1894).

[119]*Holy Spirit Power* (New Kensington PA: Whitaker House, 1996); *Spurgeon on the Holy Spirit* (New Kensington PA: Whitaker House, 2000).

[120]*Satan* (Pasadena, TX: Pilgrim Publications, n.d.).

[121]Drummond, *Spurgeon: Prince of Preachers*, 620-21; Gaussen, *Theopneustia: The Plenary Inspiration of the Holy Scriptures Deduced from Internal Evidence, and the Testimonies of Nature, History, and Science*, rev. ed., trans. David Scott and reedited and revised by B. W. Carr (London: Passmore and Alabaster, 1888; repr.: Chicago: Moody, n.d.).

[122]Drummond, *Spurgeon: Prince of Preachers*, 291-92.

[123]Bacon, *Spurgeon: Heir of the Puritans*, 113, 129, 139; Drummond, *Spurgeon: Prince of Preachers*, 292-94, 642-46.

[124]*Christ's Glorious Achievements*, 24-61, 81-112.

[125]*Spurgeon on the Five Points*; Drummond, *Spurgeon: Prince of Preachers*, 635-50. Drummond interpreted the fourth "point" as "effectual calling."

[126]Drummond, *Spurgeon: Prince of Preachers*, 640.

[127]Ibid., 646. Kathy Triggs, *Charles H. Spurgeon: The Boy Preacher on the Fens* (Basingstoke UK: Pickering and Inglis, 1984) 84, has concluded that Spurgeon "held with Calvin, that Christ died for all, but that he does not pray for all," but only for the elect.

"duty" while insisting that faith is "the gift of God and the work of the Holy Spirit."[128] On perseverance, it seems, there was no wavering, and Spurgeon repeatedly preached on backsliding.[129] Spurgeon acknowledged that he was a premillennialist, but his preaching focused on such eschatological themes as resurrection, second coming, judgment, heaven, and hell, he opposed efforts to predict the time of the second coming, and he held John Nelson Darby's writings in low esteem.[130] If there should be any central label that can aptly be placed on Spurgeon's theology and preaching, it would, according to his biographers,[131] be Christocentrism.

The Down Grade Controversy was not the first controversy in which Spurgeon was involved. Rather the first was with Hyper-Calvinist Particular Baptists during his first decade in London. Although treated marginally by Spurgeon's biographers,[132] this controversy has been carefully investigated by Iain H. Murray.[133] Spurgeon's principal critic was James Wells (1803–1872), pastor of the Surrey Tabernacle in London, who charged the youthful Spurgeon with teaching the error of duty-faith. Waged chiefly in the pages of the *Earthen Vessel,* edited by Charles Waters Banks (1806–1886) and circulated chiefly among the Strict and Particular Baptists,[134] the controversy evoked from Spurgeon a fourfold critique, according to Murray, of Hyper-Calvinism. First, "Hyper-Calvinism views gospel preaching solely as a means for the ingathering of God's elect" rather than as the unrestricted

---

[128] *12 Sermons on Faith,* 56, 57. Spurgeon also held that "faith and repentance are simultaneous," "like the Siamese twins," not successive. *Twelve Sermons on Repentance* (#1), 346.

[129] *Twelve Sermons on Backsliding.*

[130] Drummond, *Spurgeon: Prince of Preachers,* 650-53; Spurgeon, *Commenting and Commentaries: Lectures Addressed to the Students of the Pastors' College, Metropolitan Tabernacle: With a List of the Best Biblical Commentaries and Expositions: Also a Lecture on Eccentric Preachers* (New York: American Tract Society, 1890; repr.: Charleston SC: BiblioBazaar, 2008) 127, 183. Per W. Curtis Vaughan.

[131] Day, *The Shadow of the Broad Brim,* 219-20; Bacon, *Spurgeon: Heir of the Puritans,* 119-20; Drummond, *Spurgeon: Prince of Preachers,* 288-91.

[132] Fullerton, *C. H. Spurgeon,* 289-90; Carlile, *C. H. Spurgeon,* 123-24, 287; Drummond, *Spurgeon: Prince of Preachers,* 216-17, 558-59.

[133] *The Forgotten Spurgeon* (Edinburgh: Banner of Truth Trust, 1966), 45-66; *Spurgeon v. Hyper-Calvinism: The Battle for Gospel Preaching* (Edinburgh; Carlisle PA: Banner of Truth Trust, 1995).

[134] Murray, *Spurgeon v. Hyper-Calvinism,* 39-51.

proclamation to all. Second, it turns "individuals away from their only sure warrant for trusting in Christ, namely, the objective commands and invitations of the gospel" and toward a quest for a warrant from subjective experience. Third, it fails to recognize that humans are "wholly responsible" for their own sin and are totally responsible for their response to the gospel because of their "free agency" (not to be confused with "free will"). Fourth, it denies the love of God that desires the salvation of all humanity.[135] Thereby Spurgeon placed himself closer to Fuller than to Gill.[136]

Spurgeon in 1864 preached a sermon on "Baptismal Regeneration"[137] that triggered a controversy with the Church of England. He critiqued and rejected the Anglican doctrine that regeneration is wrought by baptism, that is, of infants or adults, asserting rather that "baptism without faith saves no one" and that "faith is the indispensable requisite to salvation." He rebuked the "immorality" or hypocritical conduct of those Evangelical Anglicans who did not believe in baptismal regeneration and yet subscribed to the Book of Common Prayer, which teaches such. Spurgeon preached other related sermons,[138] and about 150 pamphlets were published in opposition to Spurgeon.[139] High Church Anglicans defended baptismal regeneration, and Evangelical Anglicans were hurt by the charge of hypocrisy. As a consequence Spurgeon withdrew from the Evangelical Alliance, though later he rejoined.[140]

What led Spurgeon to allege in 1887 that there was a serious "down-grade" or dangerous declension in Nonconformist, including Baptist, theology? Writers about this controversy have cited Spurgeon's concern about certain denials, certain affirmations, and certain objectionable books. He seemed to allege that the following doctrines were being denied: the divine or plenary inspiration of the Bible,[141] the fall of man as historical occur

---

[135] Ibid., 52-99.

[136] Ibid., 48-51, 120, 125-31.

[137] Drummond, *Spurgeon: Prince of Preachers*, 787-802, has reprinted the text.

[138] Ibid., 483-90.

[139] Fullerton, *C. H. Spurgeon*, 306.

[140] Drummond, *Spurgeon: Prince of Preachers*, 490-500; John H. Y. Briggs, *The English Baptists of the Nineteenth Century*, A History of the English Baptists 3 (Didcot UK: Baptist Historical Society, 1994) 48-50.

[141] Robert Shindler, *From the Usher's Desk to the Tabernacle Pulpit: The Life and Labors of Charles Haddon Spurgeon* (New York: A. C. Armstrong and Son, 1893) 273; Charles Ray, *The Life of Charles Haddon Spurgeon* (London: Passmore

rence,[142] the personality of the Holy Spirit,[143] the virginal conception of Jesus,[144] substitutionary atonement,[145] the resurrection of Jesus,[146] justification by faith alone,[147] and eternal punishment.[148] Moreover, certain objectionable affirmations were being made relative to Darwinian evolution,[149] "higher criticism" of the Bible and German rationalism,[150] the universal Fatherhood of God,[151] postmortal salvation,[152] conditional immortality,[153] and eschatological universalism.[154] Certain books by Nonconformist authors evoked Spurgeon's criticism[155]: especially a quarter of a century earlier the Independent pastor James Baldwin Brown's (1820–1884) *The Divine Life in Man*,[156] and later Baptist Samuel Cox's (1826–1893) *Salvator Mundi*,[157]

---

and Alabaster; Isbister and Co., 1903) 418; Bacon, *Spurgeon: Heir of the Puritans*, 129; Carlile, *C. H. Spurgeon*, 244; Ernest A. Payne, *The Baptist Union: A Short History* (London: Carey Kingsgate, 1959) 130.

[142]Ray, *The Life of Charles Haddon Spurgeon*, 424.

[143]Ibid.; Bacon, *Spurgeon: Heir of the Puritans*, 131.

[144]Bacon, *Spurgeon: Heir of the Puritans*, 129.

[145]Shindler, *From the Usher's Desk to the Tabernacle Pulpit*, 273; Carlile, *C. H. Spurgeon*, 244; Payne, *The Baptist Union*, 130; Bacon, *Spurgeon: Heir of the Puritans*, 129.

[146]Bacon, *Spurgeon: Heir of the Puritans*, 131.

[147]Ray, *The Life of Charles Haddon Spurgeon*, 424.

[148]Bacon, *Spurgeon: Heir of the Puritans*, 129, 131; Payne, *The Baptist Union*, 130.

[149]Bacon, *Spurgeon: Heir of the Puritans*, 130; Drummond, *Spurgeon: Prince of Preachers*, 616, 662-63.

[150]Bacon, *Spurgeon: Heir of the Puritans*, 129.

[151]Shindler, *From the Usher's Desk to the Tabernacle Pulpit*, 273.

[152]Ibid.; Ray, *The Life of Charles Haddon Spurgeon*, 424.

[153]Shindler, *From the Usher's Desk to the Tabernacle Pulpit*, 273.

[154]Carlile, *C. H. Spurgeon*, 244.

[155]Drummond, *Spurgeon: Prince of Preachers*, 663-65.

[156](2nd ed.: London: Ward and Co., 1860). The twenty-first century reader of these fourteen textual sermons will likely find it difficult to discern why Spurgeon found the book to be so objectionable. The clue is likely Brown's endorsement of the vicarious confession theory of J. McLeod Campbell in place of penal substitution (109-11).

[157]Subtitle: *or, Is Christ the Saviour of All Men?*, 13th ed. (London: Kegan Paul, Trench, and Co., 1889; orig., 1877). Cox, 38-39, 83, asserted that neither the word "hell" nor the word "damnation" is found in the Bible and that "Gehenna" is only a figure of speech.

which advocated eschatological universalism. Spurgeon is thought to have deplored also the contemporary departure from his own type of Calvinism.[158]

John Clifford was not so much Spurgeon's personal antagonist in the Down Grade Controversy; rather he embodied and later more fully articulated many of the viewpoints that alarmed Spurgeon.[159] A native of Derbyshire, the oldest of seven siblings, he had worked as boy twelve to fourteen hours per day in a cotton mill. Having professed Christ and been baptized in a General Baptist church at fourteen, Clifford was educated at Midland Baptist College, Leicester, and in 1858 began his only pastorate, that of Praed Street General Baptist Church, London, later extended to Westbourne Park, where he remained until 1915.

Bachelor of Arts, Bachelor of Science, Master of Arts, and Bachelor of Laws degrees he earned from the University of London, and his church with its social ministry was "probably the first 'institutional' church in London."[160] Clifford repeatedly fought against Anglican or establishment privilege in and domination of primary and secondary education.[161] He helped to lead General Baptists into the Baptist Union in 1891, having already served as its president.[162] He was president of the National Council of Evangelical Free Churches[163] and the first president (1905–1911) of the Baptist World Alliance.[164] Open to Darwinian evolution and German higher

---

[158]Bacon, *Spurgeon: Heir of the Puritans*, 129; Drummond, *Spurgeon: Prince of Preachers*, 666.

[159]Bush and Nettles, *Baptists and the Bible*, 253.

[160]James Marchant, *Dr. John Clifford, C. H.: Life, Letters, and Reminiscences* (London: Cassell and Co., 1924) 1-52, esp. 42; Charles T. Bateman, *John Clifford; M.A., B.Sc., LL.B, D.D., O.M.: Free Church Leader and Preacher* (London: National Council of the Evangelical Free Churches, 1904) 2-123, esp. 56; Denis Crane, *John Clifford: God's Soldier and the People's Tribune* (London: Edwin Dalton, 1908) 1-111; G. W. Byrt, *John Clifford: A Fighting Free Churchman* (London: Kingsgate, 1947) 11-94.

[161]Marchant, *Dr. John Clifford*, 114-54.

[162]Briggs, *The English Baptists of the Nineteenth Century*, 138-57, 107.

[163]Bateman, *John Clifford*, 220-41; Crane, *John Clifford*, 155-76; Briggs, *The English Baptists of the Nineteenth Century*, 241-44; McBeth, *The Baptist Heritage*, 295.

[164]F. Townley Lord, *Baptist World Fellowship: A Short History of the Baptist World Alliance* (Nashville: Broadman, 1955) 13, 15-42; John H. Y. Briggs, "From 1905 to the End of the First World War," in *Baptists Together in Christ, 1905–*

criticism of the Bible,[165] he espoused the "new" theology in contrast to Spurgeon's older Calvinism.[166]

According to Clifford, "we must study the contents of the Bible in the same way as we do those of any book," revelation has by evolution reached its summit in the teaching of Jesus, and biblical inspiration is "of *men*," not of their writings, so that the Bible "is the *report* of the experiences of God-inspired souls." "It is not God's way to give us an absolutely inerrant Bible," and errors in the Bible do not jeopardize "the saving ideas and central facts of the Christian revelation." Inerrancy cannot be supported by appealing to the autographs of the biblical books as inerrant, by appealing to the teaching of Jesus (Matt. 5:17-18; John 10:35) and of the apostles, or by asserting that the doctrine of inerrancy is "an indispensable postulate" of other Christian doctrines. Authority, therefore, rests in "the Christ Idea," or God's becoming incarnate to redeem, or in his "dwelling and ruling in the conscience and reason of the Christian man by and through the Scrip-

---

2005: A Hundred-Year History of the Baptist World Alliance, ed. Richard V. Pierard (Falls Church VA: Baptist World Alliance, 2005) 20-46.

[165]Brackney, *The Baptists*, 145.

[166]Clifford, *The Christian Certainties: Discourses and Addresses in Exposition and Defence of the Christian Faith* (London: Isbister and Co., 1894) 269-311. Clifford had been preceded by John Howard Hinton (1791–1873), who was secretary of the Baptist Union (1841–1863) and cosecretary of the Baptist Missionary Society (1815–1818). He advocated a two-level view of biblical inspiration (by "divine revelation" and by "the influence of Divine wisdom"), "On the divine Inspiration of the Scriptures" (1850), in *The Theological Works of the Rev. John Howard Hinton, M.A.,* 7 vols. (London: Houlston and Wright, 1864-65) 3:329-86, esp. 355; embraced a "moderate Calvinism," that stood between "Hyper-Calvinism" and "Arminianism," in "Moderate Calvinism Reexamined," in ibid., 6:329-78; rejected original sin as issuing in guilt and articulated the "dispensation of mercy," controverting James Haldane, "Theology, or An Attempt towards a Consistent View of the Whole Counsel of God," in ibid., 1:50-57, and "A Rejoinder to Mr. Haldane," in ibid., 1:129-38; expounded the necessary work of the Holy Spirit in conversion, "The Work of the Holy Spirit in Conversion," in ibid., 2:3-187; and contributed to the literature on evangelism, "Individual Effort for the Conversion of Sinners Enforced" and "The Active Christian, or Individual Effort for the Conversion of Sinners Directed," in ibid., 4:135-475. In his later years Hinton took a more "conservative stance." Ian Sellers, "John Howard Hinton, Theologian," *Baptist Quarterly* 33 (July 1989): 119-32, esp. 128-29; Brackney, *A Genetic History of Baptist Thought*, 161-63.

tures." The inspiration of persons today is possible;[167] for Jesus' method was to appeal "to the authority that speaks within the soul" or to "trust in the voice of the Spirit."[168]

Clifford's doctrine of God centered in the Fatherhood of God, interpreted as universal rather than as particular.[169] His Christology gave more attention to the teaching of Jesus than to his death and resurrection, and he would "keep severely apart, the Christ of history, and the Christ of faith, and only join them when they are radically and undeniably one."[170] Jesus' suffering stretched from being born in a manger to the cross. Sinless in and made perfect through suffering, Jesus interpreted suffering's true meaning. For Clifford, however, there was no element of penal substitution.[171]

Jesus has secured "an epoch-making ascent in the value of man as man."[172] For Clifford, the universal Fatherhood of God requires or leads to the universal brotherhood of human beings, and the church is "the home of brotherhood."[173] John H. Y. Briggs has indicted Clifford for his "diminished," "undogmatic, experience-based [and] world-encountering ecclesiology." He offers in support Clifford's subordination of the churches to the kingdom of God, practice of open membership, highly individualized view of baptism, and holding the ordinances as "mere symbols."[174]

The Down Grade Controversy became identifiable when in March, April, and June 1887 three unsigned articles—later known to have been written by Robert Shindler—appeared in *The Sword and the Trowel*. He warned that "apostasy from evangelical truth would lead to rationalism and

---

[167]*The Inspiration and Authority of the Bible*, 3rd ed. (London: James Clarke and Co., 1899; orig., 1892) 3, 15-16, 18, 49, 54, 59-78, 84, 137, 225-48. See Willis B. Glover, Jr., *Evangelical Nonconformists and Higher Criticism in the Nineteenth Century* (London: Independent, 1954) 44-45.

[168]*The Ultimate Problems of Christianity* (London: Kingsgate, James Clarke and Co., 1906), 38. See also Clifford, *The Secret of Jesus* (Manchester: James Robinson, 1908) 14, and Bush and Nettles, *Baptists and the Bible*, 253-59.

[169]*The Ultimate Problems of Christianity*, 228-65.

[170]Ibid., 58.

[171]*The Gospel of Gladness and Its Meaning for Us* (Edinburgh: T.&T. Clark, 1912) 158-71.

[172]*The Ultimate Problems of Christianity*, 283.

[173]*The Gospel of World Brotherhood according to Jesus* (London: Hodder & Stoughton, 1920) 21-46, 61-89.

[174]*The English Baptists of the Nineteenth Century*, 22, 26, 23, 53, 68, 101-102, 176.

disaster." Presbyterians, Independents, and General Baptists, he alleged, had already started "'on the downgrade,'" and Particular Baptists were about to follow. He warned of Arminianism, Baxterism, Antinomianism, Arianism, and Socinianism, and "virtually equated Calvinism with evangelical theology."[175] In August, September, and October in the same periodical three articles by Spurgeon appeared. Deploring that "'these enemies of our faith expect us to call them brethren and maintain a confederacy with them,'" Spurgeon warned that doctrinal decline would have adverse effects upon spirituality[176] and became more critical as to Baptist theological colleges and Baptist pastors without calling names.[177] Samuel Harris Booth, general secretary of the Baptist Union, had exchanged correspondence with Spurgeon concerning alarming trends but with Booth's insistence on the confidentiality of the correspondence, which Spurgeon honored.[178] On 28 October by means of a letter to Booth, Spurgeon withdrew from the Baptist Union, and the Metropolitan Tabernacle did likewise the following January.[179] On 13 December the Council of the Baptist Union adopted a declaration that included six doctrinal articles and authorized a group to confer with Spurgeon.[180] Spurgeon declined to withdraw his resignation and called for a more explicit doctrinal statement such as that of the Evangelical Alliance in his 13 January 1888 meeting with Booth, Clifford, and James Culross.[181] On 18 January the council adopted resolutions containing what has been described as a "censure" of Spurgeon. In his response in *The Sword and the Trowel*, Spurgeon asserted that he could not press specific charges since the constitution of the Baptist Union contained "'no doctrinal basis except the belief that the immersion of believers is the only Christian baptism.'"[182] On 23 April, after Spurgeon and thirty others had proposed an

---

[175] Drummond, *Spurgeon: Prince of Preachers*, 675-79.

[176] Ibid., quoting Spurgeon, "Another Word concerning the Down Grade," *The Sword and the Trowel* 23 (August 1887): 397, 398.

[177] Ibid., 680-85.

[178] Carlile, *C. H. Spurgeon*, 244-45, 252; Bacon, *Spurgeon: Heir of the Puritans*, 130-32; Underwood, *A History of the English Baptists*, 230; Drummond, *Spurgeon: Prince of Preachers*, 697, 699.

[179] Drummond, *Spurgeon: Prince of Preachers*, 686-88.

[180] Ibid., 695-98.

[181] Ibid., 698-99.

[182] Fullerton, *C. H. Spurgeon*, 311; Drummond, *Spurgeon: Prince of Preachers*, 700-703.

eleven-article "doctrines of grace" statement, the Baptist Union assembly approved the doctrinal articles which had been recommended by the Council, with a preamble on believer's baptism and the Lord's Supper, and which Spurgeon found to be less than adequate.[183] They were as follows:

1. The Divine Inspiration and Authority of the Holy Scripture as the supreme and sufficient rule of our faith and practice; and the right and duty of individual judgment in the interpretation of it.
2. The fallen and sinful state of man.
3. The Deity, the Incarnation, the Resurrection of the Lord Jesus Christ, and His Sacrificial and Mediatorial Work.
4. Justification by faith—a faith that works by love and produces holiness.
5. The work of the Holy Spirit in the conversion of sinners, and in the sanctification of all who believe.
6. The Resurrection; the Judgment at the Last Day, according to the words of our Lord in Matthew xxv.46.[184]

"Spurgeon also withdrew from the London Baptist Association which he had helped to found in 1865" and joined the Surrey and Middlesex Baptist Association, which had withdrawn from the Baptist Union.[185]

Assessments of the significance of the Down Grade Controversy tend to fall in either of two directions: to regard its outcome as more positive or to regard it as more negative. The biographers of Clifford tend to be more positive, and the biographers of Spurgeon more negative. Charles T. Bateman thought that "the great debate . . . ended in a truce."[186] For G. W. Byrt, this was "a painful, unfortunate, and unsatisfying controversy" but it

---

[183]Drummond, *Spurgeon: Prince of Preachers*, 704-707. Spurgeon might have welcomed articles on biblical inerrancy, the virginal conception of Jesus, his substitutionary atonement, the Trinity, and the second coming. Bacon, *Spurgeon: Heir of the Puritans*, 139.

[184]Carlile, *C. H. Spurgeon*, 254-55, quoting the Baptist Union Council Minutes, February 1888. In adopting these articles the Council appended to article 6 a footnote stating that some in the Union, "while . . . rejecting the dogmas of Purgatory and Universalism, have not held the common interpretation of these words of our Lord." (Carlile, 255). This seems to refer to conditional immortality or annihilationism.

[185]Drummond, *Spurgeon: Prince of Preachers*, 705, 708-11.

[186]*John Clifford*, 149.

was "settled in the best way and to the greatest degree that such a controversy could be settled."[187] Biographers of Clifford rested their assessment on Clifford's anticreedalism[188] and the good personal relations between Spurgeon and Clifford.[189] A. C. Underwood reported negatively that Spurgeon found security "in an inerrant Bible" and was blinded to the "need of theological restatement" and positively that Clifford "did not confuse the permanent element in Christianity, with its theological expression." He concluded that "the Council of the Union handled the matter in such a way that freedom of thought was preserved, and room was kept for the more progressive, as well as the more conservative, elements in the denomination."[190]

On the contrary, Charles Ray agreed with Spurgeon that standing for orthodoxy is a higher priority than denominational unity and concluded that the censure by the Baptist Union was premature.[191] George C. Lorimer called Spurgeon a "Modern Elijah" in contrast to those who "pose as theological Columbuses, finding a new way across the old ocean of divine truth."[192] According to W. Y. Fullerton, withdrawal was the only "honourable course" for Spurgeon, and "a little prescience on the part of the Union" and another general secretary such as John Howard Shakespeare (1857–1928) could have brought different results.[193] For J. C. Carlile, Spurgeon was "fully justified" in protesting contemporary teachings and "being indignant over the treatment he received" from Union leaders.[194] Lewis A. Drummond declared that Spurgeon took his stand, not for eschatological or ecclesiological doctrines or even for purely Calvinist doctrines, but for "fundamentals" or "bulwarks" of the Christian faith. He found three positive contributions of the controversy: it "helped clear up" "hazy theology"; it "interested lay people in theology"; and it "helped Spurgeon and the Baptist Union to understand one another." The actions of the Union,

---

[187]*John Clifford*, 106, 110.

[188]Bateman, *John Clifford*, 148-49; Crane, *John Clifford*, 136-37.

[189]Bateman, *John Clifford*, 149; Crane, *John Clifford*, 139; Marchant, *Dr. John Clifford*, 166.

[190]*A History of the English Baptists*, 231, 232, 230.

[191]*The Life of Charles Haddon Spurgeon*, 420, 422, 426.

[192]*Charles Haddon Spurgeon: The Puritan Preacher in the Nineteenth Century* (Boston: James H. Earle, 1892) 79, 84.

[193]*C. H. Spurgeon*, 314.

[194]*C. H. Spurgeon*, 256.

for Drummond, however, were wrong, for "history has shown Spurgeon to have taken basically the right course." The controversy thus demonstrated that "at times the majority opinion is not . . . right," that "leaders can make tragic mistakes," and that, "when truth is defeated, error will continue to grow with its deadening effect."[195] Drummond alluded to the controversy involving Michael Taylor and British Baptists in the 1970s,[196] and Thomas Jerrell Sutton compared the Down Grade Controversy with the controversy over biblical inerrancy in the Southern Baptist Convention during the early 1980s.[197]

The Changing Theological Scene

The latter nineteenth century presented to Protestants both in Great Britain and in North America, including Baptists, unprecedented intellectual and sociocultural challenges that would affect their theology, even the theology that resisted or rejected these challenges. First, Charles Darwin introduced a concept of biological evolution that impacted not only the Christian doctrines of creation and of the human but also related disciplines.[198] Second, historical criticism began to be applied to an unprecedented degree to the study of the Bible so that, while bringing significant assistance to biblical interpretation, it altered for some the doctrine of the Bible itself.[199] Third, the Industrial Revolution, which increased the role of manufacturing, caused the population growth of cities, increased conflict and economic

---

[195]*Spurgeon: Prince of Preachers*, 711-14.

[196]Ibid., 714-15. See below, 570-74.

[197]"A Comparison between the Down Grade Controversy and Tensions over Biblical Inerrancy in the Southern Baptist Convention" (Ph.D. diss., Southwestern Baptist Theological Seminary, 1982).

[198]John C. Greene, *The Death of Adam: Evolution and Its Impact on Western Thought* (Ames: Iowa State University Press, 1959) 249-339, 373-77; Bert James Loewenberg, *Darwinism Comes to America, 1859–1900*, Facet Books, Historical Series no. 13 (Philadelphia: Fortress, 1969); Philip Appleman, ed., *Darwin: A Norton Critical Edition* (New York: W. W. Norton and Co., 1970) esp. 383-457; James R. Moore, *The Post-Darwinian Controversies: A Study of the Protestant Struggle to Come to Terms with Darwin in Great Britain and America, 1870–1900* (Cambridge UK: Cambridge University Press, 1979); Michael Ruse, *The Darwinian Revolution: Science Red in Tooth and Claw*, 2nd ed. (Chicago: University of Chicago Press, 1999; orig., 1979) esp. 234-73; idem, *Darwin and Design: Does Evolution Have a Purpose?* (Cambridge MA: Harvard University Press, 2003).

[199]Glover, *Evangelical Nonconformists and Higher Criticism*.

differences between labor and management under *laissez-faire* capitalism, and affected not only Christian social ethics but also theology.[200] Fourth, in philosophy, especially in the United States, the older Scottish commonsense realism and the German and British idealism yielded to the newer American philosophies of evolution, personalism, and pragmatism.[201]

For Protestants of the Reformed variety in the United States this meant the demise of the older New England Calvinistic theology[202] and the ascendancy for at least the first third of the twentieth century of the newer theological liberalism.[203] For Baptists on both sides of the Atlantic Ocean it meant diverse responses to the challenges, and in the United States Baptists in the North would be more deeply affected during the nineteenth century and the early twentieth by these challenges than Baptists in the South.

Northern and Canadian Baptist Conservative Theologians:
Alvah Hovey (1820–1903),
George Dana Boardman Pepper (1833–1913),
Calvin Goodspeed (1842–1912),
and Adoniram Judson Gordon (1836–1895)

Some theologians in the American North responded to the new challenges to Christian theology by minimal adaptation and maximum conservation of their theological heritage. Foremost among these was Alvah Hovey, who exercised leadership among Baptists in New England. Educated at Dartmouth College and Newton Theological Institution, he taught Hebrew and church history at Newton (1849–1853) prior to his longterm professorship of theology (1855–1903) and served as Newton's president from 1868 to

---

[200]Josiah Strong, *The Challenge of the City* (New York: Young People's Missionary Movement of the United States and Canada, 1908); Henry Farnham May, *Protestant Churches and Industrial America* (New York: Octagon Books, 1963; orig., Harper & Bros., 1949).

[201]Frederick Mayer, *A History of Modern Philosophy* (New York: American Book Co., 1951) 284-85, 350-77, 445-62, 476-82, 496-98, 522-64.

[202]Frank Hugh Foster, *A Genetic History of the New England Theology* (Chicago: University of Chicago Press, 1907; New York, London: Garland Publishing, Inc., 1987) esp. 543-53.

[203]Kenneth Cauthen, *The Impact of American Religious Liberalism* (New York: Harper & Row, 1962) esp. 3-5.

1898.[204] Hovey's books included a major volume on theology and ethics[205] and a collection of essays on the same theme,[206] three monographs on eschatology,[207] one on the Bible[208] and one on Christology,[209] a commentary on the Gospel of John,[210] and biographies of two Baptist leaders.[211]

Hovey built his doctrine of the Bible on the foundation of the historical reliability of the New Testament books and went on to assert that the claims of Jesus as to his knowledge and teaching and the very nature of his teachings, augmented by fulfilled prophecies and miracles, establish his infallibility as a teacher. Moreover, Jesus promised to the apostles and other authors of New Testament books the inspiration of the Holy Spirit, and both Jesus and the apostles regarded the Old Testament books as the inspired word of God. Hence "sacred writers were moved and assisted by the Holy Spirit to put on record all which the Bible, apart from errors in the text, now contains." Hovey espoused the dynamical theory of inspiration in the sense of empowerment "to apprehend and teach religious truth without error" and

---

[204] George Rice Hovey, *Alvah Hovey: Life and Letters* (Philadelphia: Judson, 1928); Brackney, *The Baptists*, 194-95.

[205] *Manual of Systematic Theology and Christian Ethics* (Philadelphia: American Baptist Publication Society, 1877); some revision together with ecclesiology added and ethics deleted: *Manual of Christian Theology* (Boston: Silver, Burdett, and Co., 1900).

[206] *Studies in Ethics and Religion; or, Discourses, Essays, and Reviews pertaining to Theism, Inspiration, Christian Ethics, and Education for the Ministry* (Boston: Silver, Burdett, and Co., 1892).

[207] *The State of the Impenitent Dead* (Boston: Gould and Lincoln, 1859); *State of Men after Death* (Philadelphia: American Baptist Publication Society, 1874); *Biblical Eschatology* (Philadelphia: American Baptist Publication Society, 1888).

[208] *The Bible* (Philadelphia: American Baptist Publication Society, 1860).

[209] *God with Us; or, the Person and Work of Christ* . . . (Boston: Gould and Lincoln, 1872).

[210] *Commentary on the Gospel of John*, An American Commentary on the New Testament (Philadelphia: American Baptist Publication Society, 1885). Hovey was also general editor of this important commentary series, contributing esp. a 39-page "General Introduction to the New Testament" (in the first volume of the series, *Commentary on the Gospel of Matthew*, by John A. Broadus [1886] iii-xliii).

[211] *A Memoir of the Life and Times of the Rev. Isaac Backus, A.M.* (Boston: Gould and Lincoln, 1859; repr.: Harrisonburg VA: Gano Books, 1991); *Barnas Sears, a Christian Educator; His Making and Work* (Boston: Silvert, Burdett, and Co., 1902).

concluded that divine inspiration made the prophets and the apostles to be "infallible teachers of truth."[212] In hermeneutics Hovey advised restraint in the use of typology[213] and asserted that the New Testament is of great help in interpreting the Old Testament but not in respect to textual criticism or "higher criticism."[214]

The person and work of Christ were reckoned by Hovey to be doctrines which belong under soteriology. He treated the biblical witness to the deity in detail and that pertaining to Jesus' humanity quite briefly. Affirming the unity of Christ's person, Hovey found the Chalcedonian statement to represent "the facts truly" but to lack any explanation of the humiliation of the Logos. Neither Wolfgang Friedrich Gess's (1819–1891) kenotic reduction of the Logos to a human soul nor Gottfried Thomasius's (1802–1875) depotentiation of the Logos nor Isaak August Dorner's (1809–1884) gradual incarnation would suffice. Instead, for Hovey, it was a "theanthropic consciousness and experience" in which Jesus' human nature "was purified from all moral evil, or bias to moral evil, . . . at the moment of its union with the divine."[215]

Hovey levied some criticism against the various historic theories of the imputation of sin,[216] and while clearly teaching the universality of sin and human depravity, did not affirm that all humans are guilty of Adam's sin but was emphatic as to the punishment of sin.[217] Hence the groundwork was laid for Christ's work as mediator. Hovey rejected the view of those who "deny that the death of Christ has anything to do with God's readiness to save sinners" and thus reject a "vicarious," or substitutionary, atonement.[218] Particularly did Hovey refute Horace Bushnell's theory of "vicarious sacri-

---

[212]*Manual of Systematic Theology and Christian Ethics*, 43-87; *Manual of Christian Theology*, 42-106, esp. 80. See also *Studies in Ethics and Religion*, 90-217.

[213]*The Bible*, 43-47.

[214]*Studies in Ethics and Religion*, 218-31.

[215]*Manual of Systematic Theology and Christian Ethics*, 172-207; *Manual of Christian Theology*, 205-47; *God with Us; or, the Person and Work of Christ . . .* (Boston: Gould and Lincoln, 1872), 17-88.

[216]The Pelagian, Arminian, Edwardean, Placean, Augustinian, and Calvinist theories.

[217]*Manual of Systematic Theology and Christian Ethics*, 133-70; *Manual of Christian Theology*, 160-85.

[218]*Manual of Systematic Theology and Christian Ethics*, 207.

fice," for making love to be "the sum total of duty" or completely identifying love and righteousness, for teaching that right is "self-existent" apart from God, for making punishment remedial but not punitive, and for improperly divesting the term "vicarious" of its inherent meaning of substitution.[219]

In 1877 Hovey made the concept of propitiation to be the conceptual center of the atonement,[220] whereas in 1900 self-sacrifice was the principal concept with propitiation, ransom, and intercession as subtopics.[221] The atonement "was intended to secure the salvation of all the elect" and "to be a provision for the salvation of every man who would repent."[222] As to the application of Christ's atonement, which he termed "redemption," Hovey explicated regeneration, justification, and sanctification.[223]

Hovey's defense of congregational polity, the baptismal mode of immersion, baptism as symbolic, believer's baptism, and close communion followed after his Baptist predecessors, and he favored the view that the baptism by John the Baptist constituted the beginning of Christian baptism.[224]

The Newton theologian gave detailed attention to eschatology but without centering it in a millennial reign. Death as punishment for sin is primarily "inflicted upon the soul" and hence is spiritual death, or "the destruction of [the sinner's] well-being rather than of simple existence."[225] But death is also "the death of the body, considered as a living organism," the "termination of animal life," and "a separation of the soul from the body."[226] From Luke 16:19-31; 2 Cor. 5:6-8; and Phil. 1:21-24[227] Hovey contended for an intermediate state on the basis that "the resurrection of the body does not ordinarily take place at the moment of death," a position some have sought to support from Luke 20:27-40 and 2 Cor. 5:1-8. Paradise is the abode of believers during the intermediate state, and Hades the abode of unbelievers during the intermediate state, and, for Hovey, these separate

---

[219]*God with Us*, 181-221, esp. 188, 200, 203, 216; 223-27.
[220]*Manual of Systematic Theology and Christian Ethics*, 207-30.
[221]*Manual of Systematic Theology*, 252-79.
[222]*God with Us*, 166-77, esp. 169, 172.
[223]*Manual of Systematic Theology and Christian Ethics*, 242-99.
[224]Ibid., 300-44; *Manual of Systematic Theology*, 345-95.
[225]*The State of the Impenitent Dead*, 30-52, esp. 31, 32.
[226]*Biblical Eschatology*, 13-22.
[227]*The State of the Impenitent Dead*, 53-73.

destinies are fixed.[228] The intermediate state will be bodiless and conscious; believers will experience "happiness" and unbelievers "misery."[229] Building on the biblical testimony for eschatological resurrection,[230] Hovey held to one general resurrection, including both righteous and wicked, at the end of "the present order of things" in bodies that differ from yet have identity with the premortal bodies.[231] Likewise there will be one universal last judgment of all human beings conducted by Christ.[232] Heaven, sans purgatory, will afford endless, perfect, and increased blessedness "proportioned to . . . fidelity on earth."[233] On the contrary, hell will afford eternal conscious misery with degrees of punishment.[234] Hovey refuted in detail the claims of annihilationists, who misinterpret "death" and "destruction" as "the extinction of conscious being" and misuse objections from the omnipotence, righteousness, and benevolence of God.[235] Hovey rejected premillennialism, holding that both resurrections of Rev. 20:4-6 are "symbolical," but his own postmillennialism was quite vague and unspecific.[236]

Hovey not only had great influence upon the Baptist denomination, especially in New England, but also upon other Baptist theologians, most notably George Dana Boardman Pepper. A graduate of Amherst College and Newton Theological Institution, he, after a five-year pastorate in Waterville, Maine, became in 1865 a professor in the newly established Crozer Theological Seminary, first in church history and then (1868–1882) in systematic theology.[237] Pepper readily acknowledged his debt to Hovey, his teacher.

---

[228]*State of Men after Death*, 10-42, 49-79, esp. 11; *Manual of Systematic Theology*, 420-22, 444-47.

[229]*Manual of Systematic Theology and Christian Ethics*, 345-49; *Biblical Eschatology*, 79-95.

[230]*Biblical Eschatology*, 23-31.

[231]Ibid., 47-65; *Manual of Systematic Theology and Christian Ethics*, 351-54.

[232]*Manual of Systematic Theology and Christian Ethics*, 354-58; *Biblical Eschatology*, 145-55; *Manual of Christian Theology*, 438-40, 448-49.

[233]*Manual of Systematic Theology and Christian Ethics*, 362-64; *Biblical Eschatology*, 156-60; *Manual of Christian Theology*, 440-42.

[234]*Manual of Systematic Theology and Christian Ethics*, 358-62; *Biblical Eschatology*, 161-67.

[235]*The State of the Impenitent Dead*, 93-123, 142-60.

[236]*Manual of Systematic Theology and Christian Ethics*, 349-51; *Biblical Eschatology*, 65-78, esp. 68; *Manual of Christian Theology*, 432-38.

[237]Brackney, *A Genetic History of Baptist Thought*, 370.

> I think . . . that the best part of myself is not myself, but Doctor Hovey. My theology, my philanthropy, my whole life is largely he. . . .[238]

Pepper's published systematic theology, like Hovey's, did begin with the existence of God and then proceeded with an extended treatment of "bibliology," in which he declared that "the Bible, as originally written, had full authority as the Word of God," that its teaching is "infallible," and that biblical inspiration means that "God so influenced and directed" the biblical writers "as to constitute himself properly the Author of those Scriptures as originally penned."[239] But Pepper differed from Hovey in setting forth a doctrine of divine decrees, in clearly espousing the federal theory of the imputation of Adamic sin, in major use of the threefold office of Christ, and in omitting ecclesiology from his systematic theology.[240]

Contemporaneous with Hovey and Pepper was a conservative Canadian theologian, Calvin Goodspeed. A native of New Brunswick and a graduate of the New Brunswick Baptist Seminary and the University of New Brunswick, he had subsequent periods of study at Regent's Park College, London, Newton Theological Institution, and the University of Leipzig. After a brief pastorate and teaching at Woodstock College in Ontario, a pastorate in Nova Scotia, and an editorship in New Brunswick, he became professor of systematic theology and apologetics (1891–1905) in McMaster University in Toronto. Then he assumed a similar position at the newly opened Baylor Theological Seminary (1905–1908) in Waco, Texas, soon to become Southwestern Baptist Theological Seminary (1908–1910) under the presidency of B. H. Carroll.[241] Goodspeed, first in an essay[242] and later

---

[238]Quoted by George R. Hovey, *Alvah Hovey*, 192.

[239]*Outlines of Systematic Theology* (Philadelphia: James B. Rodgers Co., 1873) 1-53, esp. 24, 45-46.

[240]Ibid., 78-81, 108-13, 137-52, 185. Compare Hovey, *Manual of Systematic Theology and Christian Ethics*, 96-99, 144-51, 172-207, 300-44; *Manual of Christian Theology*, 116-20, 165-76, 205-47, 345-98.

[241]Allison A. Trites, "A Forgotten Founder: A Biographical Sketch of Professor Calvin Goodspeed," *Southwestern Journal of Theology* 30 (Summer 1988): 20-24; repr. as "A Forgotten Scholar: Professor Calvin Goodspeed," in *An Abiding Conviction: Maritime Baptists and Their World*, ed. Robert S. Wilson (Hantsport NS: Lancelot, 1988) 199-204; idem, "Calvin Goodspeed: An Assessment of His Theological Contribution," in *Costly Vision: The Baptist Pilgrimage in Canada*, ed. Jarold K. Zeman (Burlington ON: Welch Publishing Co., 1988) 38; Brackney, *A Genetic History of Baptist Thought*, 469; Robert A. Baker, *Tell the Generations*

in an introduction to a commentary on Genesis,[243] offered major criticism of the dominant historical-critical approaches to the Pentateuch/Hexateuch, defended the substitutionary view of the atonement,[244] posited a progressive doctrine of sanctification,[245] expounded the doctrine of perseverance,[246] and defended the moral imperative of Sabbath observance while refuting the seventh-day doctrine.[247] The Canadian theologian strongly, though irenically, defended the Baptist distinctives: believer's baptism, baptism by the mode of immersion, regenerate church membership, and religious liberty and separation of church and state, against the "evil" consequences of infant baptism.[248] His most extensive monograph, *Messiah's Second Advent* (1900)[249] was a refutation of premillennialism, both in its historic expression and according to what would become known as dispensationalism, and a defense of postmillennialism. Goodspeed was emphatic about no "probation" after death, not using "imminent" in reference to the second coming, one general resurrection, and one eschatological judgment, but not very specific as to the nature of the millennium.

Another conservative voice among Northern Baptists was the pastor-theologian, Adoniram Judson Gordon (1836–1895). A native of New Hampton, New Hampshire, with Calvinistic Baptist parentage, he was graduated from Brown University (1860) and Newton Theological Institu-

---

Following: A History of Southwestern Baptist Theological Seminary, 1908–1983 (Nashville: Broadman, 1983) 123, 144-45.

[242]*Some Unresolved Problems of the Higher Criticism* (Toronto: Baptist Book Room, 1894).

[243]Intro. to Goodspeed and D. M. Welton, *The Book of Genesis*, An American Commentary on the Old Testament (Philadelphia: American Baptist Publication Society, 1909) ix-xxxvii.

[244]*Vicarious Atonement* (Waco TX: Baylor University Press, n.d.).

[245]"Our Articles of Faith: Article 10: Sanctification," *Southwestern Journal of Theology* o.s. 7 (July 1923): 55-63.

[246]"Our Articles of Faith: Article 11: The Perseverance of the Saints," *Southwestern Journal of Theology* o.s. 7 (October 1923): 28-36.

[247]*The Christian Sabbath* (Saint John NB: Paterson and Co., 1895).

[248]*The Peculiar Principles of the Baptists* (Toronto: Dudley and Burns, 1878); *Baptism versus Rantism: A Reply to the Misstatements and Fallacies of Rev. W. A. McKay* (Woodstock ON: Times Book and Job Printing Office, 1880); *Baptism: An Argument and a Reply* (Saint John NB: Daily Telegraph, 1882).

[249](Toronto: William Briggs, 1900) esp. 11-43, 49-58, 139-200, 253-64. See also *Messiah's Second Advent: Reply to Reviewer* (Toronto: William Briggs, 1902).

tion (1863) and then held two pastorates, first in the Boston suburb of Jamaica Plain (1863–1869) and then of the Clarendon Street Church in Boston (1869–1895). He was a longtime member and sometime chairman (1888–1895) of the executive committee of the American Baptist Missionary Union. A loyal Baptist, Gordon embraced some views that were not prevalent among the Baptists.[250]

Early Gordon sought the vitalization of worship by magnifying congregational participation through responsive readings, congregational singing of gospel songs as well as hymns, and monetary giving.[251] Embracing a moderate or evangelical Calvinism,[252] he preached on union with Christ,[253] and cooperating with Dwight L. Moody,[254] he advocated an empowerment of the Holy Spirit for service, which was "logically if not always chronologically separate from regeneration."[255] Although Gordon "used terms—enduement, filling, sealing, baptism of the Holy Spirit—interchangeably,"[256] he came to his mature position in *The Ministry of the Holy Spirit*: the baptism in the Spirit occurred once-for-all on the day of Pentecost, 1 Cor. 12:13 being a reference to water baptism, but the enduement of the Spirit is needed for appropriation and is described in three ways: sealing, filling, and anointing.[257] Furthermore, presupposing a noncessationist view of miracles, the Boston pastor, citing Matt. 8:17, Mark 16:17-18, and James 5:14-15, identified Christ as "the sickness-bearer as well as the sin-bearer of his people," thus basing healing on the atonement.[258] In a manner similar

---

[250]Ernest B. Gordon, *Adoniram Judson Gordon: A Biography* (New York: Fleming H. Revell; Philadelphia: American Baptist Publication Society, 1896); Scott M. Gibson, *A. J. Gordon: American Premillennialist* (Lanham MD: University Press of America, 2001); Brackney, *The Baptists*, 179-80.

[251]*Congregational Worship* (Boston: Young and Bartlett, 1874); Gibson, *A. J. Gordon*, 52-61.

[252]Gibson, *A. J. Gordon*, 78, 217-18, 224.

[253]*In Christ: The Believer's Union with His Lord* (London: Pickering and Inglis, n.d.; orig., Boston, 1872).

[254]Gibson, *A. J. Gordon*, 61-66, 85-87, 200-203.

[255]*The Twofold Life: or, Christ's Work for Us and Christ's Work in Us* (New York: Fleming H. Revell Co., 1883) esp. 183-212, iii.

[256]Gibson, *A. J. Gordon*, 69.

[257](Philadelphia: American Baptist Publication Society, 1894) 55-59, 65-96.

[258]*The Ministry of Healing: Miracles of Cure in All Ages* (New York: Fleming H. Revell Co., 1882) 1-38, esp. 16.

to contemporary American Holiness leaders,[259] Gordon stressed miraculous healing through faith on the basis of the atoning work of Christ.

That eschatology was very important for Gordon and that he was a premillennialist are undisputed; Scott Gibson has claimed that the second coming was "the doctrinal center of his ministry."[260] Rejecting the postmillennialism of his Newton professors and, before leaving Jamaica Plain, being introduced to the writings of the Plymouth Brethren, with their "futurist" hermeneutic for the book of Revelation within a dispensationalist framework, Gordon came to espouse and defend instead historic premillennialism with an "historical" hermeneutic for the New Testament Apocalypse.[261] Apprehending "the blessed hope," Gordon declared, provided "the strongest and most permanent impulse" of his ministry.[262] He founded and edited (1878-95) a premillennial magazine, *The Watchword*,[263] and gave final expression to his premillennialism in *Ecce Venit: Behold He Cometh*,[264] called "the last book published by a leading American historic premillennialist" at the end of the nineteenth century. Gordon's urgency toward watchfulness for the second coming was matched by his urgency toward world missions. The Holy Spirit "dictated and revealed the programme of missions," inaugurated the "great missionary eras" of Christian history, and motivates Bible translation and distribution in papal

---

[259]Notably Albert Benjamin Simpson (1843–1919).

[260]*A. J. Gordon*, 73, 34.

[261]Ibid., 20-21, 32-36, 73-78. Gordon was dispensationalist, however, in holding to a secret rapture of the saints. C. Allyn Russell, "Adoniram Judson Gordon: Nineteenth Century Fundamentalist," *American Baptist Quarterly* 4 (March 1985): 77, 78.

[262]*How Christ Came to Church: The Pastor's Dream; A Spiritual Autobiography* (Philadelphia: American Baptist Publication Society, 1895), 46; John Bruce Behney, "Conservatism and Liberalism in the Theology of Late Nineteenth Century American Protestantism: A Comparative Study of the Basic Doctrines of Typical Representatives" (Ph.D. diss., Yale University, 1941) esp. ii, iii, 6, 468, 470, systematized the theology of Gordon, contrasted with it those aspects of the theology of W. N. Clarke that addressed the same topics, and concluded that Gordon's doctrine of the second coming, not the Scriptures as a whole, was the foundation of Gordon's theology.

[263]Gibson, *A. J. Gordon*, 163-87, esp. 165, 167.

[264](New York: Fleming H. Revell Co., 1889). The fall of the church came with Emperor Constantine and the Council of Nicaea, 96-107, the Antichrist has been the papacy, 108-31, and the "mock millennium" is the "present evil age," 147-64.

lands[265] as well as pagan lands. The church, which began on the day of Pentecost, is not only the body of Christ but also "the body of the Holy Ghost," and its mission "is not to bring all the world to Christ" but "to bring Christ to all the world."[266] Gordon's urgency was seen in his strong advocacy of women as preachers, though not as ordained pastors, which pitted him against Hovey, his Newton professor.[267] He advocated and practiced open communion.[268] He rejected the "higher criticism" as a threat to evangelism, the Christian life, and Christology but did not mount a crusade against the critics.[269] Gordon's views of the work of the Spirit, faith-healing, millennial doctrine, and women preachers were likely not those of the majority of Northern Baptists during his lifetime, but Gordon continues to warrant study.[270]

Northern Baptist Mediating Theologians:
Ezekiel Gilman Robinson (1815–1894),
George Washington Northrup (1826–1900),
Elias Henry Johnson (1841–1906),
Nathan Eusebius Wood (1849–1937),
Augustus Hopkins Strong (1836–1921),
and Ebenezer Dodge (1819–1890)

Some Baptist theologians responded to the challenges of their era by adopting a mediating posture between the old and the new, which William H. Brackney has labeled a "Critical Orthodox" position.[271] Each tended to have his own way of choosing what was to be retained and what was to be appropriated. At the fountainhead of such mediating theology was the work of Ezekiel Gilman Robinson.

---

[265]B. H. Carroll, a postmillennialist, in *Papal Fields* (Waco TX: Baptist Standard, 1893), likewise contended for missions in "papal" lands.

[266]*The Holy Spirit in Missions* (New York: Fleming H. Revell Co., 1893) 8, 47, 159-98, 23, 215, 14. Clarke would write *A Study of Christian Missions* (New York; Scribner's, 1900). See also Dana L. Robert, "The Legacy of Adoniram Judson Gordon," *International Bulletin of Missionary Research* 11 (October 1987): 176-81.

[267]Gibson, *A. J. Gordon*, 105-14.

[268]Ibid., 38-39, 50-51.

[269]Bruce Shelley, "A. J. Gordon and Biblical Criticism," *Foundations* 4 (January-March 1971): 69-77.

[270]Gibson, *A. J. Gordon*, 224.

[271]*A Genetic History of Baptist Thought*, 318.

A native of Massachusetts and baptized at fourteen, Robinson was educated at Brown University and Newton Theological Institution. After brief pastorates in Norfolk, Virginia, Cambridge, Massachusetts, and Cincinnati, Ohio, and a brief professorship in the Western Theological Institute, Covington, Kentucky, he became in 1853 professor of theology in the newly founded Rochester (NY) Theological Seminary and in 1860 became the seminary's president. From 1872 to 1889 he served as president of Brown University and also taught philosophy and ethics. Thereafter he taught briefly at Crozer Theological Seminary and the University of Chicago.[272]

W. Stacey Boutwell has identified as major influences on Robinson's theology: the moral philosophy of Francis Wayland with its emphasis on moral law, conscience, and biblical revelation; familiarity with German biblical and theological scholarship of the mediating type[273] through Horatio Balch Hackett (1808–1875) and Barnas Sears (1802–1880), his teachers at Newton; and the epistemology of William Hamilton (1788–1856) of Scotland and Henry Longueville Mansel (1820–1871) of England, who combined Scottish Realism and Kantianism so that human knowledge is genuine but not direct and complete, for God is to be believed, not conceived.[274] Boutwell concluded that "Robinson's theology was shaped by the convergence of the Reformed tradition with the American Evangelical awakenings and the Enlightenment."[275]

In some respects Robinson's theology was traditional in the sense that it was quite similar to those Baptist and Protestant theologians who preceded him. He used the theistic arguments, especially the moral argument, and defended the personality of God against pantheism and positivism. He expounded the deity and personality of the Holy Spirit without reference to spiritual gifts and held to both an economic and an immanent Trinity. Robinson had a doctrine of divine decrees, held to providence as

---

[272]*Ezekiel Gilman Robinson: An Autobiography with a Supplement by H. L. Wayland and Critical Estimates*, ed. E. H. Johnson (New York: Silver, Burdett, and Co., 1896) 1-144; W. Stacey Boutwell, "The Moral Matrix of God and Man: The Shape and Shaping of Ezekiel Gilman Robinson's Theology" (Ph.D. diss., Southwestern Baptist Theological Seminary, 1998) 7-25; Brackney, *A Genetic History of Baptist Thought*, 270-71, 318-21, 350.

[273]Especially Friedrich August Gottreu Tholuck (1799–1877) and Johann August Wilhelm Neander (1789–1850).

[274]"The Moral Matrix of God and Man," 69-100.

[275]Ibid., 241.

sustenance of the created order and as governance, and defended miracles but not as proofs. Traducian as to the origin of souls, he defined the original human state as moral innocence, not moral perfection, and the *imago Dei*, essentially that humans are free and moral beings, was not lost by the fall, which did bring the loss of "real" freedom, not of "formal" freedom. Robinson tweaked the penal substitutionary view of the atonement, did not have a rigid *ordo salutis*, and was traditional as to basic eschatology.[276]

At times Robinson's theological stance seemed to be deliberately a mediating position. He affirmed the divine inspiration of the Scriptures, critiqued various theories of inspiration, and refused to embrace any theory as to its method. He espoused the Placean view of original sin as condemnable depravity rather than either the federal view of the Princeton theologians or the depravity without guilt view of the New School theologians. In Christology he combined Chalcedonian and kenotic views.[277]

At other times Robinson took steps toward the liberal theology which came to prevail in much of American Protestantism. Experience is an important factor for Christian theology, and the sources for theology included experience, conscience, and the created order. Robinson was open to evolution but not to spontaneous generation, and he defined sin as selfishness, not sensuousness or unbelief.[278]

Robinson's theology was, in A. H. Strong's words, "critical rather than constructive."[279] "He was neither an Augustinian, nor a Calvinist, nor an Arminian. . . . He was neither old school nor new school."[280] "Having re

---

[276]Robinson, *Christian Theology* (Rochester NY: E. R. Andrews, 1894) 46-58, 61-63, 229-52, 83-88, 95-109, 118-22, 132-35, 255-95, 297-342, 344-52; Boutwell, "The Moral Matrix of God and Man," 142-46, 148-50, 215-21, 158-61, 165-66, 171-75, 180-91, 222-38. According to H. L. Wayland, *E. G. Robinson, D.D., LL.D.* (Philadelphia: American Baptist Publication Society, 1895) 13, 14, Robinson stressed "actual atonement for sins, conscienceward and Godward" and wanted "facts," not a "theory." According to Brackney, *A Genetic History of Baptist Thought*, 323, Robinson's theology of atonement was affected by his reckoning holiness as the "fount" of all the moral attributes of God.

[277]Robinson, *Christian Theology*, 33-45, 147-64, 196-229; Boutwell, "The Moral Matrix of God and Man," 129-32, 195-200, 205-13.

[278]Robinson, *Christian Theology*, 355-67, 3-4, 14-15, 90-92, 137-45; Boutwell, "The Moral Matrix of God and Man," 119-26, 128-29, 163, 192-95.

[279]"Dr. Robinson as a Theologian," in *Ezekiel Gilman Robinson*, ed. Johnson, 164; repr. in Strong, *Miscellanies* (Philadelphia: Griffith and Rowland, 1912) 2:59.

[280]A. J. F. Behrends, "Dr. Robinson as a Teacher of Theology," in *Ezekiel*

jected biblicism, he was all the more bound to biblical affirmations."[281] He has been labeled a "'conservative liberal'" and a "'liberal conservative.'"[282] His great influence in shaping Rochester Theological Seminary has been clearly recognized,[283] but those who have written on the history of liberal Protestantism in the United States have not mentioned Robinson's name.[284]

Robinson's students reflected some of his mediating tendencies. George Washington Northrup, who, after teaching briefly at Rochester, in 1867 "became the first president and professor of systematic theology at the [newly founded] Baptist Union Theological Seminary in Chicago,"[285] set forth a critique of various types of Calvinist theology: reprobation is a denial of the benevolence of God; there must be grounds for predestination/reprobation other than arbitrariness; original sin as Adamic guilt is untenable; the work of the Holy Spirit is the same among "the nonelect" and "the elect while unregenerate"; if God is not moved by love toward the nonelect, God is not acting "in good faith"; and Calvinists cannot logically teach the salvation of all infants dying in infancy.[286] Northrup also taught the universal fatherhood of God, the essence of which is God's "absolute ethical perfection" and which, not the fatherhood of Adam, is the basis for the brotherhood of man. Such fatherhood stands opposed to such "dogmas" as capricious divine sovereignty, "unconditional reprobation," "limited atonement," sin as necessary to the happiness of the elect, and creedal requirements for salvation.[287]

Gilman Robinson, ed. Johnson, 227.

[281]LeRoy Moore, Jr., "The Rise of American Religious Liberalism at the Rochester Theological Seminary, 1872–1928" (Ph.D. diss., Claremont Graduate School, 1966) 19.

[282]Boutwell, "The Moral Matrix of God and Man," 245-46.

[283]Moore, "The Rise of American Religious Liberalism," 17-18, 21, 29-30.

[284]Winfield Burggraaff, *The Rise and Development of Liberal Theology in America* (Goes, Holland: Oosterbaan & Le Cointre; New York: Board of Publication . . . of the Reformed Church of America, 1928); Cauthen, *The Impact of American Religious Liberalism*; Lloyd J. Averill, *American Theology in the Liberal Tradition* (Philadelphia: Westminster, 1967).

[285]Brackney, *A Genetic History of Baptist Thought*, 345, 346.

[286]Northrup and Robert Watts, *Sovereignty of God* (Louisville: Baptist Book Concern, 1894) part 1, 1-144; part 2, 65-67.

[287]"The Fatherhood of God," *American Journal of Theology* 5 (July 1901): 473-95.

Elias Henry Johnson, who graduated from Rochester and Brown universities and was greatly influenced by E. G. Robinson, was professor of theology in Crozer Theological Seminary from 1882 to 1906.[288] His *An Outline of Systematic Theology*[289] resembles Robinson's *Christian Theology* in both structure and theological position. Hence only his differences from Robinson need to be identified. While sharing Robinson's reticence to espouse any single theory of biblical inspiration, for such theories tend to be speculative and overvalued, Johnson did comment rather favorably about the "dynamical" theory and affirmed that the Scriptures "infallibly express what it was the will of God to declare." Less impressed with the moral argument for God's existence and more explicitly moderate Arminian as to divine decrees, Johnson clearly embraced theistic evolution and was skeptical of theories pertaining to providence. He taught the postbiblical cessation of miracles, concluded that the essence of sin is not selfishness but "abnormality," and shifted to the explanation of original sin in terms of natural headship in Christ, a view he found to be complementary to traducianism. Johnson's hesitancy about theories again surfaced in reference to the atonement. All the major theories have strengths and weaknesses and tend to be exclusive. Seeking to be biblical, Johnson set forth a more extensive constructive statement about the atonement. As to its extent, he was satisfied with the historic sufficient/efficient distinction. Grace is resistible, and repentance and faith are essentially human responses. Hence only on the atonement and on the perseverance of the regenerate was Johnson clearly a Dortian Calvinist. He provided, unlike Robinson, a detailed treatment of premillennialism and postmillennialism and concluded that "neither party has made out its case."[290] Johnson was even more expansive on sanctification and the Holy Spirit. After critiquing Wesleyan sinless perfectionism, especially in its Oberlin form, the Plymouth Brethren teaching about the old and new natures, and especially the Keswick Movement's seven steps to infilling with the Holy Spirit, he set forth a more "positive

---

[288]Brackney, *A Genetic History of Baptist Thought*, 370-71.

[289](Philadelphia: American Baptist Publication Society, 1891).

[290]Ibid., 45-48, 47, 65-68, 86-93, 97-101, 104-7, 109-11, 120, 140-43, 148-50, 200-41, 250-58, 276-78, 284-88.

and active" and spiritual gifts-oriented approach to "the highest life"[291] and expounded the work of the Spirit in relation to Jesus Christ.[292]

Hovey's successor at Newton, Nathan Eusebius Wood, pursued a mediating position, which, according to Brackney, meant continuing "in the orthodox manner of Hovey, while acknowledging the emerging trends in theology." Educated at the University of Chicago and the Baptist Union Theological Seminary, Chicago, Wood was pastor of First Church, Boston, before serving as professor of theology in and president of Newton (1899–1908).[293] His writing was focused on anthropology, Christology, and soteriology. Direct creation and evolution are "entirely different" but "not necessarily contradictory." Darwin's hypothesis is a "clever human guess." God could have used a "primordial germ," but "Christian evolution" is not "strictly scientific." Moreover, the unity of humanity derives from its single source. Wood favored dichotomy, traducianism, and a cluster-of-capacities view of the *imago Dei*. By espousing selfishness as the essence of sin, he moved toward liberalism, but on original sin he reverted to an Augustinian position: "all men were potentially in Adam," and "in his fall . . . all men have sinned."[294] Wood expounded an orthodox Christology, noting that *kenosis* does mean the loss of the divine nature and that there is no "dual consciousness" in Jesus. As to atonement, he embraced what he called "the ethical vicarious theory," by which the death of Christ "completely satisfies the ethical nature of God," that is, justice and love, and "equally satisfies man's deepest sense of ethical requirement." The Newton president emphasized that divine election was for service, although election precedes the qualities for service, gave priority to union with Christ as "mediated by the Holy Spirit acting directly in the soul," reckoned justification as forensic but more than forensic and so definable in terms of forgiveness, reconciliation, and adoption, and held to a durative view of sanctification.[295] Wood

---

[291]*The Highest Life: A Story of Shortcomings and a Goal, Including a Friendly Analysis of the Keswick Movement*, 2nd ed. (New York: A. C. Armstrong, 1901).

[292]*The Holy Spirit Then and Now* (Philadelphia: Griffith and Rowland, 1904) 76-212. Johnson was one of the first Baptist theologians to treat imagination: *The Religious Use of Imagination* (New York: Silver, Burdett, and Co., 1901).

[293]*A Genetic History of Baptist Thought*, 288. Wood was later lecturer at Gordon College of Theology and Missions (289).

[294]*Man and Sin* (N.p., 1928) 8-44, 54-73.

[295]*The Person and Work of Jesus Christ: An Exposition of Christian Doctrine* (Philadelphia: American Baptist Publication Society, n.d. [1909?]) 3-57, esp. 23-24,

reported favorably that for many contemporary Baptists inspiration was no longer "the primal attestation to revelation" but rather "revelation attests inspiration" and biblical authority rests on "the Christian consciousness." He celebrated the nineteenth-century Baptist embrace of world missions as leading to the outgrowth of a narrow sectarianism.[296]

One of Robinson's students would have a greater impact on Baptist theology than Robinson: Augustus Hopkins Strong. Robinson's influence on Strong's published systematic theology was indirect and less than intentional until about 1896 but nevertheless genuine.[297] Born in Rochester, New York, of devout Baptist parents, Strong was not converted until the end of his junior year at Yale College,[298] at which time he was persuaded that he "must preach the gospel." Following studies in Rochester Theological Seminary, Strong held two pastorates, of First Church, Haverhill, Massachusetts, and First Church, Cleveland, Ohio, before being elected in 1872 professor of biblical theology[299] in and president of Rochester Seminary, a ministry he would undertake for the next forty years.[300]

Scholars have identified shifts in or distinctive periods within the theology of Strong. Carl F. H. Henry discerned three periods: the first, "uncompromisingly fundamentalist," the second, embracing evolutionary thought, and the third, under the influence of ethical monism.[301] LeRoy

---

46-50; 114-15; 122-24; 129; 189-201, esp. 200; 203-17, esp. 205-206; 224-38.

[296]"Movements of Baptist Theological Thought during the Nineteenth Century," in *A Century of Baptist Achievement*, ed. Albert Henry Newman (Philadelphia: American Baptist Publication Society, 1901) 430, 436-37.

[297]Strong, "Dr. Robinson as a Theologian," in *Ezekiel Gilman Robinson*, ed. Johnson, 164-65, 167-68; repr.: Strong, *Miscellanies*, 2:59-60, 63-64; Carl F. H. Henry, *Personal Idealism and Strong's Theology* (Wheaton IL: Van Kampen, 1951) 20-21.

[298]The stages in that conversion Strong himself identified: fellow Yale student Wilder Smith's saying to Strong, "O Strong, I wish you were a Christian!," the Charles G. Finney evangelistic services in Rochester, his finding the grace of God, and in his first pastorate discovering union with Christ. *One Hundred Chapel-Talks to Theological Students, together with Two Autobiographical Addresses* (Philadelphia: Griffith and Rowland, 1913) 10-16, 18-19, 23.

[299]De facto, systematic theology.

[300]*Autobiography of Augustus Hopkins Strong*, ed. Crerar Douglas (Valley Forge PA: Judson, 1981) 25-256; Gregory Alan Thornbury, "Augustus Hopkins Strong," in *Theologians of the Baptist Tradition*, ed. George and Dockery, 141-46.

[301]*Personal Idealism and Strong's Theology*, 15.

Moore's three periods are not identical: first, "received orthodoxy," second, a "positive and progressive" era, and third, his "reactionary polemic."[302] Henry did not include Strong's later reaction to the liberalism of his own Rochester faculty and some missionaries. For Henry,[303] certain chapters in *Christ in Creation and Ethical Monism*[304] marked a major "turning point in Strong's theology. The concluding chapters in Strong's *A Tour of the Missions*[305] and his posthumously issued volume, *What Shall I Believe?*[306] reflect his more conservative period. The successive editions of his *Systematic Theology* from 1886 to 1907 provide evidence of some significant changes.

The first topic in Strong's *Systematic Theology* was the concept of the existence of God as a "rational intuition," coupled with a treatment of the theistic arguments for God's existence and "erroneous" worldviews, to which he added an approved treatment of "ethical monism,"[307] a term seemingly coined by Strong.[308] Such a philosophy, which later American philosophy would denominate "personalism," combines "Metaphysical Monism, or the doctrine of one substance, ground, or principle of being" with "Psychological Dualism, or the doctrine that the soul is personally distinct from matter on the one hand, and from God on the other." By regarding the universe as "a finite, partial and progressive manifestation of the divine Life," ethical monism can avoid "the two errors of Pantheism—the denial of God's transcendence and the denial of God's personality" and

---

[302]"The Rise of American Religious Liberalism," 46-47.

[303]*Personal Idealism and Strong's Theology*, 95-96.

[304](Philadelphia: American Baptist Publication Society, 1899), 1-86. These chapters had appeared as articles in *The Examiner* in 1892, 1894, and 1895. Henry, *Personal Idealism and Strong's Theology*, 95; Moore, "The Rise of American Religious Liberalism," 55.

[305]Subtitle: *Observations and Conclusions* (Philadelphia: Griffith and Rowland, 1918) 163-223.

[306]Subtitle: *A Primer of Christian Theology* (New York: Fleming H. Revell Co., 1922). Strong declared: "I hold . . . middle ground between the higher critics and the so-called fundamentalists, and believe it possible for them both to reconcile their differences by a larger view of the deity and omnipresence of Christ" (8).

[307]*Systematic Theology: A Compendium and Commonplace-Book Designed for the Use of Theological Students*, 3rd ed. (New York: A. C. Armstrong and Son, 1890) 29-57; ibid., 8th ed. (Philadelphia: American Baptist Publication Society and Judson, 1907) 52-110.

[308]Grant Wacker, *Augustus H. Strong and the Dilemma of Historical Consciousness* (Macon GA: Mercer University Press, 1985) 62.

make a significant place for God's immanence. The universe is "created, upheld, and governed" by the incarnate and crucified Logos.[309] Being "neither idealistic nor materialistic," ethical monism "is not deterministic monism" but "the monism of free-will, . . . in which personality, both human and divine, sin and righteousness, God and the world, remain . . . with their antagonisms as well as their ideal unity."[310] Strong's very frequent quotation or citation of the writings of Borden Parker Bowne (1847–1910) of Boston University, Rudolf Hermann Lotze (1817–1881) of Göttingen, and George Trumbull Ladd (1842–1921) of Yale suggests his indebtedness to them for his ethical monism, but the manner of derivation remains problematic.[311] His advocacy of ethical monism evoked the criticism from reviewers, Baptist and non-Baptist, that he had not avoided pantheism.[312]

Strong was traditional in presenting miracles and fulfilled prophecies as "attesting a divine revelation." The same was true of his use of the "genuineness" (that is, antiquity) of the biblical books, the credibility of biblical authors, the unity and morality of biblical teaching, and later results of propagating biblical doctrine.[313] Originally Strong described the dynamic theory of biblical inspiration favorably and defended the truthfulness of the Scriptures as "an infallible and sufficient rule of faith and practice" against alleged errors—scientific, historical, moral, rational, and hermeneutical.[314] In the final edition of his *Systematic Theology* he altered his definition of inspiration so as to stress the Bible's sufficiency, "when . . . interpreted by the same Spirit who inspired them, to lead every honest inquirer to Christ and salvation," concluded that no theory of the mode of inspiration is

---

[309]*Systematic Theology*, 8th ed., 105-10.

[310]*Christ in Creation and Ethical Monism*, 28, 27.

[311]*Systematic Theology*, 8th ed., 1119, 1128, 1127; Henry, *Personal Idealism and Strong's Theology*, 100; Brackney, *A Genetic History of Baptist Thought*, 331.

[312]Alvah Hovey, "Dr. Strong's Ethical Monism," *The Watchman* 75 (1894) no. 50, 10-11; no. 51, 10-11; no. 52, 10-11; B. B. Warfield, review of Strong's *Systematic Theology*, 5th ed., *Presbyterian and Reformed Review* 8 (April 1897): 358; Albert Henry Newman, "Recent Changes in the Theology of Baptists," *American Journal of Theology* 10 (October 1906): 597; Caspar Wistar Hodge, Review of Strong's *Systematic Theology*, *Princeton Theological Review* 6 (April 1908): 336.

[313]*Systematic Theology*, 8th ed., 117-95.

[314]Ibid., 3rd ed., 102-4, 95, 105-14. See also *Philosophy and Religion: A Series of Addresses, Essays and Sermons Designed to Set Forth Great Truths in Popular Form* (New York: A. C. Armstrong and Son, 1888) 148-55.

needed but, if employed, it should be inductive, and made qualifying changes as to the alleged errors in the Bible.[315] Strong consistently defended the usefulness of biblical criticism, although in later years he objected to the presuppositions used by many critics.[316] Crerar Douglas has criticized Henry's interpretation of Strong for its failure to take into account Strong's two books[317] on poetry and theology and hence Strong's belief "that Christian hermeneutics could be clarified by a thorough study of poetics."[318] Jimmy McMath Givens has probed Christ as hermeneutical reference according to Strong.[319] In his last book Strong declared that "the written word is the expression of the eternal Word" and that "the only key . . . to the meaning of the entire Scripture, is to be found in Christ."[320]

Neither Strong's elaborate classification of God's attributes with eight "absolute or immanent" attributes and eight "relative or transitive" attributes yet with holiness as "the fundamental" attribute nor his exposition of the Trinity seems to have had great significance for Baptist theology.[321] His making holiness to be fundamental seemed to draw him toward transcendence, whereas his embrace of ethical monism drew him toward immanence. Having faulted Robinson for a lack of stress on an ontological Trinity,[322] Strong seems to have supplied that need,[323] but his brief treatment of the doctrine of the Holy Spirit only as a subdivision of the Trinity, with attention only to the deity and personality of the Spirit,[324] is evidence that Strong did not theologically enter the twentieth century. Strong was

---

[315]Ibid., 8th ed., 196, 211, 226, 228, 233, 235.

[316]Norman H. Maring, "Baptists and Changing Views of the Bible, 1865–1918," part 2, *Foundations* 1 (October 1958): 39, 56-57.

[317]*The Great Poets and Their Theology* (Philadelphia: American Baptist Publication Society, 1897); *American Poets and Their Theology* (Philadelphia: Griffith and Rowland, 1916; repr.: Freeport NY: Books for Libraries, 1968).

[318]"The Hermeneutics of Augustus Hopkins Strong: God and Shakespeare in Rochester," *Foundations* 21 (January-March 1978): 71-76, esp. 72, 74.

[319]"Christ as Hermeneutical Referent: An Analysis of the Extension of Christological Motifs within the Theologies of Augustus Hopkins Strong, Edgar Young Mullins, and Walter Thomas Conner" (Ph.D. diss., Southwestern Baptist Theological Seminary, 2000).

[320]*What Shall I Believe?*, 48, 57.

[321]*Systematic Theology*, 8th ed., 243-303.

[322]"Dr. Robinson as a Theologian," 194-95.

[323]*Systematic Theology*, 8th ed., 326-43.

[324]Ibid., 315-17, 323-26.

Calvinistic in his doctrine of divine decrees, which are logically but not chronologically related and are consistent with human free agency and exertion. There is only one qualification: the "decree to permit sin is . . . not an efficient but a permissive decree."[325]

Strong consistently defined creation as "that free act of the triune God by which in the beginning for his own glory he made, without the use of preexisting materials, the whole visible and invisible universe."[326] Assurance concerning creation can be found through biblical revelation, not through "science or reason."[327] The Rochester theologian rejected metaphysical and moral dualism, emanation, creation from eternity, and spontaneous generation and opted for the "pictorial-summary" interpretation of Genesis 1, thus allowing for development and "coincidences" between Genesis 1 and "geological records."[328] He embraced the theistic evolution of human beings, whereby God (Gen. 2:7) utilized existing "animal forms" to create man, so that "man came not *from* the brute, but *through* the brute."[329] Evolution, for Strong, was much more than biological; it was progressive divine revelation with Christ as "its agent and goal."[330] Indeed, as Irwin Reist[331] has noted, his evolutionary thought had an eschatological goal, identified as Christ's second coming. Creation's goal he had clearly defined as the glory of God.[332]

---

[325]Ibid., 353-70, esp. 353, 359, 363, 365.

[326]There is ambiguity relative to "without the use of preexisting materials" in that elsewhere (*Christ in Creation and Ethical Monism*, 72, and *What Shall I Believe?*, 23) Strong denied "creation out of nothing" in language suggestive of emanation. See Arthur Lynn Allen, "A Comparative Study of the Person of Christ in Selected Baptist Theologians: Augustus H. Strong, William N. Clarke, Edgar Y. Mullins, and Walter T. Conner" (Th.D. diss., New Orleans Baptist Theological Seminary, 1979) 58.

[327]Ibid., 3rd ed., 183, 184; 8th ed., 371, 374.

[328]Ibid., 3rd ed., 186-95; 8th ed., 378-97.

[329]Ibid. (8th ed.), 465-67. See William Beryl West, "Theistic Evolution in the Writings of A. H. Strong and Bernard Ramm" (Th.M. thesis, Southwestern Baptist Theological Seminary, 1962) 28-58.

[330]Strong, "The Present Outlook in Theology," *Review and Expositor* 7 (January 1910): 139, 140.

[331]"Augustus Hopkins Strong and William Newton Clarke: A Study in Nineteenth-Century Evolutionary and Eschatological Thought," *Foundations* 13 (January-March 1970): 26-43.

[332]*Systematic Theology*, 3rd ed., 195-98; 8th ed., 397-402.

Strong opted for God's preservation of the created order rather than continuous creation, and hence, for Strong, providence was primarily divine governance vis-à-vis human events. In relation to evil human acts he specified four modes of God's providence: "preventive," "permissive," "directive," and "determinative" (or limiting). He wrote of "good angels" and "evil angels" with less attention to Satan.[333]

All human beings, according to Strong, are "the offspring" of God as Creator and as the natural Father of humanity.[334] Dichotomy and traducianism were reckoned as true positions, and the *imago Dei* was twofold: a "natural likeness" that is "personality" (with self-knowledge and self-determination) and a "moral likeness" that is "holiness." The former was retained after the fall, dominion being its result, whereas the latter was lost by the fall. While defining sin as "lacking of conformity to the moral law, either in act, disposition, or state," Strong, following Robinson, opted for selfishness as the essence of sin. Every human being "possesses a corrupted nature" that is not only "a source of actual sin" but also "itself sin." Holding to a historical Adam and a historical fall and that the fall brought both physical death and spiritual death, Strong, contrary to Robinson, concluded that the guilt for Adam's sin was imputed to the entire human race in the Augustinian sense of Adamic headship and organic unity on the ground that such a view is "the most natural interpretation" of Rom. 5:12-21. For Strong, the corporate dimension of sin applied not only to humanity's union with Adam but also to the present-day societal connectedness in sin.[335] Seemingly Strong never took note as to how the Augustinian view had so often been employed in defense of infant baptism but went on to posit that infants dying in infancy will probably be regenerated immediately after death.[336]

From the perspective of its structure Strong's exposition of Christology appears to be a combination of the Chalcedonian formulation of two natures in one person, a moderate expression of the two states of humiliation and exaltation, and the exposition of Christ's three offices, within which is

---

[333] Ibid., 8th ed., 410-64.

[334] "God's special Fatherhood" applies to the regenerated ones.

[335] John David Massey, "Solidarity in Sin: An Analysis of the Corporate Conceptions of Sin in the Theologies of Augustus Hopkins Strong and Walter Rauschenbusch" (Ph.D. diss., Southwestern Baptist Theological Seminary, 2000).

[336] *Systematic Theology*, 8th ed., 474-76, 483-97, 514-32, 549-637, 660-64.

expounded an eternal atonement theory.[337] Strong's teaching that Christ had one will and one consciousness, not two,[338] called forth Albert Henry Newman's charge that Strong embraced the Eutychian and Monothelite errors.[339] By defining the self-emptying of the Logos as "the surrender of the independent exercise of the divine attributes,"[340] the Rochester president rejected both Thomasius's view that the surrender was of the "omni" attributes and Gess's view that the Logos surrendered all the divine attributes.[341] According to Strong, the preexistent Christ "bound himself to sinful humanity in the act of creation" and hence "had to share in the sinner's punishment," assumed impersonal humanity inasmuch as his human nature "had no personality separate from the divine nature," and in his incarnate state was free from depravity but not from guilt and punishment.[342]

In earlier editions of his *Systematic Theology* Strong had expounded his "ethical theory" of the atonement in terms of sin's "ill-deserving" nature and the demand of God's holiness that sin be punished, thus entailing both "satisfaction" and "substitution," and also in terms of Christ's having fully paid in his twofold nature and by his organic union with humanity the debt for sin. He also opted for general atonement.[343] But after his embrace of ethical monism, Strong developed and asserted his eternal atonement view with greater emphasis on the love of God:

> Christ therefore, as incarnate, rather revealed the atonement than made it. The historical work of atonement was finished upon the Cross, but that historical work only revealed to men the atonement made both before and since by the extra-mundane Logos.[344]

Peter Stephen Van Pelt has dubiously alleged that all the basic principles of Protestant liberalism—continuity, autonomy, and dynamism—are clearly manifested in Strong's doctrine of the atonement and that Strong's "general

---

[337]*Systematic Theology*, 8th ed., 665-776.

[338]Ibid., 694-96.

[339]"Strong's Systematic Theology," *Review and Expositor* 2 (January 1905): 62-64; idem, "Recent Changes in the Theology of Baptists," 596-97.

[340]*Systematic Theology*, 8th ed., 703.

[341]H. R. Mackintosh, *The Doctrine of the Person of Jesus Christ*, International Theological Library (Edinburgh: T.&T. Clark, 1912) 264-69.

[342]Allen, "A Comparative Study of the Person of Christ," 33, 44, 36-40.

[343]*Systematic Theology*, 3rd ed., 409-22.

[344]*Systematic Theology*, 8th ed., 762. See also *Miscellanies* 1:460-71.

atonement moved dangerously close to the cliffs of universalism."³⁴⁵ It would seem better to critique Strong's theory—*sui generis* in Baptist theology—on the basis of the once-for-all nature of Christ's sacrifice and the lack of biblical support for Strong's presupposition, that is, the union of the Logos with humankind in creation.³⁴⁶

In his *ordo salutis*, which he denominated "reconciliation" and "the application of redemption through . . . the Holy Spirit," Strong set election and calling in a sublapsarian context—election being the fourth of the decrees, gave to union with Christ a position of emphasis, interpreted regeneration as a change of "disposition" and "the divine side" of conversion, made conversion to consist of repentance and faith, reckoned justification to be a declarative "judicial act" and sanctification to be durative, and defined perseverance as "the human side" of sanctification.³⁴⁷ Strong did allow for an "implicit faith in Christ" on the part of "those who have not heard of his manifestation in the flesh."³⁴⁸

In ecclesiology the Rochester president, asserting that polity was not unprescribed in the New Testament and is not "a matter of expediency," defended congregational polity and spelled out the duties and ordination of pastors and deacons and the nature of church discipline. Baptism has

---

³⁴⁵"An Examination of the Concept of the Atonement in Selected Northern Baptist Theologians: William Newton Clarke, Augustus Hopkins Strong, and Shailer Mathews" (Th.D. diss., Mid-America Baptist Theological Seminary, 1994) 143-46, 136.

³⁴⁶Garrett, *Systematic Theology: Biblical, Historical, and Evangelical*, 2nd ed., 2:42.

³⁴⁷*Systematic Theology*, 8th ed., 777-886. Robert Keith Parks, "A Biblical Evaluation of the Doctrine of Justification in Recent American Baptist Theology: With Special Reference to A. H. Strong, E. Y. Mullins, and W. T. Conner" (Th.D. diss., Southwestern Baptist Theological Seminary, 1954) found that originally Strong expounded a forensic view of justification on the basis of the imputation of Christ's righteousness but later likewise embraced to some extent a vital view of justification. Strong's *What Shall I Believe?*, 85-86, 91, wherein he stated that "imputation is grounded in union, not union in imputation," seems to validate Parks's conclusion. But Parks's attributing the vital element to "*ethical monism*" and to Strong's doctrine of union with Christ, which went unchanged, has hardly been established.

³⁴⁸*Systematic Theology*, 8th ed., 843. See Clark H. Pinnock, "Overcoming Misgivings about Evangelical Inclusivism," *The Southern Baptist Journal of Theology* 2 (Summer 1998): 33; Thornbury, "Augustus Hopkins Strong," 141, 158-59.

immersion as its mode, symbolism as its nature, and "only persons giving evidence of being regenerated" as its proper subjects. Strong was not influenced by the Landmark rejection of "alien" immersions. He interpreted the Lord's Supper as "symbolic" after the manner of Ulrich Zwingli and, holding that "membership in the church naturally precedes communion," warned, like Booth and Kinghorn, that open communion among Baptists logically leads to open membership.[349]

As to eschatology Strong posited conscious, bodiless intermediate states for righteous and wicked between death and resurrection, allowed for "precursors" but not date-setting for the second coming of Christ, was postmillennialist without a manifest golden age of the church, anticipated one general resurrection and one universal judgment, and taught heaven and hell while refuting annihilationism and eschatological universalism.[350]

Strong, as noted already, had his critics in his lifetime and has had his assessors in later years, notably Carl F. H. Henry and Grant Wacker. Henry, taking as his premise that Strong's embrace of "ethical monism" ca.1894 constituted the major "turning-point" in his thinking, concluded that Strong compromised his concept of biblical authority and that both liberals such as William Adams Brown (1865–1943) and conservatives began to discern the import of such compromise.[351] Wacker saw Strong as a "tragic figure" who, unable to cope with historicism, sought valiantly, if not successfully, to "hold together ancient faith and modern epistemology" or "to wed tradition and modernity."[352] Wacker found that at least four different theological labels have been put on Strong: (1) "early," "irenic," and "open-minded" "fundamentalist"; (2) a "conservative" seeking to "preserve" the basics of "the Reformed theological heritage"; (3) "a mediator between liberalism and orthodoxy"; and (4) "a closet liberal hiding behind the garments of apparent orthodoxy." The third view, Wacker reported, has been most widely held.[353] Others have come to similar conclusions about Strong's

---

[349]*Systematic Theology*, 8th ed., 887-980, esp. 896, 945, 973, 976.

[350]Ibid., 981-1056. Strong did not stress the kingdom of God in his *Systematic Theology*, but in an 1869 sermon he interpreted the kingdom as eschatological: "to be set up" in the soul of man, as "a kingdom of grace and not a kingdom of force," yet its coming "has been made dependent upon the prayers and labors" of God's people. *Philosophy and Religion*, 358-67, esp. 361, 365.

[351]*Personal Idealism and Strong's Theology*, 95, 193-98.

[352]*Augustus H. Strong and the Dilemma*, 12, 15, 9-19, xiii, 125.

[353]Ibid., 7-8.

mediating role or his effort to hold onto two worlds.[354] Wacker called him "one of the most influential conservative Protestant thinkers in the United States in the late nineteenth century,"[355] and the fact that his *Systematic Theology* remained in print throughout the twentieth century tends to corroborate that judgment.

In Robinson's orbit of influence, but not his student, was Ebenezer Dodge. "Educated at Brown University and Newton Theological Institution" and after teaching in Western Baptist Theological Institute and pastorates in New Hampshire, he entered upon a 36-year teaching career in Madison University and Hamilton Theological Seminary in Hamilton, New York.[356] In his theological lectures Dodge held the "dynamical" theory of biblical inspiration and the Scriptures as the "final court of appeal in all religious questions" but also developed the "Christian consciousness" as a source of theology.[357] The antiquity of the human race was an issue to be left to science. Whereas development has been "abundantly verified," "its extension over all human and animal life" is "a mere hypothesis," for there is "difference in mind between man and brute." Dodge like Strong, embraced the Augustinian view of original sin and defined sin as selfishness. There was "no absolute *kenosis* of the divine nature" of the Logos,[358] and Dodge seemed to embrace what he called a "realistic vicarious" view

---

[354]Cauthen, *The Impact of American Religious Liberalism*, 31; Winthrop S. Hudson, *Religion in America* (New York: Scribner's, 1965) 277; idem, *Baptists in Transition: Individualism and Christian Responsibility* (Valley Forge PA: Judson, 1979) 131-32; Nancey Murphy, *Beyond Liberalism and Fundamentalism: How Modern and Postmodern Philosophy Set the Theological Agenda* (Valley Forge PA: Trinity Press International, 1996) 60, 74, 135, 153.

[355]Wacker, *Augustus H. Strong and the Dilemma*, xiii.

[356]Brackney, *A Genetic History of Baptist Thought*, 295, 300-301. Dodge served as president of Madison University from 1868 until his death in 1890, Madison's name being changed to Colgate University in 1888, and he twice studied in Germany. Ibid.

[357]Charles Hastings Dodd, "Ebenezer Dodge: Pioneer in Experiential Theology," *Crozer Quarterly* 2 (July 1925): 283, 288, claimed that Dodge "was among the first, if not the first, of American theologians to make" Christian conversion "the determinative factor" in his theology and that Dodge helped to originate the term "Christian consciousness."

[358]According to ibid., 299, for Dodge, the incarnation "was substitutionary in its entire sweep and import" and was "the incorporation and permanent indwelling of God in human consciousness."

of the atonement, according to which Christ's self-surrendering reconciling death was the judicial revelation of the penalty for the sin of the human race. General atonement he did affirm. The church, which was inaugurated at Pentecost, is a voluntary society with independent polity. Dodge's lengthy history of the mode of baptism and lengthy treatise on the subjects of baptism were like monographs tucked into his systematic theology. He followed Calvin's spiritual presence view of the Lord's Supper and opposed open communion. The Hamilton professor rejected an intermediate state, opting for the believer's receiving his spiritual body at death, defended postmillennialism and one general judgment, and refuted universalism, "restorationism," or the view that there will be limited postmortal punishment, and annihilationism.[359]

Northern Baptist Liberal Theologians:
William Newton Clarke (1841–1912),
Harry Emerson Fosdick (1878–1969),
George Cross (1862–1929),
and Henry Clay Vedder (1853–1935)

Protestant theological liberalism in the latter nineteenth century embraced the new cultural trends: evolution, historical criticism of the Bible, the emergence of urban society, and philosophical changes. Kenneth Cauthen has contended that liberalism was subject to "three types of influences," namely, "continuity," autonomy," and "dynamism," and that there were two distinguishable types of liberals: "evangelical liberals" and "modernistic liberals."[360] A central figure in the development of liberalism, both for Protestants in general and for Baptists in particular, was William Newton Clarke.

Born in New York state and the son of a Baptist pastor, Clarke, after graduating from Madison University (1861) and Hamilton Theological Seminary (1863), was successively pastor in Keene, New Hampshire, of First Church, Newton Centre, Massachusetts, and Olivet Church, Montreal, Quebec. He briefly taught New Testament and homiletics at the Baptist Theological School, Toronto, Ontario (later McMaster University) and was

---

[359]*Lectures on Christian Theology* (Hamilton NY: University Press Print, 1883) 110, 13-15, 178-79, 228, 252, 296, 412, 398-401, 486, 492, 493, 519-725, 730, 731, 747-55, 743-47, 752-55, 757-67.

[360]*The Impact of American Religious Liberalism*, 5-30. Although Cauthen did not include Clarke among the eight theologians to be analyzed, it is obvious that Clarke should be classified as an "evangelical liberal."

pastor in Hamilton. After the death of Dodge, Clarke became Joslin Professor of Christian Theology at Hamilton (1890–1908) and subsequently lectured there (1908–1912) on Christian ethics. He died at his winter home in DeLand, Florida.[361]

That Clarke made very basic theological changes is not disputed; how and when these occurred has evoked various answers. Claude L. Howe, Jr., found that Clarke as a teenager began to select what portions of the Bible were "precious" to him, that the church in Keene "had suffered sadly from the Millerite excitement" of 1843, that at Newton Centre Clarke found discussions among pastors concerning premillennialism and postmillennialism to be inconclusive, read Horace Bushnell's *The Vicarious Sacrifice Grounded in Principles of Universal Obligation*, and began to work out his own view of the atonement.[362] William H. Brackney has emphasized the influence of Clarke's "Canadian experience," insisting that his full acceptance of historical-critical method, his turning from the dominance of Pauline theology to the Gospels, and "his openness to women in Christian leadership" occurred during the Montreal-Toronto years.[363]

Clarke's most notable book, *An Outline of Christian Theology*,[364] has been called "the first broad survey of Christian theology which frankly accepted the modern view of the world . . . and subordinated theology to the Christian religion itself"[365] and "the most widely used of liberal texts in systematic theology."[366]

---

[361]Emily S. Clarke, *William Newton Clarke: A Biography* (New York: Scribner's, 1916); Claude L. Howe, Jr., "The Theology of William Newton Clarke" (Th.D. diss., New Orleans Baptist Theological Seminary, 1959; New York: Arno, 1980) 4-25; Tull, *Shapers of Baptist Thought*, 158-59; Brackney, *The Baptists*, 143-44.

[362]"The Theology of William Newton Clarke," 7, 11-12, 14-16, based on Clarke, *Sixty Years with the Bible: A Record of Experience* (New York: Scribner's, 1909) 24-25, 63-67, 102-104, 109-20.

[363]"William Newton Clarke: A Canadian-American Cross Cultural Experience," *McMaster Journal of Theology* 3 (Spring 1993): 75-80.

[364](New York: Scribner's, 1898; only publ. for Clarke's students by J. Wilson and Son in Cambridge MA, 1894).

[365]William H. Allison, "Clarke, William Newton," *Dictionary of American Biography* (1930 ed.) 4:164.

[366]Sydney E. Ahlstrom, *A Religious History of the American People* (New Haven: Yale University Press, 1972) 777.

For Clarke, the sources for Christian theology are twofold: the "Christian revelation" and the universe, the latter consisting of "man and nature." "God's self-revelation . . . was made in life and action" before there were biblical books and has been preserved in Christian experience and in the Scriptures.[367] Clarke noted the "high exceptional quality in the contents" of the Scriptures. The biblical books are marked by "great variety" in "literary structure and style," "the individuality" of the authors, their religious views, and their degree of "spiritual intensity," are a record of "a progressive revelation of God," and "are characterized by the absence of "complete inerrancy." Clarke's statements as to biblical inspiration are less than conclusive. It is "men" that are inspired, "not writings." The writings came not by divine dictation. "Inspiration to write was not different in kind from the general inspiration of the divine Spirit." There were different degrees of inspiration. "The inspiration of the Bible does not prove its excellence, but its excellence proves its inspiration." The Bible's authority comes not by external "divine certification" but by the inherent truth of its contents.[368] According to Clarke, "the Christian element in the Scriptures" must be differentiated from the non-Christian and made to be "the indispensable and formative element in Christian theology." It is "a body of truth," that which "accords with the view of divine realities which Jesus Christ revealed." Hence "a single unequivocal standard the Bible as a book can never be."[369]

The Hamilton professor defined "the Christian conception of God" as follows: "God is the personal Spirit, perfectly good, who in holy love creates, sustains, and orders all." Seeking to balance divine immanence and divine transcendence, he held "God's method in the universe" to be "evolutionary," such method not precluding creation or miracle. God exercises sovereignty over "free spiritual creatures" through "paternal moral government." Human freedom is not destroyed by predestination, and God has not kept evil out of his created order but uses it.[370] According to Clarke, Jesus cast aside or eliminated all that was "not ethical" in the conception of God.[371] For Jesus, the term and concept of "Father" are central to the being

---

[367] *An Outline of Christian Theology*, 10-24.

[368] Ibid., 26-47.

[369] *The Use of the Scriptures in Theology* (New York: Scribner's, 1905) 17, 18, 54, 50, 56, 60, 75.

[370] *An Outline of Christian Theology*, 66, 128-34, 140-47, 153-58.

[371] *The Christian Doctrine of God*, International Theological Library (New York: Scribner's, 1909) 37-39.

of God, for "within the Fatherhood of God all his other relations to men are included." Building on the parable of the prodigal son and sidestepping the Johannine language as to new birth and the Pauline language concerning adoption as "figurative," Clarke concluded that "there is only one Fatherhood in God, and that is grounded in his creatorship and his character." But this filial relationship "may be realized in full, or only in part, or not at all on man's side."[372] Clarke used "Trinity" to refer to the Trinity of manifestation and "Triunity" to refer to an ontological Trinity, the latter being the product of the post-New Testament era, but clearly held to both.[373]

A dichotomist and a traducianist, Clarke recognized the freedom of the human will but as being limited by influences and by one's lack of harmony of his own powers. The question of the origin of the human race should be remanded to the sciences but with the possibility of the direct divine creation of the original human souls. Sin was defined as "badness," "the abnormal," "departure from the standard of duty," selfishness, and "opposition to the spirit and working of God's moral government." Ignoring the historic theories of original sin, Clarke rejected a historical fall while positing the advent of evil in humankind's evolutionary rise to accountability and, though allowing a common depravity, treated guilt and punishment individually.[374]

For Clarke an incarnation was possible "because God and man are alike," and there might well have been an incarnation if there had been no human sin. He accepted Jesus' virginal conception but did not build the doctrine of the deity of Jesus Christ upon it. Jesus' miracles were seen as compassionate "deeds of kindness," not as attestations of "his divine mission," and the factuality of Jesus' resurrection Clarke clearly affirmed. Jesus' mission was to be "the gift of the heart of God, who desires to save the world."[375] The Chalcedonian formulation did not appeal to Clarke, for it assumed that God and humanity "are essentially unlike."[376] Jesus' vital re-

---

[372]Ibid., 153-64.

[373]Ibid., 161-81. But Tull, *Shapers of Baptist Thought*, 167, mistakenly concluded that Clarke espoused "a trinity of manifestation rather than a trinity of essence." Clarke, 170-71, did hold that the term "person" had undergone a change of meaning from the patristic age to the modern era.

[374]*An Outline of Christian Theology*, 182-259.

[375]Ibid., 291-92, 295, 302-303, 264, 270, 272-75, 279.

[376]Howe, "The Theology of William Newton Clarke," 85-86. Allen, "A Comparative Study of the Person of Christ," 104-8, held that in *An Outline of*

lation both to the Father and to humanity made possible a "genuine revelation" of both God and the human and brought Jesus into "perfect sympathy" with both God and man. Clarke's chief term for the work of Christ was "reconciliation."[377] According to Van Pelt, Clarke began to abandon the penal substitutionary view of the atonement while pastor in Newton Centre and "continued to revise his concept of the atonement throughout his lifetime."[378] Clarke came to the conclusion that "the same sin cannot be both punished and forgiven," for "punishment is incompatible with forgiveness," and hence "punishment of sin" cannot "be visited upon any one else than the one who has committed it." The Father, not Jesus, "is the great sin-bearer" who "bears sin first by way of endurance, as a hater of sin and a lover of men," and second "by way of endeavor," or the work of salvation.[379] Tull concluded that Clarke essentially taught the moral influence theory without explicitly saying so,[380] and Clarke's attraction to the writing of Bushnell would tend to support that conclusion. But Van Pelt seems to identify Clarke with the example theory without clearly drawing that conclusion.[381] It seems best to conclude that Clarke's teaching does not match precisely any of the major historic theories, as Bernard Harvey Cochran's view[382] that Clarke held moral influence and governmental theories seems to suggest.

The Holy Spirit, for Clarke, was not so much the third person of the Trinity as "God working in the spirit of man, and accomplishing the results that are sought in the mission and work of Christ." The Spirit's work in the world is "convincement," his work in the church is didactic, and his work in individuals runs the gamut of what other theologians have called the *ordo*

Christian Theology, 297, Clarke clearly taught that Jesus had a single "consciousness" and "will," not two, but later in *The Christian Doctrine of God*, 22-26, 239-41, drew back from metaphysical questions.

[377] *An Outline of Christian Theology*, 305-15, 321-62.

[378] "An Examination of the Concept of the Atonement," 15-16, 60. See also Clarke, *Sixty Years with the Bible*, 110-20. Clarke, *An Outline of Christian Theology*, 335-39, was opposed to "the transactional idea," i.e., penal substitution.

[379] *An Outline of Christian Theology*, 330-31, 341-45.

[380] *Shapers of Baptist Thought*, 174.

[381] "An Examination of the Concept of the Atonement," 64, 67.

[382] "William Newton Clarke: Exponent of the New Theology" (Ph.D. diss., Duke University, 1962) 211-12.

salutis. The extraordinary gifts of the Spirit ceased after the apostolic age, and their revival is not to be sought.[383]

In his commentary on the Gospel of Mark, published during his Montreal pastorate, Clarke interpreted Mark 13 to refer to the destruction of Jerusalem in AD 70 rather than to the second coming of Christ.[384] In his system he differentiated the Synoptic expectation of Christ's coming "as kingly and judicial, near in time, associated with the fall of Jerusalem" from the Johannine expectation as "invisible and spiritual," durative in nature and associated with the work of the Holy Spirit. The apostles expected his return to be soon. The negative side of his coming was Jerusalem's fall, whereas the positive side has been his presence which began on the day of Pentecost. Hence, for Clarke, "no visible return of Christ is to be expected, but rather the long and steady advance of his spiritual kingdom." Neither premillennialism nor postmillennialism satisfied Clarke, and his language was akin to what later was called amillennialism. Clarke stressed the unlikeness of the present body and the resurrection body and held that each human will be raised immediately after death. Judgment is to be universal but at death, and annihilationism and conditional immortality are inadequate, but in positing heaven and hell the Hamilton professor found it difficult to avoid the possibility of postmortal salvation.[385]

Neither Tull[386] nor Cochran[387] regarded Clarke as a "creative" or "profoundly original" theologian; for Cochran he was the "chief systematizer and popularizer" of liberalism. Cochran's thesis that Clarke "played a positive role" in three movements, namely, theological liberalism, "the social awakening of American Protestantism," and the movement toward Christian unity, has less support for the second and third contentions.[388] Clarke gave little attention to historic Baptist ecclesiological issues. This may have been due, as Tull stated,[389] to the fact that "liberalism was self-consciously ecumenical in outlook, not to say non-denominational," or to

---

[383]*An Outline of Christian Thought*, 369-71, 376-427.

[384]*Commentary on the Gospel of Mark*, An American Commentary on the New Testament (Philadelphia: American Baptist Publication Society, 1881) 179-95.

[385]*An Outline of Christian Theology*, 436-44, 431-34, 453-66, 451-43, 466-82.

[386]*Shapers of Baptist Thought*, 178.

[387]"William Newton Clarke," abstract, 1.

[388]Ibid., abstract, 3; 223-85.

[389]*Shapers of Baptist Thought*, 179.

Clarke's deliberate ecumenism. According to Cochran,[390] Clarke looked upon "the denomination and the local church" as "merely the organizational and functional expressions of the Church universal" and was willing for Baptists to "relinquish" their separateness and become absorbed into the larger body of Christ," provided that "the distinctive [Baptist] theological insights . . . should in principle be embraced by Christianity as a whole." Clarke himself acknowledged in a letter: "I do not regard myself as a champion of denominational orthodoxy, but I do regard myself as a Baptist and as a humble champion of my Master's truth."[391]

The most celebrated and widely known of Clarke's students was Harry Emerson Fosdick. A native of Buffalo, New York, and immersed at seven, he was educated at Colgate University, Hamilton Theological Seminary, and Union Theological Seminary, New York. As pastor of First Church, Montclair, New Jersey (1904–1915) he began teaching adjunctively at Union and then joined its faculty full-time in 1915. As preaching minister of First Presbyterian Church, New York, he preached in May 1922 a sermon, "Shall the Fundamentalists Win?"[392] which triggered the Fundamentalist controversy and caused his termination by Presbyterian authorities. In 1925 Fosdick was called to the pastorate of Park Avenue Church in New York City, which church was transformed in 1931 into the nondenominational Riverside Church, which Fosdick served until 1946, the year of his concurrent retirement from the Union faculty.[393]

Against the view that Fosdick was a preacher and a pastor but not a theologian, Hardy Clemons argued that five basic theological "ideas" undergirded Fosdick's ministry,[394] and Reinhold Niebuhr declared that Fosdick

---

[390]"William Newton Clarke," 270, 274.

[391]Quoted by J. W. A. Stewart, "The Story of a Friendship," in E. Clarke, *William Newton Clarke*, 143.

[392]The text may be found in Halford R. Ryan, *Harry Emerson Fosdick: Persuasive Preacher*, Great American Orators 1 (New York: Greenwood, 1989) 79-89.

[393]Fosdick, *The Living of These Days: An Autobiography* (New York: Harper & Bros., 1956); Robert Moats Miller, *Harry Emerson Fosdick: Preacher, Pastor, Prophet* (New York: Oxford University Press, 1985); Katharine A. Bonney, "Harry Emerson Fosdick's Doctrine of Man" (Ph.D. diss., Boston University, 1958) 4-36; C. W. Brister, "The Ethical Thought of Harry Emerson Fosdick: A Critical Interpretation" (Th.D. diss., Southwestern Baptist Theological Seminary, 1957) 1-33.

[394]"The Key Theological Ideas of Harry Emerson Fosdick" (Th.D. diss., Southwestern Baptist Theological Seminary, 1966).

"profoundly influenced the theological climate of his day."[395] The Bible is not to be understood through dictational inspiration and inerrancy,[396] for Christians mistakenly take the Bible as comparable to the Koran or Joseph Smith's plates.[397] Fosdick's hermeneutic, which followed the Reformers' principle of a single sense of a biblical text,[398] was affected by his embrace of the concept of "abiding experiences and changing categories," the abiding experiences being "the essence of Christianity."[399] "The Bible is a book of vital personal religion. The reality, friendliness, and unescapableness of God are its dominant themes."[400] God is incomprehensible yet personal, one yet three-in-one, the God of "action," "power," and "history."[401]

The real humanity and historicity of Jesus of Nazareth Fosdick clearly stressed;[402] for him there was no docetism. Scholars are not agreed as to assessment of Fosdick's handling of the deity of Christ, although his antimetaphysical bent was obvious. For Kenneth Cauthen deity meant for Fosdick "the supreme instance of the immanence of God" and the Messianic agency for kingdom inauguration.[403] According to Brian Lee Harbour, Fosdick saw in Jesus a "transcendent uniqueness" and "character" that was marked by "absoluteness and finality."[404] Samuel Robert Weaver, on the

---

[395]"The Significance of Dr. Fosdick in American Religious Thought," *Union Seminary Quarterly Review* 8 (May 1953): 3-4.

[396]Clemons, "The Key Theological Ideas," 262.

[397]*The Meaning of Faith* (New York: Association, 1934; orig., 1917) 168-69.

[398]*The Modern Use of the Bible*, Lyman Beecher Lectures 1924 (New York: Macmillan Co., 1924; repr., 1925) 85-89.

[399]Ibid., 97-129, esp. 102. Isaac Massey Haldeman (1845–1933), pastor of First Church, New York City, issued a critique of Fosdick's book: *Dr. Harry Emerson Fosdick's Book: "The Modern Use of the Bible": A Review* (Philadelphia: Sunday School Times Co., 1925).

[400]*The Modern Use of the Bible*, 179.

[401]Clemons, "The Key Theological Ideas," 85-137.

[402]Ibid., 153-63; Bonney, "Harry Emerson Fosdick's Doctrine of Man," 194-98. See also Fosdick, *The Manhood of the Master* (New York: Association, 1917), and *The Man from Nazareth: As His Contemporaries Saw Him* (New York: Harper & Brothers, 1949). James Martin Gray (1851–1935), president of Moody Bible Institute, Chicago, rebutted one of Fosdick's sermons: *The Audacity of Unbelief: A Reply to Dr. Harry Emerson Fosdick's Sermon Entitled "The Peril of Worshiping Jesus"* (Chicago: Moody Bible Institute, n.d.).

[403]*The Impact of American Religious Liberalism*, 81.

[404]"The Christology of Harry Emerson Fosdick" (Ph.D. diss., Baylor

other hand, identified the "fatal" weakness in Fosdick's Christology as his "failure to acknowledge Jesus as God," because of Fosdick's "concept of natural law operating in an evolutionary framework," and concluded that Fosdick's view was "a sort of Neo-Arianism."[405] Fosdick cast doubt on the accounts of Jesus' virginal conception, was unsure of "the physical aspects of the resurrection of Christ," and did "not believe in the physical return of Jesus."[406] He clearly exhibited "antipathy" toward penal substitution[407] but was not so clear as to his own view of Jesus' "vicarious [that is, redemptive] suffering."[408]

Katharine Bonney has contended that Fosdick balanced his view of human beings as potentially good and as actually sinful. Sin, which is "the result of the misuse of freedom," is whatever "hinders the development of human personality." It came not from a historical fall, but rather both good and evil derived from man's evolutionary past.[409] For Cauthen, Fosdick was "a modern Pelagian."[410] Immortality is "the going on into the future of that quality of life" which is "called eternal" but is "known in the present."[411]

Bonney classified Fosdick as a "neo-liberal" or "realist" because of his later critique of aspects of liberalism.[412] Cauthen treated Fosdick as one of two Baptists, the other being Walter Rauschenbusch (1861–1918), who were "evangelical" liberals as distinct from "modernistic" liberals.[413] Weaver accepted the label "evangelical liberal,"[414] and Harbour alluded to "a distinctly Fosdickian type of Christocentric liberalism."[415]

Theological liberalism was fully embodied in the work of George Cross. Educated at the University of Toronto, McMaster University, and the

---

University, 1973) 183, 188, 196.

[405]"The Theology and Times of Harry Emerson Fosdick" (Th.D. diss., Princeton Theological Seminary, 1960).

[406]*The Modern Use of the Bible*, 146-47, 164, 104.

[407]Clemons, "The Key Theological Ideas," 213.

[408]*A Guide to Understanding the Bible: The Development of Ideas within the Old and New Testaments* (New York: Harper & Brothers, 1938) 193-97.

[409]"Harry Emerson Fosdick's Doctrine of Man," 185, 200-205, 73-75, 70-73.

[410]*The Impact of American Religious Liberalism*, 79.

[411]Bonney, "Harry Emerson Fosdick's Doctrine of Man," 123. See Fosdick, *The Assurance of Immortality* (New York: Macmillan Co., 1926).

[412]"Harry Emerson Fosdick's Doctrine of Man," 239-40, 245.

[413]*The Impact of American Religious Liberalism*, 61-107.

[414]"The Theology and the Times," 312-13.

[415]"The Christology of Harry Emerson Fosdick," 209.

University of Chicago, he first succeeded Nathan Wood in teaching theology at Newton and then in 1912 succeeded A. H. Strong at Rochester.[416] He published a condensation of F. D. E. Schleiermacher's *The Christian Faith*.[417] Then, asserting that the ancient creeds were "no fixed eternal standard" for later times and that there was a need for theological "revision" and "restatement," he offered Jesus as "the perfect personality," the hope of a "better world," and a transformed interpretation of nature.[418] Critiquing Roman Catholic sacramentalism in which "the ritual is the practical basis of the creed" and salvation was "a matter of governmental administration" and Reformation Protestantism's legalistic view of the divine administration justice and mercy through atonement and "assurance of personal blessedness," Cross would put in place an individualistic modern Protestant "experience of betterment" that empowers as well as delivering from guilt and that has "community-forming power" and a positive attitude toward the material world. The death of Jesus is the "one great eternal act" of "self-giving" that projects itself through the "same self-giving activity" by "his followers." The new Protestantism affirms "the supreme worth of personality," and salvation is its realization. For Cross the church is diffused in society, and universal salvation is anticipated.[419]

Henry Clay Vedder, Baptist historian,[420] editor, and professor, shifted from orthodoxy to evangelical liberalism so as to become the object of criticism by fundamentalists in the 1920s. Educated at the University of

---

[416]Brackney, *A Genetic History of Baptist Thought*, 291, 336, 338. Strong later referred to the appointment of Cross as "the greatest calamity that has come to the [Rochester] seminary since its foundation." *Autobiography of Augustus Hopkins Strong*, ed. Douglas, 357.

[417]*The Theology of Schleiermacher: A Condensed Presentation of His Chief Work, "The Christian Faith"* (Chicago: University of Chicago Press, 1911).

[418]*Creative Christianity: A Study of the Genius of the Christian Faith* (New York: Macmillan Co., 1922) esp. 26, 22. See also his *What Is Christianity? A Study in Rival Interpretations* (Chicago: University of Chicago Press, 1918) 144-71, in which he labeled modern individualistic Protestantism as "evangelicalism."

[419]*Christian Salvation: A Modern Interpretation* (Chicago: University of Chicago Press, 1925) 70-156; 180-254, esp. 80, 88, 95, 103, 118, 120-21, 191-95, 126-33, 205, 135, 153-56, 253.

[420]*The Baptists*, The Story of the Churches (New York: Baker and Taylor, 1903); *A Short History of the Baptists* (Philadelphia: American Baptist Publication Society, 1891; rev. ed., 1907; repr. with new preface, Valley Forge PA: Judson, 1969).

Rochester and Rochester Theological Seminary and having served on the editorial staff of *The Examiner*, he then taught church history at Crozer Theological Seminary from 1894 to 1926. His shift, which occurred between 1908 and 1912, involved the embrace of socialism, evolution, and pragmatism, a new interpretation of the atonement, and salvation as both individual and social. Like Rauschenbusch, he stressed the societal or corporate sins that led to Jesus' death.[421] "Jesus bore our sins, not as substitute . . . but as partner, our elder brother."[422] Furthermore, Vedder concluded that "Jesus and Paul give us quite different ideas of God," and whereas "historic Christianity has followed Paul," "the Christianity of the future must follow Jesus."[423]

Social Gospel: Walter Rauschenbusch

Akin to theological liberalism but also distinctive in nature was the Social Gospel. Identified as "America's most unique contribution to the great ongoing stream of Christianity," it arose during the "Gilded Age" (1865–1880) and "reached its climax" during the years preceding World War I.[424] Influenced by the writings of Thomas Chalmers (1780–1847) of Scotland and the English Christian Socialism of Frederick Denison Maurice (1805–1872) and Charles Kingsley (1819–1875),[425] it critiqued *laissez faire* capitalism, addressing the problems brought by the Industrial Revolution and urbanization. Its earliest pastoral exponents, Washington Gladden

---

[421]Robert B. Hanley, "Henry Clay Vedder: Conservative Evangelical to Evangelical Liberal," *Foundations* 5 (April 1962): 135-57.

[422]Ibid., 148, quoting Vedder, "My Teaching about the Atonement," *The Baptist*, November 1920, 1458.

[423]*The Fundamentals of Christianity: A Study of the Teaching of Jesus and Paul* (New York: Macmillan Co., 1923) 235. See also Dwight A. Honeycutt, *Henry Clay Vedder: His Life and Thought*, Dissertation Reprint Series (Atlanta: Baptist History and Heritage Society, 2008): a reprint of Honeycutt's dissertation originally entitled "A Study of the Life and Thought of Henry Clay Vedder" (Th.D. diss., New Orleans Baptist Theological Seminary, 1984).

[424]Charles Howard Hopkins, *The Rise of the Social Gospel in American Protestantism, 1865–1915*, Yale Studies in Religious Education 14 (New Haven CT: Yale University Press, 1940) 3.

[425]Ibid., 6-7. Willem A. Visser't Hooft, *The Background of the Social Gospel in America* (St. Louis: Bethany, 1963) 66-168, listed also as influences New England Puritanism, the Enlightenment, American revivalism, and the natural and social sciences.

(1836–1918) and Josiah Strong (1847–1916), were Congregationalists.[426] But its most influential theologian in its climactic years was a Baptist, Walter Rauschenbusch.

Born in Rochester, New York, and the son of a Lutheran immigrant from Germany who had become a Baptist and was teaching in the German department of Rochester Seminary, young Walter, converted at seventeen in a pietistic setting, was educated both in Rochester and in Germany and graduated from the University of Rochester and Rochester Seminary. A volunteer for missionary service among the Telugus in India, he was not appointed apparently because of his rejection of biblical inerrancy. Instead he became pastor of the Second German Church in New York City, located "at the edge of a depressed area known as Hell's Kitchen." Confronted there with "unemployment, poverty, wretched housing, malnutrition, disease, ignorance, and crime," Rauschenbusch became increasingly involved in reform movements. During a study leave in 1891 in England and Germany he came under the influence of Schleiermacher, especially Albrecht Ritschl, Julius Wellhausen, Adolf Harnack, and Frederick W. Robertson and shifted toward theological liberalism. In 1897 he began teaching New Testament in the German department of Rochester Seminary, and in 1902 he became professor of church history in the English faculty. The publication of his *Christianity and the Social Crisis* in 1907 afforded him greater leadership of the Social Gospel movement, and his final book, *A Theology for the Social Gospel* (1917) embodied his theology.[427]

---

[426] Hopkins, *The Rise of the Social Gospel*, 337, 350; "Gladden, Washington," *The New Schaff-Herzog Encyclopedia of Religious Knowledge* (Grand Rapids MI: Baker Book House, 1950) 4:492-93; "Strong, Josiah," ibid., 11:115.

[427] Dores Robinson Sharpe, *Walter Rauschenbusch* (New York: Macmillan, 1942) esp. 58; Paul M. Minus, *Walter Rauschenbusch: American Reformer* (New York: Macmillan, 1988) esp. 3, 44, 157; Robert T. Handy, "An Introduction" (to Walter Rauschenbusch), in *The Social Gospel in America, 1870–1920: Gladden, Ely, Rauschenbusch*, A Library of Protestant Thought (New York: Oxford University Press, 1966) esp. 253-55, 258-59; Stephen Brachlow, "Walter Rauschenbusch," in *Baptist Theologians*, ed. George and Dockery, 366, 368-71; Klaus Juergen Jaehn, *Rauschenbusch: The Formative Years* (Valley Forge PA: Judson, 1976); Christopher H. Evans, *The Kingdom Is Always but Coming: A Life of Walter Rauschenbusch* (Grand Rapids MI: Eerdmans, 2004) 19-21, 43-44, 57-83, 92-96, 175-86, 284-85, 295-303.

More ethicist than systematic theologian and the holder of a chair of church history, Rauschenbusch nevertheless took theological positions and expressed theological insights.[428] Contending that under despotic governments Christians had tended to portray God as a despot, he stated that Jesus had "democratized the conception of God" by calling him "Father."[429] Since that Fatherhood had been "distorted and obscured," the Social Gospel needed to recover it.[430] Jesus was the one "who initiated the Kingdom of God," and he needs to be seen as a true person rather than as "a part of a scheme of salvation, the second premise in a great syllogism." The work of the Holy Spirit demonstrates "the social nature of religion," for the Spirit at Pentecost "had become the common property of a group."[431]

Rauschenbusch probably contributed most to three Christian doctrines: sin, the atonement, and the kingdom of God. For him the universality and reality of present evil were more important than a historical fall. Like Robinson[432] and Strong,[433] he preferred to define sin as selfishness. He stressed a social transmission of sin while not denying a biological transmission. The potent "forces of evil" do not consist of Satan and demons but of "super-personal" forces in society. He held to personal salvation from sin through conversion, but the super-personal forces must be brought under the law of Christ and the church "is the social factor in salvation."[434]

Dissatisfied with the historic theories of the atonement because they were shaped by their social and political contexts,[435] the Rochester professor identified "six great public sins" that led to Jesus' death: "religious bigotry," "the combination of graft and political power," "the corruption of justice," "mob spirit and mob action," "militarism," and "class contempt."[436] Although his teaching is akin to the moral influence theory by stressing both the cross's "demonstration of the power of sin in human life" and its

---

[428]Tull, *Shapers of Baptist Thought*, 187; Brachlow, "Walter Rauschenbusch," 371.

[429]*A Theology for the Social Gospel* (New York: Macmillan, 1917; New York: Abingdon, 1945) 174-77.

[430]Tull, *Shapers of Baptist Thought*, 198.

[431]*A Theology for the Social Gospel*, 147-49, 188, 189.

[432]See above, 290.

[433]See above, 299.

[434]*A Theology for the Social Gospel*, 38-130.

[435]Tull, *Shapers of Baptist Thought*, 201.

[436]*A Theology for the Social Gospel*, 240-58.

being "the supreme revelation of love," as Tull declared, Rauschenbusch actually "socialized" the moral influence theory, for "the redeemed" are "to live out" Christ's "self-giving life . . . in the world."[437]

The kingdom of God "is itself the social gospel," indeed "the marrow of the gospel."[438] During Christian history this doctrine has been "attenuated and weakened" by being "superseded" by the church.[439] The kingdom is "divine in its origin, progress and consummation," having been "initiated by Jesus Christ," being "sustained by the Holy Spirit," and to "be brought to its fulfilment by the power of God in his own time." Being both present and future, it is also "humanity organized according to the will of God" and "the purpose for which the Church exists." It is "an historical force," "a vital and organizing energy now at work in humanity."[440] According to Stephen Bracklow, Rauschenbusch opted for a "multidimensional" doctrine of the kingdom that went beyond the revivalist (saved individuals), the premillennialist (future otherworldly kingdom on earth), and German liberal (present ethical human progress) views.[441]

Rauschenbusch explained that he was a Baptist by conviction for four reasons. First, Baptists magnify the primacy of "spiritual experience" for membership and for ministry. This means believer's baptism, a stress on morality rather than ritual, and a quest for "original Christianity."[442] Second, "Baptists embody Christian social principles in their church organization."[443] This means a regenerate church membership, congregational polity and autonomy, the absence of a priestly class or a ministerial hierarchy, and the separation of church and state. Third, Baptists have a superstition-free, simple worship that is to be joined to "a Christlike life." Fourth, Baptists have a growing faith that places the Bible above all creeds and confessions. He concluded: "I am a Baptist, but I am more than a Baptist. All things are mine; whether Francis of Assisi, or Luther, or Knox, or Wesley; all are mine because I am Christ's."[444]

---

[437]Tull, *Shapers of Baptist Thought*, 202-203.
[438]*A Theology for the Social Gospel*, 131.
[439]Tull, *Shapers of Baptist Thought*, 195-96.
[440]*A Theology for the Social Gospel*, 139, 140-41, 142, 143, 165.
[441]"Walter Rauschenbusch," 376-77.
[442]"Why I Am a Baptist," *Baptist Leader*, January 1958, 1-4.
[443]Tull, *Shapers of Baptist Thought*, 205.
[444]"Why I Am a Baptist," 4, 6-10.

Rauschenbusch, saddened by World War I, had both his admirers and his critics. In the larger Protestantism he was the "most brilliant and generally satisfying exponent" of "social Christianity"[445] and "still towers above the other advocates of the social gospel."[446] An "evangelical liberal," he embraced liberalism without abandoning the pietism of his youth, and while seeking to "rediscover the true meaning of ancient Christianity," he propagated "a new genre of Christianity that changed the way Christianity would be interpreted in America."[447] Among Baptists he was regarded at the same time as "a bright ornament in the history of the Baptists"[448] and "a piece of ecclesiastical nebula thrown off by the Baptist denomination as it moved through time in its orbit to complacency."[449]

Northern and Canadian Baptist Fundamentalist Theologians: William Bell Riley (1861–1947), John Roach Straton (1875–1929), Thomas Todhunter Shields (1873–1955), and Jasper Cortenus Massee (1871–1965)

Fundamentalism was the most focused and intensive response within North American Protestantism to theological liberalism and its extremity, theological modernism. Having some rootage in the prophetic and Bible conference movement during the late nineteenth century, it received an impetus from the publication of the 12-volume *The Fundamentals* (1910–1912),[450] but the term "Fundamentalist" was not coined until Curtis Lee Laws (1868–1946), the editor of the national Baptist paper, *Watchman-Examiner*, did so in 1920.[451]

---

[445]Reinhold Niebuhr, *An Interpretation of Christian Ethics* (New York: Harper & Row, 1935) preface.

[446]Handy, "An Introduction," 262.

[447]Evans, *The Kingdom Is Always but Coming*, xxviii-xxx.

[448]Tull, *Shapers of Baptist Thought*, 207.

[449]Sharpe, *Walter Rauschenbusch*, 422.

[450]Published by Lyman and Molton Stewart, brothers, in Los Angeles and edited by Amzi Clarence Dixon (vols. 1-5), Louis Meyer (vols. 6-10), and Rueben Alexander Torrey (vols. 11-12), it contained 90 articles by 64 different authors. Helen C. A. Dixon, *A. C. Dixon: A Romance of Preaching* (New York: G. P. Putnam's Sons, 1931) 184.

[451]"Convention Side Lights," *Watchman-Examiner* 8 (1 July 1920): 834; Brackney, *The Baptists*, 217-18; McBeth, *The Baptist Heritage*, 571; Bill J. Leonard, *Baptist Ways: A History* (Valley Forge PA: Judson, 2003) 399.

The essence of fundamentalism has been variously interpreted by scholars. H. Richard Niebuhr identified it as deriving from Southern rural populism,[452] a view refuted chiefly by the fact that its leaders were pastors in Northern cities, whereas, for John Dillenberger and Claude Welch, it "was essentially akin to" the Lutheran and Calvinistic scholasticism of the seventeenth and eighteenth centuries.[453] Fundamentalism, according to Ernest R. Sandeen, was "an alliance between ... dispensationalism and the Princeton Theology which, though not wholly compatible, managed to maintain a united front against Modernism until about 1918."[454] Donald G. Bloesch, modifying Sandeen, reckoned fundamentalism as "a union of scholastic orthodoxy (both Reformed and Lutheran) and latter-day Pietism, which includes both premillennial and perfectionist strands."[455] According to George M. Marsden, during the 1920s "it was militantly antimodernist Protestant evangelicalism"[456]—a definition which differentiated it from the evangelicalism that preceded it and that which succeeded it.[457]

No one of these definitions precisely located fundamentalism in the Baptist heritage. Yet Baptists were among the leaders of fundamentalism.[458]

---

[452]"Fundamentalism," *Encyclopedia of Social Sciences* (New York: Macmillan, 1931) 6:526-527.

[453]*Protestant Christianity, Interpreted through Its Development* (New York: Scribner's, 1954) 230.

[454]*The Origins of Fundamentalism: Toward a Historical Interpretation*, Facet Books, Historical Series 10 (Philadelphia: Fortress, 1968) 3; orig. publ. as "Toward a Historical Interpretation of the Origins of Fundamentalism," *Church History* 36 (March 1967): 66-83.

[455]*The Evangelical Renaissance* (Grand Rapids MI: Eerdmans, 1973) 143.

[456]*Fundamentalism and American Culture: The Shaping of Twentieth-Century Evangelicalism, 1870–1925* (New York: Oxford University Press, 1980) 4.

[457]More popular definitions of Fundamentalism include those of William Ward Ayer, that it is a "resurgence" of "slumbering apostolicism" that "began not with Luther but at Pentecost" and "lived obscurely through the ages," as quoted by Louis Gasper, *The Fundamentalist Movement* (The Hague: Mouton and Co., 1963) 2, 3, and of Jerry Falwell, Ed Dobson, and Ed Hindson, *The Fundamentalist Phenomenon: The Resurgence of Conservative Christianity* (Garden City NY: Doubleday and Co., 1981) 2, 4, as "the militant and faithful defenders of biblical orthodoxy" and "reactionary Evangelicalism."

[458]In C. Allyn Russell, *Voices of American Fundamentalism: Seven Biographical Studies* (Philadelphia: Westminster, 1967) four of the seven leaders studied were Baptists, and three were Presbyterians.

Northern Baptists and Northern Presbyterians have been identified by George M. Marsden as the two denominations most conflicted by antimodernism,[459] and Winthrop S. Hudson declared that "Northern Baptists were more deeply divided, distracted, and immobilized by the Fundamentalist controversy than any other denomination" in the United States.[460]

Whether there were five agreed upon "fundamentals" and whether the identity of the five, such as biblical inerrancy, the virginal conception of Jesus, his substitutionary atonement, his bodily resurrection, and his second coming to earth,[461] was widely agreed upon are questions which continue to be probed.[462]

Probably no Baptist exerted more influence over an extended period of time upon fundamentalism than William Bell Riley.[463] Born and reared in Kentucky, he was graduated from Hanover College and Southern Baptist Theological Seminary. After brief pastorates in Indiana and Illinois, including the Calvary Church of Chicago, he began in 1897 a forty-five year pastorate of First Church, Minneapolis, Minnesota. He was a pastor-evangelist, active in campaigns in other cities, and long engaged in the campaign against evolution. Unsuccessful in getting the Northern Baptist Convention in 1922 to recommend the New Hampshire Confession of Faith, Riley joined with T. T. Shields of Toronto and John Franklyn Norris (1877–1952), pastor of First Church, Fort Worth, Texas, in 1923 in organizing the Baptist Bible Union of North America, (BBUNA),[464] and Riley led in founding and in 1919 became the first president of the interdenominational

---

[459] *Fundamentalism and American Culture*, 164-65.

[460] *Baptists in Transition: Individualism and Christian Responsibility* (Valley Forge PA: Judson, 1979) 120.

[461] Sometimes the deity of Christ and miracles were included among the five, and antievolution was always a major consideration.

[462] James Leo Garrett, Jr., "Who Are the 'Evangelicals'?," in Garrett, E. Glenn Hinson, and James E. Tull, *Are Southern Baptists "Evangelicals"?* (Macon GA: Mercer University Press, 1983) 48-49.

[463] Russell, *Voices of American Fundamentalism*, 105, called Riley (known far and wide as "The Grand Old Man of Fundamentalism") "the most important fundamentalist minister of his generation."

[464] See Robert G. Delnay, "A History of the Baptist Bible Union" (Th.D. diss., Dallas Theological Seminary, 1963); Stewart G. Cole, *The History of Fundamentalism* (New York: Richard R. Smith, 1931; repr.: Westport CT: Greenwood, 1971) 281-94.

World's Christian Fundamentals Association.⁴⁶⁵ He founded three educational institutions in Minneapolis (1902, 1938, 1944) and near his death bequeathed them to the leadership of a young evangelist, Billy Graham. He was favorable to the formation of the Conservative Baptist Association of America and at the end of his life withdrew from the Northern Baptist Convention.⁴⁶⁶

The "Modernism" that Riley found to be a "menace" he defined as centering in the view that "the Bible is purely human in its origin and authorship" and contains errors, whereas for Riley "the Bible is divine in origin, and human in expression." The "accepted versions . . . are all substantially correct," and its "true interpretation . . . involves both the literal and the spiritual."⁴⁶⁷ He defended the Bible against the "higher critics" as to its claims as to human authors and "the historicity of recorded events." Their work, he charged in 1909, breeds "skepticism" in educational institutions and in pulpits and may warrant ecclesiastical separation. But the coming religion, he asserted, will be shaped by Christ-centered, biblical orthodoxy, not by higher criticism.⁴⁶⁸ Surprisingly in his debate with Harry

---

⁴⁶⁵The text of its nine-article, premillennial doctrinal statement has been reproduced by William Vance Trollinger, Jr., *God's Empire: William Bell Riley and Midwestern Fundamentalism* (Madison: University of Wisconsin Press, 1990) 163.

⁴⁶⁶Marie Acomb Riley, *The Dynamic of a Dream: The Life Story of Dr. William B. Riley* (Grand Rapids MI: Eerdmans, 1938); Trollinger, *God's Empire: William Bell Riley and Midwestern Fundamentalism*; Russell, *Voices of American Fundamentalism*, 79-106; Timothy P. Weber, "William Bell Riley," in *Baptist Theologians*, ed. George and Dockery, 351-56, 361-62; Ferenc Morton Szasz, "Three Fundamentalist Leaders: The Roles of William Bell Riley, John Roach Straton, and William Jennings Bryan in the Fundamentalist-Modernist Controversy" (Ph.D. diss., University of Rochester, 1969) 77-99, 377; Robert Sheldon McBirnie, "Basic Issues in the Fundamentalism of W. B. Riley" (Ph.D. diss., State University of Iowa, 1952) 45-54, 79-88, 121-26; Robert E. Wenger, "Social Thought in American Fundamentalism, 1918–1933" (Ph.D. diss., University of Nebraska, 1973) 307; Walter Edmund Warren Ellis, "Social and Religious Factors in the Fundamentalist-Modernist Schisms among Baptists in North America, 1895–1934" (Ph.D. diss., University of Pittsburgh, 1974) 96-131.

⁴⁶⁷*The Menace of Modernism* (New York: Christian Alliance Publishing Co., 1917), 7-31.

⁴⁶⁸*The Finality of the Higher Criticism, or the Theory of Evolution and False Theology* (Minneapolis: author, 1909; repr., ed. Joel A. Carpenter, New York: Garland Publishing, 1988) 9-15, 25-70, 207-23.

Rimmer, Riley defended the view that the Genesis days of creation were "aeons, ages, geological days, [or] days of God," not solar days.[469]

The authors who have written about Riley are strangely silent as to how and when Riley embraced dispensational eschatology, for he did not derive such from his seminary professors. That he affirmed key features of the Darbyite system is evident from his books. The kingdom of God, being future in nature, is to be established at the second coming of Christ, "the blessed hope."[470] The Word of God is not the kingdom in embryo, but the believer or the church is the kingdom in embryo.[471] The church will disappear with the advent of the kingdom.[472] A great apostasy is approaching,[473] and the church will be raptured in "a triumphant exit" from the earth,[474] thus escaping the great tribulation.[475] "Israelites" will be "natural citizens" of the kingdom of God, whereas "regenerate Gentiles" will be its "adopted citizens."[476] There will be two resurrections separated in time by the millennium[477] and seemingly multiple judgments.[478]

Another major defender of the fundamentals of the faith was John Roach Straton. The son of the pastor of First Church, Evansville, Indiana, who had immigrated from Scotland, and reared in Georgia and Alabama, he studied in Mercer University, during which time he was converted at eighteen and excelled in oratory, in Southern Baptist Theological Seminary, and in the Boston School of Oratory and Expression. After teaching oratory at Mercer and at Baylor University and following pastorates in Chicago, Baltimore, and Norfolk, Straton served the Calvary Church, New York City

---

[469] With Harry Rimmer, *A Debate: Resolved, That the Creative Days in Genesis Were Aeons, Not Solar Days* (N.p., 1929).

[470] *The Only Hope of Church or World: What Is It?* (London: Pickering and Inglis, 1936) 36-37, 47-54.

[471] *The Evolution of the Kingdom* (New York: Charles C. Cook, 1912) 26-30, 41-44; *Re-thinking the Church* (New York: Fleming H. Revell Co., 1940) 27-45.

[472] *The Evolution of the Kingdom*, 44-46.

[473] *The Only Hope of Church or World*, 147-51.

[474] *The Evolution of the Kingdom*, 82-85; *Is Jesus Coming Again?*, 4th ed. (Grand Rapids MI: Zondervan, n.d.) 100-103, 138-39.

[475] *Is Jesus Coming Again?*, 95-100.

[476] Ibid., 69-78.

[477] *The Only Hope of Church or World*, 71-72; *The Evolution of the Kingdom*, 78-81.

[478] *The Only Hope of Church or World*, 144; *The Evolution of the Kingdom*, 137-42.

(1918–1929), during which decade he was active in the developing Fundamentalist cause within the Northern Baptist Convention.[479]

More than any Baptist fundamentalist Straton participated in public debates. Straton challenged Harry Emerson Fosdick to a debate, but Fosdick declined. Charles Francis Potter, minister of the West Side Unitarian Church in New York City and an ex-Baptist, challenged Straton to debates, and four such were held during 1923–1924.[480] In the first such debate Straton defended the Bible as "the infallible Word of God" from its preservation and circulation, its "unique universality," its "unity in diversity," its "fulfilled prophecies," its "claims concerning itself," and its "self-authenticating authority."[481] He took the negative in the debate on the proposition "that the earth and man came by evolution" and sought chiefly to answer the claims of evolutionists and to pose as ultimate the issue of cause and design versus chance.[482] Straton's son later stated that his father "had once believed in theistic evolution" and "was primarily an orator, not a scientist."[483] In the third debate Straton affirmed the proposition "that the miraculous virgin birth of Jesus Christ is a fact and . . . is an essential Christian doctrine," arguing for its "possibility" vis-à-vis natural law, its

---

[479]Russell, *Voices of American Fundamentalism*, 48, 50; Szasz, "Three Fundamentalist Leaders," 67-70; Wenger, "Social Thought in American Fundamentalism," 309-10; Hillyer H. Straton, "John Roach Straton, Prophet of Social Righteousness: Three Decades of Protestant Activism," *Foundations* 5 (January 1962): 17-38; Ferenc M. Szasz, "John Roach Straton: Baptist Fundamentalist in an Age of Change, 1875–1929," *Quarterly Review* 34 (April-May-June 1974): 59-71; John Haynes Holmes, "Straton, John Roach," *Dictionary of American Biography* 18:125-26; Walter Ross Peterson, "John Roach Straton: Portrait of a Fundamentalist Preacher" (Ph.D. diss., Boston University, 1965) 34-38, 48-49.

[480]Hillyer H. Straton, "John Roach Straton: The Great Evolution Debate," *Foundations* 10 (April-June 1967): 138-39; Russell, *Voices of American Fundamentalism*, 65-75. Straton's side of these debates was published in Straton, *The Famous New York Fundamentalist-Modernist Debates: The Orthodox Side* (New York: George H. Doran Co., 1925). Both sides were published in four separate volumes by George H. Doran Co. in 1924 and reprinted in *Fundamentalist versus Modernist: The Debates between John Roach Straton and Charles Francis Potter*, ed. Joel A. Carpenter, Fundamentalism in American Religion, 1880–1950 (New York: Garland Publishing, 1988). Subsequent citations will be from the last named.

[481]*Fundamentalist versus Modernist*, 13-51.

[482]Ibid., 30-85.

[483]Hillyer Straton, "John Roach Straton," 137, 148.

"probability" because of Old Testament prophecies, its "positive proofs" in Matthew and Luke and in the early church fathers, and its "alone" giving "an adequate object of worship."[484] In the fourth debate Straton defended the negative on the proposition "that Jesus Christ was entirely man instead of incarnate Deity." Deploring those who would merely "compliment" Jesus, he marshaled New Testament testimony to the deity of Jesus, such as his wisdom, sinlessness, love, power, and specific claims, together with his subsequent influence.[485] Straton had other debates on evolution, the first with Henry Fairfield Osborn (1857–1935), Columbia University professor of zoology and curator of the American Museum of Natural History, and later with Kirtley Fletcher Mather (1888–1978), Harvard University geology professor and Baptist layman.[486]

Straton's change of position respecting evolution was not the only theological shift during his later years. Following A. J. Gordon, he espoused divine healing through faith, without denial of physicians or medicine, on the basis of Christ's atonement (Matt. 8:17).[487] In 1926, after bringing to the Calvary pulpit Uldine Utley, a fourteen-year-old girl evangelist from California, Straton, in response to Baptist critics, issued a defense within avowed biblical inerrancy of women preachers, though not pastors, on the basis of Joel 2:28-32; Acts 2:17-21; 1 Cor. 11:5, and Gal. 3:28 and by taking 1 Cor. 14:34-35 as protection of Corinthian Christian women "from the slanders and innuendos associated with prostitutes" and 1 Tim. 2:11-12 as protection against "female usurpers" who encroach on male authority.[488]

In his study of Straton's preaching, Walter Ross Peterson treated his theology by commencing with his view of the Bible, concluding with his opposition to evolution, and sandwiching between his espousal of the five points of fundamentalism. As to the latter, Straton gave little pulpit attention

---

[484]*Fundamentalist versus Modernist*, 11-53.
[485]Ibid., 25-65.
[486]Hillyer Straton, "John Roach Straton," 140-48.
[487]*Divine Healing in Scripture and Life* (New York: Christian Alliance Publishing, 1927) esp. 80-90, 109-27.
[488]Lee Canipe, "The Unlikely Argument of a Baptist Fundamentalist: John Roach Straton's Defense of Women in the Pulpit," *Baptist History and Heritage* 40 (Spring 2005): 64-76. The text of Straton's pamphlet "Does the Bible Forbid Women to Preach and Pray in Public?" has been reprinted in Janette Hassey, *No Time for Silence: Evangelical Women in Public Ministry around the Turn of the Century* (Grand Rapids MI: Zondervan, 1986) 189-210.

to the virgin birth or substitutionary atonement, had more to say about Jesus' resurrection, and preached most often on the second coming of Christ in the context of his espoused dispensationalism.[489]

Allied with Baptist fundamentalists in the United States was Thomas Todhunter Shields, the pastor of Jarvis Street Church, Toronto, from 1910 to 1955. A native of Bristol, England, and the son of a Primitive Methodist preacher who had become a Baptist before the family emigrated to Plattsville, Ontario, and soon became the Baptist pastor in Plattsville, the younger Shields, mentored by his father, had had several pastorates in Ontario before going to "the metropolitan church" of the Baptist denomination in Canada. Shields's contribution to Baptist fundamentalism was not so much through writings as through his activism. In 1922 he began publishing *The Gospel Witness*. In 1923 he, W. B. Riley, and J. Frank Norris led in organizing the Baptist Bible Union of North America, and Shields was named its first president. When the union took over a Northern Baptist institution, Des Moines University in Iowa, Shields chaired its board briefly before its closure in 1929. As a sequel to his criticism of liberalizing trends in McMaster University and his being censured by the Baptist Convention of Ontario and Quebec, he led in 1927 in the formation of a separatist body, the Union of Regular Baptist Churches of Ontario and Quebec, which much later after splits and merger became the Fellowship of Evangelical Baptist Churches. Shields likewise founded his own Toronto Baptist Seminary.[490] A strident controversialist, he was a moderate Calvinist[491] and rejected dis-

---

[489]"John Roach Straton: Portrait of a Fundamentalist Preacher," 51-207.

[490]Leslie K. Tarr, *Shields of Canada: T. T. Shields (1873–1955)* (Grand Rapids MI: Baker Book House, 1967) esp. 14-17, 18, 50, 91-120; Brackney, *The Baptists*, 256-57; McBeth, *The Baptist Heritage*, 557-59, 575-76, 756-57; Tarr, "Another Perspective on T. T. Shields and Fundamentalism," in *Baptists in Canada: Search for Identity amidst Diversity*, ed. Jarold K. Zeman (Burlington ON: G. R. Welch Co., 1980) 209-24; Clark H. Pinnock, "The Modernist Impulse at McMaster University, 1887–1927," in ibid., 193-207; Robert David Blackaby, "Baptist Approaches to the Issue of Church and State in Canada: Contributions and Evaluation of William Aberhart, Thomas Clement Douglas, and Thomas Todhunter Shields" (Ph.D. diss., Southwestern Baptist Theological Seminary, 1998) 107-17.

[491]*The Doctrines of Grace* (Toronto: Gospel Witness, 1955). Shields did not wish to be identified as Arminian, held to particular election, and was emphatic on perseverance but seems not to have embraced limited atonement or irresistible grace (35, 42, 100-13, 136-72).

pensationalism.[492] In the larger context, "Canadian [Baptist] fundamentalism was a coalition of Shieldsite Spurgeonic Baptists with classical Philadelphia-type Regular Baptists and with premillenarian dispensationalists influenced by the Prophetic Conference movement."[493]

On the moderate side of Northern Baptist fundamentalism was Jasper Cortenus Massee. A native of Marshallville, Georgia, whose parents had Primitive Baptist roots, and converted at nine or ten, he was graduated from Mercer University in 1892 and studied for one year at Southern Baptist Theological Seminary. Massee had a succession of brief pastorates in Florida, Kentucky, Ohio, North Carolina, and Tennessee before serving Baptist Temple, Brooklyn, New York (1920–1922) and Tremont Temple Church, Boston (1922–1929), during which time he exerted leadership in the Northern Baptist Convention. He presided over the preconvention conference on Baptist fundamentals in Buffalo in 1920 and was elected president of the Fundamental Fellowship. But by 1925 he resigned his position, for the strong fundamentalists found him to be too moderate and he found their denunciation of conservatives unwarranted. Massee remained with the Northern Baptist Convention and protested the separation of the Conservative Baptists in the 1940s.[494] Massee, who championed the fundamentals against modernism, also feared "the heresy of spirit."[495] A biographer has noted that Massee "never referred to the Scriptures as inerrant, and only on rare occasions did he speak of them as infallible," for his "view of inspiration was more pragmatic in nature."[496] Massee defended biblical miracles,"[497] interpreted the tongues of Acts 2:4 as other known languages and the other references to tongues in Acts and 1 Corinthians as "unknown tongues," and emphasized repeated fillings with the Spirit and the purging

---

[492]Tarr, "Another Perspective on T. T. Shields and Fundamentalism," 220. Tarr thinks that Shields was a "modified amillennialist." See also Donald Tinder, "Fundamentalist Baptists in the Northern and Western United States, 1920–1950" (Ph.D. diss., Yale University, 1969) 126n.4.

[493]Ellis, "Social and Religious Factors in the Fundamentalist-Modernist Schisms," 232.

[494]Russell, *Voices of American Fundamentalism*, 107-12, 119-30.

[495]Ibid., 122.

[496]Ibid., 112-13.

[497]*Conflict and Conquest in Holiness* (New York: Fleming H. Revell Co., 1924) 83-113.

and enabling fire of the Spirit.[498] Atypical of Baptists from the South, he favored open communion and the converting power of the Lord's Supper so that his view has been compared with Stoddardeanism.[499] An avowed premillennialist but not a dispensationalist, Massee stressed the present consequences of anticipating the second coming of Christ[500] and chose not to attach a "program of events" to the second coming.[501]

Baptist Congress

From 1882 to 1913 the annual Baptist Congress for the Discussion of Current Questions provided an open forum for Baptists in North America to present papers on and engage in discussion about a wide range of subjects: doctrinal, ethical, polity-related, social, and political. Diverse viewpoints were normally represented by the various presenters. The great majority of participants were Northern Baptists, but Southern Baptists were often speakers, and a few were Canadian Baptists. In the normally fraternal atmosphere increasingly theological differences and tensions became evident.[502]

---

[498] *The Holy Spirit* (New York: Fleming H. Revell, 1940) 78-97, 116-35.

[499] Russell, *Voices of American Fundamentalism*, 114.

[500] *The Second Coming* (Philadelphia: Philadelphia School of the Bible, 1919) 55-146, 191-212.

[501] *The Ten Greatest Christian Doctrines* (New York: George H. Doran Co., 1925) 181-84.

[502] William H. Brackney, "The Frontier of Free Exchange of Ideas: The Baptist Congress as a Forum for Baptist Concerns, 1881–1913," *Baptist History and Heritage* 38 (Summer/Fall 2003): 8-27. Norman Fox, one of the founders of the congress, declared that the congress "was organized upon a denial of the infallibility not only of the Church of Rome, but of the Baptist churches also," the supposition being that the majority of the Baptists "might err" and a minority "might . . . be right." Fox, "The Baptist Congress," in Newman, ed., *A Century of Baptist Achievement*, 291. Brackney, 23, attributed the demise of the congress to declining attendance and interest and to the fact that the "Baptist World Alliance had become a preferred gathering." See also Roland Tenus Nelson, "Fundamentalism and the Northern Baptist Convention" (Ph.D. diss., University of Chicago, 1964) 94-106.

Numerous discussions dealt with the Bible and religious authority: the authenticity[503] and canonicity[504] of the biblical books, the inspiration of the Bible,[505] its inerrancy,[506] modern biblical criticism,[507] whether New Testament precedent carries the authority of divine command,[508] whether apostolic teachings are of equal authority with those of Jesus,[509] the relative authority of the Bible and reason,[510] the role of tradition among Baptists,[511] the role of creeds,[512] authority in Protestantism,[513] and the authority of the Christian consciousness.[514] At times the discussions focused on the doctrine of God: God's immanence,[515] God's fatherhood as universal or particular,[516] and whether the New Testament warrants a formal doctrine of the Trinity.[517] Divine healing[518] and evolution in relation to humanity's fall received attention.[519] Relative to Jesus Christ attention was given to his deity,[520] his

---

[503] *Sixteenth Annual Session of the Baptist Congress for the Discussion of Current Questions . . . 1898* (New York: Baptist Congress Publishing Co., 1898) 73-106.

[504] *Twenty-Eight Annual Session . . . 1910* (Chicago: University of Chicago Press, 1911) 151-90.

[505] *Fifth Annual Session . . . 1886* (New York: Baptist Congress Publishing Co., 1887) 10-23.

[506] *Tenth Annual Session . . . 1892* (ibid., 1892) 62-92.

[507] *Proceedings of the Second Annual Baptist Autumnal Conference . . . 1883* (Boston: Baptist Missionary Rooms, 1883) 54-71; *Twenty-Ninth Annual Session . . . 1911* (Chicago: University of Chicago Press, 1912) 34-67.

[508] *Fourteenth Annual Session . . . 1896* (New York: Baptist Congress Publishing Co., 1897) 10-13.

[509] *Fifteenth Annual Session . . . 1897* (ibid., 1898) 8-37.

[510] *Tenth Annual Session . . . 1892*, 168-93.

[511] *Twelfth Annual Session . . . 1894* (ibid., 1895) 2-32.

[512] *Seventeenth Annual Session . . . 1899* (ibid., 1899) 152-87, 190-95.

[513] *Twenty-Third Annual Session . . . 1905* (ibid., 1906) 37-63.

[514] *Proceedings of the Eighth Congress . . . 1889* (ibid., n.d.) 76-91.

[515] *Ninth Annual Session . . . 1890* (ibid., 1890) 167-87.

[516] *Fourteenth Annual Session . . . 1896*, 106-31.

[517] *Twenty-Fourth Annual Session . . . 1906* (ibid., 1906) 65-90.

[518] *Fifth Annual Session . . . 1886*, 23-39.

[519] *Sixteenth Annual Session . . . 1898* (ibid., 1898) 6-36.

[520] *Twenty-Ninth Annual Session . . . 1911*, 8-29.

virginal conception,[521] his roles as liberator and unifier,[522] and his atonement as substitutionary in relation to modern alternative views.[523] Furthermore, treatment was afforded justification as forensic or ethical,[524] the role of penalty,[525] salvation as mediated through Christ,[526] union with Christ,[527] the baptism and the role of the Holy Spirit,[528] and prayer.[529] As expected, ecclesiological topics frequently surfaced: the purity of church membership,[530] the nature of a Baptist church,[531] valid baptism,[532] baptism and church membership,[533] baptism and participation in the Lord's Supper,[534] the ordinances in general,[535] Baptist polity,[536] organic church

---

[521]*Twenty-Fifth Annual Session . . . 1907* (New York: Baptist Congress Publishing Co., n.d.) 13-42.

[522]*Twelfth Annual Session . . . 1894*, 216-32.

[523]*Eighteenth Annual Session . . . 1900* (ibid., 1900) 85-115; *Twenty-Sixth Annual Session . . . 1908* (Chicago: University of Chicago Press, n.d.) 81-110.

[524]*Eleventh Annual Session . . . 1893* (New York: Baptist Congress Publishing Co., 1894) 52-74.

[525]*Nineteenth Annual Session . . . 1901* (ibid., 1901) 86-111.

[526]*Twenty-Seventh Annual Session . . . 1909* (Chicago: University of Chicago Press, 1909) 73-106.

[527]*Sixteenth Annual Session . . . 1898*, 164-80.

[528]*Thirteenth Annual Session . . . 1895* (New York: Baptist Congress Publishing Co., 1896) 178-97; *Nineteenth Annual Session . . . 1901*, 182-201; *Twenty-Eighth Annual Session . . . 1910* (Chicago: University of Chicago Press, 1911) 45-74.

[529]*Twenty-Eighth Annual Session . . . 1910*, 12-42.

[530]*Seventh Annual Session . . . 1888* (New York: Baptist Congress Publishing Co., 1889) 161-81.

[531]*Thirtieth Annual Session . . . 1912* (Chicago: University of Chicago Press, 1913) 39-66.

[532]*Eleventh Annual Session . . . 1893*, 79-101.

[533]*Twentieth Annual Session . . . 1902* (New York: Baptist Congress Publishing Co., 1902) 8-42.

[534]*Fifteenth Annual Session . . . 1897*, 38-73.

[535]*Twenty-Third Annual Session . . . 1905*, 96-136.

[536]*Thirteenth Annual Session . . . 1895*, 35-57; *Twenty-Second Annual Session . . . 1904* (ibid., 1905) 98-125.

union,[537] the priesthood of all believers,[538] and Sunday observance.[539] A noneschatological approach to the kingdom of God,[540] eschatological resurrection,[541] immortality vis-à-vis science,[542] and hell and its alternatives[543] were also considered.

Northern Baptist Convention Controversy, 1920–1950

After World War I theological controversy intensified in the Northern Baptist Convention (NBC), which had been constituted in 1907–1908 out of the cluster of Northern Baptist societies. In 1907 a group of Baptists in southern Illinois had organized a new state body in opposition to the retention of "theological liberals" in the old state body and the liberalizing direction of the University of Chicago and in 1910 had affiliated with the Southern Baptist Convention.[544] Moreover, conservative Northern Baptists had founded Northern Baptist Theological Seminary in Chicago in 1913 and would establish Eastern Baptist Theological Seminary in Philadelphia in 1925.[545]

In 1919 the interdenominational Interchurch World Movement, "a colossal effort both to raise money and to coordinate Protestant benevolence and missions,"[546] was launched, and Northern Baptists, with strong liberal support, affiliated under the name, the New World Movement. But conservative criticism was strong; in 1920 the NBC withdrew from its interdenominational connections, and by 1924 the movement had been com-

---

[537]*Sixth Annual Session . . . 1888* (ibid., 1888) 2-23; *Twenty-Second Annual Session . . . 1904*, 160-77; *Twenty-Sixth Annual Session . . . 1908*, 206-12, 223-34; *Twenty-Eighth Annual Session . . . 1910*, 106-50; *Twenty-Ninth Annual Session . . . 1911*, 110-17, 126-41.

[538]*Seventeenth Annual Session . . . 1899*, 196-214.

[539]*Fifth Annual Session . . . 1886*, 76-88; *Proceedings of the Eighth Congress . . . 1889*, 146-63.

[540]*Twelfth Annual Session . . . 1894*, 122-55.

[541]*Seventeenth Annual Session . . . 1899*, 11-40.

[542]*Twenty-First Annual Session . . . 1903* (ibid., 1904) 135-70.

[543]*Fifth Annual Session . . . 1886*, 92-110.

[544]Torbet, *A History of the Baptists*, 444; Baker, *The Southern Baptist Convention and Its People*, 337; McBeth, *The Baptist Heritage*, 624-25.

[545]Torbet, *A History of the Baptists*, 444, 449; McBeth, *The Baptist Heritage*, 570, 593-95.

[546]Marsden, *Fundamentalism and American Culture*, 166.

pleted.[547] Prior to the NBC session in Buffalo, New York, in 1920, a "two-day rally" of fundamentalists and conservatives led by Massee, Riley, Straton, and Laws resulted in the forming of the "Fundamental Fellowship of Northern Baptists" and to annual preconvention meetings.[548] In its 1921 preconvention meeting in Des Moines, Iowa, the Fundamental Fellowship adopted a rather general seven-article confession of faith which had been written by Frank Marsden Goodchild (1860–1928),[549] pastor of Central Church, New York City.[550] It affirmed the inspiration and authority of the Bible (art. 2), the attributes of God (art. 2), the holy history of Jesus as "God's only begotten Son" (art. 3), the work of the Holy Spirit (art. 4), sin and salvation (art. 5), the church, universal and visible, and its ordinances and mission (art. 6), and conscience, church autonomy, and church-state separation (art. 7).[551] The Goodchild confession did not address such issues as theories of biblical inspiration, theories of atonement, or millennial views.

Criticism of Northern Baptist educational institutions at Buffalo in 1920 led to the appointment of a nine-member committee, with Goodchild as chairman, to investigate such institutions as to whether they "are still loyal to the great fundamental Baptist truths."[552] Its 1921 report in Des Moines classified the institutions as to their extent of Baptist governance and commended most of them while acknowledging that a few teachers needed to be removed according to due process.[553] The NBC's Board of Education defended the schools and claimed that the charges were "'largely false.'"[554]

---

[547]Ibid., 166, 276; Torbet, *A History of the Baptists*, 408, 409, 445, 455; McBeth, *The Baptist Heritage*, 566-68, 570, 601, 756.

[548]Torbet, *A History of the Baptists*, 445; McBeth, *The Baptist Heritage*, 570-71, 756; Lumpkin, *Baptist Confessions of Faith*, 381. (The original name [1920] was the "National Federation of Fundamentalists of the Northern Baptists.")

[549]Lumpkin, *Baptist Confession of Faith*, 381.

[550]Goodchild was the author of *Can We Believe? Popular Discussions of Fundamental Christian Truths* (New York: Fleming H. Revell, 1926) and of *Around the Lord's Table: Addresses Preparatory to the Lord's Supper* (New York: Fleming H. Revell, 1927).

[551]Lumpkin, *Baptist Confessions of Faith*, 382-84; *The Chronicle* 7 (April 1944): 57-58.

[552]*Annual*, NBC, 1920, 48.

[553]*Annual*, NBC, 1921, 49-93.

[554]McBeth, *The Baptist Heritage*, 572.

In 1922, following Fosdick's May sermon, "Shall the Fundamentalists Win?," W. B. Riley moved that the NBC in Indianapolis recommend to its affiliated churches their adoption of the New Hampshire Confession (1853 edition). Cornelius Woelfkin (1859–1928), pastor of Park Avenue Church in New York City, offered a substitute motion stating that "the Northern Baptist Convention affirms that the New Testament is the all-sufficient ground of our faith and practice, and we need no other statement." Woelfkin's motion prevailed by a vote of 1,264 to 637.[555] The effort of fundamentalists to secure a recommended NBC confessional standard failed. The immediate result was that the more militant, being impatient, "followed Riley in the formation of the Baptist Bible Union [of North America]" and the more moderate such as Massee, Straton, and Goodchild sought to work within the NBC "to retain whatever influence they could."[556] According to McBeth, neither group "captured" the NBC, and "each inflicted gaping wounds which have never healed."[557]

The BBUNA adopted in Kansas City in 1923 a newly drafted eighteen-article confession of faith.[558] Article one on the Scriptures was taken from the New Hampshire Confession, and to it were added explanatory statements about the Bible as the word of God and as inerrant. The divine attributes and the Trinity (art. 2) and the divine personhood of the Holy Spirit (art. 3) were affirmed. A lengthy article on Satan (art. 4) was followed by affirmation of a historical fall and the universality of sin by choice and a denial of evolution (arts. 5-6). The "virgin birth," the sinless and obedient life, and the substitutionary death of Jesus were clearly defended (arts. 7-8). The new birth or new creation was said to be "instantaneous" and supernatural, and justification to involve the imputation of Christ's righteousness (arts. 9, 11). Moreover, nothing besides "his own inherent depravity and voluntary rejection of the gospel"—such as a decree of reprobation—can prevent

---

[555]*Annual*, NBC, 1922, 129-34; Torbet, *A History of the Baptists*, 445-46; McBeth, *The Baptist Heritage*, 576-77; Marsden, *Fundamentalism and American Culture*, 171-72.

[556]Marsden, *Fundamentalism and American Culture*, 172.

[557]*The Baptist Heritage*, 577-78. See Kendal P. Mobley, "Helen Barrett Montgomery: 'A Middle-of-the-Road Baptist' Bible Translator," *Baptist History and Heritage* 42 (Spring 2007): 55-68.

[558]Lumpkin, *Baptist Confessions of Faith*, 384, reported that Shields "was chiefly responsible" for the composing of this confession and that it is "remarkably concise and definite."

"the salvation of the greatest sinner," and repentance and faith are both "solemn obligations" and "inseparable graces" (arts. 10, 12). Language about a particular church was taken from the New Hampshire Confession, but its officers were to be "pastors, elders and deacons," and both autonomy and cooperation were affirmed (art. 13). Again the influence of the New Hampshire Confession can be seen in the emblematic view of the Lord's Supper and close communion (art. 14), in perseverance as both the endurance of true believers and the keeping of God (art. 15), as to the present differences between and the future separation of the righteous and the wicked (art. 16), and in the verbatim borrowing as to civil government (art. 17). The eschatology centered in Christ's second coming, "the resurrection of the righteous dead" so as to imply a separate resurrection of the wicked, and Christ's "reign on earth" (art. 18).[559]

In 1922 Frederick L. Anderson on behalf of the American Baptist Foreign Mission Society had explained the society's procedure in examining candidates doctrinally so as to profess "doctrinal soundness without commitment to a specific doctrinal statement."[560] The 1924 NBC session in Milwaukee adopted Massee's motion calling for a seven-member committee to investigate "the conduct, policies, and practices" of the society "in the selection of missionaries,"[561] and Anderson reported that the society granted "liberty of theological opinion" within limits but that the missionaries are teaching and preaching . . . the evangelical gospel common to our Baptist faith."[562] At Seattle in 1925 the committee in its report indicated that the society had followed an "inclusive" appointment policy within the limits of Christ, the gospel, and Baptist principles,[563] that there were a few missionaries "who apparently denied basic Baptist beliefs," and that "more careful appointment procedures" and more adequate "monitoring" of missionaries

---

[559]Ibid., 385-89. Joseph M. Stowell, *Background and History of the General Association of Regular Baptist Churches* (Hayward CA: J. F. May, 1949) 82-87, has provided a text of this confession as affirmed by the General Association of Regular Baptists which condenses articles 1, 4, 5, 11, and 14, deletes "elders" (art. 12) and close communion (art. 14), and supplies the biblical reference for each article.

[560]Torbet, *A History of the Baptists*, 446; *Annual*, NBC, 1922, 87, 561-62.

[561]*Annual*, NBC, 1924, 51.

[562]*Annual,* NBC, 1924, 50, 529-38.

[563]*Annual*, NBC, 1925, 79-94, esp. 85-86.

were needed.[564] Unsatisfied, W. B. Hinson of Portland, Oregon, moved the immediate recall of doctrinally deviant missionaries on the basis of a confession stated in his motion. An amendment by R. V. Meigs of Illinois to leave these matters to the society for implementation prevailed on a 742-574 vote.[565] The resignation of three of the society's missionaries over theological issues led in 1928 to the formation of the Association of Baptists for World Evangelism.[566]

After a period of decline for the BBUNA, its 1932 meeting in Chicago marked a significant turning point. "This meeting was to be both the last gathering of the Baptist Bible Union and the first of the General Association of Regular Baptist Churches" (GARBC).[567] The GARBC has been characterized by a firm embrace of premillennialism[568] and by a strict tenet of absolute separation from those who are in any way connected with theological liberalism.[569]

The moderate fundamentalists, or conservatives, who remained in the NBC after 1923 continued to find reasons for dissatisfaction with the direction of the NBC. The chief issues were the doctrinal convictions of foreign missionaries ("inclusive policy" instead of "evangelical policy") and what was deemed to be "an excessive denominational bureaucracy."[570] Ultimately in 1943 the Conservative Baptist Foreign Mission Society (CBFMS) was formed with an evangelical policy and as a society within the NBC. But the latter connection met with resistance from the NBC leadership; consequently in 1947 the Conservative Baptist Association of America (CBAA) was constituted. By 1950 the Conservative Baptist Home Mission Society had been incorporated.[571] The eight-article doctrinal

---

[564]McBeth, *The Baptist Heritage*, 574-75.

[565]*Annual*, NBC, 1925, 94-96, 174-75; Torbet, *A History of the Baptists*, 448-49; McBeth, *The Baptist Heritage*, 575.

[566]Torbet, *A History of the Baptists*, 411.

[567]Stowell, *Background and History*, 33; Nelson, "Fundamentalism and the Northern Baptist Convention," 385-420.

[568]Stowell, *Background and History*, 22.

[569]McBeth, *The Baptist Heritage*, 757; James Daniel Luper, "The Concept of Separation in the Regular Baptist and the Conservative Baptist Movements" (Th.M. thesis, Southwestern Baptist Theological Seminary, 1967) 38-40, 51-84.

[570]McBeth, *The Baptist Heritage*, 759-59.

[571]Ibid., 758-61; Nelson, "Fundamentalism and the Northern Baptist Convention," 421-71.

statement adopted in a somewhat creedal sense by the CBAA was "nearly the same" as one previously embraced by the CBFMS. It affirmed the inspiration, trustworthiness, and supreme authority of the Bible as "God's Word" (art. 1), acclaimed the Father as the creating, prayer-answering, and saving God (art. 2), ran the gamut of Jesus' holy history (art. 3), spoke briefly of the work of the Spirit (art. 4), and declared that humans are sinners "by nature and by choice" with the twofold destiny issuing from belief and unbelief (art. 5). The articles (6, 8) on the church described the visible church, the ordinances, and the church's mission in general terms and were more emphatic as to church autonomy and church-state separation. Indeed "every human being is responsible to God alone in all matters of faith" (art. 7), and there was no reference to last things.[572] For Conservative Baptists separation as to affiliation did not prove to be a doctrine, as was true for the GARBC, and this was a major reason why they did not join the GARBC, but neither did they embrace inclusivism vis-à-vis theological liberals.[573] Furthermore the prevalence of premillennialism in the CBAA resulted in the insertion in 1955 of the word "premillennial" in article 3.[574] Among Conservative Baptists, Earl D. Radmacher (1931–) wrote a monograph on biblical, historical, and contemporary ecclesiology in the face of ecumenical and dispensational challenges in an effort to balance the universal church and the local churches,[575] and Bruce Leon Shelley (1927–) produced theological[576] as well as historical monographs.

But the most substantive theological work emanating from Conservative Baptists has been a three-volume systematic theology[577] coauthored by

---

[572]Bruce L. Shelley, *Conservative Baptists: A Story of Twentieth-Century Dissent* (Denver: Conservative Baptist Theological Seminary, 1960) 67, 155.

[573]Ibid., 61-62, 84-89, 99-103; Luper, "The Concept of Separation in the Regular Baptist and the Conservative Baptist Movements," 40, called the Conservative Baptist movement "quasi-Separatist." See also Luper, 85-123.

[574]Shelley, *Conservative Baptists*, 89-94, 155.

[575]*The Nature of the Church* (Portland OR: Western Baptist, 1972). Radmacher was president of Western Conservative Baptist Seminary, Portland.

[576]*What Baptists Believe* (Wheaton IL: Conservative Baptist, 1973); *The Church: God's People* (Wheaton IL: SP Publications, 1978); *Christian Theology in Plain Language* (Waco TX: Word, 1985).

[577]*Integrative Theology*, vol. 1, *Knowing Ultimate Reality: The Living God* (Grand Rapids MI: Zondervan, 1987); vol. 2, *Our Primary Need: Christ's Atoning Provisions* (ibid., 1990); vol. 3, *Spirit-Given Life: God's People Present and Future* (ibid., 1994).

Gordon Russell Lewis (1926–)[578] and Bruce Alvin Demarest (1935–)[579] of Conservative Baptist Seminary, Denver, Colorado. Its significance lies chiefly in its advocacy and embrace of an "integrative" method, according to which each major theological topic is to be written with six successive components: identification of the problem, solutions offered from historical theology, findings of biblical theology, a systematic formulation, apologetic encounter with other positions, and application to life circumstances.[580] Beginning with general revelation, Lewis and Demarest represent a Bible that is fully inspired and inerrant, an atonement that centers in a "propitiation and reconciling sacrifice," a soteriology that is normally Calvinist, and an eschatology that is pretribulational and premillennial.[581] They interface with theologians of the Reformed, Anglican, Roman Catholic, and Lutheran traditions but not of the Baptist, and their relatively brief doctrine of the church offers little that is distinctively Baptist.[582] They coedited a book on biblical inerrancy.[583] Lewis wrote volumes on Christian apologetics,[584] basic

---

[578]A native of Johnson City NY, and a graduate of Gordon College (B.A., 1948), Faith Theological Seminary (M.Div., 1951), and Syracuse University (M.A., 1953; Ph.D., 1959), after a brief pastorate of a Baptist church in Delaware, Lewis taught apologetics at Baptist Bible Seminary, Johnson City (1951–1958) and since 1958 has taught systematic theology and Christian philosophy at Denver. His ordination was in the General Association of Regular Baptists, and he has served as president of the Evangelical Theological Society (1992). *Who's Who in Religion*, 2nd ed. (1977) 391; *Contemporary Authors*, new revision series, vol. 50 (1996) 259-60.

[579]A native of New York City, and a graduate of Wheaton College (B.S., 1958), Adelphi University (M.S., 1963), Trinity Evangelical Divinity School (M.A., 1969), and University of Manchester (Ph.D., 1973), Demarest helped to found a Christian college in Nigeria and lectured in Liberia before beginning in 1975 to teach theology at Denver.

[580]*Integrative Theology* 1:7-8.

[581]Ibid., esp. 1:129-71; 2:401-10; 1:291-335; 2:69-120; 3:15-69, 171-236. The coauthors did not embrace dispensationalism but affirmed multiple raptures (3:416-21) and an "institutional" role for "Israel" during the millennium (3:411-13).

[582]Ibid., 3:239-304.

[583]*Challenges to Inerrancy: A Theological Response* (Chicago: Moody, 1984).

[584]*Faith and Reason in the Thought of St. Augustine* (Ph.D. diss., Syracuse University, 1959; Ann Arbor: University Microfilms International, 1982); *Judge for Yourself: A Workbook on Contemporary Challenges to Christian Faith* (Downers Grove IL: InterVarsity, 1974); *Testing Christianity's Truth Claims: Approaches to*

theology,[585] and contemporary religious cults.[586] Demarest wrote a major monograph on general revelation[587] and books on the history of exegesis,[588] Christology,[589] and spirituality.[590]

Most of the ethnic (non-English language) Baptist bodies of European origin in the United States have had some type of cooperative relationship with "the Northern Baptist societies and after 1907" with the NBC, partly because "most points of entry" for European immigrants were in the North.[591] Theological tensions within the NBC during the 1940s led to the breaking of ties by the Baptist General Conference (Swedish-American) and, with cultural factors, by the North American Baptist Conference (German-American), whose seminary was moved from Rochester, New York, to Sioux Falls, South Dakota.[592] Among the Swedish-Americans Anders Wiberg (1816–1887), who was briefly in the United States, had written biblically and historically on baptism,[593] and John Alexis Edgren

---

Christian Apologetics (Chicago: Moody, 1976; repr.: Lanham MD: University Press of America, 1990).

[585]*Decide for Yourself: A Theological Workbook* (Downers Grove IL: InterVarsity, 1970).

[586]*What Everyone Should Know about Transcendental Meditation* (Glendale CA: G/L Publications, 1975); *Confronting the Cults*, 2nd ed. (Phillipsburg NJ: Presbyterian and Reformed, 1987).

[587]*General Revelation: Historical Views and Contemporary Issues* (Grand Rapids MI: Zondervan, 1982).

[588]*A History of Interpretation of Hebrews 7, 1-10 from the Reformation to the Present*, Beiträge zur Geschichte der Biblischen Exegese 19 (Tübingen: J.C.B. Mohr/Paul Siebeck, 1976).

[589]*Jesus Christ: The God-Man* (Wheaton IL: Victor Books, 1978).

[590]*Satisfy Your Soul: Restoring the Heart of Christian Spirituality* (Colorado Springs CO: NavPress, 1999).

[591]McBeth, *The Baptist Heritage*, 725. McBeth, 725-35, discussed nine such unions or conferences.

[592]Frank H. Woyke, *Heritage and Ministry of the North American Baptist Conference* (Oakbrook Terrace IL: North American Baptist Conference, 1979) 411-13; McBeth, *The Baptist Heritage*, 734.

[593]*Christian Baptism: Set Forth in the Words of the Bible* (Philadelphia: American Baptist Publication Society, 1852?). Wiberg, while still a Lutheran in Sweden, undertook this study in order to refute believer's baptism but instead found that the New Testament has no place for infant baptism and published his findings in Swedish in 1852 before becoming a Baptist. Adolf Olson, *A Centenary History as Related to the Baptist General Conference in America* (Chicago: Baptist

(1838–1908)[594] and C. G. Lagergren[595] had written on basic Christian doctrines and Eric Wingren on premillennial eschatology.[596] The German-Americans provided the matrix for Walter Rauschenbusch's ministry and adopted a brief eight-article confession which emphasized Baptist distinctives.[597]

Thus ended that which Jasper C. Masee described as the "thirty-years' war."[598]

In summary, serious theological controversy occurred among Baptists in England and North America from the controversy with the Campbells in 1820s and 1830s to the "thirty years' war" within the Northern Baptist Convention (ca.1920-ca.1950). The less than two-decade alliance of the followers of Alexander Campbell with the Baptists in the United States, following Alexander's embrace of believer's baptism by immersion, became increasingly controversial and was terminated by division. Campbell evoked Baptist opposition especially by his Sandemanian view of faith, accompanied by his denial of any direct work of the Holy Spirit vis-à-vis the unbeliever, his McLeanist insistence on water baptism as essential to the remission of sins, and his rejection of all confessions of faith except Simon Peter's at Caesarea Philippi. Southern Baptist authors (Broaddus, Jeter, Williams, Ray, Jarrell) explicated the doctrinal differences between Baptists and Disciples of Christ.

Baptists in England and the American North, by insisting on the translation and not the transliteration of the word "baptize" in a Bengali Bible, separated from interdenominational Bible societies and formed their own. By 1879 among Southern Baptists there was controversy surrounding C. H. Toy's historical-critical views and Darwinian evolution that led to Toy's resignation from the faculty of Southern Baptist Theological Seminary. Nearly a decade later Toy's successor, Basil Manly, Jr., published a mono-

---

Conference, 1952) 40.

[594]*Fundamentals of Faith*, trans. J. O. Backlund (Chicago: Baptist Conference, 1948).

[595]The author of a five-volume work in Swedish on biblical doctrines. Olson, *A Centenary History*, 511.

[596]In Swedish. Ibid.

[597]See above, 314-18; O. E. Krueger, *In God's Hand: The Story of the North American Baptist General Conference* (Forest Park IL: North American Baptist General Conference, 1958) 34. Per Lloyd Harsch.

[598]"The Thirty Years' War," *The Chronicle* 17 (April 1954): 106-16.

graph on the doctrine of biblical inspiration in which he defended "plenary" inspiration and which constituted the orthodox reply to Toy.

At the same time among English Baptists the Down Grade Controversy saw C. H. Spurgeon and John Clifford on opposite sides. Spurgeon, who out of a Congregationalist family had become a Baptist by choice, was the boy preacher who at nineteen had taken the pulpit of Keach, Gill, and Rippon and built up Britain's great megachurch. An evangelical Calvinist and an heir of the Puritan heritage, Spurgeon had had his clashes with Hyper-Calvinist fellow Baptist pastors and with Anglicans over baptismal regeneration. Ultimately he came to suspect that among Baptists and other Nonconformists there were those who were embracing heresies such as the denial of biblical inspiration and inerrancy or of substitutionary atonement or the affirmation of the universal fatherhood of God, Darwinian evolution, or eschatological universalism. Clifford, on the other hand, a General Baptist pastor in London, had earned university degrees and embraced historical-critical method, evolution, and "the new theology." The public controversy, set off by articles in Spurgeon's *The Sword and the Trowel*, was not handled well by the leadership of the Baptist Union, and encumbered by the promise of confidentiality in correspondence, Spurgeon ultimately resigned from the Baptist Union but led no schism from the union.

The same cultural and theological challenges (historical-critical method, Darwinian evolution, industrial revolution) provoked controversy among Baptists across the Atlantic, and Baptist theologians, particularly among Northern Baptists, responded in diverse ways to these challenges. The conservative Northern and Canadian theologians (Hovey, Pepper, Goodspeed, Gordon) offered a minimum of adaptation and as maximum of conservation. Hovey was conservative as to the doctrine of the Bible and respecting penal substitution and gave much attention to eschatology. Goodspeed defended the moral imperative of Sunday observance and postmillennialism. Gordon embraced the enduement of the Spirit for service, divine healing on the basis of Christ's atonement, historic premillennialism, and world missions.

The mediating Northern theologians (Robinson, Northrup, Johnson, Wood, Strong, Dodge) were more open to the new cultural influences while not abandoning all traditional positions. Robinson was mediating by not adhering to any theory of biblical inspiration and by holding the Placean view of original sin. He was more liberal in relying on Christian experience, defining sin as selfishness, and being open to evolution, though not to spontaneous generation. Northrup critiqued Calvinism and Johnson favored the dynamic view of inspiration and moved to semi-Arminianism. Wood was conservative in holding an Augustinian view of original sin and orthodox on Christology but liberal as to the Christian consciousness and what he called an "ethical vicarious" view of the atonement. Dodge's conservatism was coupled with his rejection of an intermediate state between death and resurrection. Strong, the most influential of the mediating theologians, reputedly made a major shift to the left in the 1890s and became more conservative in his final years. His espousal of "ethical monism" led to charges of pantheism and of having compromised biblical authority. Scholars have probed the successive editions of his *Systematic Theology* to ferret out the changes relative to the doctrine of the Bible. Strong was conservative in defense of the deity of Christ and in holding to the Augustinian view of original sin. He embraced theistic evolution and favored a pictorial-summary interpretation of Genesis 1. He came to accept an eternal atonement theory.

Among the liberal Northern theologians (Clarke, Fosdick, Cross, Vedder) there was great adaptation to the cultural challenges and the new Protestant theological trends. Clarke, whose textbook was widely used and reckoned as the epitome of theological liberalism, fully accepted historical-critical method, relied on the Bible and experience, looked for "the Christian element in the Scriptures," and affirmed the universal fatherhood of God. God was said to have used evolutionary method, and a historical fall was denied. Chalcedonian Christology Clarke reckoned as inadequate for God and man are alike. The death of Christ was not substitutionary, for there must be either punishment or forgiveness. There will be no visible second coming. Fosdick's hermeneutic centered in the concept of "abiding experiences and changing categories." He stressed the humanity of Jesus; whether he held to his deity is disputed. He was doubtful as to the virginal conception, opposed to penal substitution, and unsure of a bodily resurrection. Sin was defined as that which hinders human development. Cross, a devotee of Schleiermacher's theology, represented an anticreedal individualistic Protestantism in which salvation could be defined as the realization of the supreme worth of human personality. Vedder, having made a major shift late in life, saw the theologies of Jesus and Paul as contradictory and advocated following that of Jesus while holding that Jesus bore our sins as partner or elder brother.

Walter Rauschenbusch, having had strong German influences and a pastorate in New York City's Hell's Kitchen, became the theologian of the Social Gospel as Rochester professor and impacted American Protestantism. He sought to democratize God, explicated the social transmission of moral evil, and spelled out six public sins that led to Jesus' crucifixion. He sought to magnify the kingdom of God as both divine and human, as both present and future, and as having been displaced by the church but now a mighty force at work.

Northern and Canadian fundamentalist theologians (Riley, Straton, Shields, Massee) were militantly opposed to theological liberalism and the extreme of modernism. Riley defended the Bible against the "higher critics," sought unsuccessfully to get the NBC to recommend to the churches the New Hampshire Confession, and helped to organize the BBUNA. Straton engaged in various public debates, especially on evolution, and embraced divine healing on the basis of the atonement, and women as preachers. Shields led a separation from Canadian Baptists, whereas Massee became the leader of moderate fundamentalists in the NBC, fearing a "heresy of spirit," and favored open communion and the Lord's Supper as a converting ordinance. Riley and Straton were dispensationalists; Shields and Massee were not.

The Baptist Congress afforded for three decades a forum for discussion among Baptist leaders in North America. Soon thereafter the NBC engaged in a three-decade controversy which focused on the Baptist educational institutions, the beliefs of foreign missionaries, and an effort to embrace a confession of faith (Riley vs. Woelfkin). The BBUNA became the GARBC, with a strong separationist stance, the Conservative Baptists organized during the 1940s, and other conservatives remained in the NBC. Each of these groups produced a new confession of faith. During such controversy Swedish-American and German-American Baptists loosened their ties to the NBC.

Chapter 8

Biblical Theologians

From their earliest leaders until now Baptists have characteristically sought to base their doctrinal affirmations upon specific passages within the Bible and to preach and teach in conformity with biblical teachings. As C. H. Toy declared, Baptists "have always maintained to the full the necessity of Scriptural grounds for all beliefs and practices."[1] In that sense Baptists have characteristically sought a theology that was biblical. Second, at the end of the eighteenth century the academic discipline of "biblical theology" came into existence in a rationalist setting in Europe in order to ferret out and correlate specific biblical teachings in contrast with those of the current dogmatic theology. Later the Orthodox and the Pietists also embraced this new academic discipline.[2] Not until the twentieth century did Baptists become active participants in and authors concerning "biblical theology." Third, during the middle third of the twentieth century a concentrated or focused theological movement known as the Biblical Theology movement came to the fore and influenced Baptists who worked in the discipline of biblical theology.[3]

Some Baptist scholars who majored on the exegesis of the Old Testament and/or of the New Testament cautiously moved into aspects of biblical theology, whereas other Baptist scholars sought to address as a whole Old Testament theology, New Testament theology, or biblical theology.

Ezra Palmer Gould (1841–1900)

Seemingly the first Baptist to author a volume which could be clearly identified as following the method of biblical theology was Ezra Gould in his *The Biblical Theology of the New Testament* (1901).[4] A native of Boston and an 1861 graduate of Harvard College, Gould was professor of New Testament in Newton Theological Institution from 1868 to 1882, at which

---

[1]See above, 259.
[2]Robert C. Denton, *Preface to Old Testament Theology*, Yale Studies in Religion 14 (New Haven CT: Yale University Press, 1950) 3-48. Denton, 7-8, traced the rise of biblical theology to a Latin treatise by Johann Philipp Gabler, a German, published in 1787.
[3]Garrett, *Systematic Theology*, 2nd ed., 1:15.
[4](New York: Macmillan, 1901).

time he was dismissed under the presidency of Hovey because of his use of historical-critical method.[5]

Gould held that biblical theology should be built on criticism and exegesis and on the presupposition that biblical books differ "in the details of their doctrinal teaching." The Bible "is not a homogeneous unit, but a collection of more or less heterogeneous units." Gould differentiated five groups of New Testament books: (1) Synoptic Gospels, as to the teaching of Jesus; (2) "the early teaching of the Twelve" (Acts 1-12); (3) Paul's letters (Gal., Rom., 1 and 2 Cor., Phil., Phile., 1 and 2 Thess.); (4) "the later writings of the Twelve" (Synoptic Gospels as to the Synoptists, James, 1 Pet., Rev.); and (5) "the writings of the Alexandrian period" (1st group: Col., Eph., 1 and 2 Tim., Tit., Heb., 2 Pet., Jude) (2nd group: John, 1, 2, and 3 John).[6]

Central to the teaching of Jesus was the kingdom of God, about which Gould emphasized its membership and its freedom, not its time or its means. God is the gracious and loving Father, and "Son of God" and "Son of Man" are both "Messianic titles." Gould held that Jesus taught that there is "an affinity between the spirit of man and the truth of God" and that "human nature" is "fundamentally akin" to the kingdom of God. According to Gould, Jesus' teaching about the coming of the Son of Man is to be understood as a long process beginning with the fall of Jerusalem and continuing through the ages of human history, not a visible event at the end of human history, and likewise there will be no last judgment, but rather a succession of historical judgments.[7]

In early Acts Jesus' prophetic work during his earthly ministry has been followed by his gift of the Spirit and by Jesus' kingly role in his expected return. The apostles are witnesses to Jesus' resurrection, and his death is consistent with God's plan but not "vicarious."[8]

Paul "proclaimed the abolition" of the law, both that of Moses and that written on hearts, for law cannot procure obedience to its own provisions. According to Gould, Paul taught that guilt comes only through individual transgression and that the "flesh" is not the body but "the seat of the appetites and passions." Paul substituted the righteousness of faith for the

---

[5]*Who Was Who in America*, vol. 1, 1897–1942 (Chicago: A. N. Marquis Co., 1942) 473; Brackney, *A Genetic History of Baptist Thought*, 247, 287-88, 304.

[6]*The Biblical Theology of the New Testament*, 1, 4-5.

[7]Ibid., 10-12, 24-33, 13-23, 40-48.

[8]Ibid., 51-55.

righteousness of law, and this by grace. For Gould, "justify" meant to make righteous, not to declare righteous, and faith is the "cause" of justification, that is, the faith "that works through love" and can implant life. According to Paul, the death of Jesus was a propitiatory or expiatory sacrifice, but union with Christ was more central. Gould stressed Paul's identification of Christ and the Holy Spirit to the conclusions that the Spirit was "the form of Christ's preexistence and that Jesus was the incarnation of the Holy Spirit. A bodiless intermediate state will precede the bodily resurrection. According to Gould, the Twelve taught that Jesus' return would inaugurate his Messianic reign, whereas Paul taught that the return would end the Messianic reign.[9]

The doctrine in First Peter is a "modified Paulinism," Pauline in its universalism (Gentile privileges) and its "mystical conception" of Christ but non-Pauline in having no doctrine of justification. The Epistle of James clearly presented "*a law of liberty*" in contradistinction to Paul's "freedom from the law" and justification "by works, and not by faith only." James was "presenting the case of Judaistic Christianity *vs*. Paulinism, not from the standpoint of Pharisaism, which emphasizes the formal parts of the law, but of liberal Judaism, which stands only for the ethical contents of the law." Peter emphasized Jesus' resurrection as well as his death, seen as rescue from sinful lifestyle and an example of suffering, and this stood "midway between Paul and the earlier Jewish and apostolic Christianity."[10]

Rejecting its apostolic authorship, Gould reckoned the book of Revelation to represent "an unqualified opposition to Paul" and to the Gospel and epistles of John and a "departure from the spirit and thought of Jesus more than in any other New Testament writing." Gould indicted the author for his "revengeful" Messianism and reported his holding an essentially Arian view of Jesus as exalted creature.[11]

Colossians and Ephesians, according to Gould written by "an Alexandrian Jew," represent an "orthodox Alexandrianism" set over against a "false Alexandrianism" with its dualism of spirit and matter. In Colossians Christ, who needs not to be supplemented, is said not only to rule over angels but also to be "the medium of creation." In Ephesians Jewish and Gentile believers are united in one body "on the basis of the fullness in

---

[9] Ibid., 60-61, 63, 64, 66, 70, 72, 74, 78-79, 81-83, 96-97, 76-77, 90-91.
[10] Ibid., 105-6, 116, 115, 113, 120, 122, 124.
[11] Ibid., 125, 126, 129, 131.

Christ, who sums up all things in himself."[12] The Pastoral Epistles, marked by "a fixed type of teaching" rather than argumentation, present "a deposit to be guarded, and to be committed to faithful men who shall be able to teach others." The asceticism of Jewish Gnosticism, manifested in marriage, meats, and a spiritualized resurrection, is attacked, and the church as a "teaching body" with its bishops, elders, and deacons is acknowledged.[13] Second Peter, whose authorship by Peter Gould denied, emphasized knowledge as supplementary to faith, a knowledge derived from God through Christ, resisted the heresy of antinomianism, and coped with doubt as to Jesus' second coming. In Jude licentious behavior was not to be justified by the conduct of angels who draw near to the earth, for the latter have been cast into hell.[14] Hebrews "was meant for Hebrew Christians, probably outside of Palestine" to "save" them "from a lapse into Judaism." The danger was from priestly Judaism. Using Alexandrian allegorization centering in "types, or patterns," the author set forth the superiority over angels, Moses, and the Aaronic priesthood of the Son of God, who was high priest "after the order of Melchizedek." His real incarnation meant a genuine humanity. Gould found Jesus' obedience to be more basic to the epistle than his sacrifice, and faith "makes the invisible real, and *vice versa*."[15]

Gould, having set forth seven differences and sixteen parallels between the Synoptics and John's Gospel, found that the latter, whose "object" was to "prove" Jesus' Messiahship, presents the Son of God as "an incarnation of the Alexandrian Logos." He was preexistent and equal with God, and his work was essentially to give life to human beings, his death being an attraction, not an "appeasement." Faith is the condition of this life, and there is no antithesis between faith and works. According to Gould, the Fourth Gospel presents "transcendence in the Father, incarnation in the Son, and immanence in the Holy Spirit," but it exudes a basic pessimism concerning "the world." Such pessimism, rooted in making election and world redemption antitheses, was also found in the First Epistle of John. Gould allowed for the writer to teach propitiation and reckoned the Antichrists to be heretics who were "a sign of the immediate coming of the Antichrist."[16]

---

[12]Ibid., 138, 132, 136-37, 138, 136, 138, 139.
[13]Ibid., 143, 142, 143, 144-45, 150, 149-50.
[14]Ibid., 151, 153-56, 157-58.
[15]Ibid., 162, 161, 162-63, 165, 166-68, 163-64, 164-65, 172-73, 170.
[16]Ibid., 174-81, 182, 183, 185-87, 187-88, 190-91, 191-92, 193-94, 201, 202-204, 206, 207, 208-209.

Gould's New Testament theology was greatly shaped and overshadowed by his historical-critical views, especially the authorship and dating of New Testament books, and by his stress on diversity, not pressed overtly to contradiction, in place of unity of teaching. Most of Gould's Baptist successors in biblical theology during the twentieth century would find unity amid diversity in biblical theology.

Archibald Thomas Robertson (1863–1934)

A native of Virginia who was reared in Statesville, North Carolina, Robertson completed A.B. and A.M. degrees at Wake Forest College, where he concentrated on languages and won medals in Latin and French but not in Greek, and entered Southern Baptist Theological Seminary in 1885. Upon his graduation in 1888, he was elected to the seminary's faculty and began a 46-year teaching career. He married the daughter of his mentor, John A. Broadus, participated in the Whitsitt Controversy, and had a role in the formation of the Baptist World Alliance. He developed expertise in the language and interpretation of the New Testament, taught some 6,000 students,[17] and authored forty-two books,[18] the most notable of which was the world-acclaimed *A Grammar of the Greek New Testament in the Light of Historical Research*.[19]

Robertson did not write a comprehensive theology of the New Testament but treated various doctrinal themes from the interpretation of the New Testament. Much of this centered in Christology. According to the Gospels, Jesus and the Father not only had a "unique relation," had "an interflow of knowledge," worked "in harmony," and are "one in character" but also share an eternal divine nature.[20] All four Gospels in their respective ways

---

[17]Everett Gill, Sr., *A. T. Robertson: A Biography* (New York: Macmillan, 1943) esp. xv, 143-45; Edgar Vernon McKnight, "A. T. Robertson's Contribution to the New Testament" (Th.D. diss., Southern Baptist Theological Seminary, 1960) 45-79; Mueller, *A History of Southern Baptist Theological Seminary*, 203-206; David S. Dockery, "The Broadus-Robertson Tradition," in *Theologians of the Baptist Tradition*, ed. George and Dockery, 97-103, 107-14.

[18]McKnight, "A. T. Robertson's Contribution," 397-401. *Word Pictures of the New Testament* consisted of six volumes.

[19](New York: George H. Doran, 1914; 2nd ed., 1915; 3rd ed., 1919; 4th ed., 1923; 5th ed., 1931).

[20]*The Teaching of Jesus concerning God the Father* (New York: American Tract Society, 1904) 43-65.

bear witness to Jesus' deity.[21] Q, which Robertson equated with the *Logion of Papias*, contains "the same essential picture of Jesus as the Christ" as in "the other Gospels."[22] Even more explicit was the apostle Paul in affirming the deity of Christ.[23] Jesus' humanity Robertson also affirmed but with less specific attention.[24] He changed his understanding of Jesus' usage of the term "Son of Man." In 1906 he taught that Jesus used the term to affirm his humanity,[25] whereas in 1907 and 1924 he reckoned Jesus' usage to have been a self-identification as the Messiah.[26] As the Logos and the Light[27] the Son of God became incarnate, not after the manner of the kenotic theories of self-emptying[28] but through that which Robertson identified and defended as the "Virgin Birth."[29] The Louisville scholar delineated the life of Mary from the Gospels, partly because Roman Catholics "have deified" her and Protestants "have neglected her."[30] Robertson did not hesitate to probe the Messianic consciousness of Jesus[31] or to affirm that Jesus clearly revealed the character of God the Father.[32]

Robertson taught "the general Fatherhood of God" but thought that it was "much overworked" at the beginning of the twentieth century by those who failed to recognize that humans are "by nature children of wrath" as well as "naturally children of God." Hence the particular fatherhood

---

[21] *The Christ of the Logia* (Nashville: Sunday School Board of the SBC, 1924) 42-103.

[22] Ibid., 15-41, esp. 37.

[23] *Paul the Interpreter of Christ* (New York: George H. Doran., 1921) 50-57.

[24] *The Teaching of Jesus concerning God the Father*, 59.

[25] *Keywords in the Teaching of Jesus* (Philadelphia: American Baptist Publication Society, 1906) 31.

[26] *Epochs in the Life of Jesus: A Study of Development and Struggle in the Messiah's Work* (New York: Scribner's, 1907) 24-25; *The Christ of the Logia*, 31-33, 63-64.

[27] *The Divinity of Christ in the Gospel of John* (New York: Fleming H. Revell Co., 1916) 34-43; *The Christ of the Logia*, 94-98.

[28] *Epochs in the Life of Jesus*, 13-14; *Paul the Interpreter of Christ*, 57-58.

[29] *Epochs in the Life of Jesus*, 8-13; *The Divinity of Christ in the Gospel of John*, 44; *The Christ of the Logia*, 71-72; *The Mother of Jesus: Her Problems and Her Glory* (New York: George H. Doran Co., 1925) 26-32.

[30] *The Mother of Jesus*, esp. 69.

[31] *Keywords in the Teaching of Jesus*, 12-13, 32-34; *Epochs in the Life of Jesus*, 14-24.

[32] *The Teaching of Jesus concerning God the Father*, 24-42, 149-54.

received through the new birth must also be clearly taught.[33] Jesus used "the world" both to refer to the created order and to that which was "sinful and different from his disciples."[34] According to Robertson, the Holy Spirit is personal, even though the term "person" vis-à-vis the Father, the Son, and the Spirit is problematic, and the Spirit has distinct relationships with the Father and with the Son. We are not "to pray for the coming of the Holy Spirit," and he has taken up the struggle against the "kingdom of Satan." The Spirit is equal to the Father and the Son as to nature and personhood but inferior as to office, but "blasphemy against the Spirit is blasphemy against God." Only in a qualified sense should one speak of a dispensation of the Spirit. The New Testament, Robertson stated, contains "the fact" of the Trinity but "no technical discussion" thereof.[35] He emphasized that Jesus' teaching did not focus on the origin of sin or those concerns addressed by the historic theories of original sin but stressed the universality of sin. "The modern theory of evolution is not necessarily out of harmony with the essential fact of the fall of man" or "the inherited sin of the race." The existence of a personal Satan and demons is to be affirmed. Christ's atonement "makes possible reconciliation with the Father," but "actual reconciliation is not yet accomplished . . . till the sinner comes back to the Father with confession of sin."[36] In his exegesis of New Testament texts which some have found to support the possible apostasy of true believers, Robertson demonstrated an openness to apostasy but did "not construct a formal doctrine of apostasy." That task would be undertaken by one who would acknowledge the influence of Robertson, Dale Moody.[37] Robertson defended Matthew 28:18-20 as a true saying of Jesus but denied that it contained a precise baptismal formula.[38] For Jesus and John the Baptist "the kingdom of God" was "the comprehensive term for the work and rule [and

---

[33]Ibid., 117-22, 151-54.

[34]Ibid., 85-95.

[35]*Keywords in the Teaching of Jesus*, 93-108, esp. 95, 106, 104, 98-99; *The Teaching of Jesus concerning God the Father*, 70-84, esp. 78-80, 83-84, 70-71.

[36]*Keywords in the Teaching of Jesus*, 41-55, esp. 44-45, 52-53.

[37]Clark Richard Youngblood, "The Question of Apostasy in Southern Baptist Thought since 1900: A Critical Evaluation" (Ph.D. diss., Southern Baptist Theological Seminary, 1978) 149-50. Youngblood, 129-48, has analyzed Robertson's interpretations of both the "perseverance passages" and the "apostasy passages." See below, 382.

[38]*The Christ of the Logia*, 112-26.

reign] of God in the hearts of men." Although rooted in the Old Testament, the kingdom "could be said to begin with Jesus." Pharisees mistakenly taught that it "belonged to them by right of inheritance," and the Beatitudes describe "those who are in the kingdom." The kingdom is both present and future and hence permanent.[39] Life after death is to be real and everlasting, final judgment is certain, and heaven and hell are to continue without annihilation or universal salvation.[40]

Robertson was certainly the most eminent scholar on the grammar of the Greek New Testament among Baptists. His exegetical method and conservative theological conclusions influenced and confirmed Baptists and others during an era of theological conflict. The limits thereof have been noted by the concurrent comments of two scholars who have studied Robertson. Edgar V. McKnight concluded that Robertson "continued a "historico-linguistic method of interpretation and failed to move toward a theological method."[41] David S. Dockery, writing of John A. Broadus and of Robertson, stated:

> Their commitment to exegetical theology . . . was simultaneously a strength and a weakness. They upheld the authority of Scripture, but both were cautious at best in developing a systematic approach to theology. This approach advanced biblical theology but failed to advance a coherent Baptist theology.[42]

Henry Wheeler Robinson (1872–1945)

A native of Northampton and baptized at sixteen, educated at Edinburgh University in arts, in Mansfield College, Oxford, in divinity, and in the universities of Marburg and Strassburg, Robinson had pastorates in Pitlochry in Scotland and in St. Michael's Church in Coventry in England before serving as tutor in Rawdon College in Yorkshire (1906–1920). In 1920 he became principal of Regent's Park College in London, then in 1927–1928 moved the college to Oxford, and remained its principal until

---

[39]*Keywords in the Teaching of Jesus*, 56-77, esp. 59, 62, 67, 65, 70-74; *The Christ of the Logia*, 238-47.

[40]*Keywords in the Teaching of Jesus*, 109-21. As to Robertson's doctrine of the Bible, more implied and practiced than stated, see Dockery, "The Broadus-Robertson Tradition,", 101-102, 107-10.

[41]"A. T. Robertson's Contribution," 372.

[42]"The Broadus-Robertson Tradition," 111.

1942. A prolific author and a leader among British Baptists, Robinson became one of Britain's foremost Old Testament scholars.[43]

As an Old Testament theologian Robinson gave much attention to revelation and related themes. In 1913 he identified the media through which Yahweh revealed himself to the Israelites as theophanies, miracles, oracular guidance, the prophetic consciousness, and the written word.[44] In 1942 Robinson noted that dreams and possession, though common among other religions, were employed in the religion of Israel, elaborated on revelation in "the actuality of history," and found revelation in Christianity to be centered in the redemptive work of Christ.[45] Posthumously the Oxford scholar noted the importance of the divine election of Israel and of the day of the Lord and found revelation to have occurred through the priests, the men of wisdom, and the psalmists.[46] Robinson's emphasis on the prophetic consciousness led him to embrace the divine inspiration of the biblical writers rather than the writings, and hence, for him, "the doctrine of verbal inspiration is not simply untenable; it is irrelevant."[47] Milton U. Ferguson suggested that Robinson's doctrine of revelation through history could serve as a corrective for propositionalism's attempt "to 'absolutize' the relative and neoorthodoxy's relativizing all theological expressions, including the Bible, and as a corrective for liberalism's preoccupation with divine immanence and neoorthodoxy's preoccupation with the eternal by uniting event and faith.[48] William T. Early, on the other hand, saw Robinson

---

[43]Ernest A. Payne, *Henry Wheeler Robinson: Scholar, Teacher, Principal* (London: Nisbet and Co., 1946) 9-109; John Reumann, intro. to Robinson, *Corporate Personality in Ancient Israel*, Facet Books, Biblical Series 11 (Philadelphia: Fortress, 1964) v-xiii; Rex Mason, "H. Wheeler Robinson Revisited," *Baptist Quarterly* 37 (January 1998): 213-26; William Tracy Early, "The Doctrine of Revelation in the Theology of H. Wheeler Robinson" (Th.D. diss., Union Theological Seminary, New York, 1963) 5-16.

[44]*The Religious Ideas of the Old Testament* (London: Duckworth), 102-29.

[45]*Redemption and Revelation in the Actuality of History* (London: Nisbet and Co.) 131-38, 158-94, 228-80.

[46]*Inspiration and Revelation in the Old Testament* (Oxford: Oxford University Press, 1946) 135-59, 199-270.

[47]*The Christian Experience of the Holy Spirit* (London: Nisbet and Co., 1928) 160-83, esp. 171.

[48]"H. Wheeler Robinson's Concept of Revelation: Its Relevance for Contemporary Theology" (Th.D. diss., Southwestern Baptist Theological Seminary, 1959) 272-80.

as one who embodied "the basic values of liberal theology"—continuity, an intrinsic value view of authority, and historical-critical method, while correcting and going beyond liberalism in other ways.[49]

In the Old Testament Robinson found that Yahweh was a personal God whose sovereignty was extended from the battlefield to agricultural life and ultimately to all nations (full monotheism), whose character was most clearly manifested through the prophets—justice in Amos, lovingkindness in Hosea, and holiness in Isaiah, and who used nature as the arena for executing his purpose.[50] Nature, derived from creation as due to "the free initiative of a personal God," has both mystery and order and is sustained by the Creator, who performs nature miracles and promises its "eschatological transformation."[51]

Robinson's most important contribution may have been on the doctrine of the human. His *The Christian Doctrine of Man* (1911) was a full-orbed treatment of both the biblical understanding and of the history of the Christian doctrine from the patristic to the modern eras.[52] His forte was the Old Testament perspective. For the Hebrews human personality was "from birth to death directly dependent on God," and it is "the body, not the soul," that "affords the true approach to the Hebrew conception of personality."[53] Hebrews "started not with an indwelling soul, but with an animated body."[54] Life and consciousness "were ascribed to . . . breath," and "psychical functions were ascribed not to the brain and the nervous system, but to" various bodily organs.[55] Robinson trumpeted the idea that the Hebrews held to corporate personality as well as to individual personality.[56] The two were not to be set in antithesis to the other, and there was easy transition from one to the other. Corporate personality could be extended both to the

---

[49]"The Doctrine of Revelation," 190ff.

[50]*The Religious Ideas of the Old Testament*, 51-76.

[51]*Inspiration and Revelation in the Old Testament*, 1-48, esp. 17, 28.

[52](Edinburgh: T.&T. Clark).

[53]*Inspiration and Revelation in the Old Testament*, 69-70, 71-74.

[54]*Corporate Personality in Ancient Israel*, Facet Books, Biblical Series 11 (Philadelphia: Fortress, 1964) 22.

[55]*The Old Testament: Its Making and Its Meaning*, London Theological Library (London: University of London Press; Hodder & Stoughton, 1937) 77.

[56]*The Christian Doctrine of Man*, 27-30; *The Religious Ideas of the Old Testament*, 87-89; *The Old Testament: Its Making and Meaning*, 78-79; *Corporate Personality in Ancient Israel*, 1-20.

ancestors and the posterity and was much more than a figure of speech. Robinson applied corporate personality to the four Servant songs of Isaiah and to the use of "I" in the Psalms,[57] but not all Old Testament scholars concurred.[58]

Robinson's overarching Christological title was "the Redeemer," and "redemption" the principal identification of Christ's activity. Critical of the views of Gustav Aulén, Frederick Cyril Nugent Hicks, and Vincent Taylor, he favored the actuality of God's redemptive sufferings on the cross of Jesus in the transformation of grace.[59] That suffering had been foreshadowed by Job's innocent suffering with "a cosmic purpose," Jeremiah's "sacrificial suffering ... experienced in history," the Servant community's "vicarious" but not penal suffering, and the demonstrated reconciliation of Hosea.[60] According to the Old Testament there had been diverse purposes in suffering: "the *retributive*," the "*disciplinary*," the "*probationary*," the "*revelational*," "the *sacrificial*," and "the *eschatological*." But for Christians, suffering is not solved intellectually but experientially—"*solvitur patiendo*."[61]

Robinson's "serious illness" in 1913 led him "to seek for the lacuna in his own conception of evangelical truth." The result was a major monograph on the Holy Spirit wherein he described the Spirit's indwelling as the "Kenosis" (self-emptying) of the Holy Spirit and referred to "the history of the Church as the Spirit's *Via Dolorosa*" and to the post-Reformation "Arian controversy" of the Holy Spirit.[62] For Robinson, "Christian experience constitutes the most effective entrance into a proper understanding of

---

[57]*Corporate Personality in Ancient Israel*, 3-9, 12-17.

[58]John Reumann, intro. to *Corporate Personality in Ancient Israel*, xii-xiii.

[59]*Redemption and Revelation in the Actuality of History*, 245-80, esp. 270-72; Clyde Rolston Majors, "The Contemporary Emphasis on Transformation: Its Relation to a Christian Approach to the Problem of Suffering" (Th.D. diss., Southwestern Baptist Theological Seminary, 1973) 99-139; Russell W. McConnell, "The Passion of God as Methodological Paradigm in the Theologies of H. Wheeler Robinson and Jürgen Moltmann" (Ph.D. diss., Southwestern Baptist Theological Seminary, 1998).

[60]*The Cross in the Old Testament* (Philadelphia: Westminster, 1955) 54, 189, 111, 113; *The Cross of Hosea* (Philadelphia: Westminster, 1949) 63.

[61]*Suffering Human and Divine* (New York: Macmillan Co., 1939) 31-48, 201-24.

[62]*The Christian Experience of the Holy Spirit*, 4, 151, 259-66. See also *Redemption and Revelation in the Actuality of History*, 290-97.

the Holy Spirit."⁶³ Effort has been made to show that Robinson's employment of Christian experience had extensive "ecclesiological implications."⁶⁴

Robinson considered believer's baptism, preferably though not necessarily by immersion, to be the most basic distinctive of the Baptists.⁶⁵ Rejecting "sacramentarianism" because there must be a believer and rejecting mere symbolism because Old Testament prophetic symbolism involved something more, he opted for a sacramental view of baptism as more than symbol which would complete the dissenting or free church principles: the necessity of individual conversion, the authority of the New Testament, and the spirituality of the church.⁶⁶ He endorsed open communion, while speaking of the "peril" of open membership, took note of the "missionary spirit" of the Baptists and their passion for religious liberty, and concluded that congregational polity "is one legitimate way amongst others of expressing the fundamental idea of the Church."⁶⁷ Robinson was responsible for the five-pointed star with identifying labels displayed at Regent's Park College to encapsulate Baptist emphases: "faith," "baptism," "fellowship," "freedom," and "evangelism."⁶⁸

Robinson has been commended for his nondualistic view of human personality, his broad concept of the work of the Holy Spirit,⁶⁹ his refusing to yield to psychological or sociological explanations of Christian experience,⁷⁰ and his filling the "lacuna" in the modern Baptist doctrine of the sig-

---

⁶³James David Slover, "Representative Current Approaches to the Doctrine of the Holy Spirit" (Th.D. diss., Southwestern Baptist Theological Seminary, 1969) abstract, 2.

⁶⁴David Edwin Moore, "Ecclesiological Implications of Religious Experience in the Theologies of Edgar Young Mullins and Henry Wheeler Robinson" (Ph.D. diss., Southwestern Baptist Theological Seminary, 1999).

⁶⁵*Baptist Principles* (London: Carey Kingsgate, 1925) esp. 16, 27-28.

⁶⁶Ibid., 26, 70, 12; Stanley A. Nelson, "The Doctrine of Believers' Baptism in the Writings of H. Wheeler Robinson" (Th.D. diss., Southwestern Baptist Theological Seminary, 1973) 114-40, 72-113.

⁶⁷*The Life and Faith of the Baptists*, 2nd ed. (London: Kingsgate, 1946; orig., 1927) 100-101, 108-38, 88.

⁶⁸Robinson, "The Five Points of a Baptist's Faith," *Baptist Quarterly* 11 (January and April 1942): 4-14.

⁶⁹Mason, "H. Wheeler Robinson Revisited," 221-22.

⁷⁰Duane A. Garrett, "H. Wheeler Robinson," in *Baptist Theologians*, ed. George and Dockery, 410.

nificance of baptism.[71] Hugh T. McKinley was certain that Robinson's "theology cannot be classified into a specific niche as either liberal or conservative."[72] In addition to the rejection of his concept of corporate personality as found in the Old Testament, Robinson has been criticized for retaining the nineteenth-century evolutionary view of the history of Israel's religion from animism to monotheism,[73] with the exaltation of the prophets and denigration of Moses,[74] for neglecting the Old Testament themes of covenant and deliverance, for reckoning Jesus as a sufferer *primus inter pares*, and for forsaking classical Christology through his concept of the kinship of God and humanity and not regarding "the Old Testament Messiah" as "incarnate Deity."[75] Max Eugene Polley wrote to establish the thesis that Robinson was "one of the 'fathers' of modern Old Testament theology,"[76] whereas Rex Mason was certain that Robinson was not a forerunner of the Biblical Theology movement of the middle third of the twentieth century.[77] James Hardy LaFon sought to show that Robinson's theology could serve as a "corrective, alternative, or reply" to neoorthodoxy, theistic existentialism, demythologization, and logical empiricism.[78]

Harold Henry Rowley (1890–1969)

Born in Leicester and nurtured under the pastorate of W. Y. Fullerton, Rowley was educated in Bristol Baptist College and Bristol University, the University of London, and Mansfield College, Oxford. Under appointment of the Baptist Missionary Society he taught Old Testament in Shantung Christian University in China (1922–1929). He then taught in the University College of South Wales (1930–1935) and the University College of North Wales (1935–1945) and held the chair of Semitic languages and

---

[71]Nelson, "The Doctrine of Believers' Baptism," vii.

[72]"The Theology of H. Wheeler Robinson" (Th.D. diss., Southern Baptist Theological Seminary, 1958) 293.

[73]Mason, "H. Wheeler Robinson Revisited," 219; Garrett, "H. Wheeler Robinson," 407.

[74]Garrett, "H. Wheeler Robinson," 408.

[75]Ibid., 408, 409, 410, 411, 409.

[76]"The Contribution of H. Wheeler Robinson to the Contemporary Rebirth of Old Testament Theology" (Ph.D. diss., Duke University, 1957).

[77]Mason, "H. Wheeler Robinson Revisited," 222, 224.

[78]"The Theology of Henry Wheeler Robinson: Distinctive Emphases and Relevance for Contemporary Christian Thought" (Ph.D. diss., Emory University, 1966) esp. abstract, 1, 3; text, 199-258.

literatures in the University of Manchester (1945–1959). A prolific author, he was a respected leader in post-World War II "international Old Testament studies." His scholarship combined "evangelical zeal, missionary commitment and rigorous historical-critical method."[79]

Rowley treated the Old Testament books according to the order within the three principal divisions of the Hebrew Bible: the Law, the Prophets, and the Writings.[80] The Old Testament Apocrypha, while outside the canon for Protestants, "form a valuable bridge" between the testaments. They "are born of the Old Testament and shed light on the New," especially as to the law, angels, demons, and the hereafter.[81] Rowley was one of the earliest Baptist scholars to give serious attention to the Dead Sea Scrolls and their significance for study of the New Testament.[82]

The unity of the Bible is a theme greatly emphasized by Rowley. He began by seeking to restore the recognition of predictive Old Testament prophecy as fulfilled in the New Testament, though not always literally and though at times with a "reflex influence on the prophecies themselves," as with the Servant songs of Isaiah.[83] Then, recoiling from and seeking to correct the historical-critical conclusion that the law and the cultus came later than the prophets in Israel, and these were antithetical to one another, he sought to correlate priests and prophets, law and prophecy, and divine

---

[79] R. E. Clements, "The Biblical Scholarship of H. H. Rowley (1890–1969)," *Baptist Quarterly* 38 (April 1999): 70-82, esp. 70, 75; D. Winton Thomas, "Harold Henry Rowley," *Zeitschrift für die alttestamentliche Wissenschaft* 82 (1970): i.

[80] *The Growth of the Old Testament* (London: Hutchinson's University Library, 1950).

[81] *The Origin and Significance of the Apocrypha*, Christian Knowledge Booklets (London: S.P.C.K., 1967) esp. 10-13.

[82] *The Covenanters of Damascus and the Dead Sea Scrolls* (Manchester UK: John Rylands Library and Manchester University Press, 1952); *The Dead Sea Scrolls and Their Significance* (London: Independent, 1955); *The Dead Sea Scrolls and the New Testament* (London: S.P.C.K., 1957); *Jewish Apocalyptic and the Dead Sea Scrolls* (London: Athlone, University of London, 1957); *The Teacher of Righteousness and the Dead Sea Scrolls* (Manchester UK: John Rylands Library and Manchester University Press, 1957); *The Dead Sea Scrolls from Qumran* (Southampton UK: University of Southampton, 1958); *The Qumran Sect and Christian Origins* (Manchester UK: John Rylands Library, 1961); *From Moses to Qumran: Studies in the Old Testament* (New York: Association, 1963) 237-79.

[83] *The Re-discovery of the Old Testament* (London: James Clarke, 1945) 202-15, esp. 208.

love and divine justice.⁸⁴ In *The Unity of the Bible* Rowley developed further these concerns about prophecy and fulfillment and the law and the prophets⁸⁵ and went on to spell out the nature of the Bible's unity⁸⁶ and to show how Old Testament themes such as sacrifice and the Suffering Servant illuminate both the death of Jesus and the Christian "sacraments."⁸⁷ Keenly aware of the Biblical Theology movement, he contended that the Bible's unity must be coupled with "diversity" and not equated with "uniformity." It is "a dynamic unity and not a static unity." Christ is for Christians "the standard whereby the Old Testament must be judged." In Moses Rowley found "the seeds of monotheism," and the Decalogue "can . . . be ascribed to him." Neither allegory nor typology offers the proper key, but rather "recurring patterns." The divine and the human elements are "interwoven" in the Bible, but "the continuing thread that gives unity to the record is the divine element."⁸⁸

At mid-century Rowley argued for the "relevance" and "abiding value" of the Old Testament and indeed of the entire Bible.⁸⁹ Such significance of the Old Testament could only be realized if the religious dimension of biblical study should be recovered. Neither that religious dimension nor the use of biblical archaeology should cause a depreciation of the legitimate results of nineteenth-century historical criticism, but "revelation" must not be reduced to "discovery."⁹⁰ The Old Testament "is more than the preparation for the New," for it "is integral to the Bible of the Church."⁹¹

Rejecting the older concept of inspiration in which the activity of God was solely emphasized and inspiration was made the guarantor of the inerrancy of the Bible, Rowley cited several contradictions in the Old

---

⁸⁴*The Unity of the Old Testament* (Manchester UK: Manchester University Press and John Rylands Library, 1946).
⁸⁵(London: Carey Kingsgate, 1953) 90-121, 30-61.
⁸⁶Ibid., 1-29.
⁸⁷Ibid., 122-87.
⁸⁸Ibid., 4-6, 1-4, 29, 7, 14, 23, 21, 17-20, 16. But in 1959 Rowley still held to Julius Wellhausen's "view of the origin of the Pentateuch." *The Changing Pattern of Old Testament Studies* (London: Epworth, 1959) 12.
⁸⁹*The Re-discovery of the Old Testament*, 9-23; *The Relevance of the Bible* (London: James Clarke, 1942) 11-20, 96-123.
⁹⁰*The Re-discovery of the Old Testament*, 15, 22-23, 12-13, 17; *The Relevance of the Bible*, 15-16, 18-20, 12-13, 22-23.
⁹¹*The Re-discovery of the Old Testament*, 10.

Testament which he could not resolve but concluded that such "in no sense challenge the foundation of our faith, for that rests, not on our view of inspiration, but on a living experience of the grace of God in Jesus Christ."[92] Rowley was quite sure that revelation and inspiration were not to be equated, and the same was true of inspiration and authority. He did not embrace the partial theory of inspiration but rather the theory of different levels of inspiration, and the test for judging the levels is Jesus Christ. Biblical authority rests on biblical inspiration and is not to be "equated" with the authority of the Holy Spirit "within" or the authority of the Church but yields to the final authority of God.[93]

Revelation, according to the Old Testament, occurred through a diversity of media: nature, the casting of lots, dreams, written words on stone or in books, "outstanding personalities," and, uniquely, special events such as the Exodus and the deliverance of Jerusalem from Sennacherib.[94] "The Old Testament is not interested in" general or world history but in "the purpose of God for Israel."[95] The true prophets in Israel indeed were instruments of revelation,[96] different from the teachers of China,[97] and the authors of the apocalyptic writings accounted themselves messengers of God.[98]

In the Old Testament the human body "is perceived to be inhabited by something more than breath," that is, spirit. Anthropomorphic language was frequently used, while all images of God were strictly forbidden. According to Rowley, man's "spiritual kinship with God, making possible a real fellowship with his Maker, . . . lies behind" the *imago Dei*.[99] Sin is "fundamentally . . . disobedience to the will of God," and "all sin is sin against God."[100] The Old Testament distinction between "unwitting sins and high-

---

[92]*The Relevance of the Bible*, 21-51, esp. 21-24, 36.

[93]*The Authority of the Bible* (Birmingham UK: Overdale College, Selly Oak, 1949) 6, 11-12, 6, 8.

[94]*The Faith of Israel: Aspects of Old Testament Thought* (Philadelphia: Westminster, 1957) 23-47.

[95]*The Re-discovery of the Old Testament*, 74.

[96]Ibid., 94-113.

[97]*Prophecy and Religion in Ancient China and Israel* (New York: Harper & Bros., 1956) esp. 121-44.

[98]*The Relevance of Apocalyptic: A Study of Jewish and Christian Apocalypses from Daniel to the Revelation* (London: Lutterworth, 1944) 12-14.

[99]*The Faith of Israel*, 84, 75-79, 83.

[100]*The Relevance of the Bible*, 159, 148; *The Faith of Israel*, 88, 89.

handed sins" was not simply a matter of ignorance versus knowledge, but deliberateness was involved.[101] Punishment in the Old Testament was "disciplinary" rather than "penal." Some sacrifices were "propitiatory," but this was not true of all. Especially for the prophets no sacrifice was reckoned to effect salvation "by the mere performance of an outer rite," and "salvation from sin" was "something more inclusive than sacrifice."[102] For Rowley, "the eighth- and seventh-century prophets were [not] inflexibly opposed to the whole sacrificial cultus," but only to its abuses.[103]

Rowley was convinced that the book of Job offers no "theological or philosophical explanation of the mystery of suffering."[104] Concerning the Servant songs of Isaiah he concluded:

> I find development from the thought of Israel as the Servant to the thought of an individual Servant *par excellence*, without abandoning the thought of Israel as still the Servant. If the fourth song is dominantly individual, the mission which the Servant fulfils is still not merely his own, but Israel's, and Israel is still called to enter in some measure into it, so that the Servant may really be Israel's representative.[105]

Rowley's conclusion as to the Suffering Servant coheres with his recurrent emphasis on the Gentile-embracing nonparticularism of the prophets and the protective particularism of postexilic Judaism that led to Gentile proselytism and allowed Rowley to expound on "the missionary message" of the Old Testament.[106] In his study of the Old Testament concepts of election and covenant he saw the covenant as man's response to God's grace which must be renewed by the Israelites/Jews and concluded that any repudiation of the covenant meant a repudiation of election. Peculiar to Rowley's doctrine is the idea that election was for service, that is service to the nations, not to salvation. Thus he sought to disconnect "the biblical

---

[101] *From Moses to Qumran*, 92-94.

[102] *The Faith of Israel*, 90, 92, 95, 97.

[103] *Worship in Ancient Israel: Its Forms and Meaning* (Philadelphia: Fortress, 1967) 131-35.

[104] *From Moses to Qumran*, 175; also *The Book of Job and Its Meaning* (Manchester UK: John Rylands Library and Manchester University Press, 1958) 206-207.

[105] *The Servant of the Lord and Other Essays on the Old Testament* (London: Lutterworth, 1952) 54.

[106] *Israel's Mission to the World* (London: SCM, 1939); *The Missionary Messages of the Old Testament* (London: Carey Kingsgate, 1944).

doctrine of election" from "the theological question of predestination to salvation or damnation." But the election of "the Church" is "not a rival to that of Israel" but "the continuation of that election."[107]

Rowley connected the Day of the Lord and the Golden Age, interpreted Sheol, found necromancy to be forbidden,[108] and concluded that the anticipated resurrection from the dead "does not have the form of a universal resurrection to judgement in a spiritual realm."[109]

Eric Charles Rust (1910–1991)

One of Wheeler Robinson's students would contribute to biblical theology and other disciplines from both sides of the Atlantic Ocean. Rust, born in Gravesend, England, of devout Baptist parents and baptized at fourteen, was preparing for a scientific career, specializing in mathematics, physics, and chemistry. He received Bachelor of Science and Master of Science degrees together with honors from the Royal College of Science while serving as a lay preacher in Baptist churches. From 1932 to 1935 Rust studied theology at Oxford, and then followed three pastorates: Bath; Oxford Road Church, Birmingham; and New North Road Church, Huddersfield. In 1946, for his book *The Christian Understanding of History* Oxford University awarded him the Bachelor of Divinity degree, and Rawdon College, Leeds, called him to be the senior tutor. During 1952–1953 he was visiting professor in Crozer Theological Seminary, and in 1953 he began his longtime teaching of Christian philosophy and apologetics and Old Testament theology in Southern Baptist Theological Seminary.[110]

Rust authored three books in biblical theology at ten-year intervals during the flowering of the Biblical Theology movement. *Nature and Man in Biblical Thought*[111] was a biblical study of the realm of nature, with marginal consideration of man, written as a contribution to "the philosophy of nature, which stands on the boundary between science and religion." He

---

[107] *The Biblical Doctrine of Election* (London: Lutterworth, 1950) 48, 34, 51, 16, 147.

[108] *The Faith of Israel*, 177-201, 150-76.

[109] *The Re-discovery of the Old Testament*, 226.

[110] E. Glenn Hinson, "Eric Charles Rust: Apostle to an Age of Science and Technology," in *Science, Faith, and Revelation: An Approach to Christian Philosophy*, ed. Bob E. Patterson (Nashville: Broadman, 1979; dist. by Mercer University Press, 1986ff.) 14-18.

[111] (London: Lutterworth, 1953).

contended both that there are biblical categories and images, especially those relative to the person and mission of Christ, that ought not to be abandoned in the modern era but that "Biblical cosmology, zoology, and ethnology are not binding." The two Genesis "creation myths" are explored, especially as to the extent of influence from pagan mythologies "of the surrounding peoples" and as to whether preexisting materials are presupposed, and the witness to creation in the exilic writings was noted. Rust found in the Old Testament a "hierarchy" of nature with man as the climax, a "psychic bond between the land and the people" of Israel, "order and purpose in nature," "the conservation of nature," and "the original perfection," "curse," and "restoration" of nature. He probed the meanings of *basar* (flesh), *nephesh* (soul), and *ruach* (spirit) and noted that the Old Testament has no word for "body," for "the body was the man," as Wheeler Robinson had affirmed. After reviewing the mediation of angels and the roles of the Word of God, the Spirit of God, and the Wisdom of God vis-à-vis creation and nature and after tracing creation and nature in Rabbinic Judaism, Rust came to the New Testament. Miracles predominate in the Gospels, God the Father as Creator and Christ or the Logos as the agent of creation and sustenance in the Pauline and Johannine writings, and the restoration of fallen creation in Paul and the book of Revelation. In his own conclusion Rust affirmed the Creator as the triune God of holy love on the "presupposition that God is Creator because He is Redeemer," opted for *creation ex nihilo* and preferred continuous creation to preservation, interpreted the significance of miracles, and was ready to build bridges to the scientific community.[112]

Salvation History: A Biblical Interpretation[113] was Rust's contribution to biblical theology with respect to the "understanding of history." "Christians are bound to the particularity of history" for "the center of the Christian faith is the incarnation." Rust avowed to probe *Geschichte*, not merely *Historie*. Although he found a glimmer of hope through general revelation, he was certain that "only in salvation history does God disclose himself redemptively so that man's eyes are opened to the full truth." "God comes to us in historical dress, clothing himself in the garb of historical events, and finally in the form of a man." Although our understanding of salvation history must be under the influence of historical criticism, we

---

[112]Ibid., vii; 14-15, 17; 20-81; 95-116, esp. 104; 124-60; 168-224; 232-39; 245-303, esp. 245.
[113](Richmond VA: John Knox, 1962).

must not forget that the biblical books were written out of a living faith, a faith that centered in Jesus' resurrection. In the Old Testament salvation history involved election and the covenant, judgment and promise, the remnant, the Messiah, the Servant, the Son of Man, and the age-to-come. In the New Testament it involved Jesus' coming/incarnation in the fullness of time to proclaim the kingdom of God; universal sin, demonic bondage, and divine judgment; the death, resurrection, and ascension of Jesus; the gift of the Holy Spirit, the church, and its mission to the nations despite the civil powers; and the second coming, general resurrection, and the consummation of all things. The entire salvation history, according to Rust, rested on an "eschatological framework."[114]

Rust's *Covenant and Hope: A Study in the Theology of the Prophets*[115] treated Old Testament prophecy in general, especially the weaving together of the wilderness strand and the royal or Jerusalem strand, and then prophets in particular: "the righteousness of God and the Day of Yahweh" (Amos), Yahweh's "covenant love" (Hosea), "the Lord of history and the Holy One of Israel" (Isaiah 1–39; Micah); "the hope of an individual covenant" (Jeremiah), "the divine presence and the re-creating Spirit" (Ezekiel), "the Redeemer of Israel and the Suffering Servant" (Isaiah 40-55), and "the descent of the Spirit" and "the Son of Man" (Haggai, Zechariah, Joel, Obadiah, Malachi, Isaiah 55-66, Daniel). Through the prophets Yahweh had disclosed his nature, manifested his lordship over history, and given his to-be-fulfilled eschatological promise.[116]

Two of Rust's books can be more precisely classified under the theology of history. In the first, *The Christian Understanding of History*,[117] the first part was a theological interpretation of history in general and of salvation history in particular. In the second salvation history was interpreted from the biblical texts in both testaments. Its third part sought to correlate salvation history and world history.[118] Much of the content of this initial volume was incorporated into *Salvation History*. Much of the content of

---

[114]Ibid., 7; 12-13; 28-33, esp. 33; 35; 22; 49-129; 134-228; 244-76; 284-312; 230-44. Rust's view of the atonement, 199-219, connected the cross with the incarnation and with the resurrection and combined "the victim theme" (sacrifice) and "the victor-theme" (triumph).

[115](Waco TX: Word, 1972).

[116]Ibid.

[117](London: Lutterworth, 1947).

[118]Ibid.

these two volumes found its way into *Towards a Theological Understanding of History*.[119]

Other volumes by Rust fall outside the scope of the present investigation. He was a major author in Christian apologetics,[120] wrote on environmental theology,[121] and contributed to the theology of preaching.[122] One can scarcely find another Baptist scholar than Rust who has been equally competent in biblical theology and contemporary Christian apologetics. Some may fault his use of historical-critical method or mythological language, but others have commended his scrutiny of "the perceptions of the modern day about history and science under the searchlight of salvation history."[123]

Ralph Edward Knudsen (1897–1987)

Ralph Edward Knudsen, educated at Des Moines University, Southern Baptist Theological Seminary, and Berkeley Baptist Divinity School (Th.D., 1938), served as pastor of First Church, Bozeman, Montana (1931–1935), Central Church, San Francisco (1935–1939), and University Church, Seattle (1939–1943) before becoming professor of New Testament at Berkeley in 1943 and assuming also the deanship in 1947. He retired from Berkeley in 1964.[124]

Knudsen's *Theology in the New Testament*,[125] organized generally according to the rubrics of systematic theology rather than according to the types of New Testament writings, drew more frequently and heavily on twentieth-century European and American Protestant systematic theologians

---

[119](New York: Oxford University Press, 1963).

[120]"The Apologetic Task in the Modern Scene," *Review and Expositor* 56 (April 1959): 178-200; *Science and Faith: Towards a Theological Understanding of Nature* (New York: Oxford University Press, 1967); *Evolutionary Philosophies and Contemporary Theology* (Philadelphia: Westminster, 1969); *Positive Religion in a Revolutionary Time* (Philadelphia: Westminster, 1970); *Religion, Revelation, and Reason* (Macon GA: Mercer University Press, 1981).

[121]*Nature—Garden or Desert? An Essay in Environmental Theology* (Waco TX: Word, 1971).

[122]*Preaching in a Scientific Age* (Birmingham UK: Overdale College, Selly Oak, 1951); *The Word and Words: Towards a Theology of Preaching* (Macon GA: Mercer University Press, 1982).

[123]Hinson, "Eric Charles Rust," 24.

[124]Betty Layton to James Leo Garrett, Jr., 14 December 2005, 16 March 2006, 6 April 2006.

[125]Subtitle: *A Basis for Christian Faith* (Valley Forge PA: Judson, 1964).

than on Baptist theologians. Knudsen held that the Bible is the "record of Christian revelation," favored the dynamic theory of biblical inspiration, held that biblical infallibility applies not to "grammar," "science," or "history" but to the "presentation of Jesus Christ," and concluded that biblical authority does not preclude the authority of experience and of the church. He held to the universal Fatherhood of God through creation, his special Fatherhood through redemption, and his unique Fatherhood to Jesus the Son. The New Testament presents a "consistent portrait" of Jesus but "no *systematic* Christology." The virgin birth is "a fact" but "not a major doctrine" and dependent on the incarnation. It is difficult to convey the concept of sacrifice in the modern world, but, substitution is valid, and "expiation" is not an adequate translation of "propitiation." Knudsen was less than specific about the baptism of the Holy Spirit but was thoroughly Trinitarian. The image of God according to the Old Testament meant being God's "representative" with the corollary of maleness/femaleness, whereas in the New Testament we encounter a "new image" in Christ. Knudsen inclined to the Arminian view of original sin, whereby guilt comes only with the voluntary appropriation of depravity. He emphasized the biblical images for the church and the church as ecumenical. His eschatology embraced the kingdom of God, death, the intermediate state, the second coming, resurrection, judgment, heaven, and hell, but for him the millennium had "little or no meaning for a relevant eschatology."[126]

Ray Summers (1910–1992); Edward Allison McDowell (1898–1975)

A native Texan, graduate of Baylor University (B.A.) and of Southwestern Baptist Theological Seminary (Th.M., Th.D.), and a pastor and interim pastor of numerous Baptist churches, Summers had a teaching ministry in the field of New Testament and administrative roles in three Baptist institutions: Southwestern Baptist Theological Seminary (1938–1959); Southern Baptist Theological Seminary (1959–1964); and Baylor University (1964–1980).[127] In his commentaries he demonstrated no little interest in theologi

---

[126]Ibid., 27, 38-41, 42-46, 60-65, 94, 106-9, 132-37, 180-81, 189-206, 216-20, 256-60, 333-46, 381-84, 398-414, 376-77.

[127]"Ray Summers: A Biographical Sketch," in *New Testament Studies: Essays in Honor of Ray Summers in His Sixty-Fifth Year*, ed. Huber L. Drumwright, Jr., and Curtis Vaughan (Waco TX: Markham Press Fund of Baylor University Press, 1975) xi-xii; Russell H. Dilday, Jr., "Eulogy for Ray Summers," in *Chronos,*

cal themes, and he authored a monograph in New Testament theology.[128] His focus was on biblical hermeneutics, Christology, soteriology, and eschatology.

For Summers the "foremost task" of New Testament interpretation is the discovery of the "intention" and "thought" of the biblical writer. "Historicocritical interpretation" should not only include the "investigation of... lexical, grammatical, syntactical, comparative, and rhetorical" factors but also the "life situation" and "religious experience" of the human author. "But only by reverent commitment of faith comes acceptance of this [the Bible] as indeed God's Word to man." Form critics should "search not alone for the situation in the life of the early church but also for the situation in the life of Jesus himself." Their work has indeed confirmed "a *supernatural* Jesus." Redaction criticism Summers found to be "indispensable" for the study of New Testament parables, and the salvation-history school he treated with respect.[129] After reviewing the nature of apocalyptic literature, he strongly advocated an "historical-background" method of interpreting the book of Revelation which combined "a part of the right wing preterist method with a part of the philosophy of history" method.[130]

The Texas professor "defended the 'virgin birth' against its modern rejectors, especially as to the argument from silence in the New Testament outside Matthew and Luke and in respect to textual critical evidence." Jesus' baptism was to fulfil the Father's purpose and to show identity with John the Baptist's movement and with all humanity. The three "wilderness temptations were intended to take Jesus from the way of a suffering

---

Kairos, Christos II: Chronological, Nativity, and Religious Studies in Memory of Ray Summers, ed. E. Jerry Vardaman (Macon GA: Mercer University Press, 1998) 2-6; Henry Jackson Flanders, Jr., "Ray Summers the Man," in ibid., 12-19. Summers was director of the School of Theology at Southwestern, director of graduate studies in the School of Theology at Southern, and chairman of the Department of Religion at Baylor.

[128] James Leo Garrett, Jr., "The Writings of Ray Summers," in Vardaman, ed., *Chronos, Kairos, Christos*, 21-42.

[129] "Contemporary Approaches in New Testament Study," in *The Broadman Bible Commentary*, Clifton J. Allen, gen. ed., vol. 8, *General Articles; Matthew-Mark* (Nashville: Broadman, 1969) 48-49, 51, 57, 55-56.

[130] *Worthy Is the Lamb: An Interpretation of Revelation* (Nashville: Broadman, 1951) 3-51, esp. 45-46. For his earlier and more comprehensive treatment of method, see "The Historical Background as a Basis for Interpreting the Book of Revelation" (Th.D. diss., Southwestern Baptist Theological Seminary, 1943) 53-94.

Messiah." The "central significance of the transfiguration" was "to be his fulfillment of both the law and the prophets and his religious authority."[131] The early Christians "saw the cross and the empty tomb—the crucified Jesus and the Risen Christ—as *one* mighty redemptive act of God."[132] Differences within the Gospels as to Jesus' resurrection are "complementary," "not contradictory."[133] First identifying the Christ in John's Gospel as Logos, Leader, and Lamb,[134] Summers went on conclude that "the Lamb of God" "is an adequate clue to the theology of that gospel and to outline the entire gospel under that theme.[135]

Summers's comparative study of the Coptic Gospel of Thomas and the Synoptic Gospels included a categorizing of the sayings in Thomas and a summary of the theology of that gospel with reference to "the Father, the Holy Spirit, the Son, the world, man, sin, and salvation, and the kingdom and eschatology."[136] Summers's conclusion that Thomas's theology was "a phase of Christianity on its way" was challenged by a reviewer, E. Jerry Vardaman, who asserted instead that it was a "phase of Gnosticism on its way."[137] In his commentary on Ephesians, which he attributed to Paul but reckoned a circular letter, Summers did not follow other commentators in identifying the church as the central theme but instead, "with an eye to the historical context, . . . took redemption as the central theme."[138] In his

---

[131]Garrett, "The Writings of Ray Summers," 24-25, based on Summers, "Jesus Christ: Virgin Birth, Baptism, Temptation, [and] Transfiguration," *Encyclopedia of Southern Baptists* 1:700-702, 703-704.

[132]"The Death and Resurrection of Jesus," *Review and Expositor* 62 (Fall 1965): 480.

[133]"Jesus Christ: Resurrection," *Encyclopedia of Southern Baptists* 1:705.

[134]"The Christ of John's Gospel," *Southwestern Journal of Theology* 8 (October 1965): 35-43.

[135]Garrett, "The Writings of Ray Summers," 40-41, based on Summers, *Behold the Lamb: An Exposition of the Theological Themes in the Gospel of John* (Nashville: Broadman, 1979).

[136]Garrett, "The Writings of Ray Summers," 31-32, based on Summers, *The Secret Sayings of the Living Jesus: Studies in the Coptic Gospel according to Thomas* (Waco TX: Word, 1968) 77-93.

[137]Review of Summers, *The Secret Sayings of the Living Jesus*, in *Review and Expositor* 66 (Winter 1969): 78-79.

[138]Garrett, "The Writings of Ray Summers," 30, based on Summers, *Ephesians: Pattern for Christian Living* (Nashville: Broadman, 1960) and idem, "Teaching Outline of Ephesians" and "One Message—Redemption," *Review and Expositor*

commentary on the Gospel of Luke he utilized as the central theme Jesus as "the universal Savior."[139]

Summers's most comprehensive contribution to New Testament theology was in biblical eschatology. He

> contended that 'Jesus' view of death was revolutionary' but differentiated Jesus' use of sleep in reference to death from the modern doctrine of soul sleeping. Jesus' shrinking from death was due to his bearing the sin of the world. . . . The biblical concept of death as the penalty for sin focused on spiritual death but not to the exclusion of physical death. But . . . Paul's shrinking from a disembodied state did not alter the reality of such a state. The disembodied state . . . was defended [by Summers] against D. R. G. Owen's view of cessation of life between death and resurrection and Lewis Sperry Chafer's doctrine of an intermediate body.[140]

The second coming of Jesus was examined as to "its certainty, its manner (personal, mysterious, sudden, triumphant) its time (unexpected, imminent . . .), and the proper attitudes concerning it.[141] Summers reckoned Jesus' resurrection "as the first phase of eschatological resurrection." He "interpreted in detail four New Testament texts" concerning eschatological resurrection: "John 5:24-29, 1 Thess. 4:13-18, 1 Cor. 15, and 2 Cor. 5:1-10" and concluded in favor of one general resurrection.

> He specifically rejected both the dispensationalist . . . division of the 'first resurrection' (Rev. 20:5-6) into 'rapture' and 'revelation' and . . . [the] postmillennial interpretation of both first and second resurrections as figurative or symbolic. Then he concluded that the 'first resurrection' is 'a symbol of the triumph of the martyrs,' whereas the implied second resurrection is 'the general resurrection.'[142]

The kingdom of God is "a major eschatological theme in the Gospel of Mark." Primarily the term meant "God's 'reign' or 'rule,' not the people being ruled or any geographical territory." At first Summers identified two senses of God's kingdom: "inaugurated" and "consummated," "the latter being identifiable with heaven, or final salvation."[143] Shortly thereafter he

---

60 (Fall 1963): 372, 380-87.

[139]*Commentary on Luke: Jesus, the Universal Savior* (Waco TX: Word, 1972).

[140]Garrett, "The Writings of Ray Summers," 25-26, based on Summers, *The Life Beyond* (Nashville: Broadman, 1959) 5-29.

[141]Ibid., 27, based on *The Life Beyond*, 95-146.

[142]Ibid., 26-27, based on *The Life Beyond*, 30-94.

[143]Ibid., 25, based on Summers, "An Exegetical Approach to the Gospel of

indicated three senses: inaugurated, growing, and consummated.[144] Summers's interpretation of Rev. 20:1-10 led him to the amillennial conclusion that there is "no basis" "for a literal . . . thousand-year reign of the saints with Christ on earth either before or after his second coming."[145] He was not clear as to whether he "was opting for the Augustinian form or the Kliefothite form of amillennialism."[146] As expected, the Texas scholar opted for one general judgment and two distinct eternal states: hell and heaven.[147]

Another advocate of an amillennial interpretation of Rev. 20:1-10 among Southern Baptists was Edward Allison McDowell, a native of South Carolina and a graduate of Furman University (A.B.) and Southern Baptist Theological Seminary (Th.M., Ph.D.) who taught New Testament at Southern Baptist Theological Seminary (1935–1952) and at Southeastern Baptist Theological Seminary (1952–1964).[148]

McDowell clearly embraced the Augustinian form of amillennialism, namely, that the nonliteral thousand-year "spiritual reign" of Christ and his saints began with Jesus' "exaltation" and "will continue until the end of history." Satan's fall from heaven occurred during Jesus' earthly ministry with the casting out of demons (Luke 10:18; Rev. 12:9); his being cast "into the abyss" occurred as he worked "through the beast of imperial Rome" (Rev. 20:2); his being cast into "the lake of fire and brimstone" (20:10) will occur at the end of history. The theme of the book of Revelation is "the great drama of the sovereignty of God."[149] McDowell explored the use and meaning of Messianic, Son of Man, and Suffering Servant motifs from Jesus' wilderness temptations to his cross, with an emphasis on his messianic consciousness.[150]

Mark," *Southwestern Journal of Theology* n.s. 1 (October 1958): 42-45.

[144]*The Life Beyond*, 4n.2.

[145]*Worthy Is the Lamb*, 205. He held that "the *overthrow of Satan*, and not the reign of a thousand years, is the main theme" of Rev. 20:1-10 (202).

[146]Garrett, "The Writings of Ray Summers," 23.

[147]*The Life Beyond*, 147-207.

[148]*Who's Who in the South and Southwest*, 11th ed. (1969–1970) 667. McDowell had early pastorates in Virginia and South Carolina and in retirement was minister of teaching, First Church, Atlanta.

[149]*The Meaning and Message of the Book of Revelation* (Nashville: Broadman, 1951) 195, 188-90, 200-203, xi.

[150]*Son of Man and Suffering Servant: A Historical and Exegetical Study of Synoptic Narratives Revealing the Consciousness of Jesus concerning His Person and Mission* (Nashvlle: Broadman. 1944); republ. under title *Jesus and His Cross*

Frank Stagg (1911–2001)

Born on a rice farm in Acadia Parish, Louisiana, into a family with Cajun roots, wherein his grandfather and great uncle had left the Roman Catholic Church through Bible reading and had become Baptists, Frank Stagg was baptized at eleven and called to preach at nineteen. At Louisiana College he edited the campus newspaper and was president of the statewide Baptist Student Union. He completed Th.M. and Th.D. degrees at Southern Baptist Theological Seminary, where his focus was on the Greek New Testament. After serving as pastor of First Church, DeRidder, Louisiana (1940–1945), he was then professor of New Testament at New Orleans Baptist Theological Seminary (1945–1964) and at Southern Baptist Theological Seminary (1964–1981). Stagg's writing extended beyond the field of New Testament interpretation to systematic theology and contemporary social issues, and Stagg became a respected, if at times controversial, New Testament scholar among Southern Baptists.[151]

According to Robert B. Sloan, Stagg was "first and foremost, an exegetical theologian,"[152] and according to Malcolm Tolbert, the Synoptic Gospels were "of central interest to him," for he deplored "the tendency, which he sees in fundamentalists and critical scholars alike, to make Paul's letters rather than the Gospels the point of departure for dealing with central Christian issues."[153]

Stagg wrote little about God the Father, much about God the Son, and considerable about the Holy Spirit. In his *New Testament Theology* he concentrated on the Christocentrism in the New Testament and the various

---

(1950s?).

[151]Frank Stagg, "A Continuing Pilgrimage," in *What Faith Has Meant to Me*, ed. Claude A. Frazier (Philadelphia: Westminster, 1975) 146-56; Penrose St. Amant, "A Continuing Pilgrimage: A Biographical Sketch of Frank Stagg," *Theological Educator* 8 (Fall 1977): 34-49; Malcolm Tolbert, "Frank Stagg: Teaching Prophet," in *Perspectives on the New Testament: Essays in Honor of Frank Stagg*, ed. Charles H. Talbert (Macon GA: Mercer University Press, 1985) 1-16; Robert B. Sloan, Jr., "Frank Stagg," in *Baptist Theologians*, ed. George and Dockery, 496, 498-99; Vance Corbet Andress, "A Critical Evaluation of Frank Stagg and His *Polarities of Human Existence* with Implications for Pastoral Theology and Caregiving" (Ph.D. diss., Southwestern Baptist Theological Seminary, 1996) 1-49.

[152]"Frank Stagg," 501.

[153]"Frank Stagg: Teaching Prophet," 6; see also Stagg, "Reassessing the Gospels," *Review and Expositor* 78 (Spring 1981): 187-90.

titles or concepts ascribed to Jesus. "The New Testament is from first to last about Jesus Christ. . . . Every other person in the New Testament has importance only in relationship to Jesus."[154] His self-understanding or "filial consciousness" was explored, and "Messiah" (or "Christ"), "Servants of the Lord," "Son of Man," "Lord," "Saviour," "High Priest," "Mediator," "Lamb of God," and "Logos" were explained.[155] In *The Doctrine of Christ*,[156] Stagg expounded Jesus' authority in calling disciples, over fasting, the Sabbath, food laws, and the Temple, in forgiving sins, and over "past revelation" and gave more attention to the deity of Jesus, which he called a "nonnegotiable in the New Testament." Jesus repeatedly claimed oneness with God the Father. Although the New Testament has reflections of adoptionism, kenoticism, and docetism, it went beyond these to an incarnation, or "embodiment," that embraces "the actual humanity and the actual deity of Jesus Christ."[157]

In 1966 Stagg summarized the New Testament teaching about the Holy Spirit, making clear that the gift of the Spirit was conditioned on repentance and faith, not on water baptism or the laying on of hands and contending that modern exponents of glossolalia mistakenly confuse the "other tongues" of Acts 2:4 with the "ecstatic utterance" of Corinth.[158] Shortly thereafter he clarified the "other tongues" of Acts 2:4 as "understandable language of some kind" and the tongues at Corinth as "motor phenomena brought on under the excitement of religious experience." "The shame of Corinth is not to be cloaked with the glory of Pentecost. Babbling, ancient or modern, is Corinthian and not Pentecostal."[159] In 1973 the Louisville professor labeled all Christians as "charismatics," even as all are "saints," and identified "charismatic revival" not as "a banner to be seized by ecstatic

---

[154](Nashville: Broadman, 1962) 35.

[155]Ibid., 42-79. On Matthew's use of "Christ," "Son of Man," and "Suffering Servant," see "The Christology of Matthew," *Review and Expositor* 59 (October 1962): 462-67.

[156](Nashville: Convention, 1984).

[157]Ibid., 57-64, 91-93, 90-91, 102-108. Stagg skirted around the virginal conception (ibid., 110).

[158]"The Holy Spirit in the New Testament," *Review and Expositor* 63 (Spring): 135-47, esp. 141-43, 144-46.

[159]Stagg, "Glossolalia in the New Testament," in Stagg, E. Glenn Hinson, and Wayne E. Oates, *Glossolalia: Tongue Speaking in Biblical, Historical, and Psychological Perspective* (Nashville: Abingdon, 1967) 25-29, 38, 41.

enthusiasts" but as a movement in which "the gifts of God are received and put to their intended service," that is, "the service of humankind." Stagg was still uncertain as the nature of tongues in Acts 10:46 and Acts 19:6 but rejected "flatly the notion that 'tongues' is a necessary gift of the Spirit or necessary sign that one has been 'filled with the Holy Spirit'" and critiqued the contemporary faith-healing movement.[160]

Stagg was eager to protect Christianity from charges of ditheism and tritheism[161] and to defend its monotheism.[162] But he mistakenly interpreted all the patristic doctrine of the Trinity as becoming "an emphasis upon the threeness and increasing jeopardy to the belief in oneness."[163] He employed a modalist illustration of God (son, brother, husband, father, grandfather, minister, fisherman) and mistakenly thought that he had avoided modalism by positing these roles as simultaneous, "not just one at a time."[164] Likewise he concluded from the absence of the word "Trinity" in the New Testament that there is no Three-in-Oneness expressed in the New Testament.[165] Stagg was criticized for reckoning "the difference . . . between God the Father and God the Son" as "a matter of functional perception on the part of the believer."[166]

As to the image of God in man, Stagg, after considering its possibly being the personal, spiritual capacity of human beings or human responsibility, concluded that dominion over the rest of creation was the central idea.[167] Repeatedly he defined the biblical uses of terms such as "flesh," "spirit," "body," and "soul."[168] Clearly for Stagg, "The [human] plight is one of *sin*, not merely one of finiteness, fate, involvement in material

---

[160]*The Holy Spirit Today* (Nashville: Broadman, 1973) 24-26, 47-48, 55, 67-72; rev. ed. (Macon GA: Smyth & Helwys, 1995) 21-23, 46, 54, 68-73.

[161]*New Testament Theology*, 38-40.

[162]*The Holy Spirit Today* (1973 ed.) 9-10; (1995 ed.) 1-4.

[163]Ibid. (1973 ed.) 13-16, esp. 14; (1995 ed.) 6-9, esp. 7.

[164]Ibid. (1995 ed.) 14; also *The Doctrine of Christ*, 99.

[165]"Southern Baptist Theology Today: An Interview with Frank Stagg," *Theological Educator* 8 (Fall 1977): 26-27. When Stagg dealt with such texts, he labeled them as using "tripartite language," not "trinitarian." "The Concept of the Messiah: A Baptist Perspective," *Review and Expositor* 84 (Spring 1987): 252-54.

[166]Sloan, "Frank Stagg," 511-12.

[167]*Polarities of Man's Existence in Biblical Perspective* (Philadelphia: Westminster, 1973) 25-30.

[168]*New Testament Theology*, 25-32; *Polarities of Man's Existence*, 46-58.

substance, or ignorance." Genesis 3 "is the story of a choice," and Rom. 1:18-32 "sets forth the same truths in careful and forceful analysis."[169] Stagg contended that Adam has been overemphasized in Christian theology. "Outside Genesis 1-5, the Old Testament builds nothing theologically on Adam." "Both the prophets and Jesus dealt with sin *in extenso* and in depth, but with no traceable allusion to Adam." "Genesis 3 seems clearly to trace 'the fall' to the inclination rather than the inclination to the fall." "Adam is named in [only] five New Testament writings," and only two texts are crucial: 1 Cor. 15:22, 45 and Rom. 5:12. Augustine mistranslated and hence misunderstood Rom. 5:12c, and agreeing with Hans Conzelmann,[170] Stagg concluded "that Paul's focus" in v. 12 "is not on the origin of sin but on the origin of death." Only spiritual death, not physical death, had been the consequence of sin. The Corinthian passage "has to do with bodily death and resurrection, not with the origin of sin."[171] Human existence thus is marked by "polarities": "aspective yet holistic," "individual yet corporate," "made to become," "free yet bound," "saints yet sinners," salvation as gift and [as] demand," and "self denied yet affirmed."[172]

Treating together the death and the resurrection of Jesus, Stagg in 1962 reckoned his death "on man's side" to be "a life taken," but "on Jesus' part" to be "a life given." Historic theories of atonement contain both elements of truth and limitations, and substitution was one of several motifs associated by Stagg with Jesus' death.[173] Subsequently the Louisville scholar became increasingly critical of "transactionalism" vis-à-vis the death and resurrection of Jesus as historic events with atoning/saving significance, which Stagg associated with divine "manipulation."[174] His critics took this

---

[169]*New Testament Theology*, 13, 18; see also "The Plight of Jew and Gentile in Sin: Romans 1:18–3:20," *Review and Expositor* 73 (Fall 1976): 401-13.

[170]*An Outline of the Theology of the New Testament*, trans. John Bowden (New York: Harper & Row, 1969) 197.

[171]"Adam, Christ, and Us," in *New Testament Studies: Essays in Honor of Ray Summers*, ed, Drumwright and Vaughan, 115-16, 118, 120, 121, 126-28, 117-18, 123.

[172]*Polarities of Man's Existence*, 45-191.

[173]*New Testament Theology*, 128-35, 144-45.

[174]"Adam, Christ, and Us," 125, 130-34; "The Mind in Christ Jesus," *Review and Expositor* 77 (Summer 1980): 342; "Reassessing the Gospels," 190-92. This pejorative use of "transactionalism" had been previously made by William Newton Clarke. See above, 308n.378.

to be a rejection of penal substitution. Finally, Stagg wrote favorably of the example theory of the cross,[175] though, unlike its other exponents, he retained the deity of Christ. Stagg's critique of "transactionalism" was coupled with a view of free, unhindered salvation.[176] Indeed "throughout the Gospels Jesus is depicted as forgiving sin on the simple basis of man's willingness to receive it," and God could and did "save sinners before the event of Golgotha."[177]

Although Stagg was, like his Baptist predecessors, interested in the uses of the Greek word *ekklēsia*, his treatment of the church was built around the great metaphors: people of God, body of Christ, and *koinōnia* of the Spirit.[178] His exposition of baptism was influenced by contemporary English Baptist and other authors,[179] his declared intention to set forth fully the positive features of the Lord's Supper was hardly realized,[180] and his treatment of ministry included the entire congregation as well as those ordained.[181] In *Woman in the World of Jesus*,[182] jointly authored by his wife, Evelyn Owen Stagg, the Staggs found "solid Biblical bases for a full recognition of the freedom and responsibility of woman in ministry."

Initially, Stagg interpreted the kingdom of God as both present and future and presented "eschatology" as "the goal of history" with discussions of the second coming, resurrection, judgment, and dual destiny. He took an amillennial stance, and his view of eternity as qualitatively different from time, together with his holistic view of human beings, enabled him to posit an embodied state after death.[183] Later Stagg treated the apocalyptic aspects of eschatology and interacted with dispensationalist and liberationist views.[184]

---

[175]"The Mind in Christ Jesus," 339-47. Stagg had also written favorably of the eternal dimensions of the cross. "Salvation in Synoptic Tradition," *Review and Expositor* 69 (Summer 1972): 366-67.

[176]*New Testament Theology*, 80-121. Stagg's chapter on salvation preceded his chapter on the death and resurrection of Jesus.

[177]"Salvation in Synoptic Tradition," 360, 363.

[178]*New Testament Theology*, 170-203.

[179]Ibid., 204-34.

[180]Ibid., 235-49, esp. 236, 245.

[181]Ibid., 250-76.

[182](Philadelphia: Westminster, 1978) esp. 257.

[183]*New Testament Theology*, 149-69, 305-38; see also "The Concept of the Messiah," 254-56.

[184]"Eschatology: A Southern Baptist Perspective," *Review and Expositor* 79

Robert Sloan's strong critique of Stagg's theology included not only his antitransactional, example view of the cross, his modalist rather than Trinitarian inclination, and his alleged de-apocalypticizing of New Testament eschatology but even more importantly Sloan's charge that "Stagg has ruptured the canon of the New Testament," not in terms of its literature but in terms of its "theological unity" (of Jesus and Paul), including "the cross-resurrection theological consensus of early Christianity."[185] Vance Corbet Andress has studied the usefulness of Stagg's "polarities" of human existence for the "pastoral care and counseling movement."[186]

George Eldon Ladd (1911–1982)

A native of Alberta, Canada, who emigrated to the United States in 1922 and grew up in New Hampshire, George Ladd professed faith in Christ at age eighteen in Maine through the ministry of a woman preacher. A Th.B. graduate (1933) of Gordon College, who while a student served as a Northern Baptist pastor in Gilford, New Hampshire, and a B.D. graduate (1941) of Gordon Divinity School, Ladd had a six-year (1936–1942) pastorate of First Church, Montpelier, Vermont, before moving to the Blaney Memorial Church in Boston. After a year of graduate study in classics at Boston University, he began Ph.D. studies in classics at Harvard University, which degree he completed in 1949 after having taught concurrently, first in Gordon College and later in Gordon Divinity School. Ladd joined the faculty of the newly founded Fuller Theological Seminary in Pasadena, California, in 1950 as professor of New Testament and continued in that significant role until 1980.[187]

A prolific writer, Ladd issued a group of monographs dealing with eschatology, certain monographs on other themes, and his *magnum opus*, a comprehensive New Testament theology. Throughout his career he was

---

(Spring 1982): 381-95.

[185]"Frank Stagg," 507-12.

[186]"A Critical Evaluation," vi-x, 240-48.

[187]David Allen Hubbard, "Biographical Sketch and Appreciation," in *Unity and Diversity in New Testament Theology: Essays in Honor of George E. Ladd*, ed. Robert A. Guelich (Grand Rapids MI: Eerdmans, 1978) xi-xv; *Who's Who in Religion*, 1st ed. (1975–1976) 326; Donald A. Hagner, "George Eldon Ladd," in *Bible Interpreters of the Twentieth Century: A Selection of Evangelical Voices*, ed. Walter A. Elwell and J. D. Weaver (Grand Rapids MI: Baker, 1999) 228-43.

repeatedly making the case for his having abandoned dispensationalism and embraced historic premillennialism.

Ladd began by explaining how the different millennial views had treated the kingdom of God, establishing that the kingdom is both present and future and contending that Jesus did not postpone an offer of a Davidic kingdom, giving his premillennial exegesis of Rev. 20:1-6, and answering objections to "a literal reign of Christ between the two resurrections."[188] Then he wrote in defense of the thesis that "the Blessed Hope is the second coming of Jesus Christ and not a pretribulation rapture." Probing theological history, Ladd concluded that the early church writers did not teach pretribulationism but that the latter came with John Nelson Darby's dispensationalism. Identifying with posttribulationism, he found pretribulationism to be devoid of exegetical support.[189]

A third book offered a positive, less controversial, exposition of the kingdom of God. The millennium is to be the overlapping of "This Age" and "The Age to Come," but in a sense the inter-adventual era also involves such overlapping. The kingdom makes a demand for decision, but the church is not the kingdom; rather "God's Kingdom creates the Church and works in the world through the Church."[190] Briefly Ladd sought to show the great importance of history for Christianity and of the second coming of Christ within the Christian concept of history.[191] In his fifth eschatological monograph Ladd included the Old Testament and the Pseudepigrapha so as to provide a more comprehensive interpretation of the kingdom of God from the perspective of "Biblical Realism." The latter he defined as "the effort to understand the New Testament writings from within the mind of their authors . . . rather than to force the biblical message into modern thought forms."[192] Then appeared his commentary on the book of Revelation, in which he used a slight "blending of the preterist and the ["moder-

---

[188]*Current Questions about the Kingdom of God* (Grand Rapids MI: Eerdmans, 1952).

[189]*The Blessed Hope* (Grand Rapids MI: Eerdmans, 1956) esp. 11, 19-88.

[190]*The Gospel and the Kingdom: Scriptural Studies in the Kingdom of God* (Grand Rapids MI: Eerdmans, 1959) esp. 38, 40, 42, 96, 117.

[191]*Jesus Christ and History* (Chicago: InterVarsity, 1963).

[192]*Jesus and the Kingdom: The Eschatology of Biblical Realism* (New York: Harper & Row, 1964) esp. 41-97, xiii; later publ. as *The Presence of the Future: The Eschatology of Biblical Realism* (Grand Rapids MI: Eerdmans, 1974).

ate"] futurist methods."[193] In a debate with Herman A. Hoyt, Loraine Boettner, and Anthony A. Hoekema, Ladd defended "historic premillennialism."[194] Finally he summarized his eschatology for the lay readership.[195]

Ladd's other monographs were addressed to diverse themes: an interpretation of Rudolf Bultmann's thought together with the predictive criticism that "the existentialist interpretation of the New Testament . . . will pass away as the philosophical trends shift in years to come";[196] a carefully constructed and detailed rationale, atypical of American evangelicals, for the evangelical use, without "rationalistic presuppositions" of criticism—textual, linguistic, literary, form, historical, and comparative religious—upon the basis that "the Bible is the Word of God given in the words of men in history";[197] a brief differentiation of three "patterns of New Testament truth": the Synoptic ("the kingdom of God"), the Johannine ("eternal life"), and the Pauline ("justification and the life of the Spirit");[198] and a notable apologetic for the facticity of the resurrection of Jesus.[199]

In his *magnum opus*, *A Theology of the New Testament*,[200] Ladd, like Gould but unlike Knudsen and Stagg, organized his 632-page study according to the types of New Testament writings: the Synoptic Gospels, the Fourth Gospel, "the primitive church" (Acts), the Pauline epistles, "the

---

[193] *A Commentary on the Revelation of John* (Grand Rapids MI: Eerdmans, 1972) esp. 14. Ladd's chief example of his "blending" was his interpretation of "the beast" as "both Rome and the eschatological Antichrist—and . . . any demonic power which the church must face in her entire history" (14). Rev. 4:1 does not refer "to the rapture of the church" (72), the seven seals are "not a part of the great tribulation itself, but are preparatory and preliminary" (96), and Christ does not come again until 19:11-16 (252-56).

[194] *The Meaning of the Millennium: Four Views*, ed. Robert G. Clouse (Downers Grove IL: InterVarsity, 1977) 15-40, 93-94, 143-48, 189-91.

[195] *The Last Things: An Eschatology for Laymen* (Grand Rapids MI: Eerdmans, 1978).

[196] *Rudolf Bultmann* (Chicago: InterVarsity, 1964) esp. 40. According to Molly Marshall-Green, "George Eldon Ladd," in *Baptist Theologians*, ed. George and Dockery, 486-87, Ladd's chief criticism of Bultmann was "for mitigating the 'once for all' nature of Jesus' life" and ministry.

[197] *The New Testament and Criticism* (Grand Rapids MI: Eerdmans, 1967) esp. 10, 12.

[198] *The Pattern of New Testament Truth* (Grand Rapids MI: Eerdmans, 1968).

[199] *I Believe in the Resurrection of Jesus* (Grand Rapids MI: Eerdmans, 1975).

[200] (Grand Rapids MI: Eerdmans, 1974).

general [non-Pauline] epistles," and the Apocalypse. In it the Fuller Seminary professor brought together the findings of his other books and fleshed out other aspects of New Testament theology. He frequently quoted or cited the best-known European New Testament scholars of the twentieth century.[201] Ladd's various treatments of baptism[202] were consonant with Baptist understandings of baptism. His greater preoccupation with the kingdom of God than with the church was not typical of earlier Baptists except for Rauschenbusch. Noteworthy is Ladd's contention that "the church is not the kingdom" but rather "the kingdom creates the church," "the church witnesses to the kingdom," and the church is both "the instrument" and "the custodian" of the kingdom.[203] In Ladd's handling of Rom. 11:15-16, 25-27 there was tension between the present rejection of "literal Israel" and the future salvation of the great majority of the Jews and ambiguity as to essential unity between saved Jews and Gentile believers during the millennium.[204]

Ladd had stature among New Testament scholars and was an able exponent of historic premillennialism.

Dale Moody (1915–1992); Wayne Eugene Ward (1921–)

Occupying a chair that had been associated with systematic theology but producing his *magnum opus* written more after the methods and content of biblical theology, Dale Moody was identified with the mid-century Biblical Theology movement, especially its emphasis on salvation history.[205] Born

---

[201]Most often, Rudolf Bultmann, C. H. Dodd, Joachim Jeremias, Oscar Cullmann, Vincent Taylor, and C. K. Barrett.

[202]*A Theology of the New Testament*, 40-44, 349-50, 548-49, 600.

[203]Ibid., 111-19.

[204]"Israel and the Church," *Evangelical Quarterly* 36 (October-December 1964): 206-13; Dongsun Cho, "George Eldon Ladd on the Relationship between Israel and the Church in the Kingdom of God," Historical Theology 7682, Spring 2003, Scripta, Roberts Library, Southwestern Baptist Theological Seminary, 31-46.

[205]E. Glenn Hinson, "Dale Moody: Bible Teacher Extraordinaire," in *Perspectives on Scripture and Tradition: Essays in Honor of Dale Moody*, ed. Robert L. Perkins (Macon GA: Mercer University Press, 1987) 9-10; Moody, "Doctrines of Inspiration in the Southern Baptist Theological Tradition," 182-84. Danny R. Stiver, "Dale Moody," in *Baptist Theologians*, ed. George and Dockery, 542-54, in discussing Moody's theology, treated separately his work as a biblical theologian and as a systematic theologian. Moody's being treated as a biblical theologian

into a devout Baptist family in Stamford, Texas, but reared near Fort Worth and Dallas, Dale Moody professed his faith in Christ and was baptized at twelve and began to preach while in high school. After three years of study (1933–1936) in Baylor University, where Greek and geology attracted his attention, Moody transferred to Dallas Theological Seminary; after one year and his rejection of dispensationalism the Texan studied (1937–1940) in Southern Baptist Theological Seminary in Louisville, Kentucky, from which institution, after a year of additional study at Baylor (1940–1941) and his B.A. degree, he received Th.M. (1941) and Th.D. (1947) degrees, his chief mentor being William Owen Carver. Moody began teaching at Southern Seminary in 1945 and was elected to the faculty in 1948 after having studied with Paul Tillich at Union Theological Seminary, New York City (1944–1945), and with Emil Brunner, Karl Barth, Walther Eichrodt, and Oscar Cullmann (summer, 1948) in Switzerland. After a leave of absence he completed a D.Phil. degree (1966) at Oxford University and during 1969–1970 was visiting lecturer—the second Protestant and the first Baptist—in the Gregorian University in Rome. He was a member of the Faith and Order Commission of the World Council of Churches. Moody continued to teach theology at Southern Seminary as Joseph Emerson Brown Professor of Christian Theology until 1983.[206]

Moody, sensitive to the importance of revelation in twentieth-century Protestant theology, began *The Word of Truth* with revelation and treated the whole Bible under revelation. "Special revelation," defined broadly as "an event in which God discloses himself to those who are ready to receive him," proved to be biblical revelation. Following Emil Brunner rather than Karl Barth, he affirmed the reality of "general revelation" through the created order and through conscience, but, following John Baillie and Moody's colleague Eric Rust, Moody posited the salvific nature of general revelation. He affirmed the inspiration of holy men (2 Pet. 1:20-21) and of the Holy Scriptures (2 Tim. 3:16-17). Commenting favorably on the

---

herein is not a denial of the fact that he also utilized the materials of historical theology.

[206]Hinson, "Dale Moody: Bible Teacher Extraordinaire," 3-17; Dwight Moody, "Doctrines of Inspiration," 179-81; *Who's Who in Religion*, vol. 2 (1977) 459; Melvin Duane Blackaby, "The Nature of the Church and Its Relationship to the Kingdom of God in Baptist Theology: John Leadley Dagg, Benajah Harvey Carroll, and Dale Moody" (Ph.D. diss., Southwestern Baptist Theological Seminary, 1997) 122-32; Stiver, "Dale Moody," 539-40, 542.

dynamic theory of inspiration, Moody nevertheless called for a "comprehensive" view,[207] "broad enough to include the ordinary reflection common to the historian and the extraordinary dictation characteristic of the apocalyptist."[208] Moody wrote very little concerning biblical infallibility or inerrancy.[209] His doctrine of authority was focused on the supremacy of the Scriptures, which are the "source" for Christian theology, whereas tradition constitutes the "tributaries."[210] Rejecting the exclusivist view of Hendrik Kraemer, the Louisville theologian embraced dialogue with non-Christian religions and the possibility of salvation without specific knowledge of the gospel or the church. Likewise he fostered a positive attitude toward philosophy and sought to build bridges to historical criticism and to the natural sciences.[211]

The doctrine of God, for Moody, included the theistic arguments, the divine names, the divine attributes clustered around holiness and love, and both the economic Trinity (New Testament) and the immanent Trinity (patristic theology). As to creation, Moody began with the Creator, dealt with the consummation of creation (restoration and renewal) and the preservation of the created order, was open to integrating the beginning of creation with the sciences, affirmed the goodness of creation, and interpreted providence as the purpose of creation, with prayer, miracles, and angels as aspects of providence.[212]

Soul predominates in Moody's treatment of body, soul, and spirit, perhaps because he held that "the Scriptures seem to find the unity of the human spirit and the human body in the human soul," and conscience was treated extensively. Eden is more symbol than geographical location, Moody differentiated "collective" Adam (Gen. 1:1–2:4a, P), "representative" Adam (Gen. 2:4b–3:24; JE) and "individual" Adam (Gen. 4, J) while embracing polygenism, according to which other human beings coexisted

---

[207]*The Word of Truth: A Summary of Christian Doctrine Based on Biblical Revelation* (Grand Rapids MI: Eerdmans, 1981) 38-42, 57-62, 42-47.

[208]Dwight Moody, "Doctrines of Inspiration," 188.

[209]Dwight Moody, ibid., 190-94, esp. 191, using Dale Moody's unpublished treatise, "The Inspiration of Holy Scripture," was able to ferret out the latter's distinction between infallibility (biblical doctrines) and inerrancy ("dates," "descriptions of the universe," etc.).

[210]*The Word of Truth*, 47-52, 1-11.

[211]Ibid., 62-77.

[212]Ibid., 78-169.

with Adam, Eve, Cain, and Abel. He was open to the origin of human life more than forty thousand years ago. Man and woman, being partners in creation, are to be partners in the church, although Moody did not press the pastoral ordination of women. The *imago Dei* is essentially "man's dominion over God's creation, Moody affirmed, but Moody did not show how this conforms to the Pauline usage.[213] According to the Old Testament, sin is fleeing from God and breaking the covenant with God; according to the New Testament it is ungodliness and unrighteousness. The sin that is universal is both individual and corporate, it originates in the "flesh" and the fall, and its transmission may be biological, psychological, or social.[214] Moody was less than clear on sin's relation to physical death and spiritual death but quite specific as to Satan and demons.[215]

In Christology,[216] not separating the work and person of Christ, Moody expounded the threefold office as "prophet," "priest," and "potentate."[217] Jesus as the Suffering Servant made "the supreme sacrifice which brings man to God," he being both "sacrificial victim" and "ruling victor." Walter D. Draughon III, has identified Moody's view of the cross as that of the sacrificial theory of Vincent Taylor and John Baillie and has critiqued it for failing to explain why the life of Christ is offered to God and to deal adequately with "the objective nature of Christ's work on the cross."[218] Following F. F. Bruce and C. K. Barrett, Moody insisted upon translating *hilastērion* in Rom. 3:25 as "mercy seat," as in Heb. 9:5, not as "propitiation" or "expiation."[219] He expounded the "postexistence" of Jesus in terms

---

[213]Ibid., 170-87 (esp. 180-81), 238-53, 187-238.

[214]Mark A. Gstohl, *Southern Baptist Theologians and Original Sin*, Toronto Studies in Theology 93 (Lewiston NY: Edwin Mellen, 2004) 119-22, has criticized Moody for failing to integrate the corporate nature of sin with original sin and to emphasize sin as idolatry and for too great reliance on his own exegesis of Romans.

[215]*The Word of Truth*, 271-307.

[216]Although in *The Word of God* Moody discussed soteriology prior to Christology, here the more traditional order is followed.

[217]Ibid., 366-85.

[218]"A Critical Evaluation of the Diminishing Influence of Calvinism on the Doctrine of the Atonement in Representative Southern Baptist Theologians: James Petigru Boyce, Edgar Young Mullins, Walter Thomas Conner, and Dale Moody" (Ph.D. diss., Southwestern Baptist Theological Seminary, 1987) 227-28, 233, 236. See also Moody, "The Crux of Christian Theology," *Review and Expositor* 46 (April 1949): 164-80.

[219]"Romans," *The Broadman Bible Commentary*, ed. Clifton J. Allen, vol. 10

of descent into hell, resurrection, ascension, heavenly session, and second coming, his "preexistence" in terms of the titles, "Wisdom," "Word," and "Son of God," and the "existence" of Jesus in terms of humiliation, incarnation, and perfection. Moody's exposition of the deity of Christ extended beyond the New Testament to include patristic theology, and his exposition of the humanity to modern Christology. He found the *skēnōsis* (indwelling) model of the unity of Christ to be more satisfactory than the *gnōsis* (knowledge) or *kēnōsis* (self-emptying) models.[220] According to Moody, the RSV correctly translated John 3:16 as "only Son" rather than as "only begotten Son" (KJV), for it conveys the true meaning of *monogenēs* and the erroneous translation can be traced to Jerome.[221] The Louisville professor argued persuasively that for Protestants "miraculous conception" (later "virginal conception") is a term preferable to "virgin birth," since the miracle lay in the conception rather than in the birth.[222]

Moody surprisingly did not include a chapter on the Holy Spirit in *The Word of Truth*, but he had already issued a monograph on the biblical doctrine of the Spirit. Therein he connected the Spirit with a particular function or truth in each segment of the biblical writings. For examples, the Spirit and the Messiah in the preexilic prophets, the Spirit and justification in Galatians, the Spirit and edification in 1 and 2 Corinthians, the Spirit and *koinōnia* in 1 John, and the Spirit of prophecy in Revelation. For Moody, tongues-speaking in Acts 2:4-12 must be governed by that in 1 Corinthians 14 and hence was ecstatic utterance. Respecting 1 Cor. 12:12-13 he was so concerned to discredit the idea that "each congregation" can be "a separate body of Christ" that he bypassed the issue as to whether Paul was alluding to water baptism or to Spirit baptism.[223]

(Nashville: Broadman, 1970) 183-84.

[220] *The Word of Truth*, 386-426.

[221] "God's Only Son: The Translation of John 3:16 in the Revised Standard Version," *Journal of Biblical Literature* 72 (December 1953): 213-19.

[222] "On the Virgin Birth of Jesus Christ," *Review and Expositor* 50 (October 1953): 453-62; "The Miraculous Conception," ibid., 51 (October 1954): 495-507; 52 (January 1955): 44-54; 52 (July 1955): 310-24; *The Word of Truth*, 417-18.

[223] *Spirit of the Living God: The Biblical Concepts Interpreted in Context* (Philadelphia: Westminster, 1968) 19-27, 108-15, 87-106, 175-81, 200-207, 62-63, 96-97. Moody considered Philippians, Colossians, Ephesians, 1 and 2 Timothy, and Titus as non-Pauline as to authorship.

Soteriology was the most controversial aspect of Moody's theology and proved to be so from his student days until his retirement and after. This was not so, however, because he set forth a three-stage (past, present, future) view of salvation and of sanctification, viewed regeneration as a process, questioned whether "to justify" means strictly "to declare righteous," espoused the single (man only) view of reconciliation, or embraced the Arminian doctrine of predestination as conditioned on faith.[224] Rather the controversy centered in Moody's consistent espousal and defense of the doctrine of apostasy in confutation of the Augustinian-Calvinistic doctrine of perseverance and in a Baptist context supportive of perseverance. Moody examined at length all the New Testament passages purported to support apostasy, disregarded those purported to support perseverance, and cited A. T. Robertson as his mentor.[225] Later he pressed his case by examining all the pertinent texts in the Epistle to the Hebrews.[226] In Moody Southern Baptist theology came to the espousal of all five tenets of original Arminianism.[227]

---

[224] *The Word of Truth*, 311, 322-25, 325-28, 329-31, 341-48.

[225] Ibid., 348-65. Youngblood, "The Question of Apostasy," 150-61, 171-86, 191, reported the Mexia, Texas (1940–1941) and the Shawnee, Oklahoma (1961) phases of Moody's controversy on apostasy, analyzed Moody's interpretation of the "perseverance passages" and the "apostasy passages," and made clear that for Moody apostasy is "irremedial." Contemporaneous with Moody's espousal of apostasy was a similar action by a Southern Baptist pastor in Kansas and Missouri, Robert Lee Shank (1918–), who wrote *Life in the Son: A Study of the Doctrine of Perseverance* (Springfield MO: Westcott Publishers, 1960) and *Elect in the Son: A Study of the Doctrine of Election* (Springfield, MO: Westcott Publishers, 1970). Shank held that in some cases apostasy is remedial but in other cases irremedial. Youngblood, "The Question of Apostasy," 232-35, 237-40. On Moody's third phase of controversy concerning apostasy and his early retirement, as well as the first two phases, see Hinson, "Dale Moody: Bible Teacher Extraordinaire," 12-17.

[226] *Apostasy: A Study in the Epistle to the Hebrews and in Baptist History* (Greenville SC: Smyth & Helwys, 1991). This book was "dedicated to the memory" of John Smyth, Thomas Helwys, and Thomas Grantham. The introduction narrates the author's long controversy as to apostasy.

[227] That is, conditional election, general atonement, faith as a human decision, resistible grace, and possible apostasy. According to Douglas Clyde Walker, "The Doctrine of Salvation in the Thought of James Petigru Boyce, Edgar Young Mullins, and Dale Moody" (Ph.D. diss., Southern Baptist Theological Seminary, 1986) 328, "Moody was virtually silent on the work, power, purpose, and grace of God in salvation."

Moody's doctrine of the church began with the church's mission, defined biblically in terms of *martyria* (witness) in the Petrine tradition, *diakonia* (service) in the Pauline tradition, and *koinōnia* (fellowship) in the Johannine tradition.[228] But surprisingly Moody made no connection with modern missiology, although previously he had contended that "the *purpose* of God, through the church" should provide the "vision" for the church's mission and the Holy Spirit its power.[229] Unique indeed and quite different from traditional typologies of church polity was Moody's historical classification of the structures of the church: "the "metropolitan," the "conciliar," and the "denominational."[230] The nature of the church he explicated in terms of biblical categories: the people of God and the temple of God in relation to God the Father, the body of Christ and the bride of Christ in relation to Jesus Christ, and fellowship and ministering service in relation to the Holy Spirit.[231] The ministry of the New Testament church was based on the ministry of Christ and consisted of both charismatic and ordained leadership, and Moody found deaconesses, widows, and possibly virgins in the New Testament era.[232] He first agreed with Kurt Aland that "no direct literary evidence exists for infant baptism before around AD 200."[233] Then in his Oxford dissertation he provided a detailed treatment of

---

[228] *The Word of Truth*, 427-33.

[229] "The Holy Spirit and Missions: Vision and Dynamic," *Review and Expositor* 62 (Winter 1965): 75-81.

[230] *The Word of Truth*, 433-40. See also Moody, "The Shaping of Southern Baptist Polity," *Baptist History and Heritage* 14 (July 1979): 2-11, in which he reviewed congregational, associational, and convention developments.

[231] "The Nature of the Church," *Review and Expositor* 51 (April 1954): 204-16; repr. in *What Is the Church? A Symposium of Baptist Thought*, ed. Duke K. McCall (Nashville: Broadman, 1958) 15-27; *The Word of Truth*, 440-48. Wayne E. Ward, "Dale Moody's Ecclesiology," in *Perspectives on Scripture and Tradition*, ed. Perkins, 89-92, noted the influence of ecumenical activity and contacts and possibly the impact of Karl Barth on Moody's doctrine of the nature of the church. On the similarity between Moody's treatment of the New Testament images of the church and that by Protestant and Roman Catholic theologians, see Garrett, *Systematic Theology*, 2:513.

[232] "The Ministry of the New Testament," *Review and Expositor* 56 (January 1959): 31-42; "Charismatic and Official Ministries: A Study of the New Testament Concept," *Interpretation* 19 (April 1965): 168-81; *The Word of Truth*, 448-60.

[233] "The Origin of Infant Baptism," in *The Teacher's Yoke: Studies in Memory of Henry Trantham*, ed. E. Jerry Vardaman, James Leo Garrett, Jr., and J. B. Adair

the twentieth-century writings about baptism in the Roman Catholic, Reformed, Lutheran, Anglican, and Free Church traditions, together with his own advocacy of a "primitive wholeness" that would bring together the practitioners of infant baptism and believer's baptism.[234] Finally he interpreted New Testament baptism in relation to purification, identification, incorporation, regeneration, salvation, and illumination.[235] Concerning the Lord's Supper Moody found its present significance in relation to thanksgiving and participation, its past significance in relation to the covenant and recollection, and its future significance in relation to the kingdom of God and the coming of Christ.[236] Having examined the biblical sources and the later historical types of Christian worship, the Louisville professor concluded that "the most basic thing in Christian worship seems to be gathering together to celebrate the acts of God in creation and redemption."[237]

The Hope of Glory[238] was the fullest expression of Moody's eschatology. It represents his radical commitment to biblical theology and his adherence to historic premillennialism. Its organization is threefold: "the hope of man," "the hope of history," and "the hope of creation." Death is both destruction (*katalysis*) and departure (*analysis*), and Moody strongly defended both a disembodied intermediate state and two distinct resurrections, of the righteous and of the wicked, separated by the millennium.[239] He interpreted the kingdom of God as God's reign in a threefold manner: "the immediate reign . . . in the present known only by faith," "an imminent possibility of the future that constitutes the gospel and is confirmed by signs

---

(Waco TX: Baylor University Press, 1964) 189-202, esp. 197.

[234]*Baptism: Foundation for Christian Unity* (Philadelphia: Westminster, 1967) esp. 302.

[235]*The Word of Truth*, 460-67. See also "Baptism in Theology and Practice," in *The People of God: Essays on the Believers' Church*, ed. Paul A. Basden and David S. Dockery (Nashville: Broadman, 1991) 41-50.

[236]"The New Testament Significance of the Lord's Supper," in McCall, ed., *What Is the Church?*, 79-96. In *The Word of Truth*, 467-73, the Supper was discussed under three topics: the "sources," the "significance," and the "service" itself.

[237]*The Word of Truth*, 473-80, esp. 474; Ward, "Dale Moody's Ecclesiology," 95.

[238](Grand Rapids MI: Eerdmans, 1964).

[239]Ibid., 55-102.

in the present," and "a future inheritance experienced in the present power of the Holy Spirit and a future disclosure of the glory of God."[240] Melvin D. Blackaby, noting that Moody never mentioned "the kingdom of God in connection with the church," has explained such by the fact that, for Moody, the church and the kingdom "do not overlap but are separated by the 'two ages.'" By inference from Moody's writings Blackaby conjectures that Moody held that "the church is currently outside the kingdom, waiting to fulfill its place inside the kingdom."[241] Here the residue of Moody's early dispensationalism may be detected. The concept of a "final pleroma" (fullness), of Israel and of the Gentiles, is explicated in detail, and the coming of an end-times Antichrist affirmed. Moody's cosmic eschatology includes a re-creation of the old creation, a new heaven and a new earth, and a distinction between the awaited "heavenly Jerusalem" and the fulfilled "new Jerusalem."[242] Danny R. Stiver seems to have concluded that Moody clearly espoused conditional immortality and therefore denied everlasting punishment to all the wicked, but the evidence is not very clear.[243]

Moody, whose lifelong passion was the Greek New Testament and the use of biblical categories, fought battles against Landmarkism, Dispensationalism, and Calvinism, embraced the conclusions of historical criticism and the natural sciences and the hopes of ecumenism but found that, for many others, apostasy was his "stone of stumbling."

Moody's professorial colleague for about three decades, who became a specialist in New Testament theology, was Wayne Eugene Ward. A native of Piggott, Arkansas, converted at ten, and ordained to the ministry in 1941, Ward served in U.S. Naval Aviation throughout World War II, being discharged as lieutenant (junior grade). He was a B.A. graduate of Ouachita Baptist College (now University) and a Th.M. and Th.D. graduate of Southern Baptist Theological Seminary. His massive dissertation on "The Concept of Holy Scripture in Biblical Literature"[244] reflected the advent of

---

[240] *The Word of Truth*, 516; also *The Hope of Glory*, 115-42.

[241] "The Nature of the Church," 169-71.

[242] *The Hope of Glory*, 143-92, esp. 173; 235-80.

[243] Stiver, "Dale Moody," 554, 556, 565n.130, relied on conversation with Moody after publication of *The Word of Truth*. But in *The Word of Truth*, 514-15, Moody, while expressing a "hope for" conditional immortality, stated that "there is no clear evidence in the New Testament for either the universalist or the annihilationist conclusion."

[244] (Southern Baptist Theological Seminary, 1952).

the Biblical Theology movement. He examined each segment of the Old Testament, after the order of the Hebrew Bible (Law, Former Prophets, Latter Prophets, Writings), the Old Testament Apocrypha and Pseudepigrapha, and the New Testament, engaging in exegesis of all the passages pertinent to the nature, function, and authority of the canonical Scriptures, identifying the written sources used by biblical writers, and drawing together the elements that formed and shaped the Bible's self-testimony. Acknowledging his "essentially conservative approach" to the books of the Bible "which attempts to deal fairly with the solid gains of Biblical criticism," the Southern Seminary professor-to-be stressed both "divine origin" and "human participation" and concluded that the authority of the Scriptures is to be established in the person and work of Jesus Christ, not by an "independent theory of inspiration."[245] Restating the case for the supreme authority of the Scriptures over that of the church or experience, Ward posited a limited role for confessions of faith,[246] and he redefined Christian preaching with the help of C. H. Dodd and Karl Barth.[247] Later he traced biblical theology back to Johann Philipp Gabler, responded to *Biblical Theology in Crisis*[248] by Brevard Childs, and advocated a biblical theology that utilizes "historical exegesis," embraces the entire biblical canon, is organized according to "the literary units" within each of the testaments, and is "confessional" and not merely "descriptive."[249] Finally, after reviewing again the two-century history of biblical theology with its competing rationalistic and pietistic tendencies, Ward, with a focus on European Protestant scholarship, predicted in 1981 that Jürgen Moltmann's "theology of hope" will likely be "the theology which will dominate the years immediately ahead."[250] He also produced a summary of biblical theology with an emphasis on covenant[251] and a manual of practical hermeneu-

---

[245]Ibid., esp. 23, 440, 449.

[246]"The Authority of the Bible," *Review and Expositor* 56 (April 1959): 166-77, 171.

[247]"Preaching and the Word of God in the New Testament," ibid. 56 (January 1959): 20-30.

[248](Philadelphia: Westminster, 1970).

[249]"Towards a Biblical Theology," *Review and Expositor* 74 (Summer 1977): 371-87.

[250]"New Testament Theology: Retrospect and Prospect," ibid., 78 (Spring): 153-68.

[251]*The Drama of Redemption* (Nashville: Broadman, 1966).

tics[252] and insisted that neither "parable" nor "myth" should be applied to Genesis 1–3.[253]

Ward acknowledged values in kenotic Christology, namely, God's initiative, the voluntariness of the incarnation, Jesus' restraint in using divine power, and the reality of his humanity, but found its greatest weakness to be its trying to rationalize and find analogies for the incarnation.[254]

In his exposition of the biblical doctrine of the Holy Spirit, Ward considered the descent of the Spirit at Jesus' baptism by John to be a "confirmation," "appointment," and "anointing" of Jesus as Messiah, the blasphemy against the Spirit to be rooted in Pharisaic awareness that Jesus had bypassed them and to be "equivalent" to the "outraging" of the Spirit (Heb. 10:29), 1 Cor. 12:13 to refer to Spirit baptism rather than water baptism, and the "tongues" of Acts 2:4 to be known languages.[255]

As to Christian baptism Ward contended that it should be "closely connected" with a "public confession of Jesus Christ as Lord and Savior" and argued that a "*private* baptism" is inappropriate, any "*private interpretation*" of baptism's meaning when "contradicted by the public proclamation of the church" is invalid, immersion should not be abandoned, and infant baptism should not be "a justifiable adaptation."[256] In his exposition of the Pauline metaphor of the church as the "one body" of Christ he found the term "invisible church" to be less than useful.[257]

George Raymond Beasley-Murray (1916–2000)

One of the most influential New Testament scholars in Great Britain during the twentieth century was George R. Beasley-Murray. Born in London to parents of Irish extraction, he suffered at the age of one the death of his father, George Alfred Beasley, from a road accident as a soldier, and his

---

[252]*The Word Comes Alive* (Nashville: Broadman, 1969).

[253]"Stories that Teach," in *Is the Bible a Human Book?*, ed. Wayne E. Ward and Joseph F. Green (Nashville: Broadman, 1970) 75-79.

[254]"The Person of Christ: The Kenotic Theory," in *Basic Christian Doctrines*, ed. Carl F. H. Henry (New York: Holt, Rinehart & Winston, 1962) 131-37, esp. 136.

[255]*The Holy Spirit*, Layman's Library of Christian Doctrine (Nashville: Broadman, 1987) 58-60, 62-64, 111, 98, 130. On Acts 2:4 Ward was following Stagg rather than Moody.

[256]"Baptism in Theological Perspective," *Review and Expositor* 65 (Winter 1968): 43-52, esp. 47, 51-52.

[257]"One Body—The Church," ibid. 60 (Fall 1963): 399-413, esp. 411-12.

mother then married George Murray and later moved to Leicester. The lad had been baptized at the age of four in a Roman Catholic parish church and as a teenager seemed to be entering a career as a concert pianist. He professed faith in Christ and was baptized at fifteen in a United Free Church which had been founded by a Baptist church. Turning from a musical career by a call to ministry, Beasley-Murray entered Spurgeon's College in 1936. Alongside the college curriculum, he obtained the external B. D. degree through the University of London. From 1941 to 1948 he served as pastor of Ashurst Drive Church in the London suburb of Ilford and obtained the Th.M. degree in New Testament through King's College, London. For two years he served Zion Church, Cambridge, while studying New Testament at the university and gaining B.A. and M.A. degrees but being barred because a full-time pastor from Ph.D. studies. From 1950 to 1956 Beasley-Murray served as New Testament tutor in Spurgeon's College and concurrently completed a Ph.D. degree at the University of London under R. V. G. Tasker, his thesis being published as *Jesus and the Future*.[258] From 1956 to 1958, while he taught Greek and New Testament at the Baptist Theological Seminary, Rüschlikon, Switzerland, he met Continental scholars and was introduced to Continental Baptists and to Southern Baptists, who had established the Swiss institution after World War II. Elected principal of Spurgeon's College, he served in that capacity as well as tutor in New Testament for fifteen years. The college was strengthened academically; its principal served as president of the Baptist Union and later took a stand in the controversy centering in Michael Taylor.[259] Emigrating to the United States, Beasley-Murray served from 1973 to 1980 as professor of New Testament literature, attaining to the James Buchanan Harrison Professorship in 1977, in Southern Baptist Theological Seminary. Then his final twenty years were spent in England with a continued ministry through writing.[260]

---

[258]Subtitle: *An Examination of the Eschatological Discourse, Mark 13, with Special Reference to the Little Apocalypse Theory* (London: Macmillan, 1954).

[259]See below, 571-74.

[260]Paul Beasley-Murray, *Fearless for Truth: A Personal Portrait of the Life of George Raymond Beasley-Murray, 10 October 1916—23 February 2000* (Carlisle UK: Paternoster, 2002); J. J. Brown, "George Raymond Beasley-Murray: A Personal Appreciation," in *Mission to the World*, ed. P. Beasley-Murray, 9-19; R. Alan Culpepper, "George R. Beasley-Murray," in *Baptist Theologians*, ed. George and Dockery, 567-71.

Beasley-Murray, who wrote commentaries on Ezekiel,[261] Matthew,[262] Mark 13,[263] John,[264] 2 Corinthians,[265] Philippians,[266] James, 1 Peter, Jude, 2 Peter,[267] and Revelation (four),[268] made major contributions to New Testament theology in two areas, Christian baptism and last things.[269] Both in his early years and his later he gave much attention to matters eschatological. He began by clarifying the prophetic concept of the Day of the Lord, "which is certain, but its effects, both for judgment and blessing, depend on the attitude adopted by the subjects of prophecy, whether it be repentance or hardening of heart."[270] He made it clear that to posit a "second advent" of Jesus Christ necessarily presupposes the first advent of him who is "God *manifest* in the flesh." Indeed the "cardinal assertion" of the Christian religion is that "the crucial event which illuminates all events has already taken place." The importance of the second coming lies in the truth that "the victory of the kingdom . . . will be through the action of Christ." The second

---

[261]"Ezekiel," *The New Bible Commentary*, ed. Francis Davidson (London: InterVarsity Fellowship; Grand Rapids MI: Eerdmans, 1953) 645-67.

[262]*Matthew*, Bible Study Commentary (London: Scripture Union; Fort Washington PA: Christian Literature Crusade, 1984).

[263]*A Commentary on Mark Thirteen* (New York: Macmillan, 1957).

[264]*The Gospel of John*, Word Biblical Commentary 36 (Waco TX: Word, 1987; 2nd. ed.: Nashville: Thomas Nelson, 1999).

[265]"2 Corinthians," *Broadman Bible Commentary*, vol. 11 (Nashville: Broadman, 1971) 1-76.

[266]"Philippians," *Peake's Commentary on the Bible*, ed. Matthew Black and H. H. Rowley, 2nd. ed. (Nashville: Thomas Nelson, 1962) 985-89.

[267]*The General Epistles*, Bible Guides no. 21, ed. William Barclay and F. F. Bruce (London: Lutterworth, New York: Abingdon, 1965).

[268]"The Revelation," *The New Bible Commentary*, 1168-99; *Highlights of the Book of Revelation* (Nashville: Broadman, 1972); *The Book of Revelation*, New Century Bible (London: Marshall, Morgan and Scott, 1974); also as New Century Bible Commentary (Grand Rapids MI: Eerdmans, 1981); "Premillennialism" (with Herschel H. Hobbs and Ray Frank Robbins) *Revelation: Three Viewpoints* (Nashville: Broadman, 1977) 10-70.

[269]His first book, however, was on Jesus' resurrection: *Christ is Alive!* (London: Lutterworth, 1947) and later he issued *The Resurrection of Jesus Christ* (London: Oliphants, 1964).

[270]"Biblical Eschatology: 1. The Interpretation of Prophecy," *Evangelical Quarterly* 20 (1948): 221-29, esp. 224.

coming is authentic Christian teaching, "not mere 'Second Adventism.'"[271] In his doctoral thesis[272] Beasley-Murray reviewed meticulously the writings of the advocates of the little apocalypse theory, according to which Mark 13 and its parallels were reckoned to have been "built around the nucleus of an [essentially Jewish] apocalypse of independent origin," but special attention was given to the work of Timothy Colani, author of *Jésus Christ et les Croyances messianiques de son Temps*.[273] Colani had come to Mark 13 from having rejected any connection between Jewish Messianism and Jesus and having repudiated any idea of an apocalyptic and victorious return of Jesus. Hence Mark 13 is an "interpolation" incompatible with the true teaching of Jesus. After examining other theories relative to the origin of Mark 13 and various efforts to vindicate or authenticate this eschatological discourse, Beasley-Murray concluded that its teaching "approximates so closely to the otherwise attested teaching of our Lord as to preclude the necessity for postulating an extraneous origin for it." Moreover, Mark 13 "describes the fall of the temple, bound up with that of the city [AD 70], in the context of the woes of the End." But his taking "this generation" in Mark 3:30 to refer to the generation contemporaneous with Jesus left him in the dubious position of casting doubt on the truthfulness of Jesus.[274] This last stance "caused consternation" among British evangelicals.[275] Soon thereafter his *A Commentary on Mark Thirteen*[276] dealt with its "authenticity" "as an original discourse of Jesus" and provided "a detailed exposition of each verse."[277] In a 1993 monograph Beasley-Murray was able to bring forward his earlier history of the interpretation of Mark 13 and parallels, to supply an extensive study of those authors who wrote "since the rise of redaction criticism," and to set forth his own "fresh approach to the discourse" and incorporate his commentary on Mark 13.[278] On Mark 13:30 he indicated his change of mind so that he now reckoned "all these things"

---

[271]*The Second Coming of Christ*, Norwood Papers 3 (London: Spurgeon's College, 1951) esp. 4, 6, 7.

[272]P. Beasley-Murray, *Fearless for Truth*, 71.

[273]2nd. ed. rev. and enl. (Strasbourg: Truettel et Wurtz, 1864).

[274]*Jesus and the Future*, esp. 1, 14-18, 172, 204, 183-91.

[275]P. Beasley-Murray, *Fearless for Truth*, 72-76.

[276](London: Macmillan; New York: St. Martin's, 1957).

[277]Brown, "George Raymond Beasley-Murray," 14-15.

[278]*Jesus and the Last Days: The Interpretation of the Olivet Discourse* (Peabody MA: Hendrickson, 1993).

in correlation with Mark 13:2, 32 and Matt. 23:36/Luke 11:51 to refer to the destruction of the temple and the fall of Jerusalem.[279]

In 1948 Beasley-Murray differentiated apocalyptic from prophecy, showed how, despite some likenesses, the book of Revelation differs from Jewish apocalypses, and, after strongly critiquing both "historicist" and "futurist" methods of interpreting the book of Revelation, advocated a form of the "preterist" method by which much of the content in chapters 4-19 is identified with the inter-adventual or Christian era, but not the millennium, which is to follow on earth the second advent. He suggested the possibility that Rev. 21:9-22:5 "pertains primarily to the City in the millennial age, though naturally the City remains in the same state of perfection in the new creation" (21:1-4).[280] Subsequently he published four different commentaries on the book of Revelation: the first as part of a one-volume British Evangelical commentary, the second for an American readership, the third as a full-scale volume in the *New Century Bible*, and the last in a format shared by two Southern Baptists, one representing amillennialism and the other realized apocalypticism.[281] He also defended the New Testament Apocalypse as a genuinely Christian book.[282] Beasley-Murray, together with George E. Ladd, Dale Moody, John Paul Newport, and others, helped to make historic premillennialism normative for many in Anglo-American Baptist theology during the last half of the twentieth century.

Later the Southern Seminary professor gave attention to the kingdom of God. After explicating the kingdom according to the Gospel of Mark,[283] he published a full-scale monograph, *Jesus and the Kingdom of God*. His treatments of the Old Testament and of Jewish apocalyptic literature connected the kingdom with theophany, the Day of the Lord, Son of Man, and Messiah. In Jesus' teaching about the kingdom its coming received the major stress. Jesus' utterances were interpreted under six categories: sayings on the coming of the kingdom of God in the present, parables on the same,

---

[279]Ibid., 443-49; P. Beasley-Murray, *Fearless for Truth*, 198-99.

[280]"Biblical Eschatology: II. Apocalyptic Literature and the Book of Revelation," *Evangelical Quarterly* 20 (1948): 272-82.

[281]See above, n. 268.

[282]"How Christian Is the Book of Revelation?" in *Reconciliation and Hope: New Testament Essays on Atonement and Eschatology Presented to L. L. Morris on His 60th Birthday*, ed. Robert Banks (Exeter UK: Paternoster, 1974) 275-84.

[283]"Eschatology in the Gospel of Mark," *Southwestern Journal of Theology* 21 (Fall 1978): 37-53.

sayings on the coming of the kingdom in the future, parables on the same, Son of Man sayings, and discourses on the second coming.[284] I. Howard Marshall criticized Beasley-Murray for producing "nothing more than a commentary on the relevant texts" and failing to supply "connective tissue" for his argument.[285] This was tantamount to saying that he had not moved beyond exegesis to New Testament theology. Beasley-Murray's reply to Marshall hardly sufficed,[286] but five years later he affirmed that in respect to the kingdom Jesus was "its champion (Mark 3:27), its initiator (Matt. 11:12), its instrument (Matt. 12:28), its revealer (Luke 17:20-21), [and] its mediator (Mark 2:18-19)."[287] Challenging John Crossan and others who have trouble with the Gospels having been "written backwards (that is, from the indissolubly united death and resurrection of Jesus), he found "Son (of God)" and "Son of Man" to be closely connected in the Synoptics and used interchangeably by John and Jesus' concern throughout his ministry to have been the coming of the kingdom of God.[288]

Beasley-Murray first wrote to explicate the Pauline texts on baptism: four (Rom. 10:9-10; 6:1-11; Gal. 3:27; Col. 2:11-12) of major importance, and ten of lesser significance. He first noted that Continental exegetes were identifying "baptized into his death" (Rom. 6:3) with the death of Jesus on the cross, that British exegetes were identifying it with the believer's death to sin and resurrection to life in baptism, and that there was a third essentially ethical answer. Also he took the "circumcision of Christ" (Col. 2:11) to refer to Jesus' death, not to baptism.[289] Then he expanded his New Testament focus, raising the question of authority to baptize and suggesting

---

[284](Grand Rapids MI: Eerdmans; Exeter UK: Paternoster, 1986).

[285]Review of Beasley-Murray, *Jesus and the Kingdom of God*, *Baptist Quarterly* 32 (April 1987): 98-99.

[286]"Jesus and the Kingdom of God," ibid. 32 (July 1987): 141-47.

[287]"The Kingdom of God in the Teaching of Jesus," *Journal of the Evangelical Theological Society* 35 (March 1992): 29-30. See also "The Kingdom of God in the Old and New Testaments," in *Reclaiming the Prophetic Mantle: Preaching the Old Testament Faithfully*, ed. George L. Klein (Nashville: Broadman, 1992) 179-201.

[288]"The Kingdom of God and Christology in the Gospels," in *Jesus of Nazareth: Lord and Christ: Essays on the Historical Jesus and New Testament Christology*, ed. Joel B. Green and Max Turner (Grand Rapids MI: Eerdmans; Carlisle UK: Paternoster, 1994) 22-36.

[289]"Baptism in the Epistles of Paul," in *Christian Baptism: A Fresh Attempt to Understand the Rite in Terms of Scripture, History, and Theology*, ed. Alec Gilmore (Philadelphia: Judson, 1959) 128-49, esp. 134-36, 140.

that Pedobaptists need to face the issue of faith and that Baptists need to answer the "what" of baptism.[290] In 1962 appeared *Baptism in the New Testament*, a comprehensive study that seemed to become the most influential monograph on Christian baptism by any author during the twentieth century. He identified four possible "antecedents of Christian baptism": Old Testament lustrations, lustrations in the Qumran community, Jewish proselyte baptism, which may not have been an antecedent, and the baptism administered by John the Baptist. The foundation for Christian baptism consisted of the baptism of Jesus, in which he "took his first step in bearing the sins of the world" but which New Testament writers never connected with Christian baptism, the baptismal activity of his disciples, Jesus' symbolic use of baptism, and baptism's connection with the Great Commission. Baptism, as it emerged in the Acts of the Apostles, probably included the one confession of the name of Jesus and was closely connected with the work of the Holy Spirit. Beasley-Murray examined in detail sixteen Pauline texts, two Johannine, one Petrine, and two from the Epistle to the Hebrews and then expounded the doctrine of Christian baptism in reference to grace, faith, the Holy Spirit, the church, ethics, hope, and its own necessity. Beasley-Murray reserved his treatment of infant baptism to his final chapter. He could not find it to have been practiced in the New Testament era but to be rather the product of "alien influences." He proceeded to test the modern practice by the New Testament; thus, for example, 1 Pet. 3:21, whether taken as "appeal" or "pledge," cannot be applied to infant baptism, and there can be no death and resurrection with Christ (Rom. 6:3-4) without faith. Finally as to the contemporary "inter-church" situation Beasley-Murray lamented: "The Baptist considers the Paedo-Baptist unbaptized; the Paedo-Baptist theologian regards a submission to believer's baptism after the receiving of infant baptism to be an affront to the Word of God and nigh to blasphemy." He proposed that Paedobaptists cease to use the language of the "blasphemy" of "rebaptism" and increase their baptisms of confessing believers. He proposed that Baptist churches no longer insist on believer's baptism for those Paedobaptists who wish to become Baptists and sought to defend such practice on the ground that some Baptist churches already practice open membership.[291]

---

[290] "Baptism in the New Testament," *Foundations* 3 (January 1960): 15-31, esp. 15-18, 29-30.

[291] (London: Macmillan; New York: St. Martin's, 1963) esp. 49, 361-64, 387-93. Beasley-Murray consistently referred to baptism as a "sacrament" rather than

Before a world Baptist audience Beasley-Murray took up the challenge issued by Karl Barth, commented favorably on Paul Rowntree Clifford's distinction of pedobaptism for the larger household of faith and believer's baptism for "the inner circle," and stated that Baptists should not insist on immersion for membership and should be prepared for an "immense adjustment" respecting baptism.[292] In *Baptism Today and Tomorrow* Beasley-Murray condensed his argument, making more specific the case that baptism should not be denominated a "mere symbol," making more pointed a criticism of open membership for allowing no baptism at all, taking note of and lamenting American Landmarkism, and drawing the line for Baptist church membership between those baptized as infants who have had active church membership and those that have not.[293] The British scholar, after coming to the American scene, continued to emphasize that 1 Cor. 12:13[294] and John 3:3, 5[295] are references to water baptism and to restate his case for baptismal reform.[296]

In treating the theology of the child, Beasley-Murray took a nonimputational view of original sin while stressing the solidaritaries in Adam and in Christ, held that children "are in solidarity with Christ" until they repudiate him "by sinning and yet they thus need conversion, used 1 Cor. 7:14 to support the idea that young children with a Christian parent should be "within the sphere" of the church though not yet members of the church, and urged the use of the postbaptismal catechumenate.[297] Beasley-Murray,

---

as "ordinance." His college principal, Percy W. Evans, had published *Sacraments in the New Testament: With Special Reference to Baptism* (London: Tyndale, 1947).

[292]"Baptism and the Baptism of Other Churches," in *The Truth That Makes Men Free: Official Report of the Eleventh Congress, Baptist World Alliance, Miami Beach, Florida, U.S.A., June 25-30, 1965*, ed. Josef Nordenhaug (Nashville: Broadman, 1966) 261-73.

[293](London: Macmillan; New York: St. Martin's, 1966) esp. 32, 86-88, 145-46, 166.

[294]"The Holy Spirit, Baptism, and the Body of Christ," *Review and Expositor* 63 (Spring 1966): 177-85, esp. 179-81.

[295]"John 3:3, 5: Baptism, Spirit and the Kingdom," *Expository Times* 97 (March 1986): 167-70. In dialogue with Continental and British, but never American authors, he not so much refuted as denigrated interpretations of "born of water" other than in reference to Christian baptism.

[296]"The Authority and Justification for Believers' Baptism," *Review and Expositor* 77 (Winter 1980): 63-70, esp. 69-70.

[297]"Church and Child in the New Testament," *Baptist Quarterly* 21 (January

while acknowledging that every one of the Baptist "distinctives" had been embraced by another Christian denomination but that "what makes Baptists distinctive . . . is the coalescence of these features within one community," pled unsuccessfully with his fellow English Baptists to frame a new confession of faith.[298]

R. Alan Culpepper has asserted that Beasley-Murray "provided the definitive monograph for this generation" on the three topics to which he devoted major attention: "Jesus and the future, baptism, and the kingdom of God."[299] Beasley-Murray combined, as did few of his generation, the evangelical and the ecumenical. His views of Christian baptism would elicit scholarly support from a younger generation of English Baptists, especially his rejection of the baptismal either/or symbol or sacrament, but his proposed changes in Baptist baptism-church membership practice would not evoke concurrence by most Baptists in the United States.

Donald Guthrie (1916–1992)

Donald Guthrie's entire teaching ministry was anchored in the London Bible College. Born in Ipswich of Scottish and Dutch ancestry, he was early identified with the Strict and Particular Baptists and began preaching at nineteen. He was "invited to join the teaching staff" of the college before he "had graduated" and obtained an external B.D. from the University of London. From 1949 until retirement in 1982 he was lecturer in New Testament studies. He also served as registrar for advanced studies (1964–1979) and vice principal (1978–1982). The editor of *Vox Evangelica* (1965–1980), he was visiting lecturer in Winona Lake School of Theology, Winona Lake, Indiana, and in the Freie Theologische Akademie, Seeheim, West Germany.[300] He was a deacon in Stanmore Church.[301]

1966): 206-18, esp. 209-10, 214, 216; "The Child and the Church," in *Children and Conversion*, ed. Clifford Ingle (Nashville: Broadman, 1970) 127-41; "The Theology of the Child," *American Baptist Quarterly* 1 (October 1982): 197-202.

[298]"Confessing Baptist Identity," in *A Perspective on Baptist Identity*, ed. D. Slater (London?: Mainstream Baptists for Life and Growth, 1987) 75-85, esp. 76, 78-81, 84-85.

[299]"George R. Beasley-Murray," in *Baptist Theologians*, ed. George and Dockery, 582.

[300]Guthrie, "I Stand for Truth: The Autobiography of Donald Guthrie, 1916–1992" (unpublished, courtesy of London School of Theology) esp. 7-9, 22-23, 42, per John-Paul Lotz; Harold Hamlyn Rowdon, "Donald Guthrie: An Appreciation," in *Christ the Lord: Studies in Christology Presented to Donald Guthrie*, ed. Harold

Guthrie's 982-page *New Testament Theology*[302] combined the according-to-literature and the thematic methods of explicating the theology of the New Testament. Rejecting both Wilhelm Wrede's purely historical approach and Rudolf Bultmann's existentialist approach, the London lecturer sought a balanced historical and theological approach according to which variety in the New Testament writings reflects diversity but not contradiction. The "basic unity" of the New Testament is to be found "in him who became the centre of Christian belief," Jesus Christ. Moreover, the Old Testament and Palestinian Jewish writings outweigh Hellenistic writings as sources for New Testament theology. Atypical of Guthrie's approach was his first chapter on God, in which he treated the names and the attributes of God on the basis of the entire New Testament without distinction of its types of writing. In subsequent chapters the doctrinal topic (man and his world, Christology, mission of Christ, the Holy Spirit, the Christian life, the church, and the future) was consistently treated according to the types of New Testament writings (Synoptic Gospels, the Gospel and epistles of John, Acts, Paul, Hebrews, the rest of the epistles, Revelation). Discussion of "the world" centered on angels, demons, and Satan rather than on the created order, Christology was a study of the titles applied to Jesus together with sections on Jesus' humanity, sinlessness, virgin birth, resurrection, and ascension, and the "mission of Christ" consisted of the kingdom of God and the saving work of Christ. Under the latter Guthrie included double reconciliation and forensic justification. The "Christian life" extends from repentance, faith, and forgiveness through grace and new life to sanctification and the role of the law. The church according to "the early community" (Synoptic Gospels, the Gospel and Epistles of John, Acts) was distinguished from the church according to the "developing church" (Paul, Hebrews, James, Petrine Epistles, Revelation). "The future" consisted of the second coming, the afterlife, judgment, heaven, and hell. Guthrie included ethics, personal and social, as a subdivision of New Testament theology and concluded with a chapter on the New Testament teaching about "Scripture."[303]

Hamlyn Rowdon (Leicester UK, Downers Grove IL: InterVarsity, 1982) ix-xi; Steve Motyer, "Donald Guthrie," in *Bible Interpreters of the Twentieth Century*, ed. Elwell and Weaver, 287-98.

[301]Derek Tidball to John-Paul Lotz, 2 November 2005.

[302](Leicester UK, Downers Grove IL: InterVarsity, 1981).

[303]Ibid., 24-37, 49-57, 59-70, 75-115, 122-50, 219-407, 408-509 (esp. 486-507),

Ralph Lee Smith (1918–1999)

A native of Stonefort, Illinois, a B.Ed. graduate of the University of Southern Illinois, and a Th.M. and Th.D. graduate of Southwestern Baptist Theological Seminary, Ralph Smith contributed to Old Testament theology. He taught Hebrew and Old Testament at Southwestern from 1949 to 1989, being named distinguished professor in 1987, followed by postretirement teaching until 1996.[304] He wrote commentaries on Job,[305] Amos,[306] and the minor prophets from Micah through Malachi.[307]

Smith produced studies of the theology expressed in specific books of the Old Testament. In Exodus one finds major emphasis on the Sinai covenant and the law and this covenant's being broken and renewed.[308] Deuteronomy speaks of God's "sovereignty," "solity," "formlessness," "righteousness," and "love" as well as the covenant, the law, sin, repentance, and hope for "the latter days."[309] According to Amos, God, who exercises universal sovereignty, had chosen Israel, which had ceased to "know how to do right" (3:10), other nations, whose representative sins Amos identified, had been criminally inhumane, and God's judgment was imminent.[310] In Hosea, harlotry and love are mixed with the experiential knowledge of God, exceeding wickedness, certain judgment, and "gleams of hope."[311] For Malachi the covenant and divine judgment were emphasized, and Israel's worship and worshippers indicted.[312]

573-700, 701-89, 790-892, 893-952, 953-82.

[304]Rick L. Johnson, "Ralph Lee Smith," in *The Legacy of Southwestern: Writings that Shaped a Tradition*, ed. James Leo Garrett, Jr., et al. (North Richland Hills TX: Smithfield, 2002) 149-50.

[305]*Job: A Story in Providence and Faith* (Nashville: Convention, 1971).

[306]"Amos," in *The Broadman Bible Commentary*, vol. 7, *Hosea-Malachi* (Nashville: Broadman, 1972) 81-141.

[307]*Micah-Malachi*, Word Biblical Commentary 32 (Waco TX: Word, 1984).

[308]"Covenant and Law in Exodus," *Southwestern Journal of Theology* 20 (Fall 1977): 33-41.

[309]"Some Theological Concepts in the Book of Deuteronomy," *Southwestern Journal of Theology* 7 (October 1964): 17-32.

[310]"The Theological Implications of the Prophecy of Amos," *Southwestern Journal of Theology* 9 (Fall 1966): 49-56.

[311]"Major Motifs of Hosea," *Southwestern Journal of Theology* 18 (Fall 1975): 22-32.

[312]"The Shape of Theology in the Book of Malachi," *Southwestern Journal of*

Smith near the beginning of his teaching wrote of the "death" of Old Testament theology during the first half of the twentieth century and its "revival" at mid-century.[313] Then at the end of his career in his *Old Testament Theology: Its History, Method, and Message* he provided an extensive history of the discipline of Old Testament theology up to 1992.[314] He argued that Old Testament theology should be a "normative" rather than purely "descriptive" discipline[315] and, after identifying, as Gerhard Hasel[316] had done, ten different methods for the discipline, concluded that "some combination of all these models is" likely "necessary."[317] Smith then proposed not "to present a comprehensive treatment of the whole of Old Testament theology" but rather to offer "a *model* of how to do Old Testament theology" and to discuss "some major themes that should be included."[318] Smith's chosen themes were nine in number: the knowledge of God, election/covenant, the nature of Yahweh, mankind, sin and redemption, worship, ethics, death and beyond, and the Messianic hope and the end of history.[319] Revelation embraces the hiddenness of God, the naming of God, a "more than intellectual knowledge" of God, and the roles of theophanies, events, words, and faith. Israel's election, for Smith, was due more to God's sovereignty than to his electing love, and there were possibly six covenants mentioned in the Old Testament: with Adam (?), with Noah, with Abraham, with Israel at Sinai, with David, and the new covenant. Yahweh is a saving God, a blessing God, a creating God—but with creation "subservient to 'holy history'," a holy God, a loving God, a wrathful God, a judging God, a forgiving God, and the one and only God. Only human beings are in the image of God. Although they are not divine, they are like him, exercising "some of His power on earth" and being "responsible to Him." The Old Testament viewed humans as unitary despite its use of "flesh," "spirit," "soul," and "heart." Sin is essentially "rebellion against God" involving

---

Theology 30 (Fall 1987): 22-27.

[313]"The Revival of Old Testament Theology," *Southwestern Journal of Theology* n.s. 1 (April 1959): 35-42.

[314](Nashville: Broadman & Holman, 1993) 21-71.

[315]Ibid., 72-77.

[316]*Old Testament Theology: Basic Issues in the Current Debate*, 4th ed. (Grand Rapids MI: Eerdmans, 1991) 38-114.

[317]*Old Testament Theology: Its History, Method, and Message*, 77-93, esp. 87.

[318]Ibid., 93.

[319]Ibid., 94-435.

"the whole person," is practiced by succeeding generations, and issues in guilt and punishment. Smith did not find the concepts of propitiation or double reconciliation in the Old Testament and concluded that its concept of forgiveness was "the restoration of a relationship" and not "the remission of a penalty." The deceased are in graves and in Sheol, Enoch was translated, and three were resuscitated. The Old Testament contains two texts asserting bodily resurrection and three others making "oblique references." It also looked for "the national and political restoration of Israel" while expecting a Messianic Son of David, the Suffering Servant, and the Son of Man. For Christians the New Testament is not only "the definitive and authoritative interpretation of the Old Testament" but also "the record of the last great saving act of God in human history" in Jesus Christ.[320]

Ralph Philip Martin (1925–)

A native of Anfield, near Liverpool, and converted at seventeen, Ralph P. Martin was a B.A. (1949) and M.A. (1956) graduate of the University of Manchester with pastoral education at Manchester Baptist College and a Ph.D. (1963) graduate of the University of London. After pastorates in Gloucester and Dunstable, he was lecturer in London Bible College (1959–1964), visiting professor in Bethel Theological Seminary, St. Paul, Minnesota (1964–1965), and lecturer in New Testament in the University of Manchester (1965–1969). He became professor of New Testament in Fuller Theological Seminary, Pasadena, California, in 1969 and continued until retirement in 1988. Then he taught in the University of Sheffield, became distinguished scholar-in-residence at Fuller in 1996, and is presently teaching at Azusa Pacific University.[321]

---

[320]Ibid., 103-107, 116-21, 99-102, 107-16, 135-39, 151-63, 167-233, 237-47 (esp. 247), 260-72, 276-77, 282-83, 287, 292-97, 299-303, 308, 378-84, 387, 392-95, 406-407, 410-26, 427.

[321]*Who's Who in Religion*, vol. 1 (1975–1976) 364; vol. 2 (1977) 419; Lynn A. Losie, "Ralph Philip Martin: *Curriculum Vitae*," in *Worship, Theology, and Ministry in the Early Church: Essays in Honor of Ralph P. Martin*, ed. Michael J. Wilkins and Terence Paige, Journal for the Study of the New Testament Supplement Series 87 (Sheffield UK: Sheffield Academic, 1992) 21-32; Michael J. Wilkins, "Ralph Philip Martin," in *Bible Interpreters of the Twentieth Century*, ed. Elwell and Weaver, 356-74; James E. Bradley to Joshua Lorin, 8 December 2005; Ralph P. Martin to James Leo Garrett, 10 December 2005.

Martin has written three times on the exegetical and theological aspects of Phil. 2:5-11. First, in 1960 he issued a brief monograph in which, defending the Pauline authorship of Phil. 2:5-11, he identified the passage as "a piece of early Christian kerygmatic confession which found a place in the cultus of the primitive Church." He cited favorably Joachim Jeremias and Ernst Lohmeyer to the effect that the text was a Christological hymn and Jeremias as to its presenting the three states of Christ: preexistence, incarnation, and exaltation. Unlike the first Adam, the second Adam "refused to use his favoured position to exploit His privileges and assert Himself in opposition to His Father." His self-emptying was not the abandonment of certain divine attributes, as certain kenoticists held, but, for Martin, the divestment of divine "glory," "splendour," and "fullness."[322] In his doctoral dissertation, submitted in 1963 and published in 1967, he amplified the hymnic nature of the passage, decided after weighing the arguments against and for Pauline authorship to leave the question in a "state of decision," and reviewed more extensively twentieth-century interpretations. Presenting the scholarly alternatives, Martin concluded that the self-emptying applied to the Son's role, not to his attributes, and meant that he accepted the role of servant and hence humanity. Turning from the older "ethical" view that Paul used the hymn as an example of and incentive for Christian humility, he found the hymn's possible use in a baptismal context and its more likely portraying "a soteriological drama" rather than "Christological speculation." The self-emptying and crucified Servant has become the exalted Lord, of evil powers and astral deities. So Martin suggested Stephen as a possible Hellenistic Jewish Christian author of the hymn.[323] In 1998 Martin introduced a volume of essays on Phil. 2:5-11 which emphasized its impact on Christology.[324]

Martin presented reconciliation as the "leading theme" in the "centre" of and "an interpretative key to Paul's theology."[325] In 2 Cor. 5:18-21

---

[322]*An Early Christian Confession: Philippians 2:5-11 in Recent Interpretation* (London: Tyndale, 1960) 8-16, 22, 23-25.

[323]*Carmen Christi: Philippians 2:5-11 in Recent Interpretation and in the Setting of Early Christian Worship* (Cambridge: Cambridge University Press, 1967) 1-95; 165-96, esp. 194-95; 287-311.

[324]"*Carmen Christi* Revisited," in *Where Christology Began: Essays on Philippians 2*, ed. Ralph P. Martin and Brian J. Dodd (Louisville: Westminster/John Knox, 1998) 1-5.

[325]*Reconciliation: A Study of Paul's Theology* (Atlanta: John Knox, 1981) 1,

reconciliation, the work of God in Christ, is an "objective" and "personal" "change" of the divine-human "situation," God being the "subject" and "never the direct object" of the reconciling. In Col. 1:15-20 God's reconciling of sinners, "a datum of experience," "points back to Christ's cosmic reconciliation." In Rom. 5:1-11 reconciliation "stands in some degree of tension with both 'justification' and 'wrath,'" whereas in Romans 9-11 reference is to the reconciliation of Gentiles, along with Jewish believers. In Eph. 2:11-22 the apostle asserted "both personal and ethnic reconciliation."[326]

Martin's study of the church in the New Testament focused more upon development than on the "images" of the church. Briefly connecting with the modern scene, he sought to examine critically modern models for the church: the Protestant "'lecture room' setting," the Roman Catholic "model of the theatre," the "corporation" or "community service" model, and the fellowship model which can degenerate into a "social club."[327] Martin's monograph on 1 Corinthians 12-15 he justified for three reasons: "Paul's teaching on the church is set in a context of realistic situations" in Corinth, these chapters offer "insight . . . into the role of the Holy Spirit in the church," especially as "leader in public worship," and they present Paul in his pastoral role. The Fuller Seminary professor wrote little about tongues and healing and much about body life, prophesying, praising, and praying.[328]

In *Worship in the Early Church* Martin emphasized that the primitive church was "a worshipping community" that had a "double attitude" to the cult of the temple in Jerusalem—respectful participation and sublimation—and had the "formative influence" of Jewish synagogue worship. Early Christian worship included prayers, praises, hymns, spiritual songs, confessional statements, reading of the Old Testament, proclamation, and giving.

---

5. Herein Martin was following his teacher, Thomas Walter Manson, *On Paul and John: Some Selected Theological Themes*, ed. Matthew Black, Studies in Biblical Theology 38 (London: SCM, 1963) 50, and to a lesser extent the work of another English Baptist: Arthur B. Crabtree, *The Restored Relationship: A Study in Justification and Reconciliation* (Valley Forge PA: Judson, 1963) esp. 41-46, 63-65.

[326]*Reconciliation*, 103-10, 124-26, 147, 132-35, 193.

[327]*The Family and the Fellowship: New Testament Images of the Church* (N.p.: Paternoster, 1979; Grand Rapids MI: Eerdmans, 1980) esp. 112-21.

[328]*The Spirit and the Congregation: Studies in 1 Corinthians 12-15* (Grand Rapids MI: Eerdmans, 1984) 1-4, 19-37, 60-76.

Referring to "the gospel sacraments," Martin explained how Jesus "submitted to baptism," "sanctioned baptism," "interpreted baptism" (symbolic usage), and "commanded baptism" (Matt. 28:19-20 being dominical). Martin found conversion and baptism to be so closely related as to be "virtual synonyms" and baptism to be "no empty symbol" but "a genuine sacramental action in which God works," applying "the saving efficacy of the death and resurrection of Christ." He avoided later issues related to infant baptism and immersion. As to recent scholarly debate as to whether the Last Supper was a Passover observance, Martin cautiously concluded "that Paschal ideas were in His [Jesus'] mind as He sat down with the Twelve." His exposition of the Pauline doctrine of the Lord's Supper offered no hint of later divergent understandings of the Supper.[329] Then Martin authored "a compact guide" for public worship that he hoped would be "both theologically adequate and pastorally helpful." "Worship" was defined as "the dramatic celebration of God in his supreme worth in such a manner that his 'worthiness' becomes the norm and inspiration of human living." It "should seek comprehensively to incorporate both set forms and the freedom of the Spirit." Like Beasley-Murray, Martin was interested in the bringing together of infant baptism and believer's baptism, as in the Church of South India and the Church of North India. He offered a fourfold restatement regarding the Lord's Supper:

1. "The presence of Christ is *at* the table, not *on* the table."
2. "The Lord's Supper is the supper of the Lord."
3. "The Lord's Supper is a special means of grace, not a means of special grace."
4. "The real presence is made possible by the real absence."[330]

Edward Earle Ellis (1926–)

A native of Fort Lauderdale, Florida, who at eleven professed faith in Christ and was baptized in a Baptist church in Dania, Florida—his maternal grandparents being members of the Advent Christian Church, and at fourteen was anointed by the Holy Spirit, Earle Ellis, after serving in the U.S. Army, completed a B.S. degree at the University of Virginia and was undertaking

---

[329](Grand Rapids MI: Eerdmans, 1975; orig., by Fleming H. Revell, 1964) esp. 23, 24, 87, 91-97, 105, 113.

[330]*The Worship of God: Some Theological, Pastoral and Practical Reflections* (Grand Rapids MI: Eerdmans, 1982) ix, 4, 11, 140-44, 161-70.

studies in its Law School when his hunger for the Bible led him to enter Faith Theological Seminary in Wilmington, Delaware. Transferring to the Wheaton College Graduate School in Wheaton, Illinois, he completed there M.A. and B.D. degrees in 1953. Two years later he completed a Ph.D. degree at the University of Edinburgh. Subsequently he had postgraduate studies or fellowships in the universities of Tübingen, Göttingen, Marburg, and Basel. His teaching ministry began at Aurora College, Aurora, Illinois (1955–1958), Southern Baptist Theological Seminary (1958–1960), and Bethel Theological Seminary, St. Paul, Minnesota (1960–1961). From 1962 to 1985 he taught New Testament in New Brunswick (NJ) Theological Seminary, being named research professor in 1977. From 1985 to 1998 he was research professor of theology in Southwestern Baptist Theological Seminary, Fort Worth, Texas, and he continues to teach in retirement. Having lectured in a hundred institutions, Ellis has been active in Studiorum Novi Testamenti Societas in Europe and in 1970 led in the founding of the Institute for Biblical Research in the United States. In 2005 his personal library became the nucleus of the International Reference Library for Biblical Research in Fort Worth, Texas. Ellis has authored eleven books and edited two Festschriften.[331]

Ellis has had a deep lifelong interest in biblical hermeneutics. His Edinburgh dissertation explored the Pauline use of the Old Testament, by quotation and otherwise, in ways similar to and different from Jewish exegesis, and on a wide range of topics.[332] He then broadened his interests to include πνευματικά, or "gifts of inspired perception, verbal proclamation, and/or its interpretation," "of which προφήτης is a special type." The prophet in the New Testament, especially in Acts, "makes known . . . the meaning of the Scriptures, exhorts and strengthens the congregation, and instructs the community by revelations of the future." Hence such prophecy is a form of

---

[331]Gerald F. Hawthorne, "E. Earle Ellis: A Biographical Sketch," in *History and Exegesis: New Testament Essays in Honor of Dr. E. Earle Ellis for His 80th Birthday*, ed. S. Aaron Son (Edinburgh: T.&T. Clark, 2006) 27-39; "Edward Earle Ellis: *Curriculum Vitae*," *Tradition and Interpretation in the New Testament: Essays in Honor of E. Earle Ellis for His 60th Birthday*, ed. Gerald F. Hawthorne and Otto Betz (Grand Rapids MI: Eerdmans; Tübingen: J.C.B. Mohr, 1987) ix-xvi.

[332]"The Use of the Old Testament in the Pauline Epistles" (Ph.D. diss., University of Edinburgh, 1955); published as *Paul's Use of the Old Testament* (Grand Rapids MI: Eerdmans, 1957).

Christian exegesis.[333] Furthermore, with all the hermeneutical similarities early Christianity had with apocalyptic Judaism, the Qumran community, the Pharisaic-rabbinic party, and the Sadducean party, "Jesus and his apostles and prophets," Ellis concluded, made "their unique contribution to first-century Jewish exposition by their thoroughgoing *reinterpretation of the biblical writings to the person, ministry, death and resurrection of Jesus the Messiah*."[334] Then, rejecting the three-stage (Law, Prophets, Writings) theory of the canonization of the Old Testament and taking note as to how synagogue worship utilized the Hebrew Bible and how rewriting of biblical materials (Deuteronomy, 1 and 2 Chronicles, Daniel) and scribal copying occurred, Ellis was able to speak of canonization "as a hermeneutical process."[335] Finally Ellis addressed "Jesus' attitude towards his Bible," namely, that these books "were the expression of the mind of God through faithful prophets" and he should correct the "misunderstanding and/or misapplication" of them by his contemporaries.[336]

Ellis also had a focus on New Testament eschatology, especially with reference to the Gospel of Luke and the Pauline epistles. In 1961, relative to 2 Cor. 5:1-10, he interpreted "house in heaven" to mean the ecclesial body of Christ, nakedness to mean guilt and shame, and "away from the body" to mean the absence of the solidarity and security of earthly existence and then concluded that the passage "does not deal with the intermediate state."[337] Refuting Hans Conzelmann's view that Luke introduced "a theology of salvation history to explain the delay of the parousia" and Helmut Flender's view that Luke shifted from a "horizontal, apocalyptic,"

---

[333] *Prophecy and Hermeneutic in Early Christianity: New Testament Essays* (Grand Rapids MI: Eerdmans, 1978) 24, 25, 144, 145.

[334] "Biblical Interpretation in the New Testament Church," in *Mikra: Text, Translation, Reading and Interpretation of the Hebrew Bible in Ancient Judaism and Early Christianity*, ed. Martin Jay Mulder and Harry Sysling, Compendia Rerum Iudaicarum ad Novum Testamentum, sect. 2, vol. 1 (Assen: Van Gorcum; Philadelphia: Fortress, 1988) 691; repr. in Ellis, *The Old Testament in Early Christianity: Canon and Interpretation in the Light of Modern Research*, Wissenschaftliche Untersuchungen zum Neuen Testament 54 (Tübingen: J.C.B. Mohr, 1991) 75-121.

[335] "The Old Testament Canon in the Early Church," in *Mikra*, ed. Mulder and Sysling, 653-90; repr. in *The Old Testament in Early Christianity*, 36-50.

[336] *History and Interpretation in New Testament Perspective*, Biblical Interpretation Series 54 (Leiden: E. J. Brill, 2001) 122-26, 131-32, esp. 131.

[337] *Paul and His Recent Interpreters* (Grand Rapids MI: Eerdmans) 35-48.

two-age eschatology to a "vertical, Platonic," time versus eternity perspective, Ellis found in Luke a two-age eschatology and a monistic anthropology with the possible exception of Luke 16:19-31. Indeed Jesus and his mission defined "for Luke the nature of the *continuity* and *discontinuity* between this age and the age to come." Jesus represented "in his resurrection an individual fulfillment of the age to come."[338] From a study of the usage of *sōma* in 1 Corinthians, Ellis found in 1990 that the Pauline anthropology is utterly monistic: "both the inward and outward aspects of the person refer to physical being," and hence there is no "individual existence . . . other than physical, bodily existence." Applying this to postmortal existence, he downplayed any intermediate state for believers. The Christian dead "do not count time," and the "hiatus . . . between their death and their resurrection . . . is, in their consciousness, a tick of the clock." Ellis labeled those who affirm the survival of the human soul after death as those "with lenses ground in Athens."[339] Building on the same monistic anthropology, Ellis made an elaborate argument in favor of annihilationism. Declaring that the Old Testament "pictures the whole person as going into the grave" and claiming that Sheol was seen as "virtual annihilation," he cited Ignatius, Justin Martyr, Theophilus of Antioch, Arnobius, and Athanasius in support of annihilation before proceeding to interpret key New Testament terms similarly. For Ellis "everlasting punishment" is to be "a one-time dispensing . . . of punishment that" has "an everlasting effect." Later Platonic influence, he argued, caused Christians to reinterpret the Bible so as to posit "everlasting suffering."[340]

---

[338]*Eschatology in Luke*, Facet Books, Biblical Series 30 (Philadelphia: Fortress, 1972) esp. 5, 8-10, 11, 13, 14, 17-20. See also *Christ and the Future in New Testament History* (Boston, Leiden: Brill, 2001) 105-46.

[339]"Sōma in First Corinthians," *Interpretation* 44 (April): 132-44, esp. 135, 142-43. See also *Christ and the Future in New Testament History*, 147-78. Ellis found Paul to have taught that believers go to heaven "in Christ" and are "in Christ" and that their bodily resurrection will occur at Christ's *parousia*. Ellis posited that the believers between death and resurrection are conscious of no passage of time but that for the living such time is real. No explanatory correlation of these two was offered (176-78).

[340]"New Testament Teaching on Hell," in *"The Reader Must Understand": Eschatology in Bible and Theology*, ed. Kent E. Brower and Mark W. Elliott (Leicester UK: Apollos, 1997) 199-219, esp. 197, 211-12, 209, 207-208, 199-205, 213, 215-16. See also *Christ and The Future in New Testament History*, 179-99.

Recognizing that there are two core concepts in New Testament theology, the eschatological and the Christological, Ellis produced essays supportive of the deity-claims of Jesus.[341]

From his earliest writing on Paul's use of the Old Testament Ellis pursued the question of the use of tradition or preformed traditions in the writing of the New Testament books. The capstone of this scholarly interest came in *The Making of the New Testament Documents* (1999).[342] Positing that there were four "apostolic mission circles"—"Petrine, Pauline, Jacobean, Johannine"—that cooperatively formed and transmitted traditions from the earthly Jesus, postresurrection traditions, and epistolary traditions,[343] Ellis attributed one canonical Gospel, together with epistles, to each circle—Mark, Luke, Matthew, and John.[344] His four-circle view was specifically designed to replace Ferdinand Christian Baur's conflict-ridden, Hegelian reconstruction of early Christian history,[345] and his dating of all the New Testament books except the Gospel and Epistles of John before or by AD 70[346] was an extension of the redating efforts of John A. T. Robinson.[347] Ellis's conclusions have far-reaching implications for traditional views of individual authorship of New Testament books.[348]

Ronald Ernest Clements (1929–)

Born in Essex and early at work in banking and in post-World War II military service, Ronald Clements was encouraged toward the pastoral ministry by his pastor in South Woodford Church, Herbert Hunter. He trained at Spurgeon's College (1951–1954) and obtained the B.D. degree from the University of London. At Christ's College, Cambridge, he studied Hebrew with J. N. Schofield and D. Winton Thomas and obtained a "first-class degree" in 1956. For three years he served as pastor of Southey Green Church, Sheffield, he won the Cambridge University Hebrew Prize, and he

---

[341]*Christ and the Future in New Testament History*, 38-51, 62-88.

[342]Biblical Interpretation Series 39 (Leiden: Brill, 1999).

[343]Ibid., 45-47, 263-66.

[344]Ibid., 306-375, 404, 289, 291, 266, 306.

[345]Ibid., 435-45.

[346]Ibid., 319.

[347]*Redating the New Testament* (Philadelphia: Westminster, 1976).

[348]See also Charles H. Talbert, Review of Ellis, *The Making of the New Testament Documents*, *Catholic Biblical Quarterly* 64 (January 2002): 158-60; Stephen Travis, Review of ibid., *Evangelical Quarterly* 77 (January 2005): 76-78.

began Ph.D. studies at the University of Sheffield under F. F. Bruce. That degree was received one year after he became in 1960 assistant lecturer in Old Testament at the University of Edinburgh, having resigned a newly begun pastorate in Stratford-upon-Avon. In 1967 Clements returned to the University of Cambridge as lecturer and was affiliated with Fitzwilliam College. In 1984 he was appointed Samuel Davidson Professor of Old Testament Studies at King's College, University of London, and served until retirement.[349] A prolific author, he surveyed the interpretation of the Old Testament from 1870 to 1970 with emphasis on German scholarship[350] and wrote commentaries on Exodus,[351] Deuteronomy,[352] Isaiah 1–39,[353] Jeremiah,[354] and Ezekiel.[355] In 1990 he was called "the best known Baptist scholar of the Old Testament in Europe."[356]

In his published dissertation Clements studied the presence of Yahweh in the tabernacle, with its associations with the ark of the covenant and the cherubim, and in the temple, despite the prohibition of images and any mere localization of deity.[357] The Abrahamic covenant, "an oracle of assurance" and a "promising covenant," Clements differentiated from the "law covenant" at Mount Sinai and found to have contributed to the kingdom and covenant of David, but the preexilic prophets were silent concerning the Abrahamic covenant until the Deuteronomic reform applied the covenant

---

[349]Rex Mason, "Ronald Ernest Clements: An Appreciation," in *In Search of True Wisdom: Essays in Old Testament Interpretation in Honour of Ronald E. Clements*, ed. Edward Ball, Journal for the Study of the Old Testament Supplement Series 300 (Sheffield UK: Sheffield Academic, 1999) 15-21.

[350]*A Century of Old Testament Study* (Guildford UK: Lutterworth, 1976).

[351]*Exodus*, The Cambridge Bible Commentary (Cambridge: Cambridge University Press, 1972).

[352]*The New Interpreter's Bible*, vol. 2 (Nashville: Abingdon, 1998) 269-538.

[353]*Isaiah 1–39: Based on the Revised Standard Version*, New Century Bible Commentary (Grand Rapids MI: Eerdmans; London: Marshall, Morgan and Scott, 1980).

[354]*Jeremiah*, Interpretation: A Bible Commentary for Teaching and Preaching (Atlanta: John Knox, 1988).

[355]*Ezekiel*, Westminster Bible Companion (Louisville: Westminster/John Knox, 1996).

[356]*Wisdom for a Changing World: Wisdom in Old Testament Theology*, Berkeley Lectures 2 (Berkeley CA: BIBAL, 1990) 7.

[357]*God and Temple* (Philadelphia: Fortress, 1965) esp. 28-39, 63-78, 28, ix.

to all three patriarchs and stressed its relation to the election of Israel.[358] Furthermore, the book of Deuteronomy is a "covenant document" with "covenant theology" with a focus on the Sinai covenant, instituted by divine election and balancing law and promise.[359] In addition, "there is only one Yahweh," and purity of worship can best be secured through "one single sanctuary."[360]

In his first monograph on the Old Testament prophets, Clements sought to present "a comprehensive survey of many of the more recent studies of the prophetic writings," especially the use of form criticism and "a stronger emphasis upon the relationship of the prophets" to Israelite worship. Key to that relationship was said to be a common "concern with the covenant."[361] There followed a study of eighth-century prophets: "the broken covenant" (Amos), "the enduring love of God" (Hosea), "the Holy One of Israel" and "the rod of the divine anger" (Isaiah).[362] A third volume on Old Testament prophets attempted to explore the impact of Israelite "historical, institutional, and liturgical traditions" upon the prophets as a corrective to an earlier overemphasis on "prophetic originality."[363] Furthermore, taking certain texts in the book of Isaiah as derived from a later redactor of Isaiah's preaching and dealing with Jerusalem's deliverance from Sennacherib, Clements identified three major theological themes in the redaction: "Yahweh has not abandoned his people; there is nothing to fear from the Assyrians for their days of domination over Judah are quickly coming to an end; [and] the salvation of Israel is assured through the Davidic dynasty."[364]

---

[358]*Abraham and David: Genesis XV and Its Meaning for Israelite Tradition*, Studies in Biblical Theology, 2nd ser., vol. 5 (Naperville IL: Alec R. Allenson, 1967) esp. 19, 14, 47, 61-69.

[359]*God's Chosen People: A Theological Interpretation of the Book of Deuteronomy* (London: SCM, 1968) esp. 28, 38-40, 45-49, 113-15.

[360]*Deuteronomy*, Old Testament Guides (Sheffield UK: Sheffield Academic, 1989) 50, 60-61.

[361]*Prophecy and Covenant*, Studies in Biblical Theology 43 (London: SCM, 1965) 7-8. Clements gave special attention to the election of Israel, the law, and Israelite worship vis-à-vis the preexilic prophets.

[362]*The Conscience of the Nation: A Study of Early Israelite Prophecy*, Approaching the Bible (London: Oxford University Press, 1967).

[363]*Prophecy and Tradition*, Growing Points in Theology (Atlanta: John Knox, 1975) esp. 1.

[364]*Isaiah and the Deliverance of Jerusalem: A Study of the Interpretation of Prophecy in the Old Testament*, Journal for the Study of the Old Testament

The capstone of Clement's work on the Old Testament prophets was a volume of previously published essays.[365] For examples, the modern critical denial of the Messianic hope was reviewed, and Clements concluded on the foundation of 2 Sam. 7:16, by blending redaction criticism and canon criticism, that prophetic texts "could have a double meaning"—one "original" and "a later, spiritual, and fuller, meaning." That the author of Isaiah 40-55 utilized themes that had been expressed by Isaiah of Jerusalem can be sustained by the sure examples of "Israel's blindness and deafness" and "the divine election of Israel" and possibly by other examples. Building on the view of H. H. Rowley and David S. Russell that biblical apocalyptic "emerged on the basis of a postexilic Jewish extension and reinterpretation of earlier prophecy," Clements contended that Isa. 10:23; 28:22; and Dan. 9:27, with their common reference to "the full end that is decreed," are examples representing apocalyptic editorializing of oracles from Isaiah himself.[366] Clements also issued a study of the major verbatim prayers of the Old and New Testaments.[367]

In his most comprehensive treatment of Old Testament theology,[368] which he modestly labeled as "only a tentative essay," the Cambridge scholar sought a *via media* between those who would "offer a theological commentary on the text of its various writings" and those who would "formulate a system of [Old Testament] religious ideas . . . with almost no regard for the character of the individual writings in which they appear." He interpreted "the God of Israel," "the people of God," law, and promise. He also sought to relate Old Testament theology both to "the religions of the ancient East" and to the three great monotheistic religions of the modern world, both to biblical studies and to the wider realm of theology.[369]

Supplement Series 13 (Sheffield UK: JSOT, 1980) 92-108, esp. 93.

[365] *Old Testament Prophecy: From Oracles to Canon* (Louisville: Westminster John Knox, 1996).

[366] Ibid., 49-61 (esp. 56-59), 78-92 (esp. 83-88, 91), 182-88.

[367] *In Spirit and in Truth: Insights from Biblical Prayers* (Atlanta: John Knox, 1985); also as *The Prayers of the Bible* (London: SCM, 1986).

[368] *Old Testament Theology: A Fresh Approach*, New Foundations Theological Library (Atlanta: John Knox, 1978).

[369] Ibid., esp. ix, 32.

Richard Norman Longenecker (1930–)

A native of Mishawaka, Indiana, Richard Longenecker completed B.A. and M.A. degrees at Wheaton College and, after studying in Faith Theological Seminary and Northern Baptist Theological Seminary, obtained a Ph.D. degree in 1959 from the University of Edinburgh. He taught New Testament in Wheaton College (1954–1963), Trinity Evangelical Divinity School, Deerfield, Illinois (1963–1972), and in Wycliffe College, Toronto (1972–1994). More recently he has been distinguished professor of New Testament in McMaster Divinity College of McMaster University, Hamilton, Ontario (1994–2001), and in Bethel Theological Seminary, St. Paul, Minnesota (2002–).[370] He has been a prolific author and editor in the field of New Testament studies.

Writing after the discovery of the Dead Sea Scrolls and the Nag Hammadi Library, Longenecker defined "Jewish Christianity" "ideologically" in reference to those early Christians whose concepts and expressions were rooted in Judaism and the wider Semitic thought, "geographically" in reference to the early Christianity centered in Jerusalem and the Jerusalem church, and temporally in terms of the century between Jesus' resurrection (AD 30) and the Second Jewish War (AD 132). Distinct from both Judaism and Pauline Christianity, Jewish Christianity was influenced by "noncanonical Jewish" writings (Dead Sea Scrolls, Old Testament Apocrypha, Apostolic Fathers, Christian Apologists, Papias) and "canonical Jewish Christian writings" (Matthew, John, Hebrews, James, 1, 2, and 3 John, 1 Peter, Revelation and perhaps 2 Peter and Jude). In this Jewish Christian orbit Jesus was distinctively referred to as an angel, as the eschatological prophet (Deut. 18:14-22), and as the New Moses with a new Torah and leading a new Exodus and was being named the Righteous One, the Shepherd, the Lamb, the rejected capstone, the beginning and the firstborn, and the descending and ascending one. Shared with Gentile Christianity were other titles such as Messiah or Christ, and the Son of God, whereas Son of Man was displaced and Suffering Servant, Davidic King, and High Priest were muted. Titles such as Lord, God, Savior, and Word, as applied to Jesus, for whatever degrees of Hellenistic influence there may have been, were basically drawn from Jewish or Jewish Christian roots. Longenecker saw the category of sonship as basic and the fusion of the messianism of

---

[370] *Who's Who in Religion*, vol. 1 (1975–1976) 349; vol. 2 (1977) 400; *Curriculum Vitae*; Richard N. Longenecker to James Leo Garrett, 24 September 2007.

Jewish Christianity and the lordship of Gentile Christianity and of the functional and the ontological by the second century.[371]

Biblical Exegesis in the Apostolic Period[372] is a study of the New Testament's quotation and interpretation of Old Testament texts. Acknowledging the influence of first-century Jewish hermeneutics, Longenecker found that such New Testament exegesis was thoroughly Christocentric, but those New Testament books that were "originally addressed to Jewish or Jewish Christian audiences" contain more numerous Old Testament quotations. As to whether such interpretations of Old Testament texts by New Testament writers should be taken as normative for modern Christian exegesis, Longenecker answered "no" when the interpretations were clearly "cultural" or "circumstantial" (the Midrashic or the allegorical) and "yes" when the literal interpretation approximates modern "historicogrammatical exegesis."[373]

Longenecker has given particular attention to Paul and his theology. In *Paul: Apostle of Liberty*[374] he focused on law and liberty, in *The Ministry and Message of Paul* he included the Pauline doctrines of man, Christ, being in Christ, the church, and last things,[375] and in volumes he edited, relying more on the Pauline letters than upon Acts, he dealt with the conversion of Saul of Tarsus: its nature, its effect on his Christology, and its paradigmatic value,[376] and with the order and the spontaneity, the unity and the diversity in the formation of the Pauline churches.[377]

After reporting the findings of twentieth-century scholarship concerning confessions of faith and confessional elements in the New Testament,

---

[371] *The Christology of Early Jewish Christianity*, Studies in Biblical Theology, 2nd ser., no. 17 (Napierville IL: Alec R. Allenson, 1970) 1, 3-4, 6, 11-21, 25-156.

[372] (Grand Rapids MI: Eerdmans, 1975).

[373] Ibid., 19-50, 205-20.

[374] (New York: Harper & Row, 1964) 86-208.

[375] (Grand Rapids MI: Zondervan, 1971) 87-104.

[376] "A Realized Hope, a New Commitment, and a Developed Proclamation: Paul and Jesus," in *The Road from Damascus: The Impact of Paul's Conversion on His Life, Thought, and Ministry*, ed. Richard N. Longenecker (Grand Rapids MI, Cambridge UK: Eerdmans, 1997) 18-42.

[377] "Paul's Vision of the Church and Community Formation in His Major Missionary Letters," in *Community Formation in the Early Church and in the Church Today*, ed. Richard N. Longenecker (Peabody MA: Hendrickson, 2002) 73-88, esp. 80-83.

Longenecker examined the various New Testament books for evidence as to how these confessions were "contextualized," or culturally and situationally adapted. For examples, 2 Cor. 5:19-20 as a confessional statement is joined with the ministry of reconciliation in defense of Paul's own apostolic ministry; in Matthew Jesus is the obedient Son of God in contrast to disobedient Israel, whereas in John's Gospel Jesus is not only obedient but also the "transcendental" and "metaphysical" Son of God; and in the Apocalypse the Lamb as both "sacrificial victim" and "victorious leader" has replaced the term "cross." Longenecker then argued for the need for contextualization today, especially in the Two-Thirds World, and identified and evaluated models for contextualization: "the transferal," "the translation," "the anthropological," "the ethnological," "the transcendental," "the semiotic," and "the synergistic-developmental." Worship, preaching, and ethics need to be contextualized as well as doctrine.[378] Longenecker also explored the existence in the early church of a connected passion narrative, a connected Olivet discourse, and a sayings collection.[379]

Longenecker produced careful studies of discipleship in Luke-Acts,[380] of prayer in the Pauline epistles,[381] and of development or shifts in Paul's concept of eschatological resurrection.[382]

During the fourth century of Baptist history Baptist authors were active in the academic discipline of biblical theology. Full treatments of New Testament theology were provided by Gould, Knudsen, Stagg, Ladd, and

---

[378]*New Wine into Fresh Wineskins: Contextualizing the Early Christian Confessions* (Peabody MA: Hendrickson, 1999) 5-44, 62-63, 79-83, 117-19, 129-30, 136-73.

[379]"Christological Materials in the Early Christian Communities," in *Contours of Christology in the New Testament*, ed. Richard N. Longenecker (Grand Rapids MI, Cambridge UK: Eerdmans, 2005) 48-68.

[380]"Taking Up the Cross Daily: Discipleship in Luke-Acts," in *Patterns of Discipleship in the New Testament*, ed. Richard N. Longenecker (Grand Rapids MI, Cambridge UK: Eerdmans, 1996) 50-76.

[381]"Prayer in the Pauline Letters," in *Into God's Presence: Prayer in the New Testament*, ed. Richard N. Longenecker (Grand Rapids MI, Cambridge UK: Eerdmans, 2001) 203-27.

[382]"Is There Development in Paul's Resurrection Thought?" in *Life in the Face of Death: The Resurrection Message of the New Testament*, ed. Richard N. Longenecker (Grand Rapids MI, Cambridge UK: Eerdmans, 1998) 171-202. Of the three shifts which he claims to have validated (200-201), the most important was the shift to transformation in 1 Cor. 15:51-52 from its absence in 1 Thess. 4:13-18.

Guthrie, and full treatments of Old Testament theology were presented by Robinson, Rowley, Smith, and Clements. Gould and Ladd treated New Testament theology according to the types of New Testament writings, whereas Knudsen and Stagg followed doctrinal rubrics and Guthrie sought to combine the two methods. All four Old Testament theologians organized their monographs according to doctrinal rubrics. Smith insisted on a normative approach, and Ellis and Longenecker gave attention to the use by New Testament authors of the Old Testament, especially by quotation. All authors utilized to some degree historical-critical method. Ellis and Clements saw schools or circles—traditioning—as quite determinative for biblical books as well as individual prophets or apostles. Gould and Stagg in various ways emphasized diversity within the New Testament. Ladd and Guthrie, on the other hand, stressed the doctrinal unity within the New Testament, and Rowley the unity of the Old Testament and of the Bible. All the authors, especially Robertson, affirmed the deity of Jesus Christ. Moody and Rust affirmed an ontological Trinity, whereas Stagg veered toward modalism. Robinson, Moody, Stagg, and Ward wrote or coauthored monographs on the Holy Spirit. A unitary or nondualistic view of human beings, usually with an affirmation of the body, was set forth by Robinson, Rust, Stagg, Moody, Smith, and Ellis. Robinson stressed corporate personality in the Old Testament. As to the saving work of Christ strong defense of penal substitution was lacking among these authors, while Moody and Stagg opted for the sacrificial and the example theories respectively. Martin emphasized reconciliation and Moody taught apostasy. These authors, except for Stagg, showed little interest in the uses of *ekklēsia* in the New Testament but considerable interest in the metaphors for the church. Robinson, Beasley-Murray, and Martin affirmed a more sacramental view of baptism, Beasley-Murray and Moody proposed ecumenical middle ground for Pedobaptists and Baptists, and Ward retained the more historic Baptist stance as to baptism. Ladd, Beasley-Murray, and Moody gave major emphasis to the kingdom of God and espoused historical premillennialism, whereas Summers and McDowell embraced amillennialism, and Ellis affirmed annihilationism. Robinson explored suffering, Rowley wrote on election and covenant, Martin gave expression to the theology of worship, and Longenecker noted the importance of confessional contextualization both in the apostolic age and in the present.

Chapter 9

Twentieth-Century Southern Baptists

Southern Baptists entered the twentieth century nursing the wounds and divisions resulting from the Whitsitt Controversy and having been less impacted than Northern Baptists by the cultural forces creating a new theological and ecclesiastical climate.[1] New leadership was needed, and that leadership came from and in association with Edgar Young Mullins.

Edgar Young Mullins

A native of Franklin County, Mississippi, and the first son of a Baptist pastor who preached for fifty-seven years, Edgar at the age of eight moved with his family to Corsicana, Texas. Inspired to sound learning by his educated father, the younger Mullins worked in a print shop and as telegrapher to assist in the college expenses of his older sisters before entering the Agricultural and Mechanical College of Texas, of whose first graduating class he was a member in 1879. After again working as a telegraph operator, he decided to study law in Dallas. There at twenty he professed faith in Jesus Christ during evangelistic services conducted by William Evander Penn, was baptized by his father, and was soon called to ministry. Mullins entered Southern Baptist Theological Seminary in 1881 and became a "full graduate" in 1885. His first pastorate was in Harrodsburg, Kentucky (1885–1888), and his second, of Lee Street Church, Baltimore, Maryland (1888–1895), allowed him to study at Johns Hopkins University. After one year as associate secretary of the Foreign Mission Board (SBC), Mullins was called to be pastor of First Church, Newton Centre, Massachusetts (1896–1899), near the campus of Newton Theological Institution. Elected president of Southern Baptist Theological Seminary as the successor to Whitsitt, Mullins had a twenty-nine-year presidency which brought him to the pinnacle of leadership among Baptists. A theological journal, *Review and Expositor*, was founded in 1904, student enrollment grew to 500 and the faculty to twelve, and a new fifty-acre campus was occupied in 1926. He served as president of the Southern Baptist Convention (SBC) from 1921 to 1924, chaired its committee on the Baptist Faith and Message in 1925, and was president of the Baptist World

---

[1] Torbet, *A History of the Baptists*, 445.

Alliance from 1923 to 1928.² Mullins was the author of twelve books and numerous articles, pamphlets, and unpublished items.³

Mullins was prone to state in the prefaces of his books that he was undertaking the task of theological restatement,⁴ thus suggesting that he did not intend to reiterate his predecessors. This fact does not preclude inquiry as to the probable influences shaping the theology of Mullins. Although undoubtedly Landmarkism with its church successionism was a major influence in the Baptist life of the South during Mullins's youth and early manhood, it did not seem to have had a formative effect on Mullins except perhaps to evoke from him an alternative method of validating the Baptist position. Likewise, Calvinism, as the alternative to Arminianism, was the theology of his theology professor, James P. Boyce, but it has been often stated that Mullins held to a moderate or modified Calvinism.⁵ The German theologian, Friedrich Daniel Ernst Schleiermacher, has been posited as the

---

²Isla May Mullins, *Edgar Young Mullins: An Intimate Biography* (Nashville: Sunday School Board of the SBC, 1929); A. T. Robertson, "A Sketch of the Life of President Mullins," *Review and Expositor* 22 (January 1925): 7-10; Harold W. Tribble, "Edgar Young Mullins," *Review and Expositor* 49 (April 1952): 125-38; Gaines S. Dobbins, "Mullins, Edgar Young," *Encyclopedia of Southern Baptists* 2:930; Mueller, *A History of Southern Baptist Theological Seminary*, 179-210; John S. Moore, "Mullins, Edgar Young," *Encyclopedia of Religion in the South*, 2nd ed. rev., ed. Samuel S. Hill and Charles H. Lippy (Macon GA: Mercer University Press, 2005; orig., 1984) 525-26; William Elliott Ellis, *"A Man of Books and a Man of the People": E. Y. Mullins and the Crisis of Moderate Southern Baptist Leadership* (Macon GA: Mercer University Press, 1985); Fisher Humphreys, "E. Y. Mullins," in *Baptist Theologians*, ed. George and Dockery, 330, 332; Fletcher, *The Southern Baptist Convention*, 104, 107-108, 121, 136-43, 164-65, 189, 366-67, 397; Robert S. Wilson, "Coming of Age: The Postwar Era and the 1920s," in *Baptists Together in Christ, 1905–2005*, ed. Pierard et al., 61-65, 321.

³William D. M. Carrell, "Edgar Young Mullins and the Competency of the Soul in Religion" (Ph.D. diss., Baylor University, 1993; Ann Arbor MI: University Microfilms International, 1998) 170-75.

⁴Bill Clark Thomas, "Edgar Young Mullins: A Baptist Exponent of Theological Restatement" (Th.D. diss., Southern Baptist Theological Seminary, 1963) 12-14, 214-16.

⁵Paul Abbott Basden, "Theologies of Predestination in the Southern Baptist Tradition: A Critical Evaluation" (Ph.D. diss., Southwestern Baptist Theological Seminary, 1986) 200-204; Humphreys, "E. Y. Mullins," 332-33; Draughon, "A Critical Evaluation of the Diminishing Influence of Calvinism," 71, 134, 136.

or a source for Mullins's emphasis on Christian experience. A negative factor against such indebtedness is the fact that most of Mullins's citations of Schleiermacher were in the nature of corrections or refutations.[6] Two American authors of books on Christian experience, Lewis French Stearns[7] (1847–1892) and Frank Hugh Foster[8] (1851–1935), Mullins discussed quite favorably.[9] William James's book[10] was also given attention by Mullins, but James was not prepared to affirm that Jesus Christ is the author of Christian experience.[11] More much concurrence exists among the interpreters of Mullins that he was profoundly influenced by and adopted the philosophy of personalism. In his treatment of worldviews Mullins gave most favorable assessment to personalism.[12] According to Leo Sandon, Jr.,[13] Mullins "was attracted to personal idealism as it was expounded in the writings of Borden Parker Bowne" (1847–1910), the first of the Boston University personalists, probably during his Newton Centre pastorate. William E. Ellis thought that Mullins made a selective use of "the pragmatism of James, the experientialism of Schleiermacher, and the personalism of Bowne."[14] Bill Clark Thomas was quite certain of Mullins's adoption of Bowne's personalism both as an epistemology and especially as a metaphysic.[15] In 1908 Mullins discussed personalism in connection with pragmatism and humanism and found the other two to be strictly epistemological. Personalism, he concluded, "takes the individual and personal life of man as its starting point" and "finds a personal God as the goal of its inquiry."[16]

---

[6]Thomas, "Edgar Young Mullins," 164-68.
[7]*The Evidence of Christian Experience* (New York: Scribner's, 1893).
[8]*Christian Life and Theology* (New York: Fleming H. Revell Co., 1900).
[9]"Is Jesus Christ the Author of Religious Experience?" *Review and Expositor* 1 (April 1904): 55-70, esp. 55-57. See also Thomas, "Edgar Young Mullins," 168-73.
[10]*The Varieties of Religious Experience* (New York: Modern Library, 1902).
[11]Mullins, "Is Jesus Christ the Author of Religious Experience?," 57-59; Thomas, "Edgar Young Mullins," 160-63.
[12]*The Christian Religion in Its Doctrinal Expression* (Philadelphia: Judson, 1917) 108-21.
[13]"Boston University Personalism and Southern Baptist Theology," *Foundations* 20 (April-June 1977): 103.
[14]*"A Man of Books and a Man of the People,"* 77.
[15]"Edgar Young Mullins," 139-51, 183-97.
[16]"Pragmatism, Humanism, and Personalism: The New Philosophic Movement," *Review and Expositor* 5 (October 1908): 510, 511.

Two guiding principles, it seems, governed the theology of Mullins: Christian experience and soul competency. The one governed his exposition of Christian doctrines in general, while the other was the key to his reinterpretation of Baptist distinctives. In his textbook on systematic theology, the Louisville president, following his second chapter pertaining to the human knowledge of God, explicated in detail Christian experience in his third chapter, and again discussed Christian experience in his fourth chapter relative to "Christian and other forms of knowledge."[17] Although one may be prone to ask whether Mullins was merely using Christian experience as an apologetic means of the outset of the twentieth century or was positing Christian experience as a subordinate or secondary medium for the transmission of Christian truth, a reading of Mullins's chapters makes it difficult to avoid the conclusion that for Mullins Christian experience was a major source of Christian truth.[18] According to Mullins, Christian experience is "a transaction between the divine and human persons" having a "synthetic unity," there being a distinct difference between "the natural and the regenerate consciousness," and thus Christian experience brings one to "a certainty of facts of consciousness." Likewise it has a bearing on other disciplines: the physical sciences, psychology of religion, Christian ethics, comparative religion, and philosophy. It even enables the Christian to understand the New Testament.[19] Won Kee Lee has emphasized Mullins's verification, under the influence of pragmatism, of Christian experience.[20]

Mullins developed his concept of soul competency in relation to his "axioms" of Baptist belief and as the preferred "distinguishing mark of the Baptists."[21] He first articulated his six axioms in public addresses,[22] then

---

[17]*The Christian Religion in Its Doctrinal Expression*, 35-136.

[18]Garrett, *Systematic Theology*, 2nd ed., 1:23-24.

[19]*The Christian Religion in Its Doctrinal Expression*, 50, 54-56, 60-63, 73, 83-107, 68.

[20]"The Organic Correlation between the Historical Revelation of God and the Believer's Historic Christian Experience in Edgar Young Mullins' Experiential Theology" (Ph.D. diss., Trinity Evangelical Divinity School, 1994) 276-94. Lee utilizes Mullins's *Why Is Christianity True? Christian Evidences* (Philadelphia: American Baptist Publication Society, 1905) 286-303.

[21]*The Axioms of Religion: A New Interpretation of the Baptist Faith* (Philadelphia: Griffith and Rowland, 1908) 53-69, esp. 59.

[22]To the American Baptist Publication Society in St. Louis in May 1905 and to the first world congress of the Baptist World Alliance in London in July 1905. Thomas, "Edgar Young Mullins," 337-39; *The Baptist World Congress, London,*

added the principle of soul competency in other public addresses,[23] and finally blended th two in his 1908 book, *The Axioms of Religion*. Mullins's positing of soul competency was with the awareness that previous efforts to identify Baptist distinctives had centered in baptism, church membership, and/or the Lord's Supper.[24] Although he alluded to "soul freedom,"[25] Mullins did not precisely define the relationship between soul freedom and soul competency. He did define soul competency:

> The competency of the soul in religion . . . means a competency under God, not a competency in the sense of human self-sufficiency. There is no reference here to the question of sin and human ability in the moral and theological sense, nor in the sense of independence of the Scriptures. I am not here stating the Baptist creed. On many vital matters of doctrine, such as the atonement, the person of Christ and others Baptists are in substantial agreement with the evangelical world in general. It is the historical significance of the Baptists I am stating, not a Baptist creed.[26]

Polity issues accompanied this definition inasmuch as Mullins sought to show how the incompetency of the soul was implicit in the Roman Catholic system and found also among Pedobaptist Protestants.[27]

Mullins did not approach the doctrine of revelation from the perspective that became dominant in the later twentieth century, that is, general revelation and special revelation.[28] Rather his focus was on the special or biblical revelation. It is "primarily a revelation of God himself rather than truths about God" and "primarily a spiritual transaction rather than mere illumination of the intellect." Being "rooted in the life and needs of the people," it "evoked an active response on man's part." It is both "historical

---

July 11-19, 1905, 151-52.

[23]To the Virginia Baptist Historical Society and to the Virginia Baptist General Association late in 1906 and to the General Convention of Baptists of North America in May 1907. Thomas, "Edgar Young Mullins," 339-40.

[24]*The Axioms of Religion*, 70.

[25]Ibid., 47-48, 50-51.

[26]Ibid., 53.

[27]Ibid., 59-65.

[28]Mullins did acknowledge as a source of the knowledge of God "the facts of nature and man." *The Christian Religion in Its Doctrinal Expression*, 38-39. See also Clyde J. Hurst, "The Problem of Religious Knowledge in the Theology of Edgar Young Mullins and Walter Thomas Conner," *Review and Expositor* 52 (April 1955): 166-82.

and experiential," is "regenerative and morally transforming," progressive and supernatural, and "sufficient, certain, and authoritative for all religious ends." Although Mullins recognized a distinction among terms such as "revelation," "illumination," and "inspiration," he was reluctant to embrace any of the theories of the method of inspiration, because each, containing an element of truth, cannot be exhaustive so as to encompass all biblical data.[29] Dwight Allan Moody has claimed that Mullins actually favored the "dynamical" or "inductive" theory. Moody also has noted that for Mullins the Bible is not to be equated with revelation but is the "record" of revelation, that the Bible is a book of religion and not a book of science, and that, so far as Mullins dealt with the subject, the Bible is inerrant in religious matters.[30]

Mullins's doctrine of the person of Jesus Christ included his work as the supreme Revealer of God as well as the more classical focus on the deity and humanity of Christ. Beginning with the assertion that "Jesus Christ is the key to the interpretation of Scriptures,"[31] he proceeded to find and explicate three "stages" in the New Testament teaching about the person of the Revealer. First, the Synoptic Gospels present his humanity, "Messianic calling," sinlessness, unique relation to God the Father, and "unique relation to man, to nature, and to history." Then the Acts of the Apostles adds his resurrection, his ascension, the gift of the Holy Spirit, and his return to judge and restore all things. Finally, in the Pauline epistles and the Gospel of John, Christ is the "medium" of creation and cohering bond of the created order and the eternal and preexistent Word who became incarnate. To this Mullins added the evidences from Christian experience. The revelation of God in Christ "makes known . . . the personality of God" by demonstration, completes "the historical and objective factor in man's religious life," and completes the ideas of man, God, religion, and reality.[32]

---

[29]*The Christian Religion in Its Doctrinal Expression*, 140-42, 145-53, 142-44. Mullins in *Freedom and Authority in Religion* (Philadelphia: Griffith and Rowland, 1913) 375-93, also discussed theories of inspiration and rejected William Newton Clarke's distinction between "Christian and non-Christian elements" in the Bible.

[30]"Doctrines of Inspiration in the Southern Baptist Theological Tradition," 143, 133-34, 137-38, 144-45.

[31]See the comprehensive study by Givens, "Christ as Heremeneutical Referent."

[32]*The Christian Religion in Its Doctrinal Expression*, 154-76.

Mullins wrote more about the deity than about the humanity of Jesus but concluded that the Chalcedonian Symbol "most fully gathers up the statements of the New Testament," even though it has "speculative elements" and poses practical problems.[33] The preexistence of Christ was that of a person, not of an "ideal." Mullins opted for a modified kenoticism, according to which Christ in his incarnation voluntarily suspended "the full exercise of [his] divine attributes." The Louisville president refuted the views of certain scholars; for example, Izaac Dorner's view of the gradual incarnation of Christ, William Sanday's view that in the incarnation "the divine entered Jesus in the subconscious part of his being," and Albrecht Ritschl's view that "Jesus has for us Christians the value of God."[34]

Mullins's exposition of the doctrines of God, the Holy Spirit, and the Trinity was succinct in comparison with other doctrines. God is spirit, personal, living, supreme, infinite, one, and absolute. The divine attributes Mullins classified under two categories: "the natural (self-existence, immutability, omnipresence, omniscience, omnipotence, eternity, immensity) and the moral (holiness, righteousness, love). He summarized the Old Testament and the New Testament teachings about the Holy Spirit with no attention to contemporary issues. As to the Trinity, Mullins recognized that the term "person" had been problematic and affirmed an ontological Trinity, but, bypassing the New Testament texts, majored on the value of the doctrine and objections to it.[35]

Mullins defined creation as a result: "By creation is meant all that exists which is not God." Refuting materialism, dualism, emanationism, and eternal creation, he affirmed the origination of all things by free divine action and declared that such a doctrine of creation "is not dependent on the conclusions of physical science as these may relate to the origin of the

---

[33] Allen, "A Comparative Study of the Person of Christ," 138-41, correctly observed that for Mullins the "single personhood" of Christ rather than his two natures should be "the starting point for formulating" Christology.

[34] *The Christian Religion in Its Doctrinal Expression*, 176-202, esp. 178, 180-81, 184-85, 189-90, 199-200. For a greater systematizing of Mullins's doctrine of the person of Christ, see Julius H. Spears, "The Christology of Edgar Young Mullins" (M.A. thesis, Duke University, 1945) 21-64. Mullins's defense of the "virgin birth" of Jesus was in his chapter on the knowledge of God rather than under Christology. *The Christian Religion in Its Doctrinal Expression*, 42-43.

[35] *The Christian Religion in Its Doctrinal Expression*, 216-43, 203-13.

universe."[36] Mullins became involved in the evolution controversy of the 1920s, especially in Kentucky, but, according to William E. Ellis, shifted from his earlier seeming espousal of "Christian theistic evolution"—which he preferred to call "development"—to a denial of any form of evolution.[37] Mullins was a dichotomist but could not decide between direction creation of souls and traducianism. On the image of God in man he set forth a cluster-of-capacities view (reason, moral nature, emotions, will, self-determination, original righteousness, dominion, and immortality) that may reflect his personalist philosophy.[38] Providence "implies a divine purpose in the control of the universe" and the sovereignty of God, involves God's use of physical and moral laws and the unity of humankind, is particular as well as general, and allows for miracles, prayer, angels, and Satan.[39]

Human sin came to be, not because of man's possessing a body or because of human finitude, but "with the creation of free intellectual beings with the power of contrary choice." Sin is "selfishness," the "lack of conformity to God's moral law," "a breach of . . . personal relations with God," and "a breach of covenant relations between God and the people." Mullins briefly rejected the Augustinian and the federal theories of original sin and did not espouse another[40] but did declare that "all men actually sin when they acquire capacity for sinning."[41] Mullins was doubtful of the usefulness of the distinction between "natural ability" and "moral ability." He did affirm the universality of sin and taught that not only spiritual death and eternal death but also physical death is the "penal consequence of sin."[42]

---

[36]Ibid., 251-55.

[37]*"A Man of Books and a Man of the People,"* 164-65, 188-89, 202-4, 218. Charles Joseph Ferris, "Southern Baptists and Evolution in the 1920's: The Roles of Edgar Y. Mullins, J. Frank Norris, and William Louis Poteat" (M.A. thesis, University of Louisville, 1973) 130-87, has minimized the shift.

[38]*The Christian Religion in Its Doctrinal Expression*, 255-64.

[39]Ibid., 265-80.

[40]Ibid., 281-85, 288-89, 293.

[41]*Baptist Beliefs* (Louisville: Baptist World Publishing Co., 1912; Philadelphia: Judson, 1925), 24-25. Gstohl, *Southern Baptist Theologians and Original Sin*, 47-71, esp. 70, 52, 58-63, while recognizing "the lack of precision and clarity" in Mullins's writing, has seemingly found not only in Mullins evidence for the absence of guilt prior to the age of accountability but also evidence for guilt for inherited depravity.

[42]*The Christian Religion in Its Doctrinal Expression*, 294-95, 297-99.

In treating the saving work of Christ Mullins began with the threefold office of Christ (prophet, priest, king) and then interpreted and evaluated seven historic theories of the atonement, excluding any consideration of penal substitution. He proceeded to expound "the biblical doctrine of the atonement," stressing that its motive "was the love of God," its "end" was the salvation of humanity, and its "means" was the death of the obedient Christ, who was subjected to the law of sin and death. Insisting that there were both "vital" and "legal" elements and both "Godward" and "manward" references in the atonement, the Southern Seminary president expounded and embraced a propitiatory, substitutionary atonement, which involved both penal substitution and "substitutionary love." Citing specific New Testament texts, he briefly endorsed a general atonement.[43]

Placed after the saving work of Christ and prior to the beginnings of the Christian life, election, according to Mullins, is "God's initiative in salvation." Set in the context of God's loving, gracious purpose for humankind, it means God's choice of individual human beings for salvation but not on the basis of foreseen repentance and faith, by coercion, or by merit. It is consonant with human freedom and embraces the use of means.[44] Thomas J. Nettles acknowledged that Mullins taught "unconditional election" but then charged him with "ambivalence" on this matter. He did not define election "in terms of" God's "mere will or good pleasure" and "greatly diminished God's sovereignty." Together with his theological method, Mullins's doctrine of election, Nettles concluded, led him from the Dagg-Boyce heritage.[45]

Opting for innovative language, Mullins set forth the doctrine of "the beginnings of the Christian life," beginning with the work of the Holy Spirit, divine calling, and conviction of sin. He chose to treat repentance

---

[43]Ibid., 303-37. Draughon, "A Critical Evaluation of the Diminishing Influence of Calvinism," 135-36, has concluded that, while somewhat modifying the penal substitutionary theory, Mullins nevertheless retained some of its weaknesses; for example, punishment outweighing the destruction of the power of sin, and making God entirely the object and not sufficiently the subject of the atonement. According to James Ray Nalls, "The Concept of the Atonement in Southern Baptist Thought" (Th.D. diss., Mid-America Baptist Theological Seminary, 1986) 83-92, esp. 90-92, Mullins's doctrine of the atonement centered in "the destruction of the sin-death principle."

[44]*The Christian Religion in Its Doctrinal Expression*, 338-58.

[45]*By His Grace and for His Glory*, 246-57, esp. 246, 255, 247, 254, 246-47.

and faith before discussing the terms more strictly assigned to divine agency. Repentance and faith involve mind, emotions, and will. They are simultaneously the results of God's gracious actions and the actions of one's total human nature—graces and duties. Thereby Mullins was occupying a half-way house between Calvinism and Arminianism. Conversion was given the same divine-human interpretation. Regeneration is that instantaneous change of the "moral disposition of the soul" wrought by the Holy Spirit with truth as the means. Justification was interpreted declaratively in the classic Protestant sense, and, relative to adoption, Mullins opted for the position that "all men are constituted for sonship of God, and . . . God desires all men to become sons, but that this ideal is only made real in the new birth." Union with Christ received the attention that one would expect from a theologian of personalism.[46] Under "the continuance of the Christian life" Mullins discussed sanctification and perseverance. Rejecting both antinomianism and perfectionism, he opted for both initial (a new set-apartness) and durative (transformation of character) sanctification, and rejecting both "extreme Calvinism" (like pantheism) and "extreme Arminianism" (like deism), he sought a via media in which divine warnings and divine promises are joined.[47]

Following the pattern of Dagg and Boyce and seemingly for a curricular reason Mullins did not treat the doctrine of the church in his systematic theology. In his commentary on Ephesians and Colossians, his attention to the church was minimal.[48] His contribution to ecclesiology was indirect, namely, his restatement of Baptist distinctives in terms of six "axioms," which he hoped to be convincing to non-Baptist Christians.[49]

1. The theological axiom: The holy and loving God has a right to be sovereign.

---

[46]*The Christian Religion in Its Doctrinal Expression*, 359-416.

[47]Ibid., 417-38. Walker, "The Doctrine of Salvation in the Thought of James Petigru Boyce, Edgar Young Mullins, and Dale Moody," 122n.2, 211, found an earlier deviation from Boyce in Franklin H. Kerfoot's revision of Boyce's *Abstract of Systematic Theology* and found in Mullins's unpublished lecture notes that he considered himself to be in the Augustinian-Calvinist tradition.

[48]*Studies in Ephesians and Colossians*, Convention Series (Nashville: Sunday School Board of the SBC, 1913) 11, 38, 48, 50-51, 52-53, 55, 60-62, 87, 110-11, 133, 142, 158-59, 180.

[49]*The Axioms of Religion*, 74-75.

2. The religious axiom: All souls have an equal right to direct access to God.
3. The ecclesiastical axiom: All believers have a right to equal privileges in the church.
4. The moral axiom: To be responsible man must be free.
5. The religiocivic axiom: A free Church in a free State.
6. The social axiom: Love your neighbor as yourself.[50]

These axioms were framed in contrast to Roman Catholic positions, and axioms three and five were directed to congregational polity and to religious liberty and church-state separation. In explaining axioms two and four Mullins critiqued infant baptism. He opposed open membership among Baptist churches and was cautious about proposals for organic church union. His axiom two with its emphasis on "direct access to God through Christ" tended to regard the church as an impediment. In 1908 Mullins confidently asserted: "We are approaching the Baptist age of the world, because we are approaching the age of the triumph of democracy."[51] In *Baptist Beliefs* the Louisville theologian differentiated the universal church and the local church and presented a symbolic interpretation of baptism and the Lord's Supper.[52] In addressing the Disciples of Christ, Mullins differentiated but correlated the spiritual and the ceremonial and called baptism a "symbolic instrumental cause" of salvation.[53] In his "Why I Am a Baptist" he insisted that he was a Baptist "because . . . the Baptist interpretation of Christianity best conserves the freedom of faith."[54]

Mullins began his fully developed eschatology by affirming human immortality, differentiating the initial, the durative, and the consummative senses of the coming of the kingdom of God, positing a conscious, disembodied intermediate state, and affirming "an outward, visible, and personal return of Christ."[55] In his first book, published in 1894, Mullins refuted

---

[50]Ibid., 73-74.

[51]Ibid., 127-49, 185-200, 107-26, 157-67, 238-54, 221-34, 293-94, 94, 275.

[52]Pp. 62-71.

[53]*Baptism and the Remission of Sins: Paper Read at the National Congress of Disciples, April 25, 1906* (Philadelphia: American Baptist Publication Society, 1906?) esp. 10-11, 18-19, 22.

[54]In Gilbert K. Chesterton, Charles L. Slattery, Henry Sloan Coffin, et al., *Twelve Modern Apostles and Their Creeds* (New York: Duffield, 1926; repr.: Freeport NY: Books for Libraries Press, 1968) 89-109, esp. 92.

[55]*The Christian Religion in Its Doctrinal Expression*, 439-66.

postmillennialism and advocated historic premillennialism.⁵⁶ Later he set forth the premillennial critique of postmillennialism and the postmillennial critique of premillennialism and offered his own nonpartisan conclusion, in which he deferred to and enjoined expectancy toward the second coming.⁵⁷ In his later interpretation of eschatological resurrection he was silent as to two resurrections and stressed the connection between present spiritual resurrection (that is, regeneration) and bodily eschatological resurrection. The last judgment will have Christ as the judge and will be "the finality demanded by the kingdom of God in all its aspects." Heaven and hell were affirmed, and universalism and restorationism refuted.⁵⁸

The earliest writings about Mullins of a general nature tended to be biographical and laudatory with little effort to analyze or assess his theology.⁵⁹ In 1952, Harold W. Tribble, who had been Mullins's successor in the Joseph Emerson Brown professorship of theology at Southern Seminary, offered an assessment. Mullins's "distinction was primarily as a thinker rather than as a scholar." "His approach to a theological problem was usually apologetic rather than systematic." His central thesis, Christian experience, had as its "philosophical frame" "his own blend of empiricism."

> The flavor of William James is strong. . . . Yet it is his own interpretation and adaptation of James. The flavor of Schleiermacher is also strong, but it is the older Schleiermacher whose influence may be seen, while it is the young author of *die Reden* that Mullins refutes.⁶⁰

---

⁵⁶*Christ's Coming and His Kingdom: A Brief Study of the Literal Passages of Scripture Bearing on the Second Coming of Christ* (Baltimore: C. W. Schneidereith and Sons) 41-48. He also reckoned the Antichrist to be an individual and one yet to come (35-40).

⁵⁷*The Christian Religion in Its Doctrinal Expression*, 466-72. Emmett Howell Cantwell, "Millennial Teachings among Major Southern Baptist Theologians from 1845 to 1945" (Th.M. thesis, Southwestern Baptist Theological Seminary, 1960) 67, concluded that Mullins "clearly" placed "himself in the school of amillennialism," presumably because Mullins did not set forth a specific doctrine of the millennium.

⁵⁸*The Christian Religion in Its Doctrinal Expression*, 472-503, esp. 476, 478-79, 481.

⁵⁹Mullins did have during his lifetime fundamentalist critics, notably, J. Frank Norris, J. W. Porter, Boyce Taylor, and W. B. Riley. Ellis, *"A Man of Books and a Man of the People,"* 186-96.

⁶⁰"Edgar Young Mullins," *Review and Expositor* 49 (April 1952): 132-34.

Three doctrinal dissertations focused on Mullins approached his life and thought in a sympathetic, if not uncritical, manner. Russell Hooper Dilday, Jr., (1930–) set forth both weaknesses and strengths of Mullins's apologetic method.[61] Bill Clark Thomas, taking as his clue Mullins's penchant for theological restatement, analyzed the theology of Mullins as systematic, apologetic, and Baptistic and found that the theological climate of the 1960s was not very hospitable to the thought of Mullins.[62] William Elliott Ellis made a biographical approach, utilizing Mullins's correspondence, and concluded that at the end of his life his moderate cause lost out to fundamentalists in the SBC.[63]

Baptist authors outside the SBC were accepting, qualifying, or rejecting "soul competency" as the fundamental Baptist principle. According to William Roy McNutt (1879-?), Northern Baptist ecclesiologist, individual competency is the "womb," along with "the free association of believers as a church," that "gives birth to [Baptist] polity."[64] H. Wheeler Robinson acknowledged that Mullins's statement on soul competency would be acceptable to "most Baptists" and that stressing Christian experience does bring persons "face to face with God in Christ," but Robinson critiqued excessive individualism.[65] Arnold Theodore Ohrn (1889–1963), Norwegian-born general secretary of the Baptist World Alliance, opted for the lordship of Christ as the central Baptist principle, reckoning soul competency as too anthropocentric.[66] Paul M. Harrison, a Northern Baptist, was certain that early Baptist confessions put no "primary emphasis" on soul competency, being greatly concerned about the freedom of God or of the Holy Spirit.[67] Winthrop Still Hudson, Northern Baptist church historian, saw soul competency as "derived from the general cultural and religious climate of the nine-

---

[61] "The Apologetic Method of E. Y. Mullins" (Th.D. diss., Southwestern Baptist Theological Seminary, 1960) esp. 166-78.

[62] "Edgar Young Mullins," passim.

[63] "E. Y. Mullins: Southern Baptist Theologian, Administrator, and Denominational Leader" (Ph.D. diss., University of Kentucky, 1974) abstract, ii, iii; 248.

[64] *Polity and Practice in Baptist Churches* (Philadelphia: Judson, 1935) 21, 27.

[65] *The Life and Faith of the Baptists*, 24, 142.

[66] "Christ Only Is King," Holland Foundation Lectures, Southwestern Baptist Theological Seminary, February 1950 (TC 2596, Roberts Library, SWBTS).

[67] *Authority and Power in the Free Church Tradition: A Social Case Study of the American Baptist Convention* (Princeton NJ: Princeton University Press, 1959) 18-19.

teenth century rather than from any serious study of the Bible" and failing "to provide detailed guidance for questions of church order." Its "practical effect" was "to make every man's hat his own church."[68] On the other hand, the Mullins heritage was being extended and clarified by Tribble's 1935 condensation and revision of *The Axioms of Religion*,[69] and then by Herschel Harold Hobbs (1907–1995), who revised and updated *Axioms* in 1978.[70]

But only with the advent of the biblical inerrancy controversy[71] in the Southern Baptist Convention in 1979 and the concurrent rise of the Neo-Calvinist or founders movement did the theology of Mullins become a major bone of contention and both the target of polemical attack by his critics and the rallying point for his supporters. First, we note the defenders of Mullins. Edward Glenn Hinson (1931–) made Mullins a lynchpin in his argument that Southern Baptists are not "Evangelicals" but belong to a tradition of "voluntarism" that has been friendly toward the Enlightenment and toward Schleiermacher.[72] Hinson did not include Mullins in his treatment of the "liberal" hermeneutical tradition among Southern Baptists,[73] but Claude L. Howe, Jr., instead treated Mullins under the "moderate" hermeneutical tradition.[74] Hinson did not emphasize Mullins when sketching the background of the "moderate movement" in the SBC.[75]

---

[68]"Shifting Patterns of Church Order in the Twentieth Century" in *Baptist Concepts of the Church*, ed. Hudson (Philadelphia: Judson, 1959) 215-16; repr. in Hudson, *Baptists in Transition: Individualism and Christian Responsibility* (Valley Forge PA: Judson, 1979) 141-42.

[69]E. Y. Mullins and Harold W. Tribble, *The Baptist Faith* (Nashville: Convention Press); also in Mullins, Tribble, and W. O. Carver, *The Faith and Its Furtherance* (Nashville: Broadman, 1936) 11-130.

[70]Herschel H. Hobbs and E. Y. Mullins, *The Axioms of Religion*, rev. ed. (Nashville: Broadman).

[71]Also called "the fundamentalist takeover" and "the conservative resurgence."

[72]"Baptists and 'Evangelicals': There Is a Difference" in Garrett, Hinson, and Tull, *Are Southern Baptists "Evangelicals"?*, 129-94, esp. 133, 136-42, 178-79.

[73]"Southern Baptists and the Liberal Tradition in Biblical Interpretation, 1845–1945," *Baptist History and Heritage* 19 (July 1984): 16-20.

[74]"Southern Baptists and the Moderate Tradition in Biblical Interpretation, 1845–1945," *Baptist History and Heritage* 19 (July 1984): 25-26.

[75]"The Background of the Moderate Movement," in *The Struggle for the Soul of the SBC: Moderate Responses to the Fundamentalist Movement*, ed. Walter B. Shurden (Macon GA: Mercer University Press, 1993) 1-16.

Walter B. Shurden (1937–) did not evaluate Mullins specifically, but for his *The Baptist Identity: Four Fragile Freedoms*[76] he was said to have done for Baptists of the twenty-first century what Mullins had done for Baptists eighty years earlier in *The Axioms of Religion*.[77] William D. M. Carrell in a 1993 dissertation on Mullins's concept of soul competency found it to be for him the clue to Baptist historical identity, "the absolute presupposition of the kingdom of God," and a solution to the epistemological problem in terms of a voluntaristic and soteriological competency, but he was not sufficiently aware of the relativity of human consciousness. Carrel attempted to restate soul competency in terms of Alasdair MacIntyre's narrative epistemology, which builds from a tradition, thus avoiding both coercion and excessive individualism.[78]

The capstone of the advocacy of Mullins as guide for twenty-first century Southern Baptists was the *Review and Expositor*'s Winter 1999 issue, issued for the centennial of Mullins's election as seminary president. Hinson, having found that Mullins's *Axioms of Religion* had been needed as an alternative to Landmark church successionism and was indeed a new type of apologetic, suggested two likely impediments to the usefulness of the *Axioms* in the twenty-first century: the new century's not being an age of denominationalism, and "Mullins' pronounced individualism." Nevertheless, present-day threats to "the voluntary principle as the heart of the Baptist tradition" make imperative the extension of the Mullins heritage.[79] Dilday argued that Mullins should be "a guide for Baptist theology in the twenty-first century." He asserted that Mullins always subjected Christian experience "to the authority of the Scriptures," for experience provides no "extra-biblical knowledge of God." Dilday championed Mullins as "a centrist between the extremes," namely, fixity and change, freedom and authority, individualism and community, divine sovereignty and human free will, various millennial theories, and fundamentalism and liberalism.[80] James M. Dunn reviewed assessments of "soul competency," defined it in words from Mullins and from others, and noted certain of the criticisms before setting forth the foundational role of soul competency for religious

---

[76](Macon GA: Smyth & Helwys, 1993).

[77]James M. Dunn, on cover of *The Baptist Identity*.

[78]"Edgar Young Mullins and the Competency of the Soul in Religion."

[79]"E. Y. Mullins as Interpreter of the Baptist Tradition," *Review and Expositor* 96 (Winter 1999): 109-22.

[80]"Mullins the Theologian: Between the Extremes," ibid. 75-86.

liberty and church-state separation and acknowledging that Mullins shared the "overriding optimism" of his times.[81] Phyllis Rodgerson Pleasants sought to establish the thesis that Mullins during the SBC evolution controversy failed in his diplomatic leadership and was compelled for the sake of the seminary's financial support, especially for its new campus, to yield his position as to evolution.[82] Timothy D. F. Maddox sought to co-opt Mullins for a postmodern ethos, despite the problem of compatibility on the church as community.[83]

Second, there have been those who have critiqued Mullins's theological method and concept of soul competency but have also recognized the significance of his apologetic efforts and his denominational leadership. These authors belong to the Baptist revisioning movement. James William McClendon, Jr. (1924–2000), declared that Mullins's soul competency "is so fully shaped by nineteenth century American individualism that it cannot support the equally baptist themes of discipleship and community."[84] Curtis Wynn Freeman (1955–), with an eye to epistemology, found that both fundamentalism through commonsense realism and the Princeton theologians and liberalism through Schleiermacher and Ritschl had built on foundationalism—the one with an inerrant Bible and the other with religious experience. Mullins "followed the leftward branch of modernity at a more moderate pace by adapting the categories of evangelical piety to experiential religion." He seemed "to mediate between fundamentalism and liberalism," especially during the evolution struggle. That was his "*political strategy*," Freeman noted. But his "operative" "*theological paradigm*" was religious experience.[85] Indeed, for Freeman, unlike William Ellis, Mullins successfully "steered the Southern Baptist ship" around the dangerous rock of Scylla, fundamentalism, and very close to the swirling whirlpool of

---

[81]"Church, State, and Soul Competency," ibid., 61-73.

[82]"E. Y. Mullins: Diplomatic Theological Leader," ibid., 43-60.

[83]"E. Y. Mullins: Mr. Baptist for the 20th and 21st Century," ibid., 87-105, esp. 98-101. See also the seven articles in *Baptist History and Heritage* 43 (Winter 2008) under the issue title "E. Y. Mullins and *The Axioms of Religion*."

[84]"What Is a 'baptist' Theology?" *American Baptist Quarterly* 1 (October 1982): 24.

[85]"Can Baptist Theology Be Revisioned?" *Perspectives in Religious Studies* 24 (Fall 1997): 277-78, 290, 289, 290-91.

Charybdis, liberalism, and like Odysseus of old, listened to but passed by the enticing songs of the Sirens, or modernity.[86]

Third, with the publication in 1986 of Thomas Julian Nettles's *By His Grace and for His Glory*[87] began the strong critique of Mullins by the neo-Calvinists and others. Nettles laid the blame for originating the Southern Baptist shift from strict Calvinism[88] at the feet of two leaders: Mullins, "through his theological method," and Lee Rutland Scarborough (1870–1945), president of Southwestern Baptist Theological Seminary, "through his evangelistic method." Nettles, however, did not confine his critique to method, that is, the dominance of Christian experience. Mullins affirmed a general atonement. His doctrine of election, although it involved God's choice of particular human beings and stressed the persuasiveness of God's grace, according to Nettles, was defective by embracing "God's universal salvific intention" and by resting on God's "righteous love" rather than on God's "mere will or good pleasure." Only on the nature of repentance and faith and on perseverance could Mullins pass muster.[89] Earlier Nettles and L. Russell Bush III (1944–2008), had commended Mullins for standing for "the full truthfulness of the Scripture," although he had mistakenly taken the "plenary-verbal theory of inspiration" to be synonymous with "mechanical dictation." Bush and Nettles had concluded that Mullins was "theologically within the Calvinist Baptist tradition."[90] In a subsequent article Nettles reported that Mullins had "hesitated to identify himself with either Calvinism or Arminianism," had so strongly critiqued creeds as to weaken his support of confessions of faith, and had been "the seminal power in the procreation of a diversity [among Southern Baptists] that is in-

---

[86]"E. Y. Mullins and the Siren Songs of Modernity," *Review and Expositor* 96 (Winter 1999): 23-42.

[87]Subtitle: *A Historical, Theological and Practical Study of the Doctrines of Grace in Baptist Life* (Grand Rapids MI: Baker Book House).

[88]W. Wiley Richards, *Winds of Doctrines: The Origin and Development of Southern Baptist Theology* (Lanham MD: University Press of America, 1991) 50-59, had located the beginning of the demise of Southern Baptist Calvinism in the middle of the nineteenth century, citing Alexander Campbell and the posthumous influence of Andrew Fuller, whom he identified as a three-point Dortian Calvinist.

[89]Ibid., 244-56.

[90]*Baptists and the Bible: The Baptist Doctrines of Biblical Inspiration and Religious Authority in Historical Perspective* (Chicago: Moody, 1980) 290-300, esp. 298, 296-97, 298.

nately centrifugal."[91] Seemingly oblivious to the claims that Mullins had been influenced by Schleiermacher, W. Wiley Richards (1932–) curiously claimed that Mullins "was the forerunner of [the later] neorthodoxy" in the SBC.[92]

In the Winter 1999 issue of the *Southern Baptist Journal of Theology* R. Albert Mohler, Jr., faulted Mullins for sharing "a common starting point with modernists" by his emphasis on "religious experience" and for making revelation submissive to personal experience, for refusing to identify the Bible as revelation, and for being indecisive as to evolution.[93] According to Russell D. Moore and Gregory A. Thornbury, Mullins "never forged" his various "intellectual influences into a rigorous theological method" and "experimented with an array of distinct theological epistemologies within *The Christian Religion in Its Doctrinal Expression*." He was "a sort of 'retro-filter' in his tradition, updating a tradition that he inherited with the novel resources of modernity."[94] Sean Michael Lucas contrasted Mullins and John Gresham Machen (1881–1937), professor of New Testament in Princeton Theological Seminary, as to their approaches to modernism and to the relation of religion and science, and, favoring Machen, stridently concluded: "For over seventy years, Southern Baptists have harvested the shallow discipleship and vapid theology that resulted from sowing Mullins's theological seeds of experience."[95] In his contrast between the priesthood of all Christians according to John Smyth and according to Mullins, Malcolm Beryl Yarnell III (1962–), offered extensive critique of Mullins. Soul competency is that "preexistent, immediate access to God" that "turns the early Baptists' Christocentric and dynamic relationship between person

---

[91] "The Rise and Demise of Calvinism among Southern Baptists," *Founders Journal*, issues 19-20 (Winter/Spring 1995): 19, 18-19, 21. More recently Nettles reiterated his assessment of Mullins, adding that Francis Wayland and William Newton Clarke had represented nonconfessionalism and B. H. Carroll confessionalism: "E. Y. Mullins: Reluctant Evangelical," *Southern Baptist Journal of Theology* 3 (Winter 1999): 24-42, esp. 34-35.

[92] *Winds of Doctrine*, 151-58, esp. 156.

[93] "Baptist Theology at the Crossroads: The Legacy of E. Y. Mullins," *Southern Baptist Journal of Theology* 3 (Winter 1999): 4-22, esp. 9, 19, 11, 10.

[94] "The Mystery of Mullins in Contemporary Southern Baptist Historiography," ibid., 44-57, esp. 53, 54.

[95] "Christianity at the Crossroads: E. Y. Mullins, J. Gresham Machen, and the Challenge of Modernism," ibid., 58-78, esp. 74.

and community on its head." Thus the individual "soul is a diamond while Christ is more vaguely the sun, the kingdom of God a rainbow and the church a vacuous social expression of the rainbow." In Mullins's low Christology there is no authoritative presence of Christ in the gathered church and no "ontological unity of believers in Christ." Ecclesiology is "impoverished" with a "hostile view" of the ordained ministry. Priesthood, for Mullins, is of pagan origin, Christ's priesthood is not really needed, and human priests have no special competency. "The early Baptists were Christocentric churchmen; Mullins and his disciples are anthropocentric individualists—therein lies a world of difference."[96] According to Stephen Michael Garrett, the soul competency of Mullins is an expression of "solipsism," defined as "the doctrine that there exists a first-person perspective possessing *privileged* and *irreducible* characteristics, in virtue of which we stand in various kinds of *isolation* from other persons or external things that may exist."[97]

Thus, with the advent of the twenty-first century the method and content of Mullins's theology and apologetic had become so controversially important to theologians in the Southern Baptist Convention and the Cooperative Baptist Fellowship that one could identify as a defining question, "What do you think of E. Y. Mullins?" At the same time non-Baptist historians of religion who had earlier given little attention to Mullins[98] were finding him worthy of greater attention. Sydney E.

---

[96]"Changing Baptist Concepts of Royal Priesthood: John Smyth and Edgar Young Mullins," in *The Rise of the Laity in Evangelical Protestantism*, ed. Deryck W. Lovegrove (London, New York: Routledge, 2002) 236-52, esp. 245-47, 249.

[97]"Edgar Young Mullins and the Hermeneutics of Soul Competency" (Th.M. thesis, Southwestern Baptist Theological Seminary, 2003), esp. 4-19, 39, 42, 45, 46, 50, 54-55, 56, 58, 59. The definition is from *The Cambridge Dictionary of Philosophy*, ed. Robert Audi (New York: Cambridge University Press, 1995) 751.

[98]Mullins was not included or mentioned in the following: *Contemporary American Theology: Theological Autobiographies*, 2 vols., ed. Vergilius Ferm (New York: Round Table Press, 1932, 1933); David Wesley Soper, *Major Voices in American Theology: Six Contemporary Leaders* (Philadelphia: Westminster, 1953); Soper, *Men Who Shape Belief* (Philadelphia: Westminster, 1955); Alvin C. Porteous, *Prophetic Voices in Contemporary Theology* (Nashville: Abingdon, 1966); *Theologians of Our Time*, ed. A. W. Hastings and E. Hastings (Edinburgh: T.&T. Clark, 1966); Warren F. Groff and Donald E. Miller, *The Shaping of Modern Christian Thought* (Cleveland: World, 1968).

Ahlstrom[99] mentioned Mullins in connection with *The Fundamentals*,[100] to which Mullins had contributed a chapter on "The Testimony of Christian Experience." Harold Bloom, a literary critic, has more recently published a detailed analysis of Mullins.

> Edgar Young Mullins I would nominate as the Calvin or Luther or Wesley of the Southern Baptists, but only in the belated American sense, because Mullins was not the founder of the Southern Baptists but their refounder, the definer of their creedless faith. An endlessly subtle and original thinker, Mullins is the most neglected of major American theologians. Pragmatically he is more important than Jonathan Edwards, Horace Bushnell, and the Niebuhrs, because Mullins reformulated (perhaps even first formulated) the faith of a major denomination.

In trying to explain soul competency, Bloom connected Mullins with John Milton, declaring that "Milton's devotion to the Inner Light is at the heart of Mullins's doctrine," found an element of Gnosticism in Southern Baptists "but with the American pragmatic difference," labeled soul competency "a very rough version of Emersonian self-reliance," put on Southern Baptists Ronald Knox's label of "Mystical Enthusiast," and found "the Southern Baptist soul-initiative towards Jesus" to be "a clear analogue to [William] James's emphasis upon the purposeful will to believe." Bloom asserted that Southern Baptist controversy by 1992 had resulted in the purging of "the entire spiritual legacy of E. Y. Mullins" but also declared that Southern Baptists and Mormons "will be at the center of what is to come" in American religion.[101]

Doctrinal Statements prior to 1925

The founders of the SBC in 1845 chose not to adopt an existing confession of faith or to frame another for their own newly organized body; they even justified the absence of a "new creed" by the "Baptist aversion for all creeds but the Bible."[102] Eighty years would transpire before the SBC would adopt

---

[99]*A Religious History of the American People* (New Haven CT: Yale University Press, 1972) 815-16.

[100]Subtitle: *A Testimony to the Truth*, 12 vols., ed., A. C. Dixon, Louis Meyer, and Reuben A. Torrey (Chicago: Testimony Publishing Co., 1910–1915) 3:76-85; repr. in 4 vols. (Los Angeles: Bible Institute of Los Angeles, 1917) 4:314-23.

[101]*The American Religion: The Emergence of the Post-Christian Nation* (New York: Simon & Schuster, 1992) 199, 202, 203, 204-205, 214, 225, 191.

[102]Southern Baptist Convention, *Proceedings*, 1845, 19.

a comprehensive confession of faith.[103] Prior to 1925, however, there were several doctrinal statements framed by Southern Baptist entities. Mullins played a role in framing a majority of these.

The first of these was framed in 1914 in response to developments outside the Baptist denomination. Following the proposal by Episcopal Bishop Charles H. Brent in 1910, commissions of various American Protestant denominations had met in 1913 to foster a worldwide conference on faith (doctrine) and order (polity).[104] The SBC, having been invited to participate, in 1913 referred the matter to a newly appointed commission.[105] The eleven-member commission presented to the convention for adoption in 1914 a "Pronouncement on Christian Union and Denominational Efficiency."[106] Designed "to make clear to the world at large our position on the subject of Christian Union," it affirmed "spiritual unity and brotherhood" and identified "four things which we take for granted": the Lordship of Christ "as supreme and final," the absence of any "desire to seek Christian union by compromise of honest convictions," finding "in the New Testament alone . . . the sufficient, certain and authoritative revelation" of God's will, and the common "desire to know and obey the revealed will of Christ." Then came the elaboration of five doctrines reflecting "our understanding of the Gospel": (1) equal entitlement of all human beings to "direct access to God" with the twin corollaries of responsibility and freedom (thus negating infant baptism, proxy religion, and ecclesiastical systems); (2) regeneration by the Holy Spirit via repentance and faith (negating baptismal regeneration and priestly mediation); (3) baptism as symbolic and the mode of immersion defended; (4) the church as "the outward organization which conserves and propagates the spiritual principles" of Baptists, including congregational polity and the equality of all believer-priests; and (5) the separation of church and state, for "soul freedom and civil liberty are twin blossoms on the stalk of Christian faith."

---

[103]Southern Baptist Convention, *Annual*, 1925, 70-76.

[104]Tissington Tatlow, "The World Conference on Faith and Order," in *A History of the Ecumenical Movement, 1517–1948*, ed. Ruth Rouse and Stephen Charles Neill (London: S.P.C.K., 1954) 403-13.

[105]Southern Baptist Convention, *Annual*, 1913, 40-42; James E. Carter, "Southern Baptists' First Confession of Faith," *Baptist History and Heritage* 5 (January 1970): 25.

[106]Southern Baptist Convention, *Annual*, 1914, 73-78. The commission included E. C. Dargan, J. B. Gambrell, J. M. Frost, and E. Y. Mullins.

Acknowledging that these doctrines are those most pertinent to "organic Christian union" and that various agreed upon doctrines were not included, the commission allowed for possible Southern Baptist cooperation in "moral, social [and] civic" efforts but closed the door to organic church union at present. While developing more fully their own denominational life, Southern Baptists could possibly help to foster church union on the basis of the Holy Scriptures.[107] According to James E. Carter,

> The greatest significance of the pronouncement was in setting the precedent for the adoption of doctrinal statements by the Southern Baptist Convention. It had not settled the question of Christian union. Neither had it expressed fully Baptist theology. But it had begun the practice. . . .[108]

Secondly, the Baptist Bible Institute of New Orleans at its founding in 1917–1918 began to require its faculty to "subscribe to" "Articles of Religious Belief" which had been composed by its first president, Byron Hoover DeMent (1863–1933), and adopted by the initial board of directors.[109] These articles were ten in number. The Bible as "the Word of God" is "divinely and uniquely inspired," "is the unrivalled authority in determining the faith and practice of God's people," and has "come down to us substantially as" it was "under inspiration written." The biblical books "reveal" all necessary knowledge "of God's plan of redemption and human

---

[107]Ibid. Carter, "Southern Baptists' First Confession of Faith," 26, 28, found that Mullins wrote the doctrinal section relative to Christian union and Gambrell the section on Baptist denominational efficiency and that R. H. Pitt, editor of the *Religious Herald* (VA), questioned the authority for issuing such a statement and the setting of a precedent.

[108]"Southern Baptists' First Confession of Faith," 38.

[109]Roland Q. Leavell, "New Orleans Baptist Theological Seminary," *Encyclopedia of Southern Baptists* 2:970; William A. Mueller, *The School of Providence and Prayer: A History of the New Orleans Baptist Theological Seminary* (New Orleans: New Orleans Baptist Theological Seminary, 1969) 21. DeMent, a Th.D. graduate of Southern Baptist Theological Seminary, had been pastor in Virginia, Kentucky, Texas, and South Carolina, and had taught at Baylor University and Southern Baptist Theological Seminary. J. Wash Watts, "DeMent, Byron Hoover," *Encyclopedia of Southern Baptists* 1:357-58. The institute was initially under the governance of certain state conventions and the SBC but passed to the SBC in 1925. Barnes, *The Southern Baptist Convention*, 209-12; Baker, *The Southern Baptist Convention*, 435; Fletcher, *The Southern Baptist Convention*, 130; Mueller, *The School of Providence and Prayer*, 1-16, 24-26.

duty" and "are intended for personal study and interpretation, under the guidance of the Holy Spirit" (1). The "one only true and living God," "Creator and Sustainer," "is revealed . . . as Father, Son, and Holy Spirit." The Father is "the Head of the Trinity," the Son is the virgin-born Messiah, dying, rising, interceding, and returning. The Holy Spirit has convicting, regenerating, and didactic functions (2). Man, "created innocent," but tempted by the personal Satan, sinned—sin being "nonconformity" to God's will—and hence all human beings are "born in sin, and are by nature children of wrath" (3). The way of reconciliation "is Jesus Christ," that is, by his atoning death and by union with him. This atonement "becomes personally effective through the foreordination and grace of God, and the free choice and faith of man" (4). Since all human beings "are under condemnation through personal sin," escape from condemnation comes only by hearing and accepting the gospel of the "only and all-sufficient Savior of sinners" and not to those who have never heard and those who reject the gospel. Hence every church and every Christian are under the stewardship of a "pressing . . . obligation" "to present the gospel to all men" (5). Conversion includes repentance (change), faith (surrender), regeneration (new creation), and justification ("declared forgiven and freed"). The newborn never lose their salvation, and by faith they will be finally sanctified (6). There will be "the final resurrection of all men, both the just and the unjust" (7). A New Testament church "is a voluntary assembly . . . of baptized believers in Christ covenanted together to follow the . . . New Testament in doctrine, worship, and practice" and democratically governed. Baptism is only for "saved believers," and immersion is the only biblical mode. The Lord's Supper is basically a "memorial" of Jesus' death and expected return (8). The Lord's Day should be "a day of rest and Christian service in memory of" Jesus' resurrection. Civil government is divinely ordained, church and state should be separate, and all human beings have the "right to civil and religious liberty" (9). Baptists should be loyal to and not compromise their "distinctive truths," and any cooperation with other Christian denominations should "not affect these truths" and should be "on the basis of acceptance in full of the plain teachings" of the Bible (10).[110]

The third doctrinal statement arose out of the situation of Baptists at the end of World War I. Whatever the degree of openness toward the Faith and Order Movement there may have been in 1914, the situation was quite

---

[110] New Orleans Baptist Theological Seminary 2004–2005 catalog, 8-9.

different in 1919, for at least two reasons: the U.S. Army's providing for the spiritual needs of soldiers under three categories (Protestant, Catholic, and Jewish), and the nature and results of the Interchurch World Movement.[111] Southern Baptists were ready to intensify their relationships with other Baptists, and the postwar devastation in Continental Europe presented the opportunity. The SBC president, James Bruton Gambrell (1841–1921), challenged the messengers "to send out to their fellow Baptists everywhere a rallying call to unite to make effective in all lands the unique message of Christ and His apostles which we hold in trust for our brothers in every part of the world."[112] James Franklin Love (1859–1928), corresponding secretary of the Foreign Mission Board (SBC), presented a resolution calling for the appointment of a five-member committee and naming its members[113] "to prepare greetings . . . to the people of 'like precious faith with us' scattered abroad in all nations."[114] The committee, with Mullins as chairman, prepared and issued early in 1920 "Fraternal Address of Southern Baptists."[115]

Recognizing that "religion is an indispensable factor in the reconstruction of the world now torn by war and divided by enmity" and declaring that there is "not an article" of Baptist belief "which is not essential" to this reconstruction, the committee called for closer Baptist unity and sought to inform any lacking in such knowledge about what Southern Baptists believe and practice. Eight doctrinal statements, each having biblical citations, were made. First, God is the Creator and Governor who is revealed in the Bible as Father, Son, and Holy Spirit. Second, the Bible as the Word of God is his "authoritative message to men concerning the way of salvation" and "the sufficient, certain and authoritative revelation of God and all matters of faith and practice." It is divinely inspired as marked by progressive revelation, has unity and harmony, and has Christ as its center. Third, Jesus in his death was conqueror of sin and death, vindicator of God's righteousness,

---

[111]See the address by President J. B. Gambrell, Southern Baptist Convention, *Annual*, 1919, 17-23; Barnes, *The Southern Baptist Convention*, 280-83; James E. Carter, "The Fraternal Address of Southern Baptists," *Baptist History and Heritage* 12 (October 1977): 211-13.

[112]Southern Baptist Convention, *Annual*, 1919, 23.

[113]E. Y. Mullins, J. B. Gambrell, Z. T. Cody, L. R. Scarborough, and William Ellyson.

[114]Southern Baptist Convention, *Annual*, 1919, 75.

[115]Carter, "The Fraternal Address of Southern Baptists," 214.

substitutionary Savior, and the offerer of a once-for-all sacrifice. Risen and ascended, he now intercedes for us. Fourth, the Holy Spirit, who utilizes the gospel, is needed to effect regeneration, and justification is of a declarative nature. Fifth, the church, defined locally, is composed of "spiritual equals" and should have "no overlords," and is self-governing with the duty of obedience to Christ. It has the duty to cooperate with other churches, but missionary bodies are "voluntary bodies," and churches are not subject to them. Its officers are "bishops or elders," with teaching and preaching duties, and deacons, who are responsible for its "temporal affairs." Sixth, under "ordinances" immersion is defended and close membership and close communion are prescribed. The Lord's Supper is commemorative and declarative, the bread and "the fruit of the vine" being representative of Christ's body and blood. The ordinances are symbolic, being valuable only as "their meaning is discerned." Seventh, the individual "soul" or person has the right of access to and responsibility toward God without priestly interference. "No body of people calling itself the church of Jesus Christ has any right to limit salvation to its own members." Eighth, the "ideal" is "a free church in a free state." Civil government ought not "to control men in their religious beliefs" but rather to "protect individuals and religious denominations in the free exercise of their religious rights" so that all denominations can be equal before "the civil power." Also the church is not to try "to control the state." In an unnumbered section on "Baptists and Christian Union" Christianity is defined as "primarily the personal union of the individual with Christ by faith," Mullins's axioms are succinctly stated, and "the voluntary principle" exalted. Rejected is "any artificial joining together of alien elements in any so-called organic church union." The freedom to preach must be protected, and Baptists need to foster "a great missionary and educational program" with no compromise of gospel.[116] "The Southern Baptist Convention itself neither approved nor adopted the statement. It is not found in any *Annual* of the Convention."[117] In 1920 Love reported that 54,800 copies in English had been circulated, not counting translations into other languages, with considerable response,[118] but Carter

---

[116]*Fraternal Address of Southern Baptists* ([Nashville: Sunday School Board of the SBC?], 1920). The FMB had addressed the issue of church union as early as 1916. Southern Baptist Convention, *Annual*, 1916, 120-22; Estep, *Whole Gospel Whole World*, 192-94.

[117]Carter, "The Fraternal Address of Southern Baptists," 214.

[118]Southern Baptist Convention, *Annual*, 1920, 196, 43-44.

has declared that the address "was largely ignored."[119] Its principal effect may have been closely connected with its purpose: the opening of communications with and greater cooperation with Baptist unions and conventions in continental Europe.

The fourth statement was framed and adopted by the Foreign Mission Board (FMB). In his report to the 1920 convention J. F. Love included a section entitled "A Baptist World Program." He reported on "plans . . . to extend Southern Baptist influence" among "our people in many lands" so that there would be a "universal Baptist alliance imbued with the spirit of brotherliness," indeed "a Baptist missionary alliance," in which the "need of each other is mutual."[120] Love included the full text of a Statement of Belief which the FMB had adopted "for the guidance of young men and women" who shall be appointed. All newly appointed FMB missionaries "are expected to read carefully and subscribe to" this statement consisting of thirteen articles, though no signatures were required. Some of these articles were concise summaries of what had been stated in earlier Baptist confessions of faith: the Bible (1), the one true God (2), human depravity (4), salvation (5), repentance and faith (6), regeneration (7), sanctification (8), the ordinances (10), civil government (12), and resurrection, future judgment, heaven, and hell (13). But relative to Christ article 3 was specific as to the virgin birth, the deity, the vicarious death, the bodily resurrection, and the second coming. The church (9) is "a company of voluntarily associated baptized believers in Christ, recognizing Him as the only Head . . . , exercising only such administrative and disciplinary authority as He has committed to it, conducting holy worship, observing the ordinances as He has commanded, and seeking by cooperative effort to extend His kingdom in all the world." The Lord's Day (11) is "to be observed by all Christian believers everywhere." Appointees were expected to accept the "Pronouncement on Christian Union and Cooperation," which the FMB also had adopted. The board promised to make no territorial agreements, have no "alien practice" as to church letters, and to enter into no form of cooperation not fully "reported to" and "approved by" the SBC, so that "policy abroad" would "conform to policy at home."[121] Love suggested that

---

[119]Carter, "The Fraternal Address of Southern Baptists," 218.

[120]Since Love made no direct reference to the Baptist World Alliance, founded in 1905, one needs to assume that he envisioned some other type of alliance.

[121]See also J. F. Love, *The Union Movement* (Nashville: Sunday School Board of the SBC, 1918).

the Statement of Belief, "together with the Fraternal Address, may have value for our Baptist people everywhere" and become "a basis for Baptist federation" and missions.[122] As a result of a conference with Northern, Canadian, and British Baptist leadership in London in July 1920, the FMB agreed to take responsibility for Spain, Yugoslavia, Hungary, Romania, and Ukraine as well as Italy.[123]

The fifth[124] doctrinal statement was more limited in scope. In 1923 E. Y. Mullins as SBC president included within his presidential address a section on "Science and Religion." The convention voted that this portion of the address be "adopted as the belief of this body." It consisted of three parts. First, the role of science was addressed. It has much value, and both it and the Christian religion seek to be loyal to facts. Mullins deplored the actions of some scientists who make alleged discoveries the basis for attack upon Christianity. Scientists ought not to teach as facts what are hypotheses. Evolution is a hypothesis, for "causes of the origin of species have not been traced." There is as yet no proof to contradict direct creation by God. Evolution should not be imposed in public or denominational schools. Second, the "supernatural elements in the Christian religion," notably those associated with Jesus, are strongly affirmed. Third, adherence to these facts and truths should be a "necessary condition of service for teachers" in Baptist schools, and "all schools and teachers who are thus loyal to the facts of Christianity" are to be supported. Scientists should enjoy freedom of research, but the paramount contemporary issue is the struggle "between naturalism and supernaturalism."[125] This would not be the last occasion when the SBC would face the issue of Darwinian evolution.

The 1925 Baptist Faith and Message Statement

During the 1924 session of the Southern Baptist Convention two messengers, C. P. Stealey of Oklahoma and R. K. Maiden of Missiouri, both editors, presented resolutions proposing and offering the specific texts of doctrinal statements for adoption by the convention. The resolutions committee, chaired by John E. White of South Carolina, recommended that neither of

---

[122]Southern Baptist Convention, *Annual*, 1920, 195-200.

[123]Estep, *Whole Gospel Whole World*, 205.

[124]In 1922 the SBC declined to join with the Northern Baptist Convention in formulating and adopting a common confession of faith. Southern Baptist Convention, *Annual*, 1922, 66.

[125]Southern Baptist Convention, *Annual*, 1923, 19-20.

these resolutions be adopted on the basis that the Fraternal Address of Southern Baptists and statements by President Mullins to the convention in 1923 were "sufficiently comprehensive and definite" and "accessible." But subsequently the resolutions committee, whose report was presented by Louie D. Newton of Georgia, recommended instead "that the following brethren be appointed as a committee to consider the advisability of issuing another statement of the Baptist faith and message . . .: E. Y. Mullins, Chairman, L. R. Scarborough, C. P. Stealey, W. J. McGlothlin, S. M. Brown, E. C. Dargan, [and] R. H. Pitt."[126] Mullins, Scarborough, and McGlothlin were presidents of Baptist institutions, Stealey (Oklahoma), Brown (Missouri), and Pitt (Virginia) were editors or coeditor of state Baptist papers, and Dargan was editorial secretary of the Sunday School Board. Mullins had authored or helped to frame three of the five preceding Southern Baptist-related doctrinal statements,[127] and McGlothlin, then president of Furman University, had compiled *Baptist Confessions of Faith*[128] and been professor of church history in Southern Baptist Theological Seminary for twenty-five years.[129]

What was the occasion, the situation, or the precipitating cause of the adoption by the SBC of a doctrinal statement during 1924–1925? Answers that have been given include "'the prevalence of naturalism,'"[130] "the continuing agitation over the question of evolution,"[131] and "the fundamentalist-modernist controversy" in the United States "after World War I."[132] These answers are interlocked, for evolution was a major issue in the controversy and perceived to be an expression of naturalism. Modernism and liberalism were not impacting Southern Baptists to the extent they were Northern Baptists. Carter insisted that the issue in the SBC was "not between fundamentalists and modernists as classically defined,"

---

[126]Southern Baptist Convention, *Annual*, 1924, 70-71, 80, 95.

[127]James E. Carter, "The Southern Baptist Convention and Confessions of Faith, 1845–1945" (Th.D. diss., Southwestern Baptist Theological Seminary, 1964), 117-18.

[128](Philadelphia: American Baptist Publication Society, 1911).

[129]Kathryn McGlothlin Odell, "McGlothlin, William Joseph," *Encyclopedia of Southern Baptists* 2:841-42.

[130]Barnes, *The Southern Baptist Convention*, 119, quoting the language of the Committee on Baptist Faith and Message, *SBC Annual*, 1925, 71.

[131]Baker, *The Southern Baptist Convention*, 398.

[132]Carter, "The Southern Baptist Convention," 103.

for there was "rather general" "agreement" on "fundamentals."[133] But evolution was a major issue.

Reaction to the possibility of a doctrinal statement being adopted by the SBC was mixed. Some were favorable to such as an expression of how Southern Baptists interpreted the Bible, and some even wanted to use such a confession as the means of excluding "evolutionists and modernists." Others, including White and Pitt, being unfavorable, argued that such was not necessary, that such was not proper for a missionary body, and that such could "create distrust" and "hurt evangelism." Even Mullins saw a danger in such a confession. Some thought that the committee should only address the question of "advisability," others wanted the committee to be prepared with a draft of a confession for use if the convention should accept "advisability," and still others assumed that the committee should frame and present a confession.[134]

Pitt's proposal that Mullins, McGlothlin, and Dargan be asked to write the confession was not accepted, and Mullins proceeded to lead the process with an interchange of correspondence during the summer of 1924 and a meeting in Nashville in January 1925. Mullins presented to the committee both a brief ninefold statement which he had written and a more extended draft based on the New Hampshire Confession as modified in 1853. The committee rejected the former but was favorable to the latter. Stealey wanted his own article on evolution, Dargan advised him to submit a minority report, and Scarborough favored revision of the New Hampshire Confession. By March the committee had received copies of Mullins's draft, and in a 11 May meeting in Memphis five members of the committee agreed upon a text. Pitt, being absent, sent a disclaimer stating that he could sign but with stated reservations, and Stealey, not agreeing to the article on creation, "left the committee."[135]

---

[133]Ibid., 104. According to Norman F. Furniss, *The Fundamentalist Controversy, 1918–1931* (New Haven CT: Yale University Press, 1954) 120, "The argument [among Southern Baptists] was . . . not one between liberals and conservatives, but between conservative liberals and extreme Fundamentalists."

[134]Carter, "The Southern Baptist Convention," 110-16, 118-20. Walter B. Shurden, "Southern Baptist Responses to Their Confessional Statements," *Review and Expositor* 76 (Winter 1979): 74-77, identified four groups of responses to a possible or to the actual confession of faith of 1925: "strict confessionalists," "anticonfessionalists," "confessionalists," and apathetic "nonconfessionalists."

[135]Carter, "The Southern Baptist Convention," 118, 120-24.

The Mullins committee could have chosen to utilize the Philadelphia Confession, the Abstract of Principles of Southern Baptist Theological Seminary, or any of the five Southern Baptist-related statements framed between 1914 and 1923 as the basis for its work. But it chose instead the revised New Hampshire Confession, which had come to be widely accepted by Southern Baptist churches west of the Atlantic seaboard and to be included with church covenants. Its moderate Calvinism more consonant with Southern Baptist evangelism, its stress on the local church, and its brevity may have fostered its usage.[136]

The Mullins committee introduced its proposed confession with a preamble which identified the "occasion" for the confession as the present-day "prevalence of naturalism," and set forth a fivefold restatement "of the historic Baptist conception of the nature and functions of confessions of faith." First, confessions "constitute a consensus of opinion of some Baptist body . . . for the general instruction and guidance of our own people and others" concerning our beliefs. Second, they are not "complete," final, or infallible and are capable of being revised. Third, the right to frame and publish confessions belongs to "any group of Baptists, large or small." Fourth, the Scriptures are "the sole authority for faith and practice among Baptists," and confessions are "guides in interpretation" with "no authority over the conscience." Fifth, they are "statements of religious convictions" and should not "be used to hamper freedom of thought and investigation in other realms of life."[137]

Of the eighteen articles in the 1853 revision of the New Hampshire Confession fifteen were retained with modifications by the committee. The articles on "Harmony of the Law and the Gospel" and "Civil Government" were deleted, and the article on "The World to Come" was replaced by two new articles, one on "The Resurrection" and the other on "The Return of the Lord." In the article on "The Scriptures" the statement that the Bible is "the supreme standard of which all human conduct, creeds, and opinions should be tried" was modified to read "religious opinions." The new article on God, somewhat shortened, was more explicit about God's being personal and being Creator; instead of emphasizing the offices of the Trinity, it

---

[136]McGlothlin, *Baptist Confessions of Faith*, 300-301; Lumpkin, *Baptist Confessions of Faith*, 360-61; Fletcher, *The Southern Baptist Convention*, 142, 365-67, 373.

[137]Southern Baptist Convention, *Annual*, 1925, 71; Lumpkin, *Baptist Confessions of Faith*, 391-92.

affirmed the indivisible "essence" of God. The new article on "The Fall of Man" was more specific as to man's being "created by the special act of God," and Gen. 1:27 and 2:7 were cited, and the language was expressive of an inherited sinful nature with condemnation and voluntary transgression.[138] Inserted into the article on "The Way of Salvation" was a statement that the Son of God was "by the Holy Spirit" "born of the Virgin Mary." The definition of "Justification" was changed from "the pardon of sin and the promise of eternal life" to "God's gracious and full acquittal." Likewise the definition of "Regeneration" was shifted from the gift of "a holy disposition to the mind" to "a change of heart wrought by the Holy Spirit." Under "God's Purpose of Grace" the new article omitted the idea of diligent ascertaining of assurance by true believers. In defining "Sanctification" the new article shifted from the progressive being "made partakers" of God's holiness to "the process" of gradually attaining "to moral and spiritual perfection." The article on "A Gospel Church changed "a visible Church of Christ" to "a church of Christ." The new article on "Baptism and the Lord's Supper" deleted the statements that our faith in Christ results in "our death to sin and resurrection to a new life" and that the Lord's Supper is to be "preceded always by solemn self-examination." The old article on "The Christian Sabbath" was reentitled "The Lord's Day," which was called "a Christian institution" that "commemorates the resurrection of Christ." The old article alluded to eschatological rest, whereas the new enjoined rest "from secular employments, works of necessity and mercy only excepted."[139]

Of the eight completely new articles framed by the committee, three pertain primarily to the larger society beyond the churches and five pertain primarily to Christians and churches. Unlike the old article that emphasized the God-ordained nature of civil government and possible civil disobedience, the new article on "Religious Liberty" recognized "God alone" as "the Lord of the conscience," affirmed the institutional separation of church and state, and defined the duties of each vis-à-vis the other. The article on

---

[138]Ryan Lintelman, "Article III, 'The Fall of Man,' in the Baptist Faith and Message, 1925 to 1963" (M.A. in Th. thesis, Southwestern Baptist Theological Seminary, 2006) 23, 40-41, has rightly noted that the 1925 confession as to this doctrine followed the Abstract of Principles, which could possibly be understood as teaching the imputation of Adamic guilt, rather than the New Hampshire Confession.

[139]Lumpkin, *Baptist Confessions of Faith*, 361-67, 393-96.

"Peace and War" placed the emphasis on "the duty of Christians to seek peace with all men on principles of righteousness," "to oppose everything likely to provoke war," to "do all in their power to put an end to war," and "to pray for the reign of the Prince of Peace," whose gospel is the "true remedy" for militarism. According to the article on "Social Service," Christians are obliged to make Christ's will "regnant . . . in human society." This was meant to include opposing "every form of greed, selfishness and vice," caring for the orphans, the elderly, "the helpless, and the sick," seeking "to bring industry, government and society as a whole under the sway of the principles of righteousness, truth and brotherly love," and working toward such ends "with all men of good will." There must be no compromise of "loyalty to Christ and his truth," and all such activity depends on regenerated persons.[140]

Five other articles were addressed more specifically to Southern Baptist members and churches. Because in Christ "are hidden all the treasures of wisdom and knowledge" and "Christianity is the religion of enlightenment and intelligence," according to the article on "Education," "all sound learning is "part of our Christian heritage," those born again have "a thirst for knowledge," and churches should adequately support a "system of schools." The article on "Cooperation" stressed the obligation of church members to cooperate with other church members and of churches to cooperate through "associations and conventions" with other churches to fulfill "missionary, educational and benevolent" objectives.[141] Such general Baptist bodies "are voluntary and advisory bodies" with "no authority over each other" or over the churches. On the basis of "spiritual harmony" Baptists may cooperate with those in other Christian denominations "for common [and justifiable] ends" when there is "no violation of conscience" or "compromise of loyalty to Christ" and the New Testament. The article on "Evangelism and Missions" mandated the obligation of every Christian and every church, on the basis of Christ's commands and "a spiritual necessity of the regenerate life," "to seek to extend the gospel to the ends of the earth" and "to win the lost to Christ by personal effort and by all other methods sanctioned by the Gospel of Christ." Under "Stewardship"

---

[140] Ibid., 396, 397; Southern Baptist Convention, *Annual*, 1925, 73-74.

[141] It is probable that L. R. Scarborough influenced the inclusion and the wording of the article on "Cooperation." See Scarborough, "Is Cooperation a New Testament Doctrine?" *Southwestern Journal of Theology*, o.s. 6 (April 1922): 92-96: repr.: *Baptist Standard*, 4 May 1922, 15-16.

it was said that since God is the owner of all things and "the source of all blessings, temporal and spiritual," Christians are trustees of the gospel, spiritual debtors to humankind, and bound stewards of possessions. Christians are obligated to serve God with their "time, talents and material possessions" so as to glorify God and help other human beings. They "should cheerfully, regularly, systematically, proportionately, and liberally contribute of their means to advancing the Redeemer's cause on earth." The final article on "The Kingdom of God" defined it as "the reign of God in the heart and life of the individual in every human relationship, and in every form and institution of organized human society." Preaching and teaching are "the chief means of promoting" the kingdom, Christians ought "to pray and labor continually" for its coming, and it "will be complete when every thought and will of man shall be brought into captivity to the will of Christ." No reference was made to the advent of the kingdom with Jesus' ministry or to the eschatological fulfillment of the kingdom.[142] Mullins's statement on "Science and Religion," adopted by the SBC in 1923, was appended to the report of the committee.[143]

The 1925 convention in Memphis received the committee report, signed by five members, with no question being raised as to the committee's having authority to prepare and present such a confession.[144] Stealey, who desired a more specific rejection of evolution, offered a minority report which stated "that man came into this world by direct creation of God and not by evolution." Mullins and Stealey debated the question as to where a more explicit statement should be placed, in the body or as a supplement. Stealey's amendment lost by a 2,013 to 950 vote, and then the committee report was adopted. Two days later the convention adopted a resolution that the Baptist Faith and Message Statement cannot properly be interpreted "as an endorsement of evolution."[145] Subsequently those who did not want the convention to adopt any kind of confession complained that they had had no opportunity to speak. Those desiring a more explicit confession were unsatisfied because the adopted one "had not dealt strongly enough with"

---

[142]Southern Baptist Convention, *Annual*, 1925, 74-75; Lumpkin, *Baptist Confessions of Faith*, 396-96.

[143]Southern Baptist Convention, *Annual*, 1925, 75-76.

[144]Ibid., 76; W. W. Barnes, *The Southern Baptist Convention: A Study in the Development of Ecclesiology* (Seminary Hill TX: author, 1934) 59-60.

[145]Southern Baptist Convention, *Annual*, 1925, 76, 87; Carter, "The Southern Baptist Convention," 124-28.

evolution. Those "willing to accept a confession" "if it did not include statements on natural science" prevailed. Representatives of those perspectives continued to make known their views during 1925–1926. Mullins's supporters praised him, and his critics charged that he had taken "ambiguous middle ground" and "failed to give decisive leadership" concerning evolution.[146]

In the 1926 convention in Houston President George White McDaniel (1875–1927) of Virginia concluded his presidential acceptance speech with the following statement: "This Convention accepts Genesis as teaching that man was the special creation of God, and rejects every theory, evolution or other, which teaches that man originated in, or came by way of, a lower animal ancestry." A motion by Monroe Elmon Dodd (1878–1952), pastor of First Church, Shreveport, Louisiana, to the effect that the president's statement "on the subject of evolution and the origin of man be adopted as the sentiment of this Convention, and that from this point on no further consideration be given to this subject" was unanimously adopted.[147] On the same day the trustees of Southwestern Baptist Theological Seminary voted to add the McDaniel addendum to its own slightly altered New Hampshire Confession of Faith,[148] and Scarborough announced to the convention that the new text would be required of all officers and professors.[149] Subsequently Selsus Estol Tull (1878–1973) of Arkansas introduced to the convention a resolution requiring "all its institutions and Boards, and their missionary representatives" "to give . . . assurance of individual acceptance" of the McDaniel statement, and it was adopted.[150] In November the Oklahoma state convention voted "to withhold undesignated funds of the Cooperative Program" from those SBC "seminaries whose faculties refused to sign the McDaniel statement."[151] By 1927 Southern Baptist Theological Seminary and Baptist Bible Institute complied.[152] The Oklahoma action

---

[146]Carter, "The Southern Baptist Convention," 128-32.

[147]Southern Baptist Convention, *Annual*, 1926, 18; Carter, "The Southern Baptist Convention," 132-34.

[148]Baker, *Tell the Generations Following*, 143.

[149]Southern Baptist Convention, *Annual*, 1926, 98.

[150]Ibid.

[151]Baker, *The Southern Baptist Convention*, 399.

[152]Southern Baptist Convention, *Annual*, 1927, 98, 105; Baker, *Tell the Generations Following*, 262.

evoked a study and redefinition by the SBC Executive Committee of SBC-state convention relationships, especially as to donated funds.[153]

After 1925 churches, associations, and state conventions only rarely adopted the 1925 SBC confession,[154] and hence W. W. Barnes could write in 1934 that the churches had received it "with a tremendous outburst of silence."[155]

Walter Thomas Conner (1877–1952)

Following the death of Mullins in 1928, the leading theologian among Southern Baptists during the second quarter of the twentieth century was W. T. Conner.[156] Born in Cleveland County, Arkansas, he and his family moved when Walter was fifteen to Taylor County, near Abilene, Texas. Converted at seventeen, he soon accepted a call to preach, and soon thereafter his father died. Conner struggled financially for his education, concurrently holding Baptist pastorates, first at Simmons College and later at Baylor University, from which he received B.A. (1906) and M.A. (1908) degrees, and in Southwestern Baptist (formerly Baylor) Theological Seminary, from which he received the Th.B. degree (1908). Offered by B. H. Carroll the opportunity to teach theology in the young seminary, Conner spent 1908–1910 at Rochester Theological Seminary during the Strong presidency, earning the B.D. degree, and began his 39-year professorship at Southwestern as the seminary moved to Fort Worth in 1910. During 1914 he studied at Southern Baptist Theological Seminary and completed the Th.D. degree in 1916. Writing an additional thesis, he received the Ph.D. degree from Southern in 1931. Occupying the chair of systematic theology, Conner also taught for brief periods English New Testament, New Testament theology, and Greek New Testament exegesis.[157]

---

[153]Southern Baptist Convention, *Annual*, 1928, 32-33; Baker, *The Southern Baptist Convention*, 399-400.

[154]Carter, "The Southern Baptist Convention," 165-69.

[155]*The Southern Baptist Convention: A Study in the Development of Ecclesiology*, 8.

[156]James Leo Garrett, Jr., "W. T. Conner: Contemporary Theologian," *Southwestern Journal of Theology* 25 (Spring 1983): 43.

[157]James Leo Garrett, Jr., "The Theology of Walter Thomas Conner" (Th.D. diss., Southwestern Baptist Theological Seminary, 1954) 1-23; idem, "Conner, Walter Thomas," in *Encyclopedia of Southern Baptists* 1:310; idem, "Walter Thomas Conner," in *Baptist Theologians*, ed. George and Dockery, 419-24; idem, "Walter Thomas Conner," in *The Legacy of Southwestern*, ed. Garrett et al., 33-34;

His systematic theology first took shape in *A System of Christian Doctrine* (1924).[158] In condensation it was expressed in *Gospel Doctrines* (1925)[159] and *Christian Doctrine* (1937).[160] Conner revised the first half of *A System of Christian Doctrine* under the title *Revelation and God* (1936)[161] and the second half under the title *The Gospel of Redemption* (1945).[162] Conner authored *The Faith of the New Testament* (1940),[163] and monographs on the resurrection of Jesus,[164] sanctification,[165] the work of the Holy Spirit,[166] and the work of Christ.[167] Conner was influenced by his teachers, notably, Goodspeed, Carroll, Strong, and Mullins, and by various American and European theologians, but he wrote for the student, the pastor, and the lay person, not for the scholar.[168]

"Following the pattern laid down by George Barker Stevens[169] and Henry Clay Sheldon,[170] Conner organized" *The Faith of the New Testament* "according to the principal types of New Testament literature: Synoptic, Jewish Christian, Pauline, and Johannine." Recognizing "both unity and variety of teaching in the New Testament," he gave special attention to Jesus' wilderness temptations, Jesus' teaching about the kingdom of God and about prayer, Paul's doctrine of the universality of sin, and the

---

Stewart A. Newman, *W. T. Conner: Theologian of the Southwest* (Nashville: Broadman, 1964).

[158](Nashville: Sunday School Board of the SBC, 1924).
[159](Nashville: Sunday School Board of the SBC, 1925).
[160](Nashville: Broadman, 1937).
[161]Subtitle: *An Introduction to Christian Doctrine* (Nashville: Broadman, 1936).
[162](Nashville: Broadman, 1945).
[163](Nashville: Broadman, 1940).
[164]*The Resurrection of Jesus* (Nashville: Sunday School Board of the SBC, 1926).
[165]*What Is a Saint?* (Nashville: Broadman, 1948).
[166]*The Work of the Holy Spirit* (Nashville: Broadman, 1949).
[167]*The Cross in the New Testament*, ed. Jesse J. Northcutt (Nashville: Broadman, 1954).
[168]Garrett, "Walter Thomas Conner," *Baptist Theologians*, 424, 432, 428.
[169]*The Theology of the New Testament* (New York: Scribner's, 1899).
[170]*New Testament Theology* (New York: Macmillan, 1922).

Johannine doctrine of eternal life.[171] Conner refuted anti-Christian philosophies,[172] Christian Science,[173] and Jehovah's Witnesses.[174]

Conner's work centered in systematic theology. "It has come to pass again that men are not ashamed to be known as theologians," he wrote in the preface to *The Gospel of Redemption*[175] in 1945, also noting that "the 'science of religion' was no longer prevailing." "The rise of biblical theology and the renascence of systematic theology even affected Conner, who had never winced at being a theologian," as one may detect in *The Gospel of Redemption* more than in *Revelation and God*.[176] There are observable shifts or changes in Conner's theology. He began his systematic theology "with the doctrine of revelation rather than with the doctrine of God." He gave "particular attention to the human capability to receive divine revelation," "to know God," and to crave after the worship of God despite sin. The influence of Mullins and personalism can be seen in Conner's "characteristics of human beings as spiritual persons: intelligence, rational affection, free will, and conscience." "In 1924 Conner treated the revelation of God in Christ prior to discussion of Old Testament revelation and revelation through nature, but in 1936 revelation through nature preceded biblical revelation." "Without specifying such, Conner basically agreed with . . . John Calvin and Emil Brunner that general revelation is not salvific but the basis for human accountability and preparatory for the revelation in Jesus Christ." Following Mullins, he "clearly differentiated revelation and the Bible," the latter being "the product and record of unique and historic divine revelation and a book of religion." Following Strong and Mullins, Conner did not embrace a specific theory as to the method of biblical inspiration.[177] The Bible's "'central interest' is redemption, . . . its

---

[171]Garrett, "Walter Thomas Conner," *Baptist Theologians*, 424.

[172]*Revelation and God*, 36-41.

[173]*The Teachings of Mrs. Eddy* (Nashville: Sunday School Board of the SBC, 1926).

[174]*The Teachings of "Pastor" Russell* (Nashville: Sunday School Board of the SBC, 1926).

[175]P. ix.

[176]Garrett, "Walter Thomas Conner," *Baptist Theologians*, 424-25.

[177]Moody, "Doctrines of Inspiration," 153-57, 163-69, 178, made much of the fact that Conner wrote very little concerning inspiration and did not espouse any theory of inspiration. As to inerrancy Moody utilized some personal letters by Conner in 1948 as indication of his opposition thereto but also noted Conner's affirmation of the "infallibility" of the religious teachings of the Bible and his being

unity is found in Jesus Christ," and revelation in Christ is "final" or ultimate. "Paralleling the objective revelation in Christ is the subjective revelation through the Holy Spirit," and, for Conner, "'the authority of the Bible is the authority of Christ.'"[178]

Conner consistently treated the person of Christ prior to the doctrine of God, "probably because Christ was seen as the Revealer of God." The "person of Christ" "embraced not only the interrelation of humanity and deity" in Christ but also his "virgin birth, sinlessness, miracles, and resurrection." The Southwestern theologian "was more emphatic than Mullins on the humanity of Jesus, and, unlike Strong and Mullins, related Jesus' sinlessness to his humanity." "Various kenotic theories were rejected, but a basic condescension or self-emptying was retained." What other theologians "described as the 'natural attributes' of God" Conner "treated as 'the absoluteness of God'" or God's "'infinity.'" "As omniscient God can foresee acts that are also free acts. The moral attributes "were chiefly holiness, . . . righteousness, and love." Conner "became less certain that in the Old Testament the Spirit of God is hypostatically distinct from God but was sure that in the New Testament such distinction is clear." He stressed the various aspects of the work of the Spirit. "He did not find full-blown Trinitarian teaching in the Old Testament but was led by the deity of Jesus and the personhood of the Holy Spirit to mainstream immanental Trinitarianism in which ancient heresies are avoided and the term 'person' is used advisedly."[179]

Rejecting both idealistic and naturalistic explanations of sin, "Conner saw sin as a religious conception," veritably "willful rebellion and unbelief" that resulted from "the temptation of the personal Satan."

> Departing from Calvin's concept of depravity as hereditary corruption, he taught depravity as the inevitability of sinning. Conner refused to accept either the Augustinian or the federal theories as to "original sin" as human sharing in Adamic guilt and shifted the focus from Romans 5:12-21 to

---

a "functional inerrantist."

[178] Garrett, "Walter Thomas Conner," *Baptist Theologians*, 425. James William McClendon, Jr., "The Baptist Bible: A Study in the Development of the Doctrine of the Scriptures" (mimeographed, 1961, Golden Gate Baptist Theological Seminary) 7, 8, criticized Mullins for failing to explain "the locus and method of the Bible's authority" and Conner for the lack of a "clear account of the role of the Bible."

[179] Garrett, "Walter Thomas Conner," *Baptist Theologians*, 425-26.

Romans 1:18 to 3:20. For him a historical Adam was no problem, but human beings, while perversely affected by the sin of Adam and Eve, are guilty only for their own sin. Conner developed [idiosyncratically] the concept that suffering or natural evil could have been the "anticipative consequence" of sin.[180]

Election, being defined "in terms of God's purpose, not God's decrees," was, for Conner, "the unfolding of God's plan" for "God's people and individuals." "But it is not the self-election of believers by repentance and faith or merely God's foreknowing who would repent and believe."[181] According to Conner, election is of particular human beings, and there is an "efficacious call." "God does not choose some for destruction in the same sense that he chooses some to eternal life."[182] Hence Conner has been classified under "modified Calvinistic predestination."[183] "On the doctrine of the saving work of Christ, Conner shifted from his earlier commitment" (1924, 1925) "to a moderate form of the penal substitutionary theory" "to his later embracing [1945, 1954] of the Christ as victor theory." The work of Christ "must embrace His life and His resurrection as well as His death and cannot be separated from the person of Christ."[184] "Rather than follow the classical Protestant pattern of justification, sanctification, and glorification, Conner gave attention to the various New Testament terms used to describe one's becoming a Christian," although he used "salvation" comprehensively (past, present, future). He was "critical of the forensic doctrine of justification ('declared righteous') issuing from the Reformation and argued for a vital

---

[180]Ibid., 426. Gstohl, *Southern Baptist Theologians and Original Sin*, 85-97, has criticized Conner for his concept of punishable "sins of ignorance" and for the lack of foundation for the salvation of infants dying in infancy through the death of Christ.

[181]Garrett, "Walter Thomas Conner," *Baptist Theologians*, 426.

[182]*The Gospel of Redemption*, 61-66, esp. 63, 65.

[183]Basden, "Theologies of Predestination in the Southern Baptist Tradition," 173, 208-29.

[184]See Draughon, "A Critical Evaluation," 152-95. Nalls, "The Concept of the Atonement," 98-107, ignored Conner's *The Cross in the New Testament* and hence failed to take note of his shift to the Christ as Victor view. Jason Boone Sampler, "A Critical Analysis of the Doctrine of the Atonement within the Writings of Walter Thomas Conner" (M.A. in Th. thesis, New Orleans Baptist Theological Seminary, 2003) esp. 61-62, 71-72, 79-80, emphasizing the World War II context of Conner's shift and critical of the Christ as Victor view, asserted that no later Southern Baptist theologian has followed Conner in embracing it.

doctrine ('made righteous') which was devoid of Roman Catholic works-righteousness and closely joined to regeneration."[185] In a similar deviation from Reformation Protestantism, Conner insisted that sanctification "had initial, continuing, and consummative uses, not merely the continuing." He identified repentance and faith as "'conditions of salvation'" and interpreted the Christian life "under four themes: providence, prayer, perseverance, and growth." "On perseverance Conner clearly remained a Calvinist with no disposition to allow apostasy, but his careful definition of perseverance has led to his being identified as a 'modified Calvinist.'"[186] Advocating Christian growth, he "rejected perfectionism."[187]

Conner was not Landmark in his definition of the "church" as universal as well as local but retained the Landmark rejection of "alien immersion" and the historic Baptist commitment to close communion. Reckoning the church as "primarily fellowship rather than organization," he yet "favored democratic polity." "In 1925 he stressed edification, evangelization, benevolence, and moral dynamism as the mission of the church, whereas in 1945 he contended that 'the first business' of a church is worship."[188]

The Texas theologian "set forth a fivefold interpretation of the kingdom of God: universal sovereignty, the theocracy of Israel, the spiritual rule founded by Jesus, 'a progressive power in the world,' and the consummated or eternal kingship." "In 1924 Conner taught one general resurrection of all humans at the time of the second coming of Jesus, whereas in 1945 he," following Thomas Polhill Stafford (1866–1942),[189] "inclined toward the view that resurrection bodies are received at death and resurrection itself will accompany the second coming." Similarly, Conner in 1924 "inclined toward postmillennialism, but in 1945 he identified himself generally with amillennialism." Moreover, "final judgment will reveal human character, assign destinies, and vindicate God's dealings with humanity." "Conner affirmed heaven and hell, rejecting restorationism and annihilationism."[190]

---

[185]Parks, "A Biblical Evaluation of the Doctrine of Justification," 122-57, esp. 153-57, delineated the shift in Conner's interpretation of justification from the equality of forensic and vital elements to the predominance of the vital.

[186]See Youngblood, "The Question of Apostasy," 118-21.

[187]Garrett, "Walter Thomas Conner," *Baptist Theologians*, 426-27.

[188]Ibid.,427. See Newman, *W. T. Conner*, 128-32.

[189]*A Study of Christian Doctrines* (Kansas City MO: Western Baptist Publishing Co., 1936) 598-606.

[190]Garrett, "Walter Thomas Conner," *Baptist Theologians*, 427-28. Cantwell,

Conner did not have as much worldwide influence among Baptists as Mullins has had, his impact being among Southern Baptists and those Baptists communities served by overseas Southern Baptist missionaries.[191] Included in James W. McClendon's *Pacemakers of Christian Thought*,[192] not included in James E. Tull's *Shapers of Baptist Thought*, and included in *Baptist Theologians*, edited by George and Dockery,[193] Conner left a legacy that may best be detected in his many students. Described as a two-point Dortian Calvinist[194] and as a "conservative or constructive" evangelical,[195] Conner was said in the 1980s to be a theologian whose writings, although out of print, were still relevant to the issues facing Southern Baptists: dispensationalism, charismaticism, biblical inerrancy, and resurgent Calvinism.[196]

Doctrinal Summaries for the Laity and the Convention

Especially between the two world wars Southern Baptists produced several doctrinal summaries for the instruction of church members. Oates Charles Symonds Wallace, a native of Nova Scotia and pastor of First Church, Baltimore, Maryland, produced an interpretation of the 1853 New Hampshire Confession.[197] Harold Wayland Tribble (1899–1986), professor of theology in Southern Baptist Theological Seminary, wrote a summary in the Mullins tradition, clearly differentiating the "human side" and the "divine side of Christian experience."[198] John Clyde Turner (1878–1974), pastor of First Church, Greensboro, North Carolina, was the author of a summary of the atonement and soteriological doctrines[199] and later of a

---

"Millennial Teachings," 79, asserted that "apparently" Conner "always leaned in the direction of amillennialism, but only late in life . . . was [he] unswervingly able to state his allegiance to the position."

[191]Garrett, "The Theology of Walter Thomas Conner," 335-36.
[192](Nashville: Broadman, 1962) 54-60.
[193]Pp. 419-33.
[194]Garrett, "W. T. Conner," 59-60.
[195]Garrett, "The Theology of Walter Thomas Conner," 334.
[196]Garrett, "W. T. Conner," 50-60.
[197]*What Baptists Believe; The New Hampshire Confession: An Exposition.* See above, 132n.136. For Conner's *Gospel Doctrines*, see above, 450.
[198]*Our Doctrines* (Nashville: Sunday School Board of the SBC, 1936).
[199]*Soul-Winning Doctrines* (Nashville: Sunday School Board of the SBC, 1943).

more comprehensive summary.[200] Roy Talley Edgemon (1934–), a Sunday School Board staff member and former missionary to Japan, much later wrote a ten-chapter summary.[201]

The Southern Baptist Convention in 1946, following its centennial, adopted a "Statement of Principles" on the recommendation of a twenty-member committee, appointed in 1942,[202] chaired by Ellis Adams Fuller (1891–1950), president of Southern Baptist Theological Seminary, and consisting of numerous well-known and highly respected Southern Baptist leaders. Strictly speaking, it was not a general confession of faith. Rather it was a two-part statement of "principles," the one pertaining to the doctrine of man and the other the doctrine of the church. The exposition concerning human beings focused on creaturehood rather than sinfulness. It affirmed the "value" of the individual, the endowed "competence" of the individual "to deal with God and with his fellowmen," the natural rights of the individual and their need not to be "violated," and the "responsibility" for "full realization of his possibilities" with God and with other human beings. For the attainment of such, God has provided the regenerating power of the Holy Spirit. "Out of this doctrine of the individual," the committee declared "grows the Baptist conviction concerning all aspects of religious experience and life." Regeneration/conversion "is prerequisite to church membership." The "local church," democratically governed, "is responsible directly and only to Christ," and its leadership is to be both "divinely called" and "chosen by the church." The "one and only authority in faith and practice is the New Testament," which is "the divinely inspired record and interpretation of the supreme revelation of God through Jesus Christ." Church and state should be institutionally separate with each "free to serve in its own divinely appointed sphere." As "a basic right under God" religious liberty should include not only freedom to worship but also "the right of propaganda through evangelism, education, and . . . Christian institutions." These principles were then applied at the outset of the post-World War II era to the entire social and international order in a time of

---

[200] *These Things We Believe* (Nashville: Convention Press, 1956).

[201] *The Doctrines Baptists Believe* (Nashville: Convention Press, 1988); under title, *Foundations of the Faith: The Doctrines Baptists Believe* (Nashville: LifeWay, 1999).

[202] Southern Baptist Convention, *Annual*, 1942, 104; 1944, 147; 1945, 59-60.

"reconstruction," "rehabilitation," and "reorientation," and the imperative of Christian evangelism and missions was restated.[203]

The Elliott Controversy

During the years following World War II Southern Baptist seminaries witnessed the retirement of older professors and the advent of younger professors and concurrently the greater employment of the historical-critical method in biblical studies. During 1958–1959 a major controversy erupted within Southern Baptist Theological Seminary between thirteen professors and President Duke Kimbrough McCall (1914–) and resulted in the trustee dismissal of twelve professors. Varying interpretations of this controversy have been given. For some it was a clash—almost "demonic"—of personalities.[204] For others it was a conflict over presidential leadership or curriculum matters.[205] In neither case would it have been essentially theological. Thirdly, according to Samuel S. Hill, the controversy was an unsuccessful effort by a group of post-World War II professors "to embrace openly a more ecumenical and progressive orientation," including "world-class biblical scholarship."[206] Fourth, the conflict could be seen as involving a somewhat uncritical adoption of historical-critical methods of biblical interpretation and accompanying less than orthodox theological positions.[207]

---

[203]Southern Baptist Convention, *Annual*, 1946, 37-39; Fletcher, *The Southern Baptist Convention*, 174, 176-77. According to Fletcher, 176, this document differed "from any prior confession" by making "the doctrine of man . . . the true distinctive among Southern Baptists."

[204]This was essentially the view of McCall (with A. Ronald Tonks), *Duke McCall: An Oral History* (Brentwood TN: Baptist History and Heritage Society; Nashville: Fields Publishing, 2001) 161-211, esp. 204-205.

[205]The dismissed professors desired a return to the pre-1942 "chairman of the faculty" role for the president, whereas the trustees had mandated more of a CEO model. The professors downplayed and resisted the increasing significance of psychology of religion and pastoral care as pioneered by the prolific professor-author, Wayne Edward Oates. Wayne E. Ward to James Leo Garrett, Jr., 25 January 2006.

[206]"The Story before the Story: Southern Baptists since World War II," in *Southern Baptists Observed: Multiple Perspectives on a Changing Denomination*, ed. Nancy Tatom Ammerman (Knoxville: University of Tennessee Press, 1993) 35, 36. Some would reckon this as a shift from a denominational seminary to a divinity school after the Yale model.

[207]Herschel H. Hobbs's 1960 letters to W. Douglas Hudgins, cited by Gregory A. Willis, "Progressive Theology and Southern Baptist Conservatives of the 1950s

Although there may be elements of truth in all four, the third and fourth of these, being hermeneutical and theological, could have had a bearing on the controversy centering in Ralph Harrison Elliott (1925–).

Reared in Danville, Virginia, with service in the United States Army (1943–1945), and a graduate of Carson-Newman College (B.A.) and Southern Baptist Theological Seminary (B.D., Th.D.), Elliott taught Hebrew and Old Testament interpretation from 1953 to 1958 in the latter institution before becoming in 1958 the first faculty member to be employed by the newly established Midwestern Baptist Theological Seminary in Kansas City, Missouri.[208] Just as he was moving to Midwestern, Elliott had begun to write a book on Genesis and by the end of 1960 he had after prior encouragement and correspondence submitted it to Broadman Press and received and signed a contract for its publication. The book[209] appeared in July 1961.[210] The book committee of Broadman Press had been highly commendatory in its evaluation:

> It is . . . a careful, balanced combination of modern biblical scholarship and the conservative Christian conviction that the Bible is God's inspired Word, the message of salvation. It is the most significant and creative contribution to biblical scholarship by a Southern Baptist writer since the works of A. T. Robertson and H. E. Dana. No Southern Baptist has done a comparable work in the Old Testament field.[211]

---

and the 1960s," *Southern Baptist Journal of Theology* 7 (Spring 2003): 19, 30n.20.

[208] *Who's Who in Religion*, 4th ed., 146; Mueller, *A History of Southern Baptist Theological Seminary*, 244; Elliott, *The "Genesis Controversy" and Continuity in Southern Baptist Chaos: A Eulogy for a Great Tradition* (Macon GA: Mercer University Press, 1992) 1-8, 39; Sally Rice, "Ralph Elliott: Controversial Figure among Southern Baptists" (Duke University Department of Religion Papers, 15 April 1963) 14-16.

[209] *The Message of Genesis: A Theological Interpretation* (Nashville: Broadman, 1961).

[210] Elliott, *The "Genesis Controversy,"* 7-8; Salvador T. Martinez, "Southern Baptist Views of the Scriptures in Light of the Elliott Controversy" (Th.M. thesis, Southern Baptist Theological Seminary, 1966) 8-9.

[211] Quoted by Reuben Alley, "Evasion and Appeasement," *Religious Herald*, 8 November 1962, 10, and requoted by Martinez," Southern Baptist Views," 10.

The stated purpose of the book was "to ferret out and to underscore the foundational theological and religious principles of the stories of Genesis."[212]

Certain features of Elliott's book on Genesis tended to evoke criticism: multiple authorship as viewed from the documentary hypothesis modified by oral tradition, the days of Genesis 1 as indefinite periods, the collective Adam, the exaggeration of the age of the antediluvians, Gen. 6:1-4 as a "fragment of mythology" used "as a literary device," the flood as local rather than universal, Melchizedek as a Baalite priest, Lot's wife as not turned into salt, and the proposed sacrifice of Isaac as "the fallible human reception of an infallible divine question."[213] Probably the most serious problem with the book, however, was Elliott's taking the stories of Genesis 1–11 as analogous to Jesus' parables, thereby rendering them "symbolical" rather than strictly historical.[214] But on the positive side, according to Elliott, Abraham did have a "concept of God different from that of his pagan neighbors," the historicity of the patriarchs is to be defended, and "Genesis sounds a death blow to deism, dualism, and pantheism."[215]

Soon after its publication *The Message of Genesis* evoked criticism, especially in Kansas and Missouri and notably from John F. Havlik, W. Ross Edwards, and Mack Douglas.[216] But the most influential anti-Elliott article was seemingly that published by Kenneth Owen White (1902–1985), pastor of First Church, Houston, Texas. Focusing on Elliott's symbolic and nonhistorical approach to Genesis 1–11, he labeled the book "liberalism" and "'poison'" from the Wellhausen school and warned of a drift from "the faith of our fathers" due to liberalism. White invited "men with such views" to find a place in another denomination, asked seminary trustees to be more cautious in approving faculty members, and urged the Sunday School Board to be "alert" to "any trend in the direction of liberalism."[217]

In their late December 1961 meeting the Midwestern trustees voted 14 to 7 to approve the report of its investigative committee, chaired by

---

[212]*The Message of Genesis*, vii.
[213]Ibid., 3-7, 35, 39, 59, 62-63, 66-67, 115-16, 136, 145-46; Alan Preston Neely, "A Critical Analysis of Ralph H. Elliott's *The Message of Genesis*" (mimeographed, 1962?).
[214]*The Message of Genesis*, 15-16.
[215]Ibid., 92, 16, 20.
[216]Martinez, "Southern Baptist Views," 14-16.
[217]"Death in the Pot," *Baptist Standard*, 10 January 1962, 6.

Lafayette Demetrius Johnson (1916–1981) of Virginia, that supported Elliott on the basis that many Southern Baptists do not believe in the plenary-verbal theory. Critics of the Elliott book responded negatively, accusing the trustees of evading the "real issues." In March 1962 about one hundred pastors and laymen from eight states met in Oklahoma City to plan how to secure the election of more conservative trustees for Midwestern. Prior to the SBC annual meeting in San Francisco in June 1962, a meeting of critics of the Elliott book asked K. Owen White to frame and present to the convention a motion in response to the Elliott issue and, after the group's approval of such motion, White presented it.[218] It read as follows:

> I move that the messengers of this Convention, by standing vote, reaffirm their faith in the *entire* Bible as the authoritative, authentic, infallible Word of God, that we express our abiding and unchanging objection to the dissemination of theological views in any of our seminaries which would undermine such faith in the historical accuracy and doctrinal integrity of the Bible, and that we kindly but firmly instruct the trustees and administrative officers of our institutions and [other] agencies to take such steps as shall be necessary to remedy at once those situations where such views now threaten our historic position.[219]

Two other motions calling for the cessation of the publication and sale of *The Message of Genesis* were made; one was withdrawn and the other was defeated, and White's motion, divided into two on the insistence of the convention president, Herschel H. Hobbs, was adopted.[220] Certain trustees of Midwestern eligible for reelection were not nominated, and instead anti-Elliott trustees were named to the board. Previously, in April 1962 James L. Sullivan, executive secretary of the Sunday School Board (SBC), had ordered that there be no reprinting of Elliott's book. In its July meeting the Sunday School Board allowed Sullivan's order to stand, thus insuring that Broadman Press would not republish the disputed volume.[221] In late

---

[218]Martinez, "Southern Baptist Views," 18-25; Robert T. Latham, "Concerning the Elliott Controversy," *Baptists for Freedom*, issue 1, 1 February 1963, 4-5.

[219]Southern Baptist Convention, *Annual*, 1962, 65.

[220]Ibid., 68.

[221]It was republished in February 1963 (©1962) for Abbott Books by Bethany Press (Christian Board of Publication, Disciples of Christ). Robert T. Latham, "Southern Baptists and a Book," *Baptists for Freedom*, issue 2, April 1963, 5; Fletcher, *The Southern Baptist Convention*, 207; Elliott, *The "Genesis Controversy,"* 131.

September the Midwestern trustees heard and adopted the two recommendations of the special committee relative to the Elliott matter: to get Elliott to resign or dismiss him, and to adopt a statement favorable to the use of historical-critical interpretation. On 18 October trustee negotiators asked Elliott "voluntarily" to withhold republication; he agreed on condition that the board make an official request, and the board refused lest it have the stigma of book burning. On 25 October, a signed statement by Elliott expressing willingness to abandon republication displayed by one trustee being ignored, the board voted 22 to 7 to dismiss Elliott because "he refused to withdraw his book 'voluntarily.'" The trustees then approved a statement that the historical-critical method was "'one of the valid ways of approaching the Bible,'" and "'not in conflict with the historic position of Baptists,'" though not all conclusions reached by its practitioners are to be accepted.[222] Later interpreters of these events have insisted that Elliott was dismissed for insubordination rather than for a specific heresy.[223] Most of the Baptist state papers both before and after Elliott's dismissal carried editorials and/or articles dealing with the Elliott matter. Salvador T. Martinez found that only five of these editors were clearly pro-Elliott, and four of these were in Atlantic seaboard states. These tended to affirm biblical inspiration but limit infallibility to the message of the Bible and stress the right of private interpretation. Most of the editors in the Southwest, the Midwest, the deep South, and the West were anti-Elliott and affirmed plenary-verbal inspiration.[224] Martinez argued that Elliott's doctrine of the Scriptures was more in conformity with the positions set forth in Baptist confessions of faith and by major Baptist theologians of the past than the doctrine of his critics.[225] Some stressed that the Elliott controversy had "psychological" and

---

[222]Martinez, "Southern Baptist Views," 25-42; Latham, "Concerning the Elliott Controversy," 5-6; Rice, "Ralph Elliott," 29-74.

[223]Baker, *The Southern Baptist Convention*, 416; Fletcher, *The Southern Baptist Convention*, 207; Leonard, *Baptist Ways*, 414.

[224]Martinez, "Southern Baptist Views," 128-81.

[225]Ibid., 48-125, 181-82.

"political" aspects as well as theological.[226] In his recent study Almer Jesse Smith has reported on the epistolary responses to Elliott's book.[227]

Inasmuch as Toy's resignation had some connection with Genesis and the 1925 Baptist Faith and Message Statement of 1925 was driven by conflicting views of creation and evolution, it can be said that with the Elliott controversy Southern Baptists for the third time in less than a century were in controversy over Genesis.

The 1963 Baptist Faith and Message Statement

The proposal for another confessional statement for the Southern Baptist Convention did not originate on the floor of the convention but from a conference of three leaders. Leslie Robinson Elliott (1886–1965), librarian of Southwestern Baptist Theological Seminary, in an address[228] at Southern Baptist Theological Seminary, in January 1962 had asserted that Elliott's book had made 1961 a critical year for Southern Baptists.[229] Out of a conversation in Oklahoma City between the convention's president, Herschel Harold Hobbs, and Porter W. Routh and Albert A. McClellan, both employed by the SBC Executive Committee, came the idea for a convention committee to study the 1925 statement so as to "determine" whether the convention "was drifting to the *left*" theologically.[230]

---

[226]Ibid., 46-47. Elliott was subsequently pastor, Emmanuel Church, Albany NY, 1964–1971; First Church, White Plains NY, 1971–1977; and North Shore Church, Chicago, 1977–1989; and vice president for academic life and dean of faculty, Colgate-Rochester Divinity School, 1989–1991. *Who's Who in Religion*, 4th ed., 146; *Who's Who in the East*, 26th ed., 237. For Hobbs's assessment of the controversy at the end of his life, see his "The Elliott Controversy," appendix 1 in *The Fibers of Our Faith: The Herschel H. and Frances J. Hobbs Lectureship in Baptist Faith and Heritage at Oklahoma Baptist University*, vol. 1, ed. Dick Allen Rader (Franklin TN: Providence House Publishers, 1995) 203-14.

[227]"The Making of the 1963 Baptist Faith and Message" (Ph.D. diss., Southern Baptist Theological Seminary, 2004) 37-51.

[228]"Changing Patterns in Theological Education: From Boyce to Bultmann," Founder's Day Address, SBTS, 11 January 1962 (mimeographed) esp. 39.

[229]James E. Carter, "A Review of Confessions of Faith Adopted by Major Baptist Bodies in the United States," *Baptist History and Heritage* 12 (April 1977): 87-88.

[230]Hobbs, "The Baptist Faith and Message—Anchored but Free," *Baptist History and Heritage* 13 (July 1978): 34; Fletcher, *The Southern Baptist Convention*, 208. But David William Downs, "The Use of 'Baptist Faith and Message,'

The proposal, to be processed through the Executive Committee, called for a committee consisting of all the current presidents of state conventions that "qualified . . . for representation on Southern Baptist Convention agencies" plus the presidents of the six SBC seminaries. Such a plan, having been approved by the Executive Committee, encountered some criticism by editors of state Baptist papers at the 1962 SBC session, the argument being that if the problems were occurring in the seminaries, the presidents should not be among the investigators. The names of the presidents were dropped before the recommendation was presented, and even a motion to restore them was defeated.[231] Anxiety about the competence of the twenty-four member committee, with Hobbs as chairman, abated after it became known that except for the two laymen and two of the pastors all members "had standard degrees from various Southern Baptist seminaries" and eight "had academic doctorates."[232] The convention adopted the recommendation,[233] and the committee began its work in July with a subcommittee of five being named to study the 1925 statement.[234] The committee, according to Hobbs, had three options: to reaffirm the 1925 statement, to draw up a new statement, or to revise the 1925.[235] It chose the last option. The committee sought "to secure the opinions of lay people, pastors, and theologians regarding various items." Moreover, according to Hobbs, "Every single item in the proposed statement was adopted by unanimous vote!" After "the original draft" had been completed, copies were sent to the six seminaries and to the Sunday School Board with the request that each professor and each "Board person involved in theological literature" be "asked to study the draft and offer criticisms or suggestions."[236]

1963–1983: A Response to Pluralism in the Southern Baptist Convention" (Ph.D. diss., Southern Baptist Theological Seminary, 1984; Ann Arbor MI: University Microfilms International, 1988) 3-6, 55-102, has seen the 1963 confession not so much as the product of the Elliott Controversy per se as the result of "the new pluralism" in American society and among Southern Baptists.

[231]Hobbs, "The Baptist Faith and Message," 34.

[232]Ibid., 35; Hobbs, "Southern Baptists and Confessionalism: A Comparison of the Origins and Contents of the 1925 and 1963 Confessions," *Review and Expositor* 76 (Winter 1979): 59; Carter, "A Review of Confessions," 89.

[233]Southern Baptist Convention, *Annual*, 1962, 64.

[234]Carter, "A Review of Confessions," 89.

[235]Hobbs, "The Baptist Faith and Message," 35.

[236]Hobbs, "Southern Baptists and Confessionalism," 60.

The committee's draft reduced the 1925 confession's twenty-five articles to seventeen. "Biblical references were cited beneath each article to indicate that these beliefs were biblically based."[237] The introduction included a reaffirmation of the 1925 assertion of the "supernatural" character of Christianity, the concurring quotation of the five 1925 statements about the nature and function of Baptist confessions of faith,[238] and a new statement about the faith of Baptists. Baptists, it declared, have "a living faith," "rooted and grounded in Jesus Christ," who is "the sole authority for faith and practice," his will being "revealed in the Holy Scriptures." Their confessions of faith are not "complete," "infallible," or "mandatory," but they are compatible with the Baptist emphasis on soul competency.[239]

At least five of the new articles were completely rewritten, though usually by retaining content from the 1925 statement. To the brief 1925 article on "God" was added a detailed tripartite declaration concerning the Father, the Son, and the Holy Spirit. The paragraph on the Son extends from preexistence to second coming and final judgment, and the work of the Spirit includes inspiration of the Scriptures, illumination, conviction, regeneration, character formation, spiritual gifts, sealing, assurance, and empowerment. The 1925 article on "The Fall of Man" was rewritten under the title of "Man." Whereas the earlier article majored on "original holiness," the fall therefrom, a corrupt inherited nature, and becoming "actual trangressors," the 1963 added the image of God in man and the truth that "every man possesses dignity and is worthy of respect and Christian love."[240] The six soteriological articles (4-10) of the 1925 statement were transformed into one tripartite article on "Salvation." The committee adopted a classical Protestant and not peculiarly Baptist pattern of treatment: punctiliar regeneration, continual sanctification, and eschatologi-

---

[237] Carter, "A Review of Confessions," 90.

[238] See above, 444.

[239] Southern Baptist Convention, *Annual*, 1963, 269-70.

[240] The addition of this language was contemporaneous with racial tensions and the Civil Rights movement in the United States. Hobbs, "Southern Baptists and Confessionalism," 63; Fletcher, *The Southern Baptist Convention*, 209. Lintelman, "Article III, 'The Fall of Man,' " 56, 81, 47-48, 54-55, 73-74, has argued that soul competency necessitated a change from a Calvinist doctrine of total depravity but identified Hobbs, not Mullins, as the chief culprit. Yet he failed sufficiently to identify the nonimputation of Adamic guilt as basic to the 1963 article or to probe other possible causes of the change.

cal glorification. The earlier article on "The Way of Salvation" had traced Jesus from incarnation to ascension; the new article defined salvation in terms of the redemption of the whole man." Justification, although still defined, is subsumed under regeneration. Whereas formerly repentance and faith were called both "sacred duties" and "inseparable graces," now they are termed "inseparable experiences of grace." Glorification was a newly inserted topic. In 1925 the kingdom of God was defined as God's reign over individuals and society, promoted by preaching and teaching and to be "complete" when every human thought and will is made captive to Christ's will. The new article defined the kingdom both in terms of general sovereignty and the particular role of believers, both in terms of present entry through childlike faith and "full consummation" with Christ's return and "the end of this age."[241] The 1925 article on "Education" had emphasized that wisdom and knowledge are hidden in Christ, "sound learning" is "a part of our Christian heritage," and the new birth enables believers to thirst for knowledge; hence Christian schools are as important and worthy of support as missions and benevolence. The new article, condensing the former, added, in light of the Elliott controversy, an explicit statement on balanced academic freedom and responsibility.[242]

Some articles were combined with minimal change. The 1925 articles "God's Purpose of Grace" and "Perseverance" were combined into one article under the former title. The earlier reference to "the use of means" was deleted. More importantly the committee abandoned the 1925 (and hence the New Hampshire) article about perseverance except for one sentence and inserted instead an updated summarization of the Philadelphia Confession's article 17. This is the document's only discernible shift toward Calvinism. The three 1925 articles on "The Righteous and the Wicked," "The Resurrection," and "The Return of the Lord" were combined and condensed into one article entitled "Last Things." The new article was more explicit about the end of the age, Christ's personal and visible second coming, and hell as "everlasting punishment" and less explicit as to "a" or one "resurrection of the righteous and the wicked."[243]

Other articles had very significant and relatively brief additions. The 1925 article on "The Scriptures" was reproduced with the addition of the

---

[241]This 1963 article was taken verbatim from the text I submitted to the committee.
[242]Southern Baptist Convention, *Annual*, 1963, 271-74, 276-77, 278.
[243]Ibid., 274-75, 277-78.

words "the record of God's revelation of Himself to man,"[244] and of the following sentence: "The criterion by which the Bible is to be interpreted is Jesus Christ."[245] Hobbs connected the latter insertion with Elliott's reckoning of Melchizedek as "a priest of Baal,"[246] but it obviously carries the weight of a central hermeneutical principle. At the end of the twentieth century it would prove to be a very disputed element in the 1963 statement.[247] To the 1925 article relative to the church were added two statements. First,

> This church is an autonomous body, operating through democratic processes under the Lordship of Christ. In such . . . members are equally responsible.

Second,

> The New Testament speaks also of the church as the body of Christ which includes all of the redeemed of all the ages.[248]

The latter sentence was the only portion of the 1963 text challenged by a messenger to the 1963 session. Wendell Rone of Kentucky moved its deletion, presumably because of its non-Landmark nature, but Hobbs, with the aid of Albert McClellan, quoted from J. M. Pendleton a statement supportive of such nonlocal usage, and the amendment was defeated.[249]

Still other articles had their content inverted or substantially changed. The 1925 article on "Social Service" was reentitled "The Christian and the Social Order," and the regeneration of individuals as necessary for societal changes was moved from the end to the beginning of the article. In the article on "Baptism and the Lord's Supper" each ordinance was now also identified as "an act of obedience," baptism was said to symbolize the believer's death, burial, and resurrection, and the Lord's Supper was viewed

---

[244] This wording had been used by Mullins and by Conner. See above 420, 451.
[245] Southern Baptist Convention, *Annual*, 1963, 270.
[246] Hobbs, "Southern Baptists and Confessionalism," 62.
[247] See below, 506-507.
[248] Southern Baptist Convention, *Annual*, 1963, 275.
[249] Ibid., 63, Hobbs, "The Baptist Faith and Message," in *The Fibers of Our Faith*, ed. Rader, 71. John Allen Durden, "A Selected Issue in Southern Baptist Ecclesiology: The Nature of the Church as Reflected in the Baptist Faith and Messages of 1925 and 1963" (Th.D. thesis, Mid-America Baptist Theological Seminary, 1993) regarded this addition as expressive of the views of Dagg, Whitsitt, Dargan, Mullins, Carver, Moody, Stagg, and Theron D. Price.

as anticipating the second coming.[250] In the article on "Peace and War" the admonition to pray for world peace and "oppose everything likely to provoke war" was omitted.[251] The articles on "The Lord's Day," "Evangelism and Missions," "Stewardship," and "Cooperation" had stylistic changes, and that on "Religious Liberty" was retained verbatim.[252]

Following its adoption by the SBC,[253] the 1963 Baptist Faith and Message Statement was generally well received but evoked little discussion until 1969.[254] In 1979 Walter Shurden reported that one SBC board, four SBC seminaries, and seven related state conventions had officially adopted it as their own.[255] According to James E. Carter, writing in 1976, it had been "used more extensively than" the 1925 confession.[256] In his 1984 study David Downs indicated its use in the SBC in relation to resolutions, to the definition and enforcement of orthodoxy, and to resistance to stricter requirements, its use by state conventions for membership and by incorporation into constitutions, and its use less frequently by associations and churches.[257] Hobbs later interpreted at length[258] and provided an account of the origin and usage of[259] the 1963 confession. Even more discussion of it and debate about it would come later.

---

[250]The only debate within the committee narrated by Hobbs involved the unsuccessful effort of one member to limit participation in the Lord's Supper to the members of the observing church.

[251]Southern Baptist Convention, *Annual*, 1963, 280, 276, 280.

[252]Ibid., 276, 278, 279-80.

[253]Ibid., 63.

[254]Shurden, "Southern Baptist Responses to Their Confessional Statements," 77.

[255]Ibid., 80-82.

[256]"American Baptist Confessions of Faith: A Review of Confessions of Faith Adopted by Major Baptist Bodies in the United States," in *The Lord's Free People in a Free Land*, ed. William R. Estep, Jr. (Fort Worth TX: Faculty of the School of Theology, Southwestern Baptist Theological Seminary) 71.

[257]"The Use of the 'Baptist Faith and Message,'" 103-220.

[258]*The Baptist Faith and Message* (Nashville: Convention Press, 1971).

[259]"The Baptist Faith and Message," in *The Fibers of Our Faith*, ed. Rader, 68-73.

Herschel Harold Hobbs

The chief architect of the 1963 Baptist Faith and Message Statement was himself an influential writing theologian. Born in Coosa County, Alabama, Herschel Hobbs sustained the loss by death of his father at age two and professed faith in Christ at eleven. After he worked as a boy on the family farm, he, his mother, and his siblings moved to Birmingham in 1920. The newly married Hobbs, while working for an automobile dealership, committed himself to the pastoral ministry. He and his wife completed degrees at Howard College (now Samford University) by 1932, and then he earned Th.M. and Ph.D. degrees at Southern Baptist Theological Seminary with a dissertation on "Does the Author of the Fourth Gospel Consciously Supplement the Synoptic Gospels?" Following brief pastorates in Birmingham and Montgomery, Hobbs served as pastor of Emmanuel Church, Alexandria, Louisiana (1941–1944), Dauphin Way Church, Mobile, Alabama (1944–1949), and First Church, Oklahoma City (1949–1972). He was the president of the SBC (1961–1963), the preacher for the radio program "The Baptist Hour" (1958–1976), the writer of *Studying Adult Life and Work Lessons* each quarter for Southern Baptist Sunday School teachers (1968–1993). He was the author of numerous biblical, chiefly New Testament, commentaries, and his total number of books authored has been reported as 147. Hence his was a shaping influence on both the pastors and members of Southern Baptist churches.[260]

Being both exegete and theologian, Hobbs as a systematic theologian was thoroughly biblical.[261] His high view of the Scriptures and a relatively limited role for confessions of faith[262] helped to retain his biblical orientation. But his embrace of Mullins's emphasis on Christian experience as con-

---

[260]Hobbs, *My Faith and Message: An Autobiography* (Nashville: Broadman & Holman, 1993); David S. Dockery, "Herschel H. Hobbs," in *Theologians of the Baptist Tradition*, 217-20; repr. as "The Life and Legacy of Herschel H. Hobbs (1907–1995)," *Southern Baptist Journal of Theology* 7 (Spring 2003): 62-78; Kathy Palen, "Biographical Sketch of Herschel H. and Frances J. Hobbs," in *The Fibers of Our Faith*, ed. Rader, 215-19; *Who's Who in America*, 40th ed. (1978–1979) 1:1512-13; *Who's Who in Religion*, 4th ed. (1992–1993) 232.

[261]Dockery, "Herschel H. Hobbs," 223, 230, 358, has called him "a thoroughgoing biblicist."

[262]*The Baptist Faith and Message*, 11-16. Southern Baptists, he declared, "have a living faith rather than a creedal one." For a critique, see Garrett, *Systematic Theology*, 1st ed., 1:5; 2nd ed., 1:3, and Dockery, "Herschel H. Hobbs," 221-22.

firmatory[263] qualified the singular authority of the Scriptures. In his study of Hobbs's theological method Albert P. Hopkins, Jr. found it to be "basically exegetical" and that Hobbs used a "grammatical historical" hermeneutic, "supplemented by a contextual and theological analysis," with tradition, experience, and reason playing subordinate but "supportive" roles.[264] Hobbs clearly affirmed the inspiration, the historicity, the truthfulness, the providential survival, and the authority of the Bible.[265] He also differentiated and affirmed revelation, inspiration, and illumination.[266] Although Hobbs defined certain theories of biblical inspiration,[267] he did not clearly espouse one, not being able to decide between the verbal and the dynamic. Hobbs early stressed that the Bible's authority is as "a book of religion."[268] Later, during the SBC inerrancy controversy, he was more explicit that biblical inerrancy extends to the scientific realm.[269]

Hobbs followed Mullins in differentiating and delineating natural and moral attributes of God[270] but was more explicit than Mullins in holding strictly to the particular rather than to the universal fatherhood of God.[271] God's will is "intentional, circumstantial, and ultimate," and God is sovereign and has foreknowledge that "leaves man free and responsible in his choice."[272] "In the Old Testament God the Father is on stage. . . . In the Gospels God the Son is on stage. . . . Thereafter, God the Holy Spirit is on

---

[263]*Fundamentals of Our Faith* (Nashville: Broadman, 1960) 12-13.

[264]"An Analysis of the Theological Method of Herschel H. Hobbs and His Doctrines of Christ and Salvation" (Ph.D. diss., New Orleans Baptist Theological Seminary, 1994) 59-63, 158-59, 164.

[265]*Fundamentals of Our Faith*, 1-12.

[266]*What Baptists Believe* (Nashville: Broadman, 1964) 61-65.

[267]*Fundamentals of Our Faith*, 2; *What Baptists Believe*, 64; *The Baptist Faith and Message*, 21-22; "People of the Book: The Baptist Doctrine of the Holy Scripture," in *Baptist Why and Why Not Revisited*, ed. Timothy George and Richard D. Land, Library of Baptist Classics 12 (Nashville: Broadman & Holman, 1997) 15-16. According to Dockery, "Herschel H. Hobbs," 388n.26, Hobbs confused the dictation and the plenary-verbal theories.

[268]*Fundamentals of Our Faith*, 6-7.

[269]"People of the Book," 18-21.

[270]*Fundamentals of Our Faith*, 31-35; *What Baptists Believe*, 14; *The Baptist Faith and Message*, 36-37.

[271]*Fundamentals of Our Faith*, 35-37; *What Baptists Believe*, 17-18; *The Baptist Faith and Message*, 38-39.

[272]*What Baptists Believe*, 24, 16-17, 24-26.

stage. . . . All three Persons are present at all times. . . ."[273] Hobbs's Christology was basically an expositional tracing of Jesus' holy history from preexistence to second coming with some attention to titles[274] but only rarely a treatment of the divine and human natures.[275] In his first treatment of the neglected Holy Spirit Hobbs examined both testaments and affirmed both the personality and the deity of the Spirit but majored on the post-Pentecost workings by the Spirit.[276] In the second his focus was entirely on the so-called extraordinary spiritual gifts, some of which (tongues-speaking, interpretation of tongues, healing, prophecy) have ceased to be given and others of which (discerning of spirits, miracles) seem to persist.[277] Finally Hobbs returned in a monograph to the first approach but with a chapter on the gifts.[278]

Concerning creation Hobbs declared, "Science is concerned with the *what*; the Bible is concerned with the *Who*." Rejecting both Archbishop Ussher's dating of 2004 BC and the gap theory applied to Gen. 1:1-2, he allowed for the "days" of Genesis 1 to refer to "indefinite periods of time" and reckoned the purpose of Moses to be essentially theological, inasmuch as the Israelites ought to worship the Creator rather than, as did the Egyptians, everything in nature.[279] Hobbs followed Mullins in interpreting the *imago Dei* in terms of a cluster of capacities but put more stress on "the free will of man," defined as "freedom to act within the context of his own will and judgment." With that freedom came the power of choice, which issued in sin.[280] Allowing for fallen angels and Satan, the Oklahoma pastor spelled out the universality of sin and its resulting in death—physical, spiritual, and eternal—but he had no interest in theories of imputation.[281]

---

[273]Ibid., 15; compare *Fundamentals of Our Faith*, 30-31. Dockery, "Herschel H. Hobbs," 224, found Hobbs to be "unhesitatingly Trinitarian," but his explanation tending toward modalism.

[274]*Fundamentals of Our Faith*, 38-50; *What Baptists Believe*, 28-49; *The Baptist Faith and Message*, 39-44; *Who Is This?* (Nashville: Broadman, 1952).

[275]*What Baptists Believe*, 34-37; Hopkins, "An Analysis of the Theological Method," 64-117.

[276]*Fundamentals of Our Faith*, 51-63.

[277]*What Baptists Believe*, 50-60.

[278]*The Holy Spirit: Believer's Guide* (Nashville: Broadman, 1967) esp. 123-44.

[279]*Fundamentals of Our Faith*, 14-24; *The Origin of All Things: Studies in Genesis* (Waco TX: Word, 1975) 9-22, esp. 10.

[280]*What Baptists Believe*, 66-69.

[281]*Fundamentals of Our Faith*, 64-76; *What Baptists Believe*, 68-70. According

Hobbs reviewed the several theories of the atonement, concluding that they "are the result of building a system of thought about one biblical truth while ignoring all others." He wrote favorably of substitution but interpreted Jesus' death chiefly as an offering in which Jesus was both priest and sacrifice.[282] Soteriologically located, election is not God's choice from eternity of certain particular human individuals to be saved and the choice of others for damnation but rather "a plan of salvation" by grace "for all men" and a calling of a people for salvation and service, in which all who truly believe are elected. "God knew beforehand who would accept or reject his overture of grace."[283] Thus Hobbs was Arminian on election.[284] Salvation, for Hobbs, has three phases whether expressed as the three phases of salvation or of sanctification[285] or as regeneration, sanctification, and glorification.[286] According to Hobbs, "the priesthood of all believers" belongs under the doctrine of man[287] or the doctrine of salvation,[288] not under the doctrine of the church. It is both a privilege and a responsibility, but in his 1990 monograph on this subject Hobbs referred to "the priesthood of the believer," joined it with soul competency and direct access to God, and sought to utilize it as the touchstone for Baptist distinctives.[289] The Oklahoma City pastor held to the doctrine of perseverance[290] and hence could be reckoned a one-point Dortian Calvinist.[291]

---

to Dockery, "Herschel H. Hobbs," 226, Hobbs did not believe in total depravity.

[282]*Fundamentals of Our Faith*, 77-88, esp. 80; *What Baptists Believe*, 41-42.

[283]*Fundamentals of Our Faith*, 89-100, esp. 94; *What Baptists Believe*, 106-107.

[284]Basden, "Theologies of Predestination," 251-69, esp. 268; also Basden, "Predestination," in *Has Our Theology Changed? Southern Baptist Thought since 1845*, ed. Basden (Nashville: Broadman & Holman, 1994) 59-62.

[285]*Fundamentals of Our Faith*, 101-12, esp. 102-103, 108-109; *New Testament Evangelism: The Eternal Purpose* (Nashville: Convention Press, 1960) 106-23.

[286]*What Baptists Believe*, 93-106; *The Baptist Faith and Message*, 60-63.

[287]*What Baptists Believe*, 71-72.

[288]*Fundamentals of Our Faith*, 110-11.

[289]*You Are Chosen: The Priesthood of All Believers* (San Francisco: Harper & Row, 1990).

[290]*Fundamentals of Our Faith*, 106-7; *What Baptists Believe*, 103-104; *The Baptist Faith and Message*, 68-71.

[291]Clark R. Youngblood, "Perseverance and Apostasy," in *Has Our Theology Changed?*, ed. Basden, 128-32; Mark Coppenger, "Herschel Hobbs," in *Baptist Theologians*, ed. George and Dockery, 444.

In his doctrine of the church Hobbs recognized both general and local uses of *ekklēsia* in the New Testament and the images of "building," "temple," "body," and "bride." The "rock" of Matt. 16:18 he understood as Jesus himself. "Elder," "bishop," and "pastor" "refer to the same office," and the local church should have "democratic" polity and be missionary in function. The local church is "an earthly colony" of the kingdom of God, and "the church, general and local," is "that phase of God's kingdom charged with the extension of God's rule in men's hearts."[292] Civil government is divinely ordained, Christian citizenship is an obligation, and separation of church and state and religious liberty are to be maintained.[293] Baptism and the Lord's Supper, for Hobbs, were "ordinances," not sacraments. As his Baptist forebears, he made the case for believer's baptism and for immersion, but he was unclear on the Landmark issue of "alien immersion." The Lord's Supper is a symbolic memorial of Jesus' death, and participation therein is for those properly baptized.[294] Stewardship is giving to God the "prior claim" God has on the steward, and tithing is to be enjoined and practiced.[295] According to David S. Dockery, Hobbs "de-emphasized the corporate aspect of the church and worship," and his "doctrine of the Southern Baptist Convention" was "more fully developed" than his doctrine "of the local or universal church."[296]

In Hobbs's first treatment of last things he dealt with death, the intermediate state, one eschatological resurrection, the second coming, judgment, the eschatological kingdom, heaven and hell.[297] The second contained a separate discussion of millennium.[298] According to Dockery, Hobbs shifted from an earlier premillennialism to what Hobbs "viewed as an exe-

---

[292]*Fundamentals of Our Faith*, 125-35; *What Baptists Believe*, 74-89; *The Baptist Faith and Message*, 75-82. Hobbs's argument as to why Southern Baptist churches could not join the World Council of Churches or the National Council of Churches, namely, because membership in the latter was solely by denominational bodies, would have invalidated Southern Baptist participation in the Baptist World Alliance. *Fundamentals of Our Faith*, 133; *What Baptists Believe*, 81.

[293]*What Baptists Believe*, 119-25.

[294]*Fundamentals of Our Faith*, 113-24; *What Baptists Believe*, 82-85; *The Baptist Faith and Message*, 84-91.

[295]*The Gospel of Giving* (Nashville: Broadman, 1954) 11, 12-24.

[296]"Herschel H. Hobbs," 228-29.

[297]*Fundamentals of Our Faith*, 136-61.

[298]*What Baptists Believe*, 108-18, esp. 112-13.

getically informed amillennialism,"[299] not unlike the position of McDowell and Summers.[300]

Hobbs was the foremost exponent of the Mullins heritage during the last half of the twentieth century.[301] His first priority "was devotion to the teaching of Scripture."[302] He sought "to interpret scholars and theologians to pastors and laity and . . . to interpret pastors and laity to the theologians and scholars." A "centrist" and builder of consensus among Southern Baptists, he reckoned the 1963 Baptist Faith and Message Statement to be his greatest service to them. Commending Hobbs for his Christology, soteriology, and eschatology, Dockery has found in Hobbs an "overemphasis on individual experience" and underemphasis on "doctrinal confessions."[303]

---

[299]"Herschel H. Hobbs," 229; also Hobbs, *The Cosmic Drama: An Exposition of the Book of Revelation* (Waco TX: Word, 1971) 181-90; Malcolm O'Neal Hester, "Millennialism in Southern Baptist Thought since 1900" (Ph.D. diss., Southern Baptist Theological Seminary, 1981) 90-96. See also a monograph by a member of First Church, Oklahoma City: Jesse Wilson Hodges, *Christ's Kingdom and Coming: With an Analysis of Dispensationalism* (Grand Rapids MI: Eerdmans, 1957).

[300]Summers and Hobbs combined the preterist and the philosophy-of-history methods of interpreting the book of Revelation. James T. Spivey, "The Millennium," in *Has Our Theology Changed?*, ed. Basden, 233. Other Southern Baptist amillennialists included Russell Bradley Jones (1894–1986), chairman of the Department of Bible and religious education, Carson-Newman College, Jefferson City TN, and author of *The Things Which Shall Be Hereafter* (Nashville: Broadman, 1947); *What, Where, and When Is the Millennium?* (Grand Rapids MI: Baker, 1975), and *The Great Tribulation* (Grand Rapids MI: Baker, 1980) and Ray Frank Robbins (1915–2003), professor of New Testament in New Orleans Baptist Theological Seminary and author of *The Revelation of Jesus Christ* (Nashville: Broadman, 1975) and of "Apocalyptic" in George R. Beasley-Murray, Herschel H. Hobbs, and Robbins, *Revelation: Three Viewpoints* (Nashville: Broadman, 1977) 145-222. Jones stressed a spiritual hermeneutic and Robbins held that the book of Revelation "combines the apocalyptic view and the prophetic view" and that the binding of Satan for a thousand years will be "simultaneous with" the "time, times and half a time" (Rev. 12:14) and the "short time" of freedom (Rev. 20:3). Hester, "Millennialism in Southern Baptist Thought since 1900," 79-81, 87, 89-90.

[301]Note especially Hobbs and Mullins, *The Axioms of Religion*, rev. ed. (Nashville: Broadman, 1978).

[302]Coppenger, "Herschel Hobbs," 446.

[303]Dockery, "Herschel H. Hobbs," 229-31; also Hobbs, *My Faith and Message*, 246; and Raymond Evans Carroll, "Dimension of Individualism in Southern Baptist

Baptist Ideals

On the initiative of the SBC president, Caspar Carl Warren (1896–1973), Baptist conventions in the United States and Canada were encouraged as early as 1955 to work together to celebrate the "Third Jubilee" or 150th anniversary of the Triennial Convention (1964) through cooperative efforts between 1959 and 1963 and by means of a joint celebration in 1964,[304] which would occur in Atlantic City, New Jersey. Under the editorship of Davis Collier Woolley (1908–1971), executive secretary of the SBC's Historical Commission, the Baptist Joint Committee on Jubilee Advance produced a volume of nineteen historical essays relative to Baptists in North America.[305] Composed by a seventeen-member committee chaired by Ralph Alderman Herring (1901–1972),[306] the SBC's Jubilee Advance Committee issued in 1963 a booklet entitled *Baptist Ideals*.[307] It affirmed authority (the Lordship of Christ, the Scriptures, the Holy Spirit), the individual (his worth, competence, and freedom), the Christian life (salvation by grace, discipleship, "the priesthood of the believer," family life, citizenship), the church (its nature, membership, ordinances, polity, relation to government, relation to the world), and "our continuing task" (centrality of the individual, worship, pastoral ministry, evangelism, missions, stewardship, teaching and training, Christian higher education, self-criticism).[308]

Thought" (Th.D. diss., New Orleans Baptist Theological Seminary, 1995; Ann Arbor MI: University Microfilms International, 2002) 133-48.

[304]*SBC, Annual*, 1955, 52-53; 1956, 40-41; SBC, *Book of Reports*, 1964, 174-77. Warren, pastor of First Church, Charlotte NC, while SBC president "challenges the Convention to establish 30,000 preaching points by 1964" and "became director of the resulting '30,000 Movement.' " Mary Warren Poe and Sibyl B. Warren, "Warren, Casper Carl," *Encyclopedia of Southern Baptists* 4:2538-39.

[305]*Baptist Advance: The Achievements of the Baptists of North America for a Century and a Half* (Nashville: Broadman, 1964). On Woolley, see Lynn E. May, Jr., "Woolley, David Collier," *Encyclopedia of Southern Baptists* 3:2060-61.

[306]A graduate of Wake Forest College (B.A., 1921) and Southern Baptist Theological Seminary (Th.M., 1925; Th.D., 1929) and former pastor of First Church, Winston-Salem, NC (1936–1961), Herring was director of the Seminary Extension Department of the SBC seminaries. "Herring, Ralph Alderman," *Encyclopedia of Southern Baptists* 4:2264-65.

[307]SBC, *Book of Reports*, 1964, 175.

[308]*Baptist Ideals* (Nashville: Sunday School Board of the SBC, 1963).

Doctrinal Texts for Students and Dismissals of Professors

During the twentieth century several Southern Baptist authors produced doctrinal summaries for classroom usage, especially in Baptist colleges and universities. Josiah Blake Tidwell (1870–1946), professor of Bible in Baylor University, published an extended outline of Christian doctrines. Biblical inspiration is better judged by its results than by theories as to its method, providence is "God's wise and benevolent care of all things," the baptism of the Holy Spirit occurred once-for-all at Pentecost, election of particular human beings was affirmed without reference to the nonelect, Zwingli's view of the Lord's Supper was said to be true, giving/tithing is a doctrine, one eschatological resurrection and one final judgment were affirmed, and premillennialism and postmillennialism were found to make the millennium central instead of the second coming.[309]

William Wilson Stevens (1914–1978), professor of religion in Mississippi College, issued a textbook in the tradition of Mullins and Conner but with his own distinctives. He began with revelation and favored the dynamical theory of biblical inspiration. Jesus' preexistence was real, not ideal, and his sinlessness was placed under his humanity. The tongues of Corinth greatly differed from tongues-speaking on the day of Pentecost. Stevens was explicit as to the ontological and eternal Trinity. Humans should be viewed holistically, and their souls were derived from their parents. The image means that we are spiritual beings having dominion "over the lower orders," our "spiritual tendency" is both "inherited" and "universal," and our depravity is total. The atonement, being general, involves expiation, substitution, and subjection to the law of sin and death. Jesus' resurrection and intercession were fully treated. Election is not based on God's foreknowledge of human faith or works, is for service, and does not prescribe nonelection to damnation. Repentance and faith are human responses, and the mission is said to be that of the Christian rather than of the church. Stevens defended congregational polity but did not find church succession necessary to the proper administration of baptism. Unique among Baptist authors by having a separate chapter on "the covenant," Stevens followed Moody rather than Stagg in positing an intermediate state

---

[309]*Christian Teachings* (Grand Rapids MI: Eerdmans, 1942) 22-24, 33, 43-44, 51-54, 75, 81-87, 105-10, 101-103.

and drew no clear conclusion as to the millennium, although enamored with Strong's effort to combine premillennial and postmillennial views.[310]

Reflecting the changing cultural situation of the 1960s, Dallas M. Roark (1931–), associate professor of philosophy at Kansas State Teachers College, Emporia, Kansas, introduced his book with chapters on the theistic arguments and on Christianity vis-à-vis non-Christian religions, the latter addressing the uniqueness of Christ and the exclusivity of the gospel. He repeatedly quoted from or cited twentieth-century Protestant theologians such as Emil Brunner, Karl Barth, Paul Tillich, and Reinhold Niebuhr. Revelation was treated with the quest for authority as Roark's examination of the Inner Light, conscience, religious experience, reason, the church, and the Bible led to a cluster of authorities with Christ as the apex. The Bible is infallible as the "guide to lead us to salvation in Christ," and its modern translations are as trustworthy as the nonextant autographs. The Trinity, chief alternatives to which are Unitarianism or "vague pantheism," is basic to other doctrines. Roark, keenly sensitive to the errors of the patristic age but unwilling to embrace kenoticism, sought to explicate the two natures and their union. He differentiated valid divine healing and dubious faith healing and was not sure but that tongues at Corinth were languages. All believers have already been baptized of the Holy Spirit but need repeatedly to be filled by the Spirit. Unlike the historic theories of the atonement, Roark interpreted the life and death of Jesus as the "establishment of the new covenant." Genesis 1–3 was denominated "myth" so that it can become "the story of everyman," the six days of Genesis 1 are the "six twenty-four days in which ... in man's history God told the story of creation to man,"[311] and Adam was both generic mankind and "an individual historical man." The Kansas professor offered an extensive critique of the "faith" of evolution, identified the *imago Dei* as human accountability, and could not decide between creationism and traducianism. Roark followed Reinhold Niebuhr in identifying pride as the cause or the nature of the first sin, then opted for the coming of guilt with the age of accountability. He limited the unpardonable sin to the attribution to Satan of Jesus' exorcisms, which was

---

[310]*Doctrines of the Christian Religion* (Nashville: Broadman, 1967), 13-33, 77-78, 74, 110-11, 119-20, 134-38, 140-42, 151-53, 156-57, 191-92, 202-203, 184-88, 192-99, 206-11, 219-29, 269-72, 305-308, 337, 351-70, 376-80, 381-85.

[311]As taught by Percy John Wiseman, *Creation Revealed in Six Days: The Evidence of Scripture Confirmed by Archaeology* (London: Marshall, Morgan and Scott, 1948).

manifestly the work of the Holy Spirit. Asserting that the church is "not an institution but a fellowship,"[312] Roark offered a Protestant interpretation of the classic marks of the church: one, holy, catholic, and apostolic, and sought to revalidate congregational polity from the New Testament. His treatment of baptism was in dialogue with Karl Barth and Oscar Cullmann, and he bypassed the issue of immersion. He was typically American Protestant in dealing with eschatology in that he allowed the millennium to set the agenda, and he opted for inaugurated eschatology, which is amillennial and correlates with his meanings of the kingdom of God.[313]

Fisher Henry Humphreys (1939–), assistant professor of theology in New Orleans Baptist Theological Seminary, authored a readable introduction. He sought to reconcile the qualified understanding of biblical inerrancy held by some of its advocates and the errancy view that wrestles with specific difficulties. God "is both personal and transcendent," and man's origin does not establish his value or meaning; this is "the genetic fallacy." Rather man's significance derives from the *imago Dei*, which means being personal. Humphreys showed respect for Chalcedonian Christology, but as to the death of Christ he pursued the concept of its achieving costly forgiveness, not quantitatively but qualitatively, together with Jesus' defeat of the powers of darkness. The "most fundamental work of the Spirit is to testify to Jesus." Salvation is in three tenses, and Humphreys favored as the model for the Christian life loving gratitude to Christ the Savior. Baptism and the Lord's Supper were irenically interpreted, and the Christian hope was expressed in terms of resurrection, second coming, and heaven.[314]

Designed more for the lay readership than for students was a doctrinal introduction by Jimmy Allen Millikin (1936–), professor of biblical interpretation in Mid-America Baptist Theological Seminary, Memphis, Tennessee. Affirming the inspiration and inerrancy of the Bible, he made

---

[312]As emphasized by Emil Brunner, *The Misunderstanding of the Church*, trans. Harold Knight (London: Lutterworth, 1952) esp. 9-18, 47-54, 74-75.

[313]*The Christian Faith* (Nashville: Broadman, 1969); repr. with subtitle: *An Introduction to Christian Thought* (Grand Rapids MI: Baker, 1977) 1-75 (esp. 66), 112-13, 114-32, 138-43, 147-73, 177-80, 182-92, 195-97, 198-201, 206-209, 219-21, 252-55, 260-67, 275-78, 289-98, 310-21.

[314]*Thinking about God: An Introduction to Christian Theology* (New Orleans: Insight, 1974) 39-47, 63, 73-79, 99-102, 114-21, 126, 129, 159-65, 189-97, 202-16; rev. ed. (New Orleans: Insight, 1994).

holiness the central divine attribute, included the resurrection and ascension in Christ's redemptive work, and interpreted the baptism with the Spirit as happening "to all believers at conversion." Millikin affirmed a historical fall and total depravity, but the question of imputation of Adamic guilt was left unaddressed. He held to particular election and perseverance of all true believers but reckoned repentance and faith as essentially human responses. He offered no doctrine of the universal church but was silent on Landmark views of the ordinances, and he espoused premillennialism.[315]

Jesse Morris Ashcraft (1922–), professor of theology at Southern, Midwestern, and Southeastern Baptist seminaries, produced a monograph written in dialogue with European Protestant theologians and a sole Baptist, Dale Moody. Organized in five parts (belief in God, belief in creation, unbelief and God, belief in reconciliation, belief in the new creation), the book was entitled *Christian Faith and Beliefs*[316] so as to emphasize the difference between believing and doctrines. Ashcraft began, following his prolegomena, with Christology and held together the historical Jesus and the Christ of faith, the deity and the humanity, and Christ as contemporary and as final. Then followed the doctrine of revelation, natural and historical. Ashcraft, not willing to "reduce the question of authority" to a particular theory of inspiration, nevertheless wanted a theory that is centered in Christ, included the role of the Spirit, and embraced the contemporary hearing of the Word of God through the reading of the Scriptures. The Holy Spirit is the agent of regeneration, conviction, freedom, assurance, companionship, and fellowship. Holiness and love, for Ashcraft, are predominating attributes, and, although the doctrine of the Trinity is not "explicitly stated in the New Testament," the doctrine "is necessary and embraceable." Creation and human creatureliness were theologically espoused without interaction with evolution, and the *imago Dei* was identified both as dominion and responsibility. Ashcraft celebrated the freedom that accompanies human responsibility, favored a holistic view of the human, and rejected any female subordination. Bypassing the theories as to the fall and original sin, he offered a more existentialist understanding of sin. Ashcraft rejected the penal substitutionary theory of the atonement, denying that payment and the wrath of God are involved, and advocated the sacrificial

---

[315]*Christian Doctrine for Everyman: An Introduction to Baptist Beliefs* (Greensboro NC: Gateway Publications, 1976) 16-17, 24-29, 38-39, 50-51, 58-59, 67-68, 71-73, 68-70, 84-90, 105-106.

[316](Nashville: Broadman, 1984).

theory, which takes Jesus' death as "on behalf of" but not "instead of" humanity and reckons his sacrifice not as being "to God" but as one that draws us by faith existentially into itself. Reconciliation is the single overarching soteriological term for Ashcraft, and it tends to be conflated with forgiveness. The unity of the church and its reconciling ministry were emphasized, and the ecclesiologically based priesthood of all believers involves both access to God and service for others. The Christian life is the new creation, marked by freedom, discipleship, sanctification, assurance, and perseverance. Eschatology is the expression of Christian hope with focus on all particulars except millennium.[317]

Probably the fullest treatment of atonement or the cross by a Baptist author during the twentieth century was James E. Tull's *The Atoning Gospel*. Tull explicated the relationships of Jesus' death-resurrection to God's grace, God's judgment, justification, reconciliation, sanctification, and the church. Christ is clearly Suffering Servant, High Priest, and Risen Lord. But as to the essence of the atonement Tull wrote favorably of ransom victory over sin, death, and demons, of representation as the Second Adam, and of self-emptying love, but critically of penal substitution, propitiation as placating an angry God, the Son's endurance of the displeasure of the Father, and language of a commercial transaction.[318]

Later in the century Southern Baptist theologians wrote on eschatology without focusing on the millennium. William Boyd Hunt (1916–2007), distinguished professor of theology, emeritus, Southwestern Baptist Theological Seminary, in a volume that covered the "second half" of systematic theology explicated the kingdom of God both as present reality and as eschatological consummation. The Holy Spirit "applies redemption by effecting the kingdom present," spiritual gifts empower God's people "for kingdom life and service," the Christian life "as God's doing" is "an eschatological existence," and the church is "the sign and agent of the kingdom present." Hunt developed the major eschatological rubrics from an amillennial per-

---

[317]Ibid., 13-89 (esp. 87, 84), 94-101, 109-13, 113-17 (esp. 113, 116), 126-31, 136-39, 144-48, 149-56, 158-60, 156-57, 201-202, 170-93, 222-29, 233-36, 240-62, 236-37, 271-74, 295-97, 278-80, 306-19, 323-47. Ashcraft was the author of *Rudolf Bultmann*, Makers of the Modern Theological Mind (Waco TX: Word, 1972); *The Forgiveness of Sins* (Nashville: Broadman, 1972); *The Will of God* (Nashville: Broadman, 1980); and *The Christian Hope* (Nashville: Broadman, 1988) and editor of *Medieval Christianity*, Christian Classics (Nashville: Broadman, 1981).

[318](Macon GA: Mercer University Press, 1982) esp. 116, 129-30, 156.

spective.[319] Abda Johnson Conyers III (1944–2005), professor of theology in the George W. Truett Theological Seminary of Baylor University,[320] first published a revision of his dissertation on Jürgen Moltmann's concept of history in dialogue with Moltmann himself.[321] Then, recognizing and announcing that the modern church has lost its grip on heaven—"an essential resistance . . . to that which is at the very heart of its message"—and noting the great difference between religion as "obsession" and religion as "passion," Conyers pointed the way to the recovery of transcendence and of heaven.[322] Finally, Conyers issued a theological interpretation of Jesus' Olivet discourse (Mark 13) so that its "directness and practicality" may be recovered after having been preempted by kingdom of God or millennial systems.[323]

During the 1960s, in addition to the twelve 1959 Southern Baptist Theological Seminary professorial dismissals and the termination of Elliott at Midwestern, other Southern Baptist seminary professors were dismissed or caused to resign from their teaching posts for theological reasons. Theodore Roscoe Clark (1912–1999) associate professor of theology in New Orleans Baptist Theological Seminary, was terminated in 1960 by the

---

[319]*Redeemed! Eschatological Redemption and the Kingdom of God* (Nashville: Broadman & Holman, 1993) 73-125, 240, 39, 48, 152-53, 170-78, 241-363. A native of Creston IA, and a graduate of Wheaton College (B.A., 1939) and Southwestern Baptist Theological Seminary (Th.M., 1942; Th.D., 1945), Hunt was pastor of First Church, Houston TX (1946–1952) and taught at Southwestern during 1944–1946 and 1953–1987. Curriculum Vitae, Roberts Library Archives, Southwestern Baptist Theological Seminary.

[320]A native of San Bernardino CA, who was reared in Georgia, Conyers was a graduate of the University of Georgia (B.A., 1966) and Southern Baptist Theological Seminary (M.Div., 1971; Ph.D., 1979) and was professor of Bible, Central Missouri State University, Warrensburg (1979–1987) and professor of religion and department chairman at Charleston (SC) Southern University (1987–1994). Curriculum Vitae, Truett Theological Seminary.

[321]*God, Hope, and History: Jürgen Moltmann and the Christian Concept of History* (Macon GA: Mercer University Press, 1988).

[322]*The Eclipse of Heaven: Rediscovering the Hope of a World Beyond* (Downers Grove IL: InterVarsity, 1992) esp. 31, 121-38, 167-82; 2nd ed. (South Bend IN: St. Augustine's Press, 1999).

[323]*The End: What Jesus Really Said about the Last Things* (Downers Grove IL: InterVarsity, 1995) esp. 7-8. Conyers also authored *A Basic Christian Theology* (Nashville: Broadman & Holman, 1995).

seminary because of his book, *Saved by His Life*.[324] Taking as his purpose the legitimate goal of elevating the significance of the doctrine of the resurrection of Jesus and integrating it with his death,[325] Clark, under the influence of Paul Tillich, proceeded to reject penal substitution, to reckon the doctrine of the infallibility of the Bible as "a form of idolatry," to refuse to identify "the Living Christ-Word-Spirit" with Jesus of Nazareth, and to deplore the neglect of "the reconciling and saving role of the Church."[326] In 1965 three professors of New Testament in Southeastern Baptist Theological Seminary, Robert Cook Briggs (1915–), Harold Hunter Oliver (1930–), and William Claudius Strickland (1917–2004), after five years of controversy under pressure from the trustees resigned, for they were perceived to have "embraced the methods and conclusions of Rudolf Karl Bultmann's (1884–1976) approach to the New Testament."[327]

Wallie Amos Criswell (1909–2002)

Besides Hobbs, another pastor-theologian had a major impact on Southern Baptists during the last half of the twentieth century. W. A. Criswell, a native of Oklahoma who was reared on the Texas-New Mexico border and in Amarillo, Texas, was converted and baptized at nine and licensed for ministry at seventeen before high school graduation. At Baylor University (B.A.) he majored in English, held three student pastorates, and became known as a preacher, and at Southern Baptist Theological Seminary he completed Th.M. and Ph.D. degrees, the latter involving a dissertation on "The John the Baptist Movement in Its Relation to the Christian Move-

---

[324]Subtitle: *A Study of the New Testament Doctrine of Reconciliation and Salvation* (New York: Macmillan Co., 1959).

[325]Clark, *Saved by His Life*, 40, 45, 48, 71, 72, 77-78, 152-53; quoted or cited for support: Beasley-Murray, *Christ Is Alive!* and Conner, *The Cross in the New Testament*.

[326]*Saved by His Life*, xi, xii, 47, 125, 142-43, 168. See Willis, "Progressive Theology," 21, 23.

[327]Willis, "Progressive Theology," 22; J. Marse Grant, "Intra-Faculty Squabble Disappointing to SE Friends," *Biblical Recorder*, 9 January 1965, 3, 5; "3 Professors Resign at SE: Briggs, Oliver, Coker," *Biblical Recorder*, 9 January 1965, 4; Chauncey R. Daley, "The SE Seminary Story as Seen by Former Trustee," *Biblical Recorder*, 30 January 1965, 18-19; Thomas A. Bland, "In the Beginning," in *Servant Songs: Reflections on the History and Mission of Southeastern Baptist Theological Seminary, 1950–1988*, ed. Bland (Macon GA: Smyth & Helwys, 1994) 25-27; Donald E. Cook, " 'Our Message Be the Gospel Plain,' " in ibid., 115-16.

ment." After pastorates of First Church, Chickasha, Oklahoma (1937–1941) and of First Church, Muskogee, Oklahoma (1941–1944), he succeeded the well-known and highly respected George Washington Truett as pastor of First Church, Dallas, Texas. An expository preacher of the book-by-book type, Criswell spent seventeen and one-half years preaching through the entire Bible. He served as president of the Southern Baptist Convention (1969–1970), founded a Bible college and a radio station, and was a major shaper of the Southern Baptist "conservative resurgence" at the end of the twentieth century. Most of his fifty-two books consist of sermons preached to First Church, Dallas.[328]

The theology of Criswell, as Paige Patterson has aptly noted, was "pastoral," exegetical, and indeed homiletical. Not "the theology of the cloister—written, contemplated, and rewritten," Criswell's theology was hammered out through his weekly expository preaching to his large congregation and television audience. It followed "the paradigm of John Chrysostom, C. H. Spurgeon, G. Campbell Morgan, and Donald Gray Barnhouse."[329]

First in importance is Criswell's doctrine of the Bible. Revelation "refers to the content" of what God has unveiled. It is progressive, purposive, and congruous.[330] Normally Criswell spoke of the revelation recorded in the Bible, but occasionally he affirmed God's revelation

---

[328]Criswell, *Standing on the Promises: The Autobiography of W. A. Criswell* (Dallas: Word, 1990); Billy Keith, *W. A. Criswell: The Authorized Biography* (Old Tappan NJ: Fleming H. Revell, 1973); Robert A. Rohm, *Dr. C* (Chicago: Moody Press, 1990); *Oral Memoirs of W. A. Criswell*, interviewed by Thomas L. Charlton and Rufus B. Spain (Waco TX: Baylor University Program for Oral History, 1973); Leon McBeth, *The First Baptist Church of Dallas: Centennial History (1868–1968)* (Grand Rapids MI: Zondervan, 1968) 217-347; Paige Patterson, "The Imponderables of God," *Criswell Theological Review* 1 (Spring 1987): 237-53; repr. in *The Church at the Dawn of the 21st Century: Essays in Honor of W. A. Criswell*, ed. Paige Patterson, John Pretlove, and Luis Pantoja (Dallas: Criswell Publications, 1989) 17-33; L. Russell Bush III, "W. A. Criswell," in *Baptist Theologians*, ed. George and Dockery, 450, 452-53; Paige Patterson, "W. A. Criswell," in *Theologians of the Baptist Tradition*, ed. George and Dockery, 233-37.

[329]"W. A. Criswell," 237-38.

[330]*The Bible for Today's World* (Grand Rapids MI: Zondervan, 1965) 40-47; *Great Doctrines of the Bible*, ed. Paige Patterson, vol. 1, *Bibliology* (Grand Rapids MI: Zondervan, 1982) 94-99.

through nature, history, and conscience.[331] "Inspiration refers to the transmission of what is made known."[332] Criswell espoused what he called a *"dynamic, plenary, verbal, supernatural"* theory of inspiration, the words "plenary" and "verbal" being definitive.[333] Although he specifically rejected the mechanical dictation theory,[334] his description of his own theory almost perfectly expressed the mechanical view:

> On the original parchment every sentence, word, line, mark, point, pen stroke, jot, and tittle were put there by inspiration of God.[335]

Jesus not only utilized and expressed reverence for the Old Testament and fulfilled its Messianic prophecies[336] but also confirmed "by anticipation" (John 14:26; 16:12-13) the New Testament.[337] Old Testament prophecies were literally fulfilled, and the Bible has been confirmed by modern archaeology.[338] The Scriptures have been providentially preserved.[339] Criswell was clear and emphatic respecting the infallibility of the Scriptures.[340] His favorite biblical text was seemingly Isa. 40:8.[341]

For Criswell, atheism is folly, and God is "the first universal fact" (Gen. 1:1).[342] The Trinity, which he also called the "tripersonality of God" and the "triunity of God," was seen after the analogy of human trichotomy and

---

[331] *Great Doctrines of the Bible* 1:41-44.

[332] *The Bible for Today's World*, 41.

[333] Ibid., 49. In *Great Doctrines of the Bible* 1:101, he omitted "dynamic."

[334] *The Bible for Today's World*, 48-49; *Great Doctrines of the Bible* 1:99.

[335] *Why I Preach That the Bible Is Literally True* (Nashville: Broadman Press, 1969) 26. For a different interpretation, see Bush, "W. A. Criswell," 456-57.

[336] *Great Doctrines of the Bible* 1:83-92; *Why I Preach That the Bible Is Literally True*, 19-22.

[337] *Why I Preach That the Bible Is Literally True*, 22-24.

[338] Ibid., 30-43.

[339] *The Bible for Today's World*, 109-28; *These Issues We Must Face* (Grand Rapids MI: Zondervan, 1953) 52-61.

[340] *Why I Preach That the Bible Is Literally True*, 44-60, 95-99; *Great Doctrines of the Bible* 1:63-66.

[341] *Why I Preach That the Bible Is Literally True*, 76-80; *Great Doctrines of the Bible* 1:103-10.

[342] *Great Doctrines of the Bible*, vol. 2, *Theology Proper/Christology*, 32-39, 24-31; *Five Great Affirmations of the Bible* (Grand Rapids MI: Zondervan, 1959) 9-16; *In Defense of the Faith* (Grand Rapids MI: Zondervan, 1967) 13-23.

supported by *Elohim* as plural.[343] His Christology was within the parameters of Chalcedon, but he preached more on the deity[344] than on the humanity of Jesus.[345] The incarnation was miraculous,[346] and the virgin birth is to be defended.[347] The Dallas pastor preached on the postbiblical history of the doctrine of the Holy Spirit and emphasized the personality of the Spirit. He taught two views of the baptism by the Spirit which he never fully connected or reconciled—that it occurred once-for-all at Pentecost and all believers receive it as they are made members of the body of Christ.[348] There can and ought to be multiple or "repeated" fillings with the Spirit. Whereas the offices of apostle and prophet no longer exist, there are those with the gifts of church planting and prophecy, but "four sign gifts" are no longer given, presumably miracles, healing, tongues, and interpretation of tongues.[349]

The doctrine of creation was most fully expressed by Criswell by his refutation of Darwinian evolution. In an early sermon series in which he departed from his pattern of biblical exposition, he utilized biology, embryology, and geology in his polemic and charged that the science of anthropology had produced a series of "hoaxes."[350] As to the age of the earth he did not embrace the "young earth" theory but instead the gap theory, applied to Gen. 1:1 and 1:2, thereby accounting for "the vast ages posited by the geologists."[351] Criswell adopted the dispensationalist doctrine of Lucifer's heavenly rebellion, drawn from Isa. 14:12-20 and Ezek. 28:11-19 and his ruining of the created order to explain why a reordering or re-creation of the earth was necessary.[352] The soul is directly created by God

---

[343] *Great Doctrines of the Bible* 2:68-77.

[344] *These Issues We Must Face*, 105-13; *Five Great Affirmations of the Bible*, 17-24; *In Defense of the Faith*, 24-38; *Great Doctrines of the Bible* 2:87-96.

[345] *Great Doctrines of the Bible* 2:106-22.

[346] Ibid., 2:78-86.

[347] *These Issues We Must Face*, 73-86.

[348] Patterson, "W. A. Criswell," 248, has concluded that Criswell only taught the second view.

[349] *These Issues We Must Face*, 73-86.

[350] *Did Man Just Happen?* (Grand Rapids MI: Zondervan, 1957).

[351] Patterson, "W. A. Criswell," 244; *The Criswell Study Bible* (Nashville: Thomas Nelson, 1979) note on Gen. 1:2.

[352] Patterson, "W. A. Criswell," 244; *The Criswell Study Bible*, notes on Isa. 14:12; Ezek. 18:12; 2 Pet. 2:4; and Jude 6.

at the time of human birth.[353] Although Criswell held to the fall of man and the universality of sin, these were not the focus of Criswell's preaching.

More attention was given to the perfection of Jesus' suffering in his death, which was the means of both substitution and reconciliation and, together with his resurrection, the victory over sin, death, and Satan.[354] According to Patterson, Criswell held to a general atonement, was thus at best a four-point Dortian Calvinist, and stressed election but not reprobation.[355] Prayer,[356] sanctification, the Lord's Day, and stewardship of possessions[357] were themes preached from the Dallas pulpit.

The church is "a born-again fellowship," or congregation of believers with the Bible as its "only rule of faith and practice" and the Great Commission as its mandate. Criswell did not seek to pinpoint the time of the founding of the church by Jesus but was sure that its "endowment" by the Spirit came at Pentecost. The priesthood of all believers means unhindered access to God, the offering of spiritual sacrifices, and widespread involvement in congregational life. Criswell's baptismal teaching was clearly Baptist, the Lord's Supper was strictly a memorial, and "ordinances" were not "sacraments." He also affirmed the existence of a "modern apostate church"[358] and regarded "liberalism" and "modernism" as synonymous.[359]

Criswell's theology extended beyond his own large congregation through his writings to a vast readership of pastors and students. Although one has considered him to have been more in the train of J. Frank Norris than of George W. Truett[360] and another has emphasized how Criswell stood in the shadow of Truett,[361] his own blend of biblical authority and infallibil-

---

[353]Bush, "W. A. Criswell," 456.

[354]*Great Doctrines of the Bible* 2:123-71.

[355]Patterson, "W. A. Criswell," 247.

[356]*Great Doctrines of the Bible*, vol. 7, *Prayer, Angelology* (Grand Rapids MI: Zondervan, 1987) 11-78.

[357]Ibid., vol. 6, *Christian Life, Stewardship* (Grand Rapids MI: Zondervan, 1986) 13-20.

[358]*Great Doctrines of the Bible*, vol. 3, *Ecclesiology* (Grand Rapids MI: Zondervan, 1983) 15-23, 59-95, 115-23; *The Doctrine of the Church* (Nashville: Convention Press, 1980) 30-36, 46-47, 80-106.

[359]*These Issues We Must Face*, 41-51. For Criswell's eschatology, see below, 567-68.

[360]Rohm, *Dr. C*, 149-55.

[361]Patterson, "The Imponderables of God," 24-25.

ity, expository preaching, Baptist ecclesiology, and dispensational eschatology was distinctly Criswellian.

The Broadman Bible Commentary Controversy

For the fourth time within a century Southern Baptists engaged in controversy over the book of Genesis, this time in 1969–1970. Broadman Press had undertaken the publication of a twelve-volume biblical commentary with moderate use of historical-critical methodology under the general editorship of Clifton Judson Allen (1901–1986), former editorial secretary of the Sunday School Board. All authors were Baptists, and all but six of these were Southern Baptists.[362] The volume including the Genesis section written by Gwynne Henton Davies (1906- 1998),[363] principal of Regent's Park College, Oxford, appeared in 1969. At the 1970 SBC session in Denver, Gwin Terrell Turner (1931–) of California moved that because the new commentary "is out of keeping with the beliefs of the vast majority of Southern Baptist pastors and people this Convention request the Sunday School Board to withdraw volume 1 from further distribution and that it be rewritten with due consideration of the conservative viewpoint." The motion passed by a vote of 5,394 to 2,170.[364]

The focal point of the criticism of Davies's commentary was his treatment of the "proposed sacrifice of Isaac" (Gen. 22:1-19). At first Davies reported the possibility that this text could be taken as "a parable of [Abraham's] obedience"—"obedience unparalleled outside Gethsemane." But then, rejecting any parabolic interpretation, he took the text as "the story of something that really happened." He posited that God could not have made and hence did not make this demand of filial sacrifice. The only

---

[362]Three would be from the Baptist Union of Great Britain, two from the American Baptist Convention, and one from the Baptist Union of Scotland. Allen was a native of Latta, South Carolina, and a graduate of Furman University (B.A., 1923) and Southern Baptist Theological Seminary (Th.M., 1928; Ph.D., 1932), served as associate editorial secretary (1937–1944) and editorial secretary (1945–1968) of the SBC's Sunday School Board, and wrote *Affirmation of Our Faith* (Nashville: Broadman, 1972). *Contemporary Authors* 108:18-19.

[363]*The Broadman Bible Commentary*, vol. 1, *General Articles; Genesis, Exodus* (Nashville: Broadman Press). On Davies, see John I Durham, "Gwynne Henton Davies: A Biographical Appreciation," in *Proclamation and Presence: Old Testament Essays in Honour of Gwynne Henton Davies*, ed. Durham and J. R. Porter (Macon GA: Mercer University Press, 1983) xiii-xvii.

[364]Southern Baptist Convention, *Annual*, 1970, 63, 76, 77-78.

plausible answer, according to Davies, was that Abraham's conviction that he ought to offer Isaac was "the climax of the psychology of his life," plagued by the fear of losing his son. Then the discovered ram became "the solvent of his own mistaken conviction."[365] In July 1970 the Sunday School Board voted "to withdraw this volume from distribution" but to ask Davies to do the rewriting.[366]

In the 1971 SBC session in St. Louis, Kenneth Barnett of Oklahoma moved "that the Sunday School Board be advised that the vote of the 1970 Convention regarding the rewriting of volume 1 . . . has not been followed and that the . . . Board obtain another writer and proceed with the Commentary." Barnett's motion passed by a vote of 2,672 to 2, 298.[367] The Sunday School Board invited Clyde Taylor Francisco (1916–1981), John R. Sampey professor of Old Testament in Southern Baptist Theological Seminary, to prepare another commentary, and he did so.[368] The Sunday School Board in 1970 "established the position of a doctrinal reader," and Henry Leo Eddleman (1911–1995), former president of New Orleans Baptist Theological Seminary, became its first occupant.[369] In 1972 the title was

---

[365] *The Broadman Bible Commentary* 1:196-99.
[366] Baker, *The Southern Baptist Convention*, 416-17.
[367] Southern Baptist Convention, *Annual*, 1971, 71, 76, 80.
[368] *The Broadman Bible Commentary*, vol. 1, rev. ed.: *General Articles: Genesis, Exodus* (Nashville: Broadman, 1973). See also McBeth, *The Baptist Heritage*, 649, 680-81, who said that "Francisco's revision" used "more felicitous language" but "made only minor changes"; Fletcher, *The Southern Baptist Convention*, 237-39, who observed that the 1971 "unprecedented" action "should have clearly demonstrated the potency of the conservative bent among Southern Baptists"; Leonard, *Baptist Ways*, 414.
[369] Downs, "The Use of the 'Baptist Faith and Message,'" 134-35; "Eddleman to Fill Board's Doctrinal Reader Position," *Religious Herald*, 10 September 1970, 3; "Eddleman Joins Sunday School Board," *Baptist Standard*, 9 September 1970, 5. Born in Morgantown MS, and educated at Mississippi College (B.A., 1932) and Southern Baptist Theological Seminary (Th.M, 1935; Ph.D., 1942), Eddleman had served as a missionary of the SBC's Foreign Mission Board in the Middle East (1935–1941), pastor of Parkland Church, Louisville, Kentucky (1942–1952), teacher of Old Testament and Hebrew, Southern Seminary (1950–1954), president, Georgetown College (1954–1959), and president of New Orleans Baptist Theological Seminary (1959–1970). Later he would be president of Criswell College for Biblical Studies (1972–1975). *Contemporary Authors*, new revision series, 9:145-46.

changed to manuscript analyst,[370] and the SBC rejected by an approximate 4-1 vote Gwin Turner's motion calling for the withdrawal and rewriting of the entire *Broadman Bible Commentary* on the basis of biblical inerrancy.[371]

In addition to the *Broadman Bible Commentary*, Broadman Press published during the latter twentieth century three other series with theological significance. *Christian Classics* was a twelve-volume series of classic Christian texts from the Apostolic Fathers to the end of the nineteenth century.[372] The *Layman's Library of Christian Doctrine* was a sixteen-volume series on the basis Christian doctrines.[373] *The New American Commentary* is a yet-to-be-completed forty-five-volume commentary written with a commitment to biblical inerrancy, theological unity of the Bible, and the classical Christian tradition. Thirty-eight volumes, twenty-four on the Old Testament and fourteen on the New Testament, have been issued as of mid-2008.[374]

Adjunctive to this controversy was the publication in 1969 by Broadman Press of W. A. Criswell's *Why I Preach That the Bible Is Literally True*. Its publication by Broadman evoked not only commendation by many but sharp criticism by the Association of Baptist Professors of Religion, who alleged the book undermined the historical-critical method of interpretation. These professors and others formed the E. Y. Mullins Fellowship, put forth a candidate for the SBC presidency against Criswell, and dissolved.[375]

---

[370]"Title Changed for Doctrinal Reader," *Religious Herald*, 15 June 1972, 23. This was at the insistence of Walker N. Stockburger, pastor, Trinity Church, Norfolk VA.

[371]Southern Baptist Convention, *Annual*, 1972, 55, 71.

[372](Nashville: Broadman, 1979–1981). All editors of the twelve volumes were Baptists, and all but one were Southern Baptists. The overwhelming majority of the texts were non-Baptist in authorship.

[373](Nashville: Broadman, 1984–1988). All authors were Southern Baptists.

[374](Nashville: Broadman & Holman, 1991–). The word "new" was chosen in light of the Baptist-authored *An American Commentary*, ed. Alvah Hovey (Philadelphia: American Baptist Publication Society, 1881–1890, 1904–1939). David S. Dockery was general editor for the first six volumes of the "new" series, and E. Ray Clendenen has been general editor for the remaining volumes. The seven volumes yet to be issued will pertain to Psalms, Isaiah 40–66, 1 Corinthians, Ephesians, Hebrews, and Revelation. David S. Dockery to James Leo Garrett, Jr., 12 July 2007; E. Ray Clendenen to James Leo Garrett, Jr., 1 August 2008..

[375]Criswell, *Standing on the Promises*, 218-20; Keith, *W. A. Criswell: The*

Charismaticism

Southern Baptists were more directly influenced by the Charismatic or Neo-Pentecostal movement that occurred among mainline Protestants and Roman Catholics beginning in the 1960s than by the earlier or original Pentecostalism. Especially during the mid-1970s the practice of glossolalia, or tongues-speaking, began in certain—perhaps one hundred—Southern Baptist churches. As a result Baptist associations began to take actions.

> At least five associations in four states excluded charismatic churches from their membership, and three others adopted statements of disapproval or warning.... [T]he Dallas Baptist Association [TX] branded the movement as disruptive and the Rogers Association in Northeast Oklahoma labeled it heresy.... [In 1975] the Dallas Association proceeded to disfellowship the Beverly Hills and Shady Grove Churches.[376]

Similar exclusions occurred in Ohio, Louisiana, and Oklahoma.[377] Indicative that tongues-speaking had not become a national issue is the fact that the SBC in 1975 reaffirmed the statement on the Holy Spirit in the 1963 Baptist Faith and Message but did not "approve or condemn" glossolalia.[378] Churches sympathetic to tongues-speaking held regional meetings in Louisville, Kentucky, and West Monroe, Louisiana, and then sponsored a National Southern Baptist Charismatic Conference in Dallas in July 1976, probably the high point in the movement.[379] This development evoked books on the Holy Spirit and/or charismatic gifts by Southern Baptist authors. Previously Frank Stagg had written quite critically of tongues-speaking, sharply differentiating Acts 2:4 from 1 Corinthians 12–14,[380] whereas Dale Moody had written more sympathetically, identifying the two

---

Authorized Biography, 195-202; Fletcher, *The Southern Baptist Convention*, 237-38; Walter B. Shurden and Linda Prince, "E. Y. Mullins Fellowship," *Encyclopedia of Southern Baptists* 4:2199.

[376]Claude L. Howe, Jr., "The Charismatic Movement in Southern Baptist Life," *Baptist History and Heritage* 13 (July 1978): 26; repr. in Howe, *Glimpses of Baptist Heritage* (Nashville: Broadman Press, 1981) 129.

[377]Ibid.

[378]Southern Baptist Convention, *Annual*, 1975, 75; Downs, "The Use of the 'Baptist Faith and Message,' " 90.

[379]Howe, "The Charismatic Movement," 27; repr., 129-30.

[380]Stagg, "Glossolalia in the New Testament," in Stagg, Hinson, and Oates, *Glossolalia*, 20-44.

occurrences.[381] The onrush of pneumatological monographs during the 1970 included works by Watson E. Mills,[382] Stagg,[383] Fisher Humphreys and Malcolm Tolbert,[384] Jimmy A. Millikin,[385] Landrum P. Leavell,[386] John William MacGorman,[387] Robert L. Hamblin,[388] Ralph W. Neighbours, Jr.,[389] Jack R. Taylor,[390] Lynn P. Clayton,[391] and J. Terry Young.[392] That glossolalia did not become a greater issue for Southern Baptists has been explained by Claude L. Howe, Jr.:

> In many respects, a charismatic experience is foreign to Southern Baptist life, stressing a second blessing where Baptists prize the first. It tends to establish a spiritual elite by distinguishing between Christians who have had the experience and those who have not, while Baptists stress the equality of all believers in Christ. The focus of the charismatic tends to be inward and upon believers, whereas Southern Baptist concern is outward, directed toward the world.[393]

---

[381]*Spirit of the Living God*, 10, 61-63, 97-101.

[382]*Understanding Speaking in Tongues* (Grand Rapids MI: Eerdmans, 1972); *Speaking in Tongues: Let's Talk about It* (Waco TX: Word, 1973).

[383]*The Holy Spirit Today* (Nashville: Broadman, 1973).

[384]*Speaking in Tongues* (Zachary LA: Christian Litho, Inc., 1973).

[385]*Testing Tongues by the Word* (Nashville: Broadman, 1973).

[386]*God's Spirit in You* (Nashville: Broadman, 1974).

[387]*The Gifts of the Spirit* (Nashville: Broadman, 1974).

[388]*The Spirit-Filled Trauma* (Nashville: Broadman, 1974).

[389]*This Gift Is Mine* (Nashville: Broadman, 1974).

[390]*After the Spirit Comes* (Nashville: Broadman, 1974).

[391]*No Second-Class Christians* (Nashville: Broadman, 1976).

[392]*The Spirit within You* (Nashville: Broadman, 1977). See also John Paul Newport, "Speaking with Tongues," *Home Missions*, May 1965, 7-9, 21-26; idem, "Understanding, Evaluating, and Learning from the Contemporary Glossolalia Movement," in *Tongues*, ed. Luther B. Dyer (Jefferson City MO: LeRoi Publications, 1971) 105-27; Fred E. Meeks, "The Pastor and the Tongues Movement," *Southwestern Journal of Theology* 19 (Spring 1977): 73-85; Robert H. Culpepper, *Evaluating the Charismatic Movement: A Theological and Biblical Appraisal* (Valley Forge PA: Judson, 1977); Kenneth S. Hemphill, *Spiritual Gifts: Empowering the New Testament Church* (Nashville: Broadman Press, 1988).

[393]"The Charismatic Movement in Southern Baptist Life," 21; repr., 121-22.

The Inerrancy Controversy

The controversies relative to Elliott's book and volume 1 of the *Broadman Bible Commentary* did not yield an amicable and permanent resolution but rather led to a more prolonged, intense, and divisive controversy among Southern Baptists.[394]

After a group of conservative Southern Baptists led by Milum Oswell Owens, Jr., (1913–) of Gastonia, North Carolina, and Laverne Butler of Louisville, Kentucky, had had two annual meetings, such a group, meeting in First Church, Atlanta, Georgia, in March 1973, organized the Baptist Faith and Message Fellowship. The 1963 confession was to be the rallying point for resistance to alleged theological liberalism. The new group started *The Southern Baptist Journal*, edited by William Audrey Powell, Sr. (1925–2000), and it criticized a sermon, "Shall We Call the Bible Infallible?"[395] by William E. Hull, dean of the School of Theology of Southern Baptist Theological Seminary. The fellowship sought to publish Sunday School literature, but by the end of the decade problems related to the journal led to division in its ranks and the launching of another publication, the *Southern Baptist Advocate*. The fellowship itself—leading what David T. Morgan has called "the first crusade"—would not effect major change in the Southern Baptist Convention.[396]

---

[394]No effort will be made to identify the nontheological factors in this controversy.

[395]*Baptist Program*, December 1970, 5-6, 17-18, 21. Arguing from the absence of the terms "infallible" and "inerrant" from the Bible itself, and their scant use in Baptist confessions of faith, from the sinfulness and imperfections of biblical authors, from the unavailability of the autographs of the biblical books, and from the difficulty of securing infallible translations and infallible interpretation, Hull concluded that it is "not wise to call the Bible 'infallible' " and called for reconciliation between advocates and opponents. A native of Birmingham, Hull was a graduate of Samford University (B.A., 1951) and Southern Baptist Theological Seminary (M.Div., 1954; Ph.D., 1960). He advanced from instructor to professor in New Testament and to dean of the School of Theology and provost, Southern Seminary (1954–1975), was pastor of First Church, Shreveport, Louisiana (1975–1987), and was provost and university professor at Samford (1987–2000). He wrote the commentary on the Gospel of John in the Broadman Bible Commentary. *Who's Who in America*, 57th ed. (2003) 1:2493.

[396]McBeth, *The Baptist Heritage*, 682-85; Fletcher, *The Southern Baptist Convention*, 246-48; David T. Morgan, *The New Crusades, the New Holy Land:*

Two books by the same author during the 1970s raised considerably the level of awareness and the potential for conflict over the issue of biblical inerrancy. Harold Lindsell (1913–1998) was a New York City-born Southern Baptist who had taught missions at Columbia (SC) Bible College, Northern Baptist Theological Seminary, and Fuller Theological Seminary, and was the editor of *Christianity Today*.[397] In *The Battle for the Bible* he sought to show that biblical inerrancy was a teaching of the Bible itself,[398] traced some of the history of the doctrine, and majored on recent challenges to the doctrine in the Lutheran Church-Missouri Synod, the SBC, Fuller Theological Seminary, the Evangelical Covenant Church of America, and parachurch movements. "Orthodoxy," Lindsell asserted, and the historical-critical method are deadly enemies that are antithetical and cannot be reconciled without the destruction of one or the other." Moreover, "without a belief in inerrancy any group is bound to go astray." Lindsell advocated the "domino" theory, namely, that "once a denomination departs from a belief in biblical infallibility, it opens the floodgates to disbelief about other cardinal doctrines of the faith." He concluded that no one should be denominated an "evangelical" who denies biblical inerrancy.[399] In *The Bible in the Balance* Lindsell answered his critics and added new materials concerning the denominations previously examined, especially concerning Southern and Southwestern seminaries. Inerrancy was said to be "the watershed question of this age," and the current usage of "evangelical" was said to have become so "debased" as to warrant using instead "fundamentalist" or "Orthodox Protestant."[400]

Probably less widely circulated were two booklets by Clark Harold Pinnock (1937–), a native of Toronto and Ph.D. graduate of Manchester University who was associate professor of theology in New Orleans Baptist

---

Conflict in the Southern Baptist Convention, 1969–1991 (Tuscaloosa: University of Alabama Press, 1996) 13-36.

[397]*Who's Who in Religion*, 1st ed. (1975–1976) 345; 2nd ed. (1977) 395; 4th ed. (1992–1993) 307.

[398]This was denied by other Baptists who were reckoned to be evangelicals: Carl F. H. Henry, Bernard L. Ramm, and Clark H. Pinnock. Lindsell, *The Bible in the Balance* (Grand Rapids MI: Zondervan, 1979) 31-50; "Bible Battles," *Time*, 10 May 1976, 57.

[399](Grand Rapids MI: Zondervan, 1976) esp. 82, 143, 104, 210-11. See below, 518.

[400]Esp. 118-70, 172-75, 46, 319-21.

Theological Seminary.[401] In *A Defense of Biblical Infallibility* Pinnock argued that biblical infallibility "is a *necessary*, not merely an *optional* inference from the Biblical teaching about inspiration" and that "*Sola scriptura* cannot be sustained apart from Biblical infallibility." Infallibility pertains to the autographs, and inspiration is verbal.[402] In *A New Reformation: A Challenge to Southern Baptists* the Canadian with allusions to the Down Grade and Elliott controversies and with highly polemical rhetoric, accused professors in Southern Baptist seminaries and related colleges of holding a "scaled down" view of the Scriptures, that is, noninfallibility, and a less than orthodox Christology and called for "a new reformation."[403]

With such emphasis on biblical inerrancy among Southern Baptists prior to 1979, it is not difficult to identify inerrancy as the paramount doctrinal issue in the controversy that dominated Southern Baptist life during the last two decades of the twentieth century, even though other focal issues have been advocated.[404]

The SBC session in Houston in 1979 marked the formal beginning of what has been variously denominated as the "conservative resurgence" and the "fundamentalist takeover" of the convention, its agencies, and its institutions, or what David T. Morgan has labeled "the second crusade."[405] In some measure the Baptist Faith and Message Fellowship prepared the

---

[401]Robert V. Rakestraw, "Clark H. Pinnock," in *Baptist Theologians*, ed. George and Dockery, 660, 662; Robert K. Johnston, "Clark H. Pinnock," in *Handbook of Evangelical Theologians*, ed. Walter A. Elwell (Grand Rapids MI: Baker, 1993) 428; Barry L. Callen, *Journey toward Renewal: An Intellectual Biography* (Nappanee IN: Evangel, 2000) 16-39.

[402](Philadelphia: Presbyterian and Reformed, 1967) 10, 18, 15-18.

[403](Tigerville SC: Jewel Books, 1968) 2-3, 15, 7, 17, 6-8, 11-14. But three of the four chapters consisted of messages delivered to the Southern Baptist Pastors' Conference in 1968. Pinnock's *Biblical Revelation: The Foundation of Theology* (Chicago: Moody, 1971; repr.: Phillipsburg NJ: Presbyterian and Reformed, 1985) would reflect the bibliology of B. B. Warfield, whereas his *The Scripture Principle* (San Francisco: Harper & Row, 1984) would limit "the instructional significance of the Bible" to "matters relating to human salvation." Callen, *Journey toward Renewal*, 54, 66.

[404]For example, Helen Lee Turner, "Fundamentalism in the Southern Baptist Convention: The Crystallization of a Millennialist Vision" (Ph.D. diss., University of Virginia, 1990; Ann Arbor: University Microfilms International, 1991) esp. 3-12, has interpreted the controversy in terms of millennial expectation.

[405]*The New Crusades, the New Holy Land*, 37-107.

way. As early as 1967 two of the most significant leaders, Herman Paul Pressler III (1930–), and Leighton Paige Patterson (1942–) had bonded for the common cause through a meeting in New Orleans.[406] Pressler, a graduate of Philips Exeter Academy, Princeton University, and the University of Texas Law School, and state appeals court judge in Houston, had from his youth been committed to resisting theological liberalism,[407] and Patterson, a graduate of Hardin-Simmons University and a Th.D. candidate at New Orleans Baptist Theological Seminary,[408] had a similar commitment. The strategy was to elect successive presidents of the SBC who were committed to biblical inerrancy and who could use their appointive powers to and through the committees on committees and committees on nominations to control and change the SBC's boards and seminaries.[409] Patterson became "the movement's theological spokesman, while Pressler served as chief organizer and political strategist," but Pressler was implementing the "strategy first devised by" William Audrey Powell, Sr.[410] The "backbone of the movement" would be "a strong cadre of pastors in large, aggressive, high growth churches in metropolitan areas"[411] with great support from smaller churches. The first victory came with the 1979 election on the first ballot of Adrian Rogers, pastor of Bellevue Church, Memphis, Tennessee.[412] At the same 1979 session Larry Lynn Lewis (1935–) pastor of Tower Grove Church, St. Louis,[413] introduced a

---

[406]Paul Pressler, *A Hill on Which to Die: One Southern Baptist's Journey* (Nashville: Broadman & Holman, 1999) 59-60; Fletcher, *The Southern Baptist Convention*, 244; Morgan, *The New Crusades, the New Holy Land*, 15-16. Patterson would later be pastor of First Church, Fayetteville AR (1970–1975), president of Criswell College (1975–1992), president of Southeastern Baptist Theological Seminary (1992–2003), and president of Southwestern Baptist Theological Seminary (2003–). Per Jason Duesing.

[407]Pressler, *A Hill on Which to Die*, 13-38; Morgan, *The New Crusades, the New Holy Land*, 15; *Who's Who in the South and Southwest*, 23rd ed. (1993–1994) 648; *Who's Who in Religion*, 4th ed. (1992–1993) 414.

[408]Morgan, *The New Crusades, the New Holy Land*, 16; *Who's Who in Religion*, vol. 1 (1975–1976) 433; vol. 2 (1977) 505; vol. 4 (1992–1993) 395.

[409]Pressler, *A Hill on Which to Die*, 77-82.

[410]Morgan, *The New Crusades, the New Holy Land*, 16.

[411]Fletcher, *The Southern Baptist Convention*, 248.

[412]Southern Baptist Convention, *Annual*, 1979 43; Fletcher, *The Southern Baptist Convention*, 254.

[413]*Who's Who in the Midwest*, 20th ed. (1986–1987) 344; 21st ed. (1988–1989)

resolution "on doctrinal integrity as it relates to Convention seminaries," and William Wayne Dehoney (1918–2007), pastor of Walnut Street Church, Louisville, Kentucky, introduced a motion to reaffirm article one (on the Scriptures) in the 1963 Baptist Faith and Message. The convention chose to accept the Dehoney motion and pass a resolution of gratitude to the seminaries.[414] But in 1980 the convention adopted a resolution on doctrinal integrity which commended seminary personnel who had "taught the truth in love" and exhorted the trustees of seminaries and board to "preserve . . . doctrinal integrity" and employ only those who believe in the infallibility of the original manuscripts" of the Bible and that "the Bible is truth without any error."[415] In April 1983 a nationwide moderate or noninerrantist magazine, *SBC Today*, later named *Baptists Today*, began publication.[416]

Subsequently two books, both by Texans and graduates of Baylor University and of Southwestern Baptist Theological Seminary,[417] would make more explicit the divergence on inerrancy, although ostensibly the books pertained to biblical authority. Russell H. Dilday, Jr., Southwestern's current president, in a book designed for doctrinal study in Southern Baptist churches, after setting forth a "pattern" of authority combining the objective and the subjective, affirming the fact of biblical inspiration but not a theory as to its method, and retaining Mullins's firm separation of religion and science, concluded that in the Bible itself, in early Christian history, in the Protestant Reformation, and in most Baptist confessions of faith the language of biblical inerrancy had not been employed. Such came from Francis Turretin and the Princeton school. The Bible must be seen as a divine-human book, but seemingly its truthfulness or absolute precision extends only to the religious-ethical sphere.[418] James T. Draper, Jr. (1935–), pastor of First Church, Euless, Texas, with a preface by Hobbs, deploring

---

449.

[414]Southern Baptist Convention, *Annual*, 1979, 31, 32, 45, 55-56.

[415]Ibid., 1980, 50-51.

[416]Walker L. Knight, "Moderate Organizations Fill Vacuums in SBC," *Baptists Today*, 15 December 1992, 7; idem, "The History of *Baptists Today* (1982–1992)," in *The Struggle for the Soul of the SBC: Moderate Responses to the Fundamentalist Movement*, ed. Walter B. Shurden (Macon GA: Mercer University Press, 1993) 151-68.

[417]*Who's Who in Religion*, vol. 4 (1992–1993) 128 (Dilday), 135 (Draper).

[418]*The Doctrine of Biblical Authority* (Nashville: Convention Press, 1982) 29-30, 71-77, 95-96, 111-12, 38-58, 93-95.

the "shift away from biblical authority" due to historical-critical method, existentialism, "naturalistic, uniformitarian science," and the practice of comparative religion, offered a not so fully documented history that demonstrated biblical authority more than inerrancy but said that Jesus "believed in biblical inerrancy" and called for biblical inerrancy "in every area of knowledge." Moreover, there should be "theological parameters" for those who "teach in a Southern Baptist institution" or "write curriculum" or "have a policymaking role."[419]

In 1984 SBC moderates created the Forum as an alternate preconvention meeting to the Pastors' Conference, which was being used to advance the inerrancy movement,[420] and in 1986 a group of moderates meeting in Charlotte, North Carolina, formed the Southern Baptist Alliance, with a seven-point covenant, to preserve historic Baptist principles.[421]

At the 1985 SBC session in Dallas, Bill G. Hickem, Jacksonville, Florida, pastor, and Henry Franklin Paschall (1922–), former SBC president, co-offered a motion authorizing a special committee—later to be called "the Peace Committee"—to "determine the sources" of the controversy and "make findings and recommendations" relative to the controversy, so that Southern Baptists "might effect reconciliation." The motion, which passed, specified the members of the committee, including Charles Grantland Fuller (1931–), pastor of First Church, Roanoke, Virginia, as chairman, and limited its work to a maximum of two years.[422] In its 1986 report in Atlanta the committee asked for a year of intercessory prayer, a "moratorium on theological/political position meetings," and "deceleration" of "political power structures," restraint of "inflammatory language," fairness in journalistic reporting, and fairness in "appointments and

---

[419]*Authority: The Critical Issue for Southern Baptists* (Old Tappan NJ: Fleming H. Revell, 1984) 23-79, 91, 105-109.

[420]John H. Hewett, "The History of the SBC Forum," in *The Struggle for the Soul of the SBC*, ed, Shurden, 73-92; Fletcher, *The Southern Baptist Convention*, 280. The Forum continued through 1991.

[421]Alan P. Neely, "The History of the Alliance of Baptists," in *The Struggle for the Soul of the SBC*, ed. Shurden, 101-28; Nancy Tatom Ammerman, *Baptist Battles: Social Change and Religious Conflict in the Southern Baptist Convention* (New Brunswick NJ: Rutgers University Press, 1990) 271-85. In 1992 the Southern Baptist Alliance became the Alliance of Baptists.

[422]Southern Baptist Convention, *Annual*, 1985, 64-65.

nominations."[423] In an October 1986 meeting in Glorieta, New Mexico, involving committee members, SBC agency executives, and SBC seminary presidents, the presidents framed and adopted a ten-point statement in which they affirmed that Christianity was "supernatural in its origin and history," biblical miracles were genuine, and the 66 books of the biblical canon are "not errant in any area of reality" and have "infallible power and binding authority."[424] In 1987 in St. Louis the Peace Committee made its full report. Theologically the controversy was found to center in article 1 of the 1963 Baptist Faith and Message Statement and especially as to whether "truth without any mixture of error" applies to all areas of reality, including the historical and the scientific. Advocates of such a position, said to be the majority on the committee and among Southern Baptists, would have their views represented by four examples: (1) "Adam and Eve were real persons"; (2) "the named authors did indeed write the biblical books attributed to them by those books"; (3) biblical miracles "did indeed occur as supernatural events in history"; and (4) "the historical narratives" in the Bible "are indeed accurate and reliable." Seminary faculties were to be built so as to reflect this understanding of inerrancy. The committee recommended its extension for no more than three years in order to observe the "response" and "compliance."[425] In 1988 in San Antonio the Peace Committee reported the contributions made by the committee to the denomination and asked to be discharged.[426]

The SBC seminary presidents sponsored two study conference (1987, 1988) at Ridgecrest, North Carolina, on biblical inerrancy and biblical hermeneutics, respectively.[427] The first constituted the most comprehensive

---

[423]Ibid., 1986, 62-63, 250-57.

[424]Dan Martin, "Seminary Presidents Air 'Glorieta Statement,' " *Baptist Standard*, 29 October 1986, 5, 21. Consequently Cecil E. Sherman, pastor, Broadway Church, Fort Worth, resigned from the committee. "Sherman Resigns from Peace Committee," ibid., 4, 17.

[425]Southern Baptist Convention, *Annual*, 1987, 56-57, 232-42. Consequently W. Winfred Moore, former first vice-president of the SBC, resigned from the committee because of perceiving the extension as "policing." "Moore Resigns in Protest of Extension," *Baptist Standard*, 24 June 1987, 4.

[426]Southern Baptist Convention, *Annual*, 1988, 63-64.

[427]The program personnel and topics were selected, to a large extent, by John Paul Newport (1917–2000), academic vice-president and provost of Southwestern Baptist Theological Seminary.

forum concerning biblical inerrancy in Baptist history. Northern and Canadian Evangelical scholars presented papers on various subtopics: the history of the doctrine, chiefly in North America (Mark Noll), definition of the doctrine and adjunctive truths (Robert Preus), a truce among evangelicals (Clark Pinnock), the parameters of inerrancy (Pinnock, Kenneth S. Kantzer), inerrancy in relation to the Bible's divinity and humanity (James I. Packer, Kantzer), problem areas for both noninerrantists and inerrantists (Millard J. Erickson, Packer), and implications of inerrancy for the Christian mission (Erickson, Packer). Two responses were made to each major presentation by a Southern Baptist pastor or teacher, and seventeen seminar sessions featured papers on various related topics by Southern Baptist professors.[428] The second, less expansive conference on biblical interpretation blended sermons by Southern Baptist pastors and responses by Southern Baptists professors with lectures by visiting Evangelical scholars on: divine creation and interpretation (Packer), literary criticism and interpretation (Robert Johnston), Old Testament interpretation (Walter C. Kaiser, Jr.), interpretation relative to women (Packer), New Testament interpretation (Grant Osborne), and interpretation and eschatology (Packer).[429] John P. Newport[430] had written on the Southern Baptist controversy about the Bible,[431] on the nature of Christian doctrine,[432] and a commentary on the book of Revelation,[433] and would later issue a textbook

---

[428] *The Proceedings of the Conference on Biblical Inerrancy, 1987* (Nashville: Broadman, 1987).

[429] *The Proceedings of the Conference on Biblical Interpretation, 1988* (Nashville: Broadman, 1988).

[430] A native of Missouri, Newport was a graduate of William Jewell College, Southern Baptist Theological Seminary, the University of Edinburgh, and Texas Christian University and had previously taught at Baylor University, New Orleans Baptist Theological Seminary, and Rice University.

[431] (With William Cannon), *Why Christians Fight over the Bible* (Nashville: Thomas Nelson, 1974).

[432] *What Is Christian Doctrine?* Layman's Library of Christian Doctrine 1 (Nashville: Broadman, 1984).

[433] *The Lion and the Lamb: The Book of Revelation for Today* (Nashville: Broadman, 1986).

on philosophy of religion[434] and a monograph on the New Age movement from a biblical worldview.[435]

In 1991, after two gatherings in Atlanta, a sizeable group of Southern Baptist moderates formed the Cooperative Baptist Fellowship (CBF), to serve as a channel for gifts to SBC agencies and to support its own missionaries. It became a unifying agency for the moderate cause.[436]

The principal theologian for the CBF has been Walter Byron Shurden (1937–).[437] A native of Greenwood, Mississippi, he committed his life to Christ as a college freshman and was graduated from Mississippi College (B.A., 1958) and New Orleans Baptist Theological Seminary (B.D., 1961; Th.D., 1967). Following a year of teaching at McMaster Divinity College (1965–1966) and the pastorate of First Church, Ruston, Louisiana (1966–1969), he served as professor of religion in Carson-Newman College (1969–1976), and as professor of church history (1976–1983) and dean of the School of Theology (1980–1983) of Southern Baptist Theological Seminary. From 1983 until his retirement in December 2007, he was professor of Christianity and executive director of the Center for Baptist Studies at Mercer University.[438] Shurden has used freedom as the centerpiece in his portrayal of Baptist identity. As editor of the five-volume series, *Proclaiming the Baptist Vision*, he encouraged the teaching and preaching of the Baptist identity,[439] and in his *The Baptist Identity: Four Fragile*

---

[434]*Life's Ultimate Questions: A Contemporary Philosophy of Religion* (Dallas: Word, 1989). See esp. chaps. 4 (creation), 5 (providence), 6 (Satan and demonic powers), 7 (evil and suffering), and 8 (death and after-death).

[435]*The New Age Movement and the Biblical Worldview: Conflict and Dialogue* (Grand Rapids MI: Eerdmans, 1998).

[436]Daniel Vestal, "The History of the Cooperative Baptist Fellowship," in *The Struggle for the Soul of the SBC*, ed. Shurden, 253-74; Knight, "Moderate Organizations," 7-8; Fletcher, *The Southern Baptist Convention*, 311-12, 318, 322-24, 351-52; Cecil Edwin Sherman, *By My Own Reckoning* (Macon GA: Smyth & Helwys, 2008) 131-250.

[437]This section on Shurden has been written by John Edward Forsythe.

[438]Shurden, *Not an Easy Journey: Some Transitions in Baptist Life* (Macon GA: Mercer University Press, 2005) 2-13; Staff, *Baptist Studies, Mercer University*, 2006, "Walter B. Shurden," <http://www.mercer.edu/baptiststudies/staff/shurden.htm> (accessed May 2006).

[439]Intro. to *Proclaiming the Baptist Vision: The Priesthood of All Believers* (Macon GA: Smyth & Helwys, 1993) 1-5.

Freedoms he noted four distinctly Baptist freedoms—Bible, soul, church, and religious.[440]

Shurden has rightly recognized that "Baptists can make no exclusive claim even to those principles that help define their denominational identity," and no one denomination or group within a denomination can lay sole claim to biblical authority.[441] Bible freedom, for Shurden, means that the Bible is "*under* the Lordship of Jesus Christ," that "freedom of access to the Bible" is *for* "continuing obedience" to its teaching, that Baptists have confessions, not creeds, and that Baptists, who "have no formal or informal teaching office," recognize the freedom of each believer to interpret the Bible for himself with the use of the best aids to study. Shurden deplored recent "statements about the Bible that limit access to the Bible and that codify human understanding of biblical theology."[442]

Soul freedom, furthermore, is the "right and responsibility of every person to deal with God without the imposition of creed, the interference of clergy, or the intervention of civil government." Following Mullins,[443] Shurden asserted that "each individual is competent under God to make moral, spiritual, and religious decisions." This does not mean "human self-sufficiency," for "the *individual* [is] *in* community," but personal and convictional conversion and the baptism of believers only.[444] In his full-orbed exposition of the priesthood of believers, Shurden identified, in addition to Exod. 19:4-6, five specific New Testament references: 1 Pet. 2:5, 9; Rev. 1:5-6; 5:9-10; 20:6. He did not cite texts expressive of the offering of spiritual sacrifices but instead dwelt upon the high priestly office and sacrifice of Christ in the Epistle to the Hebrews. This led to his conclusion that the priesthood of believers is "the privilege of uncoerced personal access to God's grace for your sin." Hence salvation by grace is

---

[440]Pp. 4-5. See above, 429n.76.

[441]Shurden, introduction to *Proclaiming the Baptist Vision: The Bible*, ed. Shurden (Macon GA: Smyth & Helwys, 1994) 3.

[442]*The Baptist Identity*, 9-21.

[443]See above, 418-19.

[444]*The Baptist Identity*, 23-32.

personal and voluntary.[445] Like Hobbs,[446] Shurden regarded the priesthood of believers as foundational to Baptist emphases.[447]

"Church freedom is the affirmation that local churches are free, under the Lordship of Christ, to determine their membership and leadership, to order their worship and work, to ordain whom they perceive as gifted for ministry, male or female, and to participate in the larger Body of Christ. . . ."[448] Shurden further defined "the Baptist vision of the church" as embracing both the "divine and human," both "universal" and "local" church, members who are "both believers and disciples," polity that is "both a Christocracy and a democracy," both "individual freedom" and "communal responsibility," "roles of both laity and clergy," and mission that is "both worship and witness."[449] Congregational polity is practiced by Baptists not because it is "more efficient" or "more biblical" but "because it accents the role of the individual within community" and "provides more freedom for the Holy Spirit to guide the life of the local church." Shurden favored open communion and reported favorably on open membership. Congregationalism "does not preclude cooperation with other Baptist churches,"[450] and early Baptist associations in America called for the churches to work together "without the fear of impairing democratic processes of local congregations."[451]

Religious freedom means "freedom *of* religion, freedom *for* religion, and freedom *from* religion" on the basis "that Caesar is not Christ and Christ is not Caesar." Casting himself in the tradition of Helwys, Williams, Backus, Leland, Mullins, and Truett, Shurden cited W. R. Estep's warning[452] that the U.S. Constitution's First Amendment was now "'under

---

[445]*The Doctrine of the Priesthood of Believers* (Nashville: Convention Press, 1987) 13-17, 38-41, 33-38, 45-58.

[446]See above, 471-72.

[447]*The Doctrine of the Priesthood of Believers*, 59-142.

[448]*The Baptist Identity*, 33.

[449]Shurden, introduction to *Proclaiming the Baptist Vision: The Church*, ed. Shurden (Macon GA: Smyth & Helwys, 1996) 4-14.

[450]*The Baptist Identity*, 37, 41, 39.

[451]Shurden, "Associationalism among Baptists in America, 1707–1814" (Th.D. diss., New Orleans Baptist Theological Seminary, 1967) 88-89, 99.

[452]*Revolution within the Revolution: The First Amendment in Historical Context, 1612–1789* (Grand Rapids MI: Eerdmans, 1990) 1-19.

siege.'"[453] Baptists, he contended, have "insisted on subordination of loyalty to the state to the lordship of Christ over their lives," have advocated freedom from the religious "coercion" or "constraint" of civil government with the church and the state being "*side by side*," and have urged all Christians toward "participation in the affairs of state."[454] Shurden was alarmed that so many were embracing the concept that the United States "has been, ever was, or is now a Christian nation."[455] He contended that Baptists had come to their convictions on religious liberty and church-state separation because they had been "birthed in adversity" in England and America and because, with their biblical hermeneutics tilted to the New Testament, their beliefs about God, man, faith, and the church pointed toward freedom.[456] Shurden applied freedom to theological education, which should produce "tender hearts," "tough minds," and "trained hands." That education should be "more concerned with *how* one learns than with *what* one learns," freeing learners "from the restrictions of culture and prejudice" so that they can "become life-long learners and their own teachers."[457]

Shurden has received criticism from authors in the SBC, notably Thomas J. Nettles, who has reckoned Shurden's theology as a "historical truncation of Baptist identity [which] . . . not only fails in its grasp of the doctrinal history of Baptists but disfigures ecclesiology."[458] Quite the opposite assessment has come from the CBF. According to Charles Poole, "Shurden is one of this century's most insightful interpreters of the Baptist way."[459]

In September 1992 Homer Edwin Young (1936–), pastor of Second Church, Houston, Texas, and the SBC president, appointed, without authorization from the SBC, nine study groups or a task force to "examine 'where we've been, where we need to be'" so that "'we can come together as a

---

[453] *The Baptist Identity*, 45-54.

[454] *The Doctrine of the Priesthood of Believers*, 111-25, esp. 114, 117, 121, 122.

[455] Intro. to *Proclaiming the Baptist Vision: Religious Liberty*, ed. Shurden (Macon GA: Smyth & Helwys, 1997) 1-2.

[456] "How We Got That Way: Baptists on Religious Liberty and Separation of Church and State," in Shurden, ed., *Proclaiming the Baptist Vision: Religious Liberty*, 13-23.

[457] "Freedom for Theological Education," in *Being Baptist Means Freedom*, ed. Alan Neely (Charlotte: Southern Baptist Alliance, 1988) 57-68, esp. 61-62.

[458] *Ready for Reformation?* (Nashville: Broadman & Holman, 2005) 101.

[459] *Proclaiming the Baptist Vision: The Church*, cover.

denomination.'"[460] One of the nine was a theological group or committee, cochairmen of which were Timothy Francis George (1950–), dean of Beeson Divinity School of Samford University, Birmingham, Alabama, and Roy Lee Honeycutt (1926–2004), president of Southern Baptist Theological Seminary. Young instructed the group to "use as foundational documents the 1963 Baptist Faith and Message Statement, the 1987 report and recommendations of the SBC Peace Committee, and the 1978 and 1982 Chicago Statements" relative to biblical inerrancy and biblical hermeneutics.[461]

The SBC theology committee report, released in 1993 and adopted as a resolution at the 1994 session in Orlando, Florida, stated the committee's purpose as that of examining "those biblical truths which are most surely held among the people of God called Southern Baptists" and reaffirming their "common commitment to Jesus Christ, the Holy Scriptures, and the evangelical heritage of the Christian church." The report was said to be "not . . . a new confession of faith, but . . . a reaffirmation of major doctrinal concerns set forth in the *Baptist Faith and Message* of 1963." The committee indicated that it was attempting "to move beyond the denominational conflict of recent years toward a new consensus rooted in theological substance and doctrinal fidelity" so that there might be "healing and reconciliation." It restated the purposes of Baptist confessions of faith. The doctrinal affirmation consisted of five sections: Holy Scripture, God, the person and work of Christ, the church, and last things. The committee affirmed biblical inspiration and inerrancy, quoting from James Marion Frost (1848–1916), the first secretary of the Sunday School Board (SBC), claiming the authority of the Glorieta Statement, the Peace Committee report, and two Chicago documents, and noting the publication of the *New American Commentary*. Biblical theism was reaffirmed in that God is no "limited deity" but the "universal Creator," triune in nature, "the Father of the redeemed," and "sovereign over history, nature, time, and space." Jesus Christ is "the unique and solitary Savior," and his death involved penal substitution. Original sin was affirmed without being defined, and eschatological universalism rejected. The church was defined according to its missionary purpose. The priesthood of all believers involves both access

---

[460]Herb Hollinger, "Young Naming Task Force to Study SBC," *Baptist Standard*, 16 September 1992, 3.

[461]Linda Lawson, "Young's Study Groups to Report in April," *Baptist Standard*, 24 February 1993, 14; *Journal of the Evangelical Theological Society* 21 (December 1978): 289-96; 25 (December 1982): 397-401.

to God and ministry, service, and witness but should not be "reduced to modern individualism nor used as a cover for theological relativism." Both local church autonomy and cooperation between churches were affirmed, and religious liberty was defined chiefly and idiosyncratically as the ability of the congregation and "a general Baptist body" to "determine . . . its own doctrinal and disciplinary parameters." Only three eschatological truths were reaffirmed: the second coming, final resurrection, and heaven and hell. Annihilationism and "a temporary purgatory" were rejected.[462]

Jeff B. Pool (1951–), formerly assistant professor of theology at Southwestern Baptist Theological Seminary, issued a detailed critique of the methods employed by the committee as "manipulative," of the doctrinal formulations as reductive distortions of Baptist doctrine, and of the result as the attainment of the creedalism that Baptists had previously rejected.[463]

The product of numerous dialogue sessions, a volume of essays by eight authors representing both conservatives and moderates, focused on Bible-oriented, impasse-creating issues for Southern Baptists.[464] Fourteen authors, chiefly moderate Southern Baptists, produced a volume of essays around three themes: conversion, contemplation, and the common life.[465] Nine authors, all of whom with a single exception were moderates, authored essays on biblical criticism, authority, and inerrancy and the role of confessions of faith under the editorship of Robison B. James (1931–), professor of religion in the University of Richmond.[466] Twenty authors, mostly moderate Southern Baptists, contrary to the direction of Southern Baptist leadership, issued a volume of essays on Baptist themes under the editorship of Charles William Deweese (1944–), formerly assistant executive director of the SBC's Historical Commission.[467]

---

[462]Southern Baptist Convention, *Annual*, 1994, 102, 112-18.

[463]*Against Returning to Egypt: Exposing and Resisting Credalism in the Southern Baptist Convention* (Macon GA: Mercer University Press, 1998).

[464]*Beyond the Impasse? Scripture, Interpretation, and Theology in Baptist Life*, ed. James and Dockery.

[465]*Ties That Bind: Life Together in the Baptist Vision*, ed. Gary A. Furr and Curtis W. Freeman (Macon GA: Smyth & Helwys, 1994).

[466]*The Unfettered Word: Confronting the Authority-Inerrancy Question* (Macon GA: Smyth & Helwys, 1994).

[467]*Defining Baptist Convictions: Guidelines for the Twenty-first Century* (Franklin TN: Providence House, 1996). Deweese was the author of *A Community of Believers: Making Church Membership Meaningful* (Valley Forge PA: Judson, 1978); *The Emerging Role of Deacons* (Nashville: Broadman, 1979); *Prayer in*

The inerrancy movement carried with it satellite hermeneutical issues, notably in the area of marriage and family. Reacting against the women's liberation movement and disturbed by the breakdown of family life in the churches as well as in the larger society, the SBC leadership sought to address this doctrinal/ethical issue confessionally. Charles Lawson of Maryland successfully introduced a motion at the 1997 session authorizing the president to appoint a committee to frame and present an article on "the family" as an addendum to the 1963 Baptist Faith and Message Statement.[468] The seven-member committee, consisting of five men and two women and chaired by Anthony Lynn Jordan (1949–), executive director of the Baptist General Convention of Oklahoma, presented its recommended article and an appended commentary at the 1998 session in Salt Lake City.[469] The article stated that the family "is composed of persons related to one another by marriage, blood, or adoption" and defined marriage as "the uniting of one man and one woman in covenant commitment for a lifetime." The husband and wife were both said to be "created in God's image" and "of equal worth before God" but to have different "God-given" responsibilities, the husband that of loving provision, protection, and leadership and the wife that of loving submission to his servant leadership, household management, and child-rearing. Parents are to teach their children by precept and by example, and children, whose origin was specified as being at "the moment of conception," are to honor and obey their parents.[470] Efforts to amend the proposed article to include mutual submission (Eph. 5:21) and to include single and widowed persons were defeated.[471] Although the earliest English Baptists under Mennonite

---

Baptist Life (Nashville: Broadman, 1986); *Baptist Church Covenants* (Nashville: Broadman, 1990); and *Women Deacons and Deaconesses: 400 Years of Service* (Brentwood TN: Baptist History and Heritage Society, 2005).

[468]Southern Baptist Convention, *Annual*, 1997, 36.

[469]Ibid., 1998, 77-82; Herb Hollinger, "SBC to Consider Statement on Marriage," *Baptist Standard*, 13 May 1998, 3.

[470]Southern Baptist Convention, *Annual*, 1998, 78.

[471]Ibid., 82; Marv Knox, "SBC Puts Wives, Patterson in Place," *Baptist Standard*, 17 June 1998, 1; Bob Allen, "Mohler Defends Family Statement on National TV," ibid., 1 July 1998, 3.

influence had included marriage in certain of their confessions of faith[472] and those Baptist confessions based on the Westminster Confession had included articles on marriage and family life,[473] later Anglo-American confessions had not included marriage. Hence the 1998 SBC article on the family was seemingly the first such in a major Anglo-American Baptist confession for three centuries.

The 2000 Baptist Faith and Message Statement

But neither the Presidential Theological Study Committee's report nor the family amendment satisfied the majority of the SBC messengers as to confessions or elaborations on confessions. Hence when in 1999 T. C. Pinckney of Virginia moved that the president be authorized to "appoint a blue ribbon committee to review" the 1963 confession and "bring any recommendations" in 2000, the motion passed by a divided vote of 2,327 to 1,963.[474] The new committee, chaired by Adrian Rogers, was more diverse as to gender than previous Baptist Faith and Message committees by having two women among the fifteen members,[475] but it was less representative of the various states than the 1962-63 committee and did not have a predominance of published theologians as had the 1924–1925 committee.

In the 2000 session in Orlando, Florida, the committee report was adopted after a motion to postpone consideration for one year and three amendments were defeated.[476] In the new confession the first article on "the Scriptures" had three changes from the 1963 statement. Reference to the Bible as "the record of God's revelation" was changed to the statement that the Bible "is God's revelation," thus deleting the language of Mullins and Conner. The affirmation that "all Scripture is totally true and trustworthy" was added, and the declaration, "The criterion by which the Bible is to be

---

[472]"A Short Confession" (1610), art. 37; Propositions and Conclusions concerning True Christian Religion," arts. 13, 14, 87, 88; "The True Gospel-Faith" (1654), art. 26, in Lumpkin, *Baptist Confessions of Faith*, 112, 126, 140, 195.

[473]Second London Confession (1677), art. 25; Orthodox Creed (1678), arts. 43, 47, in ibid., 284-85, 330, 332.

[474]Southern Baptist Convention, *Annual*, 1999, 36, 87, 88; Mark Wingfield, "SBC to Review Faith and Message," *Baptist Standard*, 23 June 1999, 1, 3.

[475]*The Baptist Faith and Message: A Statement Adopted by the Southern Baptist Convention, June 14, 2000* (Nashville: LifeWay Resources of the SBC, 2000) 6.

[476]Southern Baptist Convention, *Annual*, 2000, 38, 76.

interpreted is Jesus Christ," was omitted, and in its stead was placed the statement, "All Scripture is a testimony to Christ, who is Himself the focus of divine revelation." The change was allegedly due to misuse of the former statement by moderates. In article 2 on "God" six alterations were made. "The eternal God" became "the eternal triune God." Added was a statement designed to refute the theology of the openness of God movement: "God is all powerful and all knowing; and His perfect knowledge extends to all things, past, present, and future, including the future decisions of His free creatures." Christ's "death" was said to be a "substitutionary death," the Holy Spirit was identified as "fully divine," and the Holy Spirit was described as the "guarantee" rather than the "assurance" that believers will be brought to maturity. Taking a position on a question on which Southern Baptists had been divided, the new text declared: "At the moment of regeneration He [the Holy Spirit] baptizes every believer into the Body of Christ."[477] Article 3 on "Man" was changed by the addition of two sentences: "He created them male and female. . . . The gift of gender is thus part of the goodness of God's creation." In article 4 on "Salvation" the statement "There is no salvation apart from personal faith in Jesus Christ as Lord," was added, and "perfection" was changed to "maturity."

There was reconstruction of language in article 6 on "The Church" but only three substantive changes. The words relative to Christ, "committed to His teachings" were changed to "governed by His laws." The older statement that in the congregation "members are equally responsible" was replaced by the words, "each member is responsible and accountable to Christ as Lord," a change that could be perceived as a deemphasis on congregational polity. The addition, "While both men and women are gifted for service in the church, the office of pastor is limited to men as qualified by Scripture," in effect closed the door to women pastors in the SBC. In article 8 on "The Lord's Day" the words "by refraining from worldly amusements, and resting from secular employments, work of necessity and mercy only being excepted" were replaced by the statement: "Activities on the Lord's Day should be commensurate with the Christian's conscience under the Lordship of Christ." The alteration could be seen as an accommodation to an increasingly secular society.

Two changes were made in article 11 on "Evangelism and Missions." A sentence, "The Lord Jesus Christ has commanded the preaching of the

---

[477] The other position was that the baptism by the Spirit occurred once-for-all on the day of Pentecost.

gospel to all nations," was added, and the words "win the lost to Christ by personal effort" were changed to "win the lost to Christ by verbal witness undergirded by a Christian lifestyle." In the new article 12 on "Education," four sentences taken from the 1925 statement were placed at the beginning:

> Christianity is the faith of enlightenment and intelligence. In Jesus Christ abide all the treasures of wisdom and knowledge. All sound learning is therefore, a part of our Christian heritage. The new birth opens all human faculties and creates a thirst for knowledge.

Article 15 on "The Christian and the Social Order" was modified in three ways. Both "racism" and "all forms of sexual immorality, including adultery, homosexuality, and pornography," were added to the list of vices to be opposed. Added to those to be provided for were "the abused." Inserted was the sentence, "We should speak on behalf of the unborn and contend for the sanctity of all human life from conception to natural death." Added to article 16 on "Peace and War" was the admonition, "Christian people throughout the world should pray for the reign of the Prince of Peace." The 1998 family amendment constituted the new article 17.[478]

At the end of the twentieth century Southern Baptists began to reflect on the theological changes that had occurred in their midst both in the century and a half of SBC history and by virtue of the inerrancy controversy. *Has Our Theology Changed? Southern Baptist Thought since 1845*,[479] edited by Paul Abbott Basden (1955–),[480] was a study of those

---

[478]The text was not published in the 2000 SBC *Annual* but as a pamphlet: *The Baptist Faith and Message: A Statement Adopted by the Southern Baptist Convention, June 14, 2000*. See also Herb Hollinger, "BF&M Study Has 1925, 1963 Elements, but No New Articles," *Baptist Messenger*, 25 May 2000, 1, 4; "BF&M Committee Proposes 'Significant Changes,' " *Alabama Baptist*, 25 May 2000, 1, 4; James Leo Garrett, Jr., "Theology Professor Examines Background to Statement's Changes," *Baptist Standard*, 29 May 2000, 10-12.

[479]See above, 471n.284.

[480]Basden, a native of Dallas and a graduate of Baylor University (B.A., 1977) and Southwestern Baptist Theological Seminary (M.Div., 1981; Ph.D., 1986), was pastor of First Church, Clifton TX (1983–1986) and of Valley Ranch Church, Irving TX (1986–1990), was the minister to Samford University (1990–1994), was pastor of Brookwood Church, Birmingham AL (1994–2002), and is now copastor of Preston Trail Community Church, Frisco TX (2002–). He is the author of *The Worship Maze: Finding a Style to Fit Your Church* (Downers Grove IL: InterVarsity, 1999) and coedited a festschrift for James Leo Garrett, Jr.: *The People of God*.

doctrines on which there had been discernible change since 1845. Dwight A. Moody found greater attention given to biblical inerrancy, and Basden himself made the case for change on predestination by reference to the Arminian views of Hobbs, Stagg, and Moody. Walter D. Draughon III, was able to demonstrate change as to penal substitution by noting Conner's embrace of Christ as Victor and Moody's sacrificial view, but Clark R. Youngblood had only Moody as evidence of departure from perseverance. Changes on the doctrine of the Christian life Fisher H. Humphreys found to be more diffuse, but for John Bradley Creed changes as to the nature of pastoral leadership, the role of deacons, and the role of women in the church were rather evident. For Reginald McNeal there has been ferment perhaps more than changes as to the priesthood of all Christians, and according to James T. Spivey millennial doctrine has been marked by diversity that has seen the increased acceptance or the decline of the leading positions.[481] Basden concluded that overall there had been a *"diminishing influence of Calvinism,"* the greater *"influence of modern thought,"* and the impact of *"historically and culturally defining events."* There had been *"no single 'true' Baptist theology"* but a common yearning *"to be faithful to the living and written Word of God."*[482] Fisher H. Humphreys's *The Way We Were: How Southern Baptist Theology Has Changed and What It Means to Us All*[483] was a study of the changes connected with the inerrancy controversy. Humphreys sought to produce an "archive" of pre-1979 Southern Baptist theology by setting forth "the majority tradition" or the *consensus fidelium*. Not unlike the 1963 SBC Baptist Faith and Message Statement, this consensus consisted of beliefs shared with all Christians, those shared with Protestant Christians, those unique to Baptists, and those shared with revivalist Christians. In addition, Humphreys identified six minority traditions among Southern Baptists: Anabaptist, Calvinistic, Landmark, Deeper Life, Fundamentalist, and Progressive. Finally he identified as doctrines likely to be lost by Southern Baptists: the priesthood of all Christians, congregational polity, separation of church and state, and noncreedalism.[484]

Paul A. Basden to James Leo Garrett, Jr., 21 December 2006.

[481]*Has Our Theology Changed?*, 7-158, 180-262.

[482]Ibid., 329-32.

[483](New York: McCracken Press, 1994); rev. ed. (Macon GA: Smyth & Helwys, 2002).

[484]A native of Columbus MS and a graduate of Mississippi College (B.A.,

Mullins, given to theological restatement and being under the influence of personalism, made Christian experience to be crucial to Christian theology in general and soul competency to be the key to Baptist distinctives. The Bible is the "record" of revelation, and Christ is the key to its interpretation. Mullins affirmed Chalcedonian Christology and a modified kenoticism and held to penal substitution. His modified Calvinism agreed with Dort on repentance and faith and on perseverance, and he shifted from premillennialism to less specificity. At the end of the twentieth century Mullins's theology was being scrutinized among Southern Baptists—by defenders, by a mediating school, and by opponents—even as a major literary critic was elevating Mullins's importance.

Prior to 1925 Southern Baptists framed and adopted five doctrinal statements: the five-doctrine 1914 Pronouncement on Christian Union, the ten-doctrine 1917–1918 Articles of Religious Belief of the Baptist Bible Institute (New Orleans), the eight-doctrine 1920 Fraternal Address of Southern Baptists, the thirteen-article 1920 Statement of Belief of the Foreign Mission Board, and Mullins's 1923 statement on Science and Religion.

The 1925 Baptist Faith and Message Statement, prepared in response to evolution and modernism, consisted of modifications of the 1853 revised New Hampshire Confession and eight newly written articles, five concerning churches and church members and three about the larger society. In 1926 the McDaniel statement on creation and evolution was added.

Conner, influenced by his teachers, especially Mullins, wrote a New Testament theology as well as a systematic theology and began the latter with revelation. The authority of the Bible is the authority of Christ, Jesus'

1961), New Orleans Baptist Theological Seminary (B.D., 1964; Th.D., 1972), and Oxford University (B.Litt., 1967), Humphreys taught theology at New Orleans Baptist Theological Seminary (1970–1990) and, until his retirement, was professor of divinity at Beeson Divinity School of Samford University (1990–2008). He is the author of *The Christian Church* (New Orleans: Insight, 1974); *The Death of Christ* (Nashville: Broadman, 1978); *The Heart of Prayer* (Nashville: Broadman, 1980); and *The Nature of God*, Layman's Library of Christian Doctrine (Nashville: Broadman, 1985). With Philip Wise, he coauthored *Fundamentalism* (Macon Ga: Smyth & Helwys, 2004) and coedited *A Dictionary of Doctrinal Terms* (Nashville: Broadman, 1983) and with Paul E. Robertson *God So Loved the World: Traditional Baptists and Calvinism* (New Orleans: Insight, 2000) and edited *Nineteenth Century Evangelical Theology*, Christian Classics (Nashville: Broadman, 1983). *Who's Who in Religion*, vol. 2 (1977) 314.

humanity is to be stressed, and depravity, without any imputation of Adamic guilt, to be taught. A two-point Dortian Calvinist (election, perseverance), Conner shifted from penal substitution to Christ as victor and from postmillennialism to amillennialism. Doctrinal summaries were being produced for the Baptist laity, and the 1946 SBC Statement of Principles focused on human creaturehood and competence, the church, the authority of the New Testament, and religious freedom.

Following an earlier controversy at Southern Seminary, Elliott, Midwestern Seminary's first professor, authored *The Message of Genesis*, which Broadman Press published. Designed to provide a theological interpretation of Genesis, it took the stories of chapters 1–11 to be analogous to Jesus' parables, thus employing a symbolic rather than a historical hermeneutic. Critics of the book, most notably K. Owen White, pressed for a remedy to the situation, and Midwestern's trustees, once mediation failed, dismissed Elliott, while reaffirming the rightful use of the historical-critical method. Consequently SBC leadership proposed a restudy of the 1925 statement by a committee composed of state convention presidents and chaired by Hobbs. After wide consultation the committee in 1963 proposed extensive modifications of the 1925 text. Major alterations included a Christological hermeneutical principle, a rewriting of the doctrine of God, especially as to Christ and the Holy Spirit, a more classical Protestant revision as to salvation, borrowing from the Philadelphia Confession on perseverance, an affirmation of the universal church, and a definition of academic freedom and responsibility.

Hobbs, who extended the legacy of Mullins, especially as to soul competency, through the latter twentieth century, profoundly influenced pastors and Sunday School teachers through his writings and radio preaching. A biblical-exegetical theologian and a centrist, he had a limited view of the role of confessions of faith, treated Christology as the holy history of Jesus, did not teach particular election, held that some of the extraordinary gifts of the Spirit had ceased to be given, interpreted the priesthood of the believer as access to God, and shifted from premillennialism to amillennialism. Doctrinal texts were being written for students, and especially during the 1960s other professors were being dismissed from Southern Baptist seminaries.

An exegetical, homiletical, and pastoral theologian, Criswell strongly affirmed the plenary, verbal (almost dictational) inspiration, sufficiency, authority, and infallibility of the Bible, frequently critiqued Darwinian evolution, embraced the gap theory as to Gen. 1:1-2, and held to a general atonement. He was unsure whether the baptism by the Spirit occurred once-for-all at Pentecost or occurs repeatedly at the conversion of early believer, but he was a cessationist on the extraordinary gifts. The Dallas pastor was a major influence in the SBC's conservative resurgence.

Further controversy was evoked by Henton Davies's exposition of Genesis in the *Broadman Bible Commentary*, especially his treatment of Abraham's preparation to offer his son Isaac (ch. 22). The SBC voted to withdraw this volume from the series and to have it rewritten by Clyde Francisco. Lesser controversy occurred during the 1970s as some Southern Baptist churches began to experience tongues-speaking and numerous monographs appeared on the Holy Spirit.

The first effort to resist alleged liberalism or neoorthodoxy and to advance biblical inerrancy in the SBC came with the Baptist Faith and Message Fellowship. Concurrently books by Lindsell and Pinnock gave expression to the same concern. The second and successful effort came in 1979 through the leadership of Pressler and Patterson with the election of the first of a series of SBC presidents committed to biblical inerrancy, followed by the 1980 resolution on doctrinal integrity. Dilday and Draper set forth competing views of biblical authority and inerrancy. Opposition began to coalesce, first in the Southern Baptist Alliance (1986) and later in the Cooperative Baptist Fellowship (1991). Shurden became the theological spokesperson for the CBF with his freedom-centered theology. The seminary presidents pronounced that the biblical books were "not errant in any area of reality," and the Peace Committee listed four examples of orthodoxy held by the majority: historicity of Adam and Eve, authorship of biblical books by the named authors, occurrence of biblical miracles, and reliability of biblical narratives. Seminary-sponsored conferences on biblical inerrancy and biblical hermeneutics featured Evangelical and non-Baptist scholars. President Young's Theology Study Committee's report (1994), adopted by the SBC, affirmed biblical inerrancy, biblical theism, and the sole saviorhood of Jesus. The priesthood of believers was affirmed as both access and service, and religious liberty was strangely confined to the church's freedom to determine its own doctrine and discipline. The family amendment (1998) defined marriage as between one man and one woman and for their lifetime, applied the *imago Dei* to both, enjoined the wife's submission to the "servant leadership of her husband," and spelled out duties of parents and children. The 2000 Baptist Faith and Message Statement deleted from the 1963 text reference to the Bible as the "record" of revelation and the Christological hermeneutical statement, inserted wording designed to refute the openness of God theology, specified that the baptism by the Spirit occurs at conversion, somewhat deemphasized congregational polity, stated that the office of pastor was limited to men, condemned racism, homosexual practice, and abortion, and interpreted the Lord's Day more permissively.

Southern Baptists began to reflect on how their theology had changed since 1845 and how it had changed by virtue of the inerrancy controversy. At the dawn of the twenty-first century theology, as expressed by SBC actions, was more codified and specific than at any time since 1845. Concurrently, however, alternative expressions of Baptist theology, heavily weighted toward freedom, were being expressed, especially in the Cooperative Baptist Fellowship.

Chapter 10

Recovering Evangelicalism and Reassessing the Baptist Heritage

American Fundamentalism, which, to distinguish it from the earlier Evangelicalism, George M. Marsden defined as "militantly antimodernist Protestant evangelicalism," especially between the 1870s and the 1920s,[1] between the Scopes trial (1925) and the advent of World War II had been subject to ridicule, been in confused disarray, and become increasingly alienated from American culture.[2] In the 1940s a coterie of young leaders, including Harold John Ockenga (1905–1985),[3] sought to redirect the older Fundamentalism, especially its anti-intellectualism, fractious separatism, and lack of a social ethic. Ecclesiastically the new direction took shape in the National Association of Evangelicals.[4] Theologically it centered in the Evangelical Theological Society[5] and a cluster of young theologians representing Neo-Evangelicalism. Baptists—three in particular—would be among the leading theologians of the new movement. One would come from the practice of journalism and become its most influential theologian. Another would come with graduate study in the philosophy of science. Yet another, of a later generation, would come with philosophical training and pastoral experience. Each, although to varying degrees, would be identified primarily as Evangelicals and secondarily as Baptists.

Carl Ferdinand Howard Henry (1913–2003)

Henry, born in New York City to immigrant German-American parents, the mother a nominal Roman Catholic and the father a nominal Lutheran, was baptized and confirmed but not converted as a young teenager in the Episcopal Church and after high school graduation became editor of a small newspaper on Long Island. He committed himself to Jesus Christ at age

---

[1] *Fundamentalism and American Culture*, 4.
[2] Ibid., 184-95.
[3] Harold Lindsell, *Park Street Prophet: A Life of Harold John Ockenga* (Wheaton IL: Van Kampen, 1951). Ockenga was pastor of Park Street Congregational Church in Boston.
[4] James DeForest Murch, *Cooperation without Compromise: A History of the National Association of Evangelicals* (Grand Rapids MI: Eerdmans, 1956).
[5] Joel A. Carpenter, *Revive Us Again: The Reawakening of American Fundamentalism* (New York: Oxford University Press, 1997) 207.

twenty, entered Wheaton College, Wheaton, Illinois, in 1935, and in 1937 united by immersion with a Baptist church on Long Island. After graduating from Wheaton (B.A., 1938; M.A., 1941), he completed B.D. (1941) and Th.D. (1942) degrees from Northern Baptist Theological Seminary, concurrently serving a Baptist student pastorate in Chicago. Later Henry completed a Ph.D. degree under Edgar Brightman at Boston University. After teaching theology at Northern Seminary (1942–1947), he joined the faculty of the newly opened Fuller Theological Seminary, Pasadena, California, and taught chiefly apologetics and ethics until he became the founding editor of *Christianity Today* in 1956. After twelve years his editorship came to an end. In later years he taught at Eastern Baptist Theological Seminary and under sponsorship of World Vision lectured in numerous universities and theological schools.[6] Prolific as to publications, Henry wrote at least thirty-two books and edited a dozen.

In his early writings at mid-century Henry sought to show that the "reversals," or discovered inadequacies, of modern philosophy can only be corrected by Christian theism.[7] He indicted Fundamentalism for its lack of social passion, neglect of preaching the kingdom of God, and anti-intellectualism,[8] found Emil Brunner to be deficient as to revelation, Reinhold Niebuhr on sin, and American liberals on Christology,[9] reviewed critically

---

[6]Henry, *Confessions of a Theologian: An Autobiography* (Waco TX: Word, 1986); Gabriel Fackre, "Carl F. H. Henry," in *A Handbook of Christian Theologians*, enl. ed., ed. Dean G. Peerman and Martin E. Marty (Nashville: Abingdon, 1985) 583-88; Bob E. Patterson, *Carl F. H. Henry*, Makers of the Modern Theological Mind (Waco TX: Word, 1984) 18-24; R. Albert Mohler, Jr., "Carl F. H. Henry," in *Theologians of the Baptist Tradition*, ed. George and Dockery, 279-82; John D. Woodbridge, "Carl F. H. Henry: Spokesperson for American Evangelicalism," in *God and Culture: Essays in Honor of Carl F. H. Henry*, ed. D. A. Carson and Woodbridge (Grand Rapids MI: Eerdmans; Carlisle UK: Paternoster, 1993) 378-93; *Who's Who in America*, 54th ed. (2000) 2138; *Who's Who in Religion*, 4th ed. (1992–1993) 224; Stanley J. Grenz and Roger E. Olson, *20th-Century Theology: God and the World in a Transitional Age* (Downers Grove IL: InterVarsity, 1992) 288-91.

[7]*Remaking the Modern Mind* (Grand Rapids MI: Eerdmans, 1946).

[8]*The Uneasy Conscience of Modern Fundamentalism* (Grand Rapids MI: Eerdmans, 1947).

[9]*The Protestant Dilemma: An Analysis of the Current Impasse in Theology* (Grand Rapids MI: Eerdmans, 1949).

Protestant theology during the first half of the twentieth century,[10] and posed as alternatives the Christian claim to revelation and "naturalistic nihilism," or antisupernaturalistic Protestant liberalism.[11] Some of the volumes edited by Henry were doctrinal in nature,[12] and others of his own books were addressed to the situation and need of Evangelicals.[13] Unquestionably his *magnum opus* was the magisterial six-volume *God, Revelation, and Authority*.[14]

Henry's doctrine of revelation and the Bible was predicated on his consistent rejection of Protestant Neoorthodoxy as well as Liberal Protestantism.[15] In his fifteen theses in his *magnum opus* he presented revelation as by divine initiative and for human benefit, by a God who is mysteriously transcendent. It is inherently unified yet diverse in form. It is from a personal God who names himself, using historical revelation which reached its climax in Jesus Christ, the personal incarnation of God and the mediating Logos. It is a "rational-verbal communication." Thus the Bible is the "authoritative norm" for revelation, and the Holy Spirit not only inspired the Bible but also illumines it and guides in its interpretation.[16] Henry strongly defended the propositional nature of biblical revelation and the distinction between verbal inspiration and dictation.[17] He concluded that historical criticism, when devoid of alliances with alien philosophies and when its limitations are recognized, is legitimate.[18] As to literal interpretation of the Bible, he agreed with Harold Lindsell's statement: "All that is meant by saying one takes the Bible literally is that one believes what it

---

[10] *Fifty Years of Protestant Theology* (Boston: W. A. Wilde, 1950).

[11] *The Drift of Western Thought* (Grand Rapids MI: Eerdmans, 1951).

[12] *Revelation and the Bible* (Grand Rapids MI: Baker, 1958); *Basic Christian Doctrines* (New York: Holt, Rinehart & Winston, 1962); *Jesus of Nazareth: Saviour and Lord* (Grand Rapids MI: Eerdmans, 1966); *Fundamentals of the Faith* (Grand Rapids MI: Baker, 1969).

[13] *Evangelical Responsibility in Contemporary Theology* (Grand Rapids MI: Eerdmans, 1957); *Evangelicals at the Brink of Crisis: Significance of the World Congress on Evangelism* (Waco TX: Word, 1967); *A Plea for Evangelical Demonstration* (Grand Rapids MI: Baker, 1971); *Evangelicals in Search of Identity* (Waco TX: Word, 1976).

[14] (Waco TX: Word, 1976–1983); rev. ed. (Wheaton IL: Crossway, 1999).

[15] Patterson, *Carl F. H. Henry*, 45-50.

[16] *God, Revelation, and Authority*, vols. 2, 3, 4.

[17] *God, Revelation, and Authority* 3:248-303, 386-402, 429-81; 4:137-42.

[18] *God, Revelation, and Authority* 4:75-82, 385-404.

purports to say. This means that figures of speech are regarded as figures of speech."[19] Henry's understanding of biblical inerrancy has been summarized as the teaching "that the autographs [of the Bible] are safeguarded from error in whatever they teach as doctrine—not only in theological and moral matters but also in scientific, historical, and geographical ones."[20] Henry rejected Lindsell's claim that one must hold to inerrancy to be evangelical but insisted that inerrancy, although it cannot guarantee orthodoxy on all other doctrines, is a necessary inference for the sake of "consistency," so as to protect biblical trustworthiness.[21]

According to Bob Patterson,[22] Henry's doctrine of God was constructed against process philosophy/theology, but he also wrote much against Karl Barth and Emil Brunner.[23]

> The God who is, Henry contends, is the God who stands, stoops, and stays. As the God who stands, God contains in himself the ground of his existence. As the God who stoops, God voluntarily forsakes his sovereign exclusivity to both create and redeem the cosmos. As the God who stays, God governs in providence and in eschatological consummation his plan for man and the world.[24]

Henry early opted for the priority of the particular Fatherhood of God[25] and greatly emphasized the holiness, love, and goodness of God.[26] He offered a full-blown doctrine of the Trinity, while deploring the doctrine's neglect by Evangelicals.[27] After reviewing the biblical materials related to and various modern positions concerning the person of Christ, preferring a

---

[19]*God, Revelation, and Authority* 4:103-289, esp. 104; Lindsell, *The Battle for the Bible*, 37.

[20]Fackre, "Carl F. H. Henry," 594. See also Henry, *God, Revelation, and Authority* 4:162-95.

[21]*Conversations with Carl Henry: Christianity for Today*, Symposium Series 18 (Lewiston NY: Edwin Mellen, 1986) 23-28; Mohler, "Carl F. H. Henry," 398.

[22]*Carl F. H. Henry*, 136-40.

[23]*God, Revelation and Authority*, 5:93-98, 115-19, 129, 183-85, 310-11, 365-70.

[24]Patterson, *Carl F. H. Henry*, 128-29.

[25]*Notes on the Doctrine of God* (Boston: W. A. Wilde, 1948) 92-102; see also *God, Revelation, and Authority* 6:305-23.

[26]*Notes on the Doctrine of God*, 103-13; *God, Revelation, and Authority*, 6:251-68, 324-59.

[27]*God, Revelation, and Authority* 5:165-213, esp. 212.

Christology "from above" and recognizing the value of Christological titles, Henry in 1992 defended the Chalcedonian definition and anticipated "an exciting new epoch" in Christology.[28]

In expounding the doctrine of creation he concluded that he could accept "a modified theory of evolution as long as no animal species is regarded as the progenitor of man," the idea of "an ancient earth," and a nonliteral interpretation of six 24-hour days in Genesis 1, but he insisted on a historical Adam and Eve.[29]

Henry's concept of propositional revelation has been criticized in view of the analogical nature of language and the role of personal trust. His reliance upon reason, particularly deductive argumentation, to the neglect of revelation and faith has been questioned. Has he elevated the Bible to the level of Christ?[30] By his concentration on the doctrines of revelation and God, Henry has thereby given little attention to other doctrines, notably the Holy Spirit, the Christian life, and the church.[31]

But Henry helped to reestablish "theology as a vital concern of the Christian community," aggressively engaged "the broader [non-Evangelical] theological community," and "has shaped the evangelical movement to a degree unmatched by any other evangelical theologian of the period."[32]

In his early years Henry had close ties with the Northern Baptist Convention; in his later years he was honored among Southern Baptists, especially by the establishment of the Carl F. H. Henry Institute for Evangelical Engagement at Southern Seminary[33] and the Carl F. H. Henry Institute for Intellectual Discipleship at Union University.

For Evangelicals and for Baptists Carl Henry was a major theologian on the world stage[34] for half a century.

---

[28] *The Identity of Jesus of Nazareth* (Nashville: Broadman) esp. 112.

[29] Patterson, *Carl F. H. Henry*, 145; *God, Revelation, and Authority* 6:108-228.

[30] Thomas Reginald McNeal, "A Critical Analysis of the Doctrine of God in the Theology of Carl F. H. Henry," (Ph.D. diss., Southwestern Baptist Theological Seminary, 1986) 13-109, 306-31; Patterson, *Carl F. H. Henry*, 164-67; Fackre, "Carl F. H. Henry," 605; Stanley J. Grenz, *Renewing the Center: Evangelical Theology in a Posttheological Era* (Grand Rapids MI: Baker, 2000) 100-102.

[31] Mohler, "Carl F. H. Henry," 292; Russell D. Moore, "God, Revelation, and Community: Ecclesiology and Baptist Identity in the Thought of Carl F. H. Henry," *Southern Baptist Journal of Theology* 8 (Winter 2004): 26-43.

[32] Mohler, "Carl F. H. Henry," 291.

[33] Ibid., 293.

[34] Ray S. Anderson, "Evangelical Theology," in *The Modern Theologians: An*

Bernard Lawrence Ramm (1916–1992)

Ramm, a native of Butte, Montana, who had a boyhood fascination with the natural sciences and was converted after high school graduation through the witness of his brother, graduated from the University of Washington (B.A., 1938) and Eastern Baptist Theological Seminary (B.D., 1941). Then from the University of Southern California he received M.A. (1947) and Ph.D. (1950) degrees in the philosophy of science. These studies would be reflected in his *The Christian View of Science and Scripture*.[35] He taught successively in Los Angeles Baptist Theological Seminary (1943–1944), Bible Institute of Los Angeles (1944–1951), Bethel College and Seminary (1951–1954), Baylor University (1954–1959), California Baptist Theological Seminary (1959–1974), Eastern Baptist Theological Seminary (1974–1977), and American Baptist Seminary of the West (1978–1986).[36] The author of twenty books, Ramm wrote on apologetics and ethics as well as doctrinal theology. He traced Evangelicalism to the Protestant Reformation and critiqued both liberalism and neoorthodoxy, though he found values in the latter.[37] Unlike Henry and other Evangelicals, he found the study of Karl Barth's theology to be enriching[38] and to provide "a paradigm of how best to come to terms with the Enlightenment" without "*capitulating to it.*"[39]

Introduction to Christian Theology in the Twentieth Century, ed. David F. Ford, vol. 2 (Oxford: Basil Blackwell, 1989) 141-47; 2nd ed. (Oxford: Basil Blackwell, 1997) 489-94.

[35](Grand Rapids MI: Eerdmans, 1954).

[36]R. Alan Day, "Bernard Ramm," in *Baptist Theologians*, ed. George and Dockery, 588, 590; David W. Miller, "The Theological System of Bernard L. Ramm" (Ph.D. diss., Southwestern Baptist Theological Seminary, 1982) 1-7; *Contemporary Authors*, 112:406; *Directory of American Scholars*, 6th ed., 4:345; Walter Hearn, "An Interview with Bernard Ramm and Alta Ramm," *Journal of the American Scientific Affiliation* 31 (December 1979): 179-86; Grenz and Olson, *20th-Century Theology*, 297-99.

[37]*The Evangelical Heritage* (Waco TX: Word, 1973) esp. 23-40, 75-122.

[38]Ibid., 117-18.

[39]*After Fundamentalism: The Future of Evangelical Theology* (San Francisco: Harper & Row, 1983) vii, 14. See R. Albert Mohler, "Bernard Ramm: Karl Barth and the Future of American Evangelicalism," in *Perspectives on Theology in the Contemporary World: Essays in Honor of Bernard Ramm*, ed. Stanley J. Grenz (Macon GA: Mercer University Press, 1990) 27-41.

Influenced as well by Abraham Kuyper and P. T. Forsyth,[40] Ramm belonged to the Reformed theological heritage.[41] Teaching in Baptist institutions, he seldom cited other Baptist theologians and did not address Baptist ecclesiological issues.

Ramm early addressed the issue of religious authority, that is, how God delegates the authority of truth, by opting for "a mosaic of authority." The Protestant principle of authority, he declared, is "the Holy Spirit speaking in the Scriptures, which are the product of the Spirit's revelatory and inspiring action." "No wedge can be driven between the Spirit and the Bible, the Bible and Christ, and Christ and the Spirit. They form an inseparable mosaic of divine authority."[42] Recognizing the paucity of twentieth-century writings on biblical hermeneutics, he at mid-century contributed a monograph. Needed in order "to ascertain the meaning of the Word of God," the "science and art" of biblical hermeneutics seeks "to bridge the gap between" modern minds and "the minds of the Biblical writers" and thus provide "the correct interpretation." Ramm found that both Jews and Christians had both literal and allegorical schools of interpretation, and he critically examined mystical, pietistic, liberal, and neoorthodox methods. According to Ramm, Protestant hermeneutics presupposes the divine inspiration of the Scriptures and has a threefold method: literal, cultural, and critical (or justifiable). He recognized divine accommodation, progressive revelation, singular interpretation with plural applications, and the analogy of faith. He followed Patrick Fairbairn's less restrictive view of legitimate typology rather than that of Herbert Marsh and noted certain qualifications of biblical inerrancy.[43] Following in the train of John Calvin, Ramm gave emphasis to the internal testimony of the Holy Spirit, defined as "an *absolute* persuasion" by the Spirit as to the Scriptures being "the Word of God" and the gospel of salvation being true. Calvin, according to Ramm, had opted for the *testimonium* as the true alternative to Roman Catholic, Enthusiast, and rationalist views. Moreover, Liberalism had lost the *testimonium* by making it identical with religious experience, and Fundamentalism had

---

[40]*After Fundamentalism*, 8-10.

[41]Miller, "The Theological System of Bernard L. Ramm," 7-15; Day, "Bernard Ramm," 591.

[42]*The Pattern of Authority* (Grand Rapids MI: Eerdmans, 1957) 18, 28, 46.

[43]*Protestant Biblical Interpretation: A Textbook of Hermeneutics for Conservative Protestants* (Boston: Wilde, 1950) 1, 3, 6, 20-61, 78-83, 88-91, 140-45, 125-37; 2nd ed. (Boston: Wilde, 1956); 3rd ed. (Grand Rapids MI: Baker, 1970).

neglected it by its sacramental, rather than instrumental, view of the Bible in which the coordination of Word and Spirit had been sundered.[44] Special revelation is "remedial," personal, and subject to the incomprehensibility of God. God's condescension as special revelation is characterized as both "*anthropic*," or "*marked by human characteristics throughout*," and "*analogical in form*." The modalities of such revelation were numerous: casting of the lot, Urim and Thummim, "deep sleep," dreams, visions, theophanies, and angels. Special revelation came both by divine speaking and by divine action, and its supreme focus is the incarnation. The communication of special revelation utilizes languages, affords an "ectypal knowledge of God," rightly employs concepts, and results in and continues to make use of the necessarily translated Holy Scriptures.[45]

Unlike other Baptist and Evangelical theologians, Ramm directly and substantively addressed the issues between the Christian faith and the physical sciences. Seeking to foster harmony rather than perpetuate conflict between the two, with its mistakes on both sides, he explored the character of biblical language concerning natural things, defended the view that the Bible does not have a "systematized" or "postulational" cosmology, and espoused a form of progressive creationism. For Ramm, the six days of creation meant the revelation to man concerning creation during six days,[46] and the Noahic flood was "local to the Mesopotamian valley," not universal. He affirmed the monogenetic origin of human beings about 500,000 years ago.[47]

---

[44]*The Witness of the Spirit: An Essay on the Contemporary Relevance of the Internal Witness of the Holy Spirit* (Grand Rapids MI: Eerdmans, 1959) 18, 11, 18-19, 99-105, 11-16, 62-65, 109-27.

[45]*Special Revelation and the Word of God* (Grand Rapids MI: Eerdmans, 1961) 19-27, 36-48, 53-207. R. Alan Day, "The Concept of Revelation in the Theology of Bernard Ramm" (Th.D. diss., New Orleans Baptist Theological Seminary, 1979) esp. 220, wrote appreciatively of Ramm's doctrine, asserting that he had "steered a middle course between the narrowness of fundamentalism and the recklessness of liberalism," but Kenny Regan Pulliam, "A Critique of Bernard Ramm's Doctrine of the Bible" (Ph.D. diss., Bob Jones University, 1986) esp. 280, found it to be totally "unacceptable to the orthodox, fundamental Christian."

[46]The view of P. J. Wiseman. See above, 476n.311.

[47]*The Christian View of Science and Scripture*, 17-58, 65-80, 96-102 (esp. 97), 112-17, 227-29, 293, 218-26, 229-49 (esp. 249), 306-31 (esp. 306-308, 315, 327). Bob E. Patterson, "Modern Science and Contemporary Biblical Interpretation: Ramm's Contribution," in *Perspectives on Theology*, ed. Grenz, 55-67, found that

Ramm's monograph on Christology, surely one of his best, argued that evangelical Christology "is a continuation of historic Christology," or that of the ancient creeds, in contrast to the modern rejection of that historic Christology. Ramm set out a linear Christology that extended from deity and preexistence through incarnation, virgin birth, and humanity to the cross, resurrection, and ascension and then to intercession and second coming. But he also acknowledged the place of titles in Christology and the challenge posed by modern criticism to the reliability of the Gospels and reviewed the various twentieth-century alternatives to historic Christology.[48]

In his well-crafted monograph on sin Ramm wrote insightfully as the Evangelical Reinhold Niebuhr. He took his thesis from Blaise Pascal (1623–1662); namely, that "the Christian doctrine of sin is offensive to the reason and repelled by the intelligentsia and academia"; without it "much of human life and history remains forever opaque; [and] with it a shaft of light is cast upon personal existence, social existence, and the course of history...." The Christian doctrine, more anchored in Rom. 1:18–3:20 than in Rom. 5:12-21, he argued, is a better explanation of evils than alternative views. For the author of Genesis, "a Hebrew living after the Exodus," Genesis 1–3 came by "divinely inspired reconstruction" or "theology by narration." There was generic Adam, and there was the person Adam. Biological death preceded the advent of sin and became different because of sin, and infants dying in infancy will be saved. Ramm retained original righteousness and a historical fall while also embracing the existential fall. No area of human endeavor is unaffected by sin.[49]

Ramm provided an alternative to both "scientific naturalism" and creation science but rejected Ramm's progressive creationism. A commendatory assessment of Ramm's progressive creationism had been made by William Beryl West, "Theistic Evolution in the Writings of A. H. Strong and Bernard Ramm" (Th.M. thesis, Southwestern Baptist Theological Seminary, 1962).

[48]*An Evangelical Christology: Ecumenic and Historic* (Nashville: Thomas Nelson, 1985) esp. 15.

[49]*Offense to Reason: A Theology of Sin* (San Francisco: Harper & Row, 1985) vii, 163, 42-44, 49-51, 10-37, 68-75, 112-16, 117-18, 135-40, 145-59. Ramm considered original sin an essential part of the Christian theological heritage but did not espouse one of the historic theories. In this book (113) he dated the origin of humanity as "thirty to thirty-five thousand years" ago.

Rather than develop a biblical and theological exposition of Satan, Ramm, borrowing from C. S. Lewis's *The Screwtape Letters*, exposited and critiqued the views of seven modern "Wormwoods" (Hume, Nietzsche, Freud, Wittgenstein, Heidegger, Sartre, and Camus).[50]

The Holy Spirit, whom Ramm called "the Hermes from heaven" and "the [second] divine ombudsman," is necessarily both divine and personal. The Holy Spirit "must never be separated from Christ," as in mysticism, enthusiasm, psychological introspection, or Pentecostalism. For Ramm the tongues of Acts 2:4 were foreign languages, whereas those in 1 Corinthians 12–14 were "nonlanguages," and language has an existential quality. The Spirit is needed to awaken and empower the church, for "what started as limber spirit has ended up as organizational lumber."[51]

Ramm was also unique among modern Baptist theologians by providing a monograph on the doctrine of glorification. This embraced the "glorification of the soul" (end-time moral perfection, full participation in freedom, conformity to Christ), "glorification of the body" (bodily resurrection), and "glorification and the New Jerusalem" (the new heavens and the new earth).[52] He also espoused an eschatological resolution to the problem of evil, for "no present theodicy is really satisfactory."[53]

Ramm, who in his earliest student years regarded "himself as a fundamentalist-premillennial dispensationalist," moved through what he called "'a continuous upward spiral'"[54] until he could be called by Clark Pinnock a "postfundamentalist" and a "postliberal."[55] Ramm, according to Stanley J. Grenz, distanced himself more fully than Henry from the rationalism of fundamentalism, which robbed revelation of its mystery.[56]

---

[50] *The Devil, Seven Wormwoods, and God* (Waco TX: Word, 1977).

[51] *Rapping about the Spirit* (Waco TX: Word, 1974) 84-92, 156-58, 26-35, 37-44, 113, 115, 130-36, 54-61 (esp. 55).

[52] *Them He Glorified: A Systematic Study of the Doctrine of Glorification* (Grand Rapids MI: Eerdmans, 1963) 62-115.

[53] *The God Who Makes a Difference: A Christian Appeal to Reason* (Waco TX: Word, 1972) 135. On the basis of Ramm's unpublished "An Outline of Evangelical Theology," Miller, "The Theological System of Bernard L. Ramm," 103-42, has fleshed out Ramm's entire systematic theology.

[54] Miller, "The Theological System of Bernard L. Ramm," 4.

[55] "Bernard Ramm: Postfundamentalist Coming to Terms with Modernity," in *Perspectives on Theology*, ed. Grenz, 15-26.

[56] *Renewing the Center*, 115.

Millard John Erickson (1932–)

Of a generation after Henry and Ramm, Erickson would more fully embody both Evangelical and Baptist identities. Born on a Minnesota farm near Minneapolis, with Swedish Baptist immigrant grandparents, he found his ministerial calling at Bethel College before transferring to the University of Minnesota, where he majored in philosophy. Seminary studies were begun at Bethel Seminary, where Bernard Ramm was his teacher, and completed at Northern Baptist Theological Seminary (M.Div.). While serving as pastor of Fairfield Avenue Church, Chicago, he completed the M.A. in philosophy at the University of Chicago and residency requirements for a Ph.D. under William Hordern from Garrett Theological Seminary/Northwestern University. Then while serving Olivet Church, Minneapolis, he completed that degree. Five years of teaching at Wheaton College (1964–1969) were followed by twenty-three years of teaching theology at Bethel Seminary, where he also was executive vice-president and dean. Subsequently he has taught at Southwestern Baptist Theological Seminary, Western Seminary, and Truett Theological Seminary of Baylor University.[57] Early Erickson was attracted to the theologians of the new evangelicalism,[58] and then he edited a three-volume anthology, *Readings in Christian Theology*,[59] before producing his widely used *magnum opus*, *Christian Theology*.[60] The author of at least twenty-three volumes, Erickson in his later books has tended

---

[57]David S. Dockery, "Millard J. Erickson: Baptist and Evangelical Theologian," *Journal of the Evangelical Theological Society* 32 (December 1989): 519-32; idem, "Millard J. Erickson," in *Baptist Theologians*, ed. George and Dockery, 640, 642-44; L. Arnold Hustad, "Millard J. Erickson," in *Handbook of Evangelical Theologians*, ed. Walter A. Elwell (Grand Rapids MI: Baker, 1993) 412-44; Bradley G. Green, "Millard J. Erickson," in *Theologians of the Baptist Tradition*, ed. George and Dockery, 317-22; Dockery, "Millard J. Erickson: Theologian for the Church," in *New Dimensions in Evangelical Thought: Essays in Honor of Millard J. Erickson*, ed. Dockery (Downers Grove IL: InterVarsity, 1998) 17-20; Hustad, "Bibliographic Essay on the Works of Millard J. Erickson," in ibid., 443-50.

[58]*The New Evangelical Theology* (Westwood NJ: Fleming H. Revell, 1968; London: Marshall, Morgan and Scott, 1969).

[59]*The Living God* (Grand Rapids MI: Baker, 1973); *Man's Need and God's Gift* (Grand Rapids MI: Baker, 1976); *The New Life* (Grand Rapids MI: Baker, 1979).

[60]3 vols. (Grand Rapids MI: Baker, 1983, 1984, 1985); 2nd ed. (Grand Rapids MI: Baker, 1998).

either to interpret and give counsel to Evangelicals,[61] or to focus on specific doctrines,[62] or to deal with ethics.[63]

Like Ramm, Erickson regarded theology as a "science." He set forth a detailed ninefold "process," from the biblical texts to a theological system, for carrying out the task of systematic theology. He began with the doctrine of revelation rather than the doctrine of God and chose as the "central motif" "the magnificence of God." Unlike earlier Baptist theologians, he treated biblical criticism and theological language as part of the doctrine of revelation. Following Hordern, he held that in contemporizing the Christian message we should be "translators," not "transformers." General revelation is not salvific, and special revelation is both "propositional" and "personal." Erickson inclined toward the verbal theory of inspiration and clearly gave priority to the Bible's self-testimony rather than to biblical phenomena. He embraced the theory of "full inerrancy" of translations as well as autographs so as to include historical and scientific matters and opted for the theory of

---

[61]*Evangelical Interpretation: Perspectives on Hermeneutical Issues* (Grand Rapids MI: Baker, 1993); *The Evangelical Mind and Heart: Perspectives on Theological and Practical Issues* (Grand Rapids MI: Baker, 1993); *Where Is Theology Going? Issues and Perspectives on the Future of Theology* (Grand Rapids MI: Baker, 1994); *The Evangelical Left: Encountering Postconservative Evangelical Theology* (Grand Rapids MI: Baker, 1997); *Postmodernizing the Faith: Evangelical Responses to the Challenge of Postmodernism* (Grand Rapids MI: Baker, 1998); *Truth or Consequences: The Promise and Perils of Postmodernism* (Downers Grove IL: InterVarsity, 2001).

[62]*What Does God Know and When Does He Know It? The Current Controversy over Divine Foreknowledge* (Grand Rapids MI: Zondervan, 2003); *God the Father Almighty: A Contemporary Exploration of the Divine Attributes* (Grand Rapids MI: Baker, 1998); *God in Three Persons: A Contemporary Interpretation of the Trinity* (Grand Rapids MI: Baker, 1995); *Making Sense of the Trinity: Three Crucial Questions* (Grand Rapids MI: Baker, 2000); *The Word Became Flesh* (Grand Rapids MI: Baker, 1991); *Salvation: God's Amazing Plan* (Wheaton IL: Victor Books, 1978); repr. under title *Does It Matter That I'm Saved? What the Bible Teaches about Salvation* (Grand Rapids MI: Baker, 1996); *How Shall They Be Saved? The Destiny of Those Who Do Not Hear of Jesus* (Grand Rapids MI: Baker, 1996); *A Basic Guide to Eschatology: Making Sense of the Millennium* (Grand Rapids MI: Baker, 1998).

[63]*Relativism in Contemporary Ethics* (Grand Rapids MI: Baker, 1974); *Does It Matter How I Live? Applying Biblical Beliefs to Your Daily Life* (Grand Rapids MI: Baker, 1987).

"moderate harmonization" as to biblical phenomena. Erickson retained Ramm's pattern of authority except that the witness of the Spirit is more illumination than validation.[64]

Erickson clustered the divine attributes around two foci, the greatness of God and the goodness of God, and sought to balance transcendence and immanence.[65] He found it necessary to defend the Christian doctrine of God against pluralism, process thought, and open theism.[66] First, Erickson set forth concisely the "orthodox" doctrine of the Trinity, while searching for valid analogies.[67] Later in two monographs he traced the patristic doctrine of the Trinity, though without Augustine, treated the biblical materials more fully, answered the claims of feminism and generic religion, defended the metaphysics of a social Trinity, examined the views of recent authors concerning the Trinity, and dealt with worship and prayer vis-à-vis the Trinity.[68] Rather than deal with divine decrees the Bethel theologian set forth "God's plan," thereby providing "a moderately Calvinistic model" that sought "to correlate human freedom and [divine] sovereignty."[69] Creation out of nothing Erickson reckoned to have been progressive, as Ramm had held, with microevolution but without macroevolution, and as to the age of the earth he favored a form of the age-day theory. Providence embraces both preservation of the created order and governance, within which prayer and miracles occur and angels and demons are active.[70]

Erickson opened his doctrine of humanity by reviewing modern concepts of the human and closed it by recognizing the full humanity of all races, both sexes, persons of all economic conditions, the aged, the unborn, and the unmarried. Defending the historicity of Adam and Eve, he accepted a 30,000-year span of human existence.[71] His doctrine of the *imago Dei*, which did not recognize the distinctions between Genesis and Paul, purported to be the structural view and was de facto the cluster-of-capacities

---

[64]*Christian Theology*, 1st ed., 33-36, 66-79, 30-33, 78, 81-104, 127-49, 112-20, 170-74, 191-96, 207, 214-20, 207-10, 222, 233-38, 229-33, 247-53.

[65]Ibid., 263-319.

[66]*God the Father Almighty*, 31-92. See below, 578-79.

[67]*Christian Theology*, 321-42.

[68]*God in Three Persons*, 33-93, 159-210, 139-56, 219-28, 97-11, 122-30, 214-19, 239-63, 271-78, 314-28; *Making Sense of the Trinity*.

[69]*Christian Theology*, 345-63; Dockery, "Millard J. Erickson," 650.

[70]*Christian Theology*, 367-70, 382-84, 481-84, 380-82, 388-410, 433-51.

[71]Ibid., 455-72, 541-58, 474-77, 484-87.

view.[72] More creative was Erickson's "conditional unity," or predeath "pneumopsychosomatic" monism of human beings. After a detailed review of the biblical terms for sin, he opted for the "failure to let God be God," or idolatry, as "the essence of sin." Various modern answers as to the origin of moral evil were found to be inadequate, but Erickson espoused the Augustinian or natural headship theory of the imputation of Adam's sin but modified it so that the guilt is only conditional until ratified by a person's initial sinning. The "social dimension of sin" is sustained by the biblical categories of "the world," "the powers," and corporate personality, and the "potential" of physical death and of eternal life were both in prelapsarian Adam and Eve.[73]

In his *Christian Theology* Erickson opted not for a Christology "from above" or a Christology "from below" but for one from the kerygma (preaching of the primitive church). He expounded both the deity and humanity of Jesus against heretical views, defended the virgin birth, and, completing his Chalcedonian Christology, set forth the unity of Jesus' person.[74] In a large monograph on incarnational Christology Erickson interpreted and critiqued eleven twentieth-century alternatives to an incarnational or Chalcedonian Christology and then reinterpreted and defended the latter in great detail.[75] The Bethel theologian, who redefined the threefold office as that of revealer, ruler, and reconciler, not only embraced the penal substitution theory of the atonement but contended that other theories are tenable only if based on penal substitution. He opted for universal atonement with limited application.[76] A controversial stance by Erickson has been his conclusion that Jesus' resurrection was actually a "resuscitation" and that his transformation to a spiritual body came at his ascension.[77]

Erickson set forth the classical features of the doctrine of the Holy Spirit—his deity, his personality, his role in the life of Jesus, and his work in the Christian life—and then addressed contemporary claims to tongues-

---

[72]Ibid., 495-517; Garrett, *Systematic Theology*, 2nd ed., 1:460-61.

[73]*Christian Theology*, 536-39, 564-95, 636-39, 643-55, 611-15.

[74]Ibid., 665-75, 683-722, 739-58, 723-38.

[75]*The Word Became Flesh*, 87-624.

[76]*Christian Theology*, 762-69, 802-41 (esp. 819, 835). Green, "Millard J. Erickson," 328-29, has concluded that by affirming universal atonement Erickson was sublapsarian.

[77]Ibid., 776-79; Dockery, "Millard J. Erickson," 651; idem, "Millard J. Erickson: Theologian for the Church," 29.

speaking. He found no unquestionable support for the cessation of "miraculous gifts"; neither should one reject a priori the claim to tongues-speaking.[78]

Taking "salvation" as the umbrella term for the application of the work of Christ to believers, Erickson began with the single predestination of the elect, foreknowledge being "an affirmative choice" rather than "advance knowledge." He differentiated the "subjective" aspects of initial salvation (inward change) from the "objective" (individual-God relationship). The subjective includes effectual calling by God (or illumination by the Spirit), conversion (repentance and faith as human turning), and regeneration by God. The objective embraces union with Christ, forensic justification, and adoption. Sanctification and the Christian life constitute the continuation of salvation, and perseverance and glorification its completion. Erickson rejected eschatological universalism.[79]

Beginning his doctrine of the church with the fact that the Ecumenical Movement had brought the doctrine "into the forefront of discussion," Erickson offered "empirical-dynamic" and "biblical-philological" definitions of the church and showed less interest than most of his Baptist predecessors in the local uses of *ekklēsia*. The major biblical images were interpreted, the visible/invisible distinction was "maintained, but with qualifications," and the church was said to have "originated at Pentecost." The church is "spiritual Israel," but there is to be "a future for national Israel." The church's functions are evangelism, edification, worship, and social concern. Church polity, for Erickson, cannot be determined from the New Testament because of "the lack of didactic material," but congregationalism "most nearly fulfils" the principles of good polity. He regarded baptism as "a token of salvation" or "an outward symbol" of an "inward change," opted for believer's baptism, and refuted baptismal regeneration, but he was unsure that immersion must be the normative mode today, though he called it "the most adequate." In the Lord's Supper Christ is "objectively present" by the Spirit, his presence being "influential rather than metaphysical." The Bethel professor had no reason to raise the Landmark caveat about the proper administration of baptism, but neither did he mention baptism in general or baptism by immersion in particular as

---

[78]*Christian Theology*, 845-83.

[79]Ibid., 887-1022. In *How Shall They Be Saved?*, 65-139, he differentiated and evaluated "classical universalism," "twentieth-century pluralism," "Roman Catholic inclusivism," and "Protestant inclusivism."

prerequisite to receiving the elements; hence open membership in Baptist churches seems to be allowed.[80] Erickson, having differentiated various concepts of Christian unity, utilized William R. Estep's fourfold argument for Baptist nonparticipation in councils of churches.[81]

In eschatology Erickson, rejecting soul sleep, purgatory, and "instant reclothing," opted for a disembodied intermediate state in which the unrighteous go to Hades and the righteous to Paradise. The second coming will be "personal," "physical," "visible," "unexpected," "triumphant," and "impending" (but not "imminent"), but not divided into "rapture" and "revelation," as dispensationalism teaches.[82] According to Erickson, there will be two resurrections, the first of the righteous and the second of the unrighteous.[83] He included no chapter on the kingdom of God,[84] but his chapter on the millennium manifests his commitment to historic, posttribulational premillennialism. Heaven and hell were affirmed with no allowances for any form of annihilationism.[85]

According to David S. Dockery, Erickson has been "faithful to his Baptist and evangelical heritage," providing a systematic theology that "is both orthodox and contemporary, yet it is not faddish or overly innovative." Its strengths include its "balanced theological method," its "nuanced view of Scripture," and its "doxological tone." Its weaknesses include its lack of appreciation for paradox and for anthropomorphism, its view of Jesus' resurrection body, and its lack of exposition of the kingdom of God. Dockery compared Erickson quite favorably with other past and present Baptist theologians.[86] On the contrary, Stanley J. Grenz found that, while Erickson's *Christian Theology* "displays" a "generally irenic, 'generic' neo-

---

[80]Ibid., 1025-59, 1078-82, 1083-87, 1096-1105, 1121-25.

[81]Ibid., 1135-37, 1142-45; Estep, *Baptists and Christian Unity* (Nashville: Broadman, 1966) 168-88.

[82]*Christian Theology*, 1176-84, 1188-94.

[83]Ibid., 1200, 1210-11, 1214-17.

[84]He did briefly discuss the church as "a manifestation of the kingdom" (ibid., 1041-42).

[85]Ibid., 1205-41. See also *Contemporary Options in Eschatology: A Study of the Millennium* (Grand Rapids MI: Baker, 1977); repr. under title *A Basic Guide to Eschatology: Making Sense of the Millennium* (Grand Rapids MI: Baker, 1998); *How Shall They Be Saved?*, 217-32.

[86]"Millard J. Erickson," 652-54; "Millard J. Erickson, Theologian for the Church," 30-31.

evangelicalism," the later Erickson has taken on the "mantle" of Carl Henry rather than of Bernard Ramm, has warned against younger Evangelicals who positively engage the context of postmodernism, and is "drifting to the [theological] right."[87]

Baptist Distinctives

Prior to the American Modernist-Fundamentalist controversy, among Baptists there had arisen a new genre of theological writing, the exposition and/or defense of Baptist distinctives or emphases. English Baptists since the seventeenth century had produced controversial writings, especially works on baptism against Pedobaptists, but the general exposition of Baptist distinctives had been a rarity. Beginning in the 1840s and 1850s this genre came into existence as Northern,[88] Southern,[89] English,[90] and other Baptist authors produced monographs on the distinctive principles or beliefs of Baptists.[91]

---

[87] *Renewing the Center*, 118-34 (esp. 125, 118, 130, 131, 133).

[88] For example, Thomas F. Curtis, *The Progress of Baptist Principles* (Philadelphia: American Baptist Publication Society, 1855); Alvah Hovey, *Restatement of Denominational Principles* (Philadelphia: American Baptist Publication Society, 1892); Philip L. Jones, *A Restatement of Baptist Principles* (Philadelphia: Griffith and Rowland, 1909); Winthrop Still Hudson, *Baptist Convictions* (Valley Forge PA: Judson, 1963).

[89] For example, John Albert Broadus, *The Duty of Baptists to Teach Their Distinctive Views* (Philadelphia: American Baptist Publication Society, 1881); James Madison Pendleton, *Distinctive Baptist Principles* (Philadelphia: American Baptist Publication Society, 1882); John Lansing Burrows, *What Baptists Believe* (Baltimore: H. M. Wharton, 1887); Franklin Howard Kerfoot, *Distinctive Doctrines of the Baptists* (Louisville: Baptist Argus, 1898); *Baptist Why and Why Not* (Nashville: Sunday School Board of the SBC, 1900); Jeremiah Bell Jeter et al., *Baptist Principles Reset*, 3rd ed. (Richmond VA: Religious Herald, 1902); Thomas Treadwell Eaton, *The Faith of the Baptists* (Louisville: Baptist Book Concern, 1903); William Richardson White, *Baptist Distinctives* (Nashville: Sunday School Board of the SBC, 1946).

[90] For example, Timothy Harley, *Baptist Principles* (London: Baptist Tract Depository, 1882); Robinson, *Baptist Principles*; Henry Cook, *What Baptists Stand For* (London: Kingsgate, 1947); Jack Hoad, *The Baptist: A Historical and Theological Study of the Baptist Identity* (London: Grace Publications Trust, 1986).

[91] Norman, "A Critical Analysis of the Intentional Efforts of Baptists to Distinguish Themselves Theologically from Other Christian Denominations."

Such authors, as R. Stanton Norman has observed, have tended to deal with the question of authority, to refute the teachings of other Christian denominations, to magnify ecclesiology, and to represent the Baptist passion for freedom.[92] These writers have given diverse answers as to what may be identified as the primary Baptist distinctive: the authority of the Bible or of the New Testament, either its sole authority (Broadus) or its supreme authority (Hovey); a regenerate church membership (Eaton); believer's baptism (Robinson, *Baptist Principles*); baptism by immersion (Pendleton); the lordship or sovereignty of Christ (J. D. Freeman[93]), and soul competency (Mullins, *The Axioms of Religion*).[94] Norman has argued that the most basic distinction among all these writings is between those affirming "the primacy of the Bible" and those affirming "the primacy of religious experience."[95]

Baptists, Free Churches, and Believers' Churches

In England, Baptists especially during the early twentieth century specifically identified with other Free or Nonconformist denominations, particularly through the National Council of the Evangelical Free Churches (1892) and the Federal Council of the Evangelical Free Churches (1919), which united in 1920 to form the Free Church Federal Council.[96] Such identi-

---

[92]Ibid., 11-25.

[93]"The Place of Baptists in the Christian Church," in *Baptist World Congress, London, July 11-19, 1905*, 22.

[94]Norman, "A Critical Analysis," 34-59.

[95]Ibid., 72, 88, 108, 121, 134, 147, 160, 172, 186, 195, 205, 212, 231-35. See also Norman, *More Than Just a Name: Preserving Our Baptist Identity* (Nashville: Broadman & Holman, 2001).

[96]Edward Kenneth Harry Jordan, *Free Church Unity: History of the Free Church Council Movement, 1896–1941* (London: Lutterworth Press, 1956) 21-35, 49, 127-35, 229; Ernest Alexander Payne, *The Free Church Tradition in the Life of England*, 4th ed. (London: Hodder & Stoughton, 1965) 121-22, 128-29. The Federal Council had come into existence largely through the advocacy by John Howard Shakespeare, general secretary of the Baptist Union of Great Britain and Ireland, of federation as a step toward organic union. Jordan, *Free Church Unity*, 127-34. On Shakespeare, see Peter Shepherd, *The Making of a Modern Denomination: John Howard Shakespeare and the English Baptists, 1898–1924*, Studies in Baptist History and Thought 4 (Carlisle UK, Waynesboro GA: Paternoster, 2001). On the common beliefs of the Free Churches, see Henry T. Wigley, *The Distinctive Free Church Witness To-day* (Wallington UK: Religious Education Press, 1949).

fication involved the usage of the primary and original meaning of "free church," namely, nonestablishment by the civil government. At least three other meanings of "free church"[97] came into usage. The second referred to patterns of public worship in that "free church" would mean nonliturgical, or the nonuse of written prayers and prayer books. In this respect most all Baptist churches could be considered to be "free churches." The third, meaning churches practicing congregational polity, would include Baptists. The fourth meaning of "free church" has been noncreedal or nonconfessional.[98] Inasmuch as most Baptist churches and Baptist general bodies have adopted confessions of faith, though usually without creedal enforcement, the fourth usage has not been generally applicable to Baptists.[99]

In the United States and Canada during the 1960s another term "believers' churches" came into usage and constituted the theme for a series of thirteen conferences,[100] in which Baptists participated, that stretched to the end of the century. The new coinage was designed to identify those Christian churches which believed that they should be composed solely of professed and genuine believers in Jesus Christ. Such usage tended to mean, though not absolutely, churches practicing believer's baptism. Often the covenantal nature of church membership and the practice of church discipline are associated with the term.[101] Preceded by a conference by and

---

[97]Curtis W. Freeman, "'To Feed upon by Faith': Nourishment from the Lord's Table," in *Baptist Sacramentalism*, ed. Anthony R. Cross and Philip E. Thompson, Studies in Baptist History and Thought 5 (Carlisle UK; Waynesboro GA: Paternoster, 2003) 194, has identified five meanings, including the freedom of conscience.

[98]Donald F. Durnbaugh, *The Believers' Church: The History and Character of Radical Protestantism* (New York: Macmillan, 1968) 4-8.

[99]An exception is Stewart A. Newman, *A Free Church Perspective: A Study in Ecclesiology* (Wake Forest NC: Stevens Book Press, 1986) esp. 11-61, 102-5, who interpreted the Free Churches as the result of the Renaissance's having freed Western Christianity from medieval "authoritarianism" and opened the door to the responsible individualism of modernity so that the Free Churches are the "by-products" of religious experience and foster the private nonliteral interpretation of the Bible with no reference to confessions of faith.

[100]Barry L. Callen, *Radical Christianity: The Believers Church Tradition in Christianity's History and Future* (Nappanee IL: Evangel Publishing House, 1999) 189-92; John Howard Yoder, "The Believers' Church Conferences in Historical Perspective," *Mennonite Quarterly Review* 65 (January 1991): 5-19.

[101]Durnbaugh, *The Believers' Church*, 32-33.

for the General Conference Mennonite Church in Chicago in 1955 and a peace church conference in Richmond, Indiana, in 1964 and prodded by the initiative of Johannes A. Oosterbaan, professor of theology at the Mennonite Theological Seminary, Amsterdam, and the active leadership of the American Mennonite theologian-ethicist, John Howard Yoder (1927–1997),[102] Southern Baptist Theological Seminary hosted the first interdenominational Believers' Church Conference in 1967. Some "150 voluntary, nonelected participants" drawn from more than two dozen . . . denominations which claimed affiliation with . . . the Believers' Church"[103] focused on the meaning of the concept of a believers' church. Baptists William R. Estep, Jr. and Dale Moody presented papers.[104] Canadian Baptists and Canadian Mennonites held the fifth, a strictly Canadian, conference in Winnipeg in 1978,[105] Southwestern Baptist Theological Seminary hosted the ninth conference on Balthasar Hubmaier in 1989,[106] and McMaster Divinity College hosted the twelfth conference in 1996.[107] Baptists presenting papers at other conferences have included: Jarold Knox Zeman and Edwin Scott Gaustad on restitution,[108] Clark H. Pinnock on Chalcedonian Christology,[109] Timothy George on Southern Baptists,[110] Samuel J.

---

[102]John Howard Yoder, intro. to *Baptism and Church: A Believers' Church Vision*, ed. Merle D. Strege (Grand Rapids MI: Sagamore Books, 1986) 3-4; Callen, *Radical Christianity*, 14-16.

[103]Paul A. Basden, "James Leo Garrett, Jr.," in George and Dockery, eds., *Theologians of the Baptist Tradition*, ed. George and Dockery, 302.

[104]*The Concept of the Believers' Church: Addresses from the 1967 Conference*, ed. James Leo Garrett, Jr. (Scottdale PA: Herald, 1969) esp. 35-58, 224-49.

[105]*The Believers' Church in Canada: Addresses and Papers from the Study Conference in Winnipeg, May 15-18, 1978*, ed. Jarold K. Zeman and Walter Klaasen (Brantford ON: Baptist Federation of Canada; Winnipeg: Mennonite Central Committee, 1979). At least seventeen Canadian Baptists made presentations.

[106]*Mennonite Quarterly Review* 65 (January 1991): 5-53. Baptists James W. McClendon, Jr., and H. Wayne Pipkin presented papers.

[107]*The Believers' Church: A Voluntary Church: Papers of the Twelfth Believers' Church Conference Held at McMaster Divinity College, October 17-19, 1996*, ed. William H. Brackney (Kitchener ON: Pandora Press, 1998).

[108]*Journal of the American Academy of Religion* 44 (March 1976): 7-27, 77-86.

[109]Summarized by J. Denny Weaver in "A Believers' Church Christology," *Mennonite Quarterly Review* 57 (April 1983): 126-29.

[110]*Baptism and Church: A Believer's Church Vision*, ed. Strege, 39-51.

Mikolaski on ministry in the global village,[111] Estep and William H. Brackney on the Lord's Supper,[112] David T. Priestley on congregational polity, Michael A. G. Haykin on the Scottish-born nineteenth-century Canadian Baptist pastor William Fraser, and McClendon on the viability of the "voluntary church" in the twenty-first century.[113] Stanley Allen Nelson (1931–), professor of theology in Golden Gate Baptist Theological Seminary, taught systematic theology so that each doctrine could be seen in its historical context and hence the resultant "believers' church theology" was framed by the Anabaptist, Enlightenment, and patristic stories.[114]

Southern Baptists and American Evangelicals

Concurrent with their controversy over inerrancy and the quest for the believers' church, Southern Baptists began to reconsider the question of Baptist identity, especially in relation to American Evangelicals. *Are Southern Baptists "Evangelicals"?* constituted a debate between Edward Glenn Hinson (1931–), professor of church history in Southern Baptist Theological Seminary, and James Leo Garrett, Jr. (1925–), professor of theology in Southwestern Baptist Theological Seminary, with James Estol Tull, professor of theology at Southeastern Baptist Theological Seminary, as moderator.[115] After tracing the usage of "Evangelical" in Continental Europe, the British Isles, Latin America, and the United States and defining it in terms of those who hold to the full reliability and supreme authority of the Bible, the necessity of personal conversion to Christ, or the new birth, and the urgent seeking of the conversion of others, Garrett analyzed the doctrinal history of Southern Baptists so as to conclude that *"Southern Baptists are denominational Evangelicals."*[116] Recognizing that J. R. Graves

---

[111]*Servants of the Word: Ministry in the Believers' Church; Papers from a Study Conference Held at Bethany Theological Seminary, September 2-4, 1987*, ed. David B. Eller (Elgin IL: Brethren Press, 1990) 33-49.

[112]*The Lord's Supper: Believers Church Perspective*, ed. Dale R. Stoffer (Scottdale PA, Waterloo ON: Herald Press, 1997) 46-62, 231-40.

[113]Brackney, ed., *The Believers' Church*, 9-50; 179-98.

[114]*A Believers' Church Theology*, ed. Herbert Drake and Matthew Wysocki, rev. ed. (Taejon, Korea: Widows Mite Computer Products, 1996).

[115]See above, 320n.462.

[116]Ibid., 35-63, 88-127. On his further elaboration of what "denominational" means, see Garrett, "Southern Baptists as Evangelicals," *Baptist History and Heritage* 18 (April 1983): 10-20; idem, "Who Are Southern Baptists in 1989?" *Baptist Standard*, 26 July 1989, 12; and idem, "Are Southern Baptists 'Evangelicals'? A

and E. Y. Mullins had in different ways sought to establish Baptist identity, Hinson contended that Southern Baptists belong to the "voluntarist" strand of Protestantism that has been tested by the Great Awakening, the American Revolution, organizing for missions, and the impact of "the business model" on church life and that this heritage of "voluntary and uncoerced faith" has been friendly to both the Enlightenment and to Schleiermacher. It differs from the Evangelical strand of Protestantism with its objective Scriptures and confessions. Hence Southern Baptists ought not to be reckoned Evangelicals, or "intentionalists."[117]

A broader dialogue on the Southern Baptist-Evangelical relationship in the setting of conferences held at Southern Seminary produced in 1993 a volume of essays. Participants included both non-SBC Evangelicals (George M. Marsden, Robert K. Johnston, Stanley J. Grenz, Joel A. Carpenter, and Richard Mouw) and Southern Baptists (H. Leon McBeth, David S. Dockery, John P. Newport, Richard R. Melick, Bill J. Leonard, Daniel L. Akin, David D'Amico, and R. Albert Mohler, Jr.). Papers centered on the identity of each, the dialogue between the two, and the common and differing beliefs and practices. Newport identified three "strands" among Southern Baptists: Strand A (tilting toward mainline Protestants), Strand B (relations with Evangelicals), and Strand C (old Princeton inerrancy and dispensationalism). Dockery and James Emery White found four groups among Southern Baptists (fundamentalists, conservative evangelicals, moderate evangelicals, and liberals, with the second and third more numerous) and Dockery himself to be first Southern Baptist and secondly evangelical. Mohler concluded: "The best hope for the recovery of the Southern Baptist Convention lies in the rediscovery and reclamation of an authentic and distinctive Southern Baptist evangelicalism—*genuinely Baptist*, and *genuinely evangelical*."[118]

A third round of discussion may now be surfacing. Malcolm B. Yarnell III has advocated that Southern Baptists expand their dialogue to include

---

Further Reflection" in *Southern Baptists and American Evangelicals: The Conversation Continues*, ed. David S. Dockery (Nashville: Broadman & Holman, 1993) 218-23.

[117]*Are Southern Baptists "Evangelicals"?*, 133-44, 148-64, 169-79, 186-87. See also Hinson, "One Baptist's Dream: A Denomination Truly Evangelical, Truly Catholic, Truly Baptist," in *Southern Baptists and American Evangelicals*, ed. Dockery, 201-17.

[118]Dockery, ed., *Southern Baptists and American Evangelicals*, esp. v-vi.

Fundamentalists, Roman Catholics, Eastern Orthodox, mainline Protestants, the heirs of Anabaptism, and other Baptists while continuing to dialogue with Evangelicals and represent to them the Baptist distinctives.[119] William H. Brackney has extended the label "evangelical," as either claimed by or assigned to earlier Baptists and to contemporary Baptists: ABC, Canadian, and British.[120]

James William McClendon, Jr.

Another quest for Baptist identity not unlike that pursued with believers' churches was attempted by McClendon. A native of Shreveport, Louisiana, and, after service in the US Navy, a graduate of the University of Texas (B.A., 1947), Southwestern Baptist Theological Seminary (B.D., 1950; Th.D., 1953), and Princeton Theological Seminary (Th.M., 1952), he taught theology at Golden Gate Baptist Theological Seminary (1954–1966), the University of San Francisco (1966–1969), Church Divinity School and Graduate Theological Union (1971–1990), and Fuller Theological Seminary (1990–2000).[121] He had authored a primer on twentieth-century Protestant theologians,[122] a biographical approach to theologians who were not systematicians (notably Dag Hammarskjöld, Martin Luther King, Jr., and Clarence L. Jordan),[123] and with James M. Smith a study of the nature of religious convictions[124] and had coedited a book on the concept of God.[125]

McClendon planned and completed a three-volume systematic theology, the first on ethics, the second on doctrine, and the third on "witness"

---

[119]"Are Southern Baptist Evangelicals? A Second Decadal Reassessment," *Ecclesiology* 2 (2006): 210-12.

[120]"'Are Baptists Evangelicals?' The Question Revisited," *Perspectives in Religious Studies* 33 (Spring 2006): 105-21.

[121]*Contemporary Authors*, new revision series, vol. 5 (1982) 356; *Directory of American Scholars*, 10th ed. (2002) 4:329.

[122]*Pacemakers of Christian Thought* (Nashville: Broadman, 1962).

[123]*Biography as Theology: How Life Stories Can Remake Today's Theology* (Nashville: Abingdon, 1974, 1990).

[124]*Understanding Religious Convictions* (Notre Dame IN: University of Notre Dame Press, 1977); rev. ed. with subtitle *Defusing Religious Relativism* (Valley Forge PA: Trinity Press International, 1994).

[125]*Is God God?*, ed. Axel D. Stuer and McClendon (Nashville: Abingdon, 1981). McClendon's own chapter on "The God of the Theologians and the God of Jesus Christ" (184-205) was indebted to Blaise Pascal.

(that is, a theology of culture).[126] It was intended to represent and be addressed to the "baptists" (*Täufer*), or those who are the modern heirs of the Radical Reformation of the sixteenth century. McClendon deplored that the "baptists" had not produced more theological writings, having been in the United States diverted to Calvinist-Arminian and Modernist-Fundamentalist issues. His own "quest for the baptist vision" had led him to five "persistent marks" of the "baptists": "biblicism," "mission," "God-given freedom," "discipleship," and "community."[127] He found it difficult to focus on the "baptists"[128] or to engage all the "baptists."[129]

McClendon began *Doctrine* with last things, the kingdom of God being central, and ended it with a chapter on mission, he being one of two Baptist systematic theologians before the end of the twentieth century to make such inclusion.[130] McClendon rejected the historic doctrine of original sin in favor of Rauschenbusch's doctrine of social sin and redefined sin as "refusal" (of the gospel, not of general revelation), "rupture" of community, and "reversion" from growth and development. He hoped for "consonance" between Christian doctrine and the sciences respecting creation, traced ecological concerns to Irenaeus, favored "defenses" of faith rather than formal theodicies, and reckoned suffering to be "inexplicable," punitive, or redemptive. Atonement theories, for McClendon, are Christian *midrashim*, but we must return both to the biblical metaphors and to the passion narratives of the Gospels. He opted for a "two-narrative" (*kenōsis* and *plērōsis*) Christology, combining divine self-giving and "God's self-fulfillment by way of human investment." Contending that the Christian gospel is good news about God and taking atheism seriously, McClendon advocated a

---

[126]*Systematic Theology: Ethics* (Nashville: Abingdon, 1986); *Doctrine* (Nashville: Abingdon, 1994); *Witness* (Nashville: Abingdon, 2000).

[127]*Systematic Theology: Ethics*, 19-21, 25-35. McClendon included among "baptists," *inter alia*, Mennonites, Baptists, Church of the Brethren, Disciples of Christ, Churches of Christ, Plymouth Brethren, Church of God (Anderson, Indiana), and Assemblies of God (34-35).

[128]In *Ethics*, 110-31, 187-208, 276-98, his detailed treatment of historical figures pertained to non-Baptists: Jonathan and Sarah Edwards, Dietrich Bonhoeffer, and Dorothy Day.

[129]His concentration was on sixteenth-century Anabaptists and twentieth-century Baptists and Mennonites.

[130]James Leo Garrett, Jr., "Missions and Baptist Systematic Theologies," *Baptist History and Heritage* 35 (Spring 2000): 68-69.

"narrative-based trinitarianism" that keeps close to the biblical stories. Then giving more attention to the Jewish rootage of the Christian church than most "baptists," but in connection with anti-Semitism, he revamped Leslie Newbigin's[131] third ecclesiological type, the community of the Holy Spirit, so as to be more baptistic but insisted that the local church must be related to others in the larger peoplehood of God.[132]

McClendon joined with five other Baptist scholars to frame and issue in 1997 "Reenvisioning Baptist Identity: A Manifesto for Baptist Communities in North America."[133] The document defined "freedom in Christ" as God-given rather than as derivative of "natural rights or social entitlements" and a "libertarian notion" and made five affirmations.

1. *We affirm Bible Study in reading communities* rather than relying on private interpretation or supposed 'scientific' objectivity.
2. *We affirm following Jesus as a call to shared discipleship* rather than invoking a theory of soul competency.
3. *We affirm a free common life in Christ in gathered, reforming communities* rather than withdrawn, self-chosen, or authoritarian ones.
4. *We affirm baptism, preaching, and the Lord's table as powerful signs that seal God's faithfulness in Christ and express our response of awed gratitude* rather than as mechanical rituals or mere symbols.
5. *We affirm freedom and renounce coercion as a distinct people under God* rather than relying on political theories, powers, or authorities.

Furthermore, the culture wars in North America "have overwhelmed and co-opted the agenda of the church," for "the struggle for the soul of Baptists" is one against "all" of the false gods. Both the theologies of the left (Mullins's soul competency) and those of the right (Princeton theology and *The Fundamentals*) have accommodated to modernity, the one through "autonomous moral agency and objective rationality" and the other through

---

[131]*The Household of God: Lectures on the Nature of the Church* (New York: Friendship Press, 1954) 94-122.

[132]*Systematic Theology: Doctrine*, 69-102, 417-52, 125-35, 150-54, 157-58, 171-76, 230-33, 216-29, 265-79 (esp. 275), 282-94, 307-12, 317-23, 345-61, 341-44, 363-67, 370-71.

[133]The five-page printed copy is dated 20 January 1997. The text was printed in *Baptists Today*, 26 June 1997, 8-10, but with 55 signatories.

individualistic revivalist experience and truth self-evident by commonsense reason. The original signatories[134] called upon their fellow Baptists to "*embrace neither*" but, saying farewell to modernity, to opt for "free, faithful, and communal discipleship."[135]

British Baptismal Sacramentalism

Seventeenth- and eighteenth-century English Baptist authors who addressed Christian baptism tended to focus almost entirely on the recipient of or candidate for baptism and the mode of baptism rather than on the meaning of baptism.[136] In the nineteenth and early twentieth centuries baptism, together with the Lord's Supper, was commonly identified as an "ordinance."[137] At mid-century Henry Cook (1886–1970), general superintendent of the Baptist churches of metropolitan London, reported that Baptists had preferred the term "ordinance," inasmuch as baptism had been ordained by Jesus himself, but, finding such restrictive usage "unfortunate," he advocated also the use of "sacrament" in the sense that baptism becomes a "means of grace" to the believer and is truly the door to church membership.[138] Concurrently the principal of Spurgeon's College, Percy W. Evans, had used the term "sacrament."[139] We have previously noted how Wheeler Robinson, while rejecting "sacramentarianism," opted for a sacramental, more-than-a-symbol view of baptism[140] and how George Beasley-Murray consistently used "sacrament" rather than "ordinance" and rejected the idea of baptism

---

[134]Mikael Broadway, Curtis W. Freeman, Barry Harvey, Elizabeth Newman, Philip Thompson, and McClendon.

[135]See also Curtis W. Freeman, "Can Baptist Theology Be Revisioned?," *Perspectives in Religious Studies* 24 (Fall 1997): 273-310, 273-302, who included the text of the Manifesto as an appendix.

[136]Stanley E. Porter and Anthony R. Cross, "Introduction: Baptism in Recent Debate," in *Baptism, the New Testament and the Church: Historical and Contemporary Studies in Honour of R. E. O. White*, ed. Porter and Cross, Journal for the Study of the New Testament Supplement Series 171 (Sheffield UK: Sheffield Academic Press, 1999) 33.

[137]Anthony R. Cross, *Baptism and the Baptists: Theology and Practice in Twentieth-Century Britain*, Paternoster Biblical and Theological Monographs (Carlisle UK, Waynesboro GA: Paternoster, 2000) 16.

[138]*What Baptists Stand For* (London: Kingsgate, 1947) 69-74.

[139]*Sacraments in the New Testament.*

[140]See above, 354.

Recovering Evangelicalism and Reassessing... 541

as merely a symbol.[141] Thus increasingly during the last half of the twentieth century British Baptist publications on baptism have almost uniformly expressed sacramental language and concepts regarding baptism.

Reginald Ernest Oscar White (1914–2003) wrote a major monograph, *The Biblical Doctrine of Initiation*.[142] Born to English parents in Gwent, Wales, and having studied in Porth Bible School in Rhondda, he completed by examination the University of London B. D. degree and later the M. A. at Liverpool University. His six pastorates in Wales, England, and Scotland extended over three decades. In 1966 he became tutor in New Testament in the Baptist Theological College of Scotland and became principal in 1968, retiring in 1979. His more than thirty books have included monographs on the Apostle Paul[143] and on Christian ethics.[144]

Grounding biblical initiation in the concept and experience of the covenant, White magnified proselyte baptism among the Jews and found that the baptism of Jesus "refashioned" the baptism administered by John the Baptist and was more than "the prefiguring of His death" (Oscar Cullmann) in that it provided "importance and meaning" to the baptism administered by the primitive church. Faith and Jesus' name were important to that primitive Christian baptism. White was convinced that Paul believed that "baptism *accomplishes* things" and thus held, not to a "mechanical" sacramentalism ("in the sense of *ex opera operato*"), but to a "dynamic" sacramentalism (the action of God by the Spirit and the response of faith). Likewise the Gospel of John, according to White, is characterized by sacramentalism, for the "water" in John 3:5 is taken to refer to the baptism by John the Baptist so that only Christian baptism by having both water and the Spirit is complete. Hence "primitive Christian baptism" was "confessional," "ethical," "ecclesiastical," "eschatological," Spirit-endowed,

---

[141] See above, 394, 395-96.

[142] Subtitle: *A Theology of Baptism and Evangelism* (London: Hodder & Stoughton; Grand Rapids MI: Eerdmans, 1960).

[143] *Apostle Extraordinary: A Modern Portrait of St. Paul* (London: Pickering and Inglis, 1968); *Meet St. Paul: An Introduction to the Man, His Achievement and His Correspondence* (London: Bible Reading Fellowship, 1989).

[144] *The Changing Continuity of Christian Ethics*, vol. 1, *Biblical Ethics* (Exeter UK: Paternoster, 1979); vol. 2, *The Insights of History* (Exeter UK: Paternoster, 1981); Gordon W. Martin, "Biographical Sketch: Revd R. E. O. White, BD, MA," and "Select Publications of R. E. O. White," in *Baptism, the New Testament and the Church*, ed. Porter and Cross, 18-32, 15-17.

"initiatory," and "sacramental" (in the sense that baptism is "more than the act of the baptized" and "the operation of divine regenerative power acting upon" the believer). These same characteristics, White contended, mark a proper *"recovery of the biblical doctrine of initiation"* in the modern church.[145]

Concurrent with White's monograph was a volume of thirteen essays on baptism[146] edited by Alec Gilmore (1928–), a pastor in Northampton. Stephen Frederick Winward (1911–1986) "differentiated scriptural or 'apostolic' tradition, which must be received, from 'ecclesiastical' tradition, which must be tested by apostolic tradition."[147] On the one hand, Sydney Ivor Buse (1913–1971) concluded that "baptism may have been the normal rite of admission to the Christian community in the Acts of the Apostles, but it can hardly be described as either universal or necessary for salvation" and noted that currently it was Pedobaptist scholars who were insisting that baptism in Acts was "primarily one of divine activity."[148] On the other hand, Neville Clark (1926–2002), insisting that today "the overriding appeal must always be to [Christologically oriented] New Testament theology rather than New Testament practice" and deploring the persistent Baptist myopia in respect to the prevenience of divine grace," concluded that baptism in the New Testament era "implies, embodies and effects forgiveness of sin, initiation into the church and the gift of the Holy Spirit."[149] More recently

---

[145]*The Biblical Doctrine of Initiation*, 13-43, 56-109, 146-56, 217-27 (esp. 217, 220-21), 247-64 (esp. 247, 253-55, 261-62), 270-74, 305-17.

[146]*Christian Baptism: A Fresh Attempt to Understand the Rite in Terms of Scripture, History and Theology* (London: Lutterworth; Philadelphia: Judson, 1959).

[147]James Leo Garrett, Jr., "Baptists concerning Baptism: Review and Preview," *Southwestern Journal of Theology* 43 (Spring 2001): 55, based on Winward, "Scripture, Tradition, and Baptism," in Gilmore, ed., *Christian Baptism*, 25-53 (esp. 36, 49).

[148]"Baptism in the Acts of the Apostles," in *Christian Baptism*, ed. Gilmore, 116, 125-26.

[149]"The Theology of Baptism," in ibid., 311, 323, 308. In his own monograph Clark had previously stated that New Testament baptism "is effective rather than merely symbolic," for it "accomplishes union with Christ because it gives entry into the Church which is his resurrection body." *An Approach to the Theology of the Sacraments*, Studies in Biblical Theology 17 (Chicago: Alec R. Allenson, 1956) 32, 33.

Stanley K. Fowler has reviewed both the criticisms and the defenses of *Christian Baptism*.[150]

The beginning of the twenty-first century has seen a profusion of writings by British Baptist authors reflective of the sacramentality of baptism. Anthony R. Cross produced a detailed study of the doctrine and practice of baptism of British Baptists during the twentieth century, divided into three periods: 1900-37, 1938-66, 1967-99.[151] In Cross's exposition of the "common ground" held by Baptists concerning baptism one finds as a major rubric "baptism as a means of grace," and for the second period (1938–1966) he provided a chapter on "The Consolidation of Baptist Sacramentalism" which exhibited the views of White, Beasley-Murray, Clark, and Gilmore's edited volume.[152] Throughout the volume one finds predominating evidence that ecumenical discussions, concerns, and goals constituted the most important single factor affecting the twentieth-century British Baptist doctrine and practice of baptism.[153] An American teaching in Canada, Stanley K. Fowler, in a quest for support of baptismal sacramentalism, has gathered numerous British Baptist pre-1900 quotations respecting baptism, but the relative silence of the seventeenth-century confessions and the fact that only three authors offer strong evidence of instrumental sacramentalism would seem to fall short of proof that "the dominant strain of early Baptist thought" looked on baptism as mediating "the conscious experience of entrance into a state of grace." Moreover, Fowler has conceded that for eighteenth- and nineteenth-century British Baptists baptism was essentially symbolic.[154]

In a recent volume of essays entitled *Baptist Sacramentalism* and designed to advance the view thus identified, Spurgeon could not be

---

[150]"Is 'Baptist Sacramentalism' an Oxymoron? Reactions in Britain to *Christian Baptism* (1959)," in Anthony R. Cross and Philip E. Thompson, eds., *Baptist Sacramentalism*, Studies in Baptist History and Thought 5 (Carlisle UK; Waynesboro GA: Paternoster, 2005) 140-50.

[151]*Baptism and the Baptists*.

[152]Ibid., 18-41, 210-43.

[153]Ibid., 1, 97, 127-81, 244-318, 358-64, 458-62.

[154]*More Than a Symbol: The British Baptist Recovery of Baptismal Sacramentalism*, Studies in Baptist History and Thought 2 (Carlisle UK: Waynesboro GA: Paternoster, 2002) 1-88 (esp. 5, 20-32). For Robert Garner baptism afforded assurance of forgiveness, and for William Mitchell it was a "Sign" of the remission of sins.

posthumously enlisted as a supporter, for Spurgeon had regarded baptism as a matter of conscience and of obedience and had preferred the term "ordinance."[155] But Wheeler Robinson was celebrated as the one "who did more than anyone else to help [British] Baptists rediscover the sacramental understanding of baptism, . . . and the key to his sacramentalism was the person and work of the Holy Spirit."[156] A Canadian Baptist was prepared to assert that baptism and the Lord's Supper are not only "acts of commitment" but also "identity-conveying and identity-forming" "community acts" or "rites of belonging."[157] Editors of the volume referred pejoratively to the not so sacramental Baptists as Gnostic, Zwinglian, and influenced by the Enlightenment.[158]

But the numerous writings of prolific theologians do not always coincide with the beliefs and practices of Baptist congregations. Anthony Cross concluded his twentieth-century study:

> [For British Baptists] . . . a century of baptismal debate and controversy . . . seems to have created a schizophrenic denomination. . . . Baptists are themselves no nearer consensus than they were at the beginning of the century—is baptism a mere symbol however important a one, or an effective rite? The second position now commands more respect than in earlier years, but no one side has convinced the other and Baptists are left with competing theologies and practices of baptism/initiation.[159]

Bruce Milne (1940–), on the other hand, while identifying baptism and the Supper as "sacraments of the gospel," defined the meaning of baptism as "a confession of faith in Christ," "an experience of communion with Christ," "a consecration of living for Christ," and "a promise of consummation through Christ."[160]

---

[155]Tim Grass and Ian Randall, "C. H. Spurgeon on the Sacraments," in *Baptist Sacramentalism*, ed. Cross and Thompson, 58-60, 62.

[156]Anthony R. Cross, "The Pneumatological Key to H. Wheeler Robinson's Baptismal Sacramentalism," in ibid., 174.

[157]Stanley J. Grenz, "Baptism and the Lord's Supper as Community Acts: Toward a Sacramental Understanding of the Ordinances," in ibid., 84-95.

[158]Cross and Thompson, "Introduction: Baptist Sacramentalism," in ibid., 1-2; Cross, "The Pneumatological Key," 153.

[159]"Conclusion," in ibid., 463.

[160]*Know the Truth: A Handbook of Christian Belief* (Downers Grove IL: InterVarsity, 1982) 230-33. A native of Dundee, Scotland, and a graduate of St. Andrews University (M.A., 1964), London University (B.D., 1967), and Edinburgh

Recovering Evangelicalism and Reassessing... 545

During the last half of the twentieth century Southern Baptists did not follow British Baptists in the advocacy of baptismal sacramentalism. Fewer monographs on baptism were produced, and the ecumenical influence was not so strong. Warren Tyree Carr (1917–2007) pastor of Watts Street Church, Durham, North Carolina, who called baptism both the "conscience" of the church and the "primary clue to the life and death issues" facing the church, majored on the issues between infant baptism and believer's baptism.[161] Dale Moody's post-Vatican II confessional study[162] "was primarily concerned with the infant baptism vs. believer's baptism issue and only secondarily dealt with the significance of baptism and with immersion and alternative modes."[163] William Lawrence Hendricks (1929–2002), who taught theology at Southwestern (1957–1978), Golden Gate (1978–1984), and Southern (1984–1995) seminaries and at Brite Divinity School of Texas Christian University (1995–1999), shifted the discussion of baptism and children from the age of accountability, that is, the age at which one

---

University (Ph.D., 1970), Milne was a church planter in Livingston, Scotland (1968–1974), taught in Spurgeon's College (1974–1983), and served as pastor of First Church, Vancouver, British Columbia, Canada (1984–2001). Bruce Milne to James Leo Garrett, Jr., 13 December 2006, 7 July 2007. Unique among British Baptists of the period in publishing a systematic theology, Milne held a "supervision" view of biblical inspiration, regarded men and women as "equal in value and status" and "different but complementary in function," took penal substitution as central to the atonement, was critical of the World Council of Churches, and differentiated the "invisible church" ("the total company of the elect") from the "universal church" ("all the people of God in the world at one time"). *Know the Truth*, 37-38, 99-100, 153-59, 167-70, 214, 246. He also wrote *We Belong Together: The Meaning of Fellowship* (Downers Grove IL: InterVarsity, 1978); *What the Bible Says about the End of the World* (Eastbourne UK: Kingsway, 1979); *The Message of John: Here Is Your King!* The Bible Speaks Today (Leicester UK: InterVarsity, 1993); *The Message of Heaven and Hell: Grace and Destiny* (Downers Grove IL: InterVarsity, 2002); and *Dynamic Diversity: The New-humanity Church for Today and Tomorrow* (Downers Grove IL: InterVarsity, 2006). *Know the Truth* has been translated into seventeen languages.

[161]*Baptism: Conscience and Clue for the Church* (New York: Holt, Rinehart & Winston, 1964) 12, 27, 35-79. Carr was a graduate of Transylvania College and Southern Baptist Theological Seminary and later served as pastor of Wake Forest Church, Winston-Salem NC.

[162]*Baptism: Foundations for Christian Unity*.

[163]Garrett, "Baptists concerning Baptism," 62.

becomes a sinner, to the age of respondability, that is, the age at which one can credibly repent and believe[164] and dealt with baptismal abuses such as those connected with child evangelism and "multiple same-person baptisms."[165] He was unique among Baptists in addressing "theology for children" and "theology for aging."[166] Oscar Stephenson Brooks (1928–), professor of New Testament in Golden Gate Baptist Theological Seminary, understood baptism "in reference to the 'drama of decision' called forth by the Christian gospel." To repent is "'*to make a moral decision between two alternative courses set before one*,'" that is, "a deliberate choice in favor of the kingdom" of God. Moreover, "Jesus' baptism was '*an experience of self-understanding*,'" and hence "Christian baptism is closely related to Jesus' baptism."[167]

In the new Evangelicalism, which redirected Fundamentalism and resembled the earlier Evangelicalism, Baptists were among the principal theologians. The prolific Henry defended propositional revelation by a transcendent and personal God, the particular Father of believers, who became incarnate in Jesus Christ. The Bible is, in order of priority, authoritative, inspired, and inerrant. Ramm, having engaged in bridge-building between Christian theology and the physical sciences with the days of Genesis 1 as revelatory days and progressive creation and building on the Reformed heritage, addressed biblical hermeneutics and authority and the witness of the Holy Spirit and produced notable monographs on Christology and sin. Erickson, trained in philosophy, pastoral in orientation, and specific

---

[164]"The Age of Accountability," in *Children and Conversion*, ed. Clifford Ingle (Nashville: Broadman, 1970) 84-97.

[165]"Baptism: A Baptist Perspective," *Southwestern Journal of Theology* 31 (Spring 1989): 28-30.

[166]*A Theology for Children* (Nashville: Broadman, 1980); *A Theology for Aging* (Nashville: Broadman, 1986). A native of Butte, Montana, who was reared in Wichita, Kansas, Hendricks was a graduate of Oklahoma Baptist University (B.A., 1951), Southwestern Baptist Theological Seminary (B.D., 1954; Th.D., 1958), and the University of Chicago (Ph.D., 1972). He wrote *The Letters of John: Tapestries of Faith* (Nashville: Convention Press, 1970), *The Doctrine of Man* (Nashville: Convention Press, 1977), and *Who Is Jesus Christ?*, Library of Christian Doctrine (Nashville: Broadman, 1985). William David Kirkpatrick, "William Lawrence Hendricks," in *The Legacy of Southwestern*, ed. Garrett et al., 248-61.

[167]Garrett, "Baptists concerning Baptism," 63, based on Brooks, *The Drama of Decision: Baptism in the New Testament* (Peabody MA: Hendrickson, 1987) 31, 18, 31, 39, 65.

as to theological method, held to the "full inerrancy" of the translated Bible and to both propositional and personal revelation, wrote on the Trinity, defended Chalcedonian Christology, held to a modified Augustinianism theory of the imputation of Adamic sin, interpreted Jesus' resurrection as a resuscitation, and espoused historic premillennialism. Both Henry and Erickson repeatedly wrote to advise and to warn other Evangelicals.

Beginning in the middle of the nineteenth century Baptists sought to identify, interpret, and defend the Baptist distinctives. During the first half of the twentieth century British Baptists were especially related organizationally to the other British Free Churches, and during the last third of the twentieth century Baptists in North America participated in a series of conferences pertaining to believers' churches. McClendon produced a systematic theology intended to represent the believers' churches, and he and colleagues issued at the end of the century a manifesto "reenvisioning" the Baptist identity in a postmodern setting. The question of the relationship between Southern Baptists and American Evangelicals was debated and explored toward the end of the same century. Building upon the earlier advocacy of a baptismal sacramentalism by Robinson, Clark, White, and Beasley-Murray, Cross and others at the beginning of the new century strongly defended that position. Concurrently Southern Baptists were without such a sacramental trend. All of these were efforts to reassess the Baptist heritage and identity.

Chapter 11

Incursions into Baptist Theology

Baptist theology for four centuries has been shaped both by the early Calvinist-Arminian differences of a soteriological nature and the later conservative-liberal differences that loomed large during the nineteenth and twentieth centuries and by those chiefly ecclesiological issues that have differentiated Baptists from other Christian denominations. All those differences have been stock-in-trade for Baptist theology and reflective of the diversity existent among the Baptists.

But at times other movements and teachings not so encompassed have entered into and influenced Baptist theology. These incursions often have reflected theological debates, positions, and issues that have arisen outside the Baptist movement and have not been, at least initially, germane to Baptist theology.

At least three of these incursions have already been examined. One was the unwillingness of the majority of the English General Baptists at the beginning of the eighteenth century to find Matthew Caffyn's teaching to be heterodox or to make a Trinitarian declaration, with the result that the majority became Socinian or Unitarian.[1] A second was the acceptance of the Hyper-Calvinism of Tobias Crisp and Joseph Hussey, one an Anglican and the other a Congregationalist, by certain Particular Baptists.[2] The third was the adherence to Baptist identity for nearly two decades of Campbell Restorationists, whose Sandemanian doctrine of faith and McLeanist doctrine of baptismal remission became increasingly identifiable as non-Baptist.[3]

Now it becomes necessary to explore the major incursions during the twentieth century.

Modernism

Although in sermons and popular writings[4] the terms "liberalism" and "modernism" have been frequently used as synonyms, Kenneth Cauthen, writing in 1962, clearly differentiated "evangelical liberals" and "modernis-

---

[1] See above, 44-46.
[2] See above, 89-93, 98-100.
[3] See above, 249-57.
[4] Also in scholarly usage: Tinder, "Fundamentalist Baptists in the Northern and Western United States," 47.

tic liberals."⁵ Liberalism, to use Fosdick's words, was seeking to enable one "to be both an intelligent modern and a serious Christian."⁶ Liberals held to a special or historical revelation to Israel and supremely in Christ that could in the modern era be validated by reason and by experience. Modernists, on the other hand, "had no real sense of continuing in the line of the historic faith" and adopted as "the standard" for measuring religious values "the presuppositions of modern science, philosophy, psychology, and social thought." Jesus, for them, was not "*the source*" of religious truth but "the *exemplar*" thereof.⁷ Modernists either retained some form of theism or passed through theism en route to humanism. Three Baptists who have been categorized as modernists—Shailer Mathews (1863–1941), Douglas Clyde Macintosh (1877–1948), and George Burman Foster (1858–1918)—need to be examined.

Mathews, a native of Portland, Maine, where his maternal grandfather was pastor of First Church, studied at Colby College (1880–1884), where he was influenced by Albion W. Small, a pioneer in sociology, and at Newton Theological Institution (1884–1887) before returning to Colby to teach, first rhetoric and elocution and later history and political economy. After a year of study of historiography in the University of Berlin, Mathews joined in 1894 the faculty of the University of Chicago in New Testament history. In 1906 he was transferred to theology to replace George B. Foster, in 1908 he became dean of the Divinity School, and in 1933 he retired. The author or coauthor of about twenty-eight books, the president of the Northern Baptist Convention (1915), and the president of the Federal Council of the Churches of Christ in America (1912–1916), Mathews represented the Chicago school of theology and was an advocate of modernism.⁸

---

⁵*The Impact of American Religious Liberalism*, 26-30.
⁶*The Living of These Days: An Autobiography*, vii.
⁷Cauthen, *The Impact of American Religious Liberalism*, 28-29.
⁸Mathews, *New Faith for Old: An Autobiography* (New York: Macmillan, 1936); Robert Elden Mathews, "Shailer Mathews: A Biographical Note," in *The Process of Religion: Essays in Honor of Dean Shailer Mathews*, ed. Miles H. Krumbine (New York: Macmillan, 1933) 1-14; Charles Augustus Ray, "The Life and Thought of Shailer Mathews" (Th.D. diss., New Orleans Baptist Theological Seminary, 1957) 7-44; Cauthen, *The Impact of American Religious Liberalism*, 147-50; Leslie A. Muray, "Shailer Mathews: Introduction," *The Chicago School of Theology: Pioneers in Religious Inquiry*, vol. 1, ed. W. Creighton Peden and Jerome A. Stone, Studies in American Religion 66a (Lewiston NY: Edwin Mellen Press, 1996) 119-20. Mathews's books have been classified as historical, social, and theo-

"Early in his career Mathews became convinced that Christianity is not a body of truth but a religious social movement."⁹ Three results ensued. One was that Mathews would explore the social and ethical teachings of Jesus¹⁰ and expound, as did Rauschenbusch, the social gospel.¹¹ A second was that he looked upon "theological beliefs as "the product of the dominant social mind of a period" so that "they change when the social structure changes." Third, Mathews "looked to the natural and social sciences rather than to philosophy for insight into the meaning of religious doctrines."¹² Mathews identified seven "successive social minds" that have shaped Christian doctrines: "the Semitic, the Graeco-Roman, the imperialistic, the feudal, the nationalistic, the bourgeois, and the modern or scientific-democratic."¹³ Doctrines, therefore, are necessarily changing to respond to a new social mind. For Mathews, modernism "is primarily a method and not a system of dogma."¹⁴ "*It is the use of the methods of modern science to find, state and use the permanent and central values of inherited orthodoxy in meeting the needs of a modern world.*"¹⁵

In 1910 Mathews indicated that the modern world welcomed the immanence of God rather than a "juristic" or metaphysically deduced concept

---

logical. *New Faith for Old*, ii. For Mathews's bibliography, see Robert Wesley Clark, "The Contribution of Shailer Mathews to the Social Movement in American Protestantism" (Th.D. diss., Southern Baptist Theological Seminary, 1959) 283-305, and William D. Lindsey, *Shailer Mathews's Lives of Jesus: The Search for a Theological Foundation for the Social Gospel* (New York: Lang, 1996; Albany NY: SUNY, 1997) "A Comprehensive Bibliography of Mathews's Work," 281-97.

⁹Cauthen, *The Impact of American Religious Liberalism*, 148.

¹⁰*The Social Teaching of Jesus: An Essay in Christian Sociology* (New York: Macmillan, 1897) 23-27, 198-230, in which he affirmed the unity of body and soul but with the body subordinate and wrote of "the process of social regeneration"; *Jesus on Social Institutions* (New York: Macmillan, 1928; Philadelphia: Fortress, 1971).

¹¹*The Social Gospel* (Philadelphia: Griffith and Rowland, 1910); *The Individual and the Social Gospel* (New York: Missionary Education Movement of the United States and Canada, 1914).

¹²Cauthen, *The Impact of American Religious Liberalism*, 148, 149.

¹³"Theology and the Social Mind," *The Biblical World* 46 (October 1915): 201-48; Cauthen, *The Impact of American Religious Liberalism*, 151.

¹⁴Cauthen, *The Impact of American Religious Liberalism*, 153.

¹⁵*The Faith of Modernism* (New York: Macmillan, 1924; New York: AMS Press, 1969), 23.

of God.[16] In 1923 that immanence was described as being within the evolutionary process.[17] By 1931, however, Mathews declared: *"For God is our conception, born of social experience, of the personality-evolving and personally responsive elements of our cosmic environment with which we are organically related."*[18] Kenneth Cauthen's verdict on the later Mathews was twofold: for Mathews God's personhood is only analogical, and Mathews had moved from God as an objective reality toward the world of subjectivity. Mathews's God is not Trinitarian and not clearly personal.[19]

Mathews early identified man's major enemies as physical evil, sin, and death. Mathews attributed to Jesus his own definition of sin as the "state of the soul which expresses itself in acts which are injurious to personality, his or another's, and indicate that a man is unlike and hostile to a fatherly God." Sin is both individual and social, and in an evolutionary framework it is "the backward pull" toward one's animal past.[20] Conversely, morality is "conformity with the personality-producing activities of the universe."[21] How, according to the early Mathews, do humans overcome sin and death? Through forgiveness derived from Jesus and through "the assurance of immortality" obtained by Jesus' continued existence, if not his bodily resurrection.[22] Later Mathews was less specific about Jesus' resurrection.[23] Salvation is overcoming sin's "reactionary . . . tendencies" through the teaching and example of Jesus[24] and adjusting to "a personally responsive cosmos."[25]

In 1904 Mathews in *The Messianic Hope in the New Testament* supported the messianic self-consciousness of Jesus but found messianism to be particularly Jewish. He concluded that one "may believe in him as the in-

---

[16]*The Gospel and the Modern Man* (New York: Macmillan) 43-48, 51-54.

[17]*The Faith of Modernism*, 114-15.

[18]*The Growth of the Idea of God* (New York: Macmillan), 226.

[19]*The Impact of American Religious Liberalism*, 155, 157-59.

[20]*The Gospel and Modern Man*, 147-238, esp. 163, 165-66.

[21]*Is God Emeritus?* (New York: Macmillan, 1940) 58.

[22]Cauthen, *The Impact of American Religious Liberalism*, 160; *The Gospel and the Modern Man*, 180-238.

[23]*The Faith of Modernism*.

[24]Cauthen, *The Impact of American Religious Liberalism*, 160.

[25]Ibid., 161; Mathews, "Science Gives Content to Religious Thought," in *Contributions of Science to Religion*, ed. Mathews (New York, London: D. Appleton, 1924) 413-15.

carnation of God, as the revealer of a forgiving God, as the type and teacher of the perfect human life, as the Risen One who brought life and incorruption to light, without necessarily committing himself to" strict Jewish messianism.[26] In 1910 Jesus's sinlessness was affirmed but not his virgin birth.[27] By 1924 Mathews was declaring that *"Christian salvation centers about God in a man, not in a man made into a God,"* thus denying the deity of Christ, and confessing that Jesus "revealed God as Savior."[28] In his 1930 study of atonement theology Mathews, assuming that the doctrine of the atonement has been shaped by the doctrines of God and the doctrine of God by various social patterns, traced doctrines of sacrifice, acquittal, incarnation, sovereign lordship, satisfaction of honor, exhibition of rectoral justice, payment of debt, and moral influence so as to suggest the formation of another theology of the death of Christ around the process of personality development. Easter, he concluded, "heralds the fact that Jesus, while suffering from others' maladjustment to personality-evolving forces of the cosmic process, triumphed through his own adjustment to those forces."[29]

In 1910 Mathews declared that "the first duty of the church is to turn men from sin to God."[30] In 1928 he insisted that "the church as an institution evolved from the group of revolutionists Jesus gathered to found a community of brothers" but that "the church is not an economic or political institution."[31] In 1935 Mathews recognized the dangers with the institutionalization of the church but celebrated the role of minorities.[32] In 1938 he described the churches as "religious social groups," "moral ferments," and channels of grace (worship, prayer, and sacraments).[33]

Mathews's expectation through social progress of the attainment a new social order, which he equated with the kingdom of God, was undiminished

---

[26](Chicago: University of Chicago Press, 1904) 84-133, esp. 133.

[27]*The Gospel and the Modern Man*, 116-21, 129-35.

[28]*The Faith of Modernism*, 124, 180.

[29]*The Atonement and the Social Process* (New York: Macmillan, 1930) esp. 182-89, 205. Van Pelt, "An Examination of the Concept of the Atonement," 185-91, criticized Mathews's concept of atonement for its dependence on social Darwinism and process thought and its defective understanding of sin and guilt.

[30]*The Social Gospel*, 151.

[31]*Jesus on Social Institutions*, 127, 144.

[32]*Creative Christianity* (Nashville: Cokesbury, 1935) 62-64, 74-77.

[33]*The Church and the Christian* (New York: Macmillan, 1938) 12-26, 103-38, 75-102.

by World War I.[34] Mathews's denial of a bodily second coming of Christ and its origination as a concept in noncanonical Jewish writings evoked strong criticism by premillennial authors.[35]

Leslie A. Muray[36] has favorably assessed the thought of Mathews as one of the Chicago school with no thought as to whether it was endemic to or consistent with Baptist theology. According to Stephen H. Wurster,[37] modernism as represented by Mathews was part of the American "progressive" movement and thought of itself as having an educational "mission." On the contrary, Kenneth Lee Smith,[38] writing after and in the light of the rise of Protestant Neoorthodoxy, found Mathews's "socioethical" hermeneutic to have been replaced by a more theological hermeneutic, his doctrine of the church to be too sociological, and his doctrine of the kingdom of God to be too realizable in history. Hence his "antidote" to Mathews's interpretation of religion was "the historic Judaeo-Christian faith."

Macintosh, born in Breadalbane, Ontario, was descended from a paternal line of Baptist deacons of Scottish descent and from a maternal line that stemmed from John Cotton. Having professed the Christian faith first at nine and then more firmly at thirteen, he graduated from McMaster University, where philosophical idealism was regnant in 1903 and then pursued graduate studies in theology and philosophy at the University of Chicago, where pragmatism was strong and Ritschlian value judgments were being advanced by G. B. Foster. His 1909 Ph.D. dissertation was entitled "The Reaction against Metaphysics in Theology." He was ordained by the Hyde Park Church, Chicago. After two years of teaching in Brandon College in Manitoba, Macintosh joined the faculty of Yale Divinity School in 1909

---

[34]Cauthen, *The Impact of American Religious Liberalism*, 161-62.

[35]Reuben Archer Torrey, *Will Christ Come Again? An Exposure of the Foolishness, Fallacies and Falsehoods of Shailer Mathews* (Los Angeles: Bible Institute of Los Angeles, 1918); I. M. Haldeman, *Professor Shailer Mathews's Burlesque on the Second Coming of Our Lord Jesus Christ* (New York: First Baptist Church, n.d.; Philadelphia: Philadelphia School of the Bible, 1918).

[36]"Shailer Mathews: Introduction," 123-24. Mathews, *New Faith for Old*, 283, said: "The New Testament as literature could not be a test of truth for its own formulas were relative to the world in which Jesus and the apostles lived."

[37]"The 'Modernism' of Shailer Mathews: A Study in American Religious Progressivism, 1894–1924" (Ph.D. diss., University of Iowa, 1972) 223-97, 4, 151.

[38]"Shailer Mathews: Theologian of Social Process" (Ph.D. diss., Duke University, 1959) 273-306 (esp. 279, 294-95, 293-94, 301).

and continued to teach until 1942, advancing from assistant professor to emeritus professor.[39] At Yale he moved through the maze of modern philosophy to the espousal of a critical or valuational realism with a monistic epistemology.[40]

Macintosh may be reckoned a modernist in that "present reason and experience" rather than the Bible or Christ provide the "criterion of religious truth." Seeking to apply scientific method to theology,[41] he did not hesitate to embrace a "radical" rather than a "conservative" method.[42] In his emphasis on religious experience the focus was on "those elements . . . which give knowledge of God."[43] Macintosh built his scientific theology with certain presuppositions on three levels: a body of empirical religious data, theological laws formulated thereon, and probable and permissible propositions about God (attributes, creation-providence, immortality, theodicy).[44] The Yale professor moved from declaring that "there *ought* to be a God" to stating that "there *may* be a God" to insisting that "there *must* be a God" for the sake of "moral optimism and the way of life exemplified by Jesus" to declaring that "there *is* a God" who is known through personal transformative experience.[45] Such experience as Macintosh affirms has led Kenneth Cauthen to call him "an ethical intuitionist." Although his experi-

---

[39]Macintosh, "Toward a New Untraditional Orthodoxy," in *Contemporary American Theology: Theological Autobiographies*, ed. Vergilius Ferm, vol. 1 (New York: Round Table Press, 1932) 275-319; Preston Warren, *Out of the Wilderness: Douglas Clyde Macintosh's Journeys through the Grounds and Claims of Modern Thought*, American University Studies, series 7, Theology and Religion, vol. 51 (New York: Peter Lang, 1989) 1-39, 225-27; *Who's Who in America*, 21st ed. (1940–1941), 1658; Cauthen, *The Impact of American Religious Liberalism*, 169.

[40]Warren, *Out of the Wilderness*, 41-160, esp. 143, 87; Macintosh, *The Pilgrimage of Faith in the World of Modern Thought* (Calcutta: University of Calcutta, 1931).

[41]Cauthen, *The Impact of American Religious Liberalism*, 169-71.

[42]*Theology as an Empirical Science* (New York: Macmillan, 1919) 7-9.

[43]Cauthen, *The Impact of American Religious Liberalism*, 171-72.

[44]Ibid., 172-75, based on *Theology as an Empirical Science*, 26-27, 101-229.

[45]Cauthen, *The Impact of American Religious Liberalism*, 177, based on Macintosh, "First Cycle," "Second Cycle," "Fifth Cycle," and "Sixth Cycle," in Henry Nelson Wieman, Douglas Clyde Macintosh, and Max Carl Otto, *Is There a God?* (New York: Willett, Clark & Co., 1932) 21, 58, 177, 210.

ence does not require the historical Jesus, Cauthen has concluded that Macintosh retained theism in a way that Mathews did not.[46]

Man, according to Macintosh, is a free being with an evolutionary past and personality-developing future. Sin, being a matter of "beastly impulses" and "animal greed," was never clearly connected by Macintosh with the will of God or with salvation, despite his pietistic language.[47]

Macintosh's sufficient theism and moral optimism did not require "the historic Jesus" or "any Christology." These may be "*psychologically* necessary for the Christian faith of certain persons at certain times," but "an essentially Christian faith in God and an essentially Christian experience of moral salvation through the right religious adjustment are *logically* possible without" them. Jesus' work was threefold: to be "the true moral example," "the true religious example, and the true revelation of God." Jesus he called "*divine in the quality or value of his personality*," one who "exercises the *divine function* of saving man from his sin," and divine in the sense of "a special immanence."[48] That was not, of course, the confession of Nicaea I or Chalcedon.

Only late in life did Macintosh address the topic of the church, and then in an ecumenical context,[49] and never was eschatology a subject for his serious review.[50]

Two philosophers of religion placed on Macintosh the label of "ethical intuitionist" of the philosophical type.[51] Preston Warren has more recently referred to Macintosh's "Valuational Realism."[52] In 1932 Macintosh wrote of his quest for "a new untraditional orthodoxy,"[53] and in 1942 he sought

---

[46]Cauthen, *The Impact of American Religious Liberalism*, 179-80.

[47]Ibid., 180-83.

[48]*The Reasonableness of Christianity*, 134-60, esp. 137, 139, 149, 150, 151, 153.

[49]*Personal Religion* (New York: Scribner's, 1942) 232-77.

[50]He did write an essay "Eternal Life" in *Liberal Theology: An Appraisal: Essays in Honor of Eugene William Lyman*, ed. David E. Roberts and Henry Pitney Van Dusen (New York: Scribner's, 1942) 238-54. His view of the kingdom of God was essentially internal, ethical, and social. *Social Religion* (New York, London: Scribner's, 1939) 22-38, 78-92.

[51]Henry Nelson Wieman and Bernard Eugene Meland, *American Philosophies of Religion* (Chicago: Willett, Clark & Co., 1936) 159.

[52]*Out of the Wilderness*, 143.

[53]"Toward a New Untraditional Orthodoxy," 275-318.

to set forth "a modern functional evangelicalism," emphasizing sin, Christ, redemption, conversion, and the Christian life."⁵⁴ But an evaluation that is centered on his principal, religious writings would seem to corroborate Cauthen's classification of Macintosh as a modernist.⁵⁵

Foster, born in Alderson, Virginia (now West Virginia) in 1858, suffered the loss of his mother when he was five and the loss of his father to military service in the Civil War. Ordained a Baptist minister in 1879, he, after studying at Shelton College, received B.A. (1883) and M.A. (1884) degrees from West Virginia University and then graduated from Rochester Theological Seminary in 1887. After a four-year pastorate of First Church, Saratoga Springs, New York, he studied at the universities of Göttingen and Berlin in preparation for teaching philosophy at McMaster University (1892–1895). He then became assistant professor of systematic theology in the Divinity School of the University of Chicago and was promoted to professor in 1897.⁵⁶ In the same month, January 1906, in which the founding president of the university, William Rainey Harper, died,⁵⁷ Foster published what proved to be a very controversial book, *The Finality of the Christian Religion*.⁵⁸ The Chicago Baptist Ministers' Conference voted 48 to 22 to adopt a resolution, offered by Austen Kennedy de Blois (1866–1945), which declared: "That we as a conference declare it to be our resolute conviction that the views set forth in this book are contrary to the Scriptures and that its teaching and tendency are subversive of the vital and essential truths of the Christian faith."⁵⁹ The Hyde Park Church refused to

---

⁵⁴*Personal Religion*, 107-48.

⁵⁵*The Impact of American Religious Liberalism*, 29-30, 169-87.

⁵⁶Alan Gragg, *George Burman Foster: Religious Humanist,* Perspectives in Religious Studies Special Studies Series 3 (Macon GA: Mercer University Press, 1978) 1-2; Creighton Peden, *The Chicago School: Voices in Liberal Religious Thought* (Bristol IN: Wyndham Hall Press, 1987) 24; Edgar A. Towne, "George Burman Foster: Introduction," in *The Chicago School of Theology*, ed. Peden and Stone, 1-5.

⁵⁷Charles Harvey Arnold, *Near the Edge of Battle: A Short History of the Divinity School and the "Chicago School of Theology," 1866–1966* (Chicago: Divinity School Association of the University of Chicago, 1966) 28.

⁵⁸(Chicago: University of Chicago Press, 1906; 2nd ed., 1909).

⁵⁹Quoted by Perry J. Stackhouse, *Chicago and the Baptists: A Century of Progress* (Chicago: University of Chicago Press, 1933) 169-70; see also Gragg, *George Burman Foster*, 60. The minority, including Shailer Mathews, protested against the resolution.

heed admonitions to remove Foster from its membership.[60] The controversy subsided but was again ignited by the publication in June 1909 of Foster's *The Function of Religion in Man's Struggle for Existence*.[61] Foster defended himself as "a true Baptist."

> There is no creed subscription in the Baptist church, the reason being that we have no formal creed . . . because Baptists hold to the right of private interpretation of the Scripture, freedom of thought and speech, and the privilege of every man to hold communion with God without the mediation of a priest. This is kernel of the Baptist position and this I hold with all my heart.[62]

But the Ministers' Conference promptly expelled Foster.[63] Both the Divinity School and the university administration defended him but had already moved from him in 1905 to the Department of Comparative Religion as professor of philosophy of religion. That position he retained until his death in 1918.[64] Among the long-term effects of the Foster controversy[65] were the formation in 1907 in the southern part of the state of the Illinois Baptist State Association, which in 1910 affiliated with the Southern Baptist Convention, and the founding of the conservative Northern Baptist Theological Seminary in Chicago in 1913.[66]

---

[60] Stackhouse, *Chicago and the Baptists*, 170.

[61] (Chicago: University of Chicago Press, 1909). Gragg, *George Burman Foster*, 61.

[62] *The Chicago Daily Tribune*, 14 June 1909, 1-2; quoted by Gragg, *George Burman Foster*, 62, 67.

[63] Larry E. Axel, "Conflict and Censure: The Religious Odyssey of George Burman Foster," in *Alone Together: Studies in the History of Liberal Religion*, ed. Peter Iver Kaufman and Spencer Lavan, Collegium Studies in Liberal Religion (Boston: Beacon Press, 1978) 94-95.

[64] Gragg, *George Burman Foster*, 61, 63, 2. The Foster controversy was not mentioned in the histories of the University of Chicago: Thomas Wakefield Goodspeed, *A History of the University of Chicago: The First Quarter-Century* (Chicago: University of Chicago Press, 1916); idem, *The Story of the University of Chicago, 1890–1925* (Chicago: University of Chicago Press, 1925).

[65] Edgar A. Towne, "A 'Singleminded' Theologian: George Burman Foster at Chicago," *Foundations* 20 (January-March, April-June 1977): 36-59, 163-80, has provided a detailed account of the controversy sympathetic to Foster and alleging (175) that his was a "Christian" humanism.

[66] Gragg, *George Burman Foster*, 63; McBeth, *The Baptist Heritage*, 569, 624-25.

Alan Gragg has advanced the views that Foster from his seminary student years doubted Christian orthodoxy and reacted against A. H. Strong's theology and most likely studied under Julius Kaftan (1848–1926) in Berlin, and hence his account of the dissolution of "authority-religion" was autobiographical.[67] This dissolution was accelerated by the advent of comparative religion and the raising of the question of the absoluteness of Christianity, as Ernst Troeltsch and Kaftan had recently done. It involved the Scriptures as the Word of God, the canon, the apologetic usage of miracles and predictive prophecy, and allegorical interpretation. But neither was Foster able to embrace naturalism because it denied "mystery, dependence, and teleology." Hence neither supernaturalism nor naturalism recognizes fully "the rights of personality," for indeed "the mission of man is to be neither brute nor God, *but to become personality.*" After probing the question as to what method is needed to detect "the essence of Christianity" and reviewing in detail source criticism of the Gospels, Foster rejected Jesus' teachings about angels and demons and the "immediate advent of the kingdom of God," his self-identification as Messiah, and his teachings not easily conformable to modernity. He concluded that primitive Christianity is not now normative but "a fountain of life" and, in Ritschlian fashion, that Jesus' religion was "personality-religion" and "experience-religion" but not "book-religion"—principally expressed in terms of morality": "faith in God the Father" and the infinite worth of human beings.[68]

Three years later Foster cast off all vestiges of historic Christianity and embraced religious humanism. He affirmed the human soul in "its struggle for existence in the process of human and cosmic evolution." It "generates organs and functions for self-preservation, self-expression, and self-consummation." Man has "created the gods" "in order to make himself master of his environment."[69] Foster championed soul competency or autonomy as a Baptist principle. He no longer had a place for Jesus: "We can never be satisfied with this Jesus religion as a finality. We must pass on from faith in a man to faith in a new eternal Messiah—*our* Messiah, . . . our Ideal."[70]

---

[67]*George Burman Foster*, 35-45.

[68]*The Finality of the Christian Religion*, 6-7, 279-86, 39-48, 57-75, 87-147, 196-275 (esp. 207, 270-71, 273), 291-324, 325-94, 395-418 (esp. 515, 517-18).

[69]Foster was expressing thought akin to that of Ludwig Feuerbach (1804–1872).

[70]Gragg, *George Burman Foster*, 20-25, based on Foster, *The Function of Religion in Man's Struggle for Existence*, esp. 20-25, 49-50, 55-57, 73-75, 142.

Foster's *Christianity in Its Modern Expression*,[71] posthumously edited by Macintosh and published in 1921, reflects Foster's earlier views. It is, therefore, not surprising that Macintosh held to an "oscillation" view of Foster's thought, in that he "shuttled back and forth several times" between denial of God's reality and affirming theism and that Gragg has held to a clean break view in which Foster once-for-all abandoned Ritschlian theology for religious humanism.[72] Foster continued in the membership of Hyde Park Church until his death but also preached in Unitarian pulpits as well as at Hyde Park.[73]

Baptists of the preceding centuries, despite their polemical stance toward Pedobaptist Christianity, had held to Christian orthodoxy in respect to the authority of the Bible, the person and work of Jesus Christ, and other basic Christian doctrines. Modernism at the advent of the twentieth century with its making modern thought foundational to and normative for religious truth constituted such an alien and threatening incursion into Baptist theology as to warrant rejection or resistance.

Dispensationalism

Although exponents of both premillennialism and postmillennialism can be found in the four centuries of Baptist theological history, advocates of dispensationalism among Baptists can be found only during the last one and one-half centuries. We have already noted that William Bell Riley[74] and John Roach Straton[75] were dispensationalists and that George Eldon Ladd[76] abandoned dispensationalism and spent the remainder of his life expounding an alternative historic premillennialism.

Dispensationalism can be traced to the ministry and teaching of John Nelson Darby (1800–1882), a native of London and resident of Ireland who after being ordained a deacon and a priest in the Church of England became disillusioned with the church establishment and began to meet in 1827–1828 with a group of Dublin dissenters, of whom he became the leader and

---

[71](New York: Macmillan, 1921). Gragg, *George Burman Foster*, 10, has reported that the volume consists of lectures given in 1905.

[72]Gragg, *George Burman Foster*, 32n.51. See Macintosh, *The Problem of Religious Knowledge* (New York, London: Harper & Brothers, 1940) 97-119.

[73]Towne, "A 'Singleminded' Theologian," 37, 168, 169, 172, 178n.157.

[74]See above, 322.

[75]See above, 325.

[76]See above, 375-76.

which became the Plymouth Brethren. A prolific writer, he authored some forty sizeable books. Darby's initial concern was for the doctrine of the church, and only later did eschatology become central for him.[77] Darby visited Canada and the United States, and his teaching was also disseminated through the Believers' Meetings for Bible Study (1876–1900), known also as the Niagara (Ontario) Bible Conferences, and through the International Prophecy Conferences (1878, 1886).[78]

The doctrinal distinctives of Darby's dispensationalism may be summarized as follows:

1. Preponderance of a literal hermeneutic
2. Positing of multiple—often seven—dispensations[79] in biblical history, each with its own divine mandate
3. Postponement of the kingdom of God as offered to Israel by Jesus because of Israel's rejection thereof
4. Dichotomy between Israel (Jews) and the church (Gentiles) with separate purposes and destinies for each
5. The church as a parenthesis within or interruption of the divine plan
6. Letters to the seven churches (Revelation 2–3) as symbolic of seven successive periods of church history
7. Apostate nature of present Christendom
8. Pretribulational rapture of the church
9. Two distinct comings of Jesus Christ: "the rapture" (in the air) and "the revelation" (on the earth)
10. Seven-year "Great Tribulation" during which an elect remnant of Israel will be saved and gathered
11. Millennial kingdom as a Jewish millennium
12. The new Jerusalem as an earthly city[80]

---

[77]W. G. Turner, *John Nelson Darby* (London: C. A. Hammond, 1944); Robert Henry Krapohl, "A Search for Purity: The Controversial Life of John Nelson Darby" (Ph.D. diss., Baylor University, 1988); Clarence B. Bass, *Backgrounds to Dispensationalism: Its Historic Genesis and Ecclesiastical Implications* (Grand Rapids MI: Eerdmans, 1960) 48-63, 100-40.

[78]C. Norman Kraus, *Dispensationalism in America: Its Rise and Development* (Richmond VA: John Knox Press, 1958) 46, 71-110.

[79]Darby's seven dispensations were the Paradisaical, the Noahic, the Abrahamic, the Israelite, the Gentile, the Spirit, and the Millennial. *The Collected Writings of J. N. Darby*, 34 vols. (London: G. Morrish, 1867–1900; repr.: Oak Park IL: Bible Truth Publishers, 1971) 2:568-73.

[80]Bass, *Backgrounds to Dispensationalism*, 13-47; Garrett, *Systematic Theology*, 1st ed., 2:756-57; 2nd ed., 2:832-33.

J. R. Graves the Landmarker, at least during the latter part of his life, embraced dispensationalism.[81] Such views were expressed quite often in Graves's paper, *The Baptist*, and in three books published after 1880.[82] Among the authors that seemingly influenced Graves toward dispensationalism, according to Danny E. Howe, were Adoniram Judson Frost, a Baptist pastor in Sacramento, California,[83] Joseph Augustus Seiss (1823–1904), a Lutheran pastor in Philadelphia, and David Nevins Lord (1792–1880), who advocated a literal hermeneutic.[84] There is no evidence that Graves was acquainted with or utilized the writings of Darby.[85] By 1859 Graves seems to have embraced premillennialism but not dispensationalism. By 1867 he was teaching the Great Tribulation, by 1874 a different destiny for "Israel in the flesh" and "Israel in the Spirit," by 1878 the restoration of Jews to Palestine, and by 1883 the pretribulational rapture of the pure saints.[86] According to Graves, the dispensations or ages are the Adamic, the Antediluvian, the Patriarchal, the Legal or Jewish, the Gospel, the Messianic or Millennial, and the Consummation.[87] He may have been an atypical dispensationalist in that he did not attribute to the dispensations differing methods or standards of God's dealing with humanity.[88]

---

[81]This has been recognized by four scholars: Smith, "A Critical Analysis of the Theology of J. R. Graves," 144; Sandeen, *The Roots of Fundamentalism*, 166; Tull, "A Study of Southern Baptist Landmarkism," 519-20; Danny E. Howe, "An Analysis of Dispensationalism and Its Implications for the Theologies of James Robinson Graves, John Franklyn Norris, and Wallie Amos Criswell" (Ph.D. diss., Southwestern Baptist Theological Seminary, 1988) 77-139.

[82]*The Work of Christ in the Covenant of Redemption: Developed in Seven Dispensations* (Memphis: Baptist Book House, 1883); *The Dispensational Expositions of the Parables and Prophecies of Christ* (Memphis: Graves and Mahaffy, 1887); *John's Baptism: Was It from Moses or Christ? Jewish or Christian? Objections to Its Character Answered* (Memphis: J. R. Graves and Son, 1891).

[83]On Frost, see George W. Dollar, *A History of Fundamentalism in America* (Greenville SC: Bob Jones University Press, 1973) 64-66.

[84]"An Analysis of Dispensationalism," 93-104.

[85]Sandeen, *The Roots of Fundamentalism*, 166; Smith, "A Critical Analysis of the Theology of J. R. Graves," 144.

[86]Howe, "An Analysis of Dispensationalism," 81, 84-85, 85-87, 102; *The Work of Christ in the Covenant of Redemption*, 406-22.

[87]*The Work of Christ in the Covenant of Redemption*, 168-76, 177-82, 186-217, 218-43, 423-60, 461-530, 544-55.

[88]Howe, "An Analysis of Dispensationalism," 114.

According to Graves, two seeds were promised to Abraham, one a natural seed and the other the Son of God. The covenant of circumcision for Jews was distinct from the covenant of redemption for Gentiles. The Gospel dispensation is for Gentiles and is closed to the Jews so that there need be no prayers for Jews to be converted to Christ. A second atypical feature of Graves's dispensationalism was his final teaching that only the most devout Christians will be raptured and that second- and third-class Christians will endure the Great Tribulation. The reign of the Antichrist, that is, the pope, during the Great Tribulation, is to bring persecution to Christians and deception to the Jews. Pedobaptists are to be among the apostate Christians, and Baptists are to be infiltrated, according to the parables of the leaven and the mustard seed. Armageddon will pit the Antichrist against England. The second coming of Christ will deliver the Jews from the Antichrist, bring the judgment of the nations, and inaugurate the millennium. The restoration of Jews having the faith of Abraham to Palestine will be completed, and the millennium will be marked by the massive conversion of Jews to Christ and by the separate governance of Jews and Gentiles.[89]

Another exponent of dispensationalism in the Southern Baptist context was John Franklyn Norris.[90] A native of Dadeville, Alabama, Norris moved at eleven with his alcoholic father and devout Christian mother to Hubbard, Texas. Amid poverty he was converted at twelve, survived a bullet intended for his father, and was baptized and called to preach at seventeen. From 1898 to 1903 he studied at Baylor University (B.A.). Then he studied at Southern Baptist Theological Seminary, graduating in 1905 with the Th.M. degree and as valedictorian. For two years he was pastor of McKinney Avenue Church, Dallas, and for two years he was identified with the *Baptist Standard*, first as business manager and then as owner, before accepting the pastorate of First Church, Fort Worth, in 1909, where he would continue apart from certain interregna until his death in 1952. The church's condition as a congregation of cattle barons and professional people and a Kentucky revival meeting in 1911 caused Norris to turn to sensational methods and to Baptist populism, with the ensuing exodus of 600 members to other Baptist churches. Confronting the city's business and civic leadership over "Hell's Half Acre" and acquitted of arson, Norris initially had the support of fellow Baptists. But after he began attacking Baptist leaders, institutions,

---

[89]Ibid., 109, 111, 115-16, 121-22, 125-27, 128-29, 130-31, 132-33, 107, 109-10, 135, 133-35.
[90]See above, 320, 325.

and conventions, controversy led to the church's being disfellowshiped by the local association and the state convention, and to his adversarial role vis-à-vis the Southern Baptist Convention. Increasingly he identified with Northern and Canadian Fundamentalists and was acquitted in the shooting death of a protégé of the city's Roman Catholic mayor. From 1935 to 1950 Norris concurrently served as pastor of Temple Church, Detroit, Michigan, which he led out of the Northern Baptist Convention, and in 1935 he gathered a group of churches into the Premillennial Baptist Missionary Fellowship, renamed in 1950 the World Baptist Fellowship. A break with his associate, George Beauchamp Vick, in 1950 led to the latter's organizing the Baptist Bible Fellowship International.[91]

None of Norris's college or seminary professors would have likely encouraged him toward dispensationalism, for they were mostly postmillennialists. His embrace of dispensationalism was seemingly a process, beginning with his tenure at the *Baptist Standard*. The writing of I. M. Haldeman he acknowledged as an influence, several dispensational speakers were brought to the Fort Worth church as early as 1917, and Norris used the *Scofield Reference Bible*.[92] By 1929 he had adopted Scofield's seven

---

[91]Louis Entzminger, *The J. Frank Norris I Have Known for 34 Years* (Fort Worth TX: Fundamental Publishing, 1947); Wilburn S. Taylor, "Norris, John Franklyn," *Encyclopedia of Southern Baptists* 2:983; E. Ray Tatum, *Conquest or Failure? Biography of J. Frank Norris* (Dallas: Baptist Historical Foundation, 1966); Clovis Gwin Morris, "He Changed Things: The Life and Thoughts of J. Frank Norris" (Ph.D. diss., Texas Tech University, 1973); Roy Emerson Falls, *A Biography of J. Frank Norris, 1877–1952* (Euless TX: author, 1975); Royce Lee Measures, "Men and Movements Influenced by J. Frank Norris" (Th.D. diss., Southwestern Baptist Theological Seminary, 1976) 1-77; Russell, *Voices of American Fundamentalism*, 20-46; Bobby D. Compton, "J. Frank Norris and Southern Baptists," *Review and Expositor* 79 (Winter 1982): 63-84; Lee Roy McGlone, "The Preaching of J. Frank Norris: An *Apologia* for Fundamentalism" (Ph.D. diss., Southern Baptist Theological Seminary, 1983; Ann Arbor MI: University Microfilms International, 1985) 30-90; McBeth, *The Baptist Heritage*, 671, 677, 679-80, 762-68; Howe, "An Anaysis of Dispensationalism," 140-58; Homer G. Ritchie, *The Life and Legend of J. Frank Norris: "The Fighting Parson"* (Fort Worth TX: author, 1991) esp. 196-207; Barry Hankins, *God's Rascal: J. Frank Norris and the Beginnings of Southern Fundamentalism* (Lexington: University Press of Kentucky, 1996).

[92]Howe, "An Analysis of Dispensationalism," 161-70. In 1934 Norris debated Foy E. Wallace of the Churches of Christ, taking the affirmative on the return of the

dispensations (Innocence, Conscience, Human Government, Promise, Law, Grace, and Kingdom),[93] but within a decade he had reduced the dispensations to three: Law or Israel, Church or Grace, and Kingdom.[94] Building on the Bible as inspired, inerrant, perspicuous, and to be interpreted literally, Norris identified the true church as within the professing church but utterly different from the apostate church and differentiated the true church from Israel. The postponed kingdom he defended from Dan. 9:24-27. The pretribulational rapture is to be "neither secret nor partial." During the Great Tribulation, depicted in Revelation 5-19 but not limited to seven years, the apostate church is to suffer, the marriage supper of the Lamb is to occur in heaven, elect Jews will return to Palestine, and angels are to preach "the everlasting gospel" of judgment. Norris even differentiated the gospel of the kingdom and the gospel of grace. The Antichrist, the false prophet, and Satan form a "diabolic trinity." The Battle of Armageddon is to include an Anglo-Jewish alliance. During the millennium all Jews will return to Palestine, the tabernacle will be rebuilt and sacrifices resumed, Christ will reign over Israel and the nations with Jerusalem as the world's capital, and Israel and the church will be forever separate. After Satan's final rebellion and suppression, the wicked will be raised and be subject to the great white throne judgment.[95]

Another Baptist dispensationalist who would have an interdenominational ministry was John Richard Rice (1895–1980). Born in Cooke County,

---

Jews as a nation to Palestine at the second coming of Christ and their conversion to Christ and on Christ's literal millennial throne in Jerusalem. *Norris-Wallace Debate: Delivered in Fort Worth, Texas, November 5th, 6th, and 7th 1934* (Fort Worth: Fundamentalist Publishing, 1935) 7-82.

[93]Cyrus Ingerson Scofield, *Rightly Dividing the Word of Truth* (Philadelphia: Philadelphia School of the Bible, 1921; orig., 1896) 20-25; Howe, "An Analysis of Dispensationalism," 179, based on Norris, "The Abrahamic Covenant," *The Fundamentalist*, 22 February 1929, 2.

[94]Howe, "An Analysis of Dispensationalism," 179-80, based on Norris, "The Second Coming of Christ," *The Fundamentalist*, 4 March 1939, 1.

[95]Howe, "An Analysis of Dispensationalism," 171-75, 177-78, 175-76, 185-88, 177, 181, 182, 183-84, 188-91, 184-85, 194-95, 194, 195-96, 197-99. See Norris, "Fifteen Signs of the Second Coming of Christ" and "The Battle of Armageddon" in *The Battle of Armageddon* (Fort Worth TX: Calvary Publications, n.d.) 3-26, 166-81; idem, "The Great White Throne of Judgment," in *The Four Horsemen Are Riding Fast and Five Other Outstanding Messages* (Plano TX: Calvary Baptist Church, n.d.) 30-46.

Texas, and having professed Christ at nine, Rice was educated at Decatur Baptist College and Baylor University (B.A., 1920). While in graduate study in education at the University of Chicago, he was called to preach at Pacific Garden Mission. After two years of study at Southwestern Baptist Theological Seminary and an associate pastorate and pastorate in Plainview and Shamrock, Texas, he entered full-time evangelism with residence in Fort Worth. Preaching in Norris's pulpit and on his radio station led to tensions with the Southern Baptist leaders, and in 1927 Rice left the Southern Baptist Convention.[96] He founded and pastored the Fundamental Baptist Tabernacle, Dallas (1932–1940), during which time he founded a weekly paper, *The Sword of the Lord* (1934). His subsequent interdenominational evangelistic and publishing ministry was located in Wheaton, Illinois (1940–1963) and Murfreesboro, Tennessee (1963–1980). He authored nearly 200 books and booklets.[97]

By Rice's 1930s pastorate in Dallas he had embraced dispensationalism. He acknowledged that all his teachers had been postmillennialists.[98] Rice's biographers offer no clue as to how he came to such views, but it is not difficult to posit some influence from Norris. In 1935 he debated W. L. Oliphant, minister of the Oak Cliff Church of Christ, defending the propositions that "the Jews as a nation will return to Palestine when Christ returns to the earth and then will be converted to Christ" and that "Christ will establish a literal throne in Jerusalem and will reign over the whole earth for a . . . thousand years."[99] Turning to the book of Daniel, Rice interpreted the image (2:31-35) as indicating "the decay of human government and institutions" and concluded that "the smiting stone has not yet fallen," for "the utter destruction of Gentile rule" did not occur "at the first coming of Christ" and twentieth-century churches "have not fulfilled this prophecy." "Not a single government . . . is controlled on Christian

---

[96] Rice became the lifelong critic of the Southern Baptist Convention. See his *Southern Baptist Leaders Now Committed Liberals* (Murfreesboro TN: Sword of the Lord, 1970).

[97] Robert Leslie Sumner, *Man Sent from God: A Biography of Dr. John R. Rice* (Grand Rapids MI: Eerdmans, 1959); Viola Walden, *John R. Rice: "The Captain of Our Team"* (Murfreesboro TN: Sword of the Lord, 1990).

[98] *The Coming Kingdom of Christ* (Wheaton IL: Sword of the Lord, 1945) 8.

[99] *The Oliphant-Rice Debate . . . Conducted at Dallas, Texas, January 15, 16, 17, 18, 1935 and January 22, 23, 24, 25, 1935* (Austin TX: Firm Foundation Publishing House, 1935) 9-270.

principles. There are no Christian nations. . . . Gentile powers are still ruling." Daniel 9, for Rice, applied not to the time of Antiochus Epiphanes or to the first advent of the Messiah but to the second advent. The great parenthesis between the sixty-nine weeks and the seventieth is identified with the Christian era, the coming ruler (v. 26) is to be the Antichrist, and the Great Tribulation is to be the last half of the seventieth week. This is joined to a pretribulational rapture, which Rice found in the New Testament.[100] Rice was confident that the kingdom of heaven had been postponed (Matt. 23:37-39) and that the Jews will "possess Canaan forever."[101] All these teachings Rice systematized in *The Coming Kingdom of Christ*[102] together with specifics as to signs of Jesus' second coming. Rice interpreted Matt. 10:17-23 as having a "double meaning," namely, referring to the tour of the Twelve and to the Great Tribulation, and likewise Matthew 24, as referring both to the destruction of Jerusalem in AD 70 and to Christ's "revelation" on the Mount of Olives at the end of the Great Tribulation.[103] Rice differed with Scofield by rejecting the idea that the seven churches (Revelation 2–3) "represent seven periods of church history" and as a futurist as to Revelation 4–19 allowed for a nonlinear repetition of teachings from chs. 6–11 to chs. 12–19.[104]

Like Norris, W. A. Criswell's teachers had been postmillennialists or possibly amillennialists. By the early years of his Dallas pastorate he had endorsed dispensationalism.[105] Criswell asserted that he became a premillennialist when he began to do expository preaching near the end of his Muskogee pastorate and that he developed his premillennial views from his literal interpretation of the Bible, not from others.[106] Howe's research, however, has led him to two specific sources for Criswell's dispensational-

---

[100]*The Second Coming of Christ in Daniel* (Dallas: author, n.d.) 8-16, 28-44.

[101]*Christ's Literal Reign on Earth from David's Throne at Jerusalem* (Grand Rapids MI: Zondervan, 1939) 12, 7-8.

[102]*The Coming Kingdom of Christ*, esp. 130-43.

[103]*The King of the Jews: A Verse-by-Verse Commentary on the Gospel according to Matthew* (Wheaton IL; Sword of the Lord, 1955) 157-59, 366-99 (esp. 368-74).

[104]*"Behold, He Cometh!" A Verse-by-Verse Commentary on the Book of Revelation* (Murfreesboro TN: Sword of the Lord, 1977) 26-32, 107-291 (esp. 147).

[105]But Ray Summers testified that as a university student Criswell had begun to preach as a premillennialist. Howe, "An Analysis of Dispensationalism," 217-18.

[106]Ibid., 216-17.

ism: the teachings and library of his deceased pastoral predecessor at Muskogee, Aldis Norton Hall, and the book, *God's Eternal Purpose Revealed*,[107] by Abb L. Goodwin, a pastor in Oklahoma, New Mexico, and Florida whose son joined First Church, Dallas, in 1949.[108]

By the early 1950s Criswell was preaching on the "error of postmillennialism" and declaring that true Christians will be raptured and not have "to bear the terrible judgments of God," that is, the Great Tribulation.[109] In expository sermons on Revelation delivered during the 1960s Criswell preached on two eschatological comings of Christ by joining Rev. 16:15 with Rev. 1:7, interpreted the letters to the seven churches as symbolic of seven periods of church history, and took Rev. 1:19 to be the divinely given outline (past, present, future) of the entire book, so as to validate a futurist interpretation of chs. 4-19.[110] Later he depicted Jesus as the "rejected" and "exiled king" of a postponed kingdom, identified the church as a "mystery," "not mentioned in the Old Testament" but taken "out of the side of our crucified Lord," and posited a twofold coming of Christ, the first as "a thief in the night" and the second openly and visibly.[111] Indeed Christ will come for his bride.[112] Criswell defended the "premillennial faith" but was reluctant to label it as "dispensational."[113]

The "classical" dispensationalism of Darby and Scofield yielded somewhat during the 1950 and 1960s to a "revised" or "essentialist" dispensationalism, espoused by Alva J. McClain (1888–1968), Charles Caldwell Ryrie (1925–), John Flipse Walvoord (1910–2002), and J. Dwight Pentecost (1915–), three of whom were affiliated with Dallas Theological Semi-

---

[107](Jacksonville, FL: Direct Mail Advertising, 1948).

[108]Howe, "An Analysis of Dispensationalism," 218-31. Criswell wrote a preface to the 1973 edition of Goodwin's book and announced that it "would be the first official textbook of the Criswell Bible Institute." Ibid., 230.

[109]*These Issues We Must Face*, 121-23, 134-35.

[110]*Expository Sermons on Revelation*, 5 vols. in 1 (Grand Rapids MI: Zondervan, 1969) 1:106-15; 2:34-44; 1:173-84.

[111]*With a Bible in My Hand* (Nashville: Broadman, 1978) 153-55, 123-25, 157-58.

[112]*The Doctrine of the Church*, 111-12.

[113]*Great Doctrines of the Bible*, vol. 8, *Eschatology* (Grand Rapids MI: Zondervan, 1989) 95-104; Hester, "Millennialism in Southern Baptist Thought since 1900," 113-14, 121, 190-200, has interpreted Criswell's eschatology as "dispensationalist."

nary. They abandoned "the *eternal* dualism of heavenly and earthly peoples," gave more emphasis to the social nature of the church during the present dispensation, embraced the view that the new covenant of Jer. 31:31-34 is the covenant operative under the present dispensation, dropped the sharp differentiation between "kingdom of God" and "kingdom of heaven" and began to speak of a present spiritual kingdom, and held that Israel and the church will have the same kind of eternal state.[114] Similarly Ryrie summarized revised dispensationalism more succinctly in terms of three essentials: the abiding distinction between Israel and the church, a "literal" or "normal" or "plain," as distinct from "allegorical," hermeneutic, and a single doxological theology of history.[115]

Then, during the 1990s, a third form of dispensationalism called "progressive" was espoused, and one of its leading exponents has been a Baptist. Craig Alan Blaising (1949–), a native of San Antonio, Texas, holds the B.S. degree in aerospace engineering from the University of Texas at Austin, the Th.M. (1976) and Th.D. (1979) degrees from Dallas Theological Seminary, and the Ph.D. degree (1988) from the University of Aberdeen. He taught systematic theology in Dallas Seminary (1980–1989), did likewise at Southern Baptist Theological Seminary (1993–2001), where he was Joseph Emerson Brown Professor of Christian Theology, and since 2002 has been executive vice president and provost and professor of theology at Southwestern Baptist Theological Seminary. During 2004–2005 he was national president of the Evangelical Theological Society.[116]

Building on revised dispensationalism rather than classical dispensationalism, progressive dispensationalists have adopted the term "progressive" because "of the way in which" they view "the interrelationship of

---

[114]Craig A. Blaising, "The Extent and Varieties of Dispensationalism," in *Progressive Dispensationalism*, ed. Blaising and Darrell L. Bock (Grand Rapids MI: Baker, 2000; orig., 1993) 31-32, 33-34, 37-39, 32-33; Blaising and Bock, "Dispensationalism, Israel and the Church: Assessment and Dialogue," in *Dispensationalism, Israel and the Church: The Search for Definition*, ed. Blaising and Bock (Grand Rapids MI: Zondervan, 1992) 377-79.

[115]*Dispensationalism Today* (Chicago: Moody, 1965), 44-47; Blaising, "Dispensationalism: The Search for Definition," in *Dispensationalism, Israel and the Church*, 23-30.

[116]*Who's Who in Religion*, 4th ed. (1992–1993) 44; *Who's Who in America*, 54th ed. (2000) 424; Curriculum Vitae, Southwestern Baptist Theological Seminary, 2006.

divine dispensations in history, their overall orientation to the eternal kingdom of God . . . , and the reflection of these . . . relations in the literary features of Scripture."[117] Blaising and others articulated the progressive view in terms of a "more developed" and "more consistent" "historical-literary" hermeneutic, the dispensations as *"successive"* and not merely "different," "a more unified view of the biblical covenants," "a *holistic and unified* view of eternal salvation," "the church as a *new manifestation of grace*," being not "an anthropological category" but "redeemed humanity" consisting of both Jews and Gentiles, and continuity between the millennium and the eternal state.[118] Although the progressives apply the "Israel-church distinction" to the Mosaic and the present dispensations, respectively,[119] Jewish Christians of the present dispensation claim the promises to national Israel.[120] Hence with these numerous modifications of earlier forms of dispensationalism, the progressives retain the *sine qua non* of all dispensationalism: a significant distinction between Israel and the Church.

Baptists of the preceding centuries had affirmed eschatological doctrines such as the second coming of Christ, resurrection, judgment, hell, and heaven, and among them were to be found both postmillennialists and premillennialists, but eschatology had never been the arena for differentiating Baptists from other Christian denominations. Dispensationalism as a system of teaching provides not only specific and peculiar eschatological teachings but also a distinctive hermeneutic and periodization for the Old and New Testaments. The embrace of dispensationalism by certain Baptist leaders, especially in the twentieth century, was at times divisive. Its utter separation of Israel and the Church threatened the reconciliation of believing Jews and Gentiles in the "one body" of Christ and the creation of "one new man" (Eph. 2:14-18, NIV).

The English Christological Controversy

When Christological controversy erupted among British Baptists in 1971–1972, there were already other divergences within the Baptist Union of Great Britain. The Baptist Revival Fellowship, which had been formed in

---

[117]Blaising and Bock, "Dispensationalism, Israel and the Church: Assessment and Dialogue," 380.

[118]Ibid., 380-85; Blaising and Bock, *Progressive Dispensationalism*, 46-54.

[119]Blaising and Bock, "Dispensationalism, Israel and the Church: Assessment and Dialogue," 383.

[120]Blaising and Bock, *Progressive Dispensationalism*, 50.

1938, was strongly evangelical and had already considered forming a separate denominational body.[121] Some churches and ministers sympathetic to charismatic practice had withdrawn from the Baptist Union.[122] Some more ecumenically inclined formed in 1968 the Baptist Renewal Group.[123]

As one of four doctrinal messages to the April 1971 assembly of the Baptist Union Michael Hugh Taylor (1936–), the principal of Northern Baptist College,[124] spoke on "The Incarnate Presence: How Much of a Man Was Jesus?" He declared:

> I am not content to say he was an extraordinary man. I believe that in the man Jesus we encounter God. I believe that God was active in Jesus, but it will not quite do to say categorically: Jesus is God. Jesus is unique, but his uniqueness does not make him different in kind from us. He is the same sort of animal. He is fully and unambiguously a man. The difference between him and ourselves is not in the manner of God's presence of Jesus. The difference is in what God did in and through this man and the degree to which this man responded and cooperated with God.[125]

Taylor went on to declare, "I do not say that Jesus is God, but I do say with the New Testament that God was in Christ or that I encounter God in Jesus." Furthermore, Jesus is "a unique example of what human life becomes when lived in cooperation with God," and he "acted in a unique and decisive way for our salvation."[126]

Responses to Taylor's message were prompt and diverse, including both criticism and commendation. Some found him to have denied the deity of Christ and called for the termination of his principalship and his removal from the list of accredited ministers. Others commended his creativity or de-

---

[121]Ian M. Randall, *The English Baptists of the Twentieth Century*, vol. 4, A History of the English Baptists (Didcot UK: Baptist Historical Society, 2005) 203, 230, 232, 344.

[122]Ibid., 324-27.

[123]Ibid., 336-37, 342-43.

[124]Taylor, a native of Northampton and a graduate of the University of Manchester (B.A., B.D., M.A.) and of Union Theological Seminary, New York (S.T.M.), had been pastor of North Shields Church (1961–1966) and Hall Green Church, Birmingham (1966–1969) and was concurrently lecturer in theology and ethics in the University of Manchester. *Who's Who*, 150th ed. (1998) 1949; *International Who's Who*, 64th ed. (2001) 1521.

[125]Mimeographed copy, 1.

[126]Ibid., 2, 4.

fended his right to speak freely.[127] In September the London Association's council approved by a vote of 43 to 15 a resolution by Cyril Black indicating that Taylor's address seemed "'to throw doubt upon the Authority, Deity and Sinlessness of Jesus Christ'" and defeated by 43 to 20 a resolution that would have commended Taylor for seeking "'to restate traditional doctrine in contemporary terms.'"[128] On 5 October the General Purposes and Finance Committee of the Baptist Union refused by a vote of 14 to six to accept George Beasley-Murray's resolution that Taylor's address "'does not apparently do justice to the teaching of the New Testament concerning our Lord Jesus Christ'" and instead spoke more positively of Taylor's effort while urging the Union's Council to reaffirm the deity of Christ.[129] David Pawson, pastor of Commercial Road Church, Guildford, in a late October address to a London gathering on "How Much of a God Is Jesus?" contended for the deity of Christ from the three-year experience of his disciples, the explicit doctrine of the apostles, and the affirmation of the Nicene Creed.[130] In its November meeting the Union's Council strongly resisted the efforts of Stanley Voke and Beasley-Murray to get the council to acknowledge that Taylor had not squared with the teaching of the New Testament but allowed a defeated amendment by Ernest Payne on Baptist liberty to stand as an addendum to its resolution.[131] Beasley-Murray resigned as chairman of the council.

Shortly thereafter the Baptist Revival Fellowship declared by a vote 155 to 14 with 24 abstentions the inability of its members "'in conscience'" to "'remain associated with the life of a Union which has decided to tolerate the denial of the Deity of our Lord Jesus Christ amongst its accredited ministers.'" Eighteen ministers resigned before the end of the year, and in 1972 the Association of Evangelical Baptist Churches was formed. The appeal by David Russell, general secretary of the Baptist Union, not to withdraw was

---

[127]Randall, *The English Baptists of the Twentieth Century*, 367-71.

[128]Ibid., 371-72, based on *Baptist Times*, 30 September 1971, 12.

[129]Ibid., 373-74, based on Minutes of the Baptist Union General Purposes and Finance Committee, 5 October 1971.

[130]*How Much of a God Is Jesus? An Address Given . . . at Bloomsbury Central Church, London, on 2 October 1971* (Littlehampton UK: D. J. Moon, 1971).

[131]Randall, *The English Baptists of the Twentieth Century*, 374-75, based on Minutes of the Baptist Union Council, 9-10 November 1971, and Paul Beasley-Murray, *Fearless for Truth*, 148-50.

not being heeded.[132] Early in 1972 Beasley-Murray, having been refused publication in the *Baptist Times*, published and sent to all accredited ministers in the Baptist Union a pamphlet entitled *The Christological Controversy in the Baptist Union*.[133] Therein he found Taylor to have taken the position "that the belief that Jesus is truly God and truly man is a contradiction." Moreover, Taylor has rejected the uniqueness of Jesus as the Son of God and the doctrine of the incarnation. This leads logically to rejection of the doctrine of the Trinity and of union with Christ and abandonment of our Christian worship and hymnody, baptism, and the Lord's Supper. Hence, to take Taylor's position to its logical conclusion, he argued, there would remain no "justification . . . for the continuance of the Baptist denomination," and Christianity should be reduced to Reformed Judaism.[134] At the Union's assembly on 25 April 1972, after various amendments were defeated, Black's motion was approved by a vote of 1,800 to 46 with 72 abstentions.[135] It affirmed that "the Declaration of Principle represents the basic requirements for fellowship in the Baptist denomination" and that accredited ministers "are required to accept" it. Furthermore it affirmed "the unacceptability of any interpretation of the person and work of Jesus Christ our Lord which would obscure or deny the fundamental tenet of the Christian faith that Jesus Christ is Lord and Saviour, truly God and truly Man."[136] Taylor, being supported by associations in the north of England, continued in his principalship until 1985,[137] but his 1977 anti-incarnational pamphlet, *The Plain Man's Guide to the Incarnation*,[138] did not evoke

---

[132]Ibid., 375-76, 377, based on Baptist Revival Fellowship Statement, adopted at Swansea, 15-18 November 1971.

[133](Rushden UK: Stanley L. Hunt, 1972).

[134]Ibid.

[135]Randall, *The English Baptists of the Twentieth Century*, 381-82.

[136]*Baptist Times*, 27 April 1972, 7, as quoted in ibid., 381.

[137]Randall, *The English Baptists of the Twentieth Century*, 452; Geoffrey R. Breed to James Leo Garrett, Jr., 30 May 2006. Subsequently Taylor was director of Christian Aid (1985–1997), president of Selly Oak Colleges, Birmingham (1998–1999), professor of social theology, University of Birmingham (2000–2001), and director of World Faiths Development Dialogue (2002–2004). He has authored *Variations on a Theme* (1971), *Sermon on the Mount* (1982), *Learning to Care* (1983), *Good for the Poor* (1990), *Christianity and the Persistence of Poverty* (1991), *Not Angels but Agencies* (1995), and *Jesus and the Financial Institutions* (1996). *Who's Who*; *International Who's Who*.

[138](Loughbrough UK: ONE Publications, 1977).

controversy, for, as Ian Randall has observed, the "Christological orthodoxy of the Union was widely regarded as settled."[139] As a result of this controversy evangelical conviction and commitment were strengthened within the Baptist Union, as demonstrated by the movement known as Mainstream.[140]

Open Theism

Historically most Christians in general and Baptists in particular have affirmed as one of the attributes of God the omniscience, or complete knowledge, of God, including his knowledge of all future happenings. Although during Christian history Christians have differed in their explanations as to how God knows future things, they have been virtually united in holding to God's complete knowledge of the future as well as of the past and the present.

At the end of the twentieth century there arose in North America out of an Arminian-Wesleyan context[141] a theological school, consisting of both Baptists and non-Baptists, that denies God's complete foreknowledge of all future events. The school or movement has been identified as the openness of God movement,[142] open theism,[143] or free will theism.[144]

Classical Christian theology has provided three principal answers as to how God knows all things, including the future. First, from the time of the sixth-century Christian philosopher Boethius some have explained God's foreknowledge in terms of his eternity. Consequently God as eternal can see everything—the past, the present, and the future, as if present. Second,

---

[139]Randall, *The English Baptists of the Twentieth Century*, 416.

[140]Ibid., 414-15, 440-43, 468-69, 496-99; Geoffrey R. Breed to James Leo Garrett, Jr., 30 May 2006.

[141]Bruce A. Ware, *God's Lesser Glory: The Diminished God of Open Theism* (Wheaton IL: Crossway Books, 2000) 31-32; Clark H. Pinnock, *Most Moved Mover: A Theology of God's Openness* (Grand Rapids MI: Baker; Carlisle UK: Paternoster, 2001) 106.

[142]Clark Pinnock, Richard Rice, John Sanders, William Hasker, and David Basinger, *The Openness of God: A Biblical Challenge to the Traditional Understanding of God* (Downers Grove IL: InterVarsity Press; Carlisle UK: Paternoster, 1994).

[143]Gregory A. Boyd, "The Open-Theism View," in *Divine Foreknowledge: Four Views*, ed. James K. Beilby and Paul R. Eddy (Downers Grove IL: InterVarsity, 2001) 13-47.

[144]William Hasker, "A Philosophical Perspective," in Pinnock et al., *The Openness of God*, 134-35; Pinnock, "Systematic Theology" in ibid., 117.

following John Calvin, others have identified foreknowledge and predetermination. Thus God foreknows future events because he also predetermines them.[145] Third, from Luis de Molina (1536–1600), a Spanish Jesuit theologian, came the theory of "middle knowledge." Accordingly, logically prior to his decree to create all things, God knew "the range of possible worlds," knew what would be "the actual world," and, via media, knew "the range of feasible worlds." But God providentially arranged his creatures so that they would freely choose what would fulfill God's ultimate purpose.[146]

Open theism was, strictly speaking, not a *de novo* development in doctrine, inasmuch as Marcion in the second century, Calcidius in the fifth, Faustus Socinus in the sixteenth, John Biddle in the seventeenth, Jules Lequyer and Otto Pfleiderer in the nineteenth, and Edgar Sheffield Brightman and Charles Hartshorne in the twentieth seem to have denied the complete divine foreknowledge of future events.[147]

Non-Baptist advocates of open theism include Richard Rice, John Sanders, William Hasker, and David Basinger. The Baptist advocates have been Clark H. Pinnock and Gregory A. Boyd (1955–). Pinnock, after his early defense of biblical infallibility at New Orleans Baptist Theological Seminary,[148] taught at Trinity Evangelical Divinity School (1969–1974) and Regent College (1974–1977) before becoming professor of theology in McMaster Divinity College (1977–2002).[149] He shifted from an Augustinian-Calvinist stance to an Arminian position during the 1970s. Then he

---

[145]Garrett, *Systematic Theology*, 2nd ed., 1:255-56.

[146]William Lane Craig, "The Middle-Knowledge View," in *Divine Foreknowledge*, ed. Beilby and Eddy, 120-23.

[147]Millard J. Erickson, *What Does God Know and When Does He Know It? The Current Controversy over Divine Foreknowledge* (Grand Rapids MI: Zondervan, 2003) 111-31; Garrett, *Systematic Theology*, 2nd ed., 1:256; Boyd, *Trinity and Process: A Critical Evaluation and Reconstruction of Hartshorne's Di-Polar Theism towards a Trinitarian Metaphysics*, American University Studies, series 7, Theology and Religion, vol. 119 (New York: Peter Lang, 1992) 296; Robert A. Morey, *Battle of the Gods: The Gathering Storm in Modern Evangelicalism* (Southbridge MA: Crown Publications, 1989) 62-67.

[148]See above, 493.

[149]Clark H. Pinnock to James Leo Garrett, Jr., 20 July 2006; Barry L. Callen, "Clark H. Pinnock: His Life and Work," in *Semper Reformandum: Studies in Honour of Clark H. Pinnock*, ed. Stanley E. Porter and Anthony R. Cross (Carlisle UK: Paternoster, 2003) 1-15.

moved during the 1980s from Arminianism to "free will theism."[150] Boyd's spiritual roots were in the United Pentecostal Church International, and his first postdoctoral book was a critique of its modalist "heresy."[151] A graduate of the University of Minnesota (B.A.), Yale University Divinity School (M.Div.), and Princeton Theological Seminary (Ph.D.), he was first ordained by the Christian Church (Disciples of Christ). Concurrently he has taught theology in Bethel College and been pastor of Woodland Hills Church (Baptist General Conference), St. Paul, Minnesota.[152] He has authored a detailed critique of the Jesus Seminar, especially the thesis of John Dominic Crossan and Burton Mack that Jesus was "a Cynic philosopher,"[153] and two substantive volumes in defense of a "warfare worldview" rather than a "blueprint worldview" as a Christian theodicy,[154] and coauthored a review of eighteen disputed issues among Evangelicals.[155]

Proponents of open theism have presented a multifaceted case for their position. Love is the supreme or predominant attribute of God. Stress is laid on the emotions of God (that is, joy, grief, anger, jealousy, regret) as expressed in the Old Testament, for these emotions are closely connected with God's changes of mind. The "repent" (KJV)/"relent" (NIV) passages relative to God are cited, and open theists argue that God changes his decisions, not his character. Num. 23:19 and 1 Sam. 15:29, texts which seem to teach the changelessness of God, are interpreted as connected with lying and constituting exceptions to the prevailing Old Testament pattern

---

[150]*Grace Unlimited*, ed. Pinnock (Minneapolis: Bethany Fellowship, 1975); "From Augustine to Arminius: A Pilgrimage in Theology," in *The Grace of God, the Will of Man: A Case for Arminianism*, ed. Pinnock (Grand Rapids MI: Zondervan, 1989) 15-30; Roger E. Olson, "Postconservative Evangelical Theology and the Theological Pilgrimage of Clark Pinnock," in *Semper Reformandum*, ed. Porter and Cross, 16-37.

[151]*Oneness Pentecostals and the Trinity* (Grand Rapids MI: Baker, 1992) 14.

[152]Boyd's earliest espousal of God's limited knowledge of the future seems to have been Gregory A. Boyd and Edward K. Boyd, *Letters from a Skeptic* (Colorado Springs CO: Cook Communications, 1994) 30-31.

[153]*Cynic Sage, or, Son of God?* (Wheaton IL: Victor Books, 1995).

[154]*God at War: The Bible and Spiritual Conflict* (Downers Grove IL: InterVarsity, 1997); *Satan and the Problem of Evil: Constructing a Trinitarian Warfare Theodicy* (Downers Grove IL: InterVarsity, 2001).

[155]Boyd and Paul R. Eddy, *Across the Spectrum: Understanding Issues in Evangelical Theology* (Grand Rapids MI: Baker, 2002).

represented by such texts as Jer. 18:7-11.[156] God speaks conditionally (Exod. 4:1-9; Matt. 26:39) and tests his people to discern their faithfulness (Gen. 22:12; Deut. 8:2; 13:1-3; 2 Chr. 32:31).[157] The suffering of God is affirmed,[158] and Jesus' predictions of Peter's denial (Matt. 26:33-35) and Judas's betrayal (John 6:64, 70-71; 13:18-19; 17:12) are treated in the light of Peter and Judas being "predictable characters."[159] The model of God as a "caring parent" is preferred to that of an "aloof monarch," the social or relational view of the Trinity is taught, and the balancing of immanence and transcendence is declared to be the intention of open theists.[160] The influence of Greek philosophy upon Christian theology is deplored,[161] God's election is reckoned to be corporate,[162] and "God exercises sovereignty by sharing power, not by domination," and hence his sovereignty is "partly unilateral and partly bilateral."[163] All these considerations lead open theists to the conclusion that God knows "all [future] things that can be known," but some future things God cannot know lest there be "a fixity of events" and the loss of human libertarian freedom.[164]

Baptist critics of open theism have responded with monographs. Bruce Allen Ware (1953–), professor of Christian theology in Southern Baptist Theological Seminary,[165] began by noting the benefits which open theists

---

[156]Pinnock, *Most Moved Mover*, 81-83, 126-29; Richard Rice, "Biblical Support for a New Perspective," in Pinnock et al., *The Openness of God*, 18-35, 46-50; Boyd, "The Open-Theism View," 26-30, 33-37.

[157]Boyd, "The Open-Theism View," 30-33.

[158]Pinnock, *Most Moved Mover*, 56-60.

[159]Boyd, *God of the Possible: A Biblical Introduction to the Open View of God* (Grand Rapids MI: Baker, 2000) 35-39; idem, "The Open-Theism View," 20-23.

[160]Pinnock, "Systematic Theology," in Pinnock et al., *The Openness of God*, 103-104, 107-109, 104-7, 111-13; idem, *Most Moved Mover*, 83-84.

[161]John Sanders, "Historical Considerations," in Pinnock et al., *The Openness of God*, 59-87; Pinnock, *Most Moved Mover*, 65-73.

[162]Rice, "Biblical Support for a New Perspective," 56-57.

[163]Pinnock, *Most Moved Mover*, 92-96 (esp. 93), 53-56 (esp. 53).

[164]Pinnock, "Systematic Theology," in Pinnock et al., *The Openness of God*, 121-24.

[165]A native of Spokane, Washington, Ware was graduated from Whitworth College (B.A., 1975), Western Conservative Baptist Seminary (M.Div., 1978, Th.M., 1980), the University of Washington (M.A., 1981), and Fuller Theological Seminary (Ph.D., 1984) and has taught at Bethel Theological Seminary, Western Conservative Baptist Seminary, and Trinity Evangelical Divinity School. He is the

have claimed for their position: upholding "the *real* relationship that exists between God and others," the genuine risk God took in the creation of freedom-possessing humans, divine repentance, divine assessment, and great sensitivity to human suffering. Then Ware sought to show the inadequacies of the so-called "straight forward" interpretation of biblical texts by open theists, both the "growth-in-knowledge" by God texts and the divine repentance texts. Num. 23:19 and 1 Sam. 15:29 are not exceptions to the biblical pattern but central texts. On the positive side Ware used especially Isaiah 40-48, Psalm 139, and several chapters in Daniel to build his case for a biblical doctrine of "exhaustive divine foreknowledge." Jer. 18:5-10, for Ware, is not about divine change but about *"God's constancy"* in making appropriate responses "to the moral situations that he faces." Open theism's emphasis on God's risk-taking is an "assault on God's wisdom," and the God of limited knowledge of the future is harmful to prayer and seeking God's guidance.[166]

Millard Erickson, relying heavily on the commentaries by Carl Friedrich Keil (1807–1888) and Franz Delitzsch (1813–1890) and Hebrew and Greek lexicons, argued that the repentance texts connote emotional pain, not change of mind, and that the change of mind texts do not involve a divine change of mind. God tested persons to humble them and not to discover their devotion or character. Open theists have claimed too much about so-called failed prophecies, the lack of God's knowledge of the future, divine frustration, and conditional statements. Like Ware, Erickson magnified Isaiah 41-48 as repeatedly portraying divine foreknowledge but thought Ware had claimed too much for Psalm 139. He set forth prophetic narratives that "preidentified individuals" by name and "specific actions of individuals" and differentiated "unilateral divine action" prophecies, "conditional prophecies," and predictions "based on knowledge of the past and present." Open theists never explain "how God could know the character of Peter and Judas so well but not the character of Abraham." Erickson's hermeneutic involved a dependence on anthropomorphism and anthropopathism when open theists were insisting on a more literal hermeneutic.

---

author of *Their God Is Too Small: Open Theism and the Undermining of Confidence of God* (2003), *God's Greater Glory: The Exalted God of Scripture and the Christian Faith* (2004), and *Father, Son, and Holy Spirit: Relationships, Roles and Relevance* (2005). Curriculum vitae, Southern Baptist Theological Seminary.

[166]*God's Lesser Glory: The Diminished God of Open Theism* (Wheaton IL: Crossway Books, 2000).

Erickson went beyond Ware by identifying certain predecessors of open theists from the second to the twentieth centuries. He sought to alleviate open theism's charge that the traditional view of divine foreknowledge had been heavily influenced by Greek philosophy and/or Thomistic philosophy by challenging as "exaggerated" the distinction between "biblical" and "Greek" thinking and by noting that Karl Barth and Emil Brunner had resisted philosophical influences while holding to the classical doctrine of divine foreknowledge. On the contrary he traced the influence of process thought on the open theists, especially as to the dynamic nature of reality and the presumed commonsense or libertarian view of freedom. Open theism, as Ware noted, is unsettling for prayer and divine guidance, and, furthermore, it has a "finitist" approach to the problem of evil. Erickson took note of Pinnock's embrace of inclusivism, or the salvation by implicit faith in Christ,[167] of postmortem evangelism,[168] and of annihilationism.[169] Finally, Erickson concluded that although each view had its weaknesses and strengths—open theism having the advantage on practical issues and traditional theism on biblical and historical considerations, traditional theism "appears to have considerably more cogent intellectual support and fewer difficulties" than open theism.[170]

John Stephen Piper (1946–), pastor for preaching of Bethlehem Church, Minneapolis, Minnesota, coedited a volume of essays designed to refute open theism. Identifying the essence of the movement an "its denial of the exhaustive, definite foreknowledge of God," on the basis "that humans and angels can be morally responsible only if they have ultimate self-determination," he noted that for open theists "God can know ahead of time what he *intends to do his in freedom, but not what we* intend to do in our future." Piper set forth fifteen propositions, biblical, theological, and practical, in order to warn of the dangers of open theism.[171]

---

[167]*A Wideness in God's Mercy: The Finality of Jesus Christ in a World of Religions* (Grand Rapids MI: Zondervan, 1992) 20-35, 92-113. Pinnock referred to "pagan saints outside the church."

[168]Ibid., 168-72.

[169]"The Destruction of the Finally Impenitent," *Criswell Theological Review* 4 (Spring 1990): 243-59.

[170]*What Does God Know and When Does He Know It?*, passim, esp. 57-59, 56, 256.

[171]*Beyond the Bounds: Open Theism and the Understanding of Biblical Christianity*, ed. Piper, Justin Taylor, and Paul Kjoss Helseth (Wheaton IL: Crossway,

Modernism, as represented by Mathews, Macintosh, and Foster, abandoned any normative role for biblical revelation and substituted modern thought—scientific, philosophical, psychological, and sociological—as the standard for determining religious truth and values. Consequently its advocates, most of whom continued in Baptist ranks, hovered between theism and humanism and could hardly be said to have retained the historic core of Christianity.

Less destructive to the Baptists was dispensationalism, as espoused by Graves, Norris, Rice, Criswell, and Blaising. It did represent a radical differentiation between Israel and the church uncommon to earlier Baptists as well as a hermeneutic, biblical periodization, and distinctive eschatological beliefs.

Michael Taylor brought to British Baptists in the 1970s a Christological challenge by refusing to affirm the deity of Jesus Christ. Although he was allowed to retain his college principalship, the controversy served to awaken and strengthen evangelicals among British Baptists.

Open theism introduced at the end of the twentieth century to some segments of Baptist life a new and controversial view as to limitations of God's knowledge of the future, the consequences of which are still being played out.

2003) 9-11, 371-84. See also six articles in *Perspectives in Religious Studies* 34 (Summer 2007) under the issue title "Baptists and Open Theism."

Chapter 12

Missions, Ecumenism, and Globalization

William Carey, a Baptist, was in the vanguard of Protestant missiology, when he issued his *Enquiry* in 1792.[1] The nineteenth century became what the Baptist historian of missions, Kenneth Scott Latourette (1884–1968), called "the great century" in the expansion of Christianity.[2] Baptist missionaries from Europe and North America during the nineteenth century established Baptist congregations in various nations of Asia, Africa, and Latin America. In 1905 worldwide Baptist church membership had not quite reached seven and a half million.[3] Evangelization by existing churches and more extensive missionary labor on all continents during the twentieth century led to a worldwide Baptist membership total in 1998 for conventions and unions affiliated with the Baptist World Alliance of more than 42 million.[4]

Missiology of William Owen Carver (1868–1954)

Missions did not become a theological discipline for study by Baptists until the advent of the twentieth century; the first chair of missions among Baptists was inaugurated at Southern Baptist Theological Seminary in 1900 with William Owen Carver as its occupant.[5] A native of Wilson County,

---

[1]See above, 174-75.

[2]Three of Latourette's seven volumes were devoted to the nineteenth century. *A History of the Expansion of Christianity*, vols. 4, 5, and 6 (New York, London: Harper & Brothers, 1941, 1943, 1944).

[3]*The Baptist World Congress, London, July 11-19, 1905*, 343-44.

[4]*"Jesus Christ Forever. Yes!": Official Report of the Eighteenth Baptist World Congress, Melbourne, Australia, January 5-9, 2000* (Nashville: Fields Publishing, 2000) 233. But *Baptists around the World: A Comprehensive Handbook*, ed. Albert W. Wardin (Nashville: Broadman & Holman, 1995) 473, had reported only 37 million members for all Baptist bodies.

[5]Carver, *The Course of Christian Missions: A History and an Interpretation* (New York: Fleming H. Revell, 1939) 312; Mueller, *A History of Southern Baptist Theological Seminary*, 198; Olav Guttorm Myklebust, *The Study of Missions in Theological Education*, 2 vols., Studies of the Egede Institute 6 (Oslo: Forlaget Land og Kirke, 1955–1957) 1:376-77; Hugo H. Culpepper, "The Scholar and Missiologist," in *God's Glory in Missions: In Appreciation of W. O. Carver*, ed. John N. Jonsson (Louisville: priv. publ., 1985) 1, 11n.1. The first chair of missions in the United States was founded at Cumberland University, Lebanon TN, in 1884 and

Tennessee, and a graduate of Richmond College (later University of Richmond) (B.A.; M.A., 1891) and of Southern Baptist Theological Seminary (Th.M., 1895; Th.D., 1896). Carver began teaching New Testament and homiletics before assuming comparative religion and missions. He helped to found the Woman's Missionary Union Training School (1907), toured mission fields in Europe, South America, and Asia, was managing editor of *Review and Expositor* (1920–1942), led in the formation of the Southern Baptist Historical Society (1938) and of the SBC's Historical Commission (1947), and wrote twenty-one books, nine of which pertain to missions.[6] Carver wrote commentaries on Acts,[7] which he called "the gospel of the Holy Spirit," and on Ephesians, which he reckoned to be "the greatest piece of writing in all history."[8] In later years he taught philosophy of religion as well as comparative religion and missions and retired in 1943.[9]

In his inaugural address, *Missions and the Kingdom of Heaven*, Carver affirmed that "*the aim of missions*" is "*the extension of the kingdom*" and divergences as to premillennialism or postmillennialism should not hinder the missionary task. He interpreted "the end" in Matt. 24:14 as the destruction of Jerusalem in AD 70. If the nineteenth century was a time of evangelization, the twentieth needs to be that of discipleship or Christianization. While affirming that missions is the work of the church, Carver contended, probably against Crawford's Gospel Missionism,[10] that "the individual" is "the unit in missionary extension of the kingdom." The society method

---

was occupied by Claiborne H. Bell, but it was terminated in 1909 when he died (Myklebust, 374-75). Hence the Southern Seminary chair is the oldest in continuous existence in the United States.

[6]George A. Carver and H. Cornell Goerner, "Carver, William Owen," *Encyclopedia of Southern Baptists* 1:236; Culpepper, "The Scholar and Missiologist," 1-13; Mueller, *A History of Southern Baptist Theological Seminary*, 196-203; Robert Vernon Forehand, "A Study of Religion and Culture as Reflected in the Thought and Career of William Owen Carver" (Th.D. diss., Southern Baptist Theological Seminary, 1972) 11-14, 267.

[7]*The Acts of the Apostles* (Nashville: Sunday School Board, SBC, 1916) esp. 3.

[8]*The Glory of God in the Christian Calling: A Study of the Ephesian Epistle* (Nashville: Broadman, 1949) esp. 1.

[9]H. Cornell Goerner, "The Greatest Teacher I Knew," in *God's Glory in Missions*, ed. Jonsson, 20-22; Dale Moody, "Holding Fast That Which Is Good," in ibid., 85, 92-93.

[10]See above, 230-31.

prevailed for the early Carver. Carey was not "the father of modern missions" but rather "the father of organized missions, the father of the missionary society."[11] In 1906 Carver posited that due to world conditions and the religious situation Baptists had their "greatest opportunity in history," especially because of "the Baptist principle of *individualism*," notably *"regenerate individualism under the lordship of Jesus Christ."*[12] In *Missions in the Plan of the Ages* he presented missions as "the extensive realization of God's redemptive purpose in Christ by means of human messengers" and "the proclamation of the Good News of the kingdom where it is *news*." The Bible is the textbook of missions that spells out the meaning of missions to God the Father, to Jesus, to the Christian, to the church, and to the world. The message is salvation/reconciliation, the means include attraction, permeation, and conquest, and the power comes from the Holy Spirit through prayer.[13]

"Carver answered modern objections to missions by pointing to the history of missions and to the nature of Christianity as universal . . . and by acknowledging the shift in missionary motivation from patronizing and iconoclastic rescue to loving and adaptable witness."[14] "The doctrine of election must no longer, as it was for a thousand years, be misused so as to relieve Christians of the imperative of world evangelization, for election 'is a method of God and not an end' and biblically is more related to service than to salvation."[15] "From the patriarchs to Patmos the Bible contains a missionary message."[16] "The mission of Christianity is grounded in the mission of the Son of God, Messiah, and Saviour."[17] In his history of Christian

---

[11]Subtitle: *The Inaugural Address of William Owen Carver . . . in the Southern Baptist Theological Seminary, October 1, 1898* (Louisville KY: John P. Morton, 1898) esp. 5, 7, 8, 14, 15-16, 18.

[12]*Baptist Opportunity* (Philadelphia: American Baptist Publication Society, 1907) 15-45, 11, 19, 22.

[13]Subtitle: *Bible Studies in Missions* (New York: Fleming H. Revell, 1909) 11, 20-26, 27-226.

[14]James Leo Garrett, Jr., "Theologians, Baptist," in *Encyclopedia of Southern Baptists* 3:2023, based on Carver, *Missions and Modern Thought* (New York: Macmillan, 1910).

[15]Ibid., based on Carver, *All the World in All the Word* (Nashville: Sunday School Board, SBC, 1918) 16-18.

[16]Ibid., based on Carver, *The Bible a Missionary Message* (New York: Fleming H. Revell, 1921).

[17]Ibid., based on Carver, *The Self-Interpretation of Jesus* (Nashville: Sunday

missions the Southern Seminary professor declared: "Whenever and in what measure the Church of Christ has been Christian, it has been missionary." Moreover, the "unity of the human race was a central teaching of apostolic Christianity, as it is now coming to be a cardinal doctrine of modern humanitarianism. . . . One God and one human race can mean nothing else than one religion. . . ."[18] In 1935 Carver "indicted the Laymen's Inquiry on Foreign Missions[19] for its misunderstanding of the missionary enterprise"[20] and extolled denominational missions, noting also that *"the Baptist denominations . . . all owe their existence as unitary groups . . . to the missionary enterprise."*[21] According to Carver in 1942, "Christianity as the coming into the world of God's Son is a unique factor in world order and has as its purpose more than the formation of 'Christendom,' however expanded."[22] "Through his Chosen People, despite their failures, and through his servant Son, God is achieving salvation and its product, righteousness."[23]

Concurrently with his unfolding missiology Carver was engaged in theological controversy on three fronts: against Landmarkism, against Dispensationalism, and against Fundamentalism.[24]

Carver has been described as being negative toward confessions of faith, creeds, and theological systems,[25] as embracing panentheism,[26] and as standing between liberalism and orthodoxy.[27] He has been praised for

---

School Board, SBC, 1926).

[18]*The Course of Christian Missions*, 9, 12.

[19]Latourette, *A History of the Expansion of Christianity*, vol. 7 (New York, London: Harper & Brothers, 1945) 51-53.

[20]Garrett, "Theologians, Baptist," 2023, based on Carver, *The Furtherance of the Gospel* (Nashville: Sunday School Board, SBC) 106-14.

[21]*The Furtherance of the Gospel*, 72-74.

[22]Garrett, "Theologians, Baptist," 2023, based on Carver, *Christian Missions in Today's World* (Nashville: Broadman, 1942) 45-54.

[23]Ibid., 2023, based on Carver, *God and Man in Missions* (Nashville: Broadman, 1944).

[24]*Out of His Treasure: Unfinished Memories* (Nashville: Broadman, 1956) 59-87; Moody, "Holding Fast That Which Is Good," 85-90.

[25]William Cheney Smith, Jr., "A Critical Investigation of the Ecclesiological Thought of William Owen Carver" (Th.D. diss., Southern Baptist Theological Seminary, 1962) 61-62.

[26]Forehand, "A Study of Religion and Culture," 77-78, 88.

[27]Ibid., 132, 202.

emphasizing the biblical basis of missions and criticized for a too this worldly view of the kingdom of God and for acknowledging revelation through non-Christian religions that goes beyond general revelation.[28] One passage in Carver has been interpreted to mean that he taught the salvation of the unevangelized while he was noting the shift from the dominance of the avoidance of hell as the motivation for missions.[29] According to Dale Moody, Carver "lived on the frontier of thought,"[30] and according to Ellis, he was "a man ahead of his times,"[31] but, for Smith, Carver was "an anachronism theologically" in that he remained in nineteenth-century evangelicalism" and made only a "negligible" "contribution to theological scholarship."[32]

European Confessions of Faith

Most Baptist unions or conventions in Continental Europe, unlike England and Wales, adopted full-length confessions of faith during the nineteenth or twentieth centuries.[33] The unions of Denmark and Italy and the Örebro Mission in Sweden did not.[34] These confessions were often framed for presentation to civil authorities in nations having established churches so as to foster religious freedom for Baptists.[35] They were understood as confessions of faith, not as creeds to be applied coercively.[36] G. Keith Parker identified three types of European confessions: (1) the "traditional," treating a rather full list of doctrinal topics, as had the Anglo-American confessions; (2) the "comprehensive," which has treated doctrinal topics under a few major divisions in a narrative style" (the 1977 confession of the German-speaking unions); and (3) the brief, focusing usually on the Baptist distinctives (Great

---

[28]Curtis Ray Ellis, "The Missionary Philosophy of William Owen Carver" (Th.D. diss., New Orleans Baptist Theological Seminary, 1968) 18, 126, 127-28.

[29]*Missions and Modern Thought*, 297-303, as interpreted by Smith, "A Critical Investigation," 34-35.

[30]"William Owen Carver: His Remembrance and Relevance," unpublished Founder's Day address, Southern Baptist Theological Seminary, 1968, 3, as quoted by Forehand, "A Study of Religion and Culture," 4.

[31]"The Missionary Philosophy," 125.

[32]"A Critical Investigation," 86, 104.

[33]G. Keith Parker, *Baptists in Europe: History and Confessions of Faith* (Nashville: Broadman, 1982) passim.

[34]Ibid., 94, 117, 104.

[35]Ibid., 19-20, 25-26.

[36]Ibid., 11-12, 20-21.

Britain, Scotland, Norway).[37] The Baptist unions of Spain, Portugal, and Greece and the European Baptist Convention adopted the SBC's Baptist Faith and Message (1963).[38] The great majority of the confessions of the first and second types begin with the doctrine of the Bible.[39] A few begin with the doctrine of God,[40] a few commence with Christology,[41] and one starts with the fall of humanity.[42]

Continental confessions normally have affirmed the divine inspiration of the Scriptures, by the agency of the Holy Spirit,[43] and the Bible's role as "rule," "norm," "guide," "touchstone," "regulator," or "signpost."[44] Only the Irish confession has affirmed "verbal inspiration," and the recent confession of German-speaking unions by its insistence on the "obligation" of "the historical understanding of the Bible" seems to have advocated the historical-critical method.[45] Only the Polish confession named all 39 books of the Bible, the Hungarian confession stated that the Bible had been providentially "saved . . . from all essential errors," and both the Hungarian confession and that of the Evangelical Association of French-Speaking Baptist Churches affirmed the Holy Spirit's guidance of the canonization of the New Testament.[46] Only the Norwegian confession affirmed the "content" of the Apostles' and Nicene creeds.[47]

Most Continental confessions have affirmed that there is one true God who has revealed himself as Father, Son, and Holy Spirit but with little elaboration.[48] The confession of the Baptist Union of Sweden affirmed the equality of the three persons, and the Polish confession denied tritheism.[49] For the Finnish-speaking Baptists in Finland, the work of the Father is

---

[37] Ibid., 23-24.

[38] Ibid., 24, 119, 121, 145, 236.

[39] Ibid., 50, 97, 100-101, 106, 170, 173-74, 188-89, 205, 206-207, 218.

[40] The confessions of the two French bodies of Belgium and of the Evangelical Christians-Baptists in the Soviet Union; ibid., 125, 134, 137, 154.

[41] The confession of German-speaking unions and that of Czechoslovakia; ibid., 57-58, 201.

[42] Netherlands; ibid., 88.

[43] Ibid., 100-101, 106, 137-38, 154, 173-74, 188-89, 206, 218.

[44] Ibid., 97, 100-101, 106, 126, 137-38, 170, 173-74, 188-89, 205, 218.

[45] Ibid., 50, 63-64.

[46] Ibid., 173-74, 188-89, 137-38.

[47] Ibid., 97.

[48] Ibid., 101, 106, 125, 137, 154, 189, 207, 218.

[49] Ibid., 101, 174.

creation, the work of the Son is redemption, and that of the Holy Spirit is consecration or separation, whereas in the Soviet Union the Father is called Creator, the Son Savior, and the Holy Spirit Comforter.[50]

Frequently the confessions have affirmed Christ's complete deity and complete humanity,[51] and sometimes they have delineated the "holy history" of Jesus from virgin birth through temptations and sinlessness to death, resurrection, ascension, heavenly session, intercession, and second coming.[52] A few confessions have declared Jesus' "active" obedience through his perfect fulfillment of the law and his "passive" obedience by his death.[53] His death was called a "perfect sacrifice," an "atoning death," and a "vicarious death," but only the Irish confession referred to his "substitutionary sacrifice."[54]

Only the Yugoslav confession referred to the Holy Spirit as "the third person of the God-head,"[55] whereas the Hungarian confession described him as "the carrier of the personal presence of God in the created World." Moreover, the Spirit strengthened Jesus to become victor, and through him "the redemption of Christ becomes accessible for man."[56] He "initiates in the believer a new life" and becomes advocate and helper.[57]

Repeatedly the Continental confessions have affirmed that human beings were created in the image of God, though usually not defining the image.[58] Only the Hungarian and the Polish confessions declared that the image was lost by the fall of humanity,[59] and only the confession of German-speaking Baptists alluded to creation of all things "out of nothing."[60] The fall was normally said to be that of Adam and Eve, but the lengthy confession of German-speaking Baptists made no reference to an aboriginal or

---

[50] Ibid., 106, 154.

[51] Ibid., 50, 101, 107, 138-39, 175-76, 189, 207-8. The Polish Confession, 175-76, declared that Jesus had a "real human soul and body."

[52] Ibid., 88, 126, 138-39, 175-76, 207-208.

[53] Ibid., 101, 107, 175-76.

[54] Ibid., 176, 101, 107, 58, 50.

[55] Ibid., 208.

[56] Ibid., 189-90.

[57] Ibid., 60.

[58] Ibid., 101, 155, 175, 190, 208, 219. The Hungarian confession, 190, did connect the image with dominion.

[59] Ibid, 175, 190.

[60] Ibid., 61.

historical fall.[61] The fall was declared to be both "voluntary" and "self-willed"[62] and due to Satan's "intervention"/temptation/seduction.[63] It resulted in the loss of the original human state[64] and ultimately eternal death.[65] Meanwhile all human beings as descendants of Adam and Eve have inherited a fallen or sinful nature, or depravity, with the implication that only by actual sinning do they acquire guilt.[66] "Sin is nonconformity to the moral law of God in action, disposition, or attitude."[67] Satan is occasionally said to be personal and to be a rebellious angel expelled from heaven.[68]

Diverse soteriological terms have been employed: salvation,[69] new birth,[70] justification,[71] adoption,[72] forgiveness,[73] and liberation.[74] Characteristic of most of these confessions has been the clear identification of repentance and faith as the two essential conditions of salvation.[75] Little has been said in reference to election or predestination.[76] Sanctification is durative with the goal of Christlikeness or "moral and spiritual perfection."[77] For the Baptist Union of Sweden there is a third use of the law, namely, as "a rule for the walk of believers."[78] The Hungarian and the Polish confessions contain articles on prayer.[79] On the one hand the Hungarian confession affirmed the Spirit's providential preservation of those born anew to final salvation, and on the other hand the Romanian confession declared that the

---

[61] Ibid., 101, 126, 155, 175, 190, 219, 61-62.
[62] Ibid., 101, 126, 138, 209.
[63] Ibid., 138, 155, 175.
[64] Ibid., 126, 138.
[65] Ibid., 101, 125, 138, 155.
[66] Ibid., 50, 88, 101, 126, 138, 155, 175. No clear espousal of a theory of imputation of Adamic guilt to the human race can be detected.
[67] Ibid., 219.
[68] Ibid., 50, 138, 208-209.
[69] Ibid., 88, 176, 190-91, 209, 219-20.
[70] Ibid., 126-27, 139, 155, 176-77, 191, 209-10.
[71] Ibid., 50, 126-27, 139, 176-77, 192, 209-10.
[72] Ibid, 155, 192.
[73] Ibid., 60, 176-77, 209-10.
[74] Ibid., 60.
[75] Ibid., 101, 126-27, 139, 155, 191, 220.
[76] Ibid., 101.
[77] Ibid., 139, 155, 177, 192, 210.
[78] Ibid., 101-102.
[79] Ibid., 196-97, 225-26.

saved are kept in grace only "until the moment of disbelief," that is, when they "freely choose to have this keeping."[80]

As one would expect, European confessions have given major attention to ecclesiology. Confessions derived from the Soviet Union, Poland, Hungary, Yugoslavia, and Romania have specifically affirmed both the universal church and the local churches.[81] The local church ought to be composed solely of converted and baptized ones.[82] Its polity should be "congregational" or "independent" or that of "autonomous democracy,"[83] and it should practice church discipline[84] and pastoral financial support by the congregation.[85] The church's head is Jesus Christ, according to the Polish and the Romanian confessions, and, according to the Romanian, all members of the congregation are "equal" as to "rights and obligations."[86] The Romanian confession and that of German-speaking Baptists have affirmed the priesthood of all believers.[87] Ordinarily two ordained ministries have been identified: that of elder/bishop/pastor/teacher understood as synonymous, and that of deacons.[88] The Hungarian confession has differentiated "pastors" and "elders," that of the Soviet Union declared that all of the offices mentioned in Eph. 4:11 are still given, and the confessions of both French Baptist bodies acknowledged both deacons and deaconesses.[89]

Baptism is defined as immersion in/into the name of the Father, the Son, and the Holy Spirit[90]—indeed singular immersion[91]—of confessed believers, or "those who have professed repentance towards God and faith in our Lord Jesus Christ."[92] It should be preceded by gospel proclamation and should occur at the time of conversion.[93] It is "the first proof of a man's

---

[80]Ibid., 192, 227-28.
[81]Ibid., 155-56, 179-80, 194-95, 211-12, 221-22.
[82]Ibid., 108, 127, 211.
[83]Ibid., 97, 127, 221-22.
[84]Ibid., 68, 195-96, 213, 225.
[85]Ibid., 132, 143.
[86]Ibid., 180, 212, 222.
[87]Ibid., 67, 223. The latter (67, 68) also affirmed spiritual gifts and asserted that pastoral care ought to be "entrusted to the entire congregation."
[88]Ibid., 127-28, 130-31, 142-43, 180, 212, 223.
[89]Ibid., 195, 156, 131, 143.
[90]Ibid., 36, 39, 46, 65-66, 177-78, 193, 210.
[91]Ibid., 177-78, 210.
[92]Ibid., 97, 177-78, 210, 36, 39, 40.
[93]Ibid., 157, 97.

faith in Christ . . . [and] the first step of obedience" and, not reckoning infant baptism, an unrepeatable ordinance.[94] It is a symbol of the baptizand's "burial" or "entombment" and resurrection with Jesus, of "the burial of the old man and the resurrection of the new man," of "the washing away" or "purification" of sins, and of "regeneration."[95] The Lord's Supper is a "memorial" or act of remembrance or "commemoration" or "proclamation" of the death of Christ.[96] It symbolizes his body and blood or can be called a spiritual reception of his body and blood or "spiritual, heavenly food."[97] It is to be preceded by self-examination and to be observed until the second coming of Christ.[98] English Baptists have had from the eighteenth century churches practicing open communion,[99] and the confession of Scottish Baptists enjoined welcoming "believers of all backgrounds" to the Lord's table as a demonstration of Christian unity.[100] But Soviet Union and Romanian Baptists seem to restrict participation to properly baptized believers.[101]

Baptists in Eastern Europe and Scandinavia have included articles on the Lord's Day in their confessions. It is to be observed on the first day of the week, Sunday, because of Jesus' resurrection and the coming of the Holy Spirit at Pentecost.[102] It should be characterized by rest from labor,[103] corporate worship and spiritual meditation,[104] and necessary things and works of mercy.[105] Likewise, the Eastern confessions normally included articles on marriage. Accordingly, marriage has been ordained by God[106] and confirmed by Christ[107] and is to be the union of one man and one

---

[94]Ibid., 178, 179, 224.

[95]Ibid., 128, 140, 157, 224, 140, 157, 193. According to the Scottish confession (40), baptism "is a sacrament of divine grace," is the "seal of the work of the Holy Spirit," and "denotes" incorporation into the church.

[96]Ibid., 194, 157, 210-11, 140.

[97]Ibid., 128, 140-41, 157.

[98]Ibid., 179, 210-11, 179.

[99]See above, 170, 193-94.

[100]Parker, *Baptists in Europe*, 40.

[101]Ibid., 156-57, 224-25.

[102]Ibid., 102, 108-109, 181-82, 197, 213, 225.

[103]Ibid., 197, 213, 225.

[104]Ibid., 102, 108-109, 197, 213, 225.

[105]Ibid., 181-82, 197, 213, 225.

[106]Ibid., 157, 182-83, 197, 213-14, 226.

[107]Ibid., 157.

woman for life.[108] Christians should only marry fellow Christians.[109] Divorce is allowable only for adultery (U.S.S.R., Hungary, Yugoslavia)[110] or only for adultery or "malicious desertion" (Poland, Romania).[111]

The prevailing pattern in European confessions has been for certain eschatological doctrines to be briefly affirmed: the second coming of Christ, the general resurrection, the last judgment, heaven, and hell (or the new heaven and the new earth).[112] The Hungarian and the Romanian confessions affirmed the intermediate state and the Polish confession the rapture.[113] Quite different was the confession from the Soviet Union in that it specified the great tribulation and two distinct resurrections and two distinct judgments separated by Christ's millennial reign.[114]

Baptists and Ecumenism

The Ecumenical Movement was the great new ecclesial fact of the twentieth century. The idea that various churches of different confessions, scattered throughout the known world (*oikoumenē*), could relate to one another in positive ways and strive for greater unity—whether spiritual unity or federal union or organic union—gained momentum. Baptists responded in diverse ways to this movement.

English Baptists individually had had experience in relating to other Evangelical Christians through the Evangelical Alliance and as to other free churches or denominations in free church structures.[115] The Northern Baptist Convention (USA) became a member body of the Federal Council of the Churches of Christ in America when it was organized in 1908, whereas the Southern Baptist Convention never became a member body.[116]

---

[108]Ibid., 157, 182-83, 213-14, 226.
[109]Ibid., 182-83, 227.
[110]Ibid., 157, 197-98, 213-14.
[111]Ibid., 182-83, 226-27.
[112]Ibid., 50, 72-75, 102, 109, 128, 139, 141, 184, 198-99, 214-15, 228-30.
[113]Ibid., 198-99, 228-29, 184.
[114]Ibid., 158.
[115]See above, 532-33; also Randall, *The English Baptists of the Twentieth Century*, 6, 46-49.
[116]Torbet, *A History of the Baptists*, 460; Baker, *The Southern Baptist Convention*, 305; McBeth, *The Baptist Heritage*, 563, 585, 601; Leonard, *Baptist Ways*, 407.

During World War I John Howard Shakespeare[117] in *The Churches at the Cross-Roads*,[118] after identifying the gains and losses of denominationalism, argued that a federation of the Free Churches or even of the Free Churches and the Church of England would not be adequate and that organic union, not merely Christian or spiritual unity, should be the goal. But English Baptists did not accept their leader's proposal, following rather the antiorganic union stance of Terrot Reaveley Glover (1869–1943), a Baptist classical scholar.[119] Discussion of church union continued during the early 1920s, especially in response to the Anglican Lambeth Conference's *Appeal to All Christian People* (1920).[120] But Anglican insistence that Free Church ministers receive Episcopal ordination met Baptist resistance,[121] and in 1927 two English Baptists attended the World Conference on Faith and Order in Lausanne, Switzerland, but not as "official delegates" of the Baptist Union of Great Britain and Ireland.[122] Baptist distinctives were again emphasized after the world congress of the Baptist World Alliance in Stockholm, Sweden (1923), and the election of Melbourn Evans Aubrey (1885–1957) as general secretary of the Baptist Union (1925).[123]

W. O. Carver in his later years explicated the doctrine of the church vis-à-vis the developing ecumenism. From its inception in 1939 "he was a member of the American Theological Committee, a subsidiary of the World Conference on Faith and Order."[124] Carver employed "church" in three senses: (1) the whole number of spiritual, regenerate believers," constituting "the Body of Christ" and incapable of being "ecclesiastically organized"; (2) "the organized church" or "the functioning body of Christian believers," which is "limited to a community in which convenient assembling and

---

[117]See above, 277.

[118](London: Williams and Norgate, 1918). On Shakespeare's previous advocacy of federation, see Randall, *The English Baptists of the Twentieth Century*, 94-98.

[119]Randall, *The English Baptists of the Twentieth Century*, 98-99, 113.

[120]Ibid., 114-19.

[121]T. R. Glover, *The Free Churches and Reunion* (Cambridge: W. Heffer and Sons, 1921) esp. 34-56.

[122]Randall, *The English Baptists of the Twentieth Century*, 119.

[123]Ibid., 126-30; Robinson, *Baptist Principles*; James Henry Rushbrooke et al., *The Faith of the Baptists* (London: Kingsgate, 1926); Robinson, *The Life and Faith of the Baptists* (London: Kingsgate, 1927).

[124]Carver and Goerner, "Carver, William Owen," 236.

functioning are possible"; and (3) the church in the "abstract" or "generic sense." In connection with the first of these usages Carver affirmed that the Church is the "continuation of the Incarnation," while acknowledging that this was not commonly held by Baptists. The organized or local church ought, according to Baptists, to receive as members "those, only, who have made a credible profession of faith in Jesus Christ as Lord and Saviour." Carver held to believer's baptism and favored close communion. Although three types of church polity may claim some rootage in the New Testament, the congregational seems to embody best "the central and essential concepts of the Christian faith."[125] But Carver quite clearly opposed the efforts to achieve organic church union, especially by the Faith and Order leadership, for church history demonstrates how the "Institutional Church [has] displaced the Church of the Spirit."[126]

In succession to Dagg and Dargan as Southern Baptist ecclesiologists, Harvey Eugene Dana (1888–1945), professor of New Testament in Southwestern Baptist Theological Seminary (1919–1938) and president of Central Baptist Theological Seminary (1938–1945), wrote on ecclesiology during the time when Southern Baptists were deciding not to join the WCC. Dana asserted that Paul in Ephesians and Colossians viewed the *ekklēsia* "in its spiritual relation to the person of Christ" as "spiritual Israel"—not as "an ecclesiastical organization" but as "an ideal, spiritual body in sacred and vital connection with Christ . . . as its head." He criticized the Ecumenical Movement as being based on "the unscriptural theory of an organized Universal Church."[127]

---

[125]Carver, "Baptist Churches," in *The Nature of the Church: Papers Presented to the Theological Commission Appointed by the Continuation Committee of the World Conferences on Faith and Order*, ed. R. Newton Flew (London: SCM Press, 1952) 289, 293, 292, 296-97, 291; idem, *The Glory of God in the Christian Calling*, 43-61.

[126]*The Glory of God in the Christian Calling*, 61-79, esp. 63, 74.

[127]With L. M. Sipes, *A Manual of Ecclesiology*, 2nd ed. (Kansas City KS: Central Seminary Press, 1944; orig., 1941) 53, 56, 168-91 (esp. 190). Ecclesiology had been a lifelong interest of Dana; see his "Ecclesia in the New Testament and Early Christian Literature" (Th.D. diss., Southwestern Baptist Theological Seminary, 1920) and *Christ's Ecclesia* (Nashville: Sunday School Board of the SBC, 1926). Concerning Dana's many writings on the New Testament, see Mark E. Taylor, "Harvey Eugene Dana," in *The Legacy of Southwestern*, ed. Garrett et al., 79-81; and Ray Earl Bennett, "The Contribution of H. E. Dana to the Southern Baptist Understanding of the Historical-Critical Method of New Testament

In 1942 the British Council of Churches was formed in a meeting held in the Baptist Church House in London, and the Baptist Union of Great Britain and Ireland continued to participate in this "central British ecumenical body." M. E. Aubrey chaired a Faith and Order group that "recommended the formation of the World Council of Churches," Union delegates participated in the constituting assembly of the World Council of Churches in Amsterdam in 1948, and Ernest Alexander Payne (1902–1980) was a member of its Central Committee, serving as vice chairman from 1954 to 1968, and was elected one of its six presidents in 1968. Two English Baptists, Glenn Garfield Williams and Keith W. Clements, have served as general secretary of the Conference of European Churches.[128]

The American Baptist Churches, USA (formerly the Northern Baptist Convention and the American Baptist Convention) has had an extended record of interdenominational activity and ecumenical relationships.

> American Baptists helped to form the American Bible Society (1816), the Sunday and Adult School Union (1817), the International Council of Religious Education (1922, dating back through the International Sunday School Association to the National Sunday School Convention of 1832), the Foreign Missions Conference of North America (1893), the Missionary Education Movement (1902), the Federal Council of Churches (1908), the Home Missions Council of North America (1908), the National Protestant Council on Higher Education (1911), the United Stewardship Council (1920), and the United Council of Church Women (1940), most of which . . . are now in the National Council of the Churches of Christ in the U.S.A.[129]

The Northern Baptist Convention had been a charter member of the World Council of Churches.[130] There was also recurring criticism of these conciliar affiliations.[131]

Interpretation" (Ph.D. diss., Baylor University, 1974) 209-13.

[128]Randall, *The English Baptists of the Twentieth Century*, 252, 205, 254, 286, 340-41; as to criticism of membership in the WCC, see ibid., 337-45; Payne, *The World Council of Churches, 1948–1969* (London: Baptist Union of Great Britain and Ireland, 1970) 2.

[129]W. Hubert Porter, "Ecumenical Concerns among American Baptists," in *Baptists and Ecumenism*, ed. William Jerry Boney and Glenn A. Igleheart (Valley Forge PA: Judson, 1980) 21.

[130]Ibid., 28; Torbet, *A History of the Baptists*, 461.

[131]William R. Estep, Jr., *Baptists and Christian Unity* (Nashville: Broadman, 1966) 137-41.

Three Afro-American Baptist conventions, the National Baptist Convention, Inc., the National Baptist Convention of America, and the Progressive National Baptist Convention, have been member bodies in the World Council of Churches (WCC) and the National Council of the Churches of Christ in the U.S.A.[132] The same was true for a time of the Seventh-Day Baptist General Conference.[133]

Baptist unions or conventions outside the United States and Great Britain[134] that have held membership in the WCC are:

Africa
- Baptist Union of Western Congo [Democratic Republic of Congo]
- Episcopal Baptist Community [Democratic Republic of Congo]
- Native Baptist Church of Cameroon
- Union of Baptist Churches of Cameroon
- Nigerian Baptist Convention

Asia
- Bangladesh Baptist Sangha
- Baptist Union of New Zealand
- China Baptist Council
- Myanmar Baptist Convention
- Samavesam of Telugu Baptist Churches [India]

Caribbean
- Jamaica Baptist Union

Europe
- Baptist Union of Denmark
- Baptist Union of Hungary
- Evangelical Christian-Baptist Union of the U.S.S.R.
- Union of Baptist Congregations in the Netherlands

Latin America
- Baptist Convention of Nicaragua.

The associate member bodies have included:
- Baptist Association of El Salvador

---

[132]J. Deotis Roberts, "Ecumenical Concerns among National Baptists," in *Baptists and Ecumenism*, ed. Boney and Igleheart, 48.

[133]Estep, *Baptists and Christian Unity*, 141.

[134]The Baptist Union of Wales and Monmouthshire and the Baptist Union of Scotland became member bodies in 1948 but soon thereafter withdrew. Estep, *Baptists and Christian Unity*, 133.

Bengal-Orissa-Bihar Baptist Convention [India]
Evangelical Baptist Union of Italy.[135]

Following the suggestion of Thomas Treadwell Eaton, editor of the *Western Recorder*, the Southern Baptist Convention (SBC) in 1890 proposed a gathering of scholars from the various American Protestant denominations to study afresh the Bible with reference to their differing beliefs, but only the Disciples of Christ responded, and communications about such a conference played out after five years.[136] From 1911 to 1918 the SBC was open to discussion in response to overtures from the Faith and Order movement, and the SBC Foreign Mission Board participated in the Foreign Missions Conference of North America from 1893 to 1919 and from 1938 to 1950.[137] But beginning in 1919 under the presidency of James Bruton Gambrell and following the wartime ministry to Protestant soldiers and the ill-fated Interchurch World Movement, it turned toward strict denominationalism and away from interdenominational relationships. The SBC president, John Richard Sampey (1863–1946), and three others did represent the convention at the Faith and Order and Life and Work conferences in 1937.[138] In 1939 and 1940 the SBC declined membership in the about-to-be-formed World Council of Church, citing "the lack of ecclesial authority," "the danger of centralization of power in religion," and the desirability of "spiritual fellowship." Nineteen messengers presented a minority report favorable to WCC membership. In 1948 the SBC declined to send an official observer to the first WCC assembly. "During 1950–1953 the convention took no action favorable to its membership in the newly formed National Council of the Churches of Christ in the U.S.A. but continued to receive reports strongly opposed to such." The SBC never considered

---

[135]These lists are based on the lists of "member churches" and "associate member churches" that appear in the report volumes for the assemblies of the WCC from Amsterdam (1948) through Harare (1998).

[136]Raymond O. Ryland, "Southern Baptist Convention (U.S.A.)," in *Baptist Relations with Other Christians*, ed. James Leo Garrett, Jr. (Valley Forge PA: Judson, 1974) 67-70; SBC, *Annual*, 1890, 22.

[137]Ibid., 70-75; James Leo Garrett, Jr., "Are Southern Baptists 'Evangelicals'?," in *Are Southern Baptists "Evangelicals"?* by Garrett, Hinson, and Tull, 106; Ernest A. Payne, *Free Churchmen, Unrepentant and Repentant and Other Papers* (London: Carey Kingsgate, 1965) 125.

[138]Ryland, "Southern Baptist Convention (U.S.A.)," 75-78; Garrett, "Are Southern Baptists 'Evangelicals'?," 107-108.

membership in the National Association of Evangelicals, although a few individual Southern Baptists participated initially.[139]

The most articulate and visible spokesperson of English Baptists in behalf of conciliar ecumenism has been Payne. A native of London and a graduate in philosophy from King's College, London, who trained for overseas missions at Regent's Park College, and received the B.Lit. degree from Oxford, he was pastor in Northamptonshire and young people's secretary and editorial secretary for the Baptist Missionary Society before becoming a tutor at Regent's Park College in 1940. From 1950 to 1967 he served as general secretary of the Baptist Union.[140] Payne wrote extensively on the modern Protestant, especially Baptist, missionary movement[141] and on the English Free Church tradition.[142]

In 1951, Payne alerted world Baptists to the criticisms of infant baptism made by Karl Barth and Emil Brunner but insisted that the need for the Baptist denomination continues, for "Brunner and Barth have not yet become Baptists."[143] He explained and advocated the integration of the WCC

---

[139]Garrett, "Are Southern Baptists 'Evangelicals'?," 108, 51; Ryland, "Southern Baptist Convention (U.S.A.)," 78-79; SBC, *Annual*, 1939, 99; 1940, 99-100; 1948, 58; 1950, 37; 1951, 36; 1953, 51.

[140]Randall, *The English Baptists of the Twentieth Century*, 261, 260; R. L. Child, "Ernest Alexander Payne," in *Outlook for Christianity: Essays Presented to Dr. Ernest A. Payne on the Occasion of His Retirement from the Office of General Secretary of the Baptist Union of Great Britain and Ireland*, ed. L. G. Champion (London: Lutterworth, 1967) 1-8.

[141]*The First Generation: Early Leaders of the Baptist Missionary Society in England and India* (London: Carey, 1936?); *The Great Succession: Leaders of the Baptist Missionary Society during the Nineteenth Century* (London: Carey, 1938); *The Church Awakes: The Story of the Modern Missionary Movement* (London: Edinburgh House Press, 1942); *The Growth of the World Church: The Story of the Modern Missionary Movement* (London: Edinburgh House Press and Macmillan and Co., 1955); *The Baptists of the World and Their Overseas Missions* (London: Carey Kingsgate, 1955).

[142]*The Fellowship of Believers: Baptist Thought and Practice Yesterday and Today* (London: Carey Kingsgate, 1944; enl. ed., 1952); *The Free Church Tradition in the Life of England* (London: SCM Press, 1944); *Free Churchmen, Unrepentant and Repentant and Other Papers*.

[143]"Baptism in Present-day Theology," in *The Doctrine of Baptism* (Washington DC: Baptist World Alliance) 5-7.

and the International Missionary Council.[144] He continued to support the WCC and Baptist participation therein.[145] When the Executive Committee of the BWA was faced with the decision in 1962 as to whether to entertain favorably an invitation to send an official observer to Vatican Council II, Payne strongly advocated such an observer, but in view of strong opposition from the SBC and Latin American conventions he agreed in the interest of Baptist unity to the declination of the invitation.[146]

Even more emphatic in appealing for Baptist participation in the WCC than Payne's writings was a monograph[147] by Edward Roberts-Thomson (1908–1987), principal of the Baptist Theological College of New South Wales (1961–1964) and formerly principal of the Baptist Theological College of New Zealand (1953–1960).[148] Recalling William Carey's 1806 proposal for an international and interconfessional conference on world missions, he acknowledged that Baptist reluctance toward the WCC stemmed from the fact that the major participants were the state churches of European Protestantism. The Australian principal clearly identified as a crucial issue the question of unity or union and the significance of John 17 and concluded that Baptists have "a doctrine of the churches" but not "a satisfying doctrine of the Church."[149] The latter conclusion did not consider

---

[144]Payne and David G. Moss, *Why Integration? An Explanation of the Proposal before the World Council of Churches and the International Missionary Council* (London: Edinburgh House, 1957).

[145]"Baptists and the Ecumenical Movement," *Baptist Quarterly* 18 (April 1960): 258-67; republished in *Free Churchmen, Unrepentant and Repentant and Other Papers*, 120-29; *The World Council of Churches, 1948–1969*; "Great Britain," in *Baptist Relations with Other Christians*, ed. Garrett, 13-19.

[146]James Leo Garrett, Jr., *Baptists and Roman Catholicism* (Nashville: Broadman, 1965) 7; idem, "The Internationalization of the Alliance," 137-38; William R. Estep, Jr., *Baptists and Christian Unity*, 65-66.

[147]*With Hands Outstretched: Baptists and the Ecumenical Movement* (London: Marshall, Morgan and Scott, 1962).

[148]Born in England and reared in Tasmania, Roberts-Thomson trained at the Baptist College of Victoria, Bristol College (M.A.), and the Melbourne College of Divinity (D.D.) and served churches in Tasmania and Victoria. Rod Benson, "Dawn of a New Era or Recipe for Disaster? The Rise of and Demise of Edward Roberts-Thomson as Principal of the Baptist Theological College of New South Wales," *Baptist Recorder* 87 (2004): 5-21. Ken R. Manley to James Leo Garrett, Jr., 30 July 2006.

[149]*With Hands Outstretched*, 21, 18, 38-43, 57, 61.

that the Baptist doctrine of the universal Church had never been conceived as capable of organization and hence was not synonymous with widespread visible church union. Roberts-Thomson saw world confessional families as "dangerous" if they eclipse ecumenical bodies but on the other hand reckoned that the BWA had aided "the growing ecumenical influence which is penetrating Baptist thinking." He sought to correct the statement by George Washington Truett (1867–1944) and James Henry Rushbrooke (1870–1947) of three great Baptist ideas, "Truth, Freedom, Unity," by adding "Love." He was aware of the rise of English Baptist baptismal sacramentalism, of the recovery of a Calvinistic view of the Lord's Supper, and of the role of Baptists in forming the Church of North India.[150] He urged Australian Baptists and chided Southern Baptists (U.S.A.) toward membership in the WCC.[151]

William Roscoe Estep, Jr. (1920–2000), presented the classic statement[152] in behalf of Baptist nonmembership in the WCC. A native of Kentucky, he was a graduate of Berea College (B.A., 1942), Southern Baptist Theological Seminary (Th.M., 1945), and Southwestern Baptist Theological Seminary (Th.D., 1951) and taught church history at Southwestern from 1954 to 1990.[153] A specialist in Anabaptist and Reformation studies,[154] he also wrote on the religion clauses of the First Amendment to the United States Constitution[155] and the history of the SBC's Foreign Mission Board.[156] Estep stated that his purpose was not to write "*for* or *against* the

---

[150]Ibid., 26, 58, 37, 48, 72-88, 99-109.

[151]Ibid., 30, 120-21, 32, 56, 90-91, 93, 94, 97-98, 116, 118, 122-24. Subsequently Roberts-Thomson's principalship was terminated, and he became a Presbyterian minister. Estep, *Baptists and Christian Unity*, 142.

[152]*Baptists and Christian Unity*.

[153]Paul L. Gritz, "William Roscoe Estep, Jr.," in *The Legacy of Southwestern*, ed. Garrett et al., 221.

[154]*The Anabaptist Story* (Nashville: Broadman, 1963); 2nd ed. (Grand Rapids MI: Eerdmans, 1975); 3rd ed. with subtitle: *An Introduction to Sixteenth-Century Anabaptism* (Grand Rapids MI: Eerdmans, 1996); (editor) *Anabaptist Beginnings (1523–1533): A Source Book* (Nieuwkoop, Netherlands: B. de Graaf, 1976); (ed.) *The Reformation: Luther, the Anabaptists*, Christian Classics (Nashville: Broadman, 1979); *Renaissance and Reformation* (Grand Rapids MI: Eerdmans, 1986).

[155]*Revolution within the Revolution: The First Amendment in Historical Context, 1612–1789* (Grand Rapids MI: Eerdmans, 1990).

[156]*Whole Gospel—Whole World: The Foreign Mission Board of the Southern Baptist Convention, 1845–1995*.

ecumenical movement or any of its structures" or to "tell any Baptist body what its relationship to the various councils ought to be," but "to describe, inform, and explain the ecumenical movement for a Baptist audience." Three chapters were devoted to the centuries-long tensions between unity and schism and to the rise of the Ecumenical Movement and to the formation and work of the WCC. Roman Catholic ecumenism up to Vatican Council II was examined, and the National Association of Evangelicals (U.S.A.) and Carl McIntire's International Council of Christian Churches were described.[157] Baptist bodies that were in 1966 members of the WCC and most of those that were not were identified.[158] Finally, Estep identified four "issues" that were problematic for Baptist involvement "with contemporary ecumenical structures." First, the "theological issue" meant that Baptists insist on maintaining the lordship of Christ, the priesthood of all believers, the supreme authority of the Scriptures, regenerate membership and congregational polity, and believer's baptism by immersion and its relationship to the Lord's Supper. Second, the "ecclesiological" issue meant that many Baptists have been reluctant to attribute to associations, societies, conventions or unions, any ecclesial nature, rather restricting the term "church" to local congregations and to the nonorganizable universal church, or to reckon "denominational divisions" as "sinful per se." Third, the "methodological" issue meant that for Baptists world evangelization is a high priority, whereas conciliar ecumenism has emphasized comity agreements and sanctioned state-established churches. Fourth, the "teleological" issue meant that many Baptists were apprehensive that the goal of the WCC, despite specific denials, is the "organic union of Christendom.'"[159]

The BWA, especially during the last decades of the twentieth century, participated in various bilateral dialogues or conversations with other Christian world confessional bodies through selected teams from each body.[160] From 1974 to 1976 conversations were held with World Alliance of Reformed Churches with all European participants and all meetings in

---

[157]*Baptists and Christian Unity*, 2, 6-64, 65-126. The American Baptist Association, the General Association of Regular Baptist Churches, and the World Baptist Fellowship belonged to the ICCC (ibid., 103).

[158]Ibid., 127-67.

[159]Ibid., 168-88.

[160]For a summary interpretation of these, see Ken R. Manley, *The Baptist World Alliance and Inter-Church Relationships*, Baptist Heritage and Identity Booklet 1 (Falls Church VA: Baptist World Alliance, 2003) 13-24.

Switzerland. Here baptism surfaced as a major subject with attention also being given to the church and its mission.[161] From 1984 to 1988 conversations were conducted with the Vatican's Secretariat for Promoting Christian Unity, three meetings being in the United States and one in West Berlin. Much attention was given to commonalities—biblical revelation, Christology, conversion, *koinōnia* of the Spirit, and evangelization—with little attention to Marian dogmas and devotion and almost none to the papal office.[162] From 1986 to 1989 there were conversations with the Lutheran World Federation with meetings in West Germany, East Germany, and Denmark. These focused on the authority of the Scriptures and the role of creeds and confessions of faith, faith-baptism-discipleship, the nature and mission of the church, and the sixteenth-century Lutheran condemnation of the Anabaptists.[163] From 1989 to 1992 the BWA conducted conversations with the Mennonite World Conference, with meetings in the United States, Canada, and the Netherlands. Attention was given to historical origins and developments, religious authority, the church and its mission, and peace concerns.[164] From 1994 to 1997 preconversations were held with the Ecumenical Patriarchate in Istanbul and Oxford, but these did not eventuate in conversations with all the autocephalic Eastern Orthodox churches. Baptists were able to present their various beliefs, especially concerning the Bible and evangelism.[165] Conversations (2000–2005) were held with the Anglican Communion in six regional sessions with different regional participants (England, Myanmar, Kenya, Chile, Bahamas, Canada). Focus was upon continuity in church history, creeds and confessions of faith, mission, baptism, open membership among Baptists, the Lord's Supper, and

---

[161]*Reports of Conversations between the Baptist World Alliance and the Following: World Alliance of Reformed Churches . . . , Lutheran World Federation . . . , Vatican Secretariat for Promoting Christian Unity . . . , Mennonite World Conference* (McLean VA: Baptist World Alliance Division of Study and Research, n.d.) part one, 1-18.

[162]Ibid., part three, 1-15.

[163]Ibid., part two, 1-26.

[164]Ibid., part four, 1-26.

[165]*Papers Presented by Representatives of the Baptist World Alliance at Pre-Conversation Meetings in Istanbul, Turkey, May 10-13, 1996* (McLean VA: Baptist World Alliance, n.d.); "West Meets East," *Baptist World*, January-March 1995, 4-5; "Baptists and Orthodox Meet in Istanbul," *Baptist World*, July-September 1996, 19; "Orthodox Talks Proposed," *Baptist World*, July-September 1997, 17.

episcopacy.[166] Further, BWA conversations with the Vatican Secretariat for Promoting Christian Unity have been held during 2000–2004. *Dominus Iesus*, a recently issued Roman Catholic declaration, the nature of *koinōnia*, the role of the Virgin Mary, and baptism received attention.[167]

The SBC Home Mission Board's Interfaith Witness Department and the Bishops' Committee for Ecumenism and Interreligious Affairs of the National Conference of Catholic Bishops engaged in three rounds of dialogue, all papers from which were published in Southern Baptist journals.[168]

In Germany Erich Geldbach (1939–), a Baptist scholar, produced a body of writings on ecumenism[169] and occupied a chair of ecumenics and confessional studies in the (state) University of Bochum (1997–2004), but only after the Evangelical (Lutheran) Church of Westphalia had sought to prevent his installation because of his Baptist beliefs regarding baptism and because Baptist churches did not have "pulpit and table fellowship" with the Evangelical Church of Westphalia.[170]

The Evangelistic Theology of William Franklin (Billy) Graham, Jr. (1918–)

For most of the nineteenth and twentieth centuries Baptists understood missions as the sending of and the support and prayerful intercession for career missionaries who, crossing cultural, linguistic, and/or geographical boundaries, were seeking to make believing disciples of Jesus Christ and to constitute congregations of such. In parallel fashion, especially during the twentieth century, Baptists regarded evangelism as the deliberate efforts by

---

[166]*Conversations Around the World, 2000–2005: The Report of the International Conversations between the Anglican Communion and the Baptist World Alliance* (London: Anglican Communion Office, 2005).

[167]"BWA/Vatican Meeting," *Baptist World*, January-March 2001, 27; "Historic Meeting of Baptist and Catholic Leaders," *Baptist World*, January-March 2002, 24; "Baptist World/Catholic Consultation," *Baptist World*, April-June 2005, 19.

[168]*Review and Expositor* 79 (Spring 1982); *Southwestern Journal of Theology* 28 (Spring 1986); *The Theological Educator* no. 39 (Spring 1989).

[169]For his bibliography, see *Gemeinschaft der Kirchen und gesellschaftliche Verantwortung: Die Würde des Anderen und das Recht anders zu denken: Festschrift für Professor Dr. Erich Geldbach*, ed. Lena Lybaek, Konrad Reiser, and Stefanie Schardien, Ökumenische Studien 30 (Münster: Lit Verlag, 2004) 549-60.

[170]Charles McDaniel and Richard V. Pierard, "The Politics of Appointments to Protestant Theological Faculties in Germany: The Case of Professor Erich Geldbach," *Journal of Church and State* 46 (Winter 2004): 55-82.

Missions, Ecumenism, and Globalization 603

Christians and by churches, as led by the Holy Spirit, to present the gospel of Christ to persons chiefly within their spheres of influence.

Evangelism became a discipline within Baptist theological education when Benajah Harvey Carroll in 1908 in the founding of Southwestern Baptist Theological Seminary created a chair of evangelism,[171] to be occupied for a third of a century by Lee Rutland Scarborough,[172] who developed a literature on the practice of evangelism.[173] Michael Mark Hawley commended Scarborough for emphasizing evangelism "as both a divine work and a human discipline,"[174] whereas Thomas J. Nettles charged that Scarborough about 1924 shifted in his evangelistic method from "Calvinism to semi-Arminianism" by deemphasizing divine sovereignty, emphasizing human free will, and teaching "decisional regeneration."[175]

The best-known and most widely traveled Christian evangelist during the twentieth century was a Baptist, Billy Graham, who did not write as a doctrinal or systematic theologian but as an evangelist wrote on theological topics. Born on a dairy farm near Charlotte, North Carolina, to a family that

---

[171]Baker, *Tell the Generations Following*, 125-26, 139-41; Michael Mark Hawley, "A Critical Examination of Lee Rutland Scarborough's Concept of Evangelism" (Th.D. diss., New Orleans Baptist Theological Seminary, 1992; Ann Arbor MI: University Microfilm International, 1993) 5, 181; Roy J. Fish, "Lee Rutland Scarborough," in *The Legacy of Southwestern*, ed. Garrett et al., 20.

[172]Harvey Eugene Dana, *Lee Rutland Scarborough: A Life of Service* (Nashville: Broadman, 1942); Franklin M. Segler, "Scarborough, Lee Rutland," *Encyclopedia of Southern Baptists* 2:1186-87; Glenn Thomas Carson, *Calling Out the Called: The Life and Work of Lee Rutland Scarborough* (Austin TX: Eakin Press, 1996). A native of Louisiana, Scarborough was a graduate of Baylor University (B.A.) and Yale University (B.A.) and was pastor of First Church, Cameron TX, and First Church, Abilene TX. He served as president of Southwestern Seminary from 1915 to 1942.

[173]*With Christ after the Lost* (Nashville: Sunday School Board of the SBC, 1919); "The Doctrine of Evangelism," *Southwestern Journal of Theology* o.s. 4 (October 1920): 5-8; *Endued to Win* (Nashville: Sunday School Board of the SBC, 1922); *Christ's Militant Kingdom: A Study in the Trail Triumphant* (Nashville: Sunday School Board of the SBC, 1924); *A Search for Souls: A Study in the Finest of Fine Arts—Winning the Lost to Christ* (Nashville: Sunday School Board of the SBC, 1925); *How Jesus Won Men* (Nashville: Sunday School Board of the SBC, 1926; repr.: Grand Rapids MI: Baker, 1972).

[174]"A Critical Examination," 181.

[175]*By His Grace and for His Glory*, 246, 257-64. See below, 667-68.

regularly attended an Associate Reformed Presbyterian church, Graham was converted at sixteen during revival services conducted by Evangelist Mordecai Ham. After attending Bob Jones College, Cleveland, Tennessee, for one semester, he spent three and one-half years at the unaccredited Florida Bible Institute, near Tampa, Florida, where he surrendered to preach the gospel at nineteen, began youth work and preaching in area churches, and was immersed and ordained as a Southern Baptist in Palatka, Florida, at twenty. Following graduation in 1940, Graham entered Wheaton College, Wheaton, Illinois, as a sophomore and graduated with a major in anthropology in 1943, serving also as pastor of Wheaton's United Gospel Tabernacle.[176] A brief pastorate of a Baptist church in Western Springs, Illinois, was followed in 1945 by a staff position with the newly formed Youth for Christ, which involved preaching in various American and European cities. W. B. Riley persuaded Graham to become his successor, following his death, as president of the Northwestern Schools (1947–1952). Graham conducted several evangelistic campaigns in U.S. cities, but it was the fall 1949 Los Angeles crusade that brought Graham to national prominence. In 1950 he formed the Billy Graham Evangelistic Association and in 1953 in Chattanooga began racially nonsegregated seating for his meetings.[177] Graham's ministry extended rapidly and widely through all the continents and to nearly two hundred nations. His 1973 crusade in Seoul, Korea, was attended by one million people, at that time "the largest recorded religious gathering in history."[178] He "has probably preached, face to face, to more people than any spokesman for the faith in all Christian history."[179]

Graham did not delineate in detail his doctrine of revelation and the Bible. On the eve of his Los Angeles crusade he had made at Forest Home,

---

[176]Graham, *Just As I Am: The Autobiography of Billy Graham* (San Francisco: Harper, 1997) 3-68. John Pollock, *Billy Graham: The Authorized Biography* (New York: McGraw-Hill, 1966) 12-28; William G. McLoughlin, Jr., *Billy Graham: Revivalist in a Secular Age* (New York: Ronald Press, 1960) 25-34; William Martin, *A Prophet with Honor: The Billy Graham Story* (New York: William Morrow, 1991) 55-84.

[177]Pollock, *Billy Graham*, 28-66; McLoughlin, *Billy Graham*, 34-68; Martin, *A Prophet with Honor*, 84-141; Graham, *Just As I Am*, 69-187; Roger Bruns, *Billy Graham: A Biography* (Westport CT: Greenwood Press, 2004) 85-97.

[178]Bruns, *Billy Graham*, ix.

[179]Stanley High, *Billy Graham: The Personal Story of the Man, His Message, and His Mission* (New York: McGraw-Hill, 1956) 2.

in contrast to the view of his friend Charles Templeton, a life-determining commitment to accept by faith the Bible as the Word of God.[180] Repeatedly in his sermons he has declared, "The Bible says" or "The Word of the Lord says." According to James A. Auchmuty, Jr., the Bible is "the center and circumference" of Graham's preaching, indeed "a Book of power" and "of revealed truth." Graham seemed to allow for but never spelled out revelation through nature.[181] Larry Joe Davis has concluded that Graham's "dominant" method of interpreting the Bible has been the literal but on occasion he has employed allegorical, traditional, typological, pietistic, symbolic, and other methods.[182] Graham affirmed but not explicate the verbal inspiration of the Bible.[183]

Does the theology that undergirds the preaching of Graham have a central theme? Some would name his faith-understanding of the Bible.[184] Others have identified the cross of Christ[185] and "decision for Christ."[186] In Graham's proclamation of the good news the new birth is the most used soteriological concept.[187]

Despite his Presbyterian upbringing Graham never defended the five tenets of Dortian Calvinism,[188] and his emphasis on free will caused

---

[180]Pollock, *Billy Graham*, 52-53; Martin, *A Prophet with Honor*, 109-12; Howell Walker Burkhead, "The Development of the Concept of Sin in the Preaching of Billy Graham" (Ph.D. diss., Southwestern Baptist Theological Seminary, 1998) 88-98.

[181]"The Concept of Revelation in the Thought of Five Contemporary Southern Baptists: Billy Graham, Roland Q. Leavell, R. G. Lee, Carlyle Marney, and Eric C. Rust" (Th.M. thesis, Southeastern Baptist Theological Seminary, 1961) 4-11.

[182]"Interpretation of Scripture in the Evangelistic Preaching of William Franklin 'Billy' Graham" (Ph.D. diss., Southern Baptist Theological Seminary, 1986; Ann Arbor MI: University Microfilms International, 1987) 142-293, esp. 223, 270-76.

[183]Ibid., 247.

[184]Martin, *A Prophet with Honor*, 156.

[185]Charles T. Cook, *The Billy Graham Story: "One Thing I Do"* (London: Marshall, Morgan and Scott, 1954) 85.

[186]Charles W. Dullea, S.J., *A Catholic Looks at Billy Graham* (New York: Paulist, 1973) 32.

[187]*Peace with God* (Garden City NY: Doubleday, 1953) 133-41; *World Aflame* (New York: Doubleday, 1965) 140-42; *How to Be Born Again* (Waco TX: Word, 1977) 143-69.

[188]Dullea, *A Catholic Looks at Billy Graham*, 80, 99-100.

William G. McLoughlin, Jr., to conclude that Graham had appropriated the Arminianized Calvinism of the Second Great Awakening.[189]

But sin had a major place in Graham's theology. He explicated the seven deadly sins[190] and gave attention to the origin, the nature, and the consequences of sin.[191] Interpreting Isa. 14:12-15 and Ezek. 28:14-15 as referring to Satan/Lucifer, he identified the origin of sin in the prideful rebellion of Lucifer and other angels.[192] In the seduction of the serpent, the disobedience of Eve, and the concurrence of Adam, Graham found the origin of sin in the human race, although with no suggestion that God foreordained human sin.[193] In man's actually sinning by choice Graham found the origin of sin in individual human beings, for there was an inherited tendency to sin but no guilt for the sin of Eve and Adam.[194] According to Howell Walker Burkhead, there was development in Graham's concept of sin "within the framework of basic stability." The early Graham "emphasized the personal dimension of the nature of sin almost exclusively," whereas the later Graham made a place for "the social ramifications of sin."[195] For John Daniel Day, the very "fact of human guilt is the foundation stone for Billy Graham's preaching," because, "while guilt is individually acquired, it nevertheless is individually inevitable."[196]

Graham's exposition of the Holy Spirit was characteristically Protestant in that much more attention was given to the work of the Spirit than to his person.[197] The Spirit was not only active in the inspiration of the Bible but

---

[189] *Billy Graham*, 13, 15.

[190] *The 7 Deadly Sins* (Grand Rapids MI: Zondervan, 1955). They were pride, anger, envy, impurity, gluttony, slothfulness, and avarice.

[191] Burkhead, "The Development of the Concept of Sin," 99-112.

[192] *The 7 Deadly Sins*, 16-17; Graham, *Angels: God's Secret Agents* (New York: Doubleday, 1975) 59-65; John Daniel Day, "A Comparison of the Understandings of Guilt in Biblical Thought and in Representative Contemporary American Protestant Proclamation" (Th.D. diss., Southwestern Baptist Theological Seminary, 1973) 203; Burkhead, "The Development of the Concept of Sin," 102-104.

[193] Graham, *World Aflame*, 67-70; Burkhead, "The Development of the Concept of Sin," 104-106.

[194] *World Aflame*, 71; Day, "A Comparison of the Understandings of Guilt," 208, 222; Burkhead, "The Development of the Concept of Sin," 106.

[195] "The Development of the Concept of Sin," 3, 100.

[196] "A Comparison of the Understandings of Guilt," 220, 208-209.

[197] *The Holy Spirit: Activating God's Power in Your Life* (Minneapolis: Grason, 1978; New York: Warner Books, 1980). Contrast 21-32 with 33-328.

also in the process of canonization. The baptism with the Spirit occurs once-for-all at conversion, and the same is true with sealing by the Spirit, but there can be many fillings by the Spirit. The blasphemy against the Spirit is "the total and irrevocable rejection of Jesus Christ." Whereas for Graham the gifts of healing and of tongues are given today, he seemed to limit the gift of miracles today to "the frontiers of the Christian faith" "for the confirmation of the gospel." "God does not always choose to heal," for healing is not guaranteed by the atonement, and "Jesus did not always heal people the same way." Graham expounded the fruit of the Spirit[198] and reckoned the Holy Spirit to be essential to spiritual awakening.[199]

Graham wrote a monograph on angels when few Protestants were doing so.[200] He based his belief concerning angels on the teachings of the Bible and on his own experience of angelic presence. Angels, he affirmed, are God's agents both in providential care and in judgment, both in the biblical era and today, both in life and at death.[201]

Graham learned something of the teachings of dispensationalism from his mother, who was exposed to these views during his adolescence.[202] Nothing in his formal education seems to have turned him from dispensationalist views. His early preaching contained references to the rapture, though he did not connect the rapture with the establishment of the state of Israel.[203] In 1983 Graham, writing on Rev. 6:1-8, interpreted the rider of the white horse as Satan the deceiver, that of the red horse as war, that of the black horse as famine, and that of the pale horse as death.[204] Within a futurist hermeneutic of the book of Revelation, he concluded that "at some time in the future" these four horsemen will "trample across the stage of human history" "in an awesome act of judgment on the earth." But this judgment is somewhat "conditional," in that it might be deferred by

---

[198]Ibid., 57-59, 90, 107, 146-47, 183, 244, 256, 246-47, 240, 235-36, 239, 267-314.

[199]Ibid., 315-28; Cook, *The Billy Graham Story*, 90-101.

[200]*Angels: God's Secret Agents*, 2nd and rev. ed. (Minneapolis: Grason, 1986; repr.: Dallas: Word Publishing, 1994).

[201]Ibid. (1975 ed.), 15, 73-109, 111-31, 163-75, 147-55.

[202]Martin, *A Prophet with Honor*, 61-62, 578; Burkhead, "The Development of the Concept of Sin," 124.

[203]Martin, *A Prophet with Honor*, 125, 579.

[204]*Approaching Hoofbeats: The Four Horsemen of the Apocalypse* (Minneapolis: Grason, 1983) 73-206.

repentance, and is to be "correctional" in function.²⁰⁵ According to William Martin, the later Graham, while strongly stressing the second coming, has become less specific as to dispensationalist views, as evidenced by few references to precursory signs and to the time of the rapture.²⁰⁶ But Burkhead's tenuous conclusion that Graham has shifted to historic premillennialism may not be tenable.²⁰⁷ He seems rather to be on solid ground in noting that the later Graham has come to the view that God may show mercy to some of the unevangelized after death, particularly if God should see that such persons "would have received the gospel if they had had opportunity."²⁰⁸

Graham had his critics, especially during the early years of his ministry, on both sides of the Atlantic Ocean, both from the neoorthodox and liberal left and from the separatist fundamentalist right. Reinhold Niebuhr criticized him for oversimplifying the Christian faith in "decision for Christ" and for the lack of a social message.²⁰⁹ Joe E. Barnhart offered a series of criticisms, including the charge that Graham was not a consistent Southern Baptist.²¹⁰ Beginning with his New York crusade in 1957, separatist fundamentalists bitterly attacked Graham for including and cooperating with nonevangelical pastors and churches.²¹¹ John R. Rice charged him with being favorable to infant baptism.²¹² A South African who had participated in Graham's 1955 London crusade set forth a deliberate argument against Graham's theology and methods. He was not only cooperating with "Modernists" and Roman Catholics; by his doctrine of free will he had forsaken the Reformation soteriology and three aspects of

---

²⁰⁵Ibid., 74-77.

²⁰⁶*A Prophet with Honor*, 578.

²⁰⁷"The Development of the Concept of Sin," 124.

²⁰⁸Ibid., 121-22.

²⁰⁹Niebuhr, "Literalism, Individualism and Billy Graham," *The Christian Century*, 23 May 1956, 640-42; idem, "Proposal to Billy Graham," *The Christian Century*, 8 August 1956, 921-22; Dullea, *A Catholic Looks at Billy Graham*, 10; Martin, *A Prophet with Honor*, 202, 228.

²¹⁰*The Billy Graham Religion* (Philadelphia: Pilgrim, 1972) esp. 219-26.

²¹¹Especially Bob Jones, Sr., Bob Jones, Jr., John R. Rice, and Carl McIntyre. Dullea, *A Catholic Looks at Billy Graham*, 10; Martin, *A Prophet with Honor*, 239-41, 334-35; Bruns, *Billy Graham*, 79-83.

²¹²*Dr. Graham's Daring: Both Ways at Once!* (Swansea, Wales: D. Roberts, 1962?).

the Dortian TULIP: unconditional election, limited atonement, and irresistible grace.[213] A large volume by a British author was almost consistently negative.[214] But the attacks by Graham's critics have been increasingly dwarfed by the commendations given to this worldwide evangelist, whose long ministry has been unstained by scandal.

Graham's theology and evangelistic methods were communicated to thousands of evangelists from the Two-Thirds World through his sponsorship of world congresses on evangelism in Berlin (1966), Lausanne (1974), and Amsterdam (1983, 1986,[215] 2000[216]).

Harvey Gallagher Cox (1929–):
From the Secular City to Openness to Pentecostalism

A Baptist whose theological work has focused on society and culture, Harvey Cox has written for a general, not especially Baptist, readership. A native of Chester County, Pennsylvania, with Quaker and German Pietist ancestry, he was converted and baptized at thirteen in Malvern Baptist Church. A graduate of the University of Pennsylvania (B.A., 1951), Yale Divinity School (B.D., 1955), and Harvard University (Ph.D., 1963), he was in student ministry at Oberlin College, was an ecumenical fraternal worker in East Berlin, was jailed in a civil rights demonstration in North Carolina, and became a careful student of and participant in liberation theology. After two years of teaching at Andover Newton Theological School, he joined the faculty of Harvard Divinity School in 1965 as assistant professor of theology and culture, becoming the Victor Thomas Professor of Divinity in 1970. He has traveled widely and has deliberately remained a Baptist.[217]

Cox began by setting forth his own version of liberation theology and celebrating the secularization and urbanization taking place. The "political

---

[213]Errol Hulse, *Billy Graham: The Pastor's Dilemma* (Hounslow, Middlesex UK: Maurice Allan, 1966). See also Roland Rasmussen, *Back Billy Graham? California Pastor Says No* (Swansea, Wales: D. Roberts, 1963?).

[214]G. W. Target, *Evangelism Inc.* (London: Allen Lane/Penguin Press, 1968).

[215]Martin, *A Prophet with Honor*, 325-34; 439-55, 530-41.

[216]Per Roy J. Fish.

[217]Cox, *Just As I Am,* Journeys in Faith (Nashville: Abingdon, 1983) esp. 13-19, 51-86, 95-113; *Who's Who in Religion*, 4th ed. (1992–1993) 105; *Who's Who in America*, 46th ed. (1990–1991) 1:692; Cox, *Fire from Heaven: The Rise of Pentecostal Spirituality and the Reshaping of Religion in the Twenty-first Century* (Reading MA: Addison-Wesley, 1995) 6-14.

and secular world . . . is the sphere of God's liberating and renewing activity" and "the proper location of the Christian life." Too much is being said about the nature, renewal, and mission of the church, and the Christian life is being overspiritualized. "The biblical God recognizes no inner freedom apart from external conditions of freedom." Cox turned from defining sin as primarily prideful rebellion to sin as "apathy" or "sloth," which are suggestive of "abdication" and "irresponsibility." The gospel is to be redefined as *"shalom,"* consisting of reconciliation, freedom, and hope. Sacraments and ministry are redefined under liberation.[218]

With the publication of *The Secular City* Cox became a well-known author in the United States. Cox built on the idea that "the rise of urban civilization and the collapse of traditional religion are the two main hallmarks" of this "era and are closely related movements," they being united by secularization, or man's turning "away from worlds beyond and toward this world and this time." Secularization does not so much persecute religion as it "bypasses and undercuts religion," spawning "pluralism and tolerance." "Thus the *disenchantment of nature* begins with the Creation; the *desacralization of politics* with the Exodus; the *deconsecration of values* with the Sinai Covenant" and human anonymity with "deliverance from the law." Cox probed the church's response to the secular city. "The starting point for any theology of the church today must be a theology of social change." It is the very "idea of the secular city," despite serious objections, that constitutes the best image "by which *both* to understand . . . 'the Kingdom of God' *and* to develop a viable theology of revolutionary social change." The church, not as institution but as people, is to be "the avantgarde of the new regime" by "broadcasting the seizure of power," "healing the urban fractures," "making visible the city of man," and exorcising man's "fascination with other worlds—astrological, metaphysical, or religious." Cox concluded by answering Dietrich Bonhoeffer's question, "How do we speak in a secular fashion of God?," in three ways: as "a *sociological problem*," as a *"political issue,"* and as "a *theological question.*"[219]

Then Cox addressed the death of God movement, expressed his concern for Communist Eastern Europe, and adopted the term "post-Christian era,"

---

[218]*God's Revolution and Man's Responsibility* (Valley Forge PA: Judson, 1965) 21-29, 39-49, 57-75, 79-128.

[219]Subtitle: *Secularization and Urbanization in Theological Perspective* (New York: Macmillan, 1965) 1-3, 17-36, 46-49, 105, 110, 125, 127-48, 149-62 (esp. 154), 241-68.

calling for a "new breed" of American churches that are politically and socially active.[220] In a different vein, picking up on the medieval holiday known as the Feast of Fools, he sought to reintroduce "festivity and fantasy" so as "close the gap" between "the world-changers and the life-celebrators."[221] As sociologist of religion the Harvard professor explored popular religious movements and the new technology.[222]

In 1977 Cox turned to non-Christian, especially Eastern, religions. First he offered a tour of encounters with proponents of non-Christian religions and proposed a Christian "spirituality of the secular."[223] A second book, with other detailed accounts of such encounters, focused on the nature of interreligious dialogue. All religions, Cox contended, have universal and particular features. Dialogue should retain both, but Cox charged that the particular was being neglected in contemporary dialogue. Christians should not downplay in dialogue the issue of Jesus, for even non-Christians want to address it. Cox did not directly discuss the salvation of the unevangelized, but his treatment of John 14:2 and John 14:6 so that the "mansions" could be occupied by Hindus and Buddhists would seem to suggest pluralism or inclusivism. For Cox, liberation theology should help to advance interreligious dialogue.[224]

Taking the fundamentalist rejection of modernity as represented by Jerry Falwell (1933–2007), pastor, Thomas Road Baptist Church, Lynchburg, Virginia, and the liberationist rejection of modernity as represented by Ernesto Cardenal (1925–), mystic Roman Catholic revolutionary in Mexico, as prelude, Cox suggested the contours of a postmodern theology that would be liberationist, pluralist, feminist, and populist.[225] In great detail Cox narrated the summons to Rome and the ten-month silencing of Leonardo Boff (1938–), Brazilian Franciscan liberation theologian, on

---

[220]*On Not Leaving It to the Snake* (New York: Macmillan, 1967).

[221]*The Feast of Fools: A Theological Essay on Festivity and Fantasy* (Cambridge MA: Harvard University Press, 1969) esp. 3-4, vii-viii.

[222]*The Seduction of the Spirit: The Use and Misuse of People's Religion* (New York: Simon & Schuster, 1973).

[223]*Turning East: The Promise and Peril of the New Orientalism* (New York: Simon & Schuster).

[224]*Many Mansions: A Christian's Encounter with Other Faiths* (Boston: Beacon Press, 1988) 1-19 (esp. 10), 162-79.

[225]*Religion in the Secular City: Toward a Postmodern Theology* (New York: Simon & Schuster, 1984).

account of his book, *Church: Charism and Power*,[226] by the Congregation for the Doctrine of the Faith, headed by Joseph Cardinal Ratzinger, now Pope Benedict XVI. Boff represents theologizing from the perspective of the poor, "the grassroots religious energy," the "'de-Europeanization' of theology," and resistance to Vatican centralization. For Cox, "The trial of this theologian is also the trial of liberation theology."[227]

Hardly to be expected from his previous books was Cox's *Fire from Heaven* (1995), a sympathetic investigation of the origin and spread of Pentecostalism, American and worldwide, as well as the narration of his numerous visits to Pentecostal churches. Cox acknowledged that instead of the advent of the postreligious age, which he had anticipated in *The Secular City*, "a religious renaissance of sorts is under way all over the globe." Of this Pentecostalism is one notable example. Cox went back to Azusa Street in Los Angeles in 1906 for the origin of "this new upsurge of primal spirituality with its celebration of mysticism, ecstatic praise, and radical hope." Endemic to the movement has been its "*primal speech*," glossolalia, its "*primal piety*," "trance, vision, healing, dreams, [and] dance," and its "*primal hope*," millennial expectation, if not the age of the Spirit. Pentecostals, Cox found, had thrived on opposition and on division and had utilized "the prevailing popular culture . . . , while . . . raising questions about that culture." But Cox was adamant that Pentecostalism as an expression of experientialism and Fundamentalism are distinctly different movements, not to be confused or identified, vying with one another.[228] He did not allow for the possibility that both may to a degree rest under the umbrella of Evangelicalism, even as he has bypassed doctrinal considerations in treating Pentecostalism.

James Deotis Roberts (1927–): Afro-American Theology of Liberation/Reconciliation

Martin Luther King, Jr.'s (1928–1968) writings on applied Christian ethics[229] had theological content, but James Deotis Roberts was the chief

---

[226]Subtitle: *Liberation Theology and the Institutional Church*, trans. John W. Diercksmeier (New York: Crossroad, 1986).

[227]*The Silencing of Leonardo Boff: The Vatican and the Future of World Christianity* (Oak Park IL: Meyer-Stone, 1988) 3-9, 11, 15, 13, 16.

[228]*Fire from Heaven*, xv, xvi, 17, 81-122 (esp. 82), 77, 128, 15, 299-308.

[229]*The Message of a Man* (Philadelphia: Christian Education Press, 1959; Philadelphia: Pilgrim, 1968); *Strength to Love* (New York: Harper & Row, 1963);

Afro-American Baptist doctrinal theologian of the twentieth century. A native of Spindale, North Carolina, Roberts was graduated from Johnson C. Smith University (B.A., 1950), Shaw University (B.D., 1950), Hartford Seminary Foundation (S.T.M., 1952), and the University of Edinburgh (Ph.D., 1957) and served as pastor of Baptist churches in North Carolina and Connecticut. Roberts taught philosophy and religion and was college minister at Shaw University (1953–1958), taught philosophy of religion at Howard University (1958–1968), was dean of the School of Theology of Virginia Union University (1973–1974) but returned to serve at Howard from 1974 to 1980, was president and taught philosophical theology at Interdenominational Theological Center, Atlanta, Georgia (1980–1984), taught at Eastern Baptist Theological Seminary (1984–1998),[230] and is research professor of theology at Duke University Divinity School (1998–).

Roberts's initial publications, of his thesis and dissertation, were a brief study on faith and reason[231] and a well-researched monograph on a seventeenth-century leader of the Cambridge Platonists, Benjamin Whichcote (1609–1683).[232] Midway in his ministry he authored a brief handbook on Christian doctrine.[233] Later he produced an introduction to philosophy for theological students.[234] The remainder of his books have pertained to Afro-American liberation theology.

Why We Can't Wait (New York: Harper & Row, 1964); *Where Do We Go from Here: Chaos or Community?* (New York: Harper & Row, 1967); *The Trumpet of Conscience* (New York: Harper & Row, 1968).

[230]Gerald Thomas, "James Deotis Roberts," in *Baptist Theologians*, ed. George and Dockery, 627-28; *Who's Who in Religion*, 2nd ed. (1977) 563; *Contemporary Authors*, new revision series, 15 (1985): 382.

[231]*Faith and Reason: A Comparative Study of Pascal, Bergson, and James* (Boston: Christopher Publishing House, 1962). Roberts found that all three contributed "a faith beyond discursive reason" based on "reasons of the heart," but Pascal's faith was "deeper" in that his "mystic experience" was "personal," he built on the incarnation and "divine illumination by Grace," and he made better use of the wager argument (82-83, 14-15, 61-62, 41-43, 77).

[232]*From Puritanism to Platonism in Seventeenth Century England* (The Hague: Martinus Nijhoff, 1968).

[233]*Christian Beliefs* (Atlanta: John Colton, 1981); 3rd ed. (Silver Spring MD: J. Deotis Roberts Press, 2000).

[234]*A Philosophical Introduction to Theology* (London: SCM Press; Philadelphia: Trinity Press International, 1991).

Roberts's initial contributions to black theology coincided with black theology's "coming into its own." Indeed,

> the black man in the United States has undergone a certain kind of treatment which had produced a unique type of spiritual experience both personal and collective—an experience which deserves theological analysis and interpretation. The Negro's experience is similar to Israel's experience of Egyptian bondage. . . .[235]

Blackness for the black man is "a given thing," but his Christian faith is a matter of choice. Black theology must speak to the attributes of God, to providence and suffering, to sin as "both personal and social," and to Jesus as one who suffered as "the means to redemption." Moreover, "the beloved community must be inclusive of black men and women from all stations in life."[236] Black theology, Roberts declared, is "soul theology" and as an expression of "Afro-American Christianity" must be differentiated from African Christian theology and from "Black Power religion," many adherents of which are not Christians. "Liberation and reconciliation are the two main poles of Black Theology" and "are not antithetical." "There may . . . be revolution *without* reconciliation," "but there can be a revolution in race relations *with* reconciliation," if "sought by black and white Christians together." "Reconciliation, between blacks and whites, is a two-way street" based not on "the superordination-subordination pattern of whites *over* blacks," but on equality. "The exodus provides a central category for interpreting not only the Old Testament but the work of Jesus and the mission of the church as well. Rejecting ideas of blacks as the "chosen people" (Joseph R. Washington) and Jesus as historically "a black Messiah" (Albert Cleage), Roberts rather encouraged the black family and the black church in fostering "black peoplehood." But symbolically Roberts held to a "black Christ" who "participates in the black experience" and is to be encountered. "The black Messiah comes to his own; he calls each black man by his name." This black Messiah is prophet, priest, and king and both "Liberator" and "Reconciler." Roberts struggled to find a distinctive black eschatology and what he found was not distinctively black.[237]

---

[235]Roberts, "Introduction," to *Quest for a Black Theology*, ed. James J. Gardiner, S. A. (Philadelphia: Pilgrim, 1971) ix.

[236]Roberts, "Black Consciousness in Theological Perspective," in *Quest for a Black Theology*, ed. Gardiner, 62-64, 68-71, 76, 75.

[237]*Liberation and Reconciliation: A Black Theology* (Philadelphia: Westminster, 1971) 9, 22-23, 20-22, 26, 27, 10, 29, 53-60, 63-66, 130, 139, 141, 147-49,

In *A Black Political Theology*[238] Roberts sought to clarify the goal of liberation and to apply his black theology to social ethics. He then differentiated his own "mediating theism" from the "Christocentric theism" of James Cone and the "humanocentric theism" of William R. Jones.[239] In *Roots of a Black Future*[240] he developed and applied his concepts of the black family, the black church, and the black ministry. In dialogue with the Unification Church Roberts outlined a black hermeneutic that was universal, sensitive to human rights, and holistic,[241] and in dialogue with Roman Catholics he dealt with religious pluralism.[242] *Black Theology Today*[243] was essentially an interpretation and evaluation of the writings of other black theologians. In *Black Theology in Dialogue*[244] Roberts sought to relate Afro-American theology to global, and especially African, theological developments. In *The Prophethood of All Believers*[245] he applied black theology to the practice of ministry, both prophetic roles of social justice and teaching and the priestly roles of healing and shepherding.[246]

152, 156-74. The 2nd rev. ed. (Maryknoll NY: Orbis, 1994) was intended to reach a larger, more popular readership, to address more directly the black church, and to expedite "the global influence of Black Theology" (xiii-xiv).

[238](Philadelphia: Westminster, 1974).

[239]"Liberation Theism," in *Black Theology II: Essays on the Formation and Outreach of Contemporary Black Theology*, ed. Calvin E. Bruce and William R. Jones (Cranbury NJ: Associated University Presses, 1978) 233-46.

[240]Subtitle: *Family and Church* (Cranbury NJ: Associated University Presses, 1980).

[241]"Hermeneutics: History and Providence," in *Hermeneutics and Horizons: The Shape of the Future*, ed. Frank K. Flinn (New York: Rose of Sharon, 1982) 315-26.

[242]"Models for Christian Discipleship and Religious Pluralism: An African/Afro-American Perspective," in *Christ's Lordship and Religious Pluralism*, ed. Gerald H. Anderson and Thomas F. Stransky (Maryknoll NY: Orbis, 1981) 171-76.

[243]Subtitle: *Liberation and Contextualization* (Lewiston NY: Edwin Mellen, 1983). He had previously written "The American Negro's Contribution to Religious Thought," in *The Negro Impact on Western Civilization*, ed. Joseph S. Roucek (New York: Philosophical Library, 1970) 75-108.

[244](Philadelphia: Westminster, 1987).

[245]Subtitle: *An African American Political Theology for Ministry* (Louisville: Westminster/John Knox, 1994).

[246]*Liberation and Reconciliation*, 2nd ed., xv-xvi.

According to Gerald Thomas, Roberts, while refusing "to side with the zealots of black theology," has dealt "uncompromisingly ... with the issues of oppression and injustice." "Profound" indeed has been the "impact" of Roberts's "both/and" treatment of liberation and reconciliation. He coupled with his passion for the black church and community a caring for the white community.[247]

Osadolor Imasogie (1928–): Contextualized African Theology

That African theology could be different from Afro-American theology has been demonstrated in the work of the Nigerian Baptist theologian, Osadolor Imasogie. Born in Benin City in the state of Edo, "one of Africa's oldest cities" and "heartland of an ancient, African Kingdom," to a father who was a farmer and chief of patrician lineage who always worshipped an ancestral god and to a mother who had abandoned the worship of Olokun, god of the sea, under the impact of a non-Christian theistic sect and later in life would confess Christ. The son attended Baptist services, studied in Baptist schools, and was baptized at nineteen. He graduated from the Baptist College at Iwo in 1951 and from Nigerian Baptist Theological Seminary (Th.B.) in Ogbomoso in 1955. After a pastorate in Benin City he studied at Oklahoma Baptist University (B.A., 1963) and Golden Gate Baptist Theological Seminary (B.D., 1964). After becoming lecturer in the Nigerian Seminary (1965) he completed the Ph.D. degree in Christian philosophy at Southern Baptist Theological Seminary (1972). First vice principal, he was then named principal (later president) of the Nigerian Seminary in 1979 and served for fourteen years. Imasogie was president of the Nigerian Baptist Convention (1979-85), moderator of the Program on Theological Education of the WCC, and a vice president of the BWA (1995–2000).[248] Three of Imasogie's books were applied biblical expositions.[249]

---

[247]"James Deotis Roberts," in *Baptist Theologians*, ed. George and Dockery, 627-39, esp. 635.

[248]Dickson O. Uwagboe, *Osadolor Imasogie: Life in the Service of God: A Biography of the Professor of Religion and Philosophy Whom Many Claim to Have Holy Ghost Fire in His Bones!* (Benin City, Nigeria: Allied Press Services International, 1995) xviii-xxiii, 1-78; *Who's Who in the Commonwealth*, 2nd. ed. (1984) 239-40; "Biographical Sketch of the Rev. Prof. Osadolor Imasogie," in *The Message of God for a Time Like This: Selected Sermons of the Reverend Professor Osadolor Imasogie*, ed. Yusufu A. Obaje (Ibadan, Nigeria: Sibon Books, 1992), ix-x. Per Paul H. Miller.

[249]*Studies in 2 Corinthians 1-6* (Ibadan, Nigeria: Daystar Press, 1975); *The*

In his dissertation Imasogie set forth J. V. Langmead Casserley's (1909-1978) epistemology of more than sense data and knowledge as "the outcome of the interpretation of the knower and the known" and Casserley's views of metaphysics as an "analogical art," not a "demonstrative science," and of the revelatory nature of biblical history. Hence, for Casserley, reflection on one's encounter with Christ is the task of theology, whereas the effort to "view and interpret everything else in terms of" Christ is the task of Christian philosophy. Casserley's Christian apologetics was not only on the defensive but also on the offensive, so as to prepare for faith, especially among those who have accepted an alternative faith or philosophy. Imasogie then utilized Casserley's method to answer the death-of-God theologians—"the final capitulation . . . to secularism"—by providing new models for presenting the Christian gospel and to answer African Traditional Religion (ATR), which he identified as "bureaucratic monotheism," by pointing to the satisfying particularity of historical revelation in Christ.[250]

Imasogie has focused on the exposition of ATR and the delineation of a proper Christian apologetic method for West Africa. Hence his contribution lies more in apologetical theology than in systematic theology. Imasogie's use of "bureaucratic monotheism" in reference to ATR was based on the roles of the Supreme God as creator and sovereign and yet the divine nature of the various *divinities*, or nature gods. ATR is "a groping response for the reality manifested in Christ."[251] It finds man alienated from God, has a sacrificial system, and looks to life after death and final judgment.[252] But it was the phenomenological, not the Christian apologetical, method that Imasogie used in his study of Olokun, the wealthy oldest

---

Relevance of Prophet Amos for Our Time (Ibadan, Nigeria: Baptist Press, 1981); *First Epistle of Peter: A Model for Understanding the Christian Faith and Its Expression in Everyday Life* (Ibadan, Nigeria: Baptist Press, 1984).

[250]"Langmead Casserley's Understanding of Christian Philosophy as a Basis for Apologetics" (Th.D. diss., Southern Baptist Theological Seminary, 1972) esp. 2-3, 6, 13, 24-34, 75-76, 93-99, 179-99, 248-61, 268. See also "The Apologetic Challenge of the Radical Theological Movement," in *Science, Faith, and Revelation: An Approach to Christian Philosophy*, ed. Bob E. Patterson (Nashville: Broadman, 1979) 167-97.

[251]"African Traditional Religion and Christian Faith," *Review and Expositor* 70 (Summer 1973): 283-93.

[252]"Christian Apologetic Theology in a West African Context," *The Journal of the Interdenominational Theological Center* 7 (Spring 1980): 136.

son of the Creator God, the lord of the sea, and the god of fortune, who allegedly grants fertility (children), wealth, and general well-being. His worship, which has predominated among the Edo people in the Nigerian state of Bendel, involves primary initiations, initiations to the (commonly female) priesthood, and divination.[253] In 1980 Imasogie reported that a fourth stage in the history of the study of ATR had been reached: the *"period of reflection and utilization."*[254] This he later called "the period of the emergence of African scholars of religion." Rites of passage in ATR—child-naming, puberty, marriage, and funeral—and reliance upon divination and amulets were described.[255] ATR worship differs from Christian worship: its externals "are considered as having magical power to compel the presence of the divine," it does not enjoin a different life style or responsibility for others, and it is "not usually directed to the benevolent creator God but to the various divinities." Worship in the African Independent Churches, which originated during the first half of the twentieth century, Imasogie contended, has been heavily influenced by the ATR worship practices. But one "salutary" effect of ATR influence has been its "emphasis on the pervading reality of spiritual presence both within and outside the sanctuary and the consequent inevitability of encounter with that presence."[256]

Rejecting West African attempts to relativize all religions, to embrace eschatological universalism, or to make "a naïve indigenization of Christianity," the Nigerian theologian advocated another method that would "do justice" both to ATR and to Christianity "without compromising the uniqueness of the Christian message." He differentiated between West African traditional theology and a Christian theology expressed in a West African context."[257] This method he identified as that of "contextualization," or the "process of systematic presentation of the Christian faith that is

---

[253] *Olokun: The Divinity of Fortune* (Ibadan, Nigeria: Tokopa Enterprises, 1980).

[254] "Christian Apologetic Theology in a West African Context," 129.

[255] *African Traditional Religion* (Ibadan, Nigeria: University Press, 1982) 8-9, 59-74, 76-83, 85-88.

[256] "The Influence of African Traditional Religious Ideas of Worship on the Christian Worship Practices in Nigeria," *Ogbomoso Journal of Theology* 6 (December 1991): 17-23. "There is a very thin line between contextualization and syncretism" (23).

[257] "Christian Apologetic Theology in a West African Context," 137-38.

informed by a serious and critical consideration of the culture of a people and the world view that fashions that culture." He reminded Western theologians that they had often been blind to the cultural influences that had shaped their theological formulations. Likewise he lamented that the "mainstream Christian denominations in Africa" had not seriously undertaken contextualization and the "Independent" churches had "done so in protest" under unqualified leaders with the result often being syncretism.[258] To make his case for a satisfying African Christian theology, Imasogie reviewed the critiques of "traditional Western Christian theology" made by liberalism, by David Tracy, and by liberation theologians. He also contended that the African worldview was much more alike the biblical worldview than it was alike the "quasi-scientific" worldview of the West, especially as to evil spirits. Thus Christ's victory over "evil spiritual forces" is essential to African theology.[259] An African Christian theology that is truly incarnate in African culture should affect mission strategy and theological education.[260] The person of Christ is real and relevant in a secularistic age, and "no Christian apologist has the mandate of the church to whittle . . . down or reinterpret" the church's message about Christ "in terms consonant with the secular world view."[261] A contextualized African Christian theology should emphasize "certain themes": "the sacrificial death of Christ and his present intercessory role," Christ foremost as "Victor and Liberator par excellence," Christ as "the Cosmic Lord who supplies the total human needs," the role of the Holy Spirit in the day-to-day life of a Christian," and "the place of prayer in Christian life."[262]

---

[258]"Contextualization: Constructive Interaction between Culture, People, Church, and the Theological Programme," *East Africa Journal of Evangelical Theology* 2 (1983): 19-23.

[259]*Guidelines for Christian Theology in Africa* (Achimota, Ghana: African Christian Press, 1983) 25-66, 79-81.

[260]"The Church and Theological Ferment in Africa," *Review and Expositor* 82 (Spring 1985): 228-36.

[261]"The Person of Christ in a Secular World," in *Addresses and Papers: Baptist International Conference on Theological Education, . . . Ridgecrest, North Carolina, USA, January 14-17, 1982* (McLean VA: Baptist World Alliance, n.d.) 91-121, esp. 112-16, repr.: *Ogbomoso Journal of Theology* 5 (December 1990): 8-21, esp. 18-20.

[262]"African Theology: The Development of Theological Thought in Nigeria," *Baptist Quarterly* 34 (October 1992): 390-97.

At times Imasogie addressed ecclesiology. The church is "not a human organisation *per se*" but rather "a divine-human visible entity." Church membership should be validated "from time to time" by experiencing "the presence of the Spirit in one's life." Despite the "checkered history of the Church of God" with its worldliness, weakness, and fruitlessness, it has been promised "a triumphant future."[263] But churches cannot be "structureless and leaderless." Baptist polity should no longer be identified as "democracy" because of political connotations but rather as "*pneumatocracy*." Inter-church cooperation is needed, and the national convention serves as "trainer and spiritual overseer," "chief planner for the member-bodies," and annual reporter of its stewardship to the churches.[264] Imasogie did not hesitate to assert that pastors have a priestly role but stressed that their "Christ-centred leadership" should be marked by servanthood, be "people-centred" and "team-centred," and demonstrate "intellectual leadership," "emotional maturity," and "moral maturity."[265]

Imasogie was without a peer among black Baptist African theologians in addressing ATR and pressing for contextualization. But his theological method and its results have not gone unchallenged. Another Nigerian, Thompson Onumajuru Onyenechehie, has offered a searching critique of Imasogie's "bi-polar method," the correlation of revelation and culture. It is, he alleged, flawed by undercutting the once-for-all revelation of God in Christ through stressing the process of incarnational cultural identification, this being too dependent on the "revisionist" theology of David Tracy. It does "theology from below" and becomes relativistic. It is "side-tracked by the postcolonial intellectual and cultural hang-overs in Africa," thus failing to take into account the biblical and patristic roots of African Christianity. It denies the great religious and cultural diversity in Africa by posing one African culture and worldview. It "puts the cart" of "the existential life and problems of the African people" "before the horse" of special revelation, true Christian identity, and the one Body of Christ. For Onyenechehie, "incarnational theology in Africa," to be effective, must be more Christocentric.[266]

---

[263]"The Church of God: What Future?," *The Nigerian Pulpit* 3:7-21.
[264]"An African Christian View of Church Leadership and Polity," *Ogbomoso Journal of Theology* 2 (December 1987): 11-18.
[265]*The Message of God*, ed. Obaje, 88-89, 107-10, 91-96.
[266]"Doing Incarnational Theology in Africa: A Critique of Imasogie's Methodology" (M.A. thesis, Wheaton College Graduate School, 1993) 64-113.

South African Theologians and Doctrinal Statements

From the southern end of the African continent came another Baptist theological spokesman who would address issues of social justice and world religions. Born in the village of Paul Pietersburg in Natal province of South Africa to parents, Swedish and Norwegian, who were Lutheran missionaries among the Zulus, John Norman Jonsson (1925–) was baptized at eighteen into Central Baptist Church, Durban. After working as an electrical engineer for the South African Railways, he trained for the ministry at Spurgeon's College and later completed a B.D. degree from the University of London. Then from the University of Natal he received M.A. (1962) and Ph.D. (1966) degrees. After an associate pastorate in Johannesburg and pastorates in Durban and Pietermaritzburg, Jonsson served as principal of the Baptist Theological College of Southern Africa, Johannesburg (1966–1971). Two university lectureships in the history of religions followed: Witwatersrand University (1971–1975) and University of Natal (1976–1981). He was deeply and courageously involved in the struggle against *apartheid*. From 1982 to 1991 he taught missions and world religions at Southern Baptist Theological Seminary, occupying the W. O. Carver chair, and from 1991 to 2002 he taught world religions at Baylor University.[267] Among the authors whom Jonsson acknowledged as having influenced his thought were Gustaf Wingren (1910–2000), H. Wheeler Robinson, Frederick Cawley, E. O. James, Dietrich Bonhoeffer, Albert Schweitzer, Geo Widengren, Mohandas Gandhi, and Nicolas Berdyaev.[268]

In his graduate studies Jonsson defended the historicity or facticity of the resurrection of Jesus. First, utilizing arguments by Karl Barth, he refuted Rudolf Bultmann's denial based on demythologization.[269] Then in a study of the theology of the Swedish Lutheran theologian, Gustaf Wingren, he agreed with Wingren's affirmation and defense of the "factuality" of Jesus' resurrection, which involved the inseparable nature of Jesus' death and

---

[267]Gladys Crankshaw Jonsson, *Glimpses of John N. Jonsson's Incarnational Thought* (Waco TX: priv. prtg., 2000) 1-3, 5-8, 10-11; Curriculum Vitae: John N. Jonsson.

[268]Gladys Jonsson, *Glimpses*, 6, 8, 9, 10, 13-14; appendix by John Jonsson, 37-39; John Jonsson, *Dynamic Religion: Henry Wheeler Robinson* (1959; repr.: Waco TX: priv. prtg., 2001).

[269]"The Problem of Demythologization in the Theology of the Twentieth Century" (M.A. thesis, University of Natal, 1962) 154-61.

resurrection and differed from the motif research of Anders Nygren (1890–1978), which made theology dependent on philosophy of religion.[270]

Jonsson claimed to have an incarnational theology. This meant not only that the unseen God has been made manifest and that Jesus was fully human but also that all human beings have dignity and worth and belong to God's extended family and that Jesus has become "a participant in the sufferings of oppressed humanity," including those in South Africa. He suggested that Job's suffering might not have been bodily disease but rather the political oppression of the Jewish people in Babylon. Jesus' death was not so much substitutionary as it was identificatory.[271] Moreover, the mission of the church is more the humanization of the world than the evangelization of the world, but coupled with the glorification of Christ.[272]

Jonsson agreed with H. Wheeler Robinson's "paradoxical blend of revelation and history."[273] Coining the term, he advocated as a needed hermeneutical principle "retranspositionalization," that is, movement "from the pursuits of abstract meaning to the encounter with the concrete biblical intention in human life," or "from the secure human vantage point of detached abstractions" to "the traumatic vantage point from which the biblical text itself merged," or from a "'bird's-eye view'" to a "'worm's-eye view.'" Such a change, for Jonsson, was far more relevant than "establishing a reliable text of Scripture" or focusing on autographs. He was confident that Jesus' ascension did not mean his passing "from one geographical area to another" but rather his inability to be "localized," and hence "he has entered into the 'end-time' in which we find ourselves today."[274]

Another South African theologian, Chris William Parnell (1912–2007), was trained in Spurgeon's College, served as pastor of Central Church, Johannesburg (1951–1963), was general secretary of the Baptist Union of South Africa (1963–1973), and led the Western Province Branch of the

---

[270]"The Thought of Gustaf Wingren and Its Relationship to Some Modern Theologians" (Ph.D. diss., University of Natal, 1966) 207-19, 259-61.

[271]Gladys Jonsson, *Glimpses*, 11-15.

[272]Ibid.; "The Role of North Americans in the Future of the Missionary Enterprise: Reflections and a Response," *Review and Expositor* 81 (Spring 1984): 265-66.

[273]*Dynamic Religion*, esp. 12.

[274]"Retranspositionalization: Missiological Hermeneutics within the Socio-Human Context," *Review and Expositor* 84 (Winter 1987): 99-117, esp. 100, 101, 102, 99, 113.

Baptist Theological College of Southern Africa (1973–1980). In stating Baptist principles Parnell included the sole lordship of Christ, the Bible as the only creed, local church autonomy, the universal church, regenerate church membership, believer's baptism by immersion, religious freedom, world evangelization, care for the poor, different lifestyle, spiritual worship, open communion, fellowship, and stewardship.[275] Modern tongues-speaking, he contended, is not like the known languages of Acts 2:4, may or may not be identical with what occurred at Corinth, is not "the sure sign" of the baptism with the Holy Spirit since tongues-speaking has occurred among so many non-Christians, is a "physical phenomenon" of "disassociation" of mind and mouth, and yet it is a charismatic gift that should not lead to pride and division. Although Baptists should discourage tongues-speaking in worship services, tongues-speakers exercising their gift privately should be welcomed, and "emotional stirrings" encouraged.[276]

In 1924 the Baptist Union of South Africa (BUSA) had composed and adopted an eleven-article Statement of Belief, which declared that Adam's sin "incurred the penalty of death, physical and spiritual," but that human beings do not incur "personal guilt" until "actual transgression" (4). Both the universal church and the local church were affirmed (10), as was one general resurrection (9), and the ordinances were said to be both "acts of obedience" and "perpetual witnesses to the cardinal facts of the Christian faith" (11).[277] About 1968[278] the BUSA adopted a seven-article Statement of Baptist Principles,[279] and in 2000 it formally declared that "God has ordained marriage as a heterosexual relationship between a natural man and a natural woman."[280]

---

[275] *Being a Baptist* (Roodepoort, South Africa: Baptist Publishing House, 1980).

[276] Parnell, *Understanding Tongues-Speaking* (Johannesburg: South African Baptist Press, 1972; Nashville: Broadman, n.d.). Parnell (89-108) located baptism with the Holy Spirit at conversion. Parnell also wrote *The Holy Spirit and the Ordinary Christian* (Pretoria: author, 1990).

[277] "A Statement of Belief." Per Chris W. Parnell.

[278] Karen Viljoen to James Leo Garrett, Jr., 22 August 2006.

[279] "Statement of Baptist Principles." Per Chris W. Parnell.

[280] Addendum to "A Statement of Belief."

Latin American Confessions and Controversies

Brazil.[281] Brazilian Baptists owe their doctrinal conscience, according to Oswaldo Ferreira Bonfim, to the FMB-SBC missionaries who began work in Brazil in the 1880s. The first church organized in Brazil, at Salvador, Bahia, in 1882, adopted the 1853 New Hampshire Confession, with the translation being made by missionary Zachary Clay Taylor (1851–1919). The same confession was adopted in 1916 by the Brazilian Baptist Convention (BBC), which had been organized in 1907, and was called the Confession of Faith of the Baptist Churches of Brazil. In 1954 the BBC adopted a new translation of the same confession.[282]

Earlier, in 1951, the BBC formally requested the faculties of the South Brazil Baptist Theological Seminary, Rio de Janeiro, and the North Brazil Baptist Theological Seminary, Recife, to undertake work on a new confession of faith that would be reflective of Brazilian Baptist life.[283] Many years passed, however, before anything concrete was done. Following the preparatory work of missionary professors Rodney Bishop Wolfard (1921–2006) and Jerry S. Key (1932–) and of Brazilian professor Jose dos Reis Pereira (1916–1991) and others, the faculty of the South Brazil Seminary adopted in 1974 a new declaration of faith.[284]

As a result of a division within the BBC the National Baptist Convention (NBC) was organized in 1967.[285] The division was caused by a Pentecostal Holiness movement which developed within the BBC and was called the Spiritual Renovation (or Renewal) Movement. It emphasized the baptism with the Holy Spirit as a second experience of grace as well as such gifts of the Spirit as tongues-speaking and divine healing being realities for today's churches. In its first assembly (1967) the NBC was organized and

---

[281]This section has been written by Jerry S. Key, longtime FMB-SBC missionary professor in Brazil.

[282]"Os Caminhos de uma Declaraçao Doutrinaria" (Th.M. thesis, South Brazil Baptist Theological Seminary, 1989) 1, 11-13, 19, 23-29.

[283]BBC, *Annual*, 1986, 6, cited by Bonfim, "Os Caminhos," 23.

[284]*Bulletin of the South Brazil Baptist Theological Seminary*, 1984, 53-54; Bonfim, "Os Caminhos," 53.

[285]Wardin, ed., *Baptists around the World*, 338.

adopted the text of the 1963 SBC Baptist Faith and Message Statement as its doctrinal basis.[286]

A special BBC committee named to study and recommend a new confession reported in 1978 its appreciation for the 1974 South Brazil Seminary declaration.[287] After working for eight years, the committee presented and the BBC adopted unanimously in January 1986 a 19-article Doctrinal Declaration of the Brazilian Baptist Convention.[288] This 1986 text, like the 1974 seminary text, followed closely the 1963 SBC Baptist Faith and Message Statement, although there were other confessions consulted by the committee.[289] There were several exceptions. The 1986 text omitted from the 1963 articles on education, cooperation, and peace and war and added new articles on the ministry of the Word (11), religious education (14), the family (17), and death (18). There was some recasting concerning last things. The 1974 seminary text had not contained the articles on religious education and the family, and its article on the spiritual union of believers was not included in the 1986 text.[290] The latter, being partly motivated by the earlier Spiritual Renovation Movement, served, according to Reis Pereira, both doctrinal and polemical purposes.[291]

Mexico. Landmarkism, ecumenism, and charismaticism have affected the Baptist movement in Mexico.[292] Due to the influence of FMB-SBC missionaries in the late nineteenth and early twentieth centuries Landmark teachings and translated Landmark books had a shaping influence on Baptists, especially in northwest Mexico. Due to the presence of ABFMS missionaries, especially during the middle of the twentieth century, ecumenism and a favorable attitude to the WCC tended to prevail in

---

[286]CBN/NBC (Convençao Batista Nacional/National Baptist Convention) website: <http://www2.cbn.org.br>.

[287]CBB/BBC (Convençao Batista Brasileira/Brazilian Baptist Convention) *Annual*, 1979, 258-59. (Website is <http://www.batistas.org.br>.)

[288]Ibid., 24-26, cited by Bonfim, "Os Caminhos," 43-44.

[289]Ibid., 258-59, cited by Bonfim, "Os Caminhos," 34.

[290]Bonfim, "Os Caminhos," 50, has a chart comparing the articles in the 1986 BBC Doctrinal Confession, the 1974 South Brazil Baptist Theological Seminary Confession of Faith, and the 1963 SBC Baptist Faith and Message Statement.

[291]Ibid., 49.

[292]Dinorah Mendez, "History and Development of Baptists in Mexico," unpublished paper presented to the BWA Baptist History and Heritage Commission, Mexico City, 4 July 2006, 8.

southern Mexico, until the withdrawal of ABFMS missionaries.[293] In the latter twentieth century the exercise of gifts of tongues-speaking and healing, the authority of experiences, and more spontaneous worship became issues among Mexican Baptists.[294]

The Declaration of Faith of the National Baptist Convention of Mexico, adopted in 1970 after tensions concerning ecumenism,[295] was dependent on two English-language confessions written in the United States but also included articles composed in Spanish, presumably in Mexico. Its articles on the Holy Scriptures (1), God the Holy Spirit (2c), man (3), perseverance of the saints (10), and stewardship (20) were translations of the same articles in the SBC's Baptist Faith and Message Statement of 1963.[296] The article on law and gospel (11) was a translation of the same article in the 1853 edition of the New Hampshire Confession. The articles on the true God (2, introd.), God the Father (2a), and God the Son (2b) utilized the 1963 confession but made slight modifications—specifying that the Father, the Son, and the Spirit are "equal in every divine perfection," limiting God's Fatherhood to believers, and referring to the Son as "the unique Mediator" instead of "the one Mediator." Especially in the soteriological articles the Mexican confession utilized selectively or added to the 1853 New Hampshire text: salvation by grace (4), regeneration (5), justification (7), the purpose of divine grace (8), sanctification (9), and civil government (16).[297] The article on repentance and faith (6) made use of the 1963 confession but made significant additions as to their being both "indispensable requirements for salvation" and "the work of the Holy Spirit in the heart." The newly composed article on the Lord's Day (15) borrowed from both the 1853 and 1963 confessions.[298] The ecclesiological articles—a true church (12), Christian baptism (13), and the Lord's Supper (14)—and the eschatological articles—the second coming of Christ (17), the last judgment

---

[293]Justice C. Anderson, *An Evangelical Saga: Baptists and Their Precursors in Latin America* (Longwood FL: Xulon Press, 2005) 95-96, 118, 120, 121-22

[294]Mendez, "History and Development," 8.

[295]Dinorah Mendez to James Leo Garrett, Jr., 22 August 2006.

[296]*10 Estrategias Biblicas para Establecer Iglesias y Declaración de Fe de las Iglesias Bautistas* (N.p.: La Luz Bautista, 1982) 1, 2, 3, 5, 8. Per Dinorah Mendez. The article on stewardship (20) was also identical with that in the SBC's 1925 BF&M.

[297]Ibid., 6, 1, 2, 3-5, 7.

[298]Ibid., 4, 7.

(18), and heaven and hell (19)—do not seem to have been derived from any English-language confession but rather to have been composed in Spanish. Landmarkism was reflected in the insistence that baptism must be "executed by a proper administrator" and participation in the Lord's Supper be limited to "baptized believers who hold the same doctrine." There is to be one universal judgment.[299]

Juan Arellano Guerrero (1921–), a graduate of Mexican Baptist Theological Seminary (Th.B.) and professor and administrator in the same institution (1958–1961, 1963–1973), was pastor of First Church, Chihuahua (1973–1976), First Church, Durango (1976–1978), and First Church, Juarez (1978–1996).[300] He set forth a brief statement of Baptist beliefs under eight categories[301] with pertinent biblical texts being quoted under each subsection. The categorization of the attributes of God as either "natural" or "moral" was like that of E. Y. Mullins. Four sins against the Holy Spirit were identified: two by the unconverted (resistance, blasphemy) and two by believers (grieving, quenching). The devil is a "spiritual person," not abstract evil. Arellano quoted the definition of the Christian church framed by José M. Sanchez: "Following the New Testament, it is a body of believers in Christ, baptized after a credible profession of faith, and voluntarily united for the observance of the commands of Christ and to extend his kingdom on the earth." Its government is "theodemocratic," and baptism and the Lord's Supper, being "symbolic acts," are specifically to be called "ordinances," not "sacraments." The baptismal administrator ought to be authorized by a church and "one who believes and practices the New Testament doctrines." The church should be supported by the voluntary giving of believers, that is, tithes and offerings.[302]

Alejandro Zamora Alfaro (1935–), a graduate of Mexican Baptist Theological Seminary (Th.B.) and pastor since 1965 of Star of Bethlehem Church, Mexico City,[303] has articulated sixteen Baptist distinctives, most of

---

[299]Ibid., 6, 7-8.

[300]Dinorah Mendez to James Leo Garrett,Jr., 31 August 2006.

[301]God, the Trinity, man, the devil, salvation, holiness, the second coming of Christ, and the Christian church.

[302]"Doctrínas básicas que creen los cristianos bautistas, de acuerdo con la enseñanza que se desprende de la Biblia" (1976). Arellano also wrote a commentary on the 1970 confession (1986–1987). Per Dinorah Mendez.

[303]Dinorah Mendez to James Leo Garrett, Jr., 31 August 2006.

which are ecclesiological,[304] and has identified ten factors that have recently had a negative effect on Mexican Baptist identity. These included sending teachers "with different doctrines" to Baptist churches, the influence of some such teachers on Baptist seminarians, the lack of doctrinal teaching in many churches, and "the new theology of worship."[305] He also has pinpointed four contemporary doctrinal problems: the authority and primacy of the Bible, a full-orbed doctrine of the church as to membership, doctrines, ordinances, offerings, and Christ's headship, accountability to teachers in Baptist seminaries, and the "exaggerated emotionalism" in "charismatic congregations."[306]

Argentina. The original confession of faith of the International Baptist Theological Seminary (IBTS) in Buenos Aires was a translation of the Abstract of Principles of Southern Baptist Theological Seminary. Then after considerable preparation the faculty secured the adoption in 1968 of a modification of the SBC's Baptist Faith and Message of 1963.[307] The first seven articles were retained with only slight modifications: the sealing by the Holy Spirit was omitted, election was said to be "in Jesus Christ," the church was identified as a voluntary association whose functions include the worship of God under the "exclusive" lordship of Christ, and the connection of the Lord's Supper with the second coming was deleted.[308] Seven of the articles in the 1963 confession were omitted.[309] The articles on last things and on religious liberty were retained, and the article on the kingdom of God was reduced so as to emphasize the eschatological.[310]

Concurrently the Evangelical Baptist Convention of Argentina (EBCA) was involved in controversy over pentecostal or charismatic influences, particularly what was called the Movement for Spiritual Restoration. In November 1969 its executive commission sent an advisory letter to the

---

[304]"Distintivos de los Bautistas." Per Dinorah Mendez.

[305]"Recuperando nuestra identidad como bautistas Mexicanos" (1982). Per Dinorah Mendez.

[306]"Nuestra identidad bautista." Per Dinorah Mendez.

[307]*Articulos de Fe, Seminario Internacional Teológico Bautista, Buenos Aires, Argentina.* Per Justice C. Anderson. Stanley D. Clark to James Leo Garrett, Jr., 9 August 2006; Justice C. Anderson to James Leo Garrett, Jr., 10 August 2006.

[308]Ibid., 1-4.

[309]Those on the Lord's Day, evangelism and missions, education, stewardship, cooperation, the Christian and the social order, and peace and war.

[310]Ibid., 4.

churches. It described the movement as "antidenominational" and "pentecostalist," as an "infiltration" for "proselytizing purposes," as confusing and divisive in its effects, and as seeking to "annul all denominational cooperation." Its reliance on certain proof-texts negates consistent exegesis and the total teaching of the New Testament, and it has doctrinal errors, such as "a disproportionate emphasis on the work of the Holy Spirit," salvation through personal religious experience by subordinating the redemptive work of Christ, the Bible as a proof of experience, and errors as to baptism and the Lord's Supper. Charges were made of "excessive emotional effects," "lack of ethics," "pretended nondenominationalism," "spiritual pride," missing "fruits of the Spirit," and problems arising from similar movements in church history. Churches were advised to avoid any direct collaboration with the movement.[311] Justice Conrad Anderson (1929–) reviewed glossolalia in Christian history, stated the benefits from the perspective of sympathizers and the dangers from the standpoint of critics, and made charges of "embryonic heresy" in theology, ecclesiology, Christology, soteriology, and hermeneutics.[312] Anderson elaborated on these potential heresies which he called "theological aspects," when he addressed the leaders of all Evangelical theological education in Argentina.[313] Addressing the students of IBTS, he spelled out "ecclesiological errors" of the charismatic movement, alleging that it was based on Watchman Nee's (1903–1972) ecclesiology.[314]

The EBCA in August 1987 adopted a "Declaration of Baptist Beliefs and Practices," which was adapted from the SBC's Baptist Faith and Message Statement of 1963 with deletions and additions for the Argentine context. The article on God constituted the first article instead on that on the Scriptures. Added was the sentence," He is the Lord of history, in which he reveals his will to save humankind." The statement that the Father "is all powerful, all loving, and all wise" was deleted. Jesus was "engendered" rather than "conceived" by the Holy Spirit, and he is the "unique" rather

---

[311]"Declaración, La Comisión Ejecutiva, Convención Evangélica Bautista de la Argentina, Buenos Aires."

[312]"El Movimiento Espiritualista," *El Expositor Bautista* (October 1969): 18-24.

[313]*Aspectos Teológicos que Plantea el Movimiento Carismático leída en una reunión pública auspiciada por la Associación Teológica Evangélica en el Aula Magna de la Facultad Evangélica Unida, Junio de 1970.*

[314]"Problemas Ecclesiologicos que Plantea el Movimiento Carismático," 1971.

than the "one Mediator." More additions were made concerning the Holy Spirit. He is a "spiritual and personal Being, the third person of the divinity." His illumination enables each person "to understand his need of salvation and the truth of the gospel." He "abides in the whole man from the day in which he has accepted Christ as Lord and Savior." Spiritual gifts are given that recipients can "serve God," but the words "through His church" were deleted. Under the Spirit's "dominion and dynamism the church moves, being led to fulfil the ministry which has been conferred on it in the world."

The article on the Scriptures (2) added or modified two statements. The Bible "leads to the knowledge for salvation in Christ Jesus," and "is the supreme authority in everything pertaining to faith and ought to be interpreted in the light of the person of Christ Jesus under the guidance of the Holy Spirit." Sinful humanity (3) inherits "an environment corrupted by sin," and salvation (4) "is the personal experience in which the individual is redeemed from the control of sin and freed to live according to the purposes of God in one's life." The one who repents "embraces the grace of God," the one who believes "receives absolute pardon" by God's mercy, and the one justified has a "life transformed to reflect the principles of his righteousness." In place of the 1963 article on divine election the Argentine confession framed an article on "the scope of the grace of God" (5). "God in his infinite mercy expresses his grace to every person. He invites every one to call on the name of the Lord in order to receive the salvation of God in Christ Jesus. The work of the grace of God in the life of the redeemed is total, set to free the believer from the total control of Satan, to pardon his sins, to transform his character, and to make possible his progress to maturity and holiness." The article on the kingdom of God (6) with slight textual emendations was placed before the article on the church (7). In the latter the statement on the universal church was placed first. Members of a local church are "enabled to exercise the gifts which God distributes in the bosom of the body of Christ and to fulfil the work of the ministry for the edification of the Church, to do well in the world and to fulfill their universal mission." Moreover, congregational polity is "subject to the will and guidance of the Holy Spirit," and "all the members are equally responsible for exercising the spiritual priesthood." Baptism (8) is "assumed voluntarily by the believer," and the Lord's Supper, being a "commemorative act," "affirms the unity of the brothers in the body of Christ."

The article on evangelization and missions (11) was expanded so as to declare that "each follower of Christ" and "each church" has "the privilege to extend the kingdom of God," and the "sad reality of humanity without hope and without God makes urgent the fulfillment of the mandate of Christ." As to stewardship (13) "Christians ought to contribute joyfully and regularly through tithes and offerings for the extension of the kingdom of God, for the sustaining of the ministries of the church, and for the needs of the poor." The article on the Christian and society (15) was somewhat restated, and to the article on religious liberty (16) were added statements that "each individual as one created in the divine image is competent to respond directly to God," and there should be no "teaching of a particular religious creed in public education." The 1963 articles on education, cooperation, and peace and war were not included, and three new articles were framed and adopted. The article on worship (9) enjoined private, family, and collective worship. True worship "does not depend on ceremony or custom," but congregational worship should include "the reading of the Scriptures, the singing of hymns and spiritual songs, the sharing of testimonies, prayer in all its aspects, the surrender of offerings, and the preaching of the "Word." According to the article on Christian conduct (12) "every follower of Jesus ought to seek first the kingdom of God and his righteous purposes," be "under the command to express his faith by means of his conduct," "be honest in personal relations," "fulfil diligently one's engagements," and "oppose . . . every form of greed, selfishness, and vice." The article on the Christian and the church (14) emphasized mutual love, support amid trials, help in both spiritual and material matters, and the need to seek reconciliation when there are conflicts. The article also stated the propriety and pattern of church discipline. The unmodified article on "Last Things" (17) was appropriately placed at the end.[315]

In 1987 the EBCA also adopted a "Resolution on Our Baptist Identity," which was directed to the contemporary Argentine context. It affirmed "'the normative role of Scripture'" vis-à-vis experience and held that the presence of the Holy Spirit in the Christian results in fruitage, peace, and unity and that healing, tongues, and miracles are not "'proof'" of "'spiritual or doctrinal superiority.'" The Spirit works fully in conversion and continues to work through the gifts, the exercise of which should meet the test

---

[315]"Declaración de Creencias y Prácticas Bautistas, Convención Evangélica Bautista Argentina. Per Stanley D. Clark; Mark Steven Alexander, "Revival and Renewal in Argentine Baptist Life, 1982–1997: Identifying Presuppositions and Their Implications for Contextualization" (Ph.D. diss., Southwestern Baptist Theological Seminary, 2004) 49-54.

of 1 Cor. 14:40. Local church membership is very important. Believers cannot be demon possessed, but present-day possession, at least for some unbelievers, is to be accepted. God's ability to heal any and all diseases and the widespread existence of illness in a fallen world were affirmed, together with intercessory prayer for healing and God's use of medical means.[316]

A second charismatic controversy among Argentine Baptists began in October 1992 with the advent of Benny Hinn (1952–), Israel-born pastor of the interdenominational Orlando (FL) Christian Center, and a so-called "anointing" in the historic Central Church, Buenos Aires, in which hundreds fell to the floor and the church's copastors, Pablo Alberto Deiros (1945–) and Carlos Mraida, became exponents of the Unction Movement. Hinn was teaching three anointings: "the leper's anointing" (conversion), "the priestly anointing" (baptism with the Holy Spirit), and "the kingly anointing" (complete obedience and power to rout Satan with a word). For the Unction Movement falling under the Spirit was an "experiential sign gift" which served as a substitute for tongues-speaking.[317] As these phenomena occurred in other Baptist churches, the EBCA referred the matter to its Commission on Theological Matters with the result that it presented in 1993 a "Document on the Unction" to the convention. It presupposed that the Bible is "'the only guide of faith and practice,'" that the entire biblical witness on any given topic needs to have priority, and that there was need for revival and victorious Christian living. Contemporary anointing in the sense of an "'event'" that comes by the will and action of God can be valid, but such anointing is different from the anointing that occurs at conversion. God only imparts it, and "'pastors and ministers'" are not its "'indispensable mediators.'" The Holy Spirit does give "'special experiences'" to some, but not to all, believers. These are neither identical with baptism with the Spirit nor the assured "'key to holy Christian living.'"[318] At denominational meetings excitement about spiritual experiences mixed with concern over doctrinal issues. In 1997 the EBCA held a national encounter for dialogue and reflection so as to define the differing positions and to "'discern . . . up to what point the differences . . . are of such magnitude that they would not allow us to live in unity as a Baptist denomination.'"[319] In

---

[316] Alexander, "Revival and Renewal in Argentine Baptist Life," 55-62.
[317] Ibid., 38-41.
[318] Ibid., 69-71.
[319] Ibid., 42-44.

2001 it adopted a covenant which reaffirmed Baptist distinctives.[320] But issues related to the Unction Movement have not been fully resolved, and in 2005, in order to counter the pro-unction pastors' retreats and youth congresses of the CEBA, a group of antiunction churches formally organized the Argentine Baptist Association.[321]

Latin American Theologians: Orlando Enrique Costas (1942–1987), C. René Padilla (1932–), and Samuel Escobar (1934–)

During the last third of the twentieth century an indigenous Latin American, Spanish-language Evangelical theological movement developed in order to give expression to what was ultimately called "contextualization." Its chief representatives have been Orlando Enrique Costas (1942–1987), a native of Puerto Rico, C. René Padilla (1932–), an Ecuadorian, and Samuel Escobar (1934–), a Peruvian. These were founding members of Fraternidad Teológica Latinoamericana (FTL). They addressed and interacted critically with Roman Catholic liberation theologies in Latin America. Magnifying the incarnation, they moved from a metaphysical to a functional Christology, and focusing on the kingdom of God, inaugurated but not yet consummated, they connected the proclamation of the kingdom with the sociopolitical needs of Latin America. No one of these wrote as a systematic theologian but always "from a missiological context."[322]

Born in Ponce, Puerto Rico, to middle-class Methodist parents, Costas grew up in Bridgeport, Connecticut. Converted during the 1957 Billy Graham crusade in New York City, he attended Bob Jones Academy and Nyack Missionary College before returning to Puerto Rico, where he was ordained as a Baptist minister (American Baptist Convention) and graduated from the Inter American University (B.A., 1966). During the pastorate of Iglesia Evangélica Bautista in Milwaukee, Wisconsin (1966–1969), he studied at Trinity Evangelical Divinity School, Garrett Theological Seminary (M.Div., 1969), and Winona Lake School of Theology (M.A. in Theol., 1967). Then followed missionary service as seminary professor in

---

[320]"Pacto de la Convención Evangélica Bautista sobre principios y prácticas bautistas . . . Mayo de 2001."

[321]Stanley D. Clark to James Leo Garrett, Jr., 9 August 2006.

[322]Terrell Frank Coy, "Incarnation and the Kingdom of God: The Political Theologies of Orlando Costas, C. René Padilla, and Samuel Escobar" (Ph.D. diss., Southwestern Baptist Theological Seminary, 1999) 3-8.

Costa Rica under the Latin American Mission (1970–1973), doctoral study under Johannes Verkuyl in the Free University, Amsterdam (D.Th., 1976), and another stint in Costa Rica under the United Church of Christ (USA) (1977–1978). Returning to the United States, he taught missiology at Eastern Baptist Theological Seminary (1979–1984) and finally at Andover Newton Theological School in the Adoniram Judson chair (1984–1987), being also the academic dean. Antonio Carlos Barro has noted five "conversions" of Costas identified by Costas: (1) to Christ, (2) to Hispanic culture, (3) to the "forgotten and exploited," (4) to "Macedonia"—the United States; and (5) to North American Hispanics.[323]

Costas reckoned contextualization as doing theology "from the peculiar situation in which many Christians find themselves as they try to live out their faith and fulfil their vocation in their respective life circumstances" rather than from "the world of academia." It has been done from the "earliest moments" of Christian history, "though it has not always been acknowledged." Jesus as the incarnate Son of God is seen as one who "identified" "with the poor and the oppressed" and whose death, resurrection, and exaltation were scandalous but yet made *"God accessible to humanity"* and made *"men and women available to the kingdom of God."* The needed "fresh experience of Jesus Christ from within the harsh reality of the hurt, destitute, and marginated of the earth" must be verified as *"real"* and not distorted both from the New Testament and from "the transformation of the present situations of the oppressed."[324]

Costas's incarnational theology was strongly Trinitarian.

> The mission of the Father in the internal life of the Trinity is loving the Son. The mission of the Son is loving the Father. The mission of the Spirit is maintaining the bond of love between Father and Son. The . . .

---

[323] Antonio Carlos Barro, "Orlando Enrique Costas: Mission Theologian on the Way and at the Crossroads" (Ph.D. diss., Fuller Theological Seminary, 1993) 8-40; Costas, "Teólogo en la encrucijada," in *Hacia una teología evangélica latinoamericana: Ensayos en honor de Pedro Savage*, ed. Padilla (Miami: Editorial Caribe, 1984) 13-35; *Contemporary Authors* 101:123-24; 124: 89, new revision series, 82: 73-75; Anthony Christopher Smith, "The Essentials of Missiology from the Evangelical Perspective of the 'Fraternidad Teológica Latinoamericana'" (Ph.D. diss., Southern Baptist Theological Seminary, 1983; Ann Arbor, MI: University Microfilms International, 1985) 320-25.

[324] *Christ outside the Gate: Mission beyond Christendom* (Maryknoll NY: Orbis, 1982) 3-16.

Trinity can be described, therefore, as a holy community of love, a Tri-unity.

"The reconciling action of the Spirit" is "the power of evangelization," "the cross of Christ" is "the mediating sign of evangelization," and "the kingdom of God" is "the goal of evangelization."[325]

Sin is "disobedience to the lordship of God," "injustice" as "hatred and repudiation of the neighbor," and "unbelief" that "leads to idolatry." Sin is both "personal" and "corporate" or "structural." Costas could be quite specific. Latin America "is a continent conceived in sin" and "corrupted by idolatry" but also one "saturated with the message of salvation."[326] "The challenge that Bartolomé de Las Casas (1474–1566) posed to Spanish Christendom—that it was crucifying Christ anew by enslaving and oppressing the aboriginal population—is applicable to *all* European powers."[327]

Early in his writings Costas reviewed in detail and evaluated the recent developments in ecumenical missiology.[328] Likewise he evaluated the theologies of liberation. They have two advantages: they take "seriously man's concrete historical situation," and they emphasize "a service-oriented salvation and a salvation-oriented church." But their deficiencies are more numerous: their solitary "situational hermeneutic" has "dangerous consequences," their "Spirit-emptied Christology" is fallacious, their anthropology is neo-Pelagian, their "qualitatively defined salvation" leads to eschatological universalism, and their "unqualified open future" is too "vague."[329]

That Costas did not neglect the doctrine of the Holy Spirit is evidenced by Mark Richard McClellan's detailed comparison of his pneumatology

---

[325]*Liberating News: A Theology of Contextual Evangelization* (Grand Rapids MI: Eerdmans, 1989) 76-83.

[326]*Christ outside the Gate*, 21-26, 33-36.

[327]*Liberating News*, 106.

[328]*The Church and Its Mission: A Shattering Critique from the Third World* (Wheaton IL: Tyndale House; London: Coverdale House, 1974) 175-217, 265-301; *Theology of the Crossroads in Contemporary Latin America: Missiology in Mainline Protestantism, 1969–1974* (Amsterdam: Rodopi, 1976) 85-357.

[329]*The Church and Its Mission*, 240-64. See also *Christ outside the Gate*, 117-34. Carl F. H. Henry and Carl E. Braaten insisted on classifying Costas as a liberation theologian, but Howard A. Snyder, Barro, and Coy have more accurately concluded that his was "a thoroughly biblical theology of liberation" and "an evangelical political theology." Coy, "Incarnation and the Kingdom of God," 128-29.

with that of the Belgian-born Roman Catholic theologian in Brazil, José Comblín (1923–), both in the Latin American context.

> Costas presents the Holy Spirit as God in action, loving breath, energy, and liberating agency for the poor. The Spirit is moving the church toward the world in liberating service and holistic mission, reconciling all creation to God. There is a new spirituality, which is ethical and political.[330]

Roberto Gama utilized Costas, Padilla, and Escobar as exemplars of the model of the church as incarnation, both in regard to its nature as "a human-divine organism and its mission as ministry to the total man."[331] For Costas the mission of the church is "proclamation," "disciple making," "mobilization," "integral growth," "liberation," and "celebration."[332] He also interpreted and evaluated the Church Growth movement emanating from Fuller Theological Seminary. Positively, it has presented a "challenge to the missionary enterprise," offered "fresh insight into conversion, evangelism, and the church," and stimulated missiological studies. Negatively, it has "a shallow hermeneutic," its taking ecclesiology as its "theological 'locus'" is "questionable," its "concept of mission" is "truncated," and it "has overly depended on [the science of] anthropology" to the neglect of communication theory and other disciplines.[333]

Costas put more stress on the demands of the kingdom of God as to attitudes and actions than upon the blessings of the kingdom. He identified as kingdom practices for the Americas "affirming life and denouncing violence," "human solidarity and Christian unity," and "commitment to evangelism and church growth."[334] The signs of the kingdom include Christ, the

---

[330] "Pneumatology and Liberation in Latin America: An Analysis of the Nature and Work of the Holy Spirit in the Theologies of Orlando E. Costas and José Comblín" (Ph.D. diss., Southwestern Baptist Theological Seminary, 2000) abstract, iv.

[331] "The Concept of the Church as Expressed by Representative Latin American Theologians" (Th.D. diss., Southwestern Baptist Theological Seminary, 1977) 256-320, esp. 317.

[332] *Compromisa y Misión* (Miami: Editorial Caribe, 1979); E. T., *The Integrity of Mission: The Inner Life and Outreach of the Church* (New York: Harper & Row, 1979).

[333] *The Church and Its Mission*, 123-49.

[334] *Christ outside the Gate*, 91-98.

church, the struggles and conflicts of history, and "the poor and disenfranchised."³³⁵

Padilla, born in Quito, Ecuador, to poor Evangelical parents, spent his childhood in Colombia during the time of "the persecution of Protestants by Catholics," returned to Quito in his high school years, when he resisted the teaching of Marxist teachers and "began to preach over the radio, in jails, and on the streets." He spent six years (1953–1959) studying at Wheaton College (B.A., M.A.) and evangelizing Hispanic immigrants. From 1959 to 1963 Padilla was "traveling secretary for the International Fellowship of Evangelical Students . . . for . . . Venezuela, Colombia, Ecuador, and Peru," for which he would serve as associate general secretary for Latin America. Three years (1963–1966) went spent at the University of Manchester completing Ph.D. studies in New Testament under F. F. Bruce. Since moving in 1967 to Argentina, he directed *Ediciones Certeza* (1972–1981), "helped [to] found the Evangelical Theological Association in Buenos Aires," "helped to found and served as general secretary for FTL," led the KAIROS Fellowship in Buenos Aires, spoke at the 1974 Lausanne Congress on World Evangelization, was "founding editor of *Misión*," and has been pastor of La Lucila Evangelical Baptist Church in Buenos Aires.³³⁶

For Padilla evangelization and contextualization are interpenetrating realities. At Lausanne, after explaining the various uses of *kosmos* in the New Testament, he called for that separation from the world that differs from "secular Christianity," of which the (North) "American Way of Life" is a contemporary example, and that evangelism at the center of which is repentance and which results in Christian commitment to the neighbor and has "a social and political dimension."³³⁷ Padilla's exposition of the gospel included its fulfillment of Messianic expectation and its "not yet" fulfill-

---

³³⁵Barro, "Orlando Enrique Costas," 133-37.

³³⁶Coy, "Incarnation and the Kingdom of God," 254-56; Padilla, "siervo de la Palabra," in Padilla, ed., *Hacia una teología evangélica latinoamericana*, 113-20; Smith, "The Essentials of Missiology," 307-12.

³³⁷"Evangelism and the World," in *Let the Earth Hear His Voice: International Congress on World Evangelization, Lausanne, Switzerland*, ed. J. D. Douglas (Minneapolis: World Wide Publications, 1975) 116-46, esp. 116-29, 131, 130; repr. in *Mission between the Times* (Grand Rapids MI: Eerdmans, 1985) 1-44; S. T., *Misión integral: Ensayos sobre el Reino y la Iglesia* (Grand Rapids MI: Eerdmans, 1986).

ment, its being centered in the person and work of Jesus, and its reference to "a new soteriological order" that requires repentance and faith.[338]

> The incarnation unmistakably demonstrates God's intention to make himself known *from within* the human situation. Because of the very nature of the gospel, we know it only as a message contextualized in culture.

The interpreter of the Bible finds its difficult to free himself "from the influence of his own ecclesiastical tradition" and is greatly "conditioned by his culture." Latin American Christianity has yet to produce an indigenous theology, and contextualization should proceed in Africa and Asia as well. But evangelism and theology must not be divorced.[339]

"The authority of the Bible is derived from its connection with special revelation," the "essence" of which "is the redemptive action of God in the bosom of history." The acts of God are interpreted events. "In the New Testament the action of Christ is inseparable from apostolic doctrine," and "the authority of apostolic tradition depends on its connection with" Jesus' teaching. The Holy Spirit "energizes the objective truth of the Word." "I believe," declared Padilla, "in Jesus Christ because I believe in the authority of the Bible, and I believe in the authority of the Bible because I believe in Jesus Christ."[340] The needed biblical hermeneutic follows neither the "intuition" nor the "scientific" method but the "contextual," in which interpreters bring their "historical situation" and "world-and-life view" to the text.[341] Christian preaching rests on the scandalous particularity of revelation, on both "the historic facts of Christ and their apostolic interpreta-

---

[338]*Mission between the Times*, 62-82.

[339]"The Contextualization of the Gospel," *Journal of Theology for Southern Africa* no. 24 (September 1978): 13-30, esp. 12, 15, 20-24; repr. in *Readings in Dynamic Indigeneity*, ed. Charles H. Kraft and Tom N. Wisley (Pasadena CA: William Carey Library, 1979) 286-312; repr. in *Mission between the Times*, 83-109.

[340]"La autoridad de la Biblia en la teología latinoamericana," in *El debate contemporaneo sobre la Biblia* (Barcelona: Ediciones Evangelicas Europeas, 1972) 121-53.

[341]"Hermeneutics and Culture: A Theological Perspective," in *Down to Earth: Studies in Christianity and Culture: The Papers of the Lausanne Consultation on Gospel and Culture*, ed. Robert T. Coote and John R. W. Stott (Grand Rapids MI: Eerdmans, 1980) 63-78; repr. with modifications under title "The Interpreted Word: Reflections on Contextual Hermeneutics," *Themelios* 7 (September 1981): 18-23.

tion" and "on the contemporary proclamation of the Gospel in the power of the Holy Spirit."[342]

What kind of contextualized Christology did Padilla propose for Latin America? It should be, for Catholics as well as for Evangelicals, one with "no disjunction between the Jesus of history and the Christ of faith" and great emphasis on the complete humanity of Jesus. It should affirm that Jesus intended to present himself as "God's Messiah who . . . had come to inaugurate a new order in which God's rule of love and justice would be established in anticipation of the end." Padilla rejected Jon Sobrino's (1938–)[343] theory as to two stages in the ministry of Jesus: the kingdom and eschatological phase and the suffering Servant phase. Jesus, he argued, took up "a prophetic role" and was put to death as "a political rebel." Hence the church in Latin America needs to be prophetic, taking "'a preferential option for the poor'" and challenging "every dehumanizing power—be it militarism or consumerism, statism or materialism, legalism or hedonism."[344]

Spiritual warfare, for Padilla, against "principalities and powers" is not so much against suprahuman demons as against the "consumer society," "the offspring of technology and capitalism," by capitulation to which the church has made the gospel a product to be marketed.[345] Likewise, after examining the concept of the Antichrist in the New Testament, Padilla chose not to focus on its eschatological aspect but rather on the opposition to the gospel "between the resurrection and the second coming," whether as manifested in totalitarian government or a materialistic worldview. This Antichrist claims "to occupy the place that belongs exclusively to God,"

---

[342]"God's Word and Man's Words," *The Evangelical Quarterly* 53 (October-December 1981): 216-26.

[343]*Christology at the Crossroads: A Latin American Approach*, trans. John Drury (Maryknoll NY: Orbis, 1978) 58, 94, 362.

[344]"Toward a Contextual Christology from Latin America," in *Conflict and Context: Hermeneutics in the Americas: A Report on the Context and Hermeneutics in the Americas Conference Sponsored by Theological Students Fellowship and the Latin American Theological Fraternity, Tlayacapan, Mexico, November 24-29, 1983*, ed. Mark Lau Branson and Padilla (Grand Rapids MI: Eerdmans, 1986) 81-91.

[345]"Spiritual Conflict," in *The New Face of Evangelicalism: An International Symposium on the Lausanne Covenant*, ed. Padilla (London: Hodder & Stoughton; Downers Grove IL: InterVarsity, 1976) 205-21; repr. in *Mission between the Times*, 45-61.

seeks to "destroy the church either by . . . persecution from the outside" or by "error from within," and affords a "foretaste of the final manifestation of the Antichrist."[346]

Padilla reported on and celebrated the emergence of "grassroots ecclesial communities" in Roman Catholicism, especially in Brazil, which are gatherings of the poor that read the Scriptures "from below" and emphasize the priesthood of the laity and the prophetic mission of the church. This "new ecclesiology," he wrote in 1987, "has become the most powerful challenge to Protestant Christians in this region of the world."[347] Like Costas, Padilla offered a critique of the "homogeneous unit principle" of the Church Growth school but with a detailed New Testament study. In the apostolic age "each church was meant to portray *the oneness of its members* regardless of their racial, cultural, or social differences."[348] Padilla also called for partnership in mission in the postcultural age, a truly "universal church, in which all Christians are effectively involved in the world mission as equal members in the body of Christ."[349] The church belongs to the "already" aspect of the kingdom of God by being "the Messianic community" and "the community of the Spirit" and by being, along with the world, under the dominion of the kingdom and belongs to the "not yet" of the kingdom by being both "the heir" and "the sign" of the kingdom. Both are pertinent to the Latin American situation.[350]

Padilla engaged in his own demythologizing, that of the capitalist myth of "economic growth" and of the Marxist "myth of revolution," in order to "point to the kingdom of God, to the future that has already begun in Jesus

---

[346]"Christ and Antichrist in the Proclamation of the Gospel," *Theological Fraternity Bulletin* 1 (1981): 1-13; repr. in *Mission between the Times*, 110-28.

[347]"The New Ecclesiology in Latin America," *Evangelical Review of Theology* 11 (October): 336-54.

[348]"The Unity of the Church and the Homogeneous Unit Principle," *International Bulletin of Missionary Research* 6 (January 1982): 23-30, esp. 29; repr. in *Mission between the Times*, 142-69.

[349]"The Fullness of Mission," *Occasional Bulletin of Missionary Research* 3 (January 1979): 6-7, 9-11, esp. 9; repr. in *Mission between the Times*, 129-41.

[350]"The Kingdom of God and the Church," *Theological Fraternity Bulletin* 1 and 2 (1976): 1-23; repr.: "The Mission of the Church in Light of the Kingdom of God," *Transformation* 1 (January-March 1984): 16-20; "La mission de la iglesia a la luz del reino de Dios," *Misión* 5 (December 1986): 122-28; repr. in *Mission between the Times*, 186-99.

Christ, to the new creation that is taking shape in the womb of the old by the power of the Spirit."[351] But he also declared that the kingdom of God is mediated "through the practice of liberation" and "through the historic socialist project" as well as "through the church as the community of the Spirit."[352]

Escobar, born in Arequipa, "the Rome of Peru," educated in a British missionary school, and nurtured in the Peruvian Evangelical Church, was "converted and baptized in a Baptist church in Lima in 1951." At the historic University of San Marcos (M.A., 1956) he discovered the writings of John A. Mackay (1889–1963), Miguel de Unamuno, E. Stanley Jones, and Nicolas Berdyaev and participated in a Bible study group. In 1958 he met Padilla in Bolivia and traveled for the International Fellowship of Evangelical Students (IFES) in Argentina, Paraguay, Bolivia, and Uruguay. After brief stints in Argentina and Brazil (1960–1966), he was in doctoral studies at the University of Madrid (1966–1967). Returning "to Argentina in 1968, he became editor of *Certeza*, helped to found the FTL, and met John Howard Yoder. During 1973–1975 he was director of Inter-Varsity Fellowship for Canada in Toronto. Back in Latin America, he first did editorial work in Argentina (1975–1979) and was "regional secretary for the IFES" (1975–1979), and then, returning to Peru, served on the pastoral team of a Baptist church in Lima," and was president of the FTL (1970–1984). During recent years he has spent "six months each year" as professor of missiology at Eastern Baptist Theological Seminary, Philadelphia, and six months "teaching, writing, speaking in Peru and other Latin American countries."[353]

Escobar's contextualization has had a normative role for the Bible.

> An evangelical hermeneutics starts from a conviction about the basic unity of the text of the Bible. It refuses to begin by establishing polarities between the Old and New Testaments, between Gospel and epistle, between Jesus and Paul, between prophets of the left and kings of the right. . . . [It] does not separate a so-called 'factual core' from its interpretation. . . .[354]

---

[351]"God's Word and Man's Myths," *Themelios* 3 (September 1977): 3-9.

[352]"El reino de Dios y la historia en la teología latinoamericana," *Quadernos de Teología* 7 (1985): 5-12.

[353]Coy, "Incarnation and the Kingdom of God," 256-58; Escobar, "Heredero de la reforma radical," in Padilla, ed., *Hacia una teología evangélica latinoamericana*, 51-71; Smith, "The Essentials of Missiology," 304-307, 308.

[354]"Our Hermeneutic Task Today," in *Conflict and Context*, ed. Branson and

Bible translation and distribution have played a major role not only in the extension of Protestantism in Latin America and the more recent "Base Ecclesial Communities" among Roman Catholics but also in calling forth new indigenous Latin American theologies.[355] Discernment is needed to differentiate "Biblical content" from "Anglo-Saxon trappings" in Latin American theology.[356]

The Peruvian theologian, more fully than Costas or Padilla, gave attention to the Latin American historical context with its residual effect on the present. Whether the *real patronato*, by which the Spanish and Portuguese crowns controlled the Roman Catholic Church in their domains, or the long-term "Iberian-Anglo-Saxon confrontation," or the conditions conducive to the acceptance of Protestant Christianity, or the rapid growth of Pentecostalism, the "lessons from history" are to be remembered by today's theologians.[357] Escobar also refuted various contemporary theories as to the nature of Latin American Protestantism: the Catholic "conspiracy" theory that Protestants are agents of the CIA and U.S. imperialism, the theory of social scientists that it is "a force for modernization and democratization," and the Marxist theory that it is "an instrument of a new colonial pact." Instead he affirmed that it is a movement both religious and popular that "creates community" and "mobilizes people for mission"—a "surprising" "irruption of the poor."[358]

Escobar was keenly aware of John A. Mackay's identification of the "Creole Christ" or "Christ of Tangiers," who was depicted as either a babe in the arms of the Virgin Mary or as the bleeding victim of the cross, with

---

Padilla, 5, 6.

[355]"The Role of Translation in Developing Indigenous Theologies: A Latin American View," in *Bible Translation and the Spread of the Church the Last 200 Years*, ed. Philip C. Stine, Studies in Christian Mission 2 (Leiden: E. J. Brill, 1990) 81-94.

[356]"Biblical Content and Anglo-Saxon Trappings in Latin American Theology," *Occasional Bulletin from the Latin American Theological Fraternity* 3 (October 1972): 1-11.

[357]"The Church in Latin America after Five Hundred Years: An Evangelical Missiological Perspective," in *New Face of the Church in Latin America: Between Tradition and Change*, ed. Guillermo Cook, American Society of Missiology Series 18 (Maryknoll NY: Orbis, 1994) 21-37.

[358]"Conflict of Interpretations of Popular Protestantism,' in *New Face of the Church in Latin America*, ed. Cook, 112-34.

Missions, Ecumenism, and Globalization 643

its corresponding absence of the human and historical Jesus.[359] Indigenous Evangelical theology must be nondocetist and exhibit the fullness of Jesus' life and ministry, not merely an imported propositional Christology, whether Catholic or Protestant, and lead to social ethics and missiology.[360] Escobar emphasized the example of Christ, or *imitatio Christi*, somewhat under Anabaptist influence, finding the hope for Latin American churches to be in producing "'people like Jesus.'"[361] He likewise affirmed to North American university students that the risen Jesus is Lord of the universe and of history, not merely of the church, but that this lordship is paradoxical because of the simplicity of his advent, the reality of his suffering, and the fact that "his lordship is not entirely visible yet."[362] More recently he has written of the "missionary God" "who calls and sends," Christ as "God's best missionary," and the Holy Spirit in relation to "the growth of the church in numbers and depth."[363]

Like Costas, Escobar responded to the liberation theologies, but with less specific critique. The lack of a vigorous indigenous Evangelical theology helped to open the door to liberation theology. Evangelicals have their own *praxis* and should beware of Marxist *praxis*.[364]

Escobar was explicit about wrong conceptions of the kingdom of God: the Constantinian confusion of church and kingdom, dispensationalism's complete futurism, Marxist utopianism with a classless society, and the utopia of U.S. consumerism. He critiqued both socialism and capitalism; in comparison with Costas he was more critical of socialism and less strident

---

[359]"Evangelical Faith and the Theologies of Liberation," in *Liberation Thinking: An Evangelical Assessment*, ed. W. Dayton Roberts, MARC Resource Series 4 (Monrovia CA: World Vision International, 1987) 33-40.

[360]"Evangelical Theology in Latin America: The Development of a Missiological Christology," *Missiology* 19 (July 1991): 318-20. See also "El Cristo de Iberoamerica," in *¿Quien es Cristo hoy?*, 9-23.

[361]"Evangelical Theology in Latin America," 320-24.

[362]"Jesus Christ: Lord of the Universe," in *Jesus Christ: Lord of the Universe, Hope of the World*, ed. David M. Howard (Downers Grove IL: InterVarsity, 1974) 17-31.

[363]*The New Global Mission: The Gospel from Everywhere to Everyone* (Downers Grove IL: InterVarsity, 2003) 85-127 (esp. 86-90, 98-103, 124-26).

[364]"Beyond Liberation Theology: Evangelical Missiology in Latin America," *International Bulletin of Missionary Research* 6 (July 1982): 110-11; "Evangelical Faith and Theologies of Liberation," in *Liberation Thinking: An Evangelical Assessment*, ed. Roberts, 33-40.

against capitalism and consumerism. The church is "the sign of the kingdom," the "herald of salvation," "the way of incarnation," and "the way of the cross." For Escobar there is to be no revolutionary violence and no dichotomy between evangelism and social service, but, contra Costas, the poor do not have preferential entrance to the kingdom of God, and there are spiritually poor as well as economically poor.[365] The second coming of Christ is central to Escobar's theology, but he has been hesitant to conclude that missionary activity can accelerate its time.[366]

Mariano Avila, a Mexican Presbyterian, has found the social justice-oriented hermeneutic of the FTL theologians to be applicable to the contemporary Mexican situation and to the middle-class and upper-class evangelical "religiosity" developing in Latin America.[367] But Costas, Padilla, and Escobar were virtually silent about the Baptist distinctives.

Australia

Baptists in the Australian colonies during the nineteenth century, who derived from Particular Baptists much more than from General Baptists, had differences as to open and closed membership and open and strict communion. In South Australia open membership became the prevailing pattern. The influence of Charles H. Spurgeon through the graduates of his college was strong in Tasmania and New South Wales, and hence the pattern of close membership and open communion tended to prevail. Baptists had to defend their stance against pedobaptists. The Lord's Supper was generally understood in a memorialist or symbolic sense, and the term "ordinance" more common than "sacrament." Some Baptists held to Baptist historical succession, and Darwinian evolution and higher-critical approaches to biblical study produced tensions but not major divisions.[368]

---

[365]Coy, "Incarnation and the Kingdom of God," 202-20.

[366]"The Return of Christ," in Padilla, ed., *The New Face of Evangelicalism*, 255-64.

[367]"Towards a Latin American Contextual Hermeneutics: A Critical Examination of the Contextual Hermeneutics of the Fraternidad Teológica Latinoamericana" (Ph.D. diss., Westminster Theological Seminary, 1996) 240-58.

[368]Ken R. Manley, *From Wooloomooloo to 'Eternity': A History of Australian Baptists*, vol. 1., *Growing an Australian Church (1831–1914)*, Studies in Baptist History and Thought 16.1 (Milton Keynes UK, Waynesboro GA: Paternoster, 2006) 88, 103-104, 238-53, 277-85, 198, 382-89.

The Baptist Union of Victoria adopted in 1888 a nine-article Doctrinal Basis, which was a concise listing of basic Christian beliefs taken from the doctrinal statement of Australia's Evangelical Alliance,[369] in which only the ninth article on baptism and the Lord's Supper manifested distinctive Baptist theology.[370] The same union has also included in its constitution a nine-article statement entitled Principles and Ideals of the Baptist Faith.[371] Denying the need for infant baptism, it encouraged parental dedication of infants, defined conversion as the "acceptance of Jesus Christ as Saviour and Lord," and called for a converted church membership. Christ is the only Head and Lord of the church and of Christians. Baptists subscribe to no "formal Church Creed" and believe that "God has yet 'more light and truth to break forth from His Word.'" Functioning under congregational polity, the "Baptist minister" is to be "the spiritual leader" of the congregation, and "while he is a 'servant of the Church,' the Church is not his master." Those associated with him in "spiritual oversight" are specifically called deacons. Baptism "does not effect regeneration, and salvation is not dependent on it."

George Henry Morling (1891–1974), the principal of the Baptist Theological College of New South Wales (1923–1960), emphasized that the Holy Spirit is the Spirit of Christ, that "the baptism of the Spirit" occurs at conversion, that there is a contemporary gift of healing but not all are healed, that the gift of tongues, not given to all believers in the apostolic era, is to be treated today as it was in the New Testament, and that, having lost the fullness of the Spirit by resisting, grieving, or quenching the Spirit, believers are repeatedly to seek to be filled by the Spirit.[372]

Australian authors have recently produced significant theological monographs. The most substantive treatment of the resurrection of Jesus by any Baptist author has been that[373] by Thorwald Lorenzen (1936–).[374]

---

[369]Ibid., 206.

[370]Lumpkin, *Baptist Confessions of Faith*, 416-17.

[371]Ibid., 417-20.

[372]*Living with the Holy Spirit: Studies in the Holy Spirit*, comp. and ed. Bruce Thornton (Sydney: Morling Press, 2004) esp. 10-19, 52-56, 44-51, 64-70 (orig., Sydney: Baptist Union of New South Wales, 1972).

[373]*Resurrection and Discipleship: Interpretative Models, Biblical Reflections, Theological Consequences* (Maryknoll NY: Orbis, 1995; repr.: Eugene OR: Wipf and Stock, 2004). See also his *Resurrection–Discipleship–Justice: Affirming the Resurrection of Jesus Christ Today* (Macon GA: Smyth & Helwys, 2003).

[374]Born in Hamburg, Germany, and educated in the University of Sydney (B.A.,

Lorenzen began by rehearsing four modern theological models under which the resurrection has been interpreted: the "traditional" (C. F. H. Henry, W. Pannenberg), the "liberal" (R. Bultmann, J. Knox, D. F. Strauss, H. E. G. Paulus, R. Resch, D. Griffin), the "evangelical" (K. Barth, W. Künneth, E. Schillebeeckx), and the "liberation" (J. Moltmann, J. Sobrino). Secondly, he set forth the resurrection as "a foundational event" with attention to the action of God the Father, the appearances, the experience of the Holy Spirit, and the empty tomb. Thirdly, Lorenzen took up the multifaceted nature of faith in the risen Christ. Finally, writing vis-à-vis Christian discipleship, he spelled out the "consequence" of the resurrection for Christology, the doctrine of God, the doctrine of salvation, and the church and its mission. Lorenzen's book was highly evaluated by both Roman Catholic and Protestant reviewers. It is "a distinguished addition to exegetical and theological literature on the resurrection of Jesus" in which the author successfully "shows how resurrection faith can and should underpin Christian discipleship."[375] This "scholarly yet passionate study offers a wholesome combination of clarity and conviction," and its "discussion of 'experience, faith, praxis,' is distinctive."[376]

Ross Langmead (1949–), professor of missiology in Whitley College, Melbourne, has produced a detailed treatment of "incarnational mission" in which he has studied its diverse forms and argues for its viability. It means "following Jesus," "participation in Christ," and "joining God's incarnating mission." Langmead has investigated his theme as expressed by the Anabaptist/Mennonite tradition, by "radical evangelicals" such as Padilla, Costas, and Escobar, and by liberation theologians. Jürgen Moltmann serves as a bridge to expressions of sacramental incarnation (Roman Catholicism,

---

1965), Morling College (1962–1965), Baptist Theological Seminary, Rüschlikon, Switzerland (B.D., 1968; Th.M., 1969), and the University of Zürich (Th.D., 1971), Lorenzen was assistant professor of New Testament at Southeastern Baptist Theological Seminary, Wake Forest NC (1971–1974), associate professor (1974–1982) and professor (1982–1995) of systematic theology and ethics at Rüschlikon, and senior minister of Canberra Church, Canberra, Australia (1995–2005). Presently he is professor of theology in Charles Sturt University. Thorwald Lorenzen to James Leo Garrett, Jr., 12 October 2006.

[375]Gerald O'Collins, S.J., Review of Lorenzen, *Resurrection and Discipleship*, *Gregorianum* 78 (1997): 383.

[376]Luke Timothy Johnson, Review of Lorenzen, *Resurrection and Discipleship*, *Theological Studies* 57 (September 1996): 549, 550.

Anglo-Catholicism), God's mission to the whole of life (WCC), and Eucharistic participation with inculturation (Eastern Orthodoxy). Langmead has concluded that incarnational mission is especially suited to the secular, post-Christian, and postmodern society of contemporary Australia.[377]

Frank D. Rees (1950–), dean and professor of systematic theology at Whitley College, is the author of a monograph on the right use of doubt. Finding the approaches to doubt by John Henry Newman, Karl Barth, Harry A. Williams, and Val Webb to be less than satisfactory, he identifies with Paul Tillich's finding aspects of doubt with positive results. Adopting Walter Brueggemann's Old Testament concept of "a theology of divine conversation," Rees examines both questions asked by God and man's pleading, protest, and lament. The New Testament likewise is reviewed. Rees concludes that "faith can include doubt as well as belief" and that "doubt can help us to preserve faith as faith." Churches, therefore, should welcome the doubters.[378]

Asian Confessions and Monographs

Korea. The Korean Baptist Convention adopted in 1951 a sevenfold statement of Baptist propositions or distinctives: the final authority of the Bible, especially the New Testament; salvation through personal and convictional faith; the separation of church and state; autonomous congregationalism; cooperation through a national convention for more effective ministries of evangelism and missions; the priesthood and responsibilities of all believers; and baptism by immersion and the Lord's Supper.[379]

Professors in the Korean Baptist Theological Seminary have been recently productive of doctrinal monographs.[380] Hyunmoo Lee (1957–), professor of missiology, issued an introduction to missiology. He summed up the biblical basis, the theology, the history, cultural issues, contemporary strategies, and practical issues for the life and work of missionaries. The

---

[377]*The Word Made Flesh: Towards an Incarnational Missiology* (Lanham MD: University Press of America, 2004). Per Ken R. Manley. This was a Ph.D. dissertation at the Melbourne College of Divinity.

[378]*Wrestling with Doubt: Theological Reflections on the Journey of Faith* (Collegeville MN: Liturgical Press, 2001). Per Ken R. Manley.

[379]Samuel Byungdoo Nam to James Leo Garrett, Jr., 25 October 2005, 27 April 2006.

[380]Each of these summaries of the contents of the monographs has been written by the author himself, and they have been gathered by Samuel Byungdoo Nam.

author sought to intermingle Western missiological theories with perspectives from the Two-Thirds World.[381] Young-Cheol Park (1949–), professor of practical theology, wrote on the cell church phenomenon. He presented three principles as the theological background for the cell church: the Lordship of Christ, the ministry of every believer, and the church as the family of God. Then he explained how all groups should be organized and led, approaching the subject from theological, biblical, historical, and empirical perspectives.[382] Yong Gook Kim (1964–), assistant professor of church history, has produced a century-long history of Korean Baptist theology. Kim argued that the theology of the Korean Baptist denomination relied upon both missionary origins and Korean responses. He examined both the theologies of Korean Baptist pastors and theologians and the theologies of such missionaries as Malcolm C. Fenwick (1863–1935), the first foreign missionary to impact Korean Baptists,[383] and Albert Walter Gammage, Jr., (1929–2006), FMB-SBC missionary who significantly influenced Korean Baptist theology from 1959 to 1977. The book also dealt with the controversies about Fenwick's potential antinominianism and questionable Baptist identity.[384] A book on Korean Baptist hymnody from the 1890s to the 1950s by Nam Soo Kim (1954–), professor of music, contained frequent comments on the faith and doctrine of Fenwick.[385]

India. The various Baptist conventions in India that derive from the mission work of British Baptists, Northern (USA) Baptists, or Canadian Baptists have characteristically not adopted confessions of faith, although local churches have done so.[386] The Karnataka Baptist Convention of Churches, the product of the work of the FMB-SBC, adopted in 1976 an

---

[381] ET of Korean title: *Understanding Contemporary Christian Missions* (Daejeon, South Korea: Korea Baptist Theological Seminary Press, 2003).

[382] ET of Korean title: *Introduction to the Cell Church* (Seoul: Jordan Press, 2004).

[383] See *Baptists around the World*, ed. Wardin, 106.

[384] ET of Korean title: *A History of Korean Baptist Thought, 1889–1997* (Daejeon, South Korea: Korea Baptist Theological University/Seminary, 2005). This is a translation of the author's 2001 Ph.D. dissertation at Southern Baptist Theological Seminary.

[385] ET of Korean title: *A Study of Early Korean Baptist Hymnology: Gospel and Praise* (Daejeon, South Korea: Korea Baptist Theological University/Seminary Publication, 2005).

[386] Frederick S. Downs to James Leo Garrett, Jr., 25 August 2006.

abridged form of the 1963 SBC Baptist Faith and Message Statement with ten articles. The articles on God's purpose of grace, the kingdom of God, education, cooperation, the Christian and the social order, peace and war, and religious liberty were omitted. Also the section on repentance, faith, and justification was deleted. The incarnation was said to be "as the divine word," from the article on the Lord's Day was omitted "by refraining from worldly amusements," the righteous dwelling forever in heaven were not described as being "in their resurrected and glorified bodies," and from the article on evangelism was deleted the statement: "The birth of man's spirit by God's Holy Spirit means the birth of love for others."[387]

Philippines. The Baptist Conference of the Philippines adopted a concise but clearly worded twelve-article statement of faith. The Bible, it declared, is "fully inspired and without error in the original manuscripts," the Father is a merciful, prayer-answering God, the death of Jesus is "substitutionary," the church was defined first as universal and then as local, the closed or open communion issue was not addressed, and one general resurrection and one general judgment were affirmed.[388] In the Luzon Convention of Southern Baptist Churches, because of church growth methodologies and spiritual gifts, its 40 moderators and officers in consultation with the faculty of Philippine Baptist Theological Seminary, Baguio City, recently adopted an Affirmation of Unity. After reaffirming certain Baptist distinctives, it declared local church autonomy in respect to any methodologies that do not contravene the Scriptures, called for mutual respect between those with different views as to spiritual gifts, welcomed partnerships that do not "violate the standard functions of the convention," and appealed for Christian unity.[389]

Malaysia and Singapore. The Statement of Faith of the Malaysian Baptist Convention, adopted in 1981 after charismatic controversy,[390] was a slight alteration of the SBC's 1963 Baptist Faith and Message Statement. The major changes pertained to the Holy Spirit, education, and religious liberty. To the article on the Holy Spirit (2c) three additions were made: an

---

[387]"Karnataka Baptist Sabhegala Samaikya, Bangalore," 1-7. Per Brad Beaman.

[388]"Statement of Faith, Baptist Conference of the Philippines, Inc." Per Ildefonso Alfafara.

[389]*Luzon Convention of Southern Baptist Churches: Affirmation of Unity*, 1-2 June 2006, Baguio City. Per Precy Caronongan.

[390]Thomas Geoffrey Oey, *A History of the Baptists: From a Global, Asian Perspective* (Singapore: author, 1997; rev. ed. 2003) 67. Per Russell A. Morris.

affirmation that the baptism "with the Holy Spirit into the Body of Christ (1 Cor. 12:13)" occurs at conversion, an assurance that the Spirit will continue "to dwell in the believer as he matures," and a declaration that spiritual gifts "are to be exercised humbly and discreetly for the strengthening of the church and should never be exercised in such a way as to be divisive or destructive." The article on education (12) was entirely rewritten in order to change the focus from denominational educational institutions to the local church. From the article on religious liberty (17) two sentences on separation of church and state, two sentences on the imposition of penalties for religious opinions and of taxes for support of religion, and a half sentence on the right to religious opinions without civil interference were omitted so as to fit the needs in a predominantly Muslim nation. Other additions worthy of note are as follows: members of a church (6) "have equal rights and privileges," baptism (7) is to be "administered upon the authority of the local congregation," worldly amusements and secular employments are to be avoided on the Lord's Day (8) "in so far as possible," and contributions (13) are to be "through tithes and offerings." Changes included the deletion of a reference to laboring "that the kingdom may come" (9), the deletion of the word "heaven" (10), the change of "the new birth of man's spirit" to "the new birth of man" and "personal effort" to "personal witness" (11), the affirmation that missionary, educational, and benevolent ministries were to be done "in the Spirit of Christ" rather than "for the extension of Christ's kingdom" (14), and the declaration that "every Christian should seek to bring society as a whole under the sway of the principles of righteousness, truth, and brotherly love," not "industry, government, and society" (15).[391]

The Statement of Faith of the Singapore Baptist Convention, adopted in 1982,[392] was very similar to that of the Malaysia convention. Into the article on the Lord's Day (8) a new sentence was inserted: "It is a Christian principle based upon biblical teaching to encourage believers to meet together for regular worship, teaching of doctrines, fellowship, praying, and the observance of the ordinances," and a sentence was revised to read: "To enable members to participate in worship, resting from secular employments is encouraged." As to church members (6) "equal rights and privileges" became "equal rights, privileges, and responsibilities," members

---

[391]*Baptist Handbook* (Penang, Malaysia: Malaysia Baptist Convention, 1981) 1-30. Per Russell A. Morris.

[392]Oey, *A History of the Baptists*, 69.

through the Lord's Supper (7) were said to "proclaim" Christ's death, not to "remember and proclaim" it, and churches ought not to depend on civil government for "financial and/or human resources" (16). Added also was the statement: "The church will not receive directions from the civil power as to the attainment of its objectives" (16). The Singapore statement reverted at times to the language of the 1963 SBC confession: "to pray and to labour that the Kingdom may come" (9), a specific reference to "heaven" (10), "the new birth of man's spirit (11), no addition of "tithes and offerings" (13), and ministries "for the extension of Christ's Kingdom" (14). The article on education was reentitled "Equipping for Ministry" (12), with "training for recognised Christian leaders both independently and cooperatively" being shortened to "training for recognized leaders."[393]

Salvation of the Unevangelized?

Toward the end of the twentieth century the question of the final destiny of unevangelized human beings became an important and controversial issue in Christian theology, especially as a result of the greater confrontation with world religions. Three major positions were developed. Pluralists held that salvation is possible through non-Christian religions. Inclusivists held that salvation is only through Jesus Christ as the Logos but is attainable without special knowledge of the historical Jesus or an overt confession of faith. Exclusivists held that salvation comes only through Jesus Christ by an awareness of the Christian gospel and explicit faith in Christ. No Baptist seems clearly to have become a major exponent of pluralism, but Baptists have been exponents of inclusivism and exclusivism.

John N. Jonsson did not clarify whether he was an inclusivist or an exclusivist. Reporting the pluralist views of Alan Race and Paul Knitter and not taking sides in the John Hick-Lesslie Newbigin debate over theocentrism or Christocentrism, he noted that some Evangelical Christians were espousing exclusivism. He called for a transposition "away from detached, metaphysical constructs of Christo-orthodoxy" and was on the edge of syncretism by calling for the incorporation of "the diversities of our respective religions within a 'symphony' of common themes of human faith

---

[393]"Singapore Baptist Convention Baptist Statement of Faith," 4-5, 7, 5, 6, 5-6. Per Russell A. Morris.

and trust."³⁹⁴ But the uniqueness of the incarnation and the cruciality of Jesus' resurrection remained central for him.

Building on a "hermeneutic of hopefulness," that is, the universalist passages in both testaments, and the Logos doctrine of the early Greek fathers and deploring Augustine's interpretation of election as that of individuals and holding to the fewness of the saved, Clark Pinnock in *A Wideness of God's Mercy* espoused inclusivism. Avoiding "*relativism, universalism,* and *unitarianism,*" he retained a "high Christology" that necessarily includes the incarnation but without the fewness of those saved. Pinnock found both in Scripture and in the modern era evidence that there are false religions—"dark, deceptive, and cruel" and religions with elements of truth, notably, the line of "pagan saints" under the covenant of Noah. The latter "reflect to some degree general revelation and prevenient grace" but are not "ordinary ways of salvation." Pinnock did not hesitate to declare that religions "are caught up and involved in" the battle "between divine and demonic powers," but he also advocated "truth-seeking dialogue" that avoids both relativism and fideism and looked toward, with John Hick, "eschatological verification." "We hold out to the nations the coming feast of God, not the requirement of church membership." Pinnock advocated that form of postmortal evangelization that would enable the completion of "a faith decision already made on the basis of premessianic revelation" (cf. Job) and afford opportunity to those without opportunity but eventuate in judgment to those unwilling to change (cf. Herod and Hitler).³⁹⁵

Russell Foster Aldwinckle (1911–1992), a native of Leicester, England, was educated at the universities of London (B.A., history, 1932), Oxford (B.A., theology, 1936; M.A., 1948) and Strasbourg (Th.D., 1938), was pastor of Hearsall Church, Coventry (1939–1943) and North Finchley Church, London (1943–1947), and served for thirty years (1947–1977) as professor of systematic theology in McMaster Divinity College, Hamilton, Ontario. He chaired the Faith and Order Commission of the Canadian Council of Churches and was a member of the Faith and Order Commission of

---

³⁹⁴*Baptists and the Challenge of Inter-Faith Dialogue* (Waco TX: pvt. publ., 1997). This was a paper presented to the Commission on Doctrine and Inter-Church Cooperation, Baptist World Alliance, Hong Kong, July 1996.

³⁹⁵Subtitle: *The Finality of Jesus Christ in a World of Religions* (Grand Rapids MI: Zondervan, 1992) 20-35, 36, 43, 49-80, 85-106, 119-24, 129-38, 146, 168-75.

the WCC.³⁹⁶ Earlier the author of *Death in the Secular City*³⁹⁷ and *More than Man: A Study of Christology*³⁹⁸ and later of *The Logic of the Believing Mind*,³⁹⁹ in 1982 he authored *Jesus: A Savior or the Savior?*⁴⁰⁰

Disclaiming "methodological neutrality," Aldwinckle chose to deal with "the problem of religious pluralism" "from within the Christian faith." He sought "to defend the unique saviorhood of Christ while . . . leaving open the possibility of God's gracious activity in and through "non-Christian religions. In dialogue with contemporary Protestant and Roman Catholic theologians rather than with the Baptist community, he in probing the biblical doctrine of salvation found the issue of the salvation of modern Jews. The "uniqueness of the death of Jesus will depend upon the reality of God's action and presence of Jesus." Soteriology cannot be "developed in independence of" the incarnation. Whether Jesus' death was salvific "depends on how we consider the relation of Jesus to the Father and . . . on how we think of his person." Aldwinckle retained a penal element in the death of Jesus but not a personal Satan and connected Jesus' "unique saviorhood" with "the total facts of his life, and resurrection." Christians must accept "the scandal of particularity" vis-à-vis God's action in Christ. The McMaster professor explored evidences of divine grace in non-Christian religions. He agreed with John Hick that all humans will face "the God and Father of our Lord Jesus Christ" in judgment. He agreed with Karl Rahner that "the triune God of Christian faith" is involved in "universal salvific activity" but rejected Rahner's conclusion that physical death terminates the opportunity for salvation. Not clearly espousing inclusivism but leaning toward it, Aldwinckle sought to resolve the issue by affirming the possibility of salvation after death and by flirting with annihilationism.⁴⁰¹

---

³⁹⁶Curriculum Vitae, McMaster Divinity School. Per Sean A. Adams.

³⁹⁷Subtitle: *A Study of the Notion of Life after Death in Contemporary Theology and Philosophy* (London: Allen & Unwin, 1972; Grand Rapids MI: Eerdmans, 1974).

³⁹⁸(Grand Rapids MI: Eerdmans, 1976).

³⁹⁹Toronto Studies in Theology 60 (Lewiston NY: Edwin Mellen, 1995).

⁴⁰⁰Subtitle: *Religious Pluralism in Christian Perspective* (Macon GA: Mercer University Press, 1982).

⁴⁰¹Ibid., 2, 7, 3, 7, 19-36, 68, 107-109, 120, 92, 124, 149-72, 182, 183, 210, 183.

The published dissertation[402] of Molly Truman Marshall (1949–) on the Cyprianic formula *Extra ecclesiam nulla salus* pertained to the destiny of the unevangelized. A native of Oklahoma and a graduate of Oklahoma Baptist University (B.A., 1973) and Southern Baptist Theological Seminary (M.Div., 1976; Ph.D., 1983). She taught theology at Southern from 1984 until she was compelled to resign in 1994 because women could no longer be permitted to teach pastors to be and perhaps for alleged deviations from the Abstract of Principles. She then taught theology and spiritual formation at Central Baptist Theological Seminary from 1995 to 2004 and became president of Central in 2005.[403] After analyzing the exclusivist view of Emil Brunner, the inclusivist view of Karl Rahner, and the relativist (that is, pluralist) view of John Hick,[404] Marshall expressed her own view as being nearer that of Rahner. Post-mortal evangelization is possible. Christ is at work in non-Christian religions. Salvation is available primarily through the church, but the church is "representative rather than constitutive of salvation." A negative response is to be given to the Cyprianic formula, and it is not to be understood in the exclusive Roman Catholic sense or applied to the sum total of constituted churches.[405]

The exclusivist position was clearly stated and defended by Ronald Herman Nash (1936–2000). A native of Cleveland, Ohio, and a graduate of Barrington College (B.A., 1958), Brown University (M.A., 1960), and Syracuse University (Ph.D., 1964), Nash taught philosophy at Western Kentucky University from 1964 to 1991 and philosophy of religion in Reformed Theological Seminary, Orlando, Florida, from 1991 to his death.[406] He was the author or editor of at least twenty-five books. His philosophical writings included an introduction to philosophy[407] and treatments of world

---

[402] *"No Salvation outside the Church?" A Critical Inquiry*, NABPR Dissertation Series 9 (Lewiston NY: Edwin Mellen Press, 1993).

[403] "Molly T. Marshall: President and Professor of Theology and Spiritual Formation," Central Baptist Theologcial Seminary <http://www.cbts.edu/pdf/President%20Bio.pdf>; Pamela R. Durso, "Molly Marshall: A Woman of Faith and Courage," *Whitsitt Journal* 12 (Spring 2004): 1, 3-7; <http://www.abpnews.com/115.article>.

[404] *"No Salvation outside the Church?" A Critical Inquiry*, 79-194.

[405] Ibid., 208, 223-25, 229-30, 231, 233. Marshall also authored *What It Means to Be Human* (Macon GA: Smyth & Helwys, 1995) and *Joining the Dance: A Theology of the Spirit* (Valley Forge PA: Judson Press, 2003).

[406] *Who's Who in Religion*, 4th ed. (1992–1993) 373.

[407] *Life's Ultimate Questions: An Introduction to Philosophy* (Grand Rapids MI:

Missions, Ecumenism, and Globalization 655

views and faith and reason,[408] the nondependence of the New Testament on Greek philosophy and religion,[409] the epistemology of Augustine of Hippo[410] and of Gordon H. Clark,[411] and the philosophy of Herman Dooyeweerd.[412] Nash focused on a philosophy or theology of history.[413] His socio-ethical writings pertained to justice and poverty and to capitalism, socialism, and interventionism.[414] He wrote repeatedly about Evangelicalism.[415] Theologically Nash edited and coauthored books about liberation theolo-

---

Zondervan, 1999).

[408] *The Word of God and the Mind of Man* (Grand Rapids MI: Zondervan, 1982); *Faith and Reason: Searching for a Rational Faith* (Grand Rapids MI: Zondervan, 1988); *Worldviews in Conflict: Choosing Christianity in a World of Ideas* (Grand Rapids MI: Zondervan, 1992).

[409] *Christianity and the Hellenistic World* (Grand Rapids MI: Zondervan; Dallas: Probe, 1984); under title, *The Gospel and the Greeks: Did the New Testament Borrow from Pagan Thought?* (Dallas: Probe, 1992); 2nd ed. (Phillipsburg NJ: Presbyterian and Reformed, 2003).

[410] *The Light of the Mind: St. Augustine's Theory of Knowledge* (Lexington: University Press of Kentucky, 1969).

[411] "Gordon Clark's Theory of Knowledge," in *The Philosophy of Gordon H. Clark: A Festschrift*, ed. Nash (Philadelphia: Presbyterian and Reformed, 1968) 125-75.

[412] *Dooyeweerd and the Amsterdam Philosophy* (Grand Rapids MI: Zondervan, 1962).

[413] (ed.) *Ideas of History* (New York: E. P. Dutton, 1969); *Christian Faith and Historical Understanding* (Grand Rapids MI: Zondervan; Dallas: Probe, 1984); *The Meaning of History* (Nashville: Broadman & Holman, 1998).

[414] *Freedom, Justice and the State* (Lanham MD, London: University Press of America, 1980); *Social Justice and the Christian Church* (Milford MI: Molt Media, 1983); *Poverty and Wealth: The Christian Debate over Capitalism* (Westchester IL: Crossway, 1986); under subtitle *Why Socialism Doesn't Work* (Richardson TX: Probe, 1992).

[415] *The New Evangelicalism* (Grand Rapids MI: Zondervan, 1963); *Evangelicals in America: Who They Are, What They Believe* (Nashville: Abingdon, 1987); (ed.) *Evangelical Renewal in the Mainline Churches* (Westchester IL: Crossway, 1987); *Why the Left Is Not Right: The Religious Left: Why They Are and What They Believe* (Grand Rapids MI: Zondervan, 1996).

gy[416] and process theology[417] and wrote on the attributes of God,[418] recent theological and ethical controversies,[419] and the destiny of infants dying in infancy.[420]

In *Is Jesus the Only Savior?*[421] Nash refuted at length John Hick's pluralism, especially his "Copernican revolution" in turning from Christocentrism to theocentrism, his effort to "grade" the salvific dimensions of non-Christian religions, and his reckoning the incarnation as "myth" and rejecting the two natures of Christ. He refuted the inclusivism of Evangelicals such as John Sanders and Clark Pinnock and of the Roman Catholic Karl Rahner, contending that various texts in Acts cited by inclusivists do not support their case and that the "all men" and "whole world" texts can be understood as "all humans *without distinction*" rather than all humans "*without exception.*" More briefly Nash built his case for exclusivism around Romans 1–3, 10:9-10, John 14:6, and Acts 4:12. Nash also undertook refutation of postmortal evangelization.[422] In a debate with Sanders as an inclusivist and Gabriel Fackre as a proponent of postmortal evangelization, Nash held that neither of these positions can adequately deal with "the pesky problem of Christian missions."[423]

Textbook on Missiology

At the end of the twentieth century professors of missions in the seminaries of the SBC, together with other missiologists, issued a 42-chapter textbook on missiology which embraced the biblical and theological foundations, the history of missions, non-Christian religions, and missionary strategies. Justice C. Anderson traced the origin and meaning of the term "missiology"

---

[416](ed.) *Liberation Theology* (Milford MI: Molt Media, 1984); Humberto Belli and Nash, *Beyond Liberation Theology* (Grand Rapids MI: Baker, 1992).

[417](ed.) *Process Theology* (Grand Rapids MI: Baker, 1987).

[418]*The Concept of God* (Grand Rapids MI: Zondervan, 1983).

[419]*Great Divides: Understanding the Controversies that Come between Christians* (Colorado Springs CO: NavPress, 1993).

[420]*When a Baby Dies: Answers to Comfort Grieving Parents* (Grand Rapids MI: Zondervan, 1999). This book contains an account of Nash's trek from Arminianism to Calvinism (87-92).

[421](Grand Rapids MI: Zondervan, 1994).

[422]Ibid.

[423]Nash, "Restrictivism," in *What about Those Who Have Never Heard? Three Views on the Destiny of the Unevangelized*, ed. John Sanders (Downers Grove IL: InterVarsity, 1995) 107-39, esp. 134-36.

and surveyed missiology as an academic discipline closely allied with theology. Acknowledging that there have been various stated purposes of missions, Gerald David Wright (1949–) employed light as the unifying theme of a purpose statement. According to G. William Schweer (1926–) the missionary mandate derives from the one purposeful God—the Father, who is spirit, light, and love, the Son, and the Holy Spirit. For James Samuel Simmons (1951–), sin is the great "barrier" between God and humanity that calls for divine salvation, and salvation is the "great bridge between God and humanity." Similarly Millard J. Erickson spelled out the universality and dire consequences of human sin and the inadequacy of implicit faith, postmortal evangelism, and annihilationism. According to Ronald D. Rogers (1951–) the missionary purpose of the church is manifested through the leading New Testament metaphors for the church and includes both evangelistic mandate and the culture mandate, with priority on the former. Daniel Raul Sanchez (1936–) traced the discussions about contextualization from the 1960s. While allowing for both the "formal correspondence" and the "dynamic equivalence" methods in Bible translation, he opted for Padilla's "dialogical model" rather than the "dialectical model" of liberation theologians in contextualization.[424]

Carver, who occupied the first Baptist chair of missions, defined missions as the realization of God's saving purpose and the extension of his kingdom through human messengers. Early on he saw missions as the work of individuals and societies more than of churches. Its textbook is the Bible, and the Bible is a missionary book that sets forth the plan of the ages. Being between liberalism and orthodoxy, Carver seemed to allow for some revelation in non-Christian religions. A participant in the Faith and Order movement, he opposed organic church union but emphasized the universal church.

---

[424]*Missiology: An Introduction to the Foundations, History, and Strategies of World Missions*, ed. John Mark Terry, Ebbie C. Smith, and Justice C. Anderson (Nashville: Broadman & Holman, 1998) esp. 1-29, 97-113, 129-65, 114-28, 318-33. On the biblical foundations, see also Francis Marquis DuBose (1922–), *God Who Sends: A Fresh Quest for Biblical Mission* (Nashville: Broadman, 1983) and Roger Eugene Hedlund (1935–), *Mission to Man in the Bible* (Madras, India: Evangelical Literature Service for Church Growth Research Center, 1985); repr. under title *The Mission of the Church in the World: A Biblical Theology* (Grand Rapids MI: Baker Book House, 1991).

Most unions in Europe have adopted confessions of faith, often to be presented to civil authorities but not to be used as coercive creeds. The majority began with the Bible and affirmed its inspiration and supreme authority. They were Trinitarian but with little explication and affirmed both the deity and humanity of Jesus. The *imago Dei* was affirmed but not clearly interpreted. By Adam's fall all his descendants have inherited a fallen nature, but guilt comes only with actual sinning. Election was not emphasized, but sanctification was, and only the Romanian confession taught apostasy. Much attention was given to ecclesiology: both universal church and local church, congregational polity, church discipline, members as equal in rights and obligations, baptism as single immersion in the name of the Father, the Son, and the Spirit at the time of conversion, and the Lord's Supper as a symbolic memorial. The Lord's Day and marriage were defined, and eschatology was not specifically millennialist except in the Soviet Union.

English Baptists, after having worked closely with other Free Churches in Britain, did not follow Shakespeare, their leader, in his advocacy of organic church union but helped to found and became a member body of the WCC. Northern (USA) Baptists joined both the Federal and the World Councils, as did three African-American conventions and a few conventions on each of the continents. Southern (USA) Baptists, on the other hand, after initial openness to interdenominational discussion and the Faith and Order and Life and Work movements, decided not to join either the Federal, the World, or the later National Council. Payne became the leading British advocate of conciliar ecumenism, Roberts-Thomson took a strong stand in its favor, and Estep articulated the case for nonmembership in councils of churches. Because of contrary views among Baptists, the BWA did not encourage an invitation to send official observers to Vatican Council II, but more recently the BWA has participated in several bilateral dialogues with other world confessional bodies.

Graham, the best-known and most widely traveled Christian evangelist during the twentieth century, early made a life-determining commitment to biblical inspiration and authority. Sin, Satan, guilt, the new birth, the Holy Spirit, and angels were emphasized in his sermons and writings. His earlier dispensationalism has been less emphasized in later years, and he has not been closed to some possible postmortal evangelization. Criticized both by the liberal and neoorthodox left and by the fundamentalist and Calvinist right, Graham has embodied and fostered a vibrant evangelicalism throughout the world.

Cox began by celebrating secularization and urbanization and setting forth his own version of liberation theology with sloth or apathy as the central definition of sin. Calling for churches to be more politically and socially active and prematurely pronouncing on the collapse of traditional Christian religion, he then wrote on Eastern religions, encouraging interreligious dialogue and not being precise as to soteriological pluralism or inclusivism, encouraged a postliberal theology, and defended Boff, the Brazilian Catholic. Finally, he offered a sympathetic account of world Pentecostalism as a notable example, contrary to his own earlier dire assessment, of religious renaissance.

Roberts's work as an Afro-American coincided with the advent of black theology, which he defined as "soul theology" growing out of a unique spiritual experience. It needs to address God's attributes, providence and suffering, sin as personal and social, and Jesus as the one who suffered for our redemption. Roberts was emphatic that liberation and reconciliation must be joined together and that reconciliation is a two-way street. Blacks are not the "chosen people," and Jesus was not literally a black Messiah, but he can be symbolically.

Imasogie interpreted ATR as "bureaucratic monotheism" and attempted a proper Christian apologetical method that would address the West African context—both culture and worldview. This would be contextualization without imparting European/North American theology and without syncretism. Thus Christ is Victor, Liberator, and Cosmic Lord, and the Holy Spirit and prayer are available to Christians. A fellow Nigerian severely criticized Imasogie's method. Jonsson, while defending the historicity of Jesus' resurrection, posited an incarnational theology in which Jesus identifies with oppressed humanity and makes evident human worth and dignity. He advocated as a hermeneutical principle "retranspositionalization," or a movement from the abstract to the traumatically particular. Parnell restated Baptist emphases and made a place for the private exercise of tongues-speaking.

Brazilian Baptists first utilized the New Hampshire confession and later adopted a modification of the SBC's 1963 Baptist Faith and Message Statement after internal controversy over Pentecostal teachings and practices had resulted in the formation of a second and more charismatic national convention. Mexican Baptists have been affected by Landmarkism, ecumenism, and charismaticism and have modified the two English-language confessions mentioned above. Some Landmark influence has survived, and ecumenism was rejected, but charismaticism did not produce a major division.

In Argentina, however, charismaticism has twice produced major controversies. First, in response to the Spiritual Restoration Movement, the Argentine convention adopted modifications of the 1963 SBC text, first in 1968 and later in 1987. Second, in response to the Unction Movement, the convention issued documents concerning unction and about Baptist distinctives, but in 2005 antiunction Baptists formed another national body.

Costas, Padilla, and Escobar, fellow members of the FTL, wrote as missiologists in behalf of an indigenous and contextualized Latin American Evangelical theology. They stressed the authority and unity of the Bible, a functional Christology that focused on Jesus' humanity, life, ministry, and identification with the poor and oppressed, the kingdom of God as both inaugurated and not yet consummated, and the second coming of Christ. Evangelism is joined with theology and with social action. Critiques were offered as to the consumer society of North America, ecumenical missiology, liberation theologies, and the Fuller church growth school.

Influenced by English roots, Australian Baptists struggled over communion and membership issues. In Victoria a confession was framed and adopted in 1888. Recently, important monographs have been written on Jesus' resurrection, incarnational mission, and doubt.

In South Korea, likewise, recent monographs have been issued on missiology, the cell church phenomenon, and the history of Korean Baptist theology. A few Baptist bodies in India and the Philippines adopted confessions of faith. The Malaysian and Singapore conventions adopted revisions of the 1963 SBC text.

On the destiny of the unevangelized Jonsson was not clear as to whether he opted for inclusivism or exclusivism, Pinnock developed a detailed defense of inclusivism, Aldwinckle affirmed possible postmortal salvation and inclined toward inclusivism, Marshall was close to Rahner's inclusivism, and Nash set forth a vigorous defense of exclusivism.

At the end of the twentieth century Southern Baptist missiologists issued a comprehensive textbook.

Chapter 13

New Voices in Baptist Theology

At the beginning of the twenty-first century Baptists, especially in the Anglo-American orbit, are abundantly blessed with a body of younger writing theologians, all of whom were born after World War II and who were having an impact as the new century began. The majority of these had a clear Baptist identity, inclined more to Calvinism than to Arminianism, were more conservative or evangelical than liberal, and were academic theologians rather than pastoral theologians.

John Stephen Piper:
Edwardsean Theology of Christian Hedonism

No Baptist theologian, it seems, has been so shaped and influenced by the life and writings of Jonathan Edwards, Sr. as has John Piper. Born in Chattanooga, Tennessee, to an itinerant evangelist and his wife and reared in Greenville, South Carolina, he was educated at Wheaton College (B.A., 1968), Fuller Theological Seminary (B.D., 1971), and the University of Munich (Th.D., 1974). After serving as associate professor of Biblical Studies in Bethel College (1974–1980), he became senior pastor (now called pastor for preaching) of Bethlehem Church (BGC), Minneapolis, Minnesota, and continues in that role. He is the author of more than thirty books and has coedited two.[1] His dissertation pertaining to Jesus' commandment to love one's enemies found selective usage of similar material from the preceding Jewish and Hellenistic sources in the similar exhortations in the New Testament epistles, but that the latter rested principally on Jesus' own command, even though the gospel and epistolary traditions were different.[2]

There is a sense in which Piper's theology consists of only one doctrine: the doctrine of God. It is the supremacy and the glory of God, even more than his sovereignty, that is central to Piper's theology. In a "historical-grammatical exegesis of Rom. 9:1-23," he concluded that the

---

[1] Curriculum Vitae, Desiring God Ministries. Per Bruce H. Leafblad. Piper was introduced to Edwards's thought by Daniel Payton Fuller at Fuller Theological Seminary.

[2] *"Love Your Enemies": Jesus' Love Command in the Synoptic Gospels and in the Early Christian Paranesis: A History of the Tradition and Interpretation of Its Uses* (Cambridge: Cambridge University Press, 1979) esp. 17-18, 63-65, 171-75.

apostle Paul was not undertaking a formal theodicy for the divine predestination of some Israelites, which would be putting God "in the dock," but rather was declaring God's righteousness in the sense of "his unswerving commitment always to preserve the honor of his name and display his glory" through double predestination.[3] Christopher Jay Shirley has offered a searching critique of Piper's exegesis: it ignores Rom. 9:24-29 as well as chapters 10 and 11, it fails "to include Paul's argument for salvation by faith" and his "argument for individual responsibility," it ignores the eschatology of Rom. 11:28-32, and it fails to link Romans 9–11 and Romans 1–4. For Shirley, Romans 9–11 is "not a polemic on the righteousness of God in double predestination, but a profound statement on the righteousness of God in his eschatological election of a people to be his own."[4]

Piper produced a passionate monograph on the supremacy of God in missions.

> Missions is not the ultimate goal of the church. Worship is. Missions exists because worship doesn't. Worship is ultimate, not missions, because God is ultimate, not man. When this age is over, . . . missions will be no more. It is a temporary necessity. But worship abides forever.
> Worship, therefore, is the fuel and goal of missions.[5]

The God who is zealous for his glory would share that zeal with believers. Such zeal, together with "a servant spirit and a heart of mercy," motivates for world missions. Prayer is "God's instrument to *release* the power of the gospel," and God uses suffering and martyrdom in the mission to the nations. Piper defended the doctrine of hell against universalism and annihilationism and asserted the necessary proclamation and hearing of the gospel that centers in the name of Jesus. He was aware of the missiological shift to people groups.[6]

Likewise, in preaching God must be made supreme. Preaching's "goal" is "the glory of God," its "ground" is "the cross of Christ," and its "gift" is

---

[3] *The Justification of God: An Exegetical and Theological Study of Romans 9:1-23* (Grand Rapids MI: Baker, 1983; 2nd prtg., 1993) 1st prtg., 69-79, 201-205; 2nd prtg., 91-101, 217-20.

[4] "The Righteousness of God in Romans 9–11: A Critique of John Piper's *The Justification of God*" (M.A. in Theol. Thesis, Southwestern Baptist Theological Seminary, 2003) esp. 45-62.

[5] *Let the Nations Be Glad! The Supremacy of God in Missions* (Grand Rapids MI: Baker, 1993, also 2nd rev. ed., 2003) 1st ed., 11.

[6] Ibid., 2nd ed., 22-28, 33-35, 45-69 (esp. 64), 71-154, 157-67.

"the power of the Holy Spirit." "Gravity" and "gladness" are to be interwoven. Edwards, Piper insisted, provides superb guidance for preaching that makes God supreme.[7]

Piper held up, despite their flaws, as examples men who lived under sovereign grace and sovereign joy: Augustine of Hippo, Martin Luther, and John Calvin.[8] He held up Edwards for his "God-entranced vision of all things," with the dual theses: joy is at the heart of what it means for *God* to be God-glorifying" and "joy is at the heart of what it means for *us* to be God-glorifying." Then, using Edwards's own words, Piper answered modern objections to such a vision.[9] Piper republished the entire text of Edwards's *The End for Which God Created the World*, that is, the glory of God, together with his own reflection about Edwards.[10]

Motivated by Henry Scougal's (1650–1678) *The Life of God in the Soul of Man* (1677),[11] Piper wrote a book about the good news of God's gladness in being God," which at the same time was "a passionate defense of the freedom of grace." He spelled out the pleasure of God in Jesus his Son, in all his works, including creation and election, in the fame of his name, in the death of Jesus, in doing good for believers, in the prayers of the upright, and in personal obedience and public justice.[12] Likewise Piper wrote of the gospel as the very gift of God himself.[13]

In response to Robert H. Gundry's (1932–) call in 2001 for the abandonment of the doctrine of the imputation of Christ's righteousness, Piper

---

[7]*The Supremacy of God in Preaching* (Grand Rapids MI: Baker, 1990; rev. ed., 2004).

[8]*The Legacy of Sovereign Joy: God's Triumphant Grace in the Lives of Augustine, Luther, and Calvin*, book 1 of *The Swans Are Not Silent* (Wheaton IL: Crossway, 2000).

[9]"A God-Entranced Vision of All Things: Why We Need Jonathan Edwards 300 Years Later," in *A God Entranced Vision of All Things: The Legacy of Jonathan Edwards*, ed. Piper and Justin Taylor (Wheaton IL: Crossway, 2004) 21-34.

[10]*God's Passion for His Glory: Living the Vision of Jonathan Edwards . . .* (Wheaton IL: Crossway, 1998).

[11]*The Life of God in the Soul of Man*, ed. with a historical intro. by Winthrop S. Hudson (Philadelphia: Westminster, 1948; repr.: Classics of Devotion series, Minneapolis: Bethany Fellowship, 1976).

[12]*The Pleasures of God* (Portland OR: Multnomah, 1991; rev. ed., with subtitle *Meditations on God's Delight in Being God*, 2000).

[13]*God Is the Gospel: Meditations on God's Love as the Gift of Himself* (Wheaton IL: Crossway, 2005).

wrote a refutation, chiefly exegetical in nature, in defense of the doctrine. Gundry would limit the language of imputation to "'the imputation of our sins to Christ'" and to "'the counting of faith as righteousness'" and affirmed that faith *per se* "'*is* our righteousness.'" Gundry had come to his position by defining justification in terms of redemption as "'liberation from the slavery to sin.'" Piper, building his exegetical case from texts in the Pauline epistles, sought to demonstrate that Paul taught the imputation of the righteousness of Christ, which he "accomplished by his perfect obedience in life and death" with faith having an instrumental role. Such a doctrine of justification is "a mighty antidote to despair" for Christians and "bestows on Jesus Christ the fullest honor that he deserves."[14] Piper quite clearly has understood the death of Christ in terms of penal substitution,[15] but he has also interpreted the cross in terms of ransom,[16] demonstration of God's love,[17] reconciliation,[18] and example.[19]

How, according to Piper, ought believing humans to respond to the supremacy of God? First, he set forth a case for Christian hedonism, not in the sense of a "means to help us get worldly pleasures" or as a "'general theory of *moral justification*,'" but as the meaning of the opening statement of the Westminster Shorter Catechism when one word has been altered: "The chief end of man is to glorify God *by* enjoying him forever." Piper also posited that "God is more glorified in me when I am most satisfied in him" and applied Christian hedonism to conversion, worship, love, the Bible, prayer, money, marriage, missions, and suffering.[20] In addition he wrote for those who struggled for joy.[21]

---

[14]*Counted Righteous in Christ: Should We Abandon the Imputation of Christ's Righteousness?* (Wheaton IL: Crossway, 2002) 44-47, 53-119, 41, 124, 125.

[15]*The Passion of Jesus Christ: Fifty Reasons Why He Came to Die* (Wheaton IL: Crossway, 2004) 20-21, 32-33, 40-43, 70-71.

[16]Ibid., 34-35, 74-75, 108-109.

[17]Ibid., 30-31.

[18]Ibid., 60-61.

[19]Ibid., 92-93.

[20]*Desiring God: Meditations of a Christian Hedonist* (Portland OR: Multnomah, 1986, 1996, 2003) esp. 20, 15, 23, 9. For a condensation, see *The Dangerous Duty of Delight* (Sisters OR: Multnomah, 2001).

[21]*When I Don't Desire God: How to Fight for Joy* (Wheaton IL: Crossway, 2004).

In a book on the afflictions endured by three Christian leaders Piper illustrated how God designs affliction and how "the furnace of suffering" in these cases has "brought forth the gold of guidance and inspiration." John Bunyan had twelve years of "voluntary" imprisonment for preaching the gospel, William Cowper (1731–1800), hymn writer and poet, battled life-long depression and contemplated suicide, and David Brainerd (1718–1747), missionary to American Indians, died of tuberculosis at 29.[22]

The Minneapolis pastor enjoined fasting as "the hunger of a homesickness for God." Warning that there are dangers to fasting, especially spiritual dangers such as being seen by others (Matt. 6:16), he nevertheless pointed out that fasting is not a good work, or pay back, but a "gift of God." It is to be for God's glory, and the reward for fasting is God himself.[23]

As examples of Christian perseverance Piper studied John Newton (1725–1807) for his gratitude for the grace and providence of God, Charles Simeon (1759–1836) for his faithfulness after humiliation at Cambridge and failing health, and William Wilberforce (1759–1833) for endurance for the cause of the abolition of the slave trade and of slavery.[24]

Charging in 2002 that pastors "are being killed by the professionalizing of the pastoral ministry" and warning that the "rise of radical Islam" has ruined "professional pastoral politeness" and wrecked "relativistic pluralism," Piper called for renewed preaching of the "dishonorable, foolish, gruesome, and utterly glorious" cross of Christ and then proceeded to revisit many of his favorite themes.[25]

In 2005 Piper led the council of twenty-four elders of Bethlehem Church to recommend to the church the revision of its constitution so as to allow for a form of open membership. While rejecting baptismal regeneration and any who espouse such as candidates for church membership, the new policy would permit believers who conscientiously hold to their infant

---

[22] *The Hidden Smile of God: The Fruit of Affliction in the Lives of John Bunyan, William Cowper, and David Brainerd*, book 2 of *The Swans Are Not Silent* (Wheaton IL: Crossway, 2001) esp. 20-24, 19, 12, 9.

[23] *A Hunger for God: Desiring God through Fasting and Prayer* (Wheaton IL: Crossway, 1997) esp. 14, 126, 176-77, 179-80, 77-78.

[24] *The Roots of Endurance: Invincible Perseverance in the Lives of John Newton, Charles Simeon, and William Wilberforce*, book 3 of *The Swans Are Not Silent* (Wheaton IL: Crossway, 2002) esp. 9, 71-75, 93-96, 129.

[25] *Brothers, We Are Not Professionals: A Plea to Pastors for Radical Ministry* (Nashville: Broadman & Holman) esp. 1, ix, xi.

baptism or their sprinkling or pouring on confession of faith, though they would be encouraged toward believer's immersion, to be received as members. Regretful that the older policy would not allow Jonathan Edwards and other heroes of the Reformed tradition to be members, Piper opted for the Bunyan heritage. Piper's argument that "the local church . . . should have a front door about as wide as the door Christ has built for his own invisible church" was novel among most Baptists in North America.[26] Later "several elders changed their minds on the issue," the proposal was not presented to the congregation, and Piper expressed his "personal disappointment."[27]

John Piper, who has an expanding and far-reaching influence as a pastor-theologian in the God-glorifying school of Edwards, has increasingly demonstrated that he is first evangelical and Reformed and second Baptist.

Thomas Julian Nettles (1946–): Repristination of Biblical Inerrancy and Dortian Calvinism

Nettles, a native of Brandon, Mississippi, was graduated from Mississippi College (B.A., 1968), and Southwestern Baptist Theological Seminary (B.D., 1971; Ph.D., 1976). He taught church history at Southwestern (1976–1982), at Mid-America Baptist Theological Seminary (1982–1988), and at Trinity Evangelical Divinity School (1989–1997), and since 1997 he has been professor of historical theology in Southern Baptist Theological Seminary.[28] In addition to his authored or coauthored books, he has edited two collections of Baptist catechisms.[29]

Nettles coauthored with L. Russell Bush III, at the beginning of the SBC inerrancy controversy, an investigation of the leading Baptist theologians and confessions of faith in England and the United States as to their statements concerning the inspiration, inerrancy, and/or authority of the

---

[26]"Baptism and Church Membership at Bethlehem Baptist Church," http://www.desiringgod.org/media/pdf/baptism_and_membership.pdf. Per Bruce H. Leafblad.

[27]2005 Annual Report, Bethlehem Baptist Church, Minneapolis, 4. Per Bruce H. Leafblad. (Bethlehem Baptist Church, Minneapolis, website: <http://www.hopeingod.org>.)

[28]Curriculum Vitae; *Contemporary Authors*, vol. 117 (1986) 318-19.

[29]*Baptist Catechisms* (Fort Worth TX: author, 1982); *Teaching Truth, Training Hearts* (Amityville NY: Calvary Press Publishing, 1998).

Scriptures.³⁰ They found consistency in their trajectory from Smyth, Helwys, Bunyan, Keach, Gill, and Fuller through Dagg, Boyce, Broadus, Manly, Hovey, and Spurgeon to Strong, Carroll, Mullins, and Conner. But in Toy, Clifford, the liberals, and the modernists Nettles and Bush found disturbing deviations. Although Bush and Nettles did not draw precise conclusions, they were sympathetic with Manly's "plenary" theory of inspiration and Carroll's "grammatical-historical" hermeneutic. They were insistent on *sola Scriptura* and refused to admit that there were Baptists who held to *suprema Scriptura*. Inerrancy was to be limited to the autographs.³¹ This volume was seemingly influential in evoking a recovery or acceptance of the doctrine of biblical inerrancy among Southern Baptists. A revised edition (1999) included a new chapter reviewing the recent controversy, dealing briefly with the history of the doctrine of inerrancy, and assessing the recent writings of Baptist theologians.³²

In 1986 Nettles published a major monograph in Baptist historical theology in which he sought to prove the thesis that "the Doctrines of Grace," that is, Dortian Calvinism, "prevailed in the most influential and enduring arenas of Baptist denominational life until the end of the second decade of the twentieth century."³³ Nettles's terminal date applied to Southern Baptists, and his review marginalized the English General Baptists and ignored American Freewill/ Free Will Baptists.³⁴ Major exemplars interpreted so as to support the thesis included Keach, Bunyan, Gill, Fuller, Backus, Leland, Adoniram Judson, Wayland, Dagg, Mell, Boyce, Spurgeon, and Carroll.³⁵ Nettles laid the blame for the demise of Dortian Calvinism among Southern Baptists on E. Y. Mullins for his "theological methodology," in which experience overshadowed the Scriptures, and on L. R. Scarborough for his "evangelistic methodology," centering in what

---

³⁰*Baptists and the Bible: The Baptist Doctrines of Biblical Inspiration and Religious Authority in Historical Perspective*; see above, 431.

³¹Ibid., 212-16, 313, 410, 423, 411-13.

³²*Baptists and the Bible*, rev. and exp. ed. (Nashville: Broadman & Holman) esp. 359-88.

³³*By His Grace and for His Glory: A Historical, Theological, and Practical Study of the Doctrines of Grace in Baptist Life* (Grand Rapids MI: Baker Book House) 13.

³⁴Ibid., 17-18, 24-27, 48, 55, 57.

³⁵Ibid., 62-72, 73-130, 134-45, 148-58, 168-85, 194-205, 22-23, 27-28, 35-36, 38, 321, 324-25, 353-54, 361-62, 365-66, 420-21, 223-31.

Nettles called "decisional regeneration."³⁶ In his exposition of the doctrines of Dortian Calvinism the Mid-America professor, perhaps under the influence of the acronym TULIP, tended to conflate total depravity and irresistible grace (which he preferred to identify as "effectual calling") and had little to say about repentance and faith.³⁷ He sought to couple with Dortian Calvinism assurance, liberty of conscience, and missions and evangelism.³⁸ Nettles seemed to embrace the domino theory, that is, if the doctrines of Dortian Calvinism should be rejected and not be allowed to be the "fountainhead" of all theology, theological crises, "nonevangelical positions," and process theology would be the result.³⁹ He later wrote of "the conserving power of the doctrines of grace."⁴⁰

Nettles has increasingly issued a call to reformation among Southern Baptists. When writing on the "doctrines of grace" in 1986, he wistfully hoped for "a [needed] Reformation comparable to that which occurred in sixteenth-century Europe."⁴¹ In 1997 he reported that a "theological renewal, *in its incipient stages*, has provoked" an "expanding concern for revival" and asserted that "it is necessary that theological reformation serve as handmaid of revival."⁴² In 2005, while noting that Jerry Sutton had labeled "the conservative resurgence" in the SBC a "reformation,"⁴³ Nettles called it an "initiated" reformation yet to be completed, for "reformation involves much more . . . than the mere recovery of biblical authority."⁴⁴ He then identified in detail areas of needed reformation: authoritarianism in the denomination, the role of confessions of faith, biblical preaching, evangelistic methods, the complementarity of law and gospel, theology that is "grace-centered" and

---

³⁶Ibid., 50, 244-64 (esp. 246, 264). See above, 603.

³⁷Ibid., 267-347, esp. 285-96.

³⁸Ibid., 351-424.

³⁹Ibid., 27-28, 50-51, 425-26.

⁴⁰*A Foundation for the Future: The Southern Baptist Message and Mission* (Cape Coral FL: Founders Press, 1997) 46-51.

⁴¹*By His Grace and for His Glory*, 51. This book was designed "to aid" in such reformation. *An Introduction to the Southern Baptists* (Liverpool UK: Carey Publications, 1986) 30.

⁴²*A Foundation for the Future*, 8.

⁴³*The Baptist Reformation: The Conservative Resurgence in the Southern Baptist Convention* (Nashville: Broadman & Holman, 2000).

⁴⁴*Ready for Reformation? Bringing Authentic Reform to Southern Baptist*, 1, 2.

"Trinitarian Christ-centered," ecclesiology that is "theologically integrated," and theology adequate to sustain a viable worldview.⁴⁵

Now Nettles is producing a three-volume work in which he treats leading Baptist theologians in order to argue the tenability of a "coherent-truth" approach to Baptist identity rather than a "soul-liberty" approach, for "Baptists must be Christian and Protestant evangelical before they can be Baptist."⁴⁶

Donald Arthur Carson (1946–): Exemplar of Intelligent and Polemical Evangelicalism

A native of Quebec and the son of a Baptist pastor who had emigrated from Northern Ireland, Carson completed the B.S. degree (1967) at McGill University, the M.Div. degree (1970) at Central Baptist Seminary, Toronto, and the Ph.D. degree (1975) from the University of Cambridge. A church planter and pastor, he taught New Testament in Northwest Baptist Theological College and Seminary, Vancouver, British Columbia, from 1975 to 1978. Since then he has been associate professor, professor, and research professor of New Testament in Trinity Evangelical Divinity School, Deerfield, Illinois. Active in professional societies and a prolific author,⁴⁷ Carson has written major commentaries on Matthew and John,⁴⁸ an exposition of Philippians,⁴⁹ expositions of Matthew 8–10, John 14–17, and 2 Corinthians 10–13,⁵⁰ a coauthored New Testament introduction,⁵¹ and

---

⁴⁵Ibid.

⁴⁶*The Baptists: Key People Involved in Forming Baptist Identity*, vol. 1, *Beginnings in Britain* (Fearn, Scotland: Christian Focus Publications, 2005) esp. 13; see also vol. 2, *Beginnings in America* (2005), and vol. 3, *The Modern Era* (2007). In vol. 3 Nettles sought to establish that the SBC inerrancy controversy was also a controversy over Baptist identity.

⁴⁷Carson and John D. Woodbridge, eds., *Scripture and Truth* (Grand Rapids MI: Zondervan, 1983) 63, 117; Curriculum Vitae, Trinity Evangelical Divinity School; Andreas J. Köstenberger, "D. A. Carson," in *Bible Interpreters of the Twentieth Century*, ed. Elwell and Weaver, 423-33.

⁴⁸*Matthew*, The Expositor's Bible Commentary, vol. 8 (Grand Rapids MI: Eerdmans, 1984); *The Gospel according to John* (Grand Rapids MI: Eerdmans; Leicester UK: InterVarsity, 1991; in Pillar New Testament Commentary, 2000).

⁴⁹*Basics for Believers: An Exposition of Philippians* (Grand Rapids MI: Baker, 1996).

⁵⁰*When Jesus Confronts the World: An Exposition of Matthew 8–10* (Grand Rapids MI: Baker, 1987); *The Farewell Discourse and Final Prayer of Jesus: An*

an evaluative survey of New Testament commentaries.[52] He coedited and contributed to *New Bible Commentary: 21st Century Edition*.[53]

Although he has held a professorship of New Testament and produced distinctive writings in that discipline, Carson's greater contribution has been essentially theological in nature, for he has tended to move from exegesis to systematic theology.

Carson wrote on various aspects of the understanding of the Bible: the doctrine of the Scriptures, the relation of the two testaments, methods of biblical criticism, hermeneutics, and Bible translation. In a multifaceted essay on contemporary developments in the debate among Evangelicals about biblical inerrancy, he, for example, refuted Ian Rennie's view that "plenary" inspiration was sharply to be distinguished from "verbal" inspiration in nineteenth-century Britain, argued that the Princetonians' use of Scottish Common Sense Realism did not "make their doctrine of Scripture innovative," rejected the "faith and practice" restriction for inerrancy, and objected to Robert Gundry's midrashic and nonhistorical assessment of that in Matthew's Gospel which is not parallel to Mark and Q.[54] Rejecting Walter Bauer's[55] view that in the second century orthodox and heretical Christian movements coexisted and that the former prevailed by political means and James D. G. Dunn's[56] view that there was much theological diversity among the New Testament writings but "'no single normative form

---

Exposition of John 14–17 (Grand Rapids MI: Baker, 1980); *From Triumphalism to Maturity: An Exposition of 2 Corinthians 10–13* (Grand Rapids MI: Baker, 1984).

[51]With Douglas J. Moo and Leon Morris, *An Introduction to the New Testament* (Grand Rapids MI: Zondervan, 1992).

[52]*New Testament Commentary Survey* (Leicester UK: Theological Students Fellowship, 1977; 2nd ed., 1986; 3rd ed.: Grand Rapids MI: Baker, 1988; 4th ed.: Grand Rapids MI: Baker and Leicester UK: InterVarsity, 1993; 5th ed.: Grand Rapids MI: Baker, 2001).

[53]4th ed. (Leicester UK, Downers Grove IL: InterVarsity, 1994). Carson wrote "Approaching the Bible" (1-19) and "Reading the Letters" (1108-14).

[54]"Recent Developments in the Doctrine of Scripture," in *Hermeneutics, Authority, and Canon*, ed. Carson and John D. Woodbridge (Grand Rapids MI: Zondervan, 1986) 5-48, esp. 11-14, 15-18, 14-15, 35-36.

[55]*Orthodoxy and Heresy in Earliest Christianity*, trans. Philadelphia Seminar on Christian Origins and ed. Robert A. Kraft and Gerhard Krodel (Philadelphia: Fortress, 1971).

[56]*Unity and Diversity in the New Testament: An Inquiry into the Character of Earliest Christianity* (London: SCM, 1977).

of Christianity in the first century'" with the later canon legitimizing and setting limits to the diversity, Carson sought to show that there is enough unity in the New Testament as well as diversity to allow for the harmonization needed for construction of a systematic theology.[57] Of late, countering the "new perspective" on Paul generated by E. P. Sanders,[58] he has set forth half a dozen ways in which Pauline theology exhibits the "continuity of the Bible's story-line," leading to fulfillment, and in parallel fashion the discontinuity of the mystery, formerly hidden, being revealed in Christ.[59]

The Trinity professor criticized those who employ redaction criticism vis-à-vis the New Testament so as by differentiating the redactional from the tradition to render the redactional as inauthentic and advised caution in its use by evangelicals.[60] In dealing with the hermeneutical trends of the 1980s he avoided using "preunderstanding" of the text to mean "immutable nonnegotiables," critiqued the existentialist encounter of the text as being too subjective and not yielding any "*assured*" or commonly received meaning, rejected the "reductionism" of any "canon within the canon," and questioned the use of biblical paradigms (for example, the Exodus) without regard for the whole of salvation history.[61] Also he wrote on the use of the Old Testament by the Fourth Gospel and the epistles of John.[62] Conscious of the numerous pitfalls in biblical exegesis, Carson exposed four kinds of exegetical fallacies: word-study, grammatical, logical, and presuppositional/

---

[57]"Unity and Diversity in the New Testament: The Possibility of Systematic Theology," in *Scripture and Truth*, ed. Carson and Woodbridge, 65-95.

[58]*Paul and Palestinian Judaism: A Comparison of Patterns of Religion* (Philadelphia: Fortress, 1977).

[59]"Mystery and Fulfillment: Toward a More Comprehensive Paradigm of Paul's Understanding of the Old and the New," in *Justification and Variegated Nomism*, vol. 2, *The Paradoxes of Paul*, ed. Carson, Peter T. O'Brien, and Mark A. Seifrid, Wissenschaftliche Untersuchungen zum Neuen Testament 181 (Tübingen: Mohr/Siebeck; Grand Rapids MI: Baker Academic, 2004) 393-436.

[60]"Redaction Criticism: On the Legitimacy and Illegitimacy of a Literary Tool," in *Scripture and Truth*, ed. Carson and Woodbridge, 119-42.

[61]"A Sketch of the Factors Determining Current Hermeneutical Debate in Cross-Cultural Contexts," in *Biblical Interpretation and the Church: The Problem of Contexualization*, ed. Carson (Nashville: Thomas Nelson, 1985) 11-29.

[62]"John and the Johannine Epistles," in *It Is Written: Scripture Citing Scripture; Essays in Honour of Barnabas Lindars, S.S.F.*, ed. Carson and H. G. M. Williamson (Cambridge UK: Cambridge University Press, 1988) 245-64.

historical.⁶³ Twice Carson became involved in controversies over Bible translation. First, he refuted those who held that the King James Version is "the best English version now extant" and that such a conclusion should be made "a criterion of orthodoxy" partly by arguing against the Byzantine text-type that underlay the Textus Receptus.⁶⁴ More recently he tried to pour oil on the troubled waters of raging controversy over gender-inclusive language by evaluating specific changes and urging awareness as to how languages change.⁶⁵

Carson's rewritten and abridged Cambridge dissertation was a biblical study of the tension between divine sovereignty and human responsibility. He first examined twelve selected Old Testament passages embodying in some sense this tension and then developed various themes such as the many exhortations, commands, and calls to believe, obey, and choose on the one hand and God's personal causality and election on the other. Both election and human responsibility can be found in the Old Testament Apocrypha, but a theology of merit "is in the ascendancy." The apocalyptic literature sharpened "eschatological expectation," the Dead Sea Scrolls stressed God's election of a remnant, the targums and rabbinic writings absolutized human free will and saw Israel's election as the choice of the "most worthy," and Josephus continued the stress on human free will and the theology of merit. Carson selected the Gospel of John as the sole basis for a New Testament study. Exploring a few key texts, he then found that sovereignty-responsibility was expressed in Christology (Jesus as the God-man) and in eschatology (realized and futurist) as well as in soteriology. The Gospel of John never absolutizes free will, rejects the theology of merit, sees the hand of God for good "behind evil men and events," and affirms God's election of some. In both testaments the sovereignty-responsibility tension was treated not "as an abstract theological conundrum" but in the face of "personally painful and perplexing predicaments."⁶⁶

---

⁶³*Exegetical Fallacies* (Grand Rapids MI: Baker, 1984; 2nd ed.: Grand Rapids MI: Baker; Carlisle UK: Paternoster, 1996).

⁶⁴*The King James Version Debate: A Plea for Realism* (Grand Rapids MI: Baker, 1979).

⁶⁵*The Inclusive Language Debate: A Plea for Realism* (Grand Rapids MI: Baker, 1998).

⁶⁶*Divine Sovereignty and Human Responsibility: Biblical Perspectives in Tension* (Atlanta: John Knox, 1981) 9-19, 27-34, 45-54 (esp. 51), 201, 78, 201-202, 125-30, 146-49, 134-46, 203, 216.

The Trinity professor in treating Rom. 3:21-26, contra C. H. Dodd, translated *hilastērion* "propitiation," not "expiation," and found the meaning to be the removal of God's personal wrath, not the canceling of sin. Hence God as the subject "presented" Christ as "a propitiation," and God as the object was made propitious through the death of the Son.[67]

Carson addressed the issue of suffering, differentiating natural evils from social evils and noting, for example, that governments both prevent and perpetrate evil. Some suffering is peculiar to the people of God, and illness and death are both real and capable of being transcended, especially "from the prospect of vindication and resurrection." Carson did not hesitate to ascribe suffering to God, and he rested his case with that "compatibilism" between divine sovereignty and human accountability that is clothed in mystery.[68] Though announcing his intention to be relatively free "from the categories of systematic theology" in interpreting the Sermon on the Mount, he had to differentiate his own interpretation from others": the Schweitzerian "interim ethic" prior to an imminent but unrealized *parousia*; the existentialist view; the Sermon as pure law; the Anabaptist/Mennonite view as leading to pacifism; the Lutheran orthodox view of the impossible ideal as a call to repentance and preparation for the gospel; liberalism's blueprint for "a progressive civilization"; the catechetical manual; and dispensationalism's postponement to the millennium. Carson embodied the gospel preparation of the Lutheran view, the demand for present conformity of the Anabaptist view, the kingdom norms as witnessing the kingdom of liberalism, the probing of the existentialist view, and the urgency of the "interim ethic."[69]

In his specifically theological exposition of 1 Corinthians 12–14, the Trinity professor explored the diverse "grace-gifts" and was more concerned for the relation of the baptism "in the one Spirit" to the "one body" (12:13) than for the question of water baptism. Carson agreed mostly with Wayne Grudem's distinction between the authority of Old Testament

---

[67]"Atonement in Romans 3:21-26: 'God Presented Him as a Propitiation," in *The Glory of the Atonement: Biblical, Historical and Practical Perspectives: Essays in Honor of Roger Nicole*, ed. Charles E. Hill and Frank A. James III (Downers Grove IL: InterVarsity, 2004) 119-39 (esp. 129-35).

[68]*How Long, O Lord? Reflections on Suffering and Evil* (Grand Rapids MI: Baker, 1990).

[69]*The Sermon on the Mount: An Evangelical Exposition of Matthew 5-7* (Grand Rapids MI: Baker, 1978).

prophets and that of New Testament prophets. He regarded the tongues of Acts 2:4 as "xenoglossia—real, human language never learned by the speakers" and the tongues of 1 Cor. 12:10, 30 as "cognitive," not as "babbling," thus erasing any significant difference between the two. Going beyond 1 Corinthians, Carson refuted "second-blessing theology" and identified both strengths and weaknesses of "the charismatic movement."[70]

Worship and prayer also evoked the pen of Donald Carson. After carefully defining worship, he identified Christian worship as God-centered, Christ-centered, and Trinitarian, both individual and corporate, embracing "both adoration and action," and obligatory both because of divine command and God's worthiness.[71] Editing essays on the Lord's Day, he contributed a study of the Sabbath according to the four Gospels.[72] He edited a symposium on prayer[73] and used the prayers of the apostle Paul as a springboard for a call to contemporary spiritual reformation.[74]

Finally, Carson addressed issues related to contextualization and pluralism, and this cast him more in the role of polemicist/apologist. In detail he refuted the view of Daniel von Allmen[75] that Christian theology in Africa should today be contextualized because in the New Testament age the Hellenistic Jewish Christians engaged in contextualization, as, for example, they did in choosing "*Kyrios* [Lord] to render Hebrew *rabbi* and Aramaic *mari*." Among Carson's arguments against von Allmen were the charge that he had denied "the influence of the Aramaic-speaking apostles" and the plea that Africans should not be denied the lessons from historical theology.[76]

---

[70]*Showing the Spirit: A Theological Exposition of 1 Corinthians 12–14* (Grand Rapids MI: Baker, 1987) 31-47, 93-100, 138, 77-83 (esp. 83), 158-60, 170-83.

[71]"Worship under the Word," in *Worship by the Book*, ed. Carson (Grand Rapids MI: Zondervan, 2002) 11-63.

[72]Preface, introduction, and "Jesus and the Sabbath in the Four Gospels," in *From Sabbath to Lord's Day: A Biblical, Historical, and Theological Investigation*, ed. Carson (Grand Rapids MI: Zondervan, 1982) 11-12, 13-19, 57-95.

[73]*Teach Us to Pray: Prayer in the Bible and the World*, ed. Carson (Exeter UK; Grand Rapids MI: World Evangelical Fellowship, 1990).

[74]*A Call to Spiritual Reformation: Priorities from Paul and His Prayers* (Grand Rapids MI: Baker, 1992).

[75]"The Birth of Theology: Contextualization as the Dynamic Element in the Formation of New Testament Theology," *International Review of Mission* 64 (January 1975): 37-52.

[76]"Church and Mission: Reflections on Contextualization and the Third Horizon," in *The Church in the Bible and the World: An International Study*, ed.

Carson's initial sally into pluralism called for three definitions of "pluralism": (1) the fact of "growing diversity in Western culture"; (2) "the value" of exercising "toleration for this diversity"; and (3) a philosophy that tolerance must be "mandated" because "no religion has the right to pronounce itself true and others false." He went on to assert that "the challenges of pluralism are not new," for they existed in the history of Israel and for first-century Christianity. Central to debates over pluralism are the doctrines of God and revelation. Postmodernism has made Christian response to pluralism more difficult, but that response should stem "from a profound and deepening grasp of the Bible's entire storyline," and the arrival of pluralism and of globalization can have benefits.[77] Naming his three definitions of pluralism ("empirical pluralism," "cherished pluralism," and "philosophical or hermeneutical pluralism"), he then identified various "correlatives of pluralism in Western culture, such as secularization, "new age theosophy," baby buster pragmatism, pop culture, and rugged individualism.[78] Advice was given as to how preaching and evangelism should be undertaken in a pluralistic setting.[79] Carson wrote an analysis and critique of the "emerging church" movement centering in but not confined to Brian McLaren.[80] In his 640-page *The Gagging of God*[81] Carson gave full expression to the challenge of pluralism. In part one he analyzed the "hermeneutical morass" with the "disappearance of objective truth" and pointed to ways out of the morass. In part two, after developing more fully the authority of revelation and the Old and New Testament phases of "the Bible's plotline, the native of Quebec defended the finality of Jesus Christ against John Hick, Paul Knitter, Raimundo Panikkar, and Matthew Fox,

---

Carson (Exeter UK: Paternoster; Grand Rapids MI: Baker, 1987) 213-57, esp. 221-23, 228-32, 255.

[77]"Christian Witness in an Age of Pluralism," in *God and Culture: Essays in Honor of Carl F. H. Henry*, ed. Carson and John D. Woodbridge (Grand Rapids MI: Eerdmans; Carlisle UK: Paternoster, 1993) 31-66.

[78]"The Challenge from Pluralism to the Preaching of the Gospel," *Criswell Theological Journal* 7 (Fall 1993): 99-117.

[79]"The Challenge from the Preaching of the Gospel to Pluralism," *Criswell Theological Journal* 7 (Spring 1994): 15-39.

[80]*Becoming Conversant with the Emerging Church: Understanding a Movement with Its Implications* (Grand Rapids MI: Zondervan, 2005).

[81]Subtitle: *Christianity Confronts Pluralism* (Grand Rapids MI: Zondervan, 1996).

refuted the two-covenant (Jews, Gentiles) theory, and argued that the line must be drawn between orthodoxy and heresy. Part three allowed Carson to address the church-state, educational, and public policy aspects of pluralism, and part four explored pluralism within evangelicalism with special attention to the nature of evangelism, the doctrine of hell, as challenged by conditional immortality, and globalization and contextualization.[82]

Carson has been called "one of the last great Renaissance men in evangelical biblical scholarship" whose "prodigious output" may have limited his ability to produce "technical" monographs and whose "confrontational, direct manner" has been combined with the inseparable bonding of evangelical scholarship and deep personal faith.[83]

Paul Stuart Fiddes (1947–):
The Suffering and Trinitarian God and Ecumenical Theology

Fiddes as a theologian has addressed the wider Christian community on both general theological and specifically ecumenical issues while retaining a stance as a Baptist spokesperson. A native of Upminster, Essex, and four times a graduate of the University of Oxford (B.A., English, 1968; B.A., theology, 1970; M.A., 1972; D.Phil., 1975), he was ordained a Baptist minister in 1972 and was fellow and tutor in Christian doctrine (1972–1989) in Regent's Park College, Oxford, before becoming principal in 1989, and he continued his principalship until retirement in 2007. He has had responsibilities in the Baptist Union of Great Britain, the European Baptist Federation, and the BWA and has chaired the board of the Faculty of Theology of the University of Oxford (1996–1998).[84] Among his writings and editorial labors have been several volumes relative to the Christian faith and modern culture: specifically concerning English literature,[85] the novel,[86] death,[87] the center of culture,[88] and movies.[89]

---

[82]Ibid., 57-553.

[83]Köstenberger, "D. A. Carson," 427, 426, 430.

[84]Curriculum Vitae, Regent's Park College.

[85]*Freedom and Limit: A Dialogue between Literature and Christian Doctrine* (Macon GA: Mercer University Press, 1999).

[86]*The Novel, Spirituality and Modern Culture: Eight Novelists Write about Their Craft and Their Context*, ed. Fiddes (Cardiff: University of Wales Press, 2000).

[87]*The Promised End: Eschatology in Theology and Literature*, Challenges in Contemporary Theology (Oxford UK; Malden MA: Blackwell, 2000).

[88]*Faith in the Centre: Christianity and Culture*, ed. Fiddes (Oxford UK:

Although in 2000, in the company of other principals of Baptist theological colleges in England, he affirmed that "there is indeed a Baptist way of doing theology," not after James W. McClendon's 'baptist' way,[90] but on the basis of the experiences, the confessions, and the stories of the Baptists,[91] Fiddes in his first three books[92] had addressed and represented a wider Christian theological community without Baptist specificity.

Fiddes made a major contribution to the literature on the suffering of God. Utilizing but critiquing Jürgen Moltmann's effort to relate the particularity and uniqueness of God's suffering in the death of Jesus to the concept that all suffering is "taken up into God," he found that the longstanding doctrine of the impassibility of God had of late yielded for many to the concept of sacrificial personal love, the centrality of the cross for the Christian faith, the idea that theodicy requires the suffering of God, and the fact that the "world-picture" has shifted from "hierarchy" to "machine" to "organism." Fiddes employed, though not uncritically, process philosophy as the preferred matrix for divine suffering. Hence change in God is to be acknowledged, and the suffering God is said to come to glory and victory, though not specifically through Jesus' resurrection, and with God as somehow incomplete. God, suffering in the cross, remains God, suffering not merely in respect to the "economic" Trinity, as Karl Barth affirmed, and Christ suffered not merely in his human nature, as John Calvin held. The power of the suffering God Fiddes identified with persuasion and forgiveness but not with atonement. He felt compelled to interact at length with the death-of-God theologians and Paul Tillich.[93] Fiddes's monograph has been lauded as

---

Regent's Park College; Macon GA: Smyth & Helwys, 2001). Fiddes's chapter was "The Story and the Stories: Revelation and the Challenge of Postmodern Culture" (75-96).

[89]*Flickering Images: Theology and Film in Dialogue*, ed. Fiddes and Anthony J. Clarke (Oxford UK: Regent's Park College; Macon GA: Smyth & Helwys, 2005).

[90]See above, 538.

[91]"Theology and a Baptist Way of Community," in *Doing Theology in a Baptist Way*, ed. Fiddes (Oxford: Whitley Publications) 19-38 (esp. 19, 29, 19-27).

[92]*The Creative Suffering of God* (Oxford: Oxford University Press, 1988); *Past Event and Present Salvation: The Christian Idea of Atonement* (Louisville: Westminster/John Knox, 1989); *Participating in God: A Pastoral Doctrine of the Trinity* (London: Darton, Longman and Todd; Louisville: Westminster/John Knox, 2000).

[93]*The Creative Suffering of God*, 4-12, 16-45, 46-76, 78-88, 100-109, 91-100, 112-23, 26-28, 144-46, 157-69, 174-206, 230-60.

"the best effort to conceptualize . . . a suffering God within the last hundred years"[94] and "the best critical and constructive discussion of the problem . . . to date."[95] It has been criticized for binding God and creation too closely and thus rejecting *creatio ex nihilo*,[96] for too great dependence on process theology in ascribing "almost unbounded freedom" to humanity and all creation,[97] for holding that God only empathized with the sufferings of the man Jesus,[98] and for portraying "God's suffering as much less severe than human suffering."[99] Fiddes, revisiting H. Wheeler Robinson's *The Cross of Hosea*[100] and taking a sequential view of chapters 1 and 3, concluded that "God's own suffering predates" the Hosea-Gomer tragedy. Although suffering issues in judgment, it can in "the blend of [divine] love and wrath" also lead to transformation: empathy for Hosea and redemption for Gomer.[101]

Fiddes's *Past Event and Present Salvation*,[102] hailed by reviewers as deserving to be "a standard introduction"[103] or "a modern classic" on the atonement,[104] addressed the relationship of the death of Jesus as past event to present salvation. Taking a threefold view of the "human predicament" (estrangement, failing to attain potential, rebellion), noting the biblical correlation of creation and redemption, and opting for the "continual suffering" of God, Fiddes undertook a review of the use and later alteration of the major images/concepts of the atonement: sacrifice, justice, decisive victory, and act of love. In ways reminiscent of C. H. Dodd, the Oxford theologian opted for "expiation" and rejected "propitiation" as a concept, though not as a translation, and like William Newton Clarke and Frank Stagg, he was opposed to any "transactional view of the atonement." Jesus' dying under

---

[94]Review by Jeff B. Pool, *Journal of Religion* 70 (July 1990): 471.

[95]Review by Roger E. Olson, *Scottish Journal of Theology* 43 (1990): 115.

[96]Review by Paul R. Sponheim, *Interpretation* 43 (April 1989): 218.

[97]Review by Stanley J. Grenz, *Christian Century* 106 (22-29 March 1989): 325.

[98]Review by Richard Bauckham, *Baptist Quarterly* 33 (January 1990): 247-48.

[99]Review by Olson, 115.

[100]See above, 353n.60.

[101]"*The Cross of Hosea* Revisited: The Meaning of Suffering in the Book of Hosea," *Review and Expositor* 90 (Spring 1993): 175-90.

[102]Subtitle: *The Christian Idea of Atonement*.

[103]Review by Kenneth Surin, *Theology* 93 (September-October 1990): 400.

[104]Review by William J. Abraham, *Perkins* (School of Theology) *Journal* 43 (July-October 1990): 39.

God's judgment "does not mean . . . that God directly *inflicts* some kind of penalty upon him. It is to speak of his complete identification with humankind. . . . " God's judgment is "his personal consent to the natural outworking of people's estrangement from God and each other." Fiddes was especially drawn to the Abelardian view of the manifestation of God's costly love and the generating of a responsive love. Hence Abelard did not have a merely subjective view. Fiddes sought to balance in the atonement the objective and the subjective, past event and present experience, the action of God and the action of man, and change in God and change in human beings.[105] He was critiqued for not interacting with recent authors on the atonement: Vincent Taylor,[106] Leon Morris,[107] and John Stott.[108]

The Oxford principal in an in-depth comparison of Eastern Orthodox and Baptist understandings relative to salvation and the church noted that the Orthodox use "hypostatic" language and deification and Baptists have used "covenant" language to expose the salvation of the individual, that the two use the terms "visible church" and "invisible church" differently, and that Baptists object to Orthodoxy's "equating of visibility with *indivisibility*," that is, the Orthodox churches. Fiddes asserted the probability that the primary Baptist soteriological term had been reconciliation.[109] In a more complete statement of the Baptist understanding of salvation he noted that the Baptist bedrock commitment to the necessity of personal faith in Christ had led to believer's baptism, the church as a fellowship of believers, religious freedom, and evangelism and mission. Explicating the grace of God, he found Baptists moving away from a limited atonement and himself again resisting penal substitution. Most Baptists, he concluded, "combine a view of saving faith as an individual human response to Christ as Saviour, with an equally strong view of the sovereign initiative of God's grace"—"a kind of spiritual cocktail of dashes of Calvinism and Arminianism."[110]

---

[105]*Past Event and Present Salvation*, 3-4, 6-7, 17-24, 61-168 (esp. 68-72), 91, 110, 140-47, 153-58, 26-28. See above, 308n.378, 373.

[106]Review by Abraham, 39.

[107]Review by Charles R. Gresham, *Restoration Quarterly* 34 (1992): 188.

[108]Review by Robert H. Culpepper, *Faith and Mission* 8 (Fall 1990): 116.

[109]"The Church and Salvation: A Comparison of Orthodox and Baptist Thinking," in *Ecumenism and History: Studies in Honour of John H. Y. Briggs*, ed. Anthony R. Cross (Carlisle UK, Waynesboro GA: Paternoster, 2002) 120-48.

[110]*Tracks and Traces: Baptist Identity in Church and Theology*, Studies in Baptist History and Thought 13 (Milton Keynes UK, Waynesboro GA: Paternoster,

From his advocacy of the suffering of God and his treatment of atonement-salvation, Fiddes turned to the doctrine of the Trinity so as to provide "a pastoral doctrine" not only for ordained ministers but also for various kinds of caregivers. Noting that historically "person in relationship" had been reduced to an "individual subject," he sought to rehabilitate the concept that personhood consists of relationships. He opted for our "participation in God" rather than our "imitation" of the triune God, employing the ancient term *perichorēsis*, or "the mutual interpenetration of the persons." Thus Fiddes leans to the Eastern "social" rather than the Western or Augustinian "psychological" approach to the Trinity. He then applied his Trinitarian insights pastorally to abuses of power, intercessory prayer, suffering, forgiveness, death, spiritual gifts, and a wider sacramentality.[111]

Only by interpreting and assessing the Charismatic or Neo-Pentecostal movement has Fiddes addressed directly the doctrine of the Holy Spirit. Rather than determining by exegesis whether the claims concerning a post-conversional, postbaptismal "breakthrough" or "baptism" in the Spirit are biblically tenable, he chose rather to ask what the movement, known for elevating experience above reflective thought, has contributed to Christian theology. Nothing to Christian initiation, he concluded, but possibly Jesus as "the archetypal charismatic" and spiritual gifts.[112] He declared that according to the New Testament, "'baptism in the Spirit' belongs normatively within the event of water-baptism."[113]

Fiddes has consistently made the concept of the covenant to be central to ecclesiology. First, acknowledging that Baptist churches had often adopted covenants, he studied the biblical use of covenants. He differentiated two kinds of covenants in the Old Testament: the covenant that was a unilateral promise of "life and well-being" (Abraham, David) and the bilateral agreement with the nation (Sinai). Both called for human responses, and the human form of neither was final for a pilgrim people. The new covenant in the death and resurrection of Jesus is "new" because

---

2003) 228-48 (esp. 229-32, 235-42, 244, 246).

[111]*Participating in God: A Pastoral Doctrine of the Trinity.*

[112]"The Theology of the Charismatic Movement," in *Strange Gifts? A Guide to Charismatic Renewal*, ed. David Martin and Peter Mullen (Oxford: Basil Blackwell, 1984) 19-40, esp. 23, 20, 29, 32-36.

[113]*Charismatic Renewal: A Baptist View: A Report Received by the Baptist Union Council with Commentary by Paul S. Fiddes* (London: Baptist Union of Great Britain, 1980) 31.

"the hopes of Israel . . . had been fulfilled in Christ," because God the Son had gone to the depths of suffering and forsakenness, and because the cross "provides a universal focus for human response to God."[114] Second, writing to honor the German Baptist, Wiard Popkes (1936–2007), Fiddes took up the principal New Testament images of the church (body of Christ, temple of God indwelt by God's Spirit, and the people of God), lifted them into "participation" in the Triune God—not only "economic" Trinity but also "immanent" Trinity, and joined therewith the covenant, both in its vertical and horizontal (ecclesial) dimensions.[115] Third, delving more into Baptist history and beginning with the pre-Baptist Separatist church covenant made at Gainsborough (1606 or 1607), the Oxford theologian found four meanings of covenant in Puritan and Separatist theology: the eternal "covenant of grace" manifested in both testaments; the "transaction" among the Father, the Son, and the Holy Spirit for the salvation of the elect; God's agreement with the Church or with particular churches; and the agreement among members of a particular congregation as to how they should "walk together" in the Lord. These meanings were interwoven, and assent to the church covenant "moved participants toward a *blend* of Calvinistic insistence upon the enabling grace of God and Arminian affirmation of 'choosing' Christ." But, according to Fiddes, defining the church as a "voluntary society" as did John Locke,[116] has had an injurious effect on the true understanding of the church covenant. Yet today Fiddes would keep "distance" "between confessions and covenants," lest confessions of faith be seen as the needed "basis" for covenants.[117]

---

[114]"Covenant: Old and New," in *Bound to Love: The Covenant Basis of Baptist Life and Mission* (London: Baptist Union of Great Britain, 1985) 9-23.

[115]"Church, Trinity, and Covenant: An Ecclesiology of Participation," in *Gemeinschaft am Evangelium: Festschrift für Wiard Popkes zum 60. Geburtstag*, ed. Edwin Brandt, Fiddes, and Joachim Molthagen (Leipzig: Evangelische Verlagsanstalt, 1996) 37-54. Popkes, professor of New Testament in the Baptist Theological Seminary in Hamburg, was the author of *Abendmahl und Gemeinde: das Abendmahl in biblisch-theologischer Sicht und in evangelisch-frei kirchlichet Praxis* (Kassel: Oncken, 1983); *Gemeinde, Raum des Vertrauens: neutestamentliche Beobachtungen und freikirchliche Perspektiven* (Kassel: Oncken, 1984); and *Ein Gott und ein Herr: zum Kontext des Monotheismus im Neuen Testament* (Vluyn: Neukirchener, 2004). Per Mark Austin.

[116]See above, 157.

[117]"'Walking Together': The Place of Covenant Theology in Baptist Life Yesterday and Today," in *Pilgrim Pathways: Essays in Baptist History in Honour*

Fiddes has increasingly given attention to baptism. Under the rubric of "baptism and creation" he identified and explained "five motifs connected with water that have been important for the Judaeo-Christian tradition: birth, cleansing, conflict [with hostile powers]," journey, and refreshment. These motifs have been connected both with the created order, or nature, and salvation history and come to a focus in baptism by immersion. Preferring to call baptism a "sacrament," Fiddes stated that baptism not only "symbolizes" but also "actualizes" the atonement, and that baptism "in its sheer materiality . . . actually communicates the presence of the transcendent God." He extended sacramentality not only to the Lord's Supper but also to the church meeting of a Baptist congregation. He may have overextended his making identical those "suspicions of any 'sacramentalism'" and those who regard baptism as "merely an optional outward ceremony symbolizing an inward grace."[118]

In an ecumenical context Fiddes explored the feasibility of a "process" of Christian initiation, of which water baptism would be a part. After reviewing in detail recent ecumenical and Anglican writings relative to such a process and the alternative view that initiation is focused on baptism, he opted for the process and concluded that infant baptism/confirmation and believer's baptism have "the same journey."[119]

For a German audience the Oxford principal addressed the "conundrum" of a "close association," if not "an exact match," between being baptized in water and being made a member of the body of Christ. First, he cited examples of "an apparent mismatch" between the two within the practices of infant baptism and of believer's baptism. Then, he asserted, resolving the conundrum involves a proper recognition of the "interweaving" and mutual conditioning of the three New Testament uses of "body of Christ": the resurrection body of Jesus, the church, and the Eucharistic bread. Finally, applying his Trinitarian theology, Fiddes envisioned not so much the indwelling by the Logos or by the Spirit of the ecclesial body of

---

of B. R. White, ed. William H. Brackney and Fides with John H. Y. Briggs (Macon GA: Mercer University Press, 1999) 47-74, esp. 47, 52-55, 65, 67, 73.

[118]"Baptism and Creation," in *Reflections on the Water: Understanding God and the World through the Baptism of Believers*, ed. Fiddes (Oxford: Regent's Park College; Macon GA: Smyth & Helwys, 1996) 47-67, esp. 48, 59, 58, 52-53, 58, 63-65, 62.

[119]"Baptism and the Process of Christian Initiation," *The Ecumenical Review* 54 (January-April 2002): 48-65, esp. 63.

Christ as the dwelling of the members of that body in God. Hence "nobody can be baptized without either *becoming* a member of the body of Christ or *being immersed more deeply* into the reality of that body."[120]

Fiddes was confident that all English Baptists "affirm a communion with Christ which gives blessing" and ventured that it was "unlikely that Zwingli held . . . a bare memorialism." He continued the Bunyan-Hall-Spurgeon stance on open communion. With a "majority of churches within the Baptist Union" having open membership,[121] Fiddes was free to advocate conciliar ecumenism with "full communion," one visible ecumenical mission, an ecumenical "synodal structure," and a "common covenant" with episcopal oversight.[122]

The Oxford principal rejected both the top-down or hierarchical view of authority in the local church, including "authoritative elders," and the "from below" concept, according to which the pastor's authority is only that "delegated from the church meeting." Pastors, called by Christ, need to offer guidance and have the authority of servants, gaining trust through their service.[123]

Fiddes's prolific and excellent theological work nevertheless leaves major problems for Baptists: no penal substitution, heavy dependence on process thought, no serious employment of confessions of faith, baptism as actualizing Jesus' saving work, and open membership that elevates ecumenism above believer's baptism by immersion.

Wayne Arden Grudem (1948–): Reformed Theology with Vineyard Refinements

Grudem, a native of Chippawa Falls, Wisconsin, and a graduate of Harvard University (B.A., 1970), Westminster Theological Seminary (M.Div., 1973), and the University of Cambridge (Ph.D., 1979), has produced a bib-

---

[120]"Baptism and Membership of the Body of Christ," in *Gemeinschaft der Kirchen und gesellschaftliche Verantwortung: Die Würde des Anderen und das Recht anders zu denken: Festschrift für Professor Dr. Erich Geldbach*, 83-93. See also *Tracks and Traces*, 125-56.

[121]*Tracks and Traces*, 157-92 (esp. 163, 160, 175-82, 183).

[122]Ibid., 193-227 (esp. 194-97, 207-10, 212, 221-27).

[123]"Authority in People-Pastor Relationships," in *Baptist Faith and Witness: The Papers of the Study and Research Division of the Baptist World Alliance, 1990–1995*, ed. William H. Brackney and L. A. (Tony) Cupit (Birmingham AL: Samford University Press, 1995) 59-63. See also *Tracks and Traces*, 83-106.

lically based systematic theology upon a Reformed theological grid with certain influences from Neo-Pentecostalism. Ordained as a Baptist minister in the BGC (1974), he has later held membership in a Southern Baptist church and a Vineyard Christian Fellowship and currently belongs to a Bible church. He has served as assistant professor of theology in Bethel College, St. Paul (1977-81), as assistant professor and associate professor of New Testament and as professor of Biblical and systematic theology at Trinity Evangelical Divinity School (1981–2001) and since 2001 as research professor of Bible and theology in Phoenix Seminary, Phoenix, Arizona. He was president of the Council on Biblical Manhood and Womanhood (1989–1991) and president of the Evangelical Theological Society (1999).[124]

Grudem's fifty-seven-chapter *Systematic Theology*[125] is at the same time "systematized Bible" and, with notable exceptions, Reformed theology. The author implied that he would flesh out the principle of *sola Scriptura* and thus gave little attention to the history of Christian doctrine or to contemporary culture. His gathering and usage of biblical texts, however, show little influence of studies in biblical theology. The book consists of seven divisions (doctrines): the Word of God, God, man, Christ and the Holy Spirit, application of redemption, the church, and the future. Grudem began with a strong affirmation of the authority and the inerrancy (in all areas) of the Bible, together with expositions of the Bible's clarity, necessity, and sufficiency, but did not address inspiration. In treating creation Grudem rejected Darwinian evolution and the gap theory, found it impossible to resolve finally the issues of 24-hour days in Genesis 1 and of "old earth" versus "new earth" theories but was confident that there will be "no final conflict" between the Bible and the natural sciences. Male and female human beings are equal in personhood, but for Grudem, a complementarian, they are quite different as to roles, and women cannot be pastors or elders.[126] It was not possible for Jesus to sin, but Jesus has two wills;

---

[124]*Who's Who in Religion*, 4th ed. (1992–1993), 199; "Wayne Grudem," at <http://en.wikipedia.org/wiki/Wayne_Grudem>; and Phoenix Seminary, "Our Faculty"/"Grudem" at <www.phoenixseminary.edu>.

[125]Subtitle: *An Introduction to Biblical Doctrine* (Grand Rapids MI: Zondervan, 1994). Some of this section has been taken from my review of Grudem's *Systematic Theology*, *Southwestern Journal of Theology* 41 (Summer 1999): 134-36.

[126]*Systematic Theology*, 25, 73-138, 275-309, 273-75, 454-68, 973-44. See also Piper and Grudem, "An Overview of Central Concerns: Questions and Answers";

Chalcedon is accepted, and kenoticism rejected. Grudem criticized annihilationism but had little to say about eschatological universalism.[127]

Grudem's use of Reformed theology is especially evident in the following: the distinction between "incommunicable" and "communicable" attributes of God; God's "secret will" and "revealed will"; a dichotomous view of human nature; the imputation of Adam's sin to all humanity; the covenants of works, redemption, and grace; penal substitution as the only understanding of Jesus' death; limited atonement; common grace; the gospel call and effective calling; and perseverance. While using the term "reprobation," Grudem defined "preterition."[128] But Grudem deviated from Reformed theology at three points: by affirming a Baptist understanding of believer's baptism by immersion, by taking a noncessationist view as to present-day spiritual gifts, and by embracing historic or posttribulational premillennialism.[129]

Influence from or kinship with Neo-Pentecostal or Vineyard teaching can be seen in Grudem's theology not only in his noncessationism but also more fully in his careful studies of the New Testament role of prophets and his advocacy of the exercise of prophecy in today's churches.[130] Such prophecy, he contended, should be encouraged and regulated, for "the gift of prophecy . . . would add a rich new measure of vitality in worship, a sense of awe that comes from seeing God at work at this very moment and

---

Grudem, "Wives like Sarah and the Husbands Who Honor Them: 1 Peter 3:1-7"; Piper and Grudem, "Charity, Clarity and Hope: The Controversy and the Cause of Christ"; and Grudem, "The Meaning of *Kephalē* ("*Head*"): A Response to Recent Studies," in *Recovering Biblical Manhood and Womanhood*, ed. Piper and Grudem, 60-92, 194-208, 403-22, 425-68. As a complementarian Grudem has become heavily involved in the controversy over gender issues in Bible translation. See Vern Poythress and Grudem, *The Gender-Neutral Bible Controversy: Muting the Masculinity of God's Words* (Nashville: Broadman & Holman, 2000).

[127]*Systematic Theology*, 537-39, 560-61, 556-58, 549-52, 1149-51.

[128]Ibid., 156-225, 472-82, 494-96, 515-22, 570-86, 594-603, 657-65, 692-95, 788-806, 684-86.

[129]Ibid., 966-82, 1031-38, 16, 1127-31.

[130]*The Gift of Prophecy in 1 Corinthians* (Ph.D. diss., University of Cambridge, 1979; Washington DC: University Press of America, 1982); *The Gift of Prophecy in the New Testament and Today* (Westchester IL: Crossway, 1988).

in this very place. . . ."[131] But Grudem located the baptism with the Holy Spirit at conversion.[132]

As a Baptist Grudem denied that baptism is a "'major'" doctrine, advocated open membership in Baptist churches for reapproachment with pedobaptists, interpreted the Lord's Supper in a Calvinistic, not Zwinglian, sense, treated baptism and the Lord's Supper among eleven "means of grace within the church," and strongly advocated a plurality of governing elders in the local church.[133]

Nigel Goring Wright (1949–): Reinterpreted Baptist Convictions for Post-Christendom

A native of Manchester whose "post-Christian" family had roots in the Hutterite, Quaker, and Salvation Army movements, Nigel Wright was converted at fifteen in a coffee bar and baptized into a somewhat traditional Baptist church.[134] He was identified with the Restorationist Movement[135] and with the Charismatic movement and its tongue-speaking, about each of which he subsequently wrote,[136] before his Baptist identity was confirmed. He received the B.A. degree (1970) from the University of Leeds, with concurrent study in Spurgeon's College, the M.Th. degree (1987) from the University of Glasgow, and the Ph.D. degree (1994) from King's College, London. After thirteen years as pastor of Ansdell Church, Lytham St. Annes, Lancashire, he became in 1987 tutor in Christian doctrine in Spurgeon's College, was pastor of Altrinchan Church, Cheshire, from 1995 to 2000,

---

[131] *The Gift of Prophecy in the New Testament and Today*, 253-63, 266-67.

[132] *Systematic Theology*, 766-73.

[133] Ibid., 966-67, 982-83, 990, 995-96, 950-63, 928-35.

[134] Wright, "A Pilgrimage in Renewal," in Tom Smail, Andrew Walker, and Nigel Wright, *Charismatic Renewal: The Search for a Theology* (London: SPCK, 1993) 22-23.

[135] Not to be confused by American readers with the movement derived from Thomas and Alexander Campbell but having similarity with the ministry of Bill Gothard and also called the house church movement.

[136] *The Radical Kingdom* (Eastbourne UK: Kingsway, 1986), "a critique of Restorationism from the perspective of freedom"; Wright, "A Pilgrimage in Renewal," "The Theology and Methodology of 'Signs and Wonders,' " and "The Rise of the Prophetic," in Smail, Walker, and Wright, *Charismatic Renewal*, 22-32, 71-85, 117-22.

and since 2000 he has served as principal of Spurgeon's College. He has been president of the Baptist Union of Great Britain (2002–2003).[137]

Wright wrote seriously in 1989 about Satan and the demonic. Although personal language in reference to Satan is necessary, such usage creates a problem since "person" ought to be used only of beings created in the image of God. We must accept Satan's existence but not his validity; hence we must "disbelieve in the devil." Wright examined critically Edwin Lewis's "evil as discreativity," Karl Barth's evil as "nothingness," and Walter Wink's evil as "interiority." From Wright's own perspective, evil is most evident in sinful human behavior, humankind is "assailed by" and the "victim" of "greater powers," and human sin has derived from the "misuse of creaturely freedom." The possibility of a "premundane, angelic catastrophe" or fall should be maintained even though the biblical texts[138] stand "on the margin of Scriptures" and may be "gentle hints" rather than "committed teaching." According to the Spurgeon's tutor, "misnamed" physical evil is a "Shadow" cast across creation that is not inherently evil, for "not all 'pain' is evil, but evil uses pain as an alibi and disguises itself behind it." Much of what has been identified as demon possession has been misidentified, and exorcism or deliverance should be undertaken with great care. "Principalities and powers" may be both suprahuman demons and agents at work in human societal structures. The use of military or battle language for spiritual warfare ought not to obscure the difference between Christ's weapons and those of the world.[139]

Wright has written specifically, intentionally, and repeatedly about the renewal of "Baptist identity" and church life. In 1991 in *Challenge to Change: A Radical Agenda for Baptists*, after identifying the Baptist emphases, he proposed six shifts: in worship "from the *solemn* to the *celebratory*," in structure "from the *organisational* to the *organic*, or from the *institutional* to the *charismatic*," in government "from *constitution* to *consensus*," in evangelism from *programme* to *power*," in mood "from the

---

[137]Biography, Spurgeon's College website; Anne Niblock to James Leo Garrett, Jr., 26 July 2007.

[138]Isa. 14:12-21; Ezek. 28:1-17; Jude 6; 2 Pet. 2:4.

[139]*The Fair Face of Evil* (London: Marshall, Morgan and Scott) 28-30, 57-59, 30, 24, 33-52, 53-56, 61-62, 62-63, 92-95, 101-30, 136-40, 180-83. American edition: *The Satan Syndrome: Putting the Power of Darkness in Its Place* (Grand Rapids MI: Zondervan, 1990). Revised edition: *A Theology of the Dark Side: Putting the Power of Evil in Its Place* (Downers Grove IL: InterVarsity, 2004).

formal to the *informal*," and in lifestyle "from the *conformist* to the *Christian*." Identifying congregational polity as "the centre of gravity" for Baptists and finding that it has a basis in the New Testament, Wright found its current practice among British Baptists to be in a deplorably distorted state, primarily because of the adoption of parliamentary democracy and "adversarial politics" to the neglect of spiritual discernment, and thus he called for a shift from voting to the seeking of consensus in church meetings. Similarly Baptist associations need reform and renewal so that in the contemporary context Baptist churches may have "mutual support and correction" and new churches may be planted. Moreover, the Baptist Union is likewise in need of reform, both in terms of a clearer evangelical identity and decentralization that would yield more functions to the associations. More surprising was Wright's call for Baptist bishops, who would resemble the messengers of early General Baptists and, unlike the present superintendents, be called and supported by associations. Baptists need to recover and reapply their nonconformist heritage, and that means adhering to a "Dissenting" view of the civil state rather than the "sacral" or "Puritan" view. Wright, following in the train of E. A. Payne and W. R. Estep, insisted that today's Baptists could learn much from sixteenth-century Anabaptists about discipleship, evangelism, zeal, and peace. Baptist transformation was high priority for the end of the twentieth century and the dawn of the new millennium.[140] In 2002 in *New Baptists, New Agenda*, the principal made it clear that the "true church" was not to be found by locating its fall in the past, but rather it "*has yet to come*," called on Christians to be "modest" but not falsely modest in facing postmodernism, outlined opportunities for denominations in a so-called postdenominational age, and contended for a "sustainable evangelism" in which vocational evangelists have a leading role.[141] In 2005 *Free Church, Free State: The Positive Baptist Vision* had as its announced aim: "to set out in a systematic and contemporary way those convictions and practices which distinguished Baptist Christians." Therein Wright, adopting James McClendon's use of "baptist"[142] to embrace a wider circle, explicated a regenerate and disci-

---

[140](Eastbourne UK: Kingsway) 22-35, 57-70, 92, 114-24, 106-14, 124-26, 133-50 (esp. 138), 151-71, 172-90, 191-211 (esp. 202-209), 212-34 (esp. 228-32), 235-46.

[141](Carlisle UK: Paternoster), 1-12 (esp. 4), 28-45 (esp. 39-42), 46-63, 81-95 (esp. 88-91).

[142]See above, 538. Cf. *New Baptists, New Agenda*, 53.

plined church membership, believer's baptism, congregational polity, associations of churches, and separation of church and state. He argued for "sacraments" rather than "ordinances" or "institutions" and did not differentiate his views from those of the British baptismal-sacramental school. Immersion, for Wright, is only the preferred mode of baptism, and it is not reckoned a Baptist principle. The rite of blessing for children and the catechumenate are recommended. Zwingli's doctrine of the Lord's Supper is reduced to a "commonsense" view, and the pastoral ministry is seen as belonging to the *bene esse* rather than the *esse* of the church. Neither the doctrine of the Bible nor the supremacy of Scripture over tradition nor the elevation of the New Testament above the Old Testament is set forth as a Baptist principle. Whereas in Wright's other writings Baptist identification with Evangelicalism had been emphasized, the final chapter of this book stressed "ecumenical engagement."[143]

In 1996 Wright set forth his beliefs as a "radical evangelical." He called for Trinitarian orthodoxy in resistance to those such as John Hick who have abandoned it, and adopted a Barthian view of God's election according to which humans are either "those in whom election has been realized" in Christ or "those in whom it has yet to be realized," or "Christians in hope." The Bible needs to be supplemented by tradition and reason, and its content and purpose should receive more attention than its form, a failure of Evangelicals. For Wright its inerrancy extends only to the execution of its purpose. Its cosmology need not be retained, and Scripture is not "literal history at all points." Penal substitution was reinterpreted and supplemented by the holy love of God and the relational nature of atonement. The liberal spirit was celebrated, and liberalism's tenets denied. "Jesus was capable of innocent mistakes." Wright opted for conditional immortality in place of everlasting punishment and the possibility of "postmortem evangelism," while trying to retain the "missionary mandate."[144] For some, Wright's conclusions appear to be more "radical" than "evangelical." In 2002 Wright argued that "Baptists are inherently evangelical" so that the question is: what kind of "evangelical"? But in place of his earlier adjective "radical,"

---

[143](Milton Keynes UK: Waynesboro GA: Paternoster) xv, xxii-xxiii, xxviii, 49-69, 70-92, 115-37, 183-203, 204-27, 94-99, 87, 147-52, 140-41, 105-6, 172-73, 256-58.

[144]*The Radical Evangelical: Seeking a Place to Stand* (London: S.P.C.K., 1996) 3, 13-27, 28-43 (esp. 42), 44-57, 58-86, 87-102.

he threw out the possibility of "open," "unitive," "ecumenical," "catholic," "progressive," "mainstream," and "centrist."[145]

Wright's dissertation was a study of the theologies of John Howard Yoder (1927–1997) and Jürgen Moltmann (1926–) with reference to "the disavowal of Constantine," set forth by both theologians, in the context of a free church and a free state for post-Christendom. Writing as well in the context of historic Anabaptism, the wider "baptist" world, and the ecumenical situation and utilizing Alistair Kee's interpretation of Constantine, Wright took note of "Moltmann's belonging to the Reformed tradition with the state as a part of the cultural mandate, yet inclining to the Anabaptist vision, and being still neglectful of the centrality of ecclesiology and of Yoder's reinterpretation of the peace-oriented and prophetic-dissent dimensions of the free church. Wright concluded with 21 theses concerning the church, the state, and the social order. He acknowledged that historically "the English Baptists assumed a position between Anabaptism and Reformed Christianity with an inclination to the Reformed" but that his inclination was "towards Anabaptism."[146] Seemingly no British Baptist has written as much or as insightfully about church-state issues as Wright.

Stanley James Grenz (1950–2005): Reenvisioner of Evangelical Theology for a Postmodern Age

A native of Alpena, Michigan, and the son of a Baptist pastor who served in the North American Baptist Conference, Grenz was graduated from the University of Colorado (B.A., 1973), Denver Conservative Baptist Seminary (M.Div., 1976), and the University of Munich (Th.D., *magna cum laude*, 1980). After a brief pastorate in Winnipeg, Manitoba, he served as professor of systematic theology and Christian ethics in North American Baptist Seminary, Sioux Falls, South Dakota (1981–1990) and was then Pioneer McDonald Professor of Baptist Heritage, Theology, and Ethics in Carey Theological College, Vancouver, British Columbia, from 1990 until his death, while concurrently serving as professor of theology and ethics in Regent College, also in Vancouver.[147]

---

[145]*New Baptists, New Agenda*, 15-21.

[146]*Disavowing Constantine: Mission, Church and the Social Order in the Theologies of John Howard Yoder and Jürgen Moltmann* (Carlisle UK: Paternoster, 2000) 1, 63-67, 122, 1-4, 16-17, 157-77, 122-23, 88-93, 67-71, 179-92 (esp. 192).

[147]*Who's Who in Religion*, 4th ed. (1992–1993) 196; *Contemporary Authors*, vol. 163 (1998) 170-71.

Grenz published his dissertation on the life and thought of Isaac Backus,[148] edited a festschrift for Bernard Ramm[149] and coedited one for Vernon C. Grounds, contributing a chapter on Søren Kierkegaard,[150] produced an introduction to postmodernism,[151] and was cocompiler of a dictionary of theological terms.[152] He was prolific in the field of Christian ethics: a coauthored book on ministry to AIDS victims;[153] an important monograph/textbook on Christian sexual ethics, which included adultery, divorce, pregnancy, singleness, and homosexuality;[154] a coauthored book on pastoral sexual misconduct,[155] a textbook on Christian ethics having biblical, historical, and contemporary materials and emphasizing a "comprehensive ethic of love" in community;[156] and a mediating "welcoming but not affirming" response to homosexuals.[157]

Grenz's theological writing included interpretations of modern Christian theology. He authored for English readers "a synopsis of [Wolfhart] Pannenberg's systematic theology" under the dual themes of "reason" and "hope" and organized "under six headings": approach, theology, creation/humanity, Christology, ecclesiology, and eschatology.[158]

---

[148]*Isaac Backus—Puritan and Baptist*.

[149]*Perspectives on Theology in the Contemporary World: Essays in Honor of Bernard Ramm* (Macon GA: Mercer University Press, 1990).

[150]With Kenneth W. M. Wozniak, *Christian Freedom: Essays in Honor of Vernon C. Grounds* (Lanham MD: University Press of America, 1986) esp. 69-85.

[151]*A Primer on Postmodernism* (Grand Rapids MI: Eerdmans, 1996).

[152]With David Guretzki and Cherith Fee Nordling, *Pocket Dictionary of Theological Terms* (Downers Grove IL: InterVarsity, 1999).

[153]With Wendell W. Hoffman, *AIDS Ministry in the Midst of an Epidemic* (Grand Rapids MI: Baker, 1990).

[154]*Sexual Ethics: A Biblical Perspective* (Dallas: Word, 1990); rev. ed. with subtitle *An Evangelical Perspective* (Louisville: Westminster/John Knox, 1997).

[155]With Roy D. Bell, *Betrayal of Trust: Sexual Misconduct in the Pastorate* (Downers Grove IL: InterVarsity, 1995).

[156]*The Moral Quest: Foundations of Christian Ethics* (Downers Grove IL: InterVarsity, 1997).

[157]*Welcoming but Not Affirming: An Evangelical Response to Homosexuality* (Louisville: Westminster/John Knox, 1998), esp. 153-57. Grenz coauthored with Jay T. Smith, *Pocket Dictionary of Ethics* (Downers Grove IL: InterVarsity, 2003).

[158]*Reason for Hope: The Systematic Theology of Wolfhart Pannenberg* (New York: Oxford University Press, 1990) esp. 5-10. Pannenberg was Grenz's *Doktorvater* in Munich.

He coauthored with Roger E. Olson an interpretation of the leading Christian theologians of the twentieth century around the alternating themes of divine transcendence and immanence.[159] Similarly, Grenz coauthored with Ed. LeRoy Miller a briefer but similar interpretation but with Evangelicals such as Henry and Ramm omitted.[160]

Grenz's systematic theology, published in 1994[161] and revised in 2000,[162] took "community" as its "integrative motif" on the ground that "God's central program for creation," and presumably for redemption, is "the establishment of community." Acknowledging "the rationalist approach" of his teachers, Gordon Lewis and Pannenberg, he declared his intention in this volume "to integrate the rationalistic and pietistic dimensions of the Christian faith."[163] By utilizing six major divisions (theology, anthropology, Christology, pneumatology, ecclesiology, and eschatology), he had to disperse revelation and the knowledge of God and to treat the doctrines of the Bible and soteriology under pneumatology.[164] Giving prominence to the Trinity, the Carey professor organized the divine attributes under eternality and goodness, interpreted creation without careful attention to evolution, contended that "the concept of general revelation is valid and helpful" but "also limited," and affirmed the universal Fatherhood of God.[165] Moreover, he retained a historical Adam, opted for a "wholistic view of the human person," gave the *Imago Dei* an eschatological interpretation, affirmed both a historical fall and an individual fall, and denied that humanity is guilty of Adam's sin.[166] Developing his Christology in depth, Grenz affirmed the historicity of Jesus' virgin birth, while conceding that the doctrine "is not christologically indispensable." Hesitant about propitiation, he declared that Jesus' death was "primarily directed

---

[159] *20th-Century Theology: God and the World in a Transitional Age* (Downers Grove IL: InterVarsity, 1992).

[160] *Fortress Introduction to Contemporary Theologies* (Minneapolis: Fortress, 1998).

[161] *Theology for the Community of God* (Nashville: Broadman & Holman, 1994).

[162] (Grand Rapids MI: Eerdmans; Vancouver: Regent College Publishing, 2000).

[163] Ibid., 1st ed., ix-x.

[164] Ibid., 173-81, 54-67, 494-599.

[165] Ibid., 68-99, 118-24, 129-46, 173-81 (esp. 180), 183-85.

[166] Ibid., 192-93, 208-13 (esp. 211), 223-24, 229-33, 255-66.

toward human sin and not God's wrath." "Because the Bible is the Spirit's book, its purpose is instrumental to his mission," and the illumination of the Spirit was operative in the process of canonization. The Bible is "mediate revelation," and in dealing with biblical inerrancy Grenz wished to include an inductive approach to biblical phenomena.[167] The church is the sign of the kingdom and has as its mandates worship, edification, and outreach. Baptism and the Lord's Supper are "community acts of commitment," and congregational polity, although expressive of the priesthood of all believers, "is difficult to maintain in practice."[168] Earlier Grenz had written a small volume on Baptist congregational polity, origins, and emphases.[169] He then coauthored with Denise Muir Kjesbo a monograph that expounded and defended the "equalitarian" view of women in church ministry, including the pastoral ministry, over against the "complementarian" view espoused by Piper and Grudem. They argued that "in the church we can best reflect the liberating significance of Jesus' incarnation as a male by following the principle of egalitarian mutuality that he pioneered."[170] Grenz opted for an intermediate state, "amillennial realism," and eternal hell.[171] Grenz had written also an informative review and assessment of the major millennial views at the end of the twentieth century in which he narrated his own trek from dispensationalism through historic premillennialism to amillennialism and on to a modification which included the new heaven and the new earth.[172] Compensating for Grenz's truncated treatment of soteriology was his monograph on prayer with its emphasis on prayer according to God's will and persistently.[173] After producing his systematic theology, he wrote with Roger Olson an introduction to the theological task,[174] authored a brief

---

[167] Ibid., 319-423 (esp. 422), 451-53, 495, 505, 517, 522-23.

[168] Ibid., 614-20, 637-64, 665-704, 720-25 (esp. 724).

[169] *The Baptist Congregation: A Guide to Baptist Belief and Practice* (Valley Forge PA: Judson, 1985).

[170] *Women in the Church: A Biblical Theology of Women in Ministry* (Downers Grove IL: InterVarsity, 1995) esp. 209.

[171] *Theology for the Community of God*, 766-75, 805-6, 835-39.

[172] *The Millennial Maze*, esp. 9-11, 214.

[173] *Prayer: The Cry for the Kingdom* (Peabody MA: Hendrickson, 1988; rev. ed., Grand Rapids MI: Eerdmans, 2005).

[174] *Who Needs Theology? An Invitation to the Study of God* (Downers Grove IL: InterVarsity, 1996).

statement of Christian beliefs,[175] and produced a "distillation" of his theology as the foundation for Christian living for a lay readership.[176]

During his last fifteen years Grenz intentionally and concertedly set out to reinterpret his Evangelical and Baptist heritage vis-à-vis the contemporary cultural scene, especially the postmodern age. In 1993 he sought to "revision" Evangelicalism by shifting its identity from the predominance of doctrine to equality with spirituality and its theological method from propositions to include narrative and the faith community, by strengthening "the link between the Holy Spirit and Scripture," and by opting for the loving community of God rather than the kingdom of God as the integrative motif.[177] In 2000 Grenz portrayed Carl Henry and Bernard Ramm as representative of the right wing and the left wing, respectively, of twentieth-century American Evangelicalism, posited Millard Erickson as Henry's successor and Clark Pinnock as a "theological pilgrim" on the left, and suggested Wayne Grudem as the likely successor to Erickson and John Sanders to Pinnock. Then he sought to move Evangelical epistemology from foundationalism toward "a Christian belief-mosaic," to move the science and religion discussion toward ontology and eschatology, to suggest a providential role for non-Christian religions, to nudge Evangelicals from preoccupation with parachurch practice toward a "communitarian" ecclesiology, and to call for a renewed "evangelical center ... characterized by a "'generous orthodoxy.'"[178] In 2001 he coauthored with John R. Franke a volume that sought to set forth more completely a postfoundationalist theology on the basis of three sources—Scripture, tradition, and culture—and with a focus on the Trinity, the church, and last things.[179]

Grenz began a six-volume series entitled "The Matrix of Christian Theology" and designed to utilize the Scriptures, Christian tradition, and contemporary culture as a "trialogue" for "an exercise in constructive

---

[175]*What Christians Really Believe—and Why* (Louisville: Westminster/John Knox, 1998).

[176]*Created for Community: Connecting Christian Belief with Christian Living* (Grand Rapids MI: Baker, 1996) esp. 12.

[177]*Revisioning Evangelical Theology: A Fresh Agenda for the 21st Century* (Downers Grove IL: InterVarsity), esp. 31, 39, 45, 70, 72-73, 113, 147-61.

[178]*Renewing the Center: Evangelical Theology in a Post-Theological Era* (Grand Rapids MI: Baker).

[179]*Beyond Foundationalism: Shaping Theology in a Postmodern Context* (Louisville: Westminster/John Knox).

theology" so as to meet the needs of the postmodern age. Each volume was to build on the doctrine of the Trinity.[180] Grenz lived to complete only two volumes. The first to be published, anthropological in nature and using a social view of the Trinity, interpreted the *imago Dei* not in structural or relational terms but in terms of eschatological destiny, with consequence for human sexuality and the self-in-community.[181] The second, focused on the doctrine of God, sought to undo the modern secularization of being and to re-Christianize being in a Trinitarian manner and thus move "from onto-theology to theo-ontology."[182]

Like certain previous Baptist theologians, Grenz evoked both commendation and criticism. According to Roger E. Olson, Grenz made a fourfold contribution to evangelical theology: "a call to radical centrism and away from cultural accommodation"; advocacy of "ongoing reform" of evangelicalism "tied to the great tradition but open to new ways of thinking"; "exposure of evangelical theological accommodation to the [E]nlightenment"; and "the elevation of community and narrative over individualism and rationalism in theology, as well as in worship and piety."[183] On the contrary, R. Albert Mohler, Jr., found Grenz's shift from a "'creed-based' identity" to a "'spirituality-based' identity" to leave "the truth question . . . ill-defined" and to provide "a convenient way out of the pattern of debates and controversies over the inerrancy and inspiration of Scripture." Moreover, he asserted, Grenz's proposal for revisioning was similar to that of the "cultural-linguistic" or postliberal Yale school of George Lindbeck and others with its "abdication of the universal truth claim." Hence, according to Mohler, Grenz's proposal "cannot result in a genuinely evangelical system."[184] Carson found Grenz's inclusion of culture as one of three sources for theology—to be "decidedly unhelpful" and "astonishing."

---

[180]*The Social God and the Relational Self: A Trinitarian Theology of the Imago Dei* (Louisville: Westminster/John Knox, 2001) ix-x.

[181]Ibid., esp. 14-20, 23-57, 141-82, 267-336.

[182]*The Named God and the Question of Being: A Trinitarian Theo-Ontology* (Louisville: Westminster/John Knox, 2005).

[183]"Stanley J. Grenz's Contribution to Evangelical Theology," *Princeton Theological Review* 12 (Spring 2006): 27-28, 40 (esp. 40).

[184]"The Integrity of the Evangelical Tradition and the Challenge of the Postmodern Paradigm," in *The Challenge of Postmodernism: An Evangelical Engagement*, ed. David S. Dockery (Grand Rapids MI: Baker, 1997; rev. ed., 2001; orig., Wheaton IL: Victor Books, 1995) 78-81.

Hence he "cannot see how Grenz's approach to Scripture can be called 'evangelical' in any useful sense."[185]

Timothy Francis George: Evangelical/Calvinist and Baptist Historical Theologian

Born in Chattanooga, Tennessee, and educated at the University of Tennessee at Chattanooga (B.A., 1972) and Harvard University (M.Div., 1975; Th.D., 1979), George taught church history and historical theology at Southern Baptist Theological Seminary from 1978 to 1988. Then he became the founding dean of and professor of divinity in Beeson Divinity School of Samford University in Birmingham, Alabama, a multiconfessional evangelical school in a Baptist university. He continues to serve there with teaching and writing focused especially on general church history, Reformation theology, and Evangelicalism. He has served as a senior editor (1983–2000) and an executive editor (2000–) of *Christianity Today* and has been an irenic bridge-builder among Evangelicals and between Evangelicals and Roman Catholics. He has had leadership roles in the SBC and the BWA.[186]

George coedited a festschrift for his Harvard mentor,[187] George Huntston Williams, and wrote subsequently about him.[188] He wrote a readable, well-documented biography of William Carey[189] and the volume on Galatians in *The New American Commentary*.[190] With David S. Dockery he coedited an extensive volume on various Baptist theologians in two

---

[185]*The Gagging of God*, 481.

[186]Curriculum Vitae, Beeson Divinity School.

[187]With F. Forrester Church, *Continuity and Discontinuity in Church History: Essays Presented to George Huntston Williams on the Occasion of His 65th Birthday* (Leiden: E. J. Brill, 1979).

[188]"George Huntston Williams: A Historian for All Seasons," *American Journal of Theology and Philosophy* 7 (May 1986): 75-93; repr. in *The Contentious Triangle: Church, State, and University: A Festschrift in Honor of Professor George Huntston Williams*, ed. Rodney L. Petersen and Calvin Augustine Pater, Sixteenth Century Essays and Studies 51 (Kirksville MO: Thomas Jefferson University Press, 1999) 15-34; "Keeping Truth Alive as a Holy Calling," *Harvard Divinity Bulletin* 29 (Winter 2001): 4-6.

[189]*Faithful Witness: The Life and Mission of William Carey* (Birmingham AL: New Hope, 1991).

[190]*Galatians*, The New American Commentary 30 (Nashville: Broadman & Holman, 1994).

editions.[191] George republished selected sermons of James P. Boyce with his own introductory biographical essay,[192] and together with his wife Denise Wyse George, he coedited the twelve-volume Library of Baptist Classics.[193] He coauthored books on racial reconciliation[194] and on the mark of Christ upon the Christian,[195] edited a book on Dwight L. Moody[196] and essays on Evangelicals in relation to other Christian groupings,[197] and coedited a volume on Evangelical spirituality.[198]

George's more systematic expressions of theology grew out of his expertise in historical theology. His published dissertation was a detailed study of the English Separatist, John Robinson (1575–1625), whose theology had its "controlling dynamic" in "the tension between... sectarian ecclesiology ... and a high predestinarian theology."[199] His *Theology of the Reformers*[200] was a study of the theology of four of the Protestant Reformers: Martin Luther, with emphasis on justification, predestination, *sola Scriptura*, the church, word and sacrament, priesthood of all believers, and civil government; Huldrych Zwingli; with emphasis on creation, providence, baptism, and the Lord's Supper; John Calvin, with emphasis on the Trinity, creation, providence, sin, Christology, life in the Spirit, and the

---

[191]*Baptist Theologians*; *Theologians of the Baptist Tradition*. The theologians included tended to be Calvinist rather than Arminian and more Southern Baptist than Northern Baptist. George wrote chapters on John Gill (*BT*, 77-101; *TBT*, 11-33) and J. P. Boyce (*BT*, 249-66; *TBT*, 73-89).

[192]*James Petigru Boyce: Selected Writings* (Nashville: Broadman, 1989).

[193]Broadman & Holman published these under their respective titles between 1995 and 1997.

[194]With Robert Smith, Jr., *A Mighty Long Journey: Reflections of Racial Reconciliation* (Nashville: Broadman & Holman, 2000).

[195]With John D. Woodbridge, *The Mark of Jesus* (Chicago: Moody, 2005).

[196]*Mr. Moody and the Evangelical Tradition* (London: T.&T. Clark, 2004).

[197]*Pilgrims on the Sawdust Trail: Evangelical Ecumenism and the Quest for Christian Identity* (Grand Rapids MI: Baker, 2004). George's chapter (125-37) dealt with Evangelicals and Roman Catholics.

[198]With Alister E. McGrath, *For All the Saints: Evangelical Theology and Christian Spirituality* (Louisville: Westminster/John Knox, 2003).

[199]*John Robinson and the English Separatist Tradition*, National Association of Baptist Professors of Religion Dissertation Series 1 (Macon GA: Mercer University Press, 1982) esp. viii. See also "Predestination in a Separatist Context: The Case of John Robinson," *Sixteenth-Century Journal* 15 (Spring 1984): 73-85.

[200](Nashville: Broadman, 1988).

church; and Menno Simons, with emphasis on regeneration, the Scriptures, the incarnation, the church, its ordinances, and its discipline, and persecution.

George's theological writing has largely focused on theology (God), soteriology, and ecclesiology. Following the United States crisis of 11 September 2001, the Beeson dean produced a small, tightly written book[201] designed to answer whether "the Father of Jesus" is the same as "the God of Muhammad." He offered two answers: "yes" "in the sense that the Father of Jesus is the only God there is" and "no" because "Muslim theology rejects the fatherhood of God, the deity of Jesus Christ, and the personhood of the Holy Spirit," and hence the Trinity. Shared monotheism is not sufficient to make Christianity and Islam "sister religions." Muslims reject a "concocted tritheism." "God is one but not alone," "is love," "is free to be gracious," "is personal," and "is sufficiently sovereign to come as well as to send." The real stone of stumbling is Jesus' death on the cross, for the Koran teaches that someone else died in his place. Humans need atonement, grace, forgiveness, and reconciliation, not merely guidance, to follow the "strait path."

George, writing primarily for a wide Southern Baptist readership, sought to explain his beliefs as "a Reformed Baptist theologian." First laying out the doctrine of providence, which he differentiated from deism, pantheism, fatalism, and process theism, he then took Augustine's side against Pelagius, Luther's side against Erasmus, the Synod of Dort's side against the Arminians, and George Whitefield's side against John Wesley. At the same time he warned of "the quagmire of Hyper-Calvinism" and identified with the Calvinism of Carey and Spurgeon. Evidently desiring to diversify the theological garden, George offered in place of the acronym TULIP that of ROSES: "radical depravity," "overcoming grace," "sovereign election," "eternal life," and "singular redemption."[202] The Beeson dean also defended "particularism" (or exclusivism) over against pluralism and exclusivism in the debate as to the destiny of the unevangelized.[203]

---

[201] *Is the Father of Jesus the God of Muhammad?* (Grand Rapids MI: Zondervan, 2002) 69-75, 57-59, 81-87, 97-103, 135-37, 113-21.

[202] *Amazing Grace: God's Initiative—Our Response* (Nashville: LifeWay, 2000) 11, 26-45 (esp. 35-38), 48-62, 89-107, 59-60, 71-83.

[203] "The *SBJT* Forum: Responses to Inclusivism," *Southern Baptist Journal of Theology* 2 (Summer 1998): 50-52.

In interpreting John Gill's ecclesiology, George found its "fundamental impulse" to be "a peculiar correlation" of "the basis of saving faith and the locus of the true visible church." He seemed to resonate with the truth that "the church... transcends the categories of time and space in that it derives from the eternal purpose of God" and with commencing with the "invisible church" rather than the local congregation.[204] Building on a BWA response to the Faith and Order document, *Baptism, Eucharist and Ministry*,[205] George identified several "reservations" which "most Baptists and evangelicals" have to "describing the church itself as a sacrament," but then offered four legitimate meanings: the incarnational nature of Christ's presence "in the work and witness of His people on earth," a needed alternative to "sacramental individualism," the church's witnessing to Christ's work and being "the custodian and interpreter" of the Bible, and the *ecclesia in via*, or a community that "points beyond itself."[206] Recognizing Evangelicalism's neglect of ecclesiology, the Samford professor offered an Evangelical reinterpretation of the historic four marks of the true church: "one," even though Evangelicals have both reformational and restitutionist roots; "holy," but in distinction from God's holiness; "catholic," in view of the worldwide extent of Evangelicalism; and "apostolic," though inscripturated gospel rather than episcopal succession.[207]

In a Believers' Church conference in 1984, George, representing Southern Baptists, identified five "pastoral problems" relative to baptism: the residual "legacy of Landmarkism," "the proper age for baptism" ("toddler baptism"), the rebaptizing of those who have had believer's baptism at non-Baptist hands, the lack of instruction, and the lack of a positive baptismal theology.[208] Then in a Presbyterian journal he delineated "the Reformed [or earlier Baptist] doctrine of believers' baptism" in contrast both to pedo-

---

[204]"The Ecclesiology of John Gill," in *The Life and Thought of John Gill (1697–1771): A Tercentenary Appreciation*, ed. Michael A. G. Haykim (Leiden: Brill, 1997) 225-36 (esp. 226, 227).

[205]Faith and Order Paper no. 111 (Geneva: World Council of Churches, 1982).

[206]"The Sacramentality of the Church," in *Baptist Sacramentalism*, ed. Cross and Thompson, 21-35.

[207]"Toward an Evangelical Ecclesiology," in *Catholics and Evangelicals: Do They Share a Common Future?*, ed. Thomas P. Rausch, S.J. (Downers Grove IL: InterVarsity, 2000) 122-48.

[208]"The Southern Baptists," in *Baptism and Church: A Believer's Church Vision*, ed. Strege, 39-51.

baptism and to "the attenuated meaning of baptism in many modern [especially Baptist] churches." He approvingly noted that Particular Baptists taught that God effectively called elect infants dying in infancy to salvation and called for "a proper theology of children."[209]

Reacting against the Baptist tendency to regard the Lord's Supper as "merely a symbol," George advocated "a robust doctrine of the real spiritual presence of Christ in the Lord's Supper" that would reflect Calvin's "middle way between Zwingli's minimalism and Luther's literalism" and the teachings of the Second London Confession (1677, 1689) and of Spurgeon.[210]

When the doctrine was highly controverted in the SBC, George reinterpreted the priesthood of all believers by disconnecting it from soul competency and religious liberty, by placing it in the context of a healthy confessionalism that stops short of creedalism, by revisiting its collective significance by reviewing Luther and Calvin, and by warning against its being trivialized by being equated "with modern individualism or theological minimalism."[211]

George explicated the Baptist-espoused Christian ideal of "a free Church in a free state" on the eve of a national election[212] by restating the early General Baptist case for religious freedom which he had more fully researched.[213]

---

[209] "The Reformed Doctrine of Believers' Baptism," *Interpretation* 47 (July 1993): 242-54 (esp. 243, 245, 252); repr. as "Believers' Baptism: More than American Individualism," *Modern Reformation* 6 (May-June 1997): 41-47.

[210] "The *SBJT* Forum: The Lord's Supper," *Southern Baptist Journal of Theology* 6 (Fall 2002): 100-102.

[211] "The Priesthood of All Believers and the Quest for Theological Integrity," *Criswell Theological Review* 3 (Spring 1989): 283-94; repr. in *The People of God: Essays on the Believers' Church*, ed. Basden and Dockery, 85-95.

[212] "Practicing the Two Kingdoms: The Baptist Ideal of a Free Church in a Free State," *Modern Reformation* 9 (September-October 2000): 29-31, 51.

[213] "Between Pacifism and Coercion: The English Baptist Doctrine of Religious Toleration," *Mennonite Quarterly Review* 58 (January 1984): 30-49.

Roger Eugene Olson (1952–): Evangelical Arminianism and the History of Christian Doctrine

Born in Des Moines, Iowa, and the son of an Open Bible Standard[214] pastor, Olson was educated at Open Bible College (B.A., 1974), North American Baptist Seminary (M.A., 1982), and Rice University (M.A., 1982; Ph.D., 1984) with studies in the University of Munich (1981–1982). He was ordained in 1975 by Open Bible Standard Churches, and that ordination has been recognized by churches affiliated with the American Baptist Churches (USA), the BGC and the BGCT. After teaching for two years in Oral Roberts University (1982–1984), he taught theology at Bethel College, St. Paul, MN (1984–1989) before becoming professor of theology in the George W. Truett Theological Seminary of Baylor University, where he has specialized in historical theology.[215]

Olson's first solely authored book[216] was a readable one-volume history of Christian doctrine.[217] Intending to tell this history as a "story," he did not, however, clarify the method to be employed. Nearly one-half of the book is devoted to the patristic age, and there Olson followed the organic method—men, movements (including heresies), councils, and creeds. Later he tended to allow major theologians to represent movements; for example, Anselm of Canterbury, Abelard, and Thomas Aquinas as representative of Scholasticism, Hubmaier and Menno of the Radical Reformation, Jonathan Edwards of Puritanism, John Toland and Matthew Tindal of Deism, and Karl Rahner of recent Roman Catholic theology. Olson chose not to treat Eastern Orthodox theology after 1054, Roman Catholic theology between the Council of Trent and Vatican Council II, or twentieth-century Pentecostalism. He clearly explained new or distinctive doctrinal interpretations.

---

[214]Open Bible (Standard) Churches, Inc., is a Pentecostal denomination resulting from the merger in 1935 of two groups, one of which derived from the Apostolic Faith, Portland, Oregon. Among their beliefs are "healing in the Atonement" and "speaking in tongues as the initial physical evidence of the baptism in the Holy Spirit." *Dictionary of Pentecostal and Charismatic Movements*, ed. S. M. Burgess, G. B. McGee, and P. H. Alexander (Grand Rapids MI: Zondervan, 1988) 652-53. Per Paul L. Gritz. See <www.openbible.org>.

[215]Curriculum Vitae, Truett Theological Seminary; *Contemporary Authors*, vol. 223 (2004) 284-86.

[216]For his books coauthored with Grenz, see above, 692, 693-94.

[217]*The Story of Christian Theology: Twenty Centuries of Tradition and Reform* (Downers Grove IL: InterVarsity, 1999).

He tilted in favor of the legacy of "synergism" with its stress on human responsibility (Semi-Pelagians, Gregory the Great, Erasmus, Anabaptists, Melanchthon, Hooker, Arminians, Pietists, and Wesley) rather than the legacy of "monergism" with its emphasis on divine sovereignty (Augustine of Hippo, Thomas Aquinas, Luther, Zwingli, Calvin, Barth).[218]

Shortly thereafter Olson produced a similar but different volume.[219] Taking a dozen Christian doctrines from systematic theology, he gathered under each pertinent materials from the history of Christian doctrine. Each chapter follows the same pattern: first the leading issues or polarities are identified, then a "Christian consensus" on the doctrine is stated, subsequently the alternative views and diversities are explored, and finally Olson discusses the possibility of a "unified Christian view." On authority he opts for the Wesleyan Quadrilateral, on general revelation he gains consensus by excluding Barth, and on the Bible both Thomas Jefferson and John R. Rice are outside the consensus. The consensus on the Trinity is more expressive of the Cappadocian threeness than the Augustinian oneness, but Olson insists that "the social analogy needs to be corrected, balanced and supplemented by the psychological analogy." Diversities as to providence include meticulous providence, limited providence, and open theism. Olson's affirmation of the "goodness" of humanity turns out to be having the *imago Dei*, but the consensus centers in inherited depravity, not Adamic guilt. Christological consensus is Chalcedonian, though the better forms of kenoticism are acceptable. Surprisingly there is no chapter on the Holy Spirit. The death of Jesus provides "reconciliation," not specifically atonement, and the consensus on salvation sees it as both "gift" and "task." Charles G. Finney is the great modern Semi-Pelagian. Concerning the church the Anabaptist-free church-Baptist heritage is weakly represented as if its only concern were baptism and the Lord's Supper. Olson notes that there have been few eschatological "heresies," though much diversity. His synergistic sympathy is less apparent in this volume.[220]

---

[218] See the present author's review of this book: *Southwestern Journal of Theology* 42 (Summer 2000): 96-97. The Baptists treated by Olson were Walter Rauschenbusch, W. B. Riley, Curtis Lee Laws, John R. Rice, Carl F. H. Henry, and Billy Graham.

[219] *The Mosaic of Christian Belief: Twenty Centuries of Unity and Diversity* (Downers Grove IL; Leicester UK: InterVarsity, 2002).

[220] Ibid., esp. 26-27, 56-57, 73-77, 95, 98, 135-41, 153, 189-96, 204-11, 226-31, 239-40, 251, 267-75, 302, 344-45.

Having written his Rice dissertation as a critical examination of Wolfhart Pannenberg's effort to combine eschatology and the Trinity in the framework of reason and revelation with a resultant "eschatological panentheism,"[221] Olson has coauthored with Christopher Hall[222] a concise and balanced history of the doctrine of the Trinity.

In his *The Westminster Handbook to Evangelical Theology*[223] the Truett professor gave much attention to parachurch movements while virtually ignoring evangelical denominations, included as "key figures" in Evangelicalism five Baptists (Billy Graham, Carl Henry, Clark Pinnock, Bernard Ramm, A. H. Strong), and omitted water baptism from a group of fourteen issues in contemporary evangelical theology. His coauthored *Pocket History of Theology*, carrying again the "story" motif, devotes two chapters to the patristic age and one each to the medieval, the Reformation, and the modern eras. The only Baptist mentioned is W. B. Riley.[224]

With the publication of *Arminian Theology: Myths and Realities*,[225] Olson has attained the undisputed status of the leading Baptist theological advocate of Arminianism in the United States.[226] Noting that he has been a lifelong Arminian, he set out to demythologize ten misconceptions of Arminian theology. The idea that Arminianism is "the opposite " of Calvinism is erroneous because Arminius belonged to the Reformed tradition and there is common ground between the two systems. The idea that a "hybrid"—Calminianism—is possible is refuted by Olson, for the "gap" is too "wide and deep," despite common ground. The idea that Arminianism "is not an orthodox Evangelical option" can be disproved on the basis of Arminian teachings concerning the Scriptures, the Trinity and Christology. The heart of Arminian theology is not free will; rather it is "God's good character, . . . manifested in love and justice." Moreover, the

---

[221]"Trinity and Eschatology: The Historical Being of God in the Theology of Wolfhart Pannenberg" (Ph.D. diss., Rice University, 1984; Ann Arbor: University Microfilms International, 1988).

[222]*The Trinity* (Grand Rapids MI: Eerdmans, 2002).

[223](Louisville: Westminster/John Knox, 2004) 67-100, 101-39, 287-328.

[224]With Adam C. English (Downers Grove IL: InterVarsity, 2005).

[225](Downers Grove IL: InterVarsity, 2006).

[226]He had previously (2002) defended Arminianism in a Mormon context: "Confessions of an Arminian Evangelical," in *Salvation in Christ: Comparative Christian Views*, ed. Roger R. Keller and Robert L. Millet (Provo UT: Religious Study Center, Brigham Young University, 2005) 183-203.

idea that Arminians deny the sovereignty of God is untrue; they only resist a meticulous providence and want to differentiate "the antecedent and the consequent wills of God." Accused of having "a human-centered theology," Arminians deny such, for Arminius believed in total depravity and sought to distance "himself as far as possible from Pelagianism and semi-Pelagianism." Furthermore, the charge that Arminianism "is not a theology of grace" can be refuted from "the all-important Arminian concept of prevenient grace" and the strong doctrine of grace in Arminius and his modern successors. The accusation that Arminians "do not believe in predestination" is not true, for they, as did Wesley, hold rather a view that includes God's foreknowledge of the faith of believers. Arminians do not deny, but rather uphold justification by grace through faith alone, and not all Arminians hold to the governmental theory of the atonement, for some embrace the penal substitution theory.[227] Unmentioned in Olson's list is the assertion that Arminians teach the final apostasy of some true believers, presumably because such is no "myth."

David Samuel Dockery (1952–):
Evangelical-Calminian Baptist and the Doctrine of the Bible

A native of Tuscaloosa, Alabama, baptized at nine and ordained at 28, Dockery is a graduate of the University of Alabama at Birmingham (B.S., 1975), Grace Theological Seminary (M.Div., 1979), Southwestern Baptist Theological Seminary (M.Div., 1981), Texas Christian University (M.A., 1985), and the University of Texas at Arlington (Ph.D., 1988). After the pastorate of Metropolitan Church, Brooklyn, New York (1981–1984), and teaching theology and New Testament at Criswell College, Dallas (1984–1988), he then became associate professor and then professor of New Testament theology at Southern Baptist Theological Seminary (1988–1990, 1992–1996), and following a two-year period as general editor of *New American Commentary* for the Sunday School Board (SBC), rejoined the Southern faculty, becoming dean of the School of Theology (1992–1996) and vice-president of academic administration (1993–1996). In 1996 he became president of Union University, Jackson, Tennessee, and professor of

---

[227]*Arminian Theology: Myths and Realities*, 7-8, 43, 44-60, 63, 67-77, 82-93, 102-105, 114, 130-31, 123-24, 141-46, 159-61, 163-64, 166-78, 187-88, 202-207, 220, 225-29, 231-37, 240-41.

Christian studies and has presided over the expansion of this historic institution.[228]

Dockery has done considerable work as editor and coeditor of books. He has edited a work on the relationship of Southern Baptists to American Evangelicals,[229] a book of Evangelical responses to postmodernism,[230] and a festschrift for Millard J. Erickson.[231] He has coedited two editions of a volume interpreting Baptist theologians,[232] a festschrift for James Leo Garrett, Jr.,[233] a volume of nineteen essays on the different methods of biblical criticism and various issues for New Testament interpretation,[234] a book consisting of divergent views as to the Scriptures among Southern Baptists,[235] a comprehensive textbook on biblical hermeneutics,[236] a volume on the nature and future of Christian higher education,[237] and a volume concerning a Christian worldview for Christian higher education.[238] He was the general editor of *Holman Bible Handbook*[239] and of *Holman Concise*

---

[228]Curriculum Vitae, Union University; *Who's Who in Religion*, 4th ed. (1992–1993) 130; *Contemporary Authors*, vol. 223 (2004) 114-15.

[229]*Southern Baptists and American Evangelicals: The Conversation Continues.* See above, 535-36n.116.

[230]*The Challenge of Postmodernism: An Evangelical Engagement.* See above, 696n.184.

[231]*New Dimensions in Evangelical Thought: Essays in Honor of Millard J. Erickson.* See above, 525n.57.

[232]With Timothy George, *Baptist Theologians*; *Theologians of a Baptist Tradition*.

[233]With Paul A. Basden, *The People of God: Essays on the Believers' Church*.

[234]With David Alan Balck, *New Testament Criticism and Interpretation* (Grand Rapids MI: Zondervan, 1991); rev. ed. entitled *Interpreting the New Testament: Essays on Method and Issues* (Nashville: Broadman & Holman, 2001).

[235]With Robison B. James, *Beyond the Impasse? Scripture, Interpretation, and Theology in Baptist Life*. See above, 257n.55; 504n.464.

[236]With Kenneth A. Mathews and Robert B. Sloan, *Foundations for Biblical Interpretation* (Nashville: Broadman & Holman, 1994).

[237]With David P. Gushee, *The Future of Christian Higher Education* (Nashville: Broadman & Holman, 1999). Dockery was the author of three chapters.

[238]With Gregory Alan Thornbury, *Shaping a Christian Worldview: The Foundations of Christian Higher Education* (Nashville: Broadman & Holman, 2002).

[239](Nashville: Holman Bible Publishers, 1992).

Bible Commentary[240] and the compiler of *The Best of A. T. Robertson*.[241] He has been a consulting editor of *Christianity Today* since 1992.

Dockery's doctrine of the Christian Scriptures included that which serves as prolegomena: the self-testimony of the Bible and its relationship to divine revelation and to Jesus Christ. "Both Testaments view the words of Scripture as God's own words," and Psalm 119 "exemplifies" this attitude. The New Testament introduces quotations from the Old Testament by formulas such as "God says," "the Holy Spirit says," and "it is written." The Old Testament prophets had employed "the word of the Lord came to me saying" and "thus says the Lord." References to the need for and fact of fulfilled Old Testament prophecy are also a part of the self-testimony of the Scriptures. The Bible alludes to general revelation and embodies special or particular revelation, which is progressive, personal, and propositional. Jesus not only taught his disciples "that His life and ministry fulfilled the [Old Testament] Scriptures" but also provided a new Christological method of interpreting the Old Testament, that is, "in light of Himself." The New Testament is a body of "Spirit-directed writings that focused on the life, ministry, death, resurrection, and exaltation of Christ."[242]

The Old Testament contains references to the transmission or preservation of portions of the law and the prophets, and collections of the Gospels and of the Pauline epistles existed in the second century AD "The whole Bible existed in at least seven versions [languages] by the sixth century AD" Dockery was agreeable to recent scholarship in positing the closure of the Old Testament canon "by the time of Jesus," if not as early as 165 BC, but he retained the traditional view that "the decisive period in the history of the New Testament canon was AD 140-200."[243]

Dockery sought to explicate "the two-sided character of the Bible as a divine-human book" so as to avoid an "ebionitic" conclusion that the Bible is only a human book and a "docetic" conclusion that is only a divine book. 2 Tim. 3:16-17 alludes to the divine inspiration of the writings, not merely

---

[240](Nashville: Broadman & Holman, 1998).

[241](Nashville: Broadman & Holman, 1996).

[242]*The Doctrine of the Bible* (Nashville: Convention Press, 1991) 39-51 (esp. 41), 11-26, 27-37 (esp. 30, 35). See also *Christian Scripture: An Evangelical Perspective on Inspiration, Authority, and Interpretation* (Nashville: Broadman & Holman, 1995) 15-35.

[243]*The Doctrine of the Bible*, 95-109 (esp. 101, 105, 106). See also *Christian Scripture*, 77-96.

the writers, whereas the Bible obviously "is composed of different types of literature." After defining and evaluating the dictation, illumination, encounter [Karl Barth], and dynamic theories of biblical inspiration, Dockery clearly opted for the plenary theory as the one that "best accounts for the divine character of Scripture and the human circumstances of . . . [its] composition." Such inspired Scripture has the possibility of being both "normative" and "inerrant."[244]

Dockery's greatest specialization has come in biblical hermeneutics, beginning with his doctoral dissertation.[245] Commencing with Jesus' Christological interpretation of the Old Testament and that of the apostles and Jewish hermeneutical methods, he traced the functional or worship-oriented interpretation by the Apostolic Fathers and the more authoritarian response to heresies by Irenaeus and Tertullian before contrasting the Alexandrian allegorical (Clement, Origen) method and the Antiochene literal-historical and typological (Theodore of Mopsuestia, John Chrysostom) methods. "Canonical and Catholic hermeneutics" was represented by Jerome, Augustine of Hippo, and Theodoret of Cyrus. Dockery traced the medieval fourfold sense of Scripture to John Cassian.[246] Erasmus,[247] Calvin, and Luther were seen as the major Reformation contributors to hermeneutics, and in the post-Reformation era Protestant scholasticism employed a dogmatic hermeneutic with Aristotelian influence. Pietism produced Johann Albrecht Bengel, and rationalistic tendencies paved the way for the historical-critical method.[248] J. S. Semler's strictly historical method was

---

[244]"The Divine-Human Authorship of Inspired Scripture," in *Authority and Interpretation: A Baptist Perspective*, ed. Duane A. Garrett and Richard R. Melick, Jr. (Grand Rapids MI: Baker, 1987) 13-43. See also *The Doctrine of the Bible*, 53-77, where he also refuted feminist and liberation theologies, and *Christian Scripture*, 37-60.

[245]"An Examination of Hermeneutical Development in Early Christian Thought and Its Contemporary Significance" (Ph.D. diss., University of Texas at Arlington, 1988).

[246]*Biblical Interpretation Then and Now: Contemporary Hermeneutics in the Light of the Early Church* (Grand Rapids MI: Baker, 1992) 23-154, 158-60.

[247]"The Foundations of Reformation Hermeneutics: A Fresh Look at Erasmus," in *Evangelical Hermeneutics*, ed. Michael Bauman and David W. Hall (Camp Hill PA: Christian Publications, 1995) 53-75.

[248]"New Testament Interpretation: A Historical Survey," in *New Testament Criticism and Interpretation*, ed. Black and Dockery, 47-50; also in *Interpreting the New Testament*, ed. Black and Dockery, 26-28. See also "The History of Pre-

followed by F. C. Baur's "tendency criticism" and the first "quest" for the historical Jesus. Dockery made a place for the "grammatical-historical exegesis" of the Princeton school and of Baptist exegetes in America.[249] He wrote in depth about John A. Broadus and A. T. Robertson.[250] Relative to contemporary hermeneutics Dockery not only surveyed the major options, namely, author-oriented (E. D. Hirsch), reader-oriented (Hans-Georg Gadamer), and text-oriented (Paul Ricoeur), but also proposed a synthesis. Accordingly, he used the text which has "contextual keys," to bridge the "gulf" between reader and author and resurrected *sensus plenior*, or "a fuller meaning in the text than the author intended," to bring together "historical meaning" and "contemporary understanding."[251] Dockery also advocated the proper, nonabusive contemporary use of the typological method, for thereby Jesus and the apostles interpreted the Old Testament "Christologically" and therewith the unity of the two testaments can be more clearly seen.[252]

Dockery was deeply involved in the more reflective aspects of the SBC inerrancy controversy. He began in 1985 by affirming a "critical inerrancy" view of the autographs "not only in matters of salvation, but in all matters of ethics and issues of life."[253] Then he defined and explained seven different views of biblical inerrancy and two of noninerrancy as espoused by various recent evangelical authors and concluded that there was something to be learned from most of the views about inerrancy.[254] In 1988 he differentiated four groups of Southern Baptists in respect to the question of bibli-

---

Critical Biblical Interpretation," *Faith and Mission* 10 (Fall 1992): 3-33.

[249]"New Testament Interpretation: A Historical Survey," in *Interpreting the New Testament*, ed. Black and Dockery, 28-34.

[250]"John Albert Broadus," in *Bible Interpreters of the Twentieth Century*, ed., Elwell and Powell, 37-49; "The Broadus-Robertson Tradition," in *Theologians of the Baptist Tradition*, ed. George and Dockery, 90-114.

[251]"Author? Reader? Text? Toward a Hermeneutical Synthesis," *Theological Educator* 38 (1988): 7-16; *Biblical Interpretation Then and Now*, 168-83.

[252]"Typological Exegesis: Moving beyond Abuse and Neglect," in *Reclaiming the Prophetic Mantle: Preaching the Old Testament Faithfully*, ed. George L. Klein (Nashville: Broadman, 1992) 161-78, esp. 162, 163, 174-75. With George H. Guthrie he coauthored a handbook for lay readers: *The Holman Guide to Interpreting the Bible* (Nashville: Broadman & Holman, 2004).

[253]"Can Baptists Affirm the Reliability and Authority of the Bible?," *SBC Today* 2 (March 1985): 16.

[254]"Variations on Inerrancy," *SBC Today* 4 (May 1986): 10-11.

cal inerrancy (fundamentalists, evangelicals, moderates, and liberals) and concluded that evangelicals and moderates were more numerous. He noted that inerrancy had been erroneously identified with the mechanical dictation theory and with a strictly literal interpretation of the Bible. He called for the recognition of "the mystery of inspiration" and the use of canonical criticism and asserted that inerrancy is "the proper implication of the result of scripture's inspiration."[255] The same year he refuted Gordon James's *Inerrancy in the Southern Baptist Convention*.[256] Later, after the subsiding of the most heated controversy, the Union president reflected on the views of the Scriptures held by Boyce, Manly, Carroll, Mullins, and Conner, reviewed Southern Baptist theological development from 1952 to 1979 and the subsequent controversy, and restated biblical inerrancy with a view toward a more complete "evangelical orthodox consensus."[257] Recently Dockery proposed a way forward for Southern Baptists by reclaiming the Baptist heritage.[258]

Dockery did not hold to a strict *sola Scriptura* position inasmuch as he emphasized the role of confessions of faith as "secondary or tertiary."[259] Furthermore he was confident that Baptists needed to retain and reaffirm the patristic orthodoxy relative to the Trinity and Christology.[260] On soteriology he has espoused a Calminian or Amyraldian position between Calvinism and Arminianism—which Olson has declared impossible.[261] He holds to unlimited atonement and affirms that "the convicting grace of God's Spirit can be rejected." "God is the sole efficient cause of salvation," but "there are

---

[255]"Biblical Inerrancy: Pro or Con?" *Theological Educator* no. 37 (1988): 15-36 (esp. 22-24).

[256](Dallas: Southern Baptist Heritage Press, 1986). Dockery, "On Houses on Sand, Holy Wars and Heresies: A Review of the Inerrancy Controversy in the SBC," *Criswell Theological Review* 2 (Spring 1988): 391-401.

[257]"The Crisis of Scripture in Southern Baptist Life: Reflections on the Past, Looking to the Future," *Southern Baptist Journal of Theology* 9 (Spring 2005): 36-53.

[258]*Southern Baptist Consensus and Renewal: A Biblical, Historical, and Theological Proposal* (Nashville: Broadman & Holman, 2008).

[259]"Herschel H. Hobbs," 221-22.

[260]"Blending Baptist with Orthodox in the Christian University," in *The Future of Baptist Higher Education*, ed. Donald D. Schmeltekopf and Dianna Vitzana (Waco TX: Baylor University Press, 2006) 83-97, esp. 87-88.

[261]See above, 703.

also secondary and tertiary causes."[262] Faith is both "altogether brought about by God" and "altogether the human response."[263]

Dockery's writing on baptism has been focused on baptism in the New Testament without attention to historic Baptist or contemporary issues,[264] but on the Lord's Supper he has strongly advocated going beyond a "memorial-only" view by recovering the spiritual presence of Christ as affirmed by the Second London Confession and more frequent observance following self-examination and in the context of worship.[265]

Relative to eschatology the Union president, writing at the turn of the twenty-first century for Baptist church members, stressed the eschatological aspect of the kingdom of God[266] while reviewing mistaken expectations of that kingdom throughout church history, was certain that physical as well as spiritual death was the penal consequence of sin, held to an intermediate state, and critiqued reincarnation. After reviewing the various millennial views, he opted for historic premillennialism of the posttribulational type. He affirmed final judgment, hell, and heaven, refuting annihilationism and universalism and affirming exclusivism relative to the unevangelized.[267]

Baptist theologians of the baby-boom generation were characterized by both commonalities and differences. All engaged in the theological task with a high degree of intensity. Some had distinctive doctrinal emphases: Piper on worship for the pleasure of God, Fiddes on the suffering of God, Carson on the theological unity of the New Testament, Grudem on the contemporary gift of prophecy, and Dockery on the doctrine of the Bible.

---

[262]*The Gospel of Jesus Christ: By Grace through Faith* (Jackson TN: Union University, 2004).

[263]*Basic Christian Beliefs*, Shepherd's Notes; Bible Summary series (Nashville: Broadman & Holman, 2000) 52.

[264]"Baptism," in *Dictionary of Jesus and the Gospels*, ed. Joel B. Green and Scot McKnight (Downers Grove IL; Leicester UK: InterVarsity Press, 1992) 55-58; "Baptism in the New Testament," *Southwestern Journal of Theology* 43 (Spring 2001): 4-16.

[265]"The Lord's Supper in the New Testament and in Baptist Worship," *Search* 19 (Fall 1988): 38-48.

[266]But Dockery and David E. Garland held that the Sermon on the Mount is presently "obligatory on all citizens of the kingdom." *Seeking the Kingdom: The Sermon on the Mount Made Practical for Today* (Wheaton IL: Harold Shaw, 1992) 9.

[267]*Our Christian Hope* (Nashville: LifeWay Press, 1998) 8-24, 28-29, 35-38, 42-43, 67-85, 92-126. See also *Basic Christian Beliefs*, 79-88.

Some were very pronounced Calvinists: Piper, Nettles, and George. Others were moderate Calvinists: Carson and Grudem. Dockery was Calminian, and Fiddes, Wright, and Grenz were not so clearly positioned, whereas Olson was strongly Arminian. Carson and Dockery were biblically oriented theologians, while Nettles, George, and Olson were historically oriented theologians. Nettles, Dockery, Fiddes, and Wright at times wrote specifically for a Baptist readership; Piper, Carson, Grudem, and Olson wrote especially for an evangelical readership. Piper, Carson, and Olson wrote little about Baptist distinctives. On gender issues Piper and Grudem were complementarians, whereas Grenz was an equalitarian. Fiddes has been an advocate of conciliar ecumenism; Wright has sought to be both evangelical and ecumenical; George and Dockery have been representative of evangelical ecumenism. Only Fiddes has been anticonfessional. Grenz has been most adaptive to postmodernism, and Piper and Wright are the only pastor-theologians in the group.[268]

---

[268] Another generation of Baptist theologians who give serious attention to Baptist concerns is beginning to produce its corpus of writings. Notable among these are Daniel L. Akin, Paul Abbott Basden, Chad Owen Brand, Anthony R. Cross, Mark E. Dever, Curtis W. Freeman, John S. Hammett, Steven Ray Harmon, Kenneth Keathley, Jason K. Lee, R. Albert Mohler, Jr., Russell D. Moore, Robert Stanton Norman, Harry L. Poe, Robert B. Stewart, Gregory Alan Thornburg, Thomas White, and Malcolm B. Yarnell III.

Conclusion

Baptists retained a patristic heritage of Trinitarian and Christological orthodoxy and a Reformation heritage of justification by grace through faith while being sympathetic to renewal or restitutionist movements. Hence they were able slowly but surely to identify the denial of the deity of Jesus Christ as heresy.

The Baptist movement was born in the matrix of Separatist Puritanism, and its earliest internal differences reflected the soteriological differences between Particular, Calvinistic predestinationism and General, Arminian freewillism: (1) whether faith and repentance are gifts of God or responsibilities of human beings; (2) whether God's election consists of his choosing from eternity of particular human beings unto salvation with the rest of humankind being passed over; (3) whether the death of Christ was intended to be efficacious for the sins of God's elect only or to be potentially efficacious for the sins of all humanity; (4) whether God's grace operates irresistibly or resistibly; and (5) whether all of God's elect humans will be eschatologically saved or only some of the elect.

Concurrently the Baptist movement's distinctive differences from other Christian denominations were essentially ecclesiological and often, but not always, were comparable to the teachings of the sixteenth-century Continental Anabaptists—believer's baptism by immersion, the true church consisting only of those professedly and evidently regenerate, congregational polity, the priesthood of all believers (disciples), congregational discipline, and the separation of the churches and civil government, with religious freedom for all and with church members allowed to serve as civil officers. The Anabaptist kinship did not extend to immersion as the mode of baptism, Christians as civil office holders, and military service by Christians. Some Baptists espoused the observance of the seventh-day Sabbath but enlisted few followers; others embraced eschatological universalism but were reckoned as being outside the Baptist fold.

The General Baptists gave to Baptists their earliest confessions of faith—those adopted by the congregations led by Smyth and Helwys and those adopted by several congregations, normally brief, with accompanying biblical citations, and emphasizing general atonement, liberty of conscience, and believer's baptism. They also produced Baptists' first systematic theologian, Grantham (1678). Monck accused Caffyn of teaching the celestial flesh of Christ—a denial of Christ's full humanity—and of teaching that the divine nature of the eternal Logos was turned into a creature—a denial of his deity. But it was the latter that would lead most original General Baptists into Unitarianism.

From the Particular Baptists came the most distinctive Baptist confession—the First London Confession (1644). Designed to refute charges of Arminian/Pelagian and Anabaptist heresy, it had major differences from Separatism's *A True Confession* (1597) and was the first confession in all Christian history "to prescribe a single immersion as the form of baptism." The Second London Confession (1677), modeled after the Westminster and Savoy confessions, set forth the Calvinistic spiritual presence view of the Lord's Supper as well as the Zwinglian memorialist view. Kiffin defended close communion on the basis of the rightful sequence of the two ordinances, whereas Bunyan defended open communion by stressing Spirit-baptism more than water baptism and by making holiness, not water baptism, essential for church membership. Having rejected the Inner Light of the Quakers, Bunyan was infralapsarian, emphasized the imputation of Christ's righteousness to believers, and reckoned the Christian life as pilgrimage. Knollys was prone to eschatological vagaries, and Keach labored for the acceptance of congregational hymn singing in public worship. In America from the matrix of awakening Backus combined Dortian Calvinism with freedom of conscience. Dagg, Mell, and Boyce represented Southern Calvinism.

The eighteenth century brought to some Particular Baptists Hyper-Calvinism, whose tenets were: (1) a supralapsarian order of divine decrees; (2) an eternal Trinitarian covenant of redemption; (3) eternal justification which is only manifested in time; (4) no general offers of grace; and (5) antinomianism. Brine, Skepp, and Gill embraced it to varying degrees. Baptists' most prolific theologian, Gill, wrote both a verse-by-verse commentary on the entire Bible and a systematic theology. Strongly Trinitarian, he defended immersion and refuted infant baptism while reckoning baptism as not a church ordinance. Treating the seven letters of Revelation 2–3 as symbolic of ages within church history, Gill thought that he was living in the age of Sardis.

From the slumber of Hyper-Calvinism Particular Baptists were awakened by the elder Hall's *Help to Zion's Travellers* (1781), by Fuller's indiscriminate gospel preaching of the duties of repentance and faith as embodied in his *The Gospel Worthy of All Acceptation* (1785), and by Carey's *Enquiry* (1792). Wooed to the embrace of general atonement by Taylor, a General Baptist, Fuller nevertheless adhered to particular atonement. To his nuanced doctrine of penal substitution he added aspects of the governmental theory of the atonement. Fuller provided as an alternative to Gill's theology a more gospel-offered Calvinism, but Gadsby and the Strict and Particular Baptists opted for Gill and not for Fuller. Booth, a General Baptist, made a conscientious shift to the Particular position, the younger Hall continued to defend open communion, and Kinghorn and Ivimey expounded the case for close communion. Primitive Baptists in the United States opposed organized Baptist efforts on a national scale to undertake foreign missions, and Parker's opposition in particular may have been wrongly attributed to his somewhat unrelated two-seed doctrine.

Landmarkism, a development particular to the American South, though alleging to be a return to the early Baptist ecclesiology, was actually an innovation in Baptist ecclesiology. Triggered by opposition to the acceptance of "alien" or non-Baptist-administered immersions, the movement under Graves refused to recognize non-Baptist bodies as "churches" or their ministers as "gospel ministers," denying them access to Baptist pulpits. Graves embraced Baptist church succession from the New Testament era, opposed the board method of conducting foreign missions, and repeatedly sought to modify the basis of representation in the Southern Baptist Convention. Pendleton emphasized nonpulpit affiliation and opposed alien immersions as did Dayton. Graves also engaged in heavy polemics against Methodism, Presbyterians, the Roman Catholic Church, Alexander Campbell's doctrine of baptism, eschatological universalism, Spiritism, and Swedenborgianism. Graves held to the plenary-verbal theory of biblical inspiration, taught that the Father-Son-Spirit relationships are not eternal and that Jesus had no human soul, and embraced a form of dispensationalism. With full-orbed Landmarkism the kingdom of God is composed of true (Baptist) churches, and the Lord's Supper is to be partaken only by local church members. Four allegedly Landmark controversies were waged: Crawford's Gospel Missionism in North China, the new historiography of Whitsitt, the Hayden controversy in Texas, and the Bogard schism from the SBC. Extensive non-Landmark ecclesiologies were written by Dagg and by Dargan, the former providing a fully developed doctrine of the universal church. Lingering Landmark influence upon Southern Baptists during the first two-thirds of the twentieth century could be seen in the widely accepted nonalien immersion practice, the altered basis of representation in the SBC, nonmembership in councils of churches, and great denominational solidarity and loyalty.

Controversies other than the Landmark occurred among Baptists during the nineteenth and early twentieth centuries, but these centered not on Calvinist-Arminian issues or on Baptist distinctives, but on the Bible, creation/evolution, Christology, and aspects of soteriology. The uneasy alliance between followers of the Campbells and the Baptists in the United States came to an end once the differences became more apparent: the Sandemanian view of faith as bare belief of the record, the McLeanist view of water baptism as essential to remission of sins, and the Campbellite anticonfessionalism and opposition to organized Baptist missionary work. On both sides of the Atlantic Baptists formed denominational Bible societies so that Bible translations using the equivalent of "immerse" could be published. Toy's resignation from the faculty of Southern Baptist Theological Seminary was precipitated by his embrace of the Graf-Kuenen-Wellhausen theory of the Pentateuch, Darwinian evolution, and other positions thought to be contrary to the doctrine of biblical inspiration. Toy's successor, Manly, gave full expression to and defense of the plenary theory of biblical inspiration. The English Baptist Down Grade Controversy had as its chief opponents Spurgeon and Clifford. Early Spurgeon, Calvinist and Puritan, had been in controversy with Hyper-Calvinist pastors in London and then with Anglicans over baptismal regeneration. He feared a declension of orthodoxy among Baptists and Independents and, unable to persuade the Baptist Union to adopt a full-orbed confession, withdrew from the union. Clifford, long-term pastor of a General Baptist church in London and university graduate in arts, science, and law, embraced the "new theology"—inspiration of persons but not of writings, the Bible as errant, the authority of "the Christ Idea," the universal fatherhood of God, denial of penal substitution, and the like.

What Spurgeon feared to have arrived was indeed the new theological response to the changed intellectual and sociocultural factors of the latter nineteenth century: Darwinian evolution, historical criticism applied to the Bible, industrialization and urbanization under *laissez faire* capitalism, and changes in philosophy. More conservative responses to these cultural factors were made by Hovey, who combined a dynamical view of biblical inspiration, an emphasis on the deity of Christ and the incarnation, and a developed eschatology, by Goodspeed, who expounded postmillennialism and critiqued the historical-critical method, and by Gordon, who as a loyal Baptist espoused historic premillennialism, divine healing on the basis of the atonement, and the Spirit's enduement. Mediating Northern theologians included Robinson, who was traditional, mediating, and literal on different

Conclusion 717

subjects, and successors such as Northrup, Johnson, and Wood. But by far the most influential mediating theologian was Strong. Changes in Strong's theology have been noted, notably the influence of "ethical monism" (ca.1894) and travels to mission fields (1920s). Changes as to the nature of the Bible have been cited in various editions of his *Systematic Theology*. Drawn to transcendence by making holiness to be central and drawn to immanence by his embrace of ethical monism, Strong opted for theistic evolution, a pictorial-summary interpretation of Genesis 1, and the Augustinian theory of Adamic headship. The cross of Christ revealed rather than made the atonement. Liberal Baptist theologians adapted to the new climate with its emphasis on continuity, autonomy, and dynamism yet desired to retain the kernel of original Christianity. Clarke, whose text was the most widely used liberal text among American Protestants, looked for "the Christian element" in the errant Scriptures, eliminated the nonethical from the doctrine of God, regarded the incarnation as possible because God and humans are alike, and took reconciliation as the chief work of Christ. Fosdick rejected "dictational inspiration and inerrancy" and emphasized "abiding experiences and changing categories." For him there was no docetism, and no penal substitution. Rauschenbusch as a convinced Baptist was the most influential theologian in the climactic stage of the Social Gospel. Influenced by Hell's Kitchen and by studies in Germany, he stressed the social transmission of sin, identified six public sins that led to Jesus' death, and reckoned the kingdom of God, although divine in origin, as humanity organized noneschatologically according to the will of God. For three decades the Baptist Congress for the Discussion of Current Questions afforded a public forum for discussion and debate. Fundamentalist Baptists waged spiritual warfare against liberals and modernists. Riley, an evangelist and antievolutionist, sought unsuccessfully to get the Northern Baptist Convention to recommend the New Hampshire Confession to its affiliated churches. With Shields and Norris he organized the Baptist Bible Union of North America, which later became the General Association of Regular Baptists. Straton, given to public debates, taught divine healing on the basis of the atonement. Massee was a more moderate fundamentalist. Riley and Straton were dispensationalists; Shields and Massee were not. Modernists would have Baptists cut the cord of their connection with patristic orthodoxy; fundamentalists were inept in reconnecting therewith.

For thirty years (1920–1950) the NBC was engaged in theological controversy. This included the formation of the Fundamental Fellowship (1920) and its adoption of the Goodchild Confession, the investigation of educational institutions, and the probing of the beliefs of foreign missionaries and foreign mission appointees. It embraced two major separations from the NBC—that of the General Association of Regular Baptists in the 1930s and that of the Conservative Baptists in the 1940s. Among the latter Lewis and Demarest have produced a three-volume systematic theology following an "integrative" method.

Baptists became heavily involved in biblical theology during the twentieth century. Gould, Knudsen, Stagg, Ladd, and Guthrie produced full treatments of New Testament theology; Robinson, Rowley, Smith, and Clements set forth considerable treatments of Old Testament theology. Rust addressed the theology of both testaments. Gould was heavily influenced by contemporary historical-critical method, and he and Stagg emphasized diversity within the New Testament. On the contrary Ladd and Guthrie stressed the unity amid diversity, and Rowley contended for the unity of the Old Testament and of the two testaments. Robertson magnified the deity of Christ more than his humanity and the universality of sin more than its origin, while being open to the possibility of the apostasy of true believers. For Robinson the Hebrew concepts of corporate personality, wholistic human nature, and election and covenant were important, and he probed suffering and the Holy Spirit. Rust represented well the Biblical Theology movement of the middle third of the twentieth century, and he and Knudsen interacted with American and European systematic theologians. Summers and McDowell advocated amillennialism, whereas Ladd, Moody, and Beasley-Murray espoused historic premillennialism. Ladd was diligent in the critique of dispensationalism and defended the proper use—without "rationalist presuppositions"—of historical criticism of the Bible. Shifting from Paul to the Synoptics, Stagg inclined to modalism, branded penal substitution with the pejorative label "transactionalism," opted for the example view of the cross, and contrasted the "glory of Pentecost" with "the shame of Corinth." Moody held to the salvific nature of general revelation, advocated polygenism, held a sacrificial view of the death of Christ, rightly denominated the virgin birth "the virginal conception," sought rapproachment with pedobaptists, but found that apostasy, which he affirmed, was not acceptable to his fellow Baptists. The author of the twentieth century's most important book on baptism, Beasley-Murray, developed a strongly sacramental view of baptism within an open membership setting and defended the Little Apocalypse (Mark 13) as authentic teaching of Jesus. Ward was more defensive of the traditional Baptist doctrine of baptism. Martin, who took the self-emptying (Phil. 2:5-11) of Christ to be divestiture of glory instead of attributes and who found reconciliation to be the center of Paul's theology, was clearly a theologian of worship. Ellis pursued a lifelong interest in hermeneutics, drew from a monistic anthropology conclusions that denied a noncorporeal intermediate state and affirmed annihilationism, and developed a theory of New Testament origins centering in four "apostolic mission circles." Longenecker probed the contextualization of confessional elements in the New Testament as a basis for present-day use of contextualization in the Two-Thirds World. Baptist biblical theologians demonstrated considerable diversity in their conclusions. Although one can argue for the salutary or purifying effects of such biblical theologies upon Baptist systematic theologies, engagement in biblical theology by Baptists was no guarantee of orthodoxy or adherence to truth.

At the beginning of the twentieth century Mullins was in theological leadership among Southern Baptists, and his influence spread among other Baptist bodies. Influenced by personalism and possibly also by pragmatism, he used Christian experience in the exposition of Christian doctrine and employed soul competency as the distinguishing mark of the Baptists. The Bible is the record of divine revelation, a book of religion and not of science. Affirming the Chalcedonian Symbol, he yet held to a modified kenoticism. Seemingly he shifted from Christian theistic evolution to a denial of any form of evolution. Mullins held to a propitiatory, substitutionary atonement, general in nature, and repentance and faith result from divine and from human action. The Mullins heritage was extended by Tribble and Hobbs, and at the end of twentieth century Mullins's theology had become the controversial touchstone for controverted Southern Baptists. Prior to the SBC's Baptist Faith and Message Statement of 1925 five doctrinal statements were composed and in varying degrees adopted by SBC entities: the 1914 statement of beliefs related to Christian unity, the articles adopted (1917–1918) by what would become New Orleans Baptist Theological Seminary, the 1920 "Fraternal Address of Southern Baptists" addressed to Continental Baptists, the 1920 FMB statement of beliefs, and Mullins's 1923 statement on "Science and Religion." The 1925 confession, a revision of the 1853 edition of the New Hampshire Confession, had a preamble that spelled out the nature and functions of Baptist confessions, modified numerous articles from the New Hampshire, and consisted of eight entirely new articles. Conner continued but modified the Mullins tradition between the two world wars. He shifted from penal substitution to Christ as victor, from one general resurrection to the attainment of the resurrection body at death, and from postmillennialism to amillennialism. The SBC's

1946 Statement of Principles stressed the value and competence of human beings and the role of the church, and the later *Baptist Ideals* had a similar twofold focus. Elliott's *The Message of Genesis* evoked controversy, especially over his taking the stories of Genesis as symbolical and not historical, and as a consequence the SBC adopted another Baptist Faith and Message Statement in 1963, which had been written by a committee of state convention presidents chaired by Hobbs. Christ was said to be hermeneutical principle for the Scriptures, and the universal church was affirmed. Hobbs, a prolific pastor-theologian, had a high view of the Bible and limited use for confessions, was Arminian on election and hence a one-point Dortian Calvinist, and shifted from premillennialism to amillennialism. Other seminary professors besides Elliott were removed from their professorships for theological reasons, and doctrinal texts were produced for students. Criswell, another influential pastor-theologian, affirmed the plenary-verbal theory of inspiration so as to border on the dictational theory and the inerrancy of the Bible, creation with the denial of evolution, the cessationist view of many spiritual gifts, and dispensationalist eschatology. Controversy again erupted in the SBC (1970–1971) over the Genesis section of volume 1 of the *Broadman Bible Commentary*, and it resulted in the rewriting of that section and of one of the general articles by different authors. The Charismatic Movement particularly affected Southern Baptists during the 1970s, but charismatic gifts did not become a major or long-disputed issue. Rather it was biblical inerrancy that would prove to be the catalyst for a major divisive controversy during the last two decades of the century. The first but not successful effort to redirect the SBC was led by the Baptist Faith and Message Fellowship. Lindsell's two books on inerrancy, embracing the domino theory as to the effect of the loss of inerrancy on the Christian doctrines and denying the name "Evangelical" to noninerrantists, and Pinnock's two booklets aroused interest concerning inerrancy. Later the books by Dilday and by Draper would sharpen the differences. Organizationally begun in 1979, the "conservative resurgence" or "fundamentalist takeover" proceeded to place all SBC boards and agencies under the governance of persons committed to biblical inerrancy. Some noninerrantists formed the Southern Baptist Alliance in 1986, while the SBC's Peace Committee was attempting to resolve the controversy and the SBC seminary presidents were affirming inerrancy. These seminaries sponsored national conferences on biblical inerrancy and biblical hermeneutics, and in 1991 other noninerrantists or "moderates" formed the Cooperative Baptist Fellowship. Its chief theologian, Shurden, explicated four Baptist freedoms—"Bible, soul, church, and religious." Study groups appointed by Young, the SBC president, recommended doctrinal affirmations that were more specific than the 1963 confession. In 1995 the SBC added to the 1963 text a new article on the family, and in 2000 a new Baptist Faith and Message Statement was adopted. It removed the Mullins-Conner language from the article on the Bible, refuted open theism, specified that baptism by the Holy Spirit occurs at conversion and that only males may be senior pastors, and added to the list of vices.

Evangelicalism, which both grew out of American Fundamentalism and had earlier and wider roots, had three theologians during the last half of the twentieth century who had both Evangelical and Baptist identity. Henry, with writing and editorial skills, critiqued modern philosophy and theological movements such as Protestant Neoorthodoxy and Liberal Protestantism and explicated propositional revelation and the inspiration and authority of the Scriptures. Ramm, trained in the philosophy of science, addressed creation and the sciences, set forth a pattern of authority, treated hermeneutics and special revelation, and wrote significantly on sin and Christology. Erickson gave attention to theological method, took as a central motif "the magnificence of God," sought to retain Trinitarian and Christological orthodoxy, was a modified Augustinian on the imputation of Adam's sin, and made penal substitution foundational to any other view of Christ's death. For a century (ca.1850-ca.1950) Baptists produced writings that represented the new genre of Baptist distinctives. Baptists in Britain found relations with other "free churches" to be significant, whereas some Baptists in the United States and Canada pursued the nature and function of "believers' churches." Toward the end of the twentieth century Southern Baptists explored their relationships with American Evangelicals, and McClendon pursued "baptists" (*Taüfer*) and, with others, called for a "reenvisioning" of Baptist identity that differed both from Mullins's soul competency and the fundamentalist right in the context of postmodernity. Certain British Baptists increasingly explicated and defended a sacramental and more-than-symbolic view of baptism.

Following upon earlier Socinian, Hyper-Calvinist, and Campbellite incursions into Baptist theology, Baptists of the twentieth century encountered other incursions. Modernism found religious authority to be located in modern thought so as to dispense with essentials of the historic Christian faith. For Mathews religious beliefs had been shaped in each historical period by its dominant social mind; hence modernism sought to effect that change for the twentieth century. For Mathews God was not clearly personal and not Trinitarian. Macinotsh gradually moved toward affirming the necessity of belief in the existence of God and was able to retain a form of theism. Denying the finality of the Christian religion, Foster ended a humanist, defending his views of the basis of Baptist noncreedalism and soul competency and evoking strong opposition among Chicago Baptist pastors. Dispensationalism, traceable to the life and teachings of John Nelson Darby, made its way into Baptist theology through leaders such as Graves, Norris, Rice, Criswell, and Blaising. It constituted not only a fourth major millennial view to be found among Baptists but also a distinctive hermeneutic, a distinctive biblical periodization, and a distinctive view of Israel and the Church. In 1971–1972 Taylor's seeming denial of the deity of Christ, long considered a Christian heresy, resulted in a stalemate among English Baptists in that the Baptist Union rebuked Taylor's position while Taylor was allowed to retain his college principalship, but Christological orthodoxy seemed to be reacknowledged. Open theism resurfaced in North America at the end of the twentieth century and claimed Baptists among its advocates: Pinnock and Boyd. Questioning the omniscience of God vis-à-vis future matters, it majored on God's love and emotions and contended that God changes his decisions. God, it was argued, cannot know in advance all future events because of human freedom. Among open theism's critics, Ware took Jer. 18:5-10 to teach God's constancy, not his changing, and Erickson contended that the repentance texts were not change-of-mind texts.

Missiology became an academic discipline for Baptists when Carver assumed the chair of missions at Southern Seminary in 1900. For Carver missions was central to God's "plan of the ages" and to the entire Bible. Early inclined to stress the role of the individual Christian and the missionary society, he increasingly pointed to the church and denominational missions. A majority of the Continental European confessions began with the doctrine of God but were rather specific about the Scriptures and emphatic on the Trinity and Christology. These confession tended to elaborate on ecclesiology and to treat eschatology briefly. Baptists differed in their responses to the Ecumenical Movement. Shakespeare tried unsuccessfully to get English Baptists to endorse organic union, and Payne became a leading figure in the WCC. But Carver, fully committed to the Body of Christ as the whole number of believers, opposed contemporary efforts for organic church union. British and Northern Baptists, together with a significant number of Baptist conventions/unions, were strongly committed to conciliar ecumenism, especially the WCC, and Southern Baptists and a majority of Baptist unions/conventions did not join the WCC or national councils. The debate focused on Roberts-Thomson (pro-) and Estep (con-). Though declining to encourage official representation at Vatican Council II, the BWA has engaged in bilateral conversations with the Roman Catholic Church and various Protestant confessional bodies. Evangelism became an academic discipline for Baptist seminaries at Southwestern Seminary in 1908, but the most universal Baptist emphasis on evangelism came through the ministry of Graham, whose congresses brought together thousands of evangelists from the Two-Thirds World. The Bible as the Word of God, the cross of Christ, the new birth or decision for Christ, and angels were themes emphasized by Graham. Very different was Cox, who celebrated secularization, developed a liberation theology, explored Eastern religions, and defended Leonardo Boff before finally making a sympathetic approach to Pentecostalism. Roberts, theologizing out of the American black experience, not the Black Power movement, was emphatic that liberation must be accompanied by reconciliation. In the Nigerian context Imasogie made a phenomenological approach to African Tradition Religion, which he reckoned as "bureaucratic monotheism," but he used neither West African indigenization nor Western Christian theology but rather his own contextualization as the basis for an African Christian theology. In South Africa Jonsson, active in the struggle against *apartheid*, defended the historicity of Jesus' resurrection and applied the incarnation to the attainment of human dignity, while being indecisive as to the salvation of the unevangelized, whereas Parnell reinterpreted Baptist distinctives and allowed the private exercise of tongues. Brazilian Baptists, initially shaped by the New Hampshire Confession, in the late twentieth century found it necessary to frame and adopt indigenous confessions reflective of their divisions and charismaticism, but even so they used the 1963 SBC Baptist Faith and Message Statement. In Mexico Southern Baptist missionaries introduced Landmark teaching and Northern Baptist missionaries reflected a proecumenical stance. Mexican Baptists in writing their own confession drew heavily from the New Hampshire and 1963 SBC confessions. Similar dependence on Southern Baptist confessions was evident in Argentina, but two charismatic movements (1969–1971, 1992ff.) that were divisive continue to impact Argentine Baptists. Three Spanish-language Baptist and Evangelical theologians, Costas, Padilla, and Escobar, all members of the Fraternidad Teológica Latinoamericana, wrote as missiologists both in Spanish and English. A high view of the Scriptures, the centrality of the cross and resurrection, evangelism, application to the social needs of Latin America, and the second coming marked these writings. Critical of ecumenical missiologists, liberation theologies, and the Fuller Seminary Church Growth movement, they were more open to the grassroots ecclesial communities in Latin American Catholicism. Australian Baptists early dealt with the ecclesiological issues that derived from Britain, but of late their theologians have written on Jesus' resurrection, incarnational mission, and doubt. Korean Baptist theology, early shaped by their pioneer Fenwick, was later influenced by both missionary and national leaders, and their theologians have written monographs on missiological topics and historical theology. Asian conventions which derive from the work of British, Northern, and Canadian Baptists tend not to have adopted confessions of faith, whereas those originating from Southern or Baptist General Conference (Swedish) or Conservative Baptists tend to have adopted such. Examples of the latter can be seen in Malaysia, Singapore, the Philippines, and Karnataka (India) as well as South Korea. Baptists became participants in the end-of-the-century reopening of the issue of the destiny of unevangelized human beings. Pinnock and Marshall clearly espoused an inclusivist position, Aldwinckle was not clear but inclined to inclusivism, but Nash was decisively an exponent of exclusivism. Southern Baptist missiologists produced at the turn of the century a sizeable, multiauthored textbook on missiology that included the biblical and theological foundations, the history of missions, non-Christian religions, and missionary strategies. If in 1900 Baptist theology had been seen as a British and North American enterprise, by 2000 it had become much more international or global.

At the outset of the twenty-first century Baptists had a significant number of younger writing theologians. Piper, a pastor-theologian, had chosen Jonathan Edwards as his primary mentor, and hence the glory and supremacy of God were magnified and man's response is said to be to enjoy or find pleasure in God (Christian hedonism). Nettles as a historical theologian has sought to restore Dortian Calvinism among Southern Baptists, with Bush gave Baptist historical support to the doctrine of biblical inerrancy, and continues to call for spiritual renewal. Carson, a New Testament scholar who has moved toward systematics, has been prodigious, prolific, and polemical, treating diverse subjects from biblical criticism to pluralism. Fiddes, working in the Oxford context, produced monographs on the suffering of God, atonement, and the Trinity before addressing more specifically the Baptist community. Strongly ecumenical, he magnified the church covenant while taking a nonconfessional stance. Grudem's theology is basically a Reformed theology with Baptist and Vineyard refinements. In the context of a free church in a free state for post-Christendom Wright restated a renewed Baptist congregationalism with a theology not as evangelical as claimed. Grenz, a prolific author, and an explicit Baptist, sought to reenvision Evangelical theology so as to be favorable to a postmodern context. In doing so he elicited both supporters and critics. George as a historical theologian has written on general church history, Reformation theology, and evangelicalism. Like Nettles, he has reinterpreted John Gill and supported a restoration of Dortian Calvinism among Southern Baptists and has been a bridge builder between Southern Baptists and American Evangelicals and between Southern Baptists and Roman Catholics. Olson, with Pentecostal roots and collaborating with Grenz, has presented the history of Christian doctrine as "story" from an Arminian perspective and has become the most explicit present-day Baptist defender of Arminianism. Dockery, prolific as both author and editor, has contributed significantly to the doctrine of the Scriptures, especially in hermeneutics, and has set forth a Calminian position. The majority of these theologians are Calvinistic, moderately Calvinistic, or Calminian, not Arminian; the majority are evangelical rather than ecumenical.

As the Baptist quadricentennial (2009) approaches, one can discern that the Calvinist-Arminian soteriological issues that sought to balance doctrinal sovereignty and human accountability and that dominated much of Baptist theological writing during the seventeenth and eighteenth centuries have again attained contemporary importance. Moreover, the modernist/liberal-conservative/fundamentalist issues that were so central to Baptist theology during much of the nineteenth and twentieth centuries, though by no means absent from the Baptist scene, do not seem today to evoke clearly modernist or stridently liberal advocates. Furthermore, those doctrines which Baptists have shared with other Christians (Trinity, Christology) and with Reformation Protestants (justification, priesthood of all Christians) continue to be of great importance and to be productive at times of controversy. Finally, the Baptist (ecclesiological) distinctives, which were so strongly defended by the earliest Baptist authors, produced its own genre of writings (ca.1850-ca.1950) and, especially believer's baptism by immersion, were adopted by various newly formed Protestant denominations in the United States, have, after the diminishing influence of Landmarkism among Southern Baptists and the impact of ecumenism on English Baptists, come into a state of comparative neglect or assumed irrelevance. Spurgeon's question was whether anything besides immersion held the English Baptists together. Today's question may be whether Baptists hold to and clearly affirm and practice their distinctives—a question raised when a majority of the professing Christians in the world still practice infant baptism.

Index of Persons

Abel, 380
Abelard, Peter, 679, 701
Abraham, 25, 66, 85, 157, 206, 244, 398, 459, 487, 563, 578, 680
Adam, 19, 29, 35, 38, 40, 54, 60, 61, 75, 77, 96, 122, 127, 130, 131, 141-42, 149, 171, 209, 222, 227, 244, 291, 293, 299, 372, 379-80, 394, 398, 400, 453, 459, 476, 497, 512, 519, 523, 527, 528, 587-88, 606, 623, 658, 685, 692, 721
Aërius, 6
Ahlstrom, Sydney E., 433-34
Ainsworth, Henry, 18, 19
Akin, Daniel L., 536, 711
Aland, Kurt, 383
Aldwinckle, Russell Foster, 652-53, 660, 724
Alexander, 136
Allen, Arthur Lynn, 421
Allen, Clifton Judson, 486
Ames, William, 58
Ammon, Christoph Friedrich, 202
Anderson, Frederick L., 333
Anderson, Justice Conrad, 629, 656-57
Andress, Vance Corbet, 374
Anselm of Canterbury, 97, 223, 701
Apollinarius of Laodicea, 1
Arellano Guerrero, Juan, 627
Arius, 1
Arminius, James, 27, 81
Armitage, Thomas, 104
Arnobius, 405
Asbury, Francis, 218
Ascol, Thomas Kennedy, 182
Ashcraft, Jesse Morris, 478-79
Athanasius, 405
Aubrey, Melbourn Evans, 592, 594
Auchmuty, James A., Jr., 605

Augustine of Hippo, 4, 5, 96, 372, 527, 652, 655, 663, 698, 702, 707
Aulén, Gustav, 353
Avila, Mariano, 644
Ayer, William Ward 319

Backus, Isaac, 154-62, 210, 501, 667, 691, 714
Bacon, Ernest, 265
Baillie, John, 378, 380
Bampfield, Francis, 70
Bancroft, George, 113
Banks, Charles Waters, 269
Barak, 88
Barber, Christopher Bart, 239
Barclay, Robert, 233
Barebone, Praisegod, 58, 233
Barnes, William Wright, 213, 231, 236, 449
Barnett, Kenneth, 487
Barnhart, Joe E., 608
Barnhouse, Donald Gray, 482
Baro, Peter, 28
Barrett, Charles Kingsley, 377, 380
Barro, Antonio Carlos, 634, 635
Barrow, Henry, 18, 112
Barth, Karl, 378, 386, 394, 476, 477, 518, 520, 579, 597, 621, 646, 647, 677, 687, 702, 707
Bascom, Henry Bidleman, 219-20
Basden, Paul Abbott, 508-509, 711
Basinger, David, 575
Bastwick, John, 62
Bateman, Charles T., 276
Bauer, Walter, 670
Baur, Ferdinand Christian, 406, 707-708
Baxter, Richard, 86
Beasley, George Alfred, 387

Beasley-Murray, George Raymond, 387-95, 402, 413, 540, 547, 572, 573, 718
Bebbington, David, 166
Beebe, Gilbert, 210
Beecher, Edward, 203
Behney, John Bruce, 287
Bell, Claiborne H., 581-82
Bellamy, Joseph, 180, 183
Bengel, Johann Albrecht, 707
Berdyaev, Nicolas, 621, 641
Bernard, Richard, 25
Beza, Theodore, 220
Biddle, John, 575
Black, Cyril, 572, 573
Blackaby, Melvin D., 385
Blacklock, ?, 52
Blaising, Craig Alan, 569-70, 580, 722
Blaurock, George, 10
Bloesch, Donald George, 319
Bloom, Harold, 434
Blunt, Richard, 52, 233
Boethius, 574
Boettner, Loraine, 376
Boff, Leonardo, 611-12, 659, 723
Bogard, Benjamin Marquis, 239-41, 248, 255-56, 715
Bolingbroke, Henry St. John, 177
Bonfim, Oswaldo Ferreira, 624, 625
Bonhoeffer, Dietrich, 538, 610, 621
Bonney, Katharine, 312
Booth, Abraham, 173, 185-93, 200, 211, 243, 302, 715
Booth, Samuel Harris, 264, 275
Boutwell, W. Stacey, 289
Bowne, Borden Parker, 296, 417
Boyce, Gilbert, 153
Boyce, James Petigru, 134, 145-46, 148, 151, 242-43, 416, 423, 424, 667, 697, 709, 714
Boyd, Gregory A., 575-76, 522
Braaten, Carl E., 635
Bracklow, Stephen, 317

Brackney, William Henry, 28, 288, 290, 293, 305, 327, 535, 537
Bradwardine, Thomas, 7
Brainerd, David, 174, 665
Brand, Chad Owen, 711
Brantly, William Theophilus, Sr., 148, 150
Breed, Geoffrey R., 200
Brent, Charles H., 435
Briggs, John H. Y., 274
Briggs, Robert Cook, 481
Brightman, Edgar Sheffield, 516, 575
Brine, John, 89, 92-93, 99, 107-108, 168, 210, 714
Broaddus, Andrew, Sr., 255, 256, 338
Broadus, John Albert, 260, 347, 350, 532, 667, 708
Broadway, Mikael, 540
Brooks, Oscar Stephenson, 546
Brown, James Baldwin, 271-72
Brown, John Newton, 128-29, 151
Brown, Raymond, 90
Brown, S. M., 442
Brown, William Adams, 302
Browne, Robert, 17, 18
Brownlow, William G., 220
Bruce, Frederick Fyrie, 380, 406-407, 637
Brueggemann, Walter, 647
Brunner, Heinrich Emil, 378, 451, 476, 477, 516, 518, 579, 597, 654
Bucer, Martin, 7, 22
Bullinger, Henry, 69
Bultmann, Rudolf Karl, 376, 377, 396, 481, 621, 646
Bunyan, John, 66, 67-71, 107, 176, 191, 196, 665, 666, 667, 683, 714
Burkhead, Howell Walker, 606, 608
Burrage, Champlin, 16
Burrows, John Lansing, 244, 248
Burruss, John C., 221-22
Buse, Sydney Ivor, 542

Indexes

Bush, Luther Russell III, 431, 483, 666-67, 724
Busher, Mark Leonard, 15, 16, 34, 233
Bushnell, Horace, 281-82, 305, 308, 434
Bustin, Dennis C., 64
Butler, John Jay, 122-23, 150-51
Butler, Laverne, 491
Button, William, 182-83, 211
Byrd, James P., Jr., 112
Byrt, G. W., 276-77

Caffyn, Matthew, 39, 44-45, 49, 549, 713
Cain, 380
Calcidius, 575
Calvin, John, 7, 22, 69, 96, 112, 142-43, 159, 187, 208, 220, 265, 304, 434, 451, 521, 574-75, 663, 677, 697, 700, 702, 707
Campbell, Alexander, 147, 208, 212, 221, 249-57, 338, 686, 715, 716
Campbell, John McLeod, 271
Campbell, Thomas, 249-53, 254, 257, 686, 716
Camus, Alfred, 524
Cantwell, Emmett Howell, 426, 454-55
Cardenal, Ernesto, 611
Carey, William, 61, 168, 169, 172, 173-75, 189, 200, 209, 211, 212, 581, 583, 598, 696, 698, 714
Carlile, J. C., 265-66, 277
Carmichael, Robert, 250
Carpenter, C. H., 230
Carpenter, Joel A., 536
Carr, Warren Tyree, 545
Carrell, William D. M., 429
Carroll, Benajah Harvey, 235-36, 237, 238, 248, 284, 432, 449, 450, 603, 667, 709
Carroll, B. H., Jr., 206
Carson, Alexander, 200-203, 212

Carson, Donald Arthur, 669-76, 695-96, 710, 711, 724
Carter, James E., 436, 439-40, 467
Carver, William Owen, 6, 378, 466, 581-85, 592-93, 621, 657, 722
Casserley, J. V. Langmead, 617
Cassian, John, 707
Cathcart, William, 105
Cauthen, Kenneth, 304, 311, 312, 549-50, 552, 555-56
Cawley, Frederick, 621
Chafer, Lewis Sperry, 367
Chalmers, Thomas, 314
Chamberlen, Peter, 70
Charles I, King, 113
Charles II, King, 37, 42, 71
Chelčický, Peter, 6
Childs, Brevard, 386
Christian, John Tyler, 233-34, 248
Clark, Gordon Haddon, 655
Clark, Neville, 542, 543, 547
Clark, Peter, 157
Clark, Theodore Roscoe, 480-81
Clark, William Allen, 239
Clarke, John, 115
Clarke, Samuel, 44
Clarke, William Newton, 287, 304-10, 340, 372, 420, 432, 678, 717
Clayton, Lynn P., 490
Cleage, Albert, 614
Clements, Keith W., 594
Clements, Ronald Ernest, 406-409, 413, 718
Clemons, Hardy, 310
Clendenen, E. Ray, 488
Clifford, John, 264, 272-77, 339, 667, 716
Clifford, Paul Rowntree, 394
Clifton, Richard, 25
Cocceius, Johannes, 141
Cochran, Bernard Harvey, 308, 309-10
Cody, Zechariah Thornton, 148, 438
Coggins, James R., 28

Coke, Thomas, 218
Colani, Timothy, 390
Collier, Jay T., 53, 57
Collier, Thomas, 60, 80-83, 101, 107
Collins, William, 72
Comblin, José, 635-36
Cone, James, 615
Conner, Walter Thomas, 449-55, 506, 510-11, 667, 709, 719
Constantine, Emperor, 162, 287, 690
Conyers, Abda Johnson III, 480
Conzelmann, Hans, 372, 404-405
Cook, Henry, 15, 540
Costas, Orlando Enrique, 633-37, 640, 642, 643, 644, 646, 660, 723
Cotton, John, 112, 554
Cowper, William, 665
Cox, Harvey Gallagher, 609-12, 659, 723
Cox, Joseph P., 263-64
Cox, Samuel, 271-72
Coxe, Benjamin, 66
Coy, Terrell Frank, 635
Crabtree, Arthur B., 401
Cranfill, James Britton, 237-38
Crawford, Nathaniel Macon, 150, 216
Crawford, Tarleton Perry, 230-31, 248, 582, 715
Creed, John Bradley, 509
Crismon, Leo T., 243
Crisp, Tobias, 89-91, 99-100, 104, 105, 107, 549
Criswell, Wallie Amos, 481-86, 488, 511-12, 567-68, 580, 720, 722
Crosby, Thomas, 52, 234
Cross, Anthony R., 543, 544, 547, 711
Cross, George, 304, 312-13, 340
Crossan, John Dominic, 392, 576
Cullmann, Oscar, 377, 378, 477
Culpepper, Richard Alan, 395
Culross, James, 65, 264, 275

Dagg, John Leadley, 134, 137-45, 151, 242, 248, 423, 424, 466, 593, 667, 714, 715
D'Amico, David, 536
Dana, Harvey Eugene, 458, 593
Daniel, 64
Daniel, Curt, 100
Darby, John Nelson, 375, 560-61, 562, 722
Dargan, Edwin Charles, 150, 245-46, 248, 435, 442, 443, 466, 593, 715
Darwin, Charles, 278, 293
David, King, 44, 88, 136, 244, 398, 407, 680
Davidson, William Franklin, 119
Davies, Gwynne Henton, 486-87, 512
Davis, Larry Joe, 605
Day, Dorothy, 538
Day, John Daniel, 606
Day, R. Alan, 522
Dayton, Amos Cooper, 143, 216, 217, 218, 227-30, 247, 248, 715
de Blois, Austen Kennedy, 557
Deborah, 88
Dehoney, William Wayne, 495
Deiros, Pablo Alberto, 632
Delitzsch, Franz, 578
Demarest, Bruce Alvin, 335-37, 718
DeMent, Byron Hoover, 436
Denck, Hans, 9
Dever, Mark E., 145, 711
Deweese, Charles William, 504
Dexter, Henry Martyn, 233
Dick, John, 202
Dilday, Russell Hooper, Jr., 427, 429, 495, 512, 720
Dillenberger, John, 319
Ditzler, Jacob, 220
Dix, Kenneth, 198
Dockery, David Samuel, 350, 455, 468, 469, 470-71, 472, 473, 488, 530, 536, 696-97, 704-10, 711, 725

Dodd, Charles Harold, 377, 386, 673, 678
Dodd, Monroe Elmon, 448
Dodge, Ebenezer, 288, 303-304, 305, 339, 340
Dodson, Ed, 319
Dooyeweerd, Herman, 655
Dorner, Isaak August, 281, 421
Douglas, Crerar, 297
Douglas, Mack, 459
Downs, David William, 462-63, 467
Draper, James T., Jr., 162, 495-96, 512, 720
Draughon, Walter D. III, 149, 380, 423, 509
Drummond, Lewis A., 265, 277-78
DuBose, Francis Marquis, 657
Dunn, James D. G., 670-71
Dunn, James M., 429-30
Durden, John Allen, 466

Early, Joseph E., Jr., 238-39
Early, William T., 351-52
Eaton, Samuel, 51
Eaton, Thomas Treadwell, 234-35, 248, 532, 596
Eddleman, Henry Leo, 487
Edgemon, Roy Talley, 456
Edgren, John Alexis, 337-38
Edward VI, King, 16
Edwards, Jonathan, Jr., 180
Edwards, Jonathan, Sr., 153, 168, 172, 176, 182, 183, 228, 434, 538, 661, 663, 666, 701, 724
Edwards, Morgan, 118, 164
Edwards, Peter, 192
Edwards, Sarah, 538
Edwards, W. Ross, 459
Eichrodt, Walther, 378
Eliot, John, 174, 176
Elizabeth I, Queen, 17
Ella, George M., 100, 106, 188-89
Elliott, Leslie Robinson, 462

Elliott, Ralph Harrison, 457, 458-62, 491, 511, 720
Ellis, Curtis Ray, 585
Ellis, Edward Earle, 402-406, 413, 718-19
Ellis, William Elliott, 417, 422, 427, 430-31
Ellyson, William, 438
Enoch, 399
Erasmus, Desiderius, 698, 702, 707
Erickson, Millard John, 498, 525-31, 546-47, 578-79, 657, 694, 705, 721, 722
Ernesti, Johann August, 202
Ernst, James E., 114
Escobar, Samuel, 633, 636, 641-44, 646, 660, 723
Estep, William Roscoe, Jr., 14, 501-502, 530, 534, 535, 599-600, 658, 688, 722
Eutyches, 3, 44
Eve, 19, 54, 75, 96, 130, 131, 222, 380, 453, 497, 512, 519, 527, 528, 587-88, 606
Evans, Benjamin, 234
Evans, Percy William, 394, 540
Ewing, Greville, 203, 251

Fackre, Gabriel, 656
Fairbairn, Patrick, 521
Falwell, Jerry, 319, 611
Featley, Daniel, 58
Fenwick, Malcolm C., 648, 724
Ferguson, Duncan S., 266
Ferguson, Milton U., 351
Ferris, Charles Joseph, 422
Feuerbach, Ludwig, 559
Fiddes, Paul Stuart, 676-83, 710, 711, 724
Finney, Charles Grandison, 294, 702
Fitz, Richard, 17
Flender, Helmut, 404-405
Fletcher, Jesse C., 257, 457, 487

Forsyth, Peter Taylor, 521
Fosdick, Harry Emerson, 304, 310-12, 323, 331-32, 340, 550, 717
Foster, Frank Hugh, 417
Foster, George Burman, 550, 554, 557-60, 580, 722
Fowler, Edward, 69
Fowler, Stanley K., 542-43
Fox, Matthew, 675
Fox, Norman, 327
Francis of Assisi, 317
Francisco, Clyde Taylor, 487, 512
Franke, John R., 694
Fraser, William, 535
Freeman, Curtis Wynn, 430-31, 533, 540, 711
Freeman, J. D., 532
Frelinghuysen, Theodore, 153
Freud, Sigmund, 524
Frost, Adoniram Judson, 562
Frost, James Marion, 435, 503
Fuller, Andrew, 39, 47, 106, 145, 172, 173, 174, 175-89, 190, 198, 199, 209, 211, 212, 250, 270, 667, 715
Fuller, Charles Grantland, 496
Fuller, Ellis, Adams, 456
Fuller, Richard, 150, 228
Fullerton, W. Y., 277, 355

Gabler, Johann Phillipp, 386
Gadamer, Hans-Georg, 708
Gadsby, John, 198
Gadsby, William, 198-99, 212, 715
Gama, Roberto, 636
Gambrell, James Bruton, 435, 436, 438, 596
Gammage, Albert Walter, Jr., 648
Gandhi, Mohandas K., 621
Gano, John, 119
Gansfort, Wessel, 6
Gardin, Gilbert, 58
Gardner, Robert G., 138, 143, 145
Garland, David E., 710

Garner, Robert, 543
Garrett, James Leo, Jr., 383, 468, 535-36, 705
Garrett, John, 114
Garrett, Stephen Michael, 433
Gates, Errett, 255
Gaussen, Louis, 268
Gaustad, Edwin Scott, 110, 113, 163, 534
Geldbach, Erich, 602
George, Denise Wyse, 697
George, Timothy Francis, 17, 28, 94, 100, 105-106, 148, 257, 455, 503, 534, 696-700, 711, 725
Gernits, Lubbert, 29
Gess, Wolfgang Friedrich, 281, 300
Gibbon, Edward, 177
Gibson, Scott, 287
Gill, John, 83, 89, 90, 92, 93-106, 107-108, 118, 145, 153, 154, 157, 168, 178, 182, 186, 189, 193, 199, 200, 250, 264, 270, 339, 667, 715, 725
Gilmore, Alec, 542, 543
Gilpin, W. Clark, 113
Glas, John, 184, 249-50
Givens, Jimmy McMath, 297
Gladden, Washington, 314-15
Glover, Terrot Reaveley, 592
Going, Jonathan, 128
Goodchild, Frank Marsden, 331, 332, 717
Goodspeed, Calvin, 279, 284-85, 339, 450, 716
Goodwin, Abb L., 568
Goodwin, Thomas, 116
Gordon, Adoniram Judson, 279, 285-88, 324, 339, 716
Gothard, Bill, 686
Gould, Ezra Palmer, 343-47, 412-13, 718
Graf, K. H., 260, 716
Graham, William Franklin (Billy), Jr., 321, 602, 603-609, 658, 703, 723

Indexes

Grantham, Thomas, 37, 42-43, 45, 49, 81, 89, 382, 713
Graves, James Robinson, 214-25, 226, 227, 243, 247-48, 255-56, 535-36, 562-63, 580, 715, 722
Gray, James Martin, 311
Grebel, Conrad, 10
Green, Bradley G., 528
Greenwood, John, 18
Gregory of Nazianzus, 2
Gregory of Nyssa, 2
Gregory the Great, 702
Grenz, Stanley James, 158, 161, 524, 530-31, 536, 690-96, 711, 725
Griffin, David Ray, 646
Griffin, Edward Dorr, 215
Griffith, Benjamin, 116
Griffith, John, 36, 43, 49
Grotius, Hugo, 179
Grounds, Vernon C., 691
Grudem, Wayne Arden, 673-74, 684-86, 693, 694, 710, 711, 724
Gstohl, Mark A., 380, 422, 453
Gundry, Robert H., 663-64, 670
Guthrie, Donald, 395-96, 412-13, 718

Hackett, Horatio Balch, 289
Haldane, James Alexander, 200-201, 251, 273
Haldane, Robert, 200-201, 251
Haldeman, Isaac Massey, 311, 564
Hale, William, 210
Hall, Aldis, Norton, 568
Hall, Christopher, 703
Hall, Robert, Jr., 104, 168, 173, 176, 193-95, 196, 211, 683, 715
Hall, Robert, Sr., 166-68, 174, 188, 211, 714
Ham, Mordecai, 604
Hamblin, Robert L., 490
Hamilton, William, 289
Hammarskjöld, Dag, 537
Hammett, John S., 711

Hankins, Barry, 163
Harbour, Brian Lee, 311, 312
Harmon, Steven Ray, 711
Harnack, Adolf, 315
Harper, William Rainey, 557
Harrison, Paul M., 427
Harrison, Robert, 17
Hart, Oliver, 117-18
Hartshorne, Charles, 575
Harvey, Barry, 540
Hasel, Gerhard, 398
Hasker, William, 575
Havlik, John F., 459
Hawley, Michael Mark, 603
Hayden, Samuel Augustus, 237-39, 715
Haykin, Michael A. G., 173, 535
Heath, Jesse, 120
Hedlund, Roger Eugene, 657
Heidegger, Martin, 524
Helwys, Jane, 31
Helwys, Thomas, 12-13, 20, 23, 29, 31-34, 35, 49, 233, 382, 501, 667
Hendricks, William Lawrence, 545-46
Henry, Carl Ferdinand Howard, 294-95, 297, 302, 492, 515-19, 525, 531, 546, 547, 635, 646, 692, 694, 703, 721
Henry of Lausanne, 6
Herod the Great, 652
Herring, Ralph Alderman, 474
Hester, Malcolm O'Neal, 568
Hetzer, Ludwig, 9
Hick, John, 651, 652, 653, 654, 656, 675, 689
Hickem, Bill G., 496
Hicks, Frederick Cyril Nugent, 353
Hill, James E., Jr., 215
Hill, Samuel S., 457
Hindson, Ed, 319
Hinn, Benny, 632
Hinson, Edward Glenn, 382, 428, 429, 535-36

Hinson, W. B., 333-34
Hinton, John Howard, 273
Hirsch, Eric Donald, 708
Hiscox, Edward Thurston, 129
Hitler, Adolf, 652
Hobbs, Herschel Harold, 428, 460, 462-63, 466, 467, 468-73, 481, 495-96, 509, 511, 719, 719-20
Hodge, Charles, 148, 149-50, 151
Hodges, Jesse Wilson, 473
Hoekema, Anthony Andrew, 376
Hoen, Cornelius, 6
Hofmann, Melchior, 9, 12, 44
Holifield, E. Brooks, 138-39
Holmes, Obadiah, 115
Honeycutt, Roy Lee, 503
Hooke, Thomas, 37
Hooker, Thomas, 702
Hopkins, Albert P., Jr., 469
Hopkins, Samuel, 180, 190, 211
Hordern, William, 525, 526
Horst, Irwin B., 14
Hovey, Alvah, 279-83, 284, 339, 344, 532, 667, 716
Howe, Claude Leodis, Jr., 305, 428, 490
Howe, Danny Eugene, 562, 567-68
Howell, Robert Boyté Crawford, 218, 243-44, 248
Howson, Barry, 63, 64, 65, 103
Hoyt, Herman A., 376
Hubmaier, Balthasar, 10-11, 15, 111, 534, 701
Hudson, Winthrop Still, 133, 320, 427-28
Hugh of St. Victor, 63
Hull, William Edward, 237, 491
Hume, David, 177, 524
Humphreys, Fisher Henry, 477, 490, 509
Hunt, William Boyd, 479-80
Hunter, Herbert, 406
Huntington, William, 198, 199, 211

Huss, John, 7
Hussey, Joseph, 89-90, 91, 106, 107, 168, 549
Hymenaeus, 136

Ignatius of Antioch, 405
Imasogie, Osadolor, 616-20, 659, 723
Irenaeus, 707
Irving, Edward, 199
Isaac, 244, 459, 486, 487, 512
Isaiah, 408
Ivimey, Joseph, 65, 104, 173, 196-97, 200, 212, 715

Jacob, 244
Jacob, Henry, 17, 51, 58
James, 345
James I, King, 33
James, Edwin Oliver, 621
James, Gordon, 709
James, Robison B., 504
James, William, 417, 426, 434
Jarrel, Willis Anselm, 256, 338
Jefferson, Thomas, 114, 162, 702
Jeffrey, William, 37
Jeremias, Joachim, 377, 400
Jerome, 707
Jessey, Henry, 51
Jeter, Jeremiah Bell, 244-45, 248, 256, 338
Job, 622, 652
John, 345
John Chrysostom, 482, 707
John of Wesel, 6
John the Baptist, 8, 30, 136, 192, 194, 225, 228, 229, 282, 349-50, 393, 481-82, 541
Johnson, Elias Henry, 288, 292-93, 339, 716
Johnson, Francis, 17, 18, 24
Johnson, Lafayette Demetrius, 459-60
Johnson, Stephen M., 27, 28
Johnson, William Bullein, 228

Johnston, Robert K., 498, 536
Jonah, 206
Jones, Bob, Jr., 608
Jones, Bob, Sr., 608
Jones, Eli Stanley, 641
Jones, Jenkin, 116
Jones, Russell Bradley, 473
Jones, Samuel, 117
Jones, William R., 615
Jonsson, John Norman, 621-22, 651, 659, 723
Jordan, Anthony Lynn, 505
Jordan, Clarence L., 537
Joris, David, 9
Josephus, 102, 672
Jovinian, 6
Judah, 244
Judas Iscariot, 136, 577, 578
Judson, Adoniram, 205, 258, 634, 667
Justin Martyr, 405

Kaftan, Julius, 559
Kaiser, Walter Christian, Jr., 498
Kantzer, Kenneth Sealer, 498
Keach, Benjamin, 77, 83-89, 94, 107, 115-16, 150, 264, 339, 667, 714
Keach, Elias, 115, 116
Keathley, Kenneth, 711
Kee, Alistair, 690
Keil, Carl Friedrich, 578
Kendall, Robert Tillman, 208
Kerfoot, Franklin Howard, 150, 234-35
Key, Jerry S., 624
Kierkegaard, Søren, 691
Kiffin, William, 52, 53, 65-67, 72, 85, 107, 196, 243, 714
Kim, Nam Soo, 648
Kim, Yong Gook, 648
King, Henry Melville, 232
King, Martin Luther, Jr., 537, 612-13
Kinghorn, Joseph, 173, 194-96, 200, 211, 243, 302, 715
Kingsley, Charles, 314

Kjesbo, Denise Muir, 693
Knitter, Paul, 651, 675
Knollys, Hanserd, 62-65, 66, 89, 105, 107, 714
Knox, John (Scotland), 220, 228, 317
Knox, John (USA), 646
Knox, Ronald, 434
Knudsen, Ralph Edward, 363-64, 376, 412-13, 718
Kraemer, Hendrik, 379
Kuenen, Abraham, 260, 716
Künneth, Walter, 646
Kuyper, Abraham, 521

Ladd, George Eldon, 374-77, 391, 412-13, 560, 718
Ladd, George Trumbull, 296
LaFon, James Hardy, 355
Lagergren, C. G., 337-38
Lambert, Byron Cecil, 204
Lamkin, Adrian, Jr.,., 231
Land, Richard Dale, 82-83
Langmead, Ross, 646-47
Lard, Moses Easterly, 256
Las Casas, Bartolomé de, 635
Lasco, John a, 16
Lathrop, John, 51
Latourette, Kenneth Scott, 581
Lawrence, Joshua, 209
Laws, Curtis Lee, 318, 331
Lawson, Charles, 505
Leavell, Landrum P., 490
Lee, Hyunmoo, 647-48
Lee, Jason K., 28, 29, 711
Lee, O. Max, 206, 207-208
Lee, Won Kee, 418
Lefever, Alan J., 238
Leland, John, 162-63, 210, 501, 667
Leonard, Bill J., 536
Lequyer, Jules, 575
Lewis, Clive Staples, 524
Lewis, Edwin, 687

Lewis, Gordon Russell, 335-37, 692, 718
Lewis, Larry Lynn, 494-95
Lindbeck, George, 695
Lindsell, Harold, 492, 512, 517-18, 720
Lintelman, Ryan, 445, 464
Locke, John, 157, 252, 681
Lofton, George Augustus, 233, 248
Lohmeyer, Ernst, 400
Lombard, Peter, 181
Longan, George W., 250
Longenecker, Richard Norman, 410-12, 413, 719
Lord, David Nevins, 562
Lorenzen, Thorwald, 645-46
Lorimer, George C., 277
Lotze, Rudolf Hermann, 296
Love, James Franklin, 438, 439, 440-41
Lover, Thomas, 36
Lucas, Sean Michael, 432
Luce, Matthias, 252
Lumpkin, William Latane, 35, 38, 60, 82, 127, 132, 164, 332
Luther, Martin, 7, 22, 220, 228, 317, 434, 663, 697, 698, 700, 702, 707

Macalla, W. L., 253
McBeth, Harry Leon, 51, 90, 92, 105, 238, 241, 487, 536
McCall, Duke Kimbrough, 457
McClain, Alvah J., 568-69
McClellan, Albert Alfred, 462, 466
McClellan, Mark Richard, 635-36
McClendon, James William, Jr., 430, 452, 455, 535, 537-40, 547, 677, 688-89, 721
McDaniel, George White, 448, 510
MacDonald, Murdina D., 87
McDowell, Edward Allison, 368, 413, 473, 718

McGlothlin, William Joseph, 37, 82, 132, 236-27, 442, 443
MacGorman, John William, 490
Machen, John Gresham, 432
McIntire, Carl, 600, 608
Macintosh, Douglas Clyde, 550, 554-57, 560, 580, 721
MacIntyre, Alasdair, 429
Mack, Burton, 576
Mackay, John Alexander, 641, 642-43
McKinley, Hugh T., 355
Macklin, George Benjamin, 236
McKnight, Edgar Vernon, 350
Maclaren, Alexander, 4, 264
McLaren, Brian, 675
McLean, Archibald, 184-85, 200, 211, 250-51
McLoughlin, William G., 161, 605-606
McNeal, Reginald, 509
McNutt, William Roy, 427
Maddox, Timothy D. F., 430
Madison, James, 114, 162
Maiden, R. K., 441
Manly, Basil, Jr., 146-47, 151, 261-64, 338-39, 667, 709, 716
Manly, Basil, Sr., 148
Mansel, Henry Longueville, 289
Manson, Thomas Walter, 401
Manz, Felix, 10
Marcion, 575
Maring, Norman Hill, 178
Marlow, Isaac, 87-88
Marpeck, Pilgram, 11, 14
Marsden, George Mish, 319, 320, 515, 536
Marsh, Herbert, 521
Marshall, Daniel, 163-64, 210
Marshall, Ian Howard, 392
Marshall, Molly Truman, 654, 660, 724
Martin, John, 183, 211
Martin, Ralph Philip, 399-402, 413, 718

Martin, William, 608
Martinez, Salvador, 461
Mary, Queen, 16, 17, 28
Mary the Virgin, 2, 12, 29, 44, 55, 96, 348, 445
Mason, Rex, 355
Massee, Jasper Cortenus, 318, 326-27, 331, 332, 333, 338, 341, 717
Maston, Thomas B., 161
Mather, Cotton, 161
Mather, Kirtley Fletcher, 324
Matheson, Mark E., 139
Mathews, Shailer, 550-54, 580, 721
Maurice, Frederick Denison, 314
Meigs, R. V., 334
Melanchthon, Philip, 702
Melchizedek, 346, 459, 466
Melick, Richard R., 536
Mell, Patrick Hues, 134-37, 151, 667, 714
Mikolaski, Samuel J., 534-35
Miller, David W., 524
Miller, Ed. LeRoy, 692
Miller, Perry, 110, 113
Millikin, Jimmy Allen, 477-78, 490
Mills, Watson Early, 490
Milne, Bruce, 544-45
Milton, John, 196, 434
Mitchell, William, 543
Mogilas, Peter, 56
Mohler, Richard Albert, Jr., 432, 536, 695, 711
Molina, Luis de, 575
Moltmann, Jürgen, 386, 480, 646-47, 677, 690
Monck, Thomas, 39, 44, 713
Moody, Dale, 349, 377-85, 391, 413, 466, 475-76, 478, 489, 509, 534, 545, 585, 718
Moody, Dwight Allan, 140, 379, 420, 451-52, 509
Moody, Dwight Lyman, 286, 697
Moore, LeRoy, 294-95
Moore, Russell D., 432, 711
Moore, W. Winfred, 497
Morden, Peter J., 181, 187
More, John, 216
Morgan, Abel, 115-16
Morgan, David T., 491, 493
Morgan, Edmund S., 113
Morgan, George Campbell, 482
Morgan, Thomas, 177
Morling, George Henry, 645
Morris, Leon, 679
Moses, 77, 88, 183, 199, 346, 355, 357, 410
Mouw, Richard, 536
Mraida, Carlos, 632
Muhammad, 698
Mullins, Edgar Young, 35, 140, 150, 235, 415-34, 435, 438, 441-42, 443, 444, 447-48, 449, 450, 451-52, 466, 469, 470, 473, 488, 495, 500, 501, 506, 510, 511, 532, 535-36, 539, 627, 667, 709, 719, 721
Mumford, Stephen, 119
Müntzer, Thomas, 10
Muray, Leslie A., 554
Murray, George, 388
Murray, Iain H., 269-70
Murray, John, 125
Murton, John, 15, 34, 111

Nalls, James Ray, 423, 453
Nam, Samuel Byungdoo, 647
Nash, Ronald Herman, 654-56, 660, 724
Naylor, Peter, 106
Neander, Johann August Wilhelm, 289
Nee, Watchman, 629
Neighbours, Ralph W., Jr., 490
Nelson, Stanley Allen, 535
Nestorius, 2, 3
Nettles, Thomas Julian, 98, 99, 100, 106, 136, 145, 181, 423, 431, 432, 502, 603, 666-69, 711, 725

Nevius, John Livingston, 230-48
Newbigin, J. E. Lesslie, 651
Newman, Albert Henry, 6, 9, 204, 236, 300
Newman, Elizabeth, 540
Newman, John Henry, 647
Newman, Stewart Albert, 533
Newport, John Paul, 391, 497, 498-99, 536
Newport, Richard M., 206
Newton, John, 665
Newton, Louie D., 442
Niebuhr, Helmut Richard, 319, 434
Niebuhr, Reinhold, 310-11, 434, 476, 516, 523, 608
Nietzsche, Friedrich Wilhelm, 524
Noah, 97, 157, 223, 398, 652
Noll, Mark, 498
Norman, Robert Stanton, 532, 711
Norris, John Franklyn, 320, 325, 426, 485-86, 563-65, 717, 722
Northrup, George Washington, 288, 291, 339, 716
Nygren, Anders, 621-22

Oates, Wayne Edward, 457
Ockenga, Harold John, 515
Ohrn, Arnold Theodore, 427
Oliphant, W. L., 566
Oliver, Harold Hunter, 481
Olson, Roger Eugene, 692, 693-94, 695, 701-704, 709, 711, 725
Onyenechehie, Thompson Onumajuru, 620
Oosterbaan, Johannes A., 534
Orchard, George Herbert, 216
Origen, 707
Osborn, Henry Fairfield, 324
Osborne, Grant Richard, 498
Owen, John, 116, 170
Owen, Derwyn Randolph Grier, 367
Owens, Milum Oswell, Jr., 491

Packer, James Innell, 498
Padilla, C. René, 633, 636, 637-41, 642, 644, 646, 657, 666, 723
Paine, Thomas, 172, 177, 211
Palmer, Paul, 119
Panikkar, Raimundo, 675
Pannenberg, Wolfhart, 646, 691, 692, 703
Park, Young-Cheol, 648
Parker, Daniel, 204, 205-208, 211, 715
Parker, G. Keith, 585-86
Parks, Robert Keith, 301, 454
Parnell, Chris William, 622-23, 659, 723
Pascal, Blaise, 523, 537
Paschall, Henry Franklin, 496
Patterson, Bob E., 518, 522-23
Patterson, Leighton Paige, 141, 482, 484, 485, 494, 512
Paul (Saul of Tarsus), 160, 314, 340, 344-45, 348, 361, 366, 367, 372, 374, 381, 401, 405, 411, 527-28, 541, 641, 661-62, 664, 671, 674, 718
Paulus, Heinrich Eberhard Gottlob, 646
Pawson, David, 572
Payne, Ernst Alexander, 572, 594, 597-98, 658, 688, 722
Pearce, Samuel, 177
Pelagius, 698
Pelot, Francis, 117-18
Pendleton, James Madison, 129, 214-15, 217, 225-27, 247, 248, 466, 532, 715
Penn, William Evander, 415
Pentecost, J. Dwight, 568-69
Pepper, George Dana Boardman, 279, 283-84, 339
Perkins, William, 90
Person, I., 128
Peter, 345, 346, 577, 578
Peter de Bruys, 6
Peterson, Walter Ross, 324-25

Pfleiderer, Otto, 575
Philips, Dietrich (or Dirk), 12
Phillips, Charles D., 143
Philo, 102
Philpot, Joseph Charles, 199
Pinckney, T. C., 506
Pinnock, Clark Harold, 493-93, 498, 512, 524, 534, 575-76, 579, 652, 656, 660, 694, 703, 720, 722, 724
Piper, John Stephen, 579, 661-66, 693, 710, 711, 724
Pitt, R. H., 436, 442, 443
Pleasants, Phyllis Rodgerson, 430
Poe, Harry L., 711
Polley, Max Eugene, 355
Pool, Jeff B., 504
Poole, Charles, 502
Poole, Robert, 66
Popkes, Wiard, 681
Porter, J. W., 426
Potter, Charles Francis, 323
Powell, William Audrey, Sr., 491, 494
Pressler, Herman Paul III, 494, 512
Preus, Robert, 498
Price, Theron D., 466
Priestley, David T., 535
Priestley, Joseph, 178
Pulliam, Kenny Regan, 522

Quinby, Hosea, 121

Race, Alan, 651
Radmacher, Earl D., 335
Rahner, Karl, 653, 654, 656, 701
Ramm, Bernard Lawrence, 492, 520-24, 525, 526, 527, 531, 546, 691, 692, 694, 703, 721
Ramsey, David M., 148
Randall, Benjamin, 120-21, 154
Randall, Ian, 573-74
Ratzinger, Joseph (Pope Benedict XVI), 611-12

Rauschenbusch, Walter, 312, 314-18, 338, 340-41, 377, 538, 717
Ray, David Burcham, 256, 338
Reed, Edwin Allen, 180
Rees, Frank E., 647
Reid, Thomas, 139, 150
Reis Pereira, Jose dos, 624, 625
Reist, Irwin, 298
Relly, James, 159
Remmele, John, 159
Reneau, Russell, 135
Rennie, Ian, 670
Resch, R., 646
Rice, John Richard, 565-67, 580, 608, 702, 722
Rice, Luther, 164, 204, 205, 206, 212
Rice, Richard, 575
Richards, William Wiley, 149-50, 431-32
Richardson, Samuel, 53
Ricoeur, Paul, 708
Rideman, Peter, 13
Ries, Hans de, 26, 28, 29
Rigdon, Sidney, 257
Riley, William Bell, 318, 320-22, 325, 331, 332, 341, 426, 560, 604, 703, 717
Rimmer, Harry, 321-22
Rippon, John, 94, 100, 173, 197, 212, 264, 339
Ritschl, Albrecht, 315, 421, 430
Roach, James, 120
Roark, Dallas M., 476-77
Robbins, Ray Frank, 473
Roberts, James Deotis, 612-16, 659, 723
Roberts, R. Philip, 178, 180, 185
Roberts-Thomson, Edward, 254, 598-99, 658, 722
Robertson, Archibald Thomas, 150, 347-50, 382, 413, 458, 706, 708, 718
Robertson, Frederick W., 315

Robinson, Ezekiel Gilman, 288-91, 292, 294, 297, 299, 316, 339, 716
Robinson, Henry Wheeler, 350-55, 360, 361, 413, 427, 532, 540, 544, 547, 621, 622, 678, 718
Robinson, John, 17, 697
Robinson, John Arthur Thomas, 406
Rogers, Adrian, 494, 506
Rogers, Ronald D., 657
Rone, Wendell, 466
Routh, Eugene Coke, 246
Routh, Porter W., 462
Rowley, Harold Henry, 355-60, 409, 413, 718
Rushbrooke, James Henry, 599
Russell, C. Allyn, 319, 320
Russell, David S., 409, 572-73
Rust, Eric Charles, 360-63, 378, 413, 718
Ruysbroeck, John, 6
Ryland, John, 166, 168, 171-72, 173, 179, 211
Ryland, John Collett, 166, 168-70, 191, 211
Ryrie, Charles Caldwell, 568-69

Saltmarsh, John, 62
Sampey, John Richard, 596
Sampler, Jason Boone, 453
Sanchez, Daniel Raul, 657
Sanchez, José M., 627
Sanday, William, 421
Sandeen, Ernest Robert, 319
Sandeman, Robert, 184, 250
Sanders, E. P., 671
Sanders, John, 575, 656, 694
Sandon, Leo, Jr., 417
Sartre, Jean-Paul, 524
Sattler, Michael, 10
Scarborough, Lee Rutland, 431, 438, 442, 443, 446, 603, 667-68
Schaff, Philip, 232
Schillebeeckx, Edward C. F. A., 646

Schleiermacher, Friedrich Daniel Ernst, 202, 313, 315, 416-17, 426, 430, 432
Schofield, J. N., 406
Schweer, G. William, 657
Schweitzer, Albert, 621
Schwenckfeld, Caspar, 9
Scott, Walter, 253-54
Scougal, Henry, 663
Sears, Barnas, 289
Seiss, Joseph Augustus, 562
Sell, Alan P. F., 90, 99-100, 105
Semler, Johann Salomo, 707-708
Semple, Robert Baylor, 255
Sennacherib, 358, 408
Seymour, Robert Edward, 105
Shaftesbury, Antony Ashley Cooper, 177
Shakespeare, John Howard, 277, 592, 658, 722
Shank, Robert Lee, 382
Shantz, Douglas, 26
Sheldon, Henry Clay, 450
Shelley, Bruce Leon, 335
Shepard, Samuel, 121
Sherman, Cecil Edwin, 497
Shields, Thomas Todhunter, 318, 320, 325-26, 332, 341, 717
Shindler, Robert, 274
Shirley, Christopher Jay, 662
Shurden, Walter Byron, 429, 467, 499-502, 512, 720
Siegvolck, Paul, 124
Simeon, Charles, 665
Simmons, James Samuel, 657
Simons, Menno, 12, 58, 112, 698, 701
Skepp, John, 65, 89, 91-92, 107-108, 714
Sloan, Robert Bryan, 369, 374
Small, Albion W., 550
Smith, Almer Jesse, 462
Smith, Harold Stewart, 219, 223
Smith, James M., 537

Smith, John Pye, 202
Smith, Joseph, Jr., 311
Smith, Kenneth Lee, 554
Smith, Ralph Lee, 397-99, 413, 718
Smith, Wilder, 294
Smith, William Cheney, Jr., 585
Smyth, John, 12, 14, 14-15, 16, 18, 23-31, 35, 37, 49, 88, 233, 382, 432, 667
Snyder, Howard A., 635
Sobrino, Jon, 639, 646
Socinus, Faustus, 44, 575
Soule, Joshua, 218
Sparks, John, 164, 166
Spears, Julius H., 421
Speed, Robert, 87
Spilsbury, John, 51, 52, 53, 57-58
Spittlehouse, John, 216
Spivey, James T., 509
Spurgeon, Charles Haddon, 83, 264-72, 275-78, 339, 482, 543-44, 644, 667, 683, 698, 700, 716, 725
Spurgin, Hugh, 114
Stafford, Thomas Polhill, 454
Stagg, Evelyn Owen, 373
Stagg, Frank, 369-74, 376, 412-13, 466, 475-76, 489-90, 509, 678, 718
Stassen, Glen, 12
Stealey, C. P., 441-42, 443, 447
Stearns, Lewis French, 417
Stearns, Shubael, 163-64, 210
Stennett, Edward, 70
Stephen, 400
Stevens, George Barker, 450
Stevens, John, 199
Stevens, William Wilson, 475-76
Stewart, Robert B., 711
Stinson, Benoni, 123
Stinton, Benjamin, 94
Stiver, Danny R., 377-78, 385
Stone, Barton Warren, 255, 256-57
Stonehouse, James, 124
Stott, John Robert Walmsey, 679

Stow, Baron, 128
Stowell, Joseph M., 333
Straton, John Roach, 318, 322-25, 331, 332, 341, 560, 717
Strauss, David Friedrich, 646
Strickland, William Claudius, 481
Strong, Augustus Hopkins, 288, 290, 294-303, 313, 316, 339-40, 449, 450, 452, 559, 667, 703, 716-17
Strong, Josiah, 315
Stuart, Charles, 251
Stuart, Moses, 132, 202
Sullivan, James Lenox, 460
Summers, Ray, 364-68, 413, 473, 567, 718
Suso, Henry, 6
Sutcliff, John, 161, 172-73, 176, 211
Sutton, Thomas Jerrell, 278, 668

Tarr, Leslie K., 326
Tasker, Randolf Vincent Greenwood, 388
Tauler, John, 6
Taylor, Adam, 45
Taylor, Boyce, 426
Taylor, Dan, 46-49, 126, 151, 153, 180, 183, 185, 211, 714
Taylor, David, 46, 153
Taylor, Jack R., 490
Taylor, John, 205, 208, 212
Taylor, Michael, 278, 388, 571-74, 580, 722
Taylor, Vincent, 353, 377, 380, 679
Taylor, Zachary Clay, 624
Templeton, Charles, 605
Tertullian, 5, 102, 707
Tetzel, John, 205
Tennent, Gilbert, 153
Theodore of Mopsuestia, 707
Theodoret of Cyrus, 707
Theodosius I, Emperor, 162
Theophilus of Antioch, 405

Tholuck, Friedrich August Gottreu, 289
Thomas Aquinas, 701, 702
Thomas, Bill Clark, 417, 427
Thomas, D. Winton, 406
Thomas, Gerald, 616
Thomas, Jesse Burgess, 234, 248
Thomas, John, 174, 176, 189
Thomasius, Gottfried, 281, 300
Thompson, Philip, 540
Thornbury, Gregory Alan, 432, 711
Tidwell, Josiah Blake, 475
Tillam, Thomas, 70
Tillich, Paul Johannes, 378, 476, 481, 647, 677
Timmerman, N. D., 238
Tindal, Matthew, 177, 701
Toland, John, 93, 701
Tolbert, Malcolm, 369, 490
Toon, Peter, 89, 100
Toplady, Augustus M., 105
Toy, Crawford Howell, 258-61, 338-39, 343, 462, 667, 716
Tracy, David, 619, 620
Tribble, Harold Wayland, 426, 428, 455, 719
Trigs, Kathy, 268
Troeltsch, Ernst, 559
Truett, George Washington, 482, 485-86, 501, 599
Tull, James Estol, 31, 111, 114, 213, 226, 232, 234, 237, 257, 307, 308, 309-10, 316-17, 455, 479, 535
Tull, Selsus Estol, 448
Turner, Daniel, 170
Turner, Gwin Terrell, 486, 487-88
Turner, Helen Lee, 493
Turner, John Clyde, 455-56
Turretin, Francis, 495
Tymns, T. Vincent, 264
Tyndale, William, 69

Unamuno, Miguel de, 641

Underwood, A. C., 31, 83, 277
Ussher, James, 470
Utley, Uldine, 324

Van Pelt, Peter Stephen, 300-301, 308, 553
Vardaman, E. Jerry, 366
Vaughn, J. Barry, 83, 86
Vedder, Henry Clay, 104, 304, 313-14, 340
Venn, Henry, 189
Venner, Thomas, 71
Verkuyl, Johannes, 633-34
Vick, George Beauchamp, 564
Vidler, William, 47, 125, 187, 211
Vigilantius, 6
Visser't Hooft, Willem Adolph, 314
Voke, Stanley, 572
Voltaire, François Marie Arouet de, 177
von Allmen, Daniel, 674

Wacker, Grant, 302-303
Walker, Austin, 83
Walker, Douglas Clyde, 382, 424
Walker, John, 253
Wallace, Oates Charles Symonds, 132, 455
Waller, John Lightfoot, 213-14, 227
Walvoord, John Flipse, 568-69
Wamble, Gaston Hugh, 129, 213
Ward, Wayne Eugene, 383, 385-87, 413, 718
Wardlaw, Ralph, 203
Ware, Bruce Allen, 577-79, 722
Warren, Caspar Carl, 474
Warren, Preston, 556
Washington, Joseph R., 614
Watson, Forrest E., 162
Watts, Isaac, 89
Watts, Michael R., 28, 98
Wayland, Francis, 132-34, 150, 151, 216, 243, 289, 432, 667

Weaver, Rufus W., 236
Weaver, Samuel Robert, 311-12
Webb, Val, 647
Welch, Claude, 319
Wellhausen, Julius, 260, 315, 459, 716
Wells, James, 269
Wesley, Charles, 89
Wesley, John, 153, 154, 159, 317, 434, 698, 702, 704
West, Danny Martin, 147
West, Stephen, 180
West, William Beryl, 523
Whichcote, Benjamin, 613
Whiston, William, 44
Whitby, Daniel, 94, 98
White, Barrington R., 16, 26
White, James Emery, 536
White, Jerry Thomas, 226, 711
White, John E., 441-42, 443
White, Kenneth Owen, 459-60, 511
White, Reginald Ernest Oscar, 541-42, 543, 547
Whitefield, George, 120, 153, 154, 164, 228, 698
Whitsitt, William Heth, 231-37, 248, 250, 254, 415, 466, 715
Wiberg, Anders, 337
Widengren, Geo, 621
Wilberforce, William, 665
William of Orange, 84
Williams, Alvin Peter, 228, 256, 338
Williams, Charles, 264
Williams, David, 118
Williams, Edward, 192
Williams, George Huntston, 9, 45, 696
Williams, Glenn Garfield, 594
Williams, Harry A., 647
Williams, Roger, 109-14, 150, 232, 233, 501

Williams, William, 242-43, 248
Wilson, Daniel, 202
Wimberly, Dan B., 206
Winchester, Elhanan, 49, 124-26, 151, 159, 162
Wingren, Eric, 338
Wingren, Gustaf, 621-22
Wink, Walter, 687
Winward, Stephen Frederick, 542
Wiseman, Percy John, 476
Witherspoon, John, 139
Wittgenstein, Ludwig, 524
Woelfkin, Cornelius, 332, 341
Wolfard, Rodney Bishop, 624
Wood, Nathan Eusebius, 288, 293-94, 313, 339-40, 716
Woolley, Davis Collier, 474
Wrede, Wilhelm, 396
Wright, Gerald David, 657
Wright, Joseph, 45
Wright, Nigel Goring, 686-90, 711, 724
Wurster, Stephen H., 554
Wycliffe, John, 7

Yarnell, Malcolm Beryl III, 432-33, 536-37, 711
Yates, William, 258
Yoder, John Howard, 534, 641, 690
Young, Homer Edwin, 502-503, 512, 720-21
Young, John Terry, 490
Youngblood, Clark Richard, 382, 509

Zamora Alfaro, Alejandro, 627-28
Zanchi, Jerome, 135
Zeman, Jarold Knox, 534
Zwingli, Ulrich, 7, 22, 69, 220, 302, 683, 697, 700, 702

JAMES LEO GARRETT, JR., a Baptist theological educator for more than half a century, taught in three institutions: Southwestern Baptist Theological Seminary, Southern Baptist Theological Seminary, and Baylor University.

He is the author of numerous books and articles. Of note, he is the author of *Systematic Theology* (two volumes) and is co-author of *Are Southern Baptists Evangelicals?* (Mercer University Press, 1982).

www.ingramcontent.com/pod-product-compliance
Lightning Source LLC
Chambersburg PA
CBHW021411300426
44114CB00010B/459